ISBN 978-0-265-00691-7
PIBN 10963190

1 MONTH OF
FREE
READING

at
www.ForgottenBooks.com

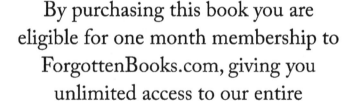

By purchasing this book you are eligible for one month membership to ForgottenBooks.com, giving you unlimited access to our entire collection of over 1,000,000 titles via our web site and mobile apps.

To claim your free month visit:
www.forgottenbooks.com/free963190

English
Français
Deutsche
Italiano
Español
Português

www.forgottenbooks.com

Mythology Photography **Fiction**
Fishing Christianity **Art** Cooking
Essays Buddhism Freemasonry
Medicine **Biology** Music **Ancient
Egypt** Evolution Carpentry Physics
Dance Geology **Mathematics** Fitness
Shakespeare **Folklore** Yoga Marketing
Confidence Immortality Biographies
Poetry **Psychology** Witchcraft
Electronics Chemistry History **Law**
Accounting **Philosophy** Anthropology
Alchemy Drama Quantum Mechanics
Atheism Sexual Health **Ancient History**
Entrepreneurship Languages Sport
Paleontology Needlework Islam
Metaphysics Investment Archaeology
Parenting Statistics Criminology
Motivational

THE

MISCELLANEOUS DOCUMENTS

OF THE

HOUSE OF REPRESENTATIVES

FOR THE

SECOND SESSION OF THE FIFTY-FIRST CONGRESS.

1890-'91.

WITH INDEX.

IN SIXTEEN VOLUMES.

WASHINGTON:
GOVERNMENT PRINTING OFFICE.
1891.

INDEX TO HOUSE MISCELLANEOUS DOCUMENTS.

CONTENTS OF THE VOLUMES.

51ST CONGRESS, ⎱ HOUSE OF REPRESENTATIVES. ⎰ MIS. DOC.
2d Session. ⎰   ⎱ No. 137.

DIGEST

OF

CONTESTED-ELECTION CASES

IN THE

FIFTY-FIRST CONGRESS.

COMPILED, UNDER RESOLUTION OF THE HOUSE,

BY

CHESTER H. ROWELL,

CLERK TO THE COMMITTEE ON ELECTIONS.

WASHINGTON:
GOVERNMENT PRINTING OFFICE.
1891.

Resolved, That there be printed and bound for the use of the House the usual number, to wit, one thousand six hundred and seven copies of the Digest of Contested Election Cases in the Fifty-first Congress, together with an index to the same, to be prepared by the clerk of the Committee on Elections, for which and for the necessary preparation and superintendence thereof there shall be paid said clerk by the Clerk of the House, out of the contingent fund, the sum of five hundred dollars; said sum to be paid when the manuscript of the work shall have been delivered to the Public Printer.

Passed the House February 5, 1891. (See Record, Fifty-first Congress, second session, pages 2198 to 2201.)

2

PREFACE.

The volumes of this series are known by custom and courtesy as " digests," but none of them have attempted to be anything more than compilations of reports, and since the volume compiled by Clarke and Hall, in 1834, none of them have been fully indexed, and most of them not indexed at all. In conformity with the plan of the series, this volume is also a compilation of reports, that is, it contains all the reports in full; but an attempt has been made to give in the index a real digest of the law points discussed in the reports. It is perhaps needless to say that committee reports, having the form of arguments addressed to the House, lend themselves much less readily to reduction to digest form than do the decisions of courts. A consideration of this difficulty will, it is hoped, explain and excuse some of the shortcomings of the digest.

On account of the unindexed condition of most of the previous volumes, I have ventured to include under each head of the digest a reference index to prior adjudications of the same question, where any exist. This list of references does not profess to be complete; it is confined to the points covered by the reports in this volume, and may not be entirely complete even as to them, but it will be found to be considerably fuller than the lists of references given in either Paine or McCrary, and, in the absence of any collected digest of all the Congressional cases, may be of some convenience in looking up precedents. No attempt has been made to analyze the decisions referred to, except to indicate the question decided, and generally whether the decision is in substantial accord with the decision in this volume or not.

In the body of the book some changes have been made from the customary form. The abstracts of law points are fuller than heretofore, and in a form more like that of court reports. The use of different sorts of type, both in the syllabi and index, will, it is hoped, facilitate rapid reference.* In addition to the statements of law points, a somewhat completer statement of facts and findings than is customary has been made. An election case, unlike most of the cases included in volumes

---

*The text of the reports being printed from stereotype plates already in existence, it was necessary to insert the new matter on separate pages, regardless of whether it would evenly fill them or not. This accounts for the gaps and blank pages between the head notes and text.

of court reports, retains an individual and historical interest, and some statement should be made in the head notes which will make it possible to see at a glance precisely what the individual features of the case are. For this reason a brief statement is made of the claims of the parties, the findings of the committee in regard to them, and the points and grounds of dissent of the minority. This is followed by an outline of the history of the case in Congress, and the syllabus of law points. At the beginning of the minority report is generally a fuller statement of the grounds of dissent, with a syllabus of law points, if any are discussed.

This statement is made on account of complaints made by members in debate in regard to the character of previous volumes, and to call attention to features of this volume which it ought perhaps to be taken for granted that any such volume would contain, but which, for some reason, have been omitted from its predecessors.

TABLE OF CASES.

All the contestees were Democrats; all the contestants, except Mr. Featherston, were Republicans. Cases 1, 2, 3, 4, 8, 9, 11, 12, 13, 14, and 15 were decided by the committee in favor of contestants; cases 5, 6, 7, 10, 16, and 17 in favor of contestees. Cases 13, 14, 16, and 17 were not reached by the House. The case of Eaton *vs.* Phelan, Tenth Tennessee, was not decided by the committee.

COMMITTEE ON ELECTIONS.

FIFTY-FIRST CONGRESS.

JONATHAN H. ROWELL, Illinois, *Chairman.*

L. C. HOUK, Tennessee.
WM. C. COOPER, Ohio.
NILS P. HAUGEN, Wisconsin.
J. F. LACEY, Iowa.
JOHN DALZELL, Pennsylvania.
C. A. BERGEN, New Jersey.
F. T. GREENHALGE, Massachusetts.

S. G. COMSTOCK, Minnesota.
CHARLES F. CRISP, Georgia.
CHARLES T. O'FERRALL, Virginia.
J. H. OUTHWAITE, Ohio.
LEVI MAISH, Pennsylvania.
L. W. MOORE, Texas.
R. P. C. WILSON, Missouri.

CHESTER H. ROWELL, *Clerk.*

6

AUTHORITIES CITED IN REPORTS.

CHARLES B. SMITH vs. JAMES M. JACKSON.

FOURTH WEST VIRGINIA.

The governor of West Virginia issued the certificate of election to Jackson. Smith claimed that the certificate of election should have been issued to him, he having a majority of the votes on the face of the returns, and also that he had received a majority of the legal votes actually cast.

Both claims are sustained by the committee, the minority dissenting from the second proposition and in part from the first. (See minority report, page 35.)

The resolutions presented by the committee were adopted by the House, February 3, 1890, by a vote of 166 to 0, and Mr. Smith was sworn in. The debate will be found on pages 948 to 1043 of the Record, but from page 948 to page 1000 it is mostly taken up with the parliamentary question of "counting a quorum."

(1) **Recount.** *When to be demanded.*

Where the statute provides for a recount at the demand of either party, this demand need not be made on the day of the announcement of the result of the first count.

(2) **Mistake.** *Power of board to correct.*

There is inherent in every body charged with the ascertainment of the popular will, whether its functions be judicial or ministerial, the power to correct an error when discovered, and to make its conclusions conform to the facts.

(3) **Abbreviation.** *The word " twe."*

Where the statute requires the return to set forth the number of votes received "in words at length," the word "twe" can not be construed to mean twelve or twenty without evidence. It should either be counted as two or the ambiguity explained by evidence.

(4) **County Court.** *Power in West Virginia to make a record.*

The county court in West Virginia has the power to make a record of its proceedings in regard to elections. "There is inherent in every such tribunal, and necessarily incident to its very purpose and existence, the power to make such record as will perpetuate and make available its legitimate action." And, aside from general principles, it appears from

an examination of the legislation of West Virginia on the subject that
the county court is more than a mere returning board.

(5) Burden of Proof.

When it is shown that the contestant was elected on the face of the
returns the burden of proof shifts to the contestee.

(6) Officers of Election. *Not sworn.*

When all the officers are not shown to have been sworn, but no harm
has resulted, it will not vitiate the election, they being *de facto* officers.
And in West Virginia, where it is provided that the fact of taking the
oath must either appear on the poll-books or be proved to the satisfaction
of the commissioners of the county court before they can count the vote
of a precinct, and the county commissioners did count the vote of a precinct where the oath was not sufficiently certified on the poll-books, it
will be presumed that they had satisfied themselves of the fact by other
evidence before counting the vote.

(7) Statutes. *Directory and mandatory.*

Statutes directing the mode of proceeding of public officers are directory merely, unless there is something in the statute itself which plainly
shows a different intent.

(8) Polling place. *Change of.*

When the election is held at a different place from that required by
law it does not vitiate the election if injury has not resulted and the
place of voting was generally understood.

(9) Vote. *Presumption of legality.*

A vote accepted by the officers holding the election is *prima facie* legal,
and can not be thrown out for illegality unless the presumption of legality
is overthrown by a clear preponderance of competent evidence.

(10) Evidence. *What competent to show how a vote was cast.*

In the absence of direct proof as to how a voter voted, evidence showing to what political party he belonged, whose election he advocated,
whose friends sustained his right to vote, and kindred testimony may
be admitted.

(11) Evidence. *Of declarations of voter.*

What the voter said at the time of voting is admissible as part of the
res gestœ ; but what he said after the day of the election either as to his
qualifications, or how he voted, or whether he voted, is inadmissible.

(12) Person of unsound mind.

A person having sufficient intelligence to make a valid will, or to bind
himself by ordinary contracts, or to be criminally responsible for his
acts, is a person of sound mind for the purposes of voting.

(13) Pauper. *Definition of.*

A pauper is one who is continuously supported in whole or in part
out of funds provided by the public authorities for that purpose.

(14) Residence. *What constitutes,*

It takes both act and intention to constitute a residence. An intention to retain a residence which has been left must be an intention actually to return to it and reside in it.

(15) Residence. *Of corporation employés.*

Where the statute provides that no person shall be deemed a resident in any county or district by reason of being employed therein by any corporation, such employment is not to be construed as *preventing* anyone from acquiring a residence at the place of his employment.

REPORT.

JANUARY 23, 1890.—Mr. DALZELL, from the Committee on Elections,
submitted the following report:

The Committee on Elections, having had under consideration the contested-election case of Charles B. Smith, contestant, against James M.
Jackson, contestee, from the fourth district of West Virginia, submit
the following report:

At an election held on the 6th day of November, 1888, James M. Jackson and Charles B. Smith were the Democratic and Republican candidates, respectively, for election as Representative to the Fifty-first Congress from the Fourth Congressional district of West Virginia. The
former obtained the governor's certificate and now holds the seat. His
right to either is contested by Smith, who claims that he was entitled
to the certificate in the first instance, and according to the votes legally
cast is now entitled to the seat.

The issue to be determined by the committee involves both these
claims.

Was the contestant elected upon the face of the returns?

It would seem that the contestee originally conceded that he was.
Contemporaneously with the issue by the governor of a certificate of
election to the contestee he made public a proclamation or declaration
not called for by any provision of law, the purpose of which evidently
was to justify his action in issuing the certificate. (See Record, p. 866.)

In this proclamation the governor says:

J. M. Jackson, who was a candidate for Representative in Congress for the Fourth
Congressional district, alleges that at two polling places at least, in Putnam County,
the election was held at other and different places than those prescribed by law, and
that motions were made before said commissioners to exclude these polls from the
count, which the commissioners refused to do, and that the majority of 171 votes in
said county in favor of C. B. Smith for said office is made up in part by the returns
from said two polling places. It is insisted by said Jackson that under our statutes
it is in the power of the governor to go behind the returns and inquire into the proceedings of the county commissioners. On the contrary it is insisted by said Smith,
through his counsel, that "the intention of the legislature was to withdraw from the
governor all power over the election returns whatsoever, except the certifying of
what appeared in the office of the executive department of the State."

The governor's decision was that he could not go behind the returns;
but it is very clear, from his statement, that prior to the issue of any
certificate, the contestee was of opinion, upon the face of the returns,
that the certificate must be issued to the contestant.

The subsequent action of the contestee is consistent with and in
affirmance of his original concession.

13

The contestant in his notice of contest (Record, p. 22) offered to rest his claim to office on the face of the returns. The issue thus tendered the contestee declined, adhering evidently to his original opinion that, tested by that standard, he had no title to the seat he now holds.

It is very plain to the committee that the contestant was elected upon the face of the returns and entitled to the certificate from the governor.

Under the laws of West Virginia (Code, sec. 22, ch. 3) it is made the duty of the commissioners of the county courts in each Congressional district, to transmit to the governor a certificate of the result of the election within their respective counties, " and in the said certificate shall be set forth, according to the truth, the full name of every person voted for, and *in words at length* the number of votes he received for any office."

The Fourth Congressional district is constituted of twelve counties, and the aggregate vote appearing from the certificates therefrom transmitted to the governor in accordance with law was, as contestant claims—

	Votes.
For Jackson	19,825
For Smith	19,837

Showing a plurality for Smith of 12 votes. According to this statement Smith, and not Jackson, was entitled to the governor's certificate of election.

But the count as made by the governor was—

	Votes.
For Jackson	19,837
For Smith	19,834

Showing a plurality for Jackson of 3 votes.

The differences between the county returns and the governor's count are confined to three counties, viz: Ritchie, Calhoun, and Pleasants.

The commissioners of Ritchie County sent two certificates. One, dated November 13, shows—

	Votes.
For Smith	1,972
For Jackson	1,405

The second, dated November 14, shows—

	Votes.
For Smith	1,973
For Jackson	1,403

The second certificate correctly represented the result of a recount of the votes, made at the instance of the contestee. The governor accepted the first and rejected the second certificate, and thus took away from Smith one vote and added to Jackson two votes.

The law of West Virginia with respect to a count and recount of returns is as follows (Code, sec. 21, ch. 3):

The commissioners of the county court shall convene in special session at the court-house on the fifth day (Sundays excepted) after every election held in their county, or in any district thereof, and the officers in whose custody the ballots, poll-books, and certificates have been placed shall lay the same before them for examination. They may, if deemed necessary, require the attendance of any of the commissioners or canvassers, or other officers or persons present at the election, to answer questions under oath respecting the same, and may make such other orders as shall seem proper to procure correct returns and ascertain the true result of the said election in their county. They may adjourn from time to time, and when a majority of the commissioners is not present their meeting shall stand adjourned till the next day, and so from day to day till a quorum be present. They shall, upon the demand of any candidate voted for at such election, open and examine any one or more of the sealed packages of ballots and recount the same, but in such case they shall seal up the same again, etc.

It seems from the second certificate from Ritchie County that the contestee was dissatisfied with the first count there made, and demanded, as he had a right to do, a recount. This certificate, so far as material, the law just quoted shows as follows:

The commissioners of the county court of Ritchie County, West Virginia, having carefully and impartially examined the returns of the election held in said county in each district thereof on the 6th day of November, 1888, upon a recount of the ballots on the demand of J. M. Jackson, candidate voted for at said election for the office of Representative in the Congress of the United States, do hereby certify that in said county for the office of Representative in the Congress of the United States for the Fourth Congressional district of West Virginia—

Charles B. Smith, of Wood County, received nineteen hundred and seventy-three (1,973) votes.

J. M. Jackson, of Wood County, received fourteen hundred and three (1,403) votes.

O. W. Smith received one vote.

Judge Jackson received one vote.

In witness whereof we, the said commissioners, have hereto signed our names this 14th day of November, A. D. 1888, &c.

This certificate the governor ignored altogether, and the contestee now seeks to justify his action by saying that upon the making of the original certificate the county court was *functus officio*, powerless even to correct an error; and that a recount can be had only when the demand therefor is made prior to the issue of a certificate. This contention is directly in the teeth of the contestee's own action in demanding the recount, and is not in the judgment of your committee tenable on any ground.

The manifest purpose of the law in providing for a recount is that errors may be corrected. There can be no recount until there has been a perfected count. Whether a recount shall be necessary can not be determined till the first count is finished. No provision is made in the law as to the time when the recount must be demanded. There is no statute of limitations on the subject. To hold that a recount must be demanded on the day of the original count leads to the manifest absurdity, of requiring the candidate to be present, in person or by proxy, in as many different places as there are county courts in his district at one and the same time. In the district in question there are twelve counties.

If the recount was lawful, as undoubtedly it was, so then was the certificate of its result, and the governor exceeded his powers in accepting the first and ignoring the second certificate from Ritchie County.

He committed a similar error with respect to Calhoun County.

The commissioners of that county also returned two certificates. The first, dated November 12, 1888, showed for Jackson 919 votes, for Smith, 630. The second, made to correct a clerical error, showed the same number of votes for Jackson, but 632 votes for Smith instead of 630, and is as follows:

(Record, p. 857.) At a regular session of the county court of Calhoun County, held at the Court House of said county on Monday, the 7th day of January, 1889, on motion of A. J. Barr, it is ordered by this court that the returns of the election held in this county on the 6th day of November, 1888, as certified by the county court, held on the 12th day of November, 1888, be corrected, it appearing to the court that there is a clerical error in the returns as certified, to wit: That the record of the result of said election for a Representative in the Congress of the United States shows that Charles B. Smith received six hundred and thirty votes, which should have been C. B. Smith received six hundred and thirty-two votes.

It is therefore ordered by this court that the record of this count be corrected, so as to show that C. B. Smith received six hundred and thirty-two votes, as shown on the face of the returns of said election, and that a copy of this order be certified to the governor of this State, and to C. B. Smith, at Parkersburg, W. Va.

The Governor ignored this second certificate and thus deprived Smith of two votes. He assigned no reason for his action, but counsel for contestee now seek to justify it on the grounds hereinbefore stated —that upon the making of the first certificate the county court was *functus officio*, and had no power to correct an error, however plain and palpable, after the certificate had been issued.

It has been held that where the judges of election discover a mistake upon a recount of the ballots, their supplemental return is entitled to be received (Archer *v.* Allen, Thirty-fourth Congress); and that errors, whether fraudulent or accidental, may be corrected at any time, even after certificate of election issued by the governor. (Butler *v.* Lahman, Thirty-seventh Congress; Morton *v.* Daily, Thirty-seventh Congress.)

It is believed that there is inherent in everybody charged with the ascertainment of the popular will, whether its functions be judicial or ministerial, the power to correct an error when discovered and to make its conclusions express the true will of the people as disclosed by their suffrages. And it is especially to be noted that there is no suggestion from any quarter that the certificates from Ritchie and Calhoun Counties, ignored by the governor, did not accurately show the exact number of votes legally cast for the respective candidates, while on the contrary it expressly appears that they did so show.

But the technicalities which unfortunately prevailed in the mind of the governor to defeat in part the true will of the voters in Ritchie and Calhoun Counties would not have affected the result had he stopped there, and they dwindle into insignificance when compared with the results of the strange mental process by which the returns from Pleasants County were perverted.

According to the returns from that county, Smith had received 697 votes and Jackson 802 votes. These 802 votes the governor raised to 812 by a most extraordinary feat of political legerdemain. We quote from his unauthorized proclamation or declaration to which we have heretofore referred, as follows:

The commissioners of Pleasants County certify as to J. M. Jackson's vote as follows: "J. M. Jackson received eight hundred and *twe* votes." The words and letters are too plain for any mistake. For the reasons heretofore given there is no authority to go behind the returns. The vote certified must be counted if enough appears to ascertain the meaning. In an action upon a note it was held: "There was no error in admitting the note sued on in evidence, because the amount thereof is written four *hund* and two and 50-100 dollars." (*Glenn* vs. *Porter*, 72 Ind., p. 525.)

So it has been held that the abbreviation in a declaration, "Damages one *thous* dollars" is not error. (1 W. L. J., Mich., 395.)

If enough appear to make the return intelligible it should be made so.

This can not be done without striking out one letter and inserting another, or by supplying the seemingly omitted letters. Acting upon the face of the paper the latter appears more in consonance with adjudged cases. The least number would give to said Jackson eight hundred and twelve votes. It will be so entered.

Thus the governor. It is difficult to treat this matter seriously. It seems like a farce to argue about it. It is hard to believe that any mature man, of ordinary intellect, and even to an extent honest, when dealing with the sacred right of suffrage could cheat himself into a justification of such conduct, much less expect to cheat anybody else. The very fact that the governor issued to the public his extraordinary proclamation explaining his reasons for granting to the contestee the certificate which plainly belonged to the contestant is a confession of guilt. The puerile reference to law cases, one bearing on the construction of a promissory note, the other on a declaration, neither of them having the remotest possible analogy to the question in hand shows the straits to which the consciously guilty party was driven. The governor knew—could not help knowing—even if a poor penman omitted to close his o so that the word looked like t-w-e, instead of t-w-o, that the word intended was *two*. Upon general principles he was bound to presume that the three letters expressed the whole word, but he was especially bound to so assume in this case, because the law, of which he pretended to be so tender, required that " the certificate shall set forth, according to the truth, the full name of every person voted for, *and in words at length the number of votes he received for any office.*"

The law, therefore, told him that the word about which he pretended to doubt was *not an abbreviation* but a number written in words *at length.* He gratuitously assumed the violation of this law by the county court making the certificate, as well as did violence to the commonest kind of common sense when he tortured these three letters into the word "twelve."

He knew furthermore that "twe" is not now, never was, and probably never will be amongst sane men an abbreviation of twelve, or of twenty, or of any number known to an American. And he knew again that the letters were intended to express a number, and that there is no number known to the English language written with three letters, the first of which is "t" and the second "w" except the single number *two*.

But even if it were conceded that there could possibly have been a doubt as to what the word meant, then it was a patent ambiguity, which any law student could have told the governor it was his duty to explain by evidence. This he was bound to do, and could very readily have done, as will clearly appear hereafter. Had it been impossible for him to do so, the only legal alternative remaining was to strike out the word altogether as insensible, and read the return 800.

Neither process would have given the certificate to the contestee. The governor therefore guessed enough to give to that gentleman three of a majority.

The true vote in Pleasants County for Jackson was 802, and not 812. Nobody now claims, nor did anybody ever claim, that it was in fact anything else.

Counsel for contestee, however, without attempting to defend a trick indefensible, ingeniously argued before the committee that the governor had no legal standard by which to explain the so-called doubtful word, and that no competent legal evidence has been produced by the contestant, to show that the true vote in Pleasants County was other than as counted by the governor.

The argument is, that under the laws of West Virginia the commissioners of the county court do not constitute in any proper sense a court of record, but are merely a returning board, having no judicial functions, except when making a recount, and no authority to evidence their action except by the issue of a single certificate, which is to be sent to and deposited with the governor.

Upon the faith of this proposition it is contended, that the only legal record evidence of the vote in Pleasants County, as ascertained by the county court, is the certificate sent to the governor, and that the certificates procured by the contestant from the clerks of the county courts and offered in evidence, showing the results of the elections in the several counties, are not competent evidence.

H. Mis. 137——2

These certificates, it is contended, were made without authority of law, and at the instance of a court having no right to make a record.

In support of this proposition counsel cited Brazie v. the Commissioners ot Fayette County, decided by the supreme court of West Virginia, and reported in 25 W. Va., p. 213. In the judgment of the committee, that case does not sustain the contention. The question material here does not seem to have been necessarily involved in the case at all. The case arose upon an application for a writ of prohibition, to restrain the commissioners of a county court from going into a judicial examination in an election case outside of the returns made to them, to ascertain whether the precinct commissioners had certified and returned certain votes not entitled to have been cast.

The court held, that the judicial functions of the county court in an uncontested election case did not extend beyond the ascertainment of the result from the papers laid before them, and whether such papers are in fact such genuine, intelligible, and substantially authenticated returns as are required by law.

True, in the course of the opinion the judge delivering it said, that if the power of the commissioners were enlarged so as to include powers beyond those mentioned they would be made a tribunal by implication only, and "a tribunal which keeps no record of its proceedings, and from whose judgment there lies no writ of error or appeal," but the case is as well decided without this sentence as with it; it has no reference to any question necessarily involved in the issue, and is the merest *dictum.* Moreover the record here referred to is not the record of what, under the court's decision, the commissioners of the county court had authority to do, but a record of what they had no power to do. It is not the existing tribunal of which the court is speaking, but of a tribunal to exist only by implication.

Even if it be conceded that the functions of the county court are ministerial, and that in their exercise it makes no such record as imparts absolute verity, and to which a bill of exceptions will lie, still it by no means follows that it makes no record at all. There is inherent in every such tribunal and necessarily incident to its very purpose and existence, the power to make such record as will perpetuate and make available its legitimate action. This is a principle of universal application.

But aside altogether from general principles it will sufficiently appear from an examination of the legislation of West Virginia on the subject of elections, taking that legislation as a whole, that the county court is more than a mere returning board.

To that court is intrusted the duty of fixing voting places. (Code, sec. 5, ch. 3.)

To it are intrusted also the power and duty of naming election commissioners. (*Ibid.*, sec. 6.)

To it are returned certificates from the district canvassers, the ballots cast, and one set of the poll-books. Its clerk is made by law the custodian of these records. (*Ibid.*, sec. 20.)

When about to exercise the functions of the county court with respect to election returns the commissioners *convene in special session.* The court so convened has power to summon witnesses, to administer oaths, "to make such orders as shall seem proper to procure correct returns, and ascertain the true result" of the election. It has power to make a recount, and is charged with the duty of so doing upon demand properly made. A court which is a mere returning board, of course, would not need to meet in *special session.* Such board necessarily would have only one kind of session, not two kinds, an *ordinary* and a *special* session.

Provision is expressly made by section 46, Acts 1881, chapter 5, for a complete record of all the proceedings of the county court, both those which relate to its general jurisdiction, exercised at its ordinary sessions, and those which relate to its exceptional jurisdiction exercised at its special sessions. The provision is:

The county court of every county shall provide two record books for the use of the court, in one of which shall be entered all the proceedings of the said court in relation to contested elections; all matters of probate; the appointment of appraisers of the estates of decedents, and the appointment and qualification of personal representatives, guardians, committees, and curators, and the settlement of their accounts; all matters relating to apprentices, *and in the other of said books shall be entered all the other proceedings of the said court.*

But in addition to the record thus provided for, there are other provisions of the law with which the position assumed by contestee's counsel and now under discussion are inconsistent.

By section 22 it is prescribed that when an election is held in a county or district for. any or all of some twenty-two different officers—State, county, and Federal—" the commissioners of the county court, or a majority of them, * * * shall carefully and impartially ascertain the result of the election in their county, and in each district thereof, and make out and sign *as many certificates thereof as may be necessary.* * * * The said commissioners shall sign *separate certificates* of the result of the election within their county *for each of the offices* specified in this section which is to be filled;" that is, *separate certificates* for *each* of the twenty different offices, State, county, and Federal.

Section 23, still preserving the plural number and speaking of certificates, makes provision for the disposition of these certificates. As to certain offices, *one* of the certificates is to go to the governor; as to certain other offices, *one* is to go to the secretary of state; as to certain offices, *one* is to go to some designated public officer; the *other* to the candidate elected.

In all cases, with respect to every office, it is the duty of the court to *sign separate certificates.* As, of the separate certificates directed to be made in the case of a candidate for Congress, *one* only is to go to the governor, and, as no provision is made for the giving of the other to the candidate or to any public officer, it necessarily remains with the clerk of the court.

By section 5 of chapter 130 (code of West Virginia)—

A copy of any record *or paper* in the clerk's office of any court, or in the office of the secretary of state, treasurer, or auditor, or in the office of surveyor of lands of any county attested by the officer in whose office the same is, may be admitted as evidence in lieu of the original.

*   *   *   *   *   *   *

Your committee are therefore clearly of the opinion that, under the laws of West Virginia, it was competent for the governor and it was his duty, to make intelligible if unintelligible the certificate as to the vote in Pleasant County, by consulting the certificate and record of that vote on file in the clerk's office of that county, and that in default of his having done so it is competent for them and is their duty now to do it.

It is conceded that ever since the passage of the West Virginia act of 1882, which we have been discussing, it has been the custom of the county court to keep on file a duplicate certificate, showing its conclusions with respect to the election of a Representative to Congress. Such being the case, even if your committee were not impressed with the belief that the argument now made by the contestee involves no more than a mere technicality without merit, they would still consider that the adoption by them now of a new construction of the law, contrary to that so long generally adhered to as the true one, would be on their part a crime not very much less than that practiced by the governor when he gave to the contestee the certificate that belonged to the contestant.

In other words, your committee believe, that if the case was one of doubt, as it is not, the practice for so many years of the parties who made the law of 1882, and of the parties for whom it was made in construction thereof, is conclusive upon them in this proceeding.

And they are of opinion that, on the face of the returns, the contestant was elected by a majority of 12, and was entitled to the governor's certificate of election.

Such being the case, the contestant is now to be treated as if he had received the certificate, and the onus is cast on the contestee to show that the returns, if truly made, would elect him. (Wallace *vs.* McKinley, Forty-eighth Congress.)

This he attempts to do in his brief submitted to the committee, by a series of propositions quite as technical and void of merit as is the contention by which he seeks to retain the benefit of the certificate wrongfully issued to him.

In eight districts, in which he had an aggregate vote of 588 and the contestant an aggregate vote of 1,083, he asks that the total vote be excluded from the count for various reasons, in one district for one reason and in another district for another. His proposition will be found to resolve itself into a demand that the voters of these eight districts shall be disfranchised for reasons with which the voters themselves had nothing at all to do, for no fault of theirs. No one will deny that to sustain this contention strong and convincing reasons must be assigned. And it is only fair to say, that the leading counsel for contestee in his argument before the committee, admitted the purely technical character of the objections to the vote in these eight precincts and declined to press them. As to one precinct only the argument was pressed by the assistant counsel of the contestee.

An examination of the reasons urged for the disfranchisement of the voters of the several precincts named, taking them in their order, will justify counsel in his concession as to their purely technical character.

The first precinct complained of is Ebenezer precinct in Calhoun County.

Here the contestant received 39 votes and the contestee 19. All are asked to be excluded because it is alleged that it does not appear that the commissioners who conducted the election were sworn.

The record shows that on the poll-book returned to the county clerk's office the oath appeared at length and in the form prescribed by law, subscribed by each and all the commissioners, but the jurat is irregular and indefinite. It reads as follows:

Subscribed and sworn to before me as one of the commissioners, L. F. Law, this —— day of November, 1888.

PETER CONLEY.

Both Law and Conley were commissioners, and either had the power to swear all the rest. It is very clear, even from the imperfect record, that all took the oath by subscribing to it, and that as to two at least the certificate is conclusive. Where part of the officers are sworn, others not, the election is valid. (Fuller *v.* Davison, 2 Bart., 126.) Two things are to be noted in this connection: first, that sworn or unsworn, all the commissioners were *de facto* election officers, and, second, that no harm resulted to any one, either the public or an individual voter, from their failure to be regularly sworn. All authorities agree that the acts of *de facto* officers are to be accepted and treated as valid so far as the public and the candidates are concerned. (Paine on Elections, sec. 373. and cases cited.) It is a well-settled principle of law, and a very ancient one, "that the act of an officer *de facto*, where it is for his own benefit, is void * * * but where it is for the benefit of strangers, or the public, who are presumed to be ignorant of such defect of title, it is good." (Cro Eliz, 699.)

It has been repeatedly held that a certificate of unsworn officers even, is prima facie, and the burden is on the contestant to show that the errors committed affected the result or rendered it uncertain. (Taylor *vs.* Taylor, 10 Min., 107; Whipley *vs.* McCune, 10 Cal., 352.)

It is contended, however, that this principle does not apply in this case because the law of West Virginia provides:

The said oath shall appear properly certified on one of the poll-books of every election, and in no case shall the vote taken at any place of voting be counted unless said oath so appears, *or unless* it be proved to the satisfaction of the commissioners of the county court, convened at the court-house, as hereinafter required, that the oath was taken before said commissioners, canvassers, and clerks entered upon the discharge of their duties.

But the contention must fail and the argument be against the contestee for the manifest reason, that unless the oath had been taken the votes at this precinct could not have been counted. The taking of the oath was to be made to appear *either* upon the poll-books *or* by proof to the satisfaction of the county commissioners. These commissioners had power, "if deemed necessary, to require the attendance of any of the commissioners or canvassers, or other officers or persons present at the election, to answer questions under oath respecting the same, and to make such other orders as shall seem proper to procure correct returns and ascertain the true result of the said election in their county."

The commissioners of the county court must be presumed to have done all things within their power necessary to be done in the performance of their duty in accordance with law. They can not be presumed to have done anything unlawful. The votes could not have been lawfully counted unless the election officers appear to have been sworn, either by the evidence of the poll-book or by other evidence satisfactory to the commissioners. The votes were counted, and if it be true that the swearing of the officers is not proven by the poll-book, it must have been otherwise proven to the satisfaction of the commissioners.

No reason, therefore, has been shown why your committee should disfranchise the voters of this district.

The next district sought to be disfranchised in the interest of the contestee is Kentuck precinct, Jackson County, where there were 152 votes for contestant and 72 for contestee.

The complaint here is that no vote was returned on the poll-books by the precinct commissioners nor any certificate in the case of the candidates for Congress.

The law of West Virginia (section 18, chapter 3, Code) requires that upon the close of the polls there shall be read from the ballots, one at a time by one of the commissioners, the designations of the offices to be filled and the names of the persons voted for for each office.

The ballot shall then be handed to another of the commissioners, who if satisfied that it was correctly read, shall string it on a thread.

The contents of the ballots as they are read shall be entered by the clerks under the supervision of the commissioners on tally papers for the purpose by suitable marks made opposite to or under the name of each person for any office to be filled.

[Sec. 20] "As soon as the results are ascertained the commissioners or a majority of them * * * at each place of voting shall make out and sign two certificates thereof [according to a prescribed form] and transmit one to the clerk of the county court. They shall also seal up the ballots, and send them with one set of the poll-books to the said clerk."

A reference to the certificate (Record, pp. 341-2-3 ; 351-2) will show that the certificates were made and signed by the commissioners holding the election, and returned to the clerks of the county and circuit court, as required by law, but that the names of contestant and contestee did not appear in said certificate, nor the office for which they were candidates and received votes. But their names were on the ballots cast at said precinct for said office, and the ballots were counted by the commissioners of election, and their names were written down by them on the tally-sheets opposite or under the designation of the office for which they received votes, and the number of votes which each received was designated on said tally-sheets, to wit, 152 for contestant and 72 for contestee, in the same manner as was done with respect to the names of all other candidates voted for at said election, and the tally-sheets were returned with the certificates and the ballots to the clerk of the county court. The aggregate votes appearing thereby to have been cast for contestant and contestee were one less than the highest number appearing to have been cast for any other two opposing candidates. When these papers reached the commissioners of the county court, counsel for contestee demanded a recount of the votes for Jackson County, as to Representative in Congress, as he had the lawful right to do. Under this demand the commissioners of the county court recounted all the ballots cast for Representative in Congress in that county, and upon that recount the number of votes appearing to have been cast for the contestant and contestee were the same as appeared upon said tally-sheets, and including these votes, the result in the county was, for contestant, 2,272 votes, and for contestee, 1,886 votes. And this result was certified to the governor.

The only irregularity here seems to have been a clerical error, in the failure of the election commissioners to insert in the certificate the result of the election at that precinct as to Representative in Congress. They did ascertain the result and wrote it correctly on the tally-sheets, and when the county commissioners counted the ballots at the demand of contestee's counsel, they obtained the same result, and the ballots were there and inspected by the commissioners, and presumably by the contestee's attorney who made the demand for recount.

But this failure of the commissioners of election to make return of the votes at this precinct could not have the effect to disfranchise the persons who voted here, and the law of West Virginia especially provides for such a case. In declaring the powers and duties of the county commissioners in ascertaining and declaring the result of the election in their respective counties, the following language is used:

They may, if deemed necessary, require the attendance of any of the commissioners or canvassers or other officers or persons present at the election, to answer questions under oath respecting the same, and may make such other orders as shall seem proper to procure correct returns and ascertain the true result of the said election in their county.

The presumption as well as the proof is, that the county commissioners ascertained, by the exercise of their powers of examination, the true result of the election, and certified accordingly. There is no pretense that they did not.

Counsel for contestee say that he, the contestee, made no demand for a recount of the vote at this precinct, and argue that the fact of such demand should appear of record. There is no law requiring the demand to be made matter of record. There is no record of demand made in any precinct, though contestee admits having made such demand in some. There is affirmative proof (Record, p. 724) that demand was made for a recount in this precinct by contestee's attorney, and neither the attorney nor the contestant was called to rebut this evidence.

The matter does not seem material, nor to merit discussion, since there is no pretense that the commissioners in the exercise of their legitimate functions did not ascertain the true vote in this precinct; no pretense that it was not truly declared; no pretense that any voter suffered anything by the alleged irregularity; in fact, nothing to take this case out of the ordinary rule of law, that statutes directing the mode of proceeding of public officers are directory merely, unless there is something in the statute itself which plainly shows a different intent.

Contestee further claims that the returns from Pine Log precinct, Jackson County, should be excluded. His charge is that "there was such misconduct and fraudulent acts upon the part of those who conducted the election as to render such poll and the votes cast respectively for contestant and for contestee null and void; that is, 139 votes for contestant and 92 votes for contestee."

From the evidence the facts appear to be as follows: Thomas Rorden, John McKown, and W. T. Dernberger were the commissioners conducting the election at this precinct. C. C. Nesselrood, a witness for contestee (p. 317-18) testifies, that the votes were counted during the night following the day of the election, and that he remained there while the vote was being counted and until it was completed; that after midnight witness went to sleep and awoke after sleeping about two hours; that when he awoke Dernberger, one of the commissioners, was asleep on a bench, and McKown, another of them, was smoking in the back part of the house; and the other commissioner, Rorden, was being assisted in the counting by W. E. Dernberger, son of the commissioner, and W. H. Rorden and Asberry Davis were stringing the votes; that Dernberger, the commissioner, and his son were both Democrats, the former being a member of the Democratic county committee; that Davis is a Democrat, and took the place of McKown in the counting. By inference, therefore, McKown is a Democrat, and Rorden was the Republican commissioner. This is the only witness who testifies as to the conduct of the election at that precinct.

The evidence does not show that the ballot-box was in the custody of any one of the commissioners so as to require it to be sealed. Even if it was out of the custody of Dernberger, from the fact that he was asleep, it was not out of that of McKown who was present in the room, and the counting proceeded under his observation, and his place was filled in the operation of counting by a Democrat. There is not the slightest evidence tending to show that there was any tampering with the ballot or returns, or any fraud of any character. All that was done was in the presence of at least two of the commissioners who were awake.

It appears from the evidence of Lemley (pp. 724-'5) that the return from this precinct did not show any votes for contestee, but 139 votes

for contestant, a mere clerical error in failing to write into the return
contestee's vote, but, under the recount which was demanded by contestee, the votes for him at this precinct were counted by the commissioners of the county court, and the number of them, 93, included in
their return to the governor.

It is to be observed that no allegation of any specific act of fraud is
alleged. Your committee are asked to presume that fraud was committed because it might have been committed, and this in the absence
of any pretense that a single legal vote was excluded from, or a single
illegal vote was included in, the result announced.

Your committee do not know of any principle of law that would
justify them in so finding. They understand the law to be as declared
in Mann v. Cassidy (1 Brewster (Penna.), 60).

An allegation of fraud committed by election officers is immaterial unless it be also
stated that the result has been affected.

The votes in Pine Log precinct should be counted as returned.

The next precinct complained of is Boyer precinct, Putnam County.
Contestee charges that the voting place in this precinct, established
by order of the county court, was McGill's post-office, but that the
election was held at Isaac's Branch school-house, from one-half to three-
quarters of a mile distant from the post-office. (Record, p. 33.) The
evidence tends to prove the above statement, but it is not claimed, nor
does the evidence tend to show that any person was deceived or prevented from voting thereby. Two witnesses only are examined by contestee in relation to this precinct, and one of them (Fowler, pp. 408–9)
says that it was his understanding from the time he knew of the election, that it was to be held at the Isaac's Branch school-house, and that
every voter in the precinct voted at said voting place, at said election,
except one, and he was too sick to go to the polls. The other witness
(Dunlap, p. 410), corroborates Fowler generally, and in addition, says
that the school election in 1887 was held at the same place. So that
contestee, by his own witnesses, proves that no voter was wronged out
of his vote, and that he was not injured by this change of voting places.

This case calls for the application of the rule which protects the
voter against disfranchisement from the default of a public officer when
such default has resulted in no injury to any one. (Farrington v. Turner, 53 Mich., 27; People v. Simonson, 5 N. Y., 22; Steele v. Calhoun,
61 Miss., 556.)

The next precinct asked to be excluded presents facts very similar to
the last, and is governed by the same principles.

Thomas School-House precinct, Putnam County: Contestee contends
that the legal voting place for this precinct was the residence of Josiah
C. Thomas, and that the election was held at the Thomas School-House,
about three-quarters of a mile distant from said residence.

Josiah C. Thomas is the only witness examined in relation to this objection and he was introduced by contestee (Record, pp. 410–11). He says
that the voting place was established at his house in 1849 or 1850 by an
act of the legislature of Virginia. This is not the way to prove an act of
the legislature. It probably amounts however to proof that this was the
voting place of the precinct by common consent, for he says they continued to vote there down to and including the Presidential election of
1880, that soon thereafter he spoke to some parties to have it changed,
that word afterwards came that it had been changed to the school-
house, that this was generally understood, and that every election since
1880, including the one in question, has been held at the school-house,

and that that has been the voting place of the precinct since that time according to common understanding.

Under this evidence, one of these places seems to have been established by custom, or common consent. At the time of the election the school-house was the legal voting place, and the subsequent order of the county court fixing it as the legal voting place was unnecessary, as it had already before that time recognized it as such by counting and considering the votes at former elections there cast. There is no possible pretext for assailing this precinct.

The contestant, in his notice of contest, specified three precincts where the election was not held at places designated by law, viz., Sandyville, Jackson County; Reedy and Curtis, in Roane County, at each of which the contestee received majorities greater in the aggregate than the majority received by contestant at the precincts challenged, for like reasons, by the contestee in his reply. The facts are about the same in the cases on both sides. No voter appears to have been deprived of an opportunity of voting by reason of the fact that the election was not held at the place designated by law.

The contestant did not press these objections made in his notice of contest. If he had they must have been overruled upon the principle already announced.

In Walton precinct, Roane County, the contestee claims that the ballot-box was in the custody of one of the commissioners of election alone, in violation of law, and that the vote at this precinct, where contestant had 131 plurality, should be rejected for this reason.

The section of the law relating to this subject is as follows (Code, ch. 3, sec. 14):

- The ballot-box shall have an aperture in the lid or top thereof to receive the ballots of voters. While the polls are open it shall be kept where it may be seen by the voters, and after the polls are closed, and until the votes are counted and the certificates of the result are signed, shall remain in the immediate custody of the commissioner, or any one of them, with the consent of the others. But it shall not be opened unless two of them at least be present, and if left at any time in the custody of one of the number, shall be carefully sealed so that it can not be opened or any ballot taken therefrom or entered therein without breaking the seal, and the others shall write their names across the place or places where it is sealed.

The facts are as follows:

The ballot-box was a firm wooden box with a sliding lid with a hole through the top to receive the ballots. There was a lock on the box but no key to it; the lid would slide easily; the lid was fastened with a nail which could be drawn out with the fingers. The commissioners of election were N. K. Walker, H. O. Rock, and J. C. Garvin; the first two Democrats and the last a Republican; on the day of the election the commissioners went to dinner at a hotel near by, and Garvin had the box; there was a seal over the aperture in the lid (p. 469); Garvin finished dinner first and took the box under his arm and went to a store about thirty or forty steps from the hotel, and in not more than five minutes Walker followed him there; contestee's witness says if box was sealed ballots could not have been put in or abstracted without the same being detected, but could if it was not sealed. They commenced counting ballots in the evening of the 6th and continued until 3 a. m., of the 7th, then took a recess until after breakfast and finished counting at 10 p. m. of the 7th. The counting was done at Mr. Riley's hotel upstairs; during the count on the 7th they halted for a rest and Walker and Rock went out and left Garvin and the two clerks with the ballot-box, which was then sealed. Walker returned in a few minutes and found only Garvin and Chris. Summers, both Republicans, in the room, standing, one on either side of the table on which the ballot-box was. Walker testifies for contestee that he saw nothing in the conduct of Garvin or Summers which led him to suppose that there had been any tampering with the ballot-box, and that there was nothing to indicate that there had been; that he knew Garvin well, and did not believe he did or would tamper with the ballot-box, or permit it to be done; that the result of the election was about as usual at that precinct, and nothing in it to indicate that there was any tampering; and that the number of ballots tallied with the number of names on the poll-books. There is a total absence of evidence tending to show any fraud or improper practices on the part of any one in conducting the election.

The evidence fails to show that the box was "left at any time in the custody of one of the number" in contemplation of the law. While they were at dinner it was as much in the custody of the one who did not have manual possession as it was in his who did. Besides, at that time it was sealed. On the other occasion it was not left in Garvin's custody in contemplation of law or in fact. The others stepped out only momentarily. The sealing was to be done only when the two turned it over to the third, thereby expressly charging him with the custody.

Besides, if there was any violation of law it was only technical, and did not tend to the injury or prejudice of the contestee, and can not deprive the voters of the right of having their votes counted as cast.

The same rule of law applied with respect to Walton precinct applies here. There was no evidence of bad faith or injurious results, nor was the result of the election rendered unreliable by reason of anything charged against the election officers.

The innocent voters of this precinct can not be disfranchised upon a mere presumption of fraud, even if the circumstances would justify it, as they do not.

The objection made to the vote of the Murphy's Mill precinct is of such a frivolous character as to merit but little discussion. It is, that the oath of the precinct commissioner does not appear properly certified on the poll-book. It was not properly certified because Marion J. Bickle, a justice of the peace who administered it, signed the jurat "Marion J. Bickle, in and for Clay district, Wood county, W. Va.," omitting the words "justice of the peace" after his name.

He was in point of fact, a justice of the peace as the evidence shows. The less comment made on this objection the better, one would think, for the contestee.

The next objection is like unto the last, and relates to Wadesville precinct, Wood County. The objection here again relates to an alleged irregularity in the *jurat.* The oath was administered by T. J. Sands, one of the commissioners of election, but he omitted to sign with his official title.

That the oath was administered by him, that he was a commissioner and by law authorized to administer it, are facts not capable of being called in question.

The matter does not seem to merit discussion.

Bearing in mind that the contestant was in the first instance entitled to the governor's certificate and had a majority of twelve, it appears from our examination of the case thus far, that he still retains that majority, and we address ourselves to the question as to whether it has been overcome by proof as to the illegal votes claimed to have been cast on both sides.

To qualify one to vote in West Virginia he must be a male citizen of the United States, twenty-one years of age, must have resided in the State for one year next preceding the election, in the county sixty days, and must be a bona fide resident of the election district in which he claims the right to vote. Paupers, convicts, and persons of unsound mind are not voters.

By the record and briefs filed in this contest, a large number of votes are attacked by both parties. In considering these votes so attacked the committee deem it proper to state generally the rules by which they have been governed in determining the question of legality or illegality, and for whom the votes were cast.

First. A vote accepted by the commissioners holding the election is *prima facie* legal. Before it can be thrown out for illegality it must be satisfactorily shown by the evidence to have been cast by one not legally qualified to vote—that is to say, the presumption of legality must be overcome by a clear preponderance of competent evidence.

By competent evidence we mean such evidence as would be admitted on the trial of the issue before a judicial tribunal, except where a relaxation of the rule is made necessary by the nature of the issue.

No provision is made by the statutes of West Virginia to ascertain what particular ballot any voter has deposited after it has been once placed in the ballot-box. Therefore in this case it becomes necessary to ascertain for which candidate a vote was given by other means than the ticket itself.

It seems to have been taken for granted by both parties that the voters themselves could not be compelled to disclose how they voted. It may be remarked in this connection that one who would knowingly cast an illegal vote ought not to be regarded as the most reliable witness. On the other hand, when he has been honestly mistaken, we can see no reason why such voter ought not to be trusted as a witness.

In order, then, to prevent illegal voting with impunity, it becomes necessary to determine what kind of testimony shall be received in ascertaining which candidate got the benefit of the illegal vote. The committee have followed the rule which appears to them to be the most reasonable, as well as the best sustained by authority.

In the absence of direct proof, evidence showing to what political party the voter belonged, whose election he advocated, whose friends maintained his right to vote, and kindred testimony, has been held admissible. Of course what the voter said at the time of voting is admissible as a part of the *res gesta*.

But what a voter said after the day of the election, either as to his qualifications, or how he voted, or whether he voted, the committee hold to be inadmissible in the absence of other testimony on the point. If such testimony can be admitted at all, which we do not concede, it certainly ought not to be received when the statement of the voter is made after the legality of his vote has been called in question. To admit this kind of testimony is to place it in the power of one not entitled to vote to have his illegal vote counted twice against the party he desires to defeat, without subjecting himself to cross-examination, and without even the formality of testifying under oath.

Again, one legally qualified may, by statements after he has voted, make himself out to be disqualified without incurring any penalty, and in that way have his legal vote given to one party counted as illegal against another party. One who has not voted at all may in the same way be proved to have voted. In a close contest, with party feeling running high—perhaps party control involved—the admission of this

kind of testimony would be doubly dangerous. It has nothing to commend it except a class of decisions whose authority has been weakened,
if not destroyed, by later and better considered adjudications. The
committee reject all such testimony as being mere hearsay of the most
dangerous kind when standing alone. When the only evidence of how
a man voted, or whether he was a legal voter, is the unsworn statement
of the voter after the election, we have let the vote stand.

In regard to what constitutes a person of unsound mind we have
adopted the rules substantially as laid down by American courts and
text-book writers and hold that a person having sufficient intelligence
to make a valid will, or to bind himself by ordinary contracts, or to be
criminally responsible for his acts, is a person of sound mind. One
whose will would be held invalid, for no other reason than mental in-
capacity, is a person of unsound mind.

In the record we find the oft-recurring question, "Was the voter in
your opinion a man of unsound mind," put to a non-professional witness without any attempt to define what was meant by unsoundness of
mind. To the answer to such question, unaccompanied by any explanation of what the witness understood by the term, we attach very little
weight.

The condition of the voter, his acts and speech, how he is regarded
by those who know him, as to his competency to contract, judicial de-
terminations, and the like evidence has been given due weight. The
term idiot is so well understood that the statement of a witness that a
person is an idiot is given more weight, as being the statement of a fact
within the knowledge of the witness, and not a mere opinion.

With these rules in view the determination of the legality of a vote
only requires a fair and intelligent consideration of the evidence. Upon
the question of what constitutes a pauper, there is some disagreement
in the authorities, but we think the following may be taken as a fair definition: A pauper is one who is continuously supported in whole or in
part out of funds provided by the public authorities for that purpose.
One who has been a public charge, and afterwards becomes self-supporting for a sufficient time before the election to show that his ability
to support himself is not a mere temporary condition, may legally vote.

One who, under temporary misfortune or sickness, receives public
aid, but is ordinarily self-supporting, is not a pauper.

The law which determines the question of residence is so well settled
that it does not need a restatement by the committee; the difficulty is
in the application of the law to the evidence.

Absence from the place claimed as a residence, for temporary purposes, does not work abandonment, but in this case some of the witnesses and some of the commissioners of election seem to have had the
view that a voting residence might be retained by the simple statement
of intention to retain a certain place as a voting residence, although an
actual residence had been taken up elsewhere, with no fixed intention
of ever again actually living at the place where the right to vote is
claimed. Others seem to think that they can establish a new residence
by intention before actually and in fact moving to the new place.

We do not concur in these views. It takes both act and intention to
establish a residence, and an intention to retain a residence which has
been left must be an intention actually to return to it and reside in it.

Some votes in this record are questioned on account of disputed or
doubtful boundary lines. The committee have not thought it their
duty to go into an investigation of disputed boundaries, but have
counted all votes as legal when the voters were otherwise qualified and

voted in good faith in the district where they believed that they had their residence, and where they had been in the habit of voting.

Applying the foregoing rules we now propose to consider the separate votes without attempting to discuss each vote at any length.

Contestee in his brief substantially concedes that the following votes cast for him were illegal and ought to be deducted from his vote.

Ephriam Hensley, non-resident.	W. W. Bromfield, Wayne County.
W. J. Gilmore, non-resident.	Alderson Watts, jr., Wayne County.
C. D. Stalnaker, minor.	William Noe, Wayne County.
Charles Reynolds, non-resident.	C. O. Bellomy, Wayne County.
John C. Deaton, pauper.	Elias Browning, Wayne County.
James Powell, unsound mind.	W. Y. Woodring, non-resident.
Henry Reynolds, non-resident.	Noble Hunter, convict.
Grant Griffith, minor.	John Cochran, pauper.
Napoleon Adkins, Wayne County.	Frederick Schwall, pauper.
W S. Napier, Wayne County.	Michael Hobart, non-resident.

making twenty conceded illegal votes, one of which, Frederick Schwall, we deduct, as the concession grows out of testimony which the committee do not consider competent.

Two or three of these votes contestee insists should not be charged against him, because not named in contestant's notice of contest.

One of them, Michael Hobart, was challenged by contestee in his reply. The vote was illegal and cast for contestee. The committee think that a vote challenged in the notice by either party is a proper subject of investigation.

Two others were not named in either notice. The pleadings in this case are more specific than the practice before the committee requires. As a general rule parties ought to be bound by their pleadings, but where neither party has been taken by surprise, and both have entered into the investigation, the rule should be relaxed in the interest of justice.

The evidence in regard to these voters was taken a month before contestee commenced examining his witnesses, the witnesses impeaching the votes were cross-examined on this branch of their testimony, and the contestee should be held to have waived his objections.

In a final summary of his claims contestant has conceded that he has failed to establish his charges with reference to a number of named voters, and that the evidence in regard to others places them in the doubtful list. As to all such we have not felt it our duty to examine the evidence, as we take the admission to amount to a waiver. Although as to some of them it may be said it takes all the benefit of presumptions to hold them valid.

Of these claimed to be fully established as having been illegally cast for contestee, the committee hold that the following should be held to have been illegally voted for contestee:

W. R. Surratt, non-resident.	Abram Jones, pauper.
Wm. Gibson, minor.	Thomas Stinson, non-resident.
John Starcher, minor.	James Dillen, non-resident.
Jacob L. Starcher, non-resident.	Walter Dillen, non-resident.
John Carney, unsound mind.	Ali Artrip, minor.
O. J. Simmons, non-resident.	John Cox, non-resident.
Oliver Burns, non-resident.	A. Kaminsky, non-resident.
Reese Stratton, unsound mind.	Lazarus Wainer, non-resident.
W. A. Palmer, non-resident.	George Dean, minor.
E. J. Long, non-resident.	Henry Yearing, non-resident.
Dr. W. S. Reese, non-resident.	Joseph Starling, non-resident.
J. D. Summers, non-resident.	E. D. Lewis, minor.
N. B. Armstrong, non-resident.	James Bolyard, minor.
John Ball, unsound mind.	

Twenty-seven in all—or forty-seven illegal ballots voted for contestee.

W. H. Surratt (Record, pp. 58–62, 269–280): This voter seems to be one of those whose residence at the place of voting was one of mere intention. His home and business were elsewhere at the time of voting and at the time of taking testimony. His intention seemed to be to retain a voting residence at his former home, without any fixed intention of ever resuming it as an actual residence.

Wm. Gibson, John Starcher, minors (Record, pp. 63–66–7, 70–1, 296, 302, 307): The most trustworthy testimony in this case, fixed by written documents, shows that these voters were minors.

Jacob L. Starcher (Record, pp. 87, 88, 89, 350) moved from West Virginia to the West in 1886 and back in 1888; claimed that he had not lost his residence; but in January, 1889, he made oath that his residence was in Minnesota on April 1, 1888, and by so doing secured a release of taxes. He can not be heard to say that he had retained a residence in West Virginia against the fact of two years' actual residence with his family in another State and his declaration on oath designed to affect his property rights.

John Carney (Record, pp. 83, 88, 89, 91, 327, 332, 336): The preponderance of evidence shows this man to be entirely irresponsible for his acts. On application of his brother a committee or conservator was appointed for him. It is said the clerk who made the appointment had no legal authority for his act. Be that as it may, it shows the estimate of his family and those who knew him best.

O. J. Simmons, non-resident (Record, pp. 83, 87, 333): Left West Virginia and moved to Ohio a year or more before the election and voted there. Claimed that his vote in Ohio was illegal, as he intended to retain a residence in West Virginia. His act was inconsistent with such intention.

Oliver Burnes: Was a resident of Ohio at the time of the election, having permanently moved from West Virginia. This does not seem to be controverted, but it is claimed that inasmuch as his name does not appear in the notice of contest the vote can not be considered. We have previously referred in this report to this class of votes, and this one falls fully within the rule announced.

Reese Stratton: This voter was not far removed from idiocy.

W. A. Palmer, non-resident (Record, pp. 97–98, 365–366): Became of age in May, 1888; lived with his father in Ohio, and moved with the family to West Virginia in March, 1888. His father rented a farm in West Virginia the previous fall and seeded it, but did not move to it until the following spring. The son helped the father do the seeding, then returned to Ohio, and went to school during the winter. There is no possible question about the illegality of this vote.

E. J. Long, non-resident: Clearly not a resident of West Virginia long enough to obtain a voting residence. Objected to on the same ground as the vote of Oliver Burns, already discussed.

Dr. W. S. Reese, non-resident: Moved to Ohio before the election with his family. His claimed intention to return to West Virginia was conditional. He not only did not carry out his claimed intention, which is a circumstance against him, but a few days after election abandoned all intention to return, and acknowledged himself a permanent resident of Ohio.

Dr. J. D. Summers (Record, pp. 146, 149, 155, 475, 476): Not a resident of the county sixty days.

The voter made arrangements to rent a house in the county on the 5th day of September, 1888, but did not move to it till the 17th.

Claimed to be a resident because of his intention to become one. It requires the conjunction of act and intention to establish a residence.

N. B. Armstrong (Record, pp. 149, 151, 155, 473): Voted in Roane County, but had not lived in the county sixty days. Had a farm in Roane County. Rented it, and moved to Wirt County in 1886. Claimed that he did not intend to abandon his residence in Roane County, but voted in Wirt County in the fall of 1886, which act concludes him to have intended to establish his residence there. He says himself that he can not say that he moved his family back sixty days before the election.

John Ball: This man was not far removed from idiocy.

John Stinson: Voted in Wayne County, and lived in Logan County. Moved from Wayne to Logan in th · spring of 1888. He was examined by the commissioners and his vote admitted on a ruling that he had not permanently abandoned his former residence. The uncontradicted testimony is against his right and the voter was not called, although it appears that he could have been. This is one of the cases in which the ruling was based upon a misunderstanding of the law, and of what kind of intention it takes to retain a residence.

James Dillen, Walter Dillen, non-residents: Father and son; moved from Kentucky less than a year before the election.

Ali Artrip, minor, (Record, pp. 179, 202, 204, 481, 486–487): We think there can be no question but that this voter was a minor. All the admissible testimony is to that effect.

John Cox, non-resident: Moved to Kentucky and engaged in business as a resident, paying taxes, working roads, etc. We think his return to West Virginia was an afterthought, arising from the gift of some land to his wife by her father. There is more doubt about this voter than any other considered, but the committee thinks it the safer rule to exclude his vote.

A. Kaminski, Lazarus Wainer, non-residents: They were Russian peddlers, naturalized in Baltimore, September, 1888, and proved that they had resided there for a year next preceding the election, as shown by the certificate of naturalization. They traveled around in West Virginia. Can not be heard to contradict their naturalization papers.

George Dean, minor: This voter swears he was of age when he voted—but the other evidence in the case shows that he did not tell the truth. He seems to have thought that he was doing.a smart thing in taking contestant by surprise, and contestee insists that contestant shall not be permitted to contradict his own witness. We do not so understand the law when applied to circumstances of this kind.

Henry Yearing, non-resident: This vote was clearly illegal, but it does not certainly appear for whom it was cast.

Joseph Starling, non-resident: Clearly illegal. Dispute as to how he voted. Considering all the legal evidence we do not think there is much room for doubt.

E. D. Lewis, minor: The most satisfactory evidence is that he was a minor.

James Bolyard, minor: Admitted that the vote was illegal, but objected to on the ground of want of notice—which we have already considered.

Deducting Yearing's vote, and it leaves 26 votes to be added to the 20 admitted; in all, 46 illegal votes cast for contestee, which, with the 12 plurality on the face of the returns, makes 58 plurality for contestant, which entitles him to a seat unless a larger number of illegal votes were cast for him.

Contestant concedes that the following votes given to him were illegal:

George Christian, non-resident.	George H. Rice, non-resident.
Isaac Dotson, pauper.	Wesley McDonald, non-resident.
P. Wayne, minor.	Henry Cunningham, non-resident.

The committee think that the following are clearly proven:

Randolph Ferrill, minor.	John Hall, convict.
J. G. Mooney, minor.	John Mitchell, non-resident.
Benjamin Singer, non-resident.	John Woernlinger, foreigner.
Robert Treet, pauper.	Peter Trent, non-resident.
B. F. Blusing, non-resident.	Spencer Dean, non-resident.
T. J. Hurlburt, non-resident.	Daniel Smith, non-resident.

Eighteen altogether.

There are others who clearly were not entitled to vote; but as to some of them, as was the case with votes charged to have been cast for contestee and not considered by the committee, it does not appear that they voted; as to others it neither appears for whom they voted nor with what party they affiliated, unless it be by what they stated after the election and after the legality of their votes had been called in question.

Fourteen other votes, laborers on a railroad, are attacked on the ground that they had not lived in West Virginia for a year, were not residents of the district where they voted, and were employés of a corporation.

As to some of them it clearly appears that they had lived in the State a sufficient time to entitle them to vote. As to none of them is it shown by competent testimony that they had not been so resident, and the presumption is in their favor.

They belonged to a construction gang which had its headquarters where they voted; to this point they constantly returned; received their mail there; had their washing done there, and had a right to fix their residence there. Their employment by a corporation did not give them a residence, but it did not prevent them from acquiring one. Some had voted there a year before. We think the presumption of legality is in no way overcome by the evidence.

William Wix, a minor, attacked by contestant and claimed by contestee to have voted for contestant is a somewhat peculiar case. His mother and sister, with whom he lived and who testify to his minority, are Democrats of a pronounced type. On the morning of the election his sister says she asked him to vote for the Democrats, but that he declared his intention to vote Republican, and on the same evening told her he had done so. It is a little strange that knowing he was a minor his mother and sister should be sending him off to the polls and urging him to vote for their candidates, considering the testimony which they subsequently gave. At the polls he was challenged by a Republican, waited until his challenger was out of the way, and while yet at the election declared he had voted the Democratic ticket.

We think it too uncertain how he voted to charge his vote to either party.

M. E. Polsne is another voter challenged by contestant. Placed on the stand by contestee to prove himself a legal voter, on cross-examination he stated such facts as showed he was not, and then volunteered the statement, not in response to any question by either party, that while voting the Democratic ticket he nevertheless voted for contestant, and upon that testimony it is now insisted that this vote ought to be charged against contestant.

This testimony was peculiar to say the least, and is subject to grave suspicion, but as the witness was not impeached by subsequent testimony we allow the charge and count the vote as illegal.

This gives 19 illegal votes for contestant, and leaves the actual plurality for contestant 39, which, in the judgment of the committee, is as near a correct statement of the true vote as can be given from all the evidence before us, and we so report.

The committee, therefore, report the following resolutions, and recommend their passage:

Resolved, That James M. Jackson was not elected as a Representative to the Fifty-first Congress from the Fourth Congressional district of West Virginia, and is not entitled to the seat.

Resolved, That Charles B. Smith was duly elected as a Representative from the Fourth Congressional district of West Virginia to the Fifty-first Congress, and is entitled to his seat as such.

H. Mis. 137——3

VIEWS OF THE MINORITY,

The various rulings of the governor of West Virginia, upon which the certificate was issued to Jackson, were in accordance with law, but there being other evidence now in the record showing that the returns counted by the committee correspond in each case to the vote actually cast, the minority so count. Believing, however, that the number of illegal votes proved by the record to have been cast for contestant in excess of the number proved to have been cast for contestee is sufficient to overcome the plurality thus indicated for contestant, the right of contestee to his seat is sustained.

35

VIEWS OF THE MINORITY.

Mr. CRISP, from the Committee on Elections, submits the following as the views of the minority:

We have heard read that portion of the report of the majority relating to the law of the case, and in the main we agree with the view therein expressed; at least in the application of the law to this case there seems to be no very important difference between us. Under the law of West Virginia the returns of the vote cast at the various precincts or voting places in each county must on the fifth day (Sundays excepted) after every election be by the officers having charge of the ballots, poll-books, and certificates placed before the commissioners of the county court, who are required to convene in special session on that day for the examination of such certificates or returns. Upon the demand of any candidate voted for, such commissioners are required to open the sealed packages of ballots and recount the same. Such commissioners shall carefully and impartially ascertain the result of the election in their county and make out and sign as many certificates thereof as may be necessary, dependent upon the number of officials voted for.

In the case of an election for Representative in Congress the commissioners transmit their certificate of the result to the governor, who ascertains who is elected and makes proclamation thereof. The certificate of the commissioners of Calhoun County under date of November 12, 1888, duly transmitted to the governor of West Virginia, show that C. B. Smith, contestant, received 630 votes. The county court of said county, on January 7, 1889, entered an order changing the vote of Smith to 632, an increase of 2 votes over the original return or certificate. The commissioners for Ritchie County sent two certificates to the governor, one dated November 13, 1888, showing that Smith received 1,972 votes, and the other dated November 14, 1888, showing that Smith received 1,973 votes, the later certificate showing one more vote for Smith than the earlier. The governor held in both these cases that he was bound to act upon the certificates earliest in date, for the reason that when the commissioners, acting as a board of canvassers under the law, made and transmitted to him their certificate of the result and adjourned their powers ceased, and both the order of the county court, correcting the first return from Calhoun County, and the second certificate from Ritchie County were illegal, unauthorized, and void.

The undersigned are inclined to think the governor was right in his view of the law; but inasmuch as we are satisfied, from other evidence contained in the record, that the later returns show the true state of the vote in these counties, and inasmuch as we are not by the law restricted in our investigation as was the governor, we accept such later returns and give to contestant all he claims, to wit; 632 votes in Calhoun County and 1,973 votes in Ritchie County.

Perhaps it should be here stated that counsel for contestant appeared before the governor and insisted that the law required the governor to determine the result of the election from the face of the returns or certificates, insisting he had no right to seek or look to any other source of information. Alter argument the governor decided this view correct, and held he could not go behind the returns.

The commissioners of Pleasant County certified to the governor that "J. M. Jackson received eight hundred and *twe* votes." On this question the governor, in his order-book declaring the result of the election, says:

The words and letters are too plain for any mistake. For the reasons heretofore given there is no authority to go behind the returns. The vote certified must be counted if enough appears to ascertain the meaning. In an action upon a note it was held: "There was no error in admitting the note sued on in evidence, because the amount thereof is written four *hund* and two and 50-100 dollars." (*Glenn* vs. *Porter*, 72 Ind., p. 525.)

So it has been held that the abbreviation in a declaration, "Damages one *thous* dollars" is not error. (1 W. L. J., Mich., 395.)

If enough appear to make the return intelligible it should be made so.

This can not be done without striking out one letter and inserting another, or by supplying the seemingly omitted letters. Acting upon the face of the paper the latter appears more in consonance with adjudged cases. The least number would give Jackson eight hundred and twelve votes. It will be so entered.

After carefully considering the evidence contained in the record—evidence wholly outside of said certificate—we think the true vote received by Jackson in Pleasants County was 802; we have therefore so counted it, thus conceding to contestant just what he claims as to the true vote in this county. Contestee averred that certain polls should be rejected because he says it does not appear the managers of election were duly sworn. In such cases the law of West Virginia imperatively says the vote shall not be counted. We are not satisfied that the evidence establishes this charge, and therefore we reject no polls on this ground, thereby again agreeing with the contention of contestant.

Contestee claimed that the vote of Walton precinct in Roane County should be excluded because there was "such misconduct and neglect and failure to discharge their duty on the part of the commissioners of election who held the election on the 6th day of November, 1888, at that precinct as amounted to fraud." It appears from the evidence that the ballot-box was an oblong, firm, wooden box, with a sliding lid, with a hole through the top to receive the ballots; there was a lock on the box, but no key; the lid would slide easily; a nail was used to keep the lid from sliding; the nail could be pushed in and pulled out with your fingers. This box in this unsecured condition was for a time in the exclusive possession of Mr. Garvin, a Republican commissioner, and Chris. Summers, another Republican. They had opportunity to have tampered with the box, and to this extent its integrity is impeached.

Mr. Garvin and Chris. Summers were not sworn by the contestant to show they did not tamper with or stuff the box. Contestant gave contestee notice that he would on the 18th day of July, 1889, examine these witnesses, but he did not do so. There may be some question of the propriety of accepting this return, but inasmuch as the only circumstance to show actual fraud was that the Republican majority was larger than was expected we do not reject the vote; thus again agreeing with the contention of contestant. The point was made in two cases that the voting place in precincts had been unlawfully changed or moved, but it appearing the vote was reasonably full, and that all parties on election day accepted the new place as legal, we see no reason for rejecting votes on this ground, again agreeing with the contention of contestant. This, we believe, disposes of all exceptions which might be by some thought technical, and we find ourselves at that point in the case where we begin to examine the evidence bearing upon the votes charged to be illegally cast for contestant, and the evidence bearing upon votes charged to be illegally cast for contestee, in full accord with the contestant as to the number of votes, including those charged to be illegal which were cast for the parties to this contest, respectively :

For Charles B. Smith .... : 19,837
For James M. Jackson 19,825

Contestant avers that 102 votes should be deducted from the 19,825 votes cast for contestee because he claims that number of said votes were illegal, naming the voters.

Contestee avers that 127 votes should be deducted from the 19,837 votes cast for contestant because he claims that number of said votes were illegal, naming the voters.

The legality or illegality of each of these votes depends upon the law of West Virginia as to the qualification of voters and the facts proven as to each voter.

First, as to the law :

The male citizens of the State shall be entitled to vote at all elections held within the counties in which they respectively reside, but no person who is a minor, or of unsound mind, or a pauper, or who is under conviction of treason, felony, or bribery in an election, or who has not been a resident of the State for one year, and of the county in which he offers to vote for sixty days next preceding such offer, shall be permitted to vote while such disability continues; but no person in the military, naval, or marine service of the United States shall be deemed a resident of this State by reason of being stationed therein. (Constitution West Virginia, Article IV, sec. 1. See published acts of 1872–'73, page 8.)

The male citizens of the State shall be entitled to vote at all elections held within the counties in which they respectively reside; but no person who is a minor, or of unsound mind, or a pauper, or who is under conviction of treason, felony, or bribery in an election, or who has not been a resident of the State for one year, and of the county in which he offers to vote for sixty days next preceding such election, and who is not, at the time of the election, an actual and bona fide resident of the district in which he offers to vote, shall be permitted to vote in such district while such disability continues. And no person in the military, marine, or naval service of the United States shall be deemed a resident of this State by reason of his being stationed therein; nor shall any person in the employ of an incorporated company, or of this State, be deemed a resident of any county, or of any district therein, by reason of being employed in said county or district. (Acts 1882, ch. 155, sec. 9. See published acts of 1882, p. 493.)

Second. As to the facts. The 229 votes assailed by the parties to this contest are attacked upon the following grounds: It is averred that some are minors, that some are non-residents of the State, that some are non-residents of the counties where they voted, that some voted without the election precinct of their residence, that some are of unsound mind, that some are paupers, and that some have been convicted of felony. To establish the charges made against the legality of these votes some 600 witnesses were examined, and their evidence appears in the record.

The undersigned believe the only correct and satisfactory way to determine who was elected to this Congress from the Fourth Congressional district of West Virginia by the legal voters thereof, was for the Committee on Elections of the House to consider each contested vote, examine all the evidence in the record bearing thereon, and then by a vote of the committee determine the legality or illegality thereof. In this way, and in this way only, the undersigned think could this case be satisfactorily determined. Certainly any court charged with the duty of deciding the question of fact presented in the record would have thus proceeded. So thinking, the undersigned proposed this method of proceeding. The majority of the committee not agreeing with this view declined so to proceed, and up to the filing of this report the undersigned are not informed as to what votes the majority determine to be legal or what votes they determine to be illegal.

The undersigned having, before the determination of this case by the committee, each separately and carefully considered all the evidence bearing upon every vote contested, have again and together reviewed and considered all the evidence bearing upon each vote challenged by either party and here present their conclusion.

We find that the following-named voters each deposited a ballot for Jackson, the contestee, and that said ballot was illegal and ought to be deducted from the vote heretofore stated as the vote for Jackson.

1. W. R. Surratt.	12. W. W. Bromfield.	23. Jas. Powell.
2. C. D. Stalnaker.	13. Alderson Watts.	24. George Dean.
3. J. L. Starcher.	14. Napoleon Adkins.	25. W. S. Wooding.
4. Charles Reynolds.	15. C. O. Bellemy.	26. Noble Hunter.
5. J. G. Armstrong	16. Wm. Noe.	27. James Bolyard.
6. J. C. Deaton.	17. Elias Browning.	28. John Cochran.
7. John Carney.	18. Abram Jones.	29. Henry Reynolds.
8. E. J. Long.	19. Jas. Dillon.	30. H. B. Armstrong.
9. J. D. Summers.	20. Walter Dillon.	31. Lewis Mattock.
10. John Ball.	21. A. Kaminsky.	
11. W S. Napier.	22. Lazrus Waines.	

We find that the following-named voters each deposited a ballot for contestant Smith, and that said ballot was illegal and ought to be deducted from the vote heretofore stated as the vote for Smith:

1. Peter Trent.	23. Thos. Burt.	45. John Mitchell.
2. Spencer Dean.	24. Lewis Mallory.	46. John Hall.
3. David Smith.	25. John Harris.	47. Wesley McDonald.
4. P. Wayne.	26. E. J. Anderson.	48. H. S. Greathouse.
5. William Wix.	27. O. Yancey.	49. P. S. Greathouse.
6. John Brannen, jr.	28. Hez. White.	50. Wm. Bradshaw.
7. John Sheets.	29. Charles Qualls.	51. John G. Dickson.
8. C. M. Messerly.	30. Marcellus Thomas.	52. Jesse Morris.
9. Henry Dye.	31. Ernest Graves.	53. H. Sheariffe.
10. I. C. Leonard.	32. Martin Wright.	54. Austin Tafferee.
11. John Davis.	33. John Diggs.	55. W H. Mamel.
12. J. T. Mooney.	34. Robt. Brown.	56. Edward Steed.
13. Wm. McCoy.	35. James Fortune	57. Henry Cunningham.
14. Robt. Treet.	36. Flem Washington.	58. George Anderson.
15. B. F. Blessing.	37. Major Jones.	59. John Woemberger.
16. Isaac Cullens.	38. W. F. Bird.	60. Israel Taylor.
17. Wm. Lee.	39. Geo. F. Jones.	61. Robert Alexander.
18. T. G. Hulbert.	40. James Parr.	62. Oscar Cunningham.
19. Geo. H. Rice.	41. Samuel Gray.	63. Wm. White.
20. E. Fletcher.	42. F. L. Johnson.	64. R. B. Mussetter.
21. Elijah Kiggins.	43. Simon Poole.	65. John Parkins.
22. J. Lute or Lub.	44. Frank Bratten.	66. N. E. Polsen.

The evidence tends to show the following-named persons voted for Smith, contestant, and that their votes were illegal; but the evidence is not so clear as in the other cases, therefore they are separated from them:

1. Geo. S. Ferrill.	8. Henry S. Poney.	15. John W. Burk.
2. Randolph Ferrill.	9. Mate Crago.	16. Perry Shriver.
3. Thos. Ferrill.	10. Wm. Crago.	17. Richard Hodgin.
4. A. H. Blackshire.	11. George Goodwin.	18. Jas. M. Cochran.
5. Charles Anderson.	12. Rufus Corbin.	19. Charles Walker.
6. Chris. Anderson.	13. A. C. Donald.	20. Isaac Davis.
7. Walter Henry.	14. H. P. Donald.	21. P. Robinson.

SUMMARY.

```
Total vote for Jackson......................................................... 19,825
Deduct illegal votes cast for him.............................................      31
                                                                             _____
    Correct vote of Jackson..................................................  19,794
                                                                             ========
Total vote for Smith..........................................................  19,837
Deduct votes clearly proved to be illegal and cast for him.............  66
Deduct those the evidence tends to show illegal........................  21
                                                                             _____
                                                                                   87
                                                                             _____
                                                                               19,750
```

On this basis the vote would be—

```
Jackson ....................................................................... 19,794
Smith.......................................................................... 19,750
                                                                             _____
    Majority for Jackson.....................................................      44
```

¯ If we deduct only those votes which are clearly and distinctly proved illegal and cast for Smith the vote would be—

```
Jackson, total vote ........................................................... 19,825
Illegal votes..................................................................      31
                                                                             _____
    Total legal vote of Jackson............................................. 19,794
Smith, total vote ...................................... 19,837
Illegal votes..........................................      66
                                                                             _____
    Total legal vote of Smith............................................... 19,771
                                                                             _____
    Clear majority for Jackson.............................................      23
```

The undersigned are therefore of the opinion that the contestee, Jackson, was duly elected, and we submit the following resolutions:

Resolved, That C. B. Smith was not elected a Representative in Congress from the Fourth district of West Virginia, and is not entitled to a seat therein.

Resolved, That James M. Jackson was duly elected a Representative in Congress from the Fourth district of West Virginia, and is entitled to retain his seat therein.

> CHARLES F. CRISP.
> JOS. H. OUTHWAITE.
> CHAS. T. O'FERRALL.
> LEVI MAISH.
> L. W. MOORE.
> R. P. C. WILSON.

GEORGE W. ATKINSON vs. JOHN O. PENDLETON.

Contestant alleged fraud pending a recount in Wetzel County, and both parties charged illegal voting. The committee find the charges as to Wetzel County sustained by the evidence. Disregarding the tainted recount in this county, and counting the votes as originally returned, the contestant has a majority on the face of the returns, and the burden of proof shifts to the contestee; he not having shown that a larger number of illegal votes were cast for contestant than for himself, but the contrary appearing from the evidence, the contestant is entitled to the seat.

The minority differ as to matters of fact only, the law as laid down by the committee in the previous case of Smith *vs.* Jackson being accepted by both sides. (See minority report, p. 61.)

The resolutions presented by the committee were adopted by the House February 27, 1890, by a vote of 162 to 0 (the Speaker announcing the names of 72 members present and not voting), and Mr. Atkinson was sworn in. The debate will be found on pages 1731 to 1781 of the Record.

(1) Fraud. *To be eliminated from the result.*

Returns which are tainted with fraud can not be made the foundation of the title to a seat in the House. The result should be purged of the fraud if practicable, and the poll only thrown out when no other alternative remains but to give effect to the fraud or to reject the poll.

(2) Recount.

The returns of election officers are *prima facie* correct, and a recount showing a different result can not be regarded unless it affirmatively appears that the ballots recounted are the same as those originally counted, and in the same condition.

(3) Burden of proof.

Contestant being shown to have been elected on the face of the returns, the burden shifts, and it devolves upon contestee to establish his right to the seat which he occupies by affirmative evidence.

43

(4) **Residence.**

The presumption should be in favor of actual residence, as ag
claimed intent to return to an abandoned residence, when the
only appears by the act of voting.

REPORT.

FEBRUARY 19, 1890.—Mr. ROWELL, from the Committee on Elections, submitted the following report:

The Committee on Elections, having had under consideration the contested-election case of George W. Atkinson *vs.* John O. Pendleton, from the First Congressional district of West Virginia, have duly considered the same and submit the following report:

By the notice of contest and answer thereto two issues are raised in the case.

One is the allegation of fraud pending a recount of the ballots in Wetzel County, and the other is the charge made by both parties, attacking a large number of votes for illegality.

By the statutes of West Virginia, after the returns have been made to the clerk of the county commissioners' court the commissioners, on demand made by any candidate, are required to recount the ballots.

The nature of the claim of contestant and its effect upon the result are correctly and succinctly stated in a brief filed in the case by contestant, from which we quote as follows:

The returns which were sent to the governor from the First Congressional district, and which included the falsified returns from Wetzel County, were, as stated by the contestee in his answer to the notice of contest, as follows:

For contestee 19,261
For contestant 19,242

Making the contestee's plurality 19

The fraud complained of is alleged to have been committed with reference to the two precincts of Martin's School-House and Archer's Fork.

The claim of the contestant is that after the ballots of these two precincts had been counted by the judges and clerks of election, and had been delivered with the poll-books to the clerk of the county court, 14 ballots of those from Martin's School-House and 10 ballots of those from Archer's Fork were changed, or "scratched," by having the contestant's name erased, so that upon the recount by the county court the votes for the contestant at Martin's School-House appeared to be 111 instead of 125 as returned by the election officers, and those at Archer's Fork 148 instead of 158.

Two of these "scratched" ballots not only had the contestant's name erased, but the contestee's inserted, so that two votes were thus improperly added to the aggregate for the contestee.

If these twenty-four votes should be restored to the contestant and these two votes deducted from the votes for the contestee, and the other

45

returns sent to the governor allowed to remain unchanged the result
would be—

For the contestant...	19,242	
Plus.........................	24	
		19,266
For the contestee..........................	19,261	
Less...	2	
		19,259

Showing a plurality for contestant of......................................   7

The rule has been announced over and over again that returns which
are tainted with fraud can not be made the foundation of the title to a
seat in the House. In the case of Washburn *vs.* Voorhees (3 Congressional Contested Election Cases, 54), a number of authorities are cited in
support of the rule which is there laid down as follows :

When the result in any precinct has been shown to be so tainted with fraud that
the truth can not be deduced therefrom, then it should never be permitted to form
a part of the canvass. The precedents, as well as the evident requirements of truth,
not only sanction but call for the rejection of the entire poll when stamped with the
characteristics here shown.

While all agree that where fraud is shown, the result of the fraud
should be in some way avoided, there has been much discussion as to
the manner in which this result is to be reached, and it may be regarded as settled that the poll will be "purged" of the fraud if that be
practicable, and only rejected when no other alternative remains but
to give effect to the fraud or to reject the poll.

In the present case it is unnecessary to enter into the discussion of this
question, for the result will be the same whether the polls in the two
disputed precincts be purged by a resort to the returns made by the
election officers, or be rejected altogether. This will be seen from the
following calculation.

At Martin's School-House the total number of votes for the contestant, as returned
by the election officers, was 125. The county court, by deducting the scratched
tickets, fourteen in number, reduced these to 111, which was the number included in
the returns sent to the governor. The number of votes for the contestee was allowed
to remain, and was certified to the governor as returned by the election officers at
134. (437.) At Archers' Fork the numbers returned by the election officers were, for
the contestant 158, and for the contestee 149. On the recount, 2 votes were added to
the contestee's and 10 deducted from the contestant's, so that the returns sent to the
governor were, for the contestant 148, and for the contestee 151. (27.) If, now, these
two precincts be entirely eliminated from the returns sent to the governor from the
entire congressional district, the result will be as follows:

For the contestant:

Returns sent to the Governor (37)............................	19,242	
Deduct Martin's School-House................................	111	
Deduct Archer's Fork.......................................	148	
		259
		18,983

For the contestee :

Returns sent to the Governor (37)............................	19,261	
Deduct Martin's school house................................	134	
Deduct Archer's Fork	151	
		285
		18,976

Showing a plurality for the contestant of................................   7

If the poll be purged by restoring to the contestant the 24 votes of which he was
fraudulently sought to be deprived, and deducting from the contestee the 2 votes

which he gained by reason of the fraud, the result, as already shown, will be the same, namely:

For the contestant:
Returns sent to the Governor (37)' 19,242
Add ....:... 24
                                                    19,266

For the contestee:
Returns sent to the Governor (37)....:........................... 19,261
Deduct 2 19,259

    Purality for contestant.. 7

The claim of the contestant is, that the ballots which were voted at these two precincts were not scratched by the voters who deposited them, and were properly counted in their true and unaltered condition by the election officers, but that after leaving the custody of these officers they were tampered with and altered. It does not devolve upon the contestant to show how or by what persons this crime was committed, nor can it be for a moment supposed that direct proof would be produced of the very fact of the alteration, testified to by persons who witnessed the actual perpetration of the fraud. Publicity would be fatal, and secrecy was essential to the success of the scheme, and unless one of the participants, as seems to have so nearly happened in this case, should himself make the disclosure resort must be had, as in other cases of fraud, to circumstantial evidence. The contestant has proved this branch of his case by showing, first, that the ballots were without blemish when they left the hands of the election officers, and, second, that the manner in which the ballots were afterwards kept, and the persons who had access to them afforded the opportunity for the crime and made its perpetration probable.

In order to authorize a recount of ballots in an election contest it must affirmatively appear that they have been kept as required by law, and that there has been no opportunity to tamper with them. (Paine on Elections, sec. 787.)

Before courts or legislative bodies can give weight to the result of a recount there must be absolute proof that the ballot-boxes containing such ballots have been safely kept and that the ballots are the identical ballots cast at the election (Paine on Elections, sec. 776, and authorities cited). An impartial public count of the ballots by sworn officers made at the close of the polls is better evidence of what the ballot-boxes then contained than a subsequent count made after a long exposure of the boxes to the tampering of dishonest partisans (Paine, sec. 787).

Taken together, the adjudications upon this question, judicial and legislative, establish conclusively the doctrine that the returns of election officers are to be held prima facie correct; that a recount changing the result will not be regarded unless it affirmatively appears that the ballots recounted are the same, and in the same condition as they were when originally counted.

An opportunity to tamper with the ballots by unauthorized persons, or a failure to keep them as the law directs, will destroy the value of the ballots as evidence when recounted and a different result reached than the one returned.

Changing ballots by scratching or by substitution, after return made, is an old method of committing fraud to change the result of elections in cases of close contest.

Even when the ballots have been in the sole custody of sworn officers of the law, it has been found practicable for dishonest men to make such changes in such a secret way as to defy detection, and on that account laws have been enacted requiring the destruction of the ballots as soon as counted, so that they could not thereafter be used to overthrow the election returns. In large cities especially, is it thought safer to risk the possibility of error in the original count than to take the chances of subsequent changes.

While in West Virginia the law makes provision for a recount, it does not dispense with the legal requirements of safe-keeping of the ballots, pending the recount.

We now consider the facts as they appear in the record with reference to the recount in Wetzel County.

We quote again from the brief of contestant as being a fair statement of the evidence in regard to original count and the recount.

The election officers at Martin's School House were three commissioners, namely: John R. Woods, Thomas H. Alley, and A. B. Streight; and two clerks, namely: William J. Wykert and W. H. Parks. Of these, Woods, Alley, and Wykert were Democrats, 'and Streight and Parks were Republicans. (355, 336, 337, 343.) The statute, after providing that every voter's name shall be entered upon the poll-books as his ballot is received, proceeds as follows (Code 1887, ch. 3, sec. 18):

"As soon as possible after the polls are closed at each place of voting for which no canvassers are appointed, the names entered on the poll-books shall be counted by the commissioners and clerks, and the number thereof be set down in words at length at the foot of the list, which shall then be signed by the inspectors and clerks; the ballot-box shall then be opened, and one of the commissioners taking therefrom one ballot at a time, in the presence of all the other officers, shall read therefrom the designations of the offices to be filled and the names of the persons voted for for each office, and hand the ballot to another of said commissioners, who, if satisfied that it was correctly read, shall string it on a thread. The contents of the ballots, as they are read, shall be entered by the clerks, under the supervision of the commissioners, on tally papers for the purpose, by suitable marks made opposite to or under the name of each person voted for, so as to show the number of votes received by every person for every office to be filled. The ballots shall be counted as they are strung upon the thread, and whenever the number shall be equal to the number of voters entered upon the poll-books, the excess, if any, remaining in the ballot-box, shall be immediately destroyed, without unfolding or unrolling the same, or allowing any one to examine or know the contents thereof."

The statute then provides (section 20) for certifying the result, sealing the ballots, poll-books, and certificates, and sending them, within four days, by the hands of one of the commissioners, to the clerk of the county court, with a duplicate of the certificates and one of the poll-books to the clerk of the circuit court. Let us see how faithfully these particular provisions of the law were complied with.

The evidence of John R. Woods, one of the Democratic commissioners, will be found on page 336 of the printed record. He says that after the polls were closed and the count commenced Streight took the ballots from the box and handed them to the witness, who read off the vote and handed the ballots to Alley, who strung them. The witness was forty-three years of age and used glasses. The greater part of the counting was done by daylight, but part of it was done by night, by lantern-light, which the witness thought was sufficient to enable him to see plainly to read the ballots. When asked whether he saw any Republican tickets on which the name of the contestant had been scratched or erased in any manner, the witness answered: "*I don't remember that I did.*" He mentions one Democratic ticket from which the contestee's name had been erased, and this accords with all of the evidence upon the subject and with the poll-books and tally-sheets, which show that the total number of votes cast was one more than the aggregate counted for the two candidates for Congress (437).

The other Democratic commissioner testifies (343) that after counting until 11 o'clock on the night of the election an adjournment was taken until next morning; that during the adjournment the commissioners kept the ballot-box and the ballots in their custody, leaving the tally-sheets with the clerks; that next morning, on resuming the count, the ballots counted the evening before were gone over again, so as to verify the accuracy of their count. On the question of the lights at night he says:

"We had good lights; we had two lights all the time, and part of the time three. *We could see plainly what we were doing;* at least I could, and I heard no complaint from others about the light." Corroborating in other particulars the testimony of Woods, he adds the significant fact that the ballots were counted twice, so far as the Congressional vote was concerned, on account of errors made by the clerks in tallying. This man had been for thirty years assisting as an officer in the holding of elections, and to the question whether it was possible that fourteen Republican ballots, from which the contestant's name had been erased, could have passed through his hands without his seeing them, he answered: "*I don't think it possible,* because *I know* he was not scratched at Martin's School House."

A. B. Streight, the Republican commissioner testifies, (335): "I took the tickets out of the box, opened them out, and gave them to John Woods, one of the other judges of said election; after I gave him the first ticket I took out of the box, I read all the balance over carefully to myself while John Woods was reading the one handed to him out loud to the tallyman; I read every ticket in the box." He saw not a single Republican ticket with the contestant's name erased. This witness corroborates Woods and Alley with reference to the light and the other particulars of the count.

The two clerks, Wykert (335) and Parks (337), did not see the ballots, but tallied them as they were read, and must in this way have been cognizant, as actors in the *res gestæ*, of any erasures which were not overlooked by the commissioners. Wykert, the Democrat, when asked whether his attention was called to any ballot from which the name of *either* of the candidates for Congress had been erased, says: "I could not be positive; I think there was one and maybe two, *but not more.*" Parks, the Republican, says that his attention was called to only one ballot which had been scratched as to the Congressional candidates, and that was the one from which the contestee's name had been erased. With reference to the lights and other particulars, the two clerks confirm what the commissioners stated.

No other witness is examined on either side with reference to the circumstances of this count, and indeed it is to be inferred, from the evidence which has been given, that no other persons were present. There is, therefore, the concurrent and uncontradicted testimony of all five witnesses to the transaction, all of whom had some, and three of whom had the best opportunities to become acquainted with the facts and three of whom were testifying against their party interests, establishing positively the fact that, when the election officers counted them these ballots were not scratched, and it is shown that the ballots were safely delivered to Snodgrass, the deputy clerk of the county court. (336.)

The election officers at Archer's Fork were three commissioners, namely: Samuel Fisher, J. D. Brookover, and Samson Starkey, and two clerks, namely, S. I. Earl and G. W. Belch. Of these, Fisher, Brookover, Earl, and Belch were Democrats, and Starkey the only Republican.

Samuel Fisher, one of the Democratic commissioners, does not remember (370) any ticket from which the name of either candidate had been scratched, though his recollection of the circumstances does not seem very clear. When asked whether he saw any ballots which had been scratched, he answers: "I did, but I don't know that there was any on Congressmen." However, he was the commissioner who strung the ballots, so that he was not required to read them all. He says, though, that he believes the returns made by the election officers at his precinct to have been correct.

J. D. Brookover, the other Democratic commissioner, testifies at page 367. Through his deposition a glimpse may be caught of the pressure under which these election officers had been placed after it began to seem as though the result of the election would turn on the question whether their evidence would overthrow that of the falsified ballots. When the witness made an affidavit stating the truth, as he understood the facts, one of his influential party friends addressed to him the remark: "Damn such a man as you are, for going back on his party as you have." When, with such a pressure upon them, these election officers come forward and give evidence in favor of the contestant, no doubt can remain of the truthfulness of their statements.

Brookover testifies that about half of the time during the count he took the ballots from the box, unfolded and inspected them, and handed them to Starkey, who called the names off to the clerks, and then passed them to Fisher, who strung them. Part of the time Starkey took the ballots from the box, inspected them, and handed them to the witness, who read th names to the clerks and handed them to Fisher. Either Brookover or Starkey read off to the clerks all of the ballots except five or six, which were read by Fisher. While they worked at night the light was at all times sufficient for them to see the names on the tickets distinctly. There was one Republican ballot with the contestant's name erased and the contestee's written upon it. He believes that the returns made from the precinct were correct. When asked whether it was possible that there could have been ten or twelve erasures of the contestant's name from Republican tickets without his seeing them, he says: "I don't think it *possible;* I don't think there could have been that many and my attention not called to it."

Samson Starkey, the Republican commissioner, corroborates (340) the testimony of Mr. Brookover with reference to the method of the count, the sufficiency of the light, and the fact that only one Republican ticket had the contestant's name erased. He says that he gave his entire attention to the counting and reading of the ballots, and that it is impossible that ten or eleven erasures of the contestant's name from Republican tickets could have escaped his notice.

The two clerks, Earl (338) and Belch (339), both Democrats, testify substantially to the same effect, so far as their opportunities for observation went, Earl stating that one ballot was scratched for each of the Congressional candidates, and Belch not remembering distinctly. but believing that there were "two or three or four" ballots with the contestant's name scratched, none of which, however, he saw. Earl

H. Mis. 137——4

thought the light was good until one of their lamps went out, after which, until daylight, he could not see any too well. Belch could see plainly all the time. Both of these witnesses were called by the contestee (951, 952) to testify that, in some instances, the commissioners, instead of calling every name upon the ballots, called them as "straight Democratic" or "straight Republican," and that when Brookover overlooked a scratch upon one ticket, though not apparently of the name of a Congressional candidate, one Wyatt, a by-stander, called his attention to it. Wyatt also testifies to these facts (953). So far from weakening, this evidence strengthens the case made for the contestant by showing that the by-standers were adding their vigilance to that of the election officers, and were quick to observe a mistake, and by showing also that, notwithstanding the presence of Democratic commissioners, clerks, and by-standers the contestee has failed to produce any evidence whatever of the making of more than one mistake, which was at once corrected, or of the presence of any scratched ballots except those which were observed and properly classified by the election officers. The ballots from this precinct, too, were carefully and safely delivered to the clerk of the county court (370).

If these ballots had really been scratched before they were deposited in the ballot-box, not only might the contestee have called the by-standers at Martin's School-House and proved the fact by them, but there was open to him one complete and satisfactory method of proving the fact of the scratching both there and at Archer's Fork. The tickets which were found, when produced before the county court, to have these scratches upon them were Republican tickets, and presumably voted by Republicans, which would have gone that far toward identifying the persons who voted them. It is not to be presumed that the twenty-four voters who must have voted the ballots, if they were voted at all, and whoby the fact of scratching expressed their desire for the contestant's defeat, would through pusillanimity or from any other motive, observe a unanimous silence through all the incidents which followed this election. Here are charges and proofs of fraud, suspicion of crime attaching to their fellow-citizens, the defeat of the candidate of their choice imminent, and all because they do not come forward and disclose the secret of their ballots. Men may, and often do, prefer to keep to themselves the names of the persons for whom they have voted, especially when they have scratched their party ticket. But this objection to making known how they vote is generally prompted rather by the desire to avoid petty annoyances and criticisms than by the fear of any serious consequences, and these reasons would readily yield when they would consider the much more serious consequences of their silence. But not one of the twenty-four has been found. And the contestee was in search of them, too, for we have the important fact developed that Mr. A. L. Mooney told Hon. Aaron Morgan that he was going to vote for Mr. Pendleton and work for him at Martin's School-House, and afterwards that he had voted for him and worked for him, "but had not got very much done for him." (940.) But Mr. Mooney's own ballot is accounted for by the one Republican vote which was found to be scratched and which was not counted by the election officers, and Mr. Mooney seems to do his testifying as the Hon. Aaron Morgan seems to do his penmanship (941) that is to say, vicariously, for he does not come upon the witness stand to testify what the little was that he had got done for the contestee.

The ballots from Martin's School House were delivered to the deputy clerk of the county court on the morning of the 8th day of November (336, 926), and those from Archer's Fork were delivered to the clerk on the 7th day of November, in the evening (390). It does not appear on what days the ballots from the other precincts throughout the county were brought in, but until all had been received those which had come in were placed in a wooden box, described as an " Arbuckle's coffee box," and allowed to remain in the clerk's office, under the clerk's desk, until all had come in, and the box was then moved into the vault (926). The box does not appear to have been nailed up during the interval between the receipt of the ballots by the clerk on the 7th and 8th days of November, and the production of the box in court on the 12th day of November.

On the 12th day of November the county court met to canvas the returns from the various voting places in the county (433). The commissioners who composed the court were Benjamin Earnshaw, T. P. Horner, and David Dulaney (426). The clerk was John C. McEldowney, and his deputy was R. E. L. Snodgrass (425, 426). All of these men were Democrats (411, 415). The ballots, poll-books, and certificates from Martin's School House had been returned in a paper sack, and those from Archer's Fork in another (426, 434). On the 12th day of November these two sacks were opened in order to permit the county court to obtain access to the poll-books and certificates (426, 434), and these sacks were not sealed up again until after the recount had been completed. but were replaced in the box unsealed (426), and so remained from the 12th day of November until the 26th day of November, when the ballots from Martin's School House were examined by the county court, and the 27th day when those from Archer's Fork were examined (434).

There are two questions of fact which have engaged the attention of the witnesses who testified upon either side with regard to the custody of these ballots. The witnesses for the contestant claim that when the ballots from these two precincts were produced before the county court to be counted, they were in confusion and appeared to have been disturbed, while the witnesses for the contestee claim that they were in good condition. The witnesses for the contestant also claim that during the recesses of the court the ballots were not replaced in the vault, as they should have been, but were allowed to lie in an open box in the clerk's office, accessible to every person who might enter (411, 415, 420). The witnesses for the contestee, on the other hand, insist that whenever the court adjourned the wooden box containing the ballots was nailed up, pieces of wood being nailed across it, and was deposited in the vault (926, 927, 425).

Another subject of controversy among the witnesses was the character of the scratching that appeared upon the ballots from these two precincts. There is no question that the scratching was of a very distinct and perceptible character (948, 434), and this makes it still more improbable that so many and such marks should have escaped the attention of the election officers. But the witnesses for the contestant claim that the ballots from Martin's School-House had been marked with a very wide black mark, made with a soft lead-pencil, and that wherever, in addition to the erasure of the contestant's name, the name of the contestee had been written upon the ballot, the writing seemed to have been done with a similar or the same pencil, and that the handwriting differed, as well as the character of the pencil marks, from the other writing and marks which in some instances appeared upon the same ballot (434). The witnesses upon the other side insist that the writing upon the tickets was not uniform (946, 947).

The county court began its sessions for the canvassing of the vote on November 12th and did not conclude its labors until November 30 (442). It is not to be inferred, however, that it labored continuously, day after day, upon the recount. On the contrary, the counting of the ballots was protracted, for no apparent reason, from day to day, and when other resources failed, a curious and suspicious scheme for postponing the conclusion of the count was resorted to. On the 21st day of November (421), Charles E. Wells and U. N. Arnett, from Marion County, were in the town of New Martinsville, where the court was in session, and Mr. Earnshaw, the president, was very late in returning to the court-room after the noon adjournment (415). Upon coming into court, Mr. Earnshaw produced a telegram purporting to be signed by Frank J. Black, a citizen of Burton (415), notifying Earnshaw that his wife was very sick. It seems that Wells and Arnett had left town upon the 2 o'clock train (420), and Wells had sent from Moundsville, in Black's name, this alarming message to Mr. Earnshaw (363). Earnshaw thereupon left, and the recount was delayed some two or three days until his return (420). As a matter of fact, Black had neither sent the telegram himself nor authorized it to be sent, and knew nothing of it until Wells himself told him, some days later, that he had used Black's name to such a message (364). Neither was Earnshaw's wife sick at the time, but on the contrary attended a merry-making on the 22d and seemed to be enjoying herself (363).

That this whole scheme was carried through by pre-arrangement with Earnshaw himself is manifest from Earnshaw's conduct after he left New Martinsville. He went to Burton, it is true, but instead of hastening home, as would have been natural if he had supposed his wife to be ill, and as he had hastened from New Martinsville, he loitered around Burton during the forenoon and then went leisurely off toward his home in the country (366). Now all this would be curious enough by itself, but when it is taken in connection with Mr. Earnshaw's explanation it becomes little less than astounding. He says (944) that Wells was in New Martinsville, and had business with him, wholly unconnected with the election; that he received the telegram already referred to, *and knew that Charles E. Wells sent it.* Then, drawing a nice distinction, he says that the telegram was not sent for the purpose of *interfering* with the recount at all, "*further than it necessarily delayed the recount*" (944). It may be taken as admitted, therefore, that the purpose of all this was to delay the recounting of the votes, and the ballots from Martin's School-house and Archer's Fork were not counted until after this delay had occurred.

It is not necessary to the case which has been made for the contestant that the committee shall find either that the ballots showed uniformity in the marking of them or that they were carelessly allowed to remain in the office of the clerk instead of in the vault; nor is it even necessary for the committee to conclude that the persons who brought about the delay in the recount by so peculiar a scheme were directly instrumental in altering the faces of the ballots. These circumstances are certainly sufficient to raise a suspicion that foul play of some kind was afoot. The evidence of these scratched ballots must be rejected, however, if not for these reasons, then for another and entirely sufficient one. Let it be assumed that from the 8th day of November until the 30th day of that month the ballots in question were kept in the vault of the clerk's office, except while they were in the court-room in the presence of the court. *Quis custodet custodes?* Who looked after the vault? Mr. R. E. L. Snodgrass tells us as much as we need wish to know about that matter. After describing the external fastenings of doors and shutters, he says that the inside door was fastened with a bolt and the outside by a combination lock; that he himself, John C. Mc-Eldowney, E. B. Snodgrass, Frank D. Young, and T. B. Jacob are all acquainted with the combination (927). Mr. McEldowney says that the combination was not only known to these persons, but also to many others, and that he did not keep the vault as a security against burglars, but as a fire-proof vault only (427).

It may be inferred from this that the keeping of the ballots in the vault, of which so much is made in the evidence for the contestee, was not so very much better than the keeping of them in the more commonly used portion of the clerk's office. Indeed, the vault seems to have been a place of safe custody not only for ballots but also for beer, and when the clerk and his friends were spending a pleasant evening together, between the sessions of the court, they went into the vault with pieces of lighted paper to look for the beer bottles (937). The point, however, that I wish to bring out, is that during all the time from the 7th and 8th days of November, when the ballots in question were delivered up by the election officers, R. E. L. Snodgrass, the deputy clerk, had free access to them at all hours of the day and night, and this whether they were in the clerk's office or in the vault. When it is considered that the unanimous testimony of all the election officers from these two precincts concurs in proving that the ballots were not scratched when they were voted and first counted, it becomes of grave importance to inquire what manner of persons had access to these ballots before the county court proceeded to count them.

The case of Kline v. Verree (2 Congressional Election Cases, 381), will be found instructive upon this point. In that case the contestant claimed that the election officers in various precincts had made mistakes in the counting, and that their returns were, therefore, inaccurate. The ballot-boxes were produced, and the ballots recounted, and it thereupon appeared that the ballots showed a different result from that which had been returned by the election officers. With regard to one precinct (page 388), it was claimed that the election officers had overlooked certain "stickers" and by mistake had counted as full ballots, ballots which had really been altered by means of these stickers. Upon an inspection of the ballots it was perceived that the stickers were upon yellow paper which had been pasted upon white ballots, making a most striking contrast. The committee in its report pertinently remarks: "None but a blind man could make the mistake of overlooking these stickers, for none other could fail to see them." The same remark might be applied to the pencil marks upon the ballots which are here in question. But I have referred to the case mainly for another purpose. When the discrepancy was discovered between the returns made by the election officers and the votes shown by the ballots as produced, inquiry was naturally made into the custody of the ballots during the interval between the two counts. The ballot-box from the third division of the Eleventh ward (page 387) had been left in the custody of Alderman Williams. It had been sealed up, and when produced was apparently in the same condition, so far as the seals were concerned, as when it had been delivered into the custody of the alderman. But the box had been kept in the office of the alderman, upon a shelf, and this office was a place of frequent resort, especially by a constable named McKinney. While it appeared that McKinney had carried this box from one place to another, and had at one time intrusted it to another man, it was not shown that McKinney had tampered with the ballot-box in any respect, but after he had been shown to have made the office a place of resort into which he could enter during the alderman's absence, the committee came to a conclusion with regard to these ballots, which they expressed as follows:

"The character of McKinney was attacked, and it appeared that he had been convicted of *extortion or obtaining money by fraud*, and had been pardoned by the governor, and since elected constable of the ward. Alderman Williams testified that he would not believe him under oath. If his character is as bad as claimed by the contestant, the committee believe him to be a very unsafe person to keep the company of ballot-boxes for three months, or be intrusted with them as he was by Alderman Williams, to carry to the magistrate's office, and would be a very suitable person to do or connive at the very thing he testifies was done. The committee could, however, place no confidence in the integrity of a ballot-box which had been in such company and keeping for three months, and when opened was found not to agree with the sworn returns received at the time of the election. By this recount the contestant gained 17 votes. As the entire recount gives him but 8 majority, it is obvious that without this correction the result can not be changed. The committee think it would be most unsafe to contest the returns by such testimony."

Let us inquire, therefore, what sort of a man it was who was keeping company with these ballots for three weeks, long enough certainly for any purpose of fraud to be accomplished. We need look no further than the testimony in this cause to ascertain that Snodgrass, if he had not been, in the language used by the committee in the case just cited, "convicted of extortion and obtaining money by fraud," was saved from the commission of such a crime not by his conscience, but by the refusal of his intended victims to be defrauded. Shortly after the recount had been concluded, and while there was yet much excitement in the public mind, over what was believed to have been a fraud, this precious deputy opened negotiations with Mr. Cowden, the chairman of the republican State executive committee for West Virginia, intimating that he knew who had scratched the ballots from Martin's School House and Archer's Fork, and that he was ready to disclose what he knew upon the payment of a sufficient consideration. Upon this intimation, Mr. Cowden, with one or two confidential friends, had an interview with Mr. Snodgrass, in which the latter gave it to be understood that he had this important information, and was ready to sell it.

It is not necessary to follow the details of the negotiation, which fell through ostensibly because the price asked was too high, but really, I suppose, because Mr. Cowden could obtain no assurance that Snodgrass was to be trusted, to comply with his part of any agreement which might be entered into (393, 414, 430). But Snodgrass has gone too far. The fact that he had been negotiating could not be kept secret. It was necessary for him to devise some explanation, and to offer some reason why he had been in consultation with the Republicans. He not only devised the explanation, but testified to it and coolly presents in his testimony a picture of himself which would scarcely be more infamous if he had confessed to have altered the ballots. His explanation is that he had arranged with one Grall to play a trick upon McIntire and Cowden, and trick them out of their money. In making the explanation he thinks, apparently, that he has satisfied the requirements of any person's conscience when he has explained that he did not tell Mr. McIntire or Mr. Cowden *that he knew* anything about the ticket scratching, but only said to them that he would tell them, for $3,000 in cash, *all he knew* about the ticket scratching (931, 933). He adds that he did not know at that time and does not know at this time anything whatever about the ticket scratching (933). He said to them, though, that in case he made a statement in relation to the matter, he would furnish circumstantial evidence that such statement, whatever it might be, was true (933). On cross-examination he was asked what his object was in telling Mr. Cowden that he was getting $60 a month, and that he might be discharged if he should tell all he knew about the ticket scratching. The portion of his deposition which immediately follows presents the whole man in his naked infamy:

"A. 15. My object was, if possible, to get him to advance the $3,000 to me for telling what I knew about the ticket scratching.

"Q. 16. Yet at that time and now you say you knew nothing about the ticket scratching. Is not that so?—A. 16. Yes, sir; I said that I knew nothing about the ticket scratching.

"Q. 17. Then your intention was to deceive Mr. Cowden to get the $3,000, or whatever sum of money you could, and give him nothing in return?—A. 17. My intention was, as I said before, to enter into a written contract, signed in duplicate, to tell all I knew about the ticket scratching, and further, I intended to comply with the conditions of the contract, and if anybody was deceived thereby I care not.

"Q. 18. But did you intend to deceive Mr. Cowden?—A. 18. I thought that if he was foolish enough to be deceived by the statement I had made him, it was all well and good so far as I was concerned.

"Q. 19. But did you not intend to deceive Mr. Cowden?—A. 19. It was my intention to deceive Mr. Cowden or any one else who were foolish enough to be deceived by statements, and it was my object to secure the $3,000 from any one who was foolish enough to pay it to me for telling what I knew about the matter."

This witness, therefore, shows himself to have been willing to commit the crime of obtaining money under false pretenses, by "extortion or obtaining money by fraud," as the committee put it in Kline v. Verree. If the constable in that case was for that reason considered bad company for the ballots, the deputy in this case must for the same reason be considered equally bad company, and the ballots themselves, to which he had constant access, are so tainted with suspicion as to make them worthless as evidence to overthrow the sworn returns of the election officers. In truth, when the matter is fairly considered, we have simply the oath of this man Snodgrass against the oath of all the election officers at these two precincts. For we only know by his oath that he really did not know anything about the scratching of the tickets, and did not engage in the scratching himself.

There are some other peculiar circumstances connected with this recount not spoken of in the brief which we have quoted.

These two precincts were not recounted until after the president of the county court had procured an adjournment by telegram referred to in the evidence and brief, known to him to be false, and designedly used by him to deceive.

This telegram was by him shown to a leading Republican, Mr. McIntyre, engaged in watching the proceedings, and his opinion asked about going home. The judge talked quite awhile about his wife's sickness and appeared to be much affected. (Record, ps. 214, 215.)

This, of course, was for a purpose, and designed to deceive. On the same day this judge had been in an upper room of a hotel in the town, in company with Wells, the sender of the false telegram, and of Lee Snodgrass, the deputy clerk. (Record p. 224.)

Up to this time the plurality for Atkinson had not been overcome and the count was nearly completed.

Previously, at a late hour of the night, that same judge had entered the vault where those ballots were kept, with one Grail and the clerk of the court, on the hunt, as he says, of a bottle of beer.

Grail was staying around the court during the recount, and remaining after the work of the day was over, usually pretty drunk; a fit tool for dirty work, if he could be trusted, and this a fit opportunity to find just where the ballot-box containing the ballots was located.

But Grail didn't sober up. Wells and Arnett visit the town. Judge Ernshaw and Lee Snodgrass have a private interview with them. Wells leaves town and sends a false telegram in another name, by previous arrangement. The court adjourns for two or three days, and then comes the recount with the extraordinary result. Ballots, too, which had been expressly forbidden to be resealed at the beginning of the recount by the same judge, over the protest of the attorney for Mr. Atkinson, who had asked that the ballots after they had been opened on the first day of the recount, might be resealed until wanted during the recount.

The false telegram, sent by Wells in the name of Black, was dated November 21, 1888. The recount did not begin again until November 23 or 24.

The connection of Wells and Arnett with this recount is shown by another telegram sent to them at New Martinsville, November 24, by which it appears that they had returned, and on business connected with the count.

The telegram may be found on page 421 of the record, and is as follows:

CHARLESTON, W. VA., *November* 24, 1888.

To C. E. WELLS or W. N. ARNETT, *New Martinsville, W. Va.:*

St. Clair says he can go to Wetzel on Monday if necessary. Have court adjourn until counsel can be heard.

McG.

Thus it is clearly made to appear that Wells and Arnett were in New Martinsville on business connected with this recount; that they helped to secure an adjournment at a critical time by deception, giving the public an apparently good reason therefor; that Judge Ernshaw and the deputy clerk were in consultation with them; that previously it took three persons, including the judge, to hunt for one bottle of beer in the ticket vault, and finally that the tickets when recounted disclosed the change heretofore shown.

Under this evidence there is no room for doubt that these ballots were fraudulently changed after the recount commenced.

They were not safely and securely kept during the count free from opportunity to tamper with them.

Some of the official custodians were improper persons, as is demonstrated, to have charge of them.

The correctness of the original count is clearly established outside of the presumption in its favor, and therefore the committee adopt the returns as a correct statement of the vote in the two precincts of Wetzel County, and hold that contestant was elected by a plurality of seven votes according to the correct returns.

By this conclusion the burden shifts, and it now devolves upon contestee to establish his right to the seat which he occupies by affirmative evidence.

This he seeks to do by charging that illegal votes were cast and counted for contestant sufficient to overcome this apparent majority and to outnumber the illegal votes alleged to have been cast and counted for contestee.

The committe have carefully examined the evidence in the record on this branch of the case, and have given due consideration to the briefs and oral arguments, and have reached the conclusion following :

For convenience we shall follow the order adopted by the parties, keeping up the numbers as we find them in the briefs.

We find that the following-named voters were not legally qualified to vote at the places where they voted, and that they voted for contestee :

No.	Name.	Remarks.
4	Clarence Tyrr	Unsound mind.
10	Calvin Ashcraft	Do.
11	Newt Wilt	Do.
12	John Furguson	Do.
13	Henry Keestemeyer	Do.
16	John Davis	Non-resident.
17	Byron Bates	Do.
19	P. H. McConaughey	Do.
26	Wm. McKinley	Do.
33	Joseph Crawford	Do.
38	Robert Dreamer	Do.
41	John C. Clowson	Do.
43	Smith Marks	Do.
44	John Gallegan	Do.
45	John W. Skinner	Do.
47	John Lodge	Do.
48	Jacob Mellbaugh	Do.
49	John F. Paugh	Do.
50	Alvin Cresswell	Do.
52	A. M. Prettyman	Do.
54	Allen Hart	Do.
56	Thomas Brothers	Do.
58	William Kidd	Do.
59	George Kidd	Do.
60	Isaac Carpenter	Do.
62	William Kleives	Do.
64	George W. Storm	Do.
65	W. A. Delaplain	Do.
66	Jack Hamilton	Do.
67	B. K. McMechen	Do.
68	George Baired, jr	Do.
70	Joseph Kress	Do.
73	Pat Williams	Do.
76	Lee Minor	Do.
79	Reuben Wade	Do.
87	Amos James	Do.
89	Lee Ganite	Do.
90	Rev. D. C. Weese	Do.
91	Lloyd Brown	Do.
92	Sandy Redman	Do.
93	Homer Griffin	Do.
94	G. A. R. Kuhn	Do
105	Isaac Woofter	Do
106	Jasper Beals	Do.
107	Silas Beals	Do.
108	Wm. O. Nitengale	Do.
109	James Hickey	Do.
116	Frederick Aushutz	Do.
118	John Mallony	Do.
156	H. C. Carrier	Do.
158	Frederick W. Bloom	Do.
196	Jesse Tuttle	Do.

No.	Name.	Remarks.
197	John M. Roberts	Non-resident.
198	J. P. Pope	Do.
199	Judson Brown	Do.
201	John Deberry	Do.
205	J. W. Squires, *alias* Wyatt	Minor.
210	Ashly Davis	Do.
213	William Weekly	Do.
215	R. L. Kidd	Do.
217	Joseph Kersey	Do.
219	Henry Beuter	Do.
220	Jacob Wertzberger	Do.
221	Henry Copps	Do.
222	Harry Noble	Do.
223	Edward Krester	Do.
225	John Roth	Do.
226	Thos. Ulman	Do.
227	Newton Johnson	Do.
228	Jerry Farreber	Do.
229	James Kimball	Do.
234	Henry Fisher	Pauper.
255	Wm. Kimney	Do.
237	Patrick Callaghan	Foreigner.
240	John Drosinski	Do.
245	John Burke	Non-resident.
249	Thos. Seaman	Do.

From Nos. 95 to 104, inclusive, are employés of the State asylum for the insane. We think the evidence shows that they have fixed their residence there and were entitled to vote.

The statute which declares that employés of the State shall not thereby become residents of the place where employed does not prevent their becoming residents if they so elect. The presumption of non-residence can be overcome by proof, as in this case.

From 120 to 154, inclusive, the voters voted at Braxton Court House, and it is insisted that the territory in which they lived had not been legally annexed to that voting district. An attempt had been made to so annex it, the residents had so voted for twelve years, and we do not think they can be disfranchised on account of technical neglect of the court, after years of acquiescence in what was supposed to be a legal order, and we hold the votes good.

From 159 to 194, inclusive, it is alleged that the voters voted out of their wards in the city of Wheeling. While from the oral evidence introduced it is quite evident that some ten or twelve of these voters voted out of their proper wards, the committee are not disposed to include them in the list of illegal voters, for the reason that no record evidence was introduced as to ward boundaries, and while both parties seemed to concede the competency of the evidence introduced, we do not feel like going into the question, in the absence of that better evidence which must have been easily accessible.

In country precincts common repute and generally acknowledged, boundaries will suffice, but the boundaries of city wards, when disputes arise about them, ought to be proven by better evidence. But for this technical neglect the committee would be obliged to find at least ten illegal votes in this list. According to our finding there were cast and counted for contestee seventy-six illegal votes, as above named. As to most of these votes there can be no doubt under the evidence. As to a very few there may be a question depending upon the weight attached to the evidence of different witnesses.

The committee have given the presumption in favor of actual residence, as against a claimed intent to return to an abandoned residence when the intent only appears by the act of voting.

We have refused to reject the votes of actual residents even when it appears that the voter had been in the habit of calling a former residence his home.

It is quite clear that at this election a strong effort was made to bring back to the State all absentees who had formerly resided in the district, and who had not lived abroad long enough to acquire a right to vote.

Some election officers seem to have adopted the erroneous view that a man retains his right to vote in his old home until he acquires a right to vote elsewhere.

Residence may be acquired in a day, but the right to vote may depend on the length of residence. There are several other illegal votes in the list challenged by contestant, but no evidence deemed admissible by the committee as to how they voted. These have been left out of consideration, the committee adhering to the rules laid down in Smith *vs.* Jackson, reported at this session.

The vote, No. 253—that of Arthur Bond—was tendered and ought to have been received, as he was clearly a legal voter. He tendered a vote for contestant and his vote should be counted against contestee.

The same is true of No. 252, Silas Friend.

Allowing these two, and there are seventy-eight votes to be deducted from contestee.

Attorneys for contestee in their brief attack 153 votes charged to have been illegally cast for contestant, and in a supplemental brief, 21 more making 174 in all.

These they have numbered 1 to 153 in original brief, and from 1 to 21 in supplemental brief.

Of these, Nos. 13 to 85, inclusive, are like those attacked by contestant at Braxton Court-House.

The attacked votes from 13 to 85 voted at Wellsburg, where they have been in the habit of voting for the last eleven years. And it is charged that they lived in a portion of the town not belonging to the Wellsburg voting precinct.

The facts are well stated in contestant's reply brief at page 16.

It seems that before the year 1887 the north line of the town of Wellsburgh and the district of the same name have been coincident, and that immediately north of the town and in Cross Creek district lived a considerable population who vote at a precinct known as "Harvey's."

In September, 1878, the circuit court of the county entered an order extending the corporate limits of the town of Wellsburgh so as to include the voting precinct at Harvey's, and so as also to include the residences of those 73 voters. * * *

The voting precinct at Harvey's was abolished and a new one opened, first at Devenney's and then at Lazarville, before the general election of 1878. This change was made because it was the understanding that the voters who resided within the recently included territory would vote in the Wellsburgh district, and the old voting place needed not therefore to be retained for their convenience, and so from that time for eleven years the voters and the county authorities have treated the region included in the town as being also a part of the district of Wellsburgh. The persons residing in this region have continuously and without objection voted in Wellsburgh.

Officers were appointed from persons residing in this territory required by law to be residents of Wellsburgh district.

In August, 1878, the county court established by an order of record a new precinct "in lieu of Harvey's, which is now within the boundaries of the district of Wellsburgh," thus recognizing this territory as being within Wellsburgh district.

It is not necessary to inquire whether all the forms of law have been complied with to take this territory into Wellsburgh district.

The court and the people recognized the fact; it was accepted as something accomplished, and the addition has been accomplished as a matter of fact.

Voters are not to be disfranchised under such circumstances any more than the acts of *de facto* officers are to be held invalid in collateral proceedings. The committee hold that these votes were legally cast, and do not enter upon any investigation of the evidence as to who got the benefit of them.

The following votes cast for contestant are held illegal:
Numbers as in contestee's brief.

No.	Name.	Remarks.
3	Frank Davis	Minor.
86	W. H. H. Smith	Non-resident.
88	Wm. Weaver	Do.
89 / 96	Frank Bowman (named twice)	Do.
90	Alfred Craft	Do.
92	C. W. Wallace	Do.
98	M. Pratt	Do.
100	Frank Justice	Do.
102	William Conners	Do.
103	George Cox*	Do.
106	Samuel Shrives*	Do.
107	Samuel Adams	Pauper.
116	Andrew Nicholson	Non-resident.
117	Jonah Dennison	Do.
121	All Ratcliff	Do.
122	George Batton	Minor.
124	Jacob Burcher	Unsound mind.
126	Samuel H. Feltro	Non-resident.
130	George Cartright	Minor.
134	John Carpenter	Convict.
135	Y. H. Branson	Minor.
131	Edgar Ewing	Non-resident.
143	Charles Vennum*	Do.
144	Thomas McCurdy*	Do.
149	—— Bundy	Do.
151	Lloyd J. Janes	Do.
153	Jacob Hall	Do.

SUPPLEMENTAL BRIEF.

No.	Name.	Remarks.
3	Charles McDonald	Non-resident.
6	Selathiel Crow	Pauper.
8	James Cunningham	Non-resident.
12	Frederick Bowers	Unsound mind.
13	G. W. Simms	Non-resident.
17	Melvin Ault	Do.
19	Lewis Barnard	

Nos. 20 and 21 are possibly illegal and the four marked with an asterisk (*) are doubtful, making in all thirty-six illegal votes cast for contestant including these doubtful votes. Josephus Daniels, No. 1, in contestee's brief, claimed to be a minor, conceded by contestant, was not a minor and his vote was legal. The concession was made by overlooking the record of the marriage of his parents, which was a year earlier than the oral testimony showed.

The result shows illegal votes cast—

For contestee	78
For contestant	36
Contestant's returned majority	7
To which add	78
	85
Subtract illegal votes for contestant	36
Balance	49

The large number of illegal votes makes it out of the question to re-view the evidence touching each vote.

The briefs filed in the case refer to the pages in the record where the evidence may be found, with a few exceptions, where attorneys seem to have overlooked some testimony in a few instances of considerable importance but only affecting two or three votes.

The committee are satisfied that a careful examination of the evidence will verify the accuracy of our findings and fully justify this report in every important particular.

In accordance with these findings, the committee propose the following resolution, and recommend its adoption:

Resolved, That George W. Atkinson was duly elected a Representative to the Fifty-first Congress from the First Congressional district of West Virginia at the election held November 6, 1888, instead of John O. Pendleton, and that said George W. Atkinson is entitled to his seat as such Representative.

VIEWS OF THE MINORITY.

The preponderance of the evidence indicates that the recount in Wetzel County properly represented the votes cast.

Applying to the testimony the law as laid down in Smith *vs.* Jackson, more illegal votes are shown to have been cast for contestant than for contestee, and contestee's right to the seat is accordingly sustained.

61

VIEWS OF THE MINORITY.

Mr. O'FERRALL, from the Committee on Elections, submitted the following as the views of the minority:

The vote in the First Congressional district of West Virginia, as returned to the governor of that State and upon which a certificate of election was issued to John O. Pendleton, the contestee, was as follows:

For John O. Pendleton, contestee... 19,261
For George W. Atkinson, contestant.. 19,242

Majority for Pendleton, contestee 19

Upon the face of the returns, it will be observed, Pendleton, the contestee, was elected and entitled to the certificate of election, and has the prima facie right to the seat he holds.

The contestant recognizing the fact that the contestee has the prima facia right has undertaken to show his superior right by alleging in his notice of contest that many persons disqualified under the constitution and laws of West Virginia voted for the contestee; that votes tendered for him, the contestant, by persons duly qualified were rejected by the officers of election; and that in the county of Wetzel fraud was committed in the recount of the ballots of 2 precincts—Martin's schoolhouse and Archer's Fork—by which he lost 14 votes at the one and 10 votes at the other, and the contestee gained 2 votes.

All these allegations are denied in the answer of the contestee; and he makes counter-charges that many illegal votes were cast for the contestant, and that legal votes tendered for him were rejected by the officers of election.

The issues then are plainly and distinctly drawn between the parties and can be readily understood.

We have not seen the report of the majority of the Committee on Elections, and we do not know upon what ground they hold that the contestant has overcome the prima facia right of the contestee and is entitled to the seat now occupied by the contestee; all we know is that they so hold, but as to what votes they exclude or count on either side, or what their conclusions are as to the alleged fraud in the recount in Wetzel County we are left in the dark.

We, therefore, are compelled to present our views sustaining the right of the contestee to the seat without any specific reference to those of the majority.

The record in this case is very voluminous, covering more than 1.500 pages of printed matter, and its examination has required much time and labor.

Adopting substantially the law laid down in the recent case of Smith vs. Jackson, so far as it applies to the questions involved in this case, we find, in our opinion, that the votes cast by the following-named parties were illegal, and that they were cast for the contestee and contestant, respectively, as follows:

For the contestee:

1. Thomas L. George.
2. Smith Marks.
3. John F. Paugh.
4. Thomas Brothers.
5. William Kidd.
6. B. K. McMechen.
7. George Baird, jr.
8. Joseph Kress.
9. Charles Rogers.
10. Isaac Woofter.
11. A. F. Wilmoth.
12. Frederick Anshurtz.
13. Thomas Marsh.
14. Frederick W. Bloome.
15. William Law Hooff.
16. J. W. Squires.
17. R. E. L. Black.
18. William Weekly.
19. Henry Benter.
20. Jacob Wiltzberger.
21. Henry Copps.
22. Harry Noble.
23. Edward Kreiter.
24. Thomas Ullum.
25. Newton Johnson.
26. Jerry Farribee.
27. Henry Fisher.
28. Patrick Callahan.

For the contestant:

1. Cephas Daniels.
2. Frank Davis.
3. Joseph Dillon.
4. J. D. Trumbo.
5. J. E. Dillon.
6. B. F. Friend.
7. G. W. Ro e.
8. J. D. Bradley.
9. Wilmer Weaver.
10. Alfred Craft.
11. Josiah Wingrere.
12. Frank Bowman.
13. Sherman Kirk.
14. Frank Justice.
15. John Ammon.
16. William Conners.
17. George Cox.
18. Michael Kelley.
19. C. B. Mills.
20. Samuel Shrives.
21. J. E. Ramsey.
22. J. J. Rogers.
23. Harvey Bee.
24. Andrew Nicholson.
25. Jesses Seeders.
26. Al Ratcliff.
27. George Batton.
28. Jacob Bencher.
29. W. E. Parrish.
30. Samuel H. Felton.
31. R. J. Ta lor.
32. Richard Johnson.
33. Geor e Cutright.
34. John Carpenter.
35. Robert Prettyman.
36. John Wise.
37. Owen McCoy.
38. J. W. Grigsby.
39. Charles Venum.
40. Thomas McCurdy.
41. J. H. Branson.
42. Joseph Shaw.
43. Arthur Wallace.
44. Samuel Murray.
45. —— Bundy.
46. J. C. Connelly.
47. Jacob Hull.
48. Dana Hubbard.
49. Charles McDonald.
50. Salathiel Crow.
51. Lindsay Hart.
52. Henry Chambers.
53. Frederick Bowers.
54. W. H. Lewis.

These voters either testified themselves for whom they voted, or it was shown satisfactorily that they were pronounced in their political opinions at the time of the election, or that they declared on the day of election which ticket they had voted or, that they were accompanied to the polls by well-known party workers, or that their votes were challenged by the supporters of one and their right to vote defended by the supporters of the other ticket, or like circumstances, raising a strong and legal presumption as to the ticket they voted and the candidate for whom they voted.

This was as much latitude as we believe the law as heretofore generally administered in this House would allow, and in our opinion, the extreme limit to which sound public policy, the security of elections, and the ends of justice in this case, as well as all others in this or future Congresses will permit.

We deduct then 28 votes from the contestee and 54 votes from the contestant.

Besides these illegal votes there were the following:

Class 1.

1. John Gilligan.
2. John Lodge.
3. Jacob Millbaugh.
4. John M. Utler.
5. William Klieves.
6. W. A. Delaplane.
7. Pat Williams.
8. Lee Minor.
9. Bode Davis.
10. John Deberry.
11. William Kimmey.
12. Thomas Seaman.
13. Reuben Wade.
14. Lloyd Brown.

Class 2.

1. W. H. H. Smith.
2. William Shriner.
3. Samuel Adams.
4. Carter Smith.
5. James Applegate.
6. M t. Jones.
7. William Bates.
8. Edgar Ewing.
9. I. H. Fitch.
10. Lloyd L. Janes.
11. Millard Stout.
12. William A. Moore.
13. Harrison Earp.
14. Alonzo Patterson.
15. Nicholas Veltz.
16. Wilson Hubbard.
17. James Cunningham.
18. Bud Layton.
19. William Myers.
20. G. W. Simms.

But we have not deducted any of these votes, for the reason that the proof as to how they voted does not come within the rule already stated. As to class 1, the testimony simply shows that they were considered or reputed to be Democrats, but when they had expressed themselves, or what opportunities the witnesses had for ascertaining their sentiments, does not appear. As to class 2, the testimony is of the same character, only differing in this that they were considered or reputed to be Republicans.

In a country like this, where the political opinions of voters are constantly changing and new issues are constantly springing up, where party votes fluctuate from year to year and majorities shift from one side to the other, where each of the two great dominant parties strain every nerve in every campaign to convert those who have been in the ranks of its enemy to its policy, and the other weaker parties seek to gather strength from both, we think it would be dangerous, indeed, to hold that a Democrat or Republican in 1884, or even later, was presumptively a Democrat or Republican in 1888. Particularly strong does this reasoning apply, in our opinion, to the election of 1888 In that election a most important issue, which had been dormant at least for years, sprung into pre-eminent prominence and became at once the shibboleth of both the Democratic and Republican parties. In many sections former party lines were broken; Republican communities became Democratic, and *vice versa*. It is a well-recognized fact that it was an election of surprises to both parties.

But without pursuing this line of argument further, we think that the authorities are almost uniform in support of the proposition that mere proof that a voter was considered or reputed to belong to a particular party is not admissible to show how he voted at an election, and certainly not unless it appear conclusively no better evidence could have been procured.

We find further that the following duly-qualified voters tendered their ballots respectively for the contestant and contestee and were rejected improperly by the officers of the election:

For contestant:

1. Silas Friend.   2. Arthur Bond.

For contestee:

1. Martin Conners.   2. B. F. Todd.

We think these votes should be added to the vote of the contestant and contestee respectively; that is, two votes to each.

The contestant charged in his notice of contest that 35 votes were cast for the contestee in Holly district, in the county of Braxton, which were illegal.

He based his charge upon the ground that in 1874 the county court of Braxton proceeded to change the boundaries of the districts and to reform them without giving the notice required by the statute, and that the 35 persons named, though living within Holly district as then formed, by the order of the county court were not legal voters in that district.

The evidence showed that these voters had voted at former elections in Holly district and many of them for years; that their votes had always been counted, and no question as to their legality had ever been raised.

The contestant also charged that 35 votes were cast in the city of Wheeling for the contestee by persons at voting places in districts or wards in which they did not reside. No record evidence as to the

H. Mis. 137——5

boundaries of said district or ward was offered; the witnesses differed
as to the limits of the districts and wards, and there appears to have
been much doubt as to the lines. The voters all believed they were
voting in the proper districts and wards, and the judges of election were
of the same opinion.

Under these circumstances we do not think these voters should be
disfranchised or that the contestee should lose their votes.

The contestee charged in his answer that 73 votes cast for the contestant in Wellsburg district, in the county of Brooke, were illegal,
and insisted they should be deducted from the vote of the contestant.

Upon an examination we found that all of these voters acted under
an honest belief that they had the legal right to vote in Wellsburg
district; that this had been the usual voting place of all the voters living within the boundaries in which they lived for years, and that it was
another case of confusion and misapprehension as to lines and orders
of the court, and under this state of facts we have determined that it
would be unjust to the voters, as well as to the contestant, to deduct
these votes.

We come now to the consideration of the recount in Wetzel County.

It is claimed by the contestant that there was no mistake made by
the officers of the election at Martin's School House and Archer's Fork
in their count, and the return they made, but that the ballots were
changed after they had been returned to the clerk's office of the county
by "scratching" his name on 24, and inserting the name of the contestee in two of them, so that he lost thereby 24 votes, and the contestee gained 2 votes.

Of course the officers of an election, unless they are corrupt, believe
that the returns they make is correct and are ready and willing to testify
to that effect. So with the officers at these precincts; they testify, and
no doubt truthfully, that they do not believe they made any mistake or
that they overlooked any "scratched" ballots, But when the recount
took place the scratched ballots referred to were found by the county
commissioners, and we must ascertain as best we can whether honest
mistakes were made by the precinct officers or the tickets were fraudulently "scratched" by some miscreant after they reached the clerk's
office.

Let us then examine the testimony.

MARTIN'S SCHOOL HOUSE.

First. The count was long and tedious.

A. B. Streight, judge (record, 335):

Ques. When was the counting done ?—Ans. Commenced counting right away after
the polls closed; counted that night until about 2 o'clock; then quit counting and got
something to eat and took us a sleep; commenced next morning; don't know exact
time, and counted on until done; only quit long enough to get something to eat.

W. H. Parks, clerk (record 337):

Quest. When was the counting done?—Ans. We commenced counting after the
polls was closed in the evening, and counted until one or two o'clock that night, and
adjourned till next morning, when we resumed count and finished late that evening.

William J. Wykert, clerk (record 335):

Quest. When was the counting done ?—Ans. On the night following the election
we counted until about midnight, and the next day from the time we got there until
9 or 10 o'clock at night.

John R. Woods, judge (record 336):

Quest. When did you commence to count and how long were you engaged ?—Ans. We began to count the night of the election day, and counted until about 9 or 10 o'clock that night, and commenced the next day about 10 o'clock, and finished that night about 9 or 10 o'clock.

Thomas H. Alley, judge (record 343):

Quest. When did you commence to count the vote cast at your election precinct on the 6th day of November, 1888, and how long were you engaged in counting it ?—Ans. We commenced about dark the day of the election; we counted on until about 11 o'clock that night, when word came that John Woods's (one of the judges) child was sick and for him to come home; we then adjourned until about 9 or 10 o'clock the next day; John Woods had then come back; we finished counting about 11 o'clock that night.

According to these statements made by the three judges and two clerks, they were engaged in receiving and counting the votes not less than thirty hours—two entire days and until late in the night of each day. These officers were men unaccustomed to such work; their usual rest was broken in upon, and it is but natural that they should have made mistakes, and that frequent mistakes were made is shown by the testimony. (Record, 337.)

Second. During the nights of the count the light was bad. There were two lamps and a lantern part of the time, and then only two lamps, and one was used by the judges and the other by the clerks (Record, 335). The judge who took the ballots from the box, and who said he read each ticket, was sixty-two years of age and a Republican (Record, 335). The judge who read off the tickets to the clerks used glasses and "usually voted the Democratic ticket;" but as to how he voted in this election he is silent (Record, 337). The judge who strung the ballots voted for the contestee, but he only examined the tickets to which his attention was called as "scratched" ballots. He was sixty-two years of age. (Record, 343.)

Streight, the Republican judge who testified with so much freedom that there was no difficulty in making the count, said when he delivered the ballots to the county clerk "that he had had trouble enough with them; that it had been an awful job to count that vote," and "told how long the commissioners had been about it, that the judges and clerks were all worn out when they got through." (Record, 948.)

His memory, too, upon the witness stand seemed to be exceedingly good, but how much reliance is to be placed in it is shown by his failure to remember how the vote stood between the contestant and contestee at his precinct when he delivered the return to the county clerk on the day after the count was concluded, and also by his statement at the same time that "almost everybody voted for the removal of the county seat; that there were only seventeen or eighteen votes against it," when the returns made by him as one of the judges at his precinct showed some sixty votes against it, and when asked if he could not be mistaken, he said "he was pretty positive." (Record, 948.)

Third. When the ballots were recounted by the county commissioners 14 Republican ballots were found upon which the name of the contestant had been scratched, and one had the name of J. W. Yeater substituted, and two had the name of J. O. Pendleton inserted. One Democratic ticket had the name of Fleming, the Démocratic candidate for governor, erased, and the name of Goff, his Republican competitor, substituted. (Record, 948.)

The scratching was done with a lead pencil; some were erased by small crosses thus × × × ×, others by straight marks. The county commissioners in considering them held them up to the light as if un-able to decide whether the ballots were scratched at all; the scratching did not appear as having been made by the same person. (Record, 947.)

We are of the opinion that all the circumstances connected with the original count at Martin's School-house, coupled with the indistinct marking of the ballots, go to show that the two judges who say they read all the ballots, in their worn and tired condition, with imperfect eye-sight and bad light, overlooked the marked or scratched ballots which were subsequently discovered, and that such was the fact no one could question for a moment, but for the charge that the ballots were tampered with after they were delivered to the clerk, and this we will hereafter consider.

ARCHER'S FORK.

At this precinct the evidence even much more strongly points to mis-takes in the count by the officers of the election. The recount discloses 10 ballots upon which the name of the contestant had been scratched.

First. The count commenced directly after dark and continued all night and until about noon the next day. (Record, 951, 952.)

Second. The light was bad. There were two lanterns and a small lamp until about 11 o'clock in the night; from 11 o'clock till 4 o'clock, one lantern and the small lamp; from 4 o'clock until daylight, only the small lamp. (Record, 953.)

Third. Two of the judges were so fatigued and worn out that they went to sleep while the count was progressing. (Record, 953.)

Fourth. There is direct evidence the judges did not observe that one ballot was scratched until their attention was called to it by a by-stander who happened to see it, and this was in broad day-light, about 10 o'clock in the morning. (Record, 952, 953, 954.)

Fifth. The proof is positive that the judge who called off the ballots for the clerks to tally did not, after the count had progressed awhile, read the names on the ballots, but would call "straight Republican ticket," "straight Democratic ticket," "straight goods," "hurrah for Harrison; all wool a yard straight goods," "hurrah for Cleveland, all wool a yard wide and straight goods," and the clerks would tally all through the long Republican or Democratic ticket as the call might in-dicate. (Record, 952, 953, 954.)

In the light of this testimony the verity of the count by the judges at this precinct is greatly shaken, and the discovery of scratched ballots by the county commissioners at the recount is not at all surprising, and would be accepted as conclusive evidence of mistakes by the judges of the precinct in the absence of proof that the ballots were tampered with after they were received by the clerk of the county court.

It appears in evidence that there was dissatisfaction expressed as to the Republican nominee for Congress, and several Republicans de-clared their intention to cut him, and one who had been an active worker declared he would injure him where he least expected. If these Republicans carried out their threats the "scratching" at Martin's School-House and Archer's Fork was the natural consequence.

CHARGE THAT BALLOTS WERE FRAUDULENTLY SCRATCHED.

As already stated, the county commissioners found 24 ballots upon which the name of the contestant had been scratched and 2 upon which his name was erased and the name of the contestee substi-tuted; this was done, the contestant charges, by R. E. L. Snodgrass, the deputy clerk, and he further charges that Benjamin Earnshaw, the president of the county court, was privy to the fraud.

The returns and ballots from these precincts were delivered to the deputy clerk (Snodgrass) in sealed packages as the law required. (Record, 426.)

The seal was not broken until the packages were opened by the commissioners and the clerk, John C. McEldowney. (Record, 426.) During the recount the ballots were in charge of the commissioners in the daytime and then locked up in the vault of the clerk's office at night by a combination lock. (Record, 427.) Surely this was all that could be expected to secure the ballots and put them beyond the reach of evil hands.

It is charged, however, that the recount was continued from day to day for a number of days with fraudulent intent, and that Benjamin Earnshaw, the president of the county court, absented himself to protract the recount, and give an opportunity to R. E. L. Snodgrass, the deputy clerk, to scratch and mutilate the ballots, and upon this charge the contestant relies to impeach the recount.

It is charged that on the 21st day of November, 1888, and during the recount, Charles E. Wells and W. W. Arnett, citizens of Marion County, appeared at the county seat of Wetzel, and that Wells had an interview with Earnshaw at dinner time; that later in the day a telegram was received by Earnshaw, sent by Wells, over the signature of a party by the name of Black, stating his (Earnshaw's) wife was sick; that thereupon the recount was adjourned until the next day; that the substance of the telegram was false and that Earnshaw knew it; and that all this was evidence of a conspiracy to perpetrate a fraud, and that it was successful.

Now, what does Earnshaw say (record, 944)?

Q. 15. State, if you remember, how many days the county count was in session for the purpose of canvassing the returns.—A. 15. I can't say positively how many days, but I believe we were here in all something like 18 days.

Q. 16. State whether or not during that session of the court you were absent; and, if so, how long?—A. 16. I was absent a time or two, but I don't remember how long I was absent.

Q. 17. State if, during the session of the county court, you remember of having seen Charles E. Wells, of Marion County, here in New Martinsville; and, if so, state, if you know, what business he was here for.—A. 17. I remember of seeing Charles E. Wells during that term of court; I understood that he was here in regard to a suit pending or to be instituted against L. G. Robinson.

Q. 18. State whether or not you had any business yourself of a public or private nature with Charles E. Wells at that time?—A. 18. *I had business of a private nature with Charles E. Wells at that time.*

Q. 19. State whether or not that business was in any way, directly or indirectly, immediately or remotely, connected with the election held in this county on the 6th of November, 1888, or in any way pertained to or affected the interests of any candidate at that election, and especially the interests of John O. Pendleton and G. W. Atkinson or A. B. Flemming or Nathan Goff, who were candidates for office at said election?—A. 19. It had *nothing to do with the election at all, and did not affect the interest of any candidate.*

Q. 20. State whether or not, on the day that C. E. Wells was here, or about that time, you received a telegram purporting to be from Frank J. Black, summoning you home; and if so, state, if you know, who sent that telegram.—A. 20. *I did receive a telegram and knew that Charles E. Wells sent it.*

Q. 21. State whether or not you left here after receiving that telegram.—A. 21. *I did.*

Q. 22. State whether or not, to your knowledge, that telegram was sent by C. E. Wells for the purpose of interfering with the recount of the votes then in progress before the county court?—A. 22. *No, sir; not at all, further than it necessarily delayed the recount: but it was not intended to interfere with the recount.*

There was no attempt to contradict this statement or to impeach the witness.

He swears positively that his business with Wells was of a private nature and had nothing whatever to do with the election, and that the telegram was not intended to interfere with the recount, further than it necessarily delayed it. If the contestant doubted the truthfulness of Earnshaw's statement, it was his duty to summons Wells. This he did not do.

There is no evidence Mrs. Earnshaw was not sick. She has been in delicate health for years, and sometimes in very bad health. (Record, 363.)

One witness testified that she attended a party at his house, "he thought" on the 22d November, but "would not be certain" (record, 363.)

We submit that there is nothing in the testimony in this case to impeach the integrity of Earnshaw and to stamp him as a man not only unworthy of the honorable position he holds but as a malefactor almost of the deepest dye.

We come now to the testimony in regard to Snodgrass, the deputy clerk, and before presenting it we desire to say that the conduct of this man after the recount was certainly not commendable. It seems that he expressed a willingness to take money from the chairman of the Republican State committee of West Virginia upon consideration that "he would tell all he knew about the ballot-scratching," when he swears he knew nothing and could not have told anything. He seems to have regarded this as a pardonable device to obtain money from the Republican party, if its chairman was "foolish" enough to pay it; but this can be said in his behalf, that it he had been corrupt and villainous enough to "scratch" the ballots, as charged, he would have been corrupt and venal enough to have made statements more direct, which, though they might have been false, it seems would have secured pecuniary benefit or bribe-money. In a word, money or positions were ready for him if he would lay the "scratching" upon some person; and if he was bad enough to commit the fraud charged, he was bad enough, for money or position, to make a false statement implicating some one else. The evidence, however, shows conclusively, we think, that he could not be led into any statement except that "he would tell all he knew;" and this not being satisfactory to the chairman of the Republican State executive committee, the negotiations ended.

This conduct upon the part of Snodgrass alone has induced the contestant to charge him with scratching the ballots, as he had access to the clerk's office. At first, J. M. McIntire, who seems to have had charge of the Republican organization in Wetzel County, suspicioned a man by the name of Null, whom he said was acting suspiciously in the clerk's office one evening, but he found he was mistaken in the man, and that "got him off his pins and he did not know what to say" (record, 937.) He then engaged a man by the name of Grall, against whom he held a bond and to whom he promised $650 or $700, "enough to square off" the bond and a position in Washington at $100 per month, for four years, to gather information for him, and suggested that Snodgrass "knew all about it." Grall went to Snodgrass and told him what McIntire had promised him, and Snodgrass told him to agree to tell all he knew about it "and then swear you know nothing" and get the money. Grall said he would not like to do that (record, 938). We give the following as the further statement of Grall in his own language:

He (Snodgrass) said I would if I could get a chance at them; I told him then I could easily enough get them on to you by telling them I believe that you knew something about it and that you would tell all you knew about it for a certain amount o.̇ money; Lee said then, all right, you do that; I went to McIntire then and told him that I believed that Lee Snodgrass knew something about the ticket-scratching and would tell all he knew for a certain sum of money; then Mr. McIntire wanted to know how much I thought he wanted; I told him I did not know, but I thought he would tell for about $2,000, or along there; then McIntire said that is a little steep, and said you see him whether or not he would not do it for less money; I told him then I would; he says, you see him and let me know and if we can make it satisfactory, the amount, that he would draw up the writings and go up to Wheeling and see Cowden; I went and saw Lee the next day after this conversation and told him what McIntire told me; and he told me then that he would rather talk to McIntire himself so they would understand each other exactly; after that I saw McIntire and told him what Lee had told me, and he says all right, you tell Lee to come to my office this evening; I told him I would see Lee and I did so.

Q. 11. When you told McIntire that you thought Lee Snodgrass knew something about the scratching of the ballots and would tell for a sum of money did you mean to state what you believed to be true or what Lee had told you to state, as you have said before?—A. 11. I just told him because Lee had told me to tell him; I did not know it was true and did not think it was.

̇Q. 11. What do you know, if anything, about such scratching of ballots as has been mentioned?—A. 11. I don't know anything.

McIntire visited the clerk's office and had an interview with Snodgrass, in which McIntire promised Snodgrass that he should not be prosecuted and should have a Government position at Washington that would pay at least $1,800 a year. Snodgrass replied he wanted no Government position, but would tell all he knew about the ticket scratching for $3,000 in cash, and that he must have the money before he made the affidavit. McIntire then wanted Snodgrass to go to Wheeling to fix the matter up, but Snodgrass declined. McIntire then proposed to Snodgrass to go to Sistersville, but Snodgrass again declined. McIntire then said he would go to Wheeling and see W. J. D. Cowden, the chairman of the executive committee of the Republican party of West Virginia, and get him to come to the county seat of Wetzel.

In a few days McIntire saw Snodgrass and told him that Cowden would be down the next evening. Cowden came and an interview was arranged between him and Snodgrass. As to what took place at this interview Cowden and Snodgrass differ. Cowden states that Snodgrass said, "Well, to cut a long story short, I will tell all about it for $3,000 cash;" to which he replied, "I can not accept any such offer." Snodgrass testifies that "Cowden said he could offer him no special inducement to make a statement, further than that he wanted me to understand that the Republican party had elected a President, also a governor of the State, and that they would remember their friends, and that they would be well provided for, and that when he said well provided for he meant amply provided for."

"Then he went on to explain the advantages of a life in Washington City, backed up with a good Government position paying from $1,800 to $2,000 per year and not much to do; and he said he could not offer me any further inducement to make the statement except that I would be exonerated from prosecution in case my statement should implicate myself; and said that the reason why he could not offer any further inducement, that it would go toward weakening my evidence before a jury, and that they wanted as strong a case as possible. I told him that as I was a Democrat I did not care to hold a Government position under a Republican administration; that I did not care to live in Washington City; but I told him, to cut the matter short, I would tell all I knew about the ticket scratching for $3,000 in cash, and would make an affidavit, but I must have the cash before the affidavit; also to have an agreement in writing, signed in duplicate, he to retain one copy and me the other, setting out what I was to do for the $3,000. Mr. Cowden said that my offer was for a large amount of money, and a fixed sum, and if that fact was made known to a jury on the trial of any indictment that might be found upon my statement it would tend to weaken my evidence very much. Then I told Mr. Cowden that when I made my statement that I would furnish evidence to prove that the statement I made was true. Mr. Cowden said that he could not make me an offer of any fixed amount of money, but would take the matter under consideration, and that I would hear from him again. .

Then I told Mr. Cowden that I would be compelled to leave. Mr. Cowden insisted on me staying and have a longer talk. I told him that I had nothing more to say about the matter, and that if he did not want the goods at the price he did not have to take them. Then it was understood all around between Cowden, McIntire, Grall, and myself that nothing would be said about our meeting. Then Mr. Cowden gave me to understand that he would further consider my proposition, and that I would hear from him soon. Then McIntire, Grall, and myself left the room."

Snodgrass is corroborated by Grall, who was present, and testified as follows:

Q. 15. Were you present at the Brast House at the time of the interview between R. E. L. Snodgrass and Mr. W. J. W. Cowden, chairman of the Republican State executive committee? And if so, state how you came to be present and what occurred between Mr. Cowden and Mr. Snodgrass; stating as fully as you can what was said by each and who were present at that interview?—A. 15. I was present; Mr. Snodgrass told me that they had made arrangements for Cowden to be here on Monday evening; I also heard the arrangements between McIntire and Snodgrass that Cowden was to be here on Monday evening; I think it was Monday evening; I am not certain; it was on the 31st day of December that he was here, and I came down street and met McIntire, and he told me that Cowden was here, and he told me that Lee wanted me to come down to the Brast House and go to Cowden's room, and I went down and McIntire and Lee Snodgrass and myself went up into the room; then McIntire introduced us to Cowden, and, after some conversation, it was either McIntire or Cowden said, "I suppose you gentlemen know what business you came here for," and Mr. Snodgrass replied, "I suppose we do;" then Mr. Cowden said, "We might as well come down to business;" says, "I understood that you, Snodgrass and McIntire, had some understanding about this matter;" he said, "Of course I can't make you no special offers or inducements to get you to give this away, as we want your evidence as strong as it can be made if it should go to any court," as near as I can remember.

Cowden said that he should be well taken care of if he should give it away; that he could get an office as clerk at Washington, that would pay him from $1,500 to $2,000 per year, and he told him that it would be much nicer to live there than here, and it would be much easier work. I can not remember word for word, but he said the streets were so much nicer there, and everything surrounding, that he, Lee, would like the city much better than he would here. Then Lee told Cowden it would not be very pleasant for him to accept a position of that kind, that he was a Democrat, and has been all his life. Cowden told him then that would not make any difference, that the Republican party would always take care of a good friend, and told him further that they had the President elected now and had a majority in the Senate and Congress both—I think that is what he said—and that he would be sure of a 4 years' job and probably longer. Then Lee told him that he did not want any office, that the only way he would tell what he knew would be for the money cash down. Cowden told him he could not do that; as he said before, they could not use his evidence in court, as it would not have any effect, or words to that effect. Then Lee told him he did not think they could come to any terms then, for that would be the only way he would tell what he knew. Lee said he would tell for $3,000, after Cowden had asked what he would want. There was present McIntire and myself and Lee Snodgrass and Cowden.

Q. 16. After Snodgrass had stated what he would take what did Cowden then say?—A. 16. He said that they could not give him any money, but he would insure him that he would be well provided for, or something to that effect; I guess that was the remark he made.

Q. 17. When the interview ended was there anything said by any one about keeping the matter secret; and, if so, by whom?—A. 17. Yes, sir; Mr. Cowden said that we would keep this meeting secret, and no one need know anything about it, or words to that effect.

From all the testimony it appears that however censurable Snodgrass's proposition may have been, he had the moral courage to resist the strong temptation held out to him to perjure himself; that though inducements of the strongest character were presented, he came forth from the interviews without perjury on his soul and without ill-gotten gains polluting his pocket. His perhaps unguarded remark and immature proposition seem to have reached the ears of men who were as willing to buy as he was to sell, but they were unwilling to pay unless they got full value.

This is all there is in reference to Snodgrass, and we submit whether a recount can be impeached by the foolish and even reprehensible conduct of a party long after it has been closed, simply because the party had, in an official capacity, possible access to the ballots during the recount. Apart from this circumstance there is not the slightest testimony which reflects in the most remote degree upon Snodgrass.

To hold that the contestee shall be deprived of the gain he made by the recount, would be to hold that an act done is fraudulent because some official connected with it and standing fair and unimpeached in the community at the time was guilty of conduct demanding censure at some period thereafter.

We believe the judges of the election at Martin's School-House and Archer's Fork precincts in Wetzel County made mistakes in counting the ballots, and that the recount subsequently made by the county commissioners was correct and truly represented the actual vote cast at these precincts.

It only remains now for us to recapitulate our conclusions.

Statement 1.

Returned vote for contestee	19,261
Add votes tendered by duly qualified voters and rejected	
	19,263
Deduct illegal votes shown by conclusive testimony to have been cast for him	28
Whole vote for contestee	19,235
Returned vote for contestant	19,242
Add votes tendered by duly qualified voters and rejected	2
	19,244
Deduct illegal votes shown by conclusive testimony to have been cast for him	54
Whole vote cast for contestant	19,190
Whole vote for contestee	19,235
Whole vote for contestant	19,190
Majority for contestee	45

This is the statement which we believe is based upon the law and sound public policy.

Statement 2.

Returned vote for contestee		19,261
Add rejected votes		2
		19,263
Deduct illegal votes in Statement 1	28	
Deduct illegal votes where evidence shows only that the voters were considered or reputed to be Democrats	14	
		42
Whole vote for contestee		19,221
Returned vote for contestant		19,242
Add rejected votes		2
		19,244
Deduct illegal votes in Statement 1	54	
Deduct illegal votes where evidence shows only that the voters were considered or reputed to be Republicans	20	
		74
		19,170
Whole vote for contestee		19,221
Whole vote for contestant		19,170
Majority for contestee		51

We make this statement for the consideration of the House in the event it is thought that proof only that a voter was considered or reputed to be a Democrat or Republican is sufficient to show how he voted.

Statement 3.

Majority for contestee under Statement 1 45
Deduct votes claimed by contestant at Martin's School-House and Archer's Fork.. 26
                                                                              ———
    Majority for contestee.. 19
                                                                              ═══
Majority for contestee under Statement 2 51
Deduct votes claimed by contestant at Martin's School-House and Archer's Fork.. 26
                                                                              ———
    Majority for contestee.. 25

This statement is presented to show that the contestee has a clear majority of 19 or 25 even after deducting all that contestant claims at Martin's School-House and Archer's Fork.

We are of the opinion that in any aspect of the case the contestee was duly elected, and we submit the following resolutions:

Resolved, That George W. Atkinson was not elected a Representative in the Fifty-first Congress from the First Congressional district of West Virginia, and is not entitled to a seat therein.

Resolved, That John O. Pendleton was duly elected a Representative in the Fifty-first Congress from the First Congressional district of West Virginia, and is entitled to his seat therein.

CHAS. O'FERRALL.
LEVI MAISH.
CHARLES F. CRISP.
JOS. H. OUTHWAITE.
L. W. MOORE.
R. P. C. WILSON.

L. P. FEATHERSTON vs. W. H. CATE.

FIRST ARKANSAS.

Contestant charged conspiracy, violence, intimidation, and fraud. The committee find frauds sufficient in amount to overturn the majority returned for contestee and to show a majority for contestant. The minority find the charges of fraud not sustained by the evidence, and that part of the testimony, being taken without legal notice, should not be considered. The case was called· up March 1, 1890, and debated until March 5, when the resolutions presented by the committee were adopted by a vote of 145 to 135, and Mr. Featherston was sworn in. The debate will be found of pages 1843 to 1955 of the Record.

(1) **Return.** *To be thrown out if false, but the votes cast not necessarily lost.*

Where the evidence shows a return to be false and not a true statement of the votes cast, such return is impeached and destroyed as evidence. But the rejection of a return does not necessarily leave the votes actually cast at a precinct uncounted. (See *ante,* Atkinson *vs.* Pendleton.) The return being shown to be false the parties are thrown back on such evidence as it may be in their power to produce to show how many votes were cast and for whom. All the votes may thus be proved and counted, but if only a part is proved, those proved are to be counted and the rest disregarded.

(2) **Suppression of testimony.**

Where one party suppresses testimony strict and technical proof will not be required of the other.

(3) **No election.**

Where no election is held votes can not be counted.

(4) **Notice of contest.**

The recitals in the notice can have none of the sanctity and binding force of an agreement or stipulation, and can not be construed into a concession.

(5) **Testimony taken without notice.** *Question of notice may be waived.*

When depositions are found in the printed record and no objection is made to the Clerk of the House or to the opposite party, the party failing to object at the earliest opportunity, or at least within reasonable time so as to put the opposite party on notice, will be deemed to have waived all question of notice, *especially* where there is no offer of proof to show a different state of facts from that shown by the depositions objected to.

75

REPORT.

FEBRUARY 19, 1890.—Mr. HOUK, from the Committee on Elections, submitted the following report:

The Committee on Elections having had under consideration the contested-election case of L. P. Featherston *vs.* W. H. Cate, from the First Congressional district of Arkansas, submit the following report:

This contest differs in one respect, at least, from all other cases of a like character pending before the House of Representatives. The contention for a seat in the House of Representatives from the First Congressional district of Arkansas is between Democrats, the contestant having veered out of the party line so far as to have become the head of an organization in that State known as "The Wheel," while the contestee continued to adhere to and was the candidate of what was known as the regular Democracy. The contestee gives the following history of the political conditions prevailing in that district prior to and about the time of the election in November, 1888:

A. Along in the year 1888 the Wheel became a factor in politics. It was supposed to be a non-political organization, formed ostensibly for the promotion of agricultural interests, and to down monopoly, and to throttle the giant corporations that were reputed to be fattening on the labor of the husbandman; to smash the trusts, abolish national banks, etc.—all very commendable, doubtless, and most certainly a labor of great magnitude, and sufficient to afford ample employment to the good Wheelers without the additional task of regulating and purifying the politics of the country.

These doctrines of the Wheel were popular, and the organization grew and became a power in the land, and thither turned their eager steps the Anarchist, the Communist, the venerable Greenbacker, the political nondescript, sorehead, and bummer of every creed and faith, and essayed to lead in the great reform. The rank and file were composed largely of the farmers, mostly Democrats—there being no doubt 10,000 of 22,000 Democrats in the district who were Wheelers—and somewhat out of temper because of the evils, real or supposed, then prevalent, and in a frame of mind to drift away from the Democratic camp and set up for themselves in a great work of reform, as they supposed.

The shrewd Republican leaders quickly took in the situation, and seeking to improve what seemed to be any opportunity to beat the Democrats in one of their strongholds, adroitly managed to have their emissaries and agents initiated into the lodge of the Wheelers, it being a secret organization.

It is needless to state that these were faithful and effective members, never failing to attend at a meeting, and always overflowing with sympathy for the poor farmer and brimful of a spirit of reform.

The candidate of the Wheelers, the contestant herein, was president of the State Wheel, which in itself gave him a powerful hold on the brethren, and it was reasonably thought he could hold the Wheelers solid for his cause, and then if the Republicans could be brought to his aid this would certainly make a combination that would overthrow the Democrats.

The scheme was not only shrewd and well-planned, but it was also comprehensive, from the fact that it was doubtless made to embrace two districts—the first and second; the agreement among the leaders being that the Republicans should support the Wheel candidate in the first, and the Wheelers should support the Republican candidate in the second.

77

Now, it must be said to the credit of the Republican leaders that they kept their part of the compact religiously to the extent of their ability. So earnest indeed were they, that ex-Governor Powell Clayton, the able and powerful leader in this State, actually came into the first district to canvass for the Wheel candidate, with the object of influencing the Republicans to support contestant and to reconcile, if possible, a strong disaffected element. (Record, page 47.)

*   *   *   *   *

It was found necessary to give the Wheel candidate official indorsements by the Republican party so as to control the voters to his support. Accordingly the district committee was called together, when it was found that a wide difference of opinion existed among them. The more intelligent argued that as the Wheel candidate and Democratic candidate had already made a canvass of the district and the lines were sharply drawn and the fight so far almost entirely within the Democratic party, it was an opportune time to run a straight Republican and capture the district. After much discussion they adjourned to October 27, when they gave the Wheel man an indorsement, etc.

We give the above quotation from contestee's brief for the purpose of showing that there was great disaffection among the Democrats in this district, and that all the other parties—Wheelers, Greenbackers, and Republicans—were supporting the contestant, who had been a Democrat and who was "in a frame of mind to drift away from the Democratic camp," and it may furnish a solution of why it was necessary for the contestee, or his friends, to overcome this defection in the strong. Republican counties.

It is clearly established by the evidence that Crittenden County is Republican, and for years has given large majorities for the Republican party.

William Royster, in speaking of the number of Republicans in Crittenden County, testified:

Q. What proportion of that vote is the Republican vote?—A. About 2,500 or 2,600. (Printed Record, page 191.)

On the same subject, Jordan Yates (col.), a witness on behalf of the contestant, being first duly sworn, testified as follows:

Q. What is your name?—A. Jordan Yates.
Q. Where do you live?—A. Live in West Memphis, Crittenden County, Ark.
Q. How old are you?—A. I am about 42.
Q. How long have you been in Arkansas?—A. Ever since 1865; Crittenden County.
Q. What is your business?—A. Farmer.
Q. You've had something to do with politics in your county?—A. Oh, yes, sir; I've had a great deal to do with it.
Q. Do you hold any official position in your county?—A. I'm chairman of the county central committee, and was also chairman of the county convention; I'm chairman now of the county central committee.
Q. Have you a pretty good idea of the number of voters, Republican voters, in your county?—A. Yes, sir; I got a pretty good idea about the number of Republican voters in the county.
Q. What's your estimate?—A. Well, sir, I think there's about 2,500; that's pretty close. I think it's close on to 2.500. (Printed record, page 192.)

On the same subject J. L. Fleming testified:

Q. Do you know whether, if there was a correct count of the actual vote in Crittenden County—whether the Republican party or Democratic party would carry the county?—A. Well, sir, if they had a correct vote, the two parties, Crittenden County is Republican by 1,800 majority; that's what I think. (Printed record, page 195.)

Wash. Deaver, on this subject, testified:

Q. Did the colored people over there take any interest in the national election?—A. Yes, sir; biggest vote was polled in that county in the national election ever I knowed, and I been there ever since the surrender.
Q. What was the vote of that county in the national election; do you know?—A. I don't know exactly.
Q. Have you any idea?—A. I think it was about 2,500.
Q. Who was that vote polled for?—A. Harrison and Featherston.

Q. Why were the colored people of that county especially anxious for a Rep. administration of national affairs ?—A. Well, sir, it was on the account of they had been pressed by this Winchester crowd this last year, and hoped to get some relief from that element. I knew years before that in the Presidential election they hardly ever paid any attention to it, scarcely polled any votes there in the county.

Q. What do you mean by being pressed ?—A. No, sir; not a fair show before the law, and the ballots never were counted; they had no show at all. The Winchester crowd just bulldozed and done as they pleased, and if they had a mayor to try him, if he was on their side they'd turn him loose, no matter what his crime was, and the other party was put in jail and prosecuted every way they could.

Q. Do you think the Rep. party of Ark. expects the national Rep. party to remedy that state of affairs ?—A. That's what they think.

Q. Was it in that hope to turn out and poll such a large vote for the national ticket ?—A. Yes, sir.

Q. If they had received a fair count, about how much plurality would they have received ?—A. About 2 thousand. (Printed record, page 224).

E. D. Sanders, on the same subject, testified as follows :

Q. What proportion of the vote in the county of Crittenden do you presume was polled for Harrison and Featherston ?—A. I think there was twenty-five hundred votes; I made an estimate of it myself.

Q. What was the proportion ?—About six to one.

Q. Did Featherston receive any other votes in the county of Crittenden in addition to those polled for Harrison ?—A. Yes, sir.

Q. Of your certain knowledge ?—A. Of my certain knowledge.

Q. In your own precinct what was the vote; were you at the polls yourself?—A. Yes, sir; I was at the Bradley precinct. I think Featherston was 195; Cate was 4.

Q. In the county precincts is that a fair proportion of the Democratic and Republican vote in Crittenden County ?—A. Well, that one wouldn't hardly be. There's two or three, Black Oak and Marion and Crawfordsville, I expect there is a little varied.

Q. I say the country precincts.—A. Yes, I reckon it would; that would be a fair sample.

Q. The falling off of your vote on account of its being a rainy day at your precinct, do you recollect what it was—what per cent.?—A. The falling off was 5 per cent.

Q. Was the interest manifested in the national election about equal all over the county ?—A. Yes, sir; well, I took really more interest myself in it than I did in the State election.

Q. And had the interest pretty generally infused all over the county ?—A. Yes, sir. (Printed record, page 200.)

David Furgeson, on the same subject, testified :

Q. The Republican vote in that county was about what, in round numbers ?—A. About 2,500.

Q. Their Democratic vote was about what?—A. About 420. (Printed record, page 208.)

It appears from the record that prior to July, 1888, the county court clerk and one other officer of this county had been indicted for drunkenness—possibly under the following statute of Arkansas:

SEC. 561. When the circuit court shall be satisfied, from its own knowledge, or from the information of others, on oath, that the clerk of such court has been guilty of any misdemeanor in office, or shall be incapable of discharging the duties of his office according to law, *or shall be a drunkard,* such court shall give notice thereof to the prosecuting attorney, stating the charges against such clerk, and requiring him to prosecute the same, and such clerk may be *suspended* from office until a trial can be had, etc. (Mansfield's Digest of Arkansas.)

SEC. 6475. Whenever any presentment of indictment be filed in any circuit court of this State against any county officer for incompetency, corruption, gross immorality, criminal conduct, etc., such circuit court shall immediately order that such officer be suspended from his office until such presentment or indictment shall be tried, etc. (Mansfield's Digest of Arkansas.)

Why the indicted officers were not suspended in compliance with these statutes, after having been indicted, is not susceptible of explanation, except upon the assumption that the judge of the circuit court did not think the indictment could be sustained, and was therefore unwilling to allow the law to be used as any part of a scheme in political

manipulations. Upon the indictment found against them these officers
were to have been tried on the 12th day of July, 1888, the court being
then in session.

On that morning something like 100 men appeared at the court-
house town armed with Winchester rifles. None of the rifles seems to
have been seen by any, except those in the plot previous to that day.

These men, thus armed with Winchester rifles, proceeded to take into
custody and force all the county officers, save the sheriff, who was of
the " Winchester-rifle crowd," to leave the county under threat of
death if they returned.

It appears from the record that this armed force conducted these
officers and others across the Mississippi River and left them in the city
of Memphis, Tenn. Had they simply exiled the officers indicted for
drunkenness, their conduct would have shown they had lost confidence
in the court, or that they did not believe the indictments could be sustained.

It seems to us that if they were simply dissatisfied with the officers
who had been indicted they would not have driven other county officers,
who were not indicted, nor private citizens from the county.

The motive for what thus took place by this process of deportation
on the 12th day of July, 1888, must be sought in something other than
a desire to rid the community of the indicted officers. We are of the
opinion that this motive may be found, and for that purpose reproduce
a portion of the testimony appearing in the printed record, stating
what was done on the morning the trial was to have taken place.

David Fergerson (col.), a witness on behalf of the contestant, being
first duly sworn, testified as follows:

Direct examine:

Q. What is your name?—A. David Fergerson.
Q. Where do you live?—A. Live now in Memphis.
Q. Where did you live at the national election last year?—A. Memphis, Tennessee.
Q. Where did you live previous to that?—A. Lived in Crittenden County, Arkansas.
Q. What was your business at the time you left Crittenden County, Ark.?—A. I
was clerk of the circuit court.
Q. How old are you?—A. 39 years old.
Q. How long have you been a citizen of Crittenden County?—A. Since 1872.
Q. You served how many times as clerk?—A. Three terms.
Q. Please state the time and manner of your leaving Crittenden County.—A. On
the morning of the 12th day of July an armed mob, composed of over a hundred men,
surrounded my office; I was in my office, and my deputy, Mr. Fleming, here. The
mob ordered us to come out, and told us that some of the white people had got anonymous letters ordering them to leave the county, and they had determined among
themselves they shouldn't leave; that we had to leave or they hoped to meet us in
heaven. I told them that I had nothing to do with writing those letters; didn't
know anything about them, and I couldn't go. They said we "had to go; if you
don't we are not responsible for you." The court was in session, Judge Riddick on
the bench, the grand jury there, and I told this armed mob that "if we had committed a crime, here's the grand jury and the court; indict us, put us in jail, and try
us." "No; you've got to leave this county; this is a white man's government, and
we are tired of negro dominations; we have been planning this for the last two years,
and no more negroes or Republicans shall hold office in this county."
Q. Did you leave them of your own accord?—A. I told them I couldn't possibly
leave; I had a bond there, and had to protect my bondsmen as well as myself, and
Col. Smith and Dr. Bingham spoke up and said, yes, we'll have to give him till evening to get out; I saw my bondsmen; they were all there with the guns in their
hands; I saw them and talked with them, and that evening I left.
Q. Were your bondsmen white or colored men?—A. They were composed of white
and colored; the white men that was on my bond was there armed.
Q. State whether there had been any charges preferred in court against you?—A.
I had a charge preferred against me there for drunkenness in office, come up for trial
that morning; they found there was nothing in it and took these steps to get us out;
said they had to control the offices, and only way to control the offices was to get us
out—by getting the leaders out they could control the balance.

Q. Had you ever had any personal trouble with any considerable number of white people?—A. I never did; in 1886 I was elected without opposition as clerk of the court.

Q. How many charges have been preferred against you since that time?—A. Been 11 charges.

Q. Upon how many have you been tried?—A. Haven't been tried on one; I took a change of venue from that county, because I couldn't get justice there, to another county in the district.

Q. State if the bond you made was accepted by the sheriff.—A. The bond that I offered was refused by the sheriff, and I had to carry my bondsmen into open court, and the bond was approved by the judge.

Q. After having been refused by the sheriff?—A. Yes, sir.

Q. Were any of the present officials, or the officials that were in office at that time, among that mob?—A. Yes, sir; W. F. Worner, sheriff, Sam Keel, clerk, S. A. Martin, county judge, W. J. Harden, assessor, C. E. Raspberry, coroner, A. H. Ferguson, treasurer.

Q. Was Worner the sheriff at that time?—A. Worner was sheriff at that time; 12 day of July, and is now present sheriff.

Q. Did he show any right or warrant or authority by which he ordered you out of the county?—A. He did not.

*　　　　　*　　　　　*　　　　　*　　　　　*

Q. What reason did they give you for not giving you a trial, when you asked it, upon the day that they ordered you out of the county; what reason did they assign to you for that action?—A. There was no reason; they said, "God damn you, you got to get out of this county. By God, you been here too long; this is a white man's country, and we will control it. We been waiting for two years for this thing, and you got to get out." I said, "Gentlemen, the court is in session and here's the grand jury." They said, "God damn that, you got to get out."

Q. The circuit court was in session?—A. Yes. sir.

Q. Was there any effort made by the circuit judge for the protection of citizens of the county that you know of?—A. None in the least.

Q. Did he know this thing was going on?—A. To the best of my knowledge and information and belief, he did.

Q. He was not present at the time, was he?—A. While they had us under arrest the capt. of the mob said, "The judge wants you to come up to the court-house and we don't want him to see us here with these men; just carry them around back of the court-house, right under a shade tree." The judge come up there and called court and took a recess, and I saw him standing in the back door of the court-house looking over there where these men were guarding myself and others.

Q. Are you satisfied that he saw you?—A. Yes, sir.

Q. Did you hear him enter any protest against that proceeding?—A. No, sir; I did not. The only thing I knowed him to do—I was indicted, as I told you before—Judge Cate and Mr. Adams, my attorneys, they come down to my house to see me, and said that Judge Riddick, if I thought it necessary, said he would get out a writ of habeas corpus for me. I told him no; I didn't think it necessary, because I wasn't under legal authority; that his court had no jurisdiction over an armed mob. I paid Judge Cate and Mr. Adams to defend me in that indictment against me.

Q. Did he abandon your case?—A. No, sir, he did not; told me he'd stick by me if I wanted to go any further in the case, but he advised me I'd better let it drop. (Printed record, page 207-8.)

The county court clerk, Furgerson, it will be seen closes his testimony by saying that contestee as his counsel advised him (Furgerson) that he "had better let it [the suit] drop." There was no way to "let it drop" except by pleading "guilty," and that would oust him from his office, which was one of the objects, no doubt, from the proof in the record, for which the conspiracy had been formed.

If the contestee had nothing to do with what transpired in Crittenden County, in July, his presence and utterances there have placed him in rather an embarrassing position. His advice to Furgerson has a significant bearing.

J. L. Fleming (col.), a witness on behalf of the contestant, being first duly sworn, testified as follows:

Q. What is your name?—A. J. L. Fleming.

Q. What is your residence?—A. I am a resident of Memphis, Tennessee.

Q. What were you at that time?—A. Resident of Marion, Crittenden County, Arkansas.

H. Mis. 137——6

Q. What is your occupation?—A. I was deputy clerk under Mr. Ferguson, and editor of the Marion Head Light.

Q. What is your age?—A. 29.

Q. How long have you lived in Marion, Ark.?—A. About four years.

Q. Did you have to leave Marion, Ark., Crittenden County, any time last year?—A. Yes, sir; on the 12 day of July, 1888, myself and ten others were brought from Marion to Mound City by an armed mob, and put on the ferry-boat at Mound City and sent over to Memphis, and guarded to Memphis; three of the men came on this side.

Q. How many men were in that mob?—A. I don't know; probably a hundred or more; more or less.

Q. What were their reasons for sending you out of the county?—A. Well, they claimed that several of the white citizens had received anonymous letters saying that they had to leave Crittenden County within five days from the time those letters were received.

Q. Do you know anything about those letters at all?—A. Yes, sir; I know some of the citizens did receive such letters.

Q. Do you know who wrote them?—A. I do not; I didn't write any of them, and knew nothing of them directly or indirectly.

Q. You say you were editor of a newspaper?—A. Yes, sir.

Q. What were the politics of that paper?—A. It was a Republican paper.

Q. Did you suffer any loss of property, time, or money in this exile?—A. Yes, sir; I suffered right smart loss of money; had some property damaged.

Q. Go on and tell about the threats that were made.—A. Well, you asked a question awile ago; didn't finish about why we were sent away; they said these letters had been written by us, myself, Ferguson, Dan Louis, and others; said we were implicated, and for that reason they came and exiled us from the county.

Q. Were there any threats made towards you?—A. Yes, sir; when they brought us away they said we were never to come back to that county any more, and if we did it would be dangerous; they meant, from what they said, they would kill us; that was the inference; never to return to Crittenden County any more.

Q. You say you have left Crittenden County?—A. Yes, sir.

Q. Why did you leave?—A. I left because they sent me away, and said I never should live there any more; and all of my business had been suspended there; and I had nothing to do there; that's one reason I have, and then, again, I don't feel safe in living there any more.

Q. You think your life is more or less in danger if you lived in Crittenden County now?—A. Yes, sir; I think some of those men there would, under some circumstances, attempt to assassinate me.

Q. Do you know whether the Republican party of Crittenden County, or Democrats, as a rule, were intimidated by the armed men in the last election there—the last national election?—A. Yes, sir; at the election in September, the State election, they were directly under the influence of that shotgun crowd—Winchester crowd; and I believe the same influence was brought to bear at the national election, though it may not have been as forcible as at the State election; but I believe the Republicans, the colored people, were under that same influence, and they wouldn't vote as freely as they had done heretofore.

*   *   *   *   *   *   .*   *

Q. You say you were exiled from Crittenden County last July?—A. Yes, sir; on the 12 day of last July.

Q. Did they accuse you of anything else, or any of your companions in exile, of any crime?—A. They had never accused me of anything; they had Mr. Ferguson and Judge Louis; they had been indicted before that; they had been indicted for intoxication in office; that was all against them. Myself they had never accused of anything—never had been convicted of any sort of crime, felony, or misdemeanor either; never have been indicted except for these anonymous letters, and never had any trial of any sort, either criminal or civil, in that county. (Printed record, page 195.)

Why they drove the Republicans out of the county.

William Royster (col.), a witness on behalf of the contestant, being first duly sworn, testified as follows:

Q. What is your name?—A. William Royster.

Q. Where do you live?—A. Live in Memphis now, sir.

Q. Where have you lived before you came to Memphis?—A. In Arkansas, Crittenden County, Marion, Ark.

Q. When did you come to Memphis?—A. Come here in September.

Q. In what year?—A. 1888.

Q. How long had you lived in Arkansas before that?—A. About 14 years ago on the 15th.

Q. How old are you?—A. I reckon I'm about 39 or 40 years old now, sir.

Q. What is your business?—A. I used to drive the stage there till the Kansas City road came through, and after that I followed up renting out horses and buggies, and farming there.

Q. Did you have a home there at the time you left?—A. I did.

Q. Have any other property in the county?—A. Yes, sir; I had 160 acres of land.

Q. Why did you leave at the time you did?—A. I voted the second or third of September, and during that day they come to me four or five different times to get Republican tickets and I wouldn't let them have it; and that night they gave me my orders to leave in ten days. Mr. Force came that night and gave me orders to leave; he come to me setting on the porch in front of my house; he said he had orders to do so; I asked him orders for what; he said, "Orders to wind up your business and leave the county." I asked what had I did; he said all I could against the white people. I said I hadn't done anything against the white people more than voted and issued the Republican ticket. He said, "Well, you got to leave or we'll kill you 'cept heaven and earth come together;" I said, "I ain't able to go." He said I could do as I damn please, stay or go; but I'd find out by waiting. I staid there till the next Monday night; the next Sunday night he shot at one of the neighbors; and Monday morning Joe Randolph was down there cleaning his horses, and he asked him how was it; and he said them that shot at him know who it were, and he said he had been to Royster and told him to leave; I told him what the consequence was and he had to go to Dr. Bingham and ask him, and Dr. Bingham was in the midst of 30 or 40 when the plot was made; and if he don't leave we will kill him 'cept heaven and earth come together. I left then; I hurried and got my clothes on; that was betwixt 12 and 1 o'clock. The train had got there before I got to the depot, and I left on my crutches and stick, and I went North and stayed there three or four days; and when I thought things had gotten quiet so I could come through the lines, I come here to Memphis.

Q. Do you know what political party Frank Force belongs to?—A. Democrats.

Q. Was the hostile demonstrations over there universal toward the colored people?—A. Yes, sir.

Q. In what way?—A. Using Winchesters and threatening them, and pretty well in every respect.

Q. Did many of them leave there in consequence of it?—A. No more than they run out of the county as I know of.

Q. Did you suffer loss in regard to your property by leaving there?—A. Yes, sir; after I left they killed one of my mules. I was offered $400 for the pair time and again; and they shot my bay more so it couldn't get about, and my house and things has all gone to destruction. I can't hear of any of them at all since I been away.

Q. Are you afraid to return there now?—A. Yes, sir.

* * * * *

Q. What act had you committed that caused Mr. Forest, as the representative of this organization, to threaten to kill you if you didn't leave the county?—A. That day at my house, of course I lived next to the court-house, I issued tickets that day. I were acquainted with the people all, you know, and generally they trusted me with the tickets; Republican tickets at the State and county elections, and I issued tickets that day, and I suppose betwixt 8 and 9 o'clock along came a young fellow, Ben Novel, and asked me for a ticket. I says, "You know you ain't going to vote this ticket; you want me to give it to you. I ain't got any to spare." About five minutes from that Mr. Cox come; I told him I ain't got tickets to spare. "Well, my wife wants to see one." "Well, I ain't got tickets to spare; I ain't got tickets for the women, I need them for the men," and I handed him a ticket, and he said, "By God you can't scare me" I said, "No I ain't scared of you," and I turned to Louis, and he said, "You'll remember this; you'll need a favor some time." I said, "I need it now," and Mr. Cox came back after dinner, again, for a ticket and I wouldn't let him have it, and about an hour after that Jim Loyd wanted one for Mr. Kelley to see, and I said, "I ain't got no tickets for Mr. Kelley now; need them for the men," and he went off and made a great bluster, and I kept the tickets till about half an hour before the election, and he come back for a ticket, and I wouldn't let him have it, and he said, "By God, you'll remember it," and that night Mr. Forest come and gave me my orders to leave.

Q. If you were in Crittenden County would you give this testimony you are giving here now?—A. No, sir; I wouldn't do it.

Q. Why not?—A. I'd be afraid.

Q. Afraid of what?—A. Afraid I'd get shot.

Q. Do you think the other witnesses would come up and testify as they have done in this investigation?—A. No, sir; they would be afraid of the Winchesters.

Q. Who has got possession of the Winchesters?—A. The Democratic party's got possession of them. (Printed record, page 189-90.)

Henry Biby (col.), a witness on behalf of contestant, being first duly sworn, deposes as follows:

Q. What is your name?—A. Henry Biby.

Q. How old are you?— A. About 26.

Q. Where do you live?—A. Been living in Marion all my life, in the county of Crittenden.

Q. What State?—A. Ark.

Q. What is your business?—A. Well, for the last year—I was deputy assessor for 4 years.

Q. How long since you left?—A. Been away since the 12th of July.

Q. Why did you leave?—A. I was at home making a recapitulation of assessments I had made on Thursday morning: 16 men come up and asked me where was Skymore; I told them I didn't know; Mr. Jim Bassett said then, "It's a damn lie, I did know," and said, "You come out, this country's getting too small for you edicated niggers and we white folks," and went on to Marion, and as we passed the sheriff's office they had a man named Dock Pointers, and the sheriff said, "Turn him loose," and they taken us, and they taken us on and under the shade tree; they searched us, and about 10 o'clock they marched us off a mile down the Milder road toward Mound City, and a wagon overtaken us, and they put us in and carried us to Mound City; there we got out and came aboard of the boat, and 9 of them got on the boat with Winchesters and horses, and when the boat landed at Hope Field I got off and 3 followed us to the foot of Jefferson street, and then told us, "Now you can go, you never have been escorted by a lot of white gentlemen before in your life, its quite a compliment to you, and unhurt, but if you ever come back to Ark. you must abide by the consequences."

Q. What position were you holding at that time?—A. Deputy assessor, under Rucks, appointed by the county judge.

Q. Had you violated the law in any way?—No, sir; I had been to the upper end of the county a day or two previous to that, and came home on summons by the circuit court as a witness in the case of Billy Shelton; that's why I was there at court at that time.

Q. What reason did these armed men give why they exiled you from the State?—A. At that time they said I was a very prominent negro in society, business, either belonged to several different societies, and afterwards they accused me of being a conspirator.

Q. Did you belong to some societies?—A. Yes, sir; the Knights of Labor and Masonic.

Q. Did they teach you to violate the law in any way?—A. No, sir; we never met and discussed religious matters or matters concerning the civil laws.

Q. Did they teach you to rob and steal and insult the white people of the country?—A. No, sir; teaches us a better grade than that.

Q. You were a member of the Knights of Labor?—A. Yes, sir.

Q. And are there some white people members of the Knights of Labor, too?—A. I suppose there are. A white gentleman, Mr. C. A. Miller, set us up, from Paragould.

Q. Do you know who Mr. C. A. Miller was?—A. Organizer of the Knights of Labor and school-teacher at Paragould.

Q. Do you know how he stood at Paragould?—A. Mr. William Stranges said he was a very intelligent man, very high in the community in which he lived.

Q. Was there any reason at any time why any member of the Knights of Labor, a white man, couldn't have come into your lodge at any time as a visiting member?—A. No, sir; while Mr. Stranges resided in Marion he very frequently visited whenever we met, and others, and the night that we were set up a good many of the prominent white citizens of Marion came down to our hall to listen to the instructions of Mr. Miller, and said they didn't see nothing in it why it shouldn't be set up.

*   *   *   *   *   *   *

Q: How many were sent away from there at the same time you were?—A. Nine outside of myself.

Q. Do you know what charges were brought against these 9?—A. No more than they were accused of being accessories, and some have been ones that is writing these anonymous letters.

Q. Do you know who wrote those anonymous letters?—A. No, sir; I do not.

Q. Had you or your friends ever heard of these anonymous letters until you were accused of having written them?—A. No, sir; not before Tuesday at 12 o'clock; the mail was distributed; the sheriff and other citizens got letters, and I heard some of them say some of the white citizens had gotten warning letters to leave the county in 5 days; well, it was a very serious charge, and a good many prominent colored men at once thought that it was expedient that they would draw up a resolution or something offering to the judge on Wednesday that he would instruct the grand jury to investigate the matter and punish the guilty ones; and Judge Lewis, he presented the petition; the judge highly complimented it; thought everything was all right, the court adjourned that evening: they all met in the court-house and Thursday about daylight about 125, more or less, armed with Winchesters, came to Marion, and about 9 o'clock they came to my house; I live in the suburbs with my mother; a place she's bought there.

Q. Did you know the men that had those Winchester rifles?—A. Pretty well all of them at that time, but since I've been here I've forgotten a great deal, but the prominent one of them I know.

Q. You saw these men with the Winchester rifles?—A. Yes, sir; I seen them; and I can name them that come over to Memphis with me; I've got a list of all of them where I'm stopping at.

Q. When they came to you did they claim to represent any legal authority; did they present any papers showing any authority for that sort of matter?—A. No, sir.

Q. Did they claim to be acting as militia?—A. No, sir.

Q. What was it that made you go?—A. I didn't know what was the matter.

Q. Under those circumstances why did you leave the county :—A. The reason why I left the county was because I saw that I had no protection, and that if I stayed there there was two chances to one that I might be killed; then they ordered me to leave. The sheriff was in the crowd and told them to take me on, that I was one of them, and he went on back in his office then. So then, on the second Monday in Feb. I went over there for trial, and Tuesday it was I went for trial; Jan. it was, and I gave $250 bond and went for trial, and the prosecuting attorney continued my case, and the evening he continued Col. J. F. Smith was sitting in front of me, and he turned back and whispered, "Henry, I think its best for you to get on the train and leave here, because some of these mischievous white boys, or some one may whip around and hurt you;" and under his advice I taken the first train coming for Memphis and been here ever since.

Q. Who was it gave you that advice?—A. Col. J. F. Smith.

Q. Have you since gone back and been tried?—A. No, sir; it was continued till July.

Q. You haven't yet been tried?—A. No, sir.

Q. Had you at any time had any special trouble with any number of the white citizens over there?—A. No, sir; some of them that morning prevailed that I should stay, and some said I was a quite peaceable boy, and others says, no, he must go just so.

Q. Have you ever had any principal difficulty with any of the white people?—A. No, sir; I was raised there among them, and never did have any difficulty with any of them.

Q. Had you considered them your friends in a business way?—A. Yes, sir; I gave them the honor that was due them.

Wash. Dever (col.), a witness on behalf of the contestant, being first duly sworn, deposes as follows:

Q. What is your name?—A. Wash. Derver.

Q. Where do you live?—A. I live here now; I used to live in Crittenden County, Marion.

Q. What State?—A. State Ark.

Q. How old are you?—A. 36.

Q. How long had you lived there before you left?—A. About 25 years.

Q. When did you leave?—A. On the 12th day of July, '88.

Q. Did you leave of your own accord?—A. No, sir.

Q. Why did you leave?—A. I was told by the sheriff to leave there; if I didn't I'de be killed on the 12th morning of July.

Q. Had you committed any crime?—A. Nothing at all, sir.

Q. Did you leave?—A. Yes, sir.

Q. You say the sheriff told you if you didn't leave there you would be killed?—A. Yes, sir; he told me that morning that he found my name to one of the notices written to the white people that they'd have to leave there in 5 days, and if I didn't leave that morning I would be killed.

Q. Did you leave by yourself?—A. No, sir; me and F. T. Moore left in company together.

Q. Did you see any armed men over there at that time?—A. Yes sir.

Q. Whereabouts were they?—A. They were in the court-house yard; there was a big crowd in the court-house yard, and then Dr. Barton and Dr. Bingham went to my house, looking for me, with their Winchester rifles.

Q. How many was in the crowd in the court-house yard?—A. It seemed to me there was 75 or 100 men; all was armed; all had Winchesters, except Chase; he had a double-barrel shotgun.

Q. What was the object of that meeting; do you know?—A. No more than what they done; they went in there and marched out Fergason and Fleming and Ramsey and Hunt and Fergason again: that was what I saw; and stood them up side of the court-house and searched them.

Q. Then what did they do?—A. Then marched them from there to the mayor's house, north of the court-house, and set them under trees, and I saw them running around looking for me, and I went off and went down in a field I was cultivating down there.

Q. Were you frightened?—A. Yes, sir; and that time I was pretty badly frightened.

Q. Did they make these other men leave the county?—A. Yes, sir; made them all leave.

Q. Were they men of family?—A. Yes, sir; most all of them.

Q. Did they have any property there?—A. Yes, sir; all, except some few.

Q. Did they have any crops?—A. Yes, sir.

Q. Were the crops injured on account of their leaving?—A. Yes, sir; all destroyed.

Q. Did you have any property there?—A. Yes, sir.

Q. Was it destroyed?—A. Yes, sir.

Q. You say you are living here now?—A. Yes, sir.

Q. Are you still afraid to return?—A. Yes, sir.

Q. Do you think if you returned your life would be in danger?—A. Yes, sir; they told me that several times.

Q. Are the others exiled with you still living here?—A. Yes, sir; afraid to go back. I don't know any that has gone back, except Dan. Lewis; he goes over there occasionally.

Q. Have you ever been convicted of any infamous offense before the law?—A. No, sir.

Q. Ever been accused of anything before the law previous to that?—A. No, sir.

Q. Have you a family?—A. Yes, sir; wife and six children; my wife is laying very low now. I had a lot and a nice orchard there, and my trees is all being destroyed nearly; I had about 90 acres in cultivation that I was running, and I had some hogs and cows and house furniture, and everything, it was all destroyed.

Q. Was the property of these other men destroyed?—A. Well, it's been injured; pretty well all destroyed; no good..

Q. Do you belong to any secret societies?—A. Yes, sir.

Q. What are they?—A. I belong to the Masonic order and the Knights of Labor.

Q. Do you think that the people who made you leave feared anything from your hands as to their lives or property at the time you left?—A. I know they didn't; no, sir. I lived there over 25 years with them, perfectly peaceable; never had no difficulty with them at all.

Q. Why did they make you leave if they didn't fear anything?—A. I only think it was a political movement; they wanted to take all the offices there was in the county.

Q. Were any men in this crowd that made you leave—were any of them officials at that time holding office there?—A. Yes, sir; the sheriff was an official; Dr. Bingham was nothing but a Dr. and Dr. Barton was a Dr., and Martin was judge, and I think that's about all.

Q. You say that you think that your exile from there was political?—A. Yes, sir.

Q. What political party do you belong to?—A. Republican party.

Q. When they ordered you out of the county, did they mention by what authority they did it?—A. No, sir; all the sheriff said to me, we find your name to one of those notices, and you must leave here to-day, don't, you'll be killed. And I asked him at that time why he wanted to drive me out of the county; I said the court's in session here, and if I violated the law or wrote any notices, why don't you try me to-day. He says, "Well, we are going to take the law in our hands to-day." That's what the sheriff said. In a few moments I went over home, and at home I saw them all go into the clerk's office, and I started to the clerk's office, and I taken another notion and went to the north part of the court-house, when I went back of the court-house, I went around that way, and they went to my house looking for me, and I just come right on around and went across the R. R. here into my field; I stayed across the R. R. till I saw them march all these men out, then I went in the field and they come on down there hunting me, and I stayed there that morning till 1 o'clock, and they rambled over my corn and cotton, everywhere, took it row by row, and stayed there till 3 o'clock in the morning, and when the 3 o'clock train came along I pitched out for Memphis.

Q. You say they claim your name was to one of those letters?—A. Yes, sir; and I asked Col. Smith that morning to let me see the letter; he said he didn't have it, Mosby had it; and I asked him to let me see it, and he claimed that Berry had it, so I never did get to see it.

Q. They never did show you the letter they claimed you wrote?—A. Never did. (Printed record, page 224.)

David Furgeson, in speaking of the condition of the county prior to the 12th of July, 1888, testified:

Q. Had the Republicans, while in authority, shown at any time a disposition to treat the white people, or the Democrats in this way, unfairly, as they believe that they are now being treated?—A. No, sir; on the contrary, we always divided all offices with them.

* * * * * * *

Q. How many of the offices had the Republicans, prior to that time, accorded the Democrats?—A. They had accorded the Democrats the sheriff, treasurer, and surveyor, county officers.
Q. You had what is generally known in Arkansas as a fusion ticket?—A. Yes, sir.
Q. Your vote was about five to one, was it?—A. About six to one.
Q. Had you seen fit to have exacted all the offices with all of the machinery in your hands at that time, would it have been possible for the white people or the Democrats to have had a single office in the county?—A. It would have been impossible for them to have had a single office in the county; if we had exacted all the offices, we could have elected every man in that county.
Q. How long had this harmonious feeling, represented by the fusion ticket, existed between the Democrats and the Republicans of that county?—A. Ever since 1880.
Q. For 8 years?—A. Yes, sir.
Q. Then I would like for you to state what seemed to be the desire of the leaders of this mob so far as future arrangements for the offices were concerned?—A. Only desire of the mob was, and the only intention was, to get control of the county so they could occupy and fill the offices.
Q. With what proportion of votes did they desire to make this control?—A. About one to six. (Printed record, page 208-9.)

George Hendley, in speaking of the demands of the negroes, testified:

Q. What do the negroes ask of the Democratic party in the way of elections?—A. Only ask for fair elections, and the enforcement of justice and law. (Printed record, page 188.)

E. D. Sanders, in speaking of why the Republican officials were driven out, testified:

Q. How, then, do you account for the action of a part of those farmers during the past election and just prior to the election?—A. Well, sir it was simply politics at the ground of it, and there was a few colored men there who held office and all of them admitted made good officers; they told me so frequently; well, they couldn't beat them and they determined to just put them out by force and take the office in opposition to the Republican party, and it is chiefly owing to the influence of unscrupulous politicians determined to advance their personal interests to the disregard of the great body of the people.
Q. Is this action of these few politicians indorsed by the better white element of Crittenden County?—A. It is not; it is the result of a political ring determined to advance personal interests, regardless of the material benefit of the population. (Printed record, page 201.)

Had the exiling been confined to persons indicted it would have indicated, as already said, a want of confidence in the courts. But it did not stop with exiling the indicted county officers. On the contrary it extended to county officers not indicted and to persons who were not county officers. In no instance was a Democrat driven out, and in every instance the exiled is found to have been either a member of "The Wheel," Union, or Knight of Labor, or Republican party.

J. P. Broadenax, after speaking of the exiling of the county assessor, testified:

J. P. Broadenax (col.), a witness on behalf of the contestant, being first duly sworn, testified as follows:

Q. Where do you live?—A. Jericho, Arkansas; Crittenden County.
Q. How long have you lived there?—A. I've been there in that county about ten years.
Q. What is your occupation?—A. Farming and merchandising, and I'm postmaster of the town.
Q. How old are you?—A. 31 years of age; will be March 6th.

Q. I want to know if you voted at the election in November ?—A. I did, sir.
Q. At what voting precinct ?—A. Bradley's.
Q. Did you hear the result of the vote announced that evening ?—A. No, sir; 1 did not.
Q. There was an election held there regularly ?—A. Yes, sir.
Q. Did you know the judges of election?—A. I did not, sir; I did, too, I think; some of them.
Q. Do you know of an organized body of men in Crittenden County armed with Winchester rifles ?—A. I've seen some there with Winchester rifles.
Q. Do you know anything of the operations of those men there last July ?—A. Some operations I know, sir.
Q. State what you know about that.—A. What I know, sir, I was on a train, on one coming down, and I seen about 30 or 40, probably more, at Marion, Arkansas.
Q. How long did the train stop ?—A. Stopped, I reckon, ten or fifteen minutes; about that time.
Q. State what you saw them do.—A. I seen them bring Assessor Rooks to the train and put him on, and two or three more men from our place down there, and they crowded them together on the train and left; O. W. Mychem was one; I don't remember just now who the others were, but there was several of them,
Q. Mr. Rooks was the assessor of your county ?—A. Yes, sir.
Q. Did he act as though he was leaving of his own accord on a pleasure trip ?—A. No, sir; he did not; he left without his accord, I think.
Q. Did you hear them say anything to him ?—A. I heard them tell him to get on and leave.
Q. He didn't get on, did he ?—A. Yes, sir.
Q. Did you see him as he came down on the train ?—A. He wasn't on the train, he got on at Marion.
Q. You didn't come on to Memphis then ?—A. Yes, sir; I did.
Q. On the train with him ?—A. Yes, sir.
Q. Did you talk to him any as you came down ?—A. I did.
Q. What did he say ?—A. I asked him what that meant; he said he didn't know; they ordered him to leave and not return any more, and didn't give him time to get his clothes or nothing else.
Q. How many were following him when you saw him ?—A. I suppose there was fifteen or twenty; I reckon about that many; I was a little excited myself; seemed to be about that many, though.
Q. He came on across the river with you ?—A. Yes, sir.
Q. Did he bring his family with him ?—A. No, sir.
Q. Do you know how long he was kept out of the county ?—A. I do not, sir.
Q. Did those gentlemen seem to be excited themselves ?—A. Well, no, sir; not very much; they seemed to be mad. (Printed record, page 196.)

J. P. Broadenax, in speaking of the Republican member of the legislature, testified:

Q. The ex-member of the legislature there, Mr. Odom, your neighbor, did he live near you ?—A. He lived about three miles from me.
Q. Did you know him well ?—A. Yes, sir.
Q. Had there ever been any complaint in the courts against him ?—A. None that I know of.
Q. Was he a good business man—considered so in the country ?—A. He was, sir; seemed to be a nice man. He was prospering, and to my notion was on good terms with his white neighbors, Mr. Martin and others. He has made some property, and represented the county in the legislature. I had heard no complaint made of him as a member of the legislature; they said he made a good one, both white and colored.
Q. Was he ordered out of the county ?—A. I don't know that he was. He told me himself he was ordered to leave, and some went out to his house after him with Winchesters.
Q. Did he leave ?—A. He did, sir.
Q. Don't you know as a matter of fact he did come back there some time in the night ?—A. Yes, sir; I do.
Q. Have you ever heard of any charge preferred against him in court in any way ?—A. Well, I have since he went away.
Q. None before that ?—A. None that I know of, sir.
Q. Had he ever been tried ?—A. Yes, sir.
Q. Sent to the penitentiary ?—A. No, sir; he was acquitted, I heard. (Printed record, page 197.)

J. W. Wymme, in speaking on this subject, testified:

Q. Did they drive any private citizens out of the county except the officers ?—A. Well, yes, sir; driven out several besides those was in office.

Q. Did these men have families?—A. Some of them did, sir.
Q. Did they own property there?—A. Yes, sir. (Printed record, page 204).

R. Y. Logan, on this subject, testified:

Q. Were there any colored people aside from these four officers exiled?—A. Oh, yes.
Q. How many?—A. Some 12 or 15 were exiled. (Printed record, page 219).

In determining the object of a conspiracy the law is that you may refer to the acts, words, and conduct of the conspirators to fathom and ascertain its existence and purpose, intent, etc. It is apparent from the evidence that a conspiracy existed and that the conspirators had made up their minds to wrest the political control of Crittenden County from the Republicans who had held it for many years.

This could not be done by obtaining a majority of the votes, for it contained a Republican majority of at least 2,000, and there was no dissension in the party.

By examining the statutes of Arkansas in relation to elections, it will be found that the county judge, the county court clerk, and the sheriff are important factors in conducting elections.

In the county judge is vested the appointment of all the judges of election. The clerk creates the county board of canvassers, and the sheriff, through his deputies, at every poll, is a power for good or evil —they can faithfully execute the law and protect the ballot-box, or they can wickedly violate the law and debauch the suffrage. That the conspirators seized upon and obtained these offices is not denied. It therefore becomes pertinent to inquire, as a means of ascertaining the purpose of the conspiracy, whether the power of these offices was exercised in accordance with the law, or as a means to aid the conspiracy to place the county under the political control of about one-sixth of its legal voters.

For this purpose we will now examine the laws of Arkansas relating to elections, and after quoting the law, try to ascertain whether it was complied with in good faith.

HOW AND BY WHOM JUDGES ARE APPOINTED.

SEC. 2654. The county court, at its last term held more than thirty days before any general election, shall appoint three discreet persons, in each township, having the qualifications of electors, to act as judges of election within the township (Mansfield's Digest of Arkansas.)

Under this provision the judges of election must be appointed at the July term of the county court. It was in July the Democrats exiled the Republican county judge, with others.

JUDGES SHALL BE OF DIFFERENT POLITICAL PARTIES.

SEC. 2757. The judges of election appointed by the county court, or chosen by the assembled electors. under the provisions of this act shall, if practicable, be from different political parties, so that each party may be represented, and they shall, in addition to the qualifications required by the constitution and this act, be able to read and write. (Mansfield's Digest of Arkansas.)

At the time the Republican county judge was exiled, he had appointed the judges of election, according to law, so that each political party was represented.

After the exiling of the Republican judge and the office had been seized and appropriated by the Democrats, the Democratic county judge, who had come into possession of the office by reason of the conspiracy, revoked these appointments, and appointed all of the judges of election from the Democratic party.

Wash Deaver, in the course of his testimony, states this significant fact:

Q. I want to know if prior to the time of your being exiled, and Judge Lewis, the county judge, being exiled, if he had appointed the judge of election for the ensuing election?—A. Yes, sir; he had,

Q. Had the notice of that fact been given to sheriff?—A. Yes, sir; put in the sheriff's box in the clerk's office.

Q. Had Judge Lewis complied with the law in Ark., by representing all political parties among the judges?—A. Yes, sir.

Q. Do you know whether or not those judges were afterwards changed?—A. Yes, sir.

Q. How do you know it?—A. I know it from the fact that Mr. Martin told me so, the judge who now holds the position, and I know that the men I know were appointed didn't serve.

Q. You say Judge Lewis appointed some Dem. at each voting place?—A. Yes, sir.

Q. Complied with the law?—A. Yes, sir.

Q. What is the general impression of the reason that prompted Judge Martin for making the changes in the judges of election?—A. To count the votes there was appointed such men as he knew would count the vote for them.

Q. Do you know in the whole county among your acquaintances of a single Rep. who served as judge of the election in Crittenden County in the last State and National election?—A. I don't know a single one, except one or two precincts where they had to arrange the election themselves, wherein the absence of the regular judges, the voters had to select judges of their own. (Printed record, page 224.)

All judges of election Democrats in the county.

E. D. Sanders, in speaking of the political status of the judges of election in Crittenden County, testified:

Q. I would like to ask whether the judges of election throughout the county, as a rule, Democrats or Republicans, or divided?—A. They were all Democrats.

Q. Does the law require in Arkansas that both political parties shall be represented by judges of election in various elections?—A. It does.

Q. What is your impression of the reason the law being violated, and almost all the judges in the entire county being selected from the Democratic ranks?—A. Well, that was very plain to me. They could defraud the Republican party out of their votes. (Printed record, page 200.)

It is not explained why it was that Judge Lewis could find two Republicans in each township who were fit to be judges of election and Judge Martin could not find any.

COUNTY COURT TO PROCURE BALLOT-BOXES.

SEC. 2676. It shall be the duty of the county court to provide, at the expense of the county, a good and sufficient ballot-box, with lock and key, for the several townships or places of voting in their respective counties for the safe-keeping of the ballots, etc. (Mansfield's Digest of Arkansas.)

SHERIFF TO DELIVER BALLOT-BOXES TO JUDGES.

SEC. 2677. It shall be the duty of the sheriff in the several counties in this State to deliver to one of the judges of election in each township the ballot-boxes so provided by the county court. (Mansfield's Digest of Arkansas.)

CLERK TO DELIVER BLANK POLL-BOOKS TO SHERIFF.

SEC. 2663. It shall be the duty of the clerk of the county court of each county, at least twenty-five days before each general election and ten days before each special election, to make out and deliver to the sheriff of his county two blank poll-books for each township, properly laid off in columns, with proper captions and forms of oaths and certificates attached thereto.

SHERIFF TO DELIVER POLL-BOOK TO THE JUDGES.

SEC. 2666. It shall be the duty of the sheriff forthwith to deliver such books to the judges of election within their respective townships. (Mansfield's Digest of Arkansas.)

Instead of the county court procuring the ballot-boxes, as the law requires, the Democratic sheriff procured fraudulent ballot-boxes, one of which is produced in evidence in this case.

Instead of delivering the poll-books, as required by law, for the November election, he neglected to perform that duty, but left that matter to the wisdom and discretion of the Democratic sheriff.

How far and how well he performed his work the testimony very explicitly shows:

R. P. James (white), a witness on behalf of the contestant, being first duly sworn, testified as follows:

Direct examination:

Q. How old are you?—A. 47 years old the 11th of this month.
Q. You are a citizen of what county?—A. Shelby County.
Q. State of Tennessee?—A. Yes, sir.
Q. We want to know if you have ever seen a box similar to the box that is marked as Exhibit "A" in a previous deposition, and is now before you, and forms a part and parcel of the testimony in this case?—A. Yes, sir.
- Q. Will you please state what you know with regard to that box, and your connection with it?—A. I know that we've made a great many boxes of that pattern—that kind; in fact, I think we made that one.
Q. We want to know if you have ever made any that were shipped to Marion, Arkansas, in Crittenden County?—A. We made, I believe it was, 21 boxes and shipped to the sheriff of Crittenden County, W. F. Werner, at Marion, Ark.; they were ordered by Mr. Werner and charged to him, I know that.
Q. Shipped on what day?—A. August 21st, 1888, as seen on page 109, ship book.
Q. How many boxes?—A. 21.
Q. Did you know anything of his official position at that time?—A. I didn't know, but I understood he was the sheriff of Crittenden County.
Q. Will you please examine that box and see if 'tis exactly the same as those 21 that you shipped to Marion for Mr. Werner, the sheriff of Crittenden County.—A. Well, I can't say that it's exactly the same, but it's almost a fac-simile.
Q. Can you see wherein it differs materially?—A. No, no; it don't differ at all, it's the same thing exactly; we don't save patterns of them at all, but I see no difference; that's the kind of box it was; there might be a little difference in dimensions, but the same thing in every other way.
Q. For what purpose were they ordered?—A. They were ordered, as I understood, for ballot-boxes.
Q. Is the entry so made on your books?—A. Yes, sir; 21 ballot-boxes.
Q. To be shipped to what point?—A. They were shipped from the store; I couldn't say positively where they were shipped to; I know they were shipped to the sheriff of Critten en County; they were charged on the books to W. F. Werner, Mound City, Arkansas.d
Q. How would you describe the boxes as made by you?—A. Well, they are made as we would generally make ballot-boxes, with that extra cap on the slot that you put the ballots in; I have no more idea what that's for than the man in the moon; it was none of my business; I made them as I was ordered; well, I have an idea, too, but at the same time I don't know.
Q. With what firm are you connected in the city of Memphis?—A. H. Wetter Manufacturing Company.
Q. In what way?—A. As foreman of the shop.
Q. As such you know the foregoing to be a correct statement of the facts?—A. Yes, sir; as near as I can get it.
Q. Were all the boxes made by you furnished with this peculiar cap which accompanies the box before you?—A. All that 21 boxes made for the sheriff of Crittenden County had that device attached to them; I had no idea I'd get into this kind of a scrape, though, when I was making them. (Printed record, page 228-9.)

Stephen James tells how the ballot-boxes returned a Democratic majority in a Republican county.

Stephen James, in speaking of the September election, says:

Q. Do you know whether the ballots were counted at the various precincts in your county according to law, or whether the boxes were carried to the county seat before being counted?—A. I can not, only from hearsay.
Q. What have you heard with regard to that?—A. At Bradley's precinct, when they got done voting, this man in Memphis remarked to the boys, "You know our orders."

My half brother was acting there that day, was representing our ticket on the outside, and when they got done voting this man remarked, "Well, boys, you know our orders," and my half brother remarked to him, "Aint you going to count them votes?" Said he, "No," and they taken the poll-boxes, two or three boys following them, and they carried it into Sam Cells' house about sundown. That was about in a mile of Marion. They never was counted at the precinct at all, and the way they kept them there, there was 220 votes cast, and the so-called Democratic party I think got eight, and when they was counted out in Marion the so-called Democratic party got 212, and the People's ticket got 8, and the man that distributed their tickets there told me he only distributed 8 tickets there that day. (Printed record, page 186.)

Having secured the appointment of Democratic judges of election the conspirators made an attempt to keep the Republicans from putting a county ticket in the field.

Jordan Yeates, in speaking of the effort on the part of the Democrats to prevent the Republicans from putting out a county ticket, testified:

Q. Have you had any trouble over there in the last few months, growing out of politics?—A. Yes, sir; we had last year, from last July up until you may say till now, we've had great trouble, sir; great trouble.

Q. Go on and state what you know about that trouble.—A. Well, they went to work, of course the Democrats did, and drive the officers, Dan Louis, Dave Furguson; that is, their intention were to get all the Republican leaders, colored, out of the county; that was their object, and they went to work and drive Dan Louis, Dave Ferguson, and a good many others, I couldn't call their names, out.

Q. What excuse did they give for that?—A. Well, the excuse they told me for it, was they had written a notice to them giving them so many days to get out the county in, certain men, and they just reversed it by making them leave before that time, in the place of them having to leave themselves.

Q. Have these same men since that time been directly charged with writing these anonymous letters?—A. Don't know, sir, whether they have or not; don't think they have.

Q. After that trouble commenced, do you know of any threats that were made as to what would be done against prominent members of your party in your county?—A. Oh, yes, sir; they were making threatenings all the time. Directly after that riot taking place, I remember they drive those men off the day that the county central committee called the convention together—that is, on Saturday were the day they were to be called—they drive them off; on Thursday I met there myself with a few more; Mr. Werner said to me, "You better not try to hold a convention here to-day, there's too much excitement; if you undertake it you will be hurt; we ain't going to have but one ticket."

Q. What ticket was that?—A. That was the Democratic ticket, and I answered him by saying we were going to hold a convention somewhere in the county to-day; he said you can't hold it here, you better not try to hold any here.

Q. Was Mr. Werner an officer in the county at that time?—A. He was the sheriff then at the time; then, of course, after I talked to him I went over to Major Crittenden, told him what Mr. Werner had said to me, then major advised me to go and hold it; that being the day set for to hold the convention for the county central committee called, to go and hold it somewhere and it would be legal. So I went up the road and got what I could together, and I didn't call the convention that time; so afterwards Mr. Werner finally agreed we could hold the convention in the court-house, but he told me that they had made one ticket, and there was going to be but that one ticket elected; that if it was elected it wouldn't do any good; that they shouldn't hold the position, and went on to make offers what he'd rather do, and so on; said he was speaking for the others; offered if I wouldn't hold the convention, $60 to each delegate; that we'd just decide on what they had done and take their men that they had appointed. I didn't agree to that, so Mr. Gus Fogalman sent for me on Saturday morning to come over there to the post-office; I went over to the post-office, and he said to me, "I want to see you to see if we can't make some arrangement to stop you all from making a ticket; I believe it would be cheaper for us for you all to do that, not to make no ticket, because if you make a ticket, if you effect it, it ain't going to do you any good, for the nominations we have made are going to be the officers; and," he said, "now, what will you charge to break up the convention? You can break it up even if the intimidation we offer of $50 a piece to each delegate; if they don't do it, why, you being chairman, you get up there, go to work, and don't heed nothing, and you'll get it done that way, if you can't do it any other way." Oh, I, of course, didn't tell him what I thought about it, because I knew I was about like the

rest; I was there amongst them Winchesters, though I told him couldn't do anything like that; that I'd tell the boys, though, what they had offered. Well, he
says, "I tell you what I'll do: We are willing to give $50 to each delegate." There
was 53, I believe, there was of us, and he says "I'll give your, prior to the rest, $250
if you'll do it,"

Q. That was Mr. Werner?—A. No, sir; that was Fogalman; he was representing the crowd; so me and him didn't agree on it, and Mr. Werner then, after that,
after we made the nomination that day, then I met him at Crawfordsville in a few
days afterwards, and he said that he had been instructed that we were going to recall to reconsider the matter, and he said if we did do it, it would be all right, and if
we didn't they were going to have the office any how, no matter how the election
went; no matter how many or how little they got, they were going to hold the office,
and if we would take their offers they would give us justice of the peace and constable, that was their offer. Really to go to work and track Mr. Werner's conversation with me from that time up, I couldn't do it because he courted me from the time
to the day of the election, but making those violent threats all the time; that we
might carry the election as we pleased, but they were going to have it.

Q. He claimed to represent the Democratic vote and you the other?—A. Yes, sir.
(Printed record, page 193.)

After the ticket was nominated the Democrats attempt to make the
candidates decline.

J. H. Williams (white), a witness on behalf of the contestant, being
first duly sworn, testified as follows:

Q. What is your name?—A. J. H. Williams.
Q. Where do you live?—A. Crittenden County.
Q. What State?—A. Arkansas.
Q. How old are you?—A. 47.
Q. How long have you lived in Arkansas?—A. 21 years 5th day of this month.
Q. Have you ever held any official position there?—A. I have.
Q. What position?—A. Squire for six years, and judge of the county and probate
court two years.
Q. What ticket were you elected on then?—A. Democratic.
Q. What have your politics been during the time you've been in Arkansas?—A.
Democratic.
Q. How long have you been farming in Arkansas?—A. 21 years.
Q. You own your home there?—A. I do; at least my wife does.
Q. Are you engaged in any other business beside farming?—A. I am, sir.
Q. What is it?—A. Merchandising.
Q. At what point?—A. Crawfordsville and Jericho.
Q. How long have you been merchandizing at both these points?—A. Well, I com-
menced in 1881 at Crawfordsville, and last spring at Jericho.
Q. About how many bales of cotton do you handle per year?—A. About 50 or 75;
I don't buy cotton; we do a cash business; we don't propose to handle cotton.
Q. Were you a candidate for a position in the last election?—A. I was.
Q. On the People's ticket?—A. Yes; I was.
Q. Do you think you were elected?—A. I was.
Q. By what vote?—A. 1,200 or 1,500 majority.
Q. Did you get the office?—A. I did not.
Q. Why not?—A. Well, I ain't been able to find out; I just seed I couldn't get
there; they said they was elected, and I couldn't get there; I don't know why.
Q. Have they ever denied that you received the plurality of votes?—A. Oh, yes;
they deny that all the time; they say they are elected, but I say they are not.
Q. What makes you think you were elected?—A. Well, sir, I was on what they
call the Republican ticket, and the majority there is generally between 1,200 and
1,500; as much as two thousand; we haven't over 400 white people in the county,
and the black man never votes any other ticket, unless he's pursuaded or paid, and
this time neither was done, that is my belief. The black people come to me and said
all I ask of you is to put your name to this ticket, we want a Democrat on this ticket,
and if you will just say you will run we'll elect you; you needn't spend a cent. And
I told them I'd serve them if they'd elect me; I didn't tell them I'd be a Republican;
I ain't a Republican, and never will be, I don't think.
Q. Were the white men that were on that ticket asked to become Republicans
when they were put on the ticket?—A. They were not; the black people asked
to have the best Democrats in the county on the ticket and they would vote for
them; they couldn't get enough of them, and put a black man on it. I rode three
weeks on my horse, and told those people that was what they ought to do, and

they wouldn't do it; I said you can go to hell; John Williams will do as he pleases.

Q. Was the disposition of the colored people to override the white people ?—A. It was not; they wanted nothing but simple quietude in every shape.

Q. Did you accept this position in the interest of the government in Crittenden County for a special desire to be judge of the county ?—A. I done it for the county's interest; not that I cared a cent for the judge's office; I wouldn't give thank you for it to-day.

Q. Does your private business require most of your time at home ?—A. Yes, sir.

Q. You say you didn't want to be nominated as judge ?—A. No, sir; the second time I wouldn't have it. I read a piece in the paper where a man had been in office 40 years, and the first hundred dollars he borrowed he never had paid it back; I said, John Williams, you go home to your wife and children.

Q. You didn't want the office of judge ?—A. I did not, sir; but when I found out that I had been nominated by the colored element on the ticket I determined to serve if I was elected, not on account of private gain to myself, but for the best interests of the people of the community.

Q. You had known of the operation of the Winchester rifle crowd at the beginning of this matter, had you ?—A. I had, sir.

Q. Did you say anything to them with regard to what would be the consequence of their way of proceeding ?—A. I said this: I said, "What you've done, you've done well enough, but don't carry it into politics." That's what I said to Dr. Bingham.

Q. Then you were looking after your own interest, and the interest of the people of the county, in a business way, when you agreed to enter this contest, and admit to all this political excitement ?—A. I was, sir; and furthermore I kept trouble down otherwise. I told them it wouldn't do. I wanted everything quiet, and told the white people and the black people that we wanted quietude, and wanted to live together.

Q. Is it your opinion, if your advice had been followed, you would have had any serious trouble in Crittenden County at this time at all ?—A. We'd have had the most prosperous country in the world, sir. They see it as well as I do now.

Q. In bringing on this trouble do you consider the mass of the colored people of that county to blame, or what is known as the Winchester element ?—A. The mass of the colored people wasn't to blame.

E. D. Sanders, after telling of the driving away of the county officials by Democrats, testified :

After that they held a convention, these same men, and made a ticket which they called a Democratic ticket; the colored people then went to make their ticket, and they forbid them to make a ticket; well, they saw they couldn't make a colored ticket, and I don't think they had any inclination to do it, and they tried very hard to get up enough white men, old farmers in there, to fill the four important offices, and they worked on this for over a week; they couldn't do it; they came to me and asked me if I would accept the nomination for sheriff, and I refused; I told them I never held any office, I didn't wish any; well, they then told me that they didn't see how they could keep down a fuss unless we would do it; unless I would get them out; I went out then and consulted with some white men about it, and they insisted that I should do it, and I told them then for the good of the county I would run; well, they met then and nominated me, and there was a delegation came out from Marion and asked me to withdraw; I asked them on what ground.

Q. Please state the names of that delegation.—A. Dr. Bingham, Major Crittenden, L. P. Berry, and Colonel Smith, John R. Chase.

Q. Were they generally considered as the leaders of the Democratic party in that movement ?—A. Yes, sir.

Q. What reason did they give you for asking you to withdraw from a nomination already tendered you ?—A. Didn't give any; I asked them to give me a reason, and they never did do it. Well, then, I proposed to them if they would do away with the ticket that they made and call a convention of the white people in the county generally and make a ticket that I would resign, I wouldn't run, and they said they couldn't do it; well, I still made another proposition; that if they would withdraw two men they had on the ticket and nominate two more that I would withdraw; said they couldn't do it; well, then I told them if they beat me they would beat me at the ballot-box, and I ran the race through and suppose I got about six votes to their one; I'm pretty certain of it, because we had outside clerks that kept every name down, but they counted us out, at least their returns—the secretary of the State counted us out.

Q. You say that your impression is, from the tally sheets kept by outside clerks friendly to your side of this cause, that you are satisfied that your ticket was elected by five or six to one ?—A. Yes; our tally sheet showed up 2,500 votes.

Q. Now what has been the proportion of the Democratic and the Republican vote in that county?—A. About one-sixth Democrats.

Q. Is it not a fact that a considerable number of men who had never before voted any other ticket but the Democratic ticket voted for your ticket?—A. They certainly did; I know that to be a positive fact. (Printed record, page 199.)

Failing to get the Republican ticket out of the way, they then commenced to threaten that they would carry the election at all hazards.

E. D. Sanders, in speaking of threats made prior to September election, testified:

Q. During the time just prior to the election did you hear any direct threats, or was there any remarks made as to the comparative value of a Winchester rifle and money in carrying elections in Arkansas?—A. I did.

Q. Please state what they were?—A. I heard, on one or two occasions, men there say that Winchester rifles were cheaper than to buy votes; and then one man told me to my face it didn't matter how the election went, they were going to have the offices.

A. Who was it that made that statement?—A. This was William Willerford (Printed record, page 199.)

Jordan Yeates, in speaking of the threats made to carry the September election, testified:

Q. And he told you that he was going to carry that election and get those officers, no matter how the vote went?—A. That's what he said, yes, sir; he certainly told me that, I reckon, more than five or six different times; he made those threats to me five or six different times; the last time was at West Memphis, and he said he wouldn't serve as sheriff with no more colored officers.

*   *   *   *   *   *   *

They made threats that they were going to carry the election, and if they had to carry it with their Winchesters; and again, now this was Mr. Jul Harden made that threat; that he thought it was cheaper to take the election with the Winchesters than it was to take it with money. I heard him make that, and I remember exactly where he was sitting when he said so; that it was cheaper for them to carry it with their Winchesters than with money; that was the evening after our convention.

Q. I want to know if some days prior to the election were they making demonstrations all around over the county with those guns—marching around with them?—A. Oh, yes, sir; they was. (Printed record, page 193.)

S. R. Rushing, on this subject, testified:

Q. Did you ever hear any threats made in regard to Republican voters voting the Republican ticket?—A. No more than the Winchester rifle crowd said there shouldn't no colored man hold office in that county; that's what they said; shouldn't no colored man hold office in that county.

Q. Have you heard any threats in regard to Republicans holding office in that county?—A. None of them shouldn't hold no office there.

Q. Who did you hear referred to on this occasion?—A. These parties that we nominated on our ticket as Republicans; Mr. James, Mr. Boon, Mr. John Williams, Jim Thompson, and Augustus. (Printed record, page 207.)

F. L. Fleming, in speaking of the ticket nominated as a fusion ticket, testified:

Q. What do you mean by a fusion ticket?—A. By giving the Democrats and Republicans part of the offices. Our method over there was to give the sheriff and treasurer to the Democrats, elect the clerk Republican, and judge Republican. Those were the four prominent positions in the county. The others were divided among the white and colored. The leading colored men of that county advocated that, and that was the kind of ticket that was elected in 1886, under our advice, and had been for several years.

Q. Did the leading colored Republicans over there, in their advice to their constituents to live in peace and amity with the white people, or not?—A. Yes, sir; they did; I ran a paper over there, and that was my advice the last issue I made over there on the 7th day of July, 1888. There was one paragraph I remember well. I asked the colored people to divide the positions between the white and colored; it wouldn't be a safe policy to advocate an entire Republican ticket or an entire black ticket. (Printed record, page 196.)

J. P. Broadenax, in speaking of what class of persons the Democrats were dissatisfied with, swears:

Q. Against whom did the armed crowd seem to be operating chiefly?—A. Against the colored, sir.

Q. That was before your county ticket was made, was it?—A. Yes, sir.

Q. You afterwards made up a county ticket upon which there was four or five responsible white men in the county, did you not?—A. Yes, sir.

Q. That was known as what ticket?—A. The Republican ticket, sir.

Q. Did you hear them say anything, or were any threats made as to that ticket or those that were on it, that you know of?—A. Well, I've heard some threats made, but they were not made directly to me.

Q. Have they seemed any kinder or more pleasant toward those white men than they have toward the colored men since that time of this opposition, seemed any kinder toward the white men that were on your ticket than they were to the colored men of the county, or have they treated them all about alike?—A. They treated them all about alike, seemed like to me as far as I've seen, the white men that was on the ticket and the colored people seemed to be treated just about alike. (Printed record, page 197.)

The Winchester rifle crowd.

William Royster, in speaking of who belonged to the Winchester rifle crowd, testified:

Q. Do you know Mr. Berry, the lawyer of Mr. Cate in this investigation?—A. Yes, sir.

Q. Do you know whether he was a member of this Winchester crowd or not?—A. Oh, yes, sir; he drilled in front of my door every night, and up-stairs in the court-house; he had the company drilling it himself; he was captain of the company in Marion; he had one company and Olie Tuck, the deputy clerk, had one.

Q. Do you know whether Mr. Kelly, the clerk of the county court, was a member of this organization or not?—A. He was then, because he guarded the jail every night to keep any troops from getting in the court-house; he kept guard while the others was out scouting.

Q. Were they officers of the county before this Winchester organization or afterwards?—A. Mr. Vance was clerk then when Kelley had the Winchesters at the court-house.

Q. Were these county officials elected in the election in which these Winchester rifles to which you refer intimidated the voters from voting?—A. Yes, sir.

Q. They were elected to their present position at that election, were they?—A. Yes, sir.

Q. So they had a personal interest, then, in this terrorizing and bulldozing?—A. Yes, sir; that morning on the 12th of July I was sitting over there in front of my house on the grocery porch, and they was down there by Mr. Chase's caucusing, and I heard Mr. Crittenden over at his office tell them they was a God damn long time doing what they promised, and they marched on to the court-house and they went off to the clerk's office and marched the men out and stood there fifteen or twenty minutes and then carried them on the north side of the court-house.

Q. Were any of the men exiled from the county by that body of men except yourself?—A. Oh, yes, sir; yes, sir; I reckon there was about fifteen or twenty of us altogether.

Q. Were they farmers and men of the county who owned property there?—A. Yes, sir, pretty well; all of them owned property, farmers and officers. (Printed record, page 190.)

J. W. Wymme, in speaking of the same subject, testified:

Q. You speak of a Winchester-rifle crowd; do you know whether that party of men claim to be Democrats or Republicans?—A. Democrats.

Q. Have you ever heard directly from them the object of their organization?—A. Never has, sir; only seen them drilling—drilling the other day.

Q. Do you know of any of the officials of Crittenden County who are members of that organization?—A. Well, yes, sir; I do.

Q. Who are they?—A. The officials are: Let me see, there is Neeley Raspberry.

Q. What position does he hold?—A. Coroner.

Q. Who else?—A. Sheriff Warner belongs to it; he's the captain, I believe, or drill-master or something.

Q. Anybody else?—A. Bob Gilliard.

Q. What position?—A. I don't know what position he holds. (Printed record, page 204.)

William Royster, in speaking of the political status of the county officers of Crittenden County, testified :

Q. You say Mr. Forest represented an organized crowd of men armed with Winchester rifles.—A. Yes, sir.

Q. Do you know who the members of that crowd were ?—A. I knew some of them.

Q. Were any of the county officials members ?—A. Yes, sir ; Mr. Warner and Julian Harden.

Q. What position did Mr. Warner hold ?—A. Mr. Warner, sheriff; Julian Hardeu, deputy sheriff; Neeley Raspberry, coroner ; and Squire Mosbey, justice of the peace ; and Squire Martin, county judge. (Printed record, page 190.)

It appears from the testimony of J. W. Wymme that the Winchester rifles were used up to the November election.

J. W. Wymme (col'd), a witness on behalf of the contestant, being first duly sworn, deposed as follows :

Q. What is your name ?—A. J. W. Wymme.

Q. Where do you live ?—A. In Crittenden County, Crawfordsville, State of Arkansas.

Q. How long have you lived there ?—A. Near twenty-three years.

Q. How old are you ?—A. 45 years old, going on 46.

Q. What is your business ?—A. Minister of the gospel.

Q. Where were you living last July ?—A. At Crawfordsville.

Q. Do you still live there ?—A. Yes, sir.

Q. You say you were living at Crawfordsville last July ?—A. Yes, sir.

Q. Do you know whether there was a political disturbance in that place at that time ?—A. There were.

Q. What was it ?—A. Well, several of our officers were put out of the country, out of the State.

Q. You say they were put out of the country; how were they put out ?—A. By guns—Winchesters—these Winchester rifles.

Q. Who had possession of those arms ?—A. There were so many that had possession of them I couldn't tell you all.

Q. Do you know any reason that was given for exiling those men to whom you refer ?—A. I do not ; only that they said they were dabbling too much in politics.

Q. What was the force of the Winchester-rifle crowd ?—A. I don't know ; I never did know how many there were.

Q. How many did you ever see ?—A. I've seen, I reckon, 18 or 20.

Q. How long did that state of affairs continue there ?—A. Well, they continued a good while. After they put those men everything become calm for a while, but they never did stop toting the guns, rifles, and one thing and another.

Q. Are they still carrying them ?—A. Yes, sir ; the day of the election, the evening after the election was over closed, I met 18 or 20 of them, all in a group, going down Marion with their rifles.

Q. What election was that ?—A. The last election we had.

Q. The election for Mr. Harrison and Mr. Featherston ?—A. Yes, sir.

Q. What effect did this state of terrorism which you refer to have upon the people of the county ?—A. Well, it had a great effect upon them, sir ; I think it scared up everybody; they were afraid to do anything ; afraid to even claim for their rights.

The contestant in his notice of contest (par. XIX) charges—

That in the county of Crittenden, in said district, there are over twenty-nine hundred (2,900) legal voters ; that not more than five hundred (500) of that number are Democrats and partisans of yours; the other twenty-four hundred (2,400) were and are friends and partisans of myself; that the county judge of said county, who is a partisan of yours, well knowing that you did not have to exceed five hundred (500) supporters in said county and that I had more than twenty-four hundred (2,400), in your interest and against mine, in violation of law appointed all of the judges of election from the political party to which you and he belong, in open and direct violation of the statute in such case made and provided, and for the purpose of producing the result herein set forth in relation to the townships of Belcher, Edmondson, Bradley, Walnut Grove, Riceville, Mound City, Scanlan, Furgeson, Crawfordsville, and Cat Island; that the sheriff of said county, who is a partisan of yours, with the intent and purpose of advancing your interests in said county and injuring mine, and with the view of preventing the holding of an election in said county on said 6th day of November, 1888, willfully failed and neglected to furnish poll-books to the judges of election in the various precincts in said county, as by law he is required to do, and but for the fact that I c used poll-books to be furnished to said judges of election no election would have been held in said county; that

H. Mis. 137——7

the county clerk of said county, who is a partisan of yours, for the purpose of aiding you and injuring me, through mistake or fraud failed to certify six hundred and twenty-one (621) votes to the secretary of state that I received in the precincts or townships of Belcher, Edmonson, Bradley, Walnut Grove, Riceville, and Furgeson, although the judges of election had made proper return thereof to him; that in the precincts last named you received only sixty-four (64) votes; that the judges of election in the precincts of Crawfordsville, Cat Island, and Walnut Grove, and all of whom are partisans of yours and creatures of the county judge, the sheriff and county clerk of said county, through mistake or fraud falsified, the returns from said last-mentioned precincts, so that they were made to appear I received four hundred and six (406) votes, whereas I received six hundred and seventy-two (672) votes in said precincts; that said falsified returns from said last-mentioned precincts show you received two hundred and eight (208) votes, whereas you received but one hundred and fifteen (115). I claim the right to show the lawlessness of your partisans in said county of Crittenden from the highest to the lowest, and any connection you may have had with them, and shall claim the right to show that their title to said offices of county judge, sheriff, and county clerk was bottomed on fraud of the character herein stated, and of ballot-box stuffing, and that said judges were selected because of their tact and talent in the business to which they were appointed, **not only** at the election held November 6th, 1888, but in that of September, 1888. **(Printed record, 6–7.)**

The lawlessness of the partisans of the contestee is fully shown; that the title to the office of the county judge, who appointed the judges of election of and from the Democratic party, was based on fraud and violence; that the county clerk, whose duty it was to certify the November vote to the secretary of state, obtained his office by the same and like means, and that the judges of election were chosen as agencies by and through which the frauds were to be committed and were committed does not admit of question, or they would not have used the fraudulent ballot-box.

We have already said the evidence fully establishes the conspiracy.

The contestant charges that the county clerk failed to certify to the secretary of state the votes cast for him in seven townships at which elections were held in Crittenden County.

The law of Arkansas in relation to counting the vote is as follows:

WHEN AND BY WHOM THE VOTE SHALL BE COUNTED.

SEC. 2695. On the fifth day after the election or sooner if all the returns have been received, the clerk of the county court shall take to his assistance two justices of the peace of the county, if they can conveniently be had, and if not then two householders having the qualifications of electors, and shall proceed to open and compare the several election returns which have been made to his office and make abstracts of the votes given for the several candidates for each office on separate sheets of paper. (Mansfield's Digest of Arkansas.)

VOTES MUST BE COUNTED REGARDLESS OF ANY INFORMALITY.

SEC. 2700. The clerks of the county courts of the several counties of this State when they shall call in two justices of the peace or householders to assist them in comparing the poll-books of the several townships shall proceed to add and count all the votes for the several persons therein voted for regardless of any informality whatever. (Mansfield's Digest of Arkansas.)

SEC. 2699. *Informality* in the certificate of the judges and clerks at any election held in any township shall not be good cause for rejecting the poll-books of said township. (Mansfield's Digest of Arkansas.)

PENALTY FOR FAILURE TO COUNT THE VOTE.

SEC. 2701. Should any clerk of the county court and the two accompanying justices, or householders, or either of them *under any circumstances* reject *or refuse to count* the vote on any poll-book of any election held by the people, such rejection or refusal by such clerk, etc., or either of them shall be deemed a high misdemeanor, etc. (Mansfield's Digest of Arkansas.)

In Patton vs. Coates, 41 Arkansas.

These sections being under construction, the supreme court of Arkansas said:
" The board of canvassers of an election have no judicial discretion whatever. They are merely for the purpose of a fair and correct computation of the votes, under public surveillance, presented to them by the clerk."

In view of these sections of the Arkansas election law, and the construction thereof by the highest court of the State, the failure of the clerk to certify the returns of the seven townships alluded to is simply a willful disregard of duty, but no greater than those indulged in by the county judge and sheriff.

For the purpose of procuring the evidence in relation to the vote of the seven townships, W. B. Eldridge, one of the attorneys of the contestant, went to the county seat of Crittenden County and obtained a certificate showing the returns were on file in [his?] office, and in speaking of his mission says:

Q. Did you go over to Marion a short time ago, and for what purpose?—A. I went there for Mr. Featherston, to procure the election returns for Crittenden County from certain townships that had not been certified up to the secretary of state from Crittenden County.

Q. Do you make this abstract Exhibit A to your deposition?—A. Yes.

[Exhibit A to deposition of W. B. Eldridge.]

Abstract of poll-books of election held on the 6th day of November, 1888, for Representative in Congress, for the 2nd Congressional district of the State of Arkansas, in Crittenden County, at the following precincts or voting places, and not certified to the secretary of the state on account of irregularities in the poll-books appearing therein, that the judges and clerks of said election were not sworn as the law directs.

	Total vote.	W. H. Cate.	L. P. Featherston.
Mound City	147	14	133
Walnut Grove	189	49	187
Bradley	208	4	195
Edmondson	90	15	75
Riceville	45	....	45
Gilmore	45	7	35
Scanlin	64	61	2

CLERK'S CERTIFICATE TO TRANSCRIPT.

STATE OF ARKANSAS, *County of Crittenden :*

I, Sam'l Keel, clerk of the circuit court, within and for the county and State aforesaid, do hereby certify that the annexed and foregoing pages contain a true and complete transcript of the above as therein set forth, and as the same appears of record, in my office at Marion, Crittenden County, Arkansas.

Witness my hand and official seal this 21st day of February, 1889.

[SEAL.] SAM'L KEEL, *Clerk.*
————— ——, *D. C.*

Q. I see from the face of the clerk's certificate that there is an assertion to the effect that the returns were not sworn to as the law directs. Please state the circumstances under which these words were put upon the face the certificate.—A. It was dictated by Mr. Berry, the lawyer of Mr. Cate in this contest, to the clerk, who wrote it word for word at his dictation, and only gave me this abstract after mature consultation with Mr. Cate's lawyer. (Printed Record, page 227-8.)

In six of the townships named, Mound City, Walnut Grove, Bradley, Edmondson, Riceville, and Gilmore, the aggregate vote was as follows :

Featherston 620
Cate 89
                                                                          ———
Majority for Featherston 531

We think this vote is sufficiently proven, and ought to be allowed the contestant.

It is conceded that the majority, on the face of the returns, for the contestee is 1,342. Deduct the 531 majority for Featherston in the six townships. This leaves Cate's majority 811.

Scanlan Township.

Scaulan Township is one of the townships included in the clerk's certificate of votes not certified to the secretary of State, and the vote in which we have not included in contestant's vote in our foregoing computation.

The testimony in relation to that township is as follows:

John Johnson (col.), a witness on behalf of the contestant, being first duly sworn, deposes as follows:

Q. What is your name?—A. John Johnson.
Q. Where do you live?—A. In Arkansas, Crittenden County.
Q. How old are you?—A. Going on forty-six.
Q. What is your business?—A. Farming.
Q. How long have you lived in Arkansas?—A. 17 years.
Q. What is your voting precinct?—A. Scanlan.
Q. Were you there at the last general election?—A. Yes, sir.
Q. What's about the usual vote of that precinct?—A. Well, from 100 to 121 or 4.
Q. How many of those are Republicans?—A. Well, about 110 or 112.
Q. How many are Democrats?—A. About 8 or 9.
Q. You say you were at the Presidential election?—A. Yes, sir; I'm at all of them, but then I was there anyhow, at that one expressly.
Q. What time did the polls open?—A. Well, they said they was to open in the morning at 9 o'clock, and close.at 4. I couldn't tell you the real hour they did open; they may have opened before 9 or after 9, that was the time set to open, at 9 o'clock.
Q. Was there some people come out to the polls that day that didn't vote?—A. They wanted to vote, but was afraid.
Q. How many people voted there?—A. I counted up 73, and they was voting on; I didn't go away, but then I went off down the river a little piece and sot around, but everybody that talked to me after I come up said they was voting Republican; there wasn't but two colored men voted the Democratic ticket, and one of them wouldn't have done it if they hadn't made him do it; he was a kind of ignorant sort of person, and they gave him the ticket and he went on and voted it.
Q. How many men did you see voto that ticket that day at the polls?—A. About 73, I think 73; I counted them particularly.
Q. Did you have the tickets in your hand?—A. Yes, sir; I had about 125 or 130 of them—150, and I reckon I give out about 30 or 40 of them that day, and saw 73 of them voted, and stood and looked at them, and saw pretty near every man that voted that day. I read the ticket and knew I was voting for Harrison.
Q. Who did you think you was voting for Congressman?—A. I just voted the straight ticket.
Q. Then this is exactly the ticket you voted?—A. Yes, sir.
Q. And this is exactly the ticket that you saw voted by 73 other men?—A. Yes, sir.
Q. And you want to file that with your testimony as the ticket that you did vote?—A. Yes, sir; marked Exhibit "A."
Q. Did the Republicans in your township vote more solidly together than usual?—A. Yes, sir; they voted solider this election than ever I known; look like the people had more privilege to vote.
Q. You mean they were more in earnest about it?—A. More in earnest, I should have said about it.
Q. What was the cause of their earnestness about voting at this time more than any other time?—A. I don't know, sir; they just thought it was a Republican election, and a great many of them was against Mr. Cleveland, and they all come together and held a meeting, and they all voted solid one way.
Q. Do you know that the returns as sent up to the clerk's office in your county only gave the Republican ticket count there two votes and the Democratic ticket 59 votes?—A. No, sir; I didn't hear anything about that; I thought that the Republicans had all that they put in, and everybody there, I reckon, thought that same thing.
Q. That is what they have returned, what do you think about that?—A. Well, I

'just think they done wrong; think they done something they had no business; I think there was a fraud in it. Any man of common sense would know as many men around the polls voting 75 or 80 or 100 men and couldn't get but two Republican tickets out of them. I'd a voted better than that if they'd had a gun on me.

Q. If the people in your township were voted properly, how many of them would turn out and swear to have voted that same ticket that you make an exhibit of, there?—A. 45 or 40 or 45.

Q. There is how many, if they were properly protected; you issued 73 yourself, you say?—A. I didn't issue that many, but I saw that many polled from other hands that was handed around, and counted them every one.

Q. If they were properly protected, are you satisfied those 73 men would turn out and testify that they did vote that ticket?—A. Yes, sir; they would; they'd come right here to-day and tell you any where.

Q. How long have you been voting at that precinct?—A. Ten years.

Q. And you say the Republican vote there, in a fair election, is about how many?—A. About 112 or 113.

Q. And how much you say the Democratic vote is?—A. About 8 or 9, some elections, in the county elections there's some 15 or 20 or 25 Democrats, 'cause they got darkies mixed in with them.

Q. Did all of the Republicans that voted vote the Republican ticket at this election?—A. Yes, sir.

Q. Was the usual number of Democrats at the polls?—A. Yes, sir; most all the white men that was there was at the polls; the biggest part of them.

Q. Can you furnish me the names, furnish me a list of these 73 voters that you speak of as having voted the Republican ticket?—A. Yes, sir; I can do it; I think I can give every man's name.

And further this deponent sayeth not. (Printed record, pages 216 217.)

Scanlan.

Willis McGee (col.), a witness on behalf of the contestant, being first duly sworn, testified as follows:

(Tin ballot-box made Exhibit A to this deposition.)

Q. What is your name?—A. Willis McGee.
Q. Where do you live?—A. Scanlan's.
Q. What county?—A. Crittenden.
Q. What State?—A. State of Arkansas.
Q. How old are you?—A. I am about 39 or 40 years old.
Q. What is your business?—A. Farming.
Q. How long have you lived there?—A. I went there in 1878, been there ever since.
(Ballot-box made Exhibit A to the deposition.)
Q. This tin box, made Exhibit A to your deposition, that I now have in my hand here, did you ever see a box like that in the State of Arkansas?—A. I did, sir.
Q. When?—A. Time the election was going on.
Q. For what purpose, if any, was the box then used?—A. To put votes in.
Q. What election is that that you refer to?—A. The Presidential election. It was used at both the elections; at the Presidential election and State and county election.
Q. Are you absolutely certain it was a box of that precise description that you saw at those two elections?—A. Yes, sir.
Q. Were the judges of that election to which you refer, at which this box or one just like it was used—were the judges of that election Democrats or Republicans?—A. Democrats.
Q. What is the usual vote in your township?—A. About 125.
Q. How many Democrats?—A. About from 25 to 30.
Q. The usual Democratic vote there is what?—A. About 25 or 30.
Q. What is the usual Republican vote of that township?—A. From 100 to 125.
Q. Do you know at that election to which you refer, do you know how many Republican votes were cast at that election?—A. No, sir; I do not know exactly how many was cast.
Q. How many did you see cast?—A. I seen about nine or ten.
Q. You are certain you saw at least nine or ten?—A. Yes, sir; I'm certain of that.
Q. Do you know the name of those parties to whom you refer that voted the Republican ticket at the national election?—A. Yes, sir.
Q. Please make a list of those names and file it as Exhibit B to your deposition.—A. I do so.
Q. Did you see those men vote that ticket?—A. I did, sir.
Q. You know it was a Republican ticket?—A. Yes, sir.

Q. Were a good many men out at the polls that day Republicans?—A. Right smart, and it was raining, and a heap didn't come.

Q. Was a good many there didn't vote?—A. Yes, sir.

Q. What was the reason?—A. The reason was they had a great time in the time of the county election, and the boys said it wasn't no use in voting; that they do just as they choose, and they didn't have no show there; they said they all voted Republican before solid out through, and they beat them at Scanlan's and every body voted Republican at Scanlan's, and they beat them.

Q. Were they counted?—A. Never were counted; that was the question.

Q. Then I want you to state the reason they didn't take any more interest, and didn't vote?—A. Because they said they all voted Republicans at the election, and when the outcry come they said everybody had voted Democratic tickets, and they said it wasn't no use for them to go there to vote; that was the reason.

Q. Are you satisfied that other people voted the Republican ticket besides those you saw vote it?—A. Yes, sir; they said so, but I knew these I did see vote it.

Q. Do you know that they returned for that township only two Republican votes?—A. No, sir.

Q. You just stated that the usual Republican vote down there was about 125 or 130?—A. Yes, sir.

Q. Usual Democratic vote is about 25?—A. Yes, sir.

Q. Your usual majority there, then, was about 100?—A. Yes, sir.

Q. You are satisfied this box was used at both elections?—A. Yes, sir.

Q. Who was the Democratic candidate for sheriff of Crittenden County?—A. Mr. Warner.

And further this deponent sayeth not.

WILLIS (his x mark) McGEE.

Deposition of E. B. Fields (col.), a witness on behalf of the contestant, being first duly sworn, testified as follows:

Q. What is your name?—A. E. B. Fields.

Q. Where do you live?—A. I live at Scanlan's, Crittenden County, Arkansas.

Q. How old are you?—A. 34.

Q. How long have you lived there?—A. Ever since 1876.

Q. Do you see this tin box that I show you here?—A. Yes, sir; I examined a box of that kind about two days before the election; helped tote it out towards where my home is.

Q. Whereabouts was that place?—A. Scanlan's.

Q. In whose possession was that box?—A. J. J. Ward, a white gentleman living down there; a Democrat.

Q. Does he hold any official position there?—A. None at all, sir.

Q. Was he one of the judges of the election there?—A. Yes, sir; he was one of the judges of election at Edmondson Station.

Q. You said that's the box he had in his possession?—A. Yes, sir.

Q. Did you vote at the Presidential election at your voting place last November?—A. Yes, sir.

Q. Do you know what disposition was made of your vote?—A. No, sir; not more than I carried my ticket in and they took it and kinder folded it up and stuck it in that box there.

Q. Put it in a box of the same appearance as that?—A. Yes, sir; same kind of tupelo as that is. I don't know what route it went, but I see them put it in at the top.

Q. Do you know what is the vote of that box over there; what is the Republican vote at your precinct?—A. About 100 and 125.

Q. What is the Democratic vote there?—A. About 25, sir.

Q. Do you know whether there was any Republican votes cast there that day or not?—A. Yes, sir; I give several of them tickets, and they sealed them up and said they was going to vote them just like they was; didn't open them at all.

Q. How many did you give tickets to?—A. I'm certain I give four; I give tickets to several, but I didn't know what they did with them; but I gave tickets to some and they held them in their hands like they were afraid they'd get away from them.

Q. Why didn't you take any more interest in the election that day?—A. In the State and county election I got disgusted, and I didn't take no more interest in it afterwards. It was the fashion to vote and I just thought I'd vote because it was a fashion; didn't do any good.

Q. Why not?—A. We usually have a great large majority, and the county election was decided, and the Democrats were 14 or 1,500 ahead, and I didn't think there was no use for voting because we always voted the same.

Q. What's the reason you didn't have any confidence in it?—A. I didn't think it was counted at all, sir.

Q. How many boxes of this description and fashion did you see over there in that election?—A. Seen two in the county election.

Q. Where were they used?—A. One was used at Scanlan's, and the other there was a tag on it for Edmondson Station. I looked at the tag myself.

Q. Do you know who sent those boxes down there, these election boxes to which you refer?—A. They said Mr. Warner sent them down there.

Q. Who said so?—A. Mr. Jerry Ward told me so.

Q. Was Mr. Warner the judge of any of the elections there?—A. No, sir; he's the sheriff of the county.

Q. Is he a Democrat or Republican?—A. He's a Democrat, I reckon. The colored people first taken him up.

Q. Were the judges and clerks of this election at which you say these Republican votes were cast Democrats or Republicans?—A. Straight-out Democrats, sir.

Q. All Democrats?—A. All Democrats, sir.

Q. Were they red-hot Democrats?—A. Right square out, sir.

Q. Were there any disturbance or rows there on the day of election?—A. When the State and county election was?

Q. Were there any in the Presidential election?—A. No, sir; it was a kind of a day like this; it was raining all day most; didn't have no fuss that day. ·

Q. If the Republican voters there had believed their votes would have been counted do you think there'd have been more people there that day than there was?—A. Yes, sir; I think there'd have been more. Always turn out in full force when they have confidence.

Q. Who was the sheriff before this election; before the last election?—A. W. F. Warner.

Q. Was he re-elected?—A. Yes, sir.

Q. On what ticket?—A. On the Democrat ticket, sir.

Q. And you say he was one of the gentlemen who had these ballot-boxes like this sent down there?—A. Yes, sir. (Printed record, page 215.)

It appears from this testimony that John Johnson saw 73 Republicans vote the Republican ticket, and that others voted after that; and that the Republican vote of the township was 112 or 113. E. B. Fields swears the judges were all Democrats and that they had the fraudulent tin box. Willis McGee swears that the judges were all Democrats, that there was a good turn-out of the Republicans, and that there was from 100 to 125 Republicans in the township. The return shows two votes for contestant.

On this state of proof the question is: How many votes should be allowed the contestant?

It was held in Bisbee *vs.* Finley that:

> Where the evidence shows a return to be false, and not a true statement of the votes cast, such return is impeached and destroyed as evidence, and the true vote may be proven by calling the electors whose names are on the poll-books as voting at such poll, and no votes not otherwise proven should be counted.

Under this rule, and we know of no exception to it, the return must be rejected.

The rejection of the return does not necessarily leave the votes actually cast at a precinct uncounted. It only declares that the returns, having been shown to be false, shall not be taken as true, and the parties are thrown back upon such other evidence as it may be in their power to produce in order to show how many votes and for whom; so that the entire vote, if sufficient pains be taken and the means are at hand, may be shown and not a single one be lost notwithstanding the falsity of the returns.

The contestant shows that he received 73, and perhaps more votes, and these, we think, should be allowed him. Deduct these from Cate's remaining majority and the vote stands thus:

Cate's majority 811
Deduct the 73
                                                                                    ———
    Leaving Cate's majority 738

The return having been overthrown, and the contestee having failed
to prove any vote in the township, is not allowed the 61 returned for
him.

Cat Island.

In relation to Cat Island precinct the testimony is as follows:

Robert Abernathy (col.), a witness on behalf of the contestant, being
first duly sworn, deposes as follows:

Q. What is your name?—A. Robert Abernathy.
Q. Where do you live?—A. I live at Cat Island.
Q. How old are you?—A. I don't know truthfully; I am something over 40, though.
Q. What is your business?—A. Well, I farm a little.
Q. Are you a planter?—A. Well, I planted last year; I reckon I will some this
year, but then I'm not an extensive farmer.
Q. Can you read and write?—A. Yes.
Q. Did you vote at the last election—the national election?—A. I did.
Q. Where did you live previous to that time?—A. Alcorn County, North Missis-
sippi.
Q. How many white people were there?—A. About twenty-five.
Q. And the rest of the voters were all colored?—A. All colored.
Q. Do you know who those colored voters voted for in the last election?—A. General Republicans; nine-tenths of them were Republicans; I heard them say prior to
the time they would vote that ticket under all hazards; then when the tickets were
issued they come there through the rain and got the tickets and went to the island,
and I seed no other ticket during the day but the Republican ticket. There was no
other exhibited publicly.
Q. How do you know the Republican ticket?—A. Well, there was Harrison and
his electors and Featherston on it; I voted it for a Republican ticket; if I failed I'm
just here under a mistake. We've had them together two or three times since, and
there was only three men that said at each meeting that they did not vote.
Q. You say you voted the Republican ticket?—A. I did.
Q. Do you know whether that ticket was put in the box or not?—A. Yes, sir; I'm
most safe in saying it were, and I seen where the chairman there couldn't see the
box. When I came up a man challenged me and says, "Has Abernathy a right to
vote?" One of the judges of election says "Yes; I have known Abernathy over two
years, he has a right to vote," and he turned and put my ticket in the box; that's
how I come to see it; if he had not turned I would not have seen it.
Q. Were there any Republican judges there at that time?—A. There was none.

George Hendley (col.) a witness on behalf of the contestant, being
first duly sworn, deposed as follows:

Q. What is your name?—A. George Hendley.
Q. Where is your residence?—A. In Crittenden County, Arkansas.
Q. What is your age?—A. 31.
Q. What is your occupation?—A. I'm a farmer and sometimes I teach school.
Q. I want to know about the usual number of voters in your township?—A.
Usually we have always voted from 196 to 200, always, in the township.
Q. What proportion of them were Democrats; about how many Democrats were in
the township?—A. Well, we have generally been known to be about from 14 to 15..
Q. How many Republicans?—A. We have been known to be from 180 to 182 and
three and four and so on.
Q. Did you vote on the November election?—A. Yes, sir; I did.
Q. Did the Republican voters in your township turn out pretty well?—A. Yes, sir;
they voted out very well.
Q. You consider it a full vote that day?—A. Yes, sir; I considered it nearly a full
vote; not quite as many as voted in the county election.
Q. Was the regular Republican ticket voted by the Republicans on that day?—A.
Yes, sir.
Q. Have you got a copy of that ticket with you?—A. I haven't one with me, but I
can describe it; it was a red ticket with a calico back to it.
Q. Did many of the Republicans scratch their tickets?—A. There didn't any scratch
it as I saw, and I don't believe any scratched it.
Q. Did any of the Republicans to your knowledge vote any other ticket?—A. None
whatever to my knowing.
Q. Were they as much as usual interested in that election?—A. Yes, sir.

Q. About what is the usual Democratic vote, did you say, of the township ?—A. It generally has been about from 13 to 15.

Q. That's about as many of the Democratic voters as you have ever known to vote there ?—A. Yes, sir.

Q. That pink ticket had who on it for Congressman ?—A. L. P. Featherston.

Q. Do you know of any of the Republicans for W. H. Cate for Congressman ?—A. I do not.

* * * * * * *

Q. Did the Republicans all vote the Republican ticket in the last election ?—A. They did as far as I know; in fact I saw most of them all vote; they all voted it; they all told me they would vote the Republican ticket; I saw a great many of them vote it, and the majority of them told me afterwards that they had voted the Republican ticket.

Q. Was there any special reason why they were more anxious that the Republican party should succeed in the last election than before ?—A. Yes, sir.

Q. What was that reason ?—A. Because there had been a great trouble occurred in the county, and the people were very much dissatisfied from the treatment; the Republicans, and more especially the colored; I know they were very much dissatisfied and they wanted all officers elected with Republican men in them.

Q. For what purpose ?—A. In order that they might get justice.

* * * * * * *

Q. Where do you live ?—A. I live in Cat Island.

Q. How long have you lived there ?—A. I been living there 7 years.

Q. What is the name of your voting precinct ?—A. Cat Island. (Printed record, page 187–8–9.)

George Hendley, in speaking of whether the judges and clerks were sworn, testifies:

Q. Do you know whether the judges and clerks of election were sworn ?—A. If they were sworn, I don't know who swore them; at that time I were acting justice of the peace there, and of course I know I didn't swear them myself, and I were the only justice of the peace that were in the township, and if they were sworn I don't know who swore them.

Q. Are you justice of the peace at present ?—A. No, sir.

Q. Were you a candidate at the last election ?—A. No, sir.

Q. You have no interest in this only to tell the truth ?—A. That's my only interest I have.

George Hendley, in speaking of the position of the ballot-box, testifies:

Q. Was the box always put where you can see all around it ?—A. No, sir; the box was in a place where I couldn't see the box; I don't remember of having seen the box.

Q. Could you see whether your ticket was put in the box or not ?—A. I never saw the box at all; I only handed my ticket in to the man that was setting in the window, or near the window, and I didn't know whether he put my ticket in the box or not.

* * * * * * *

Q. Has the custom there been to put the boxes in such a shape that the voters couldn't see it when they were voting ?—A. No, sir; it never was the case before.

Q. Was it this time ?—A. Yes, sir; it was out of sight this time: we couldn't see it. (Printed record, page 188.)

George Hendley, in speaking of the judges of election at Cat Island precinct, testifies:

Q. Who were the judges of election in your township ?—A. Dr. Stewart and Otto Sypules, and I forgotten who the others was.

Q. Were they Democrats or Republicans ?—A. They were all Democrats.

Q. Did you have any Republican judges of election the last election ?—A. No, sir; we did not.

Q. They were all Democrats ?—A. All Democrats.

Q. Do you know whether that is the condition of affairs in other parts of the county or not ?—A. I do not know, but I have heard that it was. (Printed record, page 188.)

It appears from this testimony that the Republicans turned out well; that they did not scratch the ticket; that the fraudulent ballot-box was used; that Republicans before the election had met and agreed to vote their ticket at all hazards; that there were from 180 to 182 Republicans in the township; that the judges were all Democrats; that there were not more than 14 or 15 Democrats in the township; that there was a full vote by the Republicans; that the judges were not sworn; that the ballot-box was so placed that the voter could not see it.

The return shows 120 for Featherston and 88 for contestee, and the question is, under the proof, what ought to be done?

The total vote cast is 208, and the proof is that there are but 15 Democrats in the township, and that the Republicans did not scratch their ticket. By giving the Democrats their full vote, Featherston ought to have received 193 votes out of the 208, and he is returned as receiving 120.

In view of the conduct of the partisans of the contestee in Crittenden County whereby the contestant and his attorneys were prevented from taking testimony and which will be referred to hereafter, strict and technical proof will not be required.

We think the true rule was laid down in the case of Smalls vs. Elliott, session of 1888–'89, by the minority of the committee, where it is said:

Contestee's partisan friends deliberately violate the law in suppressing the box, and contestee himself (acting through his counsel), by force and threat of violence, suppresses and hinders the judicial inquiry as to the box and its contents.

Suppressio veri — suggestio falsi. All things are presumed against him who suppresses the truth and prevents inquiry.

Shall contestee be permitted to take advantage of his own wrong, and of the willful and criminal violation of the law by his partisan friends? Is the sin of the guilty to be visited on the innocent? Shall he who suppresses the best evidence by force, fraud, and violence, stand up in the face of the court of last resort and insist that secondary evidence shall not be produced and admitted?

In this case, assuming the testimony to be true, and we do not doubt but that it is true, it appears that before the election every provision looking to a fair and honest election was violated, and that after the election every attempt to show the true vote was suppressed by the partisans of the contestee.

We think the proof clearly shows that the contestee could not have received more than 15 votes in Cat Island Township, if that many. Therefore, we give to the contestant 73 votes more than were returned for him, and deduct 73 from the vote returned for contestee. These two changes aggregate 146. The result would then stand thus:

Cate's majority	738
Deduct the	146
Leaving Cate's majority	592

Crawfordsville precinct.

In relation to the Crawfordsville precinct the testimony is as follows:

James Brown (col.), a witness on behalf of the contestant, being first duly sworn, testified as follows:

Q. What is your name?—A. James Brown.
Q. Where do you live?—A. Crawfordsville, Crittenden County, Arkansas.
Q. How long have you lived there?—A. Been living there now going on four years.
Q. What is your business?—A. Farming.
Q. How old are you?—A. The 25 of this coming month I'll be 41 years old.
Q. Did you vote for the national ticket at the election held in November for President and members of Congress in Crittenden County, Ark.?—A. Yes, sir; my intention was to vote the Republican ticket straight out.

Q. Do you know whether you did or not?—A. I don't know whether I did or not, but I voted the ticket that they gave me, that they say was Republican.

Q. Who gave you that ticket?—A. The ticket I voted I got from Henry Davis.

Q. Was he a Democrat or Republican?—A. He was claimed to be a Republican; he goes for a Republican.

Q. Do you see this box that I have in my hand here?—A. Yes, sir.

Q. With this peculiar device on top of it here?—A. Yes, sir; I see that box now.

Q. Did you ever see one like it before?—A. I didn't see one exactly like that, but it had more of a shape—come like that; they had two divisions in it. I seen the top of the box just like I look at the top of that one now. Two places cut in that box like it was cut for the tickets to go in each one of those holes; that's the way that box was; there was two places in the top of that box.

Q. Then, the box you saw was just like this one?—A. Yes, sir.

Q. You saw a box like this one, then, at Crawfordsville that was formed on top for the reception of tickets like that one is formed?—A. Yes, sir; just like that one was formed.

Q. You say your intention was to vote the Republican ticket?—A. Yes, sir.

Q. Did you cast your ballot?—A. Yes, sir; I went to the door and handed it to the man that was placed there to take the tickets.

Q. What did he do with it?—A. He cast it around to the box; I seen him carry it to the place that was to put the tickets in, but whether it went inside of the box I do not know. We all was standing out in the rain anyway, and wanted to get through as quick as we could.

Q. Was that the ballot-box?—A. Yes, sir.

Q. Was it made out of tin?—A. Yes, sir.

Q. Then, so far as you could see, it was a box constructed like that?—A. Yes, sir.

Q. You say you gave your ticket to some one. Who was that?—A. A man that was called Willis Raspberry.

Q. Was he a Democrat or Republican?—A. Well, he's a Democrat.

Q. Do you know the judges of the election that day?—A. Laurin Butler were one; Bob Jinley was the other; Jim Hooxbul was the other.

Q. Were any of those men Republicans?—A. No, sir.

Q. Were they all Democrats?—A. They were all Democrats.

Q. If this testimony that you are now giving was taken at Crawfordsville would you testify?—A. I will if I'm living and the Lord spares me.

Q. Have you ever seen any of these boxes anywhere except at Crawfordsville?—A. No, sir.

Q. Do you know what became of the ballot-box there after that day?—A. No, sir.

Q. You say your intention was to vote the Republican ticket?—A. The Republican ticket straight out, the ticket that they say Mr. Featherston was on. That was a red ticket. That's the ticket I voted.

Q. Do you know whether the negroes of that county—whether they intended to vote the Republican ticket or the Democratic ticket?—A. Their whole intention was to vote the Republican ticket straight out. Our intention was before we started, before the election come to an end—our intention was to vote the Republican ticket to beat out that Winchester crowd. That was our intention.

Q. Who was that Winchester crowd composed of?—A. Andrew Martin and Sheriff Werner.

Q. Were they Democrats or Republicans?—A. Democrats. (Printed record, page 218–19.)

Giles Shenault (col.), a witness on behalf of the contestant, being first duly sworn, tstified as follows:

Q. What is your name?—A. Giles Shenault.

Q. Where do you live?—A. Crawfordsville, about three miles southwest of Crawfordsville, Crittendon County, Arkansas.

Q. How old are you?—A. Nearly 52.

Q. How long have you been there?—A. Going on eight years.

Q. Did you vote at the last Presidential election held in the State of Ark. in November, 1888?—A. Yes, sir.

Q. Did you vote the Republican or Democratic ticket?—A. Well, I voted the red ticket they called the Republican ticket.

Q. What ticket did you intend to vote, the Republican or Democratic ticket?—A. The Republican ticket's what I was after.

Q. Do you see this tin box that I have in my hand here?—A. Yes, sir.

Q. Did you ever see one like that before?—A. I think that one we had right yonder was like that.

Q. What do you mean?—A. At Crawfordsville.

. What time did you see it there ?—A. The morning of the Presidential election.
. That took place when ?—A. In November.
Q. What year ?—A. 1888.
Q. Where did you see that box that you mention ?—A. I saw it there in the drug store.
Q. Whose drug store ?—A. Dr. Haden's.
Q. For what purpose was that box being used ?—A. They said it was a ballot-box, had the tickets in there.
Q. You say you voted the Republican ticket that day ?—A. That was my aim; I voted the ticket they called the Republican ticket.
Q. What became of that ticket ?—A. I don't know what went with it; I handed it to a man setting at the box, and he poke it down there. I don't know where it went.
Q. Was the box he put the ticket in precisely like this ?—A. I never seed nothing took off of the top like that—the mouth imitating that.

*   *   *   *   *   *

Q. Who was the gentleman you gave your ticket to, that put it in the box ?—A. Raspberry.
Q. Is he a Democrat or Republican ?—A. He's a Democrat, I reckon; what we call him.
Q. Was he one of the clerks of the election that day ?—A. Yes, sir; he was in there with them; he was constable; he was the man that showed the box, 'cause he opened it; pulled it open, and turned it over that way as you see there, and no tickets in it; that was Raspberry; he was considered to be the constable there, and I was the first man that voted, and it was raining, and I handed the ticket in to him, and stepped right back; we was very much crowded; it was pouring down rain, and he took the ticket and appeared to be putting it down in the box that way. (Printed record, page 212.)

It appears from this testimony that the fraudulent tin ballot-box was used; that the judges of election were all Democrats; that there was a good turn out, the total vote polled being 395.

It was at this township the contestant went to take testimony and was prevented from so doing by the friends of the contestee.

The nearest approximation to proof of how the vote stood, in that township, is found in the testimony of E. D. Sanders (page 200) where he says that the vote of the Republicans is about 6 to 1 of the Democrats, and when interrogated, as to Crawfordsville, he says that would not be a fair proportion for that township, nor does he say what would be.

The return from the township shows the following:

Cate	88
Featherston	147
Barrett	160
Total	395

It does not appear from the record who Barrett is, or what party put him in nomination, or whether there is any such man.

Had the contestant made proof of any vote received, as was done in Scanlan and Cat Island, we would set aside the return and give him the vote proven; but he has not done so. If we should set aside the return it would have to be done on suspicion, or from the fact that returns should not be regarded where the use of a fraudulent box is shown, and that the judges of election were all of the Democratic party in a strong Republican township. To set aside the return in a township where the contestant has a majority, but not as great as he claims it should be, in a case where he was prevented from making full proof of his vote, would be to reward the fraud complained of, and punish him for undertaking to expose it. Where there is no proof upon which we would be justified in setting aside the return, we therefore let it stand. As both parties have had credit for this vote, it having been certified to the secretary of state, it makes no change in the majority.

No election at Idlewild precinct.

. George Hendley, in speaking of the failure to hold an election at Idle-wild precinct, testifies:

Q. Is there any other voting precinct in your township?—A. Yes, sir; Idlewild.
Q. Do you know whether there was any election held at Idlewild?—A. There was not.
Q. Do you know whether the judges of election at that point were all Democrats or all Republicans?—A. They were all Democrats.
Q. What was the conclusion of the people of that precinct was the reason for not opening the polls?—A. The conclusion was because that all of the people there, the voting citizens, was going to vote the straight Republican ticket, and in order to prevent them from voting, it was supposed they wouldn't open the polls that day.
Q. Did any of the voters come down to your precinct to vote?—A. Yes, sir; about 12 or 14.
Q. Did they tell them that the polls were not open at Idlewild?—A. Yes, sir; they did.
Q. And thought that they could vote there because it was in the same township?—A. Yes, sir.
Q. Were they allowed to vote?—A. Well, I couldn't really say that they wasn't allowed, because I met them as I were coming away, but they told me that they was objected to voting.
Q. You don't know whether they voted then or not?—A. I know that they didn't vote; they said they was objected of voting by some one; I don't know who.
Q. How many men told you they were at the polls that day for the purpose of voting the Republican ticket?—A. About 26.
Q. Can you furnish their names?—A. I can.
And further this deponent sayeth not. (Printed record, page 188–9).

No polls opened in Ferguson.

Thompson Foster (col.), a witness on behalf of the contestant, being first duly sworn, testified as follows:

Q. What is you name?—A. Thompson Foster.
Q. Where do you live?—A. Crittenden County, Arkansas.
Q. How long have you lived there?—A. Ever since 1870.
Q. How old are you?—A. 28.
Q. What is your occupation?—A. Farmer.
Q. What is your usual voting precinct?—A. Ferguson precinct.
Q. Was there any election held there on the sixth day of November last?—A. No, sir.
Q. Were you at the polls to vote?—A. Yes, sir.
Q. Were the judges of election who served at the State election all Democrats or Republicans?—A. They all was supposed to be Democrats.
Q. They didn't come about the polls to open the polls during the day?—A. No, sir; not to my understanding, or not to my knowing; never saw any of them.
Q. What was the Republican majority in your precinct generally?—A. About 120 or 125.
Q. What proportion of them were at the polls during that day for the purpose of voting?—A. Off and on all day, about a hundred to my knowing.
Q. They came there for the purpose of voting?—A. Yes, sir.
Q. And the polls not being open they couldn't vote?—A. Yes, sir.

* * * * * * *

Q. About what is the Democratic vote of your township?—A. There is about six or eight.
Q. Were they out that day to vote?—A. No, sir. (Printed record, page 205.)

Furgeson.

. T. J. Jones (col.), a witness on behalf of the contestant, being first duly sworn, testified as follows:

Q. Where do you live?—A. I live in Proctor Township.
Q. Whereabouts?—A. I live there at Ferguson's.
C. What State and county?—A. Crittenden County, Arkansas.
Q. How long have you lived there?—A. About 21 years.

Q. How old are you?—A. About 29.
Q. What is your business?—A. Farming.
Q. Where is your usual voting place?—A. Ferguson's, though I vote at Jones's on the national election—Presidential election; my usual voting place is at Ferguson's.
Q. But the Presidential election you did vote at Jones's?—A. Yes, sir.
Q. Were you down at Ferguson's during the day?—A. Yes, sir; I was at Ferguson's during the day and at Jones's; was at Ferguson's first.
Q. How long were you at Ferguson?—A. About two hours, I reckon.
Q. Were there a good many people there?—A. Yes, sir.
Q. Anxious to vote?—A. Yes, sir; they were strung all around there; seemed to be.
Q. About how many came to the polls to vote at Ferguson while you were there?— A. During the day, about a hundred.
Q. Did you know all of the people?—A. No, sir; I didn't know all of them; I knew one part of them.
Q. Was that the larger part of them?—A. Yes, sir; that's a large body of them.
Q. What were their politics; were they Republicans or Democrats?—A. They all was Republicans.
Q. They all turned out to vote?—A. Yes, sir; all but about a few white men was in the crowd; they was Democrats.
Q. How many Democrats do you imagine was in the crowd?—A. I didn't see any of those white men at the polls, but in that precinct four or five of them was Democrats. All the judges, pretty well, live there in that voting precinct are Democrats, but I didn't see them all during that day.
Q. The voters that you saw at the polls then were all Republicans?—A. Yes, sir; all Republicans.
Q. You think you saw about a hundred there?—A. About a hundred.
Q. You been voting at that precinct for several years?—A. Yes, sir.
Q. The Republican vote there is usually how many?—A. Well, it's about 120.
Q. Were the judges of election for that township Democrats or Republicans?—A. They was all Democrats pretty well, I think.
Q. Did you hear any reason given for the judges not opening the polls on that day?— A. Didn't hear no reason at all; I did at one time, but I didn't pay much attention to that. Some says that Col. Armstrong wasn't there the reason the polls wasn't opened, and I understand that Col. Armstrong were in town—Memphis here—though he had been notified that he was judge of that election.
Q. Did he serve as judge in the State election?—A. In the county election he did, but not in the national election—Presidential election.
Q. If the polls had been open there all day long as they usually were and ought to have been on the day of election, from what you know of your 21 years' residence there, and of the citizens around, what would have been the majority for Harrison and Featherston in that district?—A. About 115. (Printed record, page 210.)

S. R. Rushing (col.), a witness on behalf of the contestant, being first duly sworn, deposed as follows:

Q. What is your name?—A. S. R. Rushing.
Q. What is your age?—A. About 38.
Q. Where do you live?—A. Jones's.
Q. What county?—A. Crittenden.
Q. What State?—A. Arkansas.
Q. Did you vote at the last national election?—A. No, sir; wouldn't let me vote.
Q. How did they keep you from voting?—A. Said I didn't live in that precinct.
Q. Your vote was challenged, then?—A. Yes, sir.
Q. Was the election at your regular voting place?—A. Twasn't held.
Q. Why was it not held?—A. I don't know, sir; didn't hold it there.
Q. Do you know whether the majority of voters in your precinct—how they stood —whether they were usually Democrats or Republicans?—A. All of them was Republicans but about six.
Q. You say there was no election held there at all?—A. No, sir.
Q. Was the State election held there?—A. Yes, sir.
Q. No national election?—A. No, sir.
Q. Were the judges Democrats or Republicans?—A. All of them were Democrats.
Q. You refer to the State election now?—A. Yes, sir.
Q. What is the usual number of votes polled at that township precinct?—A. About 130.
Q. What proportion of them are Republicans?—A. All of them but about five or six.
Q. Were most of them at the polls that day and anxious to vote?—A. They told me they were there all day. I was there trying to get the election held, and never got it. I was supervisor, and after I was notified that I was supervisor I went to the

polls in order to know the reason or see that there was an election held there. I was appointed by the proper authorities, and I went there for the purpose of having some kind of an election. No judges came, and there was no election held.

Q. When you got to Ferguson's and found you couldn't vote—found that the polls were not open—you went to Jones's for the purpose of voting?—A. Yes, sir.

Q. And there you were denied the right to vote?—A. Yes, sir; none of us voted at all.

Q. Were there any poll-books or a ballot-box furnished to any one that you know of in Ferguson precinct?—A. There was a ballot-box sent to me at 1 o'clock the same day; it was about 1 o'clock. I was in my store; had a clock in there, and the ballot-box come there; the fellow came; he looked like he came in haste. He come there with the ballot-box and poll-books and everything; says, "I want you to hold election at Ferguson's;" I says, "I ain't the judges." "Well," he says, "you are appointed as supervisor." I says, "I have no notice of that." "Well," he say-, "it's in this thing." And I took it and looked in there and I saw I was appointed supervisor at Ferguson's and Jones's. I thought that was a mere mistake: I don't know how I come at two places, but then my name was on at Ferguson's and Jones's, and I thought it was very necessary to vote for Harrison as President, and I wanted to vote the whole ticket, especially Featherstone; wanted to vote the whole ticket. We voted the State and county ticket solid Republican. There wan't but six men went against us at that precinct, and we voted 128 or 30 there. The reason I didn't hold the election was because I sent it to the judges of the election; I thought they were elected for a certain term under proper authorities; I sent it to them and ordered them to open the polls immediately, that I was going to hold an election. There was none held at all. There was people coming there all day; I reckon there was more than 25 or 30. I reckon there was more than them; of course I counted that many citizens of the county, and there was citizens of the United States, and we couldn't vote.

Q. If the polls had been opened there early in the morning, according to law, what would have been the majority given to Harrison and to Featherston?—A. They'd have got about 125 votes apiece.

Q. What would have been the Democratic vote there?—A. About six or eight. (Printed record, 206-7.)

The townships of Idlewild and Furgeson may be treated together. The proof shows that the judges of election at Idlewild were Democrats; that they failed to open the polls, and that the Republican majority in the precinct usually ranged from 100 to 125. It also shows that at Furgeson the judges of election were all Democrats; that they failed to open the polls, and that the Republican majority in the precinct is 115; i. e., this had been the usual Republican majority.

We know of no rule by which these votes can be counted under the state of proof as to these townships. The action of the Democratic judges in these precincts no doubt deprived the contestant of somewhere about 250 majority; but it is no worse, in fact not nearly so bad, as the conduct of the judges of election in Scanlan, Cat Island, and Crawfordville in the use and manipulation of a fraudulent ballot-box.

It is nearer on a level with the action of the county court clerk already referred to, who willfully failed to certify the vote of seven townships to the secretary of state. Nor is it quite as bad as the action of the county judge who appointed such creatures of a conspiracy as judges of election. But it does show that the conspiracy formed in July, 1888, to control the county of Crittenden politically, with less than one-sixth of the legal voters, was still alive and active in November in depriving the Republicans of their votes.

What made the Republicans poll a full vote at the November election.

Jordan Yeates, in speaking of the vote polled at the Congressional election, testified:

Q. What made them stick closer together than usual?—A. Upon the action of the Democrats with the Winchesters; that's just exactly why we stuck so close, seeing how cruel those men, undertaking to take the advantage of men, because they wanted them out of office.

Q. Do you think they stuck as closely together in the national election?—A. Yes, sir; they stuck just as close in the national election.

Q. You think they were specially anxious to see a Republican President elected?—A. Yes, sir; they had it on their minds if they carried that election they probably would be able to obtain justice.

Q. The Republican vote, then, you are satisfied, in Crittenden County, in the two last elections has been more solid than it has been for years?—A. More solid than it has been in 20 years.

Q. Repeat in as short a way as you can, your reason for thinking that?—A. My reason for thinking it was just this: It was just simply for the way that the Democrats did. They taken, for the sake of getting in possession of the office, they taken their guns, raised up an excuse against our leading men that we had there, Dave Ferguson and Dan Louis; they felt that was the only way they had to come in power, was to get up some excuse against those men to drive them away and all their followers; that was our opinion; that caused us to stick together so close; that those men did that for the purpose of frightening the election so as to frighten the others so they wouldn't try to arrest their actions at all, and we were determined to show them that it was allowed to us to vote and we intended to execute that right, and that was the feeling with the people generally, that they all turned out and voted when they had a chance, and all voted in the national election the straight Republican ticket. (Printed record, page 194.)

William Royster, in speaking on the same subject, testified:

Q. Why did the colored members of the Republican party poll such a large vote and stick so close in the national election?—A. Because the men that they had had there for leaders I suppose they had a great deal of confidence in was hurried away, and they made the brag when they got up the Winchester crowd that they had the snakes [tail] off in the morning and the head would die by sun-down; and that was the motto what drew the people together; and they said if they had cut the snake's head off they would come nearer together than they were before.

Q. What did they expect from the Republican party if it got into power?—A. I don't know, sir; they expected to get some civil law in the country; there is no law; because we expected to get some relief from the condition of affairs that prevail; to get some relief from the condition of affairs that prevail now.

And further this deponent saith not. (Printed record, page 191.)

J. L. Fleming, in speaking on this subject, testified:

Q. Do you know whether the colored people of Crittenden County vote the Republican or Democratic ticket?—A. The colored people of that county vote the Republican ticket, and they voted more solid last year than they ever did.

Q. Why?—A. Because they understood that the action of that Winchester crowd was for political purposes, and they intended to vote solid Republican—more than they ever had done before—because they saw the advantages that the whites tried to take of the colored Republicans.

Q. What were those advantages?—A. By driving the leading Republicans out of the county they thought that the colored people would have no leaders.

Q. These leaders that you speak of, did they, in their advice to the colored people, advise assassination, or incendiarism, or taking advantage of anybody?—A. No, sir; we advocated a fusion ticket in that county politics. (Printed record, page 196.)

E. D. Sanders, in speaking on this subject, testified:

Q. How was it with regard to the Republican vote; was it at all divided?—A. Not at all, sir.

Q. Was there any reason why it should have been nearer a unit than it had been in years before?—A. Yes, sir; there was, from the simple fact those men calling themselves the Democratic nominees had nominated over the Republican there, and brought out Winchester rifles; made all kind of threats that they should not even nominate a ticket, and this brought them more closely together; I know it to be a fact in the last election we had there. For several years the Republican ticket has been considerably divided, and that was done through the farmer who was controlling labor. Some of them, you know, would have a liking for the man they was working with, and would vote for him, but on this occasion they had no friends among the party at all, and therefore they consolidated and voted solidly.

Q. What was your experience as to the reliability of the nigger standing up to his friends and voting his tickets in the State election; what was your experience in this election?—A. Well, I think they stood right up and turned out fully and voted for their friends; our precinct polled a heavier vote in the State and in the last election than it has there for several years.

Q. Then you think the reason for it was to resent the unjust treatment which they considered they had received at the hands of the so-called Democratic party manipulated by the Winchester rifle crowd?—A. I do; I'm satisfied of it. (Printed record, page 199.)

The following testimony gives a detailed history of the efforts of the contestant to take proof in Crittenden County, and that he was prevented from so doing by the partisan friends of contestee.

W. B. Eldridge, being first duly sworn, testified as follows:

Q. What is your name, place of residence, age, and occupation?—A. My name is W. B. Eldridge; 28 years of age; occupation, lawyer, and residence, Memphis, Tenn.

Q. Are you a Republican or Democrat?—A. I have never voted anything, and never will vote anything but the Democratic ticket.

Q. Were you one of the attorneys for L. P. Featherston, and did you go to Crittenden County recently to take proof for him in the contest between him and Cate?—A. I was one of his attorneys and did go for that purpose.

Q. Mr. Eldridge, what sort of reception did you meet with from the people over there?—A. I was not received at all.

Q. What do you mean by saying you was not received at all; and please state how you were treated by the people over there; state fully.—A. The people seemed displeased at my presence there as the lawyer of Mr. Featherston, and I was not invited in their places of business or residences, or in any way was I shown that common politeness which the citizens of a town are supposed to extend to a stranger who is there on legitimate business.

Q. What town was this?—A. Crawfordsville, Crittenden County, Arkansas.

Q. You say you were not invited into any place of business or any house; what was the condition of the weather at this time, and did you suffer any inconvenience on account of this inhospitality?—A. My associate counsel, Mr. Henry F. Walsh, and myself were together; we remained there about two days and a night. The first day it was bitter cold, which we spent in a saloon with the doors open and no place to sit; the second day was spent under the cover of the porches of the stores. We did this because we had nowhere else to go, and no one invited us in out of the cold and weather. We had some difficulty in getting anything to eat, which we finally secured from negroes, who allowed us to eat it in an open room adjoining where it was cooked. We came very near freezing here. This was a negro eating-house; such a place I was never in before. The night coming on, we looked in vain for a place to rest, and I thought we would have to pass it in the open street. We finally induced a negro by the name of Logan to allow Mr. Walsh and myself to pass the night on a lounge in a room of his house, which was about half a mile from town. We received the only courtesy from this negro and his wife that we had there at all.

*   *   *   *   *   *   *

.Q. Mr. Eldridge, in all of your experience as a lawyer, have you ever received such impolite treatment as you experienced during your trip to Arkansas on this occasion that you speak of?—A. I never did, and hope it never will be repeated.

Q. Have you ever, in your experience as a lawyer, or in any other capacity, in traveling through the South, been forced to take your meals and lodging with negroes?—A. I never have; I was born and raised in the South, and I have never met with Southern people who did not have hospitality and common politeness before; that was the first day's experience; here's the second day's experience coming on.

Q. You speak of the second day; what happened on that day?—A. We awoke second morning and found it raining; walking through the mud back to town we got our breakfast at the same place; and standing out on the porches of the stores we had again to endure the inclemency of the weather.

Q. What sort of treatment did Mr. Featherston receive?—A. Mr. Featherstone ate with us at this negro eating-house to which I have referred; I do not know where he passed the night, as he said he had to go to the country to sleep anywhere. The people were very bitterly opposed to Mr. Featherston's making an investigation of the election, and we hourly anticipated that we would have trouble.

Q. Did you hear any threats made?—A. Yes, sir; I heard Richard Cheaton and Dr. Haden make threats.

Q. What did they say?—A. I heard them say that they did not intend to submit to an investigation of the election, and at one time I thought that Mr. Featherston would become involved in a serious difficulty with a man by the name of Dr. Haden, who seemed very much excited over our presence on the ground. I went up to the crowd where Mr. Featherston was surrounded by Dr. Hayden and his friends and carried him off to prevent a difficulty which I feared.

Q. Did any of the men about the saloon seem to be excited from drink?—A. Well, now, I don't remember whether any of them seemed to be excited or not.

Q. Were they drinking?—A. Oh, yes.

H. Mis. 137——8

Q. They were all drinking, were they?—A. Everybody was drinking pretty much.
Q. Did you all get warning from anybody over there?—A. I don't know anything about that.
Q. Did you all go over with Mr. Berry, the lawyer of Mr. Cate, and did he say anything about acting as notary public?—A. He said he would act as notary public, which afterwards he refused to do.
Q. Did you all take any depositions there?—A. We did not.
Q. What was the reason for not taking the depositions?—A. He could not get a notary public, there was a magistrate there, but he also refused to act, and Mr. Berry now refused, contrary to his promise and our expectations.
Q. Now, Mr. Eldridge, please state from your information and from what you actually observed in the conduct and the general feeling among the white people of Crawfordsville, whether there was actually danger in attempting to take depositions for Featherston?—A. I think there was danger of personal altercations which might have resulted disastrously. The people were displeased with our presence there, and I saw that if we took depositions at all we would have to do it contrary to their wishes or assistance, besides that, we could not get a notary public, and that made the taking of depositions of course impossible. (Printed record, pages 226-227.)

J. W. Wymme, on this subject, says :

Q. Do you think you would give this testimony that you are now giving if this investigation was held in Crittenden County?—A. I rather think I wouldn't, sir.
Q. Why would you not?—A. I'd be feared.
Q. Afraid of what?—A. Them fellows might kill me.
Q. What fellows?—A. Those fellows that got those guns—that military company over there.
Q. Do you think that any considerable number of voters would have given their testimony in this case if the investigation had been held at Crawfordsville?—A. No, sir; they'd have been afraid to have done so. (Printed record, page 204.)

R. Y. Logan, on this subject, testified:

Q. Do you remember advising Mr. Featherston that it would be best for him not to take testimony there in Crawfordsville at all, and to let the matter alone there?—A. Yes, sir.
Q. What was your reason for that advice?—A. Well, I knew one thing, that the people was afraid to testify.
Q. Why were they afraid to testify?—A. Well, from the general appearance of things they didn't feel free to testify.
Q. Have you heard any threats made there by the people of Crawfordsville in regard to people testifying?—A. No, sir; I didn't hear any threats made there myself, that is, from what they said ; others told me.
Q. You heard that there were threats made, you mean?—A. Yes, sir.
Q. Do you know the general feeling of the people of Crawfordsville towards Mr. Featherston?—A. No, sir; I don't really know.
Q. Do you think that Mr. Featherston could have satisfactorily carried on an examination there in this Congressional contest?—A. No, sir; I don't think he could. (Printed record, page 219.)

E. D. Hilderbrand (white), a witness on behalf of the contestant, being first duly sworn, testified as follows :

Q. What is your name?—A. E. H. Hilderbrand.
Q. Where do you live?—A. In Crittenden County, near Crawfordsville, Ark.
Q. How long have you lived there?—A. Seven years.
Q. How old are you?—A. 53.
Q. What is your business?—A. Farmer.
Q. Have you ever held any official position in that State or county?—A. Never have.
Q. Do you remember about three weeks ago when the lawyers of Mr. Featherston, Mr. Walsh and Mr. Eldridge, came to Crawfordsville with Mr. Featherston for the purpose of taking this testimony we are now taking; do you remember that time?—A. Yes, sir.
Q. Was that testimony taken at that time?—A. It was not.
Q. Why not?—A. Well, owing to the feeling of the people and the excitement that was gotten up the appearance of Mr. Featherston and his coming there created quite a commotion, when his business was known especially ; a good many were right smartly excited, but I never had heard anybody express themselves as to whether they was or was not ; I saw there was a good deal of feeling.
Q. Do you mean to say the people felt uneasy and angry on account of the appearance of Mr. Featherston and his lawyers on the ground for that purpose?—A. I judge so.

Q. Was their feeling opposed to Mr. Featherston?—A. Yes, sir; a good deal of it; there was a good deal feeling among all parties, those for and against, but that showed itself the most was those that were opposed to him.

Q. Do you know whether Mr. Featherston and his lawyers were received there with courtesy or not?—A. I do not know; I went up there that morning from home; I didn't have any idea of seeing Mr. Featherston; he was about the third man I saw after I got there; I was surprised at his coming; he had been there an hour or two when I saw him; as to how he was received, I couldn't tell you.

Q. You say that the people of Crawfordsville were very much opposed to Mr. Featherston taking his testimony there, you think, from the general manner of the population there?—A. That would be my decision.

Q. Do you think that Mr. Featherston could have induced witnesses to have testified at Crawfordsville as to his election with any degree of satisfaction?—A. No, sir; he might have gotten a few that had the nerve, the majority of them were afraid; the majority of voters that voted for him would not have went there.

Q. You say you do not think he could have procured witnesses to testify for him. Why?—A. Because they were afraid.

Q. What were they afraid of?—A. Well, sir; we are blessed with a military company in our county, and those people muster frequently and carry guns, and they show a kind of a disposition that things must go the way they say. That's what I judge. Most of the people have never had any experience in fire-arms, especially when they have them pointed at them; are a little afraid of these sorts of things.

· Q. You say you have a military organization in your county?—A. I reckon it's regularly organized; I don't know; they meet and muster regularly, and have their uniforms.

* * * * * * *

Q. Did you advise Mr. Featherston to continue that investigation or leave there?—A. My advice was to leave there. I urged the matter on him; took him home with me especially for that purpose.

Q. Why did you advise him that?—A. Because I was better acquainted with the people than he was, and I could see from the feeling and the interest that seemed to be gathering around that it was better for him to leave there. I was satisfied of one thing—that if he persisted in the course he had started out on, there would be a disturbance.

* * * * * * *

Q. Did there seem to be much drinking among the opponents of Mr. Featherston the day he was there with his attorneys?—A. There was right smart towards the middle of the day, and from that towards evening; in fact, they began to drink right smart soon after it was well understood he was in town and what his business was. There were several of them that were right smartly under the influence of whiskey.

Q. Did you at any time during that day see Mr. Featherston surrounded by the men of whom you speak, in a position that you thought was at all calculated to break the peace, and did you anticipate anything?—A. Well, I don't know hardly to answer that question; I didn't want to think that the peace would be broken, and I wasn't certain that it wouldn't be; that's just exactly the situation I was in.

Q. But you finally concluded it would be if he staid there, did you not?—A. I advised him to that effect; I believed it. (Printed record, pages 201, 202.)

J. P. Broadenax, in speaking on this subject, testified:

Q. In this county it's necessary for us to take this testimony, and we want to know if, under the feeling existing in that county, you think those people feel sufficiently and free to turn out and give evidence and appears as we are doing here? Do you think that they would like for this testimony to be taken inside of Crittenden County, and would like to come and testify?—A. They say not. There has been some talk of you coming over there and taking testimony, and a good many of them said they wouldn't turn out; thought probably there would be some trouble after it was over.

Q. Why did they imagine or think there would likely be trouble?—A. Well, from the past trouble, I suppose.

Q. Is there any evidence that those fellows intend to do any better?—A. I don't know, sir.

Q. Have you seen any evidence of it?—A. Well, no, sir; I have not.

Do you hear that they have abandoned that Winchester business, or do you know or have you heard that they are keeping it up?—A. Well, I heard that they abandoned it, sir, and I heard again that they had their Winchesters here.

Q. You think, then, that if I want to take any testimony in Crittenden County I'd better send this young gentleman with the machine and lawyer, and stay away myself?—A. Well, I don't know, Mr. Featherstone; I don't think you would be safe; still I don't know whether you would or not. (Printed record, page 198.)

116 FEATHERSTON VS. CATE.

E. D. Sanders, in speaking on this subject, testified:

Q. Under ordinary circumstances it would be necessary for us to take these depositions within Crittenden County. What is your impression as to the result of such a procedure in that county now?—A. I don't think you could possibly do it under any circumstances.

Q. Why not?—A. Simply because you would be assassinated if you attempted it. More than that, you couldn't get the men to come up there and give in their depositions.

Q. Why would they object?—A. From fear of those Winchester rifles.

Q. Where are you from?—A. Well, I was born in Tennessee, in some near county; my father moved from there to Mississippi when I was about three years old; alter that I went back to Lebanon to school, and was there four or five years. I spent all my life in Tennessee, Mississippi, and Arkansas.

Q. Are you a Republican or Democrat?—A. Well sir; from this day till I die, I'm a Republican.

Q. What have you been heretofore?—A. I've always voted the Democratic ticket, sir; ever since I first voted. (Printed record, page 200.)

Jordan Yeates, in speaking on the subject of whether witnesses would feel safe in testifying, swears:

Q. I want to ask if the mass of the voters of Crittenden County, the colored voters feel free to tell what they know, and how they voted in these past elections in Crittenden County?—A. They wouldn't feel free to do it generally, simply because they don't feel they would be safe by so doing.

Q. Do you think it would be safe for that community for us to do, either in Crittenden County in Crawfordsville, what we are doing here?—A. No, sir; I don't.

Q. What is your opinion would be the result of it?—A. Well, there'd be a great advantage taken; I don't know but what there'd be somebody killed to-night; if not they would be chased nightly; have to leave there. (Printed record, page 194.)

J. L. Fleming, in speaking on this subject, testified:

Q. Do you think it would be safe personally, for you to give this evidence now in Crittenden County, that you are giving here in Memphis, Tenn.?—A. No, sir; I wouldn't feel very safe to do it. (Printed record, page 195.)

Houston White (col.), a witness on behalf of the contestant, being first duly sworn, testified as follows:

Q. What is your name?—A. Houston White.
Q. Where do you live?—A. Crittenden County, Arkansas.
Q. How old are you?—A. About 31 years old.
Q. How long have you lived in Ark.?—A. About 19 years.
Q. What is your business?—A. Farming and preaching.
Q. Were you in Crawfordsville sometime since when Mr. Featherston and his attorneys, Mr. Walsh and Mr. Eldridge, were there for the purpose of taking investigation?—A. I was.
Q. Was that investigation taken?—A. It was not.
Q. Why not?—A. Because the threats by the white people had scared the colored population in such a way they was afraid to come and give their depositions.
Q. You think the colored people would have testified there, if that investigation had been taken?—A. No, sir; they would not.
Q. Do you think Mr. Featherston or his lawyers would have been safe if they continued there in the investigation?—A. No, sir.
Q. Why?—A. On account of the feeling of the Democratic party against them.
Q. What was that feeling?—A. They wanted Mr. Cate to have the office, and they knew Mr. Featherston had the majority of votes and they would have, everybody believed, assassinated Mr. Featherston and all his friends before they would have suffered it.
Q. Did you hear any threats that day?—A. I did.
Q. Who made it?—A. Mr. Hayden.
Q. What did he say?—A. He said the election that had been there was over and there wasn't going to be any more—no more elections nor depositions taken or nothing else, and before there would be he would see his blood in that street, and Mr. Dick Chetom said, "You bet there won't."
Q. Did you anticipate there would be a difficulty there that day when Mr. Featherston and his lawyers were there?—A. I did so, and felt very uneasy for Mr. Featherston and his lawyers, and quite uneasy about myself, because I had been a friend of Mr. Featherston's in the national election, and voted for him, and they knew it

and they seen me with him I knew they would be angry about it; they made some threats in regard to me publicly that day.

Q. What were those threats?—A. That if I didn't keep my mouth I'd have to hunt a new home.

Q. Do you know whether Mr. Featherston and his lawyers were received there politely by the people or not?—A. They were not.

Q. Where did they pass their time during their stay?—A. The lawyers with a colored man by the name of R. Y. Logan, and Mr. Featherston was at Mr. Hilderbrand's.

Q. Have you heard of any other threats having been made towards the friends of Mr. Featherston there by the Democratic party?—A. Not directly; only through other parties. I've heard some remarks that's been made that Mr. Featherston and the lawyers wasn't going to come back there any more, and they had given them a warning when they came out there; and they was gone, and the darkies needn't be expecting them or talking for them, because they wasn't coming back.

Q Who heard that statement?—A. Henry Davis.

*　　*　　*　　*　　*　　*　　*

Q. Do you think that these witnesses would have testified if this investigation had been carried on at Crawfordsville?—A. No, sir; I do not.

Q. How many witnesses do you think we could have gotten there?—A. I don't feel safe to say you would have gotten over 20 in the township. They are afraid of those Winchesters, and they say so.

Q. Who's got possession of those Winchesters?—A. The Democratic party's got possession of them. (Printed record, pages 181,182.)

Stephen James (white), a witness for the contestant, being first duly sworn, testified as follows:

Q. What is your name?—A. Stephen James.

Q. Where do you live?—A. Crittenden County, Arkansas.

Q. What is your occupation?—A. Farmer, merchant, saw-mill man, little of everything.

Q. Do you know the feeling of the people in Crittenden County towards Mr. Featherston?—A. Well, I reckon personally their feeling is good enough, but politically, I don't think it's very good.

Q. Have you ever heard any threats made toward Mr. Featherston?—A. I never heard any direct threats made.

Q. Do you know whether there was any intimidation used in Crittenden County in the Congressional election, of which Mr. Featherston was an aspirant?—A. Well, I couldn't say there was, more than the Democratic party were all under arms furnished by the Government, I suppose, or the State; I don't know whether it had any tendency to intimidate or not; I am satisfied there was intimidation done in the State election, and I was credibly informed that the people voted in the Congressional election as though they did in the State election.

Q. Do you think Mr. Featherston could, with safety to his person or with any degree of success as to the result, take testimony in Crittenden County, as to his Congressional election?—A. I have told Mr. Featherston before that I thought his safety very doubtful, and for my part, I would not take those depositions in Crittenden County; my reason for saying this is that I was a contestant for the office of county treasurer on the People's ticket, and I was repeatedly threatened with death if I continued in an investigation which I commenced.

Q. How old are you?—A. I am 60 years of age.

Q. How long have you lived in Arkansas?—A. Since the tenth of February, 1845.

Q. About how much land have you in cultivation?—A. I cultivated 800 acres in 1888.

*　　*　　*　　*　　*　　*　　*

Q. How long have you voted the Democratic ticket?—A. From James K. Polk up.

Q. Why did you oppose what claimed to be the Democratic organization of your county?—A. Because I knew that the dictatorial policy of the so-called Democratic party in the county, with their Winchester-rifle policy, would destroy the labor interests and the agricultural interests of the entire county.

*　　*　　*　　*　　*　　*　　*

Q. Do you think that the average citizens of your county feel free to express their candid opinions within the county at the present time?—A. I do not.

Q. Do you know whether this Winchester-rifle crowd is still drilling at their armory at Crawfordsville?—A. I heard that they was about a week ago, or two weeks ago. (Printed record, page 186,187.)

Rev. T. J. Jones, in speaking on this subject, testified :

Q. Have you kept pretty well posted as to the strength of the Republican party in the county ?—A. I has been, sir, for several years, though there ain't many people know it; but I has been for several years.

Q. You counted the Republican strength of the county at about what ?—A. I was supposing there was, that is, in the county something like about 1,800.

Q. 1,800 majority ?—A. Yes, sir. (Printed record, page 212.)

J. H. Williams, on this subject, testified :

Q. Do you believe it would be safe for Mr. Featherston to take testimony (contest case) inside of Crittenden County ?—A. Well, it would be owing to the precinct you were in.

Q. Say at Crawfordsville ?—A. I couldn't say that, whether he would be or not.

Q. Do you believe that the witnesses would be willing to turn out and testify at Crawfordsville ?—A. No, sir; I don't think the witnesses would come; about Featherston being safe there, I couldn't say that, but I don't think the witnesses would come there; but Featherston is different from a witness. Whether Featherston would be killed or not I couldn't say that.

Q. What is the cause of this feeling that exists among the witnesses ?—A. Well, they keep a military company there all the time. They have Winchesters at any minute, and a man going there to testify wouldn't feel safe, let him be who he would be; that's my idea about it, sir.

Q. If it was necessary for you to take the testimony of all the witnesses in your county, of all the voters that had voted for you in your county, would you persist in your contest or would you abandon it ?—A. I think it would be best to abandon it, sir.

Q. Why ?—A. My opinion is the witnesses would be afraid to turn out. (Printed record, pages 213–14.)

Thompson Foster, on this subject, testified :

Q. Do you think that the citizens of your neighborhood would feel perfectly free to turn out and testify under the circumstances that exist there now, or would they rather not do it ?—A. Well, no, sir; I don't think they really would be perfectly satisfied in doing so. I don't know about the safe part. They may be perfectly safe in doing so, but I doubt whether they'd be satisfied to do so.

Q. Why wouldn't they be satisfied ?—A. I don't know, sir; may be on account of the Winchesters.

Q. You feel now like you wouldn't like to answer too many questions about this matter ?—A. Well, of course I feel myself I am able to answer, but I wouldn't like to answer too many particular questions in regard to the Winchester rifle company. (Printed record, page 206.)

David Furgeson, on this subject, testified :

Q. From what you know of the feeling in that county that has existed from the 12th of July up to the present time, do you think that the taking of depositions would be perfectly safe in Crittenden County ?—A. I know it wouldn't be safe for Mr. Featherston, his attorney, nor his short-hand writer. (Printed record, page 209.)

Phillips County.

There is an agreement in the record as to the vote of Phillips County, whereby it is agreed that the contestant is to have 57 more votes than were returned for him, and that the contestee is to have 57 votes stricken from his returned vote, and that the contestant is to be credited with a majority of 18 in Hickory Ridge Township. These numbers added together make 132, which should be deducted from Cate's majority, and the vote would then stand thus :

Cate's majority 592
Deduct the 132
                                                                          ————
    Leaving Cate's majority... 460

Cross County.

In the township of Smith, in Cross County, Featherston is returned as receiving 15 votes and he proves up 29 votes. This overthrows the return, and leaves the parties to prove up their votes. The result is

Featherston gets 14 more votes, and Cate, not having proved any votes, loses 84, making a difference in favor of Featherston of 98. The vote would then stand thus :

Cate's majority... 460
Deduct the 98
                                                                                      ———
Leaving Cate's majority... 362

St. Francis County.

From the township of Franks the contestee is returned as receiving 269 votes and the contestant 131 votes. The proof shows that all of the judges and clerks of election were Democrats ; that the ballot-box was taken out of the presence of the United States supervisor at noon for an hour, and for an hour after the polls closed. This might have been enough to destroy the prima facie character of the return. But if it were otherwise, the testimony shows the return is false and fraudulent. The contestant, who is returned as receiving 131 votes, proves by 195 persons, whose names appear on the poll-book as voting, that they voted for him.

(Printed record, pages 47–182 ; 229–75.

The contestee who is returned as receiving 269 votes, has only proven up 112. There is hearsay testimony tending to show that 24 other persons voted for contestee. The names of the 24 persons whom it is said voted for contestee *are not on the poll-book.* There is hearsay testimony tending to show that 17 persons whose names are on the poll-book also voted for contestee.

In Wallace *vs.* McKinley, Forty-eighth Congress, it is said :

The vicious tendency of hearsay testimony in election cases needs no demonstration.

Wash Rooks, a colored man, swears there were 50 colored men voted for contestee in Franks Township. On cross-examination he was asked to name some of the 50 he saw vote for contestee. He finally named 8 ; out of the 8 named 4 of the names are not found on the poll-book ; 2 of the remaining 4 swear they voted for contestant ; aside from this the witness is successfully impeached, and it appears in testimony he was expelled from the Masonic fraternity for stealing the money of the lodge.

Upon the testimony contestee has only proven 112 votes out of the 269 returned for him. Hence, 157 votes should be deducted from the returned vote, and the vote would then stand thus:

Cate's majority 362
Deduct 157
                                                                                      ———
Leaving Cate's majority... 205

The contestant was returned as receiving 131, and has proven 195. The difference between these being 64, and this amount should be deducted from the vote of the contestee. The vote would then stand thus :

Cate's majority 205
Deduct 64
                                                                                      ———
Leaving Cate's majority... 141

Blackfish Township.

In this township no election was held. The proof shows that 29 persons having the qualification of electors attended at the voting place on the day of the election for the purpose of voting for contestant, and that the judges of election would not open the polls. This township must pass under the rule laid down as to the townships of Furgeson and Idlewild, in Crittenden County, and can not be counted.

Lee County.

In relation to Independence Township the testimony is as follows: Milton Powell, being duly sworn:

Quest. 1. Are you of lawful age?
Yes.
Quest. 2. Are you a resident of Lee County?
Yes.
Quest. 3. Are you a resident of Independence Township?
Yes.
Quest. 4. Did you vote on 6th day of Nov., 1888?
Yes.
5. Whom did you vote for Congress for the first Congressional district?—Ans. Mr. Featherston.
Quest. 6. Did you work on that day to get votes for Mr. Featherston?—Ans. I did.
Quest. 7. With what voters did you work, the Democratic or Republican voters?—Ans. With the Republican voters.
Quest. 8. What kind of tickets did you use in that election?—Ans. I used red tickets, such as I file here as an exhibit.

REPUBLICAN TICKET.

Election, Tuesday, November 6th, 1888.
For President,
BENJAMIN HARRISON,
of Indiana.
For Vice-President,
LEVI P. MORTON,
of New York.

Presidential electors.
At large—M. W. GIBBS, W. H. H. CLAYTON.

First district—GEORGE W. BELL.
Second district—A. M. MIDDLEBROOKS.
Third district—J. B. FRIEDHEIM.
Fourth district—CHAS. D. GREAVES.
Fifth district—SAMUEL MURPHY.

For Congress, First Congressional district,
L. P. FEATHERSTON,
of St. Francis County.

[Note.—The ticket submitted is printed on red paper, with a design in blue on back.]
Quest. 9. What voters voted that ticket that day?—Ans. The Republicans voted that ticket; it is a Republican ticket.
Ques. 10. What was the result of your work?—Ans. I kept count of ninety-two of those Republican tickets that went out of my hands.
Ques. 11. What was done with those tickets, ninety-two?—Ans. They were voted.
Quest. 12. How do you know they were voted?—Ans. I went with them to the ballot-box and saw them put in.
Ques. 13. How many votes were polled here that day?—Ans. Something over six hundred.
Quest. 14. What is the political complexion of this dist.; which has a majority?—Ans. The Republicans have a large majority.
Ques. 15. Can a majority of the colored people read and write?—Ans. Majority can't read and write.

Cross-examination.

Ques. 27. Did you give out more than ninety-two tickets that day to voters?—Ans. I did.
Ques. 28. How many tickets did you give out that day?—Ans. I think one hundred and twenty or twenty-five.

Ques. 35. Where were you standing when those ninety-two persons voted?—Ans. I went with each of them to the polls.

Ques. 36. Did they all vote for Mr. Featherston?—Ans. They all voted the red ticket like one filed; I saw them put it in.

Ques. 37. From the time you gave them the ticket to the time they voted did any one have the opportunity to change any name on the ticket?—Ans. No, sir.

Ques. 38. Then you positively swear that those ninety-two persons voted for Mr. Featherston?—Ans. Yes, sir; that is my belief.

Ques. 39. Are you positive or not that said ninety-two men voted for Featherston?—Ans. I am positive they voted for his name on the red ticket.

Ques. 40. Are you positive that Mr. Featherston's name was not scratched on a single one of those ninety-two tickets you gave out?—Ans. I am positive.

Ques. 41. What time of day did those ninety-two men vote?—Ans. From 9 a. m. to 5 p. m.

Ques. 42. Do you know of others voting for Mr. Featherston beside those ninety-two that day?—Ans. I do not.

Quest. 43. Can you give us some of the names of the ninety-two that voted your ticket?—Ans. Yes, sir. Anderson Powell, Wm. Otey, Milton Powell, myself, Nelse Robinson, Jordan Woodson, Burl Woodson, Tom Woodson, Jimmie Turner and son; can't think of his name. I didn't take a list of the names, but when one voted I marked it down.

Ques. 87. About how many Republican votes were cast here on the 6th of Nov. last?—Ans. There might have been two hundred and fifty or three hundred; may be not so many.

Ques. 88. How many of that number voted for Mr. Featherston?—Ans. Ninety-two, I know, cast that red ticket for him.

Redirect:

Ques. 1. In those elections in this township in which you have voted for past eight or ten years; now, have the colored people voted together or have been divided?—Ans. All voting together.

Ques. 2. How have they voted in county elections?—Ans. They have never taken any part in county elections, except a few.

Ques. 3. Have they always taken a deep interest in national elections, and for Congress?—Ans. Yes, sir; and governor.

Ques. 12. Do you know of any Republicans that have been appointed judges of the election in this county since you have been voting? (Objected to.) Ans. No, sir; I think not.

Ques. 13. Can you think of a single Republican judge that was appointed at the last election?—Ans. Can not.

Ques. 14. Who has a majority in Lee County, the Republicans or Democrats?—A. Always heard the Republicans. (Objected to as hearsay.)

Ques. 15. Did the rain keep the voters away on the last election, and was over six hundred votes a good turn-out in this township? (Objected to as leading.) Ans. Don't think the rain kept the voters away, and the vote was a good turn-out for the township.

Ques. 21. Did any Republicans canvass through here for Mr. Featherston?—Ans. None as I know of.

Ques. 22. If you have seen any thing in any papers since you were on the stand, any reference to the frauds in the elections in Lee County, state it.—Ans. I saw in a paper yesterday something in reference to it.

Ques. 23. What paper did you see it in, and what was it?—Ans. I saw that there were thirty-seven hundred voters in Lee County, and fifteen hundred Democrats achieved a victory for that party.

Ques. 24. Who did the paper say made that statement?—Ans. Judge Hutton, a member of the Democratic party and a member of the legislature. (Printed record, page 26 to 31.)

There is, under the proof, circumstances and facts sufficient to impeach the return and put the parties to proof. It is satisfactorily proven that the township is largely Republican; that 632 votes were cast, showing a full turnout; and the contestant is only returned 89 votes.

The vote for Presidential electors was as follows:

Harrison 435
Cleveland 196

Republican majority 239

Here, then, is a case where we have 239 votes not counted for any one for Congress, and this, too, in the face of testimony of witnesses saying the Republicans turned out well and were in the majority and voting the party ticket.

The contestee claims that the contestant has admitted that he received 224 votes in Independence township and cannot now invoke the protection of that rule where the return is overthrown and the parties put to proof.

The view we take of the matter renders it unnecessary to pass upon the question of estoppel.

What is claimed as a concession by the contestant, that the contestee received 224 votes in this township, is contained in the notice of contest on page 7, as follows:

> That at the precinct of Independence, in the county of Lee, in said district, at an election held on the 6th day of November, 1888, I received 397 votes and *you received 224 votes;* that the election officers of said township, who are partisans of yours, through fraud or mistake, returned that I received 89 votes, and that you received 224; that the votes as thus returned by the election officers of said township were by the county clerk of said county certified to the secretary of state, and by him laid before the governor of said State, and by him counted in determining the number of votes cast for each of us for Representative in said district. I shall therefore claim on contest that I be allowed 308 more votes than were returned and certified for me from said township.

This is not a concession that contestee received 224 *legal* votes, but is in the nature of a recital of the state of facts which he would be able to establish by proof.

This was at the inception of the contest, when contestant may not have had full information.

But be that as it may the recitals in the notice can have none of the sanctity and binding force of an agreement or stipulation and can not be construed into a concession.

The contestee did not treat this statement as a concession that he received 224 votes, but on the contrary he filed the following answer:

> As to the precinct of Independence, in the county of Lee, I deny all the charges of fraud and mistake, and say that the votes were correctly counted, returned, and certified. I deny that you received three hundred and ninety-seven (397) votes, but you received eighty-nine votes, and I received two hundred and forty-four (244) votes in said precinct or township. (Record, p. 17.)

Instead of the record making a stipulation or concession that contestee had received 224 legal votes, the number of legal votes was not admitted by contestant nor was the alleged concession accepted as such by the contestee in lieu of evidence, but he set up a claim to 244 votes instead of 224 which he now claims as having been conceded.

The parties having failed to agree upon the matter the question stands upon the proof, which shows that a fraudulent return was made by the election officers.

Only one witness was examined in Independence Township. The witness giving the testimony, on leaving the stand was arrested for perjury, and placed under $1,000 bond to answer to the State court. The attorney for contestee from that time on proclaimed he would cause the arrest of all persons who testified for contestant, if he thought they testified falsely.

After that time testimony was taken in relation to that township *outside* of the county, and Joseph Kennedy, the chairman of the Republican county committee, testified as follows:

> Int. Why do you come to this county to give your testimony in this case; is it because of threats of violence there?—Ans. So far as I am concerned I am not personally afraid, but there have been threats of violence used against Featherston men.

Int. Was not the first witness who testified in Lee Co. arrested and put under bond on account of his testimony ?—Ans. Yes, sir.

Int. Was not that witness also abused while under arrest by one Jacob Shane, and is not this a matter of common notoriety among the colored people of your Co. ?—Ans. Yes, sir.

Int. What position did this Jacob Shane occupy in the party prior to this last election ?—Ans. He was chairman of the Co. central committee, Republican.

Int. Why has he been deposed from that position ?—Ans. On account of the manner in which he had previously handled the Republican election tickets.

Int. Is it not generally understood by the Republicans of Lee Co. that Jacob Shane has proven treacherous to his party ?—Ans. Yes, sir.

Int. Of what nationality is this Jacob Shane ?—Ans. He is a Jew.

Int. How were you first induced to become favorable to Mr. Featherston ?—Ans. By the representations of this Mr. Shane. He made a speech and endorsed Mr. Featherston and urged the colored people, as there was no Republican in the field, to support Mr. Featherston. He was for Featherston up to the day before the election.

Int. What kind of a ticket was Mr. Featherston's name on ?—Ans. It was a kind of a red ticket with purple back.

Int. Was that the Presidential Republican ticket, with the President electors all on it ?—Ans. Yes, sir.

Int. Is it not a difficult matter to persuade a colored man to go back on his national ticket ?—Ans. Yes, sir; it is a difficult matter.

Int. Was it generally understood by the whole Republican party of Lee Co. that they should support Featherston ?—Ans. Yes, sir.

Int. What is the political complexion of Independence Township ?—Ans. Republican by large majority. (Printed record, page 47.)

T. F. Carter, being first duly sworn, deposes as follows:

Int. What is your name, age, and residence ?
My name is T. F. Carter; age, 27; and residence Marianna.

Int. How long had you lived in the county before the November election ?—Ans. I had lived in that township 10 months before that election, and in the State since 1885.

Int. Did you vote in that township ?—Ans. Yes, sir.

Int. For whom did you vote for Congressman, Cate or Featherston ?—Ans. Featherston.

Int. What are you, Republican or Democrat ?—Ans. I am a Republican.

Int. Was Featherston's name on the Republican national ticket ?—Ans. Yes, sir; it was.

Int. What is the political complexion of Independence, the one in which you voted ?—Ans. I know it to be a fact that is against my interests to state any further.

Int. Why is it against your interests to testify in this cause ?—Ans. My friends advised me, in view of my condition, and that as I had a little property there, to have nothing to do with the contest.

Int. Do you feel that in view of your personal and property interests there that it would be unsafe for you to testify in this case ?—Ans. Yes, sir.

Int. What position did you occupy on the day of election by appointment ?—Ans. Several told me since that I was appointed supervisor, but I knew nothing about it.

Int. Were the parties who advised you as to your safety Republican, or Democrats, and did they seem to be advising you for your personal welfare ?—Ans. Yes, sir; they advised me for my future living.

Ins. Is it not a fact that you left home the night after you were subpœnaed to testify in this case ?—Ans. Yes, sir; upon the advice of my friends I went away, as I didn't feel safe. I was not afraid that the Republicans would molest me. I know about how the vote was; but I don't care to testify.

Int. Did you take a very active part in the election and work very hard for your ticket ?—Ans. Yes, sir; I did.

Int. Are the colored people down there generally intimidated ?—Ans. I was afraid to testify there, and other colored people were influenced by the same fear. (Printed record, page 48–9.)

J. H. Cox, being first duly sworn, deposes as follows:

Int. What is your name, age, residence, and occupation ?—Ans. J. H. Cox is my name; my age is 25; my residence Independence Township, Lee Co., Ark.; I am a school teacher; I have been living 12 months in this State, 6 months in Lee Co., and 30 days in Independence Township.

Int. What are your politics ?—Ans. I am a Republican.

Int. Has the arrest of Milton Powell for testifying in this case had the effect of deterring others from testifying in the case ?—Ans. Several have told me that they would not testify because they were afraid.

Int. Why did you not return to testify after you had promised me to do so?—Ans. I was advised not to come on account of the feeling in this matter. A friend of mine informed me that Milton Powell had been arrested and said he was afraid I would be arrested and advised me to stay away, which I did. (Printed record, page 49).

The conduct of the contestee's attorney could have but one object and effect, and that was to intimidate other witnesses. There is direct testimony from one witness, and no attempt was made to impeach him, showing that 92 votes went into the box for the contestant. The returns show 89 for Featherston and 224 for the contestee. There is enough evidence to impeach the return and put the parties to proof. The friends of the contestee in Independence Township, like his friends in Crittenden County, prevented full proof being made, and can not complain if we apply the rule as to Independence Township that was applied to Scanlan and Cat Island, which we do. Full proof of the vote was not allowed to be made, and in such a case he who prevented it should suffer, if any one.

We have no hesitation in adopting this rule in relation to this township, because the contestee knew of the proof made by the contestant. He could have taken proof and shown his true vote. He elected to rely on intimidation of contestant's witnesses, and must abide the consequences of his election. He was at liberty to have shown that 319 of the persons voting at that election did not vote for either candidate for Congress, and thus have explained why it was that the contestant ran behind the Republican electors, but he has not done so.

The result is, that the contestee must lose 224 votes returned for him, and the contestant must be allowed 3 more votes than were returned for him; these two amount to 227, for which the contestant should receive credit. The vote would then stand thus:

Cate 141
Featherston 227

Making a majority for Featherston of...................................... 86

There is objection to the testimony taken before Avery, a notary public at Memphis, Tenn., which testimony we have admitted and considered as competent in arriving at a conclusion in this case. The ground of objection is, that the contestee did not have notice of the taking. The contestee does not deny that Berry, the person upon whom it is claimed notice was served, was his attorney, but his claim is the technical one that he was not his attorney for taking depositions outside of Crittenden County. The technical character of this objection is still more apparent when it is remembered that the record shows that Berry was employed to take the testimony relating to Crittenden County.

It appears from the testimony objected to that contestant, with his attorneys went to Crittenden County, and there met Berry, the attorney of contestee; that before going there an understanding existed that Berry should act as notary public to take the depositions; that in the face of this agreement he declined to so act; that a justice of the peace was asked to take the testimony and refused; that there was danger of violence, and threats were made calculated to produce the belief that bloodshed would follow; that under that state of facts Berry was notified as the attorney of contestee that the testimony in relation to that county would be taken at number 59 Madison st., Memphis, Tenn., at 9 o'clock on February 25, 1889.

We think under this state of facts notice to Berry would be sufficient, for it related to the taking of the very testimony which he was employed to take. It will not do to say that Berry's employment ended when contestee's partisan friends had succeeded in preventing the taking of testimony in Crittenden County. W. B. Eldridge (p. 226, 227) testifies:

Q. Did you all go with Berry, the lawyer of Cate, and did he say anything about acting as notary public?—A. He said he would act as notary public, which he afterwards refused to do.
Q. Did you all take any depositions there?—A. We did not.
Q. What was the reason for not taking depositions?—A. We could not get a notary public; there was a magistrate there, but he refused to act, and Mr. Berry refused, contrary to his promise and our expectations.

After detailing his treatment at Crawfordsville, in Crittenden County, in response to a question he states:

I notified L P. Berry, the attorney of Mr. Cate, that Mr. Featherston would take proof in Memphis, Tenn., at my office, on the Congressional contest; and on February 24, Walsh (an attorney) and myself both notified Mr. Berry that we would begin taking proof at 59 Madison st., Memphis, Tenn., at nine o'clock, February 25, 1889.

Contestee produces an *ex parte* affidavit from Mr. Berry, his attorney, denying notice to take depositions at Memphis, and now asks that these depositions be suppressed, and this request was made for the first time *after the printing of the record.*

The act of Congress of March 2, 1887, provides among other things that—

Before the record is printed the Clerk of the House shall notify the parties to be present at a day named at the opening of the testimony, and of agreeing upon the parts thereof to be printed; that the depositions shall be opened in the presence of the parties or their attorneys, and that such portion of the testimony as the parties may agree upon shall be printed; that in case of disagreement between the parties, the Clerk shall decide what portion of the testimony shall be printed.

The intent and object of this statute is obvious. Had it been followed the testimony now complained of might not have appeared in the printed record. Had it been followed, the objection of the contestee, now interposed, would have been made known and the contestant would have been placed in a position to elect whether he deemed the testimony of sufficient importance to make application to the committee or the House for permission and time in which to retake it. Instead of pursuing that course no objection to the printing of the testimony now objected to appears to have been made. It is said that this testimony had not been filed at the time the parties appeared before the Clerk of the House. It does appear from the Clerk's record "that on account of the non-receipt" of certain packages of testimony for contestant he was granted further time in which to file testimony.

It is not improbable, indeed it is probable, to say the least, that the attention of the contestee was at that time called to the character and contents of the testimony the contestant was thus granted leave to file.

In the case of Lowry *vs.* White, Fiftieth Congress, after the record was printed, motions were filed by both parties during the consideration of the case by the committee to exclude certain portions of the testimony, and these motions were denied, and the attention of the parties was called to this statute, and in the syllabus this language is found:

No part of the testimony submitted in a case will be suppressed where the parties fail to take advantage of the statutory provisions allowing parties to agree upon what portion of the record shall be printed prior to the hearing of the case.

In the case of a judgment by default the court will not set aside the judgment unless the defendant can show a good defense to the action.

In the case of a decree *pro confesso* the decree will not be set aside unless a meritorious defense is shown.

If the contestee had filed a motion to suppress the depositions, on the ground he was taken by surprise, and alleged that he could disprove the state of facts shown by them, he would stand in a much better light than he now does. He now makes an objection which should have been made under the act of March 2, 1887, before the record was printed. After the record was printed he must have had knowledge of these depositions. Had he then filed a motion to suppress them he would stand in a much better light, but he failed to do so and does not tender any excuse now for that failure. Had he notified the contestant, on the receipt of the printed record, of an intention to file a motion to suppress these depositions, if such was his intention, he would have performed a commendable act, and would have at that time placed the contestant on notice. Instead of doing so, however, he remained silent until after contestant filed his brief, and then, instead of filing a motion to suppress, contented himself until he could afterwards raise the question of a want of notice. Instead of coming here and insisting that he has a meritorious defense to the matters charged in relation to Crittenden County, and asking time to establish that defense by proof, he simply asks us to suppress the testimony taken by the contestant, showing and tending to show fraud, violence, and intimidation, before and at the election, and threats and danger of violence to those who proposed to make proof of the frauds.

It appears from the testimony of Eldridge, the attorney of contestant, that Berry, the attorney of contestee, was notified of the time and place at which the contestant proposed to take depositions, and it appears that a copy of the printed record was sent to the contestee on the 15th of September, 1889.

The long silence of contestee on the question of notice, after he received a copy of the printed record, and the neglect to exercise his right to object before the record was printed, and no tender of proof made to contradict what is shown by the testimony, are facts from which the inference arises that the testimony can not be contradicted, and is in the nature of a tacit admission of the existence of the state of facts shown by the depositions.

We find these depositions in the printed record, and find the contestee made no objection to them before they went there; we find that after they had appeared in the printed record he did not file any objection or protest with the Clerk of the House because they were placed there; we find that after he saw them in the printed record he failed to notify the contestant that he would object to them. Being a lawyer of experience, and having been a judge, contestee's silence and failure to offer more tangible defense than mere technical objections can only be accounted for by the assumption that he has no real defense.

In view of these facts we are of opinion that the testimony should not be suppressed. We are not deciding that testimony may be taken without notice, though there are authorities which, under the facts of this case, would justify the admission of *ex parte* evidence. We might quote to sustain even this view, from Bisbee *vs.* Finley; Buchanan *vs.* Manning; and Thoebe *vs.* Carlisle *et. al.*; but as we do not decide on the question of *ex parte* evidence, in the admission of the depositions in this case, it is unnecessary.

Under the broad provisions of the Constitution, making each House of Congress "the judge of the elections, returns, and qualifications of its own members," it would seem that we are not bound by the strict rules of evidence known to the " common law." But we are not deciding that question. What we are deciding is, that where depositions are found in the printed record, or where they appear in the printed record, and no objection is made to the Clerk of the House or to the opposite party, the party failing to object at the earliest opportunity, or at least within reasonable time, so as to put the opposite party on notice, will be deemed to have waived all question of notice, especially where there is no offer of proof to show a different state of facts than those shown by the depositions.

As already shown by the figures given, we are of opinion that the proof under the law clearly shows that contestant Featherston was elected by a majority of 86 votes.

The committee therefore report the following resolutions and recommend their passage :

Resolved, That W. H. Cate was not elected as a Representative to the Fifty-first Congress, from the First Congressional district of the State of Arkansas, and is not entitled to the seat.

Resolved, That L. P. Featherston was duly elected as a Representative from the First Congressional district of the State of Arkansas to the Fifty-first Congress, and is entitled to his seat as such.

VIEWS OF THE MINORITY.

The depositions taken without legal notice should not be considered. The charges of fraud are not sustained by the evidence.

H. Mis. 137——9

VIEWS OF THE MINORITY.

Mr. OUTHWAITE, from the Committee on Elections, submits the following as the views of the minority:

The total number of voters in this district is, in round numbers, 40,000, of which 25,000 are whites and 15,000 negroes. Twenty-two thousand are Democrats and 18,000 Republicans. It has been represented in Congress for the last ten years by a Democrat. The Republicans during that time virtually conceded it to the other party by making a nomination for Representative in Congress upon only two occasions. At a more recent State election for three judges of the supreme court, held April 2, 1889, the vote in this Congressional district was, for the leading Democratic candidate, 9,801, and for the leading Republican candidate, 8,021. The majority for the Democratic candidate was about 1,780. No one has questioned the legality or fairness of this election, nor has any one claimed that there was any fraud or intimidation anywhere throughout this Congressional district, though the total vote cast was not quite 18,000.

At the November election in 1888, 30,000 voters went to the polls and voted. On the 21st of that month the governor of the State of Arkansas, in pursuance of law, made proclamation, wherein it was alleged that W. H. Cate received 15,576 votes, and L. P. Featherston received 14,228 votes; that the former received 1,348 more votes than the latter for Representative in Congress from the First Congressional district of Arkansas. This majority is conceded by the contestant to have been shown on the face of the returns certified to the governor, in his notice of contest and in his brief.

There are seventeen counties in the district, and fraud, mistake, or improper conduct, is charged in fifteen of them. No testimony is taken or attempted to be taken except in four. The record shows that but seventeen days of the forty allowed by law (Rev. Stats., sec. 107) for taking his testimony in chief were occupied by the contestant, and that he did not avail himself in more than one instance of that other provision of the law, that testimony in contested-election cases may be taken at two or more places at the same time." (Rev. Stat., sec. 109.) No reason or excuse is given by contestant for his failure to attempt to prove the allegations of his notice and statement in some forty paragraphs concerning the election in twelve of the fifteen counties of the district. The fair inference is that there was no proof to be obtained to support his charges of fraud or misconduct in those twelve counties.

As to Phillips County, there is an agreed statement of facts (rec., pp. 183–4), admitting certain mistakes and irregularities by which it is shown that in Hicksville precinct the contestant is entitled to 33 votes and the contestee to 15 votes, which were not returned to the secretary of state for them respectively. It is further shown by said agreement that in Lake Township contestant received 127 votes and contestee received but 10 votes; but that in making the returns of said election to

131

the county clerk, the judges of said election by mistake certified that L. P. Featherston received 70 votes and W. H. Cate received 67 votes, which error was certified to the secretary of state. The correction of these errors would increase the vote of contestant 90 votes and decrease the vote of contestee 43 votes, reducing the majority of contestee by 132 votes. There is another part of said agreement that will be considered farther on in this report.

In Lee County, the testimony relates to the votes of but two townships, Independence and St. Francis. Apart from the deposition of W. T. Derrick, who simply furnishes, as county clerk, certain names taken from the lists as returned to office of the votes in Independence, Council, St. Francis, and Walnut Townships, there is the testimony of but one witness in the record, which was taken under notice. The election at Independence precinct was conducted fairly, without any intimidation or disturbance of any kind whatever. The integrity, good character and conduct of the officers of the election is not directly attacked anywhere in the record. It is ridiculous to think that Milton Powell's testimony should overthrow the sworn return of the five election officers. The testimony tends to show there were present also two Federal supervisors. The official return from this precinct, it is claimed by contestant, gave contestee 224 votes, and contestant 89 votes. Contestant claims that he received 397 votes at this precinct, but that through fraud or mistake only 89 were returned as cast for him, at the same time admitting that contestee received 224. Contestant also averred that the election officers were partisans of the sitting member. To sustain his claim he examines as a witness Milton Powell.

Powell testifies, after having identified a Republican ticket, and stating that it was printed on red paper with design in blue on the back, as follows:

Ans. 10. I kept count of 92 of those Republican tickets that went out of my hands.
Ans. 11. They were voted.
Ans. 12. I went with them to the ballot-box and saw them put in.

He says:

Ans. 30. Rainy day; after it commenced it rained steadily the remainder of the day.
Ques. 32. Were you in the rain or under shelter?—Ans. Part of the time under shelter in front of the court-house, and part of the time in the rain; I had an umbrella.

The state of the weather being very bad that day at this precinct and throughout the district, as is shown by other testimony, accounts to some extent for the falling off in the vote; but Powell's testimony on that subject here is introduced to reflect upon the accuracy of his count made under such unfavorable circumstances.

He further testifies that he does not know of others voting for Mr. Featherston, though he gave out 120 or 125 Republican tickets. In his answer No. 13, he says that something over 600 votes were polled there that day, and [Ans. 14] that the Republicans have a large majority of this district.

In answer 52 he gives his reason for saying this, but in answer 54 he says:

The county elections for the past six or eight years, it has been going Democratic.

And [Ans. 55]:

It may have been ten years; but I am positive for six or eight years.

He further testifies that Jake Shaul, the chairman of the Republican committee, and Joe Roberts and Samuel Overton, who said they were Republicans, worked for the election of Mr. Cate, the contestee.

Ques. 82. Did you see anything like intimidation or bulldozing among white or colored?—Ans. No, sir.

Ans. 85. I did not say that there was any fraud in this township. I just saw in the papers where such things were done in other counties.

Ques. 86. Have you ever seen any account in any paper, or heard from any source whatever, even an intimation of fraud in the election in this township in November last?—Ans. No, sir; I have not, as I know of.

The next two questions and answers will show what reliance is to be placed upon his previous testimony that something over 600 votes were polled in the township that day.

Ques. 87. About how many Republican votes were cast here on the 6th of November last?—Ans. There might have been 250 or 300; may be not so many.

Ques. 88. How many of that number voted for Mr. Featherston? -Ans. 92, I know, cast that red ticket for him.

This witness also testifies that of five candidates for governor since he has been a voter but one Republican had carried that township, and the Democrats the balance of the time. He shows that there was considerable disaffection among the Republicans; that the chairman of the committee was actively at work for the election of Mr. Cate, and that this support of the Democratic candidate for Congress had been so pronounced and so effective that he had recently before the time the witness was testifying been removed from his position as chairman, and another person appointed in his stead. He names three other prominent Republicans who were at these polls working for the election of Cate.

At the conclusion of his testimony, this witness was arrested for perjury in testifying that 92 votes were cast under his immediate observation for Mr. Featherston, in the face of the returns of the election officials. It is claimed on the part of the contestant that his witnesses were thus intimidated and prevented from proving his case in Lee County. It will be observed in the notice to take depositions at the time and place where Milton Powell and W. T. Derick were examined that no other names are included in the notice of the witnesses for contestant. There is nothing in the record to show that at that time and place contestant proposed to examine other witnesses as to the conduct of the election, or at any other time and place.

To sustain this pretext of intimidation, preventing the taking of testimony, there was taken, without notice to the contestee, and in another township, the testimony of two other residents of Independence Township, Lee County. In the testimony of these two men you will not find one word relating to the election or what occurred there on that day. The witnesses Carter and Cox claimed that others had been deterred from testifying in the case on account of the arrest of Milton Powell, and that they had apprehensions if they should so testify. They say as much as they possibly can of this character, well calculated to offend their political opponents, but present no facts to show that the election itself should be called in question. It is therefore not necessary to dwell longer upon the question as to what shall be done with the vote in this precinct. It should remain undisturbed as it was certified by the sworn election officers to the clerk of the circuit court of that county, and by him certified to the secretary of state. No testimony was offered tending to show that the officers of the election were not appointed according to law, and the Republican Federal supervisor of election, although he claims not to have known of his appointment, was at the election and saw nothing of which he could complain.

The next precinct to be considered is St. Francis Township, Lee County.

With regard to the vote in this township the record does not show that any testimony was ever attempted to be taken there. Notice was given by one of the attorneys of contestant that testimony would be taken before a notary named Leary at Terrell and Bond's store on February 19. Attorneys for both parties were there at the time. No witnesses were examined. None were called or sworn, and no adjournment of the hearing was had. No excuse is given anywhere for the failure to do these things. Then and there ended all legal attempts to make any proof concerning the vote in this township. In open and flagrant violation of the provisions of the law with regard to the taking of testimony in such cases, the contestant, in the absence of contestee and his attorneys, and without his knowledge, secretly and surreptitiously procured certain statements apparently made under oath before an officer not authorized by law to take testimony in contested election cases.

One of these witnesses is made to say that at the election on November 6, at this St. Francis Township, Mr. Featherston's name was on the Republican ticket, and that all the Republicans he saw vote voted the Republican ticket. Another, in answer to the question, " Did all or nearly all the Republicans vote that ticket?" says, " Nearly all I seen voted that ticket." A third, in answer to the same question, replies, " I think so." This third witness, C. B. Brown, was the Republican supervisor of election, and tells a queer story about the ballot-box being two hats, and that when the judges went to dinner one of the clerks took the ballots and put them in a large envelope and placed it in his pocket " and went about one and a half miles and ate their dinner;" that the ballots were not counted at the polling place, but at the residence of W. L. Blacher, about one mile and a half away. Neither one of these witnesses was asked a word about the politics of the judges or clerks who thus misconducted the election. As the testimony of G. T. Thompson was taken without notice, and adds to that of the other two only that there was none of his party judges or clerks of election, we give it little weight. If this vote were cast out as attainted by fraud the result would not be changed, because the returns from the precinct give each candidate an equal number of votes. There is no testimony upon which to base any different conclusion. There never was any opportunity for the contestee to take testimony contradicting this so-called testimony. Surely it is not seriously contended that any change should be made as to the vote of this township.

The contestant or his attorneys, in the case of Spring Creek Township, in Lee County, instead of taking testimony to sustain his notice and statement (record, page 7, section XXI), secretly and illegally procured so-called testimony to prove that he was prevented from securing such proof by intimidation. Why did he not interrogate the very witnesses whom he had taken out of their own county on the pretext of this intimidation as to the matters he had set out in his notice of contest. These men claimed to have been at the election, and ought to have been at the election and ought to have known something of the truth or falsity of his allegations. He sought to prove by them that the negroes feared to appear as witnesses because the attorney for contestee had said, " If they swear lies here, I will put them in the penitentiary." The contestant's attorney, in his brief, gravely says:

It was impossible to get a witness to go on the stand and testify, with the open declaration being made that he would be arrested for perjury if he testified.

He should have said "testified falsely." He contends it was useless to tell them that the State courts had no jurisdiction of such an offense. What a pity that he could not persuade those whom he seemed to have wished to do so that it was not a crime to swear falsely in a contested-election case.

Smith Township, Cross County.

In his notice contestant makes the following claim as to this township:

That at the township of Smith, in the county of Cross, in said district, at an election held on the 6th day of November, 1888, I received for Representative one hundred and fifteen (115) votes and you received eighty-four (84); that the election officers of said township, who are partisans of yours, through fraud or mistake returned that you received eighty-four (84) votes and that I received fifteen (15) votes; that the votes as thus returned were by the county clerk certified to the secretary of state and by him laid before the governor and by him counted in determining the number of votes cast for each of us in said district. I shall therefore claim on contest one hundred more votes in said township than were returned for me.

He offers no proof concerning the vote which was certified to the county clerk by the election officers and by him certified to the secretary of state.

There is no evidence showing any reason why the testimony with regard to this precinct should not have been taken in that precinct, or at least in that county. Yet twenty-nine men are called into St. Francis County as witnesses to testify concerning said election. Not one of them gives any evidence of frauds in the conduct of this election. Nearly every one of them is asked directly, " Were the judges of election in your township your political friends or enemies?" Not one of them made any reply to this question. Not one of them says the judges were partisans of the contestee. No proof is given that they were not appointed according to law from the two parties. Their integrity and their proper conduct of the election is nowhere assailed by direct evidence.

Without laying any foundation whatever to impeach the official returns of these election officers, made under oath, contestant proceeds to take the testimony of these twenty-nine men as to how they voted. Only six of them can read or write. The Republican tickets did not have Mr. Featherston's name on them at this precinct. Two of the witnesses, colored men, say that they made out the tickets, and wrote Featherston's name on for the others. There is a suspicious uniformity in the answers of about twenty of them when the question submitted to them was whether they voted for Cate or Featherston. The answer generally ran: "Featherston. Harrison for President." It is like an admission that they did not actually recollect having voted for Featherston, or did not have much interest in his election.

One of them saying he could read a little, and saw Featherston's name on his ticket, being shown W. H. Cate's name, called it "Featherston." Another said he did not vote for Congressman, but for Harrison and Morton. A third answered, "I said I voted for Cates." No testimony is given to show that contestee did not receive the full number of votes returned for him. The vote of this township should not be disturbed upon such a shallow showing.

Blackfish Township, St. Francis County.

The notice of contestant claims that at this township, by the fraudulent, illegal, and unlawful conduct of the judges of election of said township, 53 voters of said township attended at the place where such election was to be held, at the proper time for the purpose and with intention of voting for him, but were prevented from doing so by fraudulent, illegal, and unlawful conduct of said judges of election

It will be observed that contestant does not claim that the elec' officers at this precinct were partisans of contestee. The proof sh' that two of the judges were Republicans, Mr. Worley, who was sick has since died, and Ruffin Carr, a negro. The ballot-box there in the hands of a Republican Federal supervisor, a negro, named F [or Fountain] Young, and he and Carr kept the ballot-box all (Worley said his wife was sick and he could not leave home. The : had been taken off the house where the election was to have been h some weeks before, to be repaired, and had not been replaced. No o house near could be had in which to hold the election. Two are n tioned, in one of which there was cotton, and the owner objecte having an election in his cotton store-house, and the other was a n shelter with no floor.

Mr. James, the Democratic judge, was in bad health and could sit in the rain. It would have been impossible to write the name voters on the poll-books, keep tally-sheets, or, in short, conduct an (tion, and there was no force, threats, violence, or intimidation of kind used or hinted at to prevent any one who might have wishe hold an election at Blackfish that day. Mr. James told one of Republican judges to get his judges and clerks and hold an electio he wanted to.

Contestant calls some twenty witnesses. They differ materiall' their evidence as to the number of voters at the polls, and their pose. From 25 to 40 voters were there, some 15 of whom were wh and Democrats. One witness says, "I counted 35 colored people were here and coming. I counted 20 right here at the house." "TI was about 30 people, pretty much all colored people," says another. reply to the question, "If you did not vote, why did you not vot their answers ran about as follows:

"I come here to the school-house to vote, but the judges would serve." One witness said, "I started to the school-house. It was r ing hard. I could not get there. I am a Republican." Another s "I started but could not get here. I was walking and it was raini Still another said, "I understood a few days before that the judges fused to serve, and thought there was no use to go." No one else tains this notion.

Here are some specimen answers to the question:

For whom would you have voted, Cate or Featherston?
For Harrison and the Republican ticket and whatever was.
I meant to vote the Republican ticket.
Most of the colored people said they were going to vote the Republican ticket wanted to vote for Featherston for Congress and Harrison for President.
I am a Republican and wanted to vote for Harrison.
I am a Republican. I do not know who they were going to vote for for Cong
I heard some say they wanted to vote for Harrison, and some say they wante vote for Cleveland. Pretty well all of them said they would vote for Harrison. T was two or three colored people said they would vote for Cleveland.

(See record, from page 65 to page 76).

These answers are significant in the frequent omission of Mr. Fe erston's name, when it is known that there was a Republican ca date for Congress voted for in this contest of the name of W. R. I rett. It was asserted in the committee-room by Mr. Cate, in the p ence of Mr. Featherston, and not denied, that he (Featherston) a Democrat two years before this time, and had been previous ther

Is it not absurd to talk of sustaining the proposition of the contestant with regard to the vote of this township?

Attention is next directed to Frank Township, St. Francis County, where contestant makes an elaborate and desperate effort to overthrow the returns of the election officers. In his notice, speaking of this township, he says:

I received 271 and you received 129, but the election officers of said township, who are partisans of yours, through mistake, or fraud, or otherwise, returned that you received 269 votes and that I received 131.

Contestee brings as witnesses the judges and clerks of election, who account for the ballot-box during the entire period of the election, explain minutely how the election was conducted and returns made, etc. (Record, pp. 256, 259, and 76.)

He brings the Democratic supervisor, Mr. Davis, who testifies (p. 254) to the regularity of the election. He brings Andrew McGlown, the Federal supervisor for the Republican party, himself a Republican, who shows by his evidence that he was watchful and diligent in the discharge of his duty; that the box was not out of his sight but twice for not exceeding three-quarters of an hour, and then it was locked and he had the key; that when they went to dinner the Democratic supervisor had the box and he had the key; at supper he had the box and Mr. Davis the key. While the Democratic supervisor had the box at dinner it was locked in a room, and Mr. McDonald, one of the judges of election, had the key of that room. There was no chance with the Democratic officials to tamper with the ballots by taking out those which had been deposited and numbered to correspond with the name of the voter and substitute others properly marked in their places. To have done this it would have been necessary to break the lock, which was not done, or to have had another key made.

This election was held four miles in the country, where there was no locksmith or gunsmith to assist in perpetrating such a fraud. Contestant introduced proof tending to show that it was easy to duplicate a key by having one made in a few minutes on the day of the taking of testimony. It may be sufficient to say that there was no testimony tending to show that any such fraud had been perpetrated upon this ballot. The testimony shows no opportunity and no suspicious circumstances indicating any design upon the part of the officers of election. The regularly appointed officers for this precinct were not present at the time to open the polls and did not qualify, so that officers were chosen from the citizens and by them. No testimony is offered as to the facts of their election, showing that they were not chosen properly and legally, although it is claimed that the judges were all Democrats. The Republican negro who had been appointed did not come until it was late.

The election law of the State of Arkansas is as follows:

If the court shall fail to * * * appoint judges of election, or those appointed fail to act, the voters, when assembled, may appoint the judges, who shall, in all respects, perform the duties of judges of election as required by law. (Mansfield's Digest of Laws of Arkansas, section 2650.)

And it is further provided that—

The judges of election appointed by the county court, *or chosen by the assembled electors* under the provisions of this act, shall, if practicable, be from different political parties, *so that each party may be represented*, and they shall, in addition, * * * be able to read and write.

McGlow testifies (page 76):

> Mr. Jack Davis called attention of the judges and clerks, who were there, that it
> was right as the other judges and clerks   *   *   *   to elect or appoint judges in their
> places, and they went ahead and did so. There were only Mr. Hill, Mr. McDaniel,
> and Mr. Grey, and Mr. Davis, and a few other men were all that were present at this.
> None of the judges appointed by the county judge were present. Jack Bruyn, a
> colored man, was one of the regularly appointed judges. I don't know what time he
> came.

If there had been Republicans present qualified to be judges would
not this witness have so testified ? None were present—none could be
chosen. No violation of law is proven. It was shown that the box
was out of the sight of one of the federal supervisors about three-
quarters of an hour at noon and again at supper time; but never out
of sight of both federal supervisors

McGlown, this Republican negro Federal supervisor, testifies that he
saw the ballots as they were handed to the judges and deposited in the
box as they were received; that he did not change or alter the ballot of
any elector, and did not suffer his associates to do it as far as he knows;
that the ballot-box was in his sight all the time the votes were being
deposited, and also when counting out; that he examined them as they
came out of the box; they were counted correctly; he supervised the
count of the ballots by the clerk and they were correctly tallied; that
the election was conducted fairly and impartially so far as his knowledge about it was. The number of ballots taken from the ballot-box
corresponded exactly with the number of names upon the poll-books.
He never discovered any evidence of the ballot box having been tampered with when out of his sight and never saw but one key and did not
know of any other. The testimony of the two white judges sustains the
fairness, impartiality, honesty, and accuracy of the whole election proceedings at this precinct on November 6, 1888.

The contestant was present by counsel and cross-examined the witnesses when this testimony was taken. Nowhere and at no time has
he offered any testimony tending to controvert the testimony of these
election officers upon the facts to which they made oath. In contestant's brief, page 8, we find the following concerning this precinct :

> We do not claim that the box shall be thrown out or any of the voters disfranchised.
> What we claim is that the ballot-box was exposed, and that the return does not show
> the true vote, and that in such a case each party can only have the number of votes
> he proves up. We concede that poll-books duly certified and returned are prima
> facie evidence of the truth of their contents, and that the burden is upon the con-
> testant to show that they do not speak the truth.

With this burden upon himself to destroy the validity of this election, the contestant has taken the testimony of 195 men whom he claims
to have voted at that election and for him, although the preliminary
proof has not made a shadow of a case for such a course.

The county clerk of this county—a Republican—was called and examined, February 7, 1889. In his custody were the ballots of this election, each one numbered to correspond with the number of the voter on
the poll-book. They were the primary and best evidence as to how the
voter voted. No examination was made of this testimony, which had
been in the safe-keeping of one of the official partisans of contestant
from the day of election. If the ballot-box had been opened it would
have disclosed one of two things, that claim of contestant was groundless, or that the judges had made a fraudulent return. Contestee could
not safely examine this witness of the contestant.

It should be borne in mind that in this precinct and the district there
were two elections in the fall of 1888, one in September, and this one
under examination in November, and that the testimony of these wit-

nesses as to how they voted, from whom they received their tickets, and what kind of tickets they voted, is taken in February, 1889. One of the witnesses, Andy Starks, says:

I am the man who issued all the tickets. I had one man to help me issue. I can't read to amount to anything; can't write. I issued the white tickets before dinner and the red ones after dinner.

The voters in their testimony tell of getting several different colored tickets from at least ten other persons. Many of the men whose names are not on the poll-books testify to having voted for a candidate for Congress. Some swear that others voted that day whose names can not be found on the poll-books. One says he did not vote; yet he is recorded on the poll-books of that day. Some swear they voted a red ticket in the morning, when none were present to be voted, and one that he voted a blue Republican ticket before noon. Some say they voted green tickets; some yellow. One was positive that his Republican ticket was green or blue, and not white or red. More than one gave names of candidates as being on their ticket that were not upon either the Republican or Fusion ticket in November, but may have been on the county ticket in September. Some could not tell whether they voted for a Congressman at the September or the November election, or at some other time, and some did not know who they voted for for President. The names of many who swear they voted are not found on the poll-book.

One witness testifies that the Democratic ticket was blue on both sides. Several of the voters say that that was the color of the tickets they got from J. U. Jackson that day and voted them. Six of the men fix the time at which they voted for Featherston in a different month from November.

These facts are mentioned to show that very much of the evidence is weak, contradictory, and uncertain. In some instances, what the witnesses should say or do when examined appears to have been put into their minds just before they were called. Clearly is it shown that from the lapse of time many of the witnesses confused the September and November elections, and were not able to recall correctly whether they attended one or both, and what occurred at such time or times as they were there.

It is impossible from a careful examination of the testimony to show that Featherston received a single vote more than was certified for him at that precinct, to wit, 131. No pretext for disturbing the returns from this township exists.

Before passing from this county, as reflecting upon the fairness of the returns, it may be of value to notice the figures for the September election for governor, and compare the votes for President on the 6th of November with the votes for Congressman. For governor, September election, St. Francis County, James Eagle, Democrat, received 960 votes; C. N. Norwood, Fusion, received 1,570 votes, and for President, November election, St. Francis County, Grover Cleveland, Democrat, received 838 votes; Benjamin Harrison, Republican, received 923 votes; Streator, Union Labor, received 248 votes. The total vote of both candidates for President opposed to the Democratic vote is 1,171. For Congressman, November election, St. Francis County, W. H. Cate, Democrat, received 762 votes; L. P. Featherston, Republican or Fusion, received 1,231 votes. Cate received about 20 per cent. less votes than Eagle did in September, and Featherston about 20 per cent. less than Norwood did. Cate received 76 votes less than Cleveland did the 6th of November, and Featherston 60 more than both Harrison and Streator combined. Remarkably bad stormy weather in that region accounts for the falling off of the total vote in November as compared with that in September.

The last county to be considered is Crittenden. In this county, at the September election for governor, Eagle, Democrat, received 1,328 votes; Norwood, Fusion, received 1,579 votes. At the November election for President, Cleveland, Democrat, received 310 votes; Harrison, Republican, received 1,055 votes; total, 1,365 votes. For Congressman, Cate, Democrat, received 316; Featherstone, Fusion-Republican, 869 votes; Barrett, republican, 169 votes; total, 1,354 votes, but 11 less than were cast for President.

The contestant, to sustain the ninth, tenth, eleventh, twelfth, thirteenth, and fourteenth paragraphs of his notice, introduces the following exhibit, which is found on page 228 of the record:

[Exhibit A to deposition of W. B. Eldridge.]

Abstract of poll-books of election held on the 6th day of November, 1888, for Representative in Congress for the 2d Congressional district of the State of Arkansas, in Crittenden County, at the following precincts or voting places, and not certified to the secretary of the state on account of irregularities in the poll-books appearing therein, that the judges and clerks of said election were not sworn as the law directs.

	Total vote.	W. H. Cate.	L.P. Featherston.
Mound City	147	14	133
Walnut Grove	189	49	137
Bradley	208	4	195
Edmondson	90	15	75
Riceville	45	.......•	45
Gilmore	45	7	35
Scanlin	64	61	2
	788	150	624

CLERK'S CERTIFICATE TO TRANSCRIPT.

STATE OF ARKANSAS, *County of Crittenden:*

I, Sam'l Keel, clerk of the circuit court within and for the county and State aforesaid, do hereby certify that the annexed and foregoing pages contain a true and complete transcript of the above as therein set forth, and as the same appears of record in my office at Marion, Crittenden County, Arkansas.

Witness my hand and official seal this 21st day of February, 1889.

[SEAL.]   SAM'L KEEL, *Clerk.*
——— ———, *D. C.*

In regard to this contention, and in order to arrive at a proper understanding of these returns and that justice might be done all parties, the contestee, on the 16th day of January, in Little Rock, in contestant's room, proposed that in order that there should be no trouble in this matter they would both go in person to Marion, the county seat, and get thereof, to be submitted as proof in this case. It was so determined, all the facts in relation to these returns, and make an agreed statement and the Thursday week following was fixed upon as the day to meet at Marion. Contestee went on according to the agreement; contestant was not there.

While the certificate of the county clerk indicates that he did not certify to the secretary of state as part of the vote for Representative in Congress the votes from these seven precincts in this county, yet we can not concur with the committee that there is sufficient legal proof to warrant these votes being added to the respective votes for contestant and contestee in these counties. We shall consider this matter again further on.

Contestant alleges in his notice with regard to one of these precincts, viz, Scanlan, that 163 legal voters of said precinct went to said precinct at the proper time for the purpose of voting for him for Representative and were prevented from so doing by the unlawful and illegal conduct of said judges of election and by intimidation of your partisans. The so-called testimony of these men was taken in Memphis, Tenn., without notice to contestee and is offered to maintain this charge. We shall discuss the taking of this alleged testimony along with more of the same kind hereafter. Let it now be examined and applied as if it were deserving of consideration.

Willis McGee (pages 225 and 226 of the record).

Q. What is the usual vote in your township?—A. About 125.
Q. How many Democrats?—A. About 25 to 30.
Q. What is the usual Republican vote?—A. From 100 to 125,
Q. How many Republican votes were cast?—A. No, sir; I do not know exactly how many were cast. I seen about nine or ten.
Q. Please make a list of those names and file it as Exhibit B to your deposition.— A. I do so.
Q. Were a good many men out at the polls that day—Republicans?—A. Right smart, and it was raining hard and a *heap did not come.*
Q. Was there many there didn't vote?—A. Yes, sir.
Q. What was the reason?—A. The boys said it wasn't no use voting; that they do just as they choose, and they didn't have no show there. They said they all voted Republican before, solid out through, and they beat them at Scanlan's.

It may be noted here that this witness testifies—
First. To only a small number voting, and says he filed a list of their names. This he does not do for some good reason best known to himself or those concocting this testimony.
Second. It was raining and a heap of Republicans did not come to the polls.
Third. A good many of them did not vote. He does not even say he himself voted.
Finally he does not utter a word to show there was any intimidation to prevent any one from voting.
E. B. Fields (R., pp. 215, 216) says about the same as to the voters of the precinct.

Q. Do you know whether there were any Republican votes cast there that day?— A. Yes, sir; I give several of them tickets and they sealed them up and said they was going to vote them just like they was; didn't open them at all.
Q. How many did you give tickets to?—A. I am certain I give four. I give tickets to several, but I did not know what they did with them; but I give tickets to some and they held them in their hands like they were afraid they would get away from them.

When asked:

Q. Were there any disturbances or rows there in the Presidential election?—A. No, sir; it was a kind a of day like this. It was raining all day most. Didn't have no fuss that day.

No intimidation or fraud is shown by this witness. On the contrary, he denies positively the one and does not touch on the other.
John Johnson, also of Scanlan, is called to this secret Memphis examination, and his strongest statements are given below:

Q. You say you were at the Presidential election?

He had said no such thing, but answers:

Yes, sir; I'm at all them, but then I was there anyhow at that one expressly.
Q. Was there some people come out to the polls that day that didn't vote?—A. They wanted to vote but was afraid to.
Q. How many people voted there?—A. I counted off 73, and they was voting on.

I didn't go away, but then I went down the river a little piece and sot around. But everybody that talked to me after I come up said they was voting Republican.

Q. You say they voted a Republican ticket?—A. Yes, sir.

Q. How many did you see vote that ticket that day at the polls?—A. About 73; I think 73. I counted them particularly.

Q. Did you have the tickets in your hand?—A. Yes, sir; I had about 125 or 130 of them—150, and I reckon I gave out about 30 or 40 of them that day and saw 75 of them voted, and stood and looked at them and saw pretty near every man that voted that day. I read the ticket and knew I was voting for Harrison.

Q. Who did you think you was voting for Congressman?—A. I just voted the straight ticket.

Q. Then this is exactly the ticket you voted?—A. Yes, sir.

Q. And this is exactly the ticket you saw voted by 73 other men?—A. **Yes, sir.**

Q. If the people in your township were voted properly how many of **them would** turn out and swear to have voted that same ticket that you make an exhibit of there?—A. 35 or 40 or 45.

Q. There is how many if they were properly protected? You issued 73 yourself, you say?—A. I didn't issue that many, but I saw that many polled from other hands that was handed round and counted them every one.

Q. Is there any feeling of uneasiness in your community now about their election matters?—A. No, sir; I don't hear anything more than just common.

Mr. Johnson also says he can furnish a list of those who voted the Republican ticket, but he never does it. To set aside the election in this precinct upon this testimony would be an outrage upon the right of elections by the people. The testimony utterly fails to sustain the claim of contestant in whole or in the slightest part.

Cat Island Precinct, Crittenden County.

Contestant claims that he received 183 votes in this precinct and contestee only 15, and that the election officers, through fraud or mistake, returned that he, contestant, received only 120 and contestee 88. George Hendley, examined somewhere in Memphis without notice to the contestant, is made to say about as follows:

We have usually voted from 196 to 200 alway in our township; about 14 to 15 Democrats and from 180 to 182 and 3 and 4 and so on Republicans. Nearly a full vote out. Not quite as many voted in the county election. No Republican, to his knowledge scratched the ticket and none to his knowing voted any other than the Republican ticket. All told him they would vote the Republican ticket. There have been considerable uneasiness since July. The people of our community are willing to tell fully and freely all they know and other portions of the county seem to be the same way willing to tell what they have done in relation to voting in the county and how they have voted. The judges in our township were all Democrats. We could not see the box and don't know whether the judges were sworn or not.

Robert Abernethy says he voted at the national election.

Don't know how many colored votes there are in the township; there are about 25 white voters, the rest are colored. General Republicans—nine-tenths of them were Republicans. I heard them say prior to the time they would vote that ticket under all hazards. They come through the rain and got their ticket. There was no other exhibited publicly. Voted the ticket and saw it put in the box.

Nothing more is offered to afford as a pretext for sustaining the claim of the contestant as to this precinct.

Ferguson Township, Crittenden County.

Contestant claims that 109 legal voters went to the voting place in said precinct for the purpose and with the intention of voting for him for Representative and were prevented from doing so by the unlawful conduct of the judges of election, who were partisans of contestee, and by intimidation of contestee's partisans.

Thomas Foster (colored), examined in Memphis without notice, says his usual voting place is Ferguson precinct.

Judges of election at State election supposed to be Democrats. Republican majority increasing generally about 120 to 125 off and on all day. About 100 to my knowing came there for the purpose of voting and the polls not being open they could not vote. They went off elsewhere to another precinct to vote. There are about 6 or 8 Democratic votes in the township. I don't know the reason for not opening the polls. Six of the Winchester crowd came down there once during the fall and took charge of two men and put them under bonds for their appearance of the circuit court, January term. I don't think the citizens of the neighborhood would be perfectly satisfied to turn out and testify under the circumstances that exist there now. I don't know about the safe part. They may be perfectly safe in doing so, but I doubt whether they'd be satisfied to do so.

R. S. Rushing (colored), examined at Memphis without notice, lives at Jones's.

Q. Did you vote at the last national election ?—A. No, sir; wouldn't let me vote; said I didn't live in that precinct.
Q. Your vote was challenged then ?—A. Yes, sir.
Q. Was the election at your regular voting place ?—A. Wa'nt held; don't know why. All of the voters in the precinct was Republicans but about 6. Judges at State election were Democrats. I was supervisor, and after I was notified that I was supervisor I went to the polls in order to know the reason or see that there was an election held there. I was appointed by the proper authorities, and went there for the purpose of having some kind of an election. No judges came and there was no election held.
Q. When you found the polls were not open you went to Jones' for the purpose of voting ?—A. Yes, sir.
Q. And there you were denied the right to vote ?—A. Yes, sir; none of us voted at all.
Q. Were there any poll-books or a ballot-box furnished to any one that you know of in Ferguson precinct ?—A. There was a ballot-box sent to me at 1 o'clock the same day. It was about 1 o'clock. I was in my store; had a clock in there and the ballot-box come there. The fellow came; he looked like he came in haste. He came there with the ballot-box and poll-books and everything. Says, "I want you to hold election at Fergusson's." I says "I aint the judges." "Well," he says, "you are appointed as supervisor." I says, "I have no notice of that." "Well," he says, "it's in this thing." And I took it and looked in there and I saw I was appointed supervisor at Fergusson's and Jones'. I thought that was a mere mistake. I don't know how come at two places, but then my name was on at Fergusson's and Jones' and I thought it was very necessary to vote for Harrison as President, and I wanted to vote the whole ticket, especially Featherston; wanted to vote the whole ticket. We voted the State and county ticket solid Republican. There wa'nt but six men went against us at that precinct and we voted 128 or 130 there. The reason I didn't hold the election was because I sent it to the judges of the election. I thought they were elected for a certain term under proper authorities. I sent it to them and ordered them to open the polls immediately, that I was going to hold an election. There was none held at all; there was people coming there all day; I reckon there was more than 25 or 30. I reckon there was more than them. Of course I counted that many citizens of the county and there was citizens of the United States and we couldn't vote."

Rev. T. J. Jones (colored) says also at Memphis :

My usual voting place is Fergusson's, though I voted Jones' on the national election—Presidential election—voted at Jones', was at Fergusson's first about two hours, I reckon. About 100 come to Fergusson's during the day to vote. I did not know all of them. I knew one part of them. They all was Republicans.
Q. They all turned out to vote ?—A. Yes, sir; all but about a few white men was in the crowd. They was Democrats. I didn't see any of those white men at the polls, but in that precinct 4 or 5 of them was Democrats. All the judges pretty well lived there in that voting precinct are Democrats, but I didn't see them all during the day.

If there were two voting places in that township for national elections, and if these witnesses speak truth, why was not an election held at both as the law authorized, by judges chosen by the people ? The witness, Jones, gives the true state of the case. There was but one voting place for that township for national elections, which was at

Jones's. It is not necessary to guess at what might have been the result
The certified returns show that contestant received 47 votes there that
day for Representative in Congress and contestee received 5 votes. No
evidence of intimidation or fraud by partisans of contestee anywhere
appears.

Crawfordsville, Crittenden County.

Contestant's claims as to this precinct are as follows:

I received for Representative 330 votes and you received 71; that the election officers of said township, who were partisans of yours, through fraud or mistake returned
that I received only 147 votes.

Contestant, instead of taking evidence in the county to sustain this
charge, offers evidence taken in Memphis, to show that when he and
his attorney went to Crawfordsville to take testimony they were not
treated with the courtesy and politeness which the citizens of a town
are supposed to extend to a stranger who is there on legitimate business; that the people were bitterly opposed to Featherston making an
investigation of the election, and two of them made threats; that the
attorneys had to get their meals at a colored restaurant and spend the
first day in a saloon, and then had to sleep at the house of a colored
merchant; that Mr. Berry, attorney for Mr. Cate, refused to act as
notary, though he had before promised to do so; that some of the people were drinking, and friends of Featherston took him out of a crowd
to prevent difficulty, and that a majority of the voters who voted for
him would be afraid to testify there, and a mass of other matter which
in nowise relates to the merits of this contest.

We shall now discuss the question whether testimony taken as this
was should be considered by the House, and weigh it for its worth.
As we have repeated, it was taken without notice and in violation of
law.

Act of March 2, 1875 (laws 2, 43, p. 338): It is provided that the
party desiring to take depositions under the provisions of this act shall
give the opposite party notice in writing of the time and place when
and where the same will be taken; of the name of the witness to be
taken, and their places of residence, and of the name of the officer before whom the same will be taken.

To pretend not to evade these requirements of the law W. B. Eldridge says in his deposition:

I notified L. P. Berry, the attorney of Mr. Cate, that Featherston would take
proof in Memphis, Tenn., at my office on February 24, 1889. Walsh and myself both
notified Berry that we would begin taking proof at 59 Madison street, Memphis,
Tenn., February 25, 1889.

We here introduce the affidavit of Mr. Berry, which flatly contradicts
Mr. Eldridge upon this point.

STATE OF ARKANSAS, County of Crittenden:

I, L. P. Berry, an attorney at law, resident at Marion, Crittenden County, Ark.,
being sworn, do state that I have before me a printed copy of the evidence in the
case of L. P. Featherston vs. W. H. Cate in the contest for a seat in the Fifty-first
Congress of the United States from the first district of Arkansas, wherein it appears,
on page 227 of said printed record, that one W. B. Eldridge states or testifies as follows: "I notified Mr. L. P. Berry, the attorney of Mr. Cate, that Mr. Featherston
would take proof at Memphis, Tenn., at my office, on the Congressional contest; on
February 23 Mr. Henry Walsh and myself both notified Mr. Berry that we would
begin taking proof at 59 Madison street, Memphis, Tenn., at 9 o'clock on February
23, 1889," and I further state that this statement is untrue, and without any foundation in fact; that Mr. Eldridge and Mr. Walsh did not give me any such notice, nor
either of them as he states, and I never knew of evidence relating to Crittenden

County until I saw it printed in the record, nor do I to this day know at what place said supposed evidence was taken.

I further state that I was only authorized to act for Mr. Cate as his attorney in said County so far as related to taking proof in Crittenden County, Arkansas, and had no authority to represent him or take proof elsewhere, or accept, receive, or waive any notice relative to taking proof elsewhere.

L. P. BERRY.

Sworn to and subscribed before me this January 10, 1890.
[SEAL.]

SAM'L KEEL, *Clerk*,
By O. M. TUFTS, *D. C.*

If, however, there were no questions of the truthfulness of Mr. Featherston's lawyer, it is clear that the notice could not have been in writing giving contestee the material facts concerning the witnesses to be examined. It was a plain violation of the law in that respect for some covert reason.

The officer shall cause the testimony of the witnesses, together with the questions proposed by the parties or their agents, to be reduced to writing in his presence, and in the presence of the parties or their agents, if attending, and to be duly attested by the witnesses respectively (R. S., sec. 122).

The certificate of the notary, E. M. Avery (page 185 of the record), shows that this provision of law was violated. Although he attempts to give the impression that the words of the witnesses were reduced to writing by type-writer, and submitted to witnesses and attested by them, he says the short-hand reporter's notes are herewith transmitted, etc.

The performances with the witnesses he said occurred in February and early in March. His certificate is dated July 13, and upon the original papers on file in the committee room, the names are all signed by type-writer, even of those who are represented as signing their own names, except Eldridge's and one other's.

All officers taking testimony to be used in a contested election case, whether by deposition or otherwise, shall, when the taking of the same is completed and without unnecessary delay, certify and carefully seal and immediately forward the same by mail or express to the Clerk of the House of Representatives. (Act approved March 2, 1887.)

This provision of the law is also disregarded. What good reason can be given for this unlawful course? In this case the legal time for taking testimony closed April 15. As required by statute the Clerk of the House of Representatives notified parties that they should appear before him June 28, for the purpose of being present at the opening of the sealed packages of testimony and of agreeing upon the parts thereof to be printed. They came here. Only part of the depositions were in the hands of the Clerk. None of those taken in Memphis were on file.

Contestant asked for further time, which was granted, and contestee remained here waiting until July 7; but these papers were not filed. On July 21 they were at last filed. Contestee never saw them or learned their contents until a printed copy of them reached his hands late in September. The contestant and his attorneys have never attempted any explanation or offered any excuse for this extraordinary, suspicious, and illegal delay. The contestee was without any opportunity to be present and see and hear these witnesses while they were telling their tales or to cross-examine them or to bring proof subsequently to explain or contradict their statements. Their record is full of the abuses which occurred under such circumstances.

Leading questions forcing false statements from the lips of ignorance are found upon nearly every page. In more than one instance the witness has thus placed on his tongue a statement contradicting others he

H. Mis. 137——10

has just made. Perjury so striking and peculiar that it would be ridiculous if it were not pitiable, discredits more than one page. In such a way the contestant seeks to have the returns at Crawfordsville set aside and himself given the same vote as the electors for the Republican national ticket received at this precinct, although there was a regular Republican candidate for Representative, a resident of St. Francis county, who divided that vote with him.

The clerk's certificate shows that the Republican electors received 330 votes, the Democratic electors 71 votes. It also shows that W. R. Barrett, for Representative in Congress, received 160 votes; L. P. Featherston, 147 votes; Willi m H. Cate, 88 votes. The majority report has not been submitted to us, so that we do not know upon what claims the committee proposes to unseat this member of Congress duly elected by the people of one of the largest and most populous, enterprising, and intelligent of the districts of the State of Arkansas.

The contestee comes here with a certified majority of 1,348. If all that is claimed for contestant in Phillips County were allowed, which is 181, that would leave him 1,167; and then if the votes in the seven townships of Crittenden County, not certified up by the clerk were allowed as if there were no question of their legality—there would be 522 for Featherston, less 150 for Cate, or 472 more to be taken from contestee's majority, 1,167, leaving him a majority of 595, to which he is rightfully entitled.

But suppose the House should go a step further and give the contestee arbitrarily the 169 votes cast for the true Republican, Barrett, at Crawfordsville, to punish the citizens of that town for their impoliteness, discourtesy, and rudeness to contestee. that even would not obliterate the majority of the sitting member, but only reduce it to 426.

Therefore we recommend the passage of the following resolutions:

Resolved, That L. P. Featherston was not elected as a Representative to the Fifty-first Congress from the First Congressional district of Arkansas.

Resolved, That William H. Cate was duly elected and is entitled to retain his seat.

JOS. H. OUTHWAITE,
CHAS. F. CRISP,
CHAS. T. O'FERRALL,
LEVI MAISH,
L. W. MOORE,
ROBERT P. C. WILSON.

S. E. MUDD vs. BARNES COMPTON.

FIFTH MARYLAND.

Contestant claimed (1) to be elected on the face of the precinct returns, and that these returns are primary; (2) to have a majority of the legal votes after the deductions and additions required by the evidence are made; and (3) that he had been deprived of 175 votes in one precinct by violence and intimidation. All three claims are sustained by the committee, the minority dissenting both as to the law and the facts (see minority report, page 161). The resolutions presented by the committee were adopted March 20, 1890, by a vote of 159 to 145, and Mr. Mudd was sworn in. The debate will be found on pages 2392 to 2449 of the Record.

(1) **Returns.** *Which primary evidence.*

According to the law of Maryland, the duties of the presiding judges when assembled at the county seat, are purely ministerial. They are to add up the votes of the precinct returns on the books of the polls and to certify the results of this addition to the governor. They can neither throw out votes certified by the precinct judges, nor return votes not certified by the precinct judges. It is presumed, of course, that the presiding judges will do their work accurately, and that their returns to the governor will contain a correct summary of the votes in their county. This presumption is, however, merely a prima facie one, and can be rebutted at any time by showing that these returns were, in fact, not a correct summary of the precinct returns; and when this is done, the returns to the governor must be disregarded and resort had to the primary evidence of the result of the election; that is, to the precinct returns themselves.

(2) **Ballot.** *Imperfect.*

Whenever the intention of the voter is clear and unmistakable, effect should be given to it.

(3) **Burden of proof.**

When it appears that the contestant was elected on the face of the returns, the burden of showing that these returns were not correct is thrown on the contestee.

(4) **Votes unlawfully rejected.**

147

The votes of legal voters who duly offered to vote and had their votes refused, the judges truthfully or falsely alleging that some one else had previously voted on the name, should be counted for the condidate for whom it is proved they offered to vote.

(5) Votes. *Names not on poll book.*

A large number of votes was rejected because the voters who had duly applied for registration, and been registered, found their names omitted from, or inaccurately copied on, the poll books. It was claimed that these votes could not be counted, because the law of Maryland makes the poll books conclusive evidence of the right of a man to vote. *Held*, that the law simply lays down a rule of evidence for the guidance of the judges of election, so as to reduce to a minimum their judicial functions. The votes should be counted on a contest.

(6) Votes improperly rejected.

Where votes were rejected by the judges because of real or assumed doubts as to the identity of the voters presenting themselves; *held* that where their identity is clearly established, these votes must be counted for the candidate for whom they were tendered.

(7) Intimidation. *Amount of violence necessary.*

The committee holds that a citizen has a right to a free and unmolested approach to the ballot box, and is not bound to fight his way to a polling window, especially when to do so he must come into conflict with persons who claim to be officers of the law, the truthfulness of which claim he has no means of negativing, and that a candidate whose supporters have done all in their power to make voters believe that they would suffer injury if they attempted to vote, can not be heard to say that the intimidated voters should not have believed the threats made to them.

REPORT.

FEBRUARY 27, 1890.—Mr. COOPER, of Ohio, from the Committee on Elections, submitted the following report:

The Committee on Elections, having had under consideration the contested election case of Sydney E. Mudd, contestant, against Barnes Compton, contestee, from the Fifth Congressional district of Maryland, submits the following report:

At an election held on the 6th day of November, 1888, Barnes Compton and Sydney E. Mudd were, respectively, Democratic and Republican candidates for election as Representative to the Fifty-first Congress from the Fifth Congressional district of Maryland. The former obtained the governor's certificate and now holds the seat. .

His right to it is contested by the latter, who asserts—

(1) That he was elected, on the face of the returns, by a plurality of three votes, receiving in all (as appears on the precinct returns) 16,283 votes, while the contestee, as appears from the same returns, received 16,280 votes.

(2) That he was elected, if all the votes for both contestant and contestee improperly rejected are counted for them, respectively, and all votes improperly counted for them are deducted.

(3) That at the first precinct of the third district of Anne Arundel County (the vote of which was returned for contestee 168, for contestant 32) the partisans of the contestee, by violence, threats, and intimidation, prevented 175 legal voters who wished to vote for contestant from doing so.

PRIMA FACIE CASE.

The law of Maryland (Code Public General Laws, section 66, article 33, record, page 639) requires the judges of election, as soon as the ballots are read off and counted and the number for each candidate reckoned up and ascertained, to make out under their hands on the books of the polls two distinct statements and certificates of the number of votes which have been given for each candidate. The presiding judge of election (section 68, article 33, Code of Public General Laws) takes charge of these two poll-books containing these certificates and statements, and on a subsequent day, within ten days after the election, all the presiding judges of each county assemble at the Court-house of their respective county. When so assembled, (section 69, article 33, Code of Public General Laws, Record page 640), the presiding judges cast up the entire vote of all the districts or precincts of the county, and make out two distinct certificates or statements of the number of votes given in their county for each candidate. One of these certificates is then to be delivered to the clerk of the county court for the county and the other to be mailed to the governor. The governor then issues a certificate

149

to the person who, from the returns so sent to him, appears to have been elected.

According to the law of Maryland, the duties of the presiding judges when assembled at the county seat, are purely ministerial. They are to add up the votes of the precinct returns on the books of the polls and to certify the results of this addition to the governor. They can neither throw out votes certified by the precinct judges, nor return votes not certified by the precinct judges. It is presumed, of course, that the presiding judges will do their work accurately, and that their returns to the governor will contain a correct summary of the votes in their county. This presumption is, however, merely a prima facie one, and can be rebutted at any time by showing that these returns were, in fact, not a correct summary of the precinct returns; and when this is done, the returns to the governor must be disregarded and resort had to the primary evidence of the result of the election; that is, to the precinct returns themselves.

In this case the returns forwarded to the governor footed up for Barnes Compton 16,000 votes; for Compton 1 vote; for Sydney E. Mudd 15,819 votes; for S. N. Mudd 1 vote. The contestant denies the accuracy of said returns, and files duly certified copies of the precinct returns from every precinct in the Congressional district (record, pages 712 to 779), which show that the vote in the district for the contestant and the contestee was as follows:

For Sydney E. Mudd.	16,279
For S. N. Mudd	1
For S. E. Mudd	1
For Mudd	1
"One ticket upon which Sydney E. Mudd's name appeared twice and Mudd's name was not counted in the above returns"	1
Total	16,283
For Barnes Compton	16,280
Plurality for Sydney E. Mudd	3

Comparing these precinct returns with the returns made to the governor, it is found:

(1) That the returns to the governor from the counties of Howard, Anne Arundel, and Baltimore, and from the city of Baltimore, were accurate summaries of the precinct returns and were correct.

(2) That in the third district of St. Mary's County there were returned by the precinct judges 1 vote for "S. E. Mudd," and 1 vote for "Mudd," but the presiding judges did not include these votes in their return to the governor.

(3) That the returns from the fifth and ninth districts of Charles County were not included in their returns to the governor, because at the time the presiding judges made up their returns the returns from these precincts were sealed up in the boxes which the presiding judges had no authority to open. These boxes were afterwards opened by an order of court, and certified copies of the returns found in them have been filed, which show that the contestant received in these districts 432 votes and the contestee 280 votes.

(4) That the face of the precinct returns from the sixth district of Charles County shows—

There was one ticket upon which Sydney E. Mudd's name appeared twice and Mudd's name was not counted in the above returns.

(5) That in Calvert County the returns to the governor allow the contestant 1,138 votes, whereas the actual vote cast and counted in this

county, and shown by the certified copies of the precinct returns (record, pages 746 to 749), was 1,166. Mr. Mudd called the return judges of every precinct in the county (record, pages 271-275), and proved by them that the returns then on file in the clerk's office were the very returns which they made and were in no way altered. He proved by the editor of the Democratic paper in the county town that on the day the returns were made up, he copied them for his paper and that they gave the contestant 1,166 votes. He proved by the clerk of the court that immediately upon seeing it stated in the newspapers that the return to the governor gave the contestant only 1,138, he wrote to the governor stating that a mistake had been made and asking permission to correct it. The deputy clerk of the court who made up the returns to the governor, swears himself that these returns so sent on by him were erroneous and that those in the clerk's office were correct (see record, pages 271-275). If the precinct returns of any precinct had been altered, the contestee could have offered *some* evidence to show that such alterations had taken place, but he did not, in fact, take any testimony whatever upon the subject. The committee believe that the contestee is simply trying to raise a technical point of evidence to defeat the contestant's claim to 28 votes, which no one can seriously doubt the contestant received, and that the contestant's vote in Calvert County was 1,166.

(6) That in the precinct returns from Prince George's County (record, pages 762-772) there was no mention of a vote for "Compton," which the presiding judges in their return to the governor say was cast in the tenth district of the county, and consequently the presiding judges had no right to include it in their return to the governor. The contestant has, however, attempted to show that he was entitled to the vote by offering in evidence a certificate of the clerk of the court of the county (record, page 610), that on one of the tally-lists of the district there appears, "one ticket for ‘ Compton,’ not counted for Barnes Compton ;" on the other of said tally-sheets, "one ticket for Compton, torn, not counted for Barnes Compton." There is no other evidence concerning this vote. The tally lists are not a part of the certificate or statement from which the law requires the presiding judges to make up their return; and if they were, their contents are not sufficiently proved by a certificate of the clerk that such and such a thing appears upon them. Public officers prove public records, not by statements as to what their contents are, but by certified copies of the documents themselves. Moreover, it would seem, from statements quoted from one of the tally-lists referred to, that the judges may have decided that the voter intended to cancel his ticket as to candidate for Congress by tearing it.

For these reasons the committee does not think it clear that the contestee is by the evidence entitled to this vote, but thinking it likely that such a vote may have been cast, has concluded to allow it. Upon the face of the returns the committee, therefore, finds that the vote stood:

For Sydney E. Mudd	16,279
For S. E. Mudd	1
For S. N. Mudd	1
For Mudd	1
One ticket on which Mudd's name appeared twice, not counted for Mudd	1
	16,283
For Barnes Compton	16,280
For Compton	1
	16,281
Plurality for Sydney E. Mudd	2

There were no persons by the name of Mudd and Compton other than the contestant and the contestee candidates for Congress at this election; and, therefore, under the well established rule of the House, the vote for " Compton " if counted at all should be counted for the contestee, and the votes for "S. E. Mudd," for "Mudd" and for "S. N. Mudd" for the contestant. It is well settled by the authorities that the fact that the same candidate's name is on the same ticket more than once, is no reason why that ticket should not be counted, as one vote, for that candidate. It would, therefore, follow that the contestant is entitled to the one vote not counted for him, because his name is on the ticket twice. The contestee has, however, offered evidence (Record, pp. 455-457) that this ticket was not counted for the contestant, not because the name was on the ticket twice, but because the paster (upon which his name was printed) was pasted on the regular Republican ticket so as to cover up the designation of the office for which he was a candidate. If this be granted, it still remains true that whenever the intention of the voter is clear and unmistakable, effect should be given to it; and no one can have any doubt that the voter of this ticket—a straight Republican ticket—intended to vote for Mr. Mudd for the only office for which he was a candidate. No provision of a statute regulating the form of ballots will be held, or was ever intended to be held, as mandatory in contravention of such a plain and manifest intent. The committee is, therefore, of the opinion that the contestant is entitled to this vote and will count it. The face of the returns, then, in the opinion of the committee, show that the contestant was entitled to 16,283 votes, and the contestee to 16,281 votes, giving the contestant a plurality of 2 votes. Such being the case, the burden of showing that these returns (the primary evidence of the result of the election) were not correct, is thrown on the contestee.

REVIEW OF DISPUTED VOTES.

The committee holds that the votes of legal voters who duly offered to vote and had their votes refused, the judges truthfully or falsely alleging that some one else had previously voted on the name, should be counted for the candidate for whom it is proved they offered to vote. It is bad enough that a person who has no right to vote gets his vote in; it would be worse if by getting his vote in he kept an honest man's vote out.

Under this ruling the contestant gains the votes of six persons, whose names, their county and district, the allegation of the notice under which the tender and refusal of their votes was proved, and the pages of the record showing the proof, are as follows:

Name.	County and district.	Under allegation.	Pages of record.
Butler, Wm	1st precinct, 13th district, Baltimore County.	12	15, 17, 286, 288, 674.
Smith, John H	1st district, Charles County..........	24	252, 254.
Brown, Wm................	3d district, Prince George's County ..	29	259, 260.
Green, Chas. H	........do	29	260, 261.
Brown, Henry............ ..	13th district, Prince George's County.	28	261, 262, 263.
Williams, Thos..............	1st pre't, 18th ward, Baltimore County	22	37, 38, 40, 41, 320, 322, 669.

Contestee proves no votes of this class.

A large number of votes, on both sides, were rejected because the voters who had duly applied for registration and been registered found their names omitted from or inaccurately copied on the poll-books. It is urged by the contestee that the law of Maryland makes the poll-book conclusive evidence of the right of a man to vote; and that these votes can not be counted. The committee can not assent to this proposition.

The law simply lays down a rule of evidence for the judges of election, and is intended to reduce to a minimum their judicial functions. Into the qualification of voters they can not inquire. All they have the right to pass upon is the question: whether or not a person offering to vote is the person whose name is on the poll-book. This limitation is imposed upon them, because in the view of the Maryland law a polling window, on election day, is not a proper place to investigate questions of qualification. A simple rule is laid down for the guidance of the judges, and any injustice which may be done by the application of this rule can, if necessary, be corrected by the tribunal before which the contest is made. The class of cases about which we have been speaking, together with another class represented by a vote on each side in which the voter was improperly refused registration, are the very sort of cases to provide clearly for which the third section of the act of Congress of May 31, 1870, was enacted, which section read as follows:

That whenever, by or under the authority of the constitution or laws of any State or the laws of any Territory, any act is, or shall be, required to be done by any citizen as a pre-requisite to qualify or entitle him to vote, the offer of any such citizen to perform the act required to be done as aforesaid shall, if it fail to be carried into execution by reason of the wrongful act or omission of the person or officer charged with the duty of receiving or permitting such performance or offer to perform or acting thereon, be deemed and held as a performance in law of such act, and the person so offering and failing as aforesaid, and being otherwise qualified, shall be entitled to vote in the same manner and to the same extent as if he had performed such act.

The admission of such votes is in accord with the unvarying practice of Congress and the almost uniform decisions of the courts, and the committee will count all such votes properly proved on both sides.

The contestee has offered to prove a number of votes lost by because of inaccuracies on the poll-books, not otherwise referred to in his answer than by an allegation that in a very large number of other election districts he lost votes from this cause, and more votes from such cause than the contestant.

The contestant objects to the admission of this testimony on the ground that this general allegation does not, in the language of the statute governing contested elections, state "specifically the other grounds" upon which the sitting member rests the validity of his election; and the committee is inclined to agree with the contestant, but as the committee in this case has no doubt that the contestee was really entitled to some of the votes of this class which he has proved, the contestee will be allowed the votes he has proved he lost from inaccuracies of the poll-books, whether the loss of these votes was or was not specifically alleged. The committee, however, on the same principle, will allow the contestant the votes he proved in rebuttal of the contestee's allegation in paragraph 9 of his answer, that the contestee lost more votes than the contestant because of inaccuracies on the poll-books. In most cases the contestant proved how the person, whose vote he claimed to have lost in this way, would have voted had his vote been received, by the testimony of the voter himself.

The contestee, in a much larger proportion of the votes he proved, proved how they would have voted by other and less conclusive testimony, in some instances by merely proving that the voter was or had been a Democrat. The contestant objects to votes proved in this last-mentioned way being counted, on the ground that as he received a great many Democratic votes in the district, there is no certainty that these voters wanted to vote for contestee. The committee, however, has decided to allow the contestee these votes. Under these rulings, therefore, the contestant gains the votes of forty-four persons—forty under specific allegations and four in rebuttal—under general allegation above referred to.

The names of these voters, their county, and district or ward, and precinct, the allegation of the notice under which these votes were proved, and the pages of the record containing the proof, are as fol-lows :

Forty under specific allegations.

Name of voter.	Elec. dist. or pre	Under allegation.	P. of rec.
Gamble, Benjamin F......	1st pre., 13th dist., Baltimore Co......	12	11, 681, 17, 285, 291, 293, 328, 420, 501, 505, 508, 510.
Hopkins, Mal. or Melchis-edek.	1st " 13th " " "	12	13, 682, 17, 286, 291, 292.
Miller, A. W. Herman......	1st " 13th " " "	12	13, 683, 17, 286, 291, 292, 329.
Washington, Edward	1st " 13th " " "	12	14, 676, 17, 286, 292, 328, 508.
Gamble, Daniel E	1st " 13th " " "	12	18, 43, 680, 285.
Johnson, Winfield S........	1st " 17th ward, Balto. City......	15	19, 655. 20, 21, 23, 24, 42.
Wilder, John D.............	1st " 17th " " "	15	20, 22, 23, 24. 656, 42, 44.
Lutsche, George H.........	1st " 17th " " "	15	20, 22, 23, 24, 657, 41.
Virts, John R	2d " 17th " " "	16	25, 659, 26.
Taylor, John	9th " 17th " " "	17	26, 27, 661.
Kane, James E..............	9th " 17th " " "	17	27, 28, 661.
Hill, William Henry	9th " 17th " " "	17	28, 662.
Chester, Isaiah	9th " 17th " " "	17	29, 663.
Frank, Jacob	1st " 16th " " "	18	30, 31, 34, 35, 36, 395, 665.
Smith, Geo. Washington ...	1st " 16th " " "	19	31, 665, 35, 36, 307.
Brogden, William H........	1st " 16th " " "	19	32, 666.
Costen, John H	1st " 16th " " "	19	32, 33, 667, 36.
Sampson, Joseph H	1st " 16th wa·d, Balto. City	19	33, 34. 668, 36.
Allsop, William	1st " 16th " " "	18	34, 36. 43, 670.
Reed. Robert.	1st " 16th " " "	18	36, 245, 710.
Leman, David W	3d " 1st dist. Baltimore Co	13	45, 46, 677, 330, 500.
Mills, George H	1st " Howard "	23	47. 689, 297, 327.
Fishpaw, Aquilla...........	6th " " "	31	49, 51, 685, 298, 558.
Cure, Lev	6th " " "	31	49, 236, 684, 298.
Clements, James W.........	3d pre. 1st " Baltimore "	13	50, 679, 329.
Green, James W	3d " 1st " " "	13	50, 675, 330.
Thomas, John Henry	6th " Howard "	31	48, 236, 686, 298, 558.
Richardson. Wm. T........	1st " " "	23	52, 687, 327.
Gordon, Philip.............	1st " " "	23	53, 688, 327.
Kellar, Ishmael W	3d pre. 1st " Baltimore "	13	235, 678, 330.
Thomas, John F	5th " Charles "	26	216 248.
Brown, Augustin	5th " " "	26	246, 247, 251.
Thomas, James W	5th dist. Charles Co	26	247, 249.
Lyles, Philip	5th " " "	26	247, 252.
Thomas, William	5th " " "	26	248, 250.
Bowen, John T	8th " St. Mary's "	11	265, 650, 587.
Coats, Wm. Francis.........	5th " " "	10	266, 652, 587.
Brooks, David R	5th " " "	10	266, 587.
Barnes, James Henry.......	5th " " "	10	268, 269, 653.
Whittemore, Charles W	1st pre. 5th " Anne Arun. "	6	165, 672.

Four in rebuttal.

Adams, Wm	1 P. 1 D. Balt. Co.....................		393, 394, 493. 555.
Jessop, Jeremiah M.........	8 D. Anne Arundel Co		556, 792.
Holt, Levi G................	8 D. " " "		556, 557, 790.
Carter, Francis H...........	7 D. St. Mary's Co...................		575, 576, 594.

And contestee gains 17 such votes, those of Benj. F. Chappelear, B. F. Gover, Clifford Sweeney, Wm. K. Dawson, Ferdinand E. Burch, Chas. F. Burler, John E. Garnett, Jas. W. Wheatley, Dalton Howard Fisher, John H. Iglehart, Andrew M. Lainhart, Edward Woods, John M. Todd, John H. Turner, Chas. W. McCready, Richard H. Carter, John Kalb.

The committee considers there is no sufficient evidence that Albert F. Berry was a registered voter at the time he offered to vote or that he had any right to be registered ; that there is no evidence whatever that John T. Butler was not properly stricken off ; and that the very certifi cate filed by the contestee to prove that Chas. H. Soper, James R. Edelin, Wm. R. Thomas, Francis Tolson, and Andrew V. Convey were registered voters, shows, in fact, that these men never were entered by the officer of registration as qualified voters at all. The law of Maryland (Code of Public General Laws, article 33, section 14, record, pages 624–625) requires the officer of registration, so soon as an applicant of registration presents himself and before he is sworn, to write down his name. The officer then swears him and examines him, and if he finds he is qualified, he again writes his name in the column of qualified voters.

The certificate filed (record, page 586) indicates that the names of these men were not entered in this column. None of them were examined personally, and there is no evidence that they were by law entitled to registration. (See record, pages 468–70, where all the evidence concerning said persons is set forth.)

There is another class of cases in which the judges rejected votes because of real or assumed doubts as to the identity of the voters presenting themselves. Where their identity is clearly established, these votes must be counted for the candidate for whom they were tendered.

Under this ruling the contestant gains 4 votes, whose names, with similar references as above, are as follows :

Name of voter.	County, city, ward, or district.	Under allegation.	Pages of Record.
Bell, Thomas	1st pre., 13th dist. Balto. Co	12	16, 17, 673, 286, 287, 288, 289, 292, 505, 508, 510.
Booth, Samuel H	1st pre., 17th ward, Balto. City	15	20, 22, 23, 24, 658, 42, 45.
Cooper, Gustavus Elzear	5th dist. St. Mary's Co	10	267. 649, 269, 587.
Weems, Wm. Chapman	do	10	269, 270, 654, 587.

The contestee recounted the ballots at the sixth and seventh precincts of the fifteenth ward, of the first precinct of the sixteenth ward, and of the first, second, third, fourth, fifth, sixth, seventh, eighth precincts of the seventeenth ward of Baltimore City, and of the first district of Baltimore County. He asked for the recount in his answer, but with the exception of the first precinct of the first district of Baltimore County, and the first precinct of the sixteenth ward of Baltimore City, he laid no foundation for a recount by showing any ground to suppose that a mistake had been made. All the presiding judges examined by the contestee himself were Democrats, as were the majority of the judges in each of the precincts recounted. All the judges examined swore that they believed their count was correct. It is a strange circumstance that these Democratic judges should have uniformly made mistakes to the prejudice of their own candidate. The officers in whose custody the

boxes were, between the election and the recount, were all Democrats.
The contestee recounted some precinctsof a ward and not others, and
there is not a shred of evidence to show why some were recounted and
others not.   It is clear that if any one had access, even for a few moments, to the ballot-boxes, they could have been opened and their contents altered and then closed again without leaving any trace of disturbance.

The contestee gained 19 votes on the recount.   These votes we allow
him, although we feel that there is something very curious about the
whole matter.   We allow contestee's claim, based on a recount, that a
vote should be deducted from the contestant in the ninth district of
Charles County, making a loss to the contestant of 20 votes on the recount.   The committee also allows contestee a vote he claims he should
gain in the seventh district of St. Mary's County upon which his name
was written and that of the contestant is claimed to have been
scratched, although there is no allegation in the answer of contestee
under which the proof of either of these votes is strictly admissible.

We deduct from the contestee 1 vote in the second district of Calvert County, being satisfied that there was counted for the contestee a
ticket from which his name was scratched.   (Record, pages 271–273.)

Under the above rulings the

Contestant having on the face of the return..................,............................ 16,283
Gains, votes rejected because some one had illegally voted on the voter's name   6
Votes rejected because of inaccuracies of poll and registration books.........   44
Votes rejected because of a doubt as to identity of voters.....................   4
                                                                                    ————
                                                                                    16,337
And loss on recount   20
                                                                                    ————
                                                                                    16,317
                                                                                    ════
Contestee having on the face of the return..................................... 16,281
Gains, one vote in Seventh district of St. Mary's County......................   1
Votes rejected because of inaccuracies on poll or registration books   17
                                                                                    ————
                                                                                    16,299
Vote rejected because of doubt as to identity of voter   1
                                                                                    ————
                                                                                    16,300
Loss, one vote in Calvert County.......................................   1
                                                                                    ————
                                                                                    16,299

The contestant, who had two plurality on the face of the returns,
makes a net gain by correcting these individual errors of sixteen votes
and his plurality stands at eighteen votes ; this, too, after allowing the
contestee all he can possibly claim, and more than we think the strict
and perhaps safe rule of law would authorize.

Furthermore, if every one of the other votes which the contestee claims
(but which the committee does not allow him) were given him, the only
effect would be to reduce the contestant's plurality and would not affect
the final result.

INTIMIDATION OF CONTESTANT'S SUPPORTERS BY THOSE OF CON-
TESTEE.

The committee finds that the votes of the first precinct of the third district of Anne Arundel County should be thrown out.   The vote, as returned in this precinct, was 168 for the contestee and 32 for the contestant.
The undisputed facts concerning this precinct are, that there were regis-

tered therein 475 persons, 252 of whom were white and 223 colored ; that of these 475 only 206 voted, and of those who voted 191 were white men, and 15 were colored ; that when the polls opened 4 white men voted, then 15 colored men, and then 187 white men. The contestant has examined 175 colored voters of this district who did not vote ; of these 175 161 were on the polling ground ; many of these walked or rode many miles to the polls, and some who were temporarily away from home returned from Baltimore, Annapolis, Steelton, and other places to vote. All of these men swear that they wanted to vote (and most of them were at the polls with their tickets in their hands for the purpose of voting) for the contestant; 14 others swear that they started from their homes and walked a greater or less distance towards the polls and then turned back, in consequence of what they heard as to the proceedings at the polls.

There is no dispute that there were present at the polling place, from before the opening of the polls at 8 o'clock in the morning until late in the afternoon, a number of persons who were not residents of the precinct ; that those of them who were identified were residents and registered voters of Baltimore City, and that they drove down from Baltimore, reaching the polls before any of the voters, and drove back in the late afternoon; that those men, or some of them, wore badges with the words " U. S. deputy marshal" upon them, and claimed to be such ; that this claim was altogether false ; that these men were armed with pistols, which at certain periods of the day they were firing within the hearing of the polling place; that there were a number of guns in a wagon which brought them from Baltimore; that before the polls opened they placed themselves within a few feet of the window at which the citizens were to vote, and that in a very few minutes after the polls opened they seized and dragged from the line two or more colored voters (among them a man of some seventy years of age, a large property owner and tax payer, a resident of the district for twenty-five years, and a universally respected citizen), and told them that they could not vote. The person just referred to (who from age and standing was evidently the most influential colored man present) asked if the colored people were not to be allowed to vote, when the crowd from Baltimore answered, " Not a damn nigger shall vote unless he votes for Cleveland." The old colored leader then told the other colored men not to make a fuss, but as they could not vote to go away peaceably. A number of them did, but the larger number remained about the polling place for some time longer and occasionally one of them would attempt to reach the polling place.

In every such instance they were met by some one of the strangers or by one of the well-known Democratic leaders of the precinct, and told that they could not vote; and when they still pressed on, they were struck at and compelled to fall back. A number of colored voters still remained in the neighborhood of the polls, and, in order to get them away, the leader of the Baltimore gang—a man whom the witnesses all call "Tip Wells," but whose real name is proved to be John H. Wills—told a man named Ed. Pumphrey, a resident of the neighborhood, to go among the negroes, tell them that there was a gang of roughs from Baltimore there, that they had guns, and that more were coming down from Baltimore in the next train, and that they would have to fight these armed men if they wanted to vote; Pumphrey went down to where the negroes were, moved around among them, telling them what Wells directed him to tell, and adding that he was a deputy sheriff, that he could not protect them, and if they took his ad-

vice they would go home. He then came back and reported to those
who sent him what he had done. Fifty or more of the colored voters
testified that they heard Pumphrey telling them to go home; that there
was a wagon-load of roughs there with guns, and that more were coming, etc.

To rebut all this testimony the contestee produced a number of witnesses who say that they saw very little trouble; that if the colored
people had insisted on voting they think they could have done so, but
the contestee did not put upon the stand a single man whom the witnesses for the contestant identified as having interfered with the rights
of the colored Republican voters. "Tip Wells," the leader of the Baltimore gang, was appointed a few weeks after the election, by the Democratic collector of internal revenue, a store-keeper in the internal-reve-
nue service; and though he could have been summoned at any time to
deny the charges made against him, or to explain what he and his followers were doing on election day, he was not put on the stand. Frank
Chairs, another Government employé, and a resident of the precinct,
was proved to have taken part in the series of acts which intimidated
the colored voters, but he was not examined by the contestee. William
Chairs, who caught hold of one negro who went up to vote and jerked
him back, and who was the Democratic leader in the precinct, was in
the room when the testimony was being taken, coaching the counsel
for the contestee, but he was not examined.

The pseudo Deputy Sheriff Pumphrey, who played such a large part
in the plot, was not examined. These men, and these alone, could
have rebutted the grave statements made by the contestant's witnesses,
but they were not put forward to do it. The persons who interfered
with the election did so in the interest of the Democratic candidates,
and their declaration that "not a damn negro shall vote unless he votes
for Cleveland" was not an empty threat, for the Democratic negro,
Jackson, as he himself testified (record, page 148), got his ticket from
one of the gang, and according to another witness (record, page 242),
they held him up to the window to vote. The contestee claims that if
this were all so, the negroes had physical force enough to have voted
if they had persisted in doing so. The committee holds that a citizen
has a right to a free and unmolested approach to the ballot-box, and is
not bound to fight his way to a polling window, especially when to do
so he must come into conflict with persons who claim to be officers of
the law, the truthfulness of which claim he has no means of negativing,
and that a candidate whose supporters have done all in their power to
make voters believe that they would suffer injury if they attempted to
vote, can not be heard to say that the intimidated voters should not
have believed the threats made to them. The contestee's majority in
the precinct as returned was 136. The contestant proves by the voters
themselves that he lost at least 175 votes as a result of this intimidation; the intimidation existed; it changed the result in the precinct,
and the vote of the precinct must be excluded from consideration.

MISCELLANEOUS.

The evidence offered by the contestee to show that, in various precincts and districts, his colored supporters were intimidated by those of
the contestant, is of altogether too vague and unsubstantial a character
to deserve consideration. Only one colored man testified that he wanted
to vote for the contestee and was prevented from doing so by intimida-

tion; and he, on cross-examination, admitted that he intended to vote for the contestee because he had been promised $2 or $3 for so voting.

The committee can see no ground upon which the contestee's claim, that the eighth district of Anne Arundel County should be thrown out, can be sustained. It is not charged that any illegal votes were received, or counted, or that legal voters (except those whose votes were refused because of inaccuracies on the poll-books, and whose votes have already been allowed contestee and contestant respectively) were prevented from voting.

The committee, therefore, concludes that—

Contestant having on the face of the precinct returns		16,283
Gains—		
Votes of voters whose votes were refused because it was alleged that other persons had voted on their names		6
Votes of voters whose votes were refused because of inaccuracies on poll or registration books		44
Votes of voters whose votes were rejected because of doubt as to their identity		4
		16,337
Loses—		
Votes on recount	20	
Votes returned for him in first precinct, third district of Anne Arundel County	32	
		52
True vote for contestant		16,285
Contestee, having on the face of the precinct returns		16,281
Gains—		
Votes of voters whose votes were rejected because of inaccuracies on poll or registration books		17
One vote in 7th district of St. Mary's County		1
Vote of voter whose vote was rejected because of doubt as to his identity		1
		16,300
Loses—		
Votes in second district of Calvert County	1	
Vote returned for him in first precinct, third district of Anne Arundel County	168	
		169
True vote for contestee		16,131
Plurality for contestant		154

The contestant has, therefore, upon the most liberal allowance to the contestee and after the decision in contestee's favor of every doubtful point, a clear plurality of 154 votes and is entitled to his seat.

The committee, therefore, reports the following resolutions and recommends their passage:

Resolved, That Barnes Compton was not elected as a Representative to the Fifty-first Congress from the Fifth district of Maryland, and is not entitled to the seat.

Resolved, That Sydney E. Mudd was duly elected as a Representative for the Fifth Congressional district of Maryland to the Fifty-first Congress and is entitled to his seat as such.

1) **Ballots.** *Best evidence.*

The ballots, when clearly shown to be the identical ballots cast, are the best evidence of the vote.

(2) **Returns.** *Which primary evidence.*

The county returns sent to the governor are evidence of the vote of the county unless shown to be wrong by the primary evidence, either the ballots themselves or the count made by the judges of election in each precinct at the close of the election. In this case the evidence offered is insufficient to overthrow the county returns of Calvert county.

(3) **Votes.** *Improperly rejected.*

" Whenever a voter did tender his vote and his name was upon the list of voters furnished to the judges of election, although the middle name or initial might be wrongly entered, still his vote should be counted as it should have been received by the judges, the object of registration being for the purpose of identification of a voter, or if the name given by the voter was *idem sonans* with the name registered. * * * The vote of no person whose name did not appear, either properly or at least by '*idem sonans*,' could have been received by the judges, nor can they be counted by us."

(4) **Evidence.** *In rebuttal.*

Testimony in chief, offered in the time for rebuttal, should not be considered.

(5) **Intimidation.** *Amount of violence necessary.*

A poll can not be rejected for intimidation unless there was such a display of force as ought to have intimidated men of ordinary firmness. There was no such intimidation in this case.

H. Mis 137——11

VIEWS OF THE MINORITY.

Mr. MOORE, from the Committee on Elections, presented the following minority report:

The minority of your committee feel constrained to differ with the majority in their conclusions in this case, and submit the following minority report:

The undisputed facts are that by the returns made to the governor the contestee was elected by a plurality of 181 votes, and after correcting these returns by adding the votes of the sixth and ninth districts of Charles County, the plurality of the contestee was 29, as shown by the official figures.

It is also true that there was an error in the return, as made to the governor, from the first precinct of the Sixteenth ward of Baltimore City, by which the contestant was allowed 223, whereas he received but 222 votes, and his total of 15,819 is made by allowing him this vote. This is conclusively shown by the certified copy of the return of the judges. (Record, p. 609, Exhibit Compton, 14), and by the recount (pp. 319, 616).

The vote, therefore, prior to the recount, stood as follows:

Barnes Compton—official		16,000
Add vote of 5th district of Charles County		191
Add vote of 9th district of Charles County		89
Total		16,280
Sydney E. Mudd—official		15,819
Add vote of 5th district of Charles County		274
Add vote of 9th district of Charles County		158
		16,251
Deduct one vote first precinct, Sixteenth ward	1	
		16,250
Plurality for contestee		30

2. That by a recount of the ballots the contestant loses in sixth precinct of Fifteenth ward of Baltimore City 6 votes (Record, pp 616, 279, showing recount, and pp. 726, return of judges). In the seventh precinct of said ward 3 votes (Record, pp. 283, 616, 727). In the second precinct of the Seventeenth ward 1 vote (pp. 305, 616, 730). In the third precinct 5 votes (pp. 307, 616, 731). In the seventh precinct 1 vote (pp. 319, 616, 735). In the first precinct of the first district of Baltimore County 3 votes (pp. 647, 648, 741). In the ninth district of Charles County 1 vote (pp. 467, 755).

Each gained a vote in the fifth precinct of the Seventeenth ward and Compton lost 1 vote. Net loss to Mudd, 19 votes.

To recapitulate:

Vote for sitting member as above		16,280
Vote for contestant as above	16,250	
Deduct net loss on recount	19	
		16,231
Plurality for contestee after recount		49

163

The effect of the contestant has been to show, first, that there was an error of 28 votes in Calvert County; secondly, that votes were tendered for him which were refused, and should have been counted; and thirdly, that there was in the second precinct of the third election district of Anne Arundel County such intimidation as should justify the throwing out of the vote of that precinct.

THE RECOUNT.

It must be borne in mind that the precincts which were recounted (with but one single exception, that of the ninth district of Charles County) adjoined the precincts forming the Fourth Congressional district, in the city of Baltimore, in which Mr. Rayner was the Democratic candidate and Mr. Stockbridge the Republican candidate; and that the discrepancy between the vote as returned and as recounted is explained by the fact that in the hurry of the count Republican tickets, appearing not to be scratched, were counted for Mr. Mudd, while in fact on many of the tickets was printed the name of Mr. Stockbridge.

The count was made under an order of the court, as authorized by the State statutes, it was made in the presence of counsel for contestant, and every protection was thrown around it. The provisions of the State law providing for the security of the ballots are such as to insure their protection, and the evidence clearly shows that in each and every case the law was strictly followed. We can not, under the testimony, for a moment doubt that the ballots counted were the identical ballots that were cast, and when this is clearly shown the ballots are the best evidence of the vote. (McCrary, Ed. secs. 436–443, and 533 ; Paine on Elections, 759 ; Gooding vs. Wilson, 42d Congress; Smith, p. 80; Butler vs. Lehman, 1 Bartlett, 353.)

The law of the State requires the ballot-boxes to be made securely of plate glass, provided with locks ; that at the close of the count the ballot-box shall be locked, key removed therefrom and given to the minority judge; the chief judge takes the ballot-box for safe-keeping, thereupon the judges shall all write their names on a strip of paper of sufficient length for the following purpose; said strip shall be pasted over the key-hole of the ballot-box in such a manner that the signatures shall extend across the opening in the lid (where the ballots are dropped in in voting), and so that when the key is inserted it will tear the paper so pasted over the key-holes ; such paper shall be securely fastened to the box with sealing-wax or other adhesive material. Within three days the ballot-boxes and keys in Baltimore City shall be delivered to the police commissioners, and in the counties to the clerk of the circuit court, and the boxes shall not be opened for six months, except by order of the court or a judge in case of a judicial investigation or contested election. (Sections 79 and 80 of article 33 Maryland Code of Public General Laws, 1888, in Record, pp. 641 and 642.)

We submit that a compliance with these provisions preserves the ballots, and proof of compliance therewith negatives any claim of supposed tampering or handling, and is the strongest possible presumptive evidence that they are the identical ballots.

The contestee proved that each and every box was locked and sealed as required by law, delivered to the chief judge, by him carefully kept in his physical custody, and in Baltimore city delivered the next day to the police commissioners, the key delivered to the minority judge and by him delivered to said police commissioners, and in the counties delivered to the clerk of the court two days thereafter (the testimony as to these facts is found in the record, pp. 277, 278, 280, 281, 301, 304, 309, 310, 311, 312, 314, 315, 316, 447, 448). This testimony is conclusive and uncontradicted.

He examined the police commissioners of Baltimore City, the messenger or officer of the board, the clerk to the board who was in office when the boxes and keys were delivered, and his successor, who was in office at the time the recount was made, proved that the boxes were placed immediately and kept in a prison room on the second floor of the central police station intended for a cell; that the door of this cell or room was locked by a Yale lock, requiring two keys to open it; that one key was kept by the secretary of the board in the safe vault in the secretary's office; that this vault had a combination lock, and the combination was known to no one except the secretary and marshal of police; he proved by the two secretaries and the marshal of police that no one had access to the vault but themselves, and that it was never left open, and contained all the valuables belonging to the police board of the city; that the keys of the ballot-boxes were placed in this vault, and by every one who had the custody of the boxes and keys that they had not been and could not have been handled or tampered with. Also, as each box was produced, that they bore evidence of not having been tampered with. (Record, pp. 276, 280, 282, 300, 304, 308, 309, 413, 414, 415, 416, 417, 418.)

In first precinct of first district of Baltimore County, and ninth district of Charles County, substantially the same facts by the clerks, deputies, and messengers—and the clerk in Baltimore County testified that the ballot-box was carefully locked up in a press by reason of this contest (Record, pp. 444, 445, 446, 447, 448, 452, 460, 461).

If it is possible to prove anything has been carefully and securely kept, it has been proven as regards these ballots, and this having been proven, the primary and best evidence of the true vote of the precincts recounted has been given.

It manifestly appears that the judges counted for each and every Republican candidate all Republican tickets not appearing to be scratched, and thereby gave Mudd votes in cases were Stockbridge's name was printed, and which votes were by accident or design thrown away on Stockbridge.

THE VOTE OF CALVERT COUNTY.

The official returns as made to the governor gave Mr. Mudd 1,138 votes, and Mr. Compton 890 votes (see Record, p. 613, return from the judges of Calvert County). This certificate is dated two days after election and is in the exact form prescribed by the law of the State. (Sec. 69; Record, p. 640.)

It is therefore evidence of the vote of the county unless it is shown to be wrong by the primary evidence, either the ballots themselves or the count as made by the judges of election in each precinct at the close of the election.

The position was taken by the contestee that the evidence offered by the contestant to set aside this return was insufficient and inadmissible for such a purpose. The testimony of the contestant rests largely upon the recollection of the very same persons three months after the election who two days after the election certified to the governor that Mr. Mudd received but 1,138. (Record, pp. 274 and 275.)

The majority of the committee insist that the precinct returns establish the fact. (Record, pp. 746–749.)

It will be seen by the testimony (Record, pp. 274, 275) and the certificates (Record, pp. 746-749) that these copies are made from one of the books. It will be seen by reference to the law of the State (Record, p. 639, sec. 66) that it requires two plain, fair, and distinct statements and certificates of the number of votes which shall have been given " to be made out on the books of the polls," and the law requires two poll-books at each poll. These two statements and certificates on the two poll-books are duplicates; each clerk makes out one, and they should agree. A copy of one is not of itself evidence. To set aside and disprove the solemn return of the return judges nothing less than the production of the two " books" or certified copies of the duplicate returns would suffice. Besides, one of these returns is an imperfect paper in itself, and as a copy is no evidence, as it is neither certified, as required by law, nor in form and substance what the law requires (Record, pp. 747, 639, sec. 67).

As evidence it was specially excepted to by the contestee's counsel (Record, p. 779.)

It is no answer that the contestee might have shown the return wrong if such was the fact; he has a right to stand upon the return as made to the governor until successfully assailed.

And we may here remark that the return judges, who made the return to the governor, were all Republicans, and it is not to be supposed that they would have made such an error against their own candidate. And it is taxing our credulity too far to make us believe such a mistake has been made. And we further observe that in this instance the copy referred to in giving the votes is expressed only in figures, very easily changed or manufactured whilst in the custody of a Republican clerk, while the statute says it " shall be written in words at length and not in figures only."

We think it would be contrary to law and dangerous in practice to allow the judges of election three months after the election, relying on recollection alone, to vary their return based upon such imperfect and partial testimony.

REJECTED VOTES CLAIMED BY EACH SIDE.

Both the contestant and contestee claim that there were votes tendered for them respectively which were improperly rejected by the judges of election.

We have reached the conclusion that whenever a voter did tender his vote and his name was upon the list of voters furnished to the judges of election, although the middle name or initial might be wrongly entered, still his vote should be counted as it should have been received by the judges, the object of registration being for the purpose of identification of a voter, or if the name given by the voter was *idem sonans* with the name registered. By applying this rule a number of votes claimed by each side, as will be hereafter shown, must be rejected.

We base our conclusions upon the provisions of the constitution of Maryland and the acts of assembly governing elections.

The constitution of the State (article 1, section 1) prescribes the qualifications of all voters. Section 5 of the same article provides that the general assembly shall provide for a general registration of all persons possessing the qualifications prescribed by the constitution that the registration shall be conclusive evidence to the judges of the right of the person to vote, and that no person shall vote whose name does not so appear.

The legislature, in accordance with these provisions, have provided for registration, and since the adoption of the constitution of 1864, in which the same provisions appear, all elections have been held under registration laws.

The judges of election are required to take an oath to " permit all persons to vote whose names shall appear on the registry or list of voters furnished to him according to law," and that he " will not permit any one to vote whose name shall not be found upon said registry or list of voters" (record, pp. 6, 36, sec. 48).

In registering voters, the register is required to enter the name, giving at least the first Christian name in full, color, residence, etc., showing street and number, etc., of the applicant (record, p. 624, sec. 14).

The vote of no person whose name did not appear, either properly or at least by " *idem sonans*," could have been received by the judges, nor can they be counted by us.

The contestant, on pages 13 and 14 of his brief, claims forty of these votes; we allow him, for the reasons stated, the following:

M. Hopkins.	James E. Kane.	George H. Mills.
A. W. Herman Miller.	William H. Hill.	William T. Richardson.
Edward Washington.	Jacob Frank.	John T. Bowen.
Daniel E. Gamble.	George W. Smith.	William F. Coats.
Winfield S. Johnson.	William H. Brogden.	James H. Barnes.
John D. Wilder.	Joseph H. Sampson.	In all, 19.
George H. Leutsche.	William Alsop.	

We reject the following, as their names were not, by the testimony of the contestant, on the poll-book or list of voters and presented no certificate as required by law (record, p. 633, sec. 34):

John R. Vitz (25–659).	James W. Green (50).	James W. Thomas (247),
Isaiah Chester (29–67).	John Henry Thomas (48–	Philip Lyles (247).
John H. Costen (32–667).	298).	William Thomas (248).
David W. Leman (45).	Philip Gordon (53–688).	David R. Brooks (266).
Aquilla Fishpaw (49).	Ishmael W. Keller (235).	Charles W. Whittemore (165).
Lev Cure (49).	John F. Thomas (246).	In all, 18.
James W. Clements (50).	Augustin Brown (246).	

As to Benjamin F. Gamble, he does not prove an offer to vote (record, p. 11). The judge of election says he did not offer to vote (291), and his statement that he did not vote because Doctor Hall, the registration officer, said his name was not on the list is contradicted by Doctor Hall, who testifies he was not at the polls that day (328, 420).

As to John Taylor, he declined to vote as John E. Taylor, the only name corresponding to his, and clearly his vote can not be counted (record, p. 26, 27).

As to Robert Reed, he was not properly identified either as to residence by street and number or age (Record, p. 36, 710). He was registered, if at all, in October, 1888, as fifty-four years of age. This man gave his age in January, 1889, as fifty-eight years old—Robert Reed, who was registered, as fifty-four years old October, 1888.

The contestant also claims 6 votes, on page 12 of his brief, which were rejected, as he admits, because these parties had voted or others had voted on the names and they were checked off on the list of votes, namely, William Butler, John H. Smith, William Brown, Charles H. Green, Henry Brown, and Thomas Williams.

If when these parties offered to vote the names they respectively gave where checked, and either they themselves or others had voted on their names, the judges of election could not receive their votes, for the reason that otherwise they would have allowed 2 ballots to be cast by one registered voter. We therefore reject these 6 votes.

As to the 4 votes of Thomas Bell, Samuel H. Booth, Gustavus E.

Cooper, and William Chapman Weems, for reasons above given, we allow the contestant the votes of Samuel H. Booth, Cooper, and Weems, but reject the vote of Thomas Bell, because he was not identified. (Record, pp. 286, 287, 288, 289–292.)

As to the 3 votes claimed on page 22 of contestant's brief upon no principle of fairness can they be allowed.

Not only did he not claim them in his notice, but he attempted in violation of every principle of law to offer this testimony in the time allowed him for rebuttal only. (Rules, p. 4.)

This testimony was in each case specifically excepted to. (Pp. 493, 494, 556, 557.)

The attempt to make this claim in rebuttal comes directly within the case of Lynch vs. Vandiver, Mobley, p. 659, in which the committee say that "testimony offered in rebuttal which seeks to establish facts not entered into in the direct examination, is in violation of every known principle of the laws of evidence, and will not be considered."

The contestee had no opportunity to show that these parties had not tendered their votes, or any other evidence tending to deny the claim made by contestant.

The contestant in his brief relies upon the act of Congress of May 31, 1870. This act was declared unconstitutional by the Supreme Court. (United States vs. Reese, 92 U. S. Rep., p. 214.)

We therefore allow the contestant 19 of the votes claimed by him on pages 13 and 14 of his brief, and three claimed on page 16 in all, 22 votes claimed by contestee to have been wrongfully rejected.

Applying the same rule to the contestee, we allow him of the votes claimed by him on page 20 of his brief, the following: Andrew Lainhart, George H. Cummings, John E. Garnett, James W. Wheatley, John H. Iglehadt, William K. Dawson, B. L. Gover, Clifford Sweeny, Ferdinand E. Birch, and Benjamin F. Chappelear; in all, 10 votes.

We reject the following: Charles F. Buckler, Charles W. McCready, John W. Todd, John H. Turner, Richard H. Canter, John Kalb, Edward Woods, Francis Tolson, James Edelin, Andrew V. Conway, Charles Soper, Albert Berry, and Dalton H. Fisher, because their names were not on the poll-book or list of voters.

We also reject William R. Thomas, because his name had been voted; in all, 14.

VOTE NOT COUNTED FOR COMPTON IN SEVENTH DISTRICT OF ST. MARY'S COUNTY.

The contestee is clearly entitled to this vote, his name was written under Mudd's, and the writing must prevail. (McCrary, 3d edition, sec. 508.)

Mudd, therefore, loses one vote in St. Mary's, and Compton gains one.

Contestant claims that one vote for Compton in 2d district of Calvert County was scratched, the judges held differently, and properly counted the vote for Compton. (Record 271–272.)

Weight is to be given to the decision of judges of election. (McCrary, 3d ed., 465.)

Contestant claims a vote for him was wrongly rejected in the sixth district of Charles County.

A paster was pasted over the words "for Congress." The testimony of the judges, Sasscer and Cox, clearly shows this (record, pp. 456–457). Article 33, section 65, Statutes of Maryland (record, p. 639), required the ticket should be thrown out.

To recapitulate—official vote, as made to the governor:

Compton	16,000
Add vote of Charles County	191
Not before the governor	89
	280
Add vote for "Compton"	1
Add 1 vote, seventh district, St. Mary's County	1
Add votes allowed, but rejected by judges of election	10
	16,292
Mudd, official vote	15,819
Add vote of Charles County, fifth and ninth districts	432
Add votes allowed, but rejected by judges of election	22
Add vote for " Mudd," S. N. Mudd, and S. E. Mudd	3
	16,276
Deduct loss on recount	20
Deduct 1 vote, seventh district of St. Mary's County	1
	21
	16,255
Plurality for contestee	37

We allow in this enumeration the vote for " Mudd," S. N. Mudd and S. E. Mudd, to contestant's and also allow upon the same principle the vote for " Compton " in Prince George's, as it was returned to the governor, and appears on the certificate (Exhibit Compton No. 16), as filed in evidence before the committee.

FIRST PRECINCT OF THIRD ELECTION DISTRICT OF ANNE ARUNDEL COUNTY.

The effort of the contestant has been to reject the vote of this precinct upon the ground that there was such intimidation and violence as prevented a free and fair election.

The law is well settled that the poll can not be rejected unless the violence was such a display of force as ought to have intimidated men of ordinary firmness. (McCrary on Elections, sec. 416, 2d edition.)

The contestee claims, and the evidence to our mind sustains the position, that no such intimidation, force, or violence was resorted to.

The evidence shows on the part of the contestant—

(1) That the only guns on the ground that day were some guns which had been brought there by persons, some colored and some white, who were on their way gunning, it being shown to be a long-established custom of many voters in that part of the county (white and colored) to make election day a day of hunting. That the only pistol-shots fired were by some young men, nowhere near the polls, who were shooting at a mark.

(2) That instead of it being true that there were any such acts of violence as were calculated to intimidate persons of ordinary firmness, the true state of the case is just this: 1. Not long after the polls were opened (they were opened at 8 a. m.) and after some few white men had voted, a body of colored men, numbering about 100 men, who had assembled at a place called the " Mill Pond," about 100 yards from the polls, marched in a body to the polling place, and after some 15 of them had voted, 2 of their number, Hall and Andrew Sampson, who were in the line, were by some young man standing there pushed or shoved out of the line, and told they had no right to vote there, and thereupon Hall, whom the evidence shows had taken an active part in distributing tickets among the colored voters, and was looked

up to as a leader among them, after addressing certain remarks to those around, ordered, according to a large number of the witnesses, and advised, according to others, the whole line of negroes away from the polls, which order or advice was at once obeyed, and in consequence of this order or advice, which was subsequently given to others already at the polling places or on their way thereto, nearly every one if not every one of the 175 colored people referred to in contestant's allegation abstained from voting.

(3) That according to some of the witnesses it was the same young man who pushed or threw out of line both Hall and Sampson; but at all events, according to the evidence of a number of the contestant's own witnesses, the whole number of the class of persons described by some of the witnesses as "strangers," and by others as "roughs," and who are alleged to have caused the intimidation of the 175 negro voters, was but three.

(4) That according to the contestant's own proof, there were from 50 to 100 colored voters in line, when the two men, Hall and Sampson, were shoved or pushed out of line; and this number was further increased shortly after, as most did not leave the grounds till after 12 o'clock, and there were 161 on the grounds during that time.

(5) That according to the overwhelming mass of evidence, as given by the contestant's own witnesses, no blows were struck at any time, no fire-arms used or shown, no threats of personal violence made, not even the hunting guns had then been brought to the grounds when the trouble with Hall and Sampson took place.

(6) According to the contestant's own evidence none of the 175 votes were ever tendered to the judges; on the contrary the voters admit that they refused to tender their votes.

The three judges of election and two clerks were examined.

The contestant examined two of the judges of election, Hines and Jubb; Hines is a Republican, and Jubb, though professing to be a Democrat, was bitterly opposed to Mr. Compton. All the judges and clerks were appointed by the county commissioners of Anne Arundel County, all of whom were Republicans. (Page 342.)

At the close of the polls on the day of election all of the judges of election, without protest or demur of any kind, signed the certificate of election, setting forth the holding of the election and the number of votes each candidate had received. (Record, page 718.)

And on the very next day after the election Hines. the Republican judge, who was the return judge, went to Annapolis with the ballot-box and election returns, and there told Mr. Sprigg Harwood, the clerk of the circuit court for Anne Arundel County, to whom he delivered his returns and box, "that there had been no trouble about the polls; everything has passed off peaceably and quietly." (Record, page 397. See also confirmatory evidence of Woodward, page 435.)

Hines testified that he had never been judge of election before (Record, p. —). In this he is contradicted by a large number of witnesses, and it is shown that he had been judge of election three times before. He first denied he had made any statement to Mr. Harwood. He afterwards said he told Mr. Harwood the election was not fair, and when recalled testifies that he said to Mr. Harwood it was fair inside but unfair outside. He contradicted himself so much his testimony is unreliable

The contestee examined Charles H. Williams, the Democratic judge, and both clerks. Testimony of Charles H. Williams was that he was at the polls and in the room from before the polls opened till the ballots were counted; that he neither saw nor heard any disturbance. (Record, pages 342-344.)

The testimony of Dunlap (p. 453) and Heath (p. 376), the two clerks of the election, was to the same effect.

Of the five officers of election, all appointed, as shown by Williams's testimony (p. 342), by the Republican county commissioners, three testified that the election was quiet and peaceable; and two, one a bitter personal as well as political enemy of the contestee, and the other contradicting himself so frequently that his testimony is unreliable, testifying that there was a disturbance.

And here we may note a significant fact, that the contestant in an effort to sustain Jubb, his witness, called John W. Williams, who testifies that while he would believe Jubb and Hines, that in a case where Williams and others testified one way and Hines and Jubb to the contrary he would not believe Jubb and Hines. (Record, p. —.)

The testimony of this army of negroes, 175, who were there or near there, shows when carefully digested that they did not vote, because Hall, the captain, ordered them not to vote. (Record, p. 92, 97, 98, 103, 106, 107, 109, 116, 119). The following is a sample (206).

The testimony of contestee shows that Hall did give this order or advice, and for this reason they did not vote. (Evidence of Chairs, 350; Wales, 361; D. H. Williams, 366; Henry Johnson, 372; Watson, 378; S. W. Chairs, 379; Ellers, 38; Porter, 384; Brothe, 381.)

The testimony of Zachariah Gray, a constable (record p. 357), who was there all day, shows that the only pistol fired was at a mark 100 yards from the polls, and that he stopped it because it frightened the horses.

The only pistol-firing shown by contestant is the evidence of William H. Jubb (p. 242). He testifies that others were present, not one of whom, though examined by contestant, testified to the fact. His cross-examination shows him to be a man of no character.

If the principle attempted to be applied by the majority of the committee is adopted, that a district or precinct is to be thrown out because a number of voters do not attempt to exercise the right of suffrage, or because a leader insists, as Hall did, that those of his own party shall not vote, all that will be necessary in the future to deprive voters of their choice is that a few shall desist from voting, and the votes of the majority will become nugatory.

After a careful review of the entire testimony touching the matter of intimidation, we think that a candid and fair judgment of this House will be that it is insufficient to authorize us to reject the votes of those citizens who did cast their votes. And we think that the real purpose of this man Hall in collecting his negro partisans and marching to the polls at an early hour when there were but few white men at the polls, was, in fact, not to exercise his right of suffrage orderly and peacefully, but to seize any trifling circumstance which would authorize him to retire and give his orders to his followers not to vote, and in this manner to so antagonize his white neighbors as to have them disfranchised. Therefore, we recommend the passage of the following resolutions:

Resolved, That S. E. Mudd was not elected as a Representative to the Fifty-first Congress from the Fifth Congressional district of Maryland.

Resolved, That Barnes Compton was duly elected, and is entitled to retain his seat.

L. W. MOORE, of Texas.
CHARLES F. CRISP.
CHARLES T. O'FERRALL.
LEVI MAISH.
R. P. C. WILSON, of Missouri.

FRANK H. THREET vs. RICHARD H. CLARKE.

FIRST ALABAMA.

Contestant charged that the majority returned for contestee was obtained by systematic fraud on the part of the officers of election in counting for contestee votes in fact cast for contestant.

The committee find the frauds proved in the testimony insufficient to overcome the majority returned. The minority agree in the conclusion, but announce their dissent from some of the reasoning by which it is reached.

The resolutions presented were adopted by the House March 7, 1890, without debate or division. See Record page 2007.

(1) **Frauds.** *At prior elections.*

Frauds at prior elections and the obstruction to the taking of testimony in prior election contests may, and often do, throw light upon the political situation in a community, but can not be taken as an excuse for not attempting earnestly in subsequent contests to comply with the rules of evidence. Every election must rest upon its own merits.

(2) **Conspiracy.** *Partisan appointment of elections boards, evidence of.*

Where the course is systematically pursued, of appointing on the election boards to represent the minority or opposition party, persons not indorsed by that party, and as to whose loyalty to the party whose interests they are expected to guard there is a question, or of appointing persons who are unable to read and write, when there would be no difficulty in finding men well qualified in those respects, this ought of itself to be considered evidence of conspiracy to defraud on the part of the election officers.

173

REPORT.

FEBRUARY 21, 1890.—Mr. HAUGEN, from the Committee on Elections, submitted the following report:

The Committee on Elections, having had under consideration the contested election case of Frank H. Threet, contestant, against Richard H. Clarke, contestee, from the First Congressional district of Alabama, submits the following report:

The contestant and contestee were the Republican and Democratic candidates, respectively, for Representative in the Fifty-first Congress, at the election held on November 6, 1888. The contestee received the certificate of election, has duly qualified and entered upon his duties and is now occupying his seat as Representative of the district.

The certificate of the secretary of state showing the vote cast for contestant and contestee, respectively, reads as follows:

THE STATE OF ALABAMA,
OFFICE OF SECRETARY OF STATE.

From the returns made to this office by the boards of supervisors of the various counties composing the First Congressional district of Alabama, it appears that the following votes were cast for a Representative to the Fifty-first Congress from said district.

Counties.	Candidates.		
	R. H. Clarke.	Frank H. Threet.	Scattering.
Choctaw	1,382	633	
Clarke	1,564	1,234	
Marengo	3,480	1,847	
Mobile	3,220	2,408	
Monroe	1,440	766	
Washington	507	217	2
	11,593	7,105	

I, C. C. Langdon, secretary of state, do hereby certify that the foregoing is a correct statement of the returns made to my office, as required by law, of the election held on the first Tuesday after the first Monday in November, 1888, for a Representative in the Fifty-first Congress of the United States from the First Congressional district of Alabama.

Witness my hand, and the great seal of the State, at the Capitol in the city of Montgomery, this —— day of ——, 1888.

C. C. LANGDON,
Secretary of State.

[SEAL.]

A plurality for contestee of 4,488 on the face of the returns. This plurality the contestant contends was obtained by systematic frauds on the part of the inspectors and clerks of election in counting votes in fact cast for contestant as having been cast for contestee in a number of precincts, large enough to have elected him (contestant) had the returns been honestly made. The contestant in his brief describes the method pursued by his party friends at the polls, and the evidence he relies upon to establish the charges of conspiracy to defraud him as follows:

At every beat or voting precinct two or more leading Republicans would give out the Republican ballots to their Republican friends, and two or more trusted Republicans would watch and witness that they were voted; each kept an accurate account of the number of tickets he gave out and the number he saw voted. The contestant put these witnesses on the stand to prove these facts, and the vote proven was almost in the inverse ratio of the vote as counted by the precinct officers.

Such is the status of the present contest and mainly the character of the testimony of the contestant.

The charges of contestant are confined to the four counties of Choctaw, Clarke, Marengo, and Monroe, and only to those precincts in said four counties hereinafter discussed.

It appears upon examination of the evidence that the contestant has strictly confined himself to the method of proof described in his brief.

CHOCTAW COUNTY.

Mount Sterling beat.—The contestant charges that at this precinct he was deprived of fifty-nine (59) votes for the reason that the regularly appointed registrar refused to issue to that number of Republican voters proper certificates of their registration. It seems to be conceded by witnesses for contestee that 59 voters with tickets having the name of contestant upon them appeared and offered to vote, but were refused because they could not furnish certificates of registration, the registrar about 10 o'clock a. m. refusing to issue further certificates, stating that he was out of blanks, and shortly afterwards being called away; that several hours intervened before the inspectors offered to appoint another registrar, which they finally did, failing however to find any person willing to serve.

It is not charged that the registrar acted fraudulently in refusing to continue to issue certificates. His supply of blanks seems to have been exhausted, and he was called away to attend the sick-bed of his father-in-law, who, in fact, died a few days later. The probate judge of the county, who was present according to his own testimony, between 3 and 4 o'clock p. m., with the consent of the inspectors, offered to swear, orally, those who had previously voted in the precinct, and the inspectors offered to receive the votes of those so sworn.

But there is no evidence showing how many of the fifty-nine voters yet remained at the polls or how many of them, being legal voters, had previously voted at the precinct.

Section 2007, Revised Statutes of the United States, reads as follows:

Whenever under the constitution or laws of any State, or the laws of any Territory, any act is required to be done by a citizen as a prerequisite to qualify or entitle him to vote, the offer of such citizen to perform the act required to be done, shall, if it fail to be carried into execution, by reason of the wrongful act or omission of the person or officer charged with the duty of receiving or permitting such performance, or offer to perform or acting thereon, be deemed and held as a performance in law of such act; and the person so offering and failing to vote, and being otherwise qualified, shall be entitled to vote in the same manner and to the same extent as if he had in fact performed such act.

Under this law the 59 votes at the precinct under discussion must be counted for contestant.

CLARKE COUNTY.

Gainesville precinct.—The returning officer was the only officer of election who appeared at the opening of the polls on the day of election.

He proceeded, at the instance of contestant's friends, to appoint three inspectors, who were chosen from the colored party friends of contestant. These appointed two clerks.

This was in pursuance of section 262, Code of Alabama, 1876. Two of these inspectors and one of the clerks testify on behalf of contestant, and from their testimony it appears that the election proceeded quietly until about 3 o'clock p. m., when during a lull in the voting and following a seemingly well-established custom in that precinct, the election officers opened the ballot-box and proceeded to count the votes cast. It then transpired that none of the inspectors could read the ballots. This broke up the election and the ballot-box was carried off by the returning officer, seemingly without protest or objection.

One of the inspectors swears that 179 votes had been cast at the time the balloting was interrupted. His testimony also tends to show that four of these were white men and the rest colored. There is no evidence showing how these parties voted.

The voters were not called as witnesses, and no effort has been made to ascertain how the votes actually cast stood, and the committee can find no precedent for counting the 175 votes claimed by contestant for him. If these votes were cast for him, he has failed to show it, and the failure to have the true result declared was caused by no fault or fraud of contestee or his party friends, unless the failure of the regularly appointed inspectors of election to act be considered a fraud, but was occasioned wholly by the illiteracy of the party friends of contestant.

There can be no effective citizenship that is not based upon intelligence and education sufficient to take part in the active administration of the laws.

MARENGO COUNTY.

Dayton beat.—Three witnesses testify for contestant and eight for contestee in regard to this precinct.

The precinct returned 307 votes for contestee and 87 for contestant, while contestant claims that 402 votes should be returned for him, and, because of frauds committed by the partisans of contestee, none should be returned for contestee.

Doc Daniel, a witness for contestant, testifies that he is a resident of Dayton beat, has lived there three years and was present at the election in question:

Quest. Was you present at said election? And, if so, state how many votes were polled or voted by the qualified electors of said beat on said day for said office. How many of said votes were voted or polled for Frank H. Threet for said office, and how many for Richard H. Clarke?

Ans. I was present; three hundred and eighty-seven Republican votes and eighty Democratic votes were polled.

Quest. Whose name for Congress was on the 387 Republican tickets that you say were voted?—Ans. F. H. Threet.

Quest. Who distributed the ballots or votes with Frank H. Threet's name on them at said election and beat on that day, and how many were distributed?—Ans. I distributed them; I can not tell how many were distributed.

Quest. Did anybody else beside you distribute any of said votes at said precinct on that day, and, if so, who? How many did you distribute?—Ans. Yes, William Mathews and Charley Perkins; I distributed 80.

H. Mis. 137——12

Quest. Whose name for member of Congress was on these tickets that you and the other parties distributed as you say ? What was done with these ballots after they were distributed ?—Ans. F. H. Threet's name was on these ballots, and they were voted after they were distributed.

Quest. Who acted as inspectors at said election and who acted as returning officer and clerks and to what political party did they respectively belong ?—Ans. Mr. R. W. Price, H. W. Morgan, and W. W. Bruce acted as inspectors; Alec Archer and Capt. Harder were the clerks; I don't know who was the returning officer; they all belonged to the Democratic party.

Quest. State whether the votes were fairly counted at said election as cast.

Ans. I don't know, sir.

Quest. Did any one keep a list or tally of the names of the persons who voted for Frank H. Threet for said office at said election and precinct ? If yea, who kept such list ?—Ans. Nora Walton and Lee Parker kept a tally of the number, but not of the names.

Quest. How many Democrats, if you know, lived in said beat on the day of said election, and how many of them voted in said beat on that day ; and how many Republicans lived in that beat on that day, and how many of them voted at said election for Frank H. Threet ?—Ans. I don't know how many Democrats lived in said beat, and I do not know how many voted on that day ; to the best of my knowledge 460 Republicans lived in that beat on that day ; 387 of them voted for Frank H. Threet.

Quest. How many of said votes for Frank H. Threet did you see cast on that day ?—Ans. Seventy-five (75).

Quest. Was said Threet a popular or unpopular candidate ?

Ans. He was a popular candidate.

Quest. Was he not warmly supported by the Republican party in his district ?

Ans. Yes, he was warmly supported by the Republican party that day in his district.

Quest. Tell all that you know about the manner in which the election was held in your precinct; if there was any intimidation and unfair counting of the vote; tell all you know about it.

Ans. I don't know if there was any intimidation or not; I don't know if there was any unfair counting or not ; so far as I know about the conducting part, I give one man a ticket, and Israel Clarke came and took the man away from me, and took the ticket away from him and scratched something on it, and I didn't know what until he came back to me and gave the ticket back to me; Israel Clarke had scratched out two names on the ticket that I gave the man ; the names were F. H. Threet and Mr. Williams; I took the ticket from him and he went on with Israel Clarke.

Cross-examination :

Quest. How do you distinguish a Democratic ticket from a Republican ticket ?—Ans. I look at them with the names on them; one is longer than the other.

Quest. Do you tell them by the names on them, and the length, too ?—Ans. Yes.

Quest. Which is the longest, the Democratic or Republican ticket ?—Ans. The Democratic.

Quest. How many Democratic tickets did you see that day ?—Ans. About 300.

Quest. How many Republican tickets did you read that day ?

I read 75.

Quest. How far were you standing from the polls ?—Ans. About 9 to 10 steps, all day long.

Quest. Did you see Wash. Jones on that day ?—Ans. Yes, sir.

Quest. What was he doing on that day ?—Ans He was distributing tickets—Republican tickets.

Quest. How many of the tickets he distributed did you read over or measure ?—Ans. I did not read over or measure any ; but they came from the same package as those I distributed.

Quest. How far was Wash. Jones standing from the polls ?—Ans. He was standing 9 steps from the polls and about 6 steps from me, and opposite to me.

Quest. Was there not another election officer at the election at Dayton that day that you have not mentioned ?—Ans. Nary one that I remember.

Quest. Was not Jack Crawford an officer of that election ?—Ans. He was.

Quest. What are Jack Crawford's politics ?—Ans. Republican.

Quest. How long have you known Jack Crawford ?—Ans. Three years.

Quest. Do you know his general character in the community in which he lives ?—Ans. Yes, sir.

Quest. Is it good or bad ?—Ans. As far as I know it is very good.

Quest. Do you know the characters of Robt. W. Price, Henry W. Morgan, W. W. Bruce, C. H. Askew, A. H. Archer, and Capt. Harder in the community in which they live ?—Ans. I do.

Quest. Is the character of each one of them good or bad?—Ans. Very good.

Quest. Could you select from the neighborhood of Dayton beat six men that stand higher in that community as good citizens and men of integrity?—Ans. I could not.

Quest. Do you know the Rev. Mr. Moreland?—Ans. I do; I am not a member of his church.

Quest. Do you know Israel Clarke?—Ans. I do.

Quest. Do you know his general character?—Ans. Yes; he stands as high in that community as any man, colored or white.

Quest. What are his politics?—Ans. Democratic.

Quest. How long has he been a Democrat?—Ans. I don't know sir.

Quest. How did he vote in the last election?—Ans. Democrat.

Quest. What do you mean by Democrat?—Ans. He voted a Democrat ticket; one of the long tickets.

Quest. Why did he vote Democratic in this last election?—Ans. I don't know.

Quest. How has Israel Clarke voted since he was twenty-one, up to the present time?—Ans. I don't know.

Quest. How many times has Frank Threet run for Congress in this district?—Ans. I don't know.

Quest. Do you know Sam Williams?—Ans. Yes, sir.

Quest. Were you at the meeting at the church the night before the election; was Sam Williams there?
Ans. I was; I didn't see Sam there.

Quest. Was Sam Williams one of the 387 that you say voted for Threet?—Ans. He was not.

Quest. At the meeting held at the church the night before the election were not the voters present sworn to vote the Republican ticket the next day?—Ans. They were not.

Quest. How many were present?—Ans. I don't know, sir.

Quest. Who was the man that Israel Clarke took off from you that day?—Ans. Richard Nathan.

Quest. How many tickets do you say were distributed that day?—Ans. I don't know.

Rebutting questions:

Quest. Please state why you did not give the names of all the persons who distributed tickets when asked on your direct examination?—Ans. I intended to do so, but was interrupted by having another question asked me before I got through naming them all.

Quest. Did you say that Israel Clarke is Democratic in politics?—Ans. Yes, sir.

Quest. How many colored Democrats was there in Dayton beat?—Ans. I don't know, sir.

Quest. Do you know any other colored Democrat except Israel Clarke?—Ans. Yes, sir; Dick Browning.

Quest. Do you know any others besides Israel Clarke and Dick Browning?
I do not.

The testimony of this witness has been quoted at length for the reason that it does not vary materially from that offered as to other precincts in Marengo County, and discloses the general theory of contestant's case. Charles Perkins and William Mathews are offered in support of the testimony of Doc. Daniels. The former swears that he was present at the election; that about 480 votes were polled; that he does not know how many were cast for the contestant and how many for contestee; that he was issuing Republican tickets to Republican voters, and "issued" 75; "the voters put them in the window"; says about 80 Democrats and about 400 Republicans lived in the precinct; that the contestant was popular with the colored voters.

Witness saw nothing unfair about the counting. Cross-examined he testifies to the general good character of the officers conducting the election, except as to one of them, a colored Democrat, Israel Clarke; but on that point he contradicts the testimony of Doc. Daniels, given above.

William Mathews, the third witness, was chairman of the Republican executive committee for Dayton beat and distributed tickets at this election; distributed 150 tickets, and says, "They were put in the

window—voted." "About 385 Republican votes were polled there that
day, and probably 80 some odd Democratic." The colored people generally voted the Republican ticket. Like the other witnesses, he says
the contestant was a popular candidate, and was warmly supported,
and corroborates them as to the good character of the officers conducting the election. On this evidence the contestant asks that the returns
from this precinct be subverted; that 402 votes be given to him and
none to his opponent.

This evidence, standing alone and uncontradicted, would, in the opinion of the committee, overcome the prima facie character of the returns
and is competent evidence of the charge of conspiracy and fraud on the
part of the officers of the election.

But the case does not rest here.

The contestee calls as a witness J. Crawford, the United States supervisor, a Republican, appointed on the recommendation and at the
request of contestant, who testifies to his constant presence at the
polls during the voting and the count, and who swears unqualifiedly
that the election was fairly conducted and the returns honestly made.
He is corroborated by R. W. Price, the Democratic United States supervisor, as to the fairness and honesty of the election.

Israel C. Clark, Richard Browning, and John H. Webb, colored men
(two swearing they are Republicans), testify that they supported the
contestee, and that contestant did not enjoy the full confidence of his
colored Republican brethren.

Frauds at prior elections and the obstruction to the taking of testimony in prior election contests may, and often do, throw light upon the
political situation in a community, but cannot be taken as an excuse
for not attempting earnestly in subsequent contests to comply with the
rules of evidence. Every election must rest upon its own merits. The
honesty of the election officers testified to by contestant's witnesses is
wholly inconsistent with his theory of a conspiracy carried out by those
very officers to defraud him.

Faunsdale beat.—Two witnesses were called for contestant. Their
testimony tends to show that they distributed the Republican tickets at
the polls; that five of the officers of election were Democrats and two
Republicans; that the witnesses were distributing tickets at the front
end of the building, at the rear end of which the voters handed in their
ballots through a window, and that from the position of the witnesses
the window could not be seen; that no one was permitted to remain at
the back of the house except the voters and the police. This is certainly very slight evidence upon which to rest the charge of conspiracy
and fraud. The contestee called as witnesses the Republican United
States supervisor, appointed at the instance of contestant, and the Republican chairman of the executive committee of the precinct, who both
testify to the regularity and fairness of the election. They are supported by the evidence of seventeen other witnesses called by contestee. These witnesses stand unimpeached. The individual voters were
not called, and the returns must stand as made.

It should be stated that under the law of Alabama each political
party is entitled to challengers at or near the polls, but no other person
is permitted within 30 feet of the polls.

Magnolia or Hamden beat.—Ben Craig swears that Jack Northrup
distributed the Republican tickets; that witness kept a list of them,
and gives the names of 85 voters to whom Republican tickets were delivered; that he saw these voters go to the polls with these tickets;

that his view of the polls was unobstructed; that he and Northrup were "not over 20 yards" from the polls; that the votes were not fairly counted, "because they (the inspectors) reported 30 and I reported 85 Republican votes."

He is corroborated by Albert Hays, who testifies that each voter as he proceeded to the polls carried his ticket in his hand where witness could see it.

This under the rule laid down is competent evidence as to the number of Republican votes cast at this precinct, and throws upon contestee the burden of showing the fairness and legality of the proceedings. The Republican United States supervisor within the poll either failed to do his duty, or his silence must be taken as evidence of the absence of fraud. Seven witnesses for contestee, including several of the election officers, testify to the fairness of the election. Individual voters were not examined.

The evidence before the committee relative to the precincts of Jefferson, Linden, Macon, McKinley, Nixon's Store, Spring Hill, and Shiloh is substantially of the same character as that of the last three precincts.

If the results at all these polls were, as alleged by contestant, tainted by fraud and corruption to such an extent that the polls should be excluded, he has failed, in the opinion of your committee, to exercise that diligence which the law asks of every suitor before granting him the relief prayed for. Bearing in mind that the character and tendency of the proof is very similar in all these precincts, the contestant might reasonably have been expected to have, at least, in one or a few of them, called in the body of the voters of the precinct and established his claim of fraud, if fraud existed, beyond question. He does not even pretend to have made an effort to do so in this contest, but tries to excuse his want of effort in this respect because, as he alleges, in some previous contest that course had failed.

To quote from his brief:

To call the voters themselves was the best and surest means of successfully proving that the count was fraudulent. When this was attempted by the contestant the contestee would cross-examine each witness for three days, and in some instances a whole week, asking the witness all about the Bible and the history of the world from Adam down. (See testimony in the contest of McDuffie vs. Davidson, 50th Cong.) The object of this proceeding was to consume time, and as the contestant only had forty days allowed by law in which to take testimony-in-chief, it can be readily seen how difficult, if not impossible, it was to secure sufficient proof from the voters to establish the fraud, as only a few could be examined by reason of the obstructive tactics of the contestee.

It is only fair to the contestee to say that the evidence fails to disclose that any of the obstructive methods mentioned in contestant's brief were resorted to by him, and he cannot be held responsible for the sins of his predecessors. A close examination of the record bears evidence that the taking of testimony was conducted in a very leisurely manner on the part of contestant, and that, although the number of his witnesses is relatively small, his side of the case was not closed until the middle of March.

In Jefferson beat he calls three witnesses to prove the alleged frauds; contestee calls thirteen to prove the honesty and fairness of the election. So in Linden, contestant calls two witnesses, contestee twelve; in Macon, contestant two, contestee five; McKinley, contestant four, contestee three; Nixon's Store, contestant two, contestee three; Spring Hill, contestant two, contestee eight; Shiloh, contestant three, contestee eleven.

Section 259, Code of Alabama, provides:

SEC. 259. *Inspectors and precinct returning officers, how appointed.*—The judge of probate, sheriff, clerk of the circuit court, or any two of them, must, at least thirty days before the holding of any election in their county, appoint three inspectors for each place of voting, *two of which shall be members of opposing political parties, if practicable,* and one returning officer for each precinct to act at the place of holding elections in each precinct; and it shall be the duty of the sheriff to notify such inspectors and returning officers of their appointment within ten days after such appointment.

The testimony of Anthony R. Davison, chairman of the Republican executive committee of Monroe County, is to the effect that he prepared lists of inspectors in the various precincts, one for each precinct who could read and write, and who were reputed to be good Republicans, and gave the list to the sheriff, and requested the board to appoint them. They were not appointed, but men were appointed in lieu of them who could not read and write, or were not Republicans, but they were all colored men, and some of them had been recognized by Republicans as being colored Democrats for years. He says:

All the clerks and inspectors so far as I know were Democrats. There were some that were good appointments, but taking them on a whole, they were not good appointments.

This evidence is undisputed.

The committee is of the opinion that where the course is systematically pursued, of appointing on the election boards to represent the minority or opposition party, persons not indorsed by that party, and as to whose loyalty to the party whose interests they are expected to guard there is a question, or of appointing persons who are unable to read and write, when there would be no difficulty in finding men well qualified in those respects, this ought of itself to be considered evidence of conspiracy to defraud on the part of the election officers. This was clearly a violation of the law on the part of the board.

The contestant, however, has confined his proof to only two precincts in this county, viz, Monroeville and Buena Vista.

Monroeville precinct.—At this precinct the duly appointed inspectors did not qualify or serve at the election. It does not appear from the record that the three persons appointed and who did serve as inspectors, were not qualified electors of the precinct, nor that the election was not fairly and honestly conducted.

Buena Vista precinct.—Nelson Burgess testifies that, during the counting of the ballots, he was watching the proceedings with others, through the window; that one of the supervisors, George Lyons, was seen to crumple up several tickets—as high as sixty—and throw them on the floor; that there were two Republican officials in the room, one a United States supervisor and supporter of contestant, but they were crowded away from the table where the count was conducted and unable to see what was being done; that several other parties witnessed the misconduct of the inspector and commented upon it at the time. There is no evidence as to the actual number of votes cast for contestant and contestee respectively at this precinct. One hundred and thirty-five were returned for contestee and 38 for contestant.

The facts testified to by Nelson Burgess stand uncontradicted, and this poll should be excluded from the count.

Disregard and violation of the election laws appear to have taken place in various precincts in this district, but the record fails, in the opinion of the committee, to disclose that the number of votes counted for contestee illegally, or as the result of such frauds, changed the result of the election. The committee has not, therefore, in this report entered into a minute discussion of all the precincts called in question by contestant in his brief and in the argument of his counsel.

The committee is anxious to do justice to the parties coming before it, appreciating the importance of a correct decision on its part, not only to the contesting parties, but to the district where the contest arose, the people of which are entitled to have the case decided upon its merits, and not upon a too technical construction of the law.

After a fair and liberal consideration of this case, the committee is of the opinion that the contestant has failed to prove the charges contained in his notice and his right to the seat now occupied by his adversary.

The committee recommends the adoption of the following resolution :

Resolved, that Richard H. Clarke was duly elected a Representative to the Fifty-first Congress of the United States from the First Congressional district of Alabama at an election held November 6, 1888, and is entitled to a seat therein, and that Frank H. Threet was not elected a Representative at said election.

VIEWS OF THE MINORITY.

MARCH 7, 1890.—Mr. CRISP, from the Committee on Elections, submitted the following as the views of the minority:

The undersigned, members of the Committee on Elections, never having seen, or had an opportunity of seeing, the report filed in the above-stated case until after the same was reported to the House and printed, were unable to ascertain upon what grounds the committee would in such report base its judgment.

Having examined such report, we find ourselves unable to agree to the reasoning therein, and this is intended to express such disagreement.

We concur in said report only so far as the same recommends the adoption of a resolution declaring that Threet was not elected and that Clarke was.

CHARLES F. CRISP.
JOS. H. OUTHWAITE.
R. P. C. WILSON.
CHAS. T. O'FERRALL.
LEVI MAISH.
L. W. MOORE.

185

FRANCIS B. POSEY vs. WM. F. PARRETT.

FIRST INDIANA.

Illegal voting was alleged by both sides. Charges of bribery were also made in the pleadings, but no evidence presented to sustain them. The committee find some illegal votes, but not sufficient to change the plurality returned for contestee.

The resolutions presented were adopted April 16, 1890, by a vote of 125 to 4 (on division). The debate will be found on pages 3444 to 3451.

(1) **Evidence.** *In chief taken in time for rebuttal.*

The rights of the House under the Constitution are not abridged by the act regulating the manner of taking testimony in contested-election cases, but each Congress in enforcing those rights will not depart from the terms of the act except for cause. Where no reasons are presented for taking testimony in chief during the time for rebuttal, the committee will not consider such testimony.

(2) **Residence.** *Of students in college.*

Residence is a mixed question of fact and intention; the fact without also the intention is not sufficient of itself to establish a legal residence. And it is a well settled principle of the cases that one who leaves his home to go to college for the purpose of an education does not from continuance there the required time gain a residence. On the contrary, the very object of his stay raises a presumption against such result. The question in regard to students is " whether they have ever given up their last residence and undertaken to acquire another at the college. To do so they must either directly have renounced their former home and assumed the obligations of citizens in their place of adoption, or done acts, open and acknowledged, inconsistent with the one and assertive of the other." The students having testified that they had made the college town their residence, and their being no evidence that this intention was not formed and acted on in good faith, the committee would not be justified, under the state of the evidence in this case, in rejecting their votes.

187

REPORT.

APRIL 3, 1890.—Mr. BERGEN, from the Committee on Elections, submitted the following report:

The Committee on Elections, having had under consideration the case of Francis B. Posey, contestant, against William F. Parrett, contestee, from the First Congressional district of Indiana, submits the following report:

At an election held on the 6th of November, 1888, the contestant was the Republican candidate and the contestee was the Democratic candidate for Representative from the district to this Congress. The contestee, on the face of the official returns, had a plurality of 20 votes over the contestant and is in possession of the seat. His right to the seat, notwithstanding the notice and answer, is contested solely on the ground of illegal votes—that certain votes cast for him should be deducted from the number reported in his favor. This is resisted on his part, and to the claim he makes a counter-claim that certain other votes cast for contestant should be deducted from the number contestant claims to have received. There are thus 105 votes brought in question by the contestant and 75 by the contestee. The grounds relied upon by the parties in their objections to these votes are either non-residence, minority, insanity, drunkenness, marked tickets, or bribery.

The only evidence of bribery in the case is produced on the part of the contestant to prove that three Republican voters were approached by Democrats and their votes bought. The effort is unsuccessful and the charges are not sustained. It is matter of congratulation for the country, that in the First district, against which, with the whole State of Indiana, much has been said in the press, notwithstanding numerous charges of bribery in contestant's notice and counter-charges in contestee's answer and every position has been pressed acrimoniously, neither party has been able to support the charge. The only proper inference is that no such evidence was available and the charges were unfounded.

It is proper to observe here that much of the testimony in the case has been taken out of time, or to speak more accurately, in rebuttal, when by its substance it is evidence in chief. This is in violation of the act of Congress, and was at the time objected to on the part of the contestee, who though present also refused to cross-examine on that ground. No reasons for this course on the part of the contestant have been presented to the committee, and the committee has felt itself bound to exclude such evidence from its consideration of the case. It believes that the rights of the House under the Constitution are not abridged by the act referred to, but that each Congress in enforcing those rights will not depart from the terms of the act except for cause. This disposes of all

189

questions in the case except that of non-residence, for all others are supported only by such evidence.

There are two classes of voters brought in question in this case under the head of non-residents: those known as the St. Meinrad voters and the Kentucky voters, though the last description is not accurate for not all included under it are spoken of as from Kentucky.

The St. Meinrad votes were thirty in number and were cast for the contestee by students of the college or seminary at St. Meinrad. These students were young men there solely for the purpose of an education in preparation for the priesthood. They had come mostly from Indiana, but many of them from other States and some of them from foreign countries. Their tuition and support were furnished to them by their respective bishops. They all testified that their residence was at St. Meinrad. It might well be doubted if they meant more by this than that they had been at that place the time necessary to make it their home. A proper cross-examination would probably have disclosed the misunderstanding of the witnesses. But we must consider the case as it is presented. No one doubts the evidence of these very respectable gentlemen that they had been at the institution most of the time for a number of years and sufficiently long to have gained a residence if that were the only requisite. But residence is a mixed question of fact and intention; the fact without also the intention is not sufficient of itself to establish a legal residence. And it is a well-settled principle of the cases that one who leaves his home to go to college for the purpose of an education does not from continuance there the required time gain a residence. On the contrary, the very object of his stay raises a presumption against such result. This is not because the law adopts a rule in the case of students different from that in other cases, but because it also reasons from analogy and must in all cases be consistent.

The votes of those who in this case have been described as " Kentucky voters" depend upon the same principles of law as those of the St. Meinrad students, and both depend upon solving the problem whether the individual voter ever in contemplation of law changed his place of residence from that last had to that now insisted upon or opposed.

The law places a child's residence with his parents, not because they are his parents but because theirs is the home into which he is born; so also with his guardian if his is his actual home. There he has the right to vote the day he becomes of age and there he has the protection of law, the right of support if ill-health, misfortune, or poverty overtakes him whether in infancy or mature years; there a citizenship, which he has the right to prove and the flag to defend and against which simple actual absence, no matter how long, will be no defense. Nor does such residence depend upon the maintenance of the parental roof. (Fry's Elec. Cases, 71 Penn. St., 302.) It moves with it only when the law from other circumstances concludes the child is still a component part. The homestead may have disappeared and yet the legal right of the child or man be unaffected. The State will not disown its son, and it recognizes the family when a component part but not its sole dependence.

The intention of the voter is an important factor in determining the place of residence, and the proper way is to examine the surrounding circumstances to discover that intention. Plainly one who is a student at a college or toiler in Kentucky may be a voter, but he may not more than any other citizen have two places at either of which according to whim or convenience he may on election morning determine to vote. The law does not mean that a matter so vital to the rights of others shall be concealed and hidden within the single breast of one of the parties. Residence at the college, or in Kentucky, like residence at any other place gives and takes away the right to vote, but when of a person simply for the purpose of an education as in the case of the St. Meinrad students or of labor as with many of the "Kentucky voters," it raises a presumption of want of *bona fides* and necessity for other proof to show that it was the intention of the voter it should have such effect.

The student voters were Catholics, and the form benefactions took with them was from the bishop, and from this it was argued that the bishop stood *in loco parentis*. Even if granted, it would not affect the question involved, nor have more to do with it than if the students had been in a Protestant college, there supported, as is commonly the case, by their churches for the Protestant ministry. The question would still be, not whether their residence was that of the church by which they were supported, but whether they had ever given up their last residence and undertaken to acquire another at the college. To do so they must either directly have renounced their former home and assumed the obligations of citizens in their place of adoption, or done acts, open and acknowledged, inconsistent with the one and assertive of the other. Every one has a well-recognized right to change his place of residence, and may do so if he proceed in consonance with known principles.

Contestant's case must fail in regard to the students, not so much because in fact they were entitled to vote, as to use the language of the supreme court of Indiana, in Pedigo v. Grimes (112 Ind., 148), "because there is no evidence that this (their intention of making that place their residence) was not their intention formed and acted upon in good faith." Each party at the hearing relied upon this case to support his position. It is sufficient to say, while thus citing from it, that it will not bear the extreme construction put upon it by contestee. That would not only do violence to its language but place it in opposition to the trend of decisions elsewhere upon which it claims to rest.

An application of these principles to the other votes brought in question shows that the following were improperly cast and counted for the contestee and should be deducted from his number, to wit: Solon Hedges, Neeley Borden, Samuel Bogan, J. Nickens, A. Nickens, Thomas Hampton, Harry Hampton, Dink Miller, Frank Wiseman, Homer Campbell, E. T. Conway, John Oaks, Thomas Crosnow, and Stephen Winters—total, 14; and that the following were improperly cast and counted for the contestant and should be deducted from his number, to wit: James Smith, James Eskridge, Alex. Boyd, Philip Dailey—total, 4.

This still leaves the contestee with a plurality of ten (20—14+4=10).

The committee is of the opinion that the certificate of election was rightfully issued to William F. Parrett, and that he is entitled to the seat. It therefore submits the following resolutions, and recommends their adoption :

Resolved, That Francis B. Posey is not entitled to a seat in the Fifty-first Congress as Representative from the First Congressional district of Indiana.

Resolved, That William F. Parrett is entitled to a seat in the Fifty-first Congress as Representative from the First Congressional district in Indiana.

HENRY BOWEN vs. JOHN A. BUCHANAN.

NINTH VIRGINIA.

Contestant charged illegal voting, bribery, intimidation, illegal action of election officers, and a general conspiracy on the part of friends of contestee to defeat an honest expression of the will of the people.

The committee find some illegal voting, as well as some bribery and violence, but not sufficient to vitiate the election or overcome the majority returned for contestee. The minority agree in the conclusion, and also in finding some bribery and violence, but protest that the people among whom these acts were committed were not responsible for them and should not be censured.

The resolutions presented were adopted by the House April 16, 1890, without debate or division. (Record, 3451.)

(1) **Returning board.** *Power to correct return.*

Where a county returning board in making out their abstract accidentally omitted one precinct, but before forwarding their returns discovered and corrected their mistake, *held* that this was just what ought to have been done, and if this precinct return had been omitted it would have been the duty of the committee to include it in the total vote. The vote of a county can not be thrown out for such an informality.

(2) **Population.** *Not to be decided without legal determination.*

Where it was provided that in all towns of over 2,000 inhabitants a transferred voter must have his transfer recorded at least 10 days prior to the election, but in all other cases might vote without such registry, *held* that the election judges had no right to decide that a town was within the exception in the absence of any legal determination of its population.

(3) **Ballot box.** *Removal of.*

Where the poll was closed for dinner, and the box removed from the presence of the United States supervisor, *held* that but for the strong affirmative proof that no wrong was intended or done in this case the committee would unhesitatingly reject the return.

H. Mis. 137—13

(4) Intimidation.   *When return to be excluded.*

Where a small and known number of voters were intimidated to v
for contestee in a precinct where in any event he would have had
considerable majority, the return should not be rejected.   Were th
number uncertain the return would be excluded, and if a sufficient nu
ber were so intimidated as to overcome the majority of contestee
would not be entitled to retain his seat.

REPORT.

APRIL 3, 1890.—Mr. ROWELL, from the Committee on Elections, submitted the following report:

The Committee on Elections, having had under consideration the contested election case of Henry Bowen *v.* John A. Buchanan, submit the following report:

At the election held in the Ninth Congressional district of Virginia on November 6, 1888, the total vote returned for Congressman was 32,562, of which number John A. Buchanan received a majority of 478 over his Republican opponent, Henry Bowen, contestant.

The notice of contest charges, and the answer denies, illegal voting, bribery, intimidation, illegal action of election officers, and a general conspiracy on the part of friends of contestee to defeat an honest expression of the will of the people.

The evidence taken in the case affects the vote in a majority of the fourteen counties composing the district.

It is clearly shown that a number of illegal votes were cast for contestee by non-residents and other unqualified persons; but the number is comparatively small, and, in the view of the committee, a consideration of them in detail would not change the result, and for this reason we pass over this branch of the case.

The record contains considerable evidence to prove the corrupt use of money by friends of contestee.

In Russell County, the existence of a corruption fund and a willingness to use it are clearly established. Several votes were purchased and attempts were made to purchase others.. Enough appears to arouse suspicion that more votes were purchased than the evidence discloses. The committee, however, can only deal with the facts established by the evidence, however strongly they may suspect the existence of more extensive corruption than appears.

Samuel Sword was paid $6 to vote for contestee. William Sword was paid $5. The father of these two boys was offered money for his vote, but refused to sell. Pat. Robinson, who handled the corruption fund in the precinct where these men voted, claimed to be acting under the direction of one Boyd, one of the judges of election.

At another precinct in this county, George Herron, a colored man, received a pair of shoes for his vote; and Mark Price was first threatened with prosecution, and then given $2.50 to go home and not vote. James E. Boardwine was paid $5 to remain away from the polls. He would not sell his vote for money, but refrained from voting. Cumenings Thompson was offered $3 for his vote, but declined the offer. Frank Hess, James S. Hess, and Taze Honiker voted for contestee in consideration of the release of a fine which had been assessed against Frank Hess.

The bargain in this case and in some others was made with the sheriff and State's attorney of the county. Huston McNeel was induced to vote the Democratic ticket by the release of a $25 fine standing against him. William Dye and Lilburn Dye, his son, were purchased by the satisfaction of a $15 fine standing against Lilburn Dye. This purchase was made by the sheriff of the county and a satisfaction entered by him. These 10 votes were directly purchased, and no attempt is made to disprove the direct evidence establishing the fact. There is considerable circumstantial evidence tending to show that others were influenced in like manner in this county; the money was provided; the will to use it was not wanting, and, if there were other corruptible voters in the county known to the corruptors, they were undoubtedly reached in the same way and by the same representatives of the majesty of the law, the sheriff and State's attorney of Russell County. We can go no further than the evidence justifies and deduct these 10 votes from contestee's majority.

In Dickinson and Wise Counties inducements were held out to illicit distillers by United States revenue officers of immunity from prosecution for violation of the revenue laws, in consideration of support to the Democratic ticket. Three or four voters are shown to have voted for contestee on account of this kind of pursuasive argument. If others were so pursuaded it does not appear in the evidence. Altogether some twenty votes were lost to contestant in the manner above stated.

It is claimed by the contestant that several precincts in the district should be entirely rejected, and if his claim should be allowed it would be more than sufficient to overcome the majority returned for contestee. In our view of the law and evidence none of these claims can be allowed. We refer to some of them.

Giles County.—Here it is claimed that the returns from the county should be rejected, because the returning officers of the county corrected their abstract of the precinct returns after it had been made up and the board had adjourned.

It seems that in making up the abstract, by a clerical error, one precinct had been left out. Before the returns were transmitted to the Secretary of the Commonwealth, the mistake was discovered and corrected. This was just what ought to have been done, and if this precinct return had been omitted, it would have been the duty of the committee to include it in the total vote. The objection is technical and without merit.

It is further insisted that the return from Pembroke district should be rejected on account of the misconduct of the election judges.

Sometime during the day a fight took place near the polling place, and the judges of election all went out to witness it, leaving the ballot-box in the custody of the clerks, who were of opposite political faiths. During this temporary absence the Democratic clerk was seen to push a ticket into the box, and it is claimed that this circumstance proves that other ballots than those of the voters were deposited in the box. The circumstance is explained in a manner quite consistent with the honesty of the clerk. Just as the fight commenced, one of the judges had received a ballot and attempted to deposit it in the box, but in his hurry did not quite succeed, leaving the ballot in the opening, and the clerk pushed it down with his pencil. During the absence of the judges no one interfered with the box, no one was prevented from voting by the delay, and there is no evidence to impeach the return. Two or three illegal votes were cast at this poll, but there is nothing to show unfairness on the part of the judges.

Tazewell County.—At Pocahontas precinct, Tazewell County, 40 votes tendered for contestant, were in our view illegally rejected. By the statutes of Virginia it is provided that in all towns of over 2,000 inhabitants a transferred voter must have his transfer recorded at least ten days prior to the election. At all other precincts a transferred voter may vote without such registry. It was claimed by the election officers that Pocahontas was a town of over 2,000 inhabitants, and these forty voters were denied the right to vote because they had failed to have their transfers registered. Pocahontas is a new mining town; no census, state or national, has disclosed the number of its inhabitants, and there is a difference of opinion among the inhabitants as to the number of people. In the absence of any legal determination of the number, we do not think the election judges had any right to decide that this town was within the exception.

Contestee lost 4 votes by the same ruling, and there was a net loss to contestant of 36 votes.

Russell County.—We are asked to reject the returns from Honaker precinct, Russell County, on account of alleged misconduct of the election officers. At this precinct the election judges adjourned for dinner and supper, and each time two of them took the ballot-box from the polling place and carried it to a private house where they went for their meals. By this conduct the box was removed from the presence of the United States supervisor, in violation of the statute. The supervisor claims that he protested against the removal, but the preponderance of the evidence is against his claim. The majority for the contestee at this precinct was 89, a large increase over former elections. This illegal act of the judges gave opportunity for fraud, such fraud as the statute was designed to prevent. In the examination of other cases we have found that adjournment and removal of the ballot-box from the presence of the supervisor is a common method resorted to when it is intended to change the ballots or the boxes. But for the strong affirmative proof that no wrong was intended or done in this case, the committee would unhesitatingly reject the return.

The increase in the Democratic majority is accounted for, to some extent, if not fully, by the existence of the corruption fund spoken of in this report.

At Loup or Johnson's Store precinct it is claimed that the returns should be rejected because of the undue and improper influence of the Stewart Land and Cattle Company over their employés, some forty or fifty in number. The proof tends to show that at previous elections these employés had been given to understand that they must vote the Democratic ticket or lose their places. It was generally understood in the community that one of the conditions of employment by this company was that the men should vote the Democratic ticket. It is unquestionably true that many of the men believed that to vote otherwise would cost them their places, and that belief undoubtedly induced some of them to vote against their convictions. But there is no direct evidence implicating any of the members of this company in an attempt to control their employés at this election other than the presence at the polls of one of their foremen distributing tickets to the men. How many men were influenced by the prevalent belief does not appear, and this supposed influence is too uncertain and indefinite to justify the rejection of this poll or other neighboring polls where some of the employés voted.

Buchanan County.—At Slate or Sander's precinct, in Buchanan County, contestee received 52 votes, and contestant none. The evidence shows that there are from ten to fifteen Republicans in the precinct; that before the election word was circulated that no Republican would be permitted to vote there; and that six or seven of them went to the polls, and were immediately assaulted by a crowd of drunken roughs. The intervention of the more peaceably inclined saved them from injury. Threats were freely made during the day against all who should attempt to vote the Republican ticket. Three of those present, did however, vote the Republican national ticket, but they voted for contestee as a measure of prudence.

The majority of the voters at this precinct were peaceably disposed, but a few vicious, drunken partisans of contestee deprived contestant of the Republican votes of the precinct Were their number uncertain, we would exclude the return, but as their number is not a matter of uncertainty, and as contestee would have had a considerable majority in this precinct, in any event, it is not in accordance with the precedents to reject the return, if a sufficient number were so intimidated as to overcome the majority of contestee, the committee would hold that he had no right to retain his seat.

Dickinson County.—Colly precinct: At this precinct the vote was 92 for contestee and 16 for contestant. In past years it has been dangerous for a Republican to attempt to vote in this district. In 1834 only eight voted, and some of these were badly whipped before they left the polls. Previous to the day of the election in 1888 a political meeting was held, at which a Democrat and a Republican spoke, as soon as the Republican commenced to speak the disorder commenced, and one or two Republicans were assaulted. Order was only secured by the efforts of the Democratic speaker. After the meeting several Republicans were assaulted. To protect the voters a United States supervisor was appointed at this poll, and the feeling of security which resulted brought the Republicans to the polls.

Sixteen votes were cast for the Republican ticket, which, so far as appears from the evidence, was the full Republican strength. Around the polls there was plenty of fighting and drinking, but no attempt to keep any one from voting. It is a very hard neighborhood; illicit distillers abound; ignorance and vice prevail to an alarming extent, and the prejudice against the Republican party is so strong that it can not be said that a free expression of the popular will is possible. There are few Republicans in the neighborhood, but those who are there are not different in character from their Democratic neighbors, and some of them are not averse to taking a hand in the violent demonstrations which seem to be an accompaniment of elections. It does not appear that either party lost any votes because of this violence.

Wise County—Pond precinct. This is another precinct where it is claimed the returns ought to be rejected on account of violence at the polls. An armed band of illicit distillers was at the polls during the afternoon, drinking, shooting, and threatening; but the Republican vote had all been cast before the violence commenced, and no one was prevented from voting. For what purpose these men came to the polls armed does not appear. They were law-breakers, accustomed to look for attempts to arrest them, and to defend themselves, and it is probable that they did not venture far from home, even to attend an election, without carrying arms.

It seems from the evidence that in this section of Virginia election day furnishes the occasion for drinking, fighting, and settling feuds; that the peaceably-inclined understand the disposition of the more vicious, and do not fear personal injury; and that the rougher characters of both political parties are perfectly willing to take their chances on election day. Conduct which would drive the mass of voters from the polls in other communities does not seem seriously to affect the result here, and it is for this reason that we do not reject returns where so much violence prevails.

Smythe County.—At Chatham Hill, Smythe County, complaint is made of Mr. Baker, one of the judges, that he manifested a disposition to examine the tickets to see how men voted. A fight took place at this poll between whites and negroes, and there were other irregularities common to the section, but nothing to affect the integrity of the returns.

Wise County—Clay House precinct. Here frauds upon the registration are alleged. The registrar was away when he ought to have been at his office, and three or four failed to register on that account. He was active in getting Democrats on the register, and quite willing that Republicans should fail to qualify. It does not appear that any were registered who were not residents, and not more than four failed to register on account of the misconduct of the office.

It is also claimed that between one hundred and two hundred colored employés on the railroad were cheated out of their votes by failure to procure transfers from their former homes. There is nothing in this claim. These men trusted to others to procure them transfers, and neglected to do what was required of them. Trusting to others was their misfortune, but it does not excuse their own neglect. Besides, none of them tendered their ballots, and there is no sufficient evidence that they were residents in the precinct.

In Halsten, Washington County, several persons were permitted to vote for contestee without transfers or registration. This was true in one or two other places, by which illegal voting contestee's majority was increased by fourteen.

Other complaints were made, and evidence introduced to sustain them, but we have referred to the more flagrant charges, and do not deem it necessary to review the evidence further. Our conclusion is, that the majority of contestee is reduced to the extent of some 200 votes by the various frauds, irregularities, and illegal votes proved by the evidence; but this leaves him a majority of over 200 under a liberal construction of the law, and a fair consideration of all the evidence. The committee therefore submit the following resolutions:

Resolved, That John A. Buchanan was duly elected to the Fifty-first Congress from the Ninth Congressional district of Virginia, and is entitled to retain his seat.

Resolved, That Henry Bowen was not elected a Representative to the Fifty-first Congress from the Ninth Congressional district of Virginia, and is not entitled to the seat.

VIEWS OF THE MINORITY.

APRIL 7, 1890.—Mr. O'FERRALL, from the Committee on Elections, submitted the following views of the minority:

We concur in the foregoing report in so far as it declares that the sitting member is entitled to retain his seat, but with many of its statements and with much of its reasoning we do not concur. We will, however, only call attention specially to two or three points of disagreement.

First. The criticism made upon the people of several counties of said district, we think, is unjust and uncalled for. It is true that a few persons under the influence of intoxicating liquors attempted to interfere with, and in a few instances did interfere with, voters in the exercise of their right of suffrage; and it is also true that in a few instances money or other thing of value was used improperly to influence voters .in casting their ballots. But whilst these things are true and the conduct of the persons engaged in said wrongful acts should be condemned, we do not think that the people among whom these wrong-doers lived should be censured for wrongs they did not commit and for which they were not responsible. Neither do we think that one political party should be criticised for the misconduct of men, some of whom belonged to one party and some to the other, when said misconduct was not approved by either.

Second. After the committee had determined that the sitting member was entitled to retain his seat upon the contestant's own showing, we do not think it was necessary to ascertain whether the sitting member's majority was greater or less than that shown for him by the returns, but if this was to be done, justice, in our opinion, demands that the errors committed in the conduct of said election to the prejudice of the sitting member as well as to the prejudice of the contestant should have been considered and corrected. This was not done, yet it is said in the report that the majority of the sitting member was some two hundred less than that returned for him. This statement is clearly incorrect. We are satisfied if all errors to the prejudice of either party was corrected that the majority of the sitting member would be as much if not more than that returned for him.

CHAS. T. O'FERRALL.
CHARLES F. CRISP.
J. H. OUTHWAITE.
R. P. C. WILSON.
L. W. MOORE.
LEVI MAISH.

EDMUND WADDILL, JR., vs. GEORGE D. WISE.

THIRD VIRGINIA.

The case turned upon the disposition to be made of the votes of a large number of voters who attempted to vote for contestant in Jackson ward, Richmond. These voters were at the polling place, in line and ready to vote, on the day of election, but were still in line when the polls closed, having failed to reach the window. It was charged that that their inability to vote was due to intentionally dilatory tactics resorted to by the workers for contestee, with the aid and collusion of the officers of election. The committee find this charge sustained by the evidence, and regarding the votes as having been legally tendered and unlawfully rejected, count them as if cast. They were all for contestant, and if counted would give him a majority in the district. The minority find the charges of collusion on the part of the judges not sustained by the evidence, and that if there was any needless delay it was caused by partisans of contestant; that the law as found in the precedents is that in case the loss of votes was due to accident or misfortune, there is no remedy, and contestee should retain his seat; in case it was due to fraud the seat should be declared vacant. In this case it was not due to fraud, but the minority, not being satisfied of the justice of the established rule, and being of the opinion that the ends of justice will be subserved by unseating the contestee and ordering a new election, recommend that the seat be declared vacant. (See minority report, page 227.) The resolutions presented by the committee were adopted April 12, 1890, the first without division, and the second by a vote of 134 to 120, and Mr. Waddill was sworn in. The debate will be found on pages 3294 to 3363.

(1) **Vote.** *Improperly rejected.*

A lawful vote properly tendered and unlawfully excluded may be counted on a contest.

(2) **Tender.** *What is.*

The ability to reach the window and actually tender the ticket to the judges is not essential in all cases to constitute a good offer to vote. From the time the voter reaches the polling place and takes his position in line to secure his orderly turn in voting, he has commenced the act of voting.

(3) **Rejection.** *Constructive, by undue delay.*

"If by the wrongful act of fraudulent challenges unduly prolonged by the connivance and collusion of the judges of the election the voter is deprived of the opportunity to vote, the interest of our form of government and the purity of elections demand that the vote should be counted. If the fraudulent exclusion of votes would if successful, secure to the party of the wrongdoer, a temporary seat in Congress, and the only penalty for detection in the wrong would be merely a new election, giving another chance for the exercise of similar tactics, such practices would be at a great premium and an election indefinitely prevented. But if where such acts are done the votes are counted upon clear proof *aliunde*, the wrong is at once corrected in this House and no encouragement is given to such dangerous and disgraceful methods."

REPORT.

MARCH 31, 1890.—Mr. LACEY, from the Committee on Elections, submitted the following report:

The Committee on Elections, who have had under consideration the contested election case from the third Congressional district of Virginia, submit the following report:

At the general election held on the 6th day of November, 1888, in the third Virginia district, Edmund Waddill and George D. Wise were voted for to represent said district in the Fifty-first Congress.

The official returns show the following results:

	Wise.	Waddill.
Richmond City	8,040	6,324
Manchester	892	740
King William	739	1,099
Hanover	1,646	1,565
New Kent	365	705
Henrico	1,688	2,340
Chesterfield	1,567	1,586
Goochland	671	988
Total	15,608	15,347

Wise	15,608
Waddill	15,347
Majority for George D. Wise	261

(See Record, page 670.)

A number of votes are challenged in this contest, and irregularities and fraudulent acts complained of on both sides. The pivotal question in the case is as to whether certain votes in Jackson ward, in the city of Richmond, shall be counted. If these votes, or such of them as are clearly shown, should be counted for the contestant the contestant is entitled to the seat, but if the votes in question are not counted the contestant is not elected.

It is claimed by contestant that in Jackson ward 722 legal voters were wrongfully prevented from voting; that these voters were lawfully registered and qualified electors; that they presented themselves in line on the day of the election prepared to take their turns in voting, and had in their hands, ready to deposit, ballots properly prepared to cast for the contestant for member of Congress.

That the partisans and friends of the contestee hindered and obstructed these voters by making frivolous challenges of lawful voters, and that the judges of the election colluded with and aided the challengers in delaying the casting of the ballots by entertaining such challenges, by consuming unnecessary time in hearing and taking action upon them, and by making needless explanations to the voters as to the effect of certain constitutional amendments which were being voted

205

on at the election ; that by needless and fraudulent delays in receiving and depositing the ballots, these 722 voters were prevented from casting their votes for contestant. Contestant further claims that 557 of said voters thus prevented from voting remained in line at the time of the closing of the polls, and that thereupon United States commissioners prepared ballot-boxes and received the ballots of such voters and deposited the same in the boxes and preserved the same, which ballots were in evidence before the committee.

The votes thus in controversy are confined to three precincts of Jackson ward. Of these voters 457 were examined as witnesses.

In the first precinct contestant claimed that 255 of such votes were deposited, and examined 199 of the alleged voters. The names and pages of the record upon which their evidence may be found is here set out :

Joshua Coles, 238 to 240.
William Branch, 240 to 241.
Beverly Travers, 242 to 243.
Clarence Peyton, 243 to 245.
Beverly Brooks, 247 to 248.
Thomas Furm, 248 to 250.
Jerry Turner, 250 to 251.
William Marshall, 251 to 263.
Augustus Anderson, 253 to 254.
William Armstead, 254 to 255.
Charles Butler, 255 to 257.
John Bolden, 257 to 258.
Jacob Bryce, 258 to 259.
David Robinson, 259 to 260.
B. W. Rivers, 260 to 261.
Robert Bentley, 262 to 263.
W. J. Barcroft, 263 to 264.
Abram Booker, 264 to 266.
James Braxton, 266 to 267.
G. C. Booker, 268 to 269.
Joshua Bowman, 269 to 271.
William Billups, 271 to 272.
Isaac Clark, 273 to 274.
W. M. Clark, 274 to 277.
Daniel Clark, 277 to 279.
Thomas Anderson, 279 to 282.
D. Cheatham, 282 to 283.
Thomas Chatman, 284 to 285.
Henry Carter, 285 to 287.
Briscoe Cherry, 287 to 289.
Samuel Claxton, 289 to 292.
W. W. Scott, 292 to 293.
Henry Cooper, 294.
Robert Harris, 294 to 295.
Mordecai Brown, 295 to 298.
Emanuel Baker, 298 to 300.
Joseph Hennyman, 300 to 302.
Robt. B. Taylor, 302 to 304.
Madison Banks, 304 to 306.
Braxton Smith, 306 to 308.
Jesse Coy, 308 to 310.
Peter Henley, 310 to 312.
Reuben Jones, 312 to 314.
Henry Harris, 314 to 316.
C. M. Kemp, 316 to 318.
Wilson Thomas, 318 to 320.
John Robertson, 320 to 321.
W. C. Scott, 321 to 323.
William Lewis, 323 to 325.
Charles H. Muse, 325 to 327.
Thos. D. Payne, 327 to 330.
W. N. Rivers, 330 to 331.
Robt H. Taylor, 332 to 334.
Marcellus Puryear, 334 to 336.
Reuben Lewis, 336 to 338.
Charles H. James, 338 to 339.
Scott Jackson, 340 to 341.
Thaddeus Bolling, 341 to 343.
Nelson Ross, 343 to 345.
Geo. Hunt, 345 to 346.
W. S Banks, 346 to 348.
Frank Terrill, 348 to 349.
Edward Johnson, 349 to 350.
Abram Kinney, 350 to 351.
Geo. Taylor, 352 to 353.
Thomas Lee, 353 to 354.

W. P. Burrell, 355 to 358.
Gilliam Jones, 359 to 360.
Stonewall Jackson, 360 to 361.
Joseph Brown, 361 to 363.
Cassandrow Banks, 363 to 364.
Wm. Crump, 364 to 366.
William Scott, 366 to 368.
Charles Scott, 368 to 369.
W. T. Taylor, 369 to 371.
Ryland Lewis, 371.
Lewis Jackson, 372 to 373.
Major Johnson, 373 to 374.
Ned Stanton, 374 to 376.
Albert Jackson, 376 to 378.
Jones Allen, 378 to 379.
William Richardson, 379 to 380.
Abram Tinsley, 380 to 382.
Oscar Taylor, 382 to 383.
James E. Taylor, 383 to 384.
Geo. Selden, 384 to 385.
Geo. Mimms, 386 to 387.
E. C. Smith, 387 to 388.
Charles Rainey, 392 to 393.
David Strother, 395.
Benj. Thompson, 396 to 397.
Edward Jones, 397 to 398.
James Johnson, 398 to 400.
John Johnson, 400 to 401.
Daniel Reynolds, 406 to 407.
Henry Venable, 407 to 409.
James Vaughn, 109 to 410.
Patrick Jackson, 410 to 411.
Seymour Johnson, 412 to 414.
Royal White, 420 to 421.
Joseph Wilkinson, 421 to 422.
Robt. Lynch, 422 to 423.
Cornelius Dabney, 423 to 425.
Geo. Dawson, 425 to 426.
Anthony Gray, 426 to 427.
Thomas Jefferson, 427 to 428.
Robt. Johnson, 429 to 430.
John W. Jackson, 430 to 431.
Joseph Harris, 431 to 432.
A. D. Price, 433 to 434.
John Martin, 434 to 435.
Henry Dedman, 435 to 437.
Mac Frayser, 437 to 438.
Jonas Epps, 438 to 439.
Peter Hall, 439 to 440.
Russell Foster, 440 to 441.
Peyton H. Green, 442.
William Davis, 443 to 444.
Jack Hayes, 444 to 445.
Wilson Louey, 445 to 448.
Nelson Lee, 448 to 449.
Eugene Garrison, 449 to 450.
Isaac Johnson, 451 to 452.
M. C. Methord, 452 to 454.
Lewis Green, 454 to 455.
Geo. Mayo, 455 to 456.
Van Washington, 456 to 457.
Jas R. Gross, 457 to 458.
Washington Cootes, 458 to 459.
Wm. D. Poindexter, 460 to 461.
James Wren, 461 to 463.
Richard Morton, 463 to 464.
J. A. Moss, 464 to 465.

Madison Pendleton, 465 to 467.
Sam'l Wade, 467 to 468.
Geo. Wood, 468 to 469.
Benjamin Wray, 469 to 471.
William H. Pollard, 471 to 472.
R. W. Edward, 472 to 473.
W. H. Massey, 473 to 475.
Grantland Marks, 475 to 476.
Giles Willis, 476 to 477.
Collin Yates, 478 to 480.
Archer Woodson, 480 to 481.
Geo. Washington, 481 to 482.
John Lewis, 482 to 484.
Jesse Williams, 484 to 486.
James Morris, 486 to 488.
Robt. Maston, 488 to 489.
Fleming Glover, 489 to 490.
Robt. Yancey, 490 to 492.
S. L. Leftwitch, 492 to 493.
Emanual Williams, 493 to 494.
Joe Wormley, 495 to 496.
Edward Williams, 496 to 497.
John Wallace, 497 to 498.
Albert Wray. 498 to 499.
Alex. Gaines, 500 to 501.
Joseph Fortune. 501 to 502.
Henry Willis, 502 to 503.
J. H. D. Wingfield, 503 to 505.
Robt. Dickerson, 505 to 506.
A. R. Lucado, 506 to 507.
Armstead Miller, 507 to 508.
John White, 509 to 511.
William H. Frayser, 513 to 515.
Jeff Mitchell, 516 to 517.
William Fox, 520.
Fielding Hundley, 521 to 523.
William Fauntleray, 523 to 524.
J. H Cox, 530 to 5 1.
Joseph Woodfolk, 531 to 532.
Peter Chandler, 670 to 672.
Robt. H. Hill, 672.
Andrew Jackson, 673.
John Bolling, 673 to 674.
Moses Peters, 674 to 675.
Emanuel T. Jenkins, 675.
Enos Johnson, 67 to 676.
Paul Ballow, 676 to 677.
Richard L. Harris, 677 to 678.
Joseph Bell, 678 to 679.
Geo. O. Brown, 679 to 680.
Joshua Hendley, 680.
Archer Harris, 680 to 681.
Jas. H. Pride, 681 to 682.
Anthony M. Reed, 682 to 683.
Geo. E. Burke, 683.
Mark A. Ball, 683 to 684.
Albert Hooper, 684 to 685.
Alexander Holmes, 685 to 686.
Jas. E. Brooks, 687.
Jas. Thomas Carter, 687 to 688.
Henry Johnson, 688 to 689.
Albert A. Harris, 689.
Preston Hopkins, 690.
Jacob Brown, 690 to 691.
Stirling Pleasants, 691 to 692.
Jas. T. Brooks, 692 694.

In the third precinct contestant claimed that 168 ballots were deposited there with a United States commissioner, and of these voters 136 were examined. We give their names and the pages of the record where their evidence may be found: •

William Bolling, 533 to 535.
Payton Brooks, 535 to 537.
H. M. Booth, 537⅟to 538.
Cornelius Palmer, 538 to 540.
Edward Black, 540 to 541.
Reuben T. Hill, 542 to 543.
Marcus Bowles, 543 to 544.
Alexander Allen, 544 to 545.
Valvin T. Mann, 545 to 546.
Carter Marshall, 546 to 547.
Frank E. Black, 548.
Jas. Anderson, 548 to 549.
James Bell, 550 to 552.
Abner Cooley, 552 to 554.
Jas. J. Foster, 554 to 555.
Geo. M. Booker, 555 to 557.
Joseph Baker, 557 to 558.
Geo. Duncan, 558 to 559.
Albert Hundley, 559 to 560.
Wesley Harris, 560 to 562.
Osborn Holmes. 562 to 564.
William H. Hall, 564 to 565.
William H. Hope, 565 to 566.
Henry N. Dyson, 567.
Robt. Hawkins, 568 to 569.
James Jackson, 569 to 570.
Geo. Jackson, 570 to 571.
Collin T. Payne, 571 to 573.
Geo. D. Jimmerson, 573 to 574.
Robt. E. Johnson, 574 to 575.
Henry Chiles, 575 to 576.
Spencer Johnson, 576 to 577.
Andrew J. Carr, 577 to 578.
Joseph Canthorn, 578 to 579.
Israel Meriweather, 579 to 582.
Geo. H. Chiles, 582 to 584.
Andrew Dabney, 584.
Scott Freeland, 585 to 586.
Tim Flood, 586 to 587.
Charles Frayser, 587 to 589;
Gilbert Murrell, 589 to 591.
Jas. H. Fauntleroy, 591 to 594.
Moses Page, 594 to 595.
Thos. D. Harris, 596 to 597.
Jacob Taylor, 597 to 598.
Theophilus Winston, 598 to 599.

William M. Scott, 599 to 601.
And'w J. Rutherford, 601 to 602.
Archer Thomas, 602 to 603.
John H. Phinney, 603.
England Thornton, 605 to 606.
Thomas Stuedley, 606 to 607.
John Mitchell, 607.
Parker Eliett, 607 to 608.
Gilmore Robinson, 608 to 609.
Shirley C. Williams, 609.
Joseph Ward, 610.
Thomas Curd, 610 to 611.
Wm. E. Thomas, 612 to 613.
Otway Dandridge, 614.
Samuel Walton, 614 to 615.
John Duncan, 615 to 616.
Jesse Williams, 616 to 617.
Wm. W. Clay, 617 to 619.
Geo. Seay, 619 to 620.
Mason Harris, 620.
John Allen, 621.
James Dell, 621 to 622.
Lawrence Latney, 622 to 623.
Samuel Tinsley, 623.
Thos. Tinsley, 623 to 624.
Archer Smith, 624 to 625.
Albert Johnson, 625 to 626.
John T. Glasgow, 627 to 628.
John Logan, 626 to 632.
Robt. Green, 628.
James E. Woodson, 629.
Wilkins Harris, 629 to 630.
Jacob Jordan, 630 to 631.
Charles Claybrook, 631 to 632.
Moses Harris, 633.
Robt. R Spencer, 634.
Albert T. Scott, 634 to 635.
Junius R. Smith, 635 to 636.
Walter Daniel, 636 to 637.
John W. Williams, 637 to 638.
Richard Taylor, 638 to 639.
William Carrington, 639 to 642.
John Jasper. 642 to 643.
David Lee, 643 to 644.
Beverly Branch, 644 to 646.
Albert Jones, 646.

Albert Bundy, 646 to 647.
Charles H. Thompson, 647 to 648.
Geo. L. Motley, 648 to 649.
Henderson J. Brown, 650 to 651.
Peter W. Taylor, 652.
John D. Frayser, 652 to 653.
James Armstrong, 695 to 697.
W. B. F. Thompson, 699 to 702.
Isaiah Taylor, 702 to 705.
T. M. Perkins, 706 to 707.
Wm. H. Taylor, 707 to 711.
Randolph Taylor, 711 to 713.
Ambrose McKinney, 713 to 714.
Louis Christain. 715 to 716.
Samuel Cox, 716 to 717.
Thomas Thompson, 717 to 718.
B. S. Garnett, 718 to 720.
Matt Taylor, 720 to 721.
W. H. Johnson. 721 to 722.
Robt. McKenny, 722 to 723.
Robt. Coleman, 723 to 724.
Wm. H. Mosby, 724 to 725.
Henry Gray, 725 to 727.
I. H. Scott, 727 to 728.
J. M. Williams, 728 to 729.
Samuel Mayo, 729 to 730.
Thomas Graham, 730 to 731.
Samuel D. Payne, 731 to 733.
Henry O. Payne, 734.
S. M. Ellington, 734 to 737.
Robinson Lucas, 738 to 741.
Geo. W. Leake, 741 to 743.
Geo, Mimms, 743 to 747.
William Stanton, 747 to 750.
William W. Hill, 750 to 752.
James Russell, 752 to 754.
Samuel Richardson, 754 to 756.
Malachi Griffin, 757 to 758.
Andrew Morgan, 759 to 760.
Lewis Williams, 760 to 762.
C. Washington, 762 to 764.
Wilson E. Baker, 764 to 768.
Charles Williams, 768 to 769.
Joseph Taylor, 770 to 771.
Boston Ferrell, 771 to 773.

In the fourth precinct he also claims that 134 voters thus cast their ballots, and that 122 of these voters were examined, whose names we now give, and we refer to the record, where their depositions may be found:

Green Robinson, 773 to 775.
Henry Jones, 775 to 776.
Washington Hill, 776 to 778.
Elisha Jones, 778 to 781,
James H. Burke, 781 to 782.
Alexander McCoy, 782 to 784.
Elisha Morris, 785 to 787.
Alexander Forrester, 787 to 789.
Joseph Jefferson, 789 to 791.
Kirk Mason, 791 to 793.
Henry Brooks, 793 to 794.
Thos. M. Gaines, 794 to 796.
Dorsey Taylor, 796 to 797.
Chastine Fisher, 798 to 799.
William Jackson, 799 to 800.
John Hamm, 800 to 802.
Richard Adams, 802 to 803.
Mordecai Q. Jones, 803 to 804.
A. P. Fleet, 805 to 806.
Bright Granger, 806 to 807.
Peyton Rice, 808 to 809.
Junius Roberts, 809 to 811.
Sydney Johnson, 811 to 812.
Edmond Foster, 813 to 814.
William H. Price, 814 to 816.
John T. Allen, 816 to 818.
Sandy Robinson, 818 to 820.

James Hansbury, 820 to 821.
William Wells, 821 to 822.
Joseph Wells, 822 to 823.
Edward C Roman, 832 to 834.
Alfred T. Baker, 834 to 836.
Daniel Edmund, 836 to 838.
Thos. R. Hewlett, 838 to 839.
Cornelius L. Harris, 840 to 842.
William Braxton, 842 to 843.
Chas. Goodwin, 844 to 846.
Jack Gaines, 846 and 892.
Wellington Booker, 848 to 849.
William Bell, 851 to 853.
Stephen D. Turner, 854 to 855.
R. Emmett Harris, 855 to 857.
Gray Evans. 857 to 859.
Walter S. Howard, 860 to 861.
Robt. Crittenden, 862 to 863.
David Hill, 863 to 865.
Edward Carter, 865 to 866.
William Harris, 866 to 868.
Collin T. Valentine, 868 to 870.
Jos H. Patterson, 870 to 871.
Timothy Harris, 871 to 872.
W. P. Dabney, 873 to 875.
James Jones, 875 to 877.
John Holmes, 877 to 879.

Edward Norris, 879 to 881,
Joseph Custalo, 881 to 883.
Robert George, 883 to 885.
Washington Moody, 885 to 887.
Robert Walker, 887 to 889.
Dandridge Stevens, 890 to 892.
Wise Jackson, 892 to 893.
Chris. Blunt. 893 to 894.
Lewis Thompson, 895 to 897.
Winston Poindexter, 898 to 899.
James Thomas, 899 to 901.
James Lawson, 901 to 903.
Nathaniel White, 903 to 904.
Wm. Washington, 904 to 907.
A. Reed, 907 to 910.
W. H. Lewis, 910 to 911.
Henry Warner, 911 to 916.
Alfred Dickerson, 916 to 917.
Addison Lewis, 917 to 919.
Daniel Overton, 919 to 921.
Wyate Hubbard, 921 to 923.
Robt. Taylor, 923 to 925.
Henry Timberlake, 925 to 927.
Robt. Johnson, 927 to 928.
Allen A. Armstead, 928 to 930.
John Griffin, 930 to 932.
W. E. Hope, 932 to 934.

Robt. Beazley, 934 to 937.
Geo. F. McKenney, 937 to 940.
Charles W. Frost, 940 to 942.
Santee N. Lundy, 942 to 944.
A. A. Patterson. 944 to 946.
Frank Horton, 946 to 948.
Austin J. Miller, 948 to 95C.
Moses P. Randolph, 950 to 951.
Robert Taylor, 951 to 953.
James Wells, 953 to 955.
Lewis Trent, 955 to 957.
C. A. Booker, 957 to 958.

William Lightfoot, 958 to 959.
Dutch Kelley, 959 to 961.
Philip Daniel, 961 to 963.
John Law, 963 to 965.
James Brooks, 965 to 966.
Napoleon Jones, 967 to 968.
J. C. Harris, 968 to 970.
Wm. R. Robinson, 970 to 972.
D. E. Robinson, 972 to 973.
Philip Daniel, 974.
William Randolph, 974 to 975.
Jno. Thos. Baker, 975 to 977.

Joseph Jackson. 977 to 979.
James Morton, 979 to 980.
R. J. Allen, 981 to 984.
Frank Hicks, 984 to 986.
Moses Lewis, 986 to 988.
William Garnett, 988 to 990.
John Edmunds, 990 to 991.
Samuel Brown, 991 to 993.
Leander Waller, 993 to 995.
Jos. T. Stewart, 995 to 997.
Z. Newton, jr., 998 to 999.

The evidence clearly shows that from 457 to 722 legal voters ineffectually attempted to cast their ballots for the contestant in Jackson ward. It will not be necessary to discuss the evidence as to the exact number, for if this class of votes is to be counted for contestant he would be entitled to his seat upon the smallest number that the evidence could be fairly held to show. We are of the opinion that at the least 457 of such votes are clearly shown, which is more than sufficient to overcome the majority of 261 returned for contestee.

Many of the colored voters fell in line the night before the election, prepared to vote. These three precincts were inhabited by a large colored population, and a large majority of the voters were Republicans and favorable to the contestant. A report had gone out that contestee's friends had made an arrangement to delay the vote in these precincts for the purpose of reducing the anticipated majority for the contestant. That such procedure was anticipated and feared is evident from the fact that the day before the election George Duncan, Federal supervisor, wrote to M. F. Pleasants, the chief supervisor, calling his attention to this method of obstructing the election.

We set out this correspondence from 1624, 1625 of the record :

RICHMOND, VA., Nov. 5th, 1888.

To M. F. PLEASANTS, Esq, *Chief Supervisor:*

SIR : I am Federal supervisor of election at first precinct, Jackson ward, and as such am anxious to be informed as to my duties as such supervisor at my precinct. The chief trouble is to poll our vote in consequence of the large number of persons on the registration books, and the manner in which the officers of election, and those who wish to prevent a full vote, conduct themselves ; for instance challengers who desire to prevent the polling of a full vote systematically challenge the whole colored vote as it comes to the polls by asking all sorts of ridiculous questions. For instance, of a citizen who has resided within a stone's throw of a precinct for twenty years and is seventy years old, whether he lives in the precinct, how long he has resided there, when he moved in, whether he is twenty-one years of age, when he became of age, when he was born, where his parents reside,. where was he born, and such like foolish and irrelevant questions. To the judges of election quietly listen and encourage until on an average five minutes are consumed in voting a colored man, and at sunset there is left in line a large number of qualified voters deprived of the right of suffrage and who have been in line with tickets in hand, for ten hours, seeking an opportunity to vote. Is there not some Federal statute covering this class of interference with elections and making it impossible for these colored citizens to cast their ballots ?

I am, with great respect, your obedient servant,

GEORGE DUNCAN.

RICHMOND, VA., Nov. 5th, 1888.

To GEORGE DUNCAN, Esq.,
   Supervisor of Election, First Precinct, Jackson Ward, Richmond, Va.:

SIR : In reply to your letter of this date I have no hesitation in saying that the acts referred to therein are, in my opinion, a clear violation of section 5506 of the Revised Statutes of the United States and render them perpetrators liable to the fine and imprisonment prescribed by that section. That section is as follows:

SECTION 5506. Every *person* who, by *any* unlawful means, *hinders, delays, prevents,* or *obstructs,* or combines and confederates with others to hinder, delay, prevent, or obstruct, any citizen from doing any act required to be done to qualify him to vote, *or from voting at any election* in any State, Territory, district, county, city, parish, township, school district, municipality, or other territorial subdivision, shall be *fined not less than five hundred dollars*, or be *imprisoned* not less than *one month*, nor more than *one year*, or be punished by both such fine and imprisonment.

M. F. PLEASANTS,
Chief Supervisor.

Evidence was introduced supporting the claim that there was a conspiracy to prevent the voters from casting their ballots and we give a portion of the evidence.

DAVID ROBINSON (first precinct)—p. 259-'60:

8th. Question. State whether or not you had a conversation with Mr. Cottrell, the Democratic judge of election at this precinct, and if so state when it took place and what was its purport?—Answer. The night after registration, which was ten days previous to election, I was in his bar-room. I was talking about the number of votes which would have to be cast on the day of election, and he said to me that you would not cast more than 400 votes at this poll on the day of election. I inquired of him diligently to tell me why, and he did not give me definite answer.

EDWARD THOMPSON—p. 1441:

Question 15. Heard Belvin say in the morning that he intended to hold that vote down that day within 300.

IRA BENEDICT—p. 63:

Question 2. I think on the day before the election, November the 5th, at the terminus of the Richmond Union Passenger Railway, 29th and P streets, Marshall ward; present, Mr. Timberlake, one of the judges of election, first precinct, Jackson ward, Mr. Buck Adams and Capt. Peter Smith, and good many others whose names I do not know. Mr. Adams—rather Mr. Timberlake—remarked first that he calculated having the handling of about 1,200 negro votes in Jackson ward. Mr. Adams then remarked that we will shut out about half of them. Mr. Timberlake in reply said, "Right you are, partner." I do not know whether there is anything else; but there is: I now recall another remark by one of the employés of the railroad: "Timberlake, you are a damn fool for talking that way. You will get yourself into trouble." I believe that is all I remember now.

PETER SMITH—p. 1460;

Question 3. Heard and corroborates above statement of Benedict.

M. M. WILLIAMS—p. 71:

Question 2. Timberlake said he had shut out enough votes in Jackson ward to elect Wise.

W. C. RHODES—p. 75:

6th. Question. Have you had any conversation with any of the judges of that election; if so where and what was said?—Answer. The day before the election I was in conversation with W. L. Timberlake, judge at the first precinct, Jackson ward, I think. He said, "We are going to carry Jackson ward for Cleveland, Thurman, and George D. Wise, I bet you." I said to him, "You must be crazy; how can that be done when the ward gives from 1,800 to 2,500 majority?" He says, "Well, we are going to knock them out."

H. P. HARPER—p. 69:

Question 2. Heard young man traveling with Elector Ellett and City Attorney Meredith, at first precinct, say constitutional ballots were to be used to hinder and delay the election.

GEO. DUNCAN (U. S. supervisor, first precinct), p. 1380-'81:

Question 26. Heard Cottrell and Timberlake, *judges*, and Smith and Belvin, *challengers*, during the latter part of the day congratulating themselves on the success of their efforts in keeping out votes.

EDWARD THOMPSON, p. 1443:

Question 15. Thompson was ward superintendent. "Once during the day I appealed to Mr. Belvin to allow us to poll our vote." He said, "Thompson, this is life or death with us."

JOHN H. CAMPBELL, p. 179:

Question 2. Heard a gentleman come up and ask one of the gentlemen with the disfranchised lists if he had voted that man he sent up? *He said no, but we delayed the election about ten minutes, and that was better than his vote.*

JOHN W. GRAVES, p. 138:

Question 3. When approaching polls to vote in white line was whispered to by the assistant challenger, who said, "Delay them all you can." Upon enquiring as to what was said, the challenger said, "When judge questions you in regard to the constitutional amendment, ask him what it means, what it is for, and all about it."

J. W. TYLER, p. 84:

Question 3. "Glazebrook," challenger, was challenging nearly every voter. Welford, the lawyer, remarked, "Let those vote who are entitled to it." Glazebrook winked at the time, and said the more votes that were challenged there would be shut out at the close.

FRANK MANN (fourth precinct), p. 158:

Question 6. Heard statement of Finnerty and Gentry, judges at fourth precinct, as follows: The night before the election—on Monday night—me and a friend of mine was passing down Seventeenth street, and I heard Mr. Finnerty tell Mr. Gentry to vote the niggers slow. I said to him, "Hi, Mr. Finnerty, are you going to vote us to-night?" I said to Mr. Finnerty, "I will see you to-morrow." Well, the next day when they took recess after voting up to 12 o'clock he says to me, "Frank, we've got you to-day." Then I said to him, "You recollect last night when you told Mr. Gentry to vote us all slow." I told him in the presence of Mr. Rankin and Mr. Hagan when he was coming out of Mr. Hagan's door what I have just said. He just laughed at me.

JAMES H. BARRETT, p. 209:

2d Question. Where were you on the evening before the 6th day of November last, and what occurred with reference to the election to be held the next day? Answer. I was coming down Seventeenth street between 7 and 8 o'clock in the evening, and Frank Mann overtaken me by the elevator. We were on our way to the Republican headquarters. When we arrived opposite Venable street we met Mr. Finnerty and Mr. Gentry talking. As we arrived opposite them heard Mr. Finnerty say to Mr. Gentry, "Vote these niggers slow to-morrow." His reply was, "All right." At that time I had gotten by them and did not hear any more that passed. My friend Frank Mann stopped and said something to them and then overtaken me.

Governor JAMES H. HARVEY, p. 195:

10th Question. State whether or not you heard any one say anything about the voting in Jackson Ward? Answer. I heard at the polls a great many say the voting was purposely delayed in order to hinder the colored voters from casting their ballots. After the polls were closed at night, while waiting in front of the Dispatch office, I heard a man state (I inquired his name and I was told he was Pettit) that he had had the pleasure that day of seeing 500 or 600 negroes cut out of their votes. He said he had been carrying refreshments from Binford's out to the boys in Jackson Ward.

WM. WALTER COLDWELL, p. 135.

Ans. On the night of the election, while waiting to see the returns as flashed on the canvas at the Despatch office, I heard some one say, "How are you Mr. Hughes?" The answer came back, "How are you, Harwood; how has it gone in Jackson Ward?" On that I immediately turned, and my elbow or my body touched ex-Mayor Taylor, of Manchester. Harwood replied, "We have done better than we expected." I don't mean to say these are the exact words, but they give the substance. Mr. Hughes answered, "How many have you thrown out?" Mr. Harwood replied by saying "From seven to eight hundred." Mr. Hughes inquired, "How did you do it?" Harwood's reply was, "Why, it took two hours and forty-five minutes to vote one man. I sent him to his house four times for his number. He would come back one time and I would tell him it is wrong; go back and get it again." Ex-Mayor Taylor then said to Mr. Harwood, "Was that an unavoidable delay, or a natural delay?" These are his exact words. Mr. Harwood's answer was, "We fixed everything last night, but we have done better than we thought we would." Ex-Mayor Taylor then denounced it, and said that it was an outrage, and no wonder that the Northern press denounced and condemned the Southern people for such outrage. I had no part in the conversation.

The plan complained of by Mr. Duncan was carried out fully by adherents of the contestee and resulted in the exclusion of more than enough votes for contestant to change the result. The object of the persons engaged in this mode of disfranchisement clearly appears when it is known that out of all the great number of voters who were prevented from voting none of them belonged to the political party of the contestee. The evidence upon this question is very voluminous and we will give a few brief extracts to show its general character.

B. C. STOKES, a colored election judge, testifies:

14th. Question. How did they obstruct the polls?—Answer. By crowding up on the little narrow window they voted at, occupying about half the little narrow window, and this way crowding voters and those friends; other stranger challengers, they would ask an old man about sixty years old, with gray hair, whether he was twenty-one. The old colored man would say in those cases—he would take off his hat and say, look at my bald head and see.

20th. Question. Repeat, as near as you can, the kind of questions they would ask, them.—Answer. How old are you; what is your age; where do you live; what street, number (great many questions asked at times whether they live in Chesterfield County or Henrico); how long you been living in the State, city; sometimes a man would give his number of house, and if it did not agree on his book with the name, that is the poll-book, registration-book, though it was proven that was the right man, they would send him off to get his number.

21st. Question. Do you mean that they wouldn't let a man vote if there was a difference in the number of his house on the same street between the registration-book and his answer to the question?—Answer. Yes, sir; they wouldn't let him vote.

22nd. Question. Were any objections made during the day to the occupying of the window by Mr. Belvin and others?—Answer. There was objection made by Mr. Duncan, Stokes, myself, by Mr. Allan; and the Democratic challengers threatened to have Mr. Edgar Allan arrested for objecting to their obstructing.

Answer to 25th question. Belvin was arrested.

49th. Cross-question. You have said that Mr. Belvin threatened to have Mr. Allan arrested. What called forth this remark?—Answer. Mr. Allan was instructing the voters as they came to the window to say "Presidential ticket only," in order to save dispute as to whether they wanted to vote about the constitutional question.

Answer to 1st question on re-examination. I think his questions were very unnecessary. In my judgment, to obstruct the election, that we might not have a fair representation of the vote of the precinct.

A. C. ROCKECHARLIE, who was the clerk in taking the ballots and keeping a list of persons who were prevented from voting, testifies:

Answer to 2d question. Belvin took up half the window and challenged about 70 per cent. of the voters, assisted by Smith, Briggs, and other comrades, and that Mr. Epps, sergeant of police, had the constitutional card read over twice, pretending he did not understand it, and consumed over three minutes.

4th question. Smith said he wanted to kill time.

3d. Question. Look at the said memorandum book as far as you can recollect it was made at the time, and give the names of any parties, after thus refreshing your memory, that participated in said election, and state whether and what they so did when they were engaged in an effort to facilitate the voting, or to make it impossible to poll the full vote. When this diversion in reference to the memorandum book which you have now produced took place you were giving certain names. I ask, in answer to the question, that you go on with any additional names, as far as you can do so by refreshing your memory from said book.—Answer. Hillary Jones I noted out there——

There was an Italian (or of some foreign nationality) out there named Dominici K. Perross. He was challenged by Belvin, and Cottrell asked him if he wanted to vote on the constitution. The constitutional law was read to him. Belvin, finding out how the vote stood, withdrew his objection as challenger; that is, finding out it was a Democratic ballot, he withdrew said objections. Another, named A. Perross, he called for the reading of the constitutional law, and didn't vote the ticket after it was read to him. He was prompted by Belvin as to the reading of the law. Another, named M. J. (or G.) Dugin. I am giving these names from memory. Cottrell, the judge, who took tickets—I suppose he was judge. He asked Mr. Dugin if he (Dugin) wanted to vote on the constitution and have him (Cottrell) to read and explain the law to him. I suppose between three and four minutes were consumed. There was a colored citizen named Thomas Coak, or Cork, came up to vote. Cottrell asked him his name. He said, "My name is Thomas Cork." Belvin says—I suppose you would style it judge, who was looking over the colored book—Belvin——

(The witness here desires the word "says," above in the incomplete sentence "Belvin says," struck out and changed to "hollowed at him.")

Belvin hollowed to the Judge that his name begins with a "K." Belvin knew at the time that it began with a "C," for he held his finger on the name in the challenger's book. Another, named Geo. Mimms, was rejected because he gave the wrong number of his house, though he claimed to live in the same precinct. Isaac Christian was challenged by Smith—that is, Harry Smith; peremptory was the word he used. I don't know what he means by it. Collannan was another, I believe, N.

G. He called, rather asked, that this constitutional law be explained to him. Cottrell, the judge, read the law to him; he consumed time between two and three minutes. Another named Thorps. I think Robert, I am not positive as to Chas. He was challenged by both Smith and Belvin. Belvin says, "Halloo, Jack, what kind of ticket is that you have got?" Smith says to Belvin, ask him if he was sick. Belvin did ask him the question. The time consumed was nearer four than three minutes.

Answer to 10th question. Cottrell very slow in reading the oath.

11th. Question. State whether the colored voters voted generally on the constitutional convention question or not, and state what happened in reference to their desire to vote or not to vote on said proposition if anything.—Answer. I haven't any recollection of seeing any colored voter voting on the constitutional convention. Mr. Belvin would frequently ask colored voters would they desire to vote on these. They said no, or refused. Smith, Belvin, and, I think, Briggs, would hollow, "Read the law." Mr. Belvin objected to one man getting out the line until he did vote on the constitutional question.

12th. Question. What part, if any, did Judge Cottrell take in reference to voting on the constitutional question?—Answer. Cottrell frequently asked the same question, whether he desired to vote on the constitutional question. Refused and hollowed, "No, the Presidential ticket."

13th. Question. State if you know who distributed or took part in distributing these constitutional convention tickets.—Answer. Mr. Cottrell distributed a good many, and some of the challengers; who they were I don't know.

LEWIS STEWART—page 45:

Answer to 3rd question. Belvin challenged first voter at polls and then every other man.

7th question. Smith and others had books of lists of disfranchised voters in *Henrico and Dinwiddie Counties.*

8th. Question. State, if you remember, the kind of questions put by these challengers to the voters.—Answer. I don't know how many, but can tell the character of them. First ask a man who would apply to vote, gray-headed men who looked to be fifty or sixty years old, they ask him his age, where was he born, how many children he had; have you ever been out the United States; have you ever been to the penitentiary, and many cases I heard them ask them who was their master's name.

9th. Question. Did you notice any particular conduct when white men would come up to vote?—Answer. When white men would apply to vote I heard Mr. Belvin and Mr. Smith tell them have the constitution explained to them, and delayed as much time as they could with them.

14th. Question. How did Mr. Cottrell act in receiving these ballots and in depositing them?—Answer. When a voter would apply they would ask him his name and number, and after the clerks on the inside had found his name and number and hollowed out all right, he would hold that ticket in his hands till Mr. Belvin could look over his books and tell him all right, let him vote, and then he would ask voters, "What kind of ticket is that you have got?" The voter would say, "You have no right to ask me what kind of ticket I have got;" and then he would ask him, "Do you want to vote on the constitution?" The voter would say, "No; deposit my ballot;" and then say, "Perhaps you don't understand it; I will explain it to him." Mr. Cottrell said this.

Answer to 16th question. Judge Waddill and Allan tried to put a stop to it, but could not.

Answer to 18th and 19th questions. Cottrell absent ten minutes and only one vote cast, as Belvin objected.

Answer to 23rd, 24th, and 25th questions. Allan would expedite finding names and challengers talked of having him arrested.

Answer to 27th to 30th questions. Police would not, on request, remove crowd from around the polls. Captain of police snatched scantling from Judge Waddill which would have prevented crowding.

Page 49, questions 24—5. The crowd of the voters did not delay voting.

Answer to question 55. How Mr. Allan so quickly found the names on book.

Answer to 96th question. Voters asked how many children they had.

Page 54—Re-examination by Judge Waddill:

2nd. Question. In the one hundred and twenty-seventh X.-Q. you were asked as follows: "If they were told to say, 'for President only,' to avoid that question, then is it not a fact that Mr. Cottrell did ask that question?" I now ask you to explain why it was that it became necessary that any instruction should have been given to the Republican voters as to what they should say in reference to the ticket they proposed to vote as they presented their ballot to Judge Cottrell.

Answer. Mr. Cottrell would ask every voter that applied to vote what kind of ticket is that you have, and after being told, would then ask him if he would then vote on the constitution, and offered to explain it without being asked. Then it was thought by the Republicans that it might stop Mr. Cottrell from asking that question, provided they were told before they reached the polls what kind of ticket they had; it did not, however. He continued to ask, notwithstanding he was told, "for President only.".

3rd. Question. You were asked in the one hundred and fourth X.-Q. as follows : "Are the colored people or not so ignorant as not to know the number of their houses?" And you say, "There are some colored people, old ones especially, who have never had the advantages of schooling, who know nothing whatever of numbers, and they are more than apt to forget their numbers." I now ask you to explain whether the character of questions asked by these challengers and the manner in which said challengers conducted themselves were calculated to expedite, aid, and assist this class of old, ignorant, and infirm voters in casting their ballots, or were they calculated to mix up said voters and to delay and kill as much time with them as possible on account of their ignorance and old age?

(Question objected to because it is leading, and because, while it asks the witness "to explain," it really asks him to repeat what he has already said.)

Answer. No, sir; they were not calculated to expedite or assist, but, on the contrary, they would take advantage of an old, ignorant man by asking him all sorts of foolish questions.

Answer to 4th cross-question, p. 55: Belvin sent on to United States grand jury.

Answer to 6th and 7th cross-questions: White and colored voted alternately, but no white votes left out.

WALTER R. LOMAX, p. 59:

5th. Question. State as far as you can why the said vote was not polled or anything you saw that prevented it.—Answer. The judge consumed a lot of time by holding the ballot in his hand and asking Mr. Belvin if he was ready. Every now and then Mr. Smith would hollow, "Let us read the law," and they would read the law. Mr. Belvin would take a considerable time to find a name, notwithstanding the clerk on the inside had found it. They would never vote a man until Mr. Belvin found his name on the outside.

6th. Question. State, please, who Messrs. Belvin and Smith are, to whom you have referred, and what they were doing there that day.—Answer. Mr. Belvin was a challenger, I think. I don't know what Mr. Smith was. I know he was at the polls all day interfering with the voters. They were Democrats. They seemed to be there to keep people from voting—to keep Republicans from voting.

7th. Question. Was there anything to be voted on or for other than the Presidential and Congressional election? And, if so, state whether any time was lost on that account, and how lost.—Answer. A constitutional question. Time was lost on this account: The judge was distributing these tickets every five or ten minutes to—I don't know whether he handed them out to Mr. Smith or Mr. Belvin—but he did not hand them to colored people. No colored people asked for them. When a white gentleman would come up he would get one of those constitutional tickets. Then the judge would stop and read it to them, and then Mr. Belvin would say to the judge that the voter don't understand it, and then the judge would explain it to him.

8th. Question. State if you heard Mr. Belvin or Smith say anything to the voters as they would approach the window as to what they would do in reference to the constitutional question when offering to vote.

Answer. I heard Mr. Belvin, since I come to think, tell the voters to have that constitutional question read. I didn't hear Mr. Smith say anything. I can't say I did.

9th. Question. What would the voter whom Mr. Belvin thus requested the constitution to be explained to do, and what would the judge of the election do? And tell all that would then happen.—Answer. He would have the ticket read by the judge of election. The judge would read it. Then, after he would read it, the voter would tell the judge he didn't understand it, and the judge would then explain it. This is all I can remember.

14th. Question. Did you hear Mr. Belvin say or do anything when the voter would explain that he only wanted to vote the one ticket, or when other persons explained to the voter that they should only offer to vote the one ticket?—Answer. Mr. Belvin would object to their saying the Presidential ticket only. I can't say he stopped it, but he objected.

15th. Question. Did any one, and if so who, request the voters to call for the Presidential ticket only?—Answer. I stated it myself, and several others did the same thing.

16th. Question. Did Mr. Belvin say anything to you all, and if so what?—Answer. He didn't say anything to me, but appealed to the judge. He told the judge it was not right for any one to tell the voter how he should vote.

17th. Question. Were many persons challenged on the day of election by Mr. Belvin and Mr. Smith?—Answer. Yes, sir.

18th. Question. What time did you reach the polls?—Answer. I was there before the polls opened.

Answer to 14th and 16th questions, p. 60: Belvin objected to this advice to voters.

Answer to 27th question: Belvin continually occupying the window, though often told to get away.

29th. Question. Did you observe him at all during the day looking in the alphabetical list for names, and observe where he seemed to be looking?—Answer. Some one stopped Mr. Belvin; he was looking in one letter for a name in another letter. Suppose the name began with W, he would look in the letter—any other letter—except the one he should look in. Our challenger would tell him where to look; he did tell him where to look; then he would look in there and find it. Mr. Belvin wouldn't tell or allow our challenger to look on his book. Mr. Belvin would kinder turn himself to the wall.

30th. Question. Was there much time consumed in this and other ways in the voter depositing his ballot?—Answer. Yes, there was a good deal of time consumed, because the judge wouldn't vote a man until Mr. Belvin would find his name. There might have been others, but I can't recall any just now.

Answer to question 3, p. 61: Belvin advised witness to challenge all Democratic voters.

CHARLES ROBINSON, p. 63 to 66:

Answer to 3d, 4th, and 5th questions, and 34th cross-question, p. 66: Owned and lived for five years in house from which he tried to vote; was discharged from employment because he went to vote, but was not allowed to vote by Belvin. Directory corroborated his statement. See the following:

3d. Question. Do you mean you have owned and lived in that house for five years past?—Answer. Yes, sir; and I have owned the place longer than that.

4th. Question. Were you at your precinct on the election held there on the 6th of November last; and if so, did you vote?—Answer. Yes, sir; I got there at half past six in the morning and stayed there until half-past eleven before I got to the window. I did not vote.

5th. Question. Tell what happened when you got to the window.—Answer. When I got up to the window Mr. Belvin attacked me then, and said, "Hold on; don't vote him yet," just in that manner. He asked me, "Chas., how old are you?" I told him I was going on 32 years old. He says, "Have you ever been up before court; you ever been convicted of the penitentiary?" I said, "No, sir," and he said, "I've got you down here disfranchised," and I says, "Oh, no, sir. Let me swear my name in then." He says, "They got your number down here 1248, and on the book it is 1148. Hold on; don't vote him yet;" and then he said, "Stand aside." I went home to get my number, and brought it back to show it to him. He said, "Stand aside; I have got no time to bother with any number now." Then I pitched off down the depot, and I said now I know I am going to be discharged to-day.

25th. Cross-question. When you returned to the polls with the number did you take your place again in the rear of the line of voters?—Answer. No, sir; I went right up to Mr. Belvin, and he turned and said to me, "Go away from here; I've got no time to bother with you." He spoke to me like he was speaking to a hog.

34th. Cross-question. Did you come back any more that day?—Answer. Yes, sir; after Mr. James discharged me I said to myself, "All right, I will go back and take the balance of the day at it."

JAMES CHILDRESS—page 67:

7th. Question. State now, as near as you can, what was done by Mr. Belvin and other challengers, who were present during the day representing the Democratic party, to delay and hinder the voting.—Answer. Mr. Belvin was there with a book in his hand, and every voter came up he would delay him from voting until he looked over that book, and would question them all sorts of questions. He would ask old gray-headed men how old are you, where you live, have you ever been married, and would continue to ask different questions until a person had stood there five or six minutes, and then he would smile and then allow him to be voted. This is in the early part of the day. Then, in another instance later in the day, Mr. Smith was there as challenger—H. M. Smith, jr., I think. They made it a business, it seemed, to challenge each one. Mr. Smith would challenge one and then Mr. Belvin. This applies generally, as far as I could see, while I was at the polls. One instance, a man came there and didn't have his number right, and they refused to vote him, and he went away and got his right number and came back, and Mr. Belvin positively refused to vote him, objecting, and the judge refused to vote him. I think that man was named Geo. Mimms. Belvin challenged him and would not allow him to vote, and I and a good many others in the crowd hollowed out vote him on his oath. They refused to vote him on his oath. I saw Mr. Smith challenge a man, I don't know his name, and the man demanded grounds on which he challenged him, and he refused to give grounds and offered to read the law on the subject, all of which, in my judgment, he was trying to kill time. I also saw good many white men walk up to the voting place, and while doing so several of them would ask they have the law on the constitutional question read, and the challenger, Mr. Belviu, in the morning had a long talk with the judge of election as to the right to have the law read.

Answer to 12th question, p. 68. Not a single illegal voter found amid all the challengers.

W. H. L. TILMAN—pages 76-7

4th. Question. State all you saw there in the conduct of election by the officers of election, and the length of time required to poll a vote?—Answer. I was at the polls the 6th November at 2 o'clock in the morning. When I fell in line there were thirty-three men ahead of me; when I voted it was a quarter to ten. I just could discern I was moving in the line the space of every ten minutes. A man voted before me by the name of Leigh Jinkins; his vote was challenged by Mr. Preston Belvin; he said he lived over the Branch, and said he was charged with petty larceny, and that he was disfranchised, and Jinkins said he had never been disfranchised, and to swear him on his oath and he would stand the consequence; after he voted he wasn't arrested. A man by the name of George Dawson, in line in front of me; he got out of line; he didn't vote that day till night, at Moore street; he was in line again, but the polls closed on him. My vote wasn't challenged, Another man by the name of A. Scott; his name appeared on the register M. Scott; he couldn't vote; he was flung out because his name didn't corroborate with that on the registration-book; the number was the same.

Answer to 10th question. Cottrell held his ballot for Belvin to search his list and only voted him when B. could not find his name.

JACOB MALLORY:

5th. Question. Please state what occurred at the polls while you were there in connection with the election.—Answer. The first thing I heard Mr. Belvin asked the voters unnecessary questions. He asked one old gentleman how old he was, and I replied to the old gentleman to tell him that he was old enough for to vote. I think his name was Mat. He asked him if he was born in Richmond, and he said he was not, but was born in the State; and they asked him was Richmond in the State of Virginia, and I replied to him that they had no right to ask him that, and that he shouldn't answer no such question. I think you will find his other name on the book. Then he also begin to ask questions what they were voting for, whether for President or constitutional, and good many of the voters didn't understand it, and we went down the line to instruct the voters to say for President only. Then he instructed all the white voters to ask the constitutional law to be read to them. Then my reply was to Mr. Belvin why don't you let them read it yourself, and he replied that none of these could read, and he requested the judge, Cottrell, Dem., to read it to them, and he would do so. Just about ten or half past ten o'clock we appealed to the police officers, Capt. Epps and others, to keep the crowd back from the voting window. He replied that he didn't have anything to do with it; and these officers—I mean the marshals—I asked them if they couldn't get the crowd back. They said they were doing all they could, but they were doing nothing but standing there. The way the window was blocked by these challengers—there was about a dozen of them, all Democrats—the window was about two feet, I suppose, and Mr. Belvin would occupy exactly half of the window. He was standing with his book open laying in the window, and after the person would vote it would take at least two or three minutes for the voter to get away after casting his ballot, until Mr. Allan and Mr. Waddill came up, and they put a pole—Mr. Waddill did—for to keep the crowd back; but the police officer said he was obstructing the sidewalk and made him remove it. The voting was getting on pretty fast while the pole was there. It staid there only about five minutes, and about five persons, colored, voted in that time. Towards the evening the voter would come up, his name or number would be wrong on the book, and Mr. Belvin would assist on his staying there and request to vote after knowing that he wouldn't vote. After knowing that he couldn't vote Mr. Belvin insisted on his staying there and still ask to vote. He would tell him that he had as much right to vote as anybody else.

19th. Question. Would or not a great many more votes have been cast if the pole put up by Mr. Waddill had been permitted to remain by the police?—Answer. Yes, sir.

20th. Question. Did it not greatly facilitate the voting, without injury or inconvenience to the public generally?—Answer. It was helping the vote on; it didn't interfere with the public at all.

21st. Question. Did this judge of election, Cottrell, permit the challengers to obstruct the vote as you have stated without objection on their part, or did they do anything to stop it?—Answer. Didn't do anything at all to stop it; the judge would do everything the challenger requested.

GEORGE O. CARTER—p. 245:

4th. Question. State whether you attended your voting precinct at the election held on the 6th day of November, 1888; how long you remained there in line to vote, and whether or not you succeeded in voting.—Answer. Yes, sir; I did attend. I remained there from about 6.30 a. m., and only one or two voted after I voted till the close of the polls. I did not leave the ranks during the day. I eat my breakfast and dinner in the line.

6th. Question. What questions were asked you when you were about to vote, and by whom were they asked?—Answer. I was asked if I had ever been in jail. I was challenged by a person who said he was a challenger.

7th. Question. Were you asked any other questions? And state, if you know, the name of any person who questioned you.—Answer. I was asked if I was unfranchised; if I had ever been in the penitentiary. I was asked where I was born at; if I had ever been out of the United States; how long I had been in Richmond, where I came from, when I came to Richmond, and then asked me where I lived, and then how long I had been living there; where I moved from when I came there to live. He desired to know if I had ever voted before. They told me that it was a Mr. Beverly or Mr. Belvin.

8th. Question. You say you arrived at the polls at half past 6 o'clock a. m., and did not vote until just before the close of the polls. Did you in all that time break your place in the line or allow any one to go up ahead of you?—Answer. No, sir; I did not.

9th. Question. When you were about to vote was there any pushing or shoving; and, if so, what was the cause of it?—Answer. Yes, sir; a plenty of it. There were about twenty-five or thirty white people pushing to keep the colored people from getting to the window.

H. M. SMITH—p. 1152-61:—Contestee's witnesses.

25th. Question. It has also been testified that you and Mr. Belvin not only asked the unnecessary questions I have alluded to, but you were heard to instruct Mr. Belvin to ask the voters whether they were sick; state whether you did so, and, if so, why?—Answer. That was in consequence of an astute political job put up on us by Capt. Ben Scott, a Republican. About the middle of the day Capt. Scott came to me and said that there was a poor old sick man back there in the line, who could hardly stand up, and asked me, as an act of mercy, that he might come up out of his turn and vote on the white man's side of the window. I readily and cheerfully agreed to it and the man was voted; from the success of this effort, I presume, the amount of sickness in the crowd became appalling, so much so that after four or five of them had voted out of their turn on our side of the window, with our consent, I dropped back into the crowd to reconnoiter, and I heard a colored man say, in reference to a sick man who was going up to vote, "that man ain't no sicker than I is," which confirmed my own suspicions that we were being taken advantage of, and I called to Belvin to ask him if he was sick, and after that the sick men disappeared.

43d. Cross-question. Did you not sympathize with and encourage pretty much everything you saw done at the polls on that day which in your judgment tended to lessen the Republican vote at that precinct?—Answer. I went out there to assist in preventing any illegal votes from being cast. I tried to do my duty, and did not study the consequences. I would not have cared, to be frank, how small the Republican majority was, but my sole end, aim, and object was to prevent illegal votes from being cast.

51st. Cross-question. I heard some Democrats urged to vote on constitutional question.

JAS. E. MERRIWEATHER—p. 133:

5th question. Window crowded with 25 or 50 challengers and policemen.

6th and 7th questions. Old men of 60 questioned as to age, etc., and nearly all challenged.

W. H. MULLEN—p. 136 and exhibit p. 1625:

4th. Question. Look at the paper, please, you have filed with your last answer, and give us the names of the voters by precinct, and state the length of time it took to vote them and whether they are white or colored.—Answer. At the 2d precinct Braxton Hill, colored, voted in three minutes; at the same precinct Montrose Angle, white, voted in half a minute; at the same precinct Edward Jordan, colored, three minutes; William James, colored, three minutes. At the third precinct William Hopes, colored, voted in three minutes; Henry O'Neal, white, voted in half a minute; R. H. Baylor, colored, voted in three and a half minutes. The grounds stated for questioning this voter, the challenger said, was that a real estate agent standing behind him said this voter had moved, which the voter denied. At the third precinct John Johnson, col'd, voted in three minutes; Daniel Henderson, colored, was questioned for four minutes; Robert Brown, colored, voted in two minutes; Benjamin Jackson, colored, voted in three minutes.

JOHN W. GRAVES—p. 138.

3d. Question. State, please, anything that happened at the precinct when you were there to vote, as to the polling of the vote and other circumstances; and, if so, what did happen? Answer. Well, it was between one and two o'clock when I voted. I was in line with my ballot in my hand; some gentleman, I don't who he was, stationed just behind the challenger, and acting in the capacity of .assistant, leaned over and whispered to me, "Delay them all you can." I turned to him and asked him what he said, when he repeated the remark and added, "When the judge questions you in regard to the constitutional amendments, ask him what it means and what it is for and all about it." I paid no attention to him, however, but voted. After I had voted I remained long enough, possibly four or five minutes, to see the next man vote. It happened to be a bright mulatto, apparently about 35 years of age. When his name was called the challenger promptly challenged him, and commenced to question him. One of\ the first questions asked of him was his age; he also asked him how long he had been a registered voter, and other questions as regards his right to vote. Finally some one inside of the precinct said, "Why, that man has been voting here for ten years." The judges then spoke and said, "He is all right." The man was questioned no further, but allowed to vote. It took possibly three minutes to vote him. I then left the door or the window of the precinct, and, after glancing at a.long line of voters, returned to my work.

7th question. You have spoken of what this assistant challenger, as you term him, said to you. Did the challenger himself state or do anything; and, if so, what?— Answer. The only thing that the challenger said that I can remember was when my name was called the gentleman whom I have spoken.of as assistant challenger mistook my name for Gray, and said, "What is that, Gray?" I turned and said, "No, Graves." The challenger then cautioned him to remain quiet or rather said to him, "Hush, he is all right," or words to that effect.

8th question. How many persons were there in the white line when you voted?— Answer. I don't think there was but one besides myself in the line.

9th question. Was there more than one line at this precinct—I mean was there a white and a colored line?—Answer. Yes, sir.

10th question. How did they vote from these lines?—Answer. One white and one colored, alternately.

JACKSON AKERS, or ACRES—p. 173:

6th question. What was the conduct of the judges of election and challengers for the Democratic party in connection with the receiving of the ballots during the day? —Answer. Well, the conduct of the challengers, I think, was very bad. Mr. Guigou challenged nearly every other vote whilst he was there. A good deal of time was lost by the judge asking and explaining questions on the amendment to the constitution.

7th question. How did the judges delay the election in reference to the constitutional amendments?—Answer. That was done generally by white men coming to vote. It delayed it this way: When a white man would come to vote, then the judge would delay time by telling him which line to strike out if he was opposed to the amendment or which to strike out if he was in favor of it.

8th question. What did the challengers do, and who were they, at any time during the day?—Answer. The challengers had the.disfranchisement list. They challenged very near every other man who came to vote. The voter was charged with being disfranchised. Good many of them was put on their oath and voted, but some they didn't let vote at all. They took ten to fifteen minutes on most of them. I don't know but one, that is Mr. Guigon.

JNO. H. CAMPBELL—p. 178:

2nd. Question. Mr.Meredith objected to Cunningham acting as Republican challenger; one challenge delayed seven or eight minutes; challenged about six out of ten; took pride in explaining constitutional vote; long line of voters late in the evening, waiting to vote, and the same tactics were pursued, Judge Waddill using all his efforts to get in the vote quietly and peacefully; "we delayed the election about ten minutes, and that was better than his vote."

BENJ. JACKSON—p. 185:

6th question. What was the conduct of these challengers when they were there? State what they did in connection with the voting.—Answer. From the time the polls were opened until they closed at night nearly every colored voter was challenged. When they came to the polls to vote they would give their names, and if their name was found on the poll-book, and if the parties holding the poll-book would say it was all right, the challenger would say, "Hold on, judge. I challenge that vote.". After looking over the disfranchised list they would say, "All right; go on." All this time the judge of election would be holding the ballot in his hands, and he never deposited any ballot until the challengers were satisfied. I would state that I was challenged myself by Mr. Skelton on the ground that I gave the wrong age. I voted on my oath, and this took about five minutes' time. I have lived in the precinct about fifteen years, pay taxes on about three thousand dollars' worth of property. Allen Cæsar's vote was also challenged; they say his name could not be found on the poll-book, and he did not vote. A. P. Quarls' vote was also challenged on account of his not giving the right age, I think; he did not vote at all. There was another man by the name of Braxton; his vote was also challenged and he was not allowed to vote on account of not giving the right number. A great deal of time was also taken up or lost by the police forcing the lines back, and before we could get the men regularly in line again to vote, we would lose probably five or ten minutes. There was also a great deal of time lost in explaining to each colored voter as he came up to vote whether he wanted to vote for or against the convention. The judge of election would say to each voter, "Every twenty years we have to vote for constitutional convention; this convention is to make any amendments to the constitution of the State of Virginia. If you want to vote for the convention you will mark out this bottom line, and if you don't want to vote for it you will mark out the top one." This question was put to each voter as they come by the judge of election. I think this is about all that I recollect.

J. E. FARRAR (ex-councilman), p. 193:

6th. Question. State if you saw anything remarkable about the conducting of the election on that day.—Answer. Well, on my first visit I went there as I had usually gone, about the middle of the day, to vote, as they have usually gotten through with the rush of voters by that time, and usually there is no difficulty in a man voting after that hour at that precinct. I noticed when I arrived there that there were an unusual long line of voters waiting to vote. Then I went up to the voting window where they were voting and found a number of gentlemen which I had not usually seen at that precinct, and Mr. C. V. Meredith was arguing a point of law and insisting on the judge to give his decision whether a voter should tell what was his age when he registered or his exact age when he come up to vote. I asked him what was the matter; why were they voting so slow? He stated that he only wanted to know whether the persons voting there were legal voters, and wanted the judge to decide the question whether a man should tell his age when he registered or his exact age when he came to vote. I stated to him then that I wondered if he or the judge either entertained any doubt in regard to the person then at the window endeavoring to vote, as any one could see from his appearance that he was then over 50 years of age—about as gray as I am.

7th. Question. How long a time was occupied in voting one man while you were there?—Answer. I think about eight or ten minutes.

8th. Question. Did any policeman interfere with you during this colloquy with Mr. Meredith?—Answer. When I approached the window I were attacked by a policeman; he asked me was I challenger there that day, or who did I wish to see; I stated to him that I wished to vote, and to know why the voting was being conducted so slow; that he need not bother about me, that I was for peace and business, and then passed on. He said nothing more.

9th. Question. About how many colored men were in line waiting to vote when you got there?—Answer. As near as I can judge I reckon about 125 or 150.

10th. Question. Had there ever been any trouble in getting in the whole vote at that precinct at any previous election?—Answer. Not to my knowledge.

13th. Question. You say that you have been voting at that precinct for fifteen years, and that you own three thousand dollars' worth of property in that precinct. Have you ever had any trouble in voting there before, and has there ever been any difficulty in polling the full vote at precinct at any previous election?—Answer. No, sir; I never had any trouble in voting there before. We have never had any trouble before; we generally manage to poll the full vote by 4 o'clock.

14th. Question. About how many people were at the precinct when you got there in the morning, and were they in line?—Answer. Near about 200, and they were all in line.

GEORGE A. CUNNINGHAM—p. 189-90:

After remaining at the Third for a while and witnessing the slow voting, the judge at that precinct seemed to me to take lots of time and great interest in listening to all questions raised by the challengers. When they raised any objection he would hold the ballot, listen to all of them before depositing it, which consumed from three to ten minutes with each one. He took great interest in wanting to read and reading the constitutional act which was raised out there. I saw a voter being refused to vote by the objection of one of the challengers. This colored man came to vote, but was refused on the ground that he had his number on a piece of paper, and refused to give it verbally.

A. H. KAUFMAN—(candidate for house of delegates)—p. 210 :

Part answer to sixth question. I drove to the third precinct, and got there just as a man by the name of George Jackson was about to cast his ballot. I found considerable delay occasioned by one of the judges of election at that precinct voluntarily explaining to the voter the law bearing upon the vote for a call for a convention. He explained that law to that particular voter three times successively, consuming sufficient time to have voted three or four voters in an ordinary manner. I was right behind the voter, and knowing him personally I knew be was fully competent to cast his vote without the aforesaid explanation. I could not help, from the circumstances, to become aware that the judge of election had an understanding with the challengers at the polls in making this explanation so repeatedly for the purpose of delay and consumption of time. I remarked to the voter, the aforesaid Mr. Jackson, that he seemed to be very hard of understanding to-day, knowing him to be as intelligent as he was. He finally voted and went away, after consuming between six and eight minutes of time. The next voter that presented himself, a colored man, was challenged by two or three challengers. I do not know the merits of the challenging, but I saw conclusivsly that all of it was done for the purpose of delay, intimidation, and consumption of time. While this was going on a question arose between the Republican United States supervisor and some of the challengers as to their respective rights, when Colonel Tazewell Ellett came up flourishing a paper and stated in a loud voice calculated to inspire with awe any timid voter, that he had just come from the office of the secretary of the commonwealth and held the law from him; that they (the Democratic challengers) could have the United States supervisor arrested. This declaration on the part of Colonel Ellett caused considerable excitement at the polls, and consumed a great deal of time.

DAN'L HENDERSON—p. 221 :

2nd to 5th question. Owns twelve houses, six of them in Jackson ward; resided there twelve years; identified by the judges, but challenge insisted on and he had to take the oath before voting.

CHARLES FRAYSER—p. 588 :

10th. Question. Why did you not vote your ballot at the regular polls? How near to the ballot-box did you get to the regular polls, and why were you not allowed to vote there?—Answer. I was challenged there for some cause or another, I don't know what. I got right up to it, and handed my ballot in, and when they called my name a gentleman challenged my vote, and then they asked me if that was all my name, and I told them yes, except when I was a child the children used to call me Charles Heury Fraysier. The gentlemen then said I had no right to vote as my name was on the book Charles Fraysier; and then the polls closed before I got away.

11th. Question. What length of time passed from the time you got to the ballot-box and offered your ballot to vote and the time the polls closed? Answer. As near as I can come at it it must have been not less than ten minutes.

THOMAS H. BRIGGS :

29th. Cross-question. Please state some of the questions usually asked a voter by the challengers.—Answer. Asked them their names; where do you say you live; what is your number; did you say 1714? No, sir; I said 1417. Ever been to jail; wasn't you arrested for stealing last year; what did you say your name was, John Robertson; how you spell it? Robtson. Did you say Robson? No, sir. Well, didn't you used to live at number 506? No, sir. Well, here's another man the same name, I think that must be you. And all sorts such questions as that they would ask; more so on that day than I have ever known.

I. W. CARTER (councilman)—p. 170 :

3d. Question. State, please, anything that you saw or that happened at the said precinct on the said day, if anything did happen, by which the vote of said precinct was not polled.—Answer. I was at the door, and the voters came to a halt, and I happened to look in there to see what was the matter, and I went on inside and I saw Mr. Kolbe, I think, a supervisor, and a man was there who wanted to vote. He asked him his name, and he told him. He asked him his age, and he told him. His residence, and he told him; and then he asked him was he married, he answered yes; and then he asked did he have any children, and he said yes; then he asked him how many, and he told him; then he asked him how old was the oldest, and he told him; then he asked him how old was the youngest, and he told him, At this point I interfered with the question as to the age of the children. Then he stopped then and had some words with me about it, and said he could do as he pleased; that I had nothing to do with it. Then I gave up, and the man went on answering his unnecessary questions. I went out and stood at the door. About ten minutes was consumed with that one man. This man was the one they had the most trouble with. This was a well man, but sick did come during the day, and I asked the policeman to admit them, as was the custom, and the policeman said he would nto admit them unless somebody would give way in the ranks. So I said to him, you had as well try to move a brick house as to try to move a man out of ranks, and he said, well, if he was sick let him go home and go to bed; that that was the best place for him. All these things would delay the voting for about ten minutes for one man to vote. That is about all.

Question 15. Gentry would look through all the J's before allowing a man named John to vote, and would pay no attention to voter's finding his own name.

JACOB CROSS—p. 181:

Question 6, p. 182. Gentry would find name John Smith, a voter, with *right number, age, and all*, but would not allow him to vote until he had looked entirely through the list of Smiths. * * * One Morracco Smith also offered to vote; I found name and informed Gentry of it; he said it was none of my business, stand back, and would not allow him to vote until he had looked entirely through the S's. * * * Gentry had to have his attention called two or three times to voters *offering to vote before you could make him hear*. He was leaning on the book, which was open a part of the time, *and then in conversation with the other challengers* during the day.

Question 7. Kolbe was the Democratic supervisor. Asked man how long he had been married, how many children he had, etc. Thinks Kolbe was under the influence of liquor.

FRANCIS E. BURKE—p. 183:

Questions 3 and 5. Was ticket-holder for Republicans. * * * Voted more votes in the morning.

Question 9. Would have polled the vote if white and colored had been treated alike.

10th. Cross-question. Was that practice kept up until all the white men had voted?—Answer. Yes, sir.

11th. Cross-question. After the polls closed was there any general proclamation made by the United States commissioner, or any one else, so that all voters could hear, that all parties who had not voted would be allowed to do so before him at some particular place named within the limits of the precinct?—Answer. Yes, sir; I heard Judge Waddill tell them all to stay in line; that were all going to be voted by the United States commissioner.

12th. Cross-question. Who did Judge Waddill tell this to?—Answer. He was not telling it to anybody particular, but telling them all along the line. He told me to help to keep them in line; that he had a United States commissioner there and he was going to vote every one of them.

Governor JAMES H. HARVEY (ex-member legislature of Kansas, State senator, ex-United States Senator, and ex-governor of that State), p. 195:

Question 4, p. 195. Men in line had tickets in hand and complained about not being able to vote. The voting seemed to me to be exceedingly slow. * * * *Could not get in the voting-room*, but looked through window, and it seemed as if there were a great many questions being asked, and the man that I saw vote had to stand in front of the ballot-box a long time before he was permitted to vote. I saw a number of deputy United States marshals in the neighborhood of the polls and some policemen.

10th. Question. I heard at the polls a great many say the voting was purposely delayed in order to hinder the colored voters from casting their ballots.

26th. Cross-question. Were the men whom you heard say the voting was purposely delayed in order to hinder the colored voters from casting their ballots white men or colored men, Republicans or Democrats?—Answer. Some white men and some colored men. Some of them were Republicans, and some, I think, were Democrats, because they attempted to justify it.

JAMES A. DUFFY (was Republican challenger)—p. 204:

7th. Question. Why were they voted slower in the afternoon or evening?—Answer. Well, by little after 11 o'clock Mr. Randolph came down there and had a consultation with the Democratic judge, Gentry, and then Mr. Purcell; he came down there with a book, he said, with proper oath in it to administer to the voters who were sworn. He gave it to the judge and told him that that was the proper oath to administer to a party who had been sworn. The Democratic supervisor he came around and asked the voters the same questions the challengers had just asked. First one and then another of the challengers would question a man about his age, residence, and last place he voted, if he had ever been convicted of petit larceny, if he had ever been in jail, how long he had been in the city, didn't he vote in the county, didn't he move from the county to the city. After the challengers got through with a man the supervisor then would go over the same questions. They had two men arrested in the evening on account of numbers of their residence being wrong on the registration-books. These men were delayed some time at the box, and were then sent to get their right number; then after they come back they was challenged again. They were sworn then and voted. Then the Democratic supervisor ordered their arrest.

11th. Question. Which judge of election had charge of the colored book, and what was his conduct?—Answer. Mr. William Gentry. When a man came in and gave his name, he would find his name on the book, and then would look all over the book to see if he could find another name similar to the man that was standing there before he would vote him. He would close the book after a voter had voted, and when the next voter would come in he would have to open the book and look for the place again. When I would tell him the number where he would find the man's name, he would tell me that he was attending to that book, and to attend to my own business. Several times while the book was closed his attention would have to be called to a voter standing waiting to vote.

A. H. KAUFMAN—p. 210:

Question 6. I then drove down to the Fourth precinct in Jackson Ward, and when I arrived there I saw a large string of voters, all colored, on the sidewalk approaching the polling-place. In front of the line at the door of the said polling-place was a tall policeman with his club stretched perpendicular across the man's breast who was in front of the line, not allowing him or any one in the line to move either one way or the other towards the polling-place, keeping the voter entirely ignorant as to when his next turn would come, which in itself was calculated to make impatient voters leave their position in line. I saw no line of white men, and hence realize no good reason why these colored voters should be held back in that manner. I went into the room where the voting was done, and just as I came in a colored man who it seems had been sent out with a policeman to verify the number of his residence about which there had been some controversy between the voter and the Democratic United States supervisor, the question involved being the difference of a number or two from that which was on the registration-books. After informing myself of the above facts I requested the judge of election to swear the voter, which would entitle him to vote. He did so, and the man was voted, after which the Democratic United States supervisor called in a marshal and ordered the arrest of that voter, who was carried off to jail. I asked the supervisor, who at that time was standing upon a box behind one of the judges of the election, who had charge of the ballot-box and seemed to take entire control of the polling-place, why he had that man arrested. He answered me, he knew his business. I reiterated that he was drunk, and ought to have been arrested himself. Mr. James C. Smith, who was present, told me then that he had been acting that way the whole evening, and that he ought to have a warrant sworn out against him. I reiterated that I was going to swear out a warrant for the Democratic supervisor, whereupon the said Democratic supervisor said to me, "Go and have me arrested; my name is Henry Kolbe." The entire deportment of the aforesaid supervisor was dictatorial and calculated to impress with fear any timid voter that would present himself. The scene above described in itself caused a long delay in cousuming a great deal of time. I was very much incensed at the deportment and actions of the Democratic challengers and supervisors in taking the advantage of having a large majority at this polling-place, which in itself was calculated to hinder and delay the voting, so much so that I left there to go to the United States commissioner and swear out a warrant against the said Henry Kolbe, but was advised not to do so, as such a course would have necessitated the closing of that precinct.

JAMES C. SMITH (ex city sergeant, councilman, etc.), p. 236:

Question 11. They would ask a colored man if he wanted to vote on the constitutional amendment. After the colored man declined to vote on the amendment Mr. Finnerty would then read it over to him slow. In one instance a man came in by the name of Harris, about 50 years old. He was asked if he was 21 by challenger, Mr. Grymes, what year he was born in, where his mother lived, and if the last freshet had washed the dung off his house. The objection was made to this man's voting on account of his residence; the judges sent some men with him to see if he lived where he said he lived. They came back and reported to the judges that it was all right. There was some question then about his voting, and this supervisor, Kolbe, said he be damned to hell if he should vote, and said he would sit on the ballot-box first. I remarked to Kolbe that he was drunk and not fit to be there. He said it was none of my business, called in a policeman, and told him to arrest the nigger and lock him up. I told him it was a shame; that a drunken loafer like him ought to be locked up instead of the nigger. Then he took out his bottle and took another drink. He said, "I would like to see you have me arrested." When a colored man would come in I would get his name; I would go to a copy of the registration-books which we had there in the room; I would go the judge and point out the same number that corresponded with the man's name on their book. The judge, Mr. Gentry, in a friendly manner, said, "Mr. Smith, I am keeping these books," and would go up and down over the names on the books. I made the remark to him, what was the use in going all over the names when I had just pointed out the name to him. He remarked that he wanted to see if there was any more on the books, and to see if the man's name corresponded with his residence as he gave it in.

JOHN J. REILEY (Republican supervisor)—p. 148:

Questions 3 and 4. Reached polls before sunrise, and there seemed between two and three hundred voters in line.

Question 6, p. 149. This line was kept up during the day.

The voters were divided into two lines, white and colored, and the great majority of the voters were colored.

The colored voters and white voters took equal turns in voting. The white voters resident in the first precinct were 132 and colored 883; third precinct, white voters, 254, colored, 797; fourth precinct, white voters, 392, colored, 692. See record, 1635. By voting alternately the white voters were all enabled to cast their votes, leaving the excluded voters at the rear end of the long colored line. No clearer illustration of the situation could be given than the statement made by contestee's witness, H. M. Smith, above quoted, that some of the colored men, under pretence of sickness, got into the white line, and were there permitted to vote, whereupon he says the "amount of sickness in the crowd became appalling." But this ruse of the colored men to secure an opportunity to vote was stopped after a few votes were thus permitted. But when the polls closed these obstructive tactics had been successful in preventing the casting of enough Republican votes to give a majority of 261 to the Democratic contestee.

It has been held in New York, Alabama, and California that a vote lawfully tendered and not received should not be counted, but if the result was changed thereby that a new election should be ordered. (See State vs. Judge, 13 Ala., 805; Hartt vs. Harvey, 19 Howard's Practice, N. Y., 245; Webster vs. Byrnes, 34 Cal., 273.)

But this rule we think is not founded in reason and is against the weight of authority. It was seemingly though not directly sanctioned in the Nineteenth Congress in case of Biddle vs. Wing, Clarke and Hall, 504.

The Revised Statutes of the United States, section 2007, provides:

That whenever, by or under the authority of the constitution or laws of any State or the laws of any Territory, any act is, or shall be, required to be done by any citizen as a prerequisite to qualify or entitle him to vote, the offer of any such citizen to perform the act required to be done as aforesaid shall, if it fail to be carried into execution by reason of the wrongful act or omission of the person or officer charged with the duty of receiving or permitting such performance or offer to perform or acting thereon, be deemed and held as a performance in law of such act, and the person so offering and failing as aforesaid, and being otherwise qualified, shall be entitled to vote in the same manner and to the same extent as if he had performed such act.

The offer to perform the prerequisites to the right to vote is by this statute made equivalent to a performance of the act itself, where the wrongful act or omission of an officer prevents carrying such offer into execution.

This carries the doctrine of tender back one step further, and makes a tender of registration or other prerequisite sufficient to entitle the citizen to the right to vote. The doctrine that such votes should be counted is strengthened by this statute.

If the voter, in the language of the statute, "shall be entitled to vote," the right would be a very barren one if the vote tendered and refused could not be counted.

So far as Congressional elections are concerned, the offer by a voter otherwise legally qualified to perform any act which is a prerequisite to voting will be in law a performance of the act. (Paine on Elections, p. 519.)

This House has uniformly, since the Nineteenth Congress, recognized the rule that a legal vote lawfully tendered and unlawfully rejected shall be counted and given the same force and effect as if actually cast.

Whatever the rule may be in any of the States of the Union this principle is well settled as a rule of Congress.

The present Congress has recognized and followed the same doctrine, and the majority and minority reports of the committees in Atkinson vs. Pendleton both expressly recognize this rule of law.

See also the cases of Smith vs. Jackson, Mudd vs. Compton, and Featherstone vs. Cate, Fifty-first Congress.

As to the duty of Congress to count all votes legally offered and unlawfully rejected, see Sessinghaus vs. Frost (2 Ellsworth, 380); Frost vs. Metcalf (1 Ellsworth, 289); Bisbee vs. Finley (2 Ellsworth, 172); Covode vs. Foster (2 Bartlett, 600, 611); Taylor vs. Reading (2 Bartlett, 661); Porterfield vs. McCoy (Clarke and Hall, 267); Buchanan vs. Manning (2 Ellsworth, 287); Bell vs. Snyder (Smith, 247.)

The same rule prevails in England (Heywood, 5 ed., 500).

It is now an established rule of the House of Representatives of the United States that a vote duly offered and unlawfully rejected, at the polls, will be counted in a contest (Paine on Elections, Sec. 517.)

When a legal voter offers to vote for a particular candidate and uses due diligence in endeavoring to do so, and is prevented by fraud, violence, or intimidation from depositing his ballot, his vote should be counted. (Niblack vs. Walls, 42 Cong., 104; Smith, 101.)

In Sessinghaus v. Frost (2 Ellsworth, 380), decided in 1883, votes offered but not cast were counted in the Forty-seventh Congress.

In Yeates v. Martin, decided in 1881, the same rule is stated:

The soundness of this rule is indisputable; otherwise the door is open for unmeasured frauds. Suppose, for instance, in a heated election, one party should by accident be prevented from polling its heavy vote until late in the afternoon, how easy would it be for a partisan board of managers to defeat a man who otherwise would be the choice of the people. And, again, by delaying to open the polls at the time fixed by law in the forenoon of election day, and by delaying for three or four hours, and systematically challenging the voters, and consuming as much time as possible with each voter, it would be easy to procrastinate, so the hour of closing the polls should arrive and a large vote remain unpolled. (Ellsworth, Digest Election Cases 45 and 46 Congress, pp. 386-7. See, also, Bisbee vs. Finlay, Digest Election Cases 47 Congress, pp. 173-174, and views of the minority, p. 227.)

The same rule was laid down in Frost v. Metcalf in 1879, and the following is the language of the committee's report:

If contestant had proved that any man's vote was rejected by reason of his name not being on the poll-books, whose name was on the registration lists, and that his vote was offered by him *and not counted*, then he is entitled to the benefit of it. (P. 290.)

In Bradley v. Slemons, decided in 1880, the committee say:

We concede there may be circumstances under which a legal voter being deprived of the privilege of casting his ballot, it may nevertheless be counted, and (quoting from Judge McCrary) "to require each voter belonging to a class of excluded voters to go through the form of presenting his ballot, and having a separate ruling in each case, would be an idle and useless formality." (Digest Election Cases, 1875 to 1880, p. 312.)

In this case, however, the votes claimed were not counted, because no fraud, intimidation, or other misconduct was alleged or proven.

Indeed we do not understand that any of the committee question the rule laid down in this report that a lawful vote properly tendered and unlawfully excluded may be counted, and that the remedy in such a case is not to set aside the election.

But it is claimed by a minority of the committee that under the facts of the present case there has been no such an offer to vote on the part of the several hundred voters as would entitle them to have their votes counted. This brings us to the discussion of what constitutes a tender or offer to vote.

It is eminently proper in approaching the polls where there are a large number of voters that the voters should form a line and take their orderly turns in voting. To prevent any race troubles it is not unusual in many places to form two lines, one white and one colored, approaching the polls in their order and casting their ballots in regular turns or rotation.

Is the ability to reach the window and actually tender the ticket to the judges essential in all cases to constitute a good offer to vote? A voter, who is at the polling place in due time, and has taken his place in the line, ticket in hand, offering to vote, and by the wrong of the judges is prevented from reaching the window, surely has as much right on principle to have his vote counted as the voter who happens to be further up in the line and actually reaches the window and is there refused.

From the time the voter reaches the voting place and takes his position in line to secure his orderly turn in voting the elector has commenced the act of voting. It is a continuous act, and if by the wrongful act of fraudulent challenges unduly prolonged by the connivance and collusion of the judges of the election the voter is deprived of the opportunity to vote we think that the interest of our form of government and the purity of elections demand that the vote should be counted. If the fraudulent exclusion of votes would, if successful, secure to the party of the wrong-doer a temporary seat in Congress, and the only penalty for detection in the wrong would be merely a new election, giving another chance for the exercise of similar tactics, such practices would be at a great premium and an election indefinitely prevented. But if where such acts are done the votes are counted upon clear proof *aliunde*, the wrong is at once corrected in this House and no encouragement is given to such dangerous and disgraceful methods. Where an illegal vote is tendered and cast it is universally conceded that it should be excluded in a contest, and the result declared the same as if such vote had not been cast.

It is clear upon principle that where a legal vote is offered and excluded it should be counted upon furnishing proof as satisfactory as that upon which an unlawful vote is eliminated from the count. There is no more difficulty or uncertainty in the proof in the one case than in the other. We are not disposed in the present case to treat the deposit of the votes in the box of the United States commissioners as a casting of the ballots. But such fact is strong corroborating evidence and is entitled to weight in determining the purpose of the voters, and is further of value in preserving the ballots which the voters say they actually intended to have cast. These ballots were at once deposited in a safe receptacle and preserved until they were delivered into the custody of the House. Over four hundred of the voters testify to the deposit of these ballots, and that they were the same ballots which they were prevented from casting.

If a number of persons desirous of making a tender of money at a bank should form in line during banking hours, with their money in hand, and the officers of the bank should purposely delay the transaction of business in such a way as to prevent a large number of the persons desiring to make the tender from reaching the receiving teller's window during banking hours, there would be no question, we apprehend, but that this would be a good tender of money. In the present instance the voters in depositing their tickets in a separate box in the custody of a United States commissioner were attempting to carry the analogy further by making their tender good.

The voter who was standing at the window, ticket in hand, and offering it at sundown when the window was closed in his face, had done no more to have his vote cast than the next man in the line or the other voters standing ready to the extreme rear of the line. They were all doing their best to exercise their constitutional rights.

It is the duty of the judges to afford every reasonable facility to the voters in casting their ballots. We think that all these votes were tendered or offered within the fair and reasonable meaning of the law and that they should be counted, and that the action of the judges in delaying the election was equivalent in law to a refusal to receive the ballots.

We therefore recommend the passage of the following resolution:

Resolved, That George D. Wise was not elected as a member of the Fifty-first Congress from the Third district of Virginia, and is not entitled to a seat therein.

Resolved, That Edmund Waddill, jr., was elected as a member of Congress from the Third district of Virginia and is entitled to a seat therein.

H. Mis. 137——15

VIEWS OF THE MINORITY.

(1) **Tender.** *What necessary.*

"To hold that anything short of an actual tender of the ballot to the election of officers and a rejection by them was an offer to vote, would be a most dangerous and uncertain rule and one to which we can not give our sanction. Where the evidence plainly establishes the fact that a legal voter offers his ballot to the election officers and they unlawfully reject the same, under the precedents heretofore established such vote may be counted for the candidate for whom the voter offered to vote."

(2) **Votes.** *Not cast through lack of time.*

If all that is claimed by the contestant be conceded for the sake of argument, still the votes in question can not be counted, there having been no *actual* tender and rejection; "they have not been *offered* and *rejected,* and the most that can be claimed under this assumed state of facts is that there has been no fair and full election within the meaning of the law, and that neither party shall be adjudged entitled to the seat."

But the minority insist that the delay in voting was *not* caused by the partisans of contestee or the collusion of the judges, and "under such a state of facts, the courts determine the result by the vote actually cast. The enforcement of that rule in this case would give the seat to the sitting member.

"But we are not satisfied of the justice of such rule * * but are of the opinion that the ends of justice will be subserved by remitting the election to the people of the district."

227

VIEWS OF THE MINORITY.

APRIL 5, 1890.—Mr. CRISP, from the Committee on Elections, submitted the following as the views of the minority:

The contestant in his notice of contest charged intimidation upon the part of the partisans of the contestee at the polls and by the Democratic employers of the colored voters. He also charged that many illegal votes had been cast for the contestee.

In the argument of his counsel before the committee all these charges were abandoned, and in the report of the majority of this committee no reference whatever is made to them.

We can, therefore, dismiss them with the simple remark that the proof utterly failed to sustain them, but on the contrary the evidence discloses the fact that the election was quiet and orderly, and that Democratic employers allowed their colored employés every opportunity to vote, in many instances giving them the entire day of the election without "docking" them in their wages.

The vote returned for the parties to this contest, and upon which the certificate of election was issued to the sitting member, was as follows:

	George D. Wise.	Edmund Waddill, jr.
Chesterfield County	1,567	1,586
Goochland	671	988
Hanover	1,646	1,565
Henrico	1,688	2,340
King William	739	1,099
New Kent	365	705
Manchester City	892	740
Richmond City	8,040	6,324
Total	15,608	15,347

Showing a majority of 261 votes for George D. Wise, the sitting member.

It is admitted that the returns were all regular and that the certificate of election was properly issued to the sitting member, Mr. Wise.

The majority of the Committee on Elections insist, however, that there was a conspiracy upon the part of the Democratic managers and the Democratic judges of election to carry the election for Mr. Wise by the suppression of legal colored Republican votes, and that in furtherance of this conspiracy Democratic challengers were present at the first, third, and fourth precincts of Jackson ward in the city of Richmond, where the colored voters largely predominate, and by

unnecessary and unreasonable challenges of the colored voters, con-
nived at by the Democratic judges of election, consumed so much time
that 255 colored voters at the first precinct, 168 at the third precinct,
and 134 at the fourth precinct, making in all 557 voters, were deprived
of an opportunity to vote for the contestant and that in this way the
contestant was defeated and the contestee elected.'

Of this number 457 were examined as witnesses, and they testify that
they were legal voters, that they were present at the polls with their
ballots in hand for the contestant endeavoring to vote, but failed, as they
allege, by reason of the great consumption of time by the Democratic
challengers in challenging the colored voters, and by the Democratic
judges in receiving them, and the majority of the committee insist that
these 457 votes that were not cast or tendered should be counted for the
contestant, thereby overcoming the returned majority of the contestee
of 261 votes and electing the contestant.

CONSPIRACY.

In arriving at the conclusion that there was a conspiracy upon the
part of the Democratic managers and Democratic judges of election to
carry the election by the suppression of the colored vote the majority of
the committee rely upon the testimony of certain witnesses introduced
by the contestant, and we will now refer to some of them to give the
character of the evidence relied upon to prove a conspiracy as charged.

A. C. ROCKECHARLIE, p. 38:
Question 4. Heard Smith say he wanted to delay time. *Whether his remarks alluded
to the election or not I can't say.*

W. A. BENEDICT, p. 63:
Question 2. I think on the day before the election, November the 5th, at the terminus of the Richmond Union Passenger Railway, 29th and P streets, Marshall ward;
present, Mr. Timberlake, one of the judges of election, first precinct, Jackson ward,
Mr. Buck Adams and Capt. Peter Smith, and good many others whose names I do not
know. Mr. Adams—rather Mr. Timberlake—remarked first that he calculated having the handling of about 1,200 negro votes in Jackson ward. Mr. Adams then remarked that we will shut out about half of them. Mr. Timberlake, in reply, said,
"Right you are, partner." I do not know whether there is anything else; but there
is: I now recall another remark by one of the employees of the railroad: "Timberlake, you are a damn fool for talking that way. You will get yourself into
trouble." I believe that is all I remember now.

WILLIAM L. TIMBERLAKE, p. 1090
*60th. Ques. Mr. Ira Benedict, who testified on behalf of Judge Waddill, stated, as well
as I can recollect, that a day or two after the election he had a conversation with you near
the eastern terminus of the electric line, and that in that conversation you boasted that you
and the other Democratic judge had shut out or kept from voting two or three hundred colored
voters in the first precinct of Jackson ward; did you make that statement, or one similar to
it; if not, state the conversation as well as you can recollect.—Ans. I did not make that
statement. Capt. Sullivan, Mr. Benedict, and myself were talking over there one evening
about shutting out of voters, and Capt. Sullivan said, " Timberlake, how many were shut
out in your precinct?" I said, "About two or three hundred." Mr. Benedict said, "What
was the cause? how were they shut out?" I told him, " It was due to the fact that the Republican judge and Republican supervisor delayed the voting by taking so long to find the name
of the voters and by making speeches out of the window."*

H. P. HARPER, p. 69:
1. Q. State your name, age, residence, and occupation.—Ans. H. P. Harper, 48 yrs.
4 mos. 13 days; 304 West Clay; in little wood and coal business.
2. Q. Were you at the 1st precinct of Jackson ward on the 6th of Nov. last? If so,
please state at what time, and what you heard in connection with the election, if anything.—Ans. I was at the precinct cor. Gilmer and Leigh. I got there seven or little
after seven. I rent a place next door to the polls. I was there off and on all day; my
business is there. During the morning—I don't know exactly what part of the day—
on or about eight o'clock, I asked a gentleman, "What is this that you are springing

on us now ?" and he said that this is the ballot (it is impossible for me to get the exact words), the constitutional ballot to be voted on every twenty years; but there were some points about it that had not been settled by law, or never been exactly understood, or some way like that, but that Mr. Barbour and Gen'l Mahone had had an understanding that they would make no point upon that question. They are used more, he told me, in this ward than any other. I don't say positive that is the exact word, but what he did say was to the effect that they were to hinder and delay the election by asking questions and having them read.

LEWIS STUART, p. 45:
Question 10. Heard Belvin say, "We intend to hold them down to-day."

EDWARD THOMPSON, p. 1441:
Question 15. Heard Belvin say in the morning that he intended to hold that vote down that day within 300.

This man had been guilty of embezzling funds belonging to the post-office while employed in it. What weight is to be given to his testimony we leave the House to determine.

JOHN B. NEWELL, p. 73:
Question 12. Heard Henry Charters, a Federal office-holder at Washington, and an appointee of contestee, say at First Clay precinct, "By God! we have knocked the niggers out of 300 votes in Jackson ward, and Yankee Allan is raising hell about it."

JOHN W. GRAVES, p. 138:
Question 3. When approaching the polls to vote in white line was whispered to by the assistant challenger, who said, "Delay them all you can." Upon enquiring as to what was said, the challenger said, "When judge questions you in regard to the constitutional amendment, ask him what it means; what it is for, and all about it."
29. X Q. Is it not a well-known fact among the white Democrats of Richmond that you were a prominent candidate for the legislature on the Republican or Coalition ticket in the fall of '87?—Ans. I suppose so.
30. X Q. Do you think it probable that under these circumstances a Dem. would have been foolish enough to instruct you as to how you should vote and how you should cast your ballot at the next succeeding election?—Ans. I am positive that the gentleman who advised me did not know me nor my name. That is, I judge so from his expression. He advised me before my name was called, and after I announced my name to the judge he did not seem to recognize me nor did I know him. I presumed he was a Republican. I did not know positively that he was one.

JAMES H. HARVEY—p. 195:
10th question. State whether or not you heard any one say anything about the voting in Jackson Ward?—Answer. I heard at the polls a great many say the voting was purposely delayed in order to hinder the colored voters from casting their ballots. After the polls were closed at night, while waiting in front of the Dispatch office, I heard a man state (I inquired his name and I was told he was Petit) that he had had the pleasure that day of seeing 500 or 600 negroes cut out of their votes. He said he had been carrying refreshments from Binford's out to the boys in Jackson ward.
27th. X Q. Had you ever seen the man whom you heard make the statement in front of the Dispatch office on the night of the election before?—Ans. Not to know him.
28th. X Q. Do you know anything of him?—Ans. No, sir.

JAMES H. BARRETT, p. 209:
2d. Question. Where were you on the evening before the 6th day of November last, and what occurred with reference to the election to be held the next day?—Answer. I was coming down Seventeenth street between 7 and 8 o'clock in the evening, and Frank Mann overtaken me by the elevator. We were on our way to the Republican headquarters. When we arrived opposite Venable street we met Mr. Finnerty and Mr Gentry talking. As we arrived opposite them heard Mr. Finnerty say to Mr. Gentry, "Vote these niggers slow to-morrow." His reply was, "All right." At that time I had gotten by them and did not hear any more that passed. My friend, Frank Mann, stopped and said something to them and then overtaken me.

Other testimony of a similar nature appears in the record, but we do not think it necessary to give it. It all consists of loose, vague statements of disconnected parts of conversations or an occasional remark made by some excited or enthusiastic partisan, such as may be heard in the heat and excitement of any election, and is refuted by the evidence as to what actually transpired at the polls on the day of election.

The charge that the judges of elections purposely and deliberately retarded and obstructed the voting is not sustained.

At the first precinct it is shown that the colored registration-book was in the hands of the colored Republican judge; that he was an intelligent man and a merchant, and that he was assisted during the entire day in his labors by the Republican Federal supervisor, a white man, and that if there was delay in voting it was caused in great measure by the tardiness of this Republican judge and Republican Federal supervisor in finding the names of the voters on the registration-book.

It also appears that this Republican Federal supervisor was an excitable and irascible man, and that he persisted in raising objections to the challenging of voters and in presenting his views at length upon every question which was raised, thereby consuming much time; that he was very offensive in his language and conduct to the Democrats, and did more than all others to irritate and produce bad feeling.

We here refer to the following depositions to show that much delay was caused as we have just stated.

LOUIS B. SCHUTTE, one of the clerks, page 1106:

1st. Ques. What is your name, age, residence, and occupation?—Ans. My name is Louis B. Schutte; my age is 34 years; my residence is No. 550 Brooke avenue, Richmond, Va., and I am a machinist.

2nd. Ques. On the 6th of last November were you one of the clerks at the 1st precinct, Jackson, and did you act in that capacity during the entire day?—Ans. Yes, sir.

3rd. Ques. As such what duties did you perform?—Ans. To see that the names were properly recorded upon the poll-book.

4th. Ques. Who held the registration-book for the colored voters at this precinct?—Ans. Bedford C. Stokes.

5th Ques. To what political party do you belong, and to what does said Stokes belong?—Ans. I belong to the Democratic party and Stokes to the Republican.

6th. Ques. How long have you acted as clerk at this precinct?—Ans. I think four years. I remember having been clerk on three occasions. It may have been more than four years.

7th. Ques. How long has said Stokes been clerk at said precinct?—Ans. About four or five years.

8th. Ques. What is his business?—Ans. He keeps a small store on Brooke avenue.

9th. Ques. Are his customers mostly white or colored?—Ans. I don't?

10th. Ques. Have you any personal acquaintance with any large number of colored voters at that precinct?—Ans. Yes, sir; I know a good many of them.

14th. Ques. State who was in the polling-room from the opening to the closing of the polls on the day of the last election, and give their official positions on that day.—Ans. R. J. Cottrell, registrar and judge; W. L. Timberlake and Bedford C. Stokes, judges; Louis B. Schutte and S. D. Chamberlayne, clerks; George Duncan and Samuel Britton, supervisors; these were all.

15th. Ques. State whether or not Mr. Chamberlayne was on that day deaf, and if deaf, whether to such an extent that he could not hear any discussion that might have taken place between the officials inside of the room and parties on the outside of the room.

(Excepted to by the contestant, because leading and because Chamberlayne is not only the best evidence of the facts inquired into, but is the only evidence; the witness Schutte can't possibly know those facts.)

Ans. In answer I would say that in speaking loudly to Mr. Chamberlayne he can hear, but I know him to be very deaf. I can't answer as to what he heard. I am positive that he could not hear.

16th. Ques. Is Mr. Duncan a Republican or a Democrat?—Ans. He is a Republican.

17th. Ques. Were the ballots received through a window or a door?—Ans. Through a window.

18th. Ques. Was the window in the length or width of the room?—Ans. In the length of the room about the center.

19th. Ques. How wide was the window?—Ans. About three feet.

20th. Ques. Describe the location of the ballot-boxes, and of all the parties in the room.—Ans. The ballot-box was near the center of the table, about a foot and a half or two feet from the window. Mr. Cottrell was right at the ballot-box; he received the ballots and put them in the ballot-box. Mr. Timberlake was just opposite Mr. Cottrell and also near the center of the table; he was judge and had charge of the white registration-book. Stokes was seated at the north end of the table near Mr. Timberlake, and had charge of the colored registration book. Louis B. Schutte, myself, was seated just opposite Stokes, near the window, and had charge of one of the poll-books. Mr. Chamberlayne was seated on my right; he also had charge of one of the poll-books. Mr. Britton was standing near to and behind Mr. Stokes; he was the Democratic supervisor. *Mr. Duncan—I will state that his position was very irregular during the day; he was sometimes at the window and sometimes and very often at the colored registration book.*

21st. Ques. Could you or not, from the position you occupied, see what was going on in the room?—Ans. Yes, sir.

22nd. Ques. Could you or not see what took place from the front of the window on the outside?—Ans. Yes sir.

23rd. Ques. Did Mr. Britton, during the day, take any part in the election, except being present; if so, state what he did or said?—Ans. He did not take any part in the election, except when the obstruction was made there by Ben. Scott, and he ordered him to take it away, and if he did not he said he would have him arrested.

24th. Ques. Who was Ben. Scott, what were his politics, and what was the character of his obstruction?—Ans. Ben. Scott is a colored man, and as far as I know he is a Republican. His obstruction was a scantling, I think, that was about to be placed across the street, and Mr. Britton ordered him to take it away.

25th. Ques. Did Mr. Britton, at the time, give any reason for ordering the scantling to be taken away; if so, state what he said?—Ans. He said it had no business there, and I further think he said it was an obstruction.

26th. *Ques. Did Mr. Duncan take any part in that election, besides being present? If so, state, as well as you can, what he said or did during the day.—Ans. Well, yes, he took part in election; he would get up in the window oftentimes during the day, telling the crowd "for God's sake to get back; if they did not they could not vote;" he would go from the window to the registration book, held by Mr. Bedford C. Stokes, trying to help or helping him to find the names of the voters; I would state also that he was a great annoyance to Mr. Stokes, and at times got him so excited that he did not know what he was doing; instead of saying that he did not know what he was doing, say that he did not know what name he was looking for; I also remember that in looking for the name of Scott, I think, not finding Scott, Duncan said "you are foolish; you have got the wrong name; look in the M's." I also remember the name of Washington being called, and he was looking under the B's for the name of Bunn; they were looking for the name of Quarles for about three or four minutes, and said they could not find it, but subsequently found his name. He further objected to Cottrell's reading the constitutional ballots, that is, for or against the constitution; he would frequently pull out his watch and time Mr. Cottrell, saying, this took you 2¼, sometimes 2¾, and sometimes 3 minutes; I think he had a blank upon which he kept the time; I remarked to Mr. Timberlake to pull out his watch and see if this was correct; the next ballot being read, it took from ¼ to 1 minute to read it.*

(The notary makes the following note: Both witness, in answering the foregoing question, several times mentioned in the name Mimms in connection with the name Scott, and at the suggestion of Judge Waddill the notary was requested to interline what the witness said: The notary then asked the witness what he wanted added in his answer in connection with the name Scott, and understood the witness to say, add the words "look in the M's;" Judge Waddill said he understood the witness to say "look in the M's for Mimms;" thereupon the notary asked the witness which he said, and he replied that the interlineation as made by the notary, to wit, "look in the M's," was what he said and was what he wanted added.)

27th. Ques. Where at the window did Mr. Belvin stand—on the side where the colored voters were or on the side where the white voters were?—Ans. On the side where the white voters were.

28th. Ques. How much of the window did he occupy?—Ans. I can't say he occupied any; he was standing on the side, and sometimes he would look around it and put his head into it.

29th. Ques. When a white voter came up, would Mr. Belvin step aside and let him vote or force the voter to go around him?
(Excepted as clearly leading.)
Ans. *To the best of my recollection he forced the voter to go around him.*

30th. Ques. *Did Mr. Belvin's position or conduct, as Democratic challenger, in any way prevent the colored voters from getting up to the window on their side?—Ans. It did not; but on the contrary he showed a kindness to both white and colored so as to let them vote.*

31st. Ques. Did Mr. Duncan at any time during the day interfere with Mr. Belvin in the performance of his duties as Democratic challenger?—Ans. He did.

32nd. Ques. What was the character of this interference?—Ans. The only recollection I have is that Mr. Duncan threatened to have'him arrested on several occasions and had him arrested.

33rd Ques. (By same.) When Mr. Belvin would challenge a voter at any time during the day, did you hear the challenge except during the half hour when you were absent?—Ans. Yes, sir.

34th Ques. (By same.) State whether or not he challenged only those that he had grounds to suspect had no right to vote, or whether he challenged unnecessarily and by unreasonable questions?

(The contestant excepts to this question, and asked that the witness would be sent out the room during the time it was being stated, which was accordingly done. The question is clearly leading and indicates to the witness the answer he is expected to give. It moreover asks the witness to state what he can not know, namely, whether Belvin only challenged persons whom he suspected. The witness can not know his suspicions.)

Ans. I think he had a right to challenge those whom he did challenge.

35th Ques. (By same.) State as well as you can what Mr. Duncan would say when he would make a speech to the voters on the outside and to whom his remarks were addressed, the white or colored men present?

(At the request of Judge Waddill the witness is sent out of the room in order that Judge Waddill may except to the foregoing question.

The contestant excepts to the foregoing question on the ground that the witness has nowhere stated that Duncan made a speech to any one, either white or colored.

The counsel for contestee says that the witness, in answer to question 26, has said that Duncan got up and would go to the window and make statements and remarks to the crowd.)

Ans. As to the exact language, I don't know what he said more than I said in the offset, that was when he got after the crowd to keep back, and on a great many occasions threatened to arrest Mr. Belvin. I don't know exactly to whom he allude to, but as to the keeping of the crowd back, he alluded to the colored people; they were the only ones that were shoving up against the window.

36th. Ques. (By same.) *Were these speeches or talks frequently or rarely made during the day?*—Ans. *Frequently.*

37th. Ques. (By same.) *Were they short or of considerable duration? State about how long he would occupy the window on such occasions.*

(This and the last preceding question excepted to by the contestant because clearly leading.)

Ans. *I would state that sometimes they were of considerable duration, but as to the exact time I am unable to give you that.*

38th. Ques. (By same.) Would the voting go on at these times, or would it be stopped until Mr. Duncan had concluded his remarks and gotten out of the window?—Ans. *It would be stopped by Mr. Duncan.*

39th. Ques. (By same.) Did the conduct of Mr. Duncan, both as regards these remarks and his conduct towards the officers of election in the polling precinct, accelerate or impede the casting of the vote?—Ans. What are you getting at now? (The notary now explains the question. Then the witness answered as follows:) *It caused delay.* I know what you are getting at now.

40th. Ques. (By same). Why did Duncan go around to help Stokes find the names? Was Stokes slow or rapid in finding the names on the registration book of the colored voters?—Ans. *Mr. Duncan went around to assist Mr. Stokes in finding the names. Mr. Stokes was very slow indeed.*

41st. Ques. (By same.) *Did you hear Duncan make any comments on Stokes during the day; if so, what did he say?*—Ans. *Yes, sir; he said on several occasions he was a foolish man*

42nd. Ques. (By same.) You have already stated that Stokes got very excited and worried; was Mr. Duncan cool or excited on that day?—Ans. Excited, more so than that of Mr. Stokes.

43rd. Ques. (By same.) Did Mr. Duncan by his interference with Stokes make him find the names faster, or did he confuse him and delay him in finding them?—Ans. He did not make him find them faster, but on the contrary delayed him.

44th. Ques. (By same.) *When a white voter asked for an explanation of the constitutional ballot, as you stated in answer to the 26th ques., would Duncan object or not; and, if so, what would he do on these occasions?*—Ans. *Yes, sir; he would object, and would tell Cottrell, the judge, he had no right to read them. He would take out his watch and time him.*

45th. Ques. (By same.) Would these wrangles between the judges and Duncan cause much delay?

(Excepted to by the contestant as leading.)

Ans. Yes, sir.

46th. Ques. (By same.) When a voter was challenged by Mr. Belvin or any other

Democratic challenger would Duncan allow him to be sworn without objection or discussion?

(Excepted to as leading by the contestant. The witness should be asked what Duncan would do under these circumstances.)

Ans. Yes, sir; he would object to his being sworn.

47th. Ques. (By same.) State, as well as you can, what objection or remarks he would make.—Ans. His remarks to Mr. Belvin would be that he had no right to swear him; that the man was a legal voter.

48th. Ques. (By same.) Was it on such occasions that he threatened to have Mr. Belvin arrested?—Ans. Not altogether on those occasions. If Mr. Belvin simply said he challenged a man he would threaten to have him arrested then.

49th. Ques. (By same.) Did he threaten to have any others arrested, and if so, who?—Ans. Yes, sir, he did; Mr. H. M. Smith, jr.; he was the only other one that I knew of.

(The witness says upon reflection that he thinks he also threatened to have Mr. Cottrell arrested when he read about the constitution.

At this time, to wit, 2.25 p. m., it was proposed to adjourn for dinner, which contestant was at first willing should be done, provided that the time might be extended, instead of to 4, as usual, to 5 o'clock, so that he might fill an engagement to take the deposition of an old gentleman from the country, which was to be taken at 3 o'clock p. m. before another notary, and at the taking of which it was important for him to be present, and that he, the contestant, would agree to work in the night, so as to make up the hour lost before this notary, from four to five; but this accommodation not being granted, contestant insisted that we should proceed with the taking of the deposition until the usual time of adjournment, said time being from three to four o'clock. The contestant further says that he thinks the examination of this witness should be concluded and cross-examination begun, if possible, while he is on the stand.)

At this point the witness says that he desires to have his answer to the 29th question corrected so as to read as follows, to wit: Mr. Belvin did not use any force towards the voter, but simply did not move out of his way, and the voter had to walk around him, Mr. Belvin pressing himself up against the wall to enable the voter to pass.

The contestant desires the notary to record the fact that he took a recess until 4 o'clock at this point, which was accordingly.

50th. Ques. (By same.) Did Mr. Duncan at any time during the day threaten to arrest Mr. Timberlake?—Ans. I think he did.

51st. Ques. (By same.) For what did he threaten to arrest him?—Ans. There was a contest going on as to whether he would allow a voter to vote or not; they finally consented to vote him.

52nd. Ques. (By same.) Several witnesses, called on behalf of Judge Waddill, testified that Mr. Belvin delayed the voting by asking such unnecessary questions as the following: "As to who owned the voter before the war?" "Whether he had any children, and how many he had?" State whether or not you heard Mr. Belvin or any Democratic challenger ask any questions similar to those.—Ans. I did not.

53rd. Ques. (By same.) Sitting, as you say you were, directly in front of the window, were you in such a position and close enough to the window to hear the questions asked of the voters by the Democratic challengers?—Ans. Yes, sir.

54th. Ques. (By same.) Do you remember what were the grounds upon which the Democratic challengers challenged the voters; and if so, mention such as you remember?—Ans. One of the principal grounds was as to their moving from one place to another; the next ground was they had a printed list of the disqualified voters from the hustings and police court of this city.

55th. Ques. (By same.) Of all the persons at the polls that day, who did most by interference with the voters, the officers of election and others to retard and obstruct the voting?—Ans. I think Mr. Duncan is one, Mr. Bedford C. Stokes in the slowness in getting the names is another, and the continued pushing of the colored voters on the outside another. I should certainly mention Mr. Geo. Duncan as the man that did the most to obstruct the voting.

56th. Ques. (By same.) You state that you have been clerk at this precinct for about five years; state whether or not the Democratic challengers did any more challenging than was absolutely necessary to find out whether or not the person offering to vote had a legal right to vote or not?—Ans. I don't know every voter in the precinct, but I don't think they did any more challenging than they ought to have done on this occasion.

57th. Ques. (By same.) Who challenged in the place of Mr. Belvin when he went away?—Ans. Mr. H. M. Smith, jr.

58th. Ques. (By same.) Did he ask any frivolous and unnecessary questions, or did he ask questions similar to those that you have said Mr. Belvin asked?—Ans. He asked questions similar to those asked by Mr. Belvin.

59th. Ques. (By same.) Several witnesses who have testified in behalf of Judge Waddill have stated that Mr. Cottrell, who received the ballots, greatly hindered and delayed the voting; did you see Mr. Cottrell during the entire day do anything to hinder or delay the voting; and if so, what?—Ans. I did not.

60th. Ques. (By same.) Did you see Mr. Cottrell do anything during the day to aid any particular voters to get in their ballots after they had been challenged; if so, what?—Ans. He did not do anything to hinder any voter from getting in his ballot, but I don't remember seeing him do anything particularly to aid any particular voter to get in their vote after they had been challenged.

61st. Ques. (By same.) If a party came to the polls who Mr. Cottrell personally knew had a right to vote, and was challeged by the challenger, would Mr. Cottrell go through the form of swearing him before permitting him to vote, or would he vote him, stating that he knew the party had a right to vote?

(Excepted to as leading by the contestant.)

Ans. I think that that happened during the day; that is, that he would vote him without swearing him.

62nd. Ques. (By same.) Did the police force of the city of Richmond, or the U. S. deputy marshals who were at at this precinct, take any part in the election, one way or another, further than to do all in their power to preserve order?—Ans. No, sir.

63rd. Ques. (By same.) Did the line of colored voters and the colored men around the voting window make any comments on Mr. Duncan's conduct?—Ans. I think they did, some of them saying that he was very much excited; and I am under the impression that I heard the remark made that he talked too much. I am not positive, but I think I heard it said by those on the outside that there are two men in there and they can't find one man's name.

From the testimony of this witness, who was present necessarily all day at the polls, and in a position to see and hear everything done by the judges and Republican Federal supervisor, we submit that the Democratic judges did nothing to impede and retard the voting; that they simply discharged their sworn duty to pass upon the legality of a vote when it was challenged. We submit further that if there was unusual delay it was caused by the Republican judge of election and Republican Federal supervisor—the slowness of one to find the names of the colored voters on the registration book, and the officiousness, assertion of authority, and ill-temper of the other.

WILLIAM L. TIMBERLAKE, one of the judges, page 1088:

27th. Ques. (By same.) Did Mr. Duncan take any part in that election besides being present? If so, state as well as you can recollect what he said or did during the day?—Ans. Yes, sir, he did. The first thing in the morning he objected to Mr. Belvin standing at the window. Every now and then he would go to the window and make a short speech to the voters on the outside. Every time a colored voter's name would be called out he would go round to Stokes, the colored judge, and help him to find the name. Every time a white voter wanted the constitution read to him he objected and made a short speech. Mr. Belvin would challenge a vote, and he said if he did it again he would have him arrested. Every now and then he would call Stokes a block-headed fool, because he could not find the names fast enough for him. When Cottrell would read the constitutional law he would tell him if he kept on doing it he would have him punished for it. He made several other remarks there, talking and blowing. I can't tell you one-half he said and did.

28th. Ques. (By same.) Where at the window did Mr. Belvin stand—on the side where the colored voters were, or on the side where the white men voted?—Ans. On the side where the white men voted.

29th. Ques. (By same.) About how much of the window did he occupy?—Ans. He occupied about 6 or 8 inches generally. Sometimes he had his whole body in front of the window, and then again he would have nothing but his head in the window.

30th. Ques. (By same.) When a white voter came up would Mr. Belvin step aside and let him vote, or force the voter to go around him?—Ans. He would shove him around in front of him.

31st. Ques. (By same.) State as well as you can what Mr. Duncan would say when he would make a speech to the voters on the outside.—Ans. He would say, "Stand back, men; for God's sake don't shove. You are wasting your own time, and I am in here to protect you;" and wind up by saying, "Now stand back."

32nd. Ques. (By same.) To whom was Mr. Duncan speaking—to colored or white men—when he urged them to stand back?—Ans. Speaking to the colored men.

33d. Ques. (By same.) Why did he go around to help. Stokes to find the names; was Stokes slow or rapid in finding the names on the registration book of the colored voters?—Ans. He said Stokes was a blockhead and too slow for that place.

34th. Ques. (By same.) You have stated what Mr. Duncan said. State of your own knowledge, if you can, whether Stokes was slow in finding the names.—Ans. He was very slow.

35th. Ques. (By same.) Was Mr. Duncan cool or excited on that day?—Ans. He was very much excited most all day.

36th. Ques. (By same.) Did Mr. Duncan speed the finding of the names by Stokes, or did he interfere with him and delay him?—Ans. I think he interfered with him very much.

37th. Ques. (By same.) Did Mr. Duncan, when so looking for the names with Stokes, always look under the right letter for the name?—Ans. No, sir.

38th. Ques. (By same.) State any instance that you can recollect where he looked under the wrong letter?—Ans. He was looking for a man named Kennedy under the letter C. Stokes was looking for the name and Mr. Duncan was looking for the street and number. He was looking for a man named Scott, and he had the letter C; he was looking for a man named Mimms, and he had the letter N. In this case he never did find him; he sent the man away without voting.

39th. Ques. (By same.) Are you certain that the names of the voters were Kennedy, Scott, and Mimms?—Ans. Yes, sir; I have a memorandum of them.

40th. Ques. (By same.) You have said that every time a white voter wanted the constitution read to him Duncan would object and make a short speech. To whom would he make a speech; to Mr. Cottrell or to the voter?—Ans. He would make it to Mr. Cottrell.

41st. Ques. (By same.) When a voter was challenged by Mr. Belvin or any other Democratic challenger, would Duncan allow him to be sworn without objection or discussion?—Ans. No, sir.

42nd. Ques. (By same.) State, as well as you can, what objection or remark he would make.—Ans. He would say that they had no right to swear him; that he had a right to vote; that he would look into the matter hereafter.

43rd. Ques. (By same.) Was it on such occasions that he threatened to have Mr. Belvin arrested?—Ans. Yes, sir.

44th. Ques. (By same.) Did he threaten to have any one else arrested? If so, whom?—Ans. Yes, sir; myself.

45th. Ques. (By same.) For what?—Ans. Because I objected to a man's voting without being sworn, and that man he would not let vote because we wanted him sworn; he turned him away. I had his name on the memorandum I have alluded to above, but I have misplaced it, and though I have looked for it I can't find it.

46th. Ques. (By same.) Had the man whom you objected to being voted without being sworn been challenged?—Ans. Yes, sir.

47th. Ques. (By same.) You have spoken of Mr. Cottrell reading something about the right to vote on the constitution. Can you tell about the substance of what he would say?—Ans. That they had a right every so many years to vote on the constitution, whether they wanted it changed or let it stand as it was.

48th. Question. (By same.) Several witnesses called on behalf of Judge Waddill testified that Mr. Belvin delayed the voting by asking such unnecessary questions as the following: "As to who owned the voter before the war?" "Whether he had any children?" "And how many he had?" State whether or not you heard Mr. Belvin or any Democratic challenger ask any such questions?—Ans. I did not.

49th. Ques. (By same.) Sitting, as you say you did, directly in front of the window, were you in such a position and close enough to the window to generally hear the questions asked of the voters by the Democratic challengers?—Ans. Yes, sir.

50th. Ques. (By same.) Do you remember what were the grounds upon which the challengers challenged the voters; if so, mention such as you remember?—Ans. They challenged them on the ground that they were disfranchised by the police and hustings courts, and some times they had the wrong No. of their house or street.

51st. Ques. (By same.) State whether or not the conduct of Mr. Duncan, which you have described above, delayed the voting?—Ans. Yes, sir; very much.

52nd. Ques. (By same.) Were any complaints made during that day by any parties of the conduct of Mr. Duncan? And, if so, were they by the white or colored men?—*Ans. You could hear the colored men out there in the line say, when he came to the window, that if he did not come there so often that they could get more votes in; that he took up so much time getting the votes in.*

53rd. Ques. (By same.) You have stated that Mr. Duncan would object to Mr. Cottrell explaining to the voter his right to vote upon the constitutional question. Did or did not such objection consume time?—Ans. Taking it as a whole, it did consume some time.

54th. Ques. (By same.) You have stated that when a Democratic challenger would challenge a vote Mr. Duncan would object and insist that he had no right to challenge him. State whether or not such objections also consumed time.—Ans. Yes, sir.

55th. Ques. (By same.) State whether or not the questions asked by the Democratic challengers were frivolous and unnecessary, such as I alluded to in the 48th question ; if not, state the nature of the questions asked as well as you can recollect them?—Ans. They were not questions of the nature referred to in your 48th question. When Mr. Belvin challenged a vote he would say, "Were not you convicted in the police court?" the voter would say, "No," then he would ask to have him sworn. He would not every time say the police court, he would sometimes say the hustings court. He would then sometimes ask a voter where he lived.

56th. Ques. (By same.) When would he ask a voter whether he had been convicted in the police or hustings court? Would it be when he had challenged the voter on the ground of being disfranchised, or because the voter did not give the number of his residence as registered?—Ans. When he would ask him if he had been in the police or hustings court, he would find his name on the disfranchised list. If he asked him about the street and number it would be when he had given a diferent number from the one on the registration book or the book he had.

57th. Ques. (By same.) Did Mr. Smith, when he challenged in the place of Mr. Belvin, did he ask any of the frivolous questions, or did he ask questions similar to those that you have said Mr. Belvin asked?—Ans. He asked questions similar to those Mr. Belvin asked.

58th. Ques. (By same.) Several of the witnesses who have testified in behalf of Judge Waddill have stated that Mr. Cottrell, the one who received the ballots, greatly hindered and delayed the voting. Did you see Mr. Cottrell during the entire day do anything to hinder or delay the voting? And, if so, state.—Ans. No, sir.

59th. Ques. (By same.) Did you see Mr. Cottrell during the day do anything to aid any particular voters to get in their ballots after they had been challenged? If so, state it.—Ans. Yes, sir; on several occasions Mr. Belvin would challenge colored voters and Mr. Cottrell would say, "I know he is all right," and would vote him without swearing him.

Here again we find this witness testifying to the same condition of affairs as that referred to by the previous witness and showing that the colored voters themselves complained that this Republican Federal supervisor was delaying the voting.

It may be said that Stokes, the colored Republican judge, was not competent to take charge of the registration book. As we have said, he was an intelligent man and a merchant, and had acted as judge on other occasions, and the colored registration book was put in his charge at the suggestion of the Republican Federal Supervisor Duncan, as well as Cottrell, one of the Democratic judges.

W. L. TIMBERLAKE, p. 1091.

4th. X Ques. (By same.) Were you anxious that all colored men entitled to vote should get in their vote?—Ans. Yes, sir; I think that every man entitled to vote should get it in if possible.

5th. X Ques. (By same.) How did this colored man, Bedford Stokes, compare in the matter of intelligence and education with yourself?—Ans. I don't know ; he might have as much sense as I have got. I think his education is very good; he could read and write.

6th. X Ques. (By same.) Then how did you construe his looking in the C's for Kennedy, in the C's for Scott, and in the N's for Mimms when you at once detected the mistake and went to help him?—Ans. Because Mr. Duncan so much confused him that he did not know what he was doing; if Mr. Duncan had not interfered with him he would have gotten on about three times as fast.

7th. X Ques. (By same.) Then what did you mean in your answer to my first question, that you would have helped Stokes in other cases than Kennedy's had not Mr. Duncan been there to help him?—Ans. Because when Mr. Duncan was with him he had hold of one side of the book and Stokes had hold of the other, and there was no chance for me to get to the book to help him.

8th. X Ques. (By same.) But you have said that Mr. Duncan was running all over the room and continually making speeches at the window to the crowd ; why did you not then help Stokes?—Ans. Because Stokes was not looking for anybody's name then.

9th. X Ques. (By same.) Then, do I understand you that, with the exception of the time you helped to find Kennedy's name, Mr. Duncan assisted Stokes in finding the names of voters?—Ans. Yes, sir; that time Mr. Duncan was arguing with Belvin ; that was the only chance I had to help him during the day.

10th. X Ques. (By same.) Did anybody help you to find the names in your book?—Ans. No, sir ; only one time Mr. Duncan started towards me to help me, but I found the name before he reached me.

11th. X Ques. (By same.) And did you find the names, with that exception, so quickly that you needed no assistance with your book?—Ans. yes, sir.

12th. X Ques. (By same.) Which book did you have at that precinct in the May election last year?—Ans. The colored book.

13th. *X Ques. (By same.) How was it and at whose suggestion, that you took the white book at the election last November, and Bedford Stokes the colored one?—Ans. At the suggestion of Mr. Cottrell and Mr. Duncan.*

14th. X Ques. (By same.) Could you not have found the names upon the colored book much quicker than Stokes?—Ans. If I had had to undergo what Stokes did, I don't think I would have found them as quick as he did. Mr. Duncan talking and whirling his hands around, I know I would not have found them as quick as he did.

15th. X Ques. (By same.) Then, if you found this delay going on by reason of Mr. Duncan's conduct, as you have stated, why did you not propose to change books with Stokes, since Mr. Duncan never interfered with you?—Ans. I thought about asking him two or three times, and the thought struck me that if I took the colored book that Mr. Duncan would come around and do the same thing to me that he did to Stokes, and that would have ended in a big fight, and I did not want to have any of that 'round there that day.

16th. X Ques. (By same.) Who would have fought and what for?—Ans. Mr. Duncan and myself would have fought if he had bothered me as much as he did Stokes that day.

17th. X Ques. (By same.) You have said that some two or three hundred men were shut out at the close of the polls; do you mean to say that the reason these men got no opportunity to vote was because of delays caused by Mr. Duncan?—Ans. Not altogether by Mr. Duncan.

18th. X Ques. (By same.) Do you mean principally by him?—Ans. Yes, sir.

19th. X Ques. (By same.) And by whom else?—Ans. By Stokes and Belvin.

20th. X Ques. (By same.) How could Stokes cause delay if he was being hindered by Duncan as you have stated?—Ans. By not finding the names.

21st. X Ques. (By same.) But you have said you could not have found the names as fast as Stokes if Duncan had bothered you as he did him. How, then, did Stokes delay the voting?—Ans. I consider that both Stokes and Duncan delayed it, because Stokes was looking for the names and could not find them, and that fretted Mr. Duncan and he would talk to Stokes and that would bother him, and he, Duncan, was looking for the number and he could not find that either, and I consider that both of them delayed time in that way.

22nd. X Ques. (By same.) Did Mr. Cottrell and yourself, forming a majority of the board of judges, use any means whatever to check the delays and obstructions of which you have spoken, so that the hundreds that did not vote might be enabled to do so?—Ans. Yes, sir; Mr. Cottrell said to Mr. Duncan several times, "Take a chair and set down, and we will get along much faster; don't run about so much and talk so much." That seemed to make him worse than ever.

We now quote from the deposition of H. M. Smith, jr., page 1153.

22nd. Ques. (By same.) It has been charged that Mr. Cottrell delayed the election by waiting after Stokes had found the name of the voter on the colored registration book for Belvin to find the same name on the copy he had; state your observations as to that course of procedure.—Ans. There is not an iota of truth in the statement, so far as my observation went, and I was very attentive. *Mr. Stokes was so slow in finding the name that Mr. Duncan, a distinguished Republican leader and the supervisor at that precinct that day, was assisting him to find the name every five minutes of the day.* Mr. Allen and Mr. Rockecharlie and Mr. Powell were assisting Mr. Belvin to find the names on his own book, by looking over his shoulder and running their eye down the names, that he could not have been slow if he had wanted to, so indefatigable were they in their exertions to assist him. The whole contest was very pleasant and we raised no objection to their having free access to our book to see the ground of our challenge, and everything else. I will state further, as it occurs to me, that we put the challenge book, the disqualified list, and what other information we had in the hands of different parties, so that they might be all looking at the same time, so as not to cause any unnecessary delay.

29th. Ques. (By same.) *State what was Mr. Duncan's conduct during the last election day.—Ans. Mr. Duncan, who was the Federal supervisor for the Republican party at this precinct, very greatly exceeded his powers and duties as supervisor, it struck me. He was the most violent and aggressive partisan that I saw present; he seemed to take charge of the whole poll over Republicans and Democrats alike—spurring on and assisting the Republicans in every conceivable manner, making speeches to them, assisting the Republican judge to find the names, holding whispered conversations with the Republican challengers on the outside, and in assisting and threatening to arrest, and in bulldozing the Democrats.*

30th. Ques. (By same.) You have spoken of his making speeches; to whom and of what nature were they?—Ans. They were speeches to the negroes, begging them to keep in line and not to shove; not to make any unnecessary noise.

31st. Ques. (By same.) While he was speaking was the voting going on or suspended?—Ans. Everything stopped when Mr. Duncan started.

32nd. Ques. (By same.) He has been described as being remarkably cool and calm that day; do you coincide with that opinion?—Ans. *On contrary, I think he was the most nervous and excited man at the precinct that day.*

33d. Ques. (By same.) Did you hear any complaints made of his conduct that day; if so, by whom?—Ans. *I am quite sure that Mr. Edgar Allen said more than once, that he was acting very indiscreetly if he wanted to facilitate the election; and I heard several negroes say, speaking of Duncan, "that man's just helping the Democrats, that's what he's doing; he is just playing right into the Democrats' hands," or words to that effect.*

Again we find positive and direct evidence that Duncan, the Republican Federal supervisor, was the great obstructionist at the first precinct.

THIRD PRECINCT.

We pass now to the third precinct.

Did the judges of the elections retard or obstruct the voting? Did they read unnecessarily or consume time in explanation of the constitutional convention question?

WILLIAM J. STEPHENS, one of the judges, p. 1142:

30th. Ques. (By same.) *It has been testified that you read to several, if not many, of the white voters the law as to voting upon the constitutional convention. State whether you did or not.*—Ans. *I did not.*

31st. Ques. (By same.) *Did you read anything except the oath on that day?*—Ans. *I did not.*

32nd. Ques. (By same.) *Did you delay the voters by intentionally reading the oath with unnecessary slowness?*—Ans. *I did not.*

33rd. Ques. (By same.) Who read any law at——

34th. Ques. (By same.) Who read anything to the voters that day, besides the oath, in your hearing?—Ans. Mr. Homer read a paper, which was handed to him by Judge Waddill; it was a clause from the Federal Constitution bearing on elections.

35th. Ques. (By same.) Was Mr. Homer asked to read the paper; if so, by whom?—Ans. He was asked to read it by Judge Waddill.

36th. Ques. (By same.) Do you remember any of the paper and the substance of it?—Ans. I know it was bearing upon the election, but I don't remember the wording of it.

37th. Ques. (By same.) Do you know why Mr. Homer, U. S. supervisor, was asked to read that paper; is he a particularly good reader?—Ans. I do not; he is a very indifferent reader.

38th. Ques. (By same.) Where was Judge Waddill when the paper was being read?—Ans. About in front from Mr. Homer and a few feet back from the window, as well as I remember.

39th. Ques. (By same.) Do you remember whether the paper read by Mr. Homer said anything about punishing any one under the U. S. law?—Ans. My impression is that it did.

40th. Ques. (By same.) Do you remember whether Judge Waddill said anything to Mr. Homer when he handed him the paper; if so, what was it?—Ans. I don't remember distinctly, but I think he said read this for the benefit of the voters.

It seems from this deposition that the contestant himself was delaying the voting by having papers read to the voters by Horner, the Republican Federal Supervisor.

The Democratic judge read nothing except the oath when administered to a voter.

WILLIAM J. O'NEILL, one of the clerks, page 1139:

17th Ques. (By same.) *State what was the conduct of Mr. W. J. Stephens during the day.*—Ans. *From what I could see of him he desired every man who was entitled to vote to do so.*

18th. Ques. (By same.) *State whether you saw anything in his conduct tending to hinder or delay the voting.*—Ans. *I did not; he did all in his power to vote every man before sunset.*

19th. Ques. (By same.) *Did you notice Mr. Homer during the day?*—Ans. *I did.*

20th. Ques. (By same.) *State as well as you can what was Mr. Horner's conduct dur-*

ing the earlier part of that day.—Ans. Mr. Homer demanded to know upon what grounds was the votes challenged.

21st. Ques. (By same.) *Did he dispute the right of the challengers to challenge?— Ans. In some cases he did.*

22nd. Ques. (By same.) *When he so denied the right to challenge, did that end the matter, or did he raise a discussion between himself and the challenger?—A. It very often raised a discussion between him and the challenger.*

23rd. Ques. (By same.) *Did such discussion consume time or speed the voting?—Ans. It consumed about one or two minutes sometimes.*

W. C. WILKINSON, page 1201 :

2nd. Qus. State if you were at either of the precincts in Jackson ward on the day of election; if so, which one?—Ans. I was at the 3rd precinct, Jackson ward.

5th. Ques. Did you observe any disorder around the polls there that day; if so, state by whom.—Ans. I don't consider there was any disorder there that day.

6th. Ques. Did you observe how the election was conducted?—Ans. I did. It was as orderly and quiet as any I ever saw.

7th. Qus. How often have you attended elections in that ward?—Ans. Several times.

8th. Qus. The contestant, Judge Waddill, in his notice of contest alleges that certain voters at the 3rd precinct of Jackson ward were prevented from voting by the connivance of the judges of election there, policemen of the city, and deputy United States marshal and others. Now will you state whether the policemen of this city at that precinct did any act to prevent, delay, or hinder any voter from casting his ballot?—Ans. None to my knowledge ; to the contrary, I think each and every one did all they could to promote the election. I do not think there was an arrest made at that precinct that day or one attempted ; if there was I was not aware of it.

9th. Ques. State what was the conduct of the judges of the election there and of the deputy United States marshals so far as they fell under your observation.—Ans. All fair and just as far as I could see.

HENRY W. RUFF, judge, page 1128, testified :

2nd. Ques. (By same.) What official position did you hold on the 6th day of last November?—Ans. I was judge of election at the 3rd precinct, Jackson ward, and held the colored registration-book.

3rd. Ques. (By same.) State who was in the polling room during that election day at that precinct.—Ans. The judges were W. J. Stephens, S. S. Richardson, the colored judge, and myself; the clerks were W. J. O'Neil and W. S. Jenkins, and the supervisors were Thomas Hill and John J. Homes, the Republican supervisor.

4th. Ques. (By same.) Were you there during the entire day?—Ans. Yes, sir.

5th. Ques. (By same.) Who held the registration-book for white voters?—Ans. S. S. Richardson, the colored judge.

6th. Ques. (By same.) State what duties were performed by Mr. Stephens.—Ans. He was the one to receive the ballots, ask the name and call it out, and place the ballot in the box.

7th. Ques. (By same.) *State whether you saw Mr. Stephens do any act to delay or hinder the voters from voting.—Ans. No, sir ; I did not.*

8th. Ques. (By same.) *State as to your conduct during the day.—Ans. I voted them all that were entitled to vote. I found all the names, with the exception of one party whose name I could not find; I looked for his name three or four times ; I don't remember his name at this time ; Mr. O'Neil helped me to look for his name also ; I don't think it was in the books.*

9th. Ques. (By same.) *State whether or not you consumed more time than was necessary in finding the names of the colored voters.—Ans. No, sir ; I did not. I voted them as fast as I found their names. I put the regular questions to them. I ask them where they lived and such as that.*

18th. Ques. (By same.) *What was the conduct of Mr. Holmes, the Republican supervisor, during that day?—Ans. It was right bad. He objected to four or five things there about challenging votes.*

19th. Ques. (By same.) *Did you see him do anything else; if so, please state it?—Ans. He got up there and read some law he got from Mr. Pleasants, I think ; this took up about five or ten minutes ; this was when Judge Waddill was present.*

20th. Ques. (By same.) *You have stated that he objected to voters being challenged; do you mean that he disputed the right of the challengers to challenge votes?—Ans. No; when anybody was on the disfranchised list and the challengers would challenge him, Mr. Holmes would say that that was not the man, or something like that.*

21st. Ques. (By same.) *Do you know how Mr. Holmes could tell whether the man offering to vote was the party who was disqualified?—Ans. I suppose he would take the voter's word for it after he would swear him.*

22nd. Ques. (By same.) *Do you know whether he had any other means for knowing him?— Ans. No. sir ; I do not.*

23rd. Ques. (By same.) *How long have you lived in Jackson ward?—Ans. About 23 years.*

H. Mis. 137——16

It appears from this evidence that the Democratic judges were guilty of no improper conduct; that they were as expeditious as possible, and that whatever unusual delay there may have been was caused by the Republican Federal Supervisor Horner and by the contestant himself.

FOURTH PRECINCT.

So far as the fourth precinct is concerned there is no evidence whatever worthy of consideration attacking the conduct of the judges. There is evidence to show that the Democratic Federal supervisor was drunk and was disposed to give trouble, but no evidence that he in any way prevented any one from voting or that he obstructed the reception of the ballots.

Having now, we think, successfully disposed of the charge against the Democratic judges of election at the three precincts in Jackson ward, not only by the judges themselves, but by the clerks and other witnesses, and shown that, whether intentionally or not, the Republican Federal supervisors at the various precincts, and the Republican judge at one, caused and promoted delay and hindered and obstructed the voting, we pass to other questions.

CHARACTER OF THE VOTERS IN JACKSON WARD.

The colored vote in this ward is, as compared with the white vote, at least three to one.

The colored registration-books contain the same names many times. It is a well-known fact that negroes are hard to identify, and that it requires perfect acquaintance and long familiarity with them to distinguish one from another.

Then when a man presented himself at the polls and his name appeared on the registration books many times, it was absolutely necessary to closely inquire as to his identity in order that his name might be checked on the registration-book, so as to prevent the reception of an illegal vote as well as fraud upon some other voter.

Again, under the laws of Virginia, conviction of petit larceny or felony works a disfranchisement of the convict. By reference to the record it will be found that the names of over 2,000 colored men stand upon the disfranchised lists of the police and hustings courts of the city of Richmond.

Under the statute the clerks of the courts are required to furnish the judges of election with these disfranchised lists.

An examination of these lists, which were in the hands of the judges of election in Jackson ward, as well as other wards, will show that about ninety names appear about five hundred times on them, or more than five times each on an average, while very many more appear two and three times each.

The judges of election then, in order to protect the ballot-box from the votes of thieves and felons, were compelled to look carefully to these lists.

Not only was it the province and duty of the judges o election to closely scrutinize the registration books and the disfranchised lists, but it was the right of the Democratic challengers, not only in order to protect their party against such votes, but as good citizens it was their duty to guard the ballot-box against pollution, by vigilantly observing that no man not properly registered and that no man who had been disfranchised should exercise the high privilege of voting.

This, then, leads to the inquiry whether the Democratic challengers were guilty, as charged, of delaying and hindering voters by unreasonable challenges and unnecessary and frivolous questions.

B. C. STOKES, Republican judge, testified:

20 Q. Repeat as near as you can the kind of questions they (the Democratic challengers) would ask them (the voters)?—A. How old are you; what is your age; where do you live; what street; number; whether they lived in Chesterfield or Henrico Counties; how long they had been living in the State.

B. C. SCHUTTE, clerk, testified:

One of the principal grounds of challenge was as to their moving from one place to another; the next ground was they had a printed list of the disqualified voters from the hustings and police courts of the city.

The Democratic challengers did no more challenging than they ought to have done on this occasion.

SPENCER JOHNSON (colored), witness for contestant, testified: He did not see anybody obstructing the voting that day.

OSBORN HOLMS (colored), witness for contestant, testified that the questions asked were as to his age, residence, and occupation, and whether he had been disfranchised.

WESLEY HARRIS (colored), witness for contestant, testified: He did not see the Democrats do anything that he thought was wrong; that he had been living in the precinct fifteen years, and that to his knowledge the elections had been fairly and honestly conducted.

GEORGE DUNCAN (colored), witness for contestant, testified:

Ques. Did you see the Democrats do anything that they ought not to have done?—Ans. Not a thing, sir; not a thing in the world.

JOSEPH BAKER (colored), witness for contestant, testified:

Ques. Was there any obstruction or molesting of voters?—Ans. I did not see any.

GILLIAM JONES (colored), witness for contestant, testifies:

Ques. On what ground were you challenged?—Ans. Because they said I did not have the right number. I was registered at 415 Baker street and gave 515 West Baker street.

JAMES R. GROSS (colored), witness for contestant, testified:

10th. Ques. Were you challenged by any one on the outside?—Ans. No, sir. I offered to swear by my ballot, and Mr. Belvin told me to get away; that my name was not on the book.

11th. Ques. Was he on the inside?—Ans. No, sir; he was standing right by me.

12th. Ques. In answer to a question put to you by Mr. Allan you said a gentleman inside the room challenged your vote. How is it that you now tell us that Mr. Belvin on the outside told you that your name was not on the book and to stand aside?—Ans. When I went to the window to hand my ballot to the gentleman he takes my ballot in his hand. Some one inside says my name wan't there on the book, and that I did not belong to that number. I asked them please to swear me; then Mr. Belvin told me to get away, my name was not there.

W. C. WILKINSON testified:

10th. Qus. Did you recognize any persons there who were acting as Democratic challengers: if so, give their names?—Ans. Mr. Glazebrook, I don't know his first name; Mr. C. V. Meredith, I think; Mayor John Hunter, and several others, I can not recollect their names. I think Rand Tucker was there awhile.

11th. Qus. Were those gentlemen there during the whole of the day of election?—Ans. I think not, some at one time and some at another; they would relieve each other.

12th. Qus. State what these parties were doing when you saw them at that precinct.—Ans. They were challenging votes; some on convictions, and some on wrong residence. Some voters when offering to vote gave their names, and when asked the number of their residences would hold up a little strip with the street and number on it, without giving the street and number.

13th. Qus. Did you hear any challenges for causes other than you have stated?—Ans. I don't recollect. There may have been others.

14th. Qus. You have referred to a convicted list; explain particularly what you mean by that.—Ans. I mean the pamphlets furnished by the courts of disfranchisements.

15th. Qus. Were these pamphlets of which you speak in the hands of challengers?—Ans. Yes, sir.

16th. Do I understand you to have said in answer to former questions that the challenges were when the person offering to vote gave a residence different from the one appearing on the registration book, or when his name appeared on the list of persons disfranchised on account of conviction for crime?—Ans. When the name of person offering to vote appeared on the disfranchised list he was then challenged until the matter could be looked into as to whether he was the man on the list or not. When the judges were satisfied that he was not the man he was permitted to vote.

17th. Qus. How did the judges satisfy themselves when there was a challenge on account of conviction?—Ans. Diff'rent ways; sometimes in the discrepancy of age, number of years of residence, and date of conviction.

18th. Qus. Have you ever been connected with the police court of the city of Richmond?—Ans. Yes, sir; four years as bailiff of that court.

19th. Qus. State whether or not that disfranchised list of which you have spoken is a large or small one.—Ans. Very large one.

20th. Qus. State whether from your experience as a policeman you have had occasion to go amongst the colored people of Jackson ward to obtain information or to find colored men there.—Ans. Yes, sir; I have.

21st. Qus. What is your experience in getting information of one colored person as to the whereabouts of another?—Ans. It is almost impossible.

22nd. Qus. State what is their habit as to residence; I mean whether they change frequently or not.—Ans. As a general rule they do.

23rd. Qus. You have told me that you were connected with the police court for about four years, and for a long number of years connected with the police force of this city; give me your opinion as to the necessity of a close canvass of Jackson ward in the interest of a fair election.—Ans. I think it absolutely necessary to come at anything like a fair election.

24th. Qus. Did you hear any questions asked by Democratic challengers on that day which you thought to be unnecessary and uncalled for; if so, state them.—Ans. I did not; I thought the questions were very reasonable and conservative.

25th. Qus. Were you during any portion of the day of election near enough to the polling window to observe and hear what passed there?—Ans. I was; but did not take any notice of anything on the inside, as there was nothing which attracted my attention particularly on the inside.

26th. Qus. Were you not near enough to hear and see the challengers and voters at the window?—Ans. Yes, sir; near enough to touch either of them most of the time.

EDWARD L. C. SCOTT testified:

7th. X Question. (By same.) Was Mr. Douglass' vote challenged?—Answer. There was some controversy, but after a full explanation his ballot was cast, the judges being satisfied that he was entitled to vote.

8th. X Question. (By same.) Did you hear the controversy?—Answer. Some portions of it.

9th. X Question. (By same.) Did you hear enough of it to find out what the real question in controversy was?—Answer. I heard Mr. Douglass tell the judges that he lived on this side of the C. and O. railroad tracks, which is the boundary line of Ashland precinct; I mean the side next to Ashland.

W. H. MASSEY (colored), witness for contestant, testified:

11th. Ques. Tell all that happened after you got to the voting window?—Ans. When I got to the voting window my name was called by some one; I don't know who. I told the gentleman what my name was. Mr. Belvin said you don't live at 311 West Duval st. I told him yes, I did live there. Some one said my name was not on the books.

12th. What did the judges of the election say?—Ans. They give my ticket back and told me to stand aside.

13th. There are three judges of election and two clerks. Was any vote taken on your right to vote?—Ans. All they said to me was to stand aside; I could not vote.

14th. Ques. I am speaking of the judges of election. Now you understand. Do you refer to them when you say they told me to stand aside?—Ans. The man that took my ticket told me to stand aside.

15th. Ques. Where did that man stand?—Ans. He was inside of the window.

GEORGE LYNCH (colored), witness for contestant, testified:

1st. Qu. Tell all that took place between you and the man you handed your ticket to at the window.—Ans. I handed the ticket to the man and he asked me what my name was, and I told him George Lynch; he said he could not find my name on that book he had; he told me to go back to the house and get the number I voted from on Brooke avenue; I went and got it and did not get to the polls any more.

2nd. Qu. (By same.) Were you sworn?—Ans. No, sir.

3rd. Qu. (By same.) Who told you to stand aside?—Ans. I don't know his name, but it was the gentleman who took my ticket.

4th. Qu. (By same.) Were you told to stand aside so that somebody else could vote?—Ans. No, sir; he just told me to get my number and come back.

RICHARD TAYLOR (colored), witness for contestant, testified:

5th. Question. (By same.) Why were you not allowed to vote; and is there anything else that you could have done that you did not do to have enabled you to vote? What ticket would you have voted—who for President and who for Congress?

(Excepted to on the ground that it assumes matter that has not been testified to by the witness, and also on the ground that it is not competent to ask a witness what ticket he would have voted.)

Answer. When I got to the window I handed the man my ticket, and he looked on the book and said my name wa'n't on the book. My ticket was handed back to me and I was told to stand aside. I went away in half an hour. I would have voted the Republican ticket. I would have voted for Harrison for President, and Waddill for Congress.

MINOR JOHNSON (colored), witness for contestant, testified:

8th X Q. You say Mr. Belvin challenged your vote, and that at the time he simply said he objected to your voting. What else took place at that time?—Ans. Well, the clerk said that he had some two or three Minors there, and Minor Johnson was not on the book.

9th. Q. What clerk told you this?—Ans. I disremember the clerk's name.

·10th. X Q. Was it the clerk of election who held the registration book of colored voters?—Ans. Yes, sir; I think it were.

11th. X Q. Did Mr. Allan pull you out of line immediately after the clerk told you this?—Ans. No, sir; I was willing to swear my name.

12th. X Q. What hour did this happen?—Ans. About 11 o'clock.

13th. X Q. Do you mean to say that Mr. Allan did not pull you out of line; or did any one do so?—Ans. He did pull me out.

14th. Q. Did you resist?—Ans. Well, I don't know.

15th. X Q. Did you quietly submit to being pulled out of line?—Ans. I did, sir.

16th. X Q. Why did you submit? And if you were willing to give up your right to vote, why did you not stand aside yourself without being pulled out of line?—Ans. Because I thought it was right after he pulled me. I didn't stand aside myself because they objected to swearing me.

17th. X Q. Had you ever met Mr. Allan before?—Ans. I had not, to know him.

18th. X Q. Would you have allowed any one else to have pulled you out of line?—Ans. I don't know, sir. I couldn't tell.

19th. X Q. Why did you allow Mr. Allan to do so?—Ans. Well, I didn't know Mr. Allan any more than any other man at that time.

WHITFIELD STEWART (colored), witness for contestant, testifies:

1st. Qu. When you handed your ticket to the judge of election and told him that your name was Whitfield Stewart, and he then told you that there was no such name as Whitfield Stewart on the books, did he tell you to stand aside so that somebody else might come up and vote?—Ans. Yes, sir.

2nd. Qu. (By same.) Did anybody else have anything to say to you there besides the judge of election?—Ans. No, sir.

3rd. Qu. (By same.) Did you see anybody there who seemed to be interfering with the voters?—Ans. There was some interruption; more than I thought was necessary.

4th. Qu. (By same.) Who was doing this?—Ans. I don't know. I was in a strange place up there. ·

GEORGE MIMMS (colored), witness for contestant, testified:

34. X Ques. Did you see any intimidation, terrorizing, or bulldozing about the polls that day? If so, tell just what it was and who was doing it.—Ans. No, sir; I did not pay any attention; I did not see any of it.

OLIVER BROWN (colored), witness for contestant, testified:

12th. X Q. While they were so looking for your name did the man who had taken your ballot stand at the window with it in his hand waiting for them to find it?—Ans. One was holding it and waiting at the window.

13th. X Q. Did anybody pull you from the window, or did you get aside yourself?—Ans. The crowd shoved me and told me to get away, and I got aside myself. Nobody pulled me away.

14th. X Q. Did you see the gentleman at the window put his head out and urge the crowd to stand back and tell them that if they did so they could vote faster?—Ans. I didn't hear him say that while I was there.

15th. X Q. Did you hear some colored men on the outside urge the colored voters not to push and crowd so, and that if they would not they could vote faster?—Ans. Yes, sir.

We give now *in extenso* the testimony of H. M. Smith, jr., who was one of the principal Democratic challengers in Jackson ward and we invoke a careful reading of it:

5th. Ques. (By same.) State, as well as you can, what you did there on that day.—Ans. When I got there there were some 600 or 800 negroes and 8 or 10 white men, possibly more, counting policemen and deputy marshals, who were not always on the spot. When I walked up I was greeted by Major Miles Cary, who I afterwards learned had charge of the Democratic forces, of the Democratic challengers and runners, at that precinct, who said, "I am very glad you came, and would be very glad if you would help Mr. Belvin as challenger at the window;" which I proceeded to do, and in which capacity I continued during the day.

6th. Ques. (By same.) About how far were you, as a general thing, from Mr. Belvin?—Ans. I presume from 6 inches to two feet; I might say from ¼ of an inch to two feet, to be more exact.

7th. Ques. (By same.) From the time you got there until the polls closed, who did the challenging?—Ans. Either Mr. Belvin or myself; no one else that I can think of on the Democratic side.

8th. Ques. (By same.) Did Mr. Belvin, while he challenged, have any book in his hand? If so, what was it?—Ans. He had the usual challenger's book, which was an alphabetical list of the colored voters in that precinct, it being a copy of the colored registration book which had been verified as far as possible by the Democratic canvassers; I mean by verified that the canvassers had made an effort to ascertain whether the voters lived in the houses or at the places where they were registered from.

9th. Ques. (By same.) State, as well as you can, the grounds of challenge made by you or Mr. Belvin.—Ans. There were several grounds of challenge: First, on account of the voter's name being called out by himself different from what it was on the registration books; second, his age being different; third, his residence being different; fourth, his name being on the disqualified list.

10th. Ques. (By same.) State as well as you can the questions that were asked upon the respective grounds of challenge.—Ans. When a voter came up to the polls he would call his name out; we would then look on our challenging book to see if he was registered; if the name was not on the registration book, it, of course, needed no challenge to keep the man from voting; but sometimes there was a name on the registration book, not the name given by the voter, but bearing some similarity to it; we would then call the judges' attention to the difference, that they might be satisfied that he was the same man whose name was registered; one of the ways of ascertaining this fact was to ask him his age, his occupation, and his residence. Again, a voter's name would be all right, but on challenge book would show that the canvasser had ascertained and made a memorandum of the fact that the voter did not live in the house to which he was credited; in such instances we would ask him where he resided; if he gave a residence different from the registered one, but within the precinct, we made no further objection; if without the precinct, we challenged him. Again, we frequently found the voter's name on the disqualified list, in which case we challenged on that ground, and would require the voter to purge himself, unless some of the judges or reputable Republicans were satisfied or assured us that it was not the same man. The questions which we asked, of course, varied with the different circumstances, but they were asked and were calculated to elicit the different phases above enumerated.

19th. Ques. (By same.) Several witnesses called on behalf of Judge Waddill have testified that both you and Mr. Belvin asked of the voters silly and unnecessary questions, some of which were as follows: "Who owned you before the war?" "Are you married? How many children have you?" State whether or not you asked any such questions yourself, or heard Mr. Belvin ask any such.—Ans. No, sir; there were no such questions asked of any voter standing ready to vote, and the judges and supervisors would not have allowed it. The Republican supervisor, Mr. Duncan, even went so far as to object to our asking what I conceive to be legitimate, relevant, and necessary questions. There was a good deal of pleasantry going on during the day back from the window between Mr. Belvin and myself on the one side, and Mr. Edgar Allen, Mr. Rockcharlie, Mr. Powell, and Capt. Ben. Scott on the other hand, during any intermission or lull in our work, and I have no doubt that if there are any witnesses who honestly and truthfully testified that such questions were asked got their impression from what was said while we were off duty, so to speak.

20th. Ques. (By same.) It has also been testified that useless questions were asked as to the voter's age, old men and men in the prime of life being asked whether they were 21 years of age.—Ans. I am certain that no such questions were asked of any such voters; I think though that I can give the grounds for that impression, and if my memory serves me right, I think some of the witnesses have admitted that it is from this source that I am about to explain that they got their impression; I refer to the oath which the voter is required to take in the event he is challenged, which oath is to the effect that is 21 years old, and is the identical person he represents himself to be, etc.

21st. Ques. (By same.) You have mentioned the names of Mr. Allen and Mr. Rockcharlie; please state their position in relation to Mr. Belvin during the day.— Ans. They stood immediately behind him and were looking at his book most of the time.

WILLIAM J. STEVENS, judge, testified:

21st. Ques. (By same.) State, as well as you can, the nature of the questions asked to the voters when challenged upon the different grounds.—Ans. They were only those allowed by law, as to their age, residence, and occupation. I remember no foolish or silly questions being asked at all.

22nd. Ques. (By same.) When challenged upon the ground of being on the disqualified list what was the nature of the questions then?—Ans. If they were the parties whose name appeared on that list.

23rd. Ques. (By same.) Did you hear or not any question asked of the voters such as, "Who owned you before the war"? "Are you married"? "How many children have you"?—Ans. None that I remember at all.

24th. Ques. (By same.) What position did the Democratic challengers occupy as to the window?—Ans. Coming from the north they were to the left of the window, that is, to my right hand.

25th. Ques. (By same.) To which side were the colored voters?—Ans. They were to my left.

26th. Ques. (By same.) How much of the window did the Democratic challengers occupy?—Ans. I suppose about one-third of it.

27th. Ques. (By same.) Did they or not prevent the colored voters from getting to the window to vote?—Ans. They did not.

HENRY W. RUFF, judge, testified:

12th. Ques. (By same.) Could you hear or not what took place at the window between the judges, the challengers, and the voters?—Ans. I could hear a good deal of it.

13th. Ques. (By same.) State as well as you can what were the nature of the questions asked during the day by the Democratic challengers.—Ans. If they found them on the disqualified list they would ask them if they had ever been found guilty of anything. I don't remember any other kind of questions.

14th. Ques. (By same.) Did you hear any challenged on the ground of residence?— Ans. Yes, sir; two or three, I reckon; I can't say how many.

15th. Ques. (By same.) Did all the colored voters that offered to vote give correctly the number of their residence?—Ans. No, sir; I don't suppose one-half of them did.

16th. Ques. (By same.) When a wrong residence was given were any questions put to the voters; and, if so, what were the nature of them?—Ans. If they gave the wrong number I would look in the book and see what was the number in the book, and I then would ask them if they ever lived at the number on the book.

17th. Ques. (By same.) Did you hear any question asked of the colored voters, as has been charged by several of the colored men, as follows: As to who owned him before the war? Whether he had any children, and how many he had?—Ans. No, sir; I did not hear anything like that.

W. L. TIMBERLAKE, judge, testified:

42nd. X Ques. About what proportion of the colored voters were challenged and sworn?—Ans. I can't tell you; I give you a rough calculation; I think about one in twenty-five or something of that kind; sometimes eight or ten would be challenged and sworn right straight along, and then there would be fifteen or twenty, and perhaps thirty or more, and no one would be challenged.

JAMES H. BRIGGS (colored), witness for contestant, testified:

28th. X Q. How far were you from the challengers that day?—Ans. Sometimes I was within 2 or 3 feet of them; sometimes further.

29th. X Q. Please state some of the questions usually asked a voter by the challengers.—Ans. Asked them their names; where do you say you live; what is your number; did you say 1714? No, sir; I said 1417. Ever been to jail; wasn't you arrested for stealing last year; what did you say your name was, John Robinson; how you spell it? Robtson. Did you say Robson? No, sir. Well, didn't you used to live at number 506? No, sir. Well, here's another man the same name, I think that must be you. And all sorts such questions as that they would ask; more so on that day than I have ever known.

30th. X Q. Do you think that the questions that you have given above fairly illustrate the character of questions asked of voters on last election day?—Ans. Yes, sir; to the best of my judgment.

We have now given the testimony of twenty-two witnesess, colored and white, including judges and clerks of election and Democratic challengers, and this number could be largely increased if we thought it necessary, as to the nature of the challenging and the character of the questions propounded, and it is hard to believe that any unbiased mind could read this testimony without being impressed with the fact that the challenges were proper, and conducted simply with a view of eliciting the truth and preventing illegal votes from being cast.

According to all this testimony not a frivolous or unnecessary question was asked.

The voters were interrogated as to their ages and residences, for the purpose of ascertaining whether they were the persons registered and whether they had been convicted of petit larceny or felony, to ascertain whether they were the parties under the same names on the disfranchised lists.

It seems to the minority of the committee that to hold that these challenges were unjustifiable would be to deter electors from guarding and protecting the ballot-box in the future from frauds and wrongs which, if permitted, would convert elections into a sham and a farce.

A critical examination of the testimony of the colored voters who were as alleged deprived of the right to vote will furnish the strongest reasons for the closest scrutiny of this class of voters. It will be found that large numbers of them in their testimony swore most recklessly and in answer to leading and suggestive questions, which seem to have been stereotyped by the contestant, absolutely perjured themselves.

Many of them, too, while swearing that they were qualified voters, made statements at variance with that fact.

Our conclusion is, that the charge that the Democratic challengers were engaged in a conspiracy to defraud the colored voters of their right to vote and that they did unnecessarily and fraudulently obstruct and hinder them is not sustained.

COMPARATIVE VOTES IN JACKSON WARD.

The number of votes cast at the first, third, and fourth precincts of Jackson ward at various elections was as follows:

Precinct.	1884 (Presidential).	1886 (liquor license).	1886 (municipal).	1889 (house of delegates).	1888 (Presidential).
First	254	282	270	638	431
Third	782	681	639	754	575
Fourth	820	742	730	768	718
	1,856	1,705	1,639	2,160	1,724

In the five elections the average vote in the three precincts was 1,816, or only 92 votes more than in 1888.

In each precinct the average was as follows:

First precinct 375, or 56 less than in 1888.
Third precinct 686, or 111 more than in 1888.
Fourth precinct 755, or 31 more than in 1888.

CALL OF CONSTITUTIONAL CONVENTION.

Article 12, section 2, of the constitution of Virginia reads as follows:

At the general election to be held in the year 1868, and in each twentieth year thereafter, and also at such time as the general assembly may by law provide, the question "Shall there be a convention to revise the constitution and amend the same?" shall be decided by the electors qualified to vote for members of the general assembly.

In pursuance of this constitutional requirement the general assembly of Virginia at its session 1886–'87 passed the following act:

Be it enacted by the general assembly of Virginia, That at the general election to be held for the election of Representatives in Congress and electors for President and Vice-President of the United States, on the first Tuesday after the first Monday in November, 1888, as required by the constitution of Virginia, there shall be submitted to the electors qualified to vote for members of the general assembly the question "Shall there be a convention to revise the constitution and amend the same?"

(2) The judges of election at each of the several voting places in this State are hereby required to provide a ballot-box separate from that in which are to be deposited the ballots cast for Representatives in Congress and electors for President and Vice-President, in which separate ballot-box so provided the judges of election shall deposit the ballots of all qualified voters voting upon the question of a convention to revise the constitution and amend the same. Said separate ballot-boxes shall be provided as ballot-boxes for other elections are provided.

(3) The ballots to be used in said election shall be separate from the ballots cast for Representatives in Congress and electors for President and Vice-President, and shall be, respectively, as follows: "For Constitutional Convention" and "Against Constitutional Convention."

(4) The manner of receiving and canvassing said ballots and making returns and abstracts thereof, shall conform in all respects to the requirements of the general election laws of the State.

Under this act it was the duty of the judges of election to furnish electors with ballots when requested, and the judges of election in Jackson ward were simply discharging their sworn duty when they furnished ballots to those who desired them.

It was also the duty of the judges to explain the object and purpose of the ballots tendered if desired, and if they had failed they would have been derelict.

Now if the votes in the three precincts of Jackson ward were not as large as the contestant contends they ought to have been, this resulted necessarily to some extent from the delay caused by the submission of this question to the people at that election.

In conclusion, we submit:

First. That the judges of election were guilty of no wrong-doing; that all they did was strictly in the line of their official duty.

Second. That the Democratic challengers were not guilty of fraudulently, unlawfully, or unnecessarily hindering or obstructing the voters in casting their ballots.

Third. That while there was some unnecessary delay and some votes were probably lost to the contestant, it was the result of the tardiness of the Republican judge at the first precinct in finding the names of voters on the registration book and the conduct of the Republican Federal supervisors at the first and third precincts.

Having thus reported our conclusions on the facts contained in the record, we proceed to an examination of the decisions of the courts and the House in similar cases.

The court of appeals of New York in Hart *vs.* Harvey, 19 Howard Pr. Reports, page 252, had before it the express question whether a vote not cast could be counted for the candidate for whom the voter intended or desired to vote, and uses the following language:

The result of the election must be determined by the vote cast. If illegal votes can be ascertained they may be rejected; but votes not received can never be made available in favor of either party.

The supreme court of California in passing upon the same question, in Webster *vs.* Byrnes, 34 Cal., page 276, say:

The court below erred in counting for contestant the supposed votes of Gonsalves, Larkin, and Haas, under the pretense that they would have voted for him had they been allowed to vote. In all contests of this character the question is, Which candidate received the highest number of legal votes? The idea that the supposed votes of persons who did not vote, but who could have voted had they taken the necessary legal steps to entitle them to do so, should be counted for the candidate for whom they would have voted, is simply preposterous.

The supreme court of Alabama in the case of the State *ex rel.* Spence *vs.* The Judge of the Ninth Judicial Circuit, 13 Ala., page 811, say:

Smoot offered to vote at the election, but his vote was not received, and he would have voted for Spence. * * * It is perhaps unnecessary to inquire whether the managers should have permitted Smoot to vote or not, for he did not vote, and even if his vote could have had any influence in changing the result of the election, as in fact it was not given, it could only have authorized the circuit judge to have declared the election void, but could not authorize him to count it as actually given to Spence.

To the same effect see Newcum *vs.* Kirtley, supreme court of Kentucky, reported in 13 B. Munroe, page 515.

It will thus be seen that the highest courts in the States of New York, California, Alabama, and Kentucky have held that even though a legal voter should tender his ballot to the managers of the election, and they should reject the same, yet such vote could never be counted for either party. The fact that the vote was illegally rejected, and that the voter declared under oath for whom he intended and desired to vote would not authorize the tribunal that must "judge" of the election to count such vote, the election must be determined by the votes actually cast; and, if it appear that a sufficient number of votes to change the result were unlawfully or improperly rejected, the effect would be to render the election void. The undersigned have not had their attention called to, nor are they aware of any decision of any court in any of the States, or of the United States, which establishes or maintains any other or different rule from that here laid down.

The first case reported to the House of Representatives in which the contention was that votes not cast should be counted was the case of Biddle and Richard *vs.* Wing, at the first session of the Nineteenth Congress. In that case the committee say:

Mr. Richard rests his claims to the seat on grounds which, to the committee, appear entirely novel, and, as they do not at all interfere with any of the matters in controversy between the other candidates, will be first examined. He does not pretend that he has received the greatest number of votes that were actually given, but that he would have received the greatest number of votes had not his friends at the election holden in the city of Detroit been intimidated from voting by reason of the interference of deputy sheriffs and constables who, it is alleged, under the pretence of keeping the peace, struck several persons on the head, and by that means prevented them, and many others, from voting for Mr. Richard. The committee are of opinion that the duty assigned them does not impose on them an examination of the causes which may have prevented any candidate from getting a sufficient number of votes to entitle him to the seat. They consider that it is only required of them to ascertain who had the greatest number of legal votes actually given at the election. An election is the act of selecting, on the part of the electors, a person for an office or trust. In case of the application of the contrary doctrine, the greatest uncertainty must necessarily prevail; and, should it be established, it would be placing in the hands of a few riotous individuals the power of defeating any election whatever. The law appoints a particular time and place for the expression of the popular voice; when that time is past it is too late to inquire who did not vote, or the reason why. The only question now to be determined is for whom the greatest number of the legal votes have been given.

The next case we find involving this question is that of Niblack *vs.* Walls, Forty-second Congress. In that case the committee departed from the rule established in the courts and the report in Biddle & Richard *vs.* Wing, and held that votes not cast or even *offered* to the managers of election might be counted. The facts of the case are reported in the following words:

We are satisfied from the evidence that there was an organized effort on the part of the friends of the contestant to prevent a full vote being cast at this poll for the sitting member, and that it was partially successful. This conspiracy was carried out by creating a disturbance at the election by threats of violence and the exhibition of deadly weapons, and particularly by crowding about the polls in such numbers as to prevent many colored voters from reaching the polls to deposit their ballots, and with this intent.

The committee then proceed to deny that rejection of the poll would be a remedy for such wrongs, and say some other remedy must be found. In these words it is presented: •

This is to be found in the rule, which is well settled, that where a legal voter offers to vote for a particular candidate, and uses due diligence in endeavoring to do so, and is prevented by fraud, violence, or intimidation from depositing his ballot, his vote should be counted. The principle is that the offer to vote is equivalent to voting.

This report we understand to be directly contrary to the decisions of the courts, and the only case which had before been presented to the House, and we are unable to ascertain in what place and before what tribunal such rule had been " well settled ; " in fact, it appears to have been set up in the case of Niblack vs. Walls for the first time, without any precedent to sustain it, and we think an examination of the cases subsequently decided by this House will show that the rule therein suggested has never in any single instance been followed.

In Frost vs. Metcalf, reported in 1879, the committee say :

While on this branch of the subject your committee will dispose of the complaint made by the contestant that by reason of the errors in copying the registration list he lost many more votes than contestee. To count votes which were never offered at any poll is carrying the doctrine further than we ever knew it. To authorize this committee to count a vote four things are requisite: first, the person offering to vote must have been a legal voter at the place he offered to vote; second, he must have offered his vote ; third, it must have been rejected, and fourth, it must be shown for whom he offered to vote.

The case of Yeates vs. Martin relied upon does not touch the question of counting votes not cast.

In the case of Bisbee vs. Finley, reported in 1882, the committee say :

As a question of law we do not understand it to be controverted that a vote *offered* by an elector and illegally *rejected* should be counted as if cast.

The committee in that case affirm that each vote counted by it was in fact by the voter actually *tendered* to the election officers, and was by such *election officers* rejected.

In Sessinghaus vs. Frost, reported in 1883, each vote counted was actually *tendered* by the voter to the election officers, and was by the *election officers* rejected.

Bell vs. Snyder, reported in 1874, was based on a failure to open the polls until three hours after the appointed time, and is no authority for counting votes not cast. Thus we see the House has never followed the rule suggested in Niblack vs. Walls; that rule is not well settled, and has never been established in this House. In Frost vs. Metcalf the House expressly refused to follow it, and the rule prescribed in the latter case has ever since been recognized as the correct one. There are objections even to the rule as there laid down; any extension of it is fraught with difficulties and dangers, and until this time, since the report in that case, no committee of this House has ventured to depart from it.

The majority of the present committee and the majority of this House in the case of Mudd vs. Compton, just decided, failed and refused to conform to or apply the rule laid down in the case of Niblack vs. Walls, which it is now sought to enforce. It was claimed in Mudd vs. Compton, that a sufficient number of legal voters to have changed the result

had they voted were standing in line at the polls for the purpose and
with the intention of voting for contestant; but were prevented from
doing so by intimidation; and yet the committee did not count such
votes as cast—it reported in favor of rejection of the polls, and the
House, after full discussion, adopted such report.

The act of Congress referred to in the report of the committee refers
only to qualification of voters and not to the act of voting. The citations
from McCrary, and Paine on elections, referred to in the report of the
committee, are based upon the decisions of the House herein reviewed,
and as we have shown are not sustained by any of the cases referred to
except Niblack *vs.* Walls, which is a departure from and contrary to
the established rule and which stands alone, unsupported, so far as we
have been able to learn, by a decision of any court or of any legislative
body in this country.

It seems to us that the rule contended for by the majority in this case
would open wide the door for fraud and invite false swearing, which the
opposing party would have no means of refuting. To hold that anything
short of an actual tender of the ballot to the election officers and a rejection by them was an offer to vote, would be a most dangerous and
uncertain rule and one to which we can not give our sanction. Where
the evidence plainly establishes the fact that a legal voter offers his ballot to the election officers and they unlawfully reject the same, under
the precedents heretofore established such vote may be counted for the
candidate for whom the voter offered to vote. Conceding for the purpose of the argument all that is claimed by the contestant in this case,
to wit, that by fraud and intentional hindrance and delay a large number of voters who intended to vote for him were unable to reach the
poll to tender their ballots, although they used diligence; that when
the polls closed a large number of voters present on the ground desiring
to vote for him had for such reasons been unable to do so, and that
thus a sufficient number of voters were prevented from voting to have
changed the result had they succeeded in voting; still, inasmuch as
there was no actual tender of their votes and rejection thereof by the
election officers, such votes can not be counted for contestant; they
have not ·been *offered* and *rejected,* and the most that can be claimed
under this assumed state of facts is that there has been no fair and full
election within the meaning of the law, and that neither party shall be
adjudged entitled to the seat.

In the case before us we have before said we do not believe there was
any considerable obstruction of the voters in their right to vote; but it
appears that at the time the polls were closed at 3 precincts of Jackson
ward there were a number of voters present at each polling place desiring and intending to vote who were prevented from doing so through
no fault of their own, and it is possible that such voters were sufficient
in number to have changed the result had they all voted for the contestant. Under these circumstances we have been somewhat embarrassed to determine what recommendation we should make to the House.
As we have shown, under such a state of facts, the courts determine the
result by the vote actually cast. The enforcement of that rule in this
case would give the seat to the sitting member.

But we are not satisfied of the justice of such rule. While it is true
that neither the contestee nor his partisans can justly be held responsible for the failure of any of the voters to exercise their right of suffrage
yet we believe that some were deprived of the opportunity to vote and
that the number might have been sufficient to change the result, and
so believing in the interest of fair play and complete justice we are

not inclined to hold the contestant responsible for the inefficiency of the Republican judge or the conduct of the Republican Federal supervisors, but are of the opinion that the ends of justice will be subserved by remitting the election to the people of the district who can, unembarrassed by the constitutional convention question, freely declare their choice, and we therefore submit the following resolution :

Resolved, That the seat now held by George D. Wise as the Representative in the Fifty-first Congress from the Third Congressional district of Virginia, be, and the same is hereby, declared vacant.

CHARLES F. CRISP.
CHAS. T. O'FERRALL.
J. H. OUTHWAITE.
R. P. C. WILSON.
LEVI MAISH.
L. W. MOORE.

JOHN V. McDUFFIE vs. LOUIS W. TURPIN.

FOURTH ALABAMA.

———

The issues in this case are almost entirely questions of fact, about the only legal questions involved being as to the admissibility of testimony and the weight of evidence.

Contestant charged that in a large number of precincts throughout the district the officers of election fraudulently counted thousands of **votes** for contestee which were in fact cast for contestant. The committee find the charge sustained by the evidence, and that to count the vote as proved to have been cast would make a change of 17,634 votes in favor of contestant. The minority find fraud proved in eight or nine precincts, and by restating the vote of these precincts according to the evidence, and counting a number of precinct returns not counted by the county canvassing boards, make a change of 4,049 votes in favor of contestant. This being less than the majority returned, and the evidence being insufficient to sustain the charges of fraud in other precincts, the right of contestee to the seat is sustained.

The resolutions presented by the committee were adopted by the House June 4, 1890, by a vote of 130 to 113, and Mr. McDuffie was sworn in. The debate will be found on pages 5512 to 5601 of the Record.

(1) **Returns.** *Their weight as prima facie evidence.*

In considering the evidence with reference to particular precinct returns it is first necessary to inquire by whom the election was held in order to determine what weight should be given to the returns. Returns are, as a rule, prima facie evidence of the result; but if the integrity of the inspectors is in any way impeached, either by showing that their character is such as to cast suspicion on their acts, or that their belief is that frauds upon elections are justifiable, or that the manner of their selection was such as to indicate a purpose to procure a false statement of results, then the returns lose much of the weight that would otherwise attach to them.

(2) **Conspiracy.** *Partisan appointment of election boards evidence of.*

When the law provides that each of the two political parties shall have representation on the election board of inspectors it is a provision to prevent dishonest partisans from making false returns; and in such

255

case the appointment of men incompetent to determine whether the
return is honest or not to represent the party opposed to the appointing
power, tends to prove an intent to prevent that watchfulness intended
to be secured by the statute, and raises a strong suspicion (if it does
not fully prove) of conspiracy to falsify the returns.

(3) **Irregular election.** *When permissible.*

" In extraordinary cases, and where it appears that in no other way
can the actual will of the voter be ascertained, a resort to methods not
technically in accordance with statutory direction may be justifiable,
and upon proof that a full, fair, and honest election has been held by
those only who are qualified voters, under these circumstances the returns from such an election, when duly proved, may be considered and
counted.

None of those guards provided by statute to secure honest results
should be neglected, but when statutory provisions designed to protect
qualified voters in the exercise of their legal rights are made use of with
deliberate purpose to suppress the will of the majority, such action will
be regarded as fraudulent."

(4) **Return.** *Neglect to make.*

Voters are not to be disfranchised by any neglect of the officers after
the election if the correct vote can be ascertained.

(5) **Evidence.** *Of vote cast.*

The evidence of persons who issued tickets and claim to know that
they were voted is admissible to prove that the vote of a precinct
differed from the return, and if sufficiently clear and convincing may
be conclusive of the falsity of the returns.

REPORT.

MAY 7, 1890.—Mr. ROWELL, from the Committee on Elections, submitted the following report:

The Committee on Elections, having had under consideration the contested-election case of John V. McDuffie *vs.* Louis W. Turpin, from the Fourth Congressional district of Alabama, submit the following report:

The Fourth district of Alabama is composed of the counties of Dallas, Hale, Lowndes, Perry, and Wilcox. At the election held November 6, 1888, Louis W. Turpin was the Democratic candidate for Representative in the Fifty-first Congress, and John V. McDuffie was the Republican candidate.

The result of the election as certified to the Secretary of State was as follows:

Counties.	Turpin.	McDuffie.
Dallas	5,705	1,706
Hale	3,170	1,220
Lowndes	2,131	1,442
Perry	2,961	650
Wilcox	4,811	607
Total	18,778	5,625

Turpin	18,778
McDuffie	5,625
Majority for Turpin	13,153

Under this return the contestee received the certificate of election, and McDuffie contests. Notice of contest was served and answer filed as provided for by statute covering all matters considered in this report.

With such a returned majority for contestee, it is apparent either that this contest is a huge farce, or that this whole district is honeycombed with fraud.

Before proceeding to consider the evidence in the record of this particular case, the committee deems it proper to review to some extent the recent political history of this district.

By the census of 1880 the population of the Fourth district was as follows:

Counties.	White.	Colored.
Dallas	8,425	40,007
Hale	4,903	21,650
Lowndes	5,645	28,528
Perry	7,156	23,591
Wilcox	6,711	25,117
Total	32,824	135,893

H. Mis. 137——17

Upon the assumption that one out of every five of the population is
a qualified voter, this would give in round numbers in the district
6,500 white voters and 27,000 colored voters, or more than four times
as many colored as white. The population of the district is comparatively stable, and it may safely be assumed that at the present time the
same relative proportion of white and colored exists, and that the increase of population is no more than normal.

At the State election in 1874 the counties comprising this district
gave a Republican majority of 14,946. This was before the "revolution" which placed all political power in the State of Alabama in the
hands of the Democratic party. At the Presidential election in 1876
the Republican electors received a majority of 9,446. At the Congressional election in 1880, for Representative in the 47th Congress,
Charles M. Shelley, Democratic nominee, was declared elected by a
majority of 2,651 over his Republican opponent, James Q. Smith; the
vote certified being:

Shelley 9,301
Smith 6,650

    Total.. 15,951

Smith contested, and the Committee on Elections of the House
found (and the House approved) the true vote to be:

Smith 11,507
Shelley 8,704

    Smith's majority... 2,803

This did not include the total vote cast, but was the vote which, in
the opinion of the committee, could be definitely ascertained. Mr.
Ranney, of the committee, stated the vote:

Smith 11,807
Shelley 8,735

    Majority for Smith... 3,072

W. J. Stephens, another Republican, received, according to the returns, 1,693 votes, making the total Republican majority 4,766.

In this case, Mr. Smith having died before its final determination,
the seat was declared vacant. Mr. Shelley went before the people again
at the November election, in 1882, as a Democratic candidate for the
unexpired term of the Forty-seventh Congress and for the Forty-eighth
Congress. He received a certificate of election to both and took his
seat at the second session of the Forty-seventh Congress and served
out his term. John W. Jones, his Republican competitor for the unexpired term of the Forty-seventh Congress, memorialized the House for
a more speedy method of determining the right to the seat than that
furnished by the statute, the time for taking testimony under existing
law extending beyond the life of that Congress. He alleged frauds
similar to those by which Shelley had obtained his first certificate.
The committee reported in favor of an investigation by a select committee, but the Congress expired by limitation before action was taken.

George H. Craig was General Shelley's Republican competitor for
the seat in the Forty-eighth Congress; and although General Shelley's
rights under his second certificate to the Forty-seventh Congress were
never directly determined, the facts as they were developed in the
Forty-eighth fully demonstrated that that certificate was obtained by
the same fraudulent and illegal methods which had given him his first
certificate.

Craig contested his right to a seat in the Forty-eighth Congress. The result of the election, as certified to the secretary of state, was:

Shelley 7,150
Craig 4,435

Total 11,605
Shelley's majority 2,715

The Committee on Elections of the House, a majority of whose members were partisan friends of General Shelley, found the true vote to be:

Craig 10,671
Shelley 7,212

Total 17,883
Craig's majority 3,450

The remarkable feat of counting Shelley in was accomplished by rejecting returns made to the various county boards by precinct officers, on account of supposed technical defects. In arriving at this result the committee did not include precinct returns, which gave Craig an additional majority of 1,338. Had these returns been counted, Craig's majority would have been 4,766. In declining to count these additional returns the committee uses this language:

It will be observed that the committee has not counted a number of districts which were returned and not counted by the board of supervisors of the several counties. This was done out of extreme caution to count no precinct except where there was oral evidence to sustain the returns of the precinct officers.

Elections were held and returns made, but, out of *extreme caution,* the committee did not count them, because contestant had failed to strengthen them by oral proof. Here was a majority of over 4,000 turned into a minority of over 2,700, and yet the committee add:

It does not criticise the action of the board of supervisors of the several counties in rejecting these precincts.

The committee, however, reports in favor of Mr. Craig, and adds:

In doing this it has not only followed the precedents established by the House of Representatives, but the decisions of the supreme court of Alabama.

Tardy justice was done to Mr. Craig, by giving him the seat to which he was elected, late in the second session; but the delay in finally determining the case kept him from prosecuting a contest which he had commenced in the Forty-ninth Congress.

It will thus be seen that General Shelley was twice certified to the Forty-seventh Congress, and once to the Forty-eighth, although in each case he had actually been defeated by large majorities.

In the Fiftieth Congress there was also a contest from this district. At the election for that Congress the certified result was as follows:

A. C. Davidson, Democrat 14,913
J. V. McDuffie, Republican 3,526
B. F. Turner, Independent Republican 2,517

Total 20,956
Davidson's plurality, 11,387.

The report in that case, made by the Democratic members of the committee, cut Davidson's plurality down to 8,890, a deduction of 2,497. The Republican minority of the committee held and reported that a fraudulent conspiracy existed in four of the five counties in the district to defeat the will of the people; that, had the vote been honestly counted, McDuffie would have been elected by a large majority, and that by the unimpeached and honest returns of contestant's own county (Lowndes) he received a majority of 1,625, and was elected. We shall have occasion to refer to this case later on.

From this account of the action of the election officers and returning boards of this district it is clearly evident that there has existed a fixed determination on the part of the Democratic managers there that the will of the majority should be disregarded, and a willingness to resort to any methods, however unlawful and criminal, to accomplish the defeat of their Republican opponents. The record in this case justifies and fully confirms the above conclusion, and shows that the same conditions continue to exist.

If the certified returns in this case are true, it follows (allowing for 500 increase in white voters since 1880, and 2,000 increase in colored) that all the white voters and at least 11,800 colored men voted for contestee, while only 5,625 voted for contestant, and more than 11,500 did not vote at all. That is to say, more than two-thirds of the colored men who cast their ballots voted for contestee, and 43 per cent. did not vote at all.

In the light of history, and of that knowledge common to all well-informed men, it is not too much to say that such a report is a self-evident falsehood, unless there is a present condition of affairs in the Fourth district of Alabama taking that district out of the rule which prevails everywhere else.

The record in this case demonstrates its falsity beyond a reasonable doubt. The evidence in this record, as in other records from the same district, shows conclusively that the great majority of the colored men there are Republicans, and that when they vote they vote the Republican ticket.

The evidence of the certified returns, on the other hand, shows that a large majority of them vote the Democratic ticket. The conflict is between the returns and the men who cast the ballots on which the returns purport to be based.

The evidence also shows that, in almost every voting district, there are a few colored Democrats, well known to both white and black. It also shows that where the whites are in a majority a greater number of colored men vote the Democratic ticket than in localities where the blacks greatly preponderate.

The evidence further discloses that the Republicans have kept up their party organization, that they continue to take great interest in elections, and as a rule are eager to exercise the right to vote. It further shows that at this election there was entire harmony in the ranks, the only exception being a so-called Republican paper of small circulation and less influence, which lent itself to the Democracy.

The evidence further establishes the fact that throughout the district there was a general belief among the Republicans that there would not be an honest count of the votes; that, whatever the actual result, contestee would be declared elected, and that it would be necessary to prove the true vote by other means than the returns, and to appeal to the House to correct the anticipated wrong to the voters. Such belief does not exist so universally without cause. The history of this district, the common knowledge of the mass of voters in it of announced results at former elections, and the action of county officers in appointing inspectors of election, fully justified the belief; and results prove that the belief was foreknowledge.

The election laws of Alabama, so far as they are necessary to understand the issue in this case, are here inserted.

SECTION 1. *Be it enacted by the General Assembly of Alabama,* That every male citizen of the United States, and every male person of foreign birth who has been naturalized, or who may have legally declared his intention to become a citizen of the United States, before he offers to vote, who is twenty-one years old or upwards, who shall have resided in the State one year, three months in the county, and thirty days in the precinct or ward next immediately preceding the election at which he offers to vote, is a qualified elector, and may vote in the precinct or ward of his actual residence, and not elsewhere, for all officers elected by the people.

* * * * * * *

Approved February 9, 1877.

SEC. 252. The courts of county commissioners may, in their respective counties, establish, change, or abolish election precincts and places of voting therein, and may change the boundary lines thereof, as the convenience of the voters in such precincts may, in their judgment, be promoted thereby; but no order under this section shall take effect unless made at least sixty days before an election, nor until three months after notice thereof has been posted up at the court door of such county.

SEC. 258. *Number of boxes and by whom provided.*—The probate judge, sheriff, and clerk of the circuit court of each county in the State shall provide one ballot-box, and where it is deemed necessary shall provide more than one, and not more than three, at each place of voting.

CHAPTER III, ARTICLE I.

SEC. 259. *Inspectors and precinct-returning officers, how appointed.*—The judge of probate, sheriff, clerk of the circuit court, or any two of them, must, at least thirty days before the holding of any election in their county, appoint three inspectors for each place of voting, two of which shall be members of opposing political parties, if practicable, and one returning officer for each precinct to act at the place of holding elections in each precinct; and it shall be the duty of the sheriff to notify such inspectors and returning officers of their appointment within ten days after such appointment.

SEC. 260. *Sheriff is county returning officer.*—The sheriff of each county, or the person discharging the duties of such office, is the returning officer of the county.

SEC. 262. *Duties of inspectors and returning officers in holding election; how places supplied on failure to attend.*—It shall be the duty of the inspectors and the returning officers appointed to meet at the place of holding elections in the several precincts for which they have been appointed by eight o'clock of the morning of the day of election, and before nine o'clock open the several polling places as designated. And on the failure of any inspector or returning officer to attend at the hour of eight o'clock, such as may be present may complete the number. If none of the inspectors appointed are present the returning officer of the precinct shall appoint three inspectors to act, who in every such instance shall be qualified electors who are entitled to vote at that polling place. And if there should be no inspectors or returning officer present by the hour of eight o'clock at any polling place, then any three qualified electors who are entitled by law to vote at that polling place, in the election to be held, may open the polls and serve as inspectors during the election.

SEC. 263. *Returning officer absent inspectors appoint.*—If the returning officer is not present at the hour appointed, the inspectors, or those acting as such, must appoint one to serve during the election.

SEC. 264. *Clerks of election.*—Inspectors, before opening the polls, must select two persons to act as clerks.

SEC. 265. *Oath of inspectors and clerks.*—Before opening the polls, the inspectors and the clerks must take an oath to perform their duties at such election, according to law, to the best of their judgment, and the inspectors must also swear that they will not themselves, or knowingly allow any other person, to compare the number of the ballots with the number of the votes enrolled, which oath may be administered by the inspectors to each other, or by the returning officer, or a justice of the peace.

SEC. 271. *Hours of opening and closing the polls.*—The polls must be opened at each voting place, in each voting precinct, between the hours of eight and nine o'clock in the morning, and be kept open, without intermission or adjournment, until the hour of five in the afternoon, and no longer.

SEC. 281. Five witnesses for each political party may attend each voting place, without restriction as to distance, for the purpose of challenging persons who may be suspected of attempting to vote illegally.

STYLE OF BALLOTS (ACTS OF ALABAMA, 1878-'79, PAGE 72).

SECTION 1. The ballot must be a plain piece of white paper, without any figures, marks, rulings, characters, or embellishments thereon, and not less than two or more than two and one-half inches wide, and not less than five or more than seven inches

long, on which must be written or printed, or partly written and partly printed, only
the names of the persons for whom the elector intends to vote, and must designate
the office for which each person so named is intended by him to be chosen, and any
ballot otherwise than described is illegal and must be rejected.
Approved February 12, 1879.

MODE OF RECEIVING BALLOTS (ACTS OF 1878-'79, PAGE 78).

SECTION 1. One of the inspectors must receive the ballot folded from the elector,
and the same passed to each of the other inspectors, and the ballot must then, without being opened or examined, be deposited in the proper ballot-box.
Approved February 8, 1879.

MANNER OF COUNTING THE VOTES (ACTS OF ALABAMA, 1878-'79, Page 73).

SECTION 1. In counting out, the returning officer or one of the inspectors must
take the ballots, one by one, from the box in which they have been deposited, at the
same time reading aloud the names of the persons written or printed thereon and the
office for which such persons are voted for. They must separately keep a calculation
of the number of votes each person receives, and for what office he receives them; and
if two or more ballots are found rolled up or folded together, so as to induce the belief that the same was done with a fraudulent intent, they must be rejected; or, if
any ballot contains the name of more than the voter had a right to vote for the first
of such names on such ticket to the number of persons the voter was entitled to vote
for only must be counted.
Approved February 13, 1879.

ARTICLE IV, CODE OF ALABAMA.

SEC. 285. *Counting out votes.*—It is the duty of all inspectors of elections in the
election precincts, immediately on the closing of the polls, to count out the ballots
so polle .
SEC. 287. *Statement of votes and one poll-list certified, sealed up in a box, and delivered
to returning officer.*—As soon as the ballots are all counted out the inspectors must
ascertain the number of votes received for each person and for what office, and must
make a statement of the same in writing, which statement must be signed by them.
They must also certify in writing on the poll-list that such poll-list is the poll-list of
the election precinct or ward at which they were inspectors, the day and year on
which election was held, and for what offices, which certificates must be signed by
them, and such statement of the poll-list and votes thus certified must be sealed up
together with the list of the registered voters in such precinct or ward at such election, on such day, in a box to be furnished by the sheriff of the county, one or more
for each precinct or ward, and to consist of wood, tin, or sheet-iron, and securely
fastened by locks, directed to the sheriff of the county, if there be one, and, if none,
then to the person discharging the duties of such office, and immediately deliver the
same to the returning officer of the precinct.

CODE OF ALABAMA (SEC. 289, PAGE 242,

Statement and poll-lists returned to county returning officer.—The statement of votes
and poll-lists delivered to the returning officer of the precinct must be delivered to
the returning officer of the county within forty-eight hours after the election.

VOTE OF THE COUNTY, ESTIMATED. (ACTS OF ALABAMA, 1876-'77, PAGE 121.)

SECTION 1. *Be it further enacted,* That on Saturday next after the election, at the
hour of 12 meridian, the returning officer of the county, in person, or by deputy, and
the probate judge and clerk of the circuit court, shall assemble at the court-house,
or if there be no such judge and clerk, or either of them fail to attend, or if either
of them be interested by reason of being a candidate at such election, his place must
be supplied by a respectable freeholder or householder of the county; and if all such
officers be of the same political party, then the said returning officer of the county
must summons three reputable persons, resident householders or freeholders of the
county, members of the opposite political party, to attend at such time and place
and in the presence of such other persons as choose to attend; and it shall be the
duty of this board of supervisors, so constituted, to make a correct statement from
the returns of the votes from the several precincts of the county of the whole num-

ber of the votes given therein for each Officer and the person to whom such votes were given.

*   *   *   *   *   *   *

Approved January 20, 1887.

SEC. 384. *Ballots and second poll-lists, how disposed of.*—The inspectors must count the ballots deposited in the box; as soon as all the ballots contained in the box are counted the inspectors shall roll up the ballots so counted, and label the same, so as to show for what officer or officers the ballots contained therein were received, and, when so rolled up and labeled, shall be securely sealed; the rejected ballots, if any, shall also be rolled up and labeled as rejected ballots and sealed up as the other parcels; and the packages so sealed up and labeled, together with one poll-list, which shall also be securely sealed up, shall be returned to and securely fastened up in the box from which such ballots were taken and counted, and which shall also be sealed and labeled, so as to show the nature of its contents, and shall be kept by one of the inspectors for sixty days; and then the packages shall be taken out of the box, without opening or unsealing the packages, and destroyed, unless within that time the inspector having them in custody is notified that the election of some officer for which the election was held will be contested, in which case he must preserve the box containing the ballots cast for such contestant until such contest is finally determined, or until such box is demanded by some other legally constituted custodian during such contest.

Attention is called to some of the features of the law.

If any of the inspectors are absent from the place of election at 8 o'clock a. m., the inspectors present may complete the number, and proceed with the election. If no inspector is present at 8 o'clock, and the returning officer is, he may organize a board of inspectors. If none of these officers are present at 8 o'clock, then any three citizens, qualified voters, may organize the board.

One ballot-box is to be provided by the sheriff, and if necessary (that is, if more than one box is necessary to receive the votes), then more than one, and not exceeding three.

A peculiar feature of the law is that each of the three inspectors must have the ballot in his hand before it is deposited in the box, a feature which seems to have been devised for the purpose of facilitating fraud and concealing it. One dishonest inspector of very ordinary skill may, without danger of detection, change a large portion of the ballots before they reach the box. The other two may honestly testify that they saw nothing wrong. So that two inspectors may be called as witnesses and testify to the honesty of the election, while the third, who perpetrated the fraud, is left in the background.

After the election and return, the ballots are to be placed in the custody of one of the inspectors, to be kept by him sixty days, and then destroyed if no notice of contest has been served on him in the mean time. No record is made, so as to be accessible, of which inspector has the ballots; nor is any means, other than sealing, provided by law for their safe-keeping so that they may thereafter be safely examined with any assurance that they are the ballots which were voted.

The inspectors appointed by the probate judge, sheriff, and circuit clerk (or any two of them), must be appointed at least thirty days before the election; and, if practicable, must be of different political parties.

The sheriff must, at a given time, summon the probate judge and circuit clerk as a board of supervisors to ascertain and certify the result of the election. If these officers are all of the same political party, then this returning officer must summon three reputable householders, citizens and voters, of the opposite political party, to make up this returning board or board of supervisors. In connection with this section of the statute it may be remarked that all the officers made returning officers by law were of one political party, but nowhere was it deemed by them or the sheriff necessary to comply with the terms of the law and summon members of the opposite political party to act as supervisors. Such little formality, designed to secure honest returns, seems to have been entirely forgotten.

The following from decisions of the supreme court of Alabama have a bearing upon the case:

It is the election which entitles the party to office, and if one is legally elected by receiving a majority of legal votes, his right is not impaired by any omission or negligence of the managers subsequent to the election. (13 Ala., 805.)

Nor will a mistake by the managers of the election in counting the votes and declaring the results vitiate the election. Such a mistake should be corrected; the person receiving the highest number of votes becomes entitled to the office. (9 Ala., 338.)

In considering the evidence with reference to particular precinct returns, it is first necessary to inquire by whom the election was held, in order to determine what weight should be given to the returns. Returns are, as a rule, prima facie evidence of the result; but if the integrity of the inspectors is in any way impeached, either by showing that their character is such as to cast suspicion on their acts, or that their belief is that frauds upon elections are justifiable, or that the manner of their selection was such as to indicate a purpose to procure a false statement of results, then the returns lose much of the weight that would otherwise attach to them. English vs. Peele, 48th Congress. In this case the committee says:

When once the taint of fraud or unreliability is attached to the official count, its value is gone, and we must look to other sources for better information.

In Lowndes County the precinct inspectors were appointed on the 25th day of September. A few days afterwards the contestee visited the county, and on the 6th day of October an entire change was made in the list of inspectors appointed to represent the Republicans. The first list was satisfactory, and made up in the greater part of intelligent men. The second list was made without any authority in the law, and its composition shows that the change was made for a dishonest purpose. Judge Coffey (Record, p. 745) says that the reason for this change was that the sheriff and several other gentlemen told him that the Republican inspectors being *school-teachers*, did not wish to serve and mix up in politics. Hence the change. Let us see whether that was the true reason.

Church Hill.—First appointee attended for the purpose of serving and was not permitted.

Gordonsville.—Same.

Farmersville.—Offered and was refused. Served at Republican box.

Hopewell.—Superseded inspector was present and served as supervisor.

Sandy Ridge.—Superseded inspector tried to serve, and was refused. Did serve as supervisor at the Republican box.

Brooks.—Inspector superseded, but actually served, and the return is not questioned.

Prairie Hill.—Superseded inspector actually served at one box.

Letohatchie.—Superseded inspector actually served at box opened by Republicans.

Steep Creek.—Superseded inspector tried to serve, and when refused kept outside list.

Pintlala.—Superseded inspector actually served and made honest return.

St. Clair.—Superseded inspector actually served and made honest return, but false return of a pretended election made. True return rejected.

White Hall.—Superseded inspector served and made honest return.

Twelve of the first list either served or tried to serve, and eight of the new list who served could neither read nor write. The reason for the removal of intelligent and trustworthy Republicans and replacing them with ignorant and unreliable men, in pretended compliance with the law, is evident from the foregoing statement, and the falsity of Judge Coffey's reason is made apparent.

That contestee had something to do with this change does not admit of much serious question.

When the law provides that each of the two political parties shall have representation on the election board of inspectors, it is a provision to prevent dishonest partisans from making false returns; and in such case the appointment of men incompetent to determine whether the return is honest or not to represent the party opposed to the appointing power, tends to prove an intent to prevent that watchfulness intended to be secured by the statute, and raises a strong suspicion (if it does not fully prove) of conspiracy to falsify the returns.

With this proposition in view, we submit the facts in regard to the inspectors appointed to represent the Republican party.

HALE COUNTY.

Greensborough precinct.—Inspector appointed as a Republican; could neither read nor write.

Cedarville precinct.—Colored inspector known to be under the control of the Democratic inspectors, and not considered a Republican.

Carthage precinct.—All the inspectors were Democrats.

Warren's store precinct.—Inspectors all Democrats.

Havana precinct.—Inspectors all Democrats.

Newborn precinct.—Inspectors all Democrats. In this precinct, there being no Republican inspector and no United States supervisor, the Republicans refused to vote, and opened a poll of their own; but the Democratic inspectors counted them as if they had voted, and as voting the Democratic ticket. The Republican box was not returned, and is not considered.

WILCOX COUNTY.

Snow Hill precinct—Inspectors all Democrats, including the colored inspector.

Pine Apple precinct.—Inspectors all Democrats, including an illiterate colored man.

Allentown precinct.—One Republican inspector who could neither read nor write.

Bethel precinct.—One Republican inspector who could neither read nor write.

White Hall precinct.—The appointed Republican inspector at this precinct happened to be intelligent and was prevented from acting. A Democrat was substituted.

Black Bluff precinct.—Inspectors all Democrats.

Mimm's precinct.—Inspectors all Democrats, one of them a colored Democrat who could neither read nor write. An outside list of Republican voters, kept by Republican watchers, was forcibly seized by the deputy sheriff.

Camden precinct.—Colored inspector says he is a Republican, but he is one of those Republicans who vote the Democratic ticket.

Prairie Bluff precinct.—Inspectors all Democrats, one of them a colored man who could not write. He testifies that he is a Democrat.

Sedan precinct.—Inspectors all Democrats.

Bailey Springs precinct.—The colored inspector could not read or write, and was understood to·be a Democrat.

Rehobeth precinct.—Republican inspector could neither read nor write.

Canton precinct.—Inspectors all Democrats.

Geesbend precinct.—Republican inspector could not write.

PERRY COUNTY.

Marion precinct.—Republican inspector refused to sign returns, and United States supervisor shows up the fraud.

Hamburg precinct.—One inspector a Republican.

Pole Cat precinct.—Same.

Uniontown precinct.—Two boxes.

Cunningham precinct.—One inspector claimed to be a Republican.

Walthall precinct.—One inspector claimed to be a Republican, but not trusted as such.

All the inspectors in this county were appointed by the Democratic county central committee.

DALLAS COUNTY.

Martin Station precinct.—Inspectors all Democrats, including the colored inspector. Fraud shown up by the United States supervisor.

Pence precinct.—All the inspectors, including the colored one, Democrats. Box carried away and not counted until the day following the election.

Mitchell's Mill precinct.—Regular Republican inspector, with two qualified electors, held election and made return. Some one else made, return of another election. Neither return counted by returning board. Here the appointing power made a mistake, and appointed a Republican inspector capable of preventing fraud. Hence the refusal of the Democratic inspectors to act with him.

Liberty Hill precinct.—Election held by Republican inspectors, Democratic inspectors failing to appear.

Burnsville precinct.—In this precinct a duplicate box was prepared, but the Republicans found it, and it disappeared. Hence the Democratic inspectors refused to count the vote until the following day, at another place. It required time to supply the place of the lost box, with desirable tickets in it.

Union precinct.—Republican inspector could neither read nor write.

Valley Creek precinct.—Republican inspector could not write. U. S. supervisor refused admission to the polling place.

Summerfield precinct.—Republican inspector could neither read nor write.

Lexington precinct.—Inspectors all Democrats, including a colored man who could neither read or write.

Smiley precinct.—Democratic inspectors failed to appear, and election held by Republican inspector as provided by law. Returns rejected by county board, but it is admitted that they ought to be counted.

Pine Flat precinct.—The man appointed to represent the Republicans says he is neither a Republican nor a Democrat, but is a "straight out." He signs his testimony with his mark.

Vernon precinct.—Republican inspector could not read or write. Box carried away before counting.

Dublin precinct.—Election held by two inspectors. Republican could not read or write.

Orville precinct.—Colored inspector regarded as a Democrat.

Selma precinct.—One Republican inspector, but has the reputation among Republicans as a tool of the Democrats in the perpetration of election frauds.

Elm Bluff precinct.—Inspectors all Democrats.

Richmond precinct.—Republican inspector could not read or write. Outside tally-keeper beaten with a club and list taken away. Arrested by deputy sheriff.

Brown's precinct.—Republican inspector could not read or write. Ballots counted by U. S. supervisor: McDuffie 265, Turpin 16. The box containing returns tampered with and returns falsified.

Chilatchie precinct.—Returns rejected by county board, but it is admitted that they ought to be counted.

River precinct.—Republican inspector could not read or write.

Carlowville precinct.—Inspectors failed to appear. Election held by electors, but not considered by county board.

Woodlawn precinct.—Republican inspector could not read or write.

Marion Junction precinct.—Republican inspector could not write.

Old Town precinct.—Inspectors all white Democrats.

ANALYSIS.

Hale County. (Seven precincts).—In four all inspectors were Democrats. In two Republican could not read or write, and in the other Republican inspector looked on as a Democrat.

Wilcox County. (Fourteen precincts).—In eight all inspectors were Democrats. In four, Republican inspectors could not read or write. In one, Republican inspector prevented from acting, and Democrat substituted; and in one, a Republican who was distrusted.

Dallas County. (Twenty-two precincts).—All Democrats in six. Republicans, who could not read or write, in ten.

Such uniform violation of the statute and such uniform pretense of complying with its terms by appointing colored Democrats to represent the party, or by appointing illiterate colored Republicans, show method in the action of the county boards, with dishonest designs behind the method.

Under these circumstances it would be safe to apply the rule adopted in regard to this district by the House Committee on Elections in the Forty-eighth Congress, and consider as trustworthy only such returns as are sustained by oral testimony. But the committee has not gone to that extent in this case.

It is worthy of remark that in almost every precinct in the fourth district there were reliable and intelligent Republicans, competent to discharge the duties of election inspectors and to protect the voters to the extent of securing an honest count and a correct return.

Another feature of the election, which can not be overlooked, was the precaution everywhere taken by the Republicans to ascertain with accuracy the number of votes cast by them, showing a universal distrust of the precinct officers. In many precincts complete poll-lists were kept by clerks selected for that purpose, voters going to the extent of refusing to vote unless such precaution was taken. On the other hand, vigorous efforts were made by the Democrats in many places to prevent the keeping of such lists, under the pretense that the keeping of such lists was intimidation. Deputy sheriffs were active in trying to suppress this attempt to keep a check upon the distrusted election officers.

In one instance the attempt of a deputy sheriff, acting under the direction of the sheriff of the county, to stop the further keeping of a poll and to secure possession of the one that had been kept, resulted in the murder of one Republican and the wounding of two others by the deputy and his supporters. The murderer has escaped even the formality of a prosecution.

These officials who were thus attempting to prevent the measures taken by the Republicans to preserve the evidence of the vote cast, well knew the purpose of these measures, for, only two years before, in the election contest of McDuffie vs. Davidson, this kind of evidence had been used all over the district to show up the frauds in the election of 1886. The conclusion is inevitable that these acts of the Democratic officials and their aiders and abettors were done in furtherance of contemplated frauds.

The printed record discloses another unpardonable attempt to suppress testimony. This attempt was the deliberate act of contestee and his attorneys. Frivolous objections, covering whole pages of the record, and cross-examinations of witnesses which would disgrace a police court shyster, were the means by which contestee and his attorneys sought to use up the time allowed to contestant in which to take testimony to prove his allegations. This conduct resulted, beyond a reasonable doubt from a deliberate purpose to suppress as much of contestant's evidence as possible, and prevent a disclosure of the whole truth.

These are some of the general features of the case proper to be considered in applying the specific evidence in regard to the various precinct returns brought into question.

The following are the findings of the committee of the true state of the vote in the precincts named, contrasted with the returns, and, so far as accessible, with the vote as found in the case of Craig vs. Shelley, in the Forty-eighth Congress. (Report of committee in Fiftieth Congress does not give precinct findings.)

LOWNDES COUNTY.

Prairie Hill:
  Counted by committee—
    Turpin 110
    McDuffie 75
  Returned—
    Turpin 110
    McDuffie 75
Gordonsville:
  Counted by committee—
    Turpin 19
    McDuffie 200
  Returned—
    Turpin 252
    McDuffie 69
  In Forty-eighth Congress—
    Democrat 0
    Republican 299

Sandy Ridge:
  Counted by committee—
    Turpin 103
    McDuffie 203
  Returned—
    Turpin 103
    McDuffie 1
  In Forty-eighth Congress—
    Democrat 96
    Republican 207
Letohatchie:
  Counted by committee—
    Turpin 20
    McDuffie 204
  Returned—
    Turpin 249
    McDuffie 19

Lowndesborough:*
  Counted by committee—
    Turpin...................... 41
    McDuffie 140
  Returned—
    Turpin...................... 320
    McDuffie 41
  In Forty-eighth Congress—
    Democrat 44
    Republican 369
  *Inconclusive evidence tends to
  show some 350 Republican votes
  in this precinct.

Steep Creek:
  Counted by committee—
    Turpin...................... 37
    McDuffie 171
  Returned—
    Turpin...................... 146
    McDuffie 62
  In Forty-eighth Congress—
    Democrat 26
    Republican 184
Church Hill:
  ,Counted by committee—
    Turpin...................... 13
    McDuffie 166
  Returned—
    Turpin...................... 117
    McDuffie 63

Haynesville:
  Counted by committee—
    Turpin...................... 54
    McDuffie 272
  Returned—
    Turpin...................... 158
    McDuffie 0
St. Clair:
  Counted by committee—
    Turpin...................... 8
    McDuffie 214
  Returned—
    Turpin...................... 8
    McDuffie 0
  In Forty-eighth Congress—
    Democrat 6
    Republican 182
Farmersville:
  Counted by committee—
    Turpin...................... 26
    McDuffie 40
  Returned—
    Turpin...................... 26
    McDuffie 0
Fort Deposit:
  Counted by committee—
    Turpin...................... 0
    McDuffie 0
  Returned—
    Turpin...................... 60
    McDuffie 0

The remaining precincts in Lowndes County are not contested. The returns are as follows:

Precincts.	Turpin.	McDuffie.
Benton	94	60
Bragg's	98	31
Hickory Hill	98	22
Hopewell	90	54
Mt. Willing	160	113
Brooks's	17	283
Pintlala	21	330
White Hall	4	215
Total vote returned	2,131	1,442

Committee's count, by above table, deducts 1,118 from Turpin's vote and adds 1,288 to McDuffie's vote, leaving the true vote: Turpin, 1,013; McDuffie, 2,730. McDuffie's majority in Lowndes County, 1,717. The certified returns from Lowndes County in 1886 gave McDuffie 1,530 majority, and the House Committee on Elections found his majority to be larger.

WILCOX COUNTY.

Snow Hill:
  Counted by committee—
    Turpin 82
    McDuffie 445
  Returned—
    Turpin 464
    McDuffie 105
  In Forty-eighth Congress—
    Democrat 0
    Republican 515
Alleuton:
  Counted by committee—
    Turpin 27
    McDuffie 316
  Returned—
    Turpin 242
    McDuffie 67
Pine Apple:
  Counted by committee—
    Turpin 180
    McDuffie 211
  Returned—
    Turpin 348
    McDuffie 33
Bethel:
  Counted by committee—
    Turpin 57
    McDuffie 343
  Returned—
    Turpin 385
    McDuffie 15
White Hall:
  Counted by committee—
    Turpin 47
    McDuffie 84
  Returned—
    Turpin 116
    McDuffie 26
  In Forty-eighth Congress—
    Democrat 25
    Republican 71
Clifton:
  Counted by committee—
    Turpin 29
    McDuffie 204
  Returned—
    Turpin 190
    McDuffie 25
  In Forty-eighth Congress—
    Democrat 5
    Republican 169

Black's Bluff:
  Counted by committee—
    Turpin ....
    McDuffie 2
  Returned—
    Turpin 2
    McDuffie ....
Prairie Bluff:
  Counted by committee—
    Turpin ....
    McDuffie 2
  Returned—
    Turpin 2
    McDuffie ....
Boiling Springs:
  Counted by committee—
    Turpin ....
    McDuffie 2
  Returned—
    Turpin 2
    McDuffie ....
Rehobeth:
  Evidence tending to show fraud-
    ulent return, but not sufficient
    to reject returns.
  Returned—
    Turpin 1
    McDuffie ....
  In Forty-eighth Congress—
    Democrat ....
    Republican 1
Canton:
  Counted by committee—
    Turpin ....
    McDuffie 1
  Returned—
    Turpin 2
    McDuffie ....
Geesbend:
  Counted by committee—
    Turpin ....
    McDuffie 1
  Returned—
    Turpin 1
    McDuffie ....
  In Forty-eighth Congress—
    Democrat ....
    Republican 1

The returned vote of Wilcox County, including precincts not name
above, gives Turpin 4,811, McDuffie 607. By our table we deduct fro
Turpin's returned vote 2,276 and add to McDuffie's returned vote 2,20

Turpin .... 4,811—2,276=2,3
McDuffie .... 607+2,200=2,8

    Majority for McDuffie in Wilcox County 2

Hamburg:
  Counted by committee—
    Turpin...................... 35
    McDuffie 256
  Returned—
    Turpin...................... 212
    McDuffie 83
Marion:
  Counted by committee—
    Turpin...................... 83
    McDuffie 583
  Returned—
    Turpin...................... 697
    McDuffie 86
Uniontown:
  Counted by committee—
    Turpin...................... 210
    McDuffie 955

Uniontown—continued:
  Return (same in two boxes).
  Counted by returning board—
    Turpin...................... 210
    McDuffie 2
Perryville:
  Counted by committee—
    Turpin...................... 0
    McDuffie 0
  Return—
    Turpin...................... 142
    McDuffie 41
  (Throw out, as neither returns nor poll-lists were signed and no proof made.)

Perry County vote as returned gives Turpin 2,961, McDuffie 650. Deduct by our table from Turpin 973 and add to McDuffie 1,582, as follows:

Turpin .... 2,761— 933 = 1,828
McDuffie .... 650 + 1,582 = 2,232

    McDuffie's majority in Perry County...................... 404

Greensborough:
  Counted by committee—
    Turpin...................... 210
    McDuffie 693
  Returned—
    Turpin...................... 577
    McDuffie 330
  Forty-eighth Congress—
    Democrat 194
    Republican 630
Hollow Square:
  Counted by committee—
    Turpin...................... 59
    McDuffie 475

Hollow Square—continued:
  Returned—
    Turpin...................... 362
    McDuffie 169
Cedarville:
  Counted by committee—
    Turpin...................... 27
    McDuffie 490
  Returned—
    Turpin...................... 364
    McDuffie 153

Returned vote of Hale County gives Turpin 3,170, McDuffie 1,220. We deduct 1,007 from Turpin and add 1,006 to McDuffie, as follows:

Turpin .... 3,170—1,007 = 2,163
McDuffie .... 1,220+1,006 = 2,226

    McDuffie's majority 63

DALLAS COUNTY.

Martin's Station:
  Counted by committee—
    Turpin 87
    McDuffie 324
  Returned—
    Turpin 383
    McDuffie 28
  Forty-eighth Congress—
    Democratic 1
    Republican 304
  Forty-seventh Congress—
    Democratic 16
    Republican 384
Pence:
  Counted by committee—
    Turpin 8
    McDuffie 219
  Returned—
    Turpin 188
    McDuffie 20
  Forty-eighth Congress—
    Democratic 0
    Republican 150
Mitchell's Mill:
  Counted by committee—
    Turpin 0
    McDuffie 345
  Returned—
    Turpin 30
    McDuffie 0
  Forty-eighth Congress—
    Democratic 0
    Republican 307
Liberty Hill:
  Counted by committee—
    Turpin 0
    McDuffie 197
  Returned—
    Turpin 0
    McDuffie 0
Burnsville:
  Counted by committee—
    Turpin 60
    McDuffie 288
  Returned—
    Turpin 475
    McDuffie 22
Union:
  Counted by committee—
    Turpin 44
    McDuffie 336
  Returned—
    Turpin 299
    McDuffie 85
  Forty-eighth Congress—
    Democratic 0
    Republican 269
Valley Creek:
  Counted by committee—
    Turpin 60
    McDuffie 382
  Returned—
    Turpin 401
    McDuffie 89
Summerfield:
  Returned—
    Turpin 162
    McDuffie 30

Summerfield—Continued.
  Forty-eighth Congress—
    Democratic...............
    Republican...........
  (We count this as returned,
    there are strong indications
    fraud.)
Smiley:
  Counted by committee—
    Turpin ....
    McDuffie ....
  Forty-eighth Congress—
    Democratic. ....
    Republican...........
  (No return counted.)
Pine Flat:
  Counted by committee—
    Turpin ....
    McDuffie.............
  Returned—
    Turpin ....
    McDuffie ....
  Forty-eighth Congress—
    Democratic.............
    Republican ....
Vernon:
  Counted by committee—
    Turpin ....
    McDuffie ....
  Returned—
    Turpin ....
    McDuffie ....
Dublin:
  Counted by committee—
    Turpin ....
    McDuffie.............
  Returned—
    Turpin...............
    McDuffie.............
Selma:
  Returned—
    Turpin....................
    McDuffie ....
  (We leave as returned, but have
    serious doubts as to the hon-
    esty of the count.)
Elm Bluff:
  Counted by committee—
    Turpin ....
    McDuffie ....
  Returned—
    Turpin....................
    McDuffie ....
  Forty-eighth Congress—
    Democratic..............
    Republican ....
Brown's:
  Counted by committee—
    Turpin ....
    McDuffie ....
  Returned—
    Turpin ....
    McDuffie ....
  Forty-eighth Congress—
    Democratic ....
    Republican..............

Chillatchie:
Counted by committee—
    Turpin................... 0
    McDuffie.................. 144
(No returns counted.)

River:
Counted by committee—
    Turpin.................... 17
    McDuffie.................. 200
Returned—
    Turpin.................... 283
    McDuffie.................. 14
Forty-eighth Congress—
    Democratic 0
    Republican............... 133

Carlowville:
Counted by committee—
    Turpin.................... 0
    McDuffie.................. 101
(No return counted. Conceded.)

Woodlawn:
Counted by committee—
    Turpin.................... 40
    McDuffie.................. 136

Woodlawn—Continued.
Returned—
    Turpin.................... 159
    McDuffie.................. 17
Marion Junction:
Counted by committee—
    Turpin.................... 9
    McDuffie.................. 72
Returned—
    Turpin.................... 72
    McDuffie.................. 27
Old Town:
Counted by committee—
    Turpin.................... 20
    McDuffie.................. 150
Returned—
    Turpin 271
    McDuffie 5
Boykins:
Counted by committee—
    Turpin.................... 17
    McDuffie.................. 110
Forty-eighth Congress—
    Democratic 0
    Republican 93
(Returns not counted by board.)

Returned vote of Dallas County gives Turpin 5,705, McDuffie 1,706. We deduct from Turpin 2,838 and add to McDuffie 3,190.

Turpin .... 5,705—2,838=2,867
McDuffie .... 1,706+3,190=4,896

McDuffie's majority 2,029

Total majority for McDuffie in the district............................ 4,481

The following is a more extended abstract of the testimony on which the above findings are based:

LOWNDES COUNTY.

Gordonsville.—In this precinct the first appointed Republican inspector was unlawfully superseded, and a Republican who could not read or write substituted. It is shown in evidence that there are from 300 to 400 Republicans in the precinct and only 20 to 25 Democrats. It is also shown that at least 200 Republicans voted the straight Republican ticket. At about 2 o'clock p. m. a recess was taken, and a Democratic inspector took the ballot-box into an adjoining room, against the protest of the United States supervisor, and remained alone with it eleven minutes by the watch. When the votes were counted there were found to be 3 less in the box than there were names on the poll-list, and three tickets were picked up from the floor and put into the box. When the tickets were counted there was found to be a large number of tickets in the box with the Republican electors and Turpin's name on them. These tickets were of a different size and on a different kind of paper from the regular Republican tickets, and were easily distinguishable.

The United States supervisor, who received the tickets from the voters a good portion of the day, swears that no such tickets were voted. The number of Republican tickets voted, the fact that these bogus tickets were in the box, although not handed in by the voters, shows that this box was stuffed, and destroys the integrity of its contents. We are left to ascertain the vote by other evidence, which shows that there were at least 200 Republican votes, and the notice of contest concedes 19 Democratic votes.

H. Mis. 137——18

No attempt was made to sustain the return. Probably the reason for stuffing the box, instead of falsifying the count, was the presence of an intelligent supervisor. The material evidence in regard to this precinct is found on pages 728, 733, 735, and 744 of the record.

Sandy Ridge.—At this precinct two polls were opened, within 75 yards of each other. The Democratic inspectors refused to allow the regularly appointed Republican inspector to act with them, and also refused to allow the United States supervisor to act; whereupon they organized a poll in conformity with the statute. The Republicans voted at one poll, the Democrats at the other, and two returns were made. The one returned by the Democratic inspectors was counted, the other not. We count both, as showing the votes cast by those entitled to vote, and hold that the circumstances as detailed in the evidence justified the action of the Republicans in holding a separate poll. The precinct has some 250 Republicans, and possibly 130 Democrats in it. The result here—and there is no conflict in the evidence—shows that when there is a fair count the Republicans are seen to adhere to their party.

Letohatchie.—As in Sandy Ridge, there were two polls at this precinct, organized under precisely similar circumstances. The Republicans had no faith in the Democratic inspectors, and the result shows that their distrust was well grounded, for at the Democratic poll the fraud is so patent that it is beyond any question. The poll-list returned proves this. It will be found on pages 679, 680 of the record. Commencing with No. 56, it shows that the remaining voters—263 being returned as voting—voted in alphabetical order, with an occasional name inserted out of order. Of course this is a bare-faced fraud, and completely destroys the integrity of this poll. It is clearly proven that numbers of the persons whose names appear on this list did not vote at the poll, and others did not then live in the beat. The truth is these clerks and inspectors simply copied the old registry, and put tickets in the box to correspond. And yet the Democratic inspectors, with this list staring them in the face, boldly swore that they held an honest election, illustrating the tone of morals in that community as applied to elections. The committee invite inspection of this poll-list.

There are in this precinct about 225 colored voters and 75 white voters. One witness, on cross-examination, when asked why he did not vote at the Democratic box, made a significant answer: "Because they always counted me out."

Lowndesborough.—The returns for this precinct were: Turpin, 320; McDuffie, 41. The evidence shows that the precinct contains about 400 colored voters and some fifty white voters, that some 350 colored men attended the election and voted, and that most of them voted the Republican ticket. One hundred and forty make affidavit that they so voted. It is true that these are *ex parte* affidavits, the introduction of which can only be justified on the ground that contestee deliberately prevented the testimony from being taken in the lawful and regular way. Other evidence shows that of the 350 who voted, a great part voted for contestant.

There being only 50 white voters in the precinct, it follows, if the returns are true, that at least 270 colored men voted Democratic, while only 41 voted Republican, or more than six to one. This of itself is almost incredible, taken in connection with the proved fact that only a few colored men vote the Democratic ticket.

The inspectors here, including the colored man, were all Democrats, in violation of the statute. None of the clerks or inspectors were called to sustain this return. Two witnesses were called to show that a good many of the colored men voted the Democratic ticket. One of them, who was active in the interest of the Democratic party, went so far as to say that he thought to the best of his belief that about as many voted for Turpin as for McDuffie. This but confesses the claim that the returns did not show the true state of the vote (p. 539.)

Steep Creek.—Returns show: Turpin, 146; McDuffie, 62.

Milton D. Alexander, an intelligent colored man, was appointed Republican inspector for this beat, but was superseded by the subsequent appointment of an illiterate colored Democrat. He went to the polls and asked to serve, but was refused. He and an assistant distributed the tickets, and at the request of the voters had a complete poll list kept of those who voted the Republican ticket, showing the Republican vote as we count it. This poll-list was introduced in evidence, and then stolen while the testimony was being taken. The reason for keeping this outside poll is thus explained by Alexander:

We were fearing to be counted out by the Democrats, * * * and we wanted to know precisely how many Republican votes were cast for him (McDuffie) in that precinct, which was our object in keeping the outside poll. * * * We expected a contest, and expected to be counted out (pages 693, 698).

James Gillind (page 707) describes fully the method of keeping the poll, and the arrangement made beforehand with the Republican voters to enable them to prove the true vote. There are from 200 to 225 colored voters and from 25 to 30 white voters in the beat; 189 colored voters of this beat make affidavit that they voted the Republican ticket.

Here we have 170 voters declaring at the polls their intention to vote the republican ticket, taking the ticket from one chosen by them to issue tickets by pre-arrangement, holding their tickets in such a way that they could be seen until voted, and then having their names registered so as to be able to prove how they voted. These acts are a part of the *res gestæ* of the election—the deliberate declaration of the voters while engaged in the act of voting, not only of how they voted but of their utter want of confidence in the election board upon which they had no representation.

In this precinct one of the inspectors was called as a witness for contestee. He shows that Cheek, the colored inspector, voted the Democratic ticket, but that to convince the Republicans that all was honest, they had this inspector, Cheek, receive and deposit in the box all the ballots. He took the ballots from the box, but another inspector, not called, read the names. The clerk who kept the tally is called. An outsider is called to show that some colored men changed their ballots after receiving them from Alexander, in which he does not agree with the inspector. The evidence of fraudulent returns, taken in conjunction with the general evidence, is conclusive, and we so find.

Church Hill.—Return: Turpin, 117; McDuffie, 63. Committee count McDuffie, 166; Turpin, 13. The evidence shows that there are only 12 to 14 white men in this beat; that formerly there were a few colored Democrats in the beat but none at the present time; that the intelligent Republican inspector first appointed was superseded and an illiterate one substituted; and that the one first appointed attended the polls and superintended the work of putting in the Republican votes, having an outside poll kept. This poll had 167 names on it, but one was erased because the watchers did not see his hand with the ticket in it from the time he started with the ticket until it was deposited with the inspector.

Several meetings were held by the Republicans before the election, at which arrangements were made as to how the voters were to act, in order that a complete record might be kept of their vote, in anticipation of the counting out process with which they were all familiar.

As an illustration of the methods employed by the Republicans here and elsewhere, to preserve the evidence of the vote, we insert the testimony of C. F. Hrubowski, the manager at this poll (page 698) :

C. F. HRUBOWSKI, being called and sworn, deposes and saith :

Q. State your name, your age, your residence, and political party to which you belong.—A. My name is Charles F. Hrubowski; my age is 43 years old ; I reside in Church Hill beat, No. 2, in Lowndes Co., Ala.; my race is colored, and I belong to the Republican party.

Q. Did you attend the election in your precinct on the 6th day of Nov., 1888, to elect a Congressman for the 51st Congress for this district, and Presidential electors ?— A. I did attend such an election.

Q. Who held that election—that is, who were the inspectors, clerks, and returning officers ?—A. Mr. J. R. Dudley, N. B. Lever, and Cap. Dudley were inspectors; W. N. May was the clerk, and the returning officer was George Earnest, and if there was any other clerk I don't know who it was.

Q. If you had any notice or information of the fact that the probate judge, the clerk of the circuit court, and sheriff of the county, or that any two of them appointed you as one of the inspectors of said election in said precinct, state how you got that information.—A. I did get it through the Hayneville Examiner, but don't know whether the sheriff's name was signed to it or not.

Q. The witness was shown exhibit A and asked if that was a substantial copy of the notice spoken of above.—A. It was.

Q. Did you as an inspector so appointed offer or prepare to assist in holding said election ?—A. I did.

Q. Why did you not assist in holding said election ? State the reason why fully.— A. I was objected by the said inspectors holding said election, that I was not one of the regular appointed that was appointed the last time, but I insisted on staying in there any way. They said that if I did they would open the door and let everybody come in.

Q. Do you know how many Republican votes were cast for J. V. McDuffie for a seat in Congress for that election on that day ? If you do, state how many.—A. I do know. There was a 166 to my certain knowledge. There was a 167 cast by one doubtful.

Q. Now commence and state in detail fully and particularly how you know this fact. . State every fact within your knowledge tending to show that 166 Republicans voted for said McDuffie on that day.—A. The way was this: We had a committee appointed to act as clerks and act as inspectors to make a list which we made outside, so that we could tell how many Republican votes were cast there, and I issued a hundred and sixty-seven (167) tickets, with the arrangement that each man or voter should carry his ticket in his hand clear from his body or pocket, so that he wouldn't have any chance to change his ticket. Even if he had one, there was no other tickets but Republican tickets used among the Republicans that day to my knowledge. We voted very slow and carefully, so that we might be able to establish the fact to that election that day. This arrangement had been made several weeks before among the Republicans and all had agreed to go into that arrangement by holding several meetings beforehand.

Q. Why did you go to this trouble to make an outside poll-list to ascertain how many Republicans voted for McDuffie there that day when the clerks in the house were making a poll-list?—A. We did, because it was said that we could never get the count of the votes that were cast there, and we wanted McDuffie to get what votes were cast for him, as he was the choice of the people there as a candidate for Congress. He, himself, was down there and they all promised him that they would vote for him.

Q. What position did you and those who made that poll-list occupy at the time said poll-list was made in reference to the door or window where the ballots were received by the inspectors, and how far it was from said window or door ?—Ans. The election was held at the Baptist Church, the ballots were taken in at the front porch of the church, beside of the front door, and where we sat to keep this list was right in front of the door or window, about 30 feet or more from the steps.

Q. At what time was the name of each voter taken down on said list in reference to the time when the ballot was given to him ; was it before or after it was given to him ?—Ans. The names were written after the tickets were given to him; each man stood there until his name was written ; his instruction was given to him as to how he should carry his ticket to the polls or to where they received them.

Q. After one of the voters received his ballot and started to deposit it at the polls did you give out any other ticket until it was handed to the inspector?—Ans. We generally waited until after he got to the window, the place where he handed in his ticket.

Q. Did you or not carefully watch the hand of the voter that held the ticket from the time that you gave him the ticket until he deposited it with the inspectors in the house?—Ans. I did; I made it my particular business to do that.

Q. You have said that you instructed each voter that you gave a ticket what position to hold his hand in which he held the ticket until he deposited the ticket; please show the commissioner what the position was he held the hand?—Ans. They carried it in their left hand out from their body.

Q. Was this the way you instructed them to hold it?—A. It was.

Q. Did you give your individual attention to each voter from the time he took the ticket until he deposited it?—A. I did to the best of my recollection.

Q. If any one or more of them disobeyed your instructions, state how many, and what you did when you detected any variation in the manner of carrying the ticket?—A. I don't know of but one, and when I saw him put his hand in his vest pocket I had his name erased from the list.

Q. Did you issue all of these 166 ballots and delivered them to the voters?—A. I don't issue them all, but was issued in my presence by a man in my presence, under my observation.

Q. Have you that poll-list with you?—A. I have.

Q. Please hand it to the commissioner.

It was handed to the commissioner and asked to be marked Exhibit C. It was marked Exhibit C by the commissioner.

Q. Is this the identical poll-list spoken of in this deposition?—A. It is.

Adjourned until to-morrow morning, Jan. 23rd, 1889.

T. L. S. GRACE,
N. P. and Commissioner.

Met pursuant to adjournment and resumed examination.

The above testimony of Charles F. Hrobowski was taken in the absence of the contestee and his attorney. J. L. Holmes, attorney for contestee, being now present and having read over all of said Charles F. Hrobowski's testimony, makes the following objections to the answer of the witness : " I got notice of my appointment as inspector through the Hayneville Examiner."

(Contestee objects on the ground that it is illegal and hearsay, said notice in said paper not being authorized by law. To the question, " Do you know how many Republican votes were cast for J. V. McDuffie for a seat in Congress, &c. ?" Contestee objects to this question on the grounds that the returns as certified to by the inspectors and the ballots themselves are the best evidence of votes cast for J. V. McDuffie; therefore, this question call for secondary, illegal, and hearsay testimony. Contestee objects to the pretended poll-list made Exhibit C, on the ground that it is the act of a private party ; that it is against the laws of Ala. to make such a list; that it is an invasion of the secrecy of the ballot; that it is not sworn to or proven by the party who made said list, nor by any attesting witness thereto ; and objects on the further grounds that said has not been in the custody of any officer, but has been since it has been made up to this day in the custody of irresponsible private parties to the contestee unknown, and on the further grounds that the poll-list made by the inspector is the official and legal poll-list, and the ballots cast at said election, being of easy access to contestant, are the best evidence of how many votes were cast and for whom they were cast.)

Cross-examination by J. L. HOLMES, attorney for contestee:

Q. What is the race and politics of each of the inspectors?—A. J. R. Dudley and H. B. Leuer are white Democrats, and Cap Dudley is a colored man, and I suppose is a Republican. I have never known him to vote any other way.

Q. Can Cap Dudley read?—A. I think he can read.

Q. Did you ever receive personally any notice from the sheriff of Lowndes Co., or any other person officially, of your appointment as inspector?—A. I did not.

Q. Have you any positive knowledge that J. V. McDuffie received 166 votes other than the knowledge you got from the list of the voters which was kept on the outside of the house?—A. I have.

Q. Who made said list of voters that was kept on the outside?—A. James Moburkie and Fred Lewis.

Q. Are James Moburkie and Fred Lewis now living in Lowndes Co.?—A. James Moburkie is, but Fred Lewis is not now, but was then.

Q. Did you actually have your eye on the hand of Fred Lewis and James Moburkie when each one of the 166 names were actually written on said list?—A. I couldn't say that I saw the hands all the time while they were writing, but was attentive as I could be all the time.

Q. Then you can't swear positively that you saw each and every one of the 166 names written on said list?—A. I couldn't say that I saw the hand that written every name, but was present all the time.

Q. How many Republican votes did you issue yourself?—A. I issued the biggest portion of the 166, but did not issue all of them.

Q. You stated in your direct examination that you issued 167 tickets, now you state that you did not issue all of the 167 tickets. Which statement is true and which is false?—A. I had control of the tickets, and I had a man to help me distribute them. I did not say in my direct examination that I distributed all of them myself.

Q. Do you swear upon your oath that you actually had your eye on the hand upon each of the 167 voters from the time said voter received said ticket, while he was having his name registered and while he was walking to the ballot-box and until he put the ticket in the hand of the inspector?

(Contestant objects to the form of the question; particularly that part, "do you swear upon your oath," on the ground that it is an attempt to bulldoze, and tends to embarrass and confuse the witness, as the witness knows he is under oath.)

A. I do swear to the best of recollection that I saw the hand of every voter until he got to the window where he handed in his ticket, but couldn't see the inspector receive it.

Q. How could you have your eye actually upon the hand of the voter in which the ticket was held and at the same time have your eye upon the hand that wrote the names down on the list kept on the outside?

(Contestant objects to the question on the ground that it assumes a fact which is false, the witness not having related it in that way; that instead of making that statement he has stated in the presence of Wm. Holmes, as the commissioner, that he could not say that he had his eye on the clerk when he wrote every name; and as further stated, that he had the name of each voter written down before the voter started to the ballot-box.)

A. The arrangement that neither voter started away from where his name was taken until the voter that was ahead of him carried his ticket to the window, and my recollection, I thought I saw the most of the transaction of the writing, but couldn't say that I saw it at all.

Q. Did you actually have your eye upon the hand of the clerk when he wrote a single one of the 166 names on that list?—A. I did; I am satisfied I saw a good many of them written.

Q. If you had your eye on the hand of the clerk when he was writing a name on said list, how could you at the same instant of time have your eye on the hand of the voter that held the ticket?—A. To the best of my recollection I had my eye on both at the same time.

Q. What man beside yourself gave out Republican tickets that day?—A. I think it was Elbert Marshall.

Q. Was Elbert Marshall distributing tickets at the same time that you was?—A. I don't think he was; when I wasn't distributing he was.

Q. Did you remain right there with the clerk the entire time, from the time the polls opened in the morning until they closed in the evening?—A. I was not right in the presence of the clerk all the time, but was on the ground all the time with the exception of a little while, and then there was no voting at that time.

Q. You stated in your direct examination that there was no tickets but the Republican tickets used among the Republicans; do you mean by this that there was positively no other or that you saw no other?—A. I saw no other to my knowledge.

Q. Could you read the names printed on the ballots from where you stood to the window where the votes were received?

(Contestant objects to this question because it calls for immaterial and irrelevant evidence.)

A. I don't suppose I could; I never tried to do it.

Q. You stated in your direct examination that each voter carried his ballot to the ballot-box in his left hand; are positive that every one of the 166 so carried their ballots?

(Contestant objects to this question on the ground that it assumes a fact that the witness has never stated; that the witness has never said that he saw the voter carry his ticket to the ballot-box.)

A. To the best of my recollection every one of them carried their tickets in their left hands; some may have had them in their right hand, but my best recollection is that they carried it in their left hand.

Q. Might not some of them have changed their tickets from the left hand to the right hand?—A. I don't think they could have done that.

Q. Is it not a fact that when colored men vote the Democratic ticket that they keep the fact a secret from the colored Republicans?—A. It is not so in our beat; we have a few colored men who used to vote the Democratic ticket, and we respected them as before; but there is none now.

Q. Are there any white Republicans in your beat?—A. Not one.

Redirect by contestant:

Q. How many Democratic votes in that beat?—A. Generally from 14 to 12.
(Contestee objects to this question and answer on the grounds that it calls for the mere opinion of the witness.)

Q. Did you have all of the tickets in your possession originally?—A. I did.

Q. You say in answer to my question that another man assisted you in distributing the tickets; were they all distributed immediately in your presence and under your instructions?—A. They was.

Q. You was asked by Mr. Holmes about Cap Dudley, one of the inspectors at that election. What is the character of the intellect of Cap Dudley? Is it weak or strong intellect; is his intellect above or below the average of his race?—A. I should say it was weak, and that it is below the average.

Q. How near was you to the clerks when they wrote the names on said poll-list? Can you say as a fact that said clerks wrote said names on said list?—A. Sometime I was right there sitting on bench, sometime I was walking about the place between them and where they were voting; it was my honest opinion that they did; nobody else had anything to do with it but them two.

(Contestee objects to the latter part of this answer because the witness gives it as his opinion, and not as a fact.)

C. F. HRUBOWSKI.

H. B. Lever, Democratic inspector at this poll, testifies to the fairness of the count. No one was present to cross-examine him, and his testimony shows that other witnesses were necessary to sustain the return, as he did not handle the tickets.

But as to the reliability of this witness we quote from the testimony of Judge McDuffie:

Question. Do you know H. B. Lever, of Lowndes County, in said district? If yea, in what voting precinct in said county does he reside in, and resided at the time of said election, and what part, if any, did he take in said election? What political party is he a member of? If he ever said anything to you about the manner in which said election was constructed in said precinct; state all that he said.—Answer. I know H. B. Lever; he resides in Church Hill precinct, said county, and resided in said precinct on the day of the election, and acted as inspector in said precinct on said day. He is a member of the Democratic party; I had a conversation with him in the city of Selma, while the examination of witnesses in this contest was going on; we discussed the election and the manner of the count, and I told him that two years ago that I helped his faction of the Democratic party in said county with the understanding that the Republicans should have an honest count in all Federal elections thereafter, and that they had not acted squarely with me in counting me out at the last election. *He replied that he did not know that the arrangement was to continue but for one year; that if he had known it he would not have counted me out, or words to that effect; that Pat Caffee, meaning Judge A. E. Caffee, probate judge of said county, ought to have let them known about it; that he had nothing in the world against me; but while he was keeping a negro woman and had six children by her he would rather die and go to hell than have the negroes get their feet on our necks; that he was an Englishman by birth and had no ties in this country.*

If the return is true, two-thirds of the colored voters of this beat voted for contestee, notwithstanding the positive proof that every one of them was a Republican, and every one took particular pains to show it at the polls, and to prove that he was such. The declaration of each of these voters, while in the act of voting, the complete registry kept at the request of the voters, the careful plans matured beforehand and carried out on election day by the voters, not only show the universal distrust of the Democratic inspectors, but conclusively show the falsity of the return, when considered in connection with all the evidence.

Haynesville.—Return from this precinct: Turpin, 158; McDuffie, 0. Counted by the committee, Turpin, 54; McDuffie, 272. In this precinct there were two boxes. The lawfully appointed Republican inspector organized a board, and in strict compliance with the law held the election, which resulted in a vote for McDuffie of 272 votes. The unlawfully appointed Democratic inspectors held another election, at another place, and made return of 158 for Turpin and none for McDuffie. It is clearly shown by the evidence that less than 60 votes were cast at the Democratic poll, and the best evidence is that not over eleven colored men voted at that poll. This is the evidence of Tony Smith, the colored inspector, who received the tickets and was supposed to represent the Republicans, but who, as shown by the returns, voted Democratic. A clerk at the election thought there might have been as many as twenty.

Neither this clerk nor the colored inspector was present at the count and the making up of the returns. There are between 300 and 400 Republicans in the beat, and not over 65 to 75 white voters. Here again is an illustration of the solidity of the Republican vote when an honest count can be had, and a further illustration of the way Democratic majorities are manufactured by taking a vote of between 50 and 60 and returning it as 158. It further illustrates the reason for the just distrust of the Democrats entertained by the Republicans. The clerks at this election were both called as witnesses, but neither testified to the correctness of the return, nor could they, because it was a clear case of returning a hundred votes that were never cast.

This precinct, taken as a whole, is a good illustration of Democratic methods in the Fourth district of Alabama. The material evidence can be found on pages 683, 688, 709, 711, 731, 739, 750.

The testimony of Varner, Democratic inspector, shows the unreliability of the Democratic returns. The poll-list of this election mysteriously disappeared, so that its padded list cannot be given.

St. Clair.—Returned and counted, Turpin 8, McDuffie 0. Counted by the committee, Turpin 8, McDuffie 214. At this precinct it is shown that there are about 260 colored Republicans and 4 white and 4 colored Democrats. When the time for opening the polls arrived the Republican inspector asked the Democratic inspectors to open the polls, and was informed that there would be no election there that day and none at Lowndesborough. Thereupon this inspector, in compliance with the law and with the assistance of the U. S. supervisor, opened the polls and held an election, and made return as the law directs, at which election the Republican ticket received 211 votes. A return is found in the clerk's office showing that an election was held in the beat and that Turpin received 8 votes; McDuffie none. That is all the evidence there is in the record about any other election in this beat than the one held by the Republican inspectors, and yet the county board counted the Democratic return and ignored the other. The Republican inspector's return is fully proved, and the two taken together show that when there is an honest count the Republicans adhere strictly to their party ticket.

Farmersville.—Returned, Turpin, 26; McDuffie, 0. Counted by committee, Turpin, 26; McDuffie, 40. Two polls were held in this precinct. At one McDuffie received 40 votes and at the other Turpin received 26 votes. Both elections were duly returned, but the county board counted only the one where the Democrats voted. The poll where the Republicans voted was duly opened by a lawfully appointed inspector, a board organized according to law, and the election held according to legal requirements. There is a dispute as to which poll was opened first.

The result of the two elections, held side by side, shows the true vote, and we count both returns. We have already stated the situation in this district and the justification and necessity for these proceedings.

Fort Deposit.—In this precinct the regularly appointed inspectors refused to open the polls, and prevented the electors present from doing so. Late in the afternoon, after the Republicans had gone home and just before the closing hour, the Democratic inspectors opened the polls and received the Democratic votes, had them returned and counted. The precinct is largely Republican, and had the polls been duly opened McDuffie would have received a majority. There was no opportunity for the voters to deposit their ballots, the pretended election was but a pretense, and we reject the return.

WILCOX COUNTY.

Snow Hill.—Returned, Turpin 464, McDuffie 103. Counted by committee, Turpin 82, McDuffie 445. The testimony in regard to this precinct can be found on pages 123–130, 130–134, 138, and 140, forcontestant, and for contestee on pages 668, 614, 615. There are 500 colored voters in the precinct, only 4 of whom are known to be Democrats. There were at the election 75 white Democrats and 1 colored Democrat. All the inspectors were Democrats. The Republicans were fully organized, tickets were given out by one appointed for the purpose. A clerk was appointed to keep a poll-list of all the Republicans who voted, the Republicans refusing to vote unless this precaution was taken to preserve the evidence of how they voted.

After some 247 had voted and had their names recorded the deputy sheriff, acting under telephone orders from the sheriff, as the sheriff himself testifies, undertook to forcibly take this list from the outside clerk who was keeping it. In doing this he was acting without legal right, was committing an outrage upon the Republican voters, for the sake of destroying evidence. The Republican clerk tried to hold on to his poll-list, and resisted the assault made upon him. In the mêlée the deputy sheriff was knocked down, as he says, and when he arose commenced firing indiscriminately, killing a Republican by the name of William Banks. One of the parties, M. Davidson, started to run away with the poll-list, and was pursued by other Democrats, who kept firing at him until they wounded and stopped him. Henry Hawkins, another colored Republican, was also wounded.

After this the Republicans were not permitted to keep a list of names, but so determined were they to be prepared to prove their exact vote, that they continued to keep tally, and the poll-list and subsequent tally are in the record, showing 445 colored men who voted the Republican ticket that day. The evidence is clear, intelligent, and conclusive as to this number, and also that only about 75 whites voted that day. If the return is true, it follows that 341 of these colored Republicans voted the Democratic ticket, together with 120 white men, 45 of whom were not at the polls.

The return requires the belief that out of this body of nearly 500 colored Republicans, who were actively proclaiming their Republicanism at the polls, who refused to vote unless an outside record was kept, who as one man were protesting against the surrender of this poll-list, who saw one of their number murdered and two others wounded in the attempt to preserve the list, three out of every four voted the Democratic ticket in some secret way not attempted to be disclosed. We count the vote as it is clearly proven in the record by competent testimony, and give to Turpin the votes conceded in the notice of contest.

These parties were not content with killing a Republican leader, but must go further and attempt to blacken the character of the witnesses to the crime. The testimony of the deputy sheriff himself shows him

to have committed the crime of murder in his attempt to pave the way
for a fraudulent return; and this is the same deputy sheriff who was so
willing to guaranty protection to contestant when he was ordered out
of Wilcox County during the taking of testimony.

Allenton.—The returns from this precinct show a total vote of 309, of
which number Turpin is given 242, and McDuffie, 67. J. L. Grace, an
intelligent colored man and a member of the Republican executive
committee, testifies on page 142, that he stood during the day from 35
to 40 feet in front of the polls and issued the Republican tickets; saw
each man vote the ticket handed to him. The voters held their tickets
so that they could be seen until they were handed to the inspector.
Three hundred and sixteen men voted the Republican ticket, and only
three colored men voted Democratic. Not over 40 or 45 white voters in
the precinct. If the return is true, over 200 of the colored men voted
Democratic, while only 64 voted Republican. No attempt is made to
contradict the testimony for contestant or to sustain the return.

· *Bethel.*—According to the return for Bethel there were 400 votes
cast, of which 385 were for contestee and only 15 for contestant. The
proof shows that McDuffie received 343 votes instead of 15. A complete list of these votes was kept by two persons selected for that purpose, standing in front of the polls. Each voter took his ticket, voted
it, and had his name registered before the next man took a ticket. The
colored men here were active and earnest Republicans. The inspectors
were Democrats, except an ignorant colored man, who could neither
read nor write.

B. W. Lewis (page 262), B. J. Dickson (page 242), and Charles Perkins (pages 257–272), all of them intelligent young men, who had had
a fair education, attended to the Republican tickets, and each saw and
testified to the whole vote. They also show that there were 57 Democrats who voted. They say there are some 77 Democrats in the precinct, but that 20 of them did not attend the election.

Every obstruction was placed in the way of taking this testimony.
In Dickson's examination-in-chief there are 70 lines of questions and
answers, and 265 lines of objections (Record, page 242). In Perkins'
examination-in-chief there are 33 lines of questions and answers, and
144 lines of objections (see page 257). No attempt is made to contradict this testimony or to sustain the return.

If the returns were true, it would follow that 328 colored men voted
the Democratic ticket and only 15 the Republican ticket, notwithstanding their compact organization and earnest Republicanism. But the
returns are not true.

White Hall.—According to the returns there were 142 votes cast at
this precinct, 116 of which were given to Turpin. The proof shows that
McDuffie received 84 votes instead of 26.

L. E. Fisher (page 251) and D. S. Robins (page 260), two educated
colored men, issued tickets and kept a complete poll-list of the Republican voters, which poll-list is in the record. They issued 85 tickets,
but one of the men did not hold his ticket so that they were certain of
his vote, and they erased his name, thus showing the care taken to
secure accuracy. The work was well organized, and the witnesses testify with an intelligence and candor which carries conviction of truthfulness.

Charles Garrison, an intelligent man, was appointed inspector for the
Republicans but was refused admission to the polls and the election
was conducted exclusively by Democrats.

As another example of the obstructive method resorted to by contestee to prevent the taking of testimony, we refer to Fisher's testimony, on page 251, where will be found 65 lines of questions and answers and 293 lines of objections.

The evidence shows that there is but one colored Democrat in this precinct, and yet, according to the returns, 58 colored men voted the Democratic ticket. No attempt is made to sustain the returns. The inspectors seem to have been willing to make a false return, but not quite willing to commit perjury to sustain it.

Clifton.—According to the returns 215 votes were cast at this precinct, of which 190 are accredited to Turpin and only 25 to McDuffie. The evidence shows that 204 votes were cast for McDuffie. The tally was kept by Frank Black (page 263), an intelligent colored man. His testimony is confirmed by James Wicker (page 264). The colored inspector, who can neither read nor write, testifies that he took the tickets, handed them to another inspector, and he to the third, and that he does not know what the third inspector did with the tickets. The inspector who deposited the tickets in the box is not called. One of the inspectors and one other witness are called to sustain the fairness of the election, but both of these witnesses were called after contestant had been driven from the county, and without notice. To sustain the return requires the belief that 179 colored men voted the Democratic ticket while only 25 voted Republican.

Black's Bluff.—According to the returns 251 votes were cast at this precinct, 213 being credited to Turpin and 38 to McDuffie. According to the evidence McDuffie received 205. Henry R. Irvin (page 265) and W. J. Shelbern (page 270) kept the tally, and Coffee Fisher (page 265) issued the tickets. The evidence is clear and convincing. Great pains were taken to secure accuracy, and there was little chance for mistake. Cross-examination brings this fact out fully. The inspectors were all Democrats—one a colored Democrat, well known for many years as such, but he was illiterate, and could not tell whether the return was correct or not.

In the absence of any one representing contestant, without notice to him, and after he had been compelled to leave the county, this colored inspector and one other were called to sustain the returns. Testimony taken in such a way is entitled to little credit, taken in connection with the other circumstances in this case, and a perusal of it will show that it would probably not have been taken had any one been present to cross-examine. To sustain this return requires the belief that 167 colored men, known as Republicans, voted the Democratic ticket, while only 38 were faithful to their party.

Prairie Bluff.—According to the return there were cast at Prairie Bluff 259 votes, of which number Turpin is credited with 245 and McDuffie with 14. Granville Bennett (page 274) stood in view of the polls and kept a list. Two hundred and forty-one Republicans voted the Republican ticket and 13 others, being the whole number of Democrats that attended the election, are credited as voting Democratic. The list is in the record. L. J. Sikes distributed the tickets, and witness saw each one voted. He was about 30 feet from the polls. Saw each of the 241 Republican ballots voted. He is intelligent, and gives particulars, showing that he had absolute knowledge of the Republican vote cast. He also says that he knows the white inspectors of the election well, and that they are not regarded as truthful, and he would not believe them under oath.

J. L. Sikes (page 278) says that he was born in the beat; that 241 votes were cast for McDuffie and 13 for Turpin. McDuffie was pop-

ular and polled the full vote of his party. The inspectors were all
Democrats.

Pat Pullom, the colored inspector, is sixty-four years old, can not write;
testifies himself that he has been a Democrat since 1880. He received
the tickets and put them in the box, and saw them taken out and
counted. Didn't see Sikes or Bennett distributing tickets.

George McCurdy (page 487) was at the election and didn't see the
witnesses, Sikes and Bennett, and says that it was a fair election. .

Joe Robinson (page 488), one of the inspectors, testifies to the same.
These witnesses were examined in the absence of any one to cross-examine them—under the circumstances heretofore detailed. The evidence is guarded and short and very unsatisfactory, besides bearing
marks of untruth.

It may be said of this precinct, as of others, that the election board
was illegally constituted, and that the returns are simply an inversion
of party strength. The Republicans took no especial pains to insure
accuracy in their list of Democrats voted, and it is probable that 14
Democratic votes were cast instead of 13, as there was one black man
who voted Democratic, and 3 votes were added for good measure.

The list of 341 black Republicans who attended and voted is in the
record. Regarding the returns as true, it follows that 327 colored
Republicans voted Democratic and only 14 were faithful to their party,
notwithstanding their expressed desire when in the act of voting to vote
the party ticket. It further follows that in a manner so secret that it
could not be observed they changed their tickets in going 30 feet, while
holding their tickets out from their bodies and in such a position that
their chosen chairman could see them and give evidence of the fact.
It is sufficient to say that the committee gives full credit to the record
kept by the Republicans to protect themselves against the well-known
methods of the Democrats.

Boiling Springs.—Two hundred and forty-two votes are returned
from this precinct, 200 for Turpin and 42 for McDuffie. James Wad-
kins testifies that as well as he can remember 239 votes were cast, 212
for McDuffie and 27 for Turpin.

C. B. Taylor (page 279) says McDuffie is popular, and that there are
two or three colored Democrats in the beat.

S. J. Dixon (page 280) testifies that 242 votes were cast, 214 for
McDuffie and 28 for Turpin. His list is in evidence (page 280), containing the names of both Republicans and Democrats in separate lists,
showing the extreme care of the Republican managers to keep an accurate record of the election.

Dixon distributed the tickets, and D. L. Moore, J. J. Carter, and J.
W. Lovett kept the poll-list. The colored inspector at this poll could
neither read nor write, and is credited in the list as having voted Democratic. Dixon is an intelligent man and stood a severe cross-examination. He could not see the inspectors because they were inside the
house. Tickets were handed through the window and he could not see
the hands of the inspector. He saw the 214 Republican tickets handed
into the window, but did not see the hand of the inspector who received
them. If it was necessary to see the hand of the inspector to know how
a man voted he could not tell how they voted.

On this slender thread the contestee hangs his case to sustain this
poll without further evidence of its correctness. This is a fair illustration of the principle underlying the cross-examinations, and of contestee's idea of destroying the reliability of a witness's knowledge.
There were six more tickets given to colored men, but as they were not
seen to vote them, their names are left off the list.

Here, then, are 214 colored men who took Republican tickets, passed them to the inspectors, and then had their names registered; but the inspectors returned but 42 of them as having been counted. Here are 27 white men at the polls and one colored man (the inspector), known as a Democrat, and yet out of this list the inspectors work out 200 Turpin tickets, but they do not venture to testify to the correctness of the count. That is to say, 178 of these colored Republicans voted against their party, against their declaration while in the act of voting, and against their assertion then and there when they required their names to be registered as having voted the Republican ticket.

The notice of contest does not permit of giving to contestant the full vote cast for him, as only 200 are there claimed, and 42 are conceded to Turpin. This was the result of mistaken information and results in depriving a number of voters of their votes, but the committee are disposed in this case to count the vote as charged in the notice.

Canton.—Two hundred and thirty-four votes were returned from Canton, of which 223 were credited to Turpin and 11 to McDuffie.

James A. Dargans (page 290), a school teacher, but not an active politician, kept the tally of the Republican votes cast at this box. Wm. Rhea distributed the tickets; 188 were voted and tallied. Every ticket given out by Rhea was shown to Dargans, then immediately taken to the inspector, and then tallied. One voter went to the polls and handed in his ticket, and when he was tallied the next voter went forward, and so on till all had voted. Tickets were handed in through the window, inspectors in sight, but not the box.

Witness watched the voter and the ticket in his hand until it was handed in to the inspector. The crowd was kept back, so that no one was between the witness and the window, and no one near the voter. The hand that held the ticket was in constant view until the ticket was voted. The witness was severely cross-examined, and contestee satisfies himself that he has discredited the witness and shown that he did not know how the voter really voted because the witness says that he could not see the ticket after the hand was put into the window, but did see it until it was handed to the inspector.

Out of 188 colored Republicans voting at this precinct, and each taking special pains to show that he voted the Republican ticket, the inspectors generously counted 11 for the Republican candidate, and with only a handful of white voters present, manage to give contestee 223. The inspectors and clerks were Democrats. None of them are called to explain or sustain this wonderful feat of turning Republican votes into Democratic ones when making up the returns.

Geesbend.—The returns of Geesbend show 205 votes cast, of which Turpin is credited with 190 and McDuffie with 15.

Isham McLaughlin (page 293) testifies that he has lived in the beat ever since the war; that he distributed and saw voted 192 Republican tickets with McDuffie's name on them, and that Sam Petway kept the poll-list. He further says that there are but 7 white voters in the beat, all of whom voted that day. The colored inspector could not read or write.

Petway testifies that McLaughlin gave out the tickets; that each ticket was brought to him and then voted, and as soon as he had voted the voter would return to him and have his name registered as voting the Republican ticket. Out of these 192 colored Republicans the inspectors generously return 15 as voting Republican, and with only 7 white men, take 190 for themselves. No attempt is made to sustain the return.

PERRY COUNTY.

Hamburg.—According to the returns there were cast at Hamburg 295 votes, of which Turpin is credited with 212 and McDuffie with 83.

J. C. Hames (page 145) testifies that Thomas Huey issued the Republican tickets, and he read them and kept the tally as fast as they were voted; saw 256 vote the Republican ticket straight. One colored man and 44 whites voted the Democratic ticket. With one exception the colored men were Republicans and warm supporters of McDuffie. The tally was kept at the request of the voters to guard against fraud, and when the result of the count was announced there was great dissatisfaction among them.

An attempt is made to sustain this return by one of the clerks of the election who says the ballots were correctly counted "as found in the box," and by a United States supervisor who says he was in and out of the room while the voting was going on. This supervisor says there are some 50 white men and 300 colored men in the beat, and that he knows of some colored men who vote the Democratic ticket, but he refuses to give any names. He was impudent in his answers, and his evidence shows that he gave opportunity to tamper with the box if the inspectors were so disposed. The language of the clerk, "As found in the box," shows careful choice of language, but even this clerk acknowledges that he did not read the tickets; he only kept tally as the tickets were read.

If the returns are true 173 colored men voted Democratic and only 83 voted Republican, although all of the 256, in the very act of voting, announced themselves as Republicans and had their names taken down as such. The witness for contestee, who claims to be well informed, a colored man himself, could not or would not name a single one of all this number who was a Democrat. The evidence satifies the committee that the return was not correct and did not represent the true state of the vote cast. We count the vote as the evidence shows it to have been cast.

Marion.—According to the returns 783 votes were cast at Marion, of which 697 are credited to Turpin, though there are about 700 colored voters and comparatively few white voters in the precinct.

According to the testimony of J. T. Wilson (page 232), confirmed by that of Mat Boyd, there were at least 583 votes cast for McDuffie. Witness saw all these voters go to the polls with Republican tickets and hand them to the inspectors. Just before reaching the window where the votes were delivered the voters had to pass behind a coal-shed, which did not cover the voter, but left his hand out of view. With this exception the voter had no chance to change tickets without being seen. No one was near enough to the voter to give him a ticket from the time he started until he voted, and none but straight Republican tickets were given to the voters or circulated among them.

There was a Republican supervisor at this poll, and when the polls were closed the Democratic inspectors refused to go on and count the ballots, but waited until dark, and then were told by the clerk of the court that he wanted that room—but we will let the witness tell the story, as an abstract would not do full justice to the evidence.

NICKOLAS STEPHENS sworn:

Q. What is your name, age, and where did you live on the 6th of November last, and how long had you lived there?—A. Nickolas Stephens is my name; am about 43 years old; I lived in Marion beat, Perry County; have lived there about 25 years.

Q. If there was an election held there that day, state for what purpose it was held, w^ho were the Republican and Democratic candidates at said election, and what connection did you have with the election.

(Contestee objects because the matters inquired about are matters of record, and the record itself is the best evidence, and a predicate has not been laid to show these facts by first showing the loss or destruction of the record.)

A. There was an election held for President and Vice-President, and Congressman from the 4th Congressional district. Judge McDuffie was the Republican candidate and Mr. Turpin was the Democratic candidate for Congress. I was U. States supervisor.

Q. Who were the inspectors and clerks of said election? And state their politics, if you know.

(Contestee objects to the first part of the question because as to who the inspectors were is a matter of record, the record itself being the best evidence.)

A. Mr. J. A. Lightsy, Jim Lockhart, and Joe Myatt were the inspectors; Mr. Straton and Mr. Woodfin were the clerks; they were all Democrats, except Joe Myatt.

Q. Were they all warm, ardent supporters of L. W. Turpin except Myatt?

(Contestee objects because it is leading and because immaterial and irrelevant.)

A. Yes, sir.

Q. At what hour did the polls close there that day?—A. At 5 o'clock.

Q. Did you witness a count of the ballots cast there that day? If so, state fully everything that occurred.—A. I witnessed the count. After the election closed, about a half hour a light was called for repeatedly, about three times; a little while after that the lamps were brought in out of the clerk's office, after which the clerk of probate came in and asked us to get out and go into the next office, that he had some valuable books that had to stay in there that night; pretty soon after this Capt. C. H. Sewell came to me with his commission as U. S. supervisor on the Democratic side, and wanted to read his commission to me; about that time the inspector had got ready to remove into the next room. Capt. Sewell was between me and Mr. J. C. Lightsy, who had the box; I told the captain that my commission read the same as his, and the inspector had taken the box and gone into the next room, and to please let me by, that I wanted to get in there; he said to me will they let us in there; I said, yes, I have been here all day; and when I got in the box was sitting on the table; it was sometime after we got in there before they commenced to count; the reason of this was that they were bothered about getting a box to count the votes out in. When they had counted to about 25 votes, Joe Myatt asked me what had become of the Republican votes; I told him I didn't know; Judge McDuffie had to come and see after the votes; the majority of the tickets that were counted were Democratic tickets and "imitation" tickets, which imitation tickets had on the Republican electors with L. W. Turpin as candidate for Congress. The whole vote was 783, and in the count there was 805; I asked the inspector how could they count more votes than was polled; at that time Mr. Dick Lightsy came in and stated that the clerks, or Joe Myatt, had made a mistake in counting the votes they run up the count again; Mr. Straton's count stood the same; then Mr. Dick Lightsy then took his pencil and paper and showed to them their mistake; then Mr. Dick Lightsy wrote another poll-list and after he got through they then called in on the inspectors to sign, and Mr. Jack Lightsy signed and Jim Lockhart signed, and Joe Myatt refused to sign, and they told him that if he didn't sign they would arrest and put him in jail, after which I asked the inspectors privilege to ask Joe Myatt a question, and they gave me leave. I asked Joe did he conscientiously believe that the box that the votes were counting out of was the box in which they were deposited, and he stated to me that the ballots wasn't changed when counted, but he couldn't believe that Judge McDuffie got as few votes as he did there; then I said to him that if he had reason to believe that the box counted out was not the box that the votes were deposited in, he had no right to sign the return. Then Mr. Dick Lightsy walked up to me, shook his fingers in my face, and called me a damned fool, and said that I had always acted as such, after which I was called in to sign those official returns, and I refused to do so.

(Contestee objects to this answer because the facts testified to are immaterial and irrelevant, and because it is hearsay; and the conclusions of the witness based not upon facts within his knowledge, but upon the vague suspicions of Joe Myatt.)

Q. Was this Dick Lightsy, of whom you have been speaking, a member of the Democratic or Republican party?—A. A member of the Democratic party.

Q. Was he one of the officers whose duty it was to hold the election in that beat on that day?—A. He was not.

Q. Did he have any connection with the election which gave him the right to be in the room or participate in the count of the vote which was cast that took place in that room on that day?—A. He had no right in there at all, but he ran the whole business.

Q. Was not the said Dick Lightsy a warm and ardent supporter of L. W. Turpin in candidacy for Congress at that election?

(Contestee objects because leading and because immaterial.)

A. He was.

Q. You have stated in your answer to a former question that the said Dick Lightsy wrote out a poll-list; do you mean to be understood as saying that he made out a different poll-list from the one kept during the day by the clerks, and that he changed

(Contestee objects because leading, in that it suggests the answer sought, and because if such a poll-list exists it is itself the best evidence as to its contents, and no predicate has been laid by showing its loss or its destruction for the introduction of secondary evidence.)

A. He wrote a return and not a poll-list; he copied one from the printed form.

Q. Did the inspector's returns as written out by the said Dick Lightly show the number of 805 votes that were found in the box, and of which the inspectors were counting?

(Contestee objects because leading.)

A. No, sir.

Q. Then the said returns or the box from which the count was made was fraudulent, wasn't it?

(Contestee objects because leading, and because the question requires as an answer a conclusion of law, and the answer when given would be but an opinion of the witness upon a legal conclusion.)

A. I refused to sign it on the grounds that I believed it was fraudulent.

Q. Did you see the box in which the ballots were placed during the entire time the voting was going on?—A. Yes, sir.

Q. Did you ever see the box in which the ballots had been placed after C. H. Sewel got between you and the room in which the said ballot-box had been carried?—A. Not until I got in the room.

Q. Was the box that you then saw there the identical box in which you had seen the ballots deposited during the day?—A. I couldn't swear it was the box.

Q. Why is it that you couldn't swear that it was the box, and did you notice any difference in the box?—A. Because the box we used all day was a new box, and the one I found in there was a new one, and I couldn't discover any difference in the box.

Q. Did you notice the way the tickets were folded when they were put into the box during the day?—A. Yes, sir.

Q. Was the tickets that you saw counted out of the box folded into the same manner as those you saw put into the box?—A. No, sir.

Q. How long was the ballot-box out of your sight after the close of the polls and before the count commenced?—A. About a minute.

Q. Could not a box that had been prepared for the purpose be substituted in place of the true box during the time it was out of your sight?

(Contestee objects because it is leading, and because the notice of contest alleges a false and fraudulent count of the vote cast and does not charge that it was done by a substitution of one box for another; wherefore contestee says the evidence here sought is not pertinent to the issue.)

A. Yes, sir.

Q. Could you see the ballots that were deposited with the officer whose duty it was to receive them on that day at that election?—A. I could.

Q. Give, as near as you can, the whole number of Republican who voted at that box on that day.—A. I think about 597.

Q. Give, as near as you can, the whole number of Democrats who voted at that box on that day.—A. About 175 or 180.

Q. Are you not well acquainted with the Republican voters who cast their ballots at that election on that day?—A. I am.

Q. Was there a single one of them who was supporting L. W. Turpin for Congress at that election?—A. I know of one.

Q. Was there any other than the one you speak of?—A. No, sir.

Q. Then were not the 597 Republicans who voted at that box on that day supporters of J. V. McDuffie in his candidacy for Congress at that election?—A. Yes, sir.

Q. Give, as near as you can, the whole number of votes received by J. V. McDuffie for Congress at that election on that day.

(Contestee objects because the poll-lists and official returns are the best evidence of the number of votes cast and for whom cast, and because the said question tends to invade the secrecy of the ballot-box, and because it is to a fact that could be but a matter of opinion and not without the knowledge of the witness.)

A. About 597.

Q. Did you make out a supervisor return of said box; and, if so, when did you make it out?

(Contestee objects because it has not been shown by competent evidence that the witness was authorized by law to make out such return.)

A. I made out such a return on the morning of the 7th.

Q. Did you give in said report anything other than a report of the count made by the inspectors of the elections?—A. I did not.

Q. Did you fill out the blank in said report for the supervisors' count ?—A. I did.

Q. Look at the paper that is now shown you and see whether or not you are mistaken when you say you filled out the blank for the supervisors' report ?—A. Yes, sir; I see my mistake.

Q. Then you did not make any count or return any as supervisors' count, did you ?—A. No, sir; I did not.

Q. Was not the reason that you failed to make a supervisors' count because you believed that a false box had been substituted for the true box in which the ballots had been placed ?

(Contestee objects because it is a leading question.)

A. Yes, sir.

Q. State whether or not you did not further believe that the ballots that were counted were other and different ones from those that had been voted by the voter.

(Contestee objects because it is leading and because founded upon an assumption that there are no facts to support.)

A. Yes, sir; I did.

Q. State whether or not you had seen any of these imitation tickets which you say were counted out of the box distributed or circulated amongst the Republican voters at that boat on that day ?—A. I did not.

Q. Was not the first knowledge that the Republicans of that beat had of the existence of those imitation tickets the time when they were counted out of the ballot-box ?—A. Yes, sir.

From this evidence the fraud is made to appear clearly. The supervisor, who had faithfully discharged his duty, had, up to the closing of the polls, effectively prevented fraud. To change this large Republican beat into a Democratic one required further work. Hence the delay in commencing the count, the demand for a change of rooms, the appearance of the Democratic supervisor in the nick of time, the removal of the box from the sight of the watchful Republican supervisor by the ruse of stopping him to see whether his associate's commission read as his did, the change of boxes, and the substitution of one already fixed for counting. The bollot-box stuffer, however, had miscalculated the number of votes which would be deposited after he had prepared his box on the basis of those already cast and his estimate of the rest, for he got into his fraudulent box 22 more than the number actually voted. Here, too, appears a large number of tickets having the names of the Republican electors on them, and the name of Turpin for Representative. No such tickets were voted or circulated among the voters.

It may be remarked here that this kind of a ticket was found in boxes in various parts of the district, and it is sought to be shown that this ticket was voted by Republicans. In many places in the record this suggestion is made by way of showing that Republicans may have been mistaken in supposing that they voted for McDuffie, that they ignorantly voted this ticket. It does not seem to have suggested itself to the attorneys taking the testimony for contestee that proof of such deception would only be additional evidence of fraudulent practices. The care taken against such fraud prevented its success, except so far as ballot-boxes were stuffed.

In this beat a man by the name of J. C. Lightsey was substituted for the regularly appointed inspector. Lightsey removed the box before the counting commenced; Lightsey and his brother, who had no business with the counting, fixed the returns and poll-lists to suit themselves, and to Lightsey were committed the ballots when the count was completed. The fraud was so apparent that the colored inspector refused to sign the returns when the count was completed, and Lightsey undertook the work of compelling him to do so, threatening him if he refused.

One of the Democratic inspectors is called as a witness, and only shows that he does not know whether the box was changed or not; but Lightsey does not appear as a witness. The cross-examination of this

H. Mis. 137——19

inspector shows both his want of knowledge and his want of candor. Neither of the clerks testified.

Of the 583 colored Republicans who voted at Marion that day, 86 only are credited to their candidate. The fraud is apparent, and we correct the return according to the best obtainable evidence. ·

Rehobeth precinct.—The committee does not change the return, although the evidence raises serious doubts as to its correctness.

Scott and *Polecat* precincts are also left as returned.

Uniontown.—There were two boxes in this beat, and returns were made by the officials holding each election. At one the Republicans voted, at the other the Democrats. The return which was counted gave Turpin 210, McDuffie, 2. The other return gave Mc-Duffie 953. Dr. J. H. Houston's testimony (306) gives the history of the election where the Republicans voted, and shows that all the forms of law were complied with. The sheriff of the county (446) shows that the returns were presented to him and he refused to receive them. The box was retained and its contents counted in the presence of the commissioner taking the testimony.

There is a dispute about the time of opening the different polls, but in our view the question is not material in this particular case. That the two polls taken together constitute an honest statement of the result of the election, and show the exact state of the legal vote, we · have no doubt. They also show that where there is an honest count the Republicans adhere to their party ticket.

The action of the election inspectors for this precinct at the election for the Fiftieth Congress justified the action of the Republicans. Indeed, it was apparently the only course left open to them to prevent their votes from being counted for the Democratic candidate. At that election the returned vote was:

Davidson (Democrat)...**720**
Turner (Independent)..**203**
McDuffie.. **65**

The majority of the committee in that case found from the evidence such frauds as destroyed the return, and from the evidence gave Mc-Duffie 400 and Davidson 8. The evidence indicated a Republican vote of over 800, but the majority of the committee found that only 400 were satisfactorily proved.

In extraordinary cases, and where it appears that in no other way can the actual will of the voter be ascertained, a resort to methods not technically in accordance with statutory direction may be justifiable, and upon proof that a full, fair, and honest election has been held by those only who are qualified voters, under these circumstances the returns from such an election, when duly proved, may be considered and counted.

None of those guards provided by statute to secure honest results should be neglected, but when statutory provisions designed to protect qualified voters in the exercise of their legal rights are made use of with deliberate purpose to suppress the will of the majority, such action will be regarded as fraudulent.

Cunningham and Walthall.—These returns are not changed by the committee. While the evidence cast some doubt upon their correctness, it is not deemed sufficient to justify their rejection.

Perryville.—Return is rejected because neither return nor poll-list is signed. If notice of contest is to be taken as conclusive upon contestant, this return should not be rejected, but 60 votes should be counted

for contestant and 123 for contestee. In that case contestant's majority
as found by the committee would be diminished by 63 votes.

HALE COUNTY.

Of the nine precincts in Hale County attacked by the evidence, the
committee find that in only three is the evidence sufficiently conclusive
to require a rejection of the returns and an ascertainment of the true
vote by other evidence.

Greensborough.—According to the returns there were 897 votes polled
at this beat, 577 of which are credited to Turpin and 320 to McDuffie.
Dave Jones (page 37), with the assistance of Armistead Hunter, kept
the poll-list of all who voted the Republican ticket. The list, containing
697 names, is in the record (page 38). These men all had their names
recorded as voting the Republican ticket, and all but two or three went
directly to the polls and voted. Matthew Morse issued the tickets.
The issuing of these tickets and keeping the list in the manner shown
by the evidence was according to prearrangement, so as to secure an
honest count. Hunter says there are 600 to 700 colored voters in the
beat, and only five or six Democrats among them. The Republicans
were warm supporters of McDuffie.

Here we have a prearranged plan for ascertaining the vote—the issuing of tickets one at a time, the going directly to the polls and voting,
and the request of each voter to put his name down as voting for Mc-
Duffie. These men were Republicans, they voted, and while in the act
of voting declared their adherence to their party.

The witnesses were cross-examined, and showed both intelligence and
carefulness to testify only to their personal knowledge.

Clark, the colored Republican inspector, could neither read nor
write. He was called as a witness for contestee and says that some of
the colored men changed their tickets, and that the election was honestly conducted. No one was present to cross-examine him. He was
too ignorant to detect false counting, and his testimony shows his evident sympathy with the Democrats, while it further discloses the fact
that the return could not be true.

M. V. Hill, a colored man, testifies that he got a ticket from Morse,
gave it to Captain Jones, and voted a Democratic ticket. The care of the
Republicans in keeping their list is shown by the fact that Hill's name
is not on it.

T. W. De Yampert (page 548), for contestee, testifies that he was registrar of voters at that beat; that he registered from 75 to 80 colored
voters on election day, and gave them Democratic tickets and saw some
of them go to the court-house with them.

C. C. Gewin (page 398) testifies that the Republican poll-keeper could
not see the ballot-box, and that Democratic tickets could be had by the
voters.

At the election for the Forty-eighth Congress this precinct gave 630
Republican votes and 194 Democratic votes. By the present return
party majorities are almost reversed.

It will be seen that the voters of this district are mostly colored, that
neither of the white inspectors or clerks is called to testify, only the
colored inspector who could not read or write, and that the only colored
man who says he changed tickets, is not on the Republican poll-list.

It is further to be observed that the colored men, with few exceptions, are Republicans, and actively testify to their loyalty to the party,
and therefore when a return shows that in addition to the colored Dem-

ocrats of the beat at least 377 of the colored Republicans voted the Democratic ticket, against their expressed determination and open declaration at the polls, it is evident that some one has been juggling with the tickets or returns, especially when we take into consideration the further fact that there was a general conspiracy on the part of the Democratic leaders throughout the district to falsify the count.

Hollow Square.—From Hollow Square beat there were returned 531 votes, of which 362 are credited to Turpin. Here, by pre-arrangement, Motley Rediford (page 48) issued the tickets, and S. J. Hunt (page 50) kept the poll-list. This list, as found in the record, contains the names of 475 voters. Each of these witnesses testifies that he saw each voter from the time he took his ticket until it was delivered to the inspectors, that the ticket was held in the voter's hand so that it could be seen from the time it was taken until it was voted, and that each name was registered at the request of the voter, that the voters fell into line behind the stand of this clerk, chosen by them, and went forward to vote one at a time. This poll-list is identified by the witness who kept it, and by a committee composed of L. B. Pierce, Perry Glow, and Alfred Borden.

Six colored men voted Democratic, only 50 whites voted that day, according to this evidence, and 475 colored men voted the Republican ticket, and yet the return gives 362 to Turpin. Here again the colored inspector was illiterate, and no attempt is made by contestee to sustain this fraudulent return.

Cedarville.—The returns from Cedarville show that 517 votes were cast, of which 364 are credited to Turpin.

James T. Fredd, a very intelligent colored man (page 56), kept a list of 490 colored men who voted for McDuffie and the Republican ticket (page 57). He testifies very positively that he was some 30 feet from the polls, and saw every ticket voted. He was subjected to a cross-examination extending through several days; 586 cross-questions were asked and answered. During all this long and largely frivolous cross-examination he kept his temper, and sustained himself as an intelligent, truthful, and painstaking witness.

The conduct of contestee's attorneys in this cross-examination can not be too severely condemned. Its purpose was, without any doubt, to use up time and prevent a full disclosure of all the frauds perpetrated in the fourth district, advantage being taken of the fact that the commissioners had no power to put an end to such reprehensible methods. This witness knew of one colored Democrat in the beat.

Dick Crook (page 80), another witness for this beat, is asked 214 cross-questions of like character with those put to Fredd and with like purpose. He issued the tickets and helped to watch the voters, and fully comfirms Fredd. He testifies that there are about 25 white voters in the beat. This would give 490 colored Republicans, 25 white and two colored Democrats. Yet the returns show, if true, that Turpin got 339 colored votes, or 3 out of every 4.

For the contestee, D. W. Ward (page 548) says he was clerk at the election, that it was held in the street with a rope stretched around, that there was a crowd around the polls, and that Crook could not see how the men voted. He says that after the polls were closed they went into a vacant store and counted the votes, and that he kept a correct tally. No friend of contestant was present to witness the count. O'Donnell, Democrat, and Van Hambright, colored Republican, counted the votes.

Van Hambright (page 550), the illiterate colored inspector, who was too ignorant to know how the votes were counted, testifies that everything was fair. Says he was a Republican, but is not asked how he voted. No one was present on the part of contestant to cross-examine him. He is, however, considered as a Republican and is recorded as such. The Democratic inspector who counted the votes is not called. The return is evidently a fraud, and we ascertain the vote by the best attainable evidence.

DALLAS COUNTY.

Martin's Station.—According to the returns 411 votes were cast at Martin's Station, 383 being credited to Turpin and 280 to McDuffie. Ned Petway (page 146), an intelligent colored man, who can read but can not write, issued and saw voted 324 Republican tickets with McDuffie's name on them. He was rigidly cross examined. Acton Mappin (page 154) kept a pole list of the 324 Republican voters, which list is in the record. He identified the list and testified that there was no chance for the voter to exchange tickets from the time the ticket was taken until it was voted. A witness for contestee names three colored men who voted the Democratic ticket. The fact that their names are not on this list helps to confirm its accuracy.

Nathan Stratton (page 153), United States supervisor, says that there are about 480 colored and 50 white voters in the beat, and that he is personally acquainted with nearly every colored man in the beat, and that about 10 of them are Democrats. He says the Republicans here were earnest McDuffie men, and gave time and money to help his canvass. The inspectors and clerks were all Democrats, including the colored inspector. Stratton says that when the count was finished, Bamberger, a Democratic inspector, announced that McDuffie had 355 votes, and he answered: "All right."

Lewis Bamberger (page 558), a witness for contestee, was one of the inspectors. He is not a citizen of the United States, but has filed his declaration of intention to become such. He says all the officers of the election voted the Democratic ticket. Martin received the tickets, handed them to Wilson, and he received them from Wilson and deposited them in the box. Says Martin called and the clerks tallied when counting out. He swears to the correctness of the return, and yet he neither kept the tally nor read the tickets to the clerks.

He avoided giving direct answers to questions about the situation of the polling-place, but after taking a rest he was obliged to own that the place was located as testified to by contestant's witnesses. The witness prevaricates, and is neither frank nor candid in his testimony. Neither of the other inspectors or clerks were sworn, and Bamberger does not deny that he announced the vote as testified to by the supervisor. Anderson, the deputy sheriff, who distributed the Democratic tickets, says there were about 50 white voters there, and that he gave Democratic tickets to some colored men, but refuses to say that he did so to a large number. He names 3 (who are not on the Republican list) and says there are 20 more. This being true, it would only make 73 Democratic votes, a long distance from 383.

Anderson testifies that Petway could not read, but Petway showed that he could by reading to the commissioners.

In the election for the Forty-seventh Congress the Republican vote of this precinct was 384, and for the Forty-eighth Congress 304, and as proven in this case 324. The supervisor knew that the vote was over 300, and when Bamberger announced it as 355, he was satisfied that the count and tally had been fair, but he did not know that when the returns reached the county board the 355 would change into 28.

Pence.—According to the returns, 208 votes were polled at Pence ; 188 for Turpin and 88 for McDuffie. Richmond Isaacs (page 152), known and called also Richmond Sanders, issued the Republican tickets at this beat and saw them voted, 219 in number. He reads and writes. Objection being made to the evidence, on account of the name being given as Sanders, he is called again (page 340), and again repeats his testimony, under difficulties, nearly two pages of objections being recorded to take up time.

C. D. Martin (page 769) was the United States supervisor at this beat. He stood at the box all day, and saw no colored man change his ballot as he came to the polls. All the inspectors and clerks were Democrats. When the polls were closed one of the inspectors took the ballot-box to his home, some 200 yards away, and when the supervisor would not go to that house to witness the count, the box was brought back, and handed to the colored Democratic inspector, and carried away, and the count was not made until the following day. This violation of the law so invalidates the returns as to require proof of their correctness. Witness says that there are only three colored Democrats in the beat, one of whom was an inspector. He estimates the colored vote of the beat at 190, it being only an estimate.

Instead of calling the officers of the election, contestee calls one William Bell (page 646), who testifies to the effect that Isaacs could not have seen the window when the tickets were taken in. He made a bad guess at population, and only estimates 30 or 40 white voters in the beat.

Remarks upon the character of the evidence and the reversal of returns in other beats will apply to this one as well. We count it according to notice of contest.

Mitchell's Mill.—There are two returns from this beat, neither of which was counted by the returning board. They are copied into the record at page 412. The facts, as established by the evidence, are that one of the regularly-appointed inspectors appeared at the polling place at the proper time ; none of the other officers appearing before 9 o'clock. He accordingly organized an election board, in strict accordance with the law. The election was held and the returns made, as the law directs, and as a result McDuffie received 345 votes. No Democrats appeared at the polls, evidently supposing that an election would not be held, or that if it was held by honest officers it would not be counted.

The correctness of the return and the regularity of the election are proved by the testimony of Abram Carson (page 157) and James Waller (page 158). Where, or by whom, any other election was held, nowhere appears in the evidence, nor are we informed anything about the other return, which gave Turpin 30 votes, except that the county board did not count it. There are about 400 colored voters in the beat and 50 whites.

Liberty Hill.—No return from this precinct is found among the records of the county. The evidence shows that the Democratic inspectors failed to appear at the polling place, nor did any of the Democrats of the beat appear during the day. It was the intention to have no election here, but the colored inspector was on hand, as was the United States supervisor. An election board was organized according to law, the election held, and 197 votes cast for McDuffie. Returns were made out according to the vote ; what became of the returns designed for the county board does not appear, but the supervisors made returns to the chief supervisor (page 763). The voters are not to be disfranchised by any neglect of the officers after the election, if the correct vote can be ascertained. In this case it is duly proved.

Burnsville.—Returns show 497 votes cast, all except 22 of them credited to Turpin. It appears that the Democrats had a ballot-box (its contents unknown) concealed in a room adjoining the polling-place, and that before the time for counting came this box was discovered by some Republicans and carried away. This interrupted the Democratic programme and forced a delay in the count to another day and place. Witnesses for contestant are H. M. Hall (pages 161, 173, 181) and Geo. Smith (pages 223, 238, Exhibit page 240). Here as elsewhere the Republicans kept an outside poll-list, which is in the record.

Hall, an educated and intelligent colored Republican, kept the tally of 288 Republican voters, who cast their votes for McDuffie, and had their names recorded as so voting, and Hall saw all but 5 put these identical ballots given them into the hands of the inspectors. He is subjected to a long and harassing cross-examination upon immaterial matters, with the apparent purpose of getting up a scare about the stolen ballot-box. Caught with a stuffed box concealed, they prevented the production of the box by making it appear to the witnesses that the man who had secured the box had committed a great crime. In almost any other part of the country the box would have been forthcoming, and instead of the man who had secured it being in danger of the penitentiary, the men who had prepared it would be prosecuted and convicted.

Smith fully confirms the testimony of Hall. He not only distributed the tickets, but helped to keep watch. It is needless to go into details, because the method here was but a repetition of the one adopted all over the district to preserve the evidence of the true vote.

P. R. King (page 555) testifies in rebuttal that he distributed Democratic tickets that day. Thinks that Hall could not see the voter all the time on account of a paling fence. Says that there are from 400 to 500 colored voters in the beat, and that he gave colored people that day from 50 to 100 tickets. Is questioned as to whether or not it is well known, and made a joke of, that the colored people are cheated out of their votes, and answers evasively, but admits that so far as he is concerned he is determined to have white supremacy, regardless of the colored majority. His testimony, on cross-examination, strengthens rather than weakens the evidence for contestant.

David Gardner, colored, United States supervisor (page 564), George R. Mason, (page 564), and R. D. Berry (page 565), white inspectors, all testify to the accuracy of the count. No one was present to cross-examine these witnesses, their testimony is exceedingly short, and does not disclose the fact that the count was made on the day after the election, at another place, nor do they attempt to account for the whereabouts of the box in the intervening time. This of course renders their evidence in regard to the count valueless. Berry, who is a lawyer, and one of the attorneys for contestee in this case, says the law requires two ballot boxes, evidently trying to excuse the presence of a concealed box; but he is mistaken in his statement of the law, and probably knew better.

The excuse given for not counting the ballots at the close of the election was that they were afraid of a large mob of negroes who were clamoring outside, and Berry tried to prove, when cross-examining Hall, that he had said he would proceed with the count if the negroes would go away and quit clamoring to have the vote counted. Probably it did not occur to Berry when getting up this excuse for removing the box, that according to his subsequent return, only 22 negroes, all told, voted the Republican ticket, and that, if his return is true, more than 400 of the negroes were Democrats. It is indeed lamentable that three inspectors, backed by from 20 to 40 white men, and 400 negroes, were afraid of 22 Republican negroes who wanted to have the vote counted before another stuffed box could be obtained. But of course there were more than 22 Republican negroes; the return was a fraud, and the committee count the vote as the evidence shows it to have been cast.

Union.—According to the returns, 384 votes were cast at Union beat, of which Turpin is credited with 299, and McDuffie with 85. The evidence in this case is that of Hector Jones (page 167), Oscar Masely (page 172) and the poll-list of Republican voters (pages 168–169–171), and also the list of Democratic voters. The evidence is of like character with that of other precincts, the keepers of the list being extremely careful, and going to the extent of keeping a list of Democratic as well as Republican votes. The list is in the record and shows 336 Republican and 33 Democratic votes. It is in no way contradicted. We count 44 votes for contestee as conceded in the notice of contest, although as a matter of fact he only received 33. The election officers at this beat were all Democrats.

Valley Creek.—According to the returns 490 votes were cast at this precinct, 401 being credited to Turpin. The evidence is of like character with that of other precincts; a complete poll-list of the Republican voters was kept and is in evidence, and shows that 382 instead of 89 votes were cast for McDuffie. C. H. Myatt (page 179) and J. H. Goldsby (page 392) were the Republican managers at the election, and furnish the proof. A Republican United States supervisor was appointed at this poll, but was not permitted to serve. He then kept the outside poll-list. John McIlwain, the returning officer, who was very actively engaged, in a way not at all to his credit, in the contest in 1886, attempted to stop the keeping of this list and threatened to have the witness arrested. The work was temporarily stopped and some votes missed, and afterwards it was kept on the backs of tickets, apparently to avoid being seen and so prevent arrest. The so-called Republican inspector was a "professional."

To sustain this return one of the clerks of the election was called and testified that everything was fair. He was sure that the count was honest, forgetting that he had no means of knowing further than that he kept a correct tally. He could not know whether the tickets were correctly read to him or correctly deposited in the box. A disreputable colored man is also called to prove that he distributed Republican tickets with Turpin's name on them. His evidence in chief amounts to very little that is material, and that little is utterly demolished by cross-examination. None of the inspectors are called as witnesses. There are between 500 and 600 voters in the beat, all but 35 or 36 being Republicans.

Smiley.—No return was counted for Smiley by the county board. Two of the regularly appointed inspectors and a United States supervisor were present at the time for opening the polls, but the Democratic inspector said he had no time to fool with the election and refused to act. Thereupon, the other inspectors organized an election board as provided by law. The election was regular in every particular. No Democrats turned out to vote, but 86 Republicans did. Returns were duly made and delivered to the sheriff but were not counted. Returns were also made to the chief supervisor (pages 194, 365). That this return should be counted is substantially conceded.

Pine Flat.—Three hundred and twenty-nine votes were returned from Pine Flat, 249 of them for Turpin. There are in the beat about 200 colored voters and 25 white voters. The inspectors were two white Democrats and one Tom Cleveland (page 428), who says he is neither a Republican nor a Democrat, but a "straight-out." He can neither read nor write, and is entirely under the control of one of the Democratic inspectors. Like satisfactory proof as in other precincts shows that 140 votes were cast for McDuffie. Ben. Brown (pages 195-7). S. Grumbles (page 377). E. Smith (page 773).

To rebut this testimony the contestee calls Tom Cleveland, the colored inspector, to swear that everything was right, although he could neither read nor write and knew nothing about whether the count was correct or not. The return for this precinct contained many more votes than there were voters in the beat.

Vernon.—One hundred and forty-seven votes are returned from Vernon, only 8 being credited to McDuffie. The proof shows that 121 colored Republicans voted for him and that 11 white and 8 colored men voted for Turpin. The Republican inspector could neither read nor write, but he was honest. He received the votes and handed them to a Democratic inspector; says the Republicans did not change their ballots when coming towards the polls. After the polls were closed the ballot-box was carried to Lawyer John's plantation, where it was counted. Neither of the white inspectors or clerks is called to sustain the return after this unlawful act of removing the box.

One J. L. Campbell is called to prove that colored men threw away their Republican tickets, and took Democratic tickets from him and voted them. He ventured to name two, and was promptly contradicted by the voters themselves, who swore they did no such thing. Lawyer John, to whose plantation the box was taken, is also examined, but not about the count. His evidence was given to show that colored men voted the Democratic ticket, and that he was active in seeing to it that the Republican managers did not interfere with the colored men. We do not think his evidence overturns the evidence given for contestant, though to some extent it weakens it. The witness was not cross-examined, and there is a dispute about notice to take his deposition.

The fact of the illegal removal of the box before counting, of the violation of the spirit of the law in the appointment of the Republican inspector, and the failure to sustain the return by oral proof, under the circumstances, leaves the return discredited, and the true vote must be ascertained by the best attainable evidence. Evidence for contestant may be found on pages 199, 201, 764-766. For contestee on pages 641-650.

Dublin.—Eighty-seven votes were returned from Dublin, 65 of the number being credited to Turpin. The evidence, of like character with that heretofore given, shows that 49 of these votes were cast for McDuffie. None of the officers of the election were called to sustain the return, but a witness is called to testify that the Republican managers, from their position, could not certainly know how the votes were cast. The return is impeached, and we count the vote as proved.

Elm Bluff.—One hundred and one votes were returned from this precinct and 73 of them credited to Turpin. The same method was pursued in this precinct as in the others. The Republican managers attended to putting in their vote, kept a complete list of all who voted

the Republican ticket and, in this precinct, of all who voted the Democratic ticket.   Seventy-six voted Republican and 15 Democratic.
There are only 15 Democrats in the beat.   The evidence is clear and
uncontradicted (pages 233, 234, 236).

Brown's.—Three hundred and twenty-five votes are returned from
this precinct, of which number Turpin is credited with 235.   There are
in the beat about 300 colored Republicans, and from 12 to 16 white
Democrats.   For the Forty-eighth Congress the vote was : Republican,
304 ; Democratic, 10.   Here the outside poll-list was kept, as in other
places, and is in evidence, containing 309 names, all who voted of both
parties according to the outside poll.   Charles Walker, the United
States supervisor, was present during the whole election, kept the
count when the votes were being counted, and testifies that the result
was : McDuffie 265, and Turpin 16 ; that the inspectors did not foot up
their tally, but simply signed a sheet of paper with the tally on it, and
delivered the tin box to the returning officer ; that he saw the box the
next day in Selma, at the sheriff's office, and that the seal had been
tampered with.

This is direct and positive testimony of the United States supervisors
as to the actual result of the count and the subsequent tampering with
the box, and that the return, or apology for a return, made out was not
the return afterwards found among the records.   None of these officers
are called to rebut this testimony, but an outsider is called to prove the
handwriting of the inspectors .The return was a fraud. (Evidence for
contestant, pages 342, 345, 348 ; for contestee, page 584.)   Attention is
called to the lengthy objections made for delay during the taking of
this testimony.

Chillatchie.—The returns from this precinct were rejected by the returning board for technical reasons, and no vote counted.   The returns
were duly proved, and it is admitted that they ought to be counted,
giving McDuffie 144 votes.   The refusal to count this return, in direct
disregard of the decision of the supreme court of the State, throws
light on the situation in the district, and the attitude of the county
returning board.

River.—Two hundred and ninety-seven votes were returned from River
beat, 283 being credited to Turpin, and only 14 to McDuffie.   The evidence shows that there are about 300 colored voters in the beat, and
25 or 26 whites, and that all of the colored men are Republicans except
two or three.   The proof shows that 200 voted the Republican ticket
and for McDuffie.   There is no attempt to rebut this evidence.

Carlowville.—Here the election was duly and lawfully held, but the
county board refused to count the returns, as in Chillatchie.   It is conceded that the return ought to be counted.   This adds 101 to McDuffie's
vote.

Woodlawn.—According to the returns, 176 votes were cast at Woodlawn, Turpin being credited with 159, and McDuffie with 17.   The un-
controverted evidence shows that 136 votes were cast for McDuffie, and
that there are only about 40 Democratic voters in the precinct.

Marion Junction and *Old Town.*—The frauds perpetrated in these two
precincts are, in like manner, fully proved, and we count them according to the evidence, as limited by the notice of contest.   At Old Town
the return was one of the boldest frauds in the whole list.

Boykins.—The returns from this precinct were not counted by the
county board.   They showed for the Republican electors 110, and for
the Democratic electors 17, but for Turpin 117, and for McDuffie 10.

This was evidently effected by taking the 1 from the 110 and placing it before the 17. The vote was evidently cast as counted by the committee.

This closes the review of the various precincts where the committee have rejected the returns and counted the vote proved.

It will be seen that the evidence throughout the district is of a similar character, the result of intelligent organization to prevent fraud and to prove the actual vote by other means than the returns. It shows the existence of a universal belief that the returns could not be relied upon, and that that belief was justifiable.

The evidence is a direct attack upon the integrity of the officers holding the election, so far as these officials were white Democrats, upon matters connected with the exercise of the right of suffrage by colored men. If these officers would falsify the returns, it follows that no reliance could be placed in the contents of the ballot-boxes left in their hands after 'the election. The law of the case is clear, provided the evidence is satisfactory and of a character relied upon by judicial tribunals.

The violation of the letter and spirit of the law in the appointment of the election officers, so universal as to show deliberate intent, the universal knowledge of the purpose of such violation, and all the various acts of the partisans of contestee, including all the officials throughout the district, are what give weight and character to the evidence which shows the results in individual precincts, or beats, as they are called in Alabama.

The admissibility of this kind of testimony has been fully recognized by the courts, and its weight in this class of cases admitted.

Judge Howell E. Jackson, late a United States Senator and now a judge of eminence, in his charge to the jury in the recent trial of Tennessee election officers for violating the Federal election laws at Memphis, Tenn., used the following language:

Said witnesses testified that the voting-population of the fourth civil district of Fayette County on November 6, 1888, numbered between 490 and 500—say about 500. That about 80 to 100 of such voters were white men or Democrats; the remainder, numbering about 400, were colored men and Republicans. That on the day of the election there was a large turn out of such voters. That the colored voters present exceeded 300 in number. John McGowan, the Republican chairman of the district, states that there were over 300 colored Republican voters present. That he directed many or most of them to go for their tickets to John C. Reeves, who occupied a position 10 or 20 steps from the voting place, and was distributing Republican tickets to Republican voters. That Reeves's position was in full view of the window at which the ballots were handed in to the officer. That he saw many of the tickets deposited or handed in to the officer holding the election, and can not swear to the actual number that voted that had Republican tickets. John C. Reeves testified before you that he was present. That he had in his possession Republican tickets, a sample of which is produced in evidence, having on it a full list of Republican candidates, from Presidential electors and Congressmen down to State and county officers. That he issued to the colored voters on that day, upon their application for the same, 325 of those tickets while at the voting place. That on his way home he met four or five other voters going to the polls, to whom he gave Republican tickets; the names of two of those voters he finds upon the poll-list at Nos. 407 and 409. Reeves further states that he saw over one hundred of those to whom he gave tickets go directly from him to the window where the votes were received and hand them in to the officer holding the election. He could not swear that they actually deposited the identical tickets received from him, but he saw no change of ticket or change of purpose on the part of the voter after procuring from himself the Republican ticket. He recognizes on the poll-list the names of about one hundred of such Republican voters. Now, gentlemen of the jury, Reeves and McGowan are in no way impeached, nor are their statements in any wise contradicted. They stand before you as in every way credible witnesses, and their testimony is entitled to full faith and credit. If the case for the prosecution stopped with Reeves and McGowan, it would present a case of circumstantial evidence as to the vote actually cast having exceeded that which was counted and returned by the election officers and judges. When circumstantial evidence is relied on to convict, as counsel for defense has suggested, it should be of such conclusive character as to exclude any remote hypothesis of innocence.

It is to be remembered that the last remark has reference to the proof required to convict in a criminal case.

Speaking in regard to individual voters who had testified to their votes, he said:

If the prosecution had simply shown that each one of these witnesses was seen going to the poll with a Republican ticket in his hand which he had received from Reeves, with a declaration of his intention to vote said ticket, such facts and acts would have constituted circumstantial evidence that they voted said ticket.

It is to be remembered that the evidence in this case is more direct and more certain than was the evidence upon which Judge Jackson's charge was based, and that the witnesses and voters take much greater pains to be able to know the exact facts.

Remembering who Judge Jackson is and what his party affiliations are, and that the men on trial were citizens of his own State and members of the political party to which he belongs, this charge will certainly be accepted as of the very highest authority.

That any one should doubt the admissibility of this kind of evidence and its sufficiency, under the circumstances surrounding this case, is somewhat surprising, and yet it was gravely argued before the committee that the evidence was not only insufficient but altogether incompetent.

The enormous frauds shown by this record, by which an honest majority of nearly 5,000 (and there are strong grounds for suspecting it to be much larger still) was turned into a minority of more than 13,000, have necessarily made this report somewhat lengthy.

The committee recommend the adoption of the following resolutions:

Resolved, That Louis W. Turpin was not elected a Representative in the Fifty-first Congress from the Fourth Congressional district of Alabama, and is not entitled to the seat as such Representative.

Resolved, That John V. McDuffie was duly elected a Representative in the Fifty-first Congress from the Fourth Congressional district of Alabama, and is entitled to his seat as such Representative.

VIEWS OF THE MINORITY.

---

1) **Evidence.**

Each party should be required to produce the highest and best evi-
lence attainable.

(2) **Evidence.** Evidence in chief taken in time of rebuttal should not
be considered.

Granting to the contestant all that he can reasonably claim (see
syllabus, p. 255), there still remains for contestee a majority of over
),000.

VIEWS OF THE MINORITY.

MAY 26, 1890.—Mr. CRISP, from the Committee on Elections, submitted the following as the views of the minority:

The undersigned not agreeing with the majority of the Committee on Elections in their finding in the above-stated case, herein express their dissent and the reasons therefor.

The majority report correctly sets out the official returns of the votes cast in the Fourth district of Alabama at the election held November 6, 1888.

To so much of the report as is devoted to what the committee denominate the "recent political history of the district" the undersigned do not deem it necessary, nor indeed proper, to reply. Under the Constitution of the United States this House must determine the "election, qualification, and return of its members." We believe such "determination" should be arrived at in accordance with the legal evidence contained in the record and the well-established principles of law.

The general rule is that the ordinary rules of evidence apply as well to election contests as to other cases. The evidence must, therefore, be confined to the point in issue, and must be relevant. The burden of proof is always upon the contestant or the party attacking the official returns or certificate. The presumption is that the officers of the law charged with the duty of ascertaining and declaring the result have discharged that duty faithfully. (McCrary on Elections, sec. 306.)

The law applicable to this case is plain and well established and is here referred to.

Section 252, Code of Alabama, authorizes the courts of county commissioners in their respective counties to establish election precincts.

Section 258 requires the probate judge, sheriff, and clerk of each county to provide one ballot-box, and, if they deem necessary, not exceeding three, for each voting place.

Section 259 requires the same officers to appoint for each voting place three inspectors, two of whom shall be members of opposing political parties, if practicable, and one returning officer.

Section 260, the sheriff is the returning officer of the county.

Section 262, the polls must be opened before 9 o'clock on the morning of the election.

Section 264, two clerks are to be appointed by the inspectors.

Section 265, before opening the polls the inspectors and clerks must take an oath to perform their duties at such election according to law.

The return must stand until such facts are proven as to clearly show that it is not true. (McCreary on Elections, 438 and authorities there cited.)

The object of this investigation should be to ascertain the truth. In all such investigations each party should be required to produce the highest and and best evidence attainable. This rule of evidence will

303

not be disputed. In the light of this rule we will proceed at once to
an examination of the facts contained in the record.

LOWNDES COUNTY.

In this county the report of the majority of the committee attacks
the appointment of the precinct inspectors.

We propose to give the conclusions of the majority in the language of
the report, and then follow with the testimony upon which they base
their judgment.

We quote from page 8 of the report:

> In Lowndes County the precinct inspectors were appointed on the 25th day of
> September. A few days afterwards the contestee visited the county, and on the 6th
> day of October an entire change was made in the list of inspectors appointed to repre-
> sent the Republicans. The first list was satisfactory, and made up in the greater part
> of intelligent men. The second list was made without any authority in the law, and
> its composition shows that the change was made for a dishonest purpose. Judge
> Coffey (Record, page 745) says that the reason for this change was that the sheriff and
> several other gentlemen told him that the Republican inspectors being *school-teachers*
> did not wish to serve and mix up in politics. Hence the change.

We quote now from the deposition of Judge A. E. Coffey (Record,
page 745):

> Q. At what time or about what time did you make said appointment of said in-
> spectors?—A. About the 25th *or 26th of September*, 1888.
> Q. If there was any other appointment made of the inspectors by your board, or
> any change made in said appointments, state about when that was done, to the best
> of your recollection.—A. The board of supervisors met again about ten days after the
> appointment of the inspectors and revised the list, making a number of changes.
> Q. At whose instance or request was this second meeting of the board, and at
> whose instance or for what reason were those changes made? Please state fully and
> particularly.—A. *The sheriff and one of the Republican inspectors and other gentlemen,
> whose names I can not remember now, informed me that a number of the Republican in-
> spectors who had been appointed declined to serve as such inspectors, on the grounds that they
> were school-teachers and did not want to mix up in politics; and the board of supervisors
> was called together to remedy this defect in the list of inspectors.*
> Q. Was there no other reason or excuse made by those persons who communicated
> those facts to you why those changes should be made? If so, what reason or excuse
> was given by them? Please state fully.—A. *No other motive prompted me to make the
> changes except as above stated.*
> Q. State whether or not Mr. L. W. Turpin was here just before or during the time
> of this session of the board at which the changes were made of the inspectors.
> Please state when it was relative to the meeting of the board, and how long he remained
> here. State fully.
> (Contestee objects to this question on the grounds that it is illegal and irrelevant.)
> A. Mr. Turpin was here on the 28th and 29th of September, 1888, which was two
> or three days after the appointment of inspectors, and seven or eight days before the
> list of inspectors was revised and changed.
> Q. Did you have any knowledge of the fact that Mr. Turpin made complaint to
> any of the board as to the inspectors that had been appointed at your first meeting
> and that he requested or solicited any member of the board to make any changes of
> the appointment of inspectors? If he did, please state all you know on the subject.—
> A. Mr. Turpin stated to me on his arrival here, on the 28th or 29th of September,
> 1888, *that he was perfectly satisfied with the list of inspectors that had been appointed and
> that he desired that there should be a school-teacher or other intelligent Republican repre-
> sentative on the board of inspectors in every beat in the district* and he did not solicit any
> changes through me or to my knowledge.

This witness was introduced by the contestant himself, and his credibility thereby vouched for by the contestant. Does his testimony
warrant the conclusion of the majority that the change was made at
the instance of the contestee and "for a dishonest purpose?" We
think not. He testifies directly that the change was made for the
sole reason that he was informed that those appointed declined to serve,
and that the contestee had nothing whatever to do with his action, but
on the contrary expressed himself as perfectly satisfied with the first

appointees, and expressed a desire that they would serve. The majority of the committee must have misread the testimony of Judge Coffey to arrive at the position set forth in their report, or else they discredit his testimony, though he holds the high and honorable position of judge of probate of Lowndes County and his truthfulness is avouched by the contestant himself.

The report further declares, inferentially at least, that while the first appointments were satisfactory to the contestant the second appointments were not, when in answer to the following question on cross-examination:

Did not J. V. McDuffie express himself as being well satisfied with the persons appointed to hold the Congressional election in 1888?

Judge Coffey replied, "He did," and in the lengthy deposition of the contestant we fail to find any denial of this expression of satisfaction upon his part with the second appointments. We must infer, therefore, that he was satisfied before the election with the character of the second appointees, and believed them to be competent and honest men.

The majority of the committee insist that the Republican inspectors last appointed were ignorant men, while those first named were intelligent. Let us see what the contestant's witness, Judge Coffey, says on this point in answer to a question propounded by the contestant's counsel (Record, page 746):

Q. How did those inspectors of the Republican party who were appointed at the first meeting of the board and were taken off and rejected by the board at the last meeting compare with those who were appointed in their place to act as inspectors in point of education, intelligence, and qualifications to act as such inspectors? Please state fully, so far as you know.—A. I do not think that there was any great difference in the intelligence and qualifications of the original Republican inspectors and those who were appointed to fill their places, except in Hayneville beat, that I am acquainted with.

There is not a particle of testimony to affect in the remotest degree the bona fides of Judge Coffee or to throw the slightest suspicion upon his action. In fact, learning as he did that the Republicans originally appointed declined to serve, it was his duty, in the interest of a fair election and in compliance with the law, to make such changes as would insure Republican representation at the ballot-boxes, and if he had not acted upon the information and thereby the Republicans were deprived of an inspector at the respective precincts, the contestant might have complained that his failure to act was caused by a "dishonest purpose" upon his part.

But without dwelling longer upon this point let us examine the testimony as to each precinct in this county.

Following the order of the majority report we will first consider—

Gordonsville precinct.—As to this precint there is no testimony whatever even tending to impeach the fairness of the election and the correctness of the returns except that which was taken in the time for rebuttal; then the contestant introduced witnesses and examined them in chief.

It is unnecessary to call attention to the statute governing contested-election cases. Under it and in accordance with the findings of the present Committee on Elections in the case of Posey *vs.* Parrett, all this evidence must be excluded, leaving the precinct unassailed. It certainly would be gross injustice to admit the depositions of these witnesses when the contestee had no opportunity to meet and contradict their testimony.

But while adhering to this position, and believing the House will not

H. Mis. 137——20

ignore the law and depart from the long line of precedents furnished by the record of contested-election cases in former Congresses, and by the very recent case of Posey *vs.* Parrett in this House, we insist that there is nothing in the testimony of any of the witnesses which is material, except the statement of the Republican Federal supervisor that at one time during the day the ballot box was removed from the polling-room into an adjoining room by one of the Democratic inspectors. This fact was introduced to cast suspicion upon the purpose for which the box was placed in the room: but this is all dispelled by the testimony not only of one of the Democratic inspectors, but by the Republican inspector as well, and the purpose fully and satisfactorily explained.

The Democratic inspectors went to dinner together, and before leaving one of them took the box, without objection upon the part of the Republican inspector or Republican Federal supervisor, and set it just inside the door of an adjoining unoccupied room, without even entering the room, leaving the Republican inspector and Republican supervisor to keep guard, and the Republican inspector swears no one entered that room while the box was in it. (Record, 518, 522.)

The majority in their report say on page 18:

The material evidence in regard to this precinct is found on pages 728, 733, 735, and 744 of the record.

That is, they consider only as "material" the evidence taken by the contestant, and that, too, taken in the last ten days, with no opportunity to the contestee to refute it, and utterly ignore as at all "material" the direct evidence of one of the Democratic inspectors and the Republican inspector, witnesses on behalf of the contestee.

Sandy Ridge precinct.—The facts in regard to this precinct can be briefly stated.

The law of Alabama requires the polls to be opened before 9 o'clock in the morning. If all of the inspectors are not present, vacancies shall be filled by those present from the qualified voters in attendance. When the time for opening the polls on the morning of the election in controversy arrived, only one of the inspectors was present and he appointed two other inspectors who were qualified voters, one a Republican and the other of unknown politics, and the three proceeded to conduct the election.

Sometime after this poll was opened a colored man associated two other colored men with him, and without a shadow of authority opened another polling place and received votes.

There is no attack made on the manner of conducting the regular poll or the correctness of the returns of the election officers, but on the contrary the witnesses introduced by the contestee prove that the election was fair and that the returns were honest.

The majority count the votes cast at this outside, irregular, and unauthorized poll. They question and discard returns from regular polling places because the officers were all Democrats, but in this instance they count the returns from an irregular and unauthorized polling place made by men, all of whom were Republicans, unsworn, ignorant, and unlettered.

Lowndesborough precinct.—This precinct is attacked by one witness, G. T. McCall, who was a Republican ticket-holder, and here is a summary of the material points in his testimony (Record, 747):

Q. You say that you were engaged in issuing tickets there at that election that day; state about how many you issued.—A. Myself and some four or five others issued, I suppose, about 350 or 360 tickets.

(Contestee moves to strike this answer from the file on the ground that it is a mere supposition of the witness.)

Q. Were you about or near the polls during the time of voting? State whether or not these tickets and others you were issuing was voted or handed in to the inspector.—A. I was near the polls all day. Right on the grounds. I seen a great part of them handed in; I didn't see them all.

'Cross-examination (Record, 748):

Q. You stated in your direct examination that you and several others issued about 350 or 360 Republican tickets on the day of the election; how many of these did you issue yourself?—A. I suppose I issued one-third of them.

Q. Do you know as a fact how many you actually issued? I do not ask for your supposition, but for what you actually know?—A. At one time I issued one-third of a hundred and fifty, and at another time I issued some more, and don't know as a fact how many I issued.

Q. How many of the voters to whom you gave Republican tickets actually voted the ticket you gave them, if you know how many?—A. I give tickets to about seventy-five or one hundred, probably more, and I would say definitely that all of them voted them.

Upon this testimony the majority proceed to set aside the returns which gave Turpin 320, McDuffie 41, and reversing the figures give Turpin 41 and McDuffie 320, and while such action is startling when considered in the light of the testimony of the one solitary witness whose statements we have quoted, yet when we look at the evidence on behalf of the contestee, which we will now give, it is no less than astounding. (Record, 536. W. H. Merrett.)

Q. What is your name, your age, and where do you reside, and how long have you resided?—A. William H. Merrett is my name; my age is thirty-four years; I reside in Lowndesboro beat, No. 18, Lowndes County, Ala.; have resided there ten years.

Q. Did you attend an election held for your beat at Lowndesboro on the 6th day of November, 1888, to elect a Congressman to represent this district in the Fifty-first Congress; and, if so, in what capacity did you attend?—A. I did attend said election, and in the capacity of register.

Q. On the morning of said election did you, or any one else in your hearing, try to induce G. T. McCall to go into the room where the election was to be held and personally supervise said election as United States supervisor? If so, state all was said.—A. I, in company with one of the inspectors, A. Douglass, saw G. T. McCall on the grounds and each of us made personal endeavors to induce him to go in and act in the capacity of United States supervisor, he being appointed in said capacity, I telling him at the time I wanted to see a fair election and a fair count, and wanted it said that Lowndesboro beat sent off her vote as cast by the voters, and that he well knew that Lowndesboro beat was largely Democratic, and that it was important to the Democratic party for him to act. Mr. Douglass, one of the inspectors, said to him in my presence, that all he could to get the said McCall to act as United States supervisor. McCall positively refused to have anything to do in the capacity he was appointed for. We made strenuous efforts on several other Republicans to get them to act, and was not able to get any other Republican than the one that served.

Q. Were you present during the entire day at the voting place?—A. Most of the time during voting hours I was within ten feet of where the vote was handed in to the inspectors.

Q. Do you know whether or not a large number of colored voters voted the Democratic ticket there that day?—A. I personally gave them Democratic tickets, and, being in close proximity to where they passed them to the inspectors, know a large number voted the Democratic ticket.

Q. Was J. V. McDuffie a popular or unpopular candidate for Congress among the colored voters of your beat at said election?—A. By leaders, who controlled the masses of the Republican party, I consider McDuffie unpopular and not their choice for Congress. I have heard the leaders of said party say as much, and that he was too close-fisted and they were tired of working for him for nothing.

Q. Was L. W. Turpin a popular or unpopular candidate for Congress among the Democrats of your beat?—A. Very popular.

Q. Do you know the general character of A. Douglass and S. A. Tyson in the community in which they live, and how long have you known them, and did they act as inspectors at said election?

(Contestant objects to this question on the ground that there is no predicate been laid to authorizing into examining of the characters of these gentlemen; that their character is not in issue in this contest; that they are not witnesses for either party, and are not parties to the contest, and that their character for truth and veracity, or any other respect, has been attacked or put in issue.)

A. I do know the character of the above gentlemen mentioned, and have known them ten years, and they did act as inspectors to said election.

Q. What is the general character of said Douglass and Tyson, and to what class of citizens do they belong ?—A. Their character is good, and equal to the best in our community, and are of the first and best families in the beat.

Q. Do you know the character of G. T. McCall in the community in which he lives; if you do, is that character good or bad for truth and veracity ?—A. I do know his character; and while he is a smart and shrewd man in rascality, I consider his moral character bad, and where he is interested in the least I would not believe him on his oath.

Q. Did you see anything there that day that indicated anything other than a free ballot and a fair count ?—A. I did not.

Q. Judging from the votes cast at your precinct for several elections past, either State or Federal, is your beat Democratic or Republican ?—A. Democratic, by a large majority.

Cross-examination by W. C. GRIFFEN, attorney for contesant:

Q. You say according to the votes cast there for the last several years past, you say that your beat is largely Democratic; can you say of your own knowledge that a majority of the votes cast at those elections were Democratic ?—A. I can say there were Democratic, having repeatedly acted as inspector both in State and Federal elections.

Q. You say that you and Mr. Archie Douglass used your influence with G. T. McCall on the day of the election on the 6th of November last, to act as United States supervisor at that election; do you know of your own knowledge that said McCall had been appointed or had any legal authority to act as United States supervisor of said election ?—A. I saw his commission the day previous to the election.

Q. Who acted as inspectors at that election and who as clerks, and give the race and politics of each of them ?—A. A. Douglass, S. A. Tyson, and Ben Gary, inspectors; first two Democratic, last one Republican. I don't know who acted as clerks.

Q. Can Ben Gary read and write ?—A. I don't know.

(Record 538.   Hon. A. E. Coffee:)

Q. What is your name, your age, and where do you reside, and how long have you resided in this county ?—A. My name is A. E. Coffee; judge of probate court of Lowndes County; I am forty years old; I reside in Lowndes County, Ala.; I have resided in the county about twenty-five years.

Q. Please tell what you know about the election that was held on the 6th day of November, 1888, at Lowndesboro precinct, held for the purpose of electing a Congressman to represent this district in the Fifty-first Congress, and Presidential election ?— A. I voted at Lowndesboro precinct on the 6th day of November, 1888, and was about or near the polls from 12 o'clock, noon, until 5 o'clock p. m.   I saw a great many colored voters cast their ballots for L. W. Turpin, including the leading and most intelligent colored men of the beat.   The colored men of Lowndesboro beat have affiliated with the Democratic party ever since 1882.   I knew the colored men voted the Democratic ticket, because they showed me their tickets, and I saw them deposited in the ballot-box.

Q. Have you not an extensive acquaintance and knowledge of the colored voters of this county as regards to their preference for voting ?   If so, state whether or not they vote solidly for one party.—A. I have considerable knowledge of the political predilection of the colored men of Lowndes County; they have never been solidly Republican since 1882; they have been divided on all opposing candidates in the county since 1882; in 1886 they voted almost solidly for the regular Democratic nominees against their opponents

Q. It seems there were two boxes from each of the following beats, to wit: Farmerville, Sandy Ridge, Hayneville, Letohatchee, and St. Clair.   Upon what grounds did the board of supervisors refuse to open and count the box from each of these beats sent up by the Republican inspectors alone ?—A. On the grounds that the returns of an election held by the regularly appointed inspectors were before the county board of supervisors, and under the law they counted the returns of the regularly qualified inspectors and refused to count any other.

Q. Do you know the general character and standing of the Democratic inspectors that held said election in each beat in this county ?   If so, state what it is.—A. I do; almost without exception they are of the best men in the county in point of integrity, and all those qualities that go to make a good citizen.

Q. Do you know anything further that would be of benefit to the contestee in this contest ?—A. I know that since 1882 the colored people of the county have manifested very little interest in the Republican aspirants for office, as evidenced by their voting the Democratic ticket openly, and the small turn-out compared to the old days when the carpet-bagger was lord of the land, and before the colored man had found out his selfishness and deceit.

(Record 539. Dr. Shirley Bragg:)

Q. What is your name, your age, where do you reside, and how long have you resided there?—A. My name is Shirley Bragg; my age is thirty-five years; I reside in Lowndesboro; I have resided in the county nearly all of my life.

Q. What office do you hold in this county?—A. Health officer and inspector of convicts.

Q. State all you know in regard to the election held at Lowndesboro precinct on the 6th day of November, 1888, for the purpose of electing a Congressman to represent this district in the Fifty first Congress of the United States.—A. I was present and was on the ground the whole day. We had a fair turn-out there, but have seen larger crowds at the polls. I saw some of colored voters vote for McDuffie and saw some of them vote for the regular Democratic ticket. My impression is that Scott Smith worked for the Democratic ticket and voted the Democratic ticket; he is a colored man.

Q. About what portion of the colored voters did you see vote for McDuffie, and about what portion did you see vote for L. W. Turpin?—A. I saw about as many vote for L. W. Turpin as voted for McDuffie, is the best of my belief.

Q. Did the colored people of your beat take much interest in said election or not?—A. Seemed to be very little interest in the election and there was no enthusiasm at a'l.

Q. Was J. V. McDuffie a popular or unpopular candidate among the colored voters of your beat at said election?—A. I don't think the rank and file of the colored people cared much for either one of them.

Cross-examination by W. C. GRIFFEN, attorney for contestant:

Q. You say in your direct examination that you saw some of the colored voters vote for McDuffie and that you saw some vote the regular Democratic ticket; please state how many you know voted the regular Democratic ticket, and give their names who so voted.—A. I can't say how many, but know that some of them voted for Turpin by there being a red ticket on the ground and knew who was on the red ticket; it was the Democratic ticket sent to me the night before the election by the chairman of the district committee, and would have been all over the county, but was received too late for distribution.

Q. What proportion of the time that the polls were open there that day at that election were you present at the polls?—A. I was there from the time they opened until they closed, with the exception of about a half an hour, when I went to dinner.

Q. You say in your direct examination that there was a fair turn-out there that day, but that the voters seemed to take very little interest in the election; you know whether or not they all voted?—A. I do not know, but know there was less enthusiasm there at that election than I ever saw in Lowndes County.

These witnesses—men of high character—testify that many colored men voted the Democratic ticket; that the officers who conducted the election were men of the strictest integrity; that McCall, the contestant's witness, refused to serve as supervisor though appointed for that purpose, and that he is a smart and shrewd rascal and not worthy of belief on oath.

Steep Creek precinct.—We find that the majority of the committee rely upon the oft-told story that a certain number of Republican tickets were issued, therefore a corresponding number of votes were cast for McDuffie and must be counted for him.

One of the witnesses upon whose testimony the contestant mainly relies was so drunk that before the cross-examination was concluded it was found necessary to suspend until the next day so that he might sober up. (Record 697.)

The testimony of this witness is specially mentioned and approved by the report of the majority.

It is shown by the contestant's witness, W. N. Wimo, that the Democratic officers at this precinct were men "whose characters are as good as any in the State of Alabama; that they are among the best citizens." (Record 672.)

Return vote: Turpin 146, McDuffie, 62.

Counted by majority of committee: Turpin 37, McDuffie 171.

Church Hill precinct.—The election at this precinct was conducted by two Democrats and one Republican. Again comes the usual cry that a given number of Republican tickets were distributed and they were necessarily cast, and one witness is relied upon to prove this predicate of the report of the majority.

On behalf of the contestee the testimony of two witnesses was taken and we here quote it. (Record, 501–503, H. B. Lever.)

Q. What is your name, age, and in what precinct, county, and district do you reside?—A. H. B. Lever; forty-eight years of age, and live in Church Hill beat, in Lowndes County, fourth district of Alabama.

Q. Was there an election held in said county in said precinct on the 6th day of November, 1888, for the purpose of electing a member of the Fifty-first Congress of the United States of America from the Fourth Congressional district of Alabama; and, if so, who was the Republican candidate, and who was the Democrat for said office? Were you an officer of said election; and, if yea, state whether you were an inspector or not, and give the names of the other inspectors.—A. There was an election held in said precinct on said day for said office; J. V. McDuffie was the Republican candidate, and L. W. Turpin was the Democratic; I was an officer in said election; Joe R. Dudly and Captain Black were inspectors.

Q. Were all the inspectors in said election Democrats, and warm friends and ardent supporters of L. W. Turpin?—A. No. Two were Democrats and one was a Republican.

Q. Were the Democratic inspectors in said election partisans of L. W. Turpin in any other sense than that of being members of the same political party? Did you and the other Democratic inspectors, acting in concert with the white voters of said precinct, enter into and form a conspiracy with Democratic inspectors and voters throughout the Fourth Congressional district for the purpose of electing L. W. Turpin regardless of how the votes were cast? How did the Republican inspector of said election compare with point of intelligence and honesty with other Republicans of said precinct?—A. No; they were not partisans of L. W. Turpin, except that they belong to the same party. No; they did not enter into or know of any conspiracy. The Republican inspector compares favorably with the other Republicans of said beat.

Q. Who received the ballot from the electors, and who deposited in the ballot-box? Was the ballot so deposited in the ballot-box the identical ballot so handed in by the electors? Could such ballot have been changed either by the inspector receiving it or by the one depositing it without your knowledge? Was it so changed?—A. J. R. Dudly received the ballots and handed it in to Captain Black, who put them in the ballot-box. Mr. Dudly or Captain Black could not have changed the ballot without my knowing it. They were not changed, and were the identical ballots cast by the electors.

Q. Was the box in which the ballots were deposited kept locked during the day; and if so, who had the key; did not the Republican inspector before any votes was deposited in the box carefully examine and lock it; was any box filled with tickets during the time the polls were open or after the close thereof substituted for the regular ballot-box?—A. The box was kept locked, and Captain Black, the Republican inspector, had the key. He examined the box; locked it; put the key in his pocket until he opened the box to count. There was no box only the regular one.

Q. Were there any ballots other than those voted by the electors of said precinct put into the ballot-box?—A. There was none.

Q. Was the ballot-box from which the inspectors took the ballots for the purpose of counting them the identical box in which ballots voted by the electors had been deposited by the inspectors?—A. It was the identical box.

Q. Were the ballots counted by the inspectors the identical ballots that were cast by the electors?—A. They were. .

Q. Did the inspectors in making such count read tickets having on them the name of John V. McDuffie as if they were the name L. W. Turpin?—A. No, they did not.

Q. Was the count made by the inspectors a fair, just, and honest one?—A. It was a fair count, just and honest one.

Q. Was the returns made out by the inspectors and forwarded to the sheriff correct and accurate?—A. It was correct.

Q. Is this a true copy of the returns made out by the inspectors, and does it contain a correct statement of the vote of said precinct?

(The paper is now handed the witness, and the contestee asks that it be attached to his testimony, which is accordingly done and marked Exhibit B.)

A. It is a true and honest copy.

Here follows a copy of the returns, giving Turpin 117 votes and McDuffie 63 votes.

Q. How many ballots were cast at said election for John V. McDuffie and how many for L. W. Turpin?—A. McDuffie received 63 votes and L. W. Turpin 117.

Q. Could the ballot-box or ballots in it have been changed from the time of the opening of the polls to the close thereof without your knowledge?—A. It could not have been changed without my knowledge.

Q. Were they or either of them changed between the opening of the polls and the count by the inspectors?—A. They were not changed.

(Record, 505. George Ernest:)

Q. What is your name, age, and what precinct, county, and Congressional district do you reside?—A. George W. Ernest; twenty-six years of age; Church Hill precinct; Lowndes County; fourth district of Alabama.

Q. Did you so reside on the 6th day of November, 1888? If so, was there an election held in said beat for a member of Congress from the fourth Congressional district of Alabama to the Fifty-first Congress of the United States of America?—A. I did reside on the 6th day of November, 1888, when said election was held for said office on said day.

Q. What official connection, if any, did you have with said election?—A. I was appointed and acted as deputy sheriff.

Q. Were you in the room while the canvass of the polls was being made by the inspectors?—A. I was in the room at the time.

Q. Did you see the inspectors making the count; and did you read the names on the tickets? And, if so, do you know of any ballots that had the name of John V. McDuffie on them being read and counted as if they bore the name of L. W. Turpin?—A. I saw the counting of the inspectors; I read the tickets, and do not know of any that contain the name of J. V. McDuffie being read and counted for L. W. Turpin.

Q. Do you know Mr. H. B. Lever and Joseph R. Dudley; and if so, how long have you known them?—A. I know both; have known them for the last fifteen years.

Q. Do you know their general character for truth and honesty in community in which they reside, and among the people with whom they associate?—A. I do.

Q. Is not their general character very good?—A. It is.

Q. Do they not belong to, associate, and mingle with the best classes of Lowndes County?—A. They do.

Q. Was there not a good deal of discontent among the Republicans of Lowndes County on account of the nomination of J. V. McDuffie?—A. There was a good deal among the negroes.

Q. Did he receive the cordial and united support of the rank and file of his party?—A. He did not.

Q. Did not this contest arise from the fact that McDuffie supported in 1886, in the county election, what is known as the regular Democracy, instead of that wing of the Democratic party commonly called in Lowndes County Mugwumps?—A. It did.

If this is the testimony of witnesses who are credible, upon what ground can it be held that the returned vote of 117 for Turpin and 63 for McDuffie should be set aside and 13 given to Turpin and 166 to McDuffie?

Haynesville precinct.—At this precinct an election was regularly held at the court-house, the usual place for holding elections. It was conducted by two of the regularly appointed inspectors and by a third selected, in accordance with the law, to supply the place of the third appointee, who did not attend; two were Democrats and one was a Republican.

The poll was opened before 9 o'clock, as required by the statute.

A colored Republican, who claimed to be an inspector by reason of an appointment which had been revoked more than thirty days before the election, upon his own motion associated with him two other colored Republicans and opened another poll some distance from the court-house, and received the ballots of all those who presented themselves.

The only attack made on the returns from the regular polling place is that made by the leader in the outside movement (W. E. Carson), who says that the colored Republican inspector (Tony Smith) at the

regular polling place was a man "whose character for sobriety was
bad, and that he was nearly all the time drunk;" to this Smith replies
that Carson "is a tramp and beats people out of everything he can."

At the regular precinct the Democrats voted but the Republicans declined; the returns were 158 for Turpin and none for McDuffie; but
the majority of the committee held that Turpin only received 54 votes,
while McDuffie received 272 votes. They count every vote which was
cast for McDuffie at this outside place, and give Turpin only 54 votes
of the 158 which he received at the regular polling place.

The Democratic inspectors were men whose characters are shown to
have been above reproach.

In order that it may be fully understood why outside polls were
opened, and further to show the bulldozing tactics of the contestants,
we here give a part of the testimony of W. E. Haynes:

Q. State what W. E. Carson said to you, if anything, about being bulldozed and
forced to sign the returns of the pretended election held at Hayneville on the 6th day
of November, 1888.

(Contestant objects to this question on the grounds that it is illegal and irrelevant,
and on the further grounds that this witness, as William E. Carson, are parties to
this contest; that it is hearsay testimony, and that there is no predicate laid to bring
this testimony in this contest for any purpose.)

A. He told me the next day after the election that J. V. McDuffie advised separate
boxes run in certain beats and that J. V. McDuffie and his gang bulldozed and forced
the colored inspectors of these beats to hold separate elections; he said he refused to
sign the returns of his box until the day after the election, and did so under threats
of McDuffie's gang.

St. Clair precinct.—The evidence as to this precinct shows that the
election was regularly held by the duly appointed inspectors, but other
parties entirely unauthorized opened polls at another place and proceeded without any registration book to go through the farce of receiving the ballot of every man who offered to vote, and according to the
statement of one of these parties 214 ballots were cast for McDuffie and
none for Turpin, and under this state of facts the majority of the committee count 214 votes for McDuffie.

We refer here to the testimony of the witness upon which this most
extraordinary action of the majority is based: (Record, 703. Robert
Adams, witness for contestant, on cross-examination.)

Q. You stated in your direct examination that all of the inspectors were Republicans; did you or any one else make any effort to get a Democrat to serve as inspector
with you?—A. I did.

Q. Who did you ask to serve?—A. C. M. Smith.

Q. What was his reply?—A. His team was already made up.

Q. Did he say anything further than the above remark?—A. He did not.

Q. Did you ask to serve with him, or he to serve with you?—A. I asked him how
long before the polls would be open.

Q. What did he reply?—A. After a while.

Q. Then what did you say?—A. Nothing.

Q. Did you ask Mr. C. M. Smith to serve with you in holding said election?—A. I
did not.

Q. In what manner, then, or in what way did you endeavor to get Mr. Smith to
serve as an inspector?—A. I asked him how long before he would open the polls.

Q. At what time was it that he made the remark that his team was made up?—A.
Before the hour of 8 o'clock on that day.

Q. What had you said to him that called forth this remark?—A. I asked him how
long before he would open the polls?

Q. In answer to your question, how long before he would open the polls, did he
then remark in reply that his team was made up?

(Contestant objects to this question on the grounds that it is irrelevant and had
nothing to do with the issue.)

A. That was before.

Q. What did Mr. C. M. Smith say to you and what did you say to him the first time
that you had a conversation with him on the morning of the election?—A. I asked

him, I says, "Well, 'squire, I suppose we holds an election here to-day." "Yes; my team is already made up."

Q. What did you say to C. M. Smith, and what did he say to you in the second conversation?—A. "'Squire, how long before you open the polls?" and he replied, "After a while."

Q. Did you have a registration list or book, furnished by A. E. Caffe, judge of probate, to the inspectors of each beat?—A. I did not.

Q. Did you or any one else register all the voters that voted at the pretended election which you held?—A. We did not register all, but did all them who had not voted there before.

Q. If you had no register of the voters how did you know who had heretofore registered, and were therefore qualified to vote and who were not?—A. I asked them before I taken their vote.

Q. Then the only evidence that you had of a voter having registered and thereby qualifying himself for voting was what the voter said himself?—A. It was.

Q. Who wrote the names of the voters on the poll-list?—A. Myself and Humphry Adams.

Q. You stated in your direct examination that you got the registration papers from J. V. McDuffie; do you mean the papers on which to register new voters or the papers on which to make a poll-list?—A. To register new voters.

. Q. Were you or any one else that participated in that so-called election appointed or authorized by W. W. Drane, the chief registrar of the county, to register the names of persons who had not heretofore registered?—A. I was not.

Q. You stated in your direct examination that two tally-sheets were made; what did you do with each one of them?—A. I put one in the ballot-box with the poll-list and certificates, and I kept the other one at home for a contest.

Q. What did you do with this ballot-box?—A. I sealed it up and give it to the returning officer.

Q. What did you do with the ballots that were cast there that day?—A. I have them at home now.

Q. Have you been served with a notice by any one to preserve or to produce said ballots?—A. I have been served with no notice to produce the ballots, and I was told by J. V. McDuffie to hold the ballot-box containing the tickets soon after the election.

. Q. Have you any information that there was an election held at St. Clair on the 6th day of November, 1888, by C. M. Smith and others?—A. I have not.

Q. Did anybody tell you on that day or since that time that C. M. Smith and others held an election there that day?—A. They did not.

Q. Did you ever hear of an election being held there that day by C. M. Smith and others before this examination commenced?—A. I have not.

(Contestant admits that C. M. Smith and others did open the polls a short time before 5 o'clock that day, but not before.)

Q. In what house is the election usually held at that place?—A. In C. M. Smith's house.

It will be observed that this witness states that one of the regularly appointed inspectors was present on the ground before 8 o'clock in the morning, and that this inspector in effect told him he was ready to proceed to hold the election. So there was no reason to believe no poll would be opened as stated by the majority in their report. He further admits that he had no registry of voters, and that he received the ballots of all who said they were registered.

Farmersville precinct.—Here again we find two polls were opened. At 8 o'clock one of the regularly appointed inspectors associated with him a Republican and a Democrat, and they opened the polls and conducted the election.

J. D. MOORER, being called by contestee, and being sworn, doth depose and saith:

Q. What is your name and your age, and where do you reside, and how long have you resided there?—A. J. D. Moorer, jr.; my age is thirty-one years; I live in Farmersville beat, No. 5, Lowndes County, Ala.; I have resided there all my life.

Q. Did you act as inspector at your precinct of an election on the 6th day of November, 1888, for electors for President and Vice-President, and for Representative in the Fifty-first Congress of the United States from the Fourth Congressional district of Alabama?—A. I did.

Q. By whom were you notified of your appointment as inspector, and about what time?—A. Mr. Haynes, the sheriff of Lowndes County, notified me; I don't recollect what time it was, but it was about ten days before the election.

Q. Who acted with you as inspectors at that election ?—A. D. G. Moorer and Harrison Coleman.

Q. To what political party did these parties belong?—A. Harrison Coleman was a Republican, and myself and D. G. Moorer were Democrats.

Q. What time on the morning of November the 6th, 1888, did you open the polls?—A. It was a little after 8 o'clock.

Q. How long did you continue to hold open the polls, and when did you close the polls?—A. We held it open from the opening to the usual hour of closing; I think it was 5 o'clock.

Q. Did you make the returns of the votes cast there that day, and to what offices did you deliver the returns?—A. We did, and delivered them to the bailiff.

(The witness was handed a paper supposed to be a certificate or returns of the election, and was asked to look at this certificate and state if it is a correct copy of the certificate or returns; and also state how many votes were cast for L. W Turpin for a Representative to the Fifty-first Congress, and how many for J. V. McDuffie as Representative to Fifty-first Congress.)

A. It is a correct copy of the returns. There was 26 votes cast there that day, and 26 for Turpin and none for McDuffie.

Q. Do you know of any other persons holding or attempting to hold in that precinct an election on that day?—A. I do.

Q. What time, if you know, did they open the poll or begin to hold their election? Was it before you and your other inspectors had opened your polls?—A. I think it was about 9 o'clock, and after we had opened our polls.

Q. Can you state about how long after you opened your polls?—A. It was about half an hour or three-quarters after we opened.

Q. At what place did they hold their election?—A. In Mr. Youngblood's cotton yard or lot.

Q. At what point did you and your inspectors hold your election?—A. We held it in Youngblood's store, in his office.

P. J. RAST, being called and being sworn, doth depose and saith:

Q. What is your name, your age, and where do you reside, and how long have you resided there?—A. P. J. Rast; my age is forty-six years; I reside in Farmersville beat, No. 5, Lowndes County, Ala.; I have resided there near eleven years.

Q. Did you act as inspector or in any other capacity at your precinct at an election on the 6th day of November, 1888, for electors for President and Vice-President, and Representative in the Fifty-first Congress from this district; if so, in what capacity?—A. I did, as United States supervisor.

Q. Who were the State inspectors of the election that day?—A. J. D. Moorer, jr., D. G. Moorer, and Harrison Coleman.

Q. To what political party do these parties belong?—A. J. D. Moorer, jr., and D. G. Moorer belong to the Democratic party, and I suppose that Harrison Coleman he belongs to the Republican party.

Q. What time on the morning of the election were the polls opened in that beat?—A. Between 8 and 9 o'clock.

Q. How long did you continue to hold open and when did you close the polls?—A. All day and until 5 o'clock in the evening.

(The certificate known as Exhibit 2 was handed to the witness and asked did he see and supervise and look at said exhibit and state whether it is a correct copy of the returns.)

A. It is.

Q. How many votes were cast there that day, and how many were cast for L. W. Turpin, and how many for J. V. McDuffie for Congress?—A. Twenty-six in all, and 26 for L. W. Turpin and none for McDuffie.

Q. What is the usual total vote cast for all political parties at your precinct?—A. About 120.

Q. Do you know of any other persons holding or attempting to hold an election there that day?—A. I know it from information, not from any personal knowledge.

Q. Do you know what time these persons began holding their election; was it before you and the inspectors had opened your polls or after that?—A. I do not; it was after we opened our polls.

Q. Can you state about how long after you opened your polls?—A. I can not.

Q. At what place did they hold their election?—A. In Youngblood's cotton yard.

Q. At what point did you and your crowd hold your election?—A. In shed-room of Youngblood & Co.'s store.

Cross-examination by W. C. GRIFFIN, attorney for contestant:

Q. Can Harrison Coleman, one of the inspectors, read and write?—A. I think not.

Q. Whilst you were in the house where the election was being held were   u in a position to see the parties who were holding the election in the cotton yard?—A. I was not.

Q. Could any of the parties who were engaged in holding the election where you were see those who were holding the election in the cotton yard?—A. They could not without leaving the room.

Q. Where were you that morning from 8 o'clock up to the time that the polls of the election that you participated in were opened?—A. In my own store.

Q. How far was your store from Youngblood's store, where you held the election; and could you see the cotton yard from your store where these other parties held their election, or was it on the other side of the house from you?—A. About 60 to 100 feet from Youngblood's store. The cotton yard was immediately in front and in full view, commencing about 60 feet, the nearest part, and running back 30 or 40 yards.

Q. About how many negroes were there that day?—A. I saw about a dozen there; may have been more.

Redirect:

Was there anybody at the place where they held their election in the cotton and when you left your store that morning to go to your polling place?—A. I saw no one there.

This testimony is not contradicted in any particular by the witnesses for the contestant.

What excuse was there for holding this irregular poll? Upon what ground can it be justified?

Without reason or excuse certain colored Republicans go through the form of receiving the ballots of all who present themselves, without any evidence as to their right to vote, and the majority of the committee count 40 votes for the contestant at this so called polling place.

Conceding all that is claimed by the majority of the committee respecting the other precincts of this county, the vote will stand as follows:

	Turpin.	McDuffie.
County vote as returned	2 131	1,442
Deduct Letohatchie precinct	249	19
	1,882	1,423
Deduct Fort Deposit	60	
	1,822	
Add Letohatchie as counted by majority of committee	20	204
	1,842	1,627
	1,627	
Majority for Turpin	215	

HALE COUNTY.

In this county three precincts, Greensborough, Hollow Square, and Cedarville, are assailed by the majority of the committee in their report.

The vote as returned by the election officers was as follows:

	Turpin.	McDuffie.
Greensborough	577	330
Hollow Square	362	169
Cedarville	364	153
	1,303	652

The vote as returned by the majority of the committee is as follows:

	Turpin.	McDuffie.
Greensborough	210	693
Hollow Square	59	475
Cedarville	27	490
	296	1,658

Greensborough precinct.--At this precinct a colored Republican swears he issued a large number of Republican tickets, and two other colored Republicans swear they took a list of 697 men who said they voted the Republican ticket. This is all the testimony for the contestant.

On behalf of the contestee the following witnesses testified:

First. Joshua Clark, colored Republican inspector. (Record, 547.)

He swears he received every ballot that was voted and saw it put in the ballot-box.

He swears that he saw the ballots counted, and he examined each one to see whether the names were properly called.

He swears that the tickets were fairly and honestly counted and that Turpin received every vote that was returned for him.

Then he testifies as follows:

23. *Q. Do not a great many of the colored people get tickets from the person who issues Republican tickets, and change said tickets for Democratic tickets, and vote the Democratic ticket secretively?—A. Yes, sir.*

24. *Q. Why do a great many of the colored people vote the Democratic ticket secretively?— A. Because they feared to do it, and are 'buked about it by some of the leaders of the colored people.*

25. *Q. Did you see any of the colored people on the 6th day of November, 1888, as they were coming to the polls with one or two tickets in their hands?—A. I seen a good many of the colored people come inside of the court-house and put the ticket that they had in their hand into their pocket, and take one out of their pocket and bring it to me to vote.*

26. *Q. Were the polls held in the court-house?—A. It was.*

27. *Q. About how many colored people did you see, as they came in the court-house, put the ticket that they had in their hands into their pockets and take another ticket out of their pockets?—A. I don't know how many, but reckon I saw fully fifty or a hundred do it.*

28. *Q. Did you watch them to see whether they changed their tickets?—A. No, sir; I was not particularly watching them.*

This witness is unimpeached and his testimony would seem to be con clusive as to the fairness of the election at this precinct.

There was a colored Republican Federal supervisor present and he "agreed that it was done fairly and squarely." (Record, 547.)

Second. Marcellus V. Hill (Record, 400):

1. Q. What is your name, age, where do you reside, and how long have you so resided?—A. Marcellus V. Hill; I am thirty-three years old; I live in beat No. 4, Hale County; have lived there all my life.

2. Q. What is your occupation?—A. Farming.

3. Q. Do you own any property? If so, what?—A. Yes, sir; land and stock; I own 185 acres of land.

4. Q. What race do you belong to?—A. To the colored race.

5. Q. Where were you on the 6th of November, 1888?—A. At Greensboro, at the election.

6. Q. Did you get a ticket from Mathew Morse or Dave Jones on that day; and, if yes, what did you do with it?—A. I got one from Mathew Morse—a Republican ticket—I gave it to Capt. Cad Jones.

7. Q. What ticket did you vote, if any, on that day?—A. I voted the Democratic ticket straight out.

8. Q. Do not a good many of the colored people of your beat get Republican tickets from the person issuing them and then vote the Democratic ticket?—A. They say they did.

 J. Q. Name those whom you heard say that they received a Republican ticket and then voted the Democratic ticket.—A. Tom Hamilton, Mose Hamilton, and Stephen Hamilton. Those are about all I had any talk with about it.

10. Q. Can you read and write?

And further this deponent sayeth not.

This man says he got a ticket from the Republican ticket-holder but voted the straight Democratic ticket, and that many colored men say they got Republican tickets and then voted the Democratic ticket.

Third. C. C. Gewin (Record, 398):

1. Q. What is your name, age, and residence, and how long have you resided there?—A. C. C. Gewin; my age is thirty-eight years; beat No. 4, Greensboro, is my residence, and has been since the 1st of September last.

2. Q. Where were you on the 6th day of last November, 1888?—A. In Greensboro at the election.

3. Q. Did you see Mathew Morse, Dave Jones, and A. B. Hunter on that day; and if so, what were they doing and where were they?—A. I did see them all; they were distributing tickets to the colored people of the beat; they were located about 10 or 15 feet in front of the court-house, a little to the west of the door.

4. Q. Where were the polls held?—A. In the court-house, in the back part of the room.

5. Q. Could the said Morse, Jones, and Hunter see the electors when they handed their ballots to the inspectors?—A. They could not from where they were located.

6. Q. Were Morse, Jones, and Hunter standing in about the same place all day?—A. They were there from the time the polls opened until they closed.

7. Q. Were there not Democratic tickets with L. W. Turpin's name as candidate for Congress on them, on the table where the polls were held?—A. There were there and at several other places in the court-house.

8. Q. Could not the electors to whom Jones, Morse, and Hunter issued tickets have changed them without being seen by Jones, Morse, and Hunter?—A. They could.

9. Q. What office do you hold in this county?—A. Sheriff's office.

10. Q. Is it not your duty as sheriff to appoint the inspectors to hold the election at all the precincts?—A. It is mine, together with the probate judge and the circuit court clerk.

11. Q. From what class of men did you appoint the inspectors at the November election, 1888?—A. We appointed the best men in the Democratic and Republican parties.

12. Q. Who were the inspectors at beat No. 4 on November 6, 1888?—A. W. H. Moore, J. M. Jefferson, and Josh Clark.

13. Q. To what party did these men belong?—A. Moore and Jefferson were known as Democrats and Clark was known as a Republican.

14. Q. Do you know Moore and Jefferson?—A. Yes, sir; I do.

15. Q. Do you know their general reputation in the community in which they live for truth and veracity; and, if yea, is it good or bad?—A. I do; it can't be excelled.

16. Q. Do you know Josh Clark's general reputation in the community in which he lives; and, if so, is it good or bad?—A. I do; it is good.

It appears from this deposition that the Republican ticket-holders were outside of the court-house when the poll was held and could not see the voters after they entered the house; that the Democratic tickets were at various places around the polls and the voters had easy access to them, and that the best men of both parties were appointed inspectors.

Fourth: T. W. DeYampert. (Record, 548).

1. Q. What is your name and age, and where do you reside, and how long have you so resided?—A. My name is T. W. De Yampert; I am fifty-three years of age; I reside in Greensboro, beat No. 4; I have so resided for the last ten years.

2. Q. Where were you on the 6th day of last November?—A. I was in beat No. 4 at the election, and acted, by request of Mr. R. B. Douglas, assistant registrar as registrar for that day.

3. Q. About how many colored electors registered there that day?—A. About seventy-five or eighty.

4. Q. Did you issue any Democratic tickets to the colored electors of said beat on that day?—A. I gave Democratic tickets to all I registered except four or five. I don't now remember more than two or three who said they did not want Democratic tickets.

5. Q. What name was on said tickets as a candidate for Congress from the Fourth district of Alabama?—A. Louis W. Turpin.

6. Q. What did the electors to whom you issued tickets, as before stated, do with said tickets?—A. I am certain and satisfied that some of them voted the said tickets, as they carried them directly from me into the court-house where the ballot-box was. I did not watch all of them, and consequently could not say as to all of them.

Here we find seventy-five or eighty colored voters, except four or five, taking Democratic tickets from one man and some going directly into the court-house with them.

If the majority conclude that because a man took a Republican ticket and then passed into the court-house he necessarily voted the Republican ticket, then why do they not hold that because these men took Democratic tickets and then passed into the court-house they necessarily voted the Democratic ticket? We leave the majority of the committee to ponder over their consistency.

We hold that there is nothing in the records to impeach the returns from this precinct.

Cedarville precinct.—Again we have presented the same idea that colored men necessarily vote the Republican ticket and that the number of Republican votes cast is gauged by the number of Republican tickets issued. Again we find a ticket-holder issuing hundreds of tickets and superintending the recording of the names of the voters, and then watching each voter as he approached the polls and swearing he cast the identical ballot he received from him, the ticket-holder. It is taxing the credulity of any man too much to believe any such unreasonable statement or any such improbable, if not impossible, thing. Common sense and common experience teach us that such statements are false.

But in this instance the falsehood is exposed by direct and positive evidence:

A colored man by the name of Crook was the ticket-holder, and he swears he issued 490 tickets, and that they were voted for McDuffie; that he was standing or sitting in a position from which he could see and did see the tickets he issued voted. He undertakes to give the manner in which many of the voters named approached the polls.

He displays a memory which was never equaled in the history of the world, and we refer to his testimony as a specimen of that relied upon by the majority in this case. ·

That Crook was untruthful, see testimony of D. D. Ward. (Record, 548):

1. Q. What is your name, age, and where do you reside, and how long have you so resided?—A. I am thirty-eight years old; my name is D. W. Ward; I reside in Cedarville, beat No. 7, and have so resided six years.

2. Q. Where were you on the 6th day of last November?—A. I was in Cedarville, Hale County, Ala., beat No. 7.

3. Q. What were you doing there at that time?—A. I was acting as clerk of the election.

4. Q. Was there any one issuing tickets to the colored electors there on that day?—A. There was; Dick Crook issued them.

5. Q. Did said Dick Crook watch every elector to whom he had issued a ticket, to see whether said elector voted the same ticket that he had given them?—A. He did not. From where I was sitting, behind the table, I could just see the top of his hat, because there was a big crowd between Dick Crook and the polls, and it was impossible for him to have watched the said electors or to know what ticket they voted.

6. Q. Was there not a large crowd standing around said Dick Crook during the time he was issuing the tickets?—A. There was a very large crowd standing around him.

7. Q. Was there not also a large crowd standing around the polls waiting for an opportunity to vote?—A. The polls were held on the public road, with ropes stretched around said polls to keep the crowd back, with only one place for the elector to hand in his vote, and there was a large crowd around pulling and scuffling to get their vote.

William H. Locke (Record, 549):

7. Q. Was there any one there on that day issuing tickets to the colored electors ; if yea, who was he?—A. There was ; Dick Crook issued tickets there on that day.

8. Q. Did Dick Crook watch the electors to whom he had given tickets to see if they voted the tickets he had given them?—A. He did not.

9. Q. How do you know that he did not watch the electors to whom he had given tickets to see if they voted the tickets he had given them?—A. I was standing in 4 or 5 feet of him most of the day, and he (Dick Crook) had his back to the polls most of the day.

10. Q. Where were you and Dick Crook sitting at on that day?—A. Within 30 or 40 feet of the polls ; he sitting on one end of a wagon-body and I standing at the other.

11. Q. Was there not a large crowd standing around Dick Crook most of the day?—A. There was.

12. Q. Was it possible for him, with the crowd standing around him, to see whether the electors voted the same tickets he gave him?—A. It was not possible for him to see it.

15. Q. Did the electors, after they had gotten a ticket from Dick Crook, go immediately to the polls?—A. No ; they did not.

Did colored men take Democratic tickets and have access to them?

William H. Locke (Record, 549):

1. Q. What is your name, age, and where do you reside, and how long have you so resided?—A. My name is William H. Locke ; I reside at Cedarville Beat No. 7, Hale County, and I have so resided about twelve years ; I am forty-eight years old.

2. Q. Where were you on the 6th day of November, 1888, and what were you doing?—A. I was at Cedarville, Beat No. 7, where the election was held.

3. Q. What did you do on that day?—A. I acted as assistant registrar.

4. Q. About how many colored electors did you register on that day?—A. About sixty.

5. Q. About how many of those you registered did you give Democratic tickets?—A. I could not say ; I issued about seventy-five tickets, mostly to those whom I registered.

6. Q. Did the tickets that you issued have L. W. Turpin's name on them as a candidate for Congress?—A. Yes, sir.

13. Q. Were there not a great many Democratic tickets on the table where the polls were held?—A. There were.

14. Q. Were there not Democratic tickets lying around the polls in several places?—A. There were.

16. Q. Could not the electors to whom Dick Crook issued tickets have voted some other ticket without his knowledge?—A. Yes.

17. Q. Do not the leading colored people of your beat abuse and vilify any colored man who votes the Democratic ticket publicly?—A. They do.

Was the election fair and the count honest (Record, 550)?

Van Hambright, being called and duly sworn, deposes and says:

1. Q. What is your name, age, and where do you reside, and how long have you so resided?—A. My name is Van Hainbught ; I am forty-seven years old ; I live in Hale County, beat No. 7, commonly called Cedarville beat ; I have so resided for the past twenty-five years.

2. Q. Are you a Democrat or a Republican?—A. I am a Republican.

3. Q. Where were you on the 6th day of November, 1888?—A. I was at Cedarville when the election was held.

4. Q. What were you doing there?—A. I was one of the inspectors of the election.

5. Q. Were you present during the entire day?—A. Yes, sir.

6. Q. Who were the other inspectors?—A. Mr. O'Donnell and Mr. Percy Waller.

7. Q. When did you count the votes or ballots?—A. Immediately after the polls were closed.

8. Q. Were you not present while the votes or ballots were being counted, and did you not assist in counting them?—A. I was present and assisted in counting the ballots.

9. Q. Were not the said ballots honestly and fairly counted as required by law?—A. Yes, sir.

10. Q. Are you a colored man or a white man?—A. I am a colored man.

This is the witness referred to in the report of the majority as "the illiterate colored inspector."

He signs his own name, and there is nothing to indicate that he is an illiterate or ignorant man. He certainly compares most favorably with

Crook, the ticket holder, upon whose testimony the majority lay so much stress, for on page 80 of the record it will be observed Crook could not write, and signed his name Dick (his x mark) Crook.

D. W. Ward (Record, 549).

This witness was one of the clerks at the election and fully corroborates the testimony of Van Hambright, the colored Republican inspector quoted and referred to above.

We sustain the returns from this precinct.

Conceding the other precincts of this county to be as claimed by the committee, the vote will stand:

	Turpin.	McDuffie.
Returned vote...	3, 170	1, 220
Deduct Hollow Square as returned	362	169
	2, 808	1, 051
Add Hollow Square as counted by committee...........................	59	475
	2, 867	1, 526
	1, 526	
Majority for Turpin	1, 341	

WILCOX COUNTY.

Allenton.—The election officers, three in number, two Democrats and one Republican, returned under oath that the number of votes cast at this precinct was 309, of which number Turpin received 242 and McDuffie received 67. The only evidence in the record respecting this precinct is that of I. L. Grace, a colored man and a member of the Republican executive committee, who testifies that he stood between 35 and 40 feet of the polls all day; that he issued to 316 colored men each a ticket with McDuffie's name on it; that he saw the voter deposit his ballot; that three colored men voted for Turpin and between forty and forty-five white voters voted there that day. On this testimony alone the majority set aside the sworn return, and count this precinct, Turpin 27, McDuffie 316. The tickets were not examined, the voters were not examined, and the testimony of the only witness that was examined gives Turpin either 16 or 21 more votes than the committee gives him. The undersigned do not believe that the official return of this precinct should be set aside.

Pine Apple.—The election officers, three in number, two white and one colored, returned under oath that the number of votes cast at this precinct was 381, of which number Turpin received 348 and McDuffie received 33. Two witnesses are examined as to this precinct; one knows nothing except that he saw a list of 211 names said to have voted for McDuffie. The list is not produced. The other testifies that he issued 211 McDuffie tickets to that many colored voters and saw them go to the polls to vote them. On this testimony alone the majority set aside the sworn return of three election officers and count this precinct, Turpin 180, McDuffie 211. Neither the tickets in the box nor the voters who voted were examined. The undersigned do not believe that the official return of this precinct should be set aside.

Clifton.—The election officers, three in number, two Democrats and one Republican, returned under oath that the number of votes cast at this precinct was 215, of which number Turpin received 190, and McDuffie received 25. Frank Black and James Wickes, colored men, swear that

233 votes were polled at the election; that 29 of them were for Turpin, and 204 were for McDuffie. Black issued 204 McDuffie tickets to colored men, and saw them voted. Dunaway, one of the inspectors of the election, swears the return was correct, and that "the votes cast by the electors were the identical votes counted." Holloman swears that neither Black nor Wickes kept any tally-list, that the character of each is bad, and that neither is worthy of credit. On this testimony the majority set aside the sworn return of the election officers and count as cast at this precinct 233 votes, of which they give to Turpin 29 and to McDuffie 204. Neither the tickets in the box nor the voters who voted were examined. The undersigned do not believe that the official return of this precinct should be set aside.

Black's Bluff.—The election officers, three in number, returned under oath that the number of votes cast at this precinct was 251, of which number Turpin received 213 and McDuffie received 38. Ervin and Fisher and Shelbourne testify to the issuing of 205 McDuffie tickets, and aver that number of votes were cast for McDuffie and 33 for Turpin. Davis, colored, swears that a great many colored people voted for Turpin; and Spencer, one of the managers of the election, swears the "votes were counted as cast." On this testimony the majority set aside the sworn return of the election officers, and count as cast at this precinct 238 votes, of which they give Turpin 33 and McDuffie 205. Neither the tickets in the box nor the voters who voted were examined. The undersigned do not believe that the official return of this precinct should be set aside.

Pairie Bluff.—The election officers, two white and one colored, under oath, returned that the number of votes cast at this precinct was 259, of which number Turpin received 245 and McDuffie received 14. Two witnesses, colored men, testify that 254 votes were polled that day; that 241 were for McDuffie and 13 for Turpin; that they distributed tickets, saw the voters go to polling place, and kept list of voters. Palhorn, the colored inspector, swears the election was fairly conducted and the tickets voted correctly counted and returned. McCurdy and Robins, managers of the election, swear the same thing. On this testimony the majority set aside the sworn return of the election officers, decide that only 254 votes were cast, and that of this number Turpin received 13 and McDuffie received 241. Neither the tickets in the box nor the voters were examined. The undersigned do not believe that the official return of the officers at this precinct should be set aside.

Canton.—The election officers, three in number, under oath, returned that the number of votes cast at this precinct was 234, of which Turpin received 223 and McDuffie received 11. One witness, a colored man, swears that 188 votes were cast by colored men for McDuffie, and about twenty-five Democrats voted there that day; witness was 75 yards from polls, and on cross-examination says he can not swear the voters deposited their ballots or that McDuffie received more than 1 vote that day. On this testimony the majority set aside the sworn return of the officers, and count this precinct Turpin 11, McDuffie 188. Neither the tickets in the box nor the voters were examined. The undersigned do not believe the official returns of the managers at this precinct should be set aside.

Geisbend.—The election officers, two Democrats and one Republican, under oath, returned that the number of votes cast at this precinct was 205, of which Turpin received 190 and McDuffie received 15. Two witnesses, colored men, swore that they distributed 192 McDuffie tickets which were voted, and that seven white men voted that day. On this

H. Mis. 137——21

testimony the majority set aside the sworn return of the election officers, and count this precinct Turpin 9, McDuffie 172. Neither the tickets nor the voters were examined. The undersigned do not believe the official returns of the managers at this precinct should be set aside.

Counting the other precincts of this county as claimed by the majority the vote of the county will stand:

	Turpin.	McDuffie.
Returned vote	4,811	607
Deduct:		
Snow Hill	464	105
Bethel	385	15
White Hall	116	26
Boiling Springs	200	42
	1,165	188
	3,646	419
Add vote as counted by committee from—		
Snow Hill	82	445
Bethel	57	343
White Hall	47	84
Boiling Springs	42	200
	228	1,072
	3,874	1,491
Majority for Turpin	1,491	....
	2,383	....

PERRY COUNTY.

Hamburg.—The election officers, two white Democrats and one colored supervisor, under oath returned that the number of votes cast at the precinct was 295, of which Turpin received 212 and McDuffie received 83. J. C. Hamer testifies that he saw issued 256 McDuffie tickets; that he saw the voters with such tickets enter the door of the voting house; that the total vote that day was 257 colored and 44 white; that one colored man he knows voted the Democratic ticket. Benjamin, colored Republican supervisor, swears that everything was regular, and there was no fraud in counting the vote. Bell, the clerk, swears the same thing substantially. On this testimony the majority set aside the sworn return of the election officers and count the vote Turpin 35, McDuffie 256. Neither the tickets nor the voters were examined. The undersigned do not believe the sworn return of this precinct should be set aside.

Marion.—Official return Turpin 697. McDuffie 86. Wilson (page 232) testifies that he issued 583 McDuffie tickets, but can not say they were voted. Matt Boyd (page 299), in his examination in chief, says that 600 McDuffie tickets were issued, and all went straight to the polls and voted except two. He does not say they voted these identical tickets; on cross-examination (page 300); he said he would not swear they did vote them. There was a house that concealed them from view on their way to polls. This is all contestant's evidence as to the number of tickets issued and voted. Nick Stephens (page 226) first swears the poll-box was changed, cross-examination takes this back, and says he knows of no change of box or fraudulent counting of returns. The contestee took the testimony of James Lockhead, inspector (page 439), and J. B. Shivers (page 443), judge of probate. They show that this election was as fairly conducted as possible; that the count was fair, correct, and legal; contradicts Nick Stephens in almost every particular. On this testimony the majority set aside the return and count the vote, Turpin 83, M. Duffie 583. Neither the tickets in the box nor the voters were examined. The undersigned do not believe the sworn returns should be set aside.

Uniontown.—The election officers, two Democrats and one Republican, under oath returned that the vote cast was 201 for Turpin and 2 for McDuffie. The officers at this poll were regularly appointed by the proper officers, opened the polls at the proper time and place, and received all legal votes tendered. The officers properly certified the return; they were properly delivered to the returning board for county and counted.

Another box or poll was opened in a remote part of the town, not the usual place of holding elections, by persons unauthorized so to do, and in this box a number of tickets were deposited, one witness says 953, another 1,153, all for McDuffie. This box was not counted by the returning board, and should not have been; there is no pretense that the regular return was not correctly counted; the majority admit this second box or voting place was not authorized by any law or statute of the State, and the evidence shows that there was no mistake or misapprehension on the part of the voters. It was deliberately done, avowedly for want of confidence in the regularly appointed and acting officials of the election. Under no view of the law or facts can the tickets deposited in this box, even if we knew how many there were, be counted for either party.

The majority count this precinct Turpin, 210, McDuffie, 955, thus including the illegal with the legal return. This can not be done, and the undersigned believe the return as made must stand.

Counting the other precincts as claimed by the majority the vote of this county stands:

	Turpin.	McDuffie.
Returned vote	2,961	650
Deduct Perryville, where returns were not signed	142	41
	2,819	609
	609	
Turpin's majority	2,210	

Let us now consider the action of the majority with regard to the vote in Dallas County.

Martin's Station.—As to this precinct the two witnesses, Ned Petway and Acton Mapping (p. 154), upon whose testimony the majority of the committee rely to change the result of the election, stood from 120 to 150 yards away from the polls, upon a porch of a store on the same side of the street. One other witness, Nathan Stratton (p. 153), the Republican United States supervisor, was in the polling-room, and admitted that he knew nothing of the number of Republican votes cast for McDuffie except as he had been told by the other two witnesses. He testified in one breath that such number was 324, and in the next that Mr. Bamberger, one of the managers, at the close of the election asserted that there were 355. To this remark he said, "That was all right." Ned Petway (p. 146) swears there were issued by him to colored Republicans 324 tickets, and only 324 colored men voted there that day. Stratton says ten of the colored men voted the Democratic ticket. Acton Mappius swears that he don't know whether the voters whose names he placed on his list voted the ticket they got from him. The officers of the election were three white men and two colored men.

Lewis Bamberger (p. 437) testifies that he was an inspector at said election; that there were cast for Turpin 383 votes and for McDuffie 28; that these votes were counted and returned as cast; that the ballot-box was not changed; that the count of the vote was fair, honest, true, and correct, and the return a true statement. He also testified that a person sitting or standing on the porch where Petway and Maffin were could not see the window at which the ballots were received, because there was and is a building between the two places.

J. M. Anderson (p. 560) corroborates Bamberger as to the above statement, and also says that he gave out a good many Democratic tickets to colored voters; names three that he recollects, and says there were fifteen or twenty more.

We think the return should stand.

Pence.—The election at this precinct was held by regularly appointed sworn officers, among whom was one colored man. The returns were correctly made and properly certified. The majority of the committee propose to set it aside upon the testimony. (R. Sanders, p. 152, and as R. Isaac, p. 340). He says he went to the polls to issue Republican tickets; had 250 of them; that Mr. Turpin's name and Mr. McDuffie's name were on them; that he had issued all of them but 31; that he issued them to colored voters. He was 50 yards from voting place. Each voter held his ticket in such a position from the time he received it until he had voted it so that he could see it. There was not anything to obstruct his view, and that he knew these 219 ballots were cast for McDuffie, but he did not know who were the officers of the election. This fair statement of this man's evidence is sufficient to reduce to absurdity the conclusion of the committee to count 219 for McDuffie and 8 for Turpin when only 208 votes were cast at that poll that day.

The contestee took the deposition of William Bell (p. 646), who was registrar, and in no way connected with the conduct of election. He testifies that Richmond Isaac could not see the voters deposit their ballots. He (Isaac) was on one side the house while the polling place was on another, and his vision would have to go round the corner and turn at right angle to see the polls.

This was all the testimony taken by contestant and contestee in relation to this precinct until the testimony in rebuttal was taken by contestant, when he examined C. D. Martin (p. 769), and by him attempts to prove that the ballots were not counted till next day; but he says the box was kept by the inspectors, or one of them, all the time. But no witnesses could be examined, under the law, by contestee, and the contestant at this period could only take testimony in rebuttal. As nothing had been said about it before, this could not be in rebuttal. The committee can not consider this testimony. If considered, it only proves that the strict letter of the law directing an immediate count was not complied with, but no effort is made to show that the inspectors tampered with this box or manipulated the returns, which must stand as the true returns of this precinct.

Liberty Hill.—No election was held at this precinct. There is testimony tending to show that five or six negroes pretended to hold one, but they never pretended to make any return of the same to the sheriff, and the witness Turner (p. 161) did not know how many votes were cast nor how many tickets he issued. After the time for the contestee to take evidence had expired, contestant called a witness, Thomas, who claimed to have been a Federal supervisor at said election and to have made a return to the chief supervisor. It is upon this alleged return the majority of the committee act, yet this return was not produced in evidence; the fair inference is that it could not be, or rather that none such was ever made. Thomas could not remember the name of any other man on the ticket, which he swore he read over 197 times in tallying the vote, and could only remember McDuffie's because he had received newspapers from him since the election and was subpœnaed to testify for him.

Burnsville precinct.—Here contestant claimed 435 votes and admitted 60 for Turpin. The returns give Turpin 475 and McDuffie 22. The majority of the committee give Turpin 60 and McDuffie 288.

The testimony shows that some Republicans claimed to have stolen a ballot-box from a room adjoining the polling-place. No witness who saw such box is called, nor is there any evidence to show whether, in fact, the stolen article was a ballot-box or a hen-coop. We have the usual story of two colored men, one issuing tickets and the other keeping a list of the names, and two others watching the voters to see that the tickets issued were voted; but the other watchers are not put on the witness stand. The list-keeper and issuer are shown to have been where they could not see the polling; the election was legally conducted by officers appointed according to law; and one colored Republican inspector and the colored Republican United States supervisor (page 564) both testify to their close and vigilant attention to the conduct of the election and to the truth and correctness of the count and returns. These witnesses are corroborated by the two white inspectors (Mason, p. 564; Berry, p. 565). But the majority of the committee disregard these facts, and count as above mentioned for McDuffie.

Union.—To set this election aside and count the votes for McDuffie which were cast for Turpin, the majority of the committee rely on the testimony of Hector Jones and Oscar Moseley. The former claims to have kept a list of the voters to whom he issued Republican tickets, and also of the white Democratic voters, that day, and to have had men to watch that the colored men voted the ticket he gave them. He admits that there were men between him and the polls, but says there were not more than ten at a time. He also watched to see that none changed their tickets, but does not know how any except himself voted. The men he had stationed to see that the voters did not change their tickets were not called as witnesses, except Oscar Moseley, who testifies that the voters could have changed their ballots without his seeing them, and that he did not see any voter at that election deposit his ballot but himself.

Valley Creek.—The majority of the committee changes the result of the election at this precinct, where 401 votes were cast for Turpin and 89 for McDuffie, so as to give the latter 382 votes and the former only 60. This is done upon the testimony of two witnesses as to a count they made, in the face of the fact that there was a Republican who could read on the board of election officers, and the conduct and action of those officers was sustained by the testimony of two witnesses, one of whom was a leading and influential life-long Republican.

Pine Flat.—Three election officers certify under oath that Turpin received 249 votes and McDuffie received 80 votes. The colored inspector

sustains under oath the correctness of the count, and there is no satisfactory evidence impeaching the correctness of the return.

Vernon.—We find that the return from this precinct has not been
successfully assailed.

Dublin.—We find that the return from this precinct has not been successfully assailed.

Elm Bluff.—We find the return from this precinct has not been successfully assailed.

River.—We find the return from this precinct has not been successfully assailed.

Wood Lawn.—Return correct.

Marion Junction.—Return correct.

Old Town.—Return correct.

Counting the other precincts as claimed by the majority (except
Boykins which does not enter into ther eturu), the vote of this county
stands as follows:

	Turpin.	McDuffie.
Returned vote	5, 705	1, 706
Deduct:		
Mitchell's Mill..	30	0
Brown's	235	90
	265	90
	5, 440	1, 616
Add:		
Mitchell's Mill...	0	345
Brown's	16	249
Smiley*	0	86
Chillatche*	0	144
Carlowville*	0	101
	16	925
	5, 456	2, 541
	2, 541	
Turpin's majority..	2, 915	

*Not counted by board.

RECAPITULATION.

County.	Turpin.	McDuffie.
Lowndes County	1, 842	1, 627
Hale County	2, 867	1, 528
Wilcox County...	3, 874	1, 491
Perry County	2, 819	606
Dallas County...	5, 496	2, 541
Total..	16, 878	7, 79
	7, 794	
Turpin's majority	9, 104	

It will thus be seen that conceding to the contestant all that he can
in reason and good conscience claim, there is still a majority against
him of more than 9,000. The majority arrive at quite a different conclusion, but in doing so we respectfully submit—an examination of the record will disclose—that they have disregarded well-established principles
of law and violated rules of evidence, the maintenance of which is es-

tial to the ascertainment of the truth. We submit the following
resolutions in lieu of those offered by the majority:

Resolved, That John V. McDuffie was not elected a Representative
in the Fifty-first Congress from the Fourth Congressional district of
Alabama, and is not entitled to a seat therein.

Resolved, That Louis W. Turpin was duly elected a Representative
in the Fifty-first Congress from the Fourth district of Alabama, and is
entitled to retain his seat.

CHARLES F. CRISP.
CHARLES T. O'FERRALL.
J. H. OUTHWAITE.
LEVI MAISH.
L. W. MOORE.
R. P. C. WILSON.

JAMES R. CHALMERS vs. JAMES B. MORGAN.

SECOND MISSISSIPPI.

Contestant charged intimidation of voters, corrupt manipulation of registration, stuffing and stealing of ballot boxes, and illegal voting. The committee find that fraud in all these forms existed, but as the number of votes affected thereby was not sufficient to overcome the majority returned, the contestee is still entitled to the seat. Mr. Houk made a minority report, contending that a conspiracy is proved which overthrows the *prima facie* of the returns. (See minority report, p. ....) The resolutions presented by the committee were adopted August ...., 1890, by a vote of 115 to 15 (on division, the Speaker "counting a quorum"). The debate will be found on pages 8758 to 8767 of the Record.

(1) Presumption of correctness of returns.

Evidence as to certain boxes can not affect others which are not assailed.

329

REPORT.

JUNE 20, 1890.—Mr. DALZELL, from the Committee on Elections, submitted the following report:

The Committee on Elections, having had under consideration the contested-election case of James R. Chalmers, contestant, *v.* James B. Morgan, contestee, from the Second Congressional district of Mississippi, reports that it is not proven by the record that the contestant was elected, nor that the contestee was not; but it is proven that the election in question was characterized by frauds disgraceful to our civilization, and such as to call for severe animadversion on the part of every honest man.

The election in question was held on the 6th day of November, 1888. The contestant was the Republican nominee for Congress and the contestee the Democratic. The latter was returned as elected by a plurality of 8,161 votes, a plurality at least four times as great as his legal plurality.

The Second Congressional district of Mississippi consists of nine counties, Benton, De Soto, La Fayette, Marshall, Panola, Tallahatchie, Tate, Tippah, and Union. No question is made as to the honesty of the election in the two last named, and no reason has been shown why the honest voters thereof should be disfranchised.

With respect to the other seven counties, there is a number of boxes as to which no testimony was taken, but it may safely be affirmed that in not one of these counties, taken as a whole, was the election an honest one. Fraud in various forms, including intimidation of voters, corrupt manipulation of registration, stuffing and stealing of ballot-boxes, and illegal voting, finds ample illustration in all of them.

If we may judge from the evidence, this state of things is to be accounted for by the existence, in that district, of a different standard of morals from that which is generally accepted as the correct one by communities recognized as moral.

Mr. A. S. Buchanan, a lawyer, a resident of this district, who "attends the circuit and chancery courts in De Soto and Tunica Counties regularly," and who also practices in Memphis, Tenn., was one of the contestee's counsel and also a witness for him. In the course of his cross-examination, he testified thus (Record, p. 837):

Q. As a Mississippi Democrat, which do you think preferable, the triumph of Republicanism or the suppression or partial suppression of negro suffrage?—A. Well, as a Miss. Democrat, I would say that I regard either of those alternatives as a very unfortunate one. I think that anything like wholesale ballot-box stuffing or fraud

331

in elections is almost, if not quite, as greatly to be deplored as Republican rule would be. I hardly know which of the two would be most to be deplored.

Q. Then, don't you think that a little retail ballot-box stuffing here and there in Miss. preferable to Republicanism ?—A. If, as a tax-payer in Miss., the two alternatives were presented to me of being ruined by taxation or having some other fellow besmirch his conscience by ballot-box stuffing, I would not interfere to prevent the success of the Democratic party by that little game on the retail plain. But, if I had to take the oath of office and perjure myself in order to procure the triumph of the Democratic party, I'd let the party go to the devil.

This is Democratic testimony.

On the other hand, Henry Wood, an old, respectable colored man and a Republican, who has labored for his party since he has been free, and has lived on the same place, near Olive Branch, in De Soto County, for forty years, says, in speaking of the men who hold elections:

No moneyed man ain't never around there; they get a few bull-dozers to stand around there; a gentleman never does nothing dirty, but he puts out his money and gets these dirty-handed men to handle dirt for him; he never does nothing dirty himself. (Record, pp. 553 and 554.)

The facts proven with respect to the election are just such as might be expected from the testimony of these two witnesses, except that they show that Mr. Buchanan was understating the situation when he spoke of "the little game" being carried on "on the retail plan."

That these two witnesses were simply making a plain statement in accordance with existing public sentiment in the section of Mississippi in which the Second Congressional district is, will further be apparent by reference to an editorial article which appeared November 15, 1888, in The Ledger, a Democratic paper, published in Tupelo, Miss., which article was in evidence as an exhibit to the deposition of W. H. Gibbs, one of contestant's witnesses. It is as follows:

THE RACE PROBLEM.

The result of the late Presidential election in the South shows very plainly that the negroes are Republicans only through prejudice and hatred toward the white people of this section, who are nearly all Democrats. They have proven conclusively in this election that they are actuated solely by a desire to antagonize the white people—the tax-paying Democrats—among whom they unfortunately live. Their old and flimsy pretext heretofore for being Republicans—that they were fearful that they would be put back into slavery—was completely exploded by the present Democratic administration, which has been more friendly to the negro's interests than the Republicans ever were.

But with all of this, the negroes in this State turned a deaf car to their best interests and voted for Harrison for President, for the sole and express purpose of being in opposition to the white people of the South.

When the race issue has reached this stage it is due time to call a halt. The negroes must remember that the white people—the Democrats—are taxed heavily to provide them with good schools, to educate their children ; they must remember that when in any kind of need they go direct to Democrats every time for help—and rarely fail to secure assistance—and now for them to persistently vote against us is simply going a little too far. They must consider that the Democrats are now running the governmental affairs of Mississippi and the South, and will continue to do so as long as they have a spark of manhood left within them, and it is astonishing to see the negroes stubbornly and vainly fighting the party and people that make the laws under which they live and are governed.

There are a few good and true negro Democrats in Mississippi, but a large majority of them are insolent, turbulent Republicans.

They are actuated firmly by prejudice against the white people, and the time has arrived for us to shut down upon them in some manner. What shall it be ?

The problem thus presented, "How to shut down upon insolent, turbulent Republicans ?" appears to have been effectively solved in the Second Congressional district of Mississippi. Several methods were put in practice, some of which we propose to describe.

One method found to be quite effective was by the organization of *"unterrified* and determined Democrats" into military companies for campaign service. This was the method followed in Hernando, De Soto County, the home of the contestee. We append an abstract from the De Soto Times of Thursday, October 11, 1888, as found on page 238 of the record:

DE SOTO TIMES, THURSDAY, OCTOBER 11, 1888.

[Published every Thursday. W. S. Slade, editor and proprietor. Subscription rates: One copy 1 year, $1.00; one copy 6 months, 60 cents; one copy 3 months, 70 cents.]

ATTENTION! ATTENTION!

HERNANDO, MISS., *Oct.* 8. 1888.

A large and enthusiastic crowd of "unterrified" and determined Democrats assembled at the court-house last night for the purpose of reorganizing the "Old Guard," the "De Soto Blues."

After a few preliminaries a call for volunteers was made, when 54 present enlisted their names as members of the "De Soto Blues." After the enlistments had taken place an election for officers was had with the following result, to wit:

D. M. Slocum, captain.	J. C. Gillespie, 3rd se'gt.
T. W. White, jr., 1st lieu't.	C. C. Kirkland, 4th se'gt.
Geo. Wood, 2d lieu't.	J. C. Ballard, 1st corp'l.
J. H. Johnson, 3rd lieu't.	Oliver Dockery, 2d corp'l.
J. W. Lauderdale, ord. se'gt.	Harry Green, 3rd corp'l.
Stephen Humphreys, 2d se'gt.	W. H. Meriwether, 4th corp'l.

The chair, upon motion, appointed a committee of five, to wit, W. S. Weissinger, E. B. Gwyn, George Wood, J. H. Johnston, and B. Goodman, to receive the names of those desiring to enlist in said company. All recruits will therefore report to either of these gentlemen.

Messrs. Payne, Gwyn, and C. Jones were appointed to select a uniform and report their selection to the company at its meeting at the court-house on Tuesday night, 9th inst., at 7½ o'clock.

Let all attend.

D. M. SLOCUMB, *Pres't.*

E. W. SMITH, *Sec'y.*

According to the testimony of D. M. Slocumb, postmaster at Hernando Court House, and captain of the "Old Guard" of "*unterrified* and determined Democrats," this company was originally organized in an election year, 1876, *reorganized* in 1884, another election year, and *reorganized* again in 1888, another election year. In answer to a question as to how it happened "that the reorganization was just a month or so prior to the election?" he explained (Record, p. 664):

Before elections we have no excitements here or disturbances. They are more likely to occur in campaigns, and, as before stated, to prevent disturbances or violations of law, riots, etc., and reorganizations were made to fill up the deficiencies and to make it effective. * * *

How "effective" such companies are in preventing "disturbances, violations of law, etc.," will be made clear from the further testimony of this same witness, who tells (Record, pp. 664–5) of a miscellaneous shooting into houses and stores in Hernando on the night before the election. He heard the shooting, saw the bullet-holes in the buildings next morning, but when asked——

Did you with your company, or did any officer in Hernando, attempt to stop the shooting that was going on here the night before the election? If so, state who made the effort, and all about it.

He made answer:

I did not, and I don't know that any officer of the company did.

Further proof of the effectiveness of an " Old Guard" of *unterrified*, (hardly, however, corroborative of its gallant captain's evidence), will be found in the testimony of Sowell Newsom, an old gentleman seventy-five years of age, who spoke as follows (Record, p. 1036):

Qu. 10th. Did you vote in the last November election ?—Ans. I did not.

Qu. 11th. Why did you not vote ?—Ans. Judge Morgan had been my attorney and I had been friendly with him and I wished him well, but I couldn't vote for him; the shooting was so heavy Monday night before the election and the next day a good deal, I was afraid to go out the next day because some stray ball might hit me. I intended to vote late in the evening when the time I thought it would be most quiet. I intended to vote for Chalmers that evening, and there was a hard rain that evening. My calculation was that the Republican vote would be throwed out as usual and it would be no good, and in pursuance of my wife's entreaties I didn't go out; she was afraid I might get hit with a stray ball.

Qu. 11th. Please tell what you know about the shooting in Hernando the night before the election.—Ans. I think the shooting commenced on Monday night before the election and continued off and on the whole night; I heard it, and I got news that they were shooting into my store and on the negro houses all around; done by that regular organized company there; I didn't see any shooting, but there were men there who saw and knew who was shooting. I was told by Austin Bell and Perry Martin they saw the men and knew who they were shooting.

Qu. 12th. Did you know of the town marshal of Hernando or of the mayor making any efforts to put a stop to this shooting ?—Ans. I was told by Bell and Martin that the mayor and the marshal was with them while they were shooting at night. I saw Mr. Woods, the marshal, after that night and talked to him about it; he said he didn't do any of the shooting, but admitted to me he was there. Says I why didn't you stop it; he said he couldn't do it. I stated to him that if we had no protection of the officers of the law we were in a bad fix.

Qu. 13th. You speak of the military companies in Hernando. What sort of uniforms did that company wear; did they have military caps and military suits?--Ans. I don't think there was any military company there, but just political; they drilled at moonshine. Mr. Newberry said he was out there and saw them drilling. They wore a kind of a hat that nobody else did'nt wear—a kind of a white hat they called the campaign hat.

This heroic method of " preventing disturbances and violations of law, etc.," in campaign time was not confined to De Soto County. It flourished elsewhere in the district.

J. E. Drake, a United States supervisor, testified (Record, p. 445):

Q. What box do you vote at ?—A. The Sherman box, in Tallahatchie County.

Q. Is the majority of voters at that box colored or white ?—A. The majority is white, I think, but we have very near as many colored as white.

Q. Was there any shooting into the voters at that box on the last election ?—A. Yes, sir.

Q. What position did you occuy there that day ?—A. U. S. supervisor.

Q. Please explain the shooting you speak of. —A. Well, there was about 20 or 30 shots. The men were on a bluff a little above the house, and the voters were about 30 or 40 feet from the house, and the shooting was done in the direction of the men, and one of the balls fell right in front of one of the voters.

Q. Were they white or colored men who did the shooting ?—A. They were white men; hid back on the bluff.

Q. How many times did they shoot—different times ?—A. Twenty or 30 different times they shot.

In Abbeville, La Fayette County, the shooting was postponed until the polls had closed, and seems to have had some bearing upon the count.

We quote from the testimony of J. W. Hines, a United States supervisor (Record, pp. 624-5):

Q. Where do you live, Mr. Hines?—A. Live in La Fayette County, Abbeyville, Miss

Q. Did you vote at the Abbeyville box at the last Nov. election ?—A. Yes, sir.

Q. What position did you hold at that election ?—A. I was U. S. supervisor.

Q. Was there any disturbance at the election at Abbeyville or not ?—A. Yes, sir.

Q. Please begin now and state what occurred that day.—A. Everything seemed to move off smoothly until after we closed the polls; I don't know, suppose it was one or two hours; we were slow counting; there was some firing of pistols or guns near the place where we were holding the election. I asked if the officers of the polls looked into the matter and arrested the parties; I don't know whether they did or not. A few minutes after there were 3 or 4 shots fired through the window and the judge and clerk were seemed to be terribly frightened. I must confess for a moment I was frightened myself. I never hid under no book or anything. I said it was a premeditated thing, and they refused to count there; said they were afraid some of us would get shot, and they said let us move to some other place, and I said all right, and they moved to A. A. Huston & Sons' store, and there we finished the counting. That was the only disturbance, and I have a book here I would like to read and let it go along with my statement.

Q. Did you keep a list of the men who offered their votes there that day?—A. Yes, sir.

Q. How many offered to vote that day?—A. 268.

Q. Were any of those voters refused, and if so, how many?—A. Well, there was 40 colored votes refused and 3 white votes.

Q. Do you know whether any of the colored men whose votes were refused were registered and duly qualified electors?—A. I do, sir; I went to Oxford myself a few days before the election. I think it was a week; can't say exactly how long. I told the colored people of that country that my beat and College Hill beat to meet me at Oxford and I would go and see that they were properly registered. I think there was 18 that appeared on my book here that was there, and I saw them register, that was scratched, that came up to vote, and their names were scratched.

Q. Are you positive that there were only 216 votes polled there that day?—A. I am.

Q. How many votes were counted out when the count was finished?—A. 247.

Q. Did you or not, on the list you kept, designate by any mark the names of those who were refused the privilege of voting?—A. Yes, sir; when they appeared scratched on the book, or when they hadn't had a transfer on our beat, I marked it all the way through, Wm. Long, colored, scratched, and so on; you will find it all the way through there so on through scratched; you will find it all the way through there.

Q. I find in this book a statement written out substantially the same as that which you have just made to which your name is signed; state whether you write and signed that statement.—A. I did.

Q. I ask that that book be marked Exhibit A, and be made a part of the witness' deposition.

Q. Will you state where, in the excitement caused by the firing of the shots on the room and the consequent moving to another place, was there any opportunity for putting other tickets in the ballot-box other than those voted?—A. Well, yes, sir; let me go behind the firing there was made that day been handed in the Democratic judges, and I supposing something, and I was holding the thing down pretty close, I wouldn't leave the box; but it came in a different way than what I expected. There was no shelter on the outside by which bystanders could protect themselves from the rain, and we had the door closed, and they ran against the door, and there was 10 or 15 which crowded around the table, and there were parties waiting and knowing that those shots were going to be fired, I think, and the box were turned over, them that had been counted and those that were on the floor; they were all thrown together, therefore we couldn't; I remarked, "I say, judge, this is an illegal thing; we have got the votes mixed." There were those that had been counted, and those that had not been counted, and we went up to A. A. Houston & Sons to finish the count, and I don't think there was any opportunity while moving to stuff the box; if there was anything done it was done when the box was turned over.

At Oxford the weapon of peaceful warfare was a cannon, which seems to have been used for the purposes of warning in advance against "disturbances, violations of law, riot, etc."

M. A. Montgomery, a lawyer, residing in Oxford, says (Record, p. 593):

Q. Did you hear any cannon fired near the polls before the election and during the election; if so, state all about that as near as you can?—A. On the evening before the election a cannon stood on South street, some distance south of the court house and where the boxes were located—ballot-boxes. The cannon was there.

Q. Was there any firing done there?—A. The cannon was fired on the evening before the election repeatedly. The cannon was removed to the southeast, below the stores, at the southeast of the court-house, because, as I am informed, the firing of the cannon at the place it was before had jarred the business houses and broken some window-lights out. Early on the morning of the election the firing was heard, and continued at intervals until much later in the day.

Q. Did you ever see any printed statements from Congressman John M. Allen as to why the Democrats had fired cannon on election day; if so, please state what it was?—
A. I have heard several persons say that they had seen a printed statement from Mr. Allen to the effect that the cannon is fired on mornings of election in order to give warning to the niggers that there is going to be a fair election.

Not to indulge in further comment on this subject, it will be manifest to any fair-minded man who will read the testimony in this case, that measures were resorted to in many places in the Second Congressional district of Mississippi at the election in question, to terrorize the colored voters and to keep them from the polls, and the record abounds in proof that many of the colored men were prevented by fear from attempting to exercise their right of suffrage. Nor is evidence wanting that this is a favorite method of long standing of "shutting down upon" the Republican voters of this district, which up until 1876, and prior to the inauguration of the "shotgun policy" was a Republican district by a large majority.

The claim that the military company at Hernando was organized to promote the peace is, of course, too transparent to fool even the most credulous. The possibility that such company, openly proclaimed to be constituted of the adherents of one political party only, and styling themselves "unterrified" and "determined," could exist under authority of, and be armed by, the State of Mississippi is a disgrace to that State.

Your committee find that there were other methods pursued in the Second Congressional district of Mississippi "to shut down" upon the Republican voters, which were in contravention of law. Among these were:

The constitution of partisan election boards having no members other than Democrats.

The appointment in many cases of parties on such boards to represent the Republicans who, by reason of ignorance and illiteracy, were not "competent and suitable men."

The unlawful removal of ballot-boxes from the polling-places and from the view of the United States supervisors.

The illegal erasure from the registration list of duly qualified and registered voters, and the refusal to permit them to vote.

The stealing of ballot-boxes.

The election laws of Mississippi, in so far as it is necessary to quote from them for present purposes, prescribe (Code of 1880):

SEC. 105. The books of registration of the electors of the several election districts in each county and the poll-books as heretofore made out shall be delivered by the county board of registration in each county, if not already done, to the clerk of the circuit court of the county, who shall carefully preserve them as records of his office, and the poll-books shall be delivered in time for every election to the commissioners of election, and after the election shall be returned to said clerk. The clerk of the circuit court of each county shall register on the registration books of the election district of the residence of such person any one entitled to be registered as an elector, on his appearing before him and taking and subscribing the oath required by Article 7 and section 3 of the constitution of this State, and printed at the top of the pages of the registration books, which subscription of the oath aforesaid shall be by the person writing his name or mark in the proper column of said book.

SEC. 121. Two months before any general election and any election of Representatives in Congress, and any election of elector of President and Vice-President of the United States, the governor and lieutenant-governor, or president of the senate if the lieutenant-governor is performing the duties of governor, or if there is no lieutenant-governer, and the secretary of state, or a majority of such officers, shall appoint in each county in this State "commissioners of election," to consist of three competent and suitable men, who shall not all be of the same political party, if such men of different political parties can conveniently be had in the county, and who, for good cause, may be removed in the same manner as they are appointed. Before acting, the said commissioners shall severally take the oath of office prescribed by the constitution and file in the office of the chancery clerk of the county, who shall preserve such oaths. While engaged in their duties the said commissioners shall be conservators of the peace, with all the powers and duties of such, in the county in which they are acting. They shall continue in office for one year, unless removed, and until successors are appointed.

SEC. 124. On the last Monday of October preceding a general election and five days before any other, the commissioners of election shall meet at the office of the clerk of the circuit court of the county and carefully revise the registration books of the county and the poll-books of registration of the several precincts, and shall erase therefrom the names of all persons improperly thereon, or who have died, removed, or become disqualified as electors from any cause, and shall register the names of all persons illegally denied. All complaint of a denial of registration may be made to, and be heard and decided by, the commissioners of elections, who shall cause the books of registration to be corrected, if necessary, so as to show the names of all qualified electors in the county, and such books shall be prima facie evidence of the names and number of the qualified electors of the county.

SEC. 125. The clerk of the circuit court shall attend such commissioners, if so requested, and shall furnish them the books of registration and the poll-books, and shall render them all needed assistance of which he is capable in the performance of the duties in revising their lists of qualified electors.

Section 133 is as follows:

Prior to any election the said commissioners of election shall appoint three persons for each election precinct to be inspectors of the election, who shall not all be of the same political party, if suitable persons of different parties are to be had in the election district, and if any person appointed shall fail to attend and serve the inspectors present, if any, may designate one to fill his place, and if such commissioners of election shall fail to make such appointment, and in case if failure of all those appointed to attend, any three qualified electors present when the polls shall be opened may act as inspectors.

Section 136 is in the following words:

All elections by the people of this State shall be by ballot. The poll shall be open by nine o'clock in the morning and be kept open until six o'clock in the evening, and no longer; and every person entitled to vote shall deliver to one of the inspectors, in the presence of the others, a ticket or scroll of paper on which shall be written or printed the names of the persons for whom he intends to vote, which ticket shall be put in the ballot-box, and at the same time the clerks shall take down on separate lists the name of every person voting; and when the election shall be closed the inspectors shall publicly open the box and number the ballots, at the same time reading aloud the names of the persons voted for, which shall be taken down by said clerks in the presence of the inspectors; and if there should be two or more tickets rolled up together, or if any ticket shall contain the names of more persons for office than such elector had a right to vote for, such ballot shall not be counted.

At Lamar, Horn Lake, Nesbitt, Eudora, Olive Branch, College Hill, Looxahoma, and Strayhorn, the election machinery was exclusively in the hands of the Democrats, in express violation of the law which required the inspectors to be "suitable persons of different parties;" or, where there was any pretense made of appointing a Republican the appointee was illiterate and disqualified to perform the duties of his office. And the evidence goes to show that such appointees were expressly selected because of their incompetency.

The law of Congress on this subject is well settled:

The appointment of the managers of election, in fairness and common decency, should be made from opposite political parties. A refusal to do so in the face of a statute directing it to be done may in some cases be evidence of fraud, and it might form an important link in a chain of circumstances tending to establish a conspiracy. (Buchanan vs. Manning, Calkins Report Dig. Elec. Cases, 1880-1882, page 297.)

In many places the ballot-boxes were removed from the presence of the United States supervisor, against his will and without pretense of justification or excuse. Every presumption arises against those guilty of such open and express violations of a statute passed in the interest

H. Mis. 137——22

of pure elections. And where, as in this case, the practice is so common, it is hard to avoid the conclusion that it is the result of concert for a fraudulent purpose.

It is contended upon the part of contestee that a custom prevails in many of the voting places in his district, to adjourn for dinner, and that it is customary to carry off the box at such adjournment. But such custom seems always to involve the taking of the box from the oversight of the United States supervisor, and it is a bad one and not to be tolerated. In many instances this excuse can not be urged in palliation of the offense against the law.

For example: J. C. Clifton was the United States supervisor at **Taylor's** box in Tate County. He testifies (Record, p. 190) that the **box** was carried off from the voting place.

It was carried 2½ or 3 miles, to the house of W. S. Bailey. I followed the **box;** Baily and Pifer drove very fast, and every time I would gain on them Baily's **stepson** would halloo. I overtook the buggy about a half mile from his house, and **rode** along with it from there to the house. When I overtook the buggy I asked **them** what in the hell or what in the thunder are you driving so fast? I won't be positive, but it seemed to me that Pifer was trying to hide something behind his coat; I don't know what it was. On arriving at his house he took his horse out and took him to the barn, where he remained long enough to have fed a dozen horses. During this time the step-son and I remained with the box, which was still in the buggy. It was Baily who went to the barn; Pifer had gone home; Baily staid in the house and got inside of his yard with the box, and I was with him. He turned around to me and says, I haven't invited you here; I don't want you to come any further. I then said to him it was my sworn duty to watch the box. He then said he would put the box down in his passage or porch, whatever you might call it, and I said, "Then I can stand at the gate and watch it;" then, as he started on into his house, he turned round to me and said, "When I get through eating, you can come round the back way, and I will give you something to eat."

This box was subsequently stolen and no returns were made of the election at Taylor's, where the evidence indicates that there was a large Republican majority. The truth is that the stealing of the box is itself persuasive proof that this was the fact.

As to the theft of the box, Clifton says (Record, p. 191):

The box was stolen, but before the box was stolen they came with a light, which was a very small brass lamp. W. S. Baily ordered the peace officers to clear the room and they would proceed to count. I said to W. S. Baily, "That is not lawful; the vote should be counted publicly;" then I proceeded to read the law, and W. S. Baily took the lamp and went about ten feet from the box, set the lamp down on a bench, and got between the light and box, and then when I commenced reading they blew the light out. That was when the box was stolen, and T. A. Hall was sitting by the box when it was stolen.

W. S. Bailey subsequently, within less than a month, shot the supervisor (Clifton) because of the difficulty which grew out of the carrying away of this box.

The only reply made by the contestee with respect to this unblushing outrage on decency is this:

In contestant's notice of contest no mention is made of this box, and no allusion to any fraud or irregularity as it appears in the pleadings. The only witness touching the matter was examined after contestant's time expired, to wit, February 22 (R., p. 191), and on a day not named in any notice. If the box was stolen, then the actual vote was open to proof. If this could not be ascertained, then the box, not the county, should be rejected.

It is to be noted that contestee's counsel attended and cross-examined this witness. Aside from any question as to the value in votes of an election *mis*conducted in this way, it would have been refreshing to have had some explanation of why such things are possible in one of the States of the United States.

Sufficient has been said to show how the United States supervisor's law was violated and the reasons for it. It may be added that the box was carried off at each of the following precincts: Hernando No. 1, Hernando No. 2, Loves, Olive Branch, Senatobia, Sherrods.

The importance to the people of the whole country of a proper observance of the provisions of the Federal statutes with respect to elections has repeatedly been affirmed by Congress and by election committees, both Republican and Democratic.

In the Forty-fifth Congress (Democratic), in the case of Dean *vs.* Fields, the following was said:

Congress, in pursuance of its constitutional power to make regulations as to the times, places, and manner of holding elections for Representatives in Congress, or to alter State regulations on the subjects, enacted the foregoing provisions. They must be held valid and binding on all the States. From the enacting of these provisions (February 28, 1871) they became a part of the election law of the State of Massachusetts, overriding all opposing State statutes made or to be made by the State, and the passage of the State law of April 20, 1876, authorizing an aldermanic count so far as it provided for the taking of the final count of the votes for the Representatives in Congress out of the supervision and scrutiny of the United States supervisors of election was an evasion, if not a nullification, of the federal law.

After Congress had provided for the appointment of two supervisors of election for each voting place, and had required such officers to count the votes for Representative in Congress and to remain with the ballot-boxes until the count was wholly completed and the certificates made out, it is not competent for any State to provide another board of canvassers who may take possession of the ballot-boxes, exclude the federal officers and secretly count the vote and declare a different result. As the counting of the votes is now admitted to be the most important function to be performed in reference to an election, laws relating to this part of the election machinery must be strictly construed and rigidly enforced. The count made by the aldermen was made in secret three or four days after the election, partly in the night time, and the United States supervisors and all other persons, except the three aldermen, were excluded from the room and were not allowed to see what was being done. A count under such circumstances is in derogation of the acts of Congress and of no validity whatever. (Dig. El. Cases 1876 to 1880, page 194.)

The same doctrine was held in the Forty-seventh Congress, which was Republican, in the case of Buchanan *vs.* Manning, as follows:

If it be shown that there was an unlawful interference with the United States supervisors of election, whereby they were prevented from discharging duties which are committed to their hands by the law of Congress, it would undoubtedly be our duty to set aside the election at such precincts. The law of Congress in respect to Congressional elections must be obeyed by the people, and nothing will tend so much to bring this Government into disgrace as to allow its will to be nullified and its officers overawed and prevented from performing their duty.

One of the most sacred duties which this House owes to the people is to see to it that its laws are enforced and obeyed. The supervisors of election are the eyes of this House. Through them it can scrutinize every election, frauds of every kind can be detected, and ballot-box stuffing can be stamped out. (Dig. El. Cases, 1880 to 1882, page 290.)

Still another method of "shutting down upon" Republicans in the Second Congressional district of Mississippi, is illustrated by what took place at Stewart's box in De Soto County.

This testimony is from the mouth of one of contestee's witnesses, R. T. Lamb, who was one of the judges of election at that box (Record, p. 682):

Int. 13. What was proposed to be done with the box after the counting out of the ballots and the result ascertained?—Ans. There were various propositions made as to who should carry the box to Hernando, and no one seemed to want to be bothered with it any longer, as the election was over and the ballots had all been counted, so there was a proposition made that Adam Rice should bring the box to Hernando, as he had been anxious to be with it all the while. He refused to have anything more to do with it, and said that he was satisfied, and the clerks went off and left the box sitting on the table in the room in which Peebles and myself slept that night,

Int. 14. What became of that box ?—Ans. During the night we heard some one in the room, and an alarm was given and we got up and struck a light to see who it was or what it was, and we found the ballot-box gone.

Int. 15. Please state the result of the election at that box.—Ans. My recollection is that it gave the Republicans 73 majority.

The neatness and dispatch with which a ballot-box containing a majority of Republican votes can be stolen, without wrangle or bloodshed, was thus demonstrated. It is hardly necessary to say that no returns were made from that voting place.

Still another peaceable method of "shutting down" upon Republican voters, as practiced in the Second Congressional district of Mississippi, is to have no election at polls where the Republicans are likely to be in the majority. An example of how this can be done is found in what took place at Early Grove box, in Marshall County.

The witness is Dr. A. M. Lyle, who says (Record, p. 187):

I am fifty-tive years old; I am a practicing physician; I have resided in Early Grove thirty-three years.

No election was held at the Early Grove precinct in November, 1888. The judges who were appointed to hold the election would not open the box to receive the votes, under the pretense that no justice was present to qualify them. I pointed out and read from the code the sections empowering one of the judges (in the absence of any one to administer an oath) competent to qualify others oath, to qualify the others and then to be qualified himself by any one of those so qualified to act. This question was debated until about 1 p. m., when the judges, one by one, left the room without informing the electors that no votes would be received, leaving the electors powerless under the law to open the polls.

There were fully one hundred voters present to cast their votes for James R. Chalmers, for Congress, seventy colored voters, and about thirty whites.

There is a majority anti-Democratic at this box when fairly counted.

For the last ten years the custom of the Early Grove box has been to open the polls when the chances indicated a Democratic majority, or the majority would be counted for that party, and if the indications pointed to a majority being cast against the Democratic, not to open the polls; or if open, and counted, and the majority found to be anti-Democratic, not to send the box up to the county court-house.

But even when elections are held, votes may be so manipulated as to control the majority for the party desired, irrespective of the party for whom the votes may have been cast. This is illustrated by what took place at Batesville, in Panola County.

There the United States supervisor was a lawyer by the name of L. B. Lester. According to his testimony (and there is no contradiction of it) the election was conducted in the most fraudulent manner. Men entitled to vote were refused upon the ground that their names were not on the registration list, when in point of fact they had been on such list and illegally stricken therefrom. But, in addition, the box was so placed by the election officers as to prevent the supervisor from seeing whether tickets were properly placed therein. The tickets were manipulated by one T. J. Mabry, one of the judges of the election, and in such a manner as to change a Republican majority into a Democratic.

Lester's testimony is important, and we quote:

Q. Will you please state your position in regard to the ballot-box and the other officers of the election on that day? State whether there was any change made in the position of the box and of the officers during the day. State fully.—A. There was a change made at noon, sir. In the morning I had a position where I could see everything. By the change made at noon I could see nothing comparatively.

Q. Which one of the judges of election on that day received the tickets from the hands of the voters?—A. A colored man by the name of Dailey Knox.

Q. Which one of the judges placed the tickets in the box?—A. Mr. T. J. Mabry.

Q. What were the politics, respectively, of those two men?—A. I couldn't tell you Mr. Mabry's politics, sir; he was a stranger in our county.

Q. Do you know which party he was representing there that day as inspector of the election?—A. Democratic party.

Q. When the transfer was made of the tickets from the hands of Dailey Knox, the negro who received the tickets, into the hands T. J. Mabry, who deposited the tickets in the box, could you, or not, see the hands of those two persons from your position?—A. I could see the tickets pass from Knox to Mabry.

Q. All day?—A. Yes, sir; all day.

Q. Could you see Mabry's hand, or not, all the time while the ticket was being transferred in it from Knox's hand to the box?—A. No, sir.

Q. Did you notice anything that day which led you to believe there was any change of tickets being made after they left Knox's hands before being deposited? -A. All the indications pointed to something, sir; I couldn't tell what. He had an opportunity of changing them, because he put his hands right behind the box every time.

Q. At whose suggestion was the change in the position of the officers of the election and of the furniture in the room where the election was being held made?—A. Made by Mr. Stone, one of the inspectors of election.

Q. What were the politics of Mr. Stone?—A. Democrat.

Q. How often has Mr Stone been an inspector of election there?—A. Well, sir, I don't know that he's been more than about once or twice before; don't remember, though

Q. Did you notice whether there was anything wrong with the registration books that day; if so, state what?—A. Well, there was about 60 names scratched off the book, sir, that applied to vote.

Q. Did you know any of the persons whose names were scratched off?—A. Yes, sir; several of them.

Q. Did you know whether they were legally qualified voters, except as to registration, of the Batesville precinct?—A. All those that I know, sir, had been voting there all the time for the last eight or ten years.

Q. What was the reason given why they were refused to vote?—A. Because their names were scratched on the poll-book, sir.

Q. Was it or not stated that some of them were dead, marked dead when they came up?—A. There was sixteen marked dead on the poll-book, sir, that applied.

Q. Were any of those persons marked dead well known in and around Batesville or not?—A. Yes, sir; there was some old colored men that's been living there all their lives.

Q. Did you, or not, see the books, or merely hear the judge's remark their names were marked?—A. I took the judge's word for it. He called them out. I couldn't see the books at all.

Q. What was the relative number of white and colored men voting there that day?—A. Nearly four to one, sir.

Q. In whose favor?—A. Colored.

Q. There has been a good deal of testimony to the effect that a great many negroes have left that part of Panola County in the vicinity of Batesville. Do you know anything of that?—A. Yes, sir; there's been a good many left there in the last three or four years, but a good many come in too, sir.

Q. Have you heard any remark made by any man in a position to know whereof he spoke in regard to the number of colored people who had moved in there?

(Objected to on the ground that the question calls for an answer founded upon hearsay.)

A. Well, Captain Knox told me—he's our assessor, sir—that there were about as many colored voters now as there were three or four years ago.

Q. Is it or not a fact that the assessor and sheriff, in his capacity as tax-collector, would be the best witnesses as to the number of colored voters in that county?—A. I should think so, sir; they have the list.

This testimony is sufficient to give rise to a strong presumption that fraud was committed at the Batesville box. But presumption ripens into certainty when we come to consider the testimony of H. C. Worsham, which is as follows (Record, p. 472):

Q. What is your name, your age, and your occupation?—A. H. C. Worsham; age, 33 years; occupation, farmer.

Q. Where do you reside?—A. My home is in Ripley, Tippah County, Miss.

Q. Did you ever see a man who held the last election at Batesville any time; if so, who was he and where did you see him?—A. I saw one Mr. T. J. Mabry in Memphis on the 11th day of January.

Q. Did you have any conversation with him about the election at Batesville?—A. I did.

Q. Who was with you when you had this conversation with him?—A. Mr. Ash Thomas, from Benton County, Miss., and Mr. Till Williams, from Tippah County.

342 CHALMERS VS. MORGAN.

Q. Where did the conversation occur?—A. It occurred in the back room of a saloon on Second street, if I am not mistaken about that, that Mr. Mabry had been running and that morning had sold out.

Q. What city was that?—A. Memphis, Tenn.

Q. How came you to go there?—A. You told me to go there; that you believed he was one of the judges of the election at Batesville and believed I could get it out of him, if I would go there and approach him right and get a confession that he stuffed the ballot-box at Batesville.

Q. You went there, then, at my instance, to act as a detective?—A. Yes, sir.

Q. State all that occurred.—A. We went to the house and the front door was closed; we went around and in at the side door; told him I wanted a drink of whisky; he said he'd sold out and could't sell whisky. I told him I believed he was a Mississippi man; he said he was. We brought up the question of what the Allens were doing. I told him I didn't think the Aliens were doing much; that they had done but one real-good thing—that was in defeating Stevens in the nomination for Congressman, giving Judge Morgan the nomination; that I thought the Lines did that, and I says to him, "It's not so bad in our county as it is in Panola County; there are but few negroes there and some white people vote the Republican ticket and we don't have to stuff the ballot-box, but we can do it if necessary;" and then he told me he was one of the judges at that election himself, and I asked him how he managed it. He said, before dinner he couldn't work it right, couldn't operate it well, Mr. Lester watched him too close; but after dinner he put the box, he said, back in the corner and got the books between he and Lester, and then he changed the votes to suit himself; and during the conversation I remarks to him: "That box is largely Republican, isn't it?" He says, "Yes, sir." Well, I then asked him how much majority Judge Morgan got there? I disremember what he said to that; I think, though, he said about 200 or more, and just at that time Mr. Williams says to him, he says, "If the election had been fair there, General Chalmers' majority would have been fully 200, would it not?" He said, "Oh, yes."

Worsham's testimony is fully corroborated by that of J. A. Thomas, one of the parties with him when he visited Mabry. Thomas's testimony, on page 166 of the Record, is this:

Ques. No. 1. Mr. Thomas, where do you reside?—Ans. Four miles east of Michigan City, in Benton Co.

Ques. No. 2. When were you in Memphis last, Mr. Thomas?—Ans. About the eleventh and twelfth of January last.

Ques. No. 3. Did you meet H. C. Worsham, Til. Williams, and Gen. Chalmers?—Ans. Yes, sir; I did.

Ques. No. 4. Where did you see those parties?—Ans. At various places in Memphis.

Ques. No. 5. On what days did you remain in Memphis, Mr. Thomas?—Ans. The eleventh and twelfth.

Ques. No. 6. I will ask you, Mr. Thomas, to state, as near as you can, where you and Mr. Worsham and Til. Williams went on the eleventh of January last in Memphis; who we saw, and relate the conversation, as near as you can.—Ans. Well, we went aboard of 2 or 3 steam-boats and talked about various things.

Ques. No. 7. Do you remember the conversation that occurred between H. C. Worsham and Mr. Mabry?—Ans. Yes; I remember the conversation that occurred—the conversation in the port.

Ques. No. 8. I will ask you, Mr. Thomas, to state what that conversation was, as near as you can.—Ans. I went with Mr. Worsham and Mr. Williams to Mr. Mabry's place of business, and the front door was closed, and we went around to the rear of his place of business. There were two young men in the room. Mr. Worsham called for Mr. Mabry. One of the young men answered to that name, and Mr. Worsham introduced himself as a Mississippian; also Mr. Williams and myself. Mr. Mabry asked—Mr. Worsham asked Mr. Mabry how the alliance was progressing in our section of county. Mr. Worsham answered and said it was getting along very well; it had done one good thing—that it had helped Morgan to defeat Stevens for the nomination. Mr. Mabry said he helped the election at Batesville, and that he had been censured for the management of the box; and some one of the party, either Mr. Worsham or Mr. Williams one, asked him how the result of the election was there at Batesville; and he said it was 200 majority for Morgan, and it would have been 200 for Chalmers if he had not fixed it; and Mr. Worsham or Mr. Williams one asked him how he managed to fix; he said they received the votes through a window; the supervisors were outside of the window, and he moved back in the corner so that the supervisor on the outside could not see him; and he notified the colored man that he was managing the business, and for the colored man to attend to his business, that he was managing that business; and Mr.

Williams asked Mr. Mabry if he understood him to say that he managed to give Morgan 200 majority when it otherwise would have been 200 for Chalmers; and he said yes, that is just what he done. This is about all I remember that occurred about Morgan and Chalmers in that conversation.

If the testimony of Lester, Worsham, and Williams is to be believed, a very practicable and effective method of "shutting down upon" the Republicans at the Batesville box was put into execution, and with profitable results.

Each of these witnesses was rigidly cross-examined, but without result as to the truthfulness of his testimony.

If these witnesses were not telling the truth they might easily have been contradicted. No attempt was made to contradict them. On the contrary, the serious charge made by their evidence is met only by abuse of Worsham by contestee's counsel, who calls him a "buck," and charges him with certain supposed-to-be disreputable things. (Contestee's brief, pp. 80–81.) But abuse is not argument, much less evidence, and fails here, as it always fails, to meet the issue.

Quite as disgraceful as the action of Mabry, if not more so, is the mean assertion of contestee's counsel, that because he (counsel) failed to find Mabry in Memphis (and we have nothing but his unsworn statement for that),

The contestant in PERSON placed a man at a saloon on Second street, near Union, *to personate* T. J. Mabry and then sent his man WORSHAM TO WORK UP THE CASE, AND HE DID SO. (Contestee's brief, p. 86.)

The italics and capitals are copied from contestee's brief. They were not needed to add emphasis to the assertion. The contemptible meanness of it would have made it impossible for any fair-minded man to have overlooked it.

At East Holly Springs, Marshall County, the United States supervisor testifies from a list that he kept that 201 Republican votes were cast, while the returns show only 93. He further testifies that he saw one of the judges

shake his sleeves and drop tickets out of his sleeve. I couldn't see what he done with the tickets; he got them away in such a way I couldn't see what he done with them; he had a pair of big cuffs on, and they rattled down his sleeve.

This testimony is uncontradicted.

Your committee have no doubt as to what the judge did with the tickets dropped from his sleeve.

At Springport, in Panola County, where the person appointed Republican inspector could neither read nor write, Manuel Jones testified (Record, p. 444) as follows:

Q. Were you at the Springport box at the last election for Congressman?—A. Yes, sir; I was there.
Q. What ticket did you try to vote?—A. Republican ticket.
Q. State now what you saw done with your ticket when you handed it in at the window?—A. Well, when I handed in the ticket at the window he took my ticket in his right hand—he was a white man—and he was standing between me and the box, the box was behind him, and when he took my ticket and turned around and put his right hand in his pocket until he got most to the box, and he put his left hand into his left pocket and then brought his left hand up to his right hand, and then with his right hand put a ticket in the box.
Q. Was anything said at the time by any one present?—A. There was a man standing behind me who said, "There, he changed that ticket sure; that makes the fifth that has been changed to-day." I didn't think he had made the exchange until the fellow said that word, and then I watched after that to see if he would change another one, and he changed another one in the same way.

This testimony is uncontradicted.

There is no doubt in the minds of your committee, from the evidence presented in this record, that immense frauds were practiced in this Congressional district by the simple device of unlawfully striking names from the registry list, and then refusing to receive votes because of alleged want of registration.

It would be tedious to go through the election districts in detail and to quote the uncontradicted evidence of witnesses to the effect that they were duly registered prior to election day, but unregistered on that day.

A sample illustration of this sort of fraud is to be found in the evidence as to the South Oxford box, in La Fayette County.

L. N. Word, who had been appointed United States supervisor for the South Oxford box, was in the office of the circuit clerk, a Democrat and the custodian of the registration and poll-books, on the Saturday before the election of Tuesday, and witnessed the following scene : The poll-books were being delivered to messengers to be carried to the various polling places in the county. Lem S. Dillard had charge of the dispatching of the books and boxes and selected the messengers. During this time Word was looking over the various poll-books to see if his own and several of his neighbors' names were properly registered, and found everything all right. He heard Dillard say that " we (the Democratic boys) will give Morgan 4,000 majority over Chalmers."

Word was at the South Oxford box on the day of the election, and 179 colored Republicans whom he knew to have been voting there for a long time and many of whose names he had seen properly registered on the poll books on the Saturday before, were not allowed to vote because their names had been scratched off. The witness himself was not allowed to vote and was told he was marked dead.

The testimony of Word is material and we therefore quote it at length :

Q Where do you live ?—A. In La Fayette County, in the State of Miss., in the Second Congressional district.

Q. The post-office address is Oxford ?—A. Oxford, Miss., sir.

Q. How long have you lived there ?—A. I was born and raised there, sir.

Q. What position did you occupy at the last election at Oxford ?—A. U. S. supervisor.

Q. I believe there are two boxes there, are there not ?—A. Yes, sir; north and south.

Q. Of which box were you supervisor ?—A. South box.

Q. Did you vote that day ?—A. No, sir.

Q. Why ?—A. My name had been erased on the poll-book.

Q. State whether or not you had been properly registered.—A. Yes, sir; I had.

Q. State whether previous to the election you had examined the poll-book to see whether your name was properly registered and when that examination was made, if at all.—A. It was my duty as supervisor to supervise the registration books as much so as the election ; I had the utmost confidence in the board of registers, at least the majority of them, and I didn't attend their meetings regularly. I were there 3 days or a part of 3 days while they were in session. I think, sir, it was on Wednesday that I examined the Oxford south book to ascertain if any of my neighbors, their names had been erased, and in looking over that poll-book I came across my own name, and names of ten or 15 that lived right in my immediate neighborhood and found them correctly registered. That was on Wednesday before the election on Tuesday.

Q. State whether any other of the names you examined besides your own on that Wednesday before the election were found erased on the day of the election.—A. Yes, sir; there were a great many names that I can't call the names to memory now, only a few of them, probably, or 15 that is right in my immediate neighborhood.

Q. State whether or not you know those men to be voters.—A. Yes, sir; I do.

Q. And at the south box ?—A. At the south box.

Q. At Oxford ?—A. At Oxford.

Q. How many colored men voted at your box that day ?—A. Well, sir; there were 8.

Q. How many offered to vote ?—A. There was—I can give you the round numbers applied to vote; it was 405, applied to vote—that is whites and colored. Out of that number there were 214 voted. There was about 112 that applied to vote that their names could not be found on the poll-book, and the balance that applied, their names had been erased.

Q. Was the number, or rather the names, of those who had been erased from the poll-book colored or white people?—A. They were colored people.

Q. Did you keep a list of that number of colored people that offered to vote that day and were refused?—A. Yes, sir; I kept a list of every man that applied, white and black, and on my book where he was allowed to vote I put it " voted," and where his name could not be found on the poll-book I put it "his name not found."

Q. When you say his name could not be found, do you mean that no name had appeared there or that it had been scratched off?—A. No name appeared there at all.

Q. How do you say your name was marked on the list?—A. My name on the poll-book it was U. N. Word, and it had been erased.

Q. Isn't it the habit there to mark dead, removed, &c.?—A. Yes, sir.

Q. What did they have on your name?—A. Well, I didn't see it dead there, but they said, L. N. Word, dead.

Q. Who said that?—A. It was one of the clerks or judges that had the poll-book.

Q. What became of that poll-book in which you had the names of those who had applied to vote and were refused?—A. We had no dinner that day and supper was brought in and we were all eager to get something to eat. We were hungry and I tried to get my book in my pocket. It was too large; I couldn't get it there. I turned around and laid it on the mantel board and proceeded to help them set the table. I suppose I was doing that about 5 or 10 minutes, and thought of my book and looked around and it was gone.

Q. Have you ever seen that book since?—A. No, sir; I have not.

Q. Did you make any effort to secure the information which that book contained?—A. Yes, sir.

Q. State what they were?—A. There was another supervisor there that set to my right and he had never acted as supervisor before and they got along very fast and he couldn't keep up, and he did his copying from my book, and after my book was missing I applied to him for his book to get a copy, as it corresponded with mine, and he says that I can't let you have it now, but will let you have it in the morning. I told him that I would only keep it a few minutes, in order to get a copy from it, and he said, well, he'd let me have it in the morning. I told him not to let any one have it; I wanted a copy of it; and he said he would not, and when he left the room he folded it up and put it in his side vest pocket. Next morning I met him on the street and asked him for it, and he said some one stole it out of his pocket or he'd lost it; he didn't know what had become of it.

Q. I don't exactly understand whether you have stated as near as you are able the number of colored men who applied to vote at the South Oxford box whose names had been erased?—A. Well, if you will give me a pencil I can make the calculation and state exactly. They were 179 that applied to vote and was rejected.

Q. In my question I ment to ask you whether the men had been refused because of their names being scratched off?—A. Yes, sir; that was the cause.

Q. Did you know any considerable number of the voters?—A. I did, sir; know the biggest part of them.

Q. Were they Rep. or Dem. voters?—A. They were Rep. voters, sir.

Q. How long had they been voting there?—A. Some of them were old men, some of them middle-aged, some young men, and it was their first attempt to vote.

Q. Where had they lived?—A. They had lived there. Some had just become of age, and some had been voting there ever since they had been free.

Q. Did you examine any other poll-book in the county of La Fayette except the South Oxford box?—A. Yes, sir; I did.

Q. What one?—A. I examined—made a partial examination of the Abbeville book.

Q. When?—A. On Saturday before the election on Tuesday.

Q. When was the next time you saw that book and examined it?—A. In the grand-jury room.

Q. State the difference between the condition of the book, so far as you examined it, of the Saturday before the election in Nov. and when you examined it after the election before the grand jury.—A. Well, I examined the book from the letter A down to the letter K. My intention was to ascertain how many names had been erased on that poll-book from a to Z. I was interrupted by a voter coming in and claiming that he had voted for a number of year sat Abbeville, and the last time that he had applied to vote there they said that his name was erased, and I only examined down to the letter K. I found 200 names had been erased down to that letter.

Q. That was on the Saturday before the election?—A. Yes, sir; and after the election, when I examined that book before the Federal grand jury, I found 223 names had been erased down to the letter K.

Q. Have you examined the Oxford books—poll-books of the two Oxford boxes since the election?—A. I have not, sir.

Q. Why have you not?—A. I applied to the clerk to examine those books and he stated that he had received a notice from Gen. Chalmers that he would want those books and he had decided that he would let no one have them until he wanted them, and after talking the matter over he agreed to let me examine those books, and—well, he partially agreed. I then applied to him again and asked him his final answer, as to whether he would let me see those books or not; he said yes, he reckoned so. "How long will you be in examining those books," I told him I was unable to say. "When do you want to examine those books?" That was last Friday. I told him that I would want to examine that book the next day, Saturday. He says, "I will be busy Saturday and I can't go to my office;" well, says I, "Monday or Tuesday or Wednesday;" well, he says, "If I am not busy I will go with you to the office." On Tuesday I was there and asked for him, and he was out at the hotel looking at some goods. I went to his office; he was not there, and I did not apply any more; I had called there repeatedly, and I didn't care to go any more.

Q. At what did he say he would be busy?—A. He's a merchant there, and he said he would be busy at the store.

Q. When you went to him on last Friday did you tell him at whose instance you went there to examine those books?—A. No, sir; I told him that I come to know his final answer as to whether he would let me examine those books or not.

Q. Well, at whose instance did you go and make that request?—A. I went at the instance of Gen. Chalmers.

Q. On the Saturday evening before the election, when you were examining those books while you were in the office of the circuit clerk, did you hear any conversation as to sending out the poll-books to the different precincts?—A. Yes, sir.

Q. I'll ask you, then, to state fully all that occurred in that conversation.—A. Well, sir, one of the commissioners remarks—think it was Haywood Stockard, that is the best of my recollection; Haywood Stockard said that—it seems that they had to go by the dictation of L. S. Dillard as to who should be messengers in carrying out those boxes, and he said that there was one there that either had written a note to him from Abbeville to come and get the box, or they had sent him word, and he said, "Mr. Dillard come in with Mr. Bucknear," and said that Mr. Bucknear must carry that box, and while I were in there examining that book, and this colored man come in to see if his name was properly registered, Haywood Stockard, one of the commissioners, went out. They had 4 or 5 congregated in the clerk's office; he came back with some cigars in his hand; Mr Dillard and Mr. Bucknear with him; he gave the cigars to Mr. Both Stowers, and he said that Mr. Bucknear was ready to take that box, and this old man that came in there to see if his name was properly registered, his name could not be found, but his son's name could be, and Mr. Bucknear left the room with the box. Mr. R. J. Stowers said in louder than an ordinary conversation that if this man didn't get to vote he was going to raise hell about it; that was as Mr. Bucknear was leaving the room with the box; spoke it louder than an ordinary conversation, and Mr. Bucknear left with the box. I still stayed at the table, and Mr. Dillard, who seemed to have been under the influence of whiskey, sat on the table, and said: "Boys, how much majority must we give Morgan in this county?" No one made any answer, and he answered it himself and said about 4,000.

Q. Who is L. Dillard?—A. He is postmaster at Oxford, Miss.

Q. Is he the same man that sent that famous telegram, "What is the latest; we are holding the county"?—A. Yes, sir.

Q. Who is R. J. Stowers?—A. Editor of the Oxford Globe, a Democratic paper. That paper has been started, though, in the last two or three weeks. He is a lawyer by profession, and a member of the legislature from our county.

Q. You say one of the commissioners remarked that Mr. Dillard had control of this, and whoever he brought in to take the poll-books must have them?—A. Yes, sir; it seems that he had control of them.

Q. Well, did it seem so in fact?—A. Every time I was there, and there was a box went out, Mr. Dillard brought in the messenger to carry it. I was present when the College Hill box was sent out; Mr. Dillard brought the men in to carry that box.

Q. Did you have any conversation with these judges of election through the county of La Fayette as to the way they proposed to carry things, and did carry them at the last election?—A. Yes, sir; yes, sir; it was since the election; I were in the back room of Brenner & Wallace's store at Oxford, and we were discussing this erasure, and Mr. McMahon, who was an inspector of the election at College Hill, walked in; I appealed to him, and asked him if he thought it was right. He said that he thought anything was right. He says, "My God, anything is right to keep ahead of the negro." "Well," I said, "there was no negro wanted in this canvass." "That don't make a damn bit of difference; the negroes voted for Chalmers, and, by God, if we can't stuff 'um out, we'll shoot 'um out; we don't give a damn how we get 'um out, but we are going to control 'um." That is his words as near exactly as I can get it; that was the meaning of them.

Q. This box, that you speak of, was that the poll-box in which the ballots were deposited; were the ballots in that box?—A. That was Saturday before the election; on Tuesday there was nothing in the boxes except the poll-book, and probably the Dem. tickets were there; I don't know.

Q. When these men came up at the South Oxford box and offered to vote, and were rejected because their names had been erased, did you ask them any questions in the

presence of the inspectors as to whether they had formerly voted in recent elections?—
A. While I did not ask that question, some of the inspectors did, and they said they had in the railroad election in March.

Q. What was that election about?—A. To vote a subscription to the R. R.

Q. Was that an election at which all the qualified voters under the laws of the State were allowed to vote?—A. Yes, sir.

To this testimony must be added that of the two Democratic commissioners of election, which proves that the poll-books were all right when they left their hands, but so many names had been erased when the books were returned that they were really not the same books.—(Record, pp. 631–955.)

Sufficient has been shown to make certain that the election methods of the Second Congressional district of Mississippi include such as, if continued, must prove destructive of popular government. Their existence calls loudly for relief by law, of such a kind as shall secure to every citizen, without distinction of race or color, his constitutional right of suffrage.

Notwithstanding these frauds, your committee are of opinion that upon the case as presented to them on the record, the proof does not sustain the contestant's claim to an election, nor does it prove that the contestee was not elected.

Applying to the evidence the well-recognized rules of law heretofore recognized by your committee, they have in all cases where satisfied that the integrity of the returns had been successfully impeached, set aside the returns and recounted the vote in accordance with the evidence.

Pursuing this method, your committee find that the contestant was not elected.

In two counties of the nine constituting this Congressional district, in which counties there are twenty-three polling places, the election is conceded to have been fair and honest. In the remaining seven counties there are ninety-seven polling places. The validity of the election is assailed at fifty-five of these, but not successfully, in the opinion of your committee at to exceed twenty-two or twenty-three.

In Benton County, for example, consisting of eleven polling places, only two are assailed, to wit, Michigan City and Lamar. No evidence has been offered which affects the legal presumption of honesty attaching to the nine unassailed boxes. So, again, in Tallahatchie County there are fourteen boxes, only two of which were assailed. This is sufficient to show that the evidence as to the assailed boxes can not affect those unassailed.

In the opinion of your committee, following the rules of law to which they have already given adherence, the conceded fairness of the election in Tippah and Union Counties, and the legal presumption in favor of the unassailed boxes, must save to the sitting member his seat, notwithstanding the fact that glaring and reprehensible frauds were committed in connection with his election.

Upon the case as presented, therefore, your committee feel themselves constrained to recommend the passage of the following resolutions:

Resolved, That James R. Chalmers was not elected a Representative in the Fifty-first Congress from the second Congressional district of Mississippi, and is not entitled to a seat therein.

Resolved, That James B. Morgan was elected a Representative in the Fifty-first Congress from the second Congressional district of Mississippi, and is entitled to retain his seat therein.

Presumption of correctness of returns.

There can be no "legal presumption in favor of the unassailed boxes," in cases where the election, taken as a whole, was not honest.

Boxes to be treated as wholes.

Where it is shown that there was a corrupt conspiracy on the part of county officers of election to have a fraudulent election held throughout the county, and where it is shown that the conspiracy was carried out in a number of precincts of the county, and there is no evidence in regard to the other precincts, the presumption of legality fails as to all the boxes, and the whole county should be thrown out.

349

VIEWS OF MR. HOUK.

Mr. HOUK, from the Committee on Elections, submitted the following minority report:

It is with regret that I find myself compelled to differ from my brethren on the Committee of Elections. and I especially regret to dissent from the able majority report in this case, because in all except its conclusions I most heartily concur, and adopt it as a part of my report.

It begins as follows :

The Committee on Elections having had under consideration the contested election case of James R. Chalmers, contestant, v. James B. Morgan, contestee, from the Second Congressional district of Mississippi, reports that it is not proven by the record that the contestant was elected nor that the contestee was not; but it is proven that the election in question was characterized by frauds disgraceful to our civilization, and such as to call for severe animadversion on the part of every honest man.

The election in question was held on the 6th day of November, 1888. The contestant was the Republican nominee for Congress, and the contestee the Democratic. The latter was returned as elected by a plurality of 8,161 votes, a plurality at least four times as great as his legal plurality.

Again, the report says :

In two counties of the nine constituting this Congressional district, in which counties there are twenty-three polling places, the election is conceded to have been fair and honest. In the remaining seven counties there are ninety-seven polling places. The validity of the election is assailed at fifty-five of these, but not successfully, in the opinion of your committee, as to exceed twenty-two or twenty-three.

This statement shows that at twenty-three boxes out of ninety-seven the committee find fraud enough to reduce the plurality returned for the contestee at least three-fourths, or, to put it in figures, from 8,161 to 2,040. So that by an examination of one-fourth of the boxes three-fourths of the returned plurality is wiped out.

I have examined thirty-eight boxes, where I think the validity of the election is successfully assailed and which wipe out the total returned majority for the contestee, and give a majority to the contestant. It is greatly to be regretted that the majority report did not give at least the names of the boxes which were considered successfully assailed, and those which they did not, so that the House could decide intelligently about the boxes upon which the majority and minority report did not agree. A detailed statement of the boxes which I consider successfully assailed will be hereafter given, together with the testimony as to each box.

The majority report then says:

The Second Congressional district of Mississippi consists of nine counties, Benton, De Soto, La Fayette, Marshall, Panola, Tallahatchie, Tate, Tippah, and Union. No question is made as to the honesty of the election in the two last named, and no reason has been shown why the honest voters thereof should be disfranchised.

With respect to the other seven counties, there is a number of boxes as to which no testimony was taken, but it may safely be affirmed that in not one of these counties, taken as a whole, was the election an honest one. Fraud in various forms, including intimidation of voters, corrupt manipulation of registration, stuffing and stealing of ballot-boxes and illegal voting find ample illustration in all of them.

And concludes as follows:

In the opinion of your committee, following the rules of law to which they have already given adherence, the conceded fairness of the election in Tippah and Union Counties, and the legal presumption in favor of the unassailed boxes, must save to the sitting member his seat, notwithstanding the fact that glaring and reprehensible frauds were committed in connection with his election.

This contains two startling conclusions, from which I am compelled to dissent.

First, I can never agree that there can be any "legal presumption in favor of the unassailed boxes" in the seven counties, where the committee say: "It may be safely affirmed, that in not one of these counties, taken as a whole, was the election an honest one."

Second, I can never agree that two little counties, casting only one-fifth of the vote, shall control seven other counties, casting four-fifths of the vote. There were cast at this election, 19,795 votes for these two candidates and of these 3,520 were cast in the two counties, of Tippah and Union, 16,275 were cast in the other seven counties.

In these seven western counties, where the contest is made, the contestee was returned a plurality of 6,465. Take from this three-fourths of the returned plurality, to wit, 6,121, which the majority report says were fraudulently returned, and it leaves to the contestee in these seven counties a plurality of only 344, where he was returned 6,465. This practically wipes out those seven counties and gives them no voice in the election. To permit him to retain his seat on this state of facts is to sustain the Mississippi plan and allow two little Democratic counties casting 3,520 votes to control the seven Republican counties casting 16,275 votes. I can never agree to this and especially in a State where it is proved that the elections are held by machine rule, which can always maintain its power if the majority report is right, by permitting fair elections in a few white counties, and at a few white boxes where they have a majority, and by utterly corrupting the ballot-boxes where the majority is against them.

The majority report again says:

Sufficient has been shown to make certain that the election methods of the Second Congressional district of Mississippi include such as, if continued, must prove destructive of popular government. Their existence calls loudly for relief by law, of such a kind as shall secure to every citizen, without distinction of race or color, his constitutional right of suffrage.

In this I most heartily concur. But I insist that before we talk about making laws to prevent such outrages in the future, we should deal with the outrages now before us, and put a stop to the further enjoyment of a seat in Congress obtained by election methods which the majority say, "if continued must prove destructive of popular government."

Again the report says:

In many places the ballot-boxes were removed from the presence of the United States supervisor, against his will and without pretence of justification or excuse.

ery presumption arises against those guilty of such open and express violations
of a statute passed in the interest of pure elections. And where, as in this case, the
practice is so common, it is hard to avoid the conclusion that it is the result of concert for a fraudulent purpose.

This is equivalent to saying, if it does not in terms say, they are
morally certain that the contestee was not elected. And the explicit
declaration here made that "every presumption arises against those
guilty of such open and express violations of the statute passed in the
interest of pure elections," completely answers and overturns the
position of the majority in regard to the presumption of verity as to
the unexamined boxes assumed by them in order to save contestee his
seat. The law says that in case of conspiracy the testimony is generally circumstantial. And the supreme court of Mississippi speaking
of circumstantial evidence on a trial for murder, said:

As mathematical certainty is not attainable in such cases, moral certainty is all the
law requires. Even direct testimony, it is said, does not afford grounds of belief of a
higher nature. Evidence which supplies the minds of the jury to this extent constitutes full proof of the fact in question before them. This moral certainty is defined
by Chief-Justice Shaw, in his charge to the jury in the Webster case, to be a certainty that convinces and directs the understanding and satisfies the reason and
judgments of those who are bound to act conscientiously upon it. (James v. The
State, 45 Miss. R., 575.)

Under the law, as I understand it, the facts of this case clearly show
that the contestee was not elected.

Now let us look to the question whether the contestant was elected.
The majority report shows that it "saves to the contestee his seat" by
a plurality of only 2,040, and that it does this on "the legal presumption in favor of the unassailed boxes." The report does not name the
unassailed boxes as they are called. But the names of forty-four boxes
and the votes returned at each are set out in this report, and the majority will admit that they were allowed by them to stand as unassailed,
and that they were not therefore included in the twenty-three boxes
which reduced the plurality of the contestee three-fourths. These boxes
where the contestant had 269 plurality over Manning give to the contestee 2,266 plurality.

Unexamined boxes.

	Morgan.	Chalmers.
Benton County :*		
Hamilton	81	13
Canaan	87	58
Salaam	40	54
Ashland	127	31
Glen's Mill	61	1
Maxey's Store	54	15
Shawnee	46	13
Hickory Flat	81	39
Pott's Camp	28	8
	605	232
De Soto County : †		
Lewisburgh	155	30
Cockrum	122	37
Pleasant Hill	159	90
Lake Cormorant	104	155
	540	312
Marshall County : ‡		
Mount Pleasant	159	151
Banesville	76	87
Oak Grove	68	57
Spring Creek	36	32
Bethlehem	172	24
Well's Store	113	55
	624	400

*Record, page 740.   † Record, page 741.   ‡ Record, page 743.

Unexamined boxes—Continued.

	Morga
Panola County:	
Eureka	1
Knight	
Benson's Mill	
Popes	
Williamson	
Pleasant Grove	1
Pleasant Mount	1
	6
Tate County:	
Evansville	
Arkabutla	2
Palestine	
Poagville	1
Looxahoma	
Tyro	1
Thyatira	1
Independence	1
	9
La Fayette County:	
La Fayette Springs	1
Dallas	
De Lay	
Paris	
Humphrey's Mill	
Taylor	
Orwood	
Clear Creek	
Free Springs	
Sanders	
Alexander	
	8
Total	4, 2
Majority for Morgan	2, 2

Take this from 2,040 left for Morgan and gives majority for Chalmers ....,.......
Add rejected votes ....

    Makes majority for Chalmers ....

    If they be rejected on the general evidence of fraud proved testant is shown to have 226 plurality. And if to this be add votes rejected outside of La Fayette County, because the na voters were unlawfully erased from the poll-books, it gives t testant 606 plurality.

    The minority would be willing right here to submit this ca court in the country with a full assurance of obtaining a jud the facts on which there is a substantial agreement. There i tial agreement that the contestee was returned as elected by a of 6,465 votes in the seven western counties, which, in a fair el largely Republican; that at 23 boxes in these counties 6,1 plurality was found to be fraudulent; that this reduces the turned plurality to 2,040; that in these seven counties "there i of boxes as to which no testimony was taken, but it may affirmed that in not one of these counties, taken as a whol election an honest one;" that at these unexamined boxes th plurality, for the contestee is 2,266; that if they be rejected a plurality for the contestee of 226; that there was a genera ing of Republican voters in this district; that counsel for stopped taking testimony at Hernando to avoid bloodshed counsel at Oxford, on account of the great excitement ther deem it prudent to take testimony at that place; that the testimony at Holly Springs was prevented by the refusal of the Democratic mayor to proceed, after he had agreed to take the testimony; that the contestant exhausted his time and took a large amount of testimony, but was delayed by dilatory cross-examinations by counsel for contestee. On this statement of facts, on which there is a substantial agreement, we confidently ask the judgment of the House in favor of the contestant.

The principle upon which the majority report gives verity to the unexamined boxes is that the precinct is the unit and each must stand or fall by itself. While this is true in Pennsylvania it is not true in Mississippi, where the proof shows a complete election machine.

The State board of election appoints the commissioners of each county. The commissioners can and do disfranchise voters at their will by erasing their names from the poll-books without notice. The commissioners appoint the inspectors, the inspectors appoint the clerks. The clerks are the tools of the inspectors, the inspectors of the commissioners, and the commissioners of the State board, and each does the bidding of his master.

The majority report admits this when it says:

Your committee find that there were other methods pursued in the Second Congressional district of Mississippi "to shut down" upon the Republican voters, which were in contravention of law. Among these were:

The constitution of partisan election boards, having no members other than Democrats.

The appointment in many cases of parties on such boards to represent the Republicans, who, by reason of ignorance and illiteracy were not "competent and suitable men."

The unlawful removal of ballot-boxes from the polling places, and from the view of the United States supervisors.

The illegal erasure from the registration list of duly qualified and registered voters, and the refusal to permit them to vote.

The stealing of ballot-boxes.

With this perfect system established it would be a refinement of legal technics to talk about the precincts being units, or about "a legal presumption in favor of" the unexamined boxes, and more especially when further examination was prevented by obstruction interposed by the friends and agents of the contestee.

The majority report not only fails to give any detailed statement of the boxes considered to be successfully assailed, but fails to state any rule of law which has governed their actions in at least their seeming departure from the rules established in Featherstone v. Cate and Threet v. Clarke.

It makes a very proper and forcible arraignment of the district for fraud, and then, without any figures, asks the House to indorse a conclusion which is apparently in direct conflict with the facts stated and with the reasoning of the report.

The failure to make a detailed statement of the frauds adjudged, leaves the contestant in doubt as to which of his charges have been sustained, leaves the contestee at a disadvantage in preparing a defense, and leaves the House without the specific information it has a right to expect from its committee.

And it leaves the minority uncertain as to which of these thirty-eight boxes adjudged fraudulent by them are included in the twenty-three boxes adjudged by the majority to have been successfully assailed.

This narrows the discussion therefore mainly to the question of law presented as to whether the import of verity shall be given or not to the acts of the election officers in this district. Upon that depends whether the unexamined boxes shall be counted or not, and whether the voters rejected outside of La Fayette County shall be counted or not.

The import of verity given to the acts of officers is a presumption of law arising from the belief that all officers do their duty, and in a community where men respect and obey the law this is a correct presumption. But in a community where those who hold the election believe that it is necessary to preserve white civilization to suppress the negro vote, or a majority composed of negroes and a few whites, and where at every box examined it is found that the election officers have fraudulently accomplished this purpose, the presumption of common law and common sense is that men who believe the same thing, who are in the same organization, who are selected for the same purpose and placed in the same circumstances, will do the same thing. Hence, fraud being found at every box examined, and further investigation being prevented by the acts of the friends of the contestee, the import of verity is taken away from the acts of the officers who made the returns from unexamined boxes and of those who erased the names of voters from the poll books.

To determine this question it is necessary to decide first whether there was or was not any fixed plan or conspiracy in Mississippi to carry the election without regard to the vote.

The evidence in support of an allegation of a conspiracy is generally circumstantial; and it is not necessary to prove any direct concert, or even any meeting of the conspirators, as the usual fact of conspiracy may be collected from the collateral circumstances of the case. Although the common design is the root of the charge, yet it is not necessary to prove that the parties came together and actually agreed in terms to have the common design, and to pursue it by common means, and so to carry it into execution, because in many cases of the most clearly-established conspiracies there are no means of proving any such thing. If, therefore, two persons pursue by their acts the same object, often by the same means, one performing one part of an act, and the other another part of the same act, so as to complete it, with a view to the attainment of the object they were pursuing, the jury are at liberty to draw the conclusion that they have been engaged in a conspiracy to effect that object. Archbold's Cr. Practice, P. L. volume 3, star page 622, note.

The fundamental question in this case is one of law and evidence.

First, as to how far the presumption of verity can sustain returns at boxes not examined for want of time and because of obstacles interposed by the contestee, when fraud is shown at every box examined.

Second, as to how far the testimony of ticket distributors can prove votes, when to guard against fraud, men are selected to issue tickets and take down the names of voters?

Common law is common sense, and a few principles of common sense applied to this case will show beyond dispute that the contestant was elected. The import of verity given to the returns made by election officers is a presumption of law arising from the belief that all officers do their duty, and in a community where law is respected and obeyed this is the correct rule.

But in a community where the party in power believes and openly declares that it is not only justifiable to suppress the negro vote, but that this is essential to preserve their civilization, and where that party, under laws evidently enacted for that purpose by a systematic plan of erasing the names of voters, and appointing all election officers, can make returns to suit themselves, common sense teaches that no import of verity can attach to such returns.

The majority report after speaking of the various frauds in this district says:

If we may judge from the evidence, this state of things is to be accounted for by the existence, in that district, of a different standard of morals from that which is generally accepted as the correct one by communities recognized as moral.

The last report of this committee, in McDuffie *vs.* Turpin, sustains this view of the law as follows:

In considering the evidence with reference to particular precinct returns, it is first necessary to inquire by whom the election was held, in order to determine what weight should be given to the returns. Returns are, as a rule, prima facie evidence of the result; but if the integrity of the inspectors is in any way impeached, either by showing that their character is such as to cast suspicion on their acts, or that their belief is that frauds upon elections are justifiable, or that the manner of their selection was such as to indicate a purpose to procure a false statement of results, then the returns lose much of the weight that would otherwise attach to them. English *vs.* Peele, Forty-eighth Congress. In this case the committee says:

. "When once the taint of fraud or unreliability is attached to the official count its value is gone, and we must look to other sources for better information."

This is true, not only as to one precinct, but as to counties, as was held by the minority report in McDufie *vs.* Davidson, and by the reports of this committee in Featherston *vs.* Cate, and Threet *vs.* Clark, as will hereafter be shown. And this view of the law is fully sustained by the supreme court of Mississippi in the case of Word *vs.* Sykes. The reporter in the statement of the case says:

The petition further alleges that by conspiracy between Sykes and the Democratic executive committee, the State board of commissioners were induced to appoint three Democrats, friends and partisans of Sykes, election commissioners for Monroe County, who appointed Democrats, friends and partisans of Sykes, election officers at each of the voting precincts of the county.

The judge delivering the opinion of the court said:

"No mere omission or irregularity on the part of the returning officers can result in setting aside the certificate. Any practice which may be thought purposely to have been resorted to for influencing the result will have that effect, if those who made the return knew of or sanctioned it. Speaking for myself alone and not for the court, I think that the prima facie presumption of correctness in the certificate fails whenever it is shown affirmatively that as alleged in this case one side only participated in making out the returns and the other side was excluded from conducting the election and making up the count; in such case, to speak more correctly, I think the prima facie presumption of correctness never attaches. We all think that it fails where it is shown that there was any intentional wrong on the part of those who made the count." (Word *vs.* Sykes, 61 Miss. 65, 666–667.)

It will be observed that the judge in his individual opinion fully sustained the report of this committee in the case of Threet *vs.* Clark, and that the whole court say, "Any practice which may be thought purposely to have been resorted to for influencing the result" will vitiate the returns. The only question, then, is in this case, Did the party in power select all the election officers to suit themselves, and deny to the other party officers asked for by them, and was this purposely done to influence the result? That the Republicans were denied any commissioners of election asked for by them, and that this has been done continuously for years, is abundantly proved; is not denied by the contestee in this case, and is admitted in the brief of another contestee from Mississippi. (See Catchings's brief, p. 260.) That the Republicans were denied the inspectors they asked for in De Soto, Tallahatchee, and Tate Counties, and that this has been constantly done for years, will be seen from the extracts of testimony which we will give when we come to speak of these counties separately.

In the case of Threet *vs.* Clark, this committee said:

The committee is of the opinion that where the course is systematically pursued of appointing on the election boards to represent the minority or opposition party persons not indorsed by that party, and as to whose loyalty to the party whose interests they are expected to guard there is a question, or of appointing persons who are unable to read and write, when there would be no difficulty in finding men well qualified in those respects, this ought of itself to be considered evidence of conspiracy to defraud on the part of the election officers. This was clearly a violation of the law on the part of the board.

The language here is strong, clear, and positive, and announces the true rule of law, as sustained by the judge in the case of Word *vs.* Sykes. But the recent report of McDuffie *vs.* Turpin modifies this slightly, as follows:

When the law provides that each of the two political parties shall have representation on the election board of inspectors, it is a provision to prevent dishonest partisans from making false returns; and in such case the appointment of men incompetent to determine whether the return is honest or not to represent the party opposed to the appointing power tends to prove an intent to prevent that watchfulness intended to be secured by the statute, and raises a strong suspicion (if it does not fully prove) of conspiracy to falsify the returns.

What, we would ask, is the practical effect of this modification, and especially what is the practical effect of it in a case like this, where the contestee is returned 8,161 majority, and where the proof taken as confessed by the majority report shows fraud sufficient to reduce that majority to 2,040, and when further proof was prevented by the intimidation of contestant's counsel and other obstructions by the friends of the contestee? It is simply to give to the contestee, instead of the contestant, the benefit of the doubt as to the boxes which could not be reached upon the presumption that the election officers here were unlike their brethren of the same party, where the frauds were clearly proven, upon a presumption of law, when common sense teaches that the proper presumption is that they were all moved by the same impulse, to count out the Republican majority. But assuming that this unfair and illegal appointment of election officers only " raises a strong suspicion (if it does not fully prove) of conspiracy to falsify the returns," this presumption is made full proof by the well-known plans in Mississippi and by the proof made in this case against the contestee himself.

As to the plan in Mississippi, it is clearly shown that the election machinery is entirely in the hands of one party, and that the law makes a fearful engine of fraud when in the hands of men who are determined to carry the election at all hazards. The election commissioners have power and do, without notice, disfranchise all the Republican voters, or as many as they may think necessary, by erasing their names from the poll-books. And the law is purposely framed to perpetrate fraud, because no notice is given to the party who is thus disfranchised. They can and do select men as inspectors who they know have no scruples against making false returns, and they can and do appoint ignorant men to represent the Republican party, and thus can and do carry the election to suit themselves. When all this is done it is proof in itself that it was done with a purpose to effect the result, and to ask further proof would be to ask us to prove an axiomatic fact. And yet the majority of this committee say they can see no evidence of conspiracy. It is well known that there is a majority of 25,000 negro voters in Mississippi, and a number of white Republicans, yet it is equally well known that Democratic officials, with this election machinery, count a majority for the Democrats of from 30,000 to 50,000 at every election. And this is indorsed by every Democratic speaker and Democratic newspaper in Mississippi upon the ground that it is essential to preserve their civilization. This of itself is evidence of a conspiracy in that State.

But, it is unnecessary to look to general proof because the proof of a conspiracy to suppress the negro vote in this district is clearly shown by the declarations of the contestee and his supporters, and by acts done by his supporters in his presence or when he was near at hand. It is proved that in a canvass for a nomination to Congress to recommend himself to the prevailing sentiment, he declared on the stump that he was as much in favor of cheating the negro out of his vote as any other man. (Rec., p. 954.) That in another speech he said that he and others, in 1875, had buckled on their six-shooters, and with clubs in their hands, had knocked down the negro leader at the polls, and he advised this to be done again. (Rec., p. 574.) It is further proved that La Fayette County was given up to be lost to the Democrats one week before the election, and that the contestee was sent there to organize it, and that he was there when the conspiracy was formed and carried out to disfranchise the Republican voters by erasing their names from the poll-books. And it is fair to presume that he was the author of or a participator in this plan, from his previous declarations and from the fact shown in the history of this district that this same outrage was praticed at his home in De Soto County in 1880, for which the election commissioners were tried and convicted in the United States Court. (See Dig. El. 1880 to '82, p. 313.)

It is further proved that at his home a military company, armed with Winchester rifles, was organized for election purposes, and that he was present when a squad of this company was sent to Nesbit's on the day of election to remain during the count, and prevent a riot of the large majority of negroes, who believed they were being falsely counted out.

The troops were telephoned for by Democrats, when if the count was fair the Democrats were in the majority and needed no help from troops. The roof shows 192 negroes and 46 white voters there and the negroes would have had no cause for riot unless they believed their votes were being stolen.

It is further proved that the certified list of voters was destroyed at his home, by one of the Democratic commissioners of election. It is further proved, by his attorney and witness, A. S. Buchanan, that he (Buchanan) believed that Republican rule in Mississippi was worse than ballot-box stuffing; or to use his own language, he says:

I think anything like wholesale ballot-box stuffing, or fraud in elections, is almost, if not quite as greatly to be deplored as Republican rule would be. (Rec., p. 837.)

And one of his inspectors of election, W. W. McMahon, who at College Hill returned 285 for Morgan and 26 for Chalmers, where 281 negroes, and only 30 white men voted, admitted on examination that he did not believe a negro should be allowed to vote. (Rec., p. 962.) But he did not deny the following conversation, which was proved on him by L. N. Word. (Rec., p. 556.)

Q. Did you have any conversation with these judges of election through the county of La Fayette as to the way they proposed to carry things, and did carry them at the last election?—A. Yes, sir; yes, sir; it was since the election; I were in the back room of Brenner & Wallace's store at Oxford, and we were discussing this erasure, and Mr. McMahon, who was an inspector of the election at College Hill, walked in; I appealed to him, and asked him if he thought it was right. He said that he thought anything was right. He says, "My God, anything is right to keep ahead of the negro." "Well," I said, "there was no negro wanted in this canvass." "That don't make a damn bit of difference; the negroes voted for Chalmers, and, by God, if we can't stuff 'um out, we'l shoot 'um out; we don't give a damn how we get 'um out, but we are going to control 'um." That is his words as near exactly as I can get it; that was the meaning of them.

With such declarations of the belief and intentions of the contestee and his supporters in this district, it would be encouraging crime to give the import of verity to returns made in such a district and by such officers at boxes not examined, when the failure to examine them was brought about by the acts of contestee and his friends.

A fair test of the injustice of relying on such a presumption is found in the three counties of La Fayette, Tallahatchie, and Tate, in two of

which, inspectors were denied to Republicans, and in the other, La Fayette, a conspiracy to erase the names of voters from the poll books was
clearly shown. In these counties the contestant is returned but 916
votes, where in 1882 at a reasonably fair election he received 3,808 votes.
In 1882 he had in these counties a majority of 643 over Manning, and
this time Morgan is counted a majority of 3,706 over him. There are .
42 boxes in these three counties, and only 12 could be examined in the
limited time allowed and under the obstructions interposed by the
friends of contestee. But in these 12 boxes fraud enough is uncovered
to add 1,350 votes to Chalmers, and take from Morgan 1,494, making a
change of 2,844. Take this from the returned majority, 3,706, and it
falls to 822. And yet it is said this 822 must be counted for the contestee on the presumption of law that the officers at the unexamined
boxes made honest returns. To do this would be to offer a premium
for fraud in proportion to its magnitude, and "save to the sitting member his seat in Congress," obtained by the suppression of Republican
votes and held by the suppression of testimony.

The minority report in McDuffie vs. Davidson, signed by three members of the majority of this committee, including the chairman, held
that where there was evidence of a conspiracy to carry the election in
four counties out of five, the four should be thrown out, and the contestant seated on the proof in the fifth. In this case there are but three
counties out of nine which were asked to be rejected, and if this is done
the contestant is elected by a large majority, as will be seen hereafter from the discussion of each county separately. But it is now said
that this decision of McDuffie vs. Davidson is wrong; that each box
must be considered separately, and that a whole county can not be
thrown out. If this was true in any other State, it can not be true in
Mississippi, where, as we have said, each county is a unit in the election
machinery, and every box is manipulated at the dictation of the county
commissioners of election, as heretofore stated.

It is manifest that the contestant took his proof and prepared his
case under the well-founded belief that the members who signed that
minority report believed it to be law, and would so hold again, and I
for one stand by it yet. This committee has twice indorsed the doctrines there held as to whole counties at this session. In the case of
Featherstone vs. Cate, the conspiracy to carry the election in Crittenden
County in September, and the procurement of fraudulent ballot-boxes
at that time, was not only held to extend to the whole county, but to
the November election, as a continuing conspiracy because some of
these same boxes were used at some of the precincts. In the case of
Threet vs. Clark, this committee held that the action of the commissioners of election of a whole county in refusing to appoint proper inspectors at each box was in itself evidence of a conspiracy to defraud.
To hold now that a county can not be rejected as a whole, or that all
the boxes in a county can not be tainted by the action of the commissioners who control the machinery of the county, is to reverse the law, as stated in all these cases, and I can not consent to it.

But it is not essential to this case that any county should be thrown
out if the rules laid down in the case of Featherstone vs. Cate are followed, as will be hereafter seen.

The report of McDuffie vs. Turpin begins with a reference to the census of 1880, to show that there are a majority of colored voters in that
district. The contest in this case is made entirely in the seven western
counties of the second district of Mississippi, and, applying the same
rule here, the census shows 2,600 majority of colored voters in these

counties, and the majority report in this case says this was a Republican district until the adoption of the shot-gun policy.

The McDuffie *vs.* Turpin report refers to the history of that district, and gives election returns before the political revolution of 1875, to show that district was then Republican. Applying the same rule here, it is shown that Grant had in these counties a majority of 3,376 in 1872, that Ames had a majority of 3,026 in 1873, and Chalmers had a majority of 3,048 over Manning in 1882. These facts and others in the record show there are a large number of white Republicans in this district. But the contestant here presents another and more recent test of the true vote in three of these seven counties. In De Soto, Marshall, and Tate there were in 1887 hotly contested primary elections for Democratic nominations which necessarily brought out the full Democratic vote, as a nomination meant that the nominee should be counted in, as was shown by the gentleman from Minnesota (Mr. Comstock) in his able speech in the McDuffie case. At these primaries there were only 3,873 Democratic votes, and yet in the same counties the next year the contestee is counted 6,253. And to show that 3,873 was the full Democratic vote of these counties, it is just 386 more votes than Colonel Manning received in the same counties at a fair election.

The report of McDuffie *vs.* Turpin refers to former contested-election cases in that district, to show fraud and a fixed purpose of the Democrats amounting to a conspiracy to defraud. Applying the same rule in this case, all manner of frauds are shown in this district in the case of Buchanan *vs.* Manning. The report in that case, presented by Mr. Thompson, and which was originally adopted as the report of the committee, sums up the frauds in that case as follows, and comparing it with the summary of frauds made in the majority report, it will be seen that most of them are repeated in this case.

(1) The action of the governor and State board, their refusal to allow the opposition party to name any of the election commissioners.

(2) The same action on the part of the county commissions in appointing the precinct inspectors.

(3) The appointment of corrupt and illiterate officers.

(4) The systematic adjournments of the election without sufficient cause.

(5) The premature closing of the registration-books and refusal to register Republican voters, the erasing of names of Republican voters already registered, and the forgery of poll books.

(6) The failure to openly count the vote at the closing of the polls.

(7) The changing of polling places.

(8) The abandonment of ballot-boxes during adjournment, and of their carrying off to private houses during adjournment.

(9) The interference with and exclusion of United States supervisors.

(10) The fact that these practices were in counties having large Republican majorities are conclusive evidence of a conspiracy to defraud.

This being a conspiracy to defraud, there being proof of fraud at a number of precincts, and the illiterate inspectors leaving the door open to unlimited fraud, and there being no proof by contestee of good faith in the election, it must be set aside. (Dig. Elect. Cases 1880 to 1882, page 337.)

The report of McDuffie *vs.* Turpin refers to the suppression of testimony in that case by dilatory cross-examinations as follows:

The printed record discloses another unpardonable attempt to suppress testimony. This attempt was the deliberate act of contestee and his attorneys. Frivolous objections, covering whole pages of the record, and cross-examinations of witnesses which would disgrace a police-court shyster, were the means by which contestee and his attorneys sought to use up the time allowed to contestant in which to take testimony to prove his allegations. This conduct resulted, beyond a reasonable doubt, from a deliberate purpose to suppress as much of contestant's evidence as possible, and prevent a disclourse of the whole truth.

OBSTRUCTIONS TO THE TAKING OF TESTIMONY.

Applying the same rule here, it will be seen that the contestant in this case suffered more from the suppression of testimony by contestee and his friends. At Nesbit's, where there was long and insulting cross-examination of the witnesses, counsel for contestee dared the officer taking testimony to go on at night (Rec., p. 1029). At Hernando, on the very day that counsel for contestant commenced taking testimony, the news came of the assassination of Clayton, which was a fearful warning to contestant and his friends as to what they might expect if they continued to prosecute his contest, and the evidence shows that the appearances of danger were so great that counsel for contestant ceased to take testimony there. (Rec., pp. 164 and 998.)

This was followed by a threatening publication in the Globe, a Democratic paper at Oxford, saying:

If Chalmers came there and did right he would have no trouble, but if he acted as he did in De Soto County, he had better pack his traps and get away. (See Rec., p. 1040.)

Mr. Montgomery, his attorney there, had been removed from a lucrative position as principal of a public school because he had made a Republican speech in Illinois, and he says the excitement against him and Chalmers there was so great that he deemed it imprudent to take testimony there (Rec., p. 593). It is proved that the circuit clerk of Tallahatchie County delayed giving him copies of the precinct returns of that county until it was too late for him to take testimony in that county. Again, his witnesses in La Fayette County were not allowed to examine the registration books that they might compare them with the mutilated poll-books until after they had testified in chief. At Holly Springs he was prevented from taking testimony by the refusal of the Democratic mayor to go on with the testimony on account of the action of the counsel for contestee; and thus, practically, his counsel were driven from the State and compelled to take testimony at Memphis, Tenn., where his witnesses had to be carried by railroad at great expense and loss of time.

In the mean time contestant was confined personally at his home in Sardis, examining into the box at Como, and by the dilatory cross-examination he was held for thirty days in the examination of only two hundred and sixty-nine witnesses from one box, Como. Notwithstanding all these obstructions, thirty-eight out of ninety-seven boxes in the seven western counties were examined into with the result hereinafter given, which shows that he was elected.

REJECTED VOTERS.

In addition to the four hundred and twenty-two voters in La Fayette County, who were disfranchised by having their names erased from the poll-books, there were three hundred and eighty rejected in five counties, Benton, De Soto, Marshall, Panola, and Tate, making eight hundred and two voters rejected, who appeared at their usual place of voting, which shows that they were not dead and had not removed.

Under the law of Mississippi the commissioners of election of each county in a star chamber proceeding can, without notice to any one, erase the names of voters from the registration books if they are dead or removed or convicted of crime, but not otherwise. As they do this without notice to the voter, and upon ex parte statements, if any at all are taken, the only presumption in favor of their action would be that they acted honestly; but when the voters appeared living, and at their usual place of voting, this would certainly overcome any presumption that they were either dead or removed, and when we look to the history of this district the presumption even of honesty is overthrown. In 1880 the commissioners of De Soto County were indicted on two charges (see Digest Election Cases, 1880–'82, pp. 315 and 316); one for making false poll-books, of which they were acquitted, and the other for fraudulently erasing the names of voters from the poll-books, for which they were convicted (see statement of case, 1774, p. 316, and statement of their conviction, p. 313, in same volume quoted above). One of these commissioners, T. A. Dodson, is still a commissioner of that county. (See Rec., p. 741, where his name is signed to the returns.)

The Commissioners of Election in Marshall County were indicted for the same thing and plead guilty (See same volume, case 1995, page 315.) That this was done in Panola also (see same volume, page 310), under registration of voters. Under this statement of the history of these counties, any presumption as to the fairness of the officers in erasing these names is done away with. And yet the majority of the committee refuse to count these votes, on the presumption the officers are presumed to do their duty. The law in failing to provide for any notice to the voter who is disfranchised shows it was intended to be an engine of fraud.

There were rejected as follows:

Michigan City, 7 (Rec., pp. 164, 165).
Hernando Depot, 17 (Rec., p. 180).
Nesbitt's, 10 (Rec., pp. 100, 119 and 134. Names given 1139 and 1145).
Love's, 6 (Rec., p. 380).
East Holly Springs, 20 (Rec., pp. 612, 577 and 588).
West Holly Springs, 23 (Rec., pp. 612, 577, and 588).
Red Banks, 27 (Rec., pp. 635, 1107).
Hudsonville,13 (Rec., pp.638,1100; names given).
Byhalia, 40 (Rec., pp. 615 and 1111; names given).
Watson, 30 (Rec., p. 559).
Wall Hill, 17 (Rec., pp. 623, 1110; names; given).

Waterford, 28 (Rec., pp. 620,621, and 1095 names given).
Chulahoma, 30 (Rec., pp. 619,1103; names given).
Laws Hill, 8 (Rec., pp. 628, 1093; names given).
Springport, 13 (Rec., pp. 442).
Batesville, 61 (Rec., p. 237; names given).
Sherrods, 20 (Rec., p. 188).
North Oxford, 200 (Rec., pp. 562, 563).
South Oxford, 179 (Rec., p. 555).
Abbeville 40 (Rec., pp. 555, 556, and 625).
Total, 802.
422 in La Fayette, 226 in Marshall, 94 in Panola, 33 in De Soto, 20 in Tate, and 7 in Benton.

That these rejected voters all wanted to vote the Republican ticket is demonstrated by their asking for and receiving Republican tickets. That they had been voters was stated by themselves at the time they were rejected. At Holly Springs, Captain Buchanan says, the 43 rejected there were known to him as Republican voters at that poll (Rec., p. 612). At Sherrods, Grayson says the same, and that some of them lived on his place.

At Olive Branch old Henry Wood says he had been marked for dead for three elections, but " riz this time."

Under this testimony the burden of proof would be on those who reject the voters, to prove that they had moved away or died, and not upon the living voter who asked to vote at his usual place to prove that he had not moved away or was not dead.

On this subject the majority report says:

There is no doubt in the minds of your committee, from the evidence presented in this record. that immense frauds were practiced in this Congressional district by the simple device of unlawfully striking names from the registry list and then refusing to receive votes because of the alleged want of registration.

And yet, notwithstanding this declaration, the majority declined to count the 380 voters who were thus rejected outside of La Fayette County.

HOW VOTE PROVED.

As to how far the testimony of the ticket distributors can prove the votes when they are selected to issue tickets and take down the names of voters under a general belief of their party that their votes will not be fairly counted is so clearly shown in the opinion of Hon. H. E. Jackson, United States circuit judge, that we give it in full:

CHARGE TO THE JURY IN THE FAYETTE COUNTY (TENN.) ELECTION CASE.

Hon. Howell E. Jackson, United States circuit judge for Tennessee, Kentucky, Ohio, and Michigan, formerly the Democratic United States Senator from this State, presided at the trial and delivered the charge to the jury in the case of the United States vs. Carpenter et al., the judges of election at Garnett's, fourth district, Fayette County, charged with fraud at the election on November 6, 1888. After some unimportant introductory remarks the judge said:

"Counsel for defendant have   *   *   *   sought to impress upon you that some great and vital question other than the guilt or innocence of the defendants on trial is involved in this suit. This is a mistake, gentlemen of the jury. In the trial and proper disposition of this case upon the evidence, the court nor the jury have anything to do with the race problem or with the question of suffrage. The colored man has been regularly invested with the right of suffrage. The constitution of this State confers the right to vote without restriction upon all male citizens twenty-one years of age who have resided twelve months in the State and six months in the county in which the right of suffrage is exercised. The colored man has the benefit of this constitutional provision; and when he has resided in the State and county the required period he has the same right before the law to cast his vote and have it properly counted that you and I have.

"This trial in no way involves the consideration of the policy or impolicy of conferring this high privilege upon the colored population.

"Fraud can rarely be established by direct testimony, to the precise manner of its accomplishment. Its perpetration does not admit witnesses to the worst act, and it is no part of the judge's province or duty in this case to inquire into or to be satisfied as to the method or plans adopted or employed to accomplish the fraudulent acts charged, if the evidence convinces you beyond a reasonable doubt that they were done or permitted by these defendants or either of them.

    *   *   *   *   *   *

"Several witnesses testified that the voting population of the fourth civil district of Fayette County on November 6, 1888, numbered between 490 and 500, say about 500; that from 80 to 100 of such votes were white and Democrats; that the remainder, numbering about 400, were colored men and Republicans; that on the day of the election there was a large turn out of such voters; that the colored voters present exceeded 300 in number.

"John McGowan, the Republican chairman of the district, testified that there were over 300 colored Republican voters present; that he directed many or most of them to go for their tickets to John C. Reeves, who occupied a position 10 or 20 steps from the voting place, and was distributing Republican tickets to Republican voters; that Reeves's position was in full view of the window at which the ballots were handed in to the election officers; that he saw many of such tickets deposited or handed in to officers holding the election, but can not swear to the exact number that actually voted such Republican ticket. John C. Reeves testified before you that he was present; that he had in his possession Republican tickets, a sample of which is produced in evidence, having on it a full list of Republican candidates from Presidential electors and Congressmen down to State and county officers; that he issued to the colored voters on that day, upon their application for the same, three hundred and twenty-five of these tickets while at the voting place; that on his way home he met four or five other voters going to the polls to whom he gave Republican tickets; the names of two of these voters he finds upon the poll-list at numbers 407 and 409. Reeves further states that he saw over one hundred of them, to whom he gave such tickets, go directly from him to the window where the votes were received and hand them to the officers holding the election.

"He could not swear that they actually deposited the identical tickets received from him, but he saw no change of ticket or change of purpose on the part of the voter after procuring from him the Republican ticket.

"He recognizes and identifies on the poll-list the names of about 100 of such Republican voters.

"Now, gentlemen of the jury, Reeves or McGowen are in no way impeached, nor are their statements in any way contradicted. They stand before you as in every way credible witnesses, and their testimony is entitled to full faith and credit.

"If the case for the prosecution stopped with the testimony of Reeves and McGowen it would present a case of circumstantial evidence as to the vote actually cast having exceeded that which was counted and returned by the election officers and judges. When circumstantial evidence is relied on to convict, as counsel for defendants have urged, it should be of such conclusive character as to exclude every reasonable hypothesis on innocence.

"But the Government's case does not stop with the circumstantial evidence detailed by Reeves and McGowen.

"In addition to their statement, one hundred and eight witnesses have one by one separately testified before you that on the day of said election they got from Reeves Republican tickets; that they each voted such ticket just as it was received from said Reeves without in any way scratching or changing the same. Besides these one hundred and eight witnesses, Allen Dodson states that he voted a straight Republican ticket which he got from Dun Bowlan, which differed somewhat in appearance from those issued by Reeves. With the exception of said Dodson, the other one hundred and eight witnesses came before you and severally state that the ticket which they respectively voted on the 6th of November, 1888, in said fourth district of Fayette County, was received from Reeves; that they each voted such ticket as it was received by them, without change or alteration of any kind; that they handed such tickets to the officer holding the election—many of them stating that defendant Carpenter was the person to whom the ticket was delivered at time of voting. The name of each of these one hundred and eight witnesses, together with that of Allen Dodson, appears upon the poll-list of the election which is introduced as evidence. It is thus shown that these one hundred and nine witnesses actually voted at said election.

"They each identify the kind of ticket they respectively voted by showing from whom they received the same, and that after receiving such ticket they voted it without change or alteration.

"These witnesses are not impeached or any way discredited. They stand before you as credible as any that have testified. They in some instances make mistakes in saying that Harrison's name was on their ticket, and fail to remember other names that were on it. But intelligent witnesses for the defense, like Esquire Mat Rhea, make similar mistakes when they say that Cleveland's name was on the ticket they voted, and also fail to remember the names of the different candidates voted for. This is not material. The controlling fact to be ascertained from the evidence is, did the one hundred and nine witnesses for the prosecution vote the Republican ticket which they received from John C. Reeves?

"The witnesses swore directly and positively to the fact. A fact resting on their own act and within their own knowledge. This is not circumstantial, but positive evidence, and if the witnesses are believed, the fact is established that at least 109 Republican votes were cast at that election in said district. The testimony of these 109 witnesses swearing directly and positively to this fact can not be properly disregarded by the jury, because such witnesses not having been impeached or contradicted, stand before you as credible as any that have testified.

"If the prosecution had simply shown that each one of these witnesses was seen going to the polls with a Republican ticket in his hands which he had received from Reeves with a declaration of his intention to vote such ticket, such facts and acts would have constituted circumstantial evidence, that they voted such ticket; but when the voter in person comes before you as a witness and swears that he put into the ballot-box or handed into officers holding the election the identical ballot that he received from Reeves, that is not circumstantial, but positive testimony, and establishes the fact if the witness is credible; and unless impeached or directly interested in the result, all witnesses are deemed credible.

"The jury should give to such positive testimony its due weight and consideration, and the facts thereby established should be followed to their logical result.

"The jury are not at liberty to infer upon the mere suggestion of counsel that other parties have committed a crime in order to shield defendants from consequences of acts which the evidence tends to establish against them.

"The jury may not indulge in any such presumptions of guilt of other persons not on trial in order to relieve defendants whose guilt or innocence must be found upon the evidence before the jury and from that alone.

"It is further suggested by counsel for the defense that those 109 voters were before or after receiving their Republican tickets bought up, and for a consideration were induced to destroy the tickets received from Reeves and vote Democratic tickets. This suggestion is open to the same observation and objection as the others.

" It is not supported by any testimony; it involves the presumption of a criminal offense committed by some unknown parties upon the mere suggestion of counsel.

" The jury is not warranted in giving any weight to this suggestion. The force of the evidence against defendants whatever it may be, can not be broken by indulging in any such presumption."

This sustains the ruling of this committee in Featherston *v.* Cate, Threet *v.* Clarke, and McDuffie *v.* Turpin. Applying the rules of law thus clearly established, we find the result to be as follows:

GENERAL EVIDENCES OF FRAUD.

Before proceeding to discuss each box, it is well to notice the general evidence of fraud in addition to that so ably stated in the majority report all over the district, which has been a Republican district at every election admitted to be fair.

Commissioners of their own choosing refused to Republicans (Gibbs' testimony).

Have always been refused. This is admitted in Catchings's brief, page 260.

Inspectors of their own choice refused to them in De Soto County. (Bell's testimony, Rec., p. 156). Have continuously been refused. (Haynie, Rec., p. 547; Colonel Jones' testimony, Rec., p. 521; Haynie, Rec., p. 547; Henry Wood, p. 551; T. W. Turner's testimony, Rec. p. 447).

Contestee openly advocated cheating negro voters. (Howry, Rec., p. 954.) Contestee openly advocated violence. (Burton, Rec., p. 574.) Military organization at his home. (Rec., pp. 238 and 664.) Plan admitted to be to obtain tremendous majority. (Rec., p. 655.)

It is proved that a Democratic inspector changed 200 tickets at Bateville, making a difference of 400 at this box. (Rec., pp. 166–168 and 472–474.)

Democratic officers changed 72 tickets at Lamar, making a difference of 144 at this box. (See Brewer's Democratic inspector *ex parte* affidavit, newly discovered evidence, filed January 29, 1890.)

The inspectors were caught changing tickets at East Holly Springs. (Rec., p. 570.)

Inspectors caught changing tickets at Longtown. (Rec., pp. 430 and 435.)

Inspectors caught changing tickets at Springport. (Rec., pp. 442 and 444.)

Inspectors caught changing tickets at Sherman's Creek. (Rec., p. 445.)

Inspectors caught attempting to change at Senatobia. (Rec., pp. 528, 529.)

Inspectors caught attempting to change at Sherrods. (Rec., p. 188.)

Inspectors caught miscounting the votes at West Holly Springs. (Rec., pp. 577, 578.)

Inspectors caught reading Republican as Democratic tickets at Nesbitt's. (Rec., p. 102.)

A marked ticket voted at Hernando Court-House but none counted. (Rec., pp. 151, 156, and 383.)

Five scratched Democratic tickets and one Prohibition ticket with Chalmers for Congress voted at Eudora; none such counted. (Rec., pp. 969 and 970.)

At Hudsonville a marked Republican ticket voted; not counted. (Rec., p. 863.)

At Byhalia three men marked voted who were not present, one who was then sick in bed and died a few days after. (Rec., pp. 616, 622, and list of voters 1,114.)

At Hudsonville seven men not present and non-residents of the State marked voted. (Rec., p. 638 and certified list of voters, not published, but filed with the committee.)

Eight hundred and two living Republicans who came up to vote were rejected as dead or removed.

Ingram's, Stewart's, and Taylor's, large Republican boxes, were stolen.

Early Grove, where there is 100 Republican majority, no election held. (Rec., p. 187.)

Thirty-one more votes than voters at Abbeville. (Rec., p. 625.)

Twenty-one more votes than voters at Graball. (Rec., pp. 448 and 451.)

In the two counties of Tippah and Union, where the election was fair, there were only 1,064 colored voters (see Rec., p. 1), and here Chalmers received 912 votes (see Rec., pp. 747, 748). In the three counties of La Fayette, Tallahatchie, and Tate there are 5,006 colored voters (see Rec., p. 1), and here Chalmers is counted only 916 votes (see Rec., pp. 742, 745, 746). In these three counties, where no election was held, at three Republican boxes in Tallahatchie County, Chalmers had a majority of 643 over Manning (see Rec., p. 733). This time Morgan is counted 3,677 majority over Chalmers (see Rec., pp. 742, 745, 746). In one of these counties, La Fayette, the Republican voters were erased from the poll-books, and in the other two Republican inspectors were denied, and it is insisted that these counties shall be thrown out. Morgan is counted 8,100 majority (see Rec., p. 4). Manning's total vote in the district was 8,749 (Rec., p. 733). That is only 688 votes less than the entire Democratic vote of the district as shown for Manning in 1882. Morgan is counted 13,978, a majority of 5,229 over Manning's vote, and to have obtained this he must have received 5,229 Republican votes against the Republican nominee, when the Republican party was well organized.

INTIMIDATION.

Houses of negroes fired into a Hernando the night before the election. (Rec., p. 157.)

Negroes beaten and houses fired into at Leverett's, and a negro woman shot. (Rec., pp. 1048, 1049.)

Negroes beaten for refusing to join Democratic club at Dogwood Flat. (Rec., p. 1050.)

Voters fired into on day of election at Sherman's Creek. (Rec., pp. 445 and 1053.)

Tickets snatched from voters at Dogwood Flat. (Rec., pp. 449 and 1054.)

Room fired into at Abbeville while votes were being counted. (Rec., p. 625.)

Armed men went from Hernando to Nesbitt's and remained until the votes were counted. (Rec., pp. 132 and 701, 702.)

At one box (Como) the fraud was thoroughly proven by examining the voters themselves.

Taking testimony delayed by dilatory cross-examinations. (See everywhere.)

Testimony stopped at Hernando by intimidation. (Rec., pp. 164 and 994.)

Testimony stopped at Holly Springs because no officer to take it. (Rec., pp. 580–582, 600–602.)

Testimony not taken at Oxford because counsel for contestant deemed it imprudent to do so. (Rec., p. 593.)

BENTON COUNTY.

Lamar.—The box here was taken from the presence of the United States supervisor, and hence the returns are vitiated.

Perry Ward, duly sworn, deposes and says as follows:

(Counsel for J. B. Morgan objects to examination of this witness, as no notice was given.)

Qu. No. 1. Where do you live?—Ans. I live on Mr. John Mason's farm.

Qu. No. 2. Did you vote at Lamar last election?—Ans. I did.

Qu. No. 3. Was you the Federal supervisor at Lamar?—Ans. I was.

Qu. No. 4. Was you in the room where the election was held all day and until the votes were counted out?—Ans. I was.

Qu. No. 5. Was you where you could see the box all the time until the polls were closed?—Ans. Yes.

Qu. No. 6. The box wasn't removed any time during the day or night?—Ans. Yes, sir.

Qu. No. 7. Where was the box carried to, and when was it removed?—Ans. It was moved at 12 o'clock, and Mr. Brewer carried it to his house.

Qu. No. 8. Did you go with Mr. Brewer and see the box?—Ans. I did not.

Qu. No. 9. I will ask you to state just what occurred, and the condition the box was in when Mr. Brewer carried it off and brought it back, and also what was said to him (supervisor.)—Ans. When we reached the box that morning it locked and sealed and he unlocked box. We voted in the door until 12 o'clock, and at 12 o'clock he said we would close for dinner, and he said, "Judge, I will give you the key and I will take the box, and don't you run off with the key." I said, "Give me the box and you take the key, for there is nothing in the key for me to run off with; you have it all in the box." He said, "Look at the box and pull it and see if it is locked." I told him it was locked. He said, "Do you see any hole in it?" I told him "No, sir; there was no hole in it," and when the box came back after dinner it was unsealed, hole was open, and he said, "We will vote in the hole this evening." (Rec., pp. 169, 170.)

• Since the taking of the evidence in this case closed, the *ex parte* statement of the "Brewer" herein referred to has been taken by contestant, and the same filed with the Election Committee January 29, 1890, and notice thereof given to contestee by the clerk of the committee.

Brewer's affidavit states that he was one of the Democratic election inspectors at Lamar at this election; that he kept an account of the vote as counted, and preserved a memorandum thereof in his memorandum book; that he signed the returns as made up by the clerk without examining the same, thinking the clerk would make a true return of the vote; that since the election he learned the returns as published were at variance with the true vote as cast, and that he has frequently so stated.

He swears that the true vote as cast at that election, according to the memoranda then and now in his possession, was, for Chalmers 149, and Morgan 29. The returns gave Chalmers 77 and Morgan 101. But, leaving out the affidavit, and counting 48 proven for Chalmers, we should take 101 from Morgan and 77 from Chalmers. The count then stands:

	Chalmers.	Morgan.
As returned	5,817	13,978
Lamar: Deduct	77	101
	5,740	13,877
Add	48	0
	5,788	13,877

DE SOTO COUNTY.

Horn Lake.—Jim Stephens, Republican inspector, could not read or write. (Rec., p. 45.) John McCain, a suitable inspector asked for by Republicans, was refused appointment by the Democrats. (Rec., p. 40.) There were 363 votes counted at this box. It is proved that 249 of these were negroes, and that all voted the Republican ticket but one.

Jim Stephens (c.), a witness on behalf of contestant, being first duly sworn, deposed as follows:

Direct examination by Gen. CHALMERS:

Q. How old are you?—A. Eighty.

Q. Can you read and write?—A. No, sir.

Q. Were you appointed the Republican judge of election here at Horn Lake at the last Congressional election?—A. Yes, sir.

Q. Did you vote?—A. Yes, sir; I voted.

Q. Who did you vote for?—A. I voted for Mr. Chalmers.

Q. How did you know that you voted for Mr. Chalmers?—A. The ticket was given to me that way.

Q. Did you ask for a Chalmers ticket?—A. Yes, sir.

Q. Your intention was to vote for Chalmers?—A. Yes, sir. I don't know whether I voted for him or not; I couldn't read. My intention was to vote for him.

Cross-examination by Mr. WATSON:

Q. What voting precinct do you live in in this Horn Lake precinct; you live here at Horn Lake, do you?—A. Oh, yes; sir.

Q. Where did Mr. Chalmers live at the time you voted for him?—A. Well, I don't know exactly where he did live then. I voted for him. I don't know where he did live at.

Q. Do you know now where he lives?—A. No, sir; I don't know now.

Q. How long have you known Mr. Chalmers?—A. I didn't know him when I seed him without somebody else telling me it was him.

Q. Who else did you vote for?—A. Nobody else; they didn't give me but the one ticket.

Q. You say you were one of the judges of the election?—A. Yes, sir.

Q. You signed the returns of the election?—A. Yes, sir.

Q. Was the election conducted fairly?—A. It was while I was sitting there; that was all I could do about it.

Q. Were you there all day?—A. Yes, sir; I was there all day, till night.

JIM (his x mark) STEPHENS.

HORN LAKE, MISS., *Jan.*, 21, '89.

Deposition of Tom McCain (col.), a witness on behalf of the contestant, being first duly sworn, deposed as follows:

Direct examination by Gen. CHALMERS:

Q. State your name and age, and where you reside.—A. Thomas McCain is my name; living here in De Soto County; been living here for nearly 50 years, I reckon; been here ever since I was a boy, and April 1st will be 62; that's my citizenship in this country.

Q. Did you ever hold any office; if so, what was it?—A. I was elected here to the legislature of Mississippi; I believe last time I run here I beat the governor; I know I did; got more votes than the governor did.

Q. When was that?—A. It was in 1874, I believe; somewhere along there.

Q. Did you vote here at the last election for Congress?—A. I did, sir.

Q. Who did you vote for?—A. I voted for Gen. Chalmers and Harrison and Morton. I think them the men, but I voted the Chalmers ticket.

Q. About how many colored men were here on that day?—A. Well, sir, there was near 250; satisfied of that. I know it because our secretary taken down the names, I think, of 49 that was here; I know that to be a fact.

Q. Do you mean 49 or 249?—A. I meant 249. Well, they was around here same as blackbirds, around the depot till dark. Every man that's here can testify; if he'll speak just like it was he'll say so too.

Q. Did you know any colored man who voted the Democratic ticket on that day?—A. Well, we had a watch, and at the best of our discovery there was one we thought that he was a little crooked.

Q. Who was he?—A. He was a little crooked-legged fellow by the name of Sam. Doyle. He took a Republican ticket, and I think he taken two; satisfied he did—

H. Mis. 137——24

took a Democratic and a Republican ticket—and we thought from the way he acted he was going to slip in a Democratic ticket. He was living around Mr. Foster's, and come here with a Cleveland hat on, and from the way he acted on the outside we thought probably he voted the Democratic ticket; at 'least we didn't have no belief in him at all. He went up with some men to vote, but he kept dodging around, and from the way he acted we thought it was a little doubtful about him voting the Republican ticket.

Q. Could you tell me how many white men were here to vote?—A. I couldn't tell correctly, but I am satisfied there was 20 to one.

Q. You mean 20 colored to one white?—A. Yes, sir; there were so many that looked dark; there was so few white men that they looked dark.

Q. The judges gave me only 106 votes and Judge Morgan 257; in your opinion, was that a fair count or not?—A. No, sir; I couldn't say that, because I knew and was satisfied the votes we cast here that it couldn't be that, just couldn't be that, that is if they counted them correctly; if the votes got to them there was something wrong.

Q. In your opinion, did they count this box fairly in 1884 when Blaine run for President and I run for Congress?—A. Well, sir, I must speak the truth 'cause I'm sworn, 'cause I've got to die; no, sir; I can't say it was a fair election, because the maneuvers, in my judgment, didn't show to be it was fair, and of course I can't say it.

Q. How long have you been voting at Horn Lake box?—A. I voted here in '66, first vote ever I cast; since I been pronounced a free man I vote right here.

Q. When was the last fair election, in your opinion, held at Horn Lake?—A. No, not '75; '69, I believe; no, we had two elections; since the surrender things went pretty well.

Q. In the race between Alcorn and Ames which occurred in 1873, who had the majority at this box, Republicans or Democrats?—A. Republicans.

(Objected to by Foster.)

Q. Who had the majority counted since 1875 at this box?—A. Well, the Republicans always have been in the majority here at this box.

(Objected to.)

Q. Have they been counted that way?—A. No, sir.

Q. It's your opinion they have always been in the majority here at this box?—A. I know it; you may call every man in this district and you'll find there is more colored people here than white people; that shows for itself.

The number of Democratic voters at this box is shown as follows:

Deposition of W. H. Bolton (white), a witness on behalf of the contestant; being first duly sworn deposed as follows;

Direct examination by Gen. CHALMERS:

Q. Are you a Democrat or a Republican?—A. Democrat, sir.

Q. You voted for Judge Morgan, did you not, at the last election?—A. Yes, sir.

Q. Here at the Horn Lake box?—A. Yes, sir.

Q. Do you remember the primary election between Slack and Oglesby and Cook and others for district attorney here in 1887?

(Objected to on the ground that he didn't allege anything in the notice of contest about the names of Slack and Oglesby and Cook.)

Q. Then I'll ask if there was not a race between five candidates for district attorney in this county?—A. Yes, sir.

Q. Was that or not an exciting contest, and did it or not bring out the full Democratic vote at this box?—A. I think it did, sir.

Q. The vote as appears from the Hernando paper at Horn Lake box was a hundred and fifteen; is not that as many as the Democrats ever polled here at any primary election?—A. I expect it is, sir.

Q. Do you know of more white people who are Democrat voters in this beat than that?—A. There might possibly be a few more than that.

Q. Did you hear any comments at the last election as to whether all the white voters were here or not?

(Objected to.)

A. I heard the conversation over there, and I heard some say there were several that did not come here—naming them—but I don't know who they are.

Now, if we take 248 from the total vote polled, 363, it leaves exactly 115, which Bolton, a Democrat, says is the full Democratic vote here. The history of this box shows that it is notorious for fraud. In the Buchanan-Manning contest the box was taken from the presence of the United States supervisor, and when he followed it he was cursed and abused and threatened with a pistol. The box was rejected for fraud by both the majority and minority reports in that case. (See Digest Election Cases, 1880-'82, pp. 296 and 325.)

Direct-examination by Gen. CHALMERS:

Q. What is your name?—A. J N. Bolton.

Q. What is your age and profession?—A. I am 59 years old ; practice physics; do most anything that comes to hand.

Q. Where do you reside?—A. I reside in the state of Horn Lake.

Q. Were you present at the Congressional election held here Nov. last?—A. I was here in the town part of the day.

Q. What is your politics?—A. I am an Old-Line Whig.

Q. Do you know any colored man at this box who votes the Democratic ticket? If so, please state what his name is.—A. I do not know one.

Q. Were you, or were you not, United States supervisor at this box in 1884?—A. Yes, sir.

Q. Do you remember what was the difference between the white and colored voters at that time?

(Objected to.)

Q. Please state as near as you can what occurred at that election, and whether in your opinion it was a fair election at Horn Lake box, and, if not, what your reasons are?—A. I don't know, Gen,, that I understand your question exactly. They went on, voted until 6 o'clock, and after they shut the box they pushed Mr. Wooldridge, put out the light, and we all came in the dark; and when they counted the box they had it very different from what I thought it would be.

Q. Explain more fully what you mean by putting out the light, and what was done at that time?—A. Well, Mr. Wooldridge said that he had promised Mr. Batte that he wouldn't have any light through the front room and he blowed the light out, and Mr. Clinton picked up the box and started out ; and Mr. Granberry pushed me out, said he'd follow the Dr. out, and they carried the box up to my house, and after supper counted it out, but I didn't think it was the box they voted in.

Q. When were the boxes changed, if they were changed?—A. As they went out.

Q. Were there or not more colored voters who voted here that day than were counted for me or for the Republican party?—A. I think there were; I stayed in the room all the time, and I think there was more colored voters than there was white men that day.

In addition to this, it is shown that the certified list of voters, which was the record of those who voted, was destroyed by the friends of contestee at his home. E. W. Smith, one of the commissioners, says:

Cross-inter. 4. What was done by the election commissioners with the returns of the last November election?—Ans. They were placed in the vault of the circuit clerk, and I afterwards, when assisting the circuit clerk in his office, had occasion to clean up the vault, emptied the ballot-boxes and burnt the contents, and replaced the boxes in order in the vault, not knowing of any law requiring us to keep the returns any definite or stated time.

Cross-inter 5. Were the lists of voters at each box among the contents of the ballot-boxes destroyed?—Ans. I don't know about that. I never examined it.

Cross-inter. 6. Do you not act as deputy circuit court clerk for De Soto County, and were you not so acting when you aided in destroying the contents of the ballot-boxes, as you have described?—Ans. I was assisting Mr. Maxwell, but not as regularly appointed deputy.

Cross-inter. 7. You destroyed all the papers and documents returned by the various inspectors from the different boxes, did you?—Ans. I emptied the ballot-boxes on the floor and destroyed the contents, with the exception of the poll-books.

Cross-inter. 8. If any list of the voters was kept at each voting place, and such lists had been returned to you or the commissioners, they would have been in the ballot-boxes with the rest of the papers, would they not?—Ans. They would.

This is certainly enough to vitiate the returns at this box. The proof of the vote is that the negroes belonged to Republican clubs and had selected two men, Joe Rutland to issue tickets, and H. H. Hill to take down the names of those who received them, in order that they might prove their vote if it was stolen. Rutland was not examined because he had gone from the State to teach school. Hill proves that 249 Republican tickets were issued by Rutland to men who went with them to the polls to vote them, and that only one was suspected of not voting them. That he and Rutland took down the names of the voters and preserved the stubs from which the tickets were taken. He swears that he knows the handwriting of Rutland, and that these names were written partly by Rutland and partly by himself. He files as exhibit to his deposition, the list of voters thus kept, and the stubs from which the tickets were taken. (See Rec., pp. 40–44.)

Tom McCain says:

Cross-examination by Mr. FOSTER:

Q. Do I understand you to say, then, that there hasn't been a fair election held here since you beat the governor?—A. Not as I know, Mr. Foster; I know this, and you may take the books and it will show up that way, there are more colored people here, and there are more of us vote here, and we are always behind; you can call it as you please.

Q. How do you know that all of these 250 negroes voted the Republican ticket?—A. We had men watching and we had Republicans giving the tickets, and saw where they carried them and saw when they handed them in, and we saw them go in at the window.

The proof shows 248 votes for Chalmers and 1 for Morgan:

From this proof the returns should be rejected, and 248 added to Chalmers, 256 taken from Morgan. The returns here were, Chalmers, 106; Morgan, 257. The count stands—

	Chalmers.	Morgan.
Brought forward	5, 788	13, 877
Horn Lake:		
Add	142	....
Deduct	....	256
	5, 930	13, 621

Nesbitt's.—W. W. Bullard, United States supervisor, says the colored inspector here was a Democrat. (Rec., pp. 130 and 131.)

Q. What name appears on the list prepared by you since the election for you to testify by?—A. Eli Walker.

Q. Is there any other difference?—A. Yes, sir; he is marked "C. D."

Q. Is there any letter "C. D." on the original list prepared by you?—A. No, sir.

Q. Is there "C. D." on the list prepared by you since the election?—A. Yes, sir.

Q. What does that "C. D." indicate?—A. It indicated that for "Colored Democrat"

Q. Isn't it a fact that you put that "C. D." there after you had been told and talked about that Eli Walker had voted the Democratic ticket?—A. Oh, no, sir.

Q. Why, then, did you not put it on the original list kept by you on that day?—A. Because I didn't see, I inquired among the ticket issuers that come up a cotact about which way he voted, and he didn't get a ticket from the one who issued Republican tickets.

Q. When did you find that out?—A. I found that out the next day.

Q. The next day after the election you found out he didn't get a ticket from the Republican bosses and then you placed him down as a colored Democrat; is that right?—A. Yes, sir; all we wouldn't count for getting a ticket we just counted them the other way.

Neither Walker himself nor any other witness is called to disprove this. Again Bullard says Walker could not read or write.

Q. Can Eli Walker read and write?—A. Not to my knowing. (Rec., p. 102.)

Neither Walker nor any other witness is called to prove that he could read or write. The Democrats refused to appoint the inspector asked for by the Republicans, and appointed this Eli Walker.

Again Bullard says:

A. The majority voted Republican for this reason: The club, it instructed that every ticket must be voted with open, and as they were handed in every colored man excepting two handed their tickets in open, and they had to be folded up after they were handed in the window.

Q. What two were they?—A. Taylor Cansellor was one that voted his ticket folded up and Eli Walker was the other. He didn't hand his ticket in; he had his ticket in the room there; he was judge.

Q. You say the Republican club had instructed all the members to vote an open ticket?—A. Yes, sir.

Q. And all the colored men, except two, did vote an open ticket?—A. Yes, sir. (Rec., p. 102.)

Vincent Smith says:

Q. Did you vote at the Nesbit box of last Nov. election for Congressman?—A. Yes, sir.

Q. Who did you vote for?—A. Gen. Chalmers.

Q. Did you watch the men voting on that day?—A. Yes, sir.

Q. How were they voting—the colored men?—A. Well, sir, they seemed to be voting the Republican ticket, sir.

Q. Did they vote an open or a closed ballot general?—A. Well, the instruction was to vote an open ticket.

Q. Did they do that?—A. As far as I seed.

Q. Did you see Taylor Castler vote?—A. Yes, sir.

Q. What ticket did he vote?—A. Republican ticket.

Q. Who did he get it from?—A. Me.

Q. Who did you get it from?—A. John Morgan.

W. W. Bullard gives the name of every voter and his color, and shows that 182 colored and only 46 white men voted at this box. The Democratic primary election here the year before showed only 48 Democratic voters at this box. No witness is called to contradict this, and the certified list of voters having been destroyed, the list kept by the United States supervisor becomes the best evidence in the case. No witness denies that there were only 46 white voters here or that 182 negroes voted open tickets as instructed by their club.

John Morgan issued the Republican tickets and saw all but one handed open to the election inspectors; ten were rejected. (Rec. p. 134.)

Noah Odum took down the names of the Republican voters and saw them go with Republican tickets open to the polls; ten were rejected. (Rec. p. 124.)

He files a list of these names and not a single man on the list is ever called to prove that he did not vote the Republican ticket.

W. W. Bullard further says:

Q. To the best of your knowledge and belief were the ballots fairly counted or not?

(Objected to.)

A. No, sir; I didn't believe they were fairly counted.

Q. What reason, if any, did you have to believe they were not fairly counted?

(Objected to by Mr. Foster.)

A. My reason was I could slightly see the stub-end ticket in counting. I can count the stub end ticket in calling out; *the notched-edged ticket was called Democrat, too.*

Q. The ticket that had notches on the ends was read as a Democrat ticket?—A. *Yes, sir.* (Rec., p. 102.)

This is the only statement made by Bullard which there is any effort to disprove.

J. C. Meharg, a witness for contestee, being duly sworn, deposeth and saith as follows:

Int. 1. What is your name, age, and occupation, and where do you reside, and how long have you resided there, and where do you vote?—Ans. My name is J. C. Meharg; 37 years old; I reside in De Soto County, 4 miles west of Nesbit, and am a farmer; I have lived there about 27 years; I vote at Nesbit's.

Int. 2. Were you, or not, at Nesbit, at the Nov. election, 1888, and what office, if any, did you hold on that day?—Ans. I was, and was an inspector of the election at that time, and at that box.

Int. 3. Were you, or not, there all the time on that day from the opening of the polls in the morning until the ballots were counted out that night, and did you see

the counting out of same?—Ans. I was there all day, and saw the ballots counted
out.

Int. 4. Did you see any one read off the Republican tickets, or any of them, and call
out Democratic names?

(Objected to by counsel of contestant as leading.)

Ans. I did not.

Int. 5. If such had been done by any person there would you not have seen and
known it?—Ans. I would.

Int. 6. Do you know Wallace Bullard, a colored man; if so, was he present at the
last election, and did he hold any office; if any place, state what?—Ans. I know
Wallace Bullard; he was present all day until the count was about half over that
night. He claimed that he was a U. S. supervisor; I never saw his commission.

Int. 7. You state he was there until the count was about half over; please state
where he was the balance of the time, if you know, and if there was any cause for
his not being there until the count was fully made.—Ans. I do not know where he
went to; I know of no cause whatever for his leaving.

Int. 8. Did he or not leave the room while the count was being made; and, if yes,
how long?—Ans. He left the room, but as to how long I couldn't say; I suppose
twenty or twenty-five minutes.

Int. 9. Was the counting out of the ballots done publicly?—Ans. It was.

Int. 10. Was not the election at that box conducted with perfect fairness to all the
candidates, and were not the ballots counted fairly?

(Objected to by counsel for contestant as leading.)

Ans. It was.

Int. 11. Did Wallace Bullard examine the tickets and read them when the count
was being made?—Ans. He did not.

Cross-examined by counsel for contestant:

Cross-int. 1. Are you a Democrat?—Ans. I am, sir.

Cross-int. 2. How many elections have you been a judge at Nesbitt box?—Ans. I
couldn't say; some eight or ten years; have been serving every election either as inspector or clerk; sometimes one, sometimes the other.

Cross-int. 3. Who were the other judges at that box on that day?—Ans. Mr.
McKnight and one Eli Walker.

Cross-int. 4. Which was the colored man?—Ans. Walker.

Cross-int. 5. What part did you perform in that election on that day in the handling of ballots?—Ans. None whatever.

Cross-int. 6. What part did you perform in the counting of the ballots?—Ans. None
whatever.

Cross-int. 7. How far were you from the ballot-box while the voting was going
on?—Ans. Some 2 feet, I suppose.

Cross-int. 8. Were you in front or behind the ballot-box?—Ans. I was sitting rather
by the side of it.

Cross-int. 9. How far was Wallace Bullard from the ballot-box during the day?—
Ans. I suppose some 2, may be 3 feet; not over 3 feet, I think, any time during the
day. (Rec., pp. 703–704.)

Cross-int. 11. Are you willing to swear that you saw everything that was done
in the voting and the counting of votes and the handling of ballots which Wallace
Bullard saw?—Ans. No; I am not willing to swear that. (Rec., p. 705.)

Here is one of the professional election officers, who has been serving
for ten years at this same box and bringing out Democratic majorities
where there are only 46 white and 192 colored voters, and where the
negroes suspected they would be cheated, and to prove their vote agreed
to vote open tickets, and did so.

Ed. Ingram, being duly sworn, deposes as follows:

Int. 1. What is your name, age, and occupation, and where do you reside and vote,
and how long have you resided there?—Ans. 1. My name is Ed. Ingram; am 34 years
of age; am a farmer, and reside and vote at Nesbitt, De Soto County, Miss., and have
resided there 3 years.

Int. 2nd. Were you at Nesbitt at the last November election? And if yea, state what
office, if any, you held on that day.?—Ans. 2nd. I was at Nesbitt at the last November
election on that day, and was one of the judges of the election.

Ques. 3rd. Were you present from the time the polls were opened in the morning
until the ballots were counted out that night?—Ans. 3rd. I was.

Q. 4th. Did one of the inspectors of election or any of the officers of election read off
Republican tickets and call out Democratic names at said election?—Ans. 4th. No, sir;
they did not.

Int. 5th. Who did the counting of the ballots, and what were you doing when the ballots were being read?—Ans. 5. Mr. McKnight did the reading of the tickets; I would take them out of the ballot-box and look at and read them, hand them to him, and he would read them off; he read them off correctly.

Int. 6. You say he read them out correctly; please state why you say that so positively.—Ans. 6th. Because I was right near him and would have seen him had he not read them correctly.

From this it will be seen that Mr. McKnight was the inspector who read the tickets, and he was never examined to prove that he read them correctly. Mr. Ingram, who was examined, was one of the clerks. (See Rec., p. 102.) It was his duty to keep the tally-list as the voters were read to him. It was no part of his duty to read the tickets or to watch the reading of them. And it is a self-evident fact that he could not discharge the duties of clerk, and record the names on the poll-book and watch the reading and examine the tickets at the same time. On the other hand, Bullard was United States supervisor, and it was his duty to watch what was being done. It was attempted to be shown that Bullard went away when the count was but half over, but Meharg says:

Int. 7. You state he was there until the count was about half over; please state where he was the balance of the time, if you know, and if there was any cause for his not being there until the count was fully made.—Ans. I do not know where he went to; I know of no cause whatever for his leaving.

Int. 8. Did he or not leave the room while the count was being made; and, if yes, how long?—Ans. He left the room, but as to how long I couldn't say; I suppose twenty or twenty-five minutes.

But the most positive evidence that a fraud was perpetrated here is found in the fact that men armed with Winchester rifles were telephoned for and brought from Hernando to keep the peace while the count was being made.

Vincent Smith says:

Q. Did you see the military that was charged that came here on that day?—A. Yes, sir.

Q. What time did you see them?—A. It was late in the evening, sir.

Q. Were you or not at the train when they came?—A. No, sir; I was standing right along here somewhere on the street.

Q. Did you hear any remark made by those men?—A. When the boys got off the train, got around here at the depot, some asked what did they want us to do? but I didn't hear any one return them any answer.

Q. At that time had the votes been counted?—A. No, sir.

Q. How many were there in that crowd?—A. I do not know, sir, exactly.

Q. About how many?—A. It seems to me might have been 8 or 10.

Q. Did they have arms?—A. I don't know exactly. It seems like the guns I've seen them handle around in Hernando there; these 16-shooters. (Rec. p. 32.)

W. H. Rollins, witness for contestee, says:

Int. 6. Did you or not, on the morning of the last election on the 6th of last November, carry a squad of men to Nesbit, in this county, and, if so, how come you to so do; for what purpose did you go; at what time did you arrive there; what was done by you and them while there; and at what time did you and they leave Nesbit and return to Hernando?—Ans. I did. There was received a telephone message here stating that they feared some trouble there; that was why I went as a peace officer, Maj. Dockery, the sheriff, being away. We arrived there just about the time the polls closed; I quartered my men in a store-house and left a guard over them about 25 yards from where the polls were; I then went to the polls and talked to both white and black. I found that there was no trouble; I then moved my men to the depot and came back on the night train about 10 o'clock.

Cross-int. 2. Who sent the telephone message from Nesbit's about there being trouble there on election day?—Ans. My understanding was that it was Jim G. Dovie. I don't know for certain.

Cross-int. 3. To whom was it sent?—Ans. I don't know; the operator told me of it. He didn't say to whom it was sent.

Cross-int. 4. How many men did you have with you?—Ans. I reckon there was between 15 and 25, probably not over 15.

Cross-int. 5. Was Judge Morgan, the contestee, aware of your intention to go to Nesbit's?—Ans. He was at the depot when I left, but I never spoke to him. I don't know that he knew anything about it. I recollect of seeing him on the platform of the depot when I got on the train.

Cross-int. 6. Was there not shooting done by your squad of men while at the depot at Nesbit's?—Ans. I can't say. There was shooting done in the depot room, and when I got in the room I had stepped out, I hollered to them to quit that, and wanted to know who it was shooting; told them they must keep quiet. Some one spoke and said that it ain't your squad. It is these other boys that is in here. There were several other boys from the neighborhood in there with them.

Cross-int. 7. Your men were armed, were they not?—Ans. They were, but only a few of them had ammunition of their own. Mr. Woods had the ammunition of the needle-guns in his charge, and I told him not to let them have any ammunition until I had ordered it, or until it was necessary.

Cross-int. 8. Is Jas. G. Dovie, the man who sent the telephone message from Nesbit, a white man and a Democrat?—Ans. He is.

Cross-int. 9. T. C. Dockery, the sheriff of this county, is a Democrat, also, is he not; you are one?—Ans. He is, and I am.

Re-examined :

Re-int. 1. Did you or not understand from the telephone message sent from Nesbit, as stated, that the colored people there were becoming turbulent without cause, and that that was the reason trouble was apprehended, and that you were wanted simply to preserve the peace if any effort was made on their part to break it?—Ans. Yes, sir.

Re-int. 2. At what time did the shooting referred to at Nesbit, in the depot, occur, and was it, or not, after you had gone to the depot to take the train for Hernando?— Ans. It occurred after we got there to take the train to come home; a short time before the arrival of the train.

Re-int. 3. Was not Mr. Ward, referred to in your answer to Cross-int. 7, marshal of Hernando, and a peace officer?—Ans. Yes, sir. (Rec., pp. 702, 703.)

The returns here gave Morgan 130 and Chalmers only 105. If these returns were true, there were forty-six white men and eighty-four colored on one side, and that they should have been so much alarmed as to telephone for armed men to help them against one hundred and five negroes is too ridiculous, especially when the proof shows that other boys from the neighborhood were there armed. See cross-interrogatory 6 and answer. If, on the other hand, the returns were not true, and the sender of the telephone message knew a fraud was about to be perpetrated, it is easy to see why forty-six white men might apprehend trouble from one hundred and ninety-two blacks who believed themselves robbed of their votes. This is certainly enough to vitiate the returns here. With the returns set aside, the proof of the vote is clearly made out that one hundred and eighty-two colored men were seen to hand open Republican tickets to the election officers. These returns should be set aside, 77 added to Chalmers and 130 taken from Morgan. If we give him the forty-six white men and one negro Democrat, the count stands:

	Chalmers.	Morgan.
Brought forward	5, 930	13, 621
Deduct returns	105	130
	5, 825	13, 491
Add (as proved)	182	47
	6, 007	13, 538

Hernando Depot.—Here it is shown that the box was taken from the presence of the United States supervisor at dinner time, and only 32 votes counted for Chalmers where 114 voters received Republican tickets and went with them to the polls. This is unquestionably enough to set aside the returns. The only question here is as to how many votes were proved for Chalmers.

Deposition **of A. D. Johnican (col.)**, a witness on behalf of the contestant, being first duly sworn, deposed as follows:

Examination by General CHALMERS:

Q. Did you vote at the Hernando Depot box in De Soto County at the last election for Congressman?—A. Yes, sir.

Q. What ticket did you vote?—A. The Republican ticket.

Q. Did you or not distribute Republican tickets there that day or not?—A. I did.

Q. What instructions, if any, did you give to those who received those tickets?—A. I issued them with this instruction " that every one of you who takes a ticket and don't want to vote it or don't vote it or can't vote it, bring it back to me, because I am ordered to return all tickets that are not voted."

(Mr. Boyce objects to this as being incompetent.)

Q. How many tickets did you issue to colored men that day?—A. I issued 114, including one white man.

Q. How many tickets were returned to you?—A. Seventeen.

Cross-examination by Mr. BOYCE:

Q. How far were you from the ballot-box when you issued the tickets you have just spoken of?—A. I was about as far as 15 feet; I reckon about 15 feet.

Q. Were you not at times when you were issuing tickets on that day much more than 15 feet from the polls?—A. After the voting ceased I was.

Q. While the voting was going on?—A. No, sir; not outside of that limit.

Q. Were you not sitting or standing near the southeast corner of the new store now being put up by Mackinvail?—A. I was there for noon after they adjourned for dinner; after the voting stopped.

Q. Were you not there at the time you issued some of the tickets?—A. I was not. Let me correct that. I issued one ticket there and the man went directly to the ballot-box and there was no one to prevent me from seeing him get there; that is, no one in the way.

Q. In what direction from the window through which the tickets were handed to the judges, on the day of the last election, were you when you issued the tickets?—A. In front of the window; north of the window.

Q. Can you say you saw every voter to whom you issued a ticket on the day of the last election vote the identical ticket you gave him?—A. Yes, sir.

Q. Is it not a fact that a great many voters were standing at the window at different times during the day with their ballots ready to vote, and was not the voting at times very rapid?—A. They were voting very rapidly.

Q. What about the crowd standing up there?—A. The crowd was there, but it was so arranged that I could see every one who put his ticket in; the marshals had a rope around near the window and each man had to come in through the east end of the rope, and of course that would allow each one to come in after the other, which enabled me to see each one distinctly.

Q. Did you see every colored man's ticket as he passed in through the opening left by this rope?—A. I did.

Q. Did you see every man's ticket that voted at the last election as it was handed in to the judges of the election?—A. At that box I did.

Q. Did you issue a ticket on the day of the last election to John Brown?—A. John Brown lives out on Mr. Boon's place? Yes, I did.

Q. Did you see him vote?—A. Yes, sir.

Q. Did you see that he voted the identical ticket you gave him?—A. Yes, sir.

Q. How far were you from him when he voted?—A. About the same place I issued tickets in; about 15 feet.

Q. Are you willing to swear that John Brown could not have voted, and did not vote, a Democratic ticket at the last election?

(Question repeated.)—A. I am willing to swear that he did not vote it.

Q. Are you willing to swear that John Brown had no other ticket in his possession on the day of the last election other than the ticket you issued to him?—A. If he had any other he voted the one I gave him.

Q. (Question repeated.)—A. I don't know; I will not swear that; he might have had one in his pocket, but voted the one I gave him.

Q. Are you willing to swear that he did not have in his possession on that day, and at the time he voted, a Democratic ticket?—A. I am willing to swear that he voted.

Q. (Question repeated.)—A. No, sir; I am not willing to swear that; I don't know what he had in his pocket.

Q. How, then, can you swear that he voted a Republican ticket and not a Democratic ticket?—A. Because I noticed him from the time I gave him the ticket go directly to the box, and he could not exchange it.

Q. Did you pay that close attention to every person to whom you issued a ticket on the day of the last election?—A. I did.

Q. Will you swear that all the voters—all the colored voters to whom you issued tickets on the day of the last election during the day didn't have in their possession and before they voted any other ticket than the one you issued to them?—A. I will swear that they voted the one I gave them. I can't swear that they didn't have any other ticket or not.

Q. Did the colored men who voted at the box spoken of by you on the day of the last election vote open or closed tickets?—A. A portion of them voted open tickets and some closed.

Q. Now, if you knew a number of the colored men who voted at the election spoken of voted closed tickets, how could you tell at a distance of 15 feet from them whether the ticket they voted was the identical ticket you gave them or not?—A. Because they folded them when I gave them to them and went directly to the box and handed them in.

Q. Have you a list of the number and of the names of the voters to whom you issued tickets on the day of the last election?—A. I have a list of some of the names.

Q. Where is that list?—A. In my pocket

Q. Produce it?

(Witness produces this list and it is ordered by the court to be made an exhibit to his deposition.)

Q. Is this list which you produced the original list that you kept on the day of the election?—A. Yes, sir.

Q. Did you write each name as it appears on this paper on this identical piece of paper on the day of the last election?—A. I did.

Q. Have you the block of stub that you kept on the day of the last election?—A. Yes, sir.

Q. Produce that.

(Witness produces the stubs.)

Q. Has this block of stubs and this list of names that you have produced here been in your possession ever since the day of the last election?—A. It has, but not in my room; it is in my place of business where I work. I left it there.

Q. In what place of business do you work?—A. It is in Austin Bell's store when I am not teaching.

Q. Did you not leave this block of stubs and this list that you have produced in Austin Bell's possession since the day of the election?—A. I left it in his store, and everything that is in his store in his charge for safe-keeping.

Q. Do you know where Austin Bell keeps the documents?—A. Yes, sir.

Q. Where?—A. He keeps them on one of the shelves, the second shelf from the top, on the south side of his building, on the east end near the stair-steps.

Q. Did you begin on the day of the election and issue tickets to voters as they are numbered upon this list?—A. No, sir.

Q. Well, then, how can you say that this list was prepared as you issued the tickets on the day of the last election?—A. That is, I had them down.

Q. What did you have them down on?—A. On a piece of paper.

Q. A piece of paper different from this?—A. Yes, sir. The paper I had was not clean paper, and was just writing hurriedly down there. Just re-wrote them off on another piece of paper.

Q. Then the fact is that the list you have produced here purports to be a copy of the list you kept on the day of the election, is that right?—A. Yes, sir; but not numbered the same.

Q. Then why did you swear just now that this list that you here produce is the identical original list that you kept on the day of the election?—A. This is the original list.

Q. (Question repeated.)—A. I thought you meant the papers that I had. You said the list. I thought you meant the lists that I had. All the papers.

Q. Then you have another list than this that you kept on the day of the election?—A. Yes, sir.

Q. Produce that list.

(Witness produces that list.)

Q. You have now produced another list of the voters kept by you and of the persons to whom you issued tickets on the day of the last election, have you?—A. Yes, sir.

Q. Is this last list that you hand me the original list that you kept on the day of the last election?—A. Yes, sir.

(Mr. Boyce hands him the last list produced, which he says is the original list of the voters to whom he issued tickets on the day of the last election.)

Q. I ask you to state now the names of how many voters appear on the list you hold.—A. Seventeen on this list.

Q. Now I will ask you to take the first list that you produced and which you also testify was the original list of the voters to whom you issued tickets on the last election, look at that and tell me the names of how many voters appear on that.—A. Eighty-four names.

Q. To how many colored voters and white voters did you issue tickets on that day of the last election?—A. One hundred and fourteen.

Q. Did you issue a ticket to *John McEntire* on the day of the last election?—A. Yes, sir.

Q. Did you see him vote the ticket you gave him?—A. If his name is not on the rejected list I saw him vote it.

Q. Then you can't say whether his name is on the rejected list or not, can you?—A. I don't recollect whether it is or not.

Q. Then I ask you the question, if you saw John McEntire vote at the last election?—A. I saw him vote if his name is not on the rejected list.

(Witness is handed the rejected list.)

Q. Now what have you got to say?—A. *He didn't vote, because I see his name is on the rejected list.*

Q. That is the only reason why you say he didn't vote is because his name appears on what you call the rejected list, then?—A. Yes, sir.

(Witness now marks the exhibits A, B, C, and D, and they are made exhibits to his deposition.)

Q. When did you deposit these papers that you have marked exhibit A, B, C, and D with Austin Bell?—A. I left them there on the day of the election.

Q. When did you first see them again after you left them there?—A. Any time I passed along up and down the counter and looked up on the shelf I would see them.

Q. When did you next examine the papers that you have marked A, B, C, and D after leaving them in the possession of Austin Bell?—A. When I found out that I had to come down here.

Q. When was that?—A. Wednesday, next day, I think. I don't recollect what day. (Rec., pp. 381-382.)

There is an effort made to show that the list of 17 voters was the list of those who voted, because it was called the original list. There were, in fact, two original lists, one of those who voted and the other those rejected. The list of those who voted was written first on a soiled piece of paper and afterwards copied. That the list of 17 was the list of rejected voters was shown by the questions asked as to the name of John McEntire. (See list Exhibits A, B, C, and D, Rec., pp., 1150, 1151.) But if there is any doubt as to the list of names the witness swears positively as to the number, and when the Democratic commissioner destroyed the certified list of voters all doubt should be resolved against them. The count here was, Chalmers, 32; Morgan, 134; 65 should be added to Chalmers and 134 taken from Morgan. And if we give to Morgan the white votes here the count stands:

	Chalmers.	Morgan.
Brought forward	6,007	13,538
Deduct returns	32	134
	5,975	13,404
Add (as proved)	97	69
	6,072	13,473

In weighing the proof as to frauds and votes at these two Hernando boxes, it is proper to remember that Hernando is the home of the "De Soto Blues," a campaign military company, composed of "unterrified and determined Democrats," the "old guard," which is re-organized for every national campaign, and was reorganized for the campaign of 1888 on October 7, 1888 with D. M. Slocumb, postmaster at Hernando, as captain. (See Exhibit B to J. R. Chalmers's deposition, Rec., p. 238; see testimony of D. M. Slocumb, Rec., p. 664, Cross-intrgs. 1 to 6; see testimony of Sowell Newsome, Rec., p. 1036, Ques. 13.)

There was continual firing of guns and pistols in Hernando on the night before the election, as well as on the day of the election, and Sowell Newsome, the oldest white Republican in the county of De Soto, was afraid to go to the polling place to vote for fear his life would be taken.

(See testimony of Austin Bell, Rec., p. 157; see testimony of Sowell
Newsome, Rec., p. 1036, Inter. 10 and Cross-inter. 1.)

It would naturally be supposed that the contestee would try by proof to
remove the stigma of such shameful violations of law from his friends and
supporters at his home, but no attempt to do so worthy of notice is disclosed in the record, and we must, therefore, either conclude that the
charges are true, or that the contestee in this matter forsook and forgot
his friends and his home, and determined to let the shame of these frauds
rest upon them and upon his certificate. He did not examine John B.
West, the Democratic inspector who bull-dozed and intimidated the
United States supervisor at the election. He did not examine Mr. Riley,
the man who voted the scratched ticket. Yet they were both—West
and Riley—within his reach any of the forty days of his time for taking
testimony. He did not explain why his Democratic inspectors on the
day of election appointed a negro to represent the Republicans, who
was ignorant and Democratic.

HERNANDO COURT-HOUSE BOX.

Evidences of fraud.—(1) There was no Republican inspector, the negro put in to represent the Republicans being illiterate and ignorant,
and voting the Democratic ticket. He did not even live in this voting
precinct. (See testimony of J. E. Walker, Rec., p. 150; see testimony
of Austin Bell, Rec., pp. 156, 157.)

(2) The ballot box was taken out of the presence of the United States
supervisor, and taken off to dinner and supper before being counted,
and the supervisor was intimidated and insulted by John B. West, one
of the Democratic inspectors, who told said supervisor he had nothing
to do with the election. (See testimony of J. E. Walker, Rec., pp. 150, 151.)

(3) One Mr. Riley, a "cussin" preacher, voted a scratched Democratic ticket, and no scratched ticket was counted out. (See testimony
of J. E. Walker, Rec., pp. 151–156; see testimony of J. J. Evans, Rec.,
p. 383.)

Proof of vote.—J. J. Evans was the challenger for the Republicans,
and stood where he could see the negroes get their Republican tickets
from Mike Robinson, and said voters, after getting their tickets, would
pass immediately by Evans and vote. In this way Evans swears he
saw 157 straight Republican tickets voted by the colored men. (See
testimony of J. J. Evans, Rec., p. 383.)

In this statement of the Republican vote Evans is fully sustained by
J. E. Walker, the United States supervisor. Walker shows that there
were between 175 and 180 colored voters who voted at this box at said
election, and he gives a list of the colored and white men who voted,
and says that only five negroes were suspected of voting the Democratic ticket; that the support of the contestant by the Republicans
was almost unanimous. (See testimony of J. E. Walker, Rec., p. 151,
and Exhibit A to his deposition, Rec., p. 1148, said exhibit showing
the respective number of colored and white voters.)

The returns here being vitiated, the account stands thus:

	Chalmers.	Morgan.
Brought forward	6,072	13,473
Hernando Court-House:		
Add	49	
Deduct		49
	6,121	13,424

This gives Morgan all the white votes and five negroes, and gives to Chalmers the vote as proved above.

LOVE'S.

Evidences of fraud.—(1) The Republican inspector could neither read nor write. (See testimony of R. G. Orr, Rec., p. 384.)

(2) The ballot-box was taken out of the presence of the United States supervisor before being counted, and carried a half mile from the polls to the house of J. D. Mosely, one of the Democratic inspectors, and the said Democratic inspector refused to allow the supervisor to follow the box. (See testimony of R. G. Orr, Rec., pp. 385, 386.)

Proof of vote.—The witness, R. G. Orr, saw 112 men vote the Republican ticket. He is supported in this by Mr. Strong, ticket distributor for the Republicans; and Strong also proves that six negroes and one white man were refused a vote on frivolous pretexts. (See testimony of R. G. Orr, Rec., p. 384; see testimony of M. Strong, p. 386.)

The certified returns gave contestant 60, and contestee 162 votes. But the above proof shows the vote should be counted as follows:

	Chalmers.	Morgan.
Brought forward	6,121	13,424
Add	52	
Deduct		162
	6,173	13,262

No votes being proved for Morgan at the above box.

OAK GROVE.

At this box, as at all others in De Soto County, the Republicans asked for suitable inspectors, and they were refused. (See Austin Bell, Rec., p. 156.) At this box it is proved that a negro who was well known as a Democrat was appointed as inspector to represent the Republicans. Dr. W. S. Weisinger, a witness for contestee, was examined to prove that there were negroes in De Soto County who were well-known Democrats. He names fifteen in the county, where are 3,000 negro voters, and among them names Jack Harris at Oak Grove. (Rec., p. 751.)

J. M. Weisinger, Democratic United States supervisor, proves that Jack Harris was one of the inspectors at that box, and the list of voters kept by both United States supervisors shows that Jack Harris voted last and just after the inspectors, clerks and United States supervisors, and was colored. All the other inspectors and clerks were white men. This refusal of the Democratic commissioner to appoint an inspector asked for by the Republicans, and the appointment of a negro Democrat, is under the rule laid down in McDuffie *vs.* Turpin enough to set aside the return here.

The Democratic supervisor says :

The election was fair and quiet, and no cheating that I know of.

Cross-int. 12. You don't pretend to say that there could not have been fraud in the election at that box on that day without your seeing it, do you?—Ans. I do pretend to say that there was no ballot-box stuffing or miscounting of the votes.

Cross-int. 13. How can you say there was no ballot-box stuffing when you say that you were out of sight of the box during the day?—Ans. Every time I left the box Conway Rutherford, the Republican surpervisor, was left in sight of it; and if he was out of sight of the box 3 minutes all day I don't know it. He denied having seen anything wrong that evening, and I saw nothing wrong.

Cross-int. 14. How do you know that Conway Rutherford was in sight of tl when you were out of sight of it?—Ans. I was not out of sight of the box onl; minute or two at a time and part of that time was in sight of Rutherford.

Cross-int. 15. How many times have you held an official position at that box election?—Ans. Several times. I couldn't be definite about it.

Cross-int. 16. Who were the judges there that day?—Ans. I think Simon W Hoyes Robinson, and Jack Harris were inspectors, and Thad. Oliver and Henry were the clerks.

Cross-int. 17. Were not the Republicans surprised at the result as announced th Ans. I think they were from what they said. (Rec., pp. 650, 651.)

This statement shows that his declaration that there was no fra made upon the ground that he saw none, and that the Repub supervisor said that evening that he saw none. But the record it case shows that the United States supervisors at Batesville, (and Longtown each said they could see no fraud. But fraud proved at each of these places. At Batesville the Democratic insp boasted that he changed 200 tickets. At Como the fraud was pi by calling the voters themselves, and at Longtown two voters sa' inspector changing their tickets. But both the United States s visors here say that they were busy writing down the names of voter examining the poll-books, and this might well prevent them from s what was done when the votes were received and put into the That some trick had been played is shown by the fact that her unusual thing was agreed on before the counting commenced of l ing the tickets to the Republican inspector to read, and then the l: ing at him when he read it.

J. H. Weisinger says:

Cross-examined by att'y for Chalmers :

Cross-int. 1. Where were you during the day?—Ans. In the school-house i day.

Cross-int. 2. Were you so situated all the day that you could see Stroud?. The seat that I occupied or was assigned by the inspectors was in plain view of Stroud was all day.

Cross-int. 3. How far were you from the box?—Ans. About 6 or 8 feet.

Cross-int. 4. It was not an impossibility for Stroud to see those to whom he tickets approach the window where the votes were being handed in, was it? No, sir; it was not impossible; he could see them until they got up to whe crowd was.

Cross-int. 5. What duties did you perform that day at the Oak Grove box as i inspector?—Ans. I examined the poll-books and saw that no name that was du istered was rejected, and assisted in keeping a list of all the votes cast, and at: to other duties ; one or the other of us was in sight of the ballot-box al' the wh

Cross-int. 6. You did not stay with the ballot-box all day yourself, did you? Yes, sir; the ballot-box was in the house all the day, and I was in sight of it all the time except when called out to attend nature's calls until it was counte

Cross-int. 7. Who did the counting of the votes?—Ans. The agreement we a when they started to counting the votes was that the inspectors of the electii the vote and hand the tickets to the Republican sup. to see that they were right ; and I kept tally-sheet to see that they were counted right.

Redirect examination:

Int. 1. You have stated that you started out on an agreement that the insp should read the ticket, hand it to the Federal Republican supervisor and th would help keep tally ; was this carried out to the end?—Ans. It was carri until we got nearly through counting the vote ; I suppose we lacked about 30 and then the United States supervisor became careless as to whether he re; tickets or not; they were all handed him however.

Recross-examined:

Recross-int. Why did the Republican supervisor quit reading the tickets, i have said he did?—Ans. Well, that is a question I can't answer; I didn't as. and don't remember of hearing him say why.

Recross-int 2. Were not the Democrats around the polls laughing at and r ing him?—Ans. They were not laughing at or ridiculing him; they were jokii in a good-natured way. They were laughing at him, and oking him in a natured way. (Rec., pp. 650–651.)

It was evidently a good joke that where 209 negroes and 50 white men voted the count should show 205 for Morgan, 54 for Chalmers, and especially when no negro is examined to prove that he voted for Morgan, and the only white man who swears anything about the negroes voting the Democratic ticket names only eight negro Democrats at Oak Grove. [Rec., p. 751.]

At this box Thomas Stroud distributed Republican tickets and kept the stub for each ticket he gave to a voter, and watched the voter go and put it in the box (see testimony of Thomas Stroud, record 391), and he exhibits with his deposition the stubs, 209 in number. (See Exhibits A and B to his deposition. Rec., p. 1151.)

Deposition of Thomas Stroud, colored, a witness in behalf of the contestant, being first duly sworn, deposed as follows:

Examined by Gen. CHALMERS:

Q. Did you vote at the Oak Grove box at the last election for Congressman?—A. Yes, sir.

Q. Did you vote the Republican or the Democratic ticket?—A. Republican ticket.

Q. Can you read and write?—A. Yes, sir.

Q. Did you distribute tickets or not?—A. I did. (Record, p. 391.)

* * * * * * *

Q. How close were you to the polls when you were distributing these tickets?—A. Well, I were told to stay 30 feet from the polls by Mr. John Walton, the deputy, and I stayed as near 20 or 30 feet as I could squeeze inside of the polls on front of the window where they were casting tickets.

Q. Did you try to see how the men voted that you gave tickets to?—A. They voted the tickets I gave them so far as I could see, and the way that I worked to see how they voted, I made them men stand behind me, behind the trees, and I would tear off one ticket at the time and give it to the man and said to hold it in your hand and not put it in the top and keep it where I can see it, if you are a Republican man, and I watched them and gave them slow so that I could see.—(Rec. pp. 391-392.)

Deposition of Conway Rutherford (col.), a witness on behalf of the contestant; being first duly sworn, deposed as follows:

Examination by Gen. CHALMERS:

Q. Did you vote at the Oak Grove box, in De Soto County, at the last election for Congressman?—A. Yes, sir.

Q. Did you vote the Republican or the Democratic ticket?—A. I voted the straight Republican ticket.

Q. Can you read and write?—A. Yes, sir.

Q. Did you occupy any official position at the last election; if so, what?—A. Well, I occupied my position inside of the house.

Q. What officer were you?—A. Supervisor; United States supervisor.

Q. Were you connected in any way with the Republican clubs in your neighborhoods?—A. I was, sir.

Q. How many clubs were they?—A. Three clubs.

Q. Have you any book showing the names of the three clubs?—A. Yes, sir; I have.

Q. Have you any list of the colored voters who voted there that day?—A. Yes, sir.

Q. Does your list show the number of white voters as well as colored?—A. Yes, sir.

Q. Please produce your list and let me examine it. The list of voters, the list you made on the day of the election, I want that if you have it.

(Witness produces a book in which he says the list is.) (Rec., p. 508.)

(See Exhibit; Rec., pp. 1135, 1136, 1137.)

Q. Do you know any white man who voted the Republican ticket there that day? If so, give his name.—A. John Hollowman to my knowledge.

Q. Do you know any colored man who voted the Democratic ticket there that day?—A. I do not, sir.

Q. Did or not all of the men whose name you have read belong to the three Republican clubs you have mentioned?—A. Excepting one, that was John Holloman; he is a white man; all these colored men that I have called belong to the club.

Q. Can you say whether they did or did not vote the Republican ticket there that day?—A. They did vote the Republican ticket.

Q. How do you know that?—A. The men that were issuing the tickets stood right there and give them their tickets and they came and all stood distinctly from the white voters, and we had a man there to see that he got no other ticket but the Republican ticket; and they come there with the tickets and their tickets were cast there. (Rec., p. 509.)

The history of this box shows that it was rejected for fraud in 1880 (see Buchanan *vs.* Manning, Digest Election Cases, 296). From this the returns should be set aside, which gave Chalmers 54, Morgan 205. Give Morgan all the whites but 1, and the negro Democrat 50. Add to Chalmers 148, take from Morgan 155, and the count stands:

	Chalmers.	Morgan.
Brought forward	6,173	13,262
Oak Grove:		
Add	148	
Deduct		155
	6,321	13,107

EUDORA.

(1) *Evidences of fraud.*—There was no United States supervisor for the Republicans, because the one appointed refused to act, for fear his life would be taken. (See testimony of W. G. Beanland, Rec., p. 1043, Re cross-inters. 1 and 2.)

(2) The negro inspector appointed to represent the Republicans could not read and write. (See testimony of Rev. Jobe Harrol, Rec., p. 969.)

Proof of vote.—According to the certified returns there were 336 votes cast—136 for contestant and 200 for contestee. (See certified returns, Rec., p. 741.)

Rev. Jobe Harral, a Democrat, and the only witness who testified as to the vote at this box, proves that not more than 60 white people voted at this election, and that there are not more than 100 entitled to vote there.

He swears that he issued five or six Democratic tickets with Morgan's name scratched and Chalmers's written on (Rec., p. 969), and that he voted a Prohibition ticket with Chalmers for Congress. No such ticket was returned. It is returned 136 for Chalmers, 200 for Morgan. The general fraud proved in this county, the failure to count the Prohibition ticket and the five scratched Democratic tickets, the refusal to allow the Republicans an inspector of their own choosing, and the appointment of an ignorant negro to represent them at this box, and the counting of 200 votes for Morgan when the Democratic primary election showed only 121 votes, and when Harrall swears only 60 white men voted, is sufficient to set aside the return. But two witnesses are examined for contestee. Nichols says it is regarded as a white box (Rec., p. 646). Dr. S. M. Watson says if all the negroes were registered and voted there would be a small Republican majority (Rec., p. 648, cross-interrogatory 20).

In 1886, when Harrall was United States superviser there, Chalmers beat Morgan more than two to one. (See returns from Rec., 735.)

Harrall declined to be United States supervisor this time, because he was afraid of his life. He furnishes two lists of the names of 219 persons to whom he and Curtis Neal issued tickets for Chalmers, and he swears he believes they were voted by them (see lists Rec., pp. 1060, 1061, 1062.) A trick was played, or attempted to be played, on Harrall by Democrats to get Republican tickets from him, with the evident purpose of showing that all who received tickets from him were not Republicans (Rec., p. 648.) Harrall knew they were Democrats, and gives their names (Rec., p. 970), and none of these names appear on the list of those he gives as voting for Chalmers. Chalmers is counted 136, when the ticket-distributors give the names of 219 who they believed voted for him. The returns being set aside, and no positive proof of the vote, the count should be, take 136 from Chalmers and take 200 from Morgan. The count then stands:

	Chalmers.	Morgan.
Brought forward...	6,321	13,108
Eudora: Deduct	136	200
	6,185	12,908

LAUDERDALE.

Evidences of fraud.—(1) The ballot-box was taken out of the presence of the Republican United States Supervisor, and carried to the house of one Lauderdale, and the said supervisor was not permitted to follow the box. (See testimony of Henry Moore, Rec. 393.)

Cross-examined by Mr. BOYCE:

Q. Were you in the room where the ballot-box was situated all day during the election while the voting was going on?—A. Yes, sir; I was there until noon, sitting right there till the box went to dinner.

Q. Where were you in the afternoon?—A. I was with the box until it went to dinner, then I didn't go any further.

Redirect examination by Mr. PATE:

Q. You said that you followed the box to the yard and was forbidden to follow it any further; who forbid you?—A. Lovey Glin, Bob Lauderdale, and Geo. Lauderdale. (Objected to.)

Q. Where was the box taken?—A. It was carried into Dr. Lauderdale's house.

W. L. Glenn, a witness for contestee, was duly sworn, and deposeth as follows, to wit:

Int. 1. What is your name, age, place of residence, and where do you vote?—Ans. My name is W. L. Glenn; age, 50 years; reside at Lauderdale, and vote at Lauderdale, De Soto Co., Miss.

Int. 2. Were you present at said box during the day of the election on the 6th of Nov., 1888?—Ans. I was.

Int. 3. Did you or not hold a position at that election, and if so, what position?—Ans. I did; was clerk of the election at that box.

Int. 4. Give the names of the U. S. supervisor and inspector of election at that box on that day for the Republicans?—Ans. Henry Moore was the U. S. supervisor and Wash Johnson was the inspector of the election for the Republicans.

Int. 5. Henry Moore stated in his examination for contestant that the ballot-box at Lauderdale was carried to the house of Dr. A. D. Lauderdale at noon on the day of said election, and that the officers of the election representing the Democratic party forbade him to follow the box. State what you know with reference to this matter, and whether or not you went with said box to said place at that time?—Ans. I was clerk there on the day of the election aforesaid, and at about 12.15 o'c. Dr. A. D. Lauderdale invited us to dinner. We then sealed and locked the box, giving the key to the Republican inspector, and went from the store to Dr. Lauderdale's house. At the gate of Dr. Lauderdale we told Moore that we intended placing the box in Dr. Lauderdale's parlor, which we did. I saw the box placed in the parlor, and told Mr. E. D. Lauderdale to take a seat in the door. We then went to dinner, and after finishing dinner, J. R. Lauderdale took the seat of E. D. Lauderdale at the gate. We told Henry Moore we had no right to ask him into a gentleman's parlor. He turned and went off among the other negroes upon the hill. The Republican inspector was sitting in the front door of the parlor with the key of the box. (Rec., p. 661.)

H. Mis. 137——25

PROOF OF VOTE CAST. ·

Henry Moore (col.), a witness on behalf of the contestant, being first duly sworn, deposes as follows:

Direct examination by Mr. PATE :

Q. Did you vote at Lauderdale box at the last Congressional election ?—A. Yes, sir.
Q. Did you vote the Rep. or Dem. ticket ?—A. The Rep. ticket.
Q. Can you read and write ?—A. Yes, sir.
Q. Did you occupy any official position at that box ?—A. Yes, sir ; I was supervisor.
Q. Do you know how many colored men voted at that election ?—A. Yes, sir.
Q. About how many ?—A. 60 colored men voted there.
Q. How many white men ?—A. I don't know.
Q. Do you know how the colored men voted ?—A. Yes, sir.
Q. How did they vote ?—A. Rep tickets.
Q. All of them ? How do you know they voted the Rep. ticket ?—A. Because we was in a club and I seen how they voted their tickets. (Rec. p. 393.)

Upon this testimony the box is vitiated and there is proved 60 votes for Chalmers and none for Morgan. The returns here were 27 for Chalmers and 111 for Morgan. Add 33 to Chalmers and take 111 from Morgan, the count would then stand :

	Chalmers.	Morgan.
Brought forward..	6,185	12,908
Lauderdale:		
Add	33	....
Deduct	....	111
	6,218	12,797

STEWART'S.

This box was stolen while in possession of the Democratic inspectors, and before it had been returned to the county election commissioners. The result was never certified or made known in any way to the county commissioners or the secretary of state. The box contained a majority of 73 for contestant.

R. T. Lamb, a witness for contestee being present, was duly sworn and examined, as follows, to wit:

Int. 1. What is your name, age, and occupation, and where do you reside and where do you vote ?—Ans. My name is R. T. Lamb ; 35 years old ; am a farmer and a Democrat, and reside near Walls Station, on the Valley Road, in De Soto County, Miss., and vote at Stewart's box, which is about 18 miles from Hernando.

Int. 2. Where were you on the day of the Congressional election in Nov., 1888 ?—Ans. I was at Stewart's box ; I served as one of the judges at that box.

Int. 3. Were you there as such judge from the time the polls were opened until they were closed and the ballots counted ?—Ans. I was.

Int. 4. Did you participate in the counting out of the ballots ?—Ans. I did.

Int. 5. Please state how many were present when the ballots were counted out, and give their names, if you can.—Ans. There were seven of us ; myself and Pete Smith as judges, Adam Rice, a U. S. supervisor of election, Walker Peebles and Will Williamson were the clerks, and Hamp Royner he was a judge also.

Int. 6. Were the votes counted out and the tally-sheets kept in the presence of those you have just mentioned ?—Ans. Yes.

Int. 7. What became of the tally-sheets and the ballots after the counting had been completed and the result ascertained ?—Ans. They were put in the box and locked up.

Int. 12. Was the result announced after the ballots had been counted out, and were all seven of these judges, clerks, and supervisors present, and did they or not hear and know the result ?—Ans. Yes.

Int. 14. What become of that box ?—Ans. During the night we heard some one in the room, and an alarm was given and we got up and struck a light to see who it was or what it was, and we found the ballot-box gone.

Int. 15. Please state the result of the election at that box.—Ans. My recollection is that it gave the Republicans 73 majority.

Cross-examined by att'y for contestant:

Cross-int. 1. There was 73 majority, as you recollect, for the whole Republican ticket, was there not?—Ans. That is my recollection.

From this 73 should be added to Chalmers and the count will then stand:

	Chalmers.	Morgan.
Brought forward	6, 218	12, 797
Add	73	
	6, 291	12, 797

INGRAM MILLS.

This box was never returned, but an election was held, and the only proof as to the vote shows that 118 colored men voted the Republican ticket with the name of contestant on it for Congress. There is no proof of any vote for contestee, and his friends having stolen the box the presumption should be all against him. We therefore claim 118 majority for contestant. (See testimony of J. W. Love, Rec., p. 389.)

Deposition of J. W. Love (colored), a witness on behalf of contestant, being first duly sworn, deposed as follows:

Examination by Gen. CHALMERS:

Q. Did you vote at the Ingram Mill box, in De Soto County, at the last election for Congressman?—A. I did.

Q. What ticket did you vote?—A. Republican ticket.

Q. Did you distribute Republican tickets at that box that day?—A. I did.

Q. How many Republican tickets did you distribute that day?—A. I distributed 119. One was rejected. All voted but one.

Q. How do you know they all voted?—A. Because I was determined; I had heard there wasn't justice done at the box and I was determined. I got just where I could see every one voted that I give one to. I kept them right in the ranks and saw them put the tickets in the box. (Rec., p. 385.)

A. D. McInnis, witness for contestee, was brought before a justice of the peace at 8 o'clock in the morning with his deposition written out before hand, and signed before counsel for contestant could get there. (See Rec., p. 793.) Mr. Haynes says of this:

Q. At what time did you reach Cockrum; what time of day?—A. At 8.32 in the morning.

Q. What did you then learn in regard to taking the testimony there?—A. When I arrived at Cockrum at 8.32 a. m. I found Mr Boyce, who said to me that court had been opened in regular form; they had taken the deposition of one witness, Esq. A. D. McGinnis, and the court was in fact then in session, although Presiding Justice Harrison was then absent, having gone home, a distance of about two miles. He also stated to me that court had been opened in regular form. When Justice Harrison returned I demanded to cross-examine the witness, but my friend, Mr. Boyce, here, was equal to the emergency, and made the record to show a very plausible excuse why I could not be permitted to do so; but again, as at Louisburg, when the court returned, Mr. Boyce moved an adjournment. They took no further testimony that day, but before final adjournment Mr. Boyce prepared a certificate for the court to sign and send up with the record, setting forth as a fact that the testimony given by the witness, McGinnis, had been written in the presence of the court; agent for contestant, knowing that if this certificate be correct the court must have been opened that morning by sunrise, asked of the court an explanation; the court replied in substance that no part of the testimony, neither the questions nor the answers, had been written in his presence while court was in session, or in his presence, and requested Mr. Boyce to correct the certificate, which I presume he did; I don't know.

Q. Is it not the fact that no other witnesses were examined at Cockrum?—A. It is. (Rec., p. 973.)

McInnis does not swear that there was a fair election.   He says:

Int. 7. State whether or not the clerks at this box at said election kept tally-sheets, as required by law, and complete returns were made out and signed by the proper officers, the vote tabulated, and the result declared. If so, and you remember, state the vote at this box for both the candidates for Congress, Morgan and Chalmers, on the day of said election.—A. 7. The said clerks did keep such tally-sheets that day. The returns of election had been made out and signed by the proper officers and certified to by them. The count had been completed and the vote tabulated, the result publicly declared, the box sealed and put away as stated. The vote for Congressmen stood as follows, to wit: J. B. Morgan received 148 votes, Jas. R. Chalmers received 63 votes; Morgan's majority, 85. (Rec., p. 792.)

The box having been stolen the presumptions are against it. The testimony of the Republican ticket distributer being positive that he saw 118 votes handed in for Chalmers, they should be so counted, as this proves he received more than the pretended count for him. No vote being proved for Morgan, the count stands:

	Chalmers.	Morgan.
Brought forward	6, 291	13, 797
Ingrams:		
Add	118	
	6, 409	13, 797

OLIVE BRANCH.

The evidences of fraud at this box are:

(1) The Republicans had no inspector of election, and no representative at all in the election. (See testimony of Charles M. Haynie, Rec., pp. 546, 547; see testimony of Henry Wood, Rec., p. 551.)

(2) The ballot-box was taken off to dinner at 12 o'clock by the peace officer, and was kept out of sight of the inspectors and supervisors for one hour and a half by H. T. Murry, peace officer. (See testimony of H. T. Murry, Rec., pp. 765, 766.)

(3) The witness, Henry Wood, testified that it has been the custom for ten or twelve years to allow one colored man, out of every four offering, to vote. He has been refused the privilege of voting for each of the three or four Presidential elections prior to election of 1888. He was told each time he was marked dead, though he had registered for each election, and had lived on the same place for forty years. (See testimony of Henry Wood, Rec., pp. 551, 552)

Proof of votes.—Ed. Brown distributed Republican tickets, and saw 119 men to whom he gave said tickets go to the polls and offer to vote them. The witness knew these to be Republican voters at that box, as they had been for years.

Henry Wood testifies that he knew these men were legal voters, many of them, and he had lived there forty years. (See testimony of Edmund Brown, Rec., pp. 549, 550; see testimony of Henry Wood, Rec., pp. 551, 552, 553.)

This renders absurd the certified vote of 185 for contestee and 19 for contestant.

These frauds have been continued for years. (See testimony of Haynie, Rec., pp. 546, 547.

Deposition of Charles M. Haynie (white), a witness on behalf of the contestant; being first duly sworn, deposed as follows:

Direct examination by Mr. PIERSON:

Q Where do you live?—A. I live in the Olive Branch precinct, in De Soto County, Mississippi.

Q. How long have you lived there?—A. Something over 20 years.

Q. Have you been familiar with political canvasses and with elections held at the Olive Branch precinct during that time?—A. I have.

Q. I'll ask you now whether in 1882, and since that time, fair elections have been held or not, and give your reason for your answer?—A. Since 1882 the opposition of the Democratic party have been totally without representaticn at the polls. Each year since that time a very large per cent. of the Republican voters have found their names erased from the poll-book, and they've been marked, others moved, dead or gone, and the rule of the inspectors has invariably been, when a voter's name was so erased or so marked they declined letting him vote; hence a very large per cent. of the opposition to the Democratic party has been virtually disfranchised.

Q. You say that the opposition to the Democratic party has not been represented at the polls. What do you mean by that?—A. I mean that they have neither been allowed an inspector or clerk, but an ignorant, illiterate colored man has been selected by the county board of inspectors to represent the Republican party, and at the last election I'm informed the man so selected voted the Democratic ticket—voted for Cleveland and Judge J. M. Morgan.

Q. Were the same conditions existing as to the manner of erasing voters' names from the poll-book and not allowing them to vote, in 1888—at the election of 1888, as you have described in your first answer?—A. I didn't see the poll-book at the last election, hence, of my own knowledge, can't say. I was present, though, when quite a number of voters, or rather, you may put that applications to vote, were refused for the reason that their names were not found on the poll-book.

Q. I'll ask you whether you knew the men who applied to vote, and whether you knew where they had voted heretofore?—A. Yes, sir; some of them I did.

Q. Where were they voters?—A. Olive Branch; men that had lived there for a number of years, and some of them men that had voted in my presence were refused to vote at this last election; just how many I couldn't say.

Q. Was there any organization of the Republican party in your precinct in the last canvass?—A. There was.

Q. Was it a good or bad organization?—A. I regarded it a good organization.

Q. Did they support the entire Republican ticket?—A. So far as I know they did. I didn't hear a single dissenting voice among Republicans.

Upon this proof the returns should be set aside and there should be added to Chalmers 100 and taken from Morgan 185, the vote returned for him. The count will then stand.

	Chalmers.	Morgan.
Brought forward	6,409	12,797
Olive Branch:		
Add	100	
Deduct		185
	6,509	12,612

COCKRUM, LAKE CORMORANT, LEWISBURG, AND PLEASANT HILL.

At these four boxes no specific proof was taken. But at these, as at every other precinct in this county, the Republicans were denied the inspectors they asked for. In the case of Threet vs. Clarke, this committee held the law to be as follows:

The committee is of the opinion that where the course is systematically pursued, of appointing on the election boards to represent the minority or opposition party, persons not indorsed by that party, and as to whose loyalty to the party whose interests they are expected to guard there is a question, or of appointing persons who are unable to read and write, when there would be no difficulty in finding men well qualified in these respects, this ought of itself be considered evidence of conspiracy to defraud on the part of the election officers. This was clearly a violation of the law on the part of the board.

. This law declares this to be evidence of a conspiracy to defraud, but it is said there must be some further evidence of fraud to set aside the returns. We have this much evidence from the history of the district. It is charged in the notice of contest, and not denied in the answer, that the Democratic vote at these boxes in the primary election in 1877 was only 371, while they are returned 538 for contestee. In addition we have the record in the case of Buchanan *vs.* Manning, which shows that Pleasant Hill box was rejected for fraud both by the majority and minority report in that case. (See Digest Election Cases, 1880–'82, p. 296.)

In the case of McDuffie *vs.* Turpin it is said: "When the law provides that each of two political parties shall have representation on the election board of inspectors, it is a provision to prevent dishonest partisans from making false returns." And the supreme court of Mississippi said: "Any practice which may be thought purposely to have been resorted to for influencing the result" will set aside the returns. (Word *vs.* Sykes, 61 M., p. 667.)

The only question, then, is, was this practice purposely resorted to at these precincts for influencing the result?

If the same thing which was done this year has been resorted to year after year for many years, this is the best evidence that it was purposely done to affect the result of the election.

Austin Bell proves that the Republicans were denied the inspectors they asked for at this election. (Rec., p. 156.)

That this refusal has been continued for years is proved by the following testimony. C. M. Haynie says:

Cross-examination by Mr. BUCHANAN:

Q. You say that since 1882 the opposition has been without representation at the polls. Do you refer to the Olive Branch precinct alone in that answer?—A. In that answer I referred to the Olive Branch precinct because the question was confined to that precinct.

Q Have not the Republicans always been allowed an inspector or judge of the election by the election commissioners?—A. They have not, but have invariably been refused the man that they requested to be appointed for each box, and some illiterate man appointed instead of the one they requested should be appointed.

Q. My question was, has not a Republican been appointed an inspector by the board? Have the board not complied with the law by appointing a Republican inspector?—A. I'm inclined to think not, because I've reliable information that the man who has served for several years voted for Cleveland and Morgan at the last election, hence I don't think he was a Republican.

Q. And because you were reliably informed that one inspector at the Olive Branch precinct at one election voted the Democratic ticket, or for the Democratic candidate for Congress, you conclude that the inspectors of election in De Soto County—I mean the commissioners of election for De Soto County—have systematically violated their duty and refused to appoint Republican inspectors, as the law requires that they shall do?—A. Oh, I didn't say anything of that kind. That question leads to a perversion of what I said.

Q. Well, I want to understand you.—A. State that question once more.

Q. The question has been read over to you; now what have you to say to it?—A. It is well known to every man who is familiar with the political methods adopted by the Democratic party not only for the precinct of Olive Branch, but for every precinct in De Soto County, that it has been deemed best for the perpetuation of the Democratic party that no man of any intellect should be permitted to represent the Republican party at any box in the county.

Q. You say it is well known as you have stated; do you know it to be a fact?—A. I do.

Q. State how you got your information on that subject?—A. From personal observation.

Q. Then state from what facts you draw that personal observation.—A. Personal interviews with members of the county board of inspectors, and from personal interviews with prominent members of the Democratic party in the county, and from a personal examination of the books.

Q. State what members of the board of commissioners ever told you that the policy of the party was as you have stated; give the time and place of such interviews; also, state what prominent members of the Democratic party ever made similar statements to you, and give the time and place of such interviews.—A. That's a far-reaching question. I will go back of 1882 in answering that question. About 1879 I was a candidate for chancery clerk on the Greenback ticket in De Soto County, and waited upon the board—I don't remember who were the members of it; Day was one of them, though—and asked for representation at each box; they refused to do it. As for the special time, I couldn't give that; I saw him at his house; I saw him with the other— I saw him with the other members of the board at the court-house in Hernando. Again, in 1881, I was a candidate for the legislature upon the same ticket, and waited in person upon each of the members of the board; couldn't specify the days; they refused again. I was in Hernando, I believe in 1876, I'm not sure, and had a talk with Mr. Dodson, and insisted that Gen. Chalmers should have representation at the boxes, and his reply was: "Oh, you have representation every time," or words to that effect, "but we'll select the men for you." Conversations that I've had with friends outside of officials as regards the appointments, either as to time or place, I don't think has anything to do with this case.

Q. So you base your conclusions that the board of commissioners have systematically violated their duty, as you have stated, upon the above interviews which you have, as stated, with members of that board, do you not?—A. I do not wholly or entirely.

Q. Well, if you do not wholly or entirely base it upon that ground state upon what ground you do base it?—A. I base it upon the ground that since 1882, so far as I have been able to learn, not a single man has been appointed that was asked for by the Republican executive committee of the county.

Q. Have you presented the names of Republicans, and asked their appointment, to the board yourself?—A. I have not.

Q. Then what you know of the matter of the action of the board is not of your own knowledge, but hearsay, is it not?—A. I have been in frequent consultations with the executive committee, and have assisted in selecting such men—the names of suitable men to represent the various boxes at the polling places in the county. Those names were presented by some one selected by the Republican executive committee to the county board, and I am personally aware of the fact that none of those names that were sent up were ever appointed—none of the persons appointed whose names were sent up. (Rec., pp. 547, 548.)

It will be observed that the Mr. Dodson who said in 1882 "We will select the men for you" is still one of the commissioners of election of this county, and his name, T. A. Dodson, appears signed to the returns. (Rec., p. 741.)

This same T. A. Dodson was one of the commissioners in 1880, as the testimony shows, in the case of Buchanan vs. Manning, when inspectors were asked for by the Republicans and refused. (See House Miscellaneous, first session Forty-seventh Congress, vol. 4, p. 25.)

In a State like Mississippi, where, as we have asserted before, the commissioners of election control the whole machinery of election in a county, the county should be treated as an entirety, and if conspiracy and fraud are shown in the action of the commissioners this should taint the election held at every box where they have denied fair representation to the other side. It should at least change the burden of proof and compel the party relying upon the returns to show something more than the mere returns themselves to sustain their validity. That the commissioners of election of De Soto County denied inspectors of their choice to the Republicans is clearly proved. That fraud was found at every box that could be examined is abundantly shown. That one of the commissioners of election destroyed the certified list of voters is admitted by himself. That counsel for contestant were prevented by intimidation from taking testimony at Hernando is also shown, and this should be considered in connection with the want of testimony as to these boxes. All these reasons taken together show sufficient grounds to throw out these boxes. This would take from Chalmers 312, from Morgan 540.

MARSHALL COUNTY.

The notice of contest says:

MARSHALL COUNTY.

I charge that you were very unpopular in the district, and especially so in Marshall Co., where you were charged with having betrayed Col. Manning in his contest with me in 1882, and that you did not receive, within 20 per cent., the Democratic vote of this county. And yet when Col. Manning received only 1,296 votes out of a total vote of 3,607, you pretended to have received 2,248 out of a total vote of 3,660. And at the East Holly Springs box, where Col. Manning lived and voted, his majority was only 37, while your pretended majority is 220. And at this box, where the two candidates for sheriff in 1887 could poll only 181 Democratic votes, you pretend to have received 350 votes. I charge that all manner of fraud was practiced at every box in this county except Early Grove, and there your friends refused to hold an election because I would have a majority there of 60 votes. I charge that in this county I have one thousand majority over you, while 885 majority was counted for you. And further to show the gross fraud of your pretended vote, I compare it with the vote for sheriff between McWilliams and Miller, two popular Democrats, who brought out the full Democratic vote of the county in 1887 in the primary election. Byhalia and Watson then voted together, but now are two boxes.

Evidences of fraud.—Brief of contestant says :

(1) Mr. A. J. Rylee, a witness for contestee, testified as follows :

Cross-inter. 4—"Is it or not a fact, Mr. Rylee, that you have upon more than one occasion stated that the means and methods adopted and carried into execution by the Democratic party of this county in the holding of elections was unfair, fraudulent and unjust as against the parties opposing them, whether that opposition was Greenbackers or Republicans?" Ans.—"I have, privately and publicly, so far as the Greenback party is concerned, or as to Republicans when acting in concert with Greenbackers."

In answer to cross-interrogatory 3 Mr. Rylee swears that in so far as his knowledge goes they (the Democrats) use all the means at their disposal for the success of their party. The witness voted for Morgan, the contestee, in the last election and has been prominent in Marshall County politics for the last ten years. (See testimony of A. J. Rylee, Rec., p. 870.)

(2) In this campaign the Democrats were apathetic and indifferent and the negroes were more alert and active and better organized than for years. See testimony of John S. Burton, record, page 573; see circular Democratic executive committee of Marshall County, record, page 673. Besides, Judge Morgan was unpopular in the county with the Democrats because he did not heartily support Colonel Manning in his canvass in 1882 against Chalmers. (See testimony of John S. Burton, Rec., pp. 573, 4, and exhibit B to his deposition, Rec., p. 574. See testimony of C. B. Howry, Rec., pp. 954, interrogatories 1 and 2.)

And while Morgan was unpopular with the Democrats, the Republicans, with a few exceptions, were hearty in their support of Chalmers. (See testimony of John S. Burton, Rec., p. 573 (testimony of Geo. M. Buchanan, Rec., pp. 607–610).

And yet Morgan professes to have received 2,248 votes out of a vote of 3,660 in the county, when Colonel Manning in 1882 could get but 1,296 votes out of a vote of 3,607 in the county, and at Colonel Manning's own box he, in 1882, received only 37 majority, and Morgan pretends to have received 257 majority. Morgan's certified vote is rendered still more ridiculous by the fact that in 1887 a primary election was held in the county between two very popular candidates to decide which should be the candidate of the Democratic party for sheriff. There was a very exciting canvass, and the full Democratic strength was voted. The two candidates only received 1645 votes in the county. Dr. Burton swears that it is impossible for Morgan to have received, in a fair election, more votes than the two candidates for sheriff did. This, of itself, shows the gross frauds in this county. (See testimony of John S. Burton, Rec., pp. 582, 583.)

The Republicans were apprehensive that these frauds would be committed, as they had been often before. They had never been allowed any election inspectors, and had only the United States supervisors to guard their rights, and if they watched the man who took the tickets from the box, when the count started, the clerks would make false tallies; if, on the other hand, he watched the clerks, the man taking tickets out of the box would change or misread the tickets. But the Republicans of this county did not intend to be thus cheated out of their rights. Chalmers had been nominated in Holly Spring, and the Republicans of Marshall had imbibed a large share of the enthusiasm which prevailed in the nominating convention. They determined to arrange a plan by which they could ascertain what proportion of the vote polled at the election was Republican. This plan is best explained by the witness who helped arrange it, Capt. George M. Buchanan. He says :

"A short time before the election our central committee agreed on this plan: That in order to ascertain as nearly as we could the votes cast by Republicans at the election, that we would have one or more intelligent men at each precinct to take charge of all the Republican tickets and distribute them to the Republicans; at the same time another man at each precinct, to take down the list of the names of the voters as the tickets were given to them. Furthermore, we agreed and did furnish from our headquarters at Holly Springs a memorandum book for each precinct, or sufficient memorandum books for each precinct, to take down these names, with the instructions to parties distributing tickets not to do any electioneering; to go to some quiet place in view of the polls where they could write unmolested; keep an accurate account, and to give no man a ticket without he came for it and announced his intention to vote it." (See testimony of George M. Buchanan, Rec., pp. 598-599.)

It will appear in the examination in detail of this county that this plan was carried out substantially at each place about which testimony was taken. It will also appear that there was no particular testimony as to several places, and the reason of this is also given in the testimony.

Contestant made arrangements to take his testimony as to Marshall County before Mayor Calhoun at Holly Springs, and gave notice to that effect; and but for the interference of contestee's counsel, as hereinafter explained, the whole vote of this county would have been thoroughly and clearly proved.

EAST HOLLY SPRINGS.

Evidence of fraud.—(1) The whole number of votes certified was 444, while the whole number of votes appearing on the certified list of voters was only 443. (See vote certified for East Holly Springs, Rec., p. 743; see clerk's certified list of voters for this box, Rec., pp. 1127, 1128, 1129, 1130.)

(2) The United States supervisor saw one of the Democratic inspectors switching tickets, those taken from the voters being run up the inspector's sleeve and afterwards falling on the floor, while others were put in the ballot-box in the place of those dropped. (See testimony of J. J. Sigman, Rec., pp. 569-670.)

Proof of vote.—J. J. Sigman, the United States supervisor, proves that he knew personally 201 persons whose names appeared on the list of voters at this box, kept by him on the day of election, to be Republicans, and believes they voted a Republican ticket. Some persons whose names appeared on his list he did not know, and at the time of his examination could not tell whether they were white or colored. (See testimony of J. J. Sigman, Rec., pp. 569-570.)

Sigman also files his list of voters, numbering 447.

United States supervisor not allowed to see count in 1880, and 30 persons not allowed to vote. (See Dig. El. cases, 1880-1882, pp. 292-293.)

As will be seen by reference to the primary election figures above referred to, page 7 of record, the Democratic strength at this box is only 181, and Dr. Burton swears that it was, in his opinion, impossible for Judge Morgan to get more votes at this box than did these two candidates for sheriff. (See testimony of John S. Burton, Rec., pp. 582, 583.)

The fraud being proven, the number of votes being proven, and the Democratic strength being shown, we submit the vote as cast is proved to be as follows:

On this proof the return should be rejected. Counting for Chalmers his vote as proved, and none being proved for Morgan, the count would then stand thus:

	Chalmers.	Morgan.
Brought forward	6,509	12,612
East Holly Springs:		
Add	128	
Deduct		350
	6,637	12,262

The explanation of the 20 illegally rejected votes is this: Ca Buchanan swears that 43 men who received Republican tickets him returned them, saying they had not been allowed to vote be their names were scratched off. (See testimony of Geo. M. Buch Rec., p. 612.)

Dr. Burton proves that 23 of these were refused their vote at the Holly Springs box, and this would leave 20 to be refused at the Holly Springs box. (See testimony of John S. Burton, Rec., pp. 576 1055 *et seq.*)

WEST HOLLY SPRINGS.

Evidences of fraud.—Dr. John S. Burton was United States s visor here, and when the count started had the tickets handed l first Republican tickets and then Democratic ones—in blocks of and he inspected each block, and then handed them to the mar called them out, Dr. Burton checking off each block as it passed thr his hands and as it was called out. He was so particular that when the inspector handed five tickets as Republican, and there two Democratic tickets in the block, and another time when a blo five tickets was called to him as Republican, and on looking over he found one Democratic ticket, Dr. Burton called attention to the and told the Democrat he was cheating himself. In this way he cou out 213 votes for Chalmers and 138 for Morgan, Chalmers runni votes ahead of his ticket. The result was called out after the c was completed, as Dr. Burton remembers, as only 35 majority for (mers. The vote was certified, 168 for Chalmers and 183 for Mo: Dr. Burton protested against the result as announced after the c but was answered by one of the inspectors: "We kept tally and s you, and you are just as liable to make mistakes as we are. (See mony of John S. Burton, Rec., pp. 577, 578; see exhibit to his de tion, Rec., pp. 1055–1059.)

Dr. Burton, in his testimony above referred to, proves that ' were 23 negroes who presented themselves at his box to vote and refused. They had been registered and voting here from three to s years.

Proof of vote.—The above evidence of fraud proves the vote, cially as there is no attempt by contestee to meet it. The vote should stand thus:

Add 30 to Chalmers and take 30 from Morgan. Add, also, to Chal 23 rejected voters. Burchard says he knew them to be voters t Burton says they also claimed at the time to be registered voters t Count then stands:

	Chalmers.	Mc
Brought forward	6,637	
West Holly Springs:		
Add	30	.....
Deduct	....	
	6,667	

RED BANKS.

Evidences of fraud.—(1) The Democrats have at Red Banks a s tricksters and ballot-box thieves, who are regularly appointed as tion officers to do such work as is necessary to secure Democratic

cess. They had a clerk of the last election, one W. M. Burtley, who
went to Red Banks from his home in Memphis to help hold the election. (See testimony of J. W. Moore, Rec., pp. 636, 637.)

(2) While two popular Democrats could get only 72 votes, Judge
Morgan pretends to have received 115 votes in the last election. (See
figures of primary vote, Rec., p. 7, and certified vote for Marshall
County, Rec., p. 743.)

And we again assert that Democratic primaries bring out a fuller
Democratic vote than do the general elections, for the reason that a
primary election is virtually the election. This is history and the present state of affairs in Mississippi, as the record shows.

Proof of vote.—The United States supervisor, J. W. Moore, the largest
planter in Marshall County, proves that he saw 133 Republican tickets
voted at this box at the last election. He also proves that 27 Republican voters were not allowed to vote because their names had been
scratched off.

He knew the 133 Republican tickets were Republican because, (1)
they were whiter in color than the Democratic tickets and had a fringe
at one end, and (2) because he knew the voters were Republicans.

The vote as shown by the certified returns was: for Morgan, 115, and
for Chalmers, 91. The above proof shows that the vote as actually cast
was: for Chalmers, 133. The returns being vitiated the count should
be—

	Chalmers.	Morgan.
Forward	6, 667	12, 232
Red Bank:		
Add	41	
Deduct	. . . .	115
	6, 708	12, 117

BYHALIA.

Evidences of fraud.—(1) Cannon Bass and Sam Chew, numbers 51
and 333 respectively on the certified list of voters at Byhalia, were
counted as having voted, when, in fact, they were not at the polls that
day, and Cannon Bass was then at home sick, unable to get to the polls,
and shortly afterwards died of his illness. (See testimony of Thomas
Guy, Rec., p. 622; James Ingram, Rec., p. 616, and certified list of
voters at Byhalia, Rec., p. 1114.)

(2) Ben Ingram is marked on the clerk's list as having voted, No.
376, when he does not live in that precinct, and did not vote at Byhalia
that day. (See testimony of James Ingram, Rec., p. 616.)

(3) Pres. Ingram's name appears twice on the clerk's list of voters,
Nos. 224 and 304. (See certified list of voters, *supra*.)

(4) The Republican inspector could not read and write. (See testimony of James Ingram, Rec., p. 616.)

(5) The certified list of voters shows the number of voters to have
been 461. (See Ex. B to James Ingram's testimony, Record, pp. 1114
to 1117.)

Proof of vote.—Two witnesses saw 240 Republican tickets given to
that many men whom they knew to be Republican voters, on the representation from those receiving them that they wanted to vote them. It
is proved that 190 thus given tickets voted them, as shown by the clerk's
list of voters, *supra,* and 50 were not allowed to vote because their
names had been scratched off after they had been registered, as they

claimed. (See testimony of James Ingram, Rec., pp. 615, 616, a
hibits A and B to his testimony, Rec., pp. 1114–1117; see testim
Thomas Guy, Rec., p. 622.)

This box has been notorious for its frauds for years. In the Buc
vs. Manning contest, both the majority and minority of the com
concurred in the opinion that the ballot-box here was stuff
twenty-nine voters illegally rejected. (See House Miscellaneou
session Forty-seventh Congress, p. 97, and Dig. El. Cases, 18
pages 296 and 322.)

In the Chalmers vs. Manning case, the Democratic inspecto
the poll books and refused to hold the election. (See testimon
Lyle in record of Chalmers against Manning.)

From this proof the returns should be set aside. Add 35 to
mers and take 302 from Morgan, and the count would stand thus

	Chalmers.	
Forward	6,708	
By balua:		
Add	35	...
Deduct		
	6,743	

WATSON.

Evidences of fraud.—(1) There were only 104 votes returned a
and 105 votes were counted out of the box. (See certified vote
Watson, Rec., 743; see testimony of J. A. Stephens, Rec., 559–6

(2) They refused to allow thirty of the negroes who were old
there to cast their ballots, and thus deprived them and the cont
of their rights under the law. (See testimony of J. A. Stephens
559, 560.

The only question here is as to counting the rejected votes an
will be reserved for future consideration.

WALL HILL.

The proof is that 107 negroes voted the Republican ticket with
mers's name on it for Congress, and the man issuing the tickets
the men who received them to be Republicans. There were 1
who were not allowed to vote, who had been properly registered.
timony of D. L. Woods, Record, 623, and Exhibit A to his depo
Rec., 1110, 1111.)

The above evidence of Woods shows that the count should
contestant actually cast, 107.

At Wall Hill, Chalmers was counted only 80 votes, where 107
cast for him, and 17 illegally rejected. Similar frauds were perpe
here in 1880. (See Buchanan vs. Manning, Dig. El. Cases, 18
page 323.)

The returns here should be set aside. Add to Chalmers 27, an
from Morgan 119, and the count will then stand thus:

	Chalmers.	
Forward	6,743	
Wall Hill:		
Add	27	...
Deduct		
	6,770	

CHULAHOMA.

Republican tickets were distributed here, as elsewhere in Marshall County, to those who announced their intention of voting them. In this way 278 Republican tickets were issued, the names of those receiving them being taken down, and the list is marked Exhibit A to the deposition of Wiley Watson, and is in the record, 1100. This list was compared with the certified list marked Exhibit B to Watson's deposition in the record, page 1103, and the names of 248 of those to whom Republican tickets had been issued, as before stated, were found on the list of those who voted at Chulahoma, as certified by the clerk in Exhibit B, Record, page 1103. And in the list, which is a part of Exhibit A, above referred to, we find the names of 30 registered voters who were refused a vote. According to the certified returns, 321 votes were cast, 121 for Morgan and 200 for Chalmers.

This is another large Republican box where frauds have been constantly practiced. In the Buchanan vs. Manning contest, the United States supervisor was ejected from the room, for which Bowen, one of the inspectors, was convicted in the United States court. (See Dig. El. Cases, 1880–'82, pages 292 and 315, and Case No. 1771, on page 322 of same volume.)

In 1882, in the Chalmers vs. Manning contest, the box was stolen and carried off, but recaptured, and when counted had 252 majority for Chalmers. (See records of supervisors, House Miscellaneous, First Session, Forty-eighth Congress, vol. 19, doc. 48, p. 4.)

The returns here should be rejected. Add 48 to Chalmers, take 121 from Morgan, and the count then stands thus:

	Chalmers.	Morgan.
Forward	6,770	11,696
Chulahoma:		
Add	48	
Deduct		121
	6,818	11,575

EARLY GROVE.

No election was held at this place because the judges, or inspectors, who were appointed to hold the election would not open the box to receive the votes under the pretense that no justice was present to qualify them. Dr. Lyle read them the law from the code of Mississippi, by which the inspectors are authorized to administer the oath to one another, but they refused to hold the election.

There were 100 voters—70 negroes and 30 whites—there who wanted to cast their ballots for James R. Chalmers for Congress.

It has been the habit of the Democrats at Early Grove for ten years to refuse to hold an election, or else refuse to return the result when the chances were for a majority against the Democrats. All this is proved by testimony of Dr. A. M. Lyle (Rec., p. 187), and ably referred to in the majority report.

LAW'S HILL.

The certified returns give 94 for Morgan and 12 for Chalmers. This is a fraud; 45 Republican tickets were issued to men on the representation that they wished to vote them. Of this number 38 did vote, and

the others were refused, as a goodly number of the Republicans we
at every precinct in this election. (See deposition of Andrew McGhe
Rec., p. 627–'9, and Exhibit A to his deposition, Rec., p. 1053.)

Similar illegal rejections of voters at this box were proved in 188

The returns should be set aside. Add 24 to Chalmers, take 94 fro
Morgan, and the count will then stand thus:

	Chalmers.	Morga
Forward	6,818	11,
Law's Hill:		
Add	24	
Deduct		
	6,842	11,

WATERFORD.

We have here the same discrepancy that we find at almost eve
box. There were 229 voters and 230 votes. (See certified list of v(
ers, pp. 1095–'6; see certified returns for Marshall County, Rec., p. 74:

There were 136 Republican tickets distributed to Republican voter
who declared they wanted to vote them, with instructions if they d
not get to vote to return the tickets. Only 28 tickets were returne
leaving 108 to be voted. The 28 denied the right to vote were refuse
because their names had been scratched from the poll-books, and tl
contestant should be allowed the benefit of their votes. (See testimon
of H C. Walton, Rec., p. 620.)

These frauds are virtually confessed by failure of contestee to mal
any proof as to the vote or count by Moses Pegues, an inspector at th
box, who was examined as a witness by the contestee. (See testimor
of Moses Pegues, Rec., p. 860.)

The returns should be set aside here. Add 40 to Chalmers and tal
162 from Morgan, and the count will then stand thus:

	Chalmers.	Morga
Forward	6,842	11,
Waterford:		
Add	40	
Deduct		
	6,882	11,

HUDSONVILLE.

Evidences of fraud.—(1) There were 6 men who were marked
voting, none of whom lived in this precinct, and 5 of whom were re
dents of the State of Tennessee, and none of whom were present. (S
testimony of Henry Reason, Rec., p. 636.)

(2) And 13 Republican voters were refused a vote, John Lewis, tl
witness, being among the number, though they had been properly re
istered. (See testimony of Henry Reason, Rec., p. 638, and testimor
of John Lewis, Rec., p. 633, and Exhibit A to his deposition, Rec.,
1099–1100.)

(3) Wesley Woodson, a colored witness for contestee, proved that
voted a national Republican ticket with Chalmers' name scratched o
(See testimony of Wesley Woodson, Rec., p. 863.)

This would make an uneven vote at this place. But turning to the certified return of Hudsonville in the record, 743, we find the Democratic electors are given 142 votes and Morgan is given 142, and the Republican electors and Chalmers each received 77 votes. And this shows that the vote was even all around; if it is to prove anything. But looking at the first and third evidences of fraud, we see that the certified returns are without any verity whatever.

The certified list of voters was by accident omitted from the printed record, but the original, which bears the seal of the court, and is clearly identified by comparing the numbers on it with the numbers on the list filed by the witnesses, John Lewis and Henry Reasons, was filed with the committee.

An examination of this certified list shows a clear case of fraud here. Seven men who the proof shows were not in the State on the day of election, and had not been for years in the vicinity of Hudsonville, are returned as having voted there at this election. This is a similar fraud to that perpetrated at Byhalia, and the returns here should be set aside.

The testimony of John Lewis and Henry Reasons shows that 91 voters received Republican tickets from them, and went with them to the polls. A list of their names is filed, as exhibits to their depositions.

The certified list of voters shows that they all voted, and only one, Wiley Woodson, who is called as a witness for contestee, says he did not vote for Chalmers. This is the only one of the several thousand names given by the ticket distributers as having voted for contestant that was called to say he did not so vote. But Woodson says he voted a Republican ticket with Chalmers's name scratched off, yet no such ticket appears in the count. Again, John Lewis proves that he had been duly registered, and offered to vote for Chalmers, but was rejected.

This supplies the place of Wiley Woodson and shows 91 votes for Chalmers where only 77 were counted for him.

The returns should be set aside. Add 14 to Chalmers and take 142 from Morgan, and the count will then stand thus:

	Chalmers.	Morgan.
Forward	6,882	11,319
Hudsonville: Add	14	
Deduct		142
	6,896	11,177

PANOLA COUNTY.

COMO.

Evidences of fraud.—It was impossible, on account of the dilatory cross-examinations by contestee, to examine all the voters in the district, hence contestant examined the ticket distributers at most of the boxes, and selected Como as a specimen box, where the voters themselves were called and examined. There were here 370 colored, and 133 white, men who voted, but the returns gave Morgan 306, and Chalmers 207.

Two hundred and sixty-nine voters were examined, and of these 257 swore they voted for Chalmers, and 10 who were registered and offered to vote for him were illegally rejected.

Two only said they voted for Morgan. Contestant was, by dila
cross-examinations, kept for thirty days, examining 269 witnesse
this box, and was proceeding to examine more when stopped by the
jection of time expired.

This precinct was selected because the fraud was so skillfully j
ticed here that the United States supervisor was unable to dete
The examination of the witnesses clearly exposed the fraud, and
may be taken as a test and sample of what was done all over the
trict.

The returns here must be set aside and the vote counted as pro
which is 267 for Chalmers and 2 for Morgan. To do this, adds (
Chalmers and takes 304 from Morgan. The count will then stand th

	Chalmers.	Mor
Brought forward	6, 896	
Como :		
Add..	60	......
Deduct...	....	
	6, 956	

SPRING PORT.

Evidences of fraud.—(1) The Republican inspector could not read
write. (See testimony of W. S. Lester, Rec., p. 442.)

(2) Manuel Jones saw an inspector change his ticket before put
it in the box, and saw another man's ticket changed in like manner
was charged at the ballot-box that the inspector had changed
tickets, and the inspector did not deny it. (See testimony of Mar
Jones, Rec., p. 444.)

Proof of vote.—W. S. Lester proved there were 93 names of no
voters on the certified list of voters at this box and that four w
men voted for Chalmers. There were 13 negroes who were deni
vote, who claimed they had been registered and their names had l
scratched off. (See testimony of W. S. Lester, Rec., pp. 442–'3–'4.)

This testimony is undisputed.

Fraud being clearly established here, the returns should be set as
Add 5 votes to Chalmers, take 97 from Morgan. The count will t
stand :

	Chalmers.	Mor
Forward	6, 956	1
Spring Port:		
Add..	5	......
Deduct...	....	
	6, 961	1

LONGTOWN.

Evidences of fraud.—(1) Two witnesses, voters at Longtown, saw t
tickets dropped on the floor and other tickets put in the box in t
stead. (See testimony of Fret Nolen, Rec., p. 430; Silas Gray, Rec
433.)

(2) The Republican inspector could not read and write. (See te
mony of John M. Hewlett, Rec., pp. 539–40.)

Proof of vote.—The total certified vote is 211—Morgan 157, Chalmers 54.

M. G. Littlejohn, United States supervisor, proves he saw a Democratic inspector receive 94 Republican tickets, but could not tell whether said tickets went into the ballot-box or not, he being behind the box, which was so high he could not see the handling of the tickets after they were received. He is sustained by John M. Hewlett. (See testimony of M. G. Littlejohn, Rec., pp. 542–3; John M. Hewlett, Rec., pp. 535–6–7–8.)

The box was taken from the presence of the United States supervisor both at dinner and supper time.

The returns here must be set aside because clearly vitiated for fraud. The proofs show that 94 votes were cast for Chalmers, while only 54 were counted. There is no proof of any vote for Morgan, therefore add 40 to Chalmers and take 157 from Morgan, the count will then stand thus:

	Chalmers.	Morgan.
Forward	6,961	10,775
Longtown:		
Add	40	
Deduct		157
	7,001	10,618

BATESVILLE.

Evidences of fraud.—(1) A Democratic inspector, T. J. Mabry, confessed he changed the votes so as to change a majority of 200 for Chalmers into a majority of 200 for Morgan. (See testimony of H. C. Worsham, Rec., p. 472; J. A. Thomas, Rec., p. 166 *et seq.*)

(2) The United States supervisor swears that he was so placed that he could not see exactly what the fraud was, but he believed it was going on. (See testimony of Lem. B. Lester, Rec., pp. 989–91.)

(3) It is proved that at this box the negroes are in a majority of two to one, and there are 30 white people who voted and worked for Chalmers. (See testimony of R. M. Kyle, Rec., p. 444.)

The returns here are clearly proved to have been fraudulent and must be set aside. According to the statement of the Democratic inspector, Mabry, there were 200 majority here for Chalmers.

As he is counted only 132 there should be added to him 68 and taken from Morgan 245.

At this box 81 colored voters were rejected who offered to vote for Chalmers, and who, when rejected, brought their tickets to contestant, who was present at this box, and gave him their names, and each stated then and there that they had been duly registered at this box. (See list of names, R., 237.) No evidence was taken to disprove this.

These 81 should also be counted for Chalmers. Add 68 to Chalmers and take 245 from Morgan and the count will then stand thus:

	Chalmers.	Morgan.
Forward	7,001	10,618
Batesville:		
Add	68	
Deduct		245
	7,069	10,373

H. Mis. 137——26

PLEASANT MOUNT.

Evidences of fraud.—(1) The Republican inspector could neither read nor write. (See testimony of J. F. Buchanan, Rec., p. 291.)

(2) There is the same discrepancy here as noticed in Marshall County. The returns, page 744 of the record, show 226 votes cast for candidates for Congress, while the certified list of voters contains only 225 names (See certified list of voters, Rec., pp. 289–290.)

Proof of vote.—J. F. Buchanan, a white man who has lived in the precinct ever since 1844, and who has been a candidate for office several times, and who therefore knows nearly all the whites and negroes personally in the precinct, on being shown the certified list of voters at the last election, proves that 122 of those whose names appear on said list are negroes and Republicans. He says, further, two white men voted for Chalmers, and one of these, J. F. Essary, testified he so voted. (See testimony of J. F. Buchanan, Rec., pp. 290–5; J. F. Essary, Rec., p. 295.)

Another witness, Lemuel Nelson, colored, gives six additional names of negroes who voted at this box for Chalmers, these names not being included in the 122 shown by Captain Buchanan. (See testimony of Lemuel Nelson, Rec., p. 295.)

The proof that the Republican inspector could neither read nor write, and his signature by a cross-mark to the certified list of voters, when followed by the testimony of J. F. Buchanan giving the politics of the voters on the certified list, is sufficient to set aside the returns at this box.

The returns being set aside takes 126 from Morgan; there is positive proof by three witnesses, J. F. Buchanan, J. F. Essary, and Lemuel Nelson, that they voted for Chalmers.

The testimony of Buchanan and of Nelson clearly shows that all the negroes whose names appear on the certified list of voters were Republican except one, and it is said of him that he sometimes votes Republican and sometimes the Democratic ticket.

From this proof it would appear that thirty votes cast for Chalmers were counted for Morgan, and this not by relying on the color line, but by the testimony of an uncontradicted witness, who had lived long in this precinct, who had been a candidate there himself, and who knew all the voters.

From this testimony the box should either be thrown out, so far as the returns are concerned, and three votes counted for Chalmers, or thirty votes should be added to Chalmers and thirty taken from Morgan, giving one, the Republican, and the other the Democratic vote as proved by Buchanan. The box being thown out, then the count would stand thus:

	Chalmers.	Morgan.
Forward	7,069	10,373
Pleasantville thrown out, deduct	97	126
	6,972	10,247

TATE COUNTY.

The notice of contest charges:

TATE COUNTY.

This is the county where, in 1882, I had a majority of 306 votes and where I was robbed of my whole vote by the celebrated fraud whereby my vote was certified to be for J. R. Chalmers and taken from me. In this county there was a primary election for the nomination of a Democratic candidate for dist. atty., in which only 1,050 Democratic votes were cast in 1887, and in 1882 Col. Manning had only 1,166, and yet you pretend to have received about 1,500 majority. The Tate County Record, speaking of the election for dist. atty., says: At Senatobia, Oglesby received 145 and Slack 10 votes, and adds: "Senatobia is Oglesby's home and this vote is a handsome compliment to his popularity and ability." And yet at Oglesby's home you pretend to have received 318 votes, where Oglesby and Slack together could only get 155 Democratic votes. I charge that this box was stuffed at dinner time when it was taken from the presence of the U. S. supervisors.

I charge that in this county the inspectors of election were all appointed in violation of law; that the ballot-boxes were taken from the presence of the U. S. supervisors wherever we had any; that there was wholesale ballot-box stuffing, and especially I charge that at Coldwater, where I had 170 votes cast for me, the box was taken to the house of one of your friends and when counted had only 7 votes for me.

I charge that the whole election in this county was a fraud and that the vote of the county should be thrown out.

All of these charges are fully sustained by the proof.

Evidences of fraud.—The election commissioners refused to appoint any of the inspectors of election recommended by Republicans and appointed all Democrats in every box but three in the county, and one of these could not read or write. (See testimony of John S. Jones, Rec., 517 and 518.)

He further says that this was repeatedly done by the commissioners of that county, and in this he is sustained by the record of Buchanan *vs.* Manning, where the same thing was done in 1880.

E. L. Weeus, one of the witnesses for contestee, not only shows that inspectors were asked for by Colonel Jones, but tells why they were not appointed, as follows:

Int. 7. Did you hear any conversation between any two members of the board of election commissioners for Tate County at or about the time they were appointing inspectors for the election of 1888 as to the fitness of men recommended for inspectors for the Republicans?—A. 7. I heard a conversation amongst all three of them while the board was in session. *Smith was not satisfied with the persons John S. Jones, chairman of the district Republican committee, had made to him personally;* he said that some of them were bad men and he could not appoint them.—Record, 909.

Smith was the commissioner appointed by Democrats to represent the Republicans.

The brief for the contestee says:

Smith is a Republican from principle, and well knowing Jones and his mercenary politics, *repudiated and spit upon his suggestion and made his own appointments.*

This is sufficient to show that he was a mere tool of the Democrats At two of three boxes where there were Republican inspectors the box was removed from the presence of the United States supervisors, and the majority threw out these two boxes.

TAYLOR'S.

At Taylor's the ballots were never counted, the box having been stolen by the friends of the contestee. But this was not done without a protest. John C. Clifton, the United States supervisor, made as gallant a fight for the box and for an honest, fair election as any man ever did. He followed the box to the house of W. S. Bailey, one of the Democratic inspectors, and was there told by said Bailey to get his dinner in the kitchen. This insult brought about a difficulty some time after the election, in which Bailey shot and wounded Clifton, who has since been confined to his bed from said wound. (See testimony of John C. Clifton, pp. 189-191.)

The legal majority against the Democrats at this box, when fairly counted, is about 100. (See testimony of John S. Jones, Rec., p. 518.)

Clifton gives the name and color of the voters—145 colored and 30 white.

This is evidence of gross fraud and, added to the refusal of the commissioners to give the Republicans any inspectors they asked for, tend to prove a conspiracy to defraud and a determination to carry the county at all hazards, and hence where any doubt arises as to the sufficiency of proof of fraud at any one box, the benefit of that doubt should be given against the fairness of the count.

The count here should be Chalmers 145 and Morgan 30.

	Chalmers.	Morgan.
Forward	6,972	
Taylor's, add	145	
Total	7,117	

COLD WATER.

At this box 165 negroes voted open tickets for Chalmers and called out the name of Chalmers when they voted.

In his speech, made shortly before the election, he asked that all who voted for him should call out his name when they voted and this was done for that reason.

The witness Dailey also voted for Chalmers. The box was taken at dinner-time to the house of a Democrat named Bailey, and when counted was returned 275 for Morgan and only 7 for Chalmers. Mr. Bailey, to whose house the box was taken for dinner, seems to have known what the count would be here, as he had offered to bet before the election that Chalmers would not get over 7 votes at this box.

Dailey voted for Chalmers and distributed tickets and saw 165 voted for him, a list of whose names he gives. (See R., 500-502.)

This box should be rejected, and, counting the vote as proved, we add 149 to Chalmers and take from Morgan 275. The count will then stand thus:

	Chalmers.	Morgan.
Forward	7,117	16,277
Cold Water:		
Add	149	
Deduct		275
	7,266	16,002

SENATOBIA.

The ballot-box here was removed at dinner time to the house of one Waite, and taken from the presence of the United States supervisor against his protest. (See testimony of G. W. Haynes, R., 525-7.)

The record of Buchanan against Manning shows that the same thing was done here in 1880, and that the box was then taken to the residence of this same man Waite. (Dig. El. Cases 1880-'82, p. 333.)

At Senatobia the contestant received, according to the certified returns, only 44 votes, and Morgan 318, out of a total of 364 votes, when it is proved that 200 or more negroes voted there, and when it is charged in the notice of contest and not denied in the answer that, in 1887 there was a primary election for the nomination of a Democratic candidate for district attorney, the contest being between two candidates, Oglesby and Slack—Oglesby receiving at Senatobia 145 votes and Slack 10; and the Tate County Record, a Democratic paper, in speaking of said election, declared: "Senatobia is Oglesby's home, and this vote is a handsome compliment to his popularity and ability."

The returns here must be rejected, and, there being no proof of the vote, none can be counted. This takes 44 from Chalmers and 318 from Morgan, and the count will thus stand:

	.	Chalmers.	Morgan.
Forward		7, 266	10, 002
Senatobia thrown out, deduct		44	318
		7, 222	9, 684

SHERROD'S.

At this box the Republican inspector was a negro, who could not read or write. The Democratic inspectors were seen changing the tickets, and the box was removed from the presence of the United States supervisor before it was counted.

Deposition of C. A. GRAYSON (white), a witness on behalf of the contestant, being first duly sworn, deposed as follows:

Examination by General CHALMERS:

Q. State your age, your occupation, and your residence.—A. I am 45 years old; my occupation is farmer and merchant; residence, in Tate County.

Q. Were you at any box at the election; if so, state what box, and what position, if any, you held there?—A. I was at Sherrod's box, Tate County. I was U. S. supervisor.

Q. Please state whether the box was taken away from your presence without your consent before it was counted.—A. Yes, sir; it was taken away at night. Carried about one and one-half miles or two miles from the voting place through the rain, and they said it was taken to the Bowdre place.

Q. Did you see anything to indicate a stuffing of the ballot-box that day? If so, please state it.—A. I saw the man that received the tickets from the voters fold a ticket and put it under his legs—slipping it under his legs to one of the clerks or inspectors of election. They had their hands together under there. I could not tell whether they changed the ticket or not. They discovered that I saw them, and brought his hand back with a ticket in his hand and put it in the box. They seemed at different times to place themselves occasionally in position between myself and the man that received the tickets, with the box setting just before him. I would move around, got up once and stood up so that I could see that the votes went into the box, when they asked me why I stood up; and one of them jerked off a board—told me to set down; there was plenty of light—so I could see. The reason I stood up was for the want of light, so they thought. Also, a colored witness by the name of Mat White, called me outside the ropes and told me that he saw them changing tickets and putting different ones in the box.

Q. Is there anything connected with the election at that place that seemed to you to be wrong?—A. It was a very unpleasant and disorderly-held election. Drinking and cursing on the part of the Democrats; a great many unnecessary questions and insulting questions asked to the niggers.

Q. Could the negro who acted as supervisor for the Republicans there that day read or write or not?—A. The colored man that was appointed inspector didn't come. They appointed another nigger, and I don't think he could either read or write. He appeared to be a very ignorant and dull nigger; but as for his reading and writing, I am not certain.

Q. What position have you held in the Republican party in your county?—A. For 6 or 8 years I was chairman for the county committee—Republican.

Q. What office have you been a candidate for in your county?—A. Sheriff.

Q. In that election when you were the Republican candidate for sheriff, please state whether any effort was made to cheat you out of your vote at the Sherrod box. State all about it.—A. Yes, sir; I was a candidate for sheriff. At 12 o'clock the Democrats insisted on taking the box and going over to a neighbor's house for dinner—about half a mile. Myself and my friends—Republicans—objected to it. .They said they were going, and we could go with them. Couple of my friends did so, one of them the inspector. When they went in to dinner my friends suggested they had better take the box in with them. The other party said no, leave it in the room. They left it in the room. When they got into the dining-room one of my friends took a seat on the far side of the table, and just as he sat down he looked back into the room he had just came out of. The door stood open about 10 inches. He saw a young lady cross to the other side of the room with the ballot-box in her hand. He jumped up and said to the boys, "There is something wrong in yonder," and ran in there just as she was handing the box out of the window to some of their Democrat friends. He turned back and ran out of the door, and run against one that had the box in his hands, and the fellow that has the box throws it down. His other comrade—Democrat—turns his coat tail over his head and runs off. My friend hollows to him and says to him, "You need not run; I know you." He picked the box up, carried into the dinner table; kept it by his side; brought it back to the voting ground; it was closely watched from that time up till the time the votes were counted, and my majority when counted out was more than 2 to one in favor of me. (Rec., pp. 187, 188.)

From this it is manifest that the returns at this box must be set aside.

Proof of vote.—C. A. Grayson says:

Q. Did you keep a list of the voters there that day; and if so, what did you do with it?—A. I did sir; and sent the list to W. G. Beanland, chief supervisor of elections at Oxford, Miss.
Q. Please state to the best of your recollection how many white and how many colored men voted there that day.—A. My recollection is about 140 colored and 40 odd whites.
Q. Is that or not about the full strength of the whole vote at that box?—A. It is of those that vote the Democratic ticket. There are a good many other white voters there, but are not Democrats; don't claim to be Democrats. I know a number of white men that said they would not go to the eletion because it was useless; because they would be counted out. The vote would not be counted properly, and it was a waste of time to go to the election.
Q. Do you know of any colored man at that box who voted the Democratic ticket?—A. I do not.
Q. To the best of your knowledge and belief, and from what you saw and heard there that day, please state what ticket was voted by the colored men.—A. One nigger came up to the polls; he is classed as a nigger, but I think he is about 7-8 white man; he lives with an uncompromising Democrat; handed in his ticket and stated that he always voted the Democratic ticket. When I said just before that I knew of no nigger that voted the Democratic ticket, I don't regard him as a nigger; his name is Woodson. I think all the niggers voted straight Republican ticket.
Q. Did you, as U. S. supervisor, object to the box being taken away from the polling place before it was counted?—A. I did.
Q. What is, in your opinion, the majority against the Democrats at Sherrod's box at a full vote and a fair count?—A. At least one hundred.
Q. Please state why you did not come down to Sardis last week to be examined.—A. I was sick.
Q. Were any colored voters at that box rejected that day? If so, state how many, if you can.—A. I think about 18 or 20; and some of them had been voting there for 10 or 12 years—in at that box—and had never moved out; one or two on my own place that had never moved out of the beat.
Q. Upon what grounds were they rejected?—A. They claimed their names were not on the books. (Rec., pp. 187-188.)

No witness is called to contradict this statement in any respect, except to excuse the removal of the box. From this proof it is evident that this was a large Republican box, and the witness says that the negroes all voted a straight Republican ticket, and that there was a majority of at least 100 here for the Republican party.

From this proof, as but 20 were counted for Chalmers, there should be added 80 votes to him, and 166 taken from Morgan.

Grayson further proves that 18 voters were rejected here, some of whom he knew had never moved out of the beat, two of them living on his own place. These 18 should also be added to Chalmers. But as this was an *ex parte* affidavit, the box is simply thrown out on the admission of the witness for contestee that it was taken from the United States supervisors.

Take from Chalmers 20, take from Morgan 166, and the count will then stand thus:

	Chalmers.	Morgan.
Brought forward	7,222	9,684
Sherwood:		
Deduct	20	166
	7,202	9,518

STRAYHORN.

We have proof from both a Democrat and a Republican that all the inspectors of this box are Democrats.

J. H. Wommack, Democrat, and one of the commissioners, says:

Int. 12. Who at Strayhorn?—Ans. 12. Pace and I voted for T. C. Brownlee, a Republican, and elected him, but Smith of our board suggested W. A. Nelson; afterward served as U. S. supervisor at that box. Afterward Z. P. Smith asked us to re-open the Strayhorn case, and he would suggest another name; and we re-opened that and he suggested J. N. Gregory. We, Pace and I, both told him Gregory was a Democrat; Smith said he preferred a good Democrat to a sorry Republican, and we then elected Gregory. (Rec., pp. 899, 900.)

This clearly shows that Smith, the so-called Republican commissioner in this county, was a mere tool of the Democrats.

Deposition of J. A. Williams (white), a witness on behalf of the contestant; being first duly sworn, deposed as follows:

Examination by Gen. CHALMERS:

Q. Please state your name, occupation, and residence.—A. My name is J. A. Williams; occupation, farmer, and merchandise a little, and residence in Strayhorn, Miss.

Q. How long have you resided there, Mr. Williams?—A. Have been there in that settlement for about 20 years.

Q. Did you vote at the Strayhorn box at the last election for Congressman?—A. I did.

Q. What ticket did you vote?—A. Voted the Republican ticket—what is called Harrison's ticket.

Q. Do you know whether the judges—inspectors of election—were or were not all Democrats?—A. They were all Democrats. I tried to get one to say he wouldn't serve—tried to get in one of our men and to keep him out. He served himself.

Q. Mr. Williams, how many colored men voted at that box that day, to the best of your knowledge and belief?—A. I don't know; to my best judgment would be 30 or 40; didn't pay much attention. There were good many there, though.

Q. Do you know of your own knowledge whether any white men at Strayhorn were supporters of mine or not?—A. Yes, sir.

Q. About how many of them, Mr. Williams?—A. Well, sir, I couldn't say how many there was; several said that they did vote. I don't know whether they did or not.

(Excepted to as hearsay testimony.)

Q. Were you an inspector at that box four years ago, Mr. Williams?—A. Yes, sir; I was.

Q. What was my vote there then?—A. 92 votes; that is my recollection now. I think it was 92. (Rec., pp. 515, 516.)

Q. You say that four years ago when you were inspector that Gen. Chalmers received 94 votes at that box; please repeat your statement.—A. I said 92 was my recollection.

Q. I stand corrected; you said 92. Was Gen. Chalmers at that time a Republican?—A. Well, he was on that list; I couldn't tell you what he was; I don't know what he was; he was on that ticket; voted for him; at least on the Republican ticket what we voted for; he was on our ticket.

Q. Who do you mean by "we?"—A. "We" the Republican party, that
Q. Whenever there is a split among the Democrats don't you vote for the w
A. Yes, sir.
Q. Wasn't Gen. Chalmers the wedge then?—A. Yes, sir, you can call him
you want to.
Q. Did you hear him make a speech in that canvass?—A. I couldn't say,
tively or not; might and might not.
Q. Did you ever hear Gen. Chalmers in a public speech declare himself to
publican?—A. I don't know that I ever did, sir.
Q. At the time, then, that Gen. Chalmers received 92 votes he was runni
independent, was he?—A. I never heard it that way.
Q. Was he not running as an independent Democrat-Greenback?—A. I didn'
he was on my ticket, the ticket I vote, and I voted for him.
Q. You are successful, then, as an election manager for the man you vote
Well, I don't know; call it successful or what not.
Q. I will ask you to state whether or not the man in opposition to the Dei
ticket ever got as much as 92 votes at Strayhorn in any election when you
the manager?—A. Yes, sir, I think they have.
Q. Name the time and place, and the man that got that many votes in op
to the Democratic ticket at Strayhorn when somebody else held the electio
think the highest vote over mine polled there over the Republican party was
sir. (Rec., p. 517.)

This witness proves that the Republican vote here, at a fair el
is 92; that thirty or forty negroes voted here that day and tha
whites besides himself voted for Chalmers, and yet he was counte
16 votes.

The contestee attempted to overcome this proof by showin
some of the negroes voted for him and introduced two witness
this purpose, one a white man, John McNeely, and the other a
Jerry Hill, and they both agree in their statement that only two n
so voted at that election. (See R. 923–924 and 928.)

This testimony strengthens that of J. A. Williams, and show
the Republican vote here was not fairly counted.

The appointment of all Democrats as inspectors was itself un
and in direct violation of the statute. And when this is follov
proof that the vote, as counted, is far below the usual Republica
at that box, when fairly counted, this is sufficient to set aside
turns.

Take from Chalmers 16 and from Morgan 223 and the vote woul
stand:

	Chalmers.	1
Brought forward	7,202	
Strayhorn:		
Thrown out (deduct)	16	
	7,186	

All the other boxes in this county should be rejected on acco
the refusal of the Democrats to allow the Republican inspectors
for, and the appointment of Democrats, and on account of the
proved. In this county, two weeks before the election, the Tate C
Record said:

What did the drum-beat mean ten or twelve years ago? It meant this—n
premacy over whites, and it means the same thing now, under the leadership
and Chalmers. Democrats of Tate, can you stand it? If not, up and at them
old-time style and with your old-time vigor. The danger is imminent. They
and active. How are you? We repeat, the danger of losing the county is gr

And yet Chalmers was returned but 435 votes in the county an
gan 1,490 majority. The proper thing to do would be to throw the

out as to the returns and count only the vote proved at Coldwater and Taylor.

LA FAYETTE COUNTY.

The notice of contest says:

LA FAYETTE COUNTY.

This is the county where the Democratic cannon was in 1880 placed in twenty steps of the court-house and fired across the crowd of negro voters until they were dispersed, and where in 1882 *L. S. Dillard illegally held back the count* for which he was indicted in the U. S. court and plead guilty and was subsequently rewarded by Mr. Cleveland with the post-office at Oxford. In this county 800 voters who desired to vote the Republican ticket for me were disfranchised by erasure from the poll-books; 400 were erased on the poll-books at the two boxes in Oxford alone, and the U. S. supervisor, who was present, was marked dead and not allowed to vote. I charge that this was done after the poll-books were delivered to messengers to be carried to the voting places, and that some, if not all, these messengers were selected by the aforesaid postmaster, L. S. Dillard, who in 1882 sent the celebrated telegram, "What is the latest? We are holding the count."

These charges are fully sustained by the proof. The history of this county shows it to be thoroughly Republican. It was the home of L. Q. C. Lamar, and yet he was defeated here for Congress by 48 votes in 1872, by a Republican. Chalmers carried the county over Manning by 366 in 1882, and it was admitted, by the Democratic district committee-man and others, one week before the election, that Chalmers would carry the county by 400 majority, unless something was done to prevent it. Something was done and what that something was is clearly shown in the majority report. It was the disfranchisement of the Republican voters by the erasure of their names from the poll-books. They were marked dead, a more merciful killing of Republican voters than is sometimes practiced in this State. That this was the result of a deliberate conspiracy, and that the contestee was in the county when it was planned is fully proved.

Faust, a white witness and a Republican, testifies as follows: (Rec., pp. 593–594).

Q. Did you hear any conversation from a leading Democrat of Oxford a short time before the election as to the probable result in that county?—A. Yes, sir.

Q. Please state as near as you can when that was, who was present, and what was said?—A. *Friday week before the election I was in Oxford*, having business with W. V. Sullivan. In presence with Mr. W. E. Avant, in conversation and probably about our business—I had but little with him—he asked me how the election was going for Congress. I stated that I supposed that Morgan would be elected. He just said, "You don't know anything about it. Chalmers will beat Morgan 400 votes in La Fayette County if there isn't something done to prevent. I have just been around, and will have a meeting in my office at 8 o'clock to-night to prevent it, if we can." That was all that was said. This conversation occurred between us after we left the office and was standing between the south portico of the court-house and the east steps. Then we branched out, Avant and him in conversation, to other matters.

He is sustained by W. E. Avent, a white witness and Democrat, as follows (Rec., p. 956):

Q. 1. State your name, age, occupation, and voting place.—W. E. Avent; 62 years old 10th of next June; farmer; La Fayette Springs, Miss.

Q. 2. State whether or not you remember a conversation which took place last fall in regard to the election a few weeks previous to the election between Mr. W. V. Sullivan, Foust, yourself. If so, state as nearly as you can what that conversation was and where the conversation took place?—A. 2. I don't remember any one being present but W. V. Sullivan, Foust, and myself. We had a conversation with regard to the coming election. The inquiry was made by Mr. Sullivan how the election was going in my part of the county. I told him I thought that there was the least excitement, it being Presidential election, I ever saw. I went on to state that I was afraid Mr. Morgan was not going to get along as well as I would like for him to do, and we all, I believe, agreed about the matter; the thing was getting on pretty slowly. I believe this was about the chat we had among us. This conversation, I think, took place in Sullivan's office. I am not certain; I suppose we were together about one hour that day.

Q. 3. State whether or not Mr. Sullivan made any further statement with regard to the matter?—A. 3. Mr. Sullivan stated that he had been around, or was going around; was going to have a meeting that might to fix up for the election. I don't know whether they had it or not.

Q. 4. Was there any request made in regard to you remaining?—A. 4. Mr. Sullivan asked me to remain, but I did not stay. I don't know whether they had it that night or whether they had it at all or not.

Who W. V. Sullivan was is thus proved by McKenzie, chairman of the Democratic Congressional committee. (Rec., p. 655.)

Cross-int. 13. Who is the member of the Dem. ex. com. in this Cong. dist. from La Fayette County?—Ans. W. V. Sullivan.

That this conspiracy was to erase the names of Republican voters from the poll-books is thus proved.

Beanland says (Rec., p. 594):

Q. Did you hear anything from any leading Democrats of the county as to the probable result of the election? And if so state who it was, when it was, and what he said.—A. On or about the 25th of Oct. *I heard Webb Harris say the niggers was organizing all over the country and were all being registered to a man, and they, the Democrats, were to meet on that night to organize and get on some plan to beat Chalmers. Something had to be done.* On or about the 27th he told me they had organized, and were to meet that night to set the ball rolling; that if the niggers were organized *they had the books and the count.* I conversed with him more or less each day up to Saturday; then he told me or I heard him say, they might all be registered, *but they could come up dead when it come to vote,* which proved to be true. On Sat. night before the election, in the post-office at Oxford, while waiting for my mail, *I heard Lem Dillard say the niggers were better organized than they had ever been, but there would be a good many of them who would come up dead, which proved true.* The general talk among the Democrats that some strenuous effort would have to be used to beat Chalmers.

That all this was done under the direction of L. S. Dillard, who was commissioner of election in 1882, and who fraudulently held back the count for which he was indicted and plead guilty in the United States court, is shown in the majority report. That the contestee was in the county when this was done is shown as follows:

D. McKenzie, witness for contestee, on cross-examination said, (Rec., p. 651):

Int. 2. What position did you occupy in the organization of the Democratic party in the election in Nov., 1888, and previous thereto?—Ans. I was chairman of the Dem. ex. com. of De Soto Co., (and also of the 2nd Cong. dist. of Miss.. The Dist. Com.)

Cross-int. 15. What information did you have as to the Democratic and Republican organization in La Fayette County?—Ans. My information was less definite as to the organization of that county than any other in the district. The Dem. party, my information is, was not organized until late, but a pretty good organization was reported to me finally. The last week or ten days of the campaign Judge Morgan spent in that county. As chairman of the dis. com. I specially requested him to give that county his attention, and he reported it in pretty good fix.

That pretty good fix was the disfranchisement of the Republican voters, and it is fair to presume that the contestee fixed it, because this same great outrage was perpetrated at his home in De Soto County in 1880. Johnson, election commissioner of that county was convicted in the United States court and fined $500 for fraudulently erasing the names of voters from the registration and poll books. (See Digest Election Cases 1880 to 1882, Buchanan v. Manning, p. 313.) In this connection attention is called to the following testimony:

By Hon. C. D. Howry, United States district attorney under Cleveland (Rec., p. 954):

· Personally came Chas. B. Howry, a witness for J. R. Chalmers, contestant, *vs.* J. B. Morgan, contestee, who, after being sworn, testifies as follows:

Q. 1. Please state name, age, place of residence, and occupation.—A. 1. Chas. B. Howry; over 21 years; live in Oxford; a lawyer.

Q. 2. Do you remember to have been present in the N. E. part of this county when Mr. Morgan delivered his speech in this canvass with Mr. Manning for the Democratic appointment at the primary, in which speech he referred to the methods of carrying elections, using some such language as the following, that he was in favor of success in the Democratic canvass, even t hough he had to resort to counting out the colored vote in order to accomplish it ? Please state in your own words.

(Objected to as irrelevant to the issue and as not having occurred in any canvass with the two parties, and if occurred at all occurred years ago.)

A. 2. In 1882 Judge Morgan was a candidate for the Democratic nomination to Congress against Col. Manning, and at Boyd's Springs in Lafayette County the judge made a speech which I heard. In that speech he had something to say about white government and the necessity for maintaining it. This was followed by a passing remark *that he was just as much in favor of taking advantage of the negro as anybody* else, *or of cheating the negroes,* if necessary, and this last remark was used in connection with what he had to say about white government. *I understood him to use the word cheating,* but can not say positively that was the precise word. *It was either that or that he was in favor of taking advantage of the negro, if necessary. That is all.*

And by the following testimony (Rec., pp. 572, 573, 574):

Q. Do you know of any other evidence of unpopularity of Judge Morgan in Marshall County ?—A. Yes, sir; when he was running there 2 years ago last fall he made a speech at Byhalia, in which he took grounds that the election should be carried, as it always had been, to buckle on a 6-shooter, as he had done, and meet the Republican voters before they got to the polls, and drive them back, or knock them down, and take their tickets away from them. He and a man named Hight got into an argument about it and Mr. Hight and Judge Morgan published cards.

Q. Have you got a copy of Hight's card ?—A. I think I have, sir.

Q. Will you please file it and mark it as Exhibit B to your deposition ?
Witness does the same.

Exhibit B.—John S. Burton.

[Cor. Memphis Avalanche.]

MR. E. M. HIGHT, THE AUTHOR OF THE BYHALIA REPORT, COMES BACK AT JUDGE MORGAN.

BYHALIA, MISS., *September 2.*

Editor Avalanche:

While greatly astonished to find in your Tuesday's paper a positive denial from Judge J. B. Morgan of the statements attributed to him in my Sunday's correspondence to your paper, I am, nevertheless, as he has done so, not surprised to see him resort to that spirit of bulldozing which characterized his most inflammatory speech in this place on the 23d of August.

In justice to myself, I desire to not only reiterate my every statement relative to his speech, but I propose to give his utterances more fully and forcibly than I did in my former letter.

My report was not given from a Republican stand-point, nor from the stand-point of any other character of partisan, but simply from the holy stand-point of truthfulness.

In the course of Judge Morgan's speech on the 23d ult. he referred to the negroes going to the polls in squads of ten and the means by which they should be dispersed, and instanced a time when he, with fifty other men, had buckled on navy sixes and with hickory clubs in their hands had met the negroes at the polls and insisted that they vote as they directed, and on their refusal to do so the negroes were knocked down and dispersed; that these means had proved effective at that time and would prove as effective now. In describing the way in which the negroes were knocked down Judge Morgan exhibited himself and used his arms to illustrate the manner in which the clubs were used and how the negroes were felled to the earth, and made use of some such expressions as "Take that, G—d d—n you !" when they knocked one down. Several times did Judge Morgan ask pardon of his audience for the use of his profanity in their presence. From this part of Judge Morgan's speech I took occasion to say in the Avalanche that he, Judge Morgan, "alluded in strong and forcible term to the means to be used in downing the negro voter. *That he had found six shooter the most effective means of driving the negroes from the polls where they refused to vote as directed, and believed that it would now prove as effective as in by-gone days.*"

In thus making this report I was certainly justified by his language, if he
it at all. Now the question come up, Did Judge Morgan say anything of th
in his speech? In his own language he says not, in the following strong state
"I desire to say to your readers that this entire statement, with regard
'means to be used in downing the negro,' is a deliberate falsehood in the wh
all parts, in its words and in the ideas intended to be conveyed. It is the u
tion of a vicious brain, whose wish was father to the thought. I never even
as alluded to 'the means of downing the negro voter.' I did not state that
found the six-shooter the most effective means of driving the negroes from t
when they refused to vote as directed, and believed that it would now prove e
as in by-gone days.' I not only did not give utterance to such words at Byba
never entertained such views in all the days of my life. Nor did I utter at
any words from which any honest man could draw such conclusions as you
spondent presented to your readers."

The above are the words in which Judge Morgan denies my report of his sp
Byhalia, which places the whole matter in one of the two lights: That Judge
never referred to the use of navy sixes as a means of driving negroes from t
in any manner, and that Marcellus willfully lied in his report of the speec
Avalanche; or, that Judge Morgan did make use of the statements attributed
and Judge Morgan has willfully lied in his positive denial.

To show that Marcellus has not lied, I desire to say that I am willing to r
matter to the people who heard the speech at Byhalia—to the people among
live—for vindication or condemnation; to the people who enjoy a reputa
honesty and integrity, to say who has told the falsehood. And as further
the truthfulness of my statements, I append statements from a number of t
men in this community—men whose integrity has never been impeached. E
the statements:

BYHALIA, MISS., Septem

Having listened to the speech delivered by Judge J. B. Morgan in Byhali
on the night of August 23, 1886, we, the undersigned citizens, hereby state tha
said, in substance, that on former occasions he, with about fifty other men, ha
led on navy sixes, and, with hickory clubs in their hands, had met the negroe
polls and insisted that they vote as they directed, and on their refusal to do
were knocked down and thus dispersed; that these means proved effective
time, and would prove as effective now.

> J. C. MOORE,
> R. J. LYLES.
> N. F. STEVEN
> ED. R. REYN
> G. W. OWENS

BYHALIA, MISS., Septem

Having heard the speech of Judge J. B. Morgan on August 23, 1886, and i
report of same in the Avalance by Marcellus, *we pronounce the said repo*
only correct in substance, but mild in the manner in which it was written compared
utterances of Judge Morgan.

> CHARLES STAN
> PRESS STANBAC
> N. F. STEVENS.

Here are the positive statements of a number of the most respectable an
worthy citizens of this community, who directly and most emphatically cor
the statements of the Democratic Congressman from the second district of Mis
These men will not misrepresent a matter, and no man dare charge them wi
conduct. In addition to this proof I will rest my statements to the honor, in
and honesty of all others who heard the speech and have read Judge M
denial.

If this testimony is not rank perjury the contestee believes in
Mississippi methods, and he was in this county and on the
when carried ont.

The contestee had more motive than any other man to ha
fraud committed, and it is proved that he was in the county w
was done, was sent there to have it fixed and reported it in a
good fix. In cases of circumstantial evidence where a man
motive to commit an offense and the opportunity to commit it,

offense is committed, this furnishes strong circumstantial evidence of his guilt.

Evidence as to erasure of names from poll-books.

Record, p. 959, contestee's witness Carothers :
Taylor's precinct—"about 400 names stricken from book at R. R. election. No complaint of election" except that both Republicans and Democratic voters' names had been erased from lists.

Record, p. 631, witness "Alexander," one of the (reluctant) Democratic county commissioners:

Q. What is your name?—A. J. P. Alexander.
Q. Where do you live?—A. At Oxford, La Fayette County, Miss.
Q. What office do you hold in La Fayette County, Miss., if any?—A. I am jailer there; I am one of the commissioners of election.
Q. What are your duties as said commissioner of election?—A. It is to inspect the books.
Q. Do you or do you not have charge of the registration books and make them up?—A. Yes, sir.
Q. Did you see the registration books of La Fayette County, Miss., before the Nov. election in 1888?—A. Yes, sir.
Q. In what condition were those books as to their correctness when you last saw them?—A. I taken them to be correct, as far as I knew.
Q. At what time before the election did you last see those books?—A. Well, sir, I saw Kee Cummings setting them out the Thursday before the election and Tuesday, and some I saw on Saturday before the election.
Q. Did you see those books after the election?—A. Yes, sir.
Q. Will you state what was their condition in comparison before the election you saw them again?—A. They were badly marked up.
(Counsel for contestee objects to this testimony, and asks that the same be excluded, because the books about which he is testifying are not produced.)
Q. What do you mean by the books being badly scratched up?—A. *There are some of the names that had been on there were marked off.*
Q. Did you see any names that had been on those books and that by right should be on there which had been marked off?—A. *Yes, sir.*

Cross-examination by Mr. BOYCE:

Q. How long have you lived in La Fayette County?—A. About forty years.
Q. When were you made one of the board of commissioners of election for that county?—A. This last fall; I don't remember the time, before the election though.
Q. What are your politics?—A. I am a Democrat.
Q. When did you last supervise the registration books to find out that names of voters which should have appeared on that book were marked off?—A. It was after the election, after they were returned to us.
Q. Did you examine carefully the name of every voter that appeared upon the registration books for La Fayette County?—A. No, sir; not after the election. There were a great many had been erased that I knew there, and the day of the election they couldn't vote, and it was just those that I examined to see if they were there.

This witness is speaking of the books generally, including *the whole county*. He was the county jailor, had lived in the county forty years, and says, "There were a great many that I knew there [in the county] could not vote on day of election; it was just those I examined to see if they were there."

Word says (Rec., p. 555):

Q. I don't exactly understand whether you have stated as near as you are able the number of colored men who applied to vote at the South Oxford box whose names had been erased?—A. Well, if you will give me a pencil I can make the calculation and state exactly. They were 179 that applied to vote and was rejected.
Q. In my question I meant to ask you whether the men had been refused because of their names being scratched off?—A. Yes, sir; that was the cause.
Q. Did you know any considerable number of the voters?—A. I did, sir; know the biggest part of them.
Q. Were they Rep. or Dem. voters?—A. They were Rep. voters, sir.
Q. How long had they been voting there?—A. Some of them were old men, some of them middle-aged, some young men, and it was their first attempt to vote.

H. Rep. 2503——6

Q. Where had they lived?—A. They had lived there. Some had just become of age, and some had been voting there ever since they had been free.

Q. Did you examine any other poll-book in the county of La Fayette except the South Oxford book?—A. Yes, sir; I did.

Q. What one?—A. I examined—made a partial examination of the Abbeville book.

Q. When?—A. On Saturday before the election on Tuesday.

Q. When was the next time you saw that book and examined it?—A. In the grand-jury room.

Q. State the difference between the condition of the book, so far as you examined it, of the Saturday before the election in Nov. and when you examined it after the election before the grand jury.—A. Well, I examined the book from the letter A down to the letter K. My intention was to ascertain how many names had been erased on that poll-book from A to Z. I was interrupted by a voter coming in and claiming that he had voted for a number of years at Abbeville, and the last time that he had applied to vote there they said that his name was erased, and I only examined down to the letter K. I found 200 names had been erased down to that letter.

Q. That was on the Saturday before the election?—A. Yes, sir; and after the election, when I examined that book before the Federal grand jury, I found 223 names had been erased down to the letter K.

Q. Isn't it the habit there to mark dead, removed, &c.?—A. Yes, sir.

Q. What did they have on your name?—A. Well, I didn't see it dead there, but they said, L. N. Word, dead.

Q. Who said that?—A. It was one of the clerks or judges that had the poll-book.

Q. What became of that poll-book in which you had the names of those who had applied to vote and were refused?—A. We had no dinner that day and supper was brought in and we were all eager to get something to eat. We were hungry and I tried to get my book in my pocket. It was too large; I couldn't get it there. I turned around and layed it on the mantel board and proceeded to help them set the table. I suppose I was doing that about 5 or 10 minutes, and thought of my book and looked around and it was gone.

Q. Have you ever seen that book since?—A. No, sir; I have not.

This day personally appeared P. L. Redwine, a witness for contestant, J. R. Chalmers, and who, after being duly sworn, testifies as follows (Rec., p. 955):

Q. 1. What is your name?—A. 1. P. L. Redwine.

Q. 2. Your age?—A. 2. I am 54 years old.

Q. 3. Your occupation?—A. 3. I am a farmer.

Q. 4. How long have you been living in La Fayette County?—A. 4. I have lived here 54 years.

Q. 5. Were you one of the commissioners of election last fall, supervising the registration and poll-books; and, as such, what were your duties?—A. 5. Yes, sir; I was guided by the statute, and had it by me all the while.

Q. 6. What were the condition of those books when you adjourned?—A. 6. So far as I knew, correct.

Q. 7. What time did your board adjourn?—A. 7. I suppose a Saturday evening.

Q. 8. Have you examined those books since the election; and, if so, what was the condition of the books compared to the condition when you left them?—A. 8. They were not the same.

Q. 9. In what respect were they not the same?—A. 9. *There was names erased that were not when I saw them last before the election.*

Q. 10. You mean, in this answer, that the books were not in same condition as when the board adjourned?—A. 10. *I do.*

Cross-examination:

Q. 1. You left Friday evening and did not return, but left the other two members of the board still in session, did you not?—A. 1. I did.

Q. 2. When was the last time before the election and the first time after the election that you examined the books?—A. 2. About Wednesday evening previous to the election we closed the inspection of the books. I think about Wednesday evening after the election we began looking over the books again.

Q. 3. In the selection of officers of election, was not a list furnished you or your board in handwriting of W. G. Beauland, giving the names of such Republican officers as were desired appointed at each box, and did your board not follow that list?—A. 3. It did verbatim.

Q. 4. You were not present when the board adjourned, were you, but these appointments had all been made, had they not?—A. 4. I was not present at the adjournment, but the appointments had all been made before I left.

Q. 5. Was there any complaint about these appointments or any of them?—A. 5. But one; Capt. G. F. Scott was complained of by both sides.

It will again be observed that this witness is speaking of the books of all the precincts in the county (as a county).

It will also be observed that contestee's counsel failed to attempt to show that the erasing of names was confined to particular precincts.

These two witnesses (Alexander and Redwine) being their trusted political friends, and contestee fails to introduce a single witness to disprove the facts proven by these two Democratic election commissioners.

Thomas Strawn (white), a deposition on behalf of the contestant; being first duly sworn, testifies as follows:

Direct examination by Mr. PIERSON:

Q. You live in the Oxford precinct in La Fayette County, Miss., do you?—A. Yes, sir.

Q. How long have you lived there?—A. I have lived there about 20 years, sir.

Q. What position did you occupy at the North Oxford box at the last election in La Fayette County?—A. I was supervisor.

Q. Did you examine the register-book there that day?—A. Yes, sir.

Q. State the condition of that book with reference to the number of Republican voters' names being scratched off.—A. Well, there was about 200 of them, to my recollection.

Q. State how many attempted to vote there that day, as near as you can, who were refused.—A. Well, sir, I set down names till I got 190, I think it is, and then I went home; the voting was near about over when I left; don't know how many after that.

Q. What time did you quit?—A. It was between 4 and 5 o'clock.

Q. Did you know personally any considerable number of the men who attempted to vote there that day?—A. Yes, sir; I knew a great many of them.

Q. Did you know whether or not they were voters at that box, or had been voters there?—A. Yes, sir; had been voters there all the while.

Q. Upon what pretense were they refused a vote?—A. Because their names were erased from the books, scratched out, sir; all that I learned. (Rec., p. 562.)

The conspiracy here is clearly established. One of the moving spirits in it seems to have been the contestee himself, who the proof shows, said he was in favor of cheating the negro out of his vote (Rec., p. 954). Another was L. S. Dillard, who was election commissioner in 1882 and was convicted of violating the election law (see notice of contest, Rec., ——), and the third, W. V. Sullivan, member of Congressional committee for that county. The principal method used was the erasure of names of Republicans from the poll-books, the same plan adopted in contestee's county in 1880, for which the commissioners of election were afterwards indicted, tried, and convicted. (See digest election cases, 80–82, Buchanan vs. Manning, p. 313).

The Republican majority in this county is at five boxes, Abbeville, Alexander's store, College Hill, North and South Oxford. The vote at these boxes in 1882 was, Chalmers 1,119 and Manning 606. They are returned this time, Chalmers 272 and Morgan 911 (Rec., p. 742). The record of Buchanan vs. Manning shows gross frauds at these same Republican boxes. That frauds have been perpetrated in pursuance of a conspiracy is evident, and the question is, what shall be done?

The contestant asks that the returns from the county be thrown out, and insists that each county should be treated as an entirety and not each box, because under the Mississippi plan each county has a returning-board with unlimited power as to erasing names from the poll-books, the appointment of inspectors of elections, and the rejection of what they regard as illegal ballots, and that their machinery can be so used as to permit fair elections at Democratic boxes and open the door for all manner of frauds at the Republican boxes. The contestee practically admits the frauds in this county, and in his brief (page 100) suggests that if the rejected votes (422) and the vote at College Hill be counted for contestant, leaving him the other boxes as returned, he will still have a majority in this county.

Looking to what is called the unexamined boxes of this county, it will be seen that they are returned for Morgan 860, Chalmers 268. Looking to page 145 of reply brief of contestant, the boxes outside of Abbeville, College Hill, North and South Oxford, gave Manning 607, Chalmers 483. It was impossible for contestant to take proof as to these boxes, growing out of the fact that the only Republican lawyer he could get here was afraid to take testimony there. (See Montgomery, Rec., p. 593.)

Q. Did I, or not, apply to you to act as my attorney to take my testimony at Oxford ?—A. You did.

Q. Did you, or not, advise me subsequently whether you considered it prudent for me to do so or not; if so, state what you said ?—A. I had conversations with you to that effect, in which I stated, that considering the late hour at which I had received the word and my previous engagements that I ought to attend to, I couldn't take the time until March 2ud for that work, but in addition to that, and especially inasmuch as there was a very strong prejudice against me at Oxford politically on account of a Republican speech made in Illinois last campaign, having caused me the loss of my situation and my entire year's work, that I didn't think it was prudent to unite two mightier elements in the taking of your testimony.

Q. What two mightier elements do you refer to ?—A. I refer to the prejudice which already existed against myself and the prejudice against Gen. Chalmers and his contest.

Beanland says:

Qu. 8th. Did you hear, or see in the newspapers published in Oxford, any expressions as to the safety of Gen. Chalmers or his friends if they came to Oxford to take testimony ? If so, state what you heard, and what you read.

(This question objected to because it calls for hearsay evidence.)

Ans. The Oxford Globe, a Democratic newspaper printed at Oxford, some time in February said, in a short squib, that if Chalmers came here and did right he would have no trouble, but if he acted as he did in De Soto County, that he had better pack up his traps and get away, or words to this effect. (Rec., p. 1041.)

But while contestant took no proof as to other boxes, there is proof made by W. H. Caruthers, witness for contestee, that 400 names were erased from the poll-books at Taylor's. He undertakes to account for this by saying the books had been purged for the railroad election by the erasure of those who had died or moved away, but he says there was complaint made that voters who came up to vote were rejected because their names were not on the books. But the Democratic commissioners, who were reluctant witnesses for contestant, Alexander and Redwine, both say the poll-books had been changed after they went from their hands. And the fact that voters came up to vote at Taylor's shows they had neither died nor removed.

Further, a comparison of the returns from Alexander's store in 1882 and 1888 shows a strong presumption that Republican voters were erased. In 1882 the vote stood Manning 99, Chalmers 124. (See Reply Brief, 145.) In 1888 the returns show Morgan 96, Chalmers 61. (Rec., p. 742.) From this it will be seen that while Morgan got 3 votes less than Manning, Chalmers is cut off 63 votes. With the proof as to the conspiracy and the proof of wholesale erasures at every box examined about, this is circumstantial evidence that the same thing was done at Alexander's store and all over the county. Thus a state of confusion is brought by the frauds committed, which makes it impossible to ascertain the true vote. Under these circumstances there is but one course left to do justice, and that is to reject the returns from every precinct in this county and count only the vote proved.

The methods in this county are well described by two witnesses on cross-examination.

Beanland says (Rec., p. 596):

Q. Please describe and detail the Miss. plan.—A. Well, I suppose you have heard, without me describing it. It is to carry it the way they want it. If they can't carry it one way, they carry it another. Can't carry it by fair, carry it otherwise, or foul. If you had been down there in that country and heard what we Republicans have you could very easily understand the Miss. plan.

Q. Where did you receive that information about carrying the election anyway; is that based upon your experience?—A. Yes, sir, it is; I know whereof I speak.

I. W. Hines says (Rec., p. 627):

Q. Can you name an instance where the gentlemen whose names you have given and denominated bulldozers put their bulldozing into operation at the election?— A. Yes; of course, we can all know; in that country, sir, at that particular box, at the time Tilden and Arthur election, they fired pistols inside of the house, struck one of the judges on the feet and the nigger ran out; the window lights were broken out, and after they got the ballot fixed up to suit them they sent for the nigger to come in; he was somewhere down the railroad.

ABBEVILLE PRECINCT.

Rec., p. 555: Witness Word, examined book for the precinct Saturday before election down to letter K for erasure of names; after the election witness examined same book to letter K, and 23 names had been erased since his examination before election.

Rec., p. 624 (Hines): Polling place fired into during counting of vote and inspectors refused to continue counting at that place, but finished the count at another house; only 216 votes polled, but 247 counted; 40 voters denied the right to vote, name being erased or not on poll-book, many of whom were known to him as Republican voters and as having registered only a few days before.

Witness shows that election has been broken up by bulldozers at this box in former years.

Returns: Morgan, 131; Chalmers, 116. The proof shows 31 fraudulent votes in excess of voters found in the box, and 43 votes illegally rejected. At this box Manning received but 92 votes, and if the 31 illegal votes be taken from the count for Morgan, it leaves him 8 more votes than Manning had. At this box Chalmers had 199 against Manning, and if the 43 illegally rejected votes be added to his, he still has 40 less than he had against Manning. The returns can not be relied on, and taking the proof, the box should be counted, Morgan 100 and Chalmers 156.

Record, page 565: Avent, College Hill precinct, appointed Republican inspector, but was not permitted to serve by Democratic inspectors; says over 200 Republican tickets issued and voted there (returns show Chalmers 26 votes). Witness (Avent) remained all day taking voters to polls; deputy sheriff says 20 or 30 whites (only) voted.

Cross-examination: Says a great many more Republicans voted, "besides those he walked up to the polls with;" shows he walked up to polls with about 75 Republicans; first election witness ever attended.

As to this box Beanland testifies as follows:

I heard W. W. M'Maan, one of the judges at College Hill, say they went there to beat anybody the damn niggers would vote for, and they did it. Had the votes been 1,500 it would have made no difference.

Q. When you say it proved true that the niggers come up dead, what do you mean by that?—A. I mean by that that they were not allowed to vote.

Q. Why?—A. Their names were scratched off the poll-books.

Q. How were they marked "dead" on the poll-books?—A. That was my information; I didn't see the books. (Rec., p. 595.)

Word says:

Q. Did you have any conversation with these judges of election through the county of La Fayette as to the way they proposed to carry things, and did carry them at the

H. Mis. 137——27

last election?—A. Yes, sir; yes, sir; it was since the election; I were in the back room of Brenner & Wallace's store at Oxford, and we were discussing this erasure, and Mr. McMahon, who was an inspector of the election at College Hill, walked in; I appealed to him, and asked him if he thought it was right. He said that he thought any thing was right. He says, "My God, any thing is right to keep ahead of the negro." "Well," I said, "there was no negro wanted in this canvass." "That don't make a damn bit of difference; the negroes voted for Chalmers, and, by God, if we can't stuff 'um out, wee'l shoot 'um out; we don't give a damn how we get 'um out, but we are going to control 'um." That is his words as near exactly as I can get it; that was the meaning of them. (Rec., p. 556.)

Mr. McMahon, the Democratic inspector, admits that one Avent was appointed, as shown by his list, but rejects this Avent on a frivolous excuse. He denies the statement of Beauland, but did not deny the statement of Word.

W. W. McMahon, a witness for contestee, next duly sworn, on oath says:

Q. Were you a judge of election in Nov., '88, at College Hill precinct, La Fayette County, Mississippi? If so, how was the election conducted, and what was the result?—A. I was. It was an orderly, fair, and impartial election in every respect, and resulted in a Democratic majority of about 280.

Q. Did you at any time, in the presence of W. G. Beauland, state in regard to the approaching election, 1888, Nov., that you thought that any person who the niggers voted for should be beaten, and that you and other Democrats at College Hill were going to beat them, no matter if they had 1,500 majority, or any thing of that kind?—Ans. I had no such conversation with him or in his presence, at or before the election. I s'd after the election, publicly, that I did not think the negro ought to be allowed to vote. A discussion was up in a crowd as to whether, as a general proposition, the negro should be allowed to vote, whether the suffrage should not be taken from him, and I expressed the view that it was a mistake that he should be clothed with the elective franchise. This in no way influenced my action in that election. I did not aid, assist, or connive at any attempt, if any was made, to keep any one from voting and his vote being counted as he wished.

Ques. Did any one prevent any Republican judge or inspector or supervisor from acting at the College Hill precinct?—Ans. One Avant presented himself claiming to have been appointed Rep. supervisor, and when asked his name it proved not to be the one who was appointed. And he was then asked what name he proposed to vote under, and he said his real name, and his name was not the name of the person who was appointed, and he then decided to vote on his name and not serve under another name as supervisor of election, and another negro was then selected as such supervisor, who was a Republican.

Q. In whose possession was the ballot-box left from the time of the closing of the polls until the voting began? And when the counting began was it continuous until it was completed, and what chance was there given for false counting?—A. It was in the joint possession of the Republican and Democratic officers, and Jim   , one of the Republican judges, kept the key to the box. They all eat at the same place and went and came together. And after supper and counting them commenced it was continuous, open, public, and no chance for false counting; Republicans as well as Democrats were present and witness the counting of the votes. (Rec., p. 962.)

OXFORD PRECINCT (NORTH BOX).

Returns (Rec., p. 742) show Chalmers 37 votes.
Supervisor Strawn (Rec., p. 562) and Beauland (p. 595.): Kept list. Two hundred Republican names erased, all former voters at that box; only about one in twenty-five colored men got to vote.

OXFORD (SOUTH BOX).

Returns (Rec., p. 742) show Chalmers 32 votes.
Supervisor Word (Rec., p. 554) and Beauland (p. 595): Only eight colored men allowed to vote. One hundred and seventy-nine Republicans did not vote, names erased, and also those whose names could not be found. Witness was marked dead and did not vote.

The vote of La Fayette County.

	As returned.		As proved.	
	Chalmers.	Morgan.	Chalmers.	Morgan.
Abbeville	116	131	156	100
College Hill	26	285	200	....
North Oxford	37	219	227	219
South Oxford	32	180	211	180
Total	211	815	794	499

The count then stands:

	Chalmers.	Morgan.
Brought forward	7,186	9,295
Abbeville:		
Add	40	....
Deduct	....	31
	7,226	9,264
Cottage Hill:		
Add	174	....
Deduct	....	285
	7,400	8,979
North Oxford:		
Add	190	....
Deduct	....	....
	7,590	8,979
South Oxford:		
Add	179	....
Deduct	....	....
Total	7,769	8,979

The unexamined boxes of this county should beyond question be rejected. If, as the proof indicates, the wholesale disfranchisement of the voters of this was planned or consented to by the friends of contestee, no court of equity or law in the world would allow them to take advantage of this wrong, and every presumption would be given against him. To talk about a presumption in favor of the unexamined boxes in this county would be most manifest injustice.

TALLAHATCHIE COUNTY.

In this county an ignorant negro, who was a Democrat, was appointed commissioner of election to represent the Republican party. T. W. Turner says:

Q. Who was the representative of the Republican party on the board of commis sioners?—A. Geo. Lee, colored man.

Q. Was he recognized by the Republicans or not?—A. He was not. To the contrary they were requested not to appoint him.

Q. Why?—A We didn't look upon him as a Republican, the man to represent our party.

Q. Was he or not known as a Democrat?—A. He was, among his own class of people.

Q. He was a colored man, was he?—A. Yes, sir.

Q. And known by the colored men to be a Democrat?—A. Yes, sir. Recognized by them to be a Democrat. I don't think he could read or write. Utterly uncapable of adding up a column of figures. (Rec., p. 447.)

Mr. Polk, a Democrat and Circuit Clerk, says:

Cross-int. 2. State, if you know, who was the representative of the Republican party on the board of commissioners, and whether or not he could read and write.

Ans. cross 2. George Lee was the representative of the Republican party on the board of election commissioners; he can read a little, but can not write his name. (Rec., p. 844.)

Mr. Byrd, a Democrat and commissioner with him, says :

Cross-inter'y 4. State, if you know, whether or not George Lee was a (
and whether or not he can read and write.—Ans. 4. George Lee is colored;
he can read or write. (Rec., p. 845.)

The Republicans have for years been persistently refused
missioner or inspector asked for by them.   T. W. Turner say

Q. Did you ask the county commissioners for a representative of the
party as inspector at each box?—A. I don't remember whether I did or n
my impression is that I asked the county commissioners or one of the cou'
sioners, the one I believe was divested of party prejudice, would be gove
oath of office, if he wouldn't see that we got one representative from the
party that could read and write as inspector at each box; that was Sam Ma
county commissioners; he said he would do the best he could; they never
me any names or asked me as chairman of the Republican executive co:
chairman of the Republican executive committee, they never asked me
inspectors to represent our party, and in past years had never given me any
officially.

Q. Have or not in past years the commissioners been asked to give a fai:
tive to the opposition party, and have they or not refused?—A. They ha
have persistently refused.   (Rec., p. 447.)

This shows a conspiracy to defraud under the rule laid dov
Duffie *sv.* Turpin.

But the most conclusive evidence of fraud is to be found in tl
themselves.

CHARLESTON, MISSISSIPPI, —

To Hon. GEO. M. GOVAN,
   Secretary of State, Jackson, Miss. :

The following are the returns of an election held in Tallahatchie Count;
day of November, A. D. 1888:

Names of candidates.	Charleston.	Center Point.	Harrison.	Boothes.	Sherman Creek.	Dogwood Flat.	Loveretta.	New Hope.	Ross Mill.	Tippo.	Graball.	Brooklyn.	Buford.	Hybernia.
For electors for President and Vice-President of the United States.														
A. J. McLaurin	182	112	66	56	65	82	33	99	124	23	61	92	26	
L. M. Southworth	182	112	66	56	65	82	33	99	124	23	61	92	26	
E. S. Candler, jr	182	112	66	56	65	82	33	99	124	23	61	92	26	
Wm. M. Strickland	182	112	66	56	65	82	33	99	124	23	61	92	26	
D. A. Scott	182	112	66	56	65	82	33	96	124	23	61	92	26	
O. F. Bledsoe	182	112	66	56	65	82	33	99	124	23	61	92	26	
W. D. Gibbs	182	112	66	56	65	82	33	99	124	23	61	92	26	
E. J. Bowers	182	112	66	56	65	82	33	99	124	23	61	92	26	
C. E. Hooker, jr	182	112	66	56	65	82	33	99	124	23	61	92	26	No returns.
H. F. Simrall									28					
R. N. Tindall									28					
W. H. Vassar									28					
G. M. Buchanan									28					
Henry Meyer									28					
L. J. Scurlock									28					
J. R. S. Pitts									28					
O. L. Garrett									28					
T. J. Jackson									28					
For Representative in the 51st Congress, 2d Congressional district.														
J. B. Morgan	180	112	66	56	65	82	33	99	126	23	61	92	26	
J. R. Chalmers	2													
James Witherspoon									28					

STATE OF MISSISSIPPI, *Tallahatchie County:*

We, the undersigned commissioners of election for Tallahatchie County, certify that the foregoing tabular statement is *a true* and *correct return* of the *whole number of votes* cast for the several offices named therein at the general election held in said county on the 6th day of November, 1888.

A. L. BYRD,
S. D. MAY,
GEORGE LEE,
Commissioners of Election.

(Rec., p. 745.)

There are two palpable frauds shown here—one false return and the other forgery.

Revised Code of Mississippi, sec. 140, p. 82, says:

The commissioners of election shall, within ten days after the election, transmit to the Secretary of State, to be filed in his office, a statement of the whole number of votes given in their county for each candidate voted for in such county for any office at such election.

This law has been construed by the United States court in Mississippi, and it was held that "A statement of the whole number of votes given" meant a return of all the votes cast, whether counted or rejected, and if rejected, a statement as to why they were rejected. A failure to do this was held to be a crime, punishable in the United States court. (See case of United States *vs.* M. B. Collins *et al.* in Buchanan *vs.* Manning, Dig. El. cases, 1880–'82, p. 314.) They were indicted for making a partial return and plead guilty. That these commissioners made a false and criminal return to the Secretary of State is clearly proved by the witnesses for contestee, who say about 600 votes for Chalmers were thrown out because they had notched edges. The return is further shown to be false by comparison with the precinct returns, which the clerk certifies and also testifies is a true copy from the certified lists on file in his office. The commissioners' return give Chalmers but 2 votes, while the precinct returns give him 533. Again, the precinct returns give Morgan but 162 at Charleston, while the commissioners give him 180. The commissioners returned 28 votes for Witherspoon for Congress at Rosses' Mill, while the precinct returns from this box give 10 to Chalmers and none to Witherspoon. This false return is concluded with forgery. The name of George Lee is signed in full to the returns, when all the witnesses say he could not write his name. The witnesses for contestee not only show that the returns of the commissioners were false, but that the returns of the inspectors at Charleston, which gave Chalmers but 2 votes, were equally false.

We have, then, in this county evidence of a conspiracy to defraud in the appointment of the commissioner and inspectors of election. We see that there were 21 more votes counted than voters at Graball. We have evidence that tickets were changed at Sherman's Creek, that tickets were snatched from the Republican distributer at Dogwood Flat, and that violence was used toward negroes for political reasons before, during, and after the election.

Contestee suggested that the ballots for contestant, which were thrown out because ot the notched edges, might be counted.

But his witnesses differ as to how many were thus thrown out. Dogan says there were about 550 (Rec., p. 841); Polk says there were 618 (Rec., p. 843); Byrd says there were about 600 (Rec., p. 845).

This confusion and uncertainty as to the true vote having been produced by the fraudulent conduct of the officers of election, showing a purpose to defraud contestant, the returns from this county should be rejected. This would take 2 from Chalmers and 1,021 from Morgan.

But if the votes of this county can be counted from the ret
the precinct officers, the result would be as follows:

As returned, Chalmers 2, Morgan 1,021.

CRABALL.

The history of this box shows it is notorious for fraud. No e
was held there in 1882, and the reason is given as follows:
Turner says:

Q. Were you or not U. S. supervisor in 1882, when I was a candidate again
ning?—A. I was.

Q. State whether any election was held at that box at that time, and if n
not?—A. There was no election held in 1882—I believe that was the year—f
fact that I was resisted as U. S. marshal, and turned back by an armed body i
ing, I think, about 18, with Winchester rifles. •

Q. Were you on your way as U. S. supervisor to attempt to hold an election
box?—A. Yes, sir; on the public road. •

Q. You state you were met by 18 men with Winchester rifles who forbade yo
to hold the election?—A. Yes, sir. (Rec., p. 446.)

No election was held there in 1886 as will be seen from the r
(Rec., p. 737.)

*Returns of election held in Tallahatchie County, Miss., on November 2d, 1886, to el
gressman for the 3rd [should be 2nd] Congressional district.*

	Candidate fo gressma	
	---	---
	J. B. Morgan.	C
Harrison	23	
Boothe's	30	
Sherman Creek	10	
Center Point	37	
Charleston	75	
New Hope	25	...
Ross' Mill	56	
Dogwood Flat	41	
Leverette	7	
Tippo		...
Hybernia	11	...
Graball		...
Brooklin		..
Buford's		..
Total	315	
Majority	184	

At this election the officers appointed by the Democrats refn
hold any election there until they saw the citizens were about t
an election themselves. Then some of those appointed agreed
and the election was held. (See Rec., p. 446.)

This election, as returned by the precinct officers, shows 21 mor
returned than there were voters. There were 211 colored voters
and Chalmers is returned 211 votes. There were only 40 white
who voted, and Morgan is returned 61. (See Rec., p. 451.) Fro
it is evident that 21 votes should be taken for Morgan here. The
then stands:

	Chalmers.	1
Brought forward	7,769	
Graball:		
Add precinct returns	211	...
Deduct stuffed		
	7,980	

SHERMAN'S CREEK.

At this box the inspectors were all Democrats. One inspector was seen changing tickets, and the voters were fired into while the election was going on.

Deposition of J. E. DRAKE (col.), a witness on behalf of the contestant, being first duly sworn, deposed as follows:

Examination by General CHALMERS:

Q. What box do you vote at?—A. The Sherman box, in Tallahatchie County.
Q. Is the majority of voters at that box colored or white?—A. The majority is white, I think, but we have very near as many colored as white.
Q. Was there any shooting into the voters at that box on the last election?—A. Yes, sir.
Q. What position did you occupy there that day?—A. U. S. supervisor.
Q. Please explain the shooting you speak of.—A. Well, there was about 20 or 30 shots. The men were on a bluff a little above the house, and the voters were about 30 or 40 feet from the house, and the shooting was done in the direction of the men, and one of the balls fell right in front of one of the voters.
Q. Were they white or colored men who did the shooting?—A. They were white men; hid back on the bluff.
Q. How many times did they shoot—different times?—A. Twenty or 30 different times they shot.
Q. Who was the Republican inspector of election there that day, or claimed to be?—A. Alfred Buckley.
Q. Could he read or write?—A. No, sir.
Q. Do you know whether he was in fact a Republican or not?—A. He was a Democrat, and always had been a Democrat, and voted Democratic that day.
Q. Did you see him vote that day?—A. Yes, sir; I seed him vote. I gave him a Republican ticket and he put it in his pocket, and when he went to vote picked up a Democratic ticket and voted it.
Q. Did you see anything that indicated fraud going on in the reception of the vote; if so, state what it was?—A. Now, what I seed, what I would call fraud, he would bring his hands together whenever a Republican voted and handed him a ticket. He would bring his right hand up to his left hand and then put a ticket into the box with his right hand.
Q. As if he was changing it?—A. Yes, sir. It looked that way to me. It was going on while I was noticing it all the while, and after a while I called Buckley's attention to it. (Rec., p. 445.)

Sam Edsington, being duly sworn, testifies as follows:

Int. 1. What is your name, color, and politics?—Ans. 1. Sam Edington; black. I have very little to do with politics, but was always Republican.
Int. 2. In what voting precinct did you live at the last election?—Ans. 2. Sherman Creek.
Int. 3. Did you vote at the last election? If so, state at what place.—Ans. 3d. I voted at Sherman Creek.
Int. 4. How long did you remain at the voting place? And state whether or not the election was peaceable and quiet.—Ans. 4. I stayed there about three-quarters of an hour. No, sir.
Int. 5. You say in answer to 4th interrogatory that the election was not peaceable. State in full how it was interfered with; tell all about it in your own language.—Ans. 5. When I got there I was making out some tickets for the boys; and they were shooting just above my head west of the voting precinct. I told the boys to sit still, I reckoned it was somebody drunk; and in about five minutes afterwards they commenced shooting again, and they drew lower down nearer the last time than they did the 1st time. I said, "Boys, this is getting mighty hot, let us get away from here." Some of us went towards the polls, the others went home. That is all I know about it.
Int. 6. How many were engaged in the shooting, and were they shooting at any one to prevent them from voting?—Ans. 6. I don't know how many; I couldn't tell.
Int. 7. What made you think it was getting too hot for you, and made you advise the boys to get away?—Ans. 7. The balls were coming right toward us, and some of them struck the ground in three feet of us.
Int. 8. How many, if any, failed to vote who went to the polls, on account of the disturbance? State as near as you can from information and belief.—Ans. From seven to eight, I think, left without voting. (Rec., p. 1053.)

This box was returned Chalmers 14, Morgan 64.

The supervisor's return of 1882 shows that Chalmers beat Manning 2 to 1 at this box. The commissioners of election gave Chalmers none here. The returns being set aside, 2 votes proved for Chalmers and none for Morgan, we should add 2 to Chalmers and take 64 from Morgan, and the account would then stand:

	Chalmers.	Morgan.
Forward	7, 980	8, 958
Sherman's Creek:		
Add	2	....
Deduct	....	65
	7, 982	8, 893

New Hope: The commissioners give Chalmers nothing, but the precinct officers return for him 37; add this to him and the count will then stand:

	Chalmers.	Morgan.
Forward	7, 982	· 8, 893
New Hope, add to Chalmers	37	....
	8, 019	8, 893

Leverett's: At this box there was a row gotten up to intimidate the voters at the polls, and violence inflicted on the negroes for political reasons afterwards.

Cary Bynum, being sworn, testifies as follows:
Int. 1. In what precinct did you live at the election of 1888?—Ans. 1. Leverett's.
Int. 2. Did you vote at the last election; if so, where did you vote?—Ans. 2. Yes; voted at Leverett's.
Int. 3. State whether or not the election was peaceable and quiet. and whether or not all were permitted to vote as they wished, without molestation?—Ans. 3. It wasn't; they started cussing and fussing, and I went away.
Int. 4. Who were they who got up the trouble; were they Republicans or Democrats, and what was the trouble about, a private matter or politics?—Ans. Turner and Pute; they were Democrats; about the box and election.
Int. 5. Did or not the officers of the election interfere to prevent the disturbance?—Ans. No, sir; Mr. Pute was the officer himself. (Rec., p. 1047.)

Louis Turner, being duly sworn, testifies as follows:
Int. 1. State your name, age, and place of residence.—Ans. 1. Louis R. Turner; thirty-six; Tallahatchee County.
Int. 2. State whether or not you was living in this county at the last election; if so, in what precinct did you live and if you voted state where you voted.—Ans. 2. Yes; Leverett precinct; did not vote.
Int. 3. State, if you know, whether or not there was any excitement about the election; if so, state as far as you know, what was done calculated to intimidate the voters; state in full your knowledge on this subject.—Ans. 3. There was a Democratic torchlight procession, I think the night before the election, around and about Leverett precinct, and there was frequent firing of pistols by those who participated in the procession.
Int. 4. State, if you know, whether or not there was any outrages or lawlessness on the part of any Democratic club, or any member of the clubs, immediately before or after the election; state in particular all you know on the subject.—Ans. 4. Saturday after the election B. F. Pute and B. M. Turner met a negro by the name of Dick Grantham in the public road near my horse-lot; they stopped Grantham and said to him, "You damned son of a bitch, hollow hurrah for Cleveland," which he did. They then told him to "sing it out louder;" he did so, and they rode on. On the same date, at night, I heard several shots fired, I thought in the direction of some negro cabins

on my place. I walked out in my yard, and in a few minutes two or three persons passed my house. I recognized B. F. Pute and B. M. Turner. In a few minutes afterwards Ely Taylor and his wife, who live on my place, came to my house and said Mr. Pute and Mr. Turner had fired into their house, and said one shot struck Martha Taylor (Ely's wife). (Rec., pp. 1048–1049.)

At this box the commissioners gave Chalmers nothing, but the precinct officers returned for him 81; add this and the count will then stand:

	Chalmers.	Morgan.
Forward	8,019	8,893
Leverett's, add	81	
	8,100	8,893

CENTER POINT.

The commissioners here gave Chalmers nothing, precinct officers returned for him 13; add this and the count will stand:

	Chalmers.	Morgan.
Forward	8,100	8,893
Center Point, add	13	
	8,113	8,893

DOGWOOD FLAT.

At this box, which is largely Republican, personal violence was inflicted on negroes for political reasons before the election, and the tickets were snatched from the hands of the Republican who was distributing them, and he was compelled to go to Charleston, a distance of 7 miles, to get more Republican tickets, and during this time many Republican voters went away.

Ben Jones says:

Int. 4. State whether or not you was solicited to join the Democratic club before the election? And, if so, state all that occurred at that time.—Ans. 4. I was asked by Mr. Borbee. He asked me down there, and I went to the door. He asked me in and asked me if I wanted to join. I asked Mr. Fedric what was it. He says, "Ben, it is a Democratic club; do you want to join?" I said no. Mr. Borbee said, "Well, Ben, get out of the door." I went out, went over to the store, and sat down. Mr. Turner (don't know his first name) was there. Me and him sot there and talked a long time. He says, "Uncle Ben, I must go get me some water." He goes on to the well and told Mr. J. Murphree. They called him in the house, and Henry Harris came on to the store and sot down there with me. We sot and talks and runs on with one another, and after while they commence speaking in the house, and Henry says, "Hardside, let's go to the window." I say "Henry, won't they trouble us?" He said no. We went as close to de window as about 13 feet. Me and Henry both war standin' in about 13 feet of de window, in plain view, lookin' in. Mr. Clarkson come to the window and told us to get away. We went right straight to our horses. By de time I got on my horse dere was a man come out de door and said stop; and I told him I was goin' on home; I didn't have no business there. We rid on den and got about a hundred yds. from de house. We looked back behind and I said, "Henry, good God, look at the white folks back behind." Henry just reched up and got his hat and commenced fixtein' his horse, and we put out. They runned us a half a mile, and when dey first caught up with me they struck me four licks across de head; and I looked 'round at him and I said, "Boss, what do you mean? We worn't meanin' any harm." And he said, "Damn you, stop de horse." I told him I wouldn't do it. After dat my horse fell down. They were in such full speed after Henry and runed over m*, and I stepped over my horse's neck and over de fence into the field, and squatted in de corner. While I was squatin' in de corner of de fence I held my hand up and found blood runnin' into it from my head. (Rec., p. 1050.)

T. W. Turner says:

Q. If there is anything else that you know and haven't answered, please state it.—
A. We would have had a much larger vote at Dogwood Flat but for a circumstance that
occurred about 12 o'clock, I think it was.   The colored man who held the Republican
tickets and was distributing the same, and whose name was Virgil Gentry, had the
tickets forcibly jerked from his hands and pocket and destroyed by a white man and
Democrat, a member of the club, whose name was Turner, the given name I don't
remember. They were from the circumstance forced to come to Charleston, a distance
of 6 or 7 miles, to procure more tickets, and I think to the best of my memory I only had
50 tickets left to give them.   I think it was only about 50 tickets. Many of our voters
leaving during the time, and some of them coming to Charleston, thinking they could
vote there. (Rec., p. 449.)

Virgil Gentry, being duly sworn, testified as follows:

Int. 1. What is your name, color, and politics?—Ans. 1. Virgil Gentry; black; Republican.

Int. 2. In what precinct did you live at the election of 1888?—Ans. 2. Dogwood
Flat.

Int. 8. Did any one interfere with you or any one else in the distribution of Republican tickets?—Ans. 8. Didn't any further than snatching the tickets out of my
pocket, and I learned afterward that his name was Mr. Turner. (Rec. p. 1054.)

The commissioners here gave Chalmers nothing. The precinct officers returned for him 93; add this and the count will stand—

	Chalmers.	Morgan.
Forward..	8, 113	8, 893
Dogwood Flat...	93	....
	8, 206	8, 893

BUFORD'S.

The commissioners here gave Chalmers nothing. The precinct officers returned for him 8; add this and the count will stand—

	Chalmers.	Morgan.
Forward..	8, 206	8, 893
Buford's, add	8	....
	8, 214	8, 893

TIPPO.

At this box the commissioners and the inspectors count 23 votes for
Morgan and none for any one else. But the precinct returns show
that 28 votes were cast, so that 5 votes are here deliberately thrown
out without any cause being assigned, and counted for no one.

BROOKLYN.

At this box the commissioners returned none for Chalmers, but the
precinct officers returned for him 48. Adding this, the count will stand
thus:

	Chalmers.	Morgan.
Forward..	8, 214	8, 893
Brooklyn, add..	48	....
	8, 262	8, 893

BOOTHES.

At this box the commissioners gave Chalmers nothing. The precinct officers returned for him 4; add this and the count will stand—

	Chalmers.	Morgan.
Forward	8,262	8,893
Boothes, add	4	
	8,266	8,893

HARRISON.

At this box the commissioners gave Chalmers nothing; the precinct officers returned for him 12; add this and the count will stand thus:

	Chalmers.	Morgan.
Forward	8,266	8,893
Harrison, add	12	
	8,278	8,893

CHARLESTON.

At this box the witnesses for the contestee show that the same false and criminal return was made by the inspectors at Charleston that was made by the commissioners. They returned only 2 votes for Chalmers at this box, as being the whole number cast for him. The witnesses for contestee show that this was false, and that a number of votes were thrown out here for him, but as to how many no witness undertakes to say. For this fraud this box must be thrown out, and as no vote was proved for Morgan there should be taken 180 from him. It is proved that 3 white men here voted for Chalmers, 2 Democrats on Democratic tickets, the only votes counted, and Captain Turner, a white Republican. It is further shown that 155 colored men voted at this box, and the testimony of Turner, Pollard, and Buckley all show that the negroes turned out better to vote and voted more enthusiastically for the Republican ticket on that day than they had done for years. They fix the number of colored men who were Democrats at that box at 5, and Pollard says he thinks 2 who had been voting the Democratic ticket did not do so that day. Captain Turner distributed the Republican tickets and testified as follows:

Q. State whether in your opinion there was ballot-box stuffing at Charleston box or not, to the best of your knowledge and belief.—A. To the best of my belief and observation the tickets were exchanged from Republicans' hands before they got to the box and Democratic tickets inserted. My reason for that belief is that I issued between 160 and 190. I dis'member the exact number, reserving the name of each voter upon the stub of the ticket which I now have in my safe, and by referring to it I can get the exact number of tickets, and I will file that stub with my deposition as Exhibit B to my deposition. I never saw during my career as member of the Republican executive committee a more united and enthusiastic gathering than there was on that day at Charleston, or a more fixed determination to vote every man his ticket. My observation was, after the tickets were issued they remained together and a large majority of them went from where they received their tickets and deposited them at the window under my observation. I was watching at the time. I can't swear to any thing positive that I saw that was wrong. But judging from the number of colored men that voted and the number of white men, observing closely each, I don't believe there were 3 out of the entire colored vote that voted the Democratic ticket.

Anthony Pollard, being duly sworn, testified as follows:

Int. 1. What is your name, color, and occupation?—Ansr. 1. A. P. Pollard; farming and teaching.

Int. 2. In what precinct did you live at the election of 1888?—Ans. 2d. Charleston beat.

Int. 3. What is your politics?—Ans. 3d. Republican.

Int. 4. State whether or not you took an active part in the election of 1888?—Ans. 4th. I made no canvass, but gave out tickets and talked about election a great deal on the day of the election.

Int. 5. State whether or not you know about the number of colored voters at this precinct, and whether or not they generally voted, and about how many voted.—Ans. 5th. I think there's about two hundred and some odd. I think there was about 180 or 190 tickets issued on day of election at this place. I mean Republican tickets.

Int. 6. About how many colored men voted in this precinct? Do you know whether all to whom tickets were given voted?—Ans. 6. I don't know whether all the tickets given out were voted or not.

Int. 7. Were you at the polls during the day of election; if so, state if you saw any conduct of the officers of the election that indicated unfairness?—Ans. 7. Yes, I was here at the election. Nothing that indicated unfairness.

In . 8. Did you see any one exchange the tickets given in by the voters?—Ans. 8. I did not.

Int. 9. Do you know Gen. J. R. Chalmers; if so, state whether or not he was generally popular with the colored people?—Ans. 9. I know him when I see him. I think he is generally popular with the white and colored people about Charleston.

Int. 10. State if you ever heard any objection urged by the colored people against Gen. Chalmers on account of his war record?—Ans. 10. Not in this last campaign.

Int. 12. State if you know which, Morgan or Chalmers, got the majority of the vote cast at this box.—Ans. 12. I don't think there was much difference, but the Republicans generally carry this box by a small majority. I think Chalmers carried this box by a small majority.

Cross-examination:

Interrog. 1. Are you well acquainted with the voters of this county, both white and black, and have you been a candidate several times in this county?—Ans. 1st. Pretty generally with them. Once a candidate for supervisor.

Interrog. 2. Have you for several years past very well understood the political workings of this county?—Ans. 2d. I have been, but not lately.

Interrog. 3. Was the Republican party in this county well organized, or not, in the year 1888, and if so, state the nature and extent of such organization?—Ans. 3. The Republicans in this county were not so well organized, but talked about political matter generally.

Interrog. 4. What portion of the colored people who voted at this place voted the Democratic ticket for J. B. Morgan? Give your best judgment.—Ans. 4. I think those who have been in the habit of voting Democratic ticket heretofore voted that way in last election, except one or two.

Interrog. 5. What portion of the colored voters in this precinct and in this county failed to go to the polls and vote in Congressional election here in 1888?—Ans. 5. About one-fourth failed to turn out in county, but at this box there was a larger turn-out than usual in last campaign.

Robert B. Buckley, being duly sworn, testified as follows:

Int. 1. State your name, age, color, and politics.—Ans. 1. Robert B. Buckley; about 34 years; colored man; Republican.

Int. 2. In what voting precinct did you vote at the election of 1888?—Ans. 2. Charleston precinct.

Int. 3. Did you vote at the last election; if so, state at what place?—Ans. 3. Yes, sir; I voted at Charleston precinct.

Int. 4. Do you know Gen. J. R. Chalmers; if so, state whether or not he was popular with the colored voters?—Ans. 4. Yes, sir; yes, sir.

Int. 5. Was the Republican party organized during the canvass and election; if so, state how it was organized, and whether or not there was any concert of action and agreement among them?—Ans. 5. They were not organized in clubs, but had a general understanding who they would vote for.

Int. 6. Was there a general turn-out of the Republican voters at your box; if so, was it in pursuance to the agreement among them?—Ans. 6. Yes, there was a general turn-out; yes, sir.

Int. 7. Were you one of the officers of the election? If so, state what was your duty.—Ans. 7. I was an inspector of the election.

Int. 8. How many Republicans were officers at your box?—Ans. 8. One.

Int. 9. State what was assigned you to do while the voting was going on.—Ans. 9.

Part of the time in the morning I was to hunt names on the poll-books; balance of the time was sitting there looking on.

Int. 10. State whether or not you was in the position to detect any fraud, if there was any, and if you detected any fraud; if so, what was it; state in full.—Ans. 10. No, sir; I was not, I was looking over the book. No fraud was perpetrated, so far as I know.

Int. 11. Do you know how many Republican votes were polled at your box? If so, state how many, as far as you know.—Ans. 11. No, sir; don't know how many there were.

Cross-examination:

Interrog. 1. Was the election for Congressman held here in 1888 peaceable, quiet, and fair over the county generally, so far as you know?—Answer 1. So far as I know, it was.

Interrog. 2. Do you know Judge J. B. Morgan, and is he popular or unpopular with the colored voters of this county and this precinct?—Answer 2. Yes, I know him; if he is popular I don't know it.

Interrog. 3. Do you know that he is unpopular with the colored voters?—Ans. 3. Personally I don't think him unpopular; politically I never heard any one decide to vote for him.

Interrog. 4. Do you not know that some colored people voted for J. B. Morgan at this place?—Answer 4. No, sir; I do not know it. No one told me that they voted for him.

Interrog. 5. Have you ever heard that some colored people voted for J. B. Morgan at this voting place at the said election?—Ans. 5. Yes, sir; I heard the boys say one voted for him, but he denied it.

Interrog. 6. Have you not heard, and is it not your understanding and information, that there are many colored people who generally vote the Democratic ticket at this place?—Anc. 6. I have heard of four or five.

Interrog. 7. What is your opinion as to the number of Democratic tickets for J. B. Morgan cast at said election at this voting place by the colored voters? My opinion is about 4, 5, or 6—somewhere about there.

Interrog. 8. How many inspectors of election were acting as such at this place with you?—Ans. 8. Three of us; two others.

Interrog. 9. When you were looking over the poll-book at said election, was not that necessary to be done by one of the inspectors to carry on the election according to law of this State, and were not the other officers at said election then busy in their official duty as to the election?—Ans. 9. Yes, sir; yes, sir.

Interrog. 10. When you were not looking over the poll-books were you not in position and have good opportunity to detect any fraudulent conduct on the part of the other officials of said election?—Ans. 10. Yes, sir.

In opposition to this the witnesses for contestee undertake to show that more negroes than are stated by the Republican witnesses voted the Democratic ticket. Dogan says: "I do not know how many colored voters voted the Democratic ticket in this county in 1888, but do know that some of the best colored men in the county are Democrats and belong to Democratic clubs" (Rec., p. 842). Neely says:

Ans. 32. I don't know exactly number of col. voters who voted the Democratic ticket in the county, but can safely testify that at least 150 or 175 voted that ticket in the county, and at least 35 or 40 at this box: I know this from personal observation and my acquaintance with the col. voters and by giving out Democratic tickets to them, and many of them voted the Democratic ticket openly and above board. (Rec., p. 840.)

Polk says:

Answer to question 32. I think at least forty colored votes was polled for Judge J. B. Morgan at Charleston precinct. As to the other precincts I am not able to say. I know it from personal observation and their statements to me as to how they would vote; a good many voted open tickets for Judge Morgan. (Rec., p. 844.)

But not a single negro was called in this county to prove that he voted the Democratic ticket, and the color of the voters, as shown in the proof of those who voted, there were 832 colored and 783 white.

Again, at Charleston the proof shows 109 whites and 155 colored voted. Three of the whites voted for Chalmers, and if we add to the 106 white men 40 colored, which is the most extravagant guess made by any Democratic witness as to the colored Democratic vote at this box, it would make but 143 where the commissioners returned 180 for Morgan. A further gross fraud is shown at this box, in this: The precinct officers returned but 162 for Morgan, while the commissioners returned 180 (see Rec. pp. 462 and 745).

Counting the vote for Chalmers here as proven by the Republican witnesses and the count will then stand:

	Chalmers.	Morgan.
Forward	8,278	8,587
Charleston:		
Add	155	
Deduct		180
	8,433	8,407
Deduct unexamined boxes:		
Benton County	232	605
	8,201	7,802
De Soto County	312	548
	7,889	7,263
La Fayette County	268	880
	7,621	6,482
Marshall County	400	622
	7,221	5,780
Panola County	313	540
	6,908	5,340
Tate	348	944
	6,560	4,296
Add rejected votes in Benton, Marshall, De Soto, Panola and Tate	380	
	6,940	
Showing plurality for contestant	2,644	

Or if Tallahatchie County be rejected the count will then stand—returning to the last count in La Fayette:

	Chalmers.	Morgan.
Forward	7,769	8,979
Tallahatchie out, deduct	2	1,031
	7,767	7,948
Deduct unexamined boxes:		
Benton County	232	605
	7,535	7,353
De Soto County	312	548
	7,223	6,813
La Fayette County	268	880
	6,955	5,953
Marshall County	400	622
	6,555	5,331
Panola County	313	540
	6,242	4,791
Tate County	348	944
	5,894	3,847
Add rejected votes in Benton, DeSoto, Marshall, Panola, and Tate	380	
	6,274	
Plurality for contestant	2,427	

RECAPITULATION.

	Chalmers.	Morgan.
....County:	5, 817	13, 978
	Deduct 77	Deduct 101
	5, 740	13, 877
........counted	Add.. 48	....
	5, 788	13, 877
....County: ....n Lake	Add... 142	Deduct 256
	5, 930	13, 621
........ittle	Deduct 105	Deduct 130
	5, 825	13, 491
....proved	Add... 182	Add... 47
	6, 007	13, 538
....nando Depot	Deduct 32	Deduct 134
	5, 975	13, 404
....proved	Add... 97	Add .. 69
	6, 072	13, 473
........e Court-House	Add... 49	Deduct 49
	6, 121	13, 424
....	Add... 52	Deduct 162
	6, 173	13, 262
....	Add... 148	Deduct 154
	6, 321	13, 108
....	Deduct 136	Deduct 200
	6, 185	12, 908
........dale	Add... 33	Deduct 111
	6, 218	12, 797
....	Add... 73	....
	6, 291	12, 797
....	Add .. 118	....
	6, 409	12, 797
Olive Branch	Add .. 100	Deduct 185
	6, 509	12, 612
....all County: East Holly Springs	Add... 128	Deduct 350
	6, 637	12, 202
West Holly Springs	Add... 30	Deduct 30
	6, 667	12, 232
Red Bank	Add... 41	Deduct 115
	6, 708	12, 117
....holls	Add... 35	Deduct 302
	6, 743	11, 815
....t Hill	Add... 27	Deduct 119
	6, 770	11, 696
....lahoma	Add... 48	Deduct 121
	6, 818	11, 575
Law's Hill	Add... 24	Deduct 94
	6, 842	11, 481
Waterford	Add... 40	Deduct 162
	6, 882	11, 319
....donville	Add... 14	Deduct 142
	6, 896	11, 177
....h County: ....ne	Add... 60	Deduct 305
	6, 956	10, 872

RECAPITULATION —Continued.

	Chalmers.	Morgan.
Panola County—continued:		
Spring Port..................................	Add... 5	Deduct 79
Longtown.....................................	6,961 Add... 40	10,777 Deduct 155
Batesville...................................	7,001 Add... 68	10,618 Deduct 245
Pleasant Mount...............................	7,069 Deduct 97	10,373 Deduct -125
Tate County:	6,972	10,247
Taylor's	Add... 145	Add... 30
Coldwater....................................	7,117 Add... 149	10,277 Deduct 275
Senatobia....................................	7,266 Deduct 44	10,002 Deduct 318
Shirods	7,222 Deduct 20	9,684 Deduct 166
Strayhorn	7,202 Deduct 16	9,518 Deduct 223
La Fayette County:	7,186	9,295
Abbeville.....................................	Add... 40	Deduct 31
College Hill..................................	7,226 Add... 174	9,264 Deduct 285
North Oxford.................................	7,400 Add... 190	8,979 ....
South Oxford	7,590 Add... 179	8,979 ....
Tallahatchie County, throw out the county........	7,769 Deduct 2	8,979 Deduct 1,021
Benton County, unexamined boxes	7,767 Deduct 232	7,958 Deduct 605
De Soto County, unexamined boxes	7,535 Deduct 312	7,353 Deduct 540
La Fayette County, unexamined boxes	7,223 Deduct 268	6,813 Deduct 860
Marshall County, unexamined boxes	6,955 Deduct 400	5,953 Deduct 622
Panola County, unexamined boxes................	6,555 Deduct 313	5,331 Deduct 540
Tate County, unexamined boxes..................	6,242 Deduct 348	4,791 Deduct 944
Benton County .. ⎫ Do Soto County.. ⎪ Marshall County. ⎬ Add rejected vote .... Panola County... ⎪ Tate County..... ⎭	5,894 380	3,847 ....
Majority for Chalmers	6,274 2,427	3,847

From this it will be seen that if the unexamined boxes be rejected and the rejected voters outside of La Fayette County be counted for contestant, it will give him 606 plurality upon the count as admitted to be made by the majority report. If they be added to the count, as made by this report, it gives to the contestant 2,427 plurality by the count leaving out Tallahatchie County, and 2,644 if Charleston box, in Tallahatchie County, be counted according to the rule, so frequently held by this committee, of rejecting the vote when fraud is proved, and counting only the vote as proved by the ticket distributers to have been issued and voted. We have given our count in detail, and we append a tabulated recapitulation for easy reference, and we challenge any one to show that in making it we have departed at any box from the rules laid down in Featherstone *v.* Cate, Threet *v.* Clarke, or McDuffy *v.* Turpin. The committee acted on these rules in all these cases, and we see no reason why we should depart from them in this case.

When the majority of the committee found fraud enough at 23 boxes to reduce the returned plurality 6,122 votes, can it be possibble that a further examination would not have shown further fraud at the unexamined boxes sufficient to give contestant even a greater majority than is here counted for him.

For this House to declare the contestee legally elected, after all the fraud shown in this report and the first sixteen pages of the majority report, with which we agree, will be to uphold and maintain a state of things disgraceful to our civilization and to encourage its continuance and repetition so that it will grow with their growth and strengthen with their strength until it becomes imbedded in the politics of that section, never to be eradicated except by revolution.

Therefore, in consideration of the premises, the minority recommend the following resolutions:

Resolved, That James B. Morgan was not elected a Representative in the Fifty-first Congress from the second Congressional district of Mississippi, and is not entitled to a seat therein.

Resolved, That James R. Chalmers was elected a Representative in the Fifty-first Congress from the second Congressional district of Mississippi, and is entitled to a seat therein.

H. Mis. 137——28

JOHN M. LANGSTON vs. E. C. VENABLE.

Contestant charged that by the false and fraudulent returns of the election officers in certain precincts he had been deprived of the benefit of a large number of votes legally cast for him. This charge the committee find sustained by the evidence as to a sufficient number of precincts to overcome the plurality returned for contestee, and show a plurality for contestant. The minority find the evidence insufficient to sustain the charges. (See minority report, page 469.) The resolutions presented by the committee were adopted September 23, 1890, the first by a vote of 151 to 1 (the Speaker "counting a quorum") and the second without division, and Mr. Langston was sworn in. The debate will be found on pages 9822 to 10339 of the Record. (The case was under consideration most of the time from September 6 to September 23.)

(1) Irregularities. *Their effect on the prima facie of the returns.*

Mere irregularities in the conduct of the election, where it does not appear that the legally expressed will of the voter has been suppressed or changed are insufficient to impeach officially declared votes. But a succession of unexplained irregularities and disregard of law on the part of intelligent officials removes from the ballot-box and the official returns that sacred character with which the law clothes them, and makes less conclusive evidence sufficient to change the burden upon the party who maintains the legality of the official count.

(2) Change of judges of election.

Unwarranted changes in judges of election, made without reason or excuse, only a few days before the election, are suspicious circumstances, but standing alone, and not supported by evidence of fraud at the polls, affecting the result of the election, are disregarded, and the certified returns permitted to stand as made.

(3) Irregularity. *In one portion of a return does not affect the rest.*

Where a precinct return was irregular as to votes cast for Presidential electors, and had been rejected entire by the county commissioners, the committee counted the vote for Representative in Congress, which was regularly returned.

(4) Excessive ballots.

Where there was an excess of 26 ballots in a vote of about 200, and the count was conducted without witnesses, and under suspicious cir-

435

cumstances, the committee held that this was sufficient to reject the return.

(5) Unsigned return.

An unsigned statement counted as a return by the county commissioners was rejected by the committee.

(6) Suppression of testimony. *By dilatory cross-examination.*

Where in one precinct contestant began taking testimony twenty-three days before the expiration of his time, in pursuance to a notice containing the names of 292 persons, who, it is claimed, would have testified that they voted for him in said precinct, and the first two witnesses, the ticket distributers, were cross-examined by the contestee throughout the entire twenty-three days, *held*, that the contestee is estopped from claiming that the evidence of these ticket distributers is insufficient unless corroborated by that of the voters themselves, he having by his own act prevented the latter testimony from being taken.

(7) Return overthrown by testimony of voters.

Where contestant was returned as having received 139 votes in a precinct, and 283 voters testified to having voted for him, and the testimony of the ticket distributers indicated a still larger number, *held*, that this is sufficient to reject the return, and count only such votes as are proved outside the return.

(8) Votes. *Not cast.*

Where there were two lines of voters, one white and one colored, and the judges required them to vote alternately, and the colored line being much the longer, there was still a large number of voters in it who had not voted at the close of the polls, and the testimony showed that most of them were intending to vote for contestant, but they themselves were not called as witnesses, *held*, that their votes could not be counted for contestant, but that if their number had equaled or exceeded the plurality returned for the contestee so that the legality of the election depended upon them, it would invalidate his election with no further proof and make a new election necessary.

(For ruling under a different state of facts, see Waddill *vs.* Wise, *supra.*)

(9) Return. *When rejected only votes proved counted.*

Where the returns were rejected for fraud, and the only votes proved aside from the returns were for contestant, *held*, that no others could be counted, for "it is evident that giving to contestee the vote not accounted for would be a direct encouragement to election frauds, as it would give him the benefit of every fraudulent vote which his friends had made it impossible for the opposition to expose, even after the proof clearly established fraud to such an extent as to destroy absolutely the integrity of the official returns. In no case has such a rule been adopted."

REPORT.

JUNE 16, 1890.—Mr. HAUGEN, from the Committee on Elections, submitted the following report:

The official returns from the Fourth Congressional district of Virginia of the election of Representative in Congress, on the 6th of November, 1888, give E. C. Venable 13,298, John M. Langston 12,657, and R. W. Arnold 3,207 votes, a plurality of 641 votes of Venable over Langston.

The contestant, Mr. Langston, claims that this is not the true vote of the district, but is the result of fraud and corruption on the part of the election officers in certain counties and at certain precincts specified in his notice of contest, and that had the vote been honestly received and honestly returned in accordance with the laws of Virginia, a clear plurality over Mr. Venable would have appeared for him—Langston.

The committee has selected from the voluminous record (which contains some 1,200 pages of closely printed matter, much of it irrelevant and tedious cross-examination) a few precincts which appear to the committee to sustain the charges of the contestant and completely overcome the plurality for contestee on the face of the returns.

Mere irregularities in the conduct of the election, where it does not appear that the legally expressed will of the voter has been suppressed or changed, is insufficient to impeach officially declared votes and have been disregarded. But a succession of unexplained irregularities and disregard of law on the part of intelligent officials removes from the ballot-box and the official returns that sacred character with which the law clothes them, and makes less conclusive evidence sufficient to change the burden upon the party who maintains the legality of the official count.

Paine on Elections, section 596, says:

While it is well settled that mere neglect to perform directory requirements of law, or performance in a mistaken manner where there is no bad faith and no harm has accrued, will not justify the rejection of an entire poll, it is equally well settled that when the proceedings are so tarnished by fraudulent, negligent, or improper conduct on the part of the officers that the result of the election is rendered unreliable, the entire returns will be rejected and the parties left to make such proof as they may of the votes legally cast for them.

The laws of Virginia recognize the weaknesses of human nature and the necessity of having friends of the candidates representing different views upon the election boards to guard against the temptation to which a board whose members all affiliate with one political party might be subject.

437

The following provisions of the Virginia law are referred to in connection with the case:

SEC. 117. *How judges of election appointed; failing to attend, who to act.*—It shall be the duty of the electoral board of each city and county, prior to the first day of March in each year, to appoint three competent citizens, being qualified voters, who shall constitute the judges of election for all elections to be held in **their** respective election districts, for the term of one year, dating from their appointment, and who shall have power to appoint two clerks for each place of voting at such election, to whom shall be administered by the judges, or either of them, the same oath as that taken by the said judges. Whenever it is possible to do so, the persons so appointed judges of election, shall be chosen for each voting place from persons known to belong to different political parties, each one of whom shall be able to read and write. The members of any electoral board who shall willfully fail to comply with this requirement, shall be deemed guilty of misdemeanor, and on conviction thereof shall be fined not less than one hundred nor more than five hundred dollars; but no election shall be deemed invalid when the judges shall not belong to different political parties, or who shall not possess the above qualifications. Should any judge of election fail to attend at any place of voting for one hour after the time prescribed by law for opening the polls at such election, it shall be lawful for the judge or judges in attendance to select from among the bystanders one or more persons possessing the qualifications of judges of election, who shall act as judge or judges of such election and who shall have all the powers and authority of judges appointed by said electoral board: *Provided, however,* That if the judge or judges present have information that the absent judge or judges will not attend, he or they need not wait for the expiration of an hour, or any other time. Should all the judges appointed for any place of voting fail to attend at the place of voting for one hour after the time prescribed by law for opening the polls at such election, it shall be the duty of any justice of the district in which the election is held, who shall be applied to for that purpose, or the mayor, if the election is in any election district is in any town or city, to appoint three judges of election for such election district, who shall possess the same qualifications and have the same powers as judges appointed by an electoral board. Should no judges of election be appointed for any county, city, or place of voting therein, or if appointed they neglect or refuse to act for one hour after the time prescribed by law for opening the polls at such election, it shall be lawful for any three qualified voters of the district, who shall be present and willing to act, upon taking the oath prescribed for judges of election, to proceed to hold conduct, and certify the election in the manner provided in this chapter, and, for that purpose, shall have all the powers and authority of judges appointed by an electoral board.

SEC. 3849. *Judge, clerk, etc., failing to attend election, how punished.*—If any judge, clerk, or commissioner of election fail to attend at the time and place appointed for such election, or to perform any of the duties imposed on him by law, without good and sufficient reason, he shall be fined not less than ten nor more than one hundred dollars.

SEC. 3850. *Officers, etc., neglecting his duty in regard to election, or doing it corruptly, how punished.*—If any officer, messenger, or other person on whom any duty is enjoined by law relative to general or special elections, be guilty of any willful neglect of such duty, or of any corrupt conduct in the execution of the same, he shall be fined not exceeding five hundred dollars, and confined in jail not exceeding one year; and if any officer be convicted as aforesaid he shall be removed from office.

It is very evident from the last two sections quoted that the law intended that no change should be made in the legally constituted board except for most urgent reasons, and that men appointed before the commencement of a heated campaign could alone be trusted with the important duties of impartially recording the votes of self-governing freemen.

SEC. 128. *How polls closed when votes canvassed and result declared.*—As soon as the polls are finally closed (of which closing proclamation shall be made by the judges fifteen minutes previous thereto), the judges shall immediately proceed to canvass the vote given at such election, and the said canvass shall be continued without adjournment until completed, and the result thereof declared.

SEC. 129. *How votes canvassed.*—The canvass shall commence by taking out of the box the ballots unopened (except so far as to ascertain whether each ballot is single), and counting the same to ascertain whether the number of ballots corresponds with the number of names on the poll books; and if two or more separate ballots are found so folded together as to present the appearance of a single ballot, they shall be laid aside until the count of the ballot is completed. If upon a comparison of the said count with the number of names of electors on the poll-books, it appears that the two ballots thus folded together were cast by the same elector, they shall be destroyed. If the ballots in the ballot-box are still found to exceed the number of names on the poll books, all of the ballots shall be replaced in the ballot-box; and after the same shall be well shaken, one of the judges of the election being blindfolded, shall draw therefrom a sufficient number of ballots to reduce the same to a number equal to the number of electors on the poll-books. The number of ballots thus being made to agree with the number of names on the poll-book, the books shall be signed by the judges and attested by the clerks, and the number of names thereon shall be set down, in words and figures at the foot of the list of electors on the poll-books, and over the signature of the judges and attestations of the clerks in the manner and form prescribed by section one hundred and twenty. Whenever the number of ballots is reduced,·by the destruction of fraudulent ballots, below the number of names of electors on the poll-books, the cause of such reduction shall be stated at the foot of the list of electors on the poll-books, before the same are signed and attested by the judges and clerks respectively.

SEC. 130. *How votes counted and returns made.*—After the poll-books are thus signed and attested, the judges shall, if desired, *in the presence of not exceeding two friends of each political party* represented by the persons voted for in such election, proceed to count and ascertain the number of votes cast for each person voted for; and the tickets or ballots shall be distinctively read, and as soon as read and canvassed shall be strung by one of the judges on a string, and the clerks shall set down on the poll-books, next after the certificate of the judges at the foot of the list of electors as the returns of the election, the name of every person voted for, written at full length, the office for which such person received such votes, and the number of votes he received; the number being expressed in figures, and also at full length in writing, in accordance with the form prescribed in said section one hundred and twenty; which said returns when so made out, shall be signed and attested as provided in said section, but no person other than the judges of the election shall handle the ballots.

There are numerous instances in the record of unwarranted changes in judges of election, made without reason or excuse only a few days before the election. These are suspicious circumstances, but standing alone and not supported by evidence of fraud at the polls, affecting the result of the election, they have been disregarded, and the certified returns permitted to stand as made. In arriving at results, specific acts at certain designated precincts are alone considered, without unnecessarily dwelling on the general political and race features of the district.

. The contestee was the candidate of the regular Democracy. The party affiliations of contestant, as far as this contest goes, are a matter of dispute. The contestee maintains that he (contestant) ran as an independent candidate in opposition to the regular Republican nominee, Mr. Arnold. Much evidence introduced by contestee deals with the regularity of the Republican convention and the questionable features of Mr. Langston's candidacy as viewed from a strict party standpoint. The question which the committee has endeavored to solve is: Which candidate received a plurality of the votes, and not who was the regular nominee? Whom did the voters of the Fourth district of Virginia elect to represent them in the Fifty-first Congress? and not what is the percentage of white and colored blood in the veins of the respective candidates. That there was marked race prejudice in localities in favor of and against Mr. Langston is apparent from the evidence. It is a matter for regret, and one not creditable to either race. Taking the evidence of contestee's witnesses alone and it clearly establishes the practically solid support of Mr. Langston by the negroes of the district. The testimony of J. H. Van Auken, A. W. Harris, W. W. Evans, and other witnesses for contestee fully proves this. Mr. Van Auken testifies, on pages 956 and 957 on cross-examination, as follows:

132d. Question. Then, explain, if you please, how with Arnold, the regular nominee of the party, supported by its entire organization in all its great influence, skill, management, and outlay, Arnold ran so poorly in the district?—Ans. For long months prior to the election, and for long months before the convention, Mr. Langston had, unopposed, been making a cauvass, in which he and his emissaries had insidiously and industriously played upon the passions and prejudices of the colored people, basing his claims to Congress largely on the fact that the negroes outnumbered tho whites very largely, and it was time for them to send a negro to Congress. He aroused even the women, got up an immense religious fervor in his favor, and aroused the prejudice of the large mass of the unthinking colored people to such an extent as I never witnessed before and hope never to witness again. It was at white heat in Sussex County the week prior to the election, so much so that I was impressed with the opinion, and expressed it, that they would not then even listen to the Lord Jesus Christ, much less vote for him, if he were a white man and appeared against Langston. This feeling was intensified largely under the teachings and leadership of young colored men, who had no memories of the past, which enabled them to properly appreciate what the Republican party had done for their race, hence no feeling of gratitude.

With such feeling in the district the election of Langston was certainly to be expected.

It was clear that Arnold, who was receiving the support of the chairman of the Republican Congressional district committee and the party organization, as far as the chairman was able to control it, was virtually distanced in the race. All the bitterness engendered against a candidate, rightfully or mistakenly, accused of opposing the regular nominee of his party, appeared in opposition to contestant by many white Republicans, and tended to draw still more sharply the color line.

With this feeling in the district, the fact that on the very eve of the election it was found convenient or necessary by the Democratic electoral commissioners to remove Republican precinct judges of election known to be friendly to contestant, and filling the vacancies with his bitter opponents, without any reason or excuse for the change, is a badge of fraud which can not be overlooked. This question will be further discussed in connection with each precinct.

The census returns for 1880 give a total population in this district of 56,194 whites and 102,071 colored.

POARCH AND ROSS ELECTION DISTRICT, BRUNSWICK COUNTY.

At this precinct 69 votes were cast for Venable and 141 for Langston, a plurality of 72 for Langston. This vote was regularly returned to the county commissioners, but not counted for the alleged reason that the same returns showed certain votes cast for candidates for President and Vice-President, instead of for electors of President and Vice-President. For this mistake of the judges not only the electoral vote of this precinct was thrown out, but the vote for every other candidate upon the ticket was rejected by the county commissioners. This fraud now stands confessed, and leaves the plurality for contestee as follows:

Returned plurality.. 641
Less plurality for Langston at Poarch and Ross precinct 72
                                                                        ———
                                                                        569

LUNENBURG COUNTY—LEWISTON.

The regularly appointed judges at this precinct, appointed January 27, 1888, were W. P. Austin, B. H. May, and T. C. Fowlkes. Austin and May were present at the opening of the polls, but did not serve as judges. Mr. May acted as one of the clerks. The acting judges were E. G. Bayne, T. F. Robertson, and E. C. Goodwin. All the judges and clerks and the United States supervisor present were political opponents of contestant. With the exception of Mr. Austin, who testifies that on account of illness it was impossible for him to serve, no explanation is given for this sudden change of judges on the very morning of election; but that it was in pursuance of prearranged plans is apparent from the presence of Mr. Robertson at sunrise on the morning of election to serve as judge, he living some 8 or 9 miles distant from the polls.

J. W. Smith, a farmer and supervisor of Lewiston district, testifies on page 814 of the record as follows:

37th. Was Captain Austin around the polls during the day? And if so, state how often, how long he remained at the polls, and what he was doing there.—Ans. He was around the polls during the day. I don't remember how often, but I saw him two or three times during the day on the election ground working in the interest of Arnold.

38th. Name the U. S. supervisors at the polls at said precinct on election day, what political party they belonged to, and what service they rendered.—Ans. W. J. Bragg was the only one I know of. He is a Mahoneite, and staid here all day until the polls were closed, and then went home immediately after the polls were closed.

39th. Were all the judges and the clerks of the election and the U. S. supervisor the friends or opponents of Jno. M. Langston for Congress?—Ans. They were his opponents.

40th. Were the polls abandoned by the judges during said election day?—Ans. They were; they adjourned for breakfast; they went out and staid at least three-quarters of an hour. They also took a recess for dinner, and went out and staid at least three-quarters of an hour or an hour, as well as I can remember.

41st. Were there Democrat, Republican, and Mahone ticket holders at the polls of your precinct on election day, November 6th, 1888?—Ans. There were.

42nd. State whether or not ballots were in the rooms where the polls were held laying loose near the ballot-box on said election day.—Ans. Yes; there was a package of Democratic ballots laying in a few feet of the ballot-box.

43d. State what was done when the polls were closed at sundown on election day, November 6th, 1888.—Ans. The clerks of election and everybody else, except the judges, were excluded from the room, and the judges immediately proceeded to open the ballot-box and count the ballots. A few minutes before the polls were closed I asked one of the judges to let me stay in and see the ballots counted. He objected, and said they did not want anybody in the room but the judges—that was just a few minutes before the polls closed. I came out then and saw Mr. May, who was one of the clerks, and asked him could I go in with him, and he said I could. We staid out I guess about half an hour, and when we went to the door to go in we had to wait at least fifteen or twenty minutes. In the mean time Mr. King rapped at the door several times, but they would not open the door. When we did go in the ballots had all been taken out of the box and were in three separate lots on the table. I asked one of the judges how the vote stood, and he replied that Langston had fifty-six, Arnold fifty, and Venable one hundred and thirty-three. The clerks then looked at the books and found that there were twenty-five more ballots than there were names on the poll-books. They then blindfolded one of the judges and drew out twenty-five ballots, thirteen of Venable's, eight of Langston's, and four of Arnold's.

44th. You have stated that two of the officers of the election, the clerks, were excluded from the room where the count of the vote was being made, by the judges of the election. State how long it was before the clerks were admitted to the room, and whether or not their said admission was obtained easily or under difficulties.—Ans. I think said clerks were out fully an hour. Their admission was not obtained easily. Mr. May went to the door and rapped good many times, and they had to wait fully fifteen minutes before they could get in, and the judges knew very well who it was, too. I mean to say the clerks were not admitted until the judges got ready to open the door. The door was locked. They then got in easily enough when the door was unlocked.

45th. How many votes were cast for Jno. M. Langston for Congress at your said precinct on said election day?—Ans. I believe there were sixty-six cast for him.

The excess of ballots appears by the return of the judges to have been 26. Mr. Smith also testifies to the fact that the polls were held in an unusual place. The customary place for holding the election at this precinct had been the court-room of the court-house. At this particular election it was found advisable to occupy a small jury room and exclude all witnesses, not excepting the clerks of election, which would have been impracticable in the large and commodious court-room.

William Smith, a farmer, sixty-two years old and a resident of

Lunenburgh county all his life, was called as a witness, and the following is quoted from his testimony:

4th. Can you state positively whether or not Captain Austin was at the polls before
the voting commenced?—Ans. Yes, sir; he was there before my work was done. He
was in the room when the judges swore themselves in; him and Mr. May both.

5th. Were Captain William P. Austin and B. H. May the judges of election at your
precinct on election day? And if they were not, please give the names of the persons who served as judges of election.—Ans. They were not the judges that conducted
the said election. E. G. Boyre, T. F. Robertson, and E. C. Goodwin were the judges
who conducted said election.

6th. Why is it that Messrs. Boyre, Robertson, and Goodwin served as judges of
election at your precinct, when Messrs. Austin and May, the two duly appointed
judges of election, were at the polls before the voting commenced?—Ans. I CAN'T
TELL YOU, WITHOUT THEY WANTED TO DO SOMETHING THAT CAPT. AUSTIN AND MR.
MAY DID NOT WANT TO GO INTO.

7th. Was there any explanation made of it at the polls?—Ans. No, sir; they just
went right in and went to work like they had been appointed by the board.

8th. What time did the polls open on the morning of the election?—Ans. The sun
was only about five minutes high when they commenced.

9th. When did Captain Austin first leave the polls after the voting had commenced?—Ans. Some eight or ten had voted when Captain Austin was inside.

10th. How often did you see Captain Austin at the polls during the day, how long
did he remain there, and what was he doing?—Ans. All day long he was on the
election grounds with his tickets in his hands.

11th. Where were the polls held? Were they held at the usual place of voting?
And, if not, describe the place where they were held, and describe the difference
between the place where they were usually held and the place where they were held
November the 6th, 1888.—Ans. The polls were held in one of the jury-rooms, not the
usual place of voting. The place where they were held was in one of the jury-rooms.
One of them is a large room and one is a small room. The room that they got in last
election was a jury-room, where the judges got in and could shut the door and
keep the people out. I told the judges of election that morning that there was
something another wrong going to be done here to-day, and some of them replied to
me, why? And I told them because they were holding the election in a room.

12th. Did you see any ballots lying loose near the ballot-box during the day?—
Ans. I did, sir. They had the door opened about ten inches, and the box was setting sorter in front of the door where we could see it, and the judge who received
the tickets he was sitting right in front of the crack of the door, and right behind the
judge sitting there laid a handful of Democratic tickets.

13th. Who were the clerks and who was the U. S. supervisor at said election?—
Ans.—Mr. B. H. May and Jno. W. Cleaton were the clerks, and W. J. Bragg was the
U. S. supervisor.

14th. Were all the officers of election friends or opponents of Jno. M. Langston for
Congress?—Ans. They were all his opponents.

15th. Were or were not the polls abandoned during the day by the judges of election?—Ans. They took a recess for breakfast and for dinner.

16th. State what happened when the polls closed.—Ans. Directly after the polls
closed the clerks came out and the supervisor and I said to Mr. Cardozo that the
supervisor had come out and gone off home, and I told him I was going after the
supervisor to come back and see the votes counted, and Mr. Cardozo said the supervisor was sick. I did not go after him. The clerks staid out, I reckon, at least an
hour, and we went to the door and asked the judges to let us come in, and they refused
to do it. And in about an hour Mr. May came back and they turned the two clerks in
and J. W. Smith.

17th. State anything else you know.—Ans. Myself and Mr. Jno. W. Cleaton, who
was one of the clerks of the election, got to talking after the election, and Mr.
Cleaton told me that the judges of election ordered them out of the room that night,
and said if they knew he had not been a good Democrat they would not have let him
serve as a clerk of the election, and he asked them why, because he told them that
he never saw them order the clerks out of the room before.

18th. Was this Mr. Cleaton an old clerk of the election at this precinct?—Ans. He
was.

19th. Under what circumstances did Mr. Cleaton make this statement to you?—
Ans. He came by my house, and got me to carry him part of the way home, and
made said statement to me in the presence of his son.

Let it be remembered that this is not disputed by evidence. Mr.
Cleaton was not called as a witness, presumably for the reason that,
if called, he would have corroborated the statements of Mr. Smith.

W. P. Austin, the supplanted judge, was called as a witness by contestee. He testifies that the judges and clerks had been sworn in before he reached the polls and before one hour after the time for opening the polls had expired. This was in direct violation of the statute quoted above. This is not disputed or explained.

T. F. Robertson was the only one of the judges sworn to sustain their acts. He guardedly swears in answer to the leading question whether the election was fair and honest, *"It was as far as I saw, sir."* He also testifies to his inexperience in election matters, and was no doubt put forth as a witness because he, of all the judges, was innocently ignorant of the illegal acts of his colleagues, whose caution kept them from taking the stand.

On cross examination Mr. Robertson says, page 1097.

28th. Please state when the canvass of the vote commenced after the polls were closed at sundown.—Ans. Just as quick as we could; no recess was taken.

29th. Where was the clerks of election, B. H. May and J. W. Clinton, when the ballot-box was opened to proceed with the count and canvass of the vote?—Ans. I don't know; they were there just then. Mr. May excused himself; said he had some business he had to attend to. Mr. Clinton excused himself, that he wanted to walk about a little, and we could go on without them as easy as we could with them. By the time we got the tickets divided they knocked at the door and we turned them in, Jno. Wm. Smith, Republican, R. J. Toone, Democrat, with them.

30th. Then it is a fact that the ballots were taken out of the ballot-box and divided into different piles during the absence of the two clerks of election, is it not?—Ans. Yes, sir; by Mr. E. G. Bayne, Republican.

31st. Please describe how the ballots were taken out of the ballot-box in order to count them.—Ans. We took the top off of the box and turned it upside down and poured them all down on the table in one pile.

32nd. Then it is a fact that the ballot-box was turned upside down and the ballots were dumped in one pile on the table, instead of taking them out from the ballot-box singly, one by one; is that so?—Ans. Yes, sir; and then they were picked up one by one and separated.

34th. How long were Clerks of Election Clinton and May absent?—Ans. Not more than fifteen or twenty minutes, I reckon.

35th. How often did they knock at the door, and how long were they knocking at the door in order to gain admission into the room?—Ans. They knocked several times; they were, sir, I reckon, something like five minutes; we were busy dividing the tickets and did not want to stop, but had it to do to get rid of their fuss.

36th. What was Mr. Bayne's, the judge of election, condition? Was he perfectly sober at this time, or was he under the influence of intoxicating liquors?—Ans. I do not know whether he was or not; he appeared to be mighty badly excited; whether he was tight or not I do not know.

37th. How many ballots were there found in the ballot-box in excess of the total number of names found on the poll-books?—Ans. Twenty-six.

38. How long did it take to canvass the vote and who called off the ballots?—Ans. I don't recollect. E. G. Bayne, with Jno. Wm. Smith to help him.

39th. Was not Mr. Bayne's condition such at this time that he required of Jno. Wm. Smith to enable him to call off the ballots?—Ans. In the beginning he seemed to be quite nervous, and after calling off the names on a dozen or so tickets, he then went on without the assistance of anybody.

40th. Who else, besides Judge of Election Bayne, handled the ballots, counted, and read off the same?—Ans. E. C. Goodwyn and myself, the two other judges, helped to count them; neither of us read off any names, but looked on, and I strung the tickets as he read them off.

41st. Which one of the judges or clerks of election, if any one of them, was friendly towards Jno. M. Langston for Congress?—Ans. All of us, I reckon, sir; I have no animosity against him, and I don't reckon the others had.

42nd. You have stated that E. G. Bayne was a Republican. How do you know that fact?—Ans. He told me so two or three weeks ago.

43rd. Please state, if you have no objection, to which political party you belong, and what candidate for Congress you supported during the last Congressional campaign.—Ans. I supported Mr. E. C. Venable, and am to-day and was born a Democrat, and am to-day, and expect to die so.

44th. To what political party did Mr. E. C. Goodwyn, the other judge of election, and Mr. B. H. May and J. W. Clinton, the last two, who were clerks of election, belong during the last Congressional campaign in this district?—Ans. I would not swear that I know what either of them are, except Mr. B. H. May, but they told me they were Democrats. Mr. May is a Democrat.

The clerks were not called as witnesses.

The only United States supervisor serving, W. J. Bragg, left immediately after the closing of the polls, not to return, and was consequently ignorant of any of the illegal acts of the judges charged. The committee is of the opinion that the excess of 26 ballots in a total vote of about 200 could not have occurred without the connivance of the judges of election, and is such evidence of fraud as must necessarily exclude this box. Contestee does not in his briefs even mention the excess of ballots. The returns awarded Venable 119, Langston 48, and Arnold 46 votes. The returns are impeached and rejected. No competent evidence was offered as to the true vote cast. The account now stands:

Plurality for Venable 569
Deduct plurality for Venable at Lewiston, which is equivalent to rejecting the poll 71
                                                                            ———
    Leaves plurality for Venable 498

MANNBORO, AMELIA COUNTY.

The electoral commissioners of Amelia County reported this precinct as having given 122 votes for Venable, and 111 for Langston. The regularity of this return was challenged by contestant in his notice of contest. The only thing in the Record bearing upon this question is found on page 173, giving the following unsigned statement:

FOR CONGRESS.

E. C. Venable rec'd (122) one hundred and twenty-two votes.
John Mercer Langston rec'd (111) one hundred and eleven votes.
R. W. Arnold rec'd (73) seventy-three votes.
After the names, etc., are all set down, and at the foot of the list, a certificate in the following form is required to be given:
We hereby certify, That ——— had ——— votes for ———; and ——— had ——— votes for ———; that ——— had ——— votes for ———, &c.

            Clerks.   Judges.

If this is the act of the officers of election it is difficult to see why the contestee did not introduce some evidence to show that fact. As it is the plurality of eleven returned for contestee must be deducted from his former vote.

Plurality for Venable... 498
Deduct plurality for Venable returned in Mannboro............................. 11
                                                                            ———
    Leaves plurality for Venable... 487

CITY OF PETERSBURG.

This brings us to the city of Petersburg, the home of contestant, and the center of population and politics of the district. And it becomes proper here to give the general plan pursued by contestant in the district to test the fairness and honesty of the election returns. There is abundant evidence that apprehension of frauds were well founded, and contestant proposed to disclose them.

M. N. Lewis, thirty years old, an editor and lawyer, residence Petersburg, had charge of the campaign of contestant as secretary of his campaign committee, and in his testimony details the methods pursued.

A circular letter issued by contestant to friends in different parts ot
the district is testified to by this witness. We quote the following extract from it, found on page 539 of the Record:

THE ELECTION.

The afternoon before the election, on Monday, November 5th next, see that the
tickets are at your precinct; and if you do not receive them or know where they are
go at once to the court-house and ascertain where they are. This is very important,
because no man can vote without a ballot. On election morning be at the polls
without fail at least fifteen minutes before sunrise. Not later than 6.30 o'clock a. m.
On November 6th the sun rises at 6.42 o'clock and sets at 5.06 o'clock.

If the judges and clerks of election are not present, send some trusted friend for
them, and if they do not come by 7.15 o'clock a, m., consult some of the respectable
white voters at the polls and take proper steps to open the polls and conduct the
election.

I presume that the white voters present will take sufficient interest to conduct the
election in the manner prescribed by law; but if they do not, send at once for some
good lawyer, engage him at a reasonable fee to come to the polls and open the polls
and conduct the election under his instruction. He will find the full instructions in
the new code, a copy of which every justice of the peace has in his possession, and
which you should borrow from him and study the registration and election laws as
soon as you receive these instructions.

On the election day the most important part of your duty is to be discharged. I send
you herewith blank book and blank returns. Yourself and another reliable intelligent man must remain at the polls all day; do not, I urge you, leave the polls for any
purpose whatever, unless you leave in your place during your absence a reliable, intelligent friend who can read and write. In the book I send you do not fail to enter
the names of every voter who casts his ballot for me on election day at your voting
precinct. This is very important, and I shall depend upon your careful attention to
it. Enter the names plainly of every man who votes for Langston. Do not fail to do
this. The record of the names of every man who votes for me may be vital to my interest. You will find printed instructions in each book, which read and carefully
follow during the day and after the polls are closed.

I ask your special attention to the "election return," as per blank form herewith.
Please read the instructions at the bottom of the same and be careful to observe them
strictly. When the polls are closed select an intelligent friend to go inside and witness the counting of the ballots, and instruct him to look and see that the returns are
all properly made out and signed by the judges and clerks of election according to
the form on the poll-books. Do not fail to realize the great importance of having
the returns made out properly; if they are not, the commissioners of election for
your county may reject them and adjourn without observing the law as to amended
returns.

On the night of election notify me in writing of every irregularity, fraud, ballot-box
stuffing, or any other violation of law on election day at your precinct, and be careful to give me full particulars.

I ask you to read these instructions over and over again. Impress every point
upon your mind, and if you do not understand them let me know.

Remember, my friend, that my election may depend upon your efforts.

Please acknowledge receipt of this circular-letter immediately, so that I may know
that you have received it and can rely upon your attention to the same.

I am, sincerely, your friend,

JNO. MERCER LANGSTON.

To ——, ——,
——, —— Precinct,
——, —— County.

At the Republican Langston clubs in the city of Petersburgh it was
agreed that every supporter of Langston should vote an open ticket;
that he should show his ticket to some reliable friend of Langston selected for the purpose of registering the names of the Langston voters
and witnessing the deposit of their ballots in the box. This plan was
very generally followed by the enthusiastic supporters of contestant,
and the results promptly reported to him after election. With this plan
of campaign in mind we will consider the election in the third and
sixth wards of Petersburgh. There seems to have been a general belief

on the part of the supporters of contestant that it would be necessary to prove the true vote by other means than the returns, and they resorted to the only means to do so within their power.

THIRD WARD.

The returns from this ward give Venable 518, Langston 174, and Arnold 105 votes.

M. N. Lewis, the witness referred to above, testifies that he was at the polls all day, from the opening of the same until long after they closed, and kept tally of the Republicans voting for Langston and Harrison, in pursuance of the instructions of his party.

The judges and clerks of election were all Democrats and bitterly opposed to contestant. Only one United States supervisor served, and he a Democrat.

The following extracts are submitted from the testimony of Mr. Lewis, which is too voluminous to quote at length:

44. Question. Do you or do you not know Wm. Crichton, Jno. F. Williams, and Virginius S. Weddell?—Answer. I do; they were the judges of election in 3rd ward.

45. Question. At what election were they the judges of the election?—Answer. Election held Nov'r 6th, 1888.

46. Question. Do you know or not R. W. Bowden and Thos. S. Griffin?—Answer. Yes, sir; they were the clerks of the election held Nov'r 6th, 1888.

47. Question. Do you or do you not know G. B. Gill?—Answer. Yes, sir; he was the U. S. supervisor at 3rd ward polls, Nov'r 6th, 1888.

48th. Question. How many U. S. supervisors were on duty at the polls in the 3rd ward, this city, on election day, Nov'r 6th, 1888?—Answer. Only one, a Democratic supervisor, Gorman B. Gill.

49th. Question. Please state what political party all the judges and clerks of election and the U. S. supervisor at the 3rd ward on election day, Nov'r 6th, 1888, belonged?—Answer. To the Democratic party; each one of whom voted the straight Democratic ticket in my presence.

50. Question. Please state whether or not all the officers of election were bitterly opposed to Prof'r Langston's election to Congress?—Answer. They were.

51. Question. Please state whether or not you know F. R. Clements, who was appointed U. S. supervisor, 3rd ward, this city, at the said election.—Answer. I do.

52. Question. Did he serve as U. S. supervisor at said ward on said election day?—Answer. No, sir; nor was he seen about the polls until late in the afternoon of election day, Nov'r 6th, 1888.

59. Question. Do you or do you not know how many colored votes were cast at the 3d ward polls on said election day for E. C. Venable for Congress?—Answer. Not more than 15.

60. Question. Do you or do you not know how many colored votes were cast at the 3d ward polls on said election day for R. W. Arnold for Congress?—Answer. About 20. There were not more than 50 ballots cast by the voters at 3rd ward polls on election day, Nov. 6th, 1888, for R. W. Arnold.

62. Question. Did you or did you not, as a friend and supporter of Prof'r. Langston's, apply to one of the judges of election to be allowed to enter the room when the polls closed at sundown in your ward at said election in order to witness the count and canvass of the vote?—Answer. I had been allowed to go into the polls of the 3d ward to witness the count of the ballots at nearly every election for the last 6 years. I applied on the 6th of Nov'r, 1888, when the polls closed, to Mr. William Crichton, one of the judges of the election, to be allowed—that since there was neither a Republican judge, clerk, or supervisor in the polls—that I be allowed to come in and witness the count of the ballots, and was refused admission. I will state further that no Republican witnessed the count of the ballots in 3rd ward on the 6th day of November, 18-8.

63. Question. How long did the said count and canvass of the vote of your ward last?—Answer. Until about 11 o'clock.

64. Question. Did you keep a record at the polls of the 3rd ward on said election day, and if so, what record?—Answer. I kept a record of the votes cast for Jno. M. Langston.

65. Question. Why was this record kept at the polls of the 3rd ward on said election day of the votes cast for Jno. M. Langston?—Answer. In order to be able to know how many votes were cast for Jno. M. Langston for Congress.

66. Question. State where you stood at the polls of the 3rd ward on election day and how long you remained there?—Answer. There were two entrances to the 3rd ward polls, one for the white voters by which they approached the ballot-box, the other by which the colored voters approached the ballot-box. I stood right at the entrance where the colored voters approached the ballot-box, and where I could see the ballots given by the voter to the judge who received the ballots and deposited them in the box. I was there from sunrise until sunset, only leaving once for about 30 minutes. I saw and read the ballot of every voter whose name I have checked on my book, and I saw the same ballot which I read in the hands of each voter deposited by the judge in the ballot-box.

67. Question. Have you the said record books in your possession?—Answer. I have.

68. Question. Are the four books you have now here before the notary public the identical four books you had at the polls in the 3d ward on election day, November the 6th, 1888?—Answer. Yes, sir.

69th. Question. Did you or did you not enter in your own handwriting the names of the colored voters in the identical four books you have now before the notary public at your ward on election day, Novr. 6th, 1888, at the time the said colored voters cast their ballots?—Answer. I entered all the names with the exception of a few that were entered during the 30 minutes I was away from the polls.

70. Question. When and under what circumstances did you particularly observe the ballot of each colored voter before recording his name in said book?—Answer. I read his ballot carefully, and after I had seen the judge, to whom he handed his ballot, deposit it in the ballot-box I then placed his name on my book.

71. Question. Please give the name of the judge or judges of election who received the ballots from the voters at the polls of your ward on said election day.—Answer. Wm. Crichton.

72. Question. Please examine the ticket I hand you and state whether or not the ballot you saw in the hands of each voter of the 3rd ward on election day, Nov'r 6th. 1888, and which was delivered to and received by the judge of election, was identically like the ballot I hand you, and did you or did you not enter upon your said books the name of each colored voter who cast a ballot identically like the one here presented to you?—Answer. This is the identical ballot voted by each voter whose name I put upon my book.

The ballot here filed is a straight Republican ballot, with Langston for Congress.

73. Question. You have stated that you stood at the polls of the 3d ward all the day of election from the opening to the closing of the same, excepting about 30 minutes, and that you were immediately at the polling place of the 3d ward in this city; that then and there you took down in the four books which you have here identified and handed to the notary public the name of every colored voter, showing you a ticket identical with the one you have just examined, and which is filed with these depositions, marked Exhibit M, after said ticket had been delivered to and received by the judge of election at said ward on election day, Nov'r 6th, 1888. Now please give the name of each voter who you so entered in said books as you have stated?

The witness here gave the names of 286 voters recorded by him as all (except two indicated) having voted for contestant, and filed the four books containing the names with the notary taking the evidence, and they are in the possession of the committee. The names appear in the record. The word "Langston" is written after each name in these books, except the names numbered 222 and 227, which are marked "Dem."

74. Question. You have stated that you occupied the position immediately at the window of the polling place in the 3d ward, on the side at which the col'd people voted, all the day of election except about 30 minutes. Please state how many names were entered upon the books you kept during your absence, if any were so entered.—Answer. 16.

These sixteen names were fully identified by Wm. J. Smith, who entered them in the absence of Mr. Lewis.

78. Question. You have stated that on election day W. J. Smith during your temporary absence from the polls, entered the names of 16 colored voters upon the 4 books which you kept. Please state, if you remember, how many names you recorded upon the said books on that day at the time and under the circumstances already testified to.—Answer. I recorded two hundred and one names. The others, with the excep-

tion of 16 names, were recorded in my presence and by my instructions by Wm. J. Smith and S. B. McE. Jones.

79. Question. Have you, since the 6th day of Nov'r, 1888, compared the 4 books as to which you have been testifying with the poll-books of the 3d ward, on deposit in the clerk's office of this city, or with either one of said poll-books, or with a certified copy thereof?—Answer. I have compared the 4 books with one of the poll-books.

80. Question. State what object you had in making such comparisons, and state the result of it.—Answer. I compared the books to ascertain if they agreed. I found that a great many of the names were misspelt, and some few whose names I took and whose ballot I saw deposited, their names do not appear on the poll-book which I examined.

81. Question. Are you able from memory, or by reference to any memoranda taken at the time of making such comparison, to say what names there were which you entered on your said books of persons whom you saw deposit their ballots at 3rd ward, and which names do not appear on the poll-book you have said you examined?—Answer. I can.

82. Question. Then please state these names.

Answer. R. P. Armistead, Richard Bragg, Solomon Crawford, Jno. Hawkes, Stephen Royd, R. W. Smith.

83. Question Do I not understand you, then, to say that with the exception of these 6 names (and making no reference to the differences in spelling) the record of names on the official poll-book of 3rd ward of the voters at the last election contains all the names of the col'd voters recorded in your 4 books as having voted on that day?—Answer. It does.

The verity of Mr. Lewis's books stands unquestioned. Not one of the 286 voters of the Third ward registered by him is called to dispute the fact that he voted as Mr. Lewis testified he saw him vote. Not one of the six men not registered by the clerks, but whom Mr. Lewis says he saw deposit their ballots, was called to testify that he did not vote on that day. This would have been a short and decisive way to have impeached the testimony of Mr. Lewis, and it was a way quickly resorted to by contestee to impeach a similar record at Columbian Grove, Lunenburgh County. In that precinct the contestant called a witness who testified that he saw 130 votes cast for contestant, and gave the names of the voters. Two of these voters were called by contestee, and testified that they did not vote for contestant. The committee has permitted the vote of Columbian Grove to stand as returned. That precinct is referred to to illustrate the alertness of contestee in similar cases to defend the returns by the oath of the voter where the facts warranted it.

On cross-examination Mr. Lewis was asked eight hundred and nine questions, covering the political history of Virginia for years; this did not in any manner weaken his testimony in chief, but corroborated and strengthened it. The cross-examination commenced February 12 and continued until February 25. We quote the following from it:

340. Question. You said in answer to the 334th question that the tally-keepers at the polls who kept the tally of votes cast for Langston were instructed to put no names on the tally-books except the names of those whom you were absolutely sure voted for him; will you please explain how any tally-keeper outside the house could be absolutely certain how a man voted?—Answer. By seeing and reading his ticket, which was in every instance which we have recorded, handed to the judge who deposited them in the box wide open, the judge folding them instead of the voter.

341. Question. Were Langston's tally-keepers also his ticket-holders at the polls?—Answer. No, sir.

342. Question. Then in each case where the name was entered on the tally-book, did the voter bring his ticket to the tally-keeper that he might inspect it?—Answer. He brought it to me.

343. Question. Was this precaution adopted at every precinct in pursuance of the confidential circular sent out by Prof'r Langston and filed as a part of this record, marked Exhibit H.?—Answer. Yes, sir.

344. Question. Did those who could read themselves bring their tickets to you?—Answer. Yes, sir.

345. Question. Then I understand you to say that in every case in which a name

was recorded in the tally-book that you kept that the ballot was brought to you, that you examined the same, and that it was voted openly?—Answer. Yes, sir.

346. Question. Was there not a press of voters at the 3rd-ward polls all day or during a greater portion of the day—Nov'r 6th, 1888?—Answer. During the morning hours the lines were continually kept up.

347. Question. Did the voters at 3rd ward approach the polls in regular lines?—Answer. Yes, sir.

348. Question. How many abreast did they approach the polls?—Answer. Single file, each line.

349. Question. Were you in a position to see the ballot voted which you had inspected?—Answer. Right in front of the door and not 4 feet from the ballot-box.

350. Question. Were you on a level with the inside of the room when the ballots were received?—Answer. The elevation of the room from the ground is not more than 6 inches.

351. Question. Then you were on a level with the voters, weren't you?—Answer. Yes, sir.

On the general subject of the conduct of the campaign, he says:

740. Question. What facilities for information upon these subjects have you had as secretary of Langston's campaign committee?—Answer. In every precinct in the district the most intelligent and enlightened men were appointed to keep Langston tally-books, and at least one book was forwarded to headquarters as soon as possible after closing their respective precincts.

741. Question. Are those books still in your possession?—Answer. They are in the possession of Prof'r Langston's leading counsel in this case.

742. Question. Is there any formal and informal affidavit of the correctness of the contents of these books made by the parties who were appointed by your campaign committee to keep said books attached thereto?—Answer. In each book pasted on a fly-leaf is a certificate as to the correctness of the book, which is signed by the person keeping said book.

743. Question. I understand, then, that such certificates are the mere unsworn statements of Prof'r Langston's campaign appointees and workers. Is this true?—Answer. Yes, sir.

744. Question. Have you no other guarantee of the accuracy of said tally-books?—Answer. No, sir.

745. Question. Have you any means of knowing whether said tally-keepers were at their post during every minute of election day?—Answer. Yes, sir; persons who were present at each precinct from which we received these books assured us of the constancy and faithfulness of these tally-keepers.

746. Question. Have you ever made any investigation of the constancy and faithfulness of these tally-keepers; and, if so, when, and what caused you to make such investigation?—Answer. We have; a few days after the election, in order to satisfy ourselves that these men had been faithful to the trust imposed in them.

747. Question. Had you any reason to doubt their faithfulness?—Answer. No, sir; but as there had been such a wide difference between their reports and the official reports we felt obliged to make investigation before entering into this contest.

748. Question. Where was this investigation held and by whom?—Answer. It was held in the different counties by Mr. Langston's trusted friends.

749. Question. Were the witnesses put upon oath?—Answer. They were not.

750. Question. Have you any personal knowledge or information received from any one who had personal knowledge of the actual transfer of votes cast for Prof'r Langston to either of the other candidates at any election precinct in the district? In other words, have you seen or has any one seen such act of misconduct on the part of the officers of election, and are not the charges that you make as to the transfer of votes based solely on the inferences which you make from the non-agreement of your tally-books and the official returns?—Answer. Of course we could not make them by any other means, because at the specific places where these transfers were made, in no instance was a friend of Mr. Langston's allowed to witness the canvass of the ballots.

754. Question. Has it been the custom in this district in previous elections for the electors to show their ballots to the party tally-keeper?—Answer. No, sir.

755. Question. Were there any steps taken previous to Nov'r 6th last, by Prof'r Langston's campaign committee to bring about a change of custom in this regard?—Answer. Yes, sir.

756. Question. What steps were so taken and for what purpose?—Answer. For the reason as I have before stated, we had every reason to believe that fraud would be committed, and in order that we might be enabled to ascertain how many ballots were cast at each precinct for Harrison, Morton, and Langston, special canvassers were sent throughout the district and instructed to closely canvass each precinct and

to urge upon the people that, as the opposing candidate would have all the officers of election, the only remedy we had for frustrating their evil designs of fraud upon the ballot-box would be for the Republican voters supporting Harrison, Morton, and Langston to show their tickets to the tally-keepers who would be supplied with books at each precinct throughout the district for the purpose of recording the name of each man who should so vote and exhibit his ballot to said tally-keeper.

W. J. Smith, a merchant of the Third Ward, city of Petersburg, corroborates the testimony of Mr. Lewis as to what took place at the polls in that ward. It is proper in this connection to call attention to the fact that the tedious, irrelevant cross-examination of these two witnesses consumed all the time allowed to contestant for taking evidence in this ward and made it impossible for him to call further witnesses.

On Saturday, the 9th day of February, contestant began taking depositions as to Third Ward of the city of Petersburg, in pursuance of notice which contained a list of 292 names of Republicans, every one of whom it is claimed would have testified that he was a qualified voter, and voted for Langston in Third Ward. (Record, pp. 514 to 516.) The first witness sworn, M. N. Lewis, was asked by the contestee's counsel 809 questions on cross-examination, and was kept on the witness stand from February 9 (p. 523) until February 25 (p. 588), both inclusive, a period of seventeen days. The second witness, W. J. Smith, was sworn Monday, February 25 (p. 588), was asked 148 cross-questions, and was kept on the witness stand until Saturday, the 2d day of March, 11 o'clock at night, a period of six days (p. 599), when the time limited by law for the contestant to take testimony expired, and the notary closed the depositions. (Record, pp. 588 to 599.) By such wanton waste of time contestant was robbed of the opportunity of examining a large number of witnesses who he claims voted for him. And contestee is estopped from claiming that the evidence of these two witnesses is insufficient, having by his own acts prevented the taking of further evidence in this ward.

The only official connected with the election who was called to sustain the official count was the United States supervisor, Mr. G. B. Gill, who in a general way testifies to the fairness of the election, and says it is impossible for a person outside to keep tally of the votes as testified to by Lewis. On his cross-examination he makes the following fatal admissions as to the fairness and impartiality of the judges, and attention is called to section 130 of the Statutes of Virginia, quoted above in this connection:

3d. Question. At the time of the closing of the said polls, or thereafter, did any of the party friends of John M. Langston make a request of the judges of said precinct or ward to be allowed to witness the count and canvass of the ballots of the vote cast at said voting precinct; that is, to be allowed to enter the room when the count of the ballots and the canvass of the vote was made?—Ans. There was such a request made, and the judges replied that there were United States supervisors appointed for that purpose to see that the ballots cast were properly counted, and that no others from either party would be admitted.

4th. Question. Then, I understand you to answer in your foregoing answer that the party friends of John M. Langston were denied by the judges of election that request or right?—Ans. Yes, sir.

5th. Question. Then, I understand you to answer further that said count and canvass without any party friends of the said John M. Langston was made without their witnessing the same?—Ans. It was made without the friends of John M. Langston, E. C. Venable, or R. W. Arnold being present.

6th. Question. Was there any other United States supervisor of election who acted with you on the said day of election; and if so, who?—Ans. There was not.

7th. Question. Were you appointed a United States supervisor as a representative of the Democratic or Republican party?—Ans. I don't know. I received a commission from the chief supervisor, and he said nothing about it.

8th. Question. If you are willing to answer, will you state for whom you voted for

Congress on said election for this 4th Congressional district of Virginia?—Ans. I decline to answer.

9th. Question. Do you know of your own knowledge whether any other United States supervisor was appointed for said voting precinct; and if so, who?—Ans. Yes; F. K. Clements was appointed.

10th. Question. Do you know of your own knowledge why he did not act as such?—Ans. I do not.

Two police officers, George W. Dunn and J. M. Young, were called to contradict Lewis as to his continuous attendance at the polls. Dunn says Lewis was at the polls only about an hour and a half in the morning and left; that he returned late in the evening. In this he contradicts not only Lewis but all the witnesses of contestee, and shows himself wholly unworthy of credit. He was himself at the polls all day. He can not name a single colored man who voted the Democratic ticket. He knows nothing of the political complexion of the police force, but can not name a Republican on it. He says no one could have seen the ballots except the judge who received them. This judge, who of all men in Petersburgh could have testified in relation to the action of Lewis on that day, was not called as a witness. Nor was either one of the other judges called to sustain his handiwork with his oath. The clerks likewise abstained from asserting on the witness stand, where they would have been subjected to a cross-examination, the legality of their acts. Two representatives of the interests of contestee kept tally of his vote at the polls; and three men represented Arnold in a similar capacity. These men were engaged in the same capacity for their candidates as Mr. Lewis was for contestant. They necessarily came in contact with Mr. Lewis during the day, but not one of them is called as a witness. Their names appear on page 571 of the record. Their silence confirms the testimony of Mr. Lewis, were confirmation necessary.

The other policeman, Mr. Young, noticed Lewis "on account of his being around there and taking an active part in the canvass and election," but says he left two or three times during the day the door where they were voting. This virtually corroborates Lewis as to his position at the door, and the only difference between them seems to be whether Lewis left the door once only, as he says, or twice, as stated by Young. He heard some colored men with folded ballots say among themselves that they were going to vote for Langston. Evidently he did not hear colored men say anything about voting for any one else, for he is silent as to that. He says Lewis was standing on a huckster bench in front of the door most of the time with his face towards the ballot-box and that there was no obstruction between him and the box. He says Dunn and Gibbons, two Democrats not officers of election, were inside of the polling place.

With the friends of contestant studiously excluded from witnessing the count, and with 284 votes proved to have been cast for him, while the returns gave him only 174, this box stands impeached and must be rejected.

In the case of Washburn vs. Voorhees (3 Congressional Election Cases, 62), it was held that "where in one precinct but 143 votes were returned, while 173 were cast for contestant (a difference of only 30 votes), and in another 20 less were returned than were proved, and the officers were shown to be violent partisans of the party in whose favor the frauds were, the whole vote of the precinct was rejected."

In the case of Bisbee vs. Finley (6 Congressional Election Cases, 177), where 259 votes were cast at one precinct for a candidate, and only 69 were returned for him, it was said in the report: "That any considerable number of votes proven for one candidate in excess of the number

returned for him, has always been regarded as evidence of fraud, and a
legitimate method of impeaching the returns. We think it is sufficient
to exclude the return from the count without further evidence."

Applying the law thus laid down and the law as quoted from Paine
on Elections, at the beginning of this report, the account will stand
thus:

Plurality for Venable, brought forward 487
Deduct plurality for Venable, Third ward returned, which is equivalent to throwing out the precinct 344

Leaves plurality for Venable 143
But Langston has proved votes cast for him at this precinct 284

The contestee has failed to prove any vote cast for him, thus making a plurality
   in favor of Langston of... 141

SIXTH WARD.

The returns in this ward give Venable 352, Arnold 160, and Langston 139 votes, a plurality in favor of Venable over Langston of 213.
In this ward the negroes have a large majority, and the evidence shows
that they were active and united supporters of contestant. The contestant placed upon the stand 283 witnesses, each of whom swears that
he is a qualified and duly registered voter of the Sixth ward, and that
he voted for contestant on November 6, 1888. Each one was cross-examined by counsel for contestee. This clearly shows that the poll must
be rejected and the parties left to other evidence than the falsified returns to establish their vote. The judges appointed in May for this
ward were all political opponents of contestant, and all served.

Not a vote was challenged on either side during the day of election.
Although the colored voters at this precinct stood to the white voters
in the ratio of nearly three to one, Mr. Akers and his associates thought
it fair to put up in front of the polls a barrier to separate the negroes
from the whites in two lines, one upon the right hand and the other
on the left hand, and then to receive the ballots from each side alternately, a white man's ballot, and then a negro's ballot; and so on
throughout the day, unless some colored man who wished to vote the
white men's ticket could get permission to fall in in the line of whites.
The plain consequence of enforcing such a rule is evidenced by the fact
that out of 265 registered white voters, all voted except 14; and out of
709 registered colored voters, there were 308 (nearly half) who did not
vote. (Aker's deposition, Record, p. 831 et seq.) Consequently, when
the polls were closed at sunset there stood in line at the door of the
polling-place 124 Republican voters with Langston ballots open in their
hands, anxious to vote, and denied their right of suffrage. (Record, pp.
196, 197.) Six others, whose names are on page 196, had become dis-
heartened and gone away.

Thomas H. Brown, witness for the contestant, being duly sworn, said:

   1st. Question. State your name, age, and residence.—Answer. Thomas H. Brown;
I am twenty-four years old, and live at No. 218 Halifax street, Petersburg, Va.
   2d. Question. Were you a voter in 6th ward on election day, Nov. 6th, 1888?—Answer. I was.
   3d. Question. If you are willing to waive your legal right, please state if you voted
for Congressman on that day; and if so, for whom?—Answer. I voted for John M.
Langston.
   4th. Question. When did you reach the polls, and how long did you remain there
during the day?—Answer. I went to the polls between half past five and six o'clock
in the morning and remained all day, except for about fifteen minutes.

5th. Question. What were you doing during the day?—Answer. Assisting keeping the books.

6th. Question. In keeping what books?—Answer. In keeping the names of the colored voters who voted for Harrison, Morton, and Langston.

7th. Question. How could you tell that they voted for Langston?—Answer. Because I saw their tickets when they were given to the judge of election, as each of them voted an open ballot.

8th. Question. Where were you standing; how far from the ballot-box, and how far from the judge who received the ballots?—Answer. I was standing within two feet of the door, and about four feet from the judge when at the ballot-box

9th. Question. Were the ballots open when handed to the judge?—Answer. Those that I refer to when I say voted for Langston.

10th. Question. Do you mean that those who voted for Langston handed their ballots open to the judge?—Answer. I do.

11th. Question. Could you see the ballot until the judge put it in the ballot-b x?—Answer. Yes, sir.

12th. Question. Were the names of the voters as they handed their open ballots to the judge recorded in your book?—Answer. They were.

13th. Question. How many names were recorded in the book as voting for John M. Langston?—Answer. Three hundred and seventy.

14th. Question. How did the voters approach the polls; that is, how were they arranged?—Answer. They formed a line.

15th. Question. Were there more than one line?—Answer. There were two lines, one on each side of a plank; one for the white or Democratic voters, the other for the colored voters.

16th. Question. Were the white and colored voters voted equally; that is, did it take any more time to vote one than it did the other?—Answer. I think not, because when the colored voter came up to vote it seemed to be a great difficulty in finding his name, and seemingly the white voters were recognized on sight.

17th. Question. About how long did it take to vote a colored voter after he had given his name?—Answer. In some cases from about one to three minutes, and in others longer.

18th. Question. About how long did it take to vote a white voter after he had given his name?—Answer. About one and a half minutes, except occasionally there would be some difficulty and it would take possibly two minutes.

19th. Question. Were you in line?—Answer. No, sir; I was not in line.

20th. Question. Were you at the polls when they closed?—Answer. I was at the polls when the judge gave notice, and a few moments the polls would be closed. Then I left my stand, which was upon a box within two foot of the door, and began to get the men to retain their places until they received from me what steps they were to take.

21st. Question. Were you there when the polls did close?—Answer. Close enough to see the doors when they were shut.

22d. Question. Were there voters in both lines?—Answer. I think not, because early in the day the line on white or Democratic side was exhausted, and the men as a general thing afterwards were voted as they came to the polls on that side.

23d. Question. What men?—Answer. The white men, or the supposed Democrats.

24th. Question. Was there anybody in the Republican line when the polls closed?—Answer. There were.

25th. Question. Do you know how many?—Answer. I could not say exactly, but there were between one hundred and one hundred and fifty.

26th. Question. How far did the line extend?—Answer. From Dr. Stillwell's office down to or below T. P. Noble's barber shop.

27th. Question. How came the line to be from Dr. Stillwell's office down to Noble's barber shop?—Answer. Because when the polls closed the men in line seemed to be anxious to deposit their ballots, so we thought in order to know who they were that wanted to vote, so we simply had them to turn the line and give their tickets, with their name on them. to Messrs. Robinson, Smith, and Brewer.

28th. Question. Did you receive any tickets, write the names of the voter on his ticket, or record the names of any of these men who had not voted?—Answer. I did not, but simply showed the leader of the line where to go.

29th. Question. Did the others who were left in the line when the polls closed follow the leader in regular order across to Dr. Stillwell's office and form the line to which you have referred?—Answer. When the polls closed all of those who had not voted seemed to be anxious, and followed as regular as they could.

Cross examination:

19th. Question. Were you close by the polls on said day from the time they were opened to the time they were closed, with the exception of the few minutes you spoke of in your direct examination?—Answer. I were.

20th. Question. You said in your direct examination that you took a list of men who voted for Langston during that day at 6th ward. Do you mean that with the exception of the few minutes above referred to you took down the names of all the men who voted for Langston at said time and place; or, in other words, that you in some way kept an accurate account of the men who voted for Langston?—Answer. I said that I assisted in keeping the book, and I say now that we kept an accurate account of the Langston vote and the whole colored vote at 6th ward in said election.

21st. Question. Whom did you assist in keeping the book?—Answer. Pleasant Goodwyn.

22d. Question. What did you do towards keeping the book?—Answer. I had a list of the colored voters in 6th ward, and as they voted Pleasant would write the name, while I would check them, but this was done alternately between him and I.

23d. Question. How many names did you have on your book referred to?—Answer. As a whole, we had four hundred and eight.

24th. Question. How many names did you have on your list of the colored voters in 6th ward?—Answer. I just said that we had four hundred and eight, as we were only keeping in that book the colored voters.

25th. Question. How many colored men voted at said polls on said day?—Answer. We recorded the names of four hundred and eight.

26th. Question. You said in your answer to the 22d question above that you had a list of the colored voters in 6th ward. How many names were on that list?—Answer. There were six hundred and forty-seven.

27th. Question. How many colored men voted during that day who did not vote for Langston?—Answer. There were 408 colored votes cast, 38 of which we are not certain who they voted for.

28th. Question. Do you wish to be understood as saying that you know that 370 votes were cast for Langston at said time and place?—Answer. I do.

29th. Question. Did every one of the 370 men vote an open ballot?—Answer. They did, except one.

30th. Question. And did you read the name of John M. Langston on each one of these ballots?—Answer. We did.

31st. Question. Is it not a fact that several colored men voted in what you have termed the white or Democratic line?—Answer. They did.

34th. Question. How many white men do you suppose voted?—Answer. I do not know.

35th. Question. Do you know of a single white man that voted for Langston?—Answer. I can't say that I do.

36th. Question. How many colored men do you suppose voted for Venable?—Answer. I can't say.

37th. Question. How many white men do you suppose voted for R. W. Arnold?—Answer. I have no idea.

38th. Question. How many colored men do you suppose voted for R. W. Arnold?—Answer. I do not know.

39th. Question. Then, for all you know or believe to the contrary, the official return of the number of votes cast for Arnold must be correct?—Answer. I don't say that either.

40th. Question. Then, for all you know to the contrary, the official return of the number of votes cast for R. W. Arnold must be correct?—Answer. I don't say that.

41st. Question. Then what do you say?—Answer. I say that we kept a record of colored men who voted for John M. Langston, and we did not keep either Venable's or Arnold's vote.

42d. Question. You said in answer to the 25th and 27th questions on cross-examination that 408 colored men voted at said polls on said day, 38 of whom you were not sure of as having voted for Langston; then must you not know with reasonable certainty how many colored men voted for Arnold?—Answer. Not necessarily.

43d. Question. How many colored men voted for either Arnold or Venable?—Answer. I did not keep the record of either Arnold or Venable vote.

44th. Question. Did you not say that you kept a record of all the colored voters who voted that day at 6th ward?—Answer. We did keep a record of the colored vote at said ward on said day.

45th. Question. Have you not stated how many colored votes were polled for Langston?—Answer. I said that we kept a record of the Langston votes and all colored voters that voted on said day at said place.

46th. Question. Was or was not this an accurate record?—Answer. We kept it accurate, according to our judgment. I mean to say that we taken the names of all colored men who voted at said poll on said day.

54th. Question. How many of them voted for John M. Langston?—Answer. Out of the 408 mentioned by me 370 were Langston ballots.

55th. Question. Were 408 all the colored men who you said voted at said polls on said day?—Answer. 408 is all I said.

56th. Question. In your answer to 53d question on cross-examination, you stated that you took the names of *all* the colored men who voted at said polls on said day. Please state unequivocally how many of those men voted for Langston?—Answer. I think I have told you in my former answer how many men that we taken as Langston votes; there may have been more.

57th. Question. I repeat the 56th question.—A. I can't tell you any nearer than I have in my former answers.

58th. Question. Were three hundred and seventy all the colored men who voted for Langston. If more voted for him state, as near as you can, how many more, and if less voted for him, state as near as you can, how many less.—Answer. I can't say that more did vote for him, because I only kept the names of those who voted an open ballot; there may have been others who voted for him.

59th. Question. During your examination you have testified more than once that those men who voted for Langston voted open ballots; then do you wish to retract that statement now?—Answer. I do not, but simply add to it by saying that we took the names of those who voted an open ballot with John M. Langston's name on it, and we can vouch for them; of course, we could not say anything about those who voted the closed ballot.

60th. Question. You have stated that you took the names of *all* the colored men who voted in 6th ward on said day; state how many of them you *know* did not vote for Langston.—Answer. One.

61st. Question. State how many of them you know did vote for Langston.—Answer. I think I have said before that 370 men were recorded by us as having voted for Langston.

62d. Question. You were not requested to say how many men were recorded by you as having voted for Langston. You were asked to state how many men *you know* voted for Langston. Please answer the question asked you and say no more.

Answer. I can tell you nothing more than what I have told you, as I think that in saying that we recorded 370 shows at once my knowledge of the Langston vote in said ward.

63d. Question. Then do you know of your own personal knowledge that Langston got 370 votes in said ward? Be kind enough to answer categorically.—Answer. He did.

64th. Question. And you do not know who received the balance of the colored votes cast in said ward (37 in number)?—Answer. I do not.

65th. Question. How many white persons, as near as you can judge, voted at said ward on said day?—Answer. I can't say.

66th. Question. You are asked for an approximate answer only?—Answer. I have no idea.

67th. Question. Did as many as 500 white persons vote at said ward on said day?—Answer. I don't know.

68th. Question. Do you mean to say that you profess to be a man of any intelligence and staying at the polls all day, as you said you did, and recording all the colored votes cast there that day, as you said you did, you do not know that as many as 500 white persons did not vote at said polls on said day?—Answer. It matters not whether I profess to have any intelligence, I did not take notice of the white vote, therefore I answered "I don't know."

69th. Question. Did as many as 500 white persons vote in said ward on said day?—Answer. I don't know.

70th. Question. Do the white voters in said ward outnumber the colored voters?—Answer. They do not.

71st. Question. Did as many as 648 white persons vote in said ward on said day?—Answer. I think not.

72d. Question. Did as many as 600?—Answer. I think not.

73d. Question. Did as many as 550?—Answer. I don't know.

74th. Question. Did more than 5 white persons vote at said ward on said day?—Answer. They must have.

75th. Question. Do you mean to say the most accurate estimate you can form as to the number of white persons who voted at said ward on said day is between 5 and 600?—Answer. I do not mean anything of the kind.

76th. Question. Then please explain what you do mean.—Answer. As I kept no record of the white vote in said ward I do not propose either by estimate or otherwise to say anything about it.

77th. Question. Counsel for contestee informs you that he has a legal right to ask you such questions as the above in order to test your credibility and the accuracy of your memory, and that if you refuse to answer them you take the law into your own hands. Do you still persist in refusing to give even an approximate estimate as to the number of white men who voted in said ward on said day?—Answer. I do not object to answering any question concerning things of which I have any knowledge, but do not think that I can do justice to myself or anybody else to try even to approximate anything that I paid no attention to.

We have given these extensive extracts from the testimony of this intelligent witness for the striking contrast it affords between a gentlemanly and courteous witness and a desperate, browbeating attorney. Much more cross-examination follows of the same character, giving grounds for suspicion that for lack of a meritorious defense contestee tried to prevent by delay as far as possible the calling of witnesses.

This testimony is corroborated by that of Pleasant Goodwyn, who said:

1st. Question. What is your name, age, and residence?—Answer. Pleasant Goodwyn; my age is 32 years, and residence 325 Federal street.

2d. Question. Were you a voter in the 6th ward, city of Petersburgh, on election-day, Nov. 6th, 1888?—Answer. Yes, sir.

3d. Question. If you are willing to waive your legal right, please state if you voted for Congressman on that day, and if so, for whom you voted.—Answer. I did, and voted for John M. Langston.

4th. Question. When did you reach the polls, and how long did you remain there during the day?—Answer. I got there about quarter to six in the morning and remained until the closing of the polls at night.

5th. Question. State how the polls were opened, that is, what was said and done by the judges.—Answer. I think the polls were opened about quarter to seven, and at that time the judge said Oh yes, Oh yes, the polls are opened, and then a strip of board was nailed across the door, and a plank extended down to divide the line. Before voting they arrested Richard Tucker from the door.

6th. Question. State fully all you saw and heard relative to the arrest of Tucker?—Answer. I saw Tucker standing at the door when the judge said you all get back; he being in front he backed backwards a short distance, and the judge said you all must get out from there, and he seemed that he could get no further back, as the crowd was behind him. Supervisor Scott called Mr. Stutz to take this man away, and he did not return no more. Then after that Mr. Berry came to the polls and said, I am supervisor of this precinct; Mr. Akers said, I don't know so much about that; Mr. Berry said, do you object to my performing my duty as supervisor? Mr. Akers says, I am informed that Mr. Minetree is the supervisor of this precinct. Mr. Berry said then, do you object to me, for I have got my papers to show that I am the supervisor of this precinct? Mr. Akers says, I don't object to you, but you can see Supervisor Scott. Mr. Berry went away, and when he came back him and Mr. Scott was together, and went into the precinct.

7th. Question. Did you see any disorderly conduct on the part of Tucker, or did he refuse to obey the judge when told to get back?—Answer. I did not.

8th. Question. Did Tucker vote at any time during the day?—Answer. No, sir.

9th. Question. When the polls opened were the ballot-boxes in sight?—Answer. Yes, sir.

10th. Question. Were the ballot-boxes opened and held up or so placed that it could be seen that they were empty?—Answer. The ballot-box was not held up and opened.

11th. Question. What were you doing at the polls all day?—Answer. I was taking the names of the colored voters who voted for John M. Langston.

12th. Question. Did you take the names of all the colored voters who voted at 6th ward on election day, Nov. 6, 1888?—Answer. I did.

13th. Question. How could you tell when a colored voter voted for John M. Langston?—Answer. Because I read the name of John M. Langston on the ticket and saw them handed to the judge and saw him put it into the box.

14th. Question. Where were you standing and how could you see each ticket?—Answer. I was standing in a chair very near the door of the precinct where I could see every man's ticket that would have it open.

15th. Question. How near were you to the ballot-box and how near to the judge who received the ballots?—Answer. I was as close to the judge as the wall of the door would permit me; between him and the box.

16th. Question. Could you see each ballot from the time it was handed to the judge until he put it into the ballot-box?—Answer. I could see every ballot that was handed to the judge that day.

17th. Question. How was it or why was it that you could see the name of John M. Langston on the ballots?—Answer. Because the ballots were open, that I could read them and see the name of John M. Langston.

18th. Question. Were these ballots opened and so held for the purpose of allowing you to see them?—Answer. They were opened for the purpose that I might see them and record their names as to whom they voted for.

19th. Question. Are you sure that the opened ballots which you saw were handed to the judge and it went into the ballot-box?—Answer. Yes, sir; I am sure that every ballot that I saw handed to the judge went in the ballot-box.

20th. Question. Did you record the name of every voter who voted an open ballot for John M. Langston?—Answer. I did record every colored voter who voted for John M. Langston at 6th ward precinct.

21st. Question. Do you mean to say that you recorded the name of every colored voter who voted for John M. Langston or the name of every colored voter who voted an open ballot for John M. Langston?—Answer. I mean to say that I recorded every name who voted an open ballot for John M. Langston, and also recorded every colored vote cast on that day.

22d. Question. In what did you record the names above referred to?—Answer. I recorded them in books used for the tellers on that day.

23d. Question. How many books did you use?—Answer. Four.

24th. Question. Have you those books in your possession?—Answer. I have.

26th. Question. Please state if these books have been in your exclusive possession since Nov. 6th, 1888, and also whether all of the names were recorded by you yourself, and whether there have been any additions to or any subtractions from the names in said books.—Answer. These books have not been in my exclusive possession since Nov. 6, but I do certify that I wrote four hundred and eight names in those books, and there have been none added to or subtracted from them. The books are here filed.

27th. Question. Please take said books and state if every name is in your own writing.—Answer. (Here witness took the books and answered as follows:) Yes, sir; I certify that all these names are my handwriting.

28th. Question. Have you seen these books before to-day?—Answer. Yes; I have.

29th. Question. Have you examined them to-day? If so, state when.—Answer. Yes; I have examined them to-day while here.

30th. Question. Did you examine them before you took the stand?—Answer. I did.

31st. Question. Please give the names of those voters whom you recorded as voting an open ballot for John M. Langston, refreshing your memory, if necessary, from the record you kept.

Answer. All the names recorded in Exhibits A, B, C, and D, and filed as part of my deposition, voted an open ballot for John M. Langston as member of Congress from this 4th Congressional district of Virginia, with the following exceptions, namely: Sip O. Watson, Sam'l Jones, Ned Patterson, Wm. E. Prichard, Abram Jones, Thos. Parham, W. T. Hicks, George Ellis, Geo. F. Hill, Wyatt Alfriend, John M. Alfriend, R. H. Smith, Emmett E. Jones, Sam'l Jackson, David Perry, Wm. N. Gunns, Pleasant Jackson, Alfred Robinson, Fed Cooper, C. H. Mabry, K. Coleman, Jas. H. Taylor, Wm. H. Jordan, Jos. Ellis, Wm. wood, Wm. H. Moore, Robt. Jones, Edward Grigs bys, Beverly Younger, Thomas Butler.

32d. Question. I see from the exhibits filed that some of the names have "D" and "A" marked after them; what does this mean?—Answer. The names that have "D" marked after them is that they were folded and marked "D" for doubtful, and also the letter "A" are for those who voted an open ticket for Arnold.

33d. Question. Were there any delays or stoppages in voting after the polls opened?—Answer. Yes, sir; there were four to my knowledge that day.

34th. Question. Please state for what they were and about how long they continued.—Answer. The first stoppage after the polls opened were for breakfast, and the time they stopped may be a half or three-quarters of an hour. They also stopped to have the crowd moved back because the colored line was doubled. The time they stopped for that I don't suppose was more than ten or fifteen minutes. They also stopped again in looking for the name of "James W. Smith." The judge says he had voted, and he referred them to his number and street, when they found he was correct and voted him. The next stoppage was for dinner, and I suppose it took about a half or three-quarters of an hour.

35th. Question. When the judges stopped for breakfast and dinner was the voting entirely suspended?—Answer. Yes.

36th. Question. You have stated that there were lines. How many and for whom were they?—Answer. There were two lines, one said to be for the white and the other for the colored; but they voted some colored on the white line.

37th. Question. Did you hear any objection raised to the voting of colored voters on that side said to be for white voters? I mean objection by the judges.—Answer. I did hear one objection, and that was to Robert H. Harris by Judge Akers. He claimed that Harris had a Republican ticket; Harris offered to bet him that it was not; then Harris says, "All you have to do is to deposit my ticket as I give it to you;" then Akers says, "You have no right on this side of the line," and deposited the ticket; Harris says, "I now bet you ten dollars that it is a Republican ticket with John M. Langston at the bottom;" Akers said, "That is all right, go on."

38th. Question. Did you see any other colored man vote from the same side as did Harris?—Answer. I did see other colored men vote on that side.

39th. Question. State who they were, and whether any objection was raised by the judges?—Answer. I will state those I can remember who voted on that side as follows: 1st. Nathaniel Robinson, Wm. E. Prichard, Robert H. Harris, Wm. Wood, Abram Jones, Sam'l Jones, Emmett Shelly, Henry Jones, Geo. Ellis, C. H. Mabry, Thos. Butler. That is all I recollect that voted on that side.

40th. Question. Could you remember any others if you referred to the record you kept? If so, please do that to refresh your memory, and give their names.—Answer. I have seen two names I recognize as voting on the white side, namely, David Perry and Thomas Parham.

41st. Question. Do you know why these men, with the exception of Rob't H. Harris, were allowed to vote on the side said to be for white voters?—Answer. No, sir.

42d. Question. Did you see any colored voter vote an open ballot for John M. Langston from that side said to be for white voters?—Answer. I did see three who voted on that side of the whites who showed me their ticket, when near the judge, and then folded it and handed it to the judge whilst my eyes was upon them.

43d. Question. Who were they?—Answer. Nathaniel Robinson, Robt. H. Harris, and Emmett Shelly.

44th. Question. Did you see any colored voter vote an open ballot from that side said to be for the white who handed his open ballot for John R. Langston to the judge open so that the judge knew it was a Langston ballot?—Answer. I saw Robert Harris, whom they thought to vote with them, hand the judge his ballot, folded once, and the judge claimed it was a Republican ticket.

45th. Question. Did you see the judge vote any colored voter from the side said to be for the white when he *knew* that the ballot was a Langston ballot?—Answer. I saw the judge vote a man from that side which he claimed to know that that was a Republican ticket which the man had just handed him.

46th. Question. Did you see any open ballots handed to the judge by the voters in the colored line?—Answer. Yes; I did see a great many ballots handed to the judge wide open, and the judge says, "You must fold your own ballots," and this was done frequently during the day.

47th. Question. Did you see any ballots handed to the judge wide open by any colored voter who voted from the line said to be for the white voters?—Answer. I did see three ballots from the white line which were open for the purpose that I may see whom they did vote for, and those ballots were folded again and were not removed from their fingers until handed to the judge.

48th. Question. You have failed to answer the question, which is this: Did you see any ballots *handed to the judge* wide open by any colored voter who voted from the line said to be for the white voters?—Answer. I did not.

49th. Question. Were there, at any time during the day, two lines of voters, one white and one colored?—Answer. It was.

50th. Question. How were the men voted from these lines; that is, how were they voted, taking into consideration the time required to vote?—Answer. These men were voted one white and one colored until the white line would become exhausted; then they would vote colored from either side, providing if they seemed to be in sympathy with their party, but if not they would claim that this is not the side for colored voters; it seems that when a colored voter would come it was very hard to find his name on the registration books, but as soon as a white voter would appear and hand his ticket and call his name the judge would very readily reply, "It is all right." So it made the voting proceed very slowly until Mr. Venable came, I think, about noonday, and says, "You all must try to vote these men." Then a long string of men were extending from the poll-door near to Market street.

51st. Question. Was the voting proceeded with any faster after the remark to which you refer was made by Mr. Venable?—Answer. It was.

52d. Question. Did it not so continue until the polls closed?—Answer. Yes.

53d. Question. Did you see any colored voter refused his vote because he was on the side said to be for white voters and sent around to the colored line?—Answer. I saw two.

54th. Question. Please give their names.—Answer. Richard Wilson and Peter T. Smith.

55th. Question. Can you state of your own knowledge that it took longer for a colored voter to vote than it did for a white voter?—Answer. I can state that I did not hear the judge stop to ask a white voter for his number and street during that day, but it were frequently done when he come to look for the name of a colored voter.

56th. Question. Did you see *any* white voter delayed or kept waiting to vote after he had given his name to the judge at any time during the day?—Answer. I did not.

57th. Question. Can you say about how long it took for a white voter to vote?—Answer. I can not specify the exact time, because I had no time to designate him, but to my best judgment I don't think it took more than 3 to 5 minutes to vote any white voter who came to the poll that day.

58th. Question. How long do you suppose it took to vote a colored voter?—Answer. I know that as soon as some of the colored voters would give their ballot to the judge and call their name the judges would immediately say, "It is all right," and others would give their ballot and call their name, and the judge would look on the books and then ask his name over again, and after asking would look again, and some cases the judge were referred to the number on the registration book, which I suppose would take a space of time from 5 to 10 minutes.

59th. Question. Do you swear that the white voters were voted much more rapidly than the colored?—Answer. I do swear that the white voters, according to my knowledge, was voted faster than the colored.

60th. Question. How long have you lived in 6th ward?—Answer. About ten years.

61st. Question. How long or in how many elections have you served around the polls?—Answer. I have served around the polls at three elections, and stayed all day each time.

62d. Question. How did the turnout of the voters in the last election compare with the previous elections you have seen?—Answer. The voters at the last election turned out fuller than I ever saw them.

63d. Question. About how many white Republican voters live in 6th ward?—Answer. I believe there are between two and three hundred.

64th. Question. About how many Democratic voters?—Answer. I believe about two hundred or more.

65th. Question. About how many colored voters?—Answer. I believe there are between 700 to 800.

66th. Question. Who were the judges at 6th ward on last election day?—Answer. Mr. Akers, Eckles, and Lewis.

67th. Question. How many Democrats and how many Republicans?—Answer. Two Democrats. Mr. Eckles claims to be a Republican.

68th. Question. Was either one of the three judges friendly to John M. Langston's candidacy?—Answer. Not that I know of.

69th. Question. Who were the clerks?—Answer. Mr. Shelly and Kidd.

70th. Question. To what party do they belong?—Answer. Democratic party.

71st. Question. Who were the supervisors?—Answer. Mr. Berry and Scott.

72d. Question. To what party do they belong?—Answer. Mr. Scott belongs to the Democratic party and Mr. Berry claims to be a Republican.

73d. Question. Was Mr. Berry friendly to the candidacy of John M. Langston?—Answer. I think he was not.

74th. Question. Was Mr. Berry at the polls when they opened? If not, state when he reached the polls.—Answer. He was not there when the polls opened, but came in the time when the judges were signing their names.

75th. Question. In what ward does Mr. Berry live, and do you know when he was appointed supervisor?—Answer. I do not know what ward he lives in, neither do I know the time he was appointed supervisor.

76th. Question. Were the tickets which you saw printed "John M. Langston" or "John Mercer Langston?"—Answer. The tickets that I saw and recorded had "John M. Langston" on them.

77th. Question. When the polls closed how many lines were in front of the door?—Answer. There was two lines.

78th. Question. What two lines?—Answer. The Democrats on one side and the Republicans on the other.

79th. Question. Was there anybody in the Democratic line when the polls closed? Answer. Yes, sir.

80th. Question. Who were they?—Answer. I could not name them personally.

81st. Question. Were they white or colored?—Answer. Both white and colored.

82d. Question. How came colored voters in the line said to be for whites?—Answer. Because it was near the closing of the polls and the people got as near as possible to see how they were voting. The reason why, because just before the closing of the polls a man said they were voting ten to one, and that caused the rush.

83d. Question. Do you mean to say there were voters in the Democratic line trying to vote when the polls closed?—Answer. I do not.

84th. Question. Were there voters in the Republican line trying to vote when the polls closed?—Answer. There were.

85th. Question. Have you any idea as to the number of men in the line who had not voted when the polls closed?—Answer. I suppose there may have been 120 or more.

86th. Question. Do you swear that these men in line had not voted during the day?—Answer. Yes; I do.

87th. Question. Did you see any voters leave the polls before voting because they were unable to vote?—Answer. I did.

88th. Question. How many and who were they?—Answer. I know one did go and not return; another one started away, I called him back and asked the man who was next to the polling place to give way for him, James H. Anderson, to vote, and he did vote. The one that went away was named Henry Moody.

89th. Question. When the polls closed what became of the line of colored voters who had failed to vote?—Answer. They were instructed to keep in line and go over to Dr. Stillwell's office and remain until their names were taken and also their tickets.

A cross-examination commencing on February 14 and continuing until February 22, and consuming all the time allowed by law to contestant to take evidence in this ward, and containing 323 questions, confirms the above, and shows that 377 voters were seen by witness to deposit ballots for contestant. Their names were filed with the notary and are found on pages 280 and 281 of the record. This evidence is further corroborated by that of Richard Townes, page 282, and J. York Harris, member of the common council and chairman of the ward, page 291.

The only officer of election called to sustain the returns is Mr. Akers, one of the judges. He excuses the delay charged upon the officers by claiming difficulty in finding names of colored men. He says the man least familiar with the work was given charge of colored registration book; why this particular man he does not say. He is unable to find on the book more than two colored men in the ward of the same name, but swears that because of the similarity of their names it is more difficult to find colored than white voters.

It is attempted by the testimony of the witness Akers to contradict and break down the facts established by seven witnesses called by contestant who were present at the polls and whom he disputes in detail, and at least 213 individual voters in excess of those returned for Langston, each of whom swears he voted for Langston.

Coming to this poll with 141 plurality, contestant's count must be increased by the plurality returned against him, which is equivalent to throwing out the poll. This adds to his total:

Vote brought forward... 141
Plurality in sixth ward returned for Venable.................................... 213
Add to this vote proved for Langston... 377

Makes a total plurality for Langston of 731

Besides the votes cast, 124 colored men were by the delay of the officers prevented from casting their ballots.

F. N. Robinson, witness for the contestant, being duly sworn, said on that subject:

1st. Question. State your age, residence, and occupation.—Answer. I am twenty-three years old; I reside at 33 Perry street, Petersburg, Virginia; I am a teacher by occupation.

2d. Question. Where were you on the 6th day of last November, election day?—Answer. Was in Petersburg, at the 6th ward most of my time.

3d. Question. State whether or not you were at 6th ward polls most of your time that day.—Answer. I was.

4th. Question. State, if you please, what occurred, if anything, at the close of the polls that day in said ward in which you took special interest and part.—Answer. When the judge of election declared the polls closed there were a line of men waiting to vote, and as they were unable their names were taken in an office in front of the polls; I mean one of the judges of election.

5th. Question. State, if you please, who took the names of the persons to whom you refer as not being able to vote.

Answer. I did, sir.

6th. Question. Were you or not assisted in that labor; if so, by whom?

Answer. I was, by Mr. Andrew J. Smith and David Brewer, one more, Brown, I don't know his first name, and Blenn, I don't know his first name.

7th. Question. State fully what was done.—Answer. When the polls closed upon a line of men, Andrew J. Smith, David Brewer, and myself, being loyal Republicans, felt it our duty to note all men that was unable to vote; we commenced by receiving the names of those who had held the ballots, counted and sealed up the same, writing the names of the persons who held the ballots on the back of the ballot, and the package and book in which I took the names were preserved.

The books containing the names of these parties were filed with the notary with the residence of each, and are in the possession of the committee, thus furnishing contestee every facility for investigating the truthfulness of contestant's witnesses.

On cross-examination the same delay was indulged in and effort to consume time in this as in the third ward.

It appears by the record (p. 191) that the contestant gave notice that on the 31st day of January, 1889, he would commence to take the depositions of one hundred and forty-nine witnesses in addition to the 283 above referred to as having been called and having sworn that they voted for him, whose names were given, mostly negroes, who were expected to testify that they were qualified voters, and that they cast their ballots for John M. Langston. The first of these witnesses, called and sworn January 31, at 12 o'clock m., was F. N. Robinson (p. 192). His direct examination was completed by eight questions. The cross-examination began the same day, January 31 (p. 197), and was prolonged until late in the day of the 5th of February—six days—(p. 223) by the asking of 316 questions, nine-tenths of which were useless, irrelevant, and frivolous, and intended without disguise or motive only to consume time.

And then occurred an outrage without a parallel in the history of election cases. Just as the witness answered the three hundred and sixteenth cross-question (p. 223) he was arrested and taken into custody by a deputy United States marshal by virtue of a warrant or capias, falsely, maliciously, and without probable cause sued out against him by two persons, attorneys-at-law, who had as counsel for the contestee appeared and participated in said cross-examination, upon their complaint on oath that the witness refused to testify in this case.

An examination of the record shows the absolute falsity of this charge. The witness maintained under the most provoking and insulting cross-examination remarkable self-possession and dignified courtesy, and the only explanation of this outrageous conduct on the part of contestee's counsel must be that they hoped by their perjury to intimidate other witnesses from taking the stand to expose the frauds by which their client obtained the certificate of election.

Having themselves stopped the cross-examination by the arrest of the witness they impudently objected to the consideration of his testimony for the reason that they had not had the opportunity to cross-examine him, and for the further reason that his deposition was not signed.

David L. Brewer, another witness, says, on this subject, page 225:

1st. Question. What is your name, age, and residence?—Answer. David L. Brewer; twenty-two years old; 62 Lombard street, Petersburg, Virginia.

2d. Question. Were you on the 6th day of November last, election day, in the city of Petersburg; and, if so, state whether or not you were at the 6th ward polls at any time during that day, and if anything special occurred at said polls state what fully, and whether you took, with others whose names you may give, any special part therein so far as the same had to do with the election then and there occurring?—Answer. I was in the city and at 6th ward polls about three hours before the closing of the polls and noticing the manner in which the men were voted, and I concluded to stay until the closing of the polls. There were one hundred and twenty-four men in line at the closing of the polls which could have voted if they only had a chance. Seeing how they were defrauded out of their votes, I walked down the line and noticed and also read every man's ballot as he had it opened, holding it up. I noticed one hundred and twenty-one ballots that one hundred and twenty-one men held was for John M. Langston for a member of Congress, and three ballots which three men had was for R. W. Arnold for member of Congress. Seeing how these men were defrauded I, in company with F. N. Robinson and A. J. Smith, invited these men across the street so as we could take their names and ballots; and if they could sign their ballots they did so, and those that could not write A. J. Smith and myself signed their ballots with their mark attached and then witnesseth it. I also noticed that they had two lines, one for the Democrats and one for the Republicans, and I also noticed that they would vote three Democrats to one Republican. After the line had swung across the street we proceeded to take the names and ballots. After taking the names and ballots the ballots were strung by me, counted by F. N. Robinson, A. J. Smith, and myself; then we proceeded and made a parcel of them and sealed them with F. N. Robinson, D. L. Brewer, and L. M. Glenn in the room, in the presence of William Wesley Brown and Drewry Batts.

3d. Question. How were the names taken and how kept by you, in list or book, or how?—Answer. The names were taken and kept by F. N. Robinson in a book, whilst Smith and I signed and witnesseth the ballots of men who could not write. Robinson took the name of each man as we called it out.

4th. Question. State whether or not you saw, examined, and know the book kept, as stated by you?—Answer. I saw and know the book.

5th. Question. Please state whether or not the book which is now handed to you and the package to which you have referred and described are the identical ones arranged and kept as described by you as having been arranged and kept on the 6th day of last November. [The package and book were handed to the witness.]—Answer. They are.

(The contestant now asks that the book and package be now filed and made a part of the testimony of the witness.)

6th. Question. State, if you please, whether or not there were differences made in the mode or manner of approach, partition or otherwise, between voters seeking to cast their ballots at the 6th ward in the city of Petersburgh on the 6th day of November, 1888?—Answer. There was a partition which divided the Republicans from the Democrats.

A. J. Smith testified, page 228, *et seq.*:

My name is A. J. Smith; I am twenty-seven years old; I live at 526 Pegram street. I was in Petersburg the 6th of November last. I was at the 6th Ward polls about two hours during the morning, and again from soon after 3 o'clock p. m. till after the polls had closed. During the progress of the election I noticed some things that I regarded as peculiar, one of which was that while all the colored voters were required to approach the polling place on one side of a plank and the white voters on another, certain colored voters were conducted to the window where the voting was going on, on the same side with the white voters, and allowed to vote. At each time during the day that I was there, there was on the side of the plank appointed for colored voters a long row of voters who complained of the delay of the election. I tried to vote in the morning, but had to leave before I succeeded. When I returned in the afternoon, about 3.15 p. m., so great was the crowd of voters on the colored side that I despaired of being able to vote. Finally, I voted by chance; the long line of voters had moved away from the plank and the short line had formed between them and the plank. I thought it a chance to get in my vote, and moved from the long line and took a place in the short line. The judges ordered the police to arrange the line; they decided to allow the persons in the short line to vote, and so I voted. If it had not been for this I would have been among the large number of persons who were in line waiting to deposit their votes when the polls closed. After I had voted I moved around about the polls, and seeing such a large number of persons who were prevented by the delay of the officers of the election from getting in their ballots, and seeing that most of these people were going to vote for the candidate for whose election I was most anxious, and knowing that most of them had been a long time in the attempt to vote, I thought that there might be a remedy for what I considered a willful suspension of their votes. I consulted with other persons who felt as I did, and we decided to take a list of persons remaining in line and their ballots. When the polls closed the persons in line were asked to remain in line and to file past Dr. Stillwell's office, where arrangements had been made to receive their names and ballots. Mr. F. N. Robinson and Mr. David L. Brower were in the office, sitting at a table by the window. Finding that they were not taking their names and ballots as fast as the people desired, I offered to assist them and did assist them. I stood by the window and took the ballots, writing the names and residences of the persons, giving them on the back of the ballots. When I commenced this I asked Freeman Jones, a voter of 6th ward, to stand at my side and see that the ballots so indorsed by me were the same ballots given me. When I had finished, and that was when no more ballots were offered, I handed them to Robinson through the window, and the names on the backs were copied on the list and the ballots strung with other ballots that they had taken. I had occasion to leave the window for a few moments, and when I returned they were preparing to seal them up in a package. I agreed that this was the proper thing to do, but I did not assist in doing this. I left and went down town. All this occurred within a short time after the closing of the polls, and was finished a long time before the judges made the return of the election.

Cross-examination:

11th. Question. In answer to a previous question you stated that a plank separated the white and colored voters at 6th ward election day, Nov. 6th, 1888. Was not that plank supposed to separate the Democrats and Republicans?—Answer. It was not supposed to separate the Democrats and Republicans. I mentioned it in order to point out a novel feature of the election. This plank has been used to separate the colored voters from the white. I can not remember ever seeing a white voter vote from the side of the plank appointed for the colored voters; but on this occasion some few colored voters were taken to the window on the side of the plank appointed for the white voters, and did vote from there. The selection of these few from among the large number of colored voters who were in line attempting to vote seemed peculiar.

12th. Question. Is it not a fact that persons who voted on one side of the plank were regarded as, and thought by the party managers on both sides to vote the Republican ticket, and those who vote on the other side of the plank as voting the Democratic ticket?—Answer. I can't see how it could be so regarded. There are white voters in 6th ward who are classed as Republicans. They all voted on the same side as other white voters. This prevents any one familiar with 6th ward election from making the distinction you suggest.

15th. Question. How many do you suppose left the polls without voting?—Answer. I can not say with certainty. I know of several who have reported that they did not vote, because they left the polls after having spent an unusually long time in trying to vote.

(The latter statement made by the witness was objected to by counsel for contestee on the ground that it is hearsay.)

16th. Question. Do you of your own personal knowledge know of any who left before the polls closed without voting?—Answer. I know of several who have said that they did. Unless I had watched a person closely and continuously I would be unable to testify of my own personal knowledge whether he had voted.

17th. Question. Please give the names of those who told you that they left before voting.—Answer. I do remember the names of two persons, others I did not know or have forgotten. The persons referred to as remembered by me are W. S. Fields and Wm. H. Reaves.

18th. Question. Please say how many you think must have left without voting.—Answer. The cases of which I learned will amount probably to twelve.

19th. Question. Is it your judgment that those twelve were all who left before the polls closed without voting?—Answer. I can not express an opinion as to whether they were all; I have not tried to ascertain; I have learned of these in general conversation about the election.

20th. Question. Did you make any attempt yourself to get into the line formed by the white voters?—Answer. I did not.

21st. Question. Did you see any one excluded who did make the attempt?—Answer. I did not see any one excluded. It was the understanding with the police that only such colored persons as were conducted by this way to the window should be allowed to approach.

22d. Question. Please explain what you mean by the words "only such colored persons as were conducted that way should be allowed to approach."—Answer. I mean that all other colored persons were restricted to the side of the plank generally used for colored persons.

23d. Question. Did you not say that some colored persons voted on the side of the plank generally used for white persons?—Answer. I did.

24th. Question. Then might not the fact that one side of the plank was generally used for colored persons have been in consequence of the preference of the colored persons themselves of that side of the plank?—Answer. I think not. I suppose that they would not prefer to remain away from the window where the votes were received rather than approach nearer on the other side.

25th. Question. You have testified substantially that you did not yourself attempt to approach the window from the other side of the plank; that you did not see any one who attempted to do so denied a place in the line on the other side, and in fact that several colored men actually entered the line and voted. Then, where was the "sinister design" that you have testified to as being manifest?—Answer. I did not attempt to approach the ballot-box on the side mentioned, but I spoke to the police authorities about this condition of things. I was led to believe that it would be useless to attempt it. The general impression was that the few colored persons voting from the white line had been induced to vote a ticket more acceptable to the managers of the election than the tickets which the majority of the voters on the other side of the plank were about to offer, and which most of them displayed open in their hands. I think this favor extended to the colored voters who voted on the other side was not so much a favor to them as an attempt to get in all of a certain kind of ballots.

26th. Question. Then, from your last answer, it is evident that if any " sinister design" was really manifest the exhibition of it is to be attributed to the city police. You surely don't mean to say that any of the police authorities of the city of Petersburg stationed themselves at the end of the line filled by white men and allowed only those colered men to enter it who had, as you say, been induced to vote the ticket which was more acceptable to the managers of the election than the ticket which the majority of the voters on the other side of the plank were about to offer ?—Answer. The police appeared to be acting under the direction of the judges of election in all their acts relative to the arranging of the lines of voters. For example ; When I had secured a place in the short line to which I have referred previously I noticed the judges of election ordered the police to arrange one line on that side of the plank. They stated that they were unable to decide which was the proper line, and suggested that those in the short line be allowed to vote. I noticed this particularly, as I was in the short line and interested in the decision of the judges. The judges decided as the police suggested. As regards the 2d part of the question, I mean to say that no colored man was allowed by the police to come very near the line referred to unless escorted by certain persons.

It appears from the above that by the intended delay 124 voters were prevented from casting their ballots, and that in all human probability 121 of them would have voted for contestant, and 3 for Mr. Arnold. The committee has not counted these votes for contestant, distinguishing between this case and the case of Waddill *vs.* Wise, decided at this session of Congress, where a somewhat similar state of affairs was presented in certain wards of the city of Richmond. But in Waddill *vs.* Wise each voter counted for contestant by the committee had been called as a witness by contestant, and had sworn to his right to vote, and that he would have voted for contestant had he been permitted to cast his ballot. This supplemental proof was not furnished in this case.

The committee is, however, of the opinion that if these 124 votes equaled or exceeded the plurality returned for the contestee so that the legality of the election depended upon them, it would invalidate his election with no further proof and make a new election necessary, and to that extent the committee agrees with the reasoning of the report of the minority in Waddill *vs.* Wise.

Taking this view of the case the 124 voters prevented from casting their ballots must be considered for the purpose of unseating the contestee only, but can not be considered in favor of contestant's right to his seat. The contestee's lack of a plurality would then be the plurality found for contestant, viz, 731 plus 124 equals 855.

Restating the vote showing the election of Langston we have :

	Venable.	Langston.
Returned vote	13, 298	12, 657
Add Poach and Ross	69	141
	13, 367	12, 798
Deduct Lewiston as returned	119	48
	13, 248	12, 750
Deduct Mannborough as returned	122	111
	13, 126	12, 639
Deduct Third Ward, Petersburg, as returned	518	174
	12, 608	12, 465
Add votes proved		284
	12, 608	12, 749
Deduct Sixth Ward, Petersburg, as returned	352	139
	12, 256	12, 610
Add votes proved		377
Making total legal vote	12, 256	12, 987
		12, 256
Showing legal plurality for Langston		731

Or, to state the account differently, for the sake of illustration, we will give Mr. Venable all the votes not accounted for in the Third Ward, and we have—

Total vote Third Ward as returned.. 797
Vote proved for Langston.. 284
Vote for Arnold, returned 105

                                                                             389
Leaves balance of vote for Venable... 408

    Total as returned 797

And in Sixth Ward, total vote returned 651
Vote proved for Langston.. 377
Vote for Arnold, returned... 160

                                                                             537
Leaves balance of vote for Venable... 114

    Total as returned.. 651

Under this plan the total vote would stand as follows:

[It is unnecessary to include the vote for Arnold, as it does not affect the result.]

	Venable.	Langston.
Total vote corrected down to Petersburgh..	13,126	12,639
Deduct returned vote Third and Sixth Wards.................................	870	313
	12,256	12,326
Add vote proved for Langston, giving to Venable vote not accounted for	522	661
Making the result..	12,778	12,987
		12,778
Or a plurality for Langston of..	....	209

Throwing out the third and sixth wards and not counting vote proved in those wards gives Langston a plurality of 70. Or take the total vote as returned from the district with the addition of Poarch and Ross precinct, which is admitted, and re-adjust it as proven in Third and Sixth wards of Petersburgh, leaving rest of district untouched, and we have the following result:

	Venable.	Langston.
Vote as returned in district including Poarch and Ross........................	13,367	12,798
Deduct returned vote Third and Sixth wards	870	313
	12,497	12,485
Add vote proved for Langston in Third and Sixth wards and giving Venable vote not accounted for..	522	661
	13,019	13,146
		13,019
This gives Langston a plurality of......................................	....	127

The committee adheres to the first of the above statements as being the legal method of ascertaining the true vote, and uses the latter illustrations simply for the purpose of demonstrating that in any view of the case the contestant is elected and entitled to his seat. It is evident that giving to contestee the vote not accounted for would be a direct encouragement to election frauds, as it would give him the benefit of

H. Mis. 137——30

every fraudulent vote which his friends had made it impossible for the opposition to expose, even after the proof clearly established fraud to such an extent as to destroy absolutely the integrity of the official returns. In no case has such a rule been adopted.

Sufficient is shown to show the election of contestant, and the committee does not by its silence indorse the fairness of the election in many precincts not discussed in this report, but challenged in contestant's notice and briefs, and as to which there was evidence of illegal practices. Neither do we approve of the dilatory tactics pursued by contestee's counsel in other than the Third and Sixth wards, Petersburgh, whereby contestant was prevented from pursuing his examination of many witnesses in such wards.

At Meherrin, Lunenburgh County, one of the judges duly appointed and friendly to contestant was illegally denied the right to serve and another substituted in his place unfriendly to contestant. There is evidence tending to show that 40 votes were cast for contestant and only 20 returned for him. But the latter fact is disputed, and the returns are permitted to stand.

At Brown's Store there was an unwarranted and unexplained change of two judges on October 30, only a few days before election, and considerable evidence of misconduct and attempts at bribery by persons outside of the polls. It is not clearly shown that the results were affected, and the returns are not disturbed.

At Columbian Grove only one of the legally-appointed judges served, the electoral board appointing two new judges without notice and without apparent cause or legal authority on October 28, immediately before the election. One of the legally-appointed judges offered to serve on the morning of election but was refused.

At Hicksford, Greensville County, there is considerable evidence tending to show that all the votes cast for contestant were not counted for him. No friend of contestant was permitted to witness the count. All the judges and clerks of election were opposed to contestant.

In no case did a substitution of judges result in placing a friend of contestant upon the local returning board, while in many instances his friends were removed and his political opponents substituted for them.

The committee desires to express its condemnation of the practice of re-adjusting legally-constituted election boards during a heated political contest without cause and without warrant of law, and for the evident purpose of placing one political party or candidate entirely in the hands of its or his political opponents. There can be but one purpose in such a change, and that a purpose to which criminally-inclined minds only will resort.

Judge Howell E. Jackson, late a United States Senator and now a judge of eminence, in his charge to the jury in the recent trial of Tennessee election officers for violating the Federal election laws at Memphis, Tenn., used the following language:

Said witnesses testified that the voting population of the fourth civil district of Fayette County on November 6, 1888, numbered between 490 and 500—say about 500. That about 80 to 100 of such voters were white men or Democrats; the remainder, numbering about 400, were colored men and Republicans. That on the day of the election there was a large turn out of such voters. That the colored voters present exceeded 300 in number. John McGowan, the Republican chairman of the district, states that there were over 300 colored Republican voters present. That he directed many or most of them to go for their tickets to John C. Reeves, who occupied a position 10 or 20 steps from the voting place, and was distributing Republican tickets to Republican voters. That Reeves' position was in full view of the window at which the ballots were handed in to the officer. That he saw many of the tickets deposited or handed in to the officer holding the election, and can not swear to the actual number that voted that had Republican tickets. John C. Reeves testified before you that he was present. That he had in his possession Republican tickets, a sample of which is produced in evidence, having on it a full list of Republican candidates, from Presidential electors and Congressmen down to State and county officers. That he issued to the colored voters on that day, upon their application for the same, 325 of those tickets while at the voting place. That on his way home he met four or five other voters going to the polls, to whom he gave Republican tickets; the names of two of those voters he finds upon the poll-list at Nos. 407 and 409. Reeves further states that he saw over one hundred of those to whom he gave tickets go directly from him to the window where the votes were received and hand them in to the officer holding the election. He could not swear that they actually deposited the identical tickets received from him, but he saw no change of ticket or change of purpose on the part of the voter after procuring from himself the Republican ticket. He recognizes on the poll-list the names of about one hundred of such Republican voters. Now, gentlemen of the jury, Reeves and McGowan are in no way impeached, nor are their statements in any wise contradicted. They stand before you as in every way credible witnesses, and their testimony is entitled to full faith and credit. If the case for the prosecution stopped with Reeves and McGowan, it would present a case of circumstantial evidence as to the vote actually cast having exceeded that which was counted and returned by the election officers and judges. When circumstantial evidence is relied on to convict, as counsel for defense has suggested, it should be of such conclusive character as to exclude any remote hypothesis of innocence.

It is to be remembered that the last remark has reference to the proof required to convict in a criminal case.

Speaking in regard to individual voters who had testified to their votes, he said:

If the prosecution had simply shown that each one of these witnesses was seen going to the poll with a Republican ticket in his hand which he had received from Reeves, with a declaration of his intention to vote said tickets, such facts and acts would have constituted circumstantial evidence that they voted said ticket.

It is to be remembered that the evidence in this case is more direct and more certain than was the evidence upon which Judge Jackson's charge was based, and that the witnesses and voters take much greater pains to be able to know the exact facts.

Remembering who Judge Jackson is and what his party affiliations are, and that the men on trial were citizens of his own State and members of the political party to which he belongs, this charge will certainly be accepted as of the very highest authority.

We therefore recommend the passage of the following resolution:

Resolved, That E. C. Venable was not elected a Representative of the Fifty-first Congress from the Fourth Congressional district of Virginia, and is not entitled to a seat therein.

Resolved, That John M. Langston was elected a Representative of Congress from the Fourth Congressional district of Virginia, and is entitled to a seat therein.

VIEWS OF THE MINORITY.

(1) **Returns.** *Irregularities in.*

The returns rejected by the county commissioners because they were not made in accordance with the directory provisions of the Virginia statutes should be counted by the committee, there being no suspicion of fraud or evidence tending to impeach their correctness.

(2) **Notice of contest.** *Parties should be bound by.*

If any question had been raised in the notice of contest in regard to the precinct from which the returns were not signed, and no evidence taken to show their correctness, the committee would be right in rejecting them, but their being no mention of this precinct in the notice of contest, the contestee should not be required to produce any evidence in regard to it.

(3) **Return.** *When rejected what votes be counted.*

If a return is to be rejected, and votes counted for contestant, the contestee should at least be given his well-defined party vote, which was cast for him.

(4) **Evidence.** *Testimony actually taken only to be considered, not what might have been taken.*

"The House of Representatives may in a proper case grant additional time to take testimony, but it will never, until all principles governing judicial procedure and the hearing and determination of causes are set aside and utterly disregarded, strengthen and bolster up a weak and feeble attempt to annul the solemn act of election officials upon the mere assertion of a party that he could, if he had been favored with more time, have proved his case."

(5) **Votes.** *Not cast.*

There is nothing to indicate that the inability of voters to cast their votes in time was due to any act of contestee or his partisans. The plan of allowing voters from the white and colored line to vote alternately was a proper one. The votes not cast cannot be counted for the benefit or injury of any one.

(6) **Excessive votes.**

The mere fact that the number of votes returned exceeds the number of names checked on the voting list does not in the absence of fraud or of a change in the result affect the validity of the election. (Paine, § 539.)

The suspicious circumstances claimed in this case are not inconsistent with the honesty of the returns.

469

VIEWS OF THE MINORITY.

Mr. O'FERRALL, from the Committee on Elections, submitted the following as the views of the minority:

We, the undersigned, members of the Committee on Elections, having duly considered the record and the briefs filed and the oral arguments of counsel in the contested election case of John M. Langston vs. Edward C. Venable, from the Fourth Congressional district of Virginia, submit the following as our views:

The Fourth Congressional district of Virginia is composed of the counties of Amelia, Brunswick, Dinwiddie, Greensville, Lunenburgh, Mecklenburgh, Nottoway, Powhatan, Prince Edward, Prince George, and Sussex, and the city of Petersburgh.

At the election in November, 1888, Edward C. Venable was the Democratic nominee, R. W. Arnold the Republican nominee, and John M. Langston an independent Republican candidate for Congress in this Congressional district.

The contest was waged with great vigor by the Democrats in their support of their nominee, Venable, and by the Republicans in support of their nominee, Arnold, and the independent candidate, Langston, respectively.

The nominee of the Democrats was a strong and popular candidate, a resident of the city of Petersburgh, a large manufacturer and employer of many hands, and he was supported most enthusiastically by his party.

Arnold, the Republican nominee, had the earnest support of General William Mahone, chairman of the Republican State Committee, a resident of Petersburgh, and the entire Republican organization of the district, and substantially all the white, and many of the colored Republicans.

Langston rallied around him the greater part of the colored voters, and being a colored man, drew "the color line" and demanded the support of his race over the regular nominee of the Republican party, who was a white man. He canvassed the district, making everywhere speeches which were calculated and intended to arouse race prejudices, denounced the Republican nominee because he was a white man, and General Mahone, chairman of the Republican State Committee, in the most violent terms.

The fight between the followers of Arnold and Langston became most intensely bitter.

From the prominent and leading colored leaders outside of the State, as well as within the district, came severe criticism of Langston's course.

Frederick Douglass, now Minister to Hayti, addressed a letter to prominent colored men in the District, in reply to a letter written by them, from which we quote the following language in reference to Langston:

I have nothing whatever to say against the ability of the gentleman who is just now making a vigorous canvass for Congressional honors in your district. You know his history. He came among you ostensibly as an educator, and not as a politician. He had acquired before he came among you considerable reputation by his ability as a speaker and by his connection with Howard University. He was on the finance committee of the Freedman's Bank when most of its bad loans were made. He was among those who insisted that the doors of the bank should be kept open when he knew that that concern was insolvent. He remained with Howard University so long as there was a chance of making himself its president. He deserted it and denounced it when the trustees of that institution refused to gratify his ambition. Coming among you as an educator, he sought the earliest opportunity to put himself in training as a politician. His high vocation as a scholar and a teacher was abandoned for the pursuit of political honors. I do not say the political sins and sinuosities of John Mercer Langston are worse than those of many other men who occupy seats in the national Congress, but I do say that they have been such as to justify the colored citizens of the 4th district of Virginia to regard his nomination as one, under the circumstances, not to be made.

His nomination of Hon. Fitzhugh Lee for the Vice-Presidency; his coquetting with the Democratic party; his leaning towards a division of the colored vote; his duplicity in keeping the name of James G. Blaine at the head of his paper in Virginia, while he frantically shouted for Sherman at the Chicago convention, clearly with the motive of making himself secure in the good graces of one or the other, if successful, proves him to be a trickster. And above all, the insolent announcement of his determination to force his nomination by threatening the Republican party with division by running for Congress, with or without the consent of that party, fairly places him beyond the pale of Republican support.

No encouragement should be given to any man whose mad political ambition would imperil the success of the Republican party in any section of the Republic.

Yours, for the triumphant election of Benjamin Harrison and Levi P. Morton,

FREDERICK DOUGLASS.

CEDAR HILL, ANACOSTIA, D. C., *August* 15, 1888.
(Record 22.)

R. L. Singleton, president of the Virginia Republican Association of the city of Washington, addressed the following letter to Perry Carson, a well-known colored leader:

HEADQUARTERS VIRGINIA REPUBLICAN ASSOCIATION,
No. 738 FOURTH STREET NORTHWEST,
Washington, D. C., October 29*th,* 1888.

Col. PERRY CARSON,
Member National Republican Committee, Washington, D. C.:

DEAR SIR: As the president of the Virginia Republican Association, numbering 200 members, through whose efforts nearly 1000 colored voters will soon be sent to the polls in Virginia, I have a right to a hearing at your hands regarding the Petersburgh Congressional embroglio in our State, where Candidate John M. Langston, lately of this district, well known to you personally and politically, is said to stand with broad-axe and bowie-knife in hand threatening with direct social and personal injury all voters of your race and mine who are not of his following in the disastrous Congressional battle which he has brought upon the party in that stronghold of Republicanism. Like myself, you, sir, are a black man and proud of the negro race. For eight years or more you have faced, and facing have overcome, all opposition to your leadership of the negro masses at the national capital. It will not be forgotten that you and that noble Irish patriot and Republican Andrew Gleason carried the banner of the "white plumed knight" to victory in this city four years ago, and also that right nobly did you and your compatriot repeat that victory in June last, when the Chicago convention saw you both, a second time, the trusted delegates of our party in that great national conclave of Republican representative men.

And when that most illustrious of Americans James G. Blaine, soon after the Chicago nomination, returned from his journey abroad, borne, as it were, in a million of Republican arms, it will not be forgotten that one of his first and most earnest inquiries, on nearing his native shores, was the one when he said to his bosom friend, Stephen B. Elkins: "Elkins, I see Gleason abroad; where is Carson?"

Now, sir, as a Virginia Republican, and like yourself a Southern born and raised black man, I want to know by what right of superiority, in any respect whatsoever, John M. Langston, who has always boasted of his white, not of his negro, blood, should have so suddenly become the Colossus and dictator of your race and mine in Virginia, stirring up strife amongst a large class of its Republican voters by appeals to their superstitions and ignorance, and riding rough-shod over our old and trusted leaders there, colored as well as white men. Why, I inquire, should the negro voters of the District be asked to walk beneath Langston's legs and meekly march, like so many sheep, to the slaughter which, without a settlement of the trouble into which he has plunged the party there, awaits us on election day?

In a brief talk with Langston a day or two ago in this city he contemptuously waved me away from him, saying I was a Mahone man and too much for white men, or words to that effect. My simple reply was, that when the colored man needed friends in Virginia he, Langston, was not on hand; that when a brave commander was wanted to lead our hosts Langston was never to be found on a single one of our many and memorable battle-fields. Our captain and leader was General William Mahone, and a right noble one he was and is.

And now saluting you, Col. Carson, in the words of Napoleon to his great field marshal, Ney, as the bravest of the brave, I want you to kindly inform me, and through me the Republicans of my State, something of the political character and record of the most overbearing and audacious man whom I have had the fortune to know since my connection with State and national politics.

Yours, sincerely,

R. L. SINGLETON,
President of the Virginia Republican Association.

(Record 25.)

To this letter Carson replied as follows:

WASHINGTON, D. C., *October 30th,* 1888.

R. L. SINGLETON, Esq.,
President, etc.

MY DEAR SIR: Your letter of yesterday touching the unfortunate condition of political affairs in your time-honored stronghold of Republicanism, the 4th Congressional district of Virginia, is before me. My reply shall be sincere and brief. I am opposed to the election of Hon. John M. Langston to a seat in Congress from that district for the very simple and proper reason that he is not the regular or lawful nominee of the party for that office, and being myself a strict party man, I unhesitatingly advise all good Republicans, without regard to race or color, to support the nomination of Judge Arnold for the position in question. From the moment Mr. Langston uttered his unfortunate declaration to the effect that he should press his candidacy for Congress, whether nominated or not by the Republican convention, I have classed him with the bolters, marplots, and other assistant Democrats, of whom our grand old party has unhappily too many. These are my primary reasons, but there are many secondary ones, a few of which I may briefly refer to.

Mr. Langston's printed utterance, made either in a speech or interview a year or more ago, wherein he substantially announced his willingness to support Governor Fitzhugh Lee, of your State, for the Vice-Presidency of the United States, fixed his status in my mind as that of a deserting Republican or a designing hypocrite having an axe to grind with the Democratic officials, to the end that thrift of some sort might come to him from desertion of his party on the one hand or flattery and hypocrisy toward Governor Lee on the other.

From all I know of his conduct whilst an official in this city and otherwise I am driven to the conclusion that he is, to all intents and purposes, a white man's man, except when he is doing what he now is, viz, soliciting colored votes for official position. In 1882, while a member of the board of health of this city, he never, though often requested, gave to a single one of his colored fellow-citizens the slightest official recognition.

I remember that James L. Bowen, a most reputable colored physician, begged the place of a ward doctor at his hands. Bowen was a graduate of medicine and had had several years' experience in the practice. Instead of helping that poor negro, he gave the appointment to a young white stripling of a doctor who had not been six months from school.

Representing us as a negro, he appointed, with perhaps a single exception, white men to office, because he was not at that time, nor never was in his taste, habits, or association, a negro at all.

He learned decidedly and openly in favor of the white man, and no one who knew him well, either then or now, will pretend that he is in any sense a reliable and fit representative of the negro race of this country.

Very truly, yours,

PERRY H. CARSON,
Carson's Hotel, Penn. Avenue, Washington, D. C.

(Record 26.)

A colored minister addressed the following letter to his congregation:

PETERSBURGH, VIRGINIA, *October 31st*, 1888.

To the members and congregation worshiping at New Hope Baptist Church (colored), Sussex County, Va.:

Beloved in Christ: Moved by a sense of duty I owe to you as your chosen pastor, I have in the past refrained from all participation in any political canvass, and my purpose to maintain a like course of conduct in the present was fixed, until matters had taken such course and reached such point that longer to hold my peace would be a dereliction of duty to myself as a man and to you as a pastor.

The enunciation lately made by Mr. Langston of war against every white in this Congressional district who should dare to cast his vote against him for Congress, first opened my eyes to the dangers to my race, which was sure to follow, if the threat of Mr. Langston was attempted to be carried out.

I could not then hold my peace, and, impelled by the love I bear you, I now do most earnestly warn you against giving your approbation to any such sentiment by affording the "aid and comfort" of your vote to the author of the sentiment. To vote Mr. Langston now would be to endorse the sentiment which you must see, of necessity, will bring upon you the indignant rebuke of every reputable white man in the district, whether he be a Democrat or Republican.

The color line could not be more distinctly drawn. To adopt the advice of Mr. Langston is to draw this line more closely than ever before, and I ask you, is it not reasonable for the white man to turn upon you the doctrine which Mr. Langston would have you apply to the white man?

You are sensible people, and you must know that, if left to yourself, warring against the white man, you must be the sufferers. It is our duty to cultivate the kindest, friendliest relations with the white man—not of war.

The Republican party has shown its disposition to recognize our race wherever, by intellect or education, any has shown himself to be capable. Can you say that the like has been done by the Democratic party?

Are you forgetful that the Virginia negroes enjoy larger political privileges, greater advantages of citizenship, than are vouchsafed to the race in any other state? And do you know that you owe this same to the very men against whom Mr. Langston would have you declare war? Do you owe Mr. Langston anything?

Have you forgotten that you owe to the very men whom Mr. Langston now vilifies the right to vote without the payment of the dollar capitation tax? Do you owe to Mr. Langston anything for this? Have you forgotten that to the very men upon whom he would have you turn your backs you are indebted for free schools, open as well to the colored child as to the white child, with colored teachers? Did Mr. Langston give you any aid in this behalf? Do you forget that you are indebted to the very men whom you are advised to ostracise for relief from the whipping-post? Do you owe Mr. Langston anything for this? Do you forget that you owe to these very men whom Mr. Langston now traduces the right to sit in the jury-box? Is this no privilege that you should cherish? Will you abandon those who invested you with this great privilege to aid Mr. Langston, to whom you owe nothing for the right? Does it show gratitude to the men who have relieved such of our race as lunatics from confinement in the common jails by providing for their exclusive use an asylum which in all its parts is the equal of the best asylum devoted to the whites by following the advice of Mr. Langston? Do you owe anything to Mr. Langston for the Colored Lunatic Asylum? Have you forgotten the magnificent Colored Normal School, near Petersburgh, by which the colored men and women are fitted to teach our colored children, and will you wage war against the men who have secured such a benefit to you? Did Mr. Langston contribute anything to this great blessing to the colored people of Virginia?

He has been the recipient of the loaves and fishes, and he has contributed nothing. Have you lost all sense of gratitude for all these things that you should turn your backs upon men who have thus proved to be your friends upon the dictation of one who seeks for his own personal ends to rouse all the worst passions, which must result to your injury and enure any good to our race?

My brethren, I beg of you to pause and consider before you shall determine to follow the advice of Mr. Langston, and imperil the best interest of our race by giving your vote to a person who has never in any wise, nor at any time, nor at any place, shown himself friendly to the colored man or to the Republican party.

I shall vote for the regular nominee of the Republican party—Judge Arnold—and I trust you will do the same.

In bonds of Christian love,

WILLIAM WALLACE,
Pastor New Hope Church, Sussex County, Virginia.

These letters were published in circular form by Langston's Republican opponents and distributed in the district.

The National Leader, a Republican paper published in Washington, on the 6th day of October, 1888, contained the following editorial:

The admirers of Mr. Langston are greatly injuring their chances of their ambitious but misguided leader by offering insult to General Mahone. It will be time enough to play the "Dead March in Saul" when Mahone is beaten, if he can be beaten, and we are not so sure that he will be. Mr. Langston should employ experienced and practical politicians to conduct his side-show in the fourth Virginia district. Their tactics, if the Lancet is to be credited, are not such to insure success to their side. It is not good politics and certainly not good sense to make a personal enemy of an influential and powerful politician like General William Mahone, who has done more for the colored people of Virginia than any white man in the State.

We are not sure that Mr. Langston is as good a friend of the negro as Mahone, for, if we remember right, he is the same Mr. Langston who, some years ago in Richmond, declared that if he believed he had one drop of negro blood in his veins he would lance the artery that contained it and let it out.

Heretofore Mr. Langston has been very white; now he is very black. We can't understand it.

General Mahone was by no means inactive while Langston was engaged in "offering insult" to him. He issued an address to the Republicans of the district, which we here give:

To the Republican voters of the Fourth Congressional district:

It is my duty to inform you that at the regular Republican convention for this district, held at Farmville on the 19th day of September, Judge R. W. Arnold, of Sussex County, a true and tried Republican, was nominated by acclamation as your candidate for Congress. This convention was composed of the following legally elected delegates:

From Sussex. S. T. Drewry, J. B. Jarratt, J. D. Neblett, W. H. Mason, Stith Parham, R. H. Lewis, John Lawhead—solid.

From Prince George: Charles Gee, James A. Young. J. R. Temple, E. T. Ellis, Nelson Hobbs, James Diggs—solid.

From Greenville: B. F. Jarratt and Le Grand Jackson—two out of the six delegates elected by the county.

From Dinwiddie: J. C. Duane; A. G. Butterworth; W. D. Falconer; Albert Johnson, by L. E. Coleman, his alternate; J. C. Spain; Robert Goodwyn, by Hon. A. W. Harris, his alternate; George W. Matthews—solid.

From Nottoway; W. H. Ash; J. E. Leath, by Charles Rowe, his alternate: Ryland Ross; S. F. Jackson; E. H. Witmer; Lewis White, by William Fitzgerald, his alternate—solid.

From Lunenburgh: T. C. Matthews; G. W. McLaughlin; C. E. May, by Henry Hicks, his alternate; Lee Davis; Junius Bagley—solid.

From Mecklenburgh: Ludd Ruffin; Charles Alexander, by Aaron Beard, his alternate; W. H. Jones; Sowney Towner; W. H. Jones, sheriff; Samuel G. Baskerville; W. H. Northington, by Gerard Baskerville, his alternate—seven out of eleven elected by the county.

From Powhatan: W. H. Flanagan, Washington Jones, Patrick Mayo, Larry Mosely —solid.

From Prince Edward: Hon. B. S. Hooper, N. M. Griggs, N. M. McGhee, Richard Woodson, Cephas Gray, Walker Blanton, Albert S. Hines, Joseph S. Doswell—solid.

In all, 52 out of 85 delegates elected to the convention, leaving only thirty-three delegates who went off and held a mass-meeting and put up Mr. J. M. Langston. Of the 33 delegates so refusing to enter the Republican convention there were 12 from the city of Petersburgh, whose seats were contested.

In this state of the case you have before you three candidates for Congress, the Hon. R. W. Arnold, the regular nominee of the Republican party, Mr. E. C. Venable, the regular nominee of the Democratic party, and Mr. John M. Langston, the candidate put up by a mass-meeting composed of misled Republicans. But one of these candidates can be elected, and it is for the thoughtful Republican to determine whether he will aid the election of the regular Democratic nominee, Mr. Venable, by throwing his vote away on Mr. Langston, or, like a loyal Republican to the Republican party, resolutely support the nominee of his party, and cast his ballot for Judge Arnold.

A vote for Langston is half a vote for Venable, and in the interest of the Democratic candidate for President.

A vote for Arnold is a whole vote for the principles of the Republican party and in support of the election of the Republican candidate for the Presidency.

Let no true Republican be drawn away from his Republican duty in this contest by any preferences he may have had for the nomination of his favorite previous to the Farmville convention, but now that it has met and given us a candidate in the person of Judge R. W. Arnold, it behooves all true Republicans to stand by him as the duly delegated standard-bearer of the Republican party of the fourth district.

WILLIAM MAHONE,
Chairman.

There were many colored men engaged in the canvass for Arnold, but they were treated rudely and threatened with violence by Langston's supporters, who were wrought up by him to a state of frenzy. Here is what A. W. Harris, one of the most intelligent and respectable colored men in Virginia and a member of the legislature of the State, says:

1. Question. What is your age, occupation, and residence?—Answer. I am 36 19th of this coming August; lawyer; in the county of Dinwiddie, about two miles from the city.

2nd. Question. Please state what office, if any, of a public character you are now occupying.—Ans. A member of the house of delegates of Virginia.

3d. Question. Please state whether you took part in the campaign which preceded the election of a member of Congress from this district on November 6th, 1888; and if you occupied any position in the campaign organization, please state what it was.—Ans. I took part in the campaign, as above suggested, as a canvasser. I occupied no other position in the campaign organization.

4th. Question. Please state to what political party you belong, what party you supported as a canvasser in the campaign above referred to, and as the nominee of what party were you elected to the house of delegates?—Ans. I belong to the Republican party. I supported the Republican party's nominee in the campaign above referred to. My last nomination to the house of delegates was by the Republican party.

5th. Question. Have you ever belonged to any other political party?—Ans. No; unless one who belonged to the fusion between the Readjusters and Republicans from '80 to '83 can be said to have belonged to other than the Republican party. In that fusion, however, I was a member of the Republican wing.

14th. Question. After the nomination of Judge Arnold by the regular Republican convention please state whether or not Judge Arnold made any canvass of this district, either personally or by his supporters.—Ans. I know that from October the 4th until the close of the canvass Judge Arnold spent nearly every day in the various counties of the district, a majority of the time making two speeches a day. I know that he made a pretty thorough canvass through his supporters; that is to say, as I now remember there were fifteen persons who spent a good portion of the time in the field as canvassers. This does not include the number of persons who did not leave their particular counties.

15th. Question. Please name as many as you can of the gentlemen who canvassed the district for Judge Arnold, and if there were both white and colored canvassers please signify that fact as you call the names.—Ans. There was W. H. Ashe, B. Baskerville, jr., W. W. Evans, J. W. Watson, H. C. Cox, J. W. Adams, J. W. Flippen, Collins Johnson, J. R. Jones, William Jones, T. S. Hamlin, C. H. Branch, Peter G. Morgan, W. H. Jordan, R. B. Baptist, and A. W. Harris. I am not supposed to give everybody in the canvass, but those I remember just now. The above list is made up entirely of colored canvassers. I have not undertaken to give any white canvassers in the above list, because I had not as much to do with them as with the colored canvassers, and therefore remember among the white canvassers only such persons as Senator Charles Gee, Jamieson of Mecklenburg, Jones of Mecklenburg, Boswell of Nottoway, Jones of Brunswick, Butterworth of Dinwiddie, and Cardoza of Lunenburg.

16th. Question. Please state, if you know, whether any of the colored canvassers mentioned have at any time occupied public positions of honor and trust in the communities in which they reside; and, if so, state who they are and what position.—Ans. W. H. Ashe is a member of the house of delegates from Nottoway and Amelia; B. Baskerville, jr., is a member of the house of delegates of Virginia from Mecklenburg County; W. W. Evans is a member of the house of delegates of Va. from Petersburg. These three gentlemen are sitting members from their respective counties. J. R. Jones is an ex-senator from the senatorial district composed of the counties of Mecklenburg and Charlotte; W. H. Jordan is an ex-member of the house of delegates from the city of Petersburgh; Peter G. Morgan is an ex-member of the Virginia legislature from the Petersburgh district, and is at present a member of the Petersburgh city council; Collins Johnson is, as I remember, an ex-member of the legislature from Brunswick County.

18th. Question. Please state what was the character of the canvass made by Professor Langston and his supporters in furtherance of his election as a Representative in Congress from the Fourth Congressional district of Virginia.—Ans. The canvass, as I saw it, was a very bitter one. Whenever it could be done successfully the persons who supported Judge Arnold were prevented from speaking and getting at the crowd in any way that Mr. Langston's friends could prevent them. The controlling element of that canvass seems to have inspired the masses with the belief that it was scarcely less than criminal to oppose the candidacy of Professor Langston. I never in all my life saw the lines drawn so tightly against a set of people who dared to differ with another set; and this condition of affairs extended even to the women. The race line was tightly drawn, and it was argued that we, the colored people, have a majority in this district, and because we have a majority we must elect Mr. Langston to Congress. It is the only canvass in which I ever took part that I have seen men on the opposite side driven from the platform. It was a canvass in which the doctrine was taught that the colored men were able to do without white Republicans, and in which the further doctrine was taught that the white or colored Republican who was not on that side might conceive that all hopes of future advancement or recognition in the lines of the Republican party were sealed. My idea of the canvass as conducted from Mr. Langston's stand-point was that no one was to have an opinion unless that opinion went to the furtherance of the aims and ends of their side. Social ostracism so far as one colored man can socially ostracise another was practiced throughout the canvass. It was a canvass which I regard as exceedingly hurtful to the relations existing between the two races of this section of Virginia, because the animosities and hatreds engendered were of such a character as to make the colored people restive in their present condition and attempt to do that by themselves which the experience of the race in every Southern State since the war has shown can only be done through the united effort of the white and colored people when they are harmoniously moving together for the accomplishment of an end. I mean to be understood by this answer as saying that no strong effective Republican party in the South can be built up upon black votes alone; that they must have the aid of white men, and those white men must be drawn from the ranks of the Democratic party, or rather from that class of white men and their sons who followed the fortunes of the ex-Confederacy, by a spirit of toleration on the part of the present members of the Republican party as one finds it in the South. Such toleration and consideration for the prejudices and education which has obtained with that class of men was not discoverable in Mr. Langston's canvass, but rather there was a disposition to say to those people, "If you can't see things as I do, and take that which I mete out to you, we don't care for you to take a position in the Republican party."

(NOTE.—The attorney for the contestant objects to so much of this answer as is hearsay, mere opinion as shown therein, and shall insist that it be stricken from the record as wholly illegal.)

19th. Question. You have stated that Mr. Langston's canvass was the only one in which you have seen speakers of the opposite side driven from the platform. Do you mean that during the canvass Judge Arnold's speakers were driven from the platform by Mr. Langston's supporters?

(NOTE.—The attorney for the contestant objects to the question both on the ground that it is leading and is in its character and effect not direct, but cross-examination.)

Ans. I do. I saw them driven from the platform at Clarksville in the county Mecklenburg.

20th question. You have stated that Mr. Langston's supporters did all they could to prevent Arnold's speakers from speaking. Please explain a little more fully how they did this.

(NOTE.—Objected to by the attorney for the contestant as leading and as being cross-examination and not direct.)

Ans. At Clarksville they were plainly told that unless they were there to talk for Mr. Langston they would be taken from the stand; and at that place they were further told that they did not intend to hear any speakers unless they were in Mr. Langston's interest. At other places they would get together a good number of people who would come near the speakers' stand, howl and shout for Langston, break up the meeting by that means if possible, or get into a general row, and thereby prevent Arnold's speakers from proceeding further.

(Record 925.)

W. W. Evans, a colored member of the legislature, a notary public of the city of Petersburgh, and editor of the Virginia Lancet, a Republican newspaper published in the city of Petersburgh, testified as follows as to Langston's incendiary speeches, his bad conduct in the canvass, the intense feeling he aroused, and the violent action of his supporters:

7. Quest. You say that your paper, the Virginia Lancet, is a Republican newspaper, published in this district. Please say how long it has been published, and what other

newspapers, published and edited by colored men in this district, were in operation
prior to the beginning of Mr. Langston's campaign for Congress?—Answer. The Virginia Lancet was started in 1882. It has been running ever since. During that time
two papers, viz, the Southern Tribune and the Star of Zion, were edited and published by colored men. At the time when Mr. Langston began his contest for Congress there was only one newspaper published and edited by a colored man in this
district.

8. Quest. During the years since its foundation what has been the object and aim
of the Virginia Lancet in reference to the colored people, and what has been its position and reputation among them?

(To which question the attorney for contestant objects, as having no relevancy to
any matter in issue in this case, and therefore as being without competency.)

Answer. The Virginia Lancet has aimed to advance the political and material interests of the colored people. It has had the reputation of being the organ of that class
of our citizens in this section.

13. Quest. Please state as fully as you can, what was the character of the canvass
made by Professor Langston and his supporters in furtherance of his election as a
Representative in Congress from the Fourth Congressional district of Virginia.

(To which question and any answer made thereto the att'y for contestant objects as
necessarily involving matter which is simply hearsay and matter of mere opinion
without reference, and so without bearing in any proper and legal sense upon any
issue involved in this contest.)

Answer. To say that it was bitter, mean, and vile will express it feebly. It was a
system of organized ostracism of every man who dared to oppose Mr. Langston's
aspirations. Mr. Langston, his friends, and his supporters throughout the district
held up to ridicule every colored man who supported Judge Arnold. Whenever
any of Judge Arnold's canvassers went into the counties to make speeches in his
behalf they were met by an organized crowd of Mr. Langston's supporters, who
used all their powers to prevent these speakers from discussing the questions which
were at issue in this district. Many of such supporters of Judge Arnold were
forced to travel many miles to secure accommodations on account of the rancor
and bad feeling which had been stirred up by Mr. Langston, his supporters, and
friends. Not only was this true, but Mr. Langston and his supporters left nothing undone to stir up bitter relations between the whites and blacks of this district. They went so far as to demand the support of every white Republican in the
district upon the penalty that they were never to be voted for by the colored voters
unless they supported him. During that canvass some of Mr. Langston's friends
and supporters made it their special duty to insult me while I passed along the streets.
whenever I appeared in a public meeting, ofttimes coming to my office for that purpose
Many of these men were good, honest, and industrious citizens who were incited to
these acts by some of the men of the colored race who claimed to be intelligent leaders.
It is known that Mr. Langston openly defied the Republican organization of the State
and nation, and that he had the support of none of the loyal Republicans of this district
after his nomination. A great many of the men who have been true to the Republican
party in the past were misled and misguided, and gave him a support which many of
them, to my own knowledge, this day regret.

14. Quest. What was the especial ground of difference between the leading colored
men who supported Judge Arnold and the supporters of Mr. Langston?—Answer. The
men who supported Judge Arnold believed that the success of the Republican party in
this district could only be effected by giving hearty and cordial support to the regular
candidate of the Republican party. Judge Arnold was the regular nominee of that
party in this district for Congress. These men believed that by supporting any independent, white or black, they would injure the chances of the success of the party. Mr.
Langston made his fight from the beginning on the ground of color. The men who supported Judge Arnold could not sympathize with such a movement because they believed
that it would be impossible to win in any way that would advance the race upon such
grounds. Prof. Langston is undoubtedly one of the most cultured of the men that has
been produced by the negro race in America. His reputation as an orator is well
known. His ability to reach the masses was well shown in the recent contest for
Congress. He, however, got on the wrong side of the question. I mean by that that
he took himself outside of the Republican party. The men who supported him did so
on account of the fact that he was a leading colored man. In this you will find, in
some measure, the reason why leading colored men differed.

15. Quest. Is Prof. Langston a man of family, and if so, where does his family live?—
Answer. Mr. Langston is a man of family. I have had the pleasure of meeting his
wife. I think his family live in Washington, D. C.

16. Quest. Has Prof. Langston any reasons for taking up a permanent residence
apart from his wife and family?—Answer. None that I know of.

17. Quest. Has Prof. Langston any permanent house and home in the State of Vir-

ginia?—Answer. When Prof. Langston came to Petersburg in 1885 I was then secretary of the Virginia Normal and Collegiate Institute. I ofttimes had reason to consult Prof. Langston, who was at that time the president of that institution. He resided then at the corner of West street and Lee avenue. I think he has called that
his home ever since. I don't know positively whether that is his home or not.
(Record, 1038).

We have now quoted sufficiently from the record in this case to
show how greatly divided the Republican party of this district was in
the fall of 1888; quite enough to indicate beyond doubt that the dis-
sentions in its ranks were of such a character as to disorganize it and
give a harmonious and well-organized opposing party, though in the
minority, every hope of success; that the Democratic nominee was in
a position to draw from both factions of the Republican party, while
Arnold could not draw from Langston, nor Langston from Arnold.

It was then no surprise to the voters of the State when the result
was announced after the returns came in that Venable had received
13,298 votes, Langston 12,657 votes, and Arnold 3,267 votes, giving
Venable a plurality of 641 votes.

The surprise comes now when the Committee on Elections of the
House of Representatives, by a vote of 5 to 4 (two Republican and
two Democratic members being absent, and two Republican members
declining to vote), finds that John M. Langston, and not Edward C.
Venable, was duly elected to a seat in the Fifty-first Congress.

As members of this committee, we had carefully examined the record
in this case; we had listened attentively to the oral arguments and
closely studied the briefs filed, and we had come to the deliberate conclusion that no partisan feeling, however intense or blinding, could so
warp the facts or exclude the testimony as to result in a finding in
favor of the contestant.

We know that we are all liable, unconsciously it may be, to be
affected by party bias and to have our judgments swayed from the
right channel by partisan prejudices; but we felt that this was a case
so plain there was no place upon which to rest even a doubt, and that
there would be an unanimous decision in favor of the contestee.

In fact, we believed that nearly if not every member of the committee had rendered a verdict against the contestant in his own mind when,
after the argument, the case was submitted, and we were astounded
when we found such a change had come over our Republican colleagues.

Usually, in fact almost universally, when a contest is made for a seat on
the floor of Congress, the contestant makes charges against the opposite political party to which he belongs.

A Republican contestant charges fraud or improper conduct upon the
part of the Democratic party, and *vice versa*. In this instance, however, the contestant, though a Republican, bases his contest almost
exclusively upon charges against the chairman, committeemen, Federal
supervisors, and election officers of his own party.

In the record, and in his briefs, he charges a conspiracy upon the
part of General Mahone, and those he terms "Mahoneites," to defraud
him, and most unmercifully does he apply the lash to them.

On page 30, of one of his many briefs, he charges General Mahone
with former frauds. He goes back to the years 1874 and 1878, and
arraigns the chairman of the State committee of his party with ballot-
box stuffing and the use of fraudulent tickets. He says:

In the year 1874, when Wm. Hodges Mann, of Nottoway County, ran against Hon.
W. H. H. Stowell for Congress, and in the year 1878, when Wm. E. Hinton, jr., of
Petersburg, ran against Hon. Joseph Jorgenseon for Congress—while General Wm.

Mahone was an active partisan leader of the Democratic party in the Congressional district of which Petersburg was a part, and before he had been refused the Democratic nomination for governor of Virginia—the district was flooded with little ballots, then called "kiss-verse tickets," bearing the names of the Democratic candidates for Congress, and resembling in size and shape and texture the *interest coupons* which in these latter days are clipped from corporation coupon bonds. A *fac-simile* of one of these ballots is produced here. The originals were printed on tissue paper.

City of Petersburgh. Virginia.
ELECTION, November 3rd, 1874.
For Representative in Congress From 4th District; Judge **WM. H. MANN,** of Nottoway County.

Again, on page 35, he says:

3. It is alleged and proved that Mahone procured and had printed and circulated a letter from Frederick Douglass, dated August 15, 1888, and addressed to George Fayerman, Peter G. Morgan, and other political intimates of Mahone, opposing the nomination of John M. Langston as a candidate for Congress, at the Republican convention then called to be held in Farmville in the month of September following. (Rec., pp. 884, 886.)

He quotes approvingly, on page 38, the following attack on General Mahone, which appeared in the columns of the New York Tribune:

General Mahone's charges about Mr. Blaine's conspiring against him in Virginia have as much truth in them as the statements just noted. It is a poor cause that stands in need of tactics like these, and Virginia Republicans will do well, in the light of this exposure, to take very little advice from General Mahone hereafter as to their conduct in national politics.

*   *   *   *   *   *   *

We take pleasure in saying that whereas we have sometimes suffered ourselves to be persuaded in the past that General Mahone was an honorable and efficient leader of Virginia Republicanism, our better judgment has always inclined us to the common belief, which has now become a settled conviction, that he is a selfish and malicious trickster, unfit for the leadership of any cause which has not for its sole motive and object the elevation of William Mahone.

Again on page 48, he says:

Proof of the enthusiastic solidarity of the colored Republicans could not further go. What chance had Arnold and Mahone, or Venable, without fraud and bribery, to get votes out of such a constituency.

The testimony in other parts of the record, and the incessant wailings of Arnold and Mahone and Venable ever since this contest began, prove that in the other counties of the district and in the city of Petersburgh the feeling was as intense, and the purpose to vote for Langston as determined, as they were in Sussex.

No, no! no!! Mahone's opposition to Langston does not give even colorable support to Mr. Venable's pretended plurality.

FALSE PRETENSES.

But, in very truth, the reason assigned by Mahone as excuse for his opposition to Langston's candidacy before the Farmville convention, was a false pretense; and the colored Republicans of the Fourth district knew it. As a pretense, it was good enough and plausible enough to deceive and mislead some Republican statesmen who were captivated by the idea of winning recruits from Democratic ranks, and, unfortunately, were persuaded to accept Mr. Mahone's assurances as evidence of truth.

Again, on page 52, he assails the great Republican leader of his party in Virginia in the following style:.

Mahone foresaw in Langston a local rival. He will endure no rivalry. He recoils from the perils of comparisons, which are to him very odious. So long as Langston might wish to be the Republican candidate for Congress from the Fourth Congressional district of Virginia there seemed to be no chance for Mahone. The thought distressed him. One can imagine Mahone in soliloquy, muttering the words which Prince Henry outspoke in the altercation with Harry Hotspur which preluded their fatal duel:

> I am the Prince of W[h]ales; and think not, [Langston],
> To share with me in glory any more..
> Two stars keep not their motion in one sphere;
> Nor can one [district] bear the double reign
> Of [John M. Langston] and the Prince of W[h]ales.

Delendo est Carthago! Langston must go under! And now, "grand, gloomy, and peculiar, he sits upon his throne a sceptered hermit, wrapped in the solitude of his own originality."

The meanness of the motive was as patent as the deceitfulness of the pretense. The negroes were not deceived. But they were deeply grieved to see a selfish and unscrupulous man—who entered the Senate of the United States in December, 1881, as a Hancock and English Democrat-Readjuster—permitted again to wield his merciless and masterful lash, and to insult, degrade, and torture the African race in the person of their Representative; and they huddled together with the instinct of self-preservation. If all the ballots which were truly cast and deposited for Langston by the colored Republicans of the district had been honestly canvassed, counted, and returned, Mr. Langston would have had a majority over both of his competitors. Mr. Langston has been assured by many colored Democrats that they voted for him.

Read here how he pours out his wrath upon the "Prince of W(h)ales," as he contemptuously terms General Mahone in his soliloquy above (page 57):

The contestee and his advocates reproach Mr. Langston for not attending a meeting at the Academy of Music, in the city of Petersburg, when Senator Blair, of New Hampshire, delivered a speech under the auspices of General Mahone. They say:
"You chose to absent yourself, and were represented at that meeting only by a crowd of your boisterous and ill-mannered followers and supporters, who offered insults to General Mahone while he was introducing Senator Blair to the audience." (See brief for contestee, near bottom of page 13.)
What tender solicitude for Mahone!
Mr. Langston was not there, and is hardly responsible for the manners of "followers," who, if they had followed him, would have been at home. As was expected, Mahone abused the confidence of Senator Blair, and tried to use his name, character, and influence for the purpose of insulting and degrading the colored men of Petersburg, and Langston as their representative. Mahone hired the hall and controlled it. White Republicans were admitted upon the main floor, to the lower portion of the house, but colored Republicans were compelled to go up in the gallery. This order was enforced by John Crosstick and E. T. Berry, two white men who had been policemen. And after the election, both of said persons were appointed by the Democratic municipal authorities of Petersburg to salaried offices. (Rec., pp. 120, 536, etc.)

But he does not stop, as we have said, in his attacks upon the chairman of the State committee of his party, but in his notice of contest and in his briefs he charges the Republican judges of election, Republican clerks of election, and Republican Federal supervisors all over the district with ballot-box stuffing, false counts, and frauds generally.

In his notice of contest he assails the returns as fraudulent, and charges the election officers with fraud at the following precincts

Lewiston, Columbian Grove, Meherrin, Brown's Store, Pleasant Grove, Rehoboth, Knight's and Oliver's Mills, and Lochleven, in Lunenburg County; Blackstone, in Nottoway County; Hicksford, Zion or Moss, Belfield and Trotter's Store, in Greenville County; Rives, in Prince George County; South Hill, in Mecklenburg County; Ballsville, in Powhatan County; Rice's and Spring Creek, in Prince Edward County; Tillman's and Edmunds' Store, in Brunswick County; New Hope, Sutherland, and Court House, in Dinwiddie County; first election district, First ward, Third Ward, Fourth ward, and Sixth ward. Petersburg City.

H. Mis. 137——31

Now let us see to what party or parties the election officers who are so vigorously assailed by the contestant belonged:

	Federal supervisors.		Judges.				Federal supervisors.		Judges.		
	Republican.	Democrat.	Republican.	Democrat.	Doubtful.		Republican.	Democrat.	Republican.	Democrat.	Doubtful.
Lewiston	1	....	1	1	1	Rives*	....	....	....	....	....
Columbian Grove	1	....	1	2	....	South Hill*	....	....	....	....	....
Meherrien	....	1	....	2	1	Ballsville*	....	....	....	....	....
Brown's Store	1	1	1	2	....	Rice's	1	....	1	2	....
Pleasant Grove*	....	....	....	....	....	Spring Creek*	....	....	....	....	....
Rehoboth*	....	....	....	....	....	Tillman & Edmunds' Store*	....	....	....	....	....
Knight's & Oliver's Mills*	....	....	....	....	....	New Hope*	....	....	....	....	....
Lochleven*	....	....	....	....	....	Sutherland*	....	....	....	....	....
Blackstone	....	....	L1	2	....	Court-House*	....	....	....	....	....
Hicksford	1	....	L1	2	....	First ward, first precinct†	1	1	1	2	....
Zion or Moss†	1	1	1	2	....	Third ward†	1	....	1	2	....
Belfield†	....	....	1	2	....	Fourth ward*†	....	....	....	....	....
Trotter's Store†	....	....	L1	2	....	Sixth ward	1	....	1	2	....

* No testimony.
† Much testimony was taken by the contestant at these precincts, but his own supporters disproved his charges, and he abandons them. His charges embraced 27 precincts, but he took no testimony to sustain his allegations at 14 of them.

It will be observed that at every precinct at which he took testimony, excepting one, there was a Republican official, and that at all but three there were Republican Federal supervisors, and two of these three precincts he abandoned. So that we have:

Precincts assailed 27
Precincts where no testimony was taken..13
Precincts where testimony was taken, at which there were Republican judges....12
Precincts where testimony was taken, at which there were Republican Federal supervisors 9

We say that the contestant has charged the election officers of his own party with the great crime of cheating and defrauding him out of his election, and that he comes before the House and country arraigning generally the election officials of the party of which he professes to be such a warm adherent, as deep-dyed criminals.

He has, however, the satisfaction of knowing that he has convicted Republican officials as well as the chairman of the Republican committee of the State of Virginia by the verdict of five Republican members of the Committee on Elections of the House of Representatives, and that while these officials and the chairman and leader of his party stand condemned, he stands approved, indorsed and sustained by this verdict of five out of nine Republican members of the committee, or five out of fifteen members composing the whole committee.

Whether the House of Representatives with its three hundred and thirty members will affirm this verdict and place its stamp of condemnation upon these men or send him away with his false clamor remains to be determined.

We propose now to refer to the positions taken by the majority in their report.

POACH AND ROSS.

They claim that the returns from Poach and Ross precinct in Brunswick County, which gave Langston 141 votes and Venable 69 votes, and which were rejected by the canvassing board, should be counted.

We find that these returns were rejected because they were not made in accordance with the directory provisions of the election statute of Virginia; and, in the absence of any suspicions of fraud, or evidence tending to impeach their correctness, we think they should be counted.

	Venable.	Langston.
Take their returned vote	13,298	12,657
Add vote at Poach and Ross	69	141
Total	13,367	12,798

Majority for Venable 569.

MANNBORO, AMELIA COUNTY.

The majority of the committee reject the vote at this precinct, which was counted by the canvassing board, upon the ground that there are no returns.

It is true the returns from this precinct were not signed by the officers of election, and if the question had been raised in the notice of contest and no evidence taken to show their correctness, we would agree with the majority that they should be rejected. But the notice of contest, will be examined in vain for any charge or reference to this precinct.

It is unnecessary to refer to a principle so well settled that a contestant must be confined to his allegations and the contestee can not be required to do more than meet them. The contestee, finding no charge as to this precinct, was justified in ignoring any attack which the contestant made on it in his testimony. The vote as counted was Venable 122, Langston 111.

SIXTH WARD OF PETERSBURGH.

According to the returns from this precinct:

	Votes.
Venable received	352
Langston received	139
Arnold received	160
Total	651

The majority of the committee propose "to readjust" the vote at this precinct by rejecting the returns as an entirety, and then giving Langston 377 votes (which they claim have been proved to have been cast for him), and Venable none.

This is at least a startling proposition. Let us examine the facts.

The election was conducted by two Democratic and *one Republican judge*, and one Democratic and *one Republican clerk*, and watched by one Democratic and *one Republican Federal supervisor*. All were intelligent white men.

B. D. Akers, one of the judges, testified that he turned the ballot-box upside down and exposed it to the judges, clerks, and United States supervisors in the morning, before the balloting commenced. (Question 16, Record, 819.)

That there were Republican tickets at the polls in circulation with Venable's name on them, similar to the regular Republican ticket and Langston ticket, and that they could not be distinguished except by reading them. (Questions 54–62, Record, 821.)

That both of the supervisors were present from the opening of the polls to the closing. (Question 75, Record, 822).

That both supervisors personally scrutinized the count and canvass of all the ballots cast. (Question 85, Record, 824.)

That during the entire day they were in a position to see all that transpired in the voting place, and that the Republican supervisor sat by the side of the ballot-box with his face to the judges and clerks, and could see the ballots as they were handed in by the voters, and as they were deposited by the judges in the ballot box. (Question 92–4, Record, 824–5.)

That there was no discrimination made between white and colored voters, and many colored voters voted in the white line; that there was no unnecessary delay in receiving the ballots, and that a vote was cast about every minute. (Question 100–110, Record, 825.)

And his examination-in-chief concludes with the following question and answer—the one as searching as possible and the other thoroughly responsive:

134. *Q. Can you or not, now that you have been fully questioned as to the election held in sixth ward, in the city of Petersburg, on the sixth day of November, 1888, state that the returns of that election, as made to the clerk of the hustings court of Petersburg and now on file in his office, contain a full, complete, and accurate statement of the number of ballots cast at sixth ward voting place on that day and of the number cast for each candidate voted for at that election?—A. Yes, sir; I can and do so state.* (Record, 827.)

Cross-examination:

37. Q. Were any other persons present in the polling-room at sixth ward on 6th of Nov., 1888, from the opening of the polls to the sealing of the poll-books and ballots, besides the judges and clerks of election and U. S. supervisors already named?—A. No, sir; excepting the boy that brought the meals.

38. Q. Were any of these persons absent from the polling-room at any time after entering upon the discharge of their duties to said sealing of the poll-books and ballots?—A. No, sir; with the exception of one time when Mr. Scott went outside to stop the loud talking and noise, he being the only one to my recollection that left the room during the day.

39. Q. Mr. E. T. Berry, U. S. supervisor, has testified that at the closing of the polls the box was opened and the ballots were dumped in a pile upon the table. Does that agree with your recollection?—A. Yes, sir.

40. Q. You have stated that the ballots were then canvassed by the judges. Were the ballots opened at this time, or counted folded. I mean just as voted?—A. Yes, sir. I canvassed them folded. No one counted them but myself, with the judges and supervisors and clerks looking on.

41. Q. Did the tickets found in the box exceed the names on the poll-books?—A. No, sir. It was short one ballot.

42. Do you remember whether there were any tickets, when the counting came to be done, having the name of one candidate for Congress scratched therefrom, and another name substituted?—A. Yes, sir. There were twelve scratched ballots. Ten of them had Langston's name scratched out and Venable's name written in pencil in place; one with Arnold's name scratched out and no name written in the place of it; one with Venable's name scratched out and no name written in place of it.

43. Q. Was there any considerable number of ballots voted openly at sixth ward on the 6th Nov., 1888?—A. There was. There was a good many white and a good many colored, and a good many of both voted their ballots folded.

44. Q. When a ballot was handed you open, did you not necessarily see what names some of them contained?—A. Yes, sir.

45. Q. You always folded a ballot before depositing it in the box, did you not?—A. Yes, sir.

46. Q. During the count of the vote to ascertain the number of votes received by each candidate, did you again count all the ballots yourself while the other officers looked on, or were the ballots divided into portions and each portion counted by a different person?—A. All three of the judges separated the ballots into piles of fifty or a hundred, dividing the Democratic ballots from the Republican. As soon as this

was done we counted the Democratic ballots to find out the number of votes cast for the electors, and Republican likewise. Then we separated the Republican ballots to get at the name of the Congressmen at the bottom, and we separated those ballots, putting the Langston ballots to themselves, the Venable ballots to themselves, and the Arnold ballots to themselves. Then we counted them and gave each candidate what those ballots called for. I counted myself all of the tickets for Congressman, and requested Mr. Berry to count them after me for fear of mistake. This being finished we examined the scratched tickets, and gave to each one what those tickets called for.

47. Q. During all this separation and counting. who, if any one, handled the ballots besides yourself, Eckles, and Lewis ?—A. No one.

48. Q. Did neither of the U. S. supervisors or clerks help to divide the ballots into piles of fifty or a hundred ?—A. No sir.

49. Q. Did not Mr. Berry handle the ballots when he counted them at your request ?—A. Yes, sir; he handled them to see if my count was correct and also to satisfy himself.

50. Q. Did Mr. Scott handle the ballots to the same extent ?—A. No, sir; he never touched a ballot during the day.

51. Q. You are certain, then, that neither of the clerks of election handled the ballots at all ?—A. Yes, sir; I am certain. (Record, 830, 831.)

This witness stands unimpeached. The contestant did not call a witness to testify that he was not a man of truth and integrity. He is an old resident of Petersburg and has held responsible positions in the city government.

We refer now to the testimony of the Republican Federal supervisor who was an office-holder for years under the Republican administration of the city.

E. T. Berry testified he was a Republican; that he was appointed Federal supervisor as a representative of the Republican party by the Chief United States supervisor, M. F. Pleasants; that he was inside the voting place every moment of the time between the opening and closing of the polls, except once about a minute, during the daytime, when he appointed some one in his stead and retired to meet a call of nature. (Questions 11, 12, 14, 15, 16, 33, Record, 843, 844.)

That he agreed to act as supervisor at the request of Harrison Waite, chairman of the Republican City Executive Committee. (Questions 42, 43, 44, Record, 844, 845.)

That he personally watched the counting of the ballots and the making of the return; *that he personally scrutinized, counted, and canvassed each ballot cast at that precinct, and that the return made by the judges and clerks is a full, fair, and accurate statement of the number of ballots cast on that day at :hat precinct, and a true and accurate statement of the number of ballots cast for each candidate voted for at that election.* (Questions 48, 49, 50, Record, 845.)

That there was no discrimination between white and colored voters; that he saw Republican tickets at the polls with Venable's name on them, and that there was no difference in the appearance of the various Republican tickets which were in circulation. (Questions 51, 58, 59, 60, 61, Record, 845.)

On cross-examination he testified that the judges, clerks, and supervisors were all present during the count and canvass of the vote. (Record, 861.)

This witness was subjected to a most severe cross-examination; no less than four hundred and thirty-four cross-questions were propounded to him, but the only effect it had was to emphasize the fact that he was an ardent and enthusiastic Republican and a close political friend of the Republican State chairman, General Mahone, and that the election was fairly conducted and the returns absolutely honest.

No witness was called to attack his character.

E. J. Bond testified that he was present at the polls when they were opened and was there all the time until they were closed, with the exception of about ten or fifteen minutes twice; that the full Demócratic vote was out; that one of the judges displayed the ballot-box to all that were present to show that it was empty before any ballots were received; that he (the witness) objected to E. T. Berry serving as Federal supervisor upon the ground that he had not been appointed for that precinct, but withdrew his objection when Berry presented his commission; that when he made his objection there were supporters of Langston at the polls and within hearing, but they made no objection to Berry; that Langston was at the polls also, but he heard of no objection to Berry upon his part; that Arnold had all the white and many of the colored Republicans supporting him at this precinct, and he saw many colored men in line with Arnold tickets in their hands; that he knew of Republicans who voted for Harrison and Morton and Venable; that he saw no discrimination upon the part of the election officers; that there were colored clubs organized for the support of Venable, and he heard of colored Arnold clubs. (Record, 870–872.)

His examination-in-chief concludes with the following questions and answers:

40. Did U. States Supervisor Berry remain inside the polling place all day?—Ans. He did, so far as I know, as I did not see him come out any time during the day.

41. After the polls had closed did you see any of the officers of election come out of the polling place before the vote had been counted?—Ans. I did not.

42. After the polls had closed, did you see any one go in while the vote was being counted and canvassed?—Ans. I did not.

43. Did you see or hear the officers of election refuse to admit any one applying for entrance?—Ans. I did not hear any one applying, therefore heard no one refused.

44. Please say whether or not any act of fraud or illegality came under your observation at 6th ward during the conduct of that election.—Ans. I did not.

45. *Was or was it not, so far as you could see, a fairly conducted election?*—Ans. *From the time that I saw them in the morning until I left at night, I saw nothing that was unfair or unlawful. Mr. Alexander Hamilton, a friend of Mr. Venable, was present some time during the day, and asked me how the voting was progressing, and I answered "Very well." He said to me, "Urge your judges to vote the voters as rapidly as they can," which I did do on more than one occasion. On the occasion of Mr. Butler Mahone's timing the voting, he said to me "A good many voters at that precinct were complaining to his father, General Mahone, that they, the voters, were being voted too slowly at 6th ward precinct, and that if they were not voted faster he would be obliged to have the judges of election arrested for unnecessarily delaying the voting." But after timing them he was satisfied, and said he would go and tell his father that he thought they were being voted as fast as possible.*

We have the sworn returns of the judges and clerks of election, Democratic and Republican, and also of the Federal supervisors, Democratic and Republican. In addition we have the depositions of one of the Democratic judges and the Republican Federal supervisor swearing unqualifiedly to the correctness and honesty of the returns, and other evidence of a corroborative character.

In election cases, however, before a return can be set aside, there must be proof that the proceedings in the conduct of the election, or in the return of the vote, were so tainted with fraud, that the truth can not be deduced from the returns. (McCrary, § 534, and seq.)

The returns must stand until such facts are proven as to clearly show that it is not true. (McCrary, § 536.)

The official acts of sworn officers are presumed to be honest and correct until the contrary is made to appear. (McCrary, § 538.)

The presumption is that an election is honestly conducted, and the burthen of proof to show it otherwise, is on the party assailing the returns. (McCrary, § 542; Paine, §§ 759, 762, 763, 764.)

The maxim that "fraud is not to be presumed" applies as well to the conduct of elections and making returns, as to transactions between individuals; and there is also a stronger presumption against fraud which arises from the acts of public officers, acting under the sanction of their official oaths; and nothing but the most *credible, positive,* and *unequivocal evidence* should be permitted to destroy official returns. It is not sufficient to cast *suspicion* upon them; they must be *proved* fraudulent before they are rejected. (6 A. and E. En. of Law. Elections, p. 354, and authorities there cited. Paine, §§ 759, 762, 763.)

How and upon what evidence do the majority of the committee in the face of the sworn returns of the officers of election sustained by the depositions of the officials just named and others, propose to set aside and discard the returns at this precinct and give Langston 377 votes and Venable none?

Ignoring completely the testimony just quoted, the majority refer to and set out *in extenso* the testimony of two witnesses, Thomas H. Brown and Pleasant Goodwyn, both colored. Brown swears that he was at the polls all day except about fifteen minutes, assisting Goodwyn in keeping the names of the colored voters who voted for Harrison, Morton, and Langston, by checking the names on a registration list as Goodwyn named them; that he could tell they voted for Langston because he saw their tickets when they were given to the judge of election, *as each* of them voted an open ballot; that he was standing within 2 feet of the door and about 4 feet from the judge when at the ballot-box, and that 370 names were recorded.

Goodwyn swears that he was engaged in recording the names of colored voters who voted for Harrison, Morton, and Langston, and that he occupied a chair nearly the entire day within 2 feet of the door of the polling place and about 4 feet from the judges who received the ballots the entire day, and that he received 408 names and that 377 of them voted for Langston.

The improbability of Brown and Goodwyn's stories is so strong that we can not see how they can be relied upon to set aside the solemn returns of election officers. Common sense and experience teach us that it was impossible for these men to observe the tickets and watch the movements of 377 men running through an entire day—from the rising to the setting of the sun—and these men mixed up and necessarily shifting their positions in a crowd of 600 or 700 voters, and at the same time record their names on one book and check them on another.

Besides, it is hard to believe that physical endurance could have been equal to the task of remaining in one position, jammed by the multitude for twelve hours without food or drink (for they had neither according to their testimony), and without nature calling them away from their post for a moment.

We say to believe such testimony, if it stood uncontradicted, and the witnesses were men whose characters were as high as any in the land, would tax human credulity too much.

But they are contradicted, in that it is shown that they were not engaged in taking and checking the names at the point they swear they occupied the entire day.

They say they were within 2 feet of the door and about 4 feet from the judge who received the ballots, and that they saw every ballot before it was deposited, and saw it handed to the judge and saw the judge deposit it in the box.

Akers, the judge who received the ballots, contradicted them:

71. Q. Did you or not see Pleasant Goodwyn and Thos. H. Brown at sixth ward voting place that day? If you did, state where you saw them.—A. I do not know Pleasant Goodwyn, and I know Thos. H. Brown by sight. I saw *Thos. H. Brown once* during the day, and he was *standing about eight feet from the door leaning up against the fence.* (Record, 822.)

75. Q. Pleasant Goodwyn, in answer to question 15, on his direct examination in behalf of the contestant, has used the following language: "I was as close to the judge as the wall of the door would permit me between him and the box." You have said that you do not know Pleasant Goodwyn by sight. Did you or not see any person in the place thus described?—A. *I did not see any one but William H. Jordan.* He was the *only* one I saw *near the door.* (Record, 822.)

Neither Townes nor Harris, the Langston ticket distributers, even mention the names of Brown and Goodwyn in their lengthy depositions, and no other witness of the many examined by the contestant refer directly or indirectly to these two men who, according to their statements, were within an arm's reach of the ballot-box every minute of the day scrutinizing the tickets in the hands of the voters, receiving and checking their names.

Could they have occupied such a conspicuous position at the polls and been visible only to each other?

We insist that the returns from this precinct can not be destroyed by such testimony, when under the law "nothing but the most *credible, positive,* and *unequivocal evidence* should be permitted."

Continuing our examination of the evidence as to this precinct, we find that Richard Townes and J. York Harris testify that they issued *all* of the Langston tickets that were placed in the hands of the voters. (Record, 283–292.)

Townes testifies he issued 150. (Record, 286.) Harris is silent as to the number he issued. (Record, 291.) So there is no proof that more than 150 Langston tickets were issued, and the returns gave him 139 votes.

But there is no evidence whatever that either Townes or Harris issued Langston tickets except what they declare themselves. Townes says he got the tickets from Colonel Brady who was Langston's manager, but Townes could not read, as will be seen from the following extract from his deposition:

25th. Question. You say that you can read enough to see that the name of John M. Langston was on your ticket. Can you spell "Langston"?—Answer. I don't say that I can spell the whole, but I can spell the first three letters in his name.
26th. Question. Can you tell a capital L from a capital T by sight?—Answer. I can't say that I can; but what I had reference to on the ticket the reading commenced with a "J."J-O-M—John—the way I spelled it.
27th. Question. Then this J-O-M was the only part of John M. Langston's name you could read, was it?—Answer. Distinctly, I meant to say and I know that there were no other John's name on the ticket who were running for Congress.
28th. Question. Can you tell me any other letters at all which followed this J-O-M on the ticket?—Answer. I can't say that I can right now.
29th. Question. You say that J-O-M was the only part of John M. Langston's name which you distinctly read. Did you read the balance of his name indistinctly?—Answer. I did not. Whenever I looked at the ticket and discovered the letters J-O-M I was satisfied it was Langston's ticket.
30th. Question. You are satisfied, then, that the ticket you voted had J-O-M on it, are you?—Answer. I am.
31st. Question. Then if J-O-M was the only part of the ticket which you could read, how can you swear that the balance of the name was the balance of John M. Langston's name?—Answer. The J-O-M I could make out on the ticket myself, and I had my brother-in-law to read the ticket from bottom to top to me before I attempted to vote; and not only him, I had the ticket read during the day by several other young men that were around, and I had no other tickets in my possession. (Rec., 286–7.)

It is a significant fact that though Colonel Brady lived in Petersburgh, he was never called as a witness to verify the statement of Townes.

We must infer that Brady's testimony would not have aided the contestant, else it would have been taken.

The witnesses who testified that they got their tickets from Townes could not read, and knew nothing but what Townes told them.

So we have simply this summary of facts : That Townes, an ignorant colored man who could not read, issued 150 tickets without any knowledge as to what was printed on them, and 150 colored men who could not read voted them without knowing what tickets they were voting except what Townes, equally as ignorant as themselves, told them. Upon this statement it is proposed to reject the returns from this precinct and "readjust" them by counting all these votes and many more for the contestant.

What a travesty upon justice !

The sworn declarations of the three judges, two clerks, and two Federal supervisors are to be set aside as false, and these officers branded as liars, perjurers, and ballot-box stuffers upon the testimony of Townes.

We can not believe the House of Representatives will perpetrate what we conceive to be so great a wrong.

But pursuing our examination of this precinct still further, we say there is no evidence that these voters who got tickets from Townes (assuming that they were Langston tickets) voted them. No one saw the tickets they actually voted, as they were handed to the judge at the ballot-box, and we have only their simple statement that they handed the ballots they received from Townes to the judge. There is no way to contradict this statement, and therefore how dangerous it is to receive such testimony to destroy the returns of public officers, in favor of which the law raises the strongest presumption. Each one of these voters stands upon his own unsupported statement, while every one of them is contradicted by all the officers of the election, so far as their testimony tends to falsify the return.

In this ward the testimony of the contestant's witnesses shows that there are at least 220 white Democratic voters and not less than 20 straight colored Democratic voters. The evidence further shows that the full Democratic vote was out at the election in question. If it is determined to give Langston 377 votes upon such testimony as that of Brown and Goodwyn, a modicum of justice at least would require that the Democratic vote of 240 (220+20) should be given to Venable.

Then up to this point the vote would stand as follows :

	Venable.	Langston.
Vote as returned...	13,298	12,657
Add vote at Poach and Ross	69	141
	13,367	12,798
Deduct returned vote Sixth ward, Petersburgh..........	352	139
	13,015	12,659
Add "reformed" vote, Sixth ward, Petersburgh	240	377
	13,255	13,036

Majority for Venable over Langston, 219 votes.

While still insisting that the effort to impeach the returned vote in this ward has utterly failed, yet if it is determined to discard the returns, the vote should at least be so "readjusted" as to give the contestee the well-defined Democratic vote which was cast for him.

THIRD WARD OF PETERSBURGH.

The vote as returned from this precinct was as follows:

	Votes.
Venable	518
Langston	174
Arnold	105
Total	797

The majority of the committee propose to reject these returns as a whole and so "readjust" them as to give Langston 284 votes and Venable none.

Against this proposition we enter a protest far stronger than even in the case of the Sixth ward.

This ward extends through the most populous, business, and residence portion of the city. It is largely a white ward and has for years been known as a reliable Democratic ward. In 1886 it elected a Democratic council ticket by a large majority. In the spring of 1888, Collier, Democrat, received 484 votes; Bolling, Republican, received 305 votes, in the mayoralty election. In neither of these elections was there even a suspicion of fraud. It is the place of residence of the great body of white Republicans, who were, according to the evidence, almost unanimously supporters of Arnold.

The majority of the committee in their report base their conclusions upon the testimony of Matt N. Lewis and W. J. Smith.

Lewis testifies he kept a record at the polls of this ward of the votes cast for Langston; that he stood right at the entrance where the colored voters approached the ballot-box, and where he could see the ballots given to the judge who received the ballots and deposited them in the box; that he was there from sunrise until sunset, only leaving once for about thirty minutes; that he saw and read the ballot of every voter whose name he checked on his book and he saw each ballot he checked deposited in the ballot-box; that he entered himself in his book, in his own handwriting, all the names with the exception of a few that were entered during the thirty minutes he was absent from the polls; that he read each ballot carefully. He gives the names of 286 voters as having been recorded by him and as having voted for Langston except two. He says 16 of the 286 were entered during his absence by Smith.

This is a full summary of this man's testimony.

Before introducing the evidence thoroughly contradicting the statements of this witness it may be well to indicate the character of man he is:

In the hustings court of the city of Petersburg, October 21, 1887, C. H. Cuthbert, foreman, W. H. Harrison, J. B. Brady, J. P. Hoag, John Berry, and John H. Bell were sworn as grand jurors for the body of this city, and having received their charge retired to their room, and after some time spent therein returned into the court and presented an indictment against Matt N. Lewis—"a true bill"—which is as follows, viz:

STATE OF VIRGINIA,
    City of Petersburg, to wit:

In the hustings court of the said city, the jurors of the Commonwealth of Virginia, in and for the body of the city of Petersburg, and now attending the said court, upon their oath present, that on the 30th day of August, in the year 1887, in said city, T. J. Jarratt was the legally qualified mayor of said city, and as such a justice of the peace thereof, and that Matt N. Lewis, on said day, in said year, in said city, being an evil disposed person, and unjustly and unlawfully intending to defame, asperse, scandalize, and vilify the character of the said T. J. Jarratt, and to insinuate, and cause it to be believed that the said T. J. Jarratt had been guilty of gross misconduct in his said office of mayor of said city and justice of the peace as aforesaid, did unlawfully, maliciously, wickedly, and scandalously compose, write, print, and publish, and did cause and procure to be composed, written, printed, and published in a certain public newspaper, entitled the "Daily Index Appeal," which newspaper was then and there circulated in said city, a certain false, wicked, mischievous, and scandalous libel of and concerning the said T. J. Jarratt, and of and concerning his official conduct in his said office of mayor of said city and justice of the peace as aforesaid, and of and concerning the administration of public justice in the mayor's court of said city whilst he, the said T. J. Jarratt, was presiding and sitting therein as mayor of said city and justice of the peace as aforesaid, which wicked, mischievous, and scandalous libel is in the words and figures as follows, to wit:

"COMMUNICATED.

"At a meeting of colored men, called on Monday evening, August 29, 1887, the following resolutions were offered and adopted:

" Whereas on Tuesday, August 23, 1887, an unsophisticated colored man (Ed. Ridley), in an unguarded moment, assaulted a lady who had first assaulted him, he was set upon by a crowd of white men and most brutally and unmercifully beaten, thereby taking the law in their own hands;

" Whereas, although he (Ed. Ridley) applied to the proper authorities for warrants for the punishment of his assailant, he was denied that right, which is common property of all American citizens, 'the right of protection by law,' and instead of being the complainant he was forced to be the defendant before the laws (he, said Matt N. Lewis, meaning one Fed Ridley, sometimes called Edward Ridley, who on the 25th day of August, in said year, was convicted before him, said T. J. Jarratt, mayor of said city and justice of the peace as aforesaid, of having made an assault in and upon one Louisa F. De Jarnette, in said city, on said 23d day of August, in said year);

" Whereas the mayor of our city, the proper person from whom all citizens expect even-handed and equal justice, has seen fit (yielding to a false and mean clamor of supposed public sentiment) to impose a most extortional fine and unprecedented sentence upon this poor colored man;

" Whereas the mayor has had numerous cases of the same nature and kind, i. e., the case of Mr. W. I. Jarratt, vs. his cook, the case of W. E. Wyatt vs. a colored woman, the case of —— Clarke vs. a colored girl in the employ of his father (T. Jeff. Clarke), and these cases were more aggravated than that of Ridley's, and the mayor never has imposed further than a small fine in either case: Therefore,

"Resolved, That we condemn his sentence in this case of Ridley as that of a prejudicial officer, a bias judge, and unqualified chief magistrate, and further characterize the whole affair as an outrage and disgrace to the civilization of the 19th century, and a travesty upon justice.

"MATT N. LEWIS,
"W. N. SMITH,
"H. C. KENNEDY,
"*Committee.*"

" an. 30–1t "

(he, said Matt N. Lewis, meaning that he, said T. J. Jarratt, was the mayor of said city referred to in said libel, and that his, said T. J. Jarratt's, sentence in said case of said Ridley, convicted as aforesaid, was the official act of a prejudiced, biased, and and unqualified mayor of said city, and as such a justice of the peace as aforesaid) to the great damage and infamy of the said T. J. Jarratt, to the great scandal and dishonor of public justice, and against the peace and dignity of the Commonwealth of Virginia.

Upon the testimony of T. J. Jarratt, D. L. Selke, and F. R. Russell, T. C. Johnson, W H. Jones, T. G. Watkins, sworn in court and sent to the grand jury to give evidence.

JOHN C. ARMISTEAD, C.

And in said court Monday, January 30, 1888.

The Commonwealth of Va., prosecuting, against Matt N. Lewis, defendant.   Ind'ct, misd'm'r.

This day came as well the attorney for the Commonwealth as the defendant in own proper person, and thereupon said defendant pleaded guilty, and a jury, to wit, G. W. Bain, J. W. Wheary, E. M. Allen, C. H. Marshall, J. T. Ashby, R. F. Hobbs, C. J.

Walthall, R. T. Coghill, A. J. Clements, E. W. Sydnor, E. J. Armstrong, and J. T. Garrett, was selected by ballot and duly sworn by consent of the defendant, and having heard the evidence of witnesses and arguments of counsel, returned their verdict as follows: We, the jury find the accused guilty, and make the fine twenty-five dollars. Therefore it is considered by the court that the Commonwealth recover against the said defendant said fine of $25 and the costs of his own prosecution.

Copies.
Teste:

RO. GILLIAM, *Clerk.*

(Record 989–991.)

This high-handed act upon the part of this man is not calculated to commend him to favorable consideration. The mayor of the city of Petersburgh, who was a Republican, was libeled by this would-be exemplar of public morals because he refused to issue a warrant for the arrest of a white lady, for "assaulting an unsophisticated colored man" who in "an unguarded moment" had committed an assault upon her.

But now to the contradictions of this witness.

German H. Gill, Federal Supervisor.

22d. Question. Do you know a colored man called Matt N. Lewis?—A. Yes.

23d. Question. Did you see him on the 6th of November, 1888; and if so, state where he was, what he was doing, and how long he staid at the 3d ward polls on that day?—Ans. I saw him. He stood just opposite the door, about 4 feet distant. He seemed to be keeping a tally of the colored. He was there about two-thirds of the time. He was away several times during the day, making in all, I should judge, about one-third of the day that he was absent.

24th. Question. It has been testified by the said Lewis in this case that he was there, *i. e.*, immediately in front of the 3d ward ballot-box, from sunrise until sunset, only leaving once about thirty minutes. Please state whether or not the said testimony is true, and your reasons for your answer?—Ans. It is not. My reason for so stating is that another took his place on more than one occasion that day, and I saw him several times walk away from his position 20 or 30 feet, and would remain away for several minutes conversing with parties around the polls.

25th. Question. Were the persons who kept his tally-book in his absence under his immediate superintendence and direction when they entered the names of voters upon their books?—Ans. No, sir.

26th. Question. There have been filed in the record as a part of the testimony of the said Lewis four books purporting to be the tally-books which he kept on November 6th, 1888, at the 3d ward polls, containing the names of more than 200 voters whose ballots he swore were given for Jno. M. Langston. In answer to the following question asked the said Lewis on his direct examination, to wit, "When and under what circumstances did you particularly observe the ballot of each colored voter before recording his name in said book," the said Lewis replied: "I read his ballot carefully, and after I had seen the judge to whom he handed his ballot deposit it in the ballot-box I then placed his name on my book." Please state whether this reply of the said Lewis is true, and give your reasons.—Ans. It can not be true. For the reasons that unless the ballots were handed by the voters to Lewis he could not read them carefully, which was not done. The voters coming up in line handed their ballots to the judge without passing them to Lewis for examination. A large number of them he could not have read at all, the parties not showing or holding them to him for that purpose; at least one-half or more voting folded or closed ballots.

27th. Question. Did you see any voter hold his ballot before Lewis for examination?—Ans. No; not directly to Lewis. I saw several hold their ballots above their heads unfolded, and it would have been impossible for Lewis to see what names were on the ballots, unless he had remarkable eye-sight. I was as near to them as he with glasses on and I could not read them.

28th. Question. Would your answers to the 26th and 27th questions apply equally to the parties who kept the books in the absence of Lewis?—Ans. They would.

29th. Question. Do you know the fact that it was suggested at the time by parties about the polls that the Langston tally-keepers were recording votes cast for one of the other candidates?—Ans. Yes; I heard the report and heard parties joking Lewis and others about it.

30th. Question. Were there any ballots distributed at the 3d ward polls bearing the Republican Presidential electors with the name of E. C. Venable for Congress?—Ans. Yes; there were ballots headed "Regular Republican ticket" which had E. C. Venable's name on them for Congress; and I believe, to the best of my knowledge, that a number of men entered by Lewis upon his books voted the said ticket.

31st. Question. Were there any ballots deposited in the box wherein the names of the Democratic candidates were written by hand; and state why such ballots were so written?—Ans. Yes; I believe that these ballots were so written, because the parties voting them wished to conceal the fact that they voted for E. C. Venable. (Record 987.)

He contradicts Lewis in his statement that he (Lewis) was at the polls all the time. He contradicts him in his statement that he examined the ballots as the voters approached the polls and shows that it was impossible for him read them. He says Lewis was at the polls about two-thirds of the day only.

Is this man of high character or Lewis to be believed? We prefer to rely upon the testimony of Gill.

Another witness contradicts Lewis.

James M. Young.

1st. Question. (By counsel for contestee.) What is your age, occupation, and residence?—Ans. I am 29 years old; my occupation, police officer for the city of Petersburg; my residence, corner Sycamore and Oak streets, 3d ward.

2d. Question. Where were you on election day, November 6th, 1888?—Ans. I was at the 3d ward precinct.

3d. Question. Were you on duty there that day?—Ans. I was.

4th. Question. What time did you get to the polls on that day and how long did you stay there?—Ans. Well, sir, I think it was after I had eaten breakfast, about 7 or 8 o'clock. I stayed there all day.

5th. Question. During the time you were at the polls did you see M. N. Lewis, a witness for the contestant in this case?—Ans. Yes, sir.

6th. Question. The said Lewis has testified upon his direct examination as follows: "I stood right at the entrance where the colored voters approached the ballot-box, where I could see the ballots given by the voter to the judge, who received the ballots and deposited them in the box. I was there from sunrise until sunset, only leaving once about thirty minutes." Please consider this statement carefully and say if you know whether it is true, and give your reasons.—Ans. He is mistaken. He left there, sir, two or three times during the day. I mean the door where they were voting. I missed him away from there. I noticed that he was gone. I noticed him on account of his being around there and taking an active part in the canvass and election. (Record, 970, 971.)

George W. Dunn, another witness, contradicts Lewis in the most emphatic manner.

1st. Question. What is your age, occupation, and residence?—Ans. Age, 36; occupation, police officer of the city of Petersburg; residence, Hotel Gary, Tabb st., 3d ward.

2d. Question. Where were you on the 6th day of November, 1888, election day?—Ans. At the 3d ward voting precinct.

3d. Question. Were you on duty during that day?—Ans. I was.

4th. Question. At what time did you go to the 3d ward polls and how long did you stay there?—Ans. I went there at sunrise and remained the whole day, with the exception of about three-quarters of an hour.

5th. Question. During the time that you were present at 3d ward polls did you see one M. N. Lewis, a witness for the contestant in this case?—Ans. I did.

6th. Question. The said Lewis has testified upon his direct examination in this case as follows: "I stood right at the entrance where the colored voters approached the ballot-box (meaning the ballot-box of 3d ward polls), where I could see the ballots given by the voter to the judge who received the ballots and deposited them in the box. I was there from sunrise until sunset, only leaving once about thirty minutes." Please consider this answer carefully and say if you know whether the same is true, and give your reasons for your answer.—Ans. *It is not true. Mr. Lewis had a position that he could see the ballot about an hour and a half. He was obstructing the voters, and I removed him from his position. He then occupied a place on an old stand, about ten feet from the judge of election. He remained in that position about half an hour. He then left the precinct. I didn't see him any more until about twelve o'clock. He was coming from towards 6th ward precinct. He then disappeared again and returned late in the evening.*

7th. Question. There have been filed in the record as a part of the testimony of the said Lewis four books purporting to be the tally-books which he kept on November 6th, 1888, at the 3d ward polls, containing the names of more than 200 voters, whose ballots he swore were given for John M. Langston. In answer to the following question asked the said Lewis on his direct examination, to wit: "When, and under what circumstances, did you particularly observe the ballot of each colored voter before recording his name in said books?" the said Lewis replied: "I read his ballot carefully, and after I had seen the judge to whom he handed his ballot deposit it in the ballot-box I then placed his name on my book." Please state whether this reply of the said Lewis is true, and give your reasons.—Ans. *It is not true. All the colored voters were in a line separate from the whites. They had several parties giving them tickets, and it was impossible for any one to tell how they were voting. The colored tally-book of 3d ward, on Mr. Langston's side was kept by two or three different parties, and the position that they held they could not have told one ticket from another.*

(NOTE.—J. M. Taylor, esq., counsel for the contestee, appeared and asked to be entered as counsel of record.)

8th. Question. Please state whether or not you have attended 3d ward polls at other elections prior to November 6th, 1888, and, if so, how many.—Ans. I have attended two others prior to the Presidential election.

9th. Question. Is it the custom at the 3d ward polls for the colored voters to vote open or folded ballots?—Ans. They have been voting to suit themselves in the last two or three elections, and they would allow no one to see their tickets; and the majority of them would allow no one to see their tickets.

10th. Question. Do you mean to say that on November 6th, 1888, the majority of the colored voters would allow no one to see their tickets?—Ans. I do. They had two or three ticket-holders, and they were giving out different kinds of tickets. After they got in line the majority of them refused to show their tickets. They did not want any one to know how they voted; for Langston, Venable, or Arnold.

11th. Question. Did you see any considerable number of colored voters show their tickets to the said Lewis, or to one W. J. Smith, or to one S. B. McE. Jones, who, as the said Lewis testified, kept his tally-books in his absence?—Ans. I did not.

12th. Question. Would you have known such a fact if it had existed?—Ans. I think I should.

13th. Question. Were there any tickets with the name of R. W. Arnold for Congress distributed to the colored voters at 3d ward polls November 6th, 1888?—Ans. There was.

14th. Question. Were there any tickets bearing the Republican Presidential electors with the name of E. C. Venable for Congress distributed to the colored voters at 3d ward polls November 6th, 1888?—Ans. There were a great many distributed of that kind.

15th. Question. Were there any tickets written by hand bearing the regular Democratic nominees distributed to the colored voters at 3d ward polls November 6th, 1888?—Ans. I didn't see any.

16th. Question. Was it possible for any person standing outside of the polls at any place to say how the colored voters cast their ballots, and give your reasons?—Ans. It was not. No one stood near enough to see the ballot, except the judge, and the greater portion of them were folded, and it was impossible for him to tell how they were voting.

17th. Question. It has been testified by the said Lewis that he knows that more than 270 ballots were cast for John M. Langston at the 3d ward polls November 6th, 1888, because that number of names appear on the four books already mentioned, kept by himself and W. J. Smith and S. B. McE. Jones. Please state whether you know the said statement of Lewis to be true or untrue, and give your reasons for your answer.—Ans. It is untrue. It was impossible for Lewis, Smith, and Jones to tell how a great portion of the colored voters voted. No man at 3d ward precinct or set of men could have told how any twenty-five or thirty men had voted, after they got in line with two or three different kinds of tickets in their hands. I saw that no one interfered with them, as I was sent there for the purpose of keeping order and not let the voters be interfered with. I carried out the order the whole day, with the exception of three-quarters of an hour. (Record, 965, 966.)

We ask that this testimony be carefully read.

Still another witness contradicts Lewis. George Fayerman, a prominent Republican, a former member of the legislature, a canvasser for honorables James H. Platt, W. H. Stowell, Joseph Jorgensen, J. D. Brady, and —— Gaines, formerly Republican members of Congress from this district.

11th. Question. Are you familiar with the Republican voters of 3d ward, in which you live?—Ans. I am, sir.

12th. Question. Please state whether or not you were present at the 3d ward polls on the 6th of November, 1888; and, if so, how long were you there and in what capacity?—Ans. I was there nearly the whole day, not being absent more than half an hour at any time. I held the colored voters' book; checked their names when they voted. When not otherwise engaged, I would be distributing tickets or influencing men to either vote for Arnold or Venable.

13th. Question. The said Matt N. Lewis mentioned above has testified that on the 6th of November, 1888, he stood immediately in front of the 3d ward ballot-box from sunrise until sunset, only leaving about thirty minutes during the day. Please state whether or not you know this testimony to be true or false.—Ans. Lewis was there for about three-quarters of the day, and when there he sat on a box in front of the judges with his back to the voters.

14th. Question. Please state whether or not it is the custom in 3d ward among the Republican voters to vote folded or open ballots.—Ans. The custom is to vote folded ballots.

15th. Question. Was the election of the 6th of November, 1888, any exception to this rule?—Ans. It was partially. A few of the men voted open ballots, between one-eighth and one-tenth of the colored voters. A great many of the colored men were very particular in guarding their ballots so that no one could see how they voted.

16th. Question. Did you see any of the supporters of Langston exhibit their tickets to the said Lewis before voting?—Ans. No, not one; they had not the means of doing it from the position that Lewis occupied.

17th. Question. If it had been the general rule for the supporters of Langston to exhibit their ballots to Lewis in order that he might record their names in a book, would you or would you not have been cognizant of such a custom?—Ans. *Certainly I would have known. The only way Lewis could have judged would have been by the men who voted; he might have surmised; still I know a great many new voters of the 3d ward who were crying Langston that either voted for Arnold or Venable.*

18th. Question. *Do you or not know the fact that at the time it was suggested to the Langston tally-keepers that they were recording on their books as voting for Langston men who in reality had cast their ballots for one of the other candidates?*

Ans. Yes, sir; several colored men have come to me at the poll and stated that they were tired of this nonsense of colored women and ministers interfering in politics; that they were never going to vote against General Mahone and his candidate; therefore they voted for Mr. Arnold in preference to Mr. Langston; and yet these very men were crying out Langston and "What's the matter with Langston," in every corner of the streets.

19th. Question. During the time or times when the said Lewis was absent from the 3d ward polls he has testified that one W. J. Smith and one S. B. Mac E. Jones assumed his position and kept his tally-books. Please state whether they enjoyed any other or better opportunities for recording the supporters of Langston, and whether or not the supporters of Langston showed them their ballots before handing them to the judge.

Ans. I did see Wm. J. Smith occupying the position where Lewis was, but I never saw Jones. Smith had no greater facility of seeing the ballot than Lewis, and I never saw any one show either Lewis or Smith a ballot.

20th. Question. There have been filed in this record as a part of the testimony of the said Lewis four books purporting to be the tally-books which he kept on the 6th of November, 1888, which he kept at the 3d ward polls, containing the names of more than 200 voters whose ballots he swore were given for John M. Langston. In answer to the following question asked the said Lewis on his direct examination, to wit, "When, and under what circumstances did you particularly observe the ballot of each colored voter before recording his name in said books?" the said Lewis replied, "I read his ballot carefully, and after I had seen the judge to whom he handed his ballot deposit it in the ballot-box, I then placed his name on my book." Please state whether or not this reply of the said Lewis is true, and give your reasons.—*Ans. It may be true so far as the one-eighth or one-tenth of the men who voted an open ticket, provided Lewis was present and was paying some attention. But with regard to the others 'tis not true, for he had not the means of knowing how they voted.*

21st. Question. From your experience in such matters, is it possible outside of the polls to keep an accurate tally of the votes cast for any particular candidate in an election conducted under the laws which regulated the election of November 6th, 1888, and give your reasons?—Ans. Not possible, except four men unite in concert in keeping an account and paying particular attention to the voters in giving and depositing their tickets. On the 6th of November Langston's friends had so many ticket-holders and so many men otherwise engaged that they were in conflict with each other, and some of these ticket-holders, *whilst pretending to be for Langston, were distributing tickets for Arnold; therefore no proper count could be kept.*

German H. Gill, Federal supervisor (Record, 986):

12th. Question. Were you present after the close of the polls and during the count and canvass of the vote?—Ans. I was present during the count and canvass of the vote, and from the time the polls closed I did not leave until the count and canvass was finished or completed, and the tally-sheets, &c., with the ballots were placed in the ballot-box and sealed by the judge.

13th. Question. How did the number of ballots found in the box correspond with the number of names on the poll-books?—Ans. They corresponded exactly. There were 797 names registered by the clerks, and the number of ballots were 797 found in the box.

14th. Question. Please describe the manner in which the ballots were canvassed and counted, and say by whom were they canvassed and counted, and, refreshing your memory from the poll-book already filed, say what was the result.

(NOTE.—Counsel for contestant now asked for an adjournment of the taking of the above deposition until 4 p. m. of this day, as he has a pressing engagement which it is impossible for him to neglect, especially, too, as there are now only three of Langston's counsel in the city, and that the other two counsel are now engaged in taking depositions in this contested-election case in other parts of the city under notice given by the contestee through his counsel.)

Ans. The ballot-box was emptied by William Crichton, judge, on the table. I saw that nothing was left in the box. The ballots were then counted by the judges, William Crichton, John T. Williams, Virginius L. Weddell, and myself, I claiming the right as United States supervisor for that precinct to count the same. The number of ballots taken from the box were 797. The ballots for each candidate were then separated and counted for each candidate. The result was: Venable, 518; Arnold, 105; Langston, 174. The ballots were separated and counted by three judges already mentioned and myself. I was present during the entire count and canvass of the vote.

15th. Question. Did you keep any record yourself during the day; and if you did, state in what manner you kept it, and how its result accorded with the number of ballots found in the box?—Ans. I kept a tally of the white and colored vote during the day upon a patent tally-sheet, which I received as an advertisement, the parties wishing to sell these sheets, and having the sheet I used it for the purpose of keeping a tally that day. My count upon this sheet summed up 5 less than the poll-book, which difference was due to the fact that I failed to make the cross-mark in the tally, thereby beginning the next tally, losing one each time I made the mistake.

16th. Question. From your experience in such matters, is it possible outside of the polls to keep with accuracy a record of the number of votes cast for any particular candidate; and give your reasons?—Ans. From my experience it is impossible to tell by any means outside of the polls how many votes are cast for any particular candidate or party. My reason for so stating is that I have frequently tried to do so at the same polling place, having an accurate copy of the registration book made myself while a registrar, and have never yet been able to tell at the close of the polls which party or candidate had the most ballots cast for them, or estimate how many had been cast for any particular candidate. I have failed to come within 150 votes between the two parties, Republican and Democrat, and found it impossible to tell anything about the number of ballots for any one candidate. The fact of the ballots, as a general thing, being folded by the voters, in my opinion, makes it impossible for a man outside of the polls to say how many ballots have been cast for any particular candidate.

17th. Question. Was the election of the 6th of November, 1888, any exception to the general rule with regard to the voting of folded ballots?—Ans. No, sir.

18th. Question. Was there any fraud or sharp practice of any kind practiced in the counting, canvassing, or returning of the vote of 3d ward polls on November 6th, 1888?— Ans. I had every opportunity to see and hear everything that was done or said in the count and canvass and return of the said vote. I saw nothing of fraud or sharp practice. If I had seen any such fraud or sharp practice I should, as United States supervisor, have stopped it at once.

19th. Question. If there had been any fraud at the 3d ward polls, would you not have been able to see and discover it?—Ans. Yes.

Could evidence be more direct?

This concludes the testimony taken as to this precinct. The case of the contestant stands upon the testimony of Lewis alone (for if it falls Smith's testimony must fall), which is overwhelmingly rebutted and contradicted by no less than four witnesses.

We have, then, the sworn returns of three judges and two clerks and one Federal supervisor and the testimony of four witnesses on the one hand and the uncorroborated and contradicted testimony of one witness (Lewis) on the other.

The majority of the committee in their report seem to regard the testimony of the contestant's witnesses as weak, and yet they treat it as conclusive proof of fraud, ballot-box stuffing, etc., and declare that the contestee has no right to complain, as he delayed the completion of the examination of these witnesses to such an extent as to prevent the taking of further evidence. In other words, the majority of the committee decide a great and important question upon the assumption that the contestant *might* have proved his case if he had not been interfered with by the contestee; they decide upon what *might* have been in the record, not upon what *is* in it. With all due deference we submit that this is hardly in the line of legal procedure and even-handed justice.

But was the contestant in fact prevented from taking other testimony by the acts of the contestee? The majority say that he was, by reason of the long cross-examination of his witnesses. Well, when it is remembered that the contestant was relying upon the testimony of these witnesses to at least lay the foundation for the rejection of a poll at which more than 700 votes were cast and a large plurality given to the contestee, the exercise of common judgment would have taught him that their testimony would be tested by the most rigid cross-examination, and if he did not prepare for such an emergency he has himself only to blame. It nowhere appears in evidence that the contestant was unable to procure legal assistance or notarial service in the taking of all the evidence he desired in the forty days allowed by law, but it appears that he had many attorneys and that much time was unoccupied by him, which could have been utilized if he had been anxious to do so. It is also charged in a letter written to him by the contestee (Record, 634) that he was in fact absent from the State of Virginia on other business a large portion of the forty days allowed him for the taking of testimony, and this charge is not denied by him in his reply to said letter. (Record, 636.)

But be all this as it may, surely we can never agree to set a precedent by which a case can be determined by what a party *might* have done "if wind and tide had been in his favor," but which he has not done.

The House of Representatives may in a proper case grant additional time to take testimony, but it will never, until all principles governing judicial procedure and the hearing and determination of causes are set aside and utterly disregarded, strengthen and bolster up a weak and feeble attempt to annul the solemn act of election officials upon the mere assertion of a party that he could, if he had been favored with more time, have proved his case.

Concluding as to this precinct, we insist that the returns are unimpeached and must stand.

DELAY OF JUDGES—NOT ENOUGH VOTING PLACES.

The contestant charges that many of his voters were hindered from voting by the delay of the judges in receiving ballots. The majority of the committee, on page 28 of their report, say that it appears 121 of Langston's voters were prevented from casting their ballots by the delay of the judges in Sixth ward.

There is not the slightest evidence whatever in our opinion to sustain this charge. At this precinct 651 votes were cast, or about one vote every minute. This was rapid voting when it is considered that the registration books and disfranchised lists had to be examined. There was no delay by challenges, as there was not a voter challenged during the day. The contestant claims that his voters were discriminated against, as the judges alternated by receiving first the ballot of a colored man and then the ballot of a white man; he thinks two colored voters should have voted to every white voter, and the majority of the committee seem to agree with him.

H. Mis. 137——32

From this position we dissent. We think a white man has as much right to tender his ballot and have it received as a colored man and *vice versa*, and that a man because his skin is white should not be required to wait at the polls until two other men had deposited their ballots because their skin is black.

If the voting facilities in the sixth ward were inadequate, neither the contestee nor his party is responsible, as will appear from the following testimony:

B. D. Akers:

77. Q. How many voting precincts were there in sixth ward at the time of the November, 1888, election, and how many had there been prior to that time ?—A. Only one.

78. Q. What party was in power in the city council of the city of Petersburg on February 1st, 1888 ?—A. Republican.

79. Q. Is it or not a fact that at that date the Republican members of said city council were in the majority ?—A. It is a fact.

80. Q. Were or not the four members of the said city council from said sixth ward all Republicans at that time?—A. Yes, sir.

81. Q. I find from the proceedings of the common council of the city of Petersburg, held February 1st, 1888, that the following members of that council voted to establish another voting place in sixth ward in addition to the one at which the election was held November 6th, 1888: Blake, Enniss, W. T. Hargrave, Epes Hargrave, Johns, Newcomb, Parham, Thweatt, Waite, and Goodwyn. Please state whether these thirteen persons whose names I have called were then and are now Republicans or Democrats ?—A. They were then and are now Republicans.

82. Q. I find from an examination of the proceedings of said city council that on March 20th, 1888, a special meeting of said council was held, in pursuance of a request therefor made by Epes Hargrave, Harrison, Waite, and eight others, and that at that meeting Mr. Enniss, one of the Republican members from sixth ward, moved a suspension of the rules in order that he might offer an ordinance to repeal the ordinance passed February 1st, 1888, dividing sixth ward into two voting precincts. I find, too, from the same proceedings that there were present at this special meeting, held March 20th, 1888, the following members of said council: E. A. Goodwyn, president, and Messrs. Blake, Ennis, Farley, Gilliam, W. T. Hargrave, Epes Hargrave, Johns, Newcomb, Osborne, Parham, Seward, Thweatt, Waite, Wilson, and Zimmer. I find further that the rules were suspended, and that the ordinance dividing sixth ward into two voting precincts was repealed. Please state what party was, on March the 20th, 1888, in the majority in the city council of Petersburg, and what were then and what or now the politics of the members of said council whose names I have last mentioned above, which names the notary will read over to you.—A. The Republicans were in power. (The notary here read the names:) E. A. Goodwyn, president, Republican; Blake, Republican; Enniss, Republican; Farley, Republican; Gilliam, Democrat; W. T. Hargrave, Republican; Epes Hargrave, Republican; Johns, Republican; Newcomb, Republican; Osborne, Democrat; Parham. Republican; Seward, Democrat; Thweatt, Republican; Waite, Republican; Wilson, Republican; and Zimmer, Democrat.

83. Q. Then what party, according to this record, is responsible for the fact that the ordinance passed Feb'y the 1st, 1888, establishing two voting precincts for sixth ward, was repealed March the 20th, 1888, at a special meeting called for that purpose, the Democratic or the Republican party in said city council?—A. The Republican.

84. Q. Have you examined a duly-certified copy of the said council proceedings showing the facts as above set forth, and if you have in your hand such a certified copy, will you please hand it to the notary to be filed as an exhibit with this your deposition?

(NOTE.—Here counsel for the contestee handed the witness the certified copy of the said proceedings, which the witness carefully examined.)

A. Yes, sir, I have examined it.

(NOTE.—And here the witness handed the notary a certified copy of said proceeding, which is marked "B D A, Exhibit A," and asked that the same be filed as an exhibit with this his deposition, which is accordingly done. Here the notary marked the same as above indicated.)

(B. D. A.) EXHIBIT A.

STATE OF VIRGINIA:

At a regular meeting of the common council of the city of Petersburg, held in the council chamber Feb'y 1st, 1888; present Capt. E. A. Goodwyn, president, and Messrs. Bagwell, Blake, Davis, Enniss, Gilliam, Hargrave, W. T., Hargrave, Epps, Harris,

Johns, Newcomb, Osborne, Markham, Smith, Seward, Thweatt, Van Auken, Wheary, and Wilson.

The ordinance, laid over from the last meeting of the council, entitled "An ordinance to amend and re-enact sec. 7 of chapter 54, printed ordinances of the city of Petersburgh," was taken up and passed by the following vote:

Ayes: Messrs. Blake, Enniss, Hargrave, W. T., Hargrave, Epps, Harris, Johns, Newcomb, Parkham, Thweatt, Van Auken, Waite, Wilson, and Goodwyn—13.

Nays: Bagwell, Davis, Gilliam, Osborne, Smith, Seward, and Wheary—7.

Ordinance 1st.—Be it ordained by the common council of the city of Petersburg, that section 7 of chapter 54, printed ordinances of the city of Petersburg, be so amended and re-enacted as to read as follows:

That 6th ward of the city be divided into two precincts. Section 7. That of said ward lying north of a line beginning at the City Hospital and running east to the intersection of West street and Lee avenue; thence east along the middle of Lee avenue to Jones street; thence south along the middle of Jones street to Cedar; thence east along the center of Cedar street to Halifax; thence south along the middle of Halifax to Porterville street; thence east along the middle of Porterville to Harding street, be known as precinct No. 1; and the voting place of said precinct No. 1 shall be at and in house No. 211 Halifax street.

And that all of said ward lying south and west of said line and not included in precinct No. 1 be known as precinct No. 2, and that the voting place for said precinct No. 2 shall be at and in the building known as Minetree's shop, on Halifax street near Melville.

At a special meeting of the common council of the city of Petersburg held in the council chamber March 20th, 1888, present, the president, and Messrs. Blake, Enniss, Farley, Gilliam, Hargrave, W. T., Hargrave, Epps, Harris, Johns, Newcomb, Osborne, Parkham, Seward, Thweatt, Waite, Wilson, and Zimmer.

The president explained why a special meeting of the council was called by reading the following:

Hon. E. A. GOODWYN,
Presiden: of the Council:

We respectfully request that you will call a special meeting of the common council, say on Tuesday night, to consider some proposed amendments to the revised ordinances before they shall be put in print.

Respect.,
E. HARGRAVE,
HARRISON WAITE (and eight others).

Mr. Ennis moved a suspension of the rules to offer an ordinance entitled "An ordinance to repeal an ordinance dividing the 6th ward into two precincts." Messrs. Gilliam and Seward excused. The rules were suspended and the ordinance read and adopted.

Ordinance.—Be it ordained that sec. 7, chapter 54 of the printed, be re-enacted so as to repeal so much of an ordinance to amend and re-enact sec. 7, chapter 54 of printed ordinances dividing 6th ward into two precincts, passed by the common council Feb'y 1st, 1888, and that the same be, and is hereby, repealed.

STATE OF VIRGINIA,
City of Petersburg, to wit:

I, J. F. McIlwaine, city auditor, and ex-officio clerk of the common council of the city of Petersburg, in the State aforesaid, do certify that the foregoing is a true transcript from the records of the common council of said city.

In testimony whereof I hereto set my hand this 16th day of February, A. D. 1889.
J. F. McILWAINE,
City Auditor and ex-officio Clerk of the Common Council of said City.

STATE OF VIRGINIA,
City of Petersburg, to wit:

I, Chas. F. Collier, mayor of the city of Petersburg, in the State aforesaid, do certify that J. F. McIlwaine, who hath given the preceding certificate, is now, and was at the time of giving the same, city auditor of the said city, and as such clerk of the common council of said city and custodian of its records, duly elected and qualified; that his signature is genuine and his attestation is in due form.

In testimony whereof I have hereto set my hand and affixed the seal of the said city, this 18th day of February, 1889.

[SEAL.]
CHARLES F. COLLIER,
Mayor of said City.

STATE OF VIRGINIA,
   City of Petersburg, to wit:

I, J. F. McIlwaine, city auditor of the city aforesaid, in the State of Virginia, do certify that Chas. F. Collier, whose genuine signature appears to the foregoing certificate, is now, and was at the time of signing the same, mayor of said city, duly elected and qualified, and authorized by law to give said certificate.

In testimony whereof I hereto set my hand this 18th day of February, A. D. 1889.
                                J. F. McILWAINE,
   City Auditor and ex-officio Clerk of the Common Council of the City of Petersburg.

(NOTE.—Counsel for the contestant objects to the filing of this certified copy, since the substance of same has already been made a matter of record in question put to the witness by counsel for the contestee.)

85. Q. Is it or not true that the 20th day of March, 1888, above mentioned, was but about two months prior to the city election, in May, 1888?—A. Yes, sir. (Record, 822, 823, 824.)

It will be observed that the city council was largely Republican; that on the 1st day of February, 1888, nine (all Republicans, all that were present) voted to establish a second precinct in the 6th ward; that on the 20th day of March, 1888, *on the motion of a Republican member,* the ordinance establishing this second precinct was *repealed,* and that there were present at this meeting 12 Republicans and 4 Democrats; that this special meeting was called at the request of Harrison Waite, chairman of the Republican city committee, E. Hargrave, another Republican, and eight other members whose names are not given.

LEWISTON PRECINCT—LUNENBURGH COUNTY.

We come now to the last precinct assailed by the report of the majority of the committee. Lewiston, Lunenburgh County.

The returns from this precinct gave:

	Votes.
Venable	119
Langston	48
Arnold	46
Total	213

This entire poll is rejected by the majority, and 313 votes absolutely disfranchised, and Venable deprived of a plurality of 73 votes.

Here is a summary of the facts:

The three judges—two Democratic and one Republican—appointed by the electoral board of the county, declined to serve, the Republican on account of ill health, one of the Democrats because he desired to go to another precinct as a worker for his party, and the other because being a ready penman it was desired that he should act as a clerk. It usually being difficult to get men to act as judges, these original appointees on the day before the election arranged for others to take their places—two Democrats and one Republican—and on the morning of the election they appeared early at the polls, took the required oath, and at sunrise opened the polls and conducted the election to the close.

A Republican Federal supervisor was appointed and acted until the polls closed, and then being sick, he went to his home and did not return. When the ballots were counted an excess of 25 were found, and one of the judges was blind-folded and drew out 13 Venable, 8 Langston, and 4 Arnold ballots. The poll was held in a jury-room adjoining and opening into the court-room.

T. F. Robertson, one of the judges, testifies that the ballot-box was in full view of the voters; that E. O. Goodwyn was the judge who received the ballots from the voters; that he saw Goodwyn deposit every ballot he received in the ballot-box; that when the polls closed the ballots were taken from the box, divided among the candidates, and counted; that a recess was taken at dinner time, the door was locked by Goodwyn, who put the key in his pocket, and they all returned together; that when the polls closed, the clerks said they were tired and went out, remaining fifteen or twenty minutes, when they returned and the canvass was commenced and concluded; that he and Goodwyn looked over the tickets as they were read by Bayne, the Republican judge. (Record, 1095-1098.)

W. J. Bragg, the Republican Federal supervisor, testified that he remained in the polling room all the time during the voting; that he watched all the proceedings as far as he could; that the election was conducted fairly so far as he knew; that the ballot-box was in full view of the voters and they could see their ballots deposited in it; that the judges took a recess for dinner, locking the door and taking the key with them; that the count-room and jury-room are in the second story of the court-house and are reached by a stairway from the front, and that during the recess he was watching and saw no one enter the court-room; that it was 20 feet from the ground and no one could have entered through a window during the recess without being detected, as the court-yard was full of people. That as he lived 4 or 5 miles from the precinct and was sick he left for home after the polls closed and took his bed. On cross-examination:

If there was any improper ballots put in the ballot-box I didn't find it out. There was no fraud practiced that I know of. I watched as well as I could, and if they got in there I didn't find it out.

He says the jury-room was a suitable place for holding the election and no objection was made to it. (Record, 1117-1120.)

The majority of the committee held:

(1) That the change from the court-room to the jury-room was a suspicious circumstance.

We do not think so. The jury-room was, in our opinion, a more suitable place than the large open court-room.

(2) That the change of judges was another suspicious circumstance.

We do not think so. One judge was sick, another preferred to work for his party at another precinct, and the third preferred to act as a clerk.

(3) That the retirement of the clerks and the delay in admitting them when they returned was another suspicious circumstance.

We do not think so. Robertson, the judge, explains that they retired because they were tired, and no doubt wanted to rest a little before they commenced the canvass of the vote; that they were not absent more than fifteen or twenty minutes, and the little delay in admitting them when they wrapped was because the judges were engaged in separating the ballots.

(4) That the judges were not appointed in accordance with the statute.

We agree with them upon this point, but the provision of the statute is not mandatory, and these judges were at least *de facto* officers, and the voters should not be made to suffer because of a mere irregularitys.

(5) That the excess of ballots in the ballot-box was a badge of fraud which, together with the above-recited circumstances, should exclude the vote at this precinct.

From this we most earnestly dissent.

The mere fact that the number of votes returned exceeds the number of names checked on the voting list does not in the absence of fraud or of a change in the result affect the validity of the election. (Paine, § 599.)

These excessive ballots could not affect the result. How they got into the box no one, so far as the record shows, can tell. Suppose they were put there by one of the judges. Should that disfranchise more than 200 voters?

There is no evidence that the Democratic vote at this precinct was unusually large or the Republican vote unusually small. In the draw Venable suffered more than Langston or Arnold, they losing, respectively, 13, 8, and 4 votes. Langston's supporter and witness (J. W. Smith) testified that he believed Langston received 66 votes (Record, 814, question 45); the return gave him 48 votes, or 18 less than his friend and worker believed he received.

Would it not be more in consonance with justice to give Langston 18 votes more and deduct them proportionately from Venable and Arnold, or even take all from Venable, than reject the entire returns? Would not that course be more equitable than depriving Venable of the entire advantage he had at this precinct? Could Langston complain?

While adhering firmly to our position that the vote at this precinct should be counted as returned, yet if it is not to stand we insist that the contestant should not have more than his worker and witness claims for him, or Venable made to lose everything.

So, giving Langston the benefit of all that can be claimed for him, the vote will stand as follows:

	Venable.	Langston.
Vote as returned..	.13,298	12,657
Add vote at Poach and Ross...........................	69	141
	13,367	12,798
Deduct returned vote, sixth ward, Petersburg............	352	139
	13,015	12,659
Add reformed vote, sixth ward, Petersburg..............	240	377
	13,255	13,036
Deduct returned vote at Lewiston.......................	119	48
	13,136	12,988
Add "reformed" vote at Lewiston.......................	101	66
	13,237	13,054

Clear majority of Venable over Langston, 183 votes.

RECAPITULATION OF STATEMENTS.

First. Adding vote at Poach and Ross: Majority for Venable 569 votes.

This we believe to be in accordance with the law and the facts.

Second. "Readjusting" the vote in sixth ward of Petersburg, and giving to Langston all he claims, and to Venable the well-known Democratic vote, which according to the testimony of Langston's witnesses was out in full force: Majority for Venable, 219 votes.

Third. "Readjusting," as above stated, the vote in the sixth ward of Petersburg, and reforming the vote at Lewiston, and giving to Langston all that his worker and witness claimed for him (66 votes), and deducting his gain of 18 votes over the returned vote for him from Venable : Majority for Venable, 183 votes.

Having conceded to the contestant far more than precedents, law, or sound policy would allow, and giving to him everything which his friends claim for him, except in the third ward of Petersburg, it will be seen that the contestee has a clear, and, it appears to us, incontestable majority of 183 votes.

As we have indicated, the majority of the committee have arrived at a conclusion entirely different, but we submit most respectfully that they have in every instance disregarded without reason the testimony of contestee's witnesses, and acted upon presumptions, not facts, and strengthened weak points in the contestant's case by drawing upon their imaginations as to what *might* have been proved if the contestant had been more active and energetic.

We submit the following resolutions in the stead of those offered by the major.ty:

Resolved, That John M. Langston was not elected a Representative in the Fifty-first Congress from the Fourth Congressional district of Virginia and is not entitled to a seat therein.

Resolved, That Edward C. Venable was duly elected a Representative in the Fifty-first Congress from the Fourth Congressional district of Virginia and is entitled to retain the seat he holds.

CHAS. T. O'FERRALL,
CHAS. F. CRISP,
L. W. MOORE,
R. P. C. WILSON,
LEVI MAISH,
JOS. H. OUTHWAITE.

THOMAS E. MILLER vs. WM. ELLIOTT.

SEVENTH SOUTH CAROLINA.

Contestant charged that by the statutes of South Carolina and the partisan manner of executing them, many voters possessing all the constitutional qualifications for voting were prevented from registering and refused the right to vote. He also charged that the judges of election in a number of precincts repeatedly shifted the ballot boxes for the purpose of deceiving the voters, and causing them to deposit their ballots in the wrong boxes, and that by this proceeding, as well as by ballot-box stuffing and other frauds, he was deprived of a large number of votes honestly cast for him by legal voters.

The committee find (1) that the registration and election laws of South Carolina are unconstitutional, and their execution partisan and illegal; (2) that the shifting of the ballot boxes being for the purpose of deception and hence unlawful, the votes lost by it should be restored; and (3) that where the ballot boxes were stuffed the returns should be rejected and the vote counted as proved to have been cast.

The minority find (1) that the registration and election laws of the State are constitutional and reasonable, and their execution fair; (2) that the shifting of the ballot boxes was a proper proceeding, and the votes found in the wrong boxes could not be counted even if the evidence showed satisfactorily their number and for whom they were cast; and (3) that there being no evidence to show by whom the boxes were stuffed, and the excess of ballots having been "purged" by the method provided for in the statutes of South Carolina, the returns should be allowed to stand. (See minority report, p. 533.)

The resolutions presented by the committee were adopted by the House September 23, 1890, by a vote of 157 to 1 (on division, the Speaker "counting a quorum"), and Mr. Miller was sworn in the next day. The case was not debated. (See Record, p. 10339.)

(1) Registration law unconstitutional.

The registration law of South Carolina is unconstitutional, because it is not a reasonable regulation of the right to vote, but is, under the pretense of regulation, an abridgment, subversion, and restraint of that right. Its unreasonable or restrictive features are (1) that it does not provide sufficient facilities for registration, and leaves to the registering officer a dangerous discretion; (2) that it attaches the penalty of permanent disfranchisement for failing for any cause to register for the

505

first election at which the citizen would be entitled to vote if registered; (3) that it affixes a like penalty for parting with or destroying a registration certificate; (4) that all applications for transfer or renewal of certificates must be made at the county seat of the county where the original certificate was issued; (5) that when the board of appeals has decided against an applicant for registration, he may appeal, but must give notice in writing within five days, and commence proceedings in court within ten days thereafter, or be forever debarred from voting. This is a special remedy with a fifteen-days statute of limitations; (6) that the supervisor is given arbitrary power to strike names from the registry list without posting the names and without notice to anybody.

(2) **Election law unconstitutional.**

The provision of the election law of South Carolina which provides for several ballot boxes, distinguished from each other only by the labels, and that no ticket found in the wrong box shall be counted, is practically an educational test, and is hence in direct violation of the constitution of the State.

(3) **Votes.** *Rejected.*

Persons otherwise qualified as voters who attempted to get certificates of registration and were prevented by the action of the register ing officers, were legal voters, and if they tendered their votes to the judges of election and were refused, their votes could be counted on a contest.

(4) **Shifting of ballot boxes.**

The shifting of ballot boxes for the purpose of deceiving voters and enforcing on them an educational test not permitted by the constitution of the State, is an unlawful and fraudulent proceeding.

" An act may not expressly be forbidden by law, but if it is done with an unlawful purpose, and succeeds in accomplishing that purpose, the act is thereby made unlawful." Under such circumstances the votes found in the wrong boxes should be counted.

" It is no answer to say that the counting of such ballots is prohibited by statute (even admitting that the statute is a reasonable regulation, which, under the peculiar circumstances in South Carolina, we do not), when the mistaken deposit has resulted from the active deception of the managers. It is a crime at common law to enter into a conspiracy to commit any offense against the purity and fairness of a public election. (Paine on Elections, section 496, and authorities cited.)"

(5) **Ballot-box stuffing.**

Where ballot boxes are proved to have been stuffed, the returns are rejected and no votes counted except those proved or conceded aside from the returns. This in spite of the fact that the excess of votes had been " purged" as provided for in the statutes of South Carolina, for "such method of disposing of extra ballots is provided for mistakes, and not for frauds."

REPORT.

JUNE 20, 1890.—Mr. ROWELL, from the Committee on Elections, submitted the following report:

The Committee on Elections have had under consideration the contested election case of Thomas E. Miller *vs.* William Elliott, from the Seventh Congressional district of South Carolina, and submit the following report:

At the election held November 6, 1888, in the Seventh Congressional district of South Carolina, for Representative in Congress, Thomas E. Miller was the candidate of the Republican party and William Elliott of the Democratic party. The certified returns gave Elliott a majority over Miller of 1,355, as shown by the following table.

Election returns, Seventh Congressional district.

Counties.	William Elliott.	Thomas E. Miller.	Robert Simmons.
Beaufort	898	2,056	
Berkeley	1,753	1,547	54
Charleston	45	143	
Colleton	652	210	
Georgetown	821	957	
Orangeburg	987	310	
Richland	367	222	2
Sumter	1,782	933	18
Williamsburg	1,053	624	
	8,358	7,003	74

The notice of contest, and answer thereto, cover all matters considered by the committee.

Before proceeding to examine the charges in detail, and the evidence introduced in regard to them, the committee deems it proper to call attention to some of the general features of the case.

In redistricting the State after the census of 1880, the legislature of South Carolina utterly ignored the Federal Statutes. The territory of the Seventh district is in no sense contiguous. It is well described in contestant's brief.

The new district—the Seventh Congressional district—was created without regard to shape, size, or contiguity of territory as required by law. To secure the appearance of the latter, it is necessary to regard a portion of the Atlantic Ocean as dry land. It extends from the capital of the State to Savannah, Ga., a distance of over 200 miles, and consists of the Republican portions of five of the original districts. It contains only three entire counties, to which is added an irregular patchwork of portions of six (6) counties, and in it is massed the population of every large colored or Republican settlement and town on the sea-coast or interior, and from it has been excluded nearly every white or Democratic settlement. In one place the district is

run into the ocean for the purpose of excluding the Democratic precincts of McClel-
lanville and Mount Pleasant, in Berkeley County, and Sullivan's Island, or Moultrie-
ville precinct, in Charleston County.

In color of population it was made as black as the deeds of the election officers, who
have violated every law and principle of justice to return contestee to Congress.

But this monstrosity can not thoroughly be understood without an
examination of a map of the district. An examination of the description of the district in the Congressional Directory will show that its
contiguity is secured by putting into it the sea beach of Charleston
County, a strip of sand a few feet wide and many miles long, covered
half of every day by the waters of the Atlantic Ocean and incapable of
human habitation. All the habitable main-land of this county is in
another district.

The following table shows the population of the district according to
the census of 1880:

SEVENTH CONGRESSIONAL DISTRICT.

Population and number of males of voting age classified by race according to census of 1880.

	Total.	White.	Colored.	Males 21 years of age and over.	
				White.	Colored.
The district..........................	187,536	31,529	156,016	7,695	32,898
Georgetown County	19,613	3,466	16,147	852	3,449
Beaufort County	30,176	2,442	27,734	693	6,127
Sumter County..........................	37,037	9,979	27,058	2,273	4,980
Orangeburg County	13,634	....	....		
Township of Amelia	3,664	629	3,035	169	609
Township of Goodby's	1,490	433	1,057	95	199
Township of Lyons	2,428	419	2,009	103	369
Township of Pine Grove	1,994	393	1,601	89	323
Township of Poplar	1,512	446	1,066	110	223
Township of Providence	1,260	387	873	83	150
Township of Vance's.................	1,286	206	1,080	47	191
Williamsburg County.....................	15,681	....	....		
Township of Anderson................	733	465	268	104	46
Township of Hope	2,326	615	1,711	128	302
Township of Indian	1,914	317	1,597	75	271
Township of King's, except the town of Kings-tree.	2,458	400	2,058	94	358
Township of Laws	1,295	208	1,087	50	198
Township of Mingo	1,371	362	1,009	89	177
Township of Penn	1,481	237	1,244	58	234
Township of Ridge	2,001	410	1,591	101	249
Township of Sutton's................	779	232	547	46	92
Township of Turkey.................	1,323	310	1,013	58	182
Colleton County.........................	12,961	....	....		
Township of Collin's	1,431	390	1,041	98	271
Township of Adam's Run..............	4,409	537	3,872	154	871
Township of Glover..................	1,337	179	1,158	45	242
Township of Fraser..................	1,708	160	1,548	46	384
Township of Lowndes.................	1,555	78	1,497	27	363
Township of Blake..........	2,521	49	2,472	28	574
Charleston County, except those portions in First district.	49,553	6,854	42,699	1,735	9,817
Richland County:					
Lower Township.......................	8,881	917	7,964	252	1,642

It will be seen that the colored men of voting age in this district outnumber the whites by more than 25,000. It is undoubtedly a misfor-
une, but it is none the less true, that political parties in this district are
divided on race lines. The colored men as a rule are Republicans, and
the white men are Democrats. That this is true is nowhere seriously
questioned in the record in this case. It is therefore safe to say, unless
the mass of colored voters have ceased to take an interest in political
matters, that with laws bearing equally on white and black, and with

anything like a fair election, the Republicans of the Seventh district would poll four times as many votes as the Democrats, and would have anywhere from 15,000 to 20,000 majority.

The history of the district as it has come before former Congresses, and as it is presented in this record, precludes the belief that its colored men have to any considerable extent ceased to be interested in elections, especially Presidential and Congressional elections. On the contrary, the colored Republicans have at all times kept up their party organization and have never failed to make a determined effort to secure a Republican Representative in Congress from the Seventh district.

The present election and registration law of South Carolina was enacted by the legislature of that State in 1881. In the brief of contestant that law is characterized in the following vigorous language:

In 1881 the election and registration law of South Carolina, the twin companion of the gerrymandering already described, was enacted by the legislature. It was the high-water mark of political ingenuity coupled with rascality, and merits its appellation, "Fraud made easy and safe." It is perfect in being entirely fair on its face, and sufficiently elastic to be susceptible to any construction in its enforcements, or to permit any species of fraud to be committed without a violation of any of its provisions. It is particularly remarkable in zealously guarding with severe penalties the transmission of the fraudulent results obtained by the local boards, while the neglect that amounts to fraud and offenses against political rights are not even made a simple misdemeanor.

As we call attention to some of the salient features of the law, it will be seen that this language is by no means too emphatic. That this law was enacted for the deliberate purpose of indirectly disfranchising, so far as possible, the colored voters of the State admits of no serious question. We give here so much of the election and registration law of South Carolina as is necessary to illustrate our views.

The constitution of the State prescribes the qualifications of voters. They must be male citizens of the United States, twenty one years of age, residents of the State one year and of the county sixty days, not inmates of almshouses or prisons, and not of unsound mind. Persons convicted of treason, murder, robbery, or dueling are disfranchised, and the legislature is expressly prohibited from disfranchising any one else.

The first section of the registration act defines the qualifications for voting as in the constitution, except that it adds a new and enlarged meaning to the term robbery.

The second section provides that no person shall be allowed to vote unless registered in the manner provided in the act.

The third section provides for the appointment, by the governor (by and with the advice and consent of the senate), of a supervisor of registration for each county on or before the 1st day of March following the passage of the act, and every two years thereafter; also for the appointment of two assistant supervisors to act with the supervisor as a board of appeals in case of refusal by the supervisor to register any applicant.

Section 4 provides for registration books, two for each precinct.

SEC. 5. After the approval of this act the supervisor of registration, in the months of May and June next, shall make a full and complete registration of all qualified voters, in the following manner: He shall give three weeks' notice of the times and places of registration, by advertising in one or more county papers, or by posting in a public place in each voting precinct where no paper is published in the county. The time for registration shall not be less than one nor more than three days at each registration precinct. Immediately after closing the registration at the precinct he shall open his books at the county seat to correct errors in registration and to register such electors as failed to register at their respective precincts, and who shall then and there present themselves for that purpose, entering the names of such voters in his book for their proper precincts. At the conclusion of the registration hereinbefore provided for the supervisor of registration shall revise the list, and in case it be made to appear to his satisfaction that there is a qualified voter in a precinct who has failed to register, he may, upon such evidence as he may think necessary in his discretion, permit the name of such voter to be placed on said list and issue a certificate therefor. That for the purpose of registration each township as now laid out and defined be, and is hereby, declared a registration precinct, and in those counties in which there are no such townships that the parish, as formerly known and defined, be, and is hereby, declared such precinct, and in the cities of Columbia and Charleston each ward shall be a registration precinct.

SEC. 6. When the said registration shall have been completed, the books shall be closed and not reopened for registration, except for the purposes and as hereinafter mentioned, until after the next general election for State officers. After the said next general election, the said books shall be reopened for registration of such persons *as shall thereafter become entitled to register* on the first Monday in each month, to and until the first Monday of July, inclusive, preceding the following general election, upon which last-named day the same shall be closed and not reopened for registration until after the said general election; and ever after the said book shall be opened for registration of such electors, on the days above mentioned, until the first day of July preceding a general election, when the same shall be closed as aforesaid until the said general election shall have taken place.

SEC. 7. Each elector in the State shall be required, at the time advertised for his precinct as hereinbefore provided, to appear before the supervisor of registration, at the place advertised, and make oath before the said supervisor, which oath the said supervisor is hereby authorized and required to administer, that the facts then and there to be stated by him as to his name, age, occupation, and place of residence, and duration of residence in the county and State are true, and thereupon the said supervisor shall enter the name, age, occupation, and place of residence of the elector in the appropriate column in his registration book. He shall make and keep a list of the contested applications for registration which he rejects, and report the same for hearing before the assistant supervisors as hereinbefore required.

SEC. 8. The supervisor of registration shall determine as to the legal qualifications of any applicant for registration by summary process, requiring oath, evidence, or both, if he deem proper, subject to revision by the assistant supervisors and himself in all cases where he has refused to register an applicant. From the decision of the supervisors of registration any applicant who is rejected shall have the right to a review thereof by the circuit court, provided he give notice in writing to the supervisor of his application for such review, and the grounds thereof, within five days from the date of his rejection, and commence his proceedings within ten days from the service of said notice.

Section 9 provides for the registration of persons coming of age.

Section 10 provides for giving a certificate of registration to each registered voter.

Section 11 provides for the renewal of certificates when worn or defaced, and, as amended, provides for renewal of lost certificates, but the applicant is obliged to make oath to the circumstances attending the loss, and "that he has not sold, bartered, or parted with the same for any pecuniary, valuable, or *other* consideration, and has not willfully destroyed the same," and the supervisor is authorized to require *such evidence as he deems necessary* as to the loss.

His decision is subject to review by the board of appeals, when a renewal certificate has been rejected, and their action is subject to review by the circuit court if notice is given within five days and proceedings commenced within ten days thereafter.

Sections 12, 13, 14, and 15 provide for the surrender of the old and the issue of new registration certificates whenever a voter changes his residence, either within the precinct or to another precinct or county. Any one so changing his residence without a transfer certificate, is debarred from the privilege of voting.

SEC. 16. The supervisor of registration shall, immediately preceding each election, revise the registration of electors and mark off the names of such electors as have died and such as have removed from one residence, precinct, parish, ward, or county, to another, without notifying him and obtaining a certificate of transfer as hereinbefore provided.

Sections 17 and 18 provide for furnishing the managers of election with copies of the registration books, and for the pay of supervisors.

It will be seen that under this act a complete precinct registration of all qualified voters who should apply was provided for, to be made in the months of May and June, 1882; the supervisors visiting each township for that purpose, after due notice, and remaining not less than one nor more than three days. In that time he was required to administer oaths to all applicants, requiring a statement of age, residence, occupation, length of residence in county and State, and to take such other evidence as he deemed fit; to make a record of these items, and to issue to each registered voter a certificate containing the same statement required to be recorded. In many of the townships of the State this was an impossibility within the limited time.

Immediately on closing the precinct registration the supervisor was required to open his books at the county seat, to correct errors and register such voters as had failed to register at the precinct registration. Having concluded his registration he is required to revise his lists, and *may, in his discretion*, permit a registration if any qualified voter has failed to register. Having completed his revision the books must be closed and not thereafter opened for registration until after the next general election, and then only for those who have become entitled to registration since the close of the first general registration. After each general election, the books are to be opened on the first Monday in each month up to and including the first Monday in July next preceding any general election, but only for the registration of those who have become entitled to register since the last closing of the books.

Under the letter of this act, any qualified elector who failed to register at the first general registration is forever thereafter debarred from registering and from voting. Any one subsequently becoming entitled to register and failing to do so before the closing of the books in July preceding the general election at which he would first be entitled to vote is forever thereafter disfranchised. A minor failing to register before the first general election following his becoming of voting age is thereafter disfranchised. Such is the letter of the law, and such, we are informed, is the universal practice of registering officers. We quote the testimony of one of them:

James S. Polk, being duly sworn, deposes and says (p. 345):

Question. What official position do you hold in Sumter County?—Answer. Supervisor of registration.

Question. How long have you held that position?—Answer. Two years last October.

Question. It has been testified by several witnesses for the contestant that you refused upon proper demand to register duly qualified Republican voters; was such the fact?—Answer. It was not; I never did.

Question. What is the provision of the registration law in regard to such persons as were refused registration?—Answer. The law provides that a man must be registered for the election preceding which he becomes twenty-one years of age; if from neglect or any cause he fails to register then, then he is debarred from registering afterwards by the terms of the law.

R. H. Richardson (p. 26) says:

Q. Do you know the supervisor of registration of this county?—A. I do.
Q. Is he a Democrat or a Republican?—A. A Democrat.
Q. Do you know that he refused upon proper demand to register Republican voters before the last election?—A. Persons who were of age at the time the general registration laws were passed he refused to register, on the ground that they had neglected their former chance of being registered in their time.

Any one parting with his certificate of registration for any consideration, or willfully destroying it, becomes thereby forever disfranchised,

and yet he has committed neither treason, murder, robbery, nor dueling, nor, indeed, has he committed any offense made a crime by the
laws of the State.   That these provisions of the registration statutes
are unconstitutional and void can not be seriously questioned.   They
attach the penalty of permanent disfranchisement for failing for any
cause to register for the first election at which the citizen would be
entitled to vote if registered.   They affix a like penalty for parting
with or destroying a registration certificate.

But they give such latitude to the supervisor of registration as will
enable him to take good care that none of his political friends shall suffer the penalty.   After the first general registration, all future registrations and changes of registration must be made at the county seat;
and all applications for transfer certificates must be made at the county
seat of the county where former registration was had, although the
voter may in the mean time have moved to the opposite end of the
State.   All applications for the renewal of worn or lost certificates must
in like manner be made at the county seat of the county where the certificate was issued; and, at the will of the supervisor, such evidence of
the circumstances of loss as he may require must be produced.

When the board of appeals has decided against an applicant for registration, he may appeal, but must give notice in writing within five
days, and commence proceedings in court within ten days thereafter,
or be forever debarred from voting.   A special remedy with a fifteen-
days statute of limitations!

Under the name of a registration law, these burdensome and unreasonable, and, therefore, unlawful barriers have been erected, to exclude from the polls a large body of citizens.

In States whose constitutions do not provide, nor authorize their legislatures to
provide, that persons shall not vote unless registered in a prescribed mode, the question whether a legislative provision to that effect is or is not of constitutional
validity always turns upon the question whether it is merely a reasonable and convenient regulation of the right to vote, or is under the pretense of regulation an
abridgment, subversion, or restraint of that right.   (Paine on Elections, section 340.)

In the case of Capen *vs.* Foster (12 Pick., 485) the supreme court of
Massachusetts said:

And this court is of opinion that, in all cases where the Constitution has conferred
a political right, or privilege, and where the Constitution has not particularly designated the manner in which that right is to be exercised, it is clearly within the
just and constitutional limits of the legislative power to adopt any reasonable and
uniform regulations in regard to the time and mode of exercising that right in a
prompt, orderly, and convenient manner.   Such a construction would afford no warrant for such an exercise of legislative power as, under the pretense and color of
regulating, should subvert or seriously restrain the right itself.

The supreme court of Pennsylvania, in the case of Page *vs.* Allen
(58 Penn. St., 338), pronounced a registry law of that State unconstitutional on the ground that it impaired the free exercise of the right of
suffrage conferred by the Constitution.   The court said:

For the orderly exercise of these (constitutional) qualifications it is admitted that
the legislature must prescribe necessary regulations as to the places, mode and manner, and whatever else may be required to secure its full and free exercise; but this
duty and right inherently imply that such regulations are to be subordinate to the
enjoyment of the right, the exercise of which is regulated.   The right must not be
impaired by the regulations; it must be regulations purely, not destruction.   If this
were not an immutable principle, elements essential to the right itself might be in-
vaded, frittered away, or entirely exscinded, under the name or pretense of regulation, and thus would the natural order of things be subverted, by making the principal subordinate to the accessory; to state is to prove this position.

To crown all, the supervisor, without notice to anybody, and without
posting the names, is required, immediately preceding any general

election, to revise the registry and strike off the names of such persons as he determines have died or have changed their residence and have neglected to notify him and obtain a transfer certificate.

When it is remembered that the white Democrats of the State are largely the property owners, having permanent places of residence, and that the colored men are poor, mostly tenants and laborers, under the necessity of frequently changing their homes the hardship and inequality of the law are more strikingly evident.

It would seem that the law placed enough obstructions in the way of registration to satisfy the most earnest believer in the disfranchisement of the colored men of South Carolina, but, as shown by the record in this case, the supervisors appointed to execute it have succeeded, in almost every instance, in erecting other and most effective barriers not provided for in the statute. They are required to keep their books at the county seat, and to open them for registration on the first Monday of certain specified months, but they are not required to give any notice of where they keep their offices or their books. In many counties a diligent search on the part of Republicans fails to discover the supervisor's office, or, when it is found, so many hindrances and obstructions are interposed that voters fail to get transfers or registry, although they apply at every opportunity, during every month of registration in the year of a general election. In some large precincts no one has been able to secure a transfer since the general registry in 1882.

Albert Beach, supervisor of registration of Colleton County, testifies (p. 293) that in Jacksonborough precinct there have been no renewals or transfers for the last four years; the same for Adams Run, for Delemars, for Gloverville, and for Green Pond.

He further says that he did not advertise where he would meet the citizens for the purpose of renewal, transfers, or original registration, because it was generally known where he would be.

In regard to the action of this same supervisor, we quote the testimony of W. F. Myers (p. 95):

Q. What facilities were afforded by the supervisor of registration in registering, renewing, and transferring certificates?—A. So far as Republicans were concerned no facilities were offered for registering those who have recently come of age, those who had removed, nor for those who desired renewal. I took over a hundred and fifty affidavits of Republicans applying for certificates, and at one time had a number of applicants to come to the court-house from a great distance to meet the supervisor, but he could never be found. On the other hand Democrats were afforded every and undue opportunities to secure theirs. I, on the 4th of November preceding the last election, in the court-room, was an unwilling listener to a conversation between Hon. C. G. Henderson and the supervisor of registration, Beach, when the former asked for those certificates. The latter replied that they were made and in his office. He went out and returned with a package and handed it to Mr. Henderson, which I supposed were the certificates. I have had two citizens, known to be Democrats, to tell me that up to the day before the election they were urgently requested to go up and get a certificate of registration that they could go up and vote on the 6th, which they declined to do.

Q. Did the supervisor have an office; if so, where was it?—A. So far as I could ascertain or find out through diligent inquiry he had not. I inquired at the offices located in the court-house, but none could or would say where he was located, excepting Auditor Smith, who said he (meaning the supervisor) came into his (Smith's) office, but he could not tell me if he had a permanent office.

J. H. Chapman, page 92 of record, corroborates Myers when questioned:

Q. Do you know if any person or persons desiring to register or have their registration certificates transferred or renewed have ever gone to the county seat at any time during 1888? If so, state the dates upon which they went.

(Objected to upon the grounds that the persons applying for renewal of certificates are the best evidence; what witness might say would be hearsay and inadmissible.)

H. Mis. 137——33

A. I do know of such persons going for the purpose of having their's renewed or transferred; on the first Monday in March, first Monday in April, first Monday in July, and after they, along with myself, got up to Walterboro. I inquired for the office of the supervisor of registration; I inquired of Mr. Myers and Jackson Grant, but I could not find the office.

Q. State into what building, if any, did you go at Walterboro to look for the office of supervisor of registration.—A. I went in the court-house and I looked on each side of the building as I passed through the passage-way for the sign of the office of supervisor of registration, and I never saw any sign of said office.

Q. State if while there looking for said office of registration if you saw the supervisor of registration.—A. I did not.

Q. Did you look into any of the rooms or offices in the court-house building for the supervisor of registration on said days?—A. I did.

W. B. Scott (page 94 of record) goes into the office the supervisor of registration claims to use on the proper day of registration, does not find him, but finds the auditor of the county, who knows nothing except "he sometimes comes in there." Scott being questioned:

Q. Have you ever gone to Walterboro and endeavored to find the office of supervisor of registration; and, if so, state what happened.—A. I went there the first Monday in last March, and as I went I took my registration certificate with me to see whether I could get it change from Jacksonboro to Green Pond, and as I went up I ask Jackson Grant what time the supervisor will be in and whereabout he held his office; he told me to go to the court-house and I would find out, and I went over and saw the auditor; Mr. Smith told me where the office of the supervisor was; he said sometimes he comes in here and moreover I have not time to bother with you. Then I came on back home and after I came back I wrote a letter to Major Myers.

Q. Did you ever go back again?—A. I went back the first Monday in June and did not see the supervisor, and I went back again in July and the supervisor was pointed out to me; I went to him where his office was and when he would be in, as they had his registrar certificate and desire to have it change from Jacksonboro to Green Pond and had forty affidavits of persons who wanted to change theirs and said he did not know when he would be in Walterboro and he had no office there.

As to Orangeburgh County, we quote from the testimony of E. A. Webster (p. 324):

Q. Are the same facilities afforded Republicans and Democrats alike in registration of voters in Orangeburgh County?—A. In the administration of the law the same facilities are not allowed to Republicans as to Democratic voters. The Republicans are not able to find the supervisor of registration for the purpose of changing certificates, registering and renewing. The supervisor residing some ten miles from the court-house, his office has not been kept open as required by law. Republicans had access only during the time his office was opened. The office on those days crowded with Republicans, and a large number were present who could not register, though they applied. The office has not been open since the first Monday in August, 1888, to Republicans previous to the election. In my judgment there were at least fifteen hundred who applied and were not registered, including necessary transfers and changes, on the last day in question. Just before the closing of the office I presented to the supervisor of registration a large number of affidavits of lost certificates collected from voters present from the Seventh Congressional district, and tendered them to the supervisor, requesting that he should issue certificates thereon, which he refused to do. I will state that while Republicans met with this embarrassment and obstruction certificates were issued to Democrats without personal application. I protested against this, as Republican county chairman, as being unfair. The supervisor, who is a Democrat, stated to me that he was not compelled under the law to make these changes and issue certificates except upon personal application, *but that if he choose to favor his political friends he should do so.* I applied to him several times after the first Monday in August—meeting him on the street—to make some changes in certificates for change of residence, and to issue in place of lost certificates upon affidavits in my possession; this he refused to do. My instructions, as county chairman, to the Republican voters who applied was to wait about or at the office until it was closed. I should judge, on the last day, that about 250 or 300 were there when the office closed; many of them from the Seventh Congressional district.

By means detailed by these witnesses, thousands of Republicans of the seventh district were deprived of such certificates of registration as the managers would recognize. Hundreds of them went to the polls and presented their old certificates, only to find their names stricken from the books. Many of them were voters who had not changed their residence, even within the precinct of their residence. Some who, after much trouble, had secured transfer certificates, went to the polls and found that the description copied into the precinct registry did not agree with the description in their certificates, and so were unable to vote.

We do not make any account of the number of these voters who failed to get certificates and who tendered their votes, because in this case it would not affect the result farther than to increase contestant's majority; but we hold that all such persons, otherwise qualified, were legal voters.

We go further, and hold that there is no valid registration law in South Carolina. The election machinery of the State, while not so bad as its registration laws, is still of a character which can not well be overlooked. All the machinery of elections is in the hands of the Democratic party. The governor appoints commissioners of election for each county, without provision for minority representation; there being two sets of these commissioners, one for State and the other for Federal elections. These in turn appoint precinct managers. To these commissioners the returns of the precinct managers are returned, to be by them canvassed and certified to a State returning board, composed of certain State officers. Both the county and State returning boards have quasi-judicial powers, instead of being limited to the canvass and certification of the vote as cast.

From seven to nine ballot boxes are required to hold an election; one for governor and lieutenant-governor, one for other State officers, one for circuit solicitor, one for state senator, one for member of the State house of representatives, one for county officers, one for representative in Congress, one for Presidential elector, and a ninth box if any special question is to be voted on at that election.

These boxes are to be labeled according to the officers, the two Federal boxes to be presided over by one set of managers, and the six or seven State boxes by another set. Polls for Federal and State elections may be widely separated. All the tickets are to be of a specified description, and none others can be counted. The voter is required to deposit his own ticket, and find out for himself the right box, the managers on demand only being required to read the names on the boxes, but there is no requirement that they shall designate the boxes while pronouncing the names, or read the names in any particular order. No other person is permitted to speak to the voter while in the polling place. No tickets found in the wrong box are to be counted.

This, in fact, makes an educational test, in direct violation of the constitution of the State. Its practical operation will be seen when we come to consider the details of this case.

In the Seventh district, except in one county, all the supervisors of registration, all the commissioners of election, and all the precinct managers, were Democrats, the Republicans being denied representation on any of the boards. The only way to have watchfulness at the election, by persons not politically hostile to contestant, was to secure the appointment of United States supervisors, one of each party, who, under the present law, are required to serve without compensation.

On the 27th day of September, 1888, the Republican executive committee of the State addressed a communication to Governor Richardson, asking for representation on the election boards. To this communication the Governor made answer, denying the request, and, among other things, said:

It will be sufficient simply to say that, in my judgment, a departure from the wisely-established methods and principles upon which these appointments are made would endanger the continuance of the perfectly free, fair, and peaceful elections—the professed object of your desire—that are the proud boast and the highest achievement of Democratic rule in this State.

This from the chief executive of the State, when denying to a party which outnumbered his party four to one in the Seventh district, a participation in the conduct of the election, a participation which is regarded almost everywhere else as necessary to honest elections, and when denied is regarded as a matter of law, as casting a suspicion upon the integrity of the election and returns.

But the governor continues:

To the eternal honor of our State and the Democratic party it can now be said that our elections are the freest and fairest in the world, and that not a single citizen of hers, no matter what his rank, color, or condition, can, under her just and equal laws, impartially administered as they are, be by any perversion or intimidation, barred at the polls from the free and full exercise of his suffrage. There is not only perfect freedom in voting, but the amplest protection afforded the voter.

From what we have said of the registration and election law and from the examples given of the conduct of supervisors of registration, it will be seen that we do not agree with the governor. We are at a loss to understand how such language could be used with sincerity. In the further examination of this case we shall show how grievously the governor was deceived as to the Seventh district, if, indeed, his answer to the executive committee had any other purpose than to mislead the people of the United States outside of South Carolina.

With this general review of the situation we come to the examination of the specific facts affecting the election.

BALLOTS IN WRONG BOXES.

The first question which we consider, which resulted in a loss of votes to contestant, is the failure to count ballots for him found in the Presidential box. As has been noted, managers of elections are prohibited from counting any ballots found in the wrong box. At the federal polls, at this election, there were two boxes, one for Presidential electors, and one for Congressman. Under the peculiar wording of the statute, unlettered voters are obliged to rely upon those of their associates who can read to learn how to deposit their tickets so as not to get them into the wrong box, and so lose their votes.

If the two boxes are put into position before the voting commences, and are permitted to remain in the same position during the day, there is little danger of any mistake, all the voters being instructed as to their position by those in whom they have confidence. But if the boxes are shifted about at intervals during the day, it follows as a matter of course that every unlettered voter who goes to the poll after the change and before its discovery deposits his ballot in the wrong box, and loses his vote so far as the count of the managers is concerned. There is no prohibition in the statute against shifting the boxes, and so it is assumed by the managers of election that they have a right to shift the boxes as often as they please, for the express purpose, as they acknowledge, of confusing the voters and causing them to deposit their ballots in the wrong box.

It was gravely argued before the committee by an eminent lawyer that there was nothing wrong in this shifting of boxes, and that contestee was entitled to all the benefits accruing to him by reason of such action. An act may not expressly be forbidden by law, but if it is done with an unlawful purpose, and succeeds in accomplishing that purpose, the act is thereby made unlawful.

At this election, in a large number of precincts, this shifting of boxes was resorted to. The facts and the motive are proven beyond a reasonable doubt. We submit a few extracts from the evidence upon this branch of the case:

Daniel Ravenel, Republican United States supervisor at Jourdin's, Williamsburgh County, says (p. 8):

Q. Was the position of the boxes changed during the progress of the election that day?—A. Yes, sir.
Q. By whom?—A. By the managers.
Q. About how many times?—A. As well as I can recollect about six or seven times.
Q. Did you show the voters or attempt to show the voters what box to deposit their ballots in?—A. I attempted to show them, but the managers objected.

M. M. Monzon, Republican United States supervisor at Kingstree, says (p. 13):

Q. How many ballots, if any, were found in the Presidential electors' box bearing the name of Thomas E. Miller for member of 51st Congress from the Seventh Congressional district?—A. Sixty-six were in the wrong boxes.
Q. What was done with those ballots; were they counted for Thomas E. Miller?—A. No, sir; they were not counted for Miller. They were destroyed by the managers.
Q. Was the position of the boxes changed that day during the election?—A. They were, a number of times.
Q. By whom were they changed?—A. By the managers of election.

Jesse S. Fulmore, Republican United States supervisor at Indiantown (p. 15), says:

Q. What was done with those 81 ballots?—A. They were taken out and destroyed.
Q. Then they were not counted for Thomas E. Miller?—A. No, sir.
Q. Who destroyed them?—A. The managers of election.
Q. Were the managers of election Republicans or Democrats?—A. They were all Democrats.
Q. Was the position of the boxes changed or shifted about that day, during the progress of the election?—A. Yes, sir; they were changed from one place to another at least five times.
Q. Who shifted or changed them about?—A. The managers of election.

B. J. Fortune, Republican United States supervisor at Corbell's Store (p. 21), says:

Q. What became of the other 29 ballots?—A. They were destroyed by the managers.
. Why were they destroyed?—A. Because they were placed into the wrong box.
Q. What box?—A. Into the Presidential box.
Q. Whose names did these ballots bear?—A. T. E. Miller.
Q. Was the position of the boxes changed during the election from the position they were in at the beginning; if so, by whom?—A. They were changed about 8 or 9 times by W. A. Cooper and Robert Wilson, the managers.
Q. Did you hear the managers making any remarks in regard to the change of the boxes?—A. I did not, although I called attention to change.
Q. To what political party did the managers belong?—A. The Democratic party.

L. R. Davis, Republican United States supervisor at Sumter (p. 24), says:

Q. Whose name did these 9 ballots bear?—A. T. E. Miller.
Q. Was the position of the boxes changed during the election from the position they were in when the voting began; if so, by whom?—A. Changed frequently by the managers.
Q. After they were so changed, and a voter would vote, what did the managers say?—A. They did not say anything, except on one or two occasions.
Q. What was said on those occasions?—A. On one occasion I wanted to vote myself; the box was shifted around, and the managers laughed and said I made him vote in the wrong box.

Q. To what political party did the managers belong?—A. The Democratic party.
Q. Did you keep a poll-list?—A. I tried to do it, but was prevented.
Q. State who prevented you from keeping a poll-list.
(Objected to as irrelevant, nothing in the ground of contest.)
A. The list I was keeping was snatched from me several times by Mr. R. D. Lee, counsel for contestee and Democratic county chairman.
(Objected to on above grounds.)
Q. Do you know what official position, if any, Mr. Lee held at the polls on that day?—A. I think he held a position as constable.
Q. Did you keep or succeed in keeping any part of the poll-list?—A. None; I tried twice; it was snatched and destroyed.
Q. Was any violence offered to you by any of the managers, if you should keep a poll-list?
(Objected to as above.)
A. I was threatened to be put out if I kept another poll-list.

M. Johnson, Republican United States supervisor at Eastover (p. 319), says:

Q. State if you can where the boxes were placed while the voting was being done, and if they were changed as to position during the day by any one.—A. The boxes were placed on board partition between the managers and the person voting, and were shuffled by the managers during the day.
Q. State if there was any object or closed partition between where the managers of election stood and where you stood while the voting was being conducted.—A. I was placed at such a position by the chairman of the board of managers from which I could see the voting, but the boxes were being changed so that I could not see them when they were handled or changed by the managers.
Q. Do you mean by above answer to say that either of the boxes was taken off of where they were placed originally, out of your sight, by any one?—A. I do, as the managers took them off from where they were originally placed; I could not see them.
Q. When they took them, or either, from where they were originally placed where would they place them? I mean, would they place them between you and any object or not? If so, state what the object was.—A. They would place them behind this board partition on a box or something of the kind, and would then change them.
Q. While the boxes or box was taken out of its original place and placed behind the board partition were you in a position to see what was done to or with the boxes or box by any one?—A. I was not from the fact that the partition prevented my seeing, and anything could have been done with the boxes while they were changing them.
Q. Why did you not go behind the partition whenever any one took a box or boxes out of your sight?—A. I was assigned to my position in the room by chairman of board, where I had to remain all day.

J. C. Eason, Democratic United States supervisor at Eastover (p. 332), says:

Q. Did the managers or any one of them in any way interfere or intermeddle with any of the voters, except to put to them certain questions required by law, while casting their votes?—A. No; they never interfered with any one.
Q. What disposition or arrangement would the managers make with reference to the boxes during the day while the election was going on?—A. The only thing I saw them do with the boxes was to change the position of the two boxes. That is, place one where the other had been. This was done openly, so Johnson and I could see it done. One box was distinctly labeled for Presidential electors and the other was distinctly labeled for member of Congress.
Q. Why was this interchange of boxes made?—A. I think the cause was that Johnson began sending out notes stating which sides the respective boxes for electors and Congressman were on.
Q. Can you say how many these shiftings of the boxes were made during the day?—A. I can not.
Q. How long were the managers in making the shifting of the boxes?—A. It was momentarily. They would pick up, move the other in its place, and put it down.
Q. In making these changes was any one of them ever taken out of Johnson's sight?—A. I could always see them myself.

And on cross-examination:

Q. The ballot-boxes, you say, were transposed several times through the day?—A. Yes.
Q. And ballots were deposited by colored voters after these changes as well as by white voters?—A. Yes.

Q. When a voter went to the boxes to deposit his ballot did anybody accompany him ?—A. No.

Q. Or did anybody explain to the voter the character of the respective boxes ?—A. No.

Q. And therefore if a voter who could not read should deposit his ballots in the boxes according to the information he had previously received as to their location, there would be no certainty of his ballots going into the boxes he had intended ?—A. No ; I think not.

Q. And is that the way it happened that there were 8 or 10 ballots in one of the boxes which the managers destroyed because they were in the wrong box ?—A. I suppose that was the way of it.

Robert Wilson, Democratic manager at Corbett's Store (p. 347), says:

Cross-examined by Mr. WHITTAKER:

Question. By whom was the position of the boxes changed ?—Answer. In some cases by myself, and in some by Mr. W. A. Cooper, one of the managers.

Question. Why was the position of the boxes changed ?—Answer. *They were changed to carry out the spirit of the law and test the intelligence of the voter.* The voters were being directed by a man who had climbed up a tree so that he could see the position of the boxes over the barricade ; the voters were coming in with their tickets and hands held upright, one in one hand and one in another, and whenever the boxes were changed the man up the tree would hollow out, " Mind dare !" " Change dem tickets !"

Question. Why were the boxes labeled ?—Answer. They were delivered to us labeled.

Question. State that law which in our State directs the managers to test the intelligence of the voter by any means.—Answer. I know of no law which directs us and none to prohibit. *We understood the spirit of the law to be that each man must read for himself the labels upon the boxes.*

Question. Does the spirit of the law prevent any person outside of the polling place directing a voter how and where to deposit his ballot ?—Answer. We think so, as it required us to put up secure barricades.

Question. Was the position of the boxes changed while the voters were in the polling place ?—Answer. In some cases it was.   * * *   The position of the boxes were changed several times that day ; I know of no law to prevent it ; Fortune objected and we told him if he would show us any law to prohibit, we would not move them again ; he examined his copy of the law carefully and told us that he saw none.

As to this witness' statement of the law for putting up "secure barricades," it may be said that the law provides that an inclosure "shall be *railed off,* or otherwise provided " (sec. 29), thus showing that the law does not contemplate a tight barricade which shall shut off the view.

C. O. Marshall, Democratic manager at Eastover (p. 336), says:

Q. Were any of these two boxes in which the election was held carried or taken by any person out of the sight of the managers ?—A. They were not.

Q. During the time of the election were these two boxes shifted or transposed on this shelf upon which they rested ?—A. They were.

Q. For what purpose were these boxes transposed and in what manner ?—A. When we made the first change Meshoch Johnson, the Republican supervisor, spoke to a voter and told him to tell them outside about the position of the boxes. I called his attention to the State law forbidding any one to speak to voters. He then got to sending notes out by voters, trying to give them to voter surreptitiously. The boxes were changed several times in consequence of this U. S. supervisor *trying to defeat the election laws,* thus trying to give his party an undue advantage.

This resulted in a net loss to contestant of over a thousand votes. This account excludes from consideration all votes in those precincts where the voters deposited the same kind of a ballot in each box, so as to make sure that one of them would be counted, and only takes into consideration those ballots which are shown by the number voting, the number of ballots in the box, or by corresponding electoral ballots in the wrong box, to have been placed in the wrong box by mistake, and against the intention of the voter.

In every instance but one, the shifting of the boxes is shown. The purpose was unlawful, the result was the failure to have counted, and the destruction of over 1,000 ballots cast for contestant by duly qualified voters.

The managers of election took no account of these ballots, immediately destroyed them under a claim that the law so directed (a claim not sustained by the statute), and as witnesses almost universally show a remarkable forgetfulness as to their number. The United States supervisors, present at all the polls when this destruction occurred, kept an account of the number, and by that means we are able to ascertain with reasonable certainty the whole number lost.

Following are the precincts where losses of this character occurred, with the net number after deducting any losses sustained by Elliott.

Williamsburg County:		Orangeburg County:	
Gourdin's	22	Washington Seminary	25
Blooming Vale	10	Fort Motte	16
Black Mingo	23	Colleton County:	
Greeleyville	128	Adams Run	95
Salters	23	Berkeley County:	
Cade's	20	Strawberry Ferry	21
Kingstree	66	Biggin Church	18
Indiantown	81	Black Oak	44
Sumter County:		Ten-Mile Hill	37
Corbett's Store	29	Calamus Pond	22
Statesburgh	3	Muster House	38
Sumter	9	Brick Church	11
Lynchburgh	29	Camp Ground	150
Raftin Creek	12	Hant Gap	61
Bethel Cross Roads	5		
Mayesville	40	Total	1,040

Making large allowance for any mistake in numbers, we add 1,000 to the returned vote for Miller, making his vote 8,003, after this addition, and leaving Elliott's majority 355.

It will hardly be claimed by any one that this unlawful attempt by the partisan friends of contestee, acting as managers of election, to disfranchise a thousand voters, ought to be permitted to succeed, in a contest. Both law and justice forbid.

If the intention of the elector can be ascertained, it is not to be defeated merely because the inspector, through mistake or fraud, deposits his ballot in the wrong box; nor because the elector himself, by mistake without fraud, places it in the wrong box. (People vs. Bates, 11 Mich., 368.)

Here the elector placed his ballot in the wrong box by mistake, the result of the unlawful and fraudulent acts of the managers of the election. It is no answer to say that the counting of such ballots is prohibited by statute (even admitting that the statute is a reasonable regulation, which, under the peculiar circumstances in South Carolina, we do not), when the mistaken deposit has resulted from the active deception of the managers. It is a crime at common law to enter into a conspiracy to commit any offense against the purity and fairness of a public election. (Paine on Elections, section 496, and authorities cited).

BALLOT-BOX STUFFING.

COLLETON COUNTY.

Gloverville precinct.—Here the whole number of votes polled for member of Congress was 134; 113 were returned for Elliott, and 20 for Miller. When the box was opened at the close of the polls it was found to contain an excess of 85 ballots, more than half as many again as were actually voted. This proves that the box was dishonestly stuffed by somebody. The managers were all Democrats and friends of contestee. It is scarcely possible that it could have been done by the voters. But the evidence leaves no doubt upon the question as to who committed the crime.

The United States supervisor went to the polling place very early in the morning, and staid in front of the usual polling place waiting for the managers to come and prepare to open the polls. Before the time for opening the polls James H. Dodd, one of the managers, came to the fire where the United States supervisor was standing, and on being asked, answered that the poll was to be held in the store.

While the supervisor and Dodd were talking the clerk of the store opened the door, where the voters afterwards entered to vote. The supervisor entered the store and asked to have the ballot-box opened before the election commenced. He was then informed that the election had already commenced, and five ballots been deposited. The time for voting had not yet arrived, the polling place had not been opened, no proclamation had been made; with the exception of Nero Williams, who was seen coming from the back door of the store, all of these first five voters slept in the store in which the poll was opened the night previous to the election. Three of the five were not registered voters and two of them were managers of the election.

Here is clear evidence of a conspiracy: The getting together the night before and sleeping in the polling place, the pretended opening of the polls before the polling place was opened and the United States supervisor admitted, and the deposit of illegal ballots so as to make an excuse for not exposing the interior of the box to the inspection of the United States supervisor, the peculiar twisted character of the tickets in the box, which could not have been placed there by the voters on account of the narrow opening, and which were not taken when the excess of ballots was drawn out under a pretense of complying with the law—all reach to the inevitable conclusion that the box was stuffed with Elliott tickets before the voting commenced. We insert here the testimony of E. M. Chisolm, United States supervisor (record, pp. 285, 286, 287):

E. M. Chisolm, being duly sworn, says:

Q. State your age, occupation, residence, and where you were on the 6th day of November, 1888.—A. I am 31 years; am a farmer; live in Gloverville Precinct; was at Gloverville acting as supervisor on November 6 last.

Q. State for whom you voted as member of Congress from the seventh district on the 6th of November, 1888.—A. For T. E. Miller.

(Objection.)

Q. State from whom did you get your ballot, if you can read, and how many ballots or tickets did you vote for Congressman at the last election.—A. From Abrahm Small, who was distributing; can read; voted one ticket for Congressman.

(Objection.)

Q. State at what precinct did you vote, and if any one read your ticket for you.—A. Gloverville; read my own ticket.

Q. How many boxes were at the poll that day?—A. Two.

Q. State the name of the person who read your ticket to you, and to what political party he belongs.—A. Abrahm Small; he is a Republican.

Q. You have stated that you were supervisor at Gloverville poll; state what time in the morning you arrived at the polls, what you saw, and what was done by you and the managers or any other persons connected with the poll.—A. I think it was about half past four when I reached the poll the morning of election; I met there Abrahm Small, Sam Hawkins, and Rob't Smalls; I inquired of them as to where the voting would take place; that was then right opposite the store where elections are generally held; as we saw none of the managers, after being there about half an hour, things being quite still; then we heard a little thumping in the store as if some one was getting up putting on their shoes, after which we saw the two so-called Democrats, Ceasar Chisolm and Nero Williams, come from the back part of the store and walk to our fire; we waited some time when Joe Dodd, another of the managers, come from behind the store with his brother, Julius Dodd; we judge they came from out of the store.

After being there a little while I said to Mr. Dodd, "Where will the poll be held to-day?" He said he was manager of the Congressional poll. I said, "That's the

poll I am asking you about." In that time the front door of the store was opened by
W. F. Hill, a clerk in the store. Mr. Dodd invited me in after I told him I was supervisor—Joe Dodd, I mean. He showed me how the voters would come in to a window. I said to him, "Mr. Dodd, the law requires me to look into the box before the
voting commences." Instead of giving me a direct answer he touched another of the
managers, Ceasar Chrisolm, and walked off; then they had a conversation, after
which he, Dodd, said, "It is too late now, you can not look in the box." Then I
said, "I will note your objections." He said, "All right." He again repeated that
"we refuse on the ground that it was too late." I asked him the hour. He said the
poll was opened at six o'clock; I said it is not now six o'clock, because we have the
time right here and it lacks now five minutes to six. Then he pulled out his watch
saying, "Gracious, it is near 7 o'clock!" He said at this juncture that they had
commenced voting; I said, "Well, I was here about two hours ago, and I saw no one
vote; if anybody has voted give me the names that I may copy them." He presented
his name (Joe Dodd) first; the next, I think, was Ceasar Chisolm, W. F. Hill, Nero
Williams, and Julius B. Dodd, which I copied.

(W. B. Gruber, counsel for contestee, objects to any conversation had between the
supervisors and the managers or any person or other persons than the managers,
upon the ground that it is irrelevant and hearsay, and therefore not admissible.)

Q. State whether the election was quiet during the day.—A. Yes, everything went
on perfectly quiet.

Q. State what was done by you or the managers at the close of the poll, relating
all the circumstances that happened during the canvassing and counting of the votes.

(Objection on ground that if the witness as Federal supervisor performed his duty
as the law required him to do and reduced to writing in the form of a report the matters he is now called upon to testify, as to that the report would be the highest and
best evidence as to what happened, and secondary evidence inadmissible.)

A. After copying the few names that was given me by Mr. Dodd, and he showed
me the window at which the people were to vote, I saw the difficulty that seemed to
be intended for fraud. I saw it was necessary the way they had it arranged to have
some one right at the window to give these men their tickets. I then choose one I
knew was competent to issue out and stand at the window. They were instructed
that as each man came up to vote Abrahm Smalls was to hand him his tickets. The
Democrats did the same, having a man on the other side of the window to hand their
tickets. This rule was observed the whole day, vote after vote, until the closing of
the poll. Then Joe Dodd, one of the managers, said that "every one of you leave the
house, and all of the white men come in." Chisolm, he said, "you can stay; I did
not mean you, and Abrahm Smalls can stay with you." Before they commenced
counting they seemed somewhat confused as to how they should count. That is, Joe
Dodd, who seemed to be the chief, and Ceasar Chisolm, they stepped off a space, holding a secret talk. They came back and suggested how they should count, which was
that they would throw all the ballots out of the small box into a larger one, which
they did. Then Ceasar Chisolm commenced to count right off; then Joe Dodd, point-
ing his finger, said, "Hold on, you must stir the votes up first; stir them up; keep
your eyes out." Then they went on; they then counted without giving candidates
any credit at all, after which they had a considerable lot of votes over the names on
the poll-list—229 in all in the box. Then they found that the total number of names
on poll-list was 134; then they proceeded to give candidates their credit. The question came up as to the excessive votes—what was to be done with them. One of the
managers then turned his back, but not his eyes. I then observed that the general
Republican votes was folded and a portion of the Democratic votes was folded and
the rest was twisted. Then they would draw one of the folded votes—the twisted votes
were never drawn—until they got down to the number on the poll-list, destroying as
they drew. The managers then suggested that we now go into a general drunk, which
was done. I refused to join, against their urgent and frequent requests. They commenced to call off the tickets. Joe Dodd would take them from the box and Ceasar
Chisolm would call the names from the tickets, giving each candidate, Miller and
Elliott, credits. He called to a certain number and stopped at the suggestion of Joe
Dodd to take another drink, seeming to be more polite to me that night than ever before; then they finished up the canvassing, giving Elliott, I think, 114 and Miller 21.

(Counsel for contestee objects on ground that result of the vote should be proved
by the written return of the managers and supervisors.)

Q. Did you observe or notice what name or names was on the ballots as they were
counted?—A. I did not, because they had the table crowded and they seemed to stand
from me while counting.

Q. What was the name of the person who called the names from the tickets, and can
he read and write?—A. Ceasar Chisolm; I suppose he can sign his name, you may
call that writing, and I suppose he could distinguish the names between Elliott and
Miller.

Q. State whether you noticed the hole or aperture in the Congressional box and whether those twisted tickets could have been voted through that hole and found in the condition which they were.—A. I did notice the hole; that's what aroused my attention to notice these twisted tickets and they could not have been voted through that hole.

Q. State the name of the person who had the key and opened the box or boxes at the close of the poll.—A. Joe Dodd.

Q. Were you in a position to know the number of Republican votes that were distributed by Smalls at the window and voted by the voters?—A. I was; I saw every person as he came and offered to vote. One man, Sam Perry, wanted to assist Smalls and I refused to allow him, as he was not competent,to distinguish the different votes. Chisolm, one of the Democratic managers, was there at different times trying to poke Democratic tickets in Republican hands. I know every man in Gloverville Township and know of only two colored men who voted the Democratic ticket.

Q. Do you know the number of white voters who are entitled to vote at that poll; if so, state that number?

· (Objected to on ground that the record as kept by the managers is the only evidence competent to prove who actually voted on that day.)

A. The Democrats as I remember now were Joe Dodd, Julius Dodd, John E. Bryan, B. G. Willis, T. S. Ackerman, W. H. Nix, P. Gatch, J. B. Glover, F. T. Glover, H. L. Ackerman, A. E. Griffith, W. F. Hill, H. H. Durant, and B. M. Williams; I think Paul McCants. I am satisfied that the whites do not cast over 21 this time including the two colored men. The total No. of white votes in Gloverville is about (25) twenty-five.

We refer also to the poll-list, page 628, and to the testimony of the registering officer of the county, page 293.

The evidence shows that a large majority of the votes at this precinct were Republican, and that not to exceed 21 voted the Democratic ticket. Inasmuch as it is impossible from the evidence to ascertain what was the true state of the vote, we reject the returns entirely. Taking 113 from Elliott, and 20 from Miller, we have: Elliott, 8,245; Miller, 7,983. Elliott's majority, 262.

Green Pond.—At this precinct the returned vote was:

Elliott 216
Miller 52

Here we have another example of ballot-box stuffing.

John F. Brown, United States supervisor (pages 294, 295, 296), gives a clear statement of the conduct here, and we quote:

Q. State your age, occupation, residence, and where you were on the 6th day of November, 1888.—A. Am about 33; lawyer; live in Green Pond precinct; was at Green Pond poll acting as supervisor on election day last.

Q. State for whom you voted as member of Congress from the 7th district on the 6th of November, 1888?—A. For T. E. Miller.

(Objection.)

Q. State from whom did you get your ballot, if you can read, and how many ballots or tickets did you vote for Congressman at the last election.—A. From J. H. Chapman; I can read; voted one on that day for Congress.

(Objected.)

Q. State at what precinct did you vote, and if any one read your ticket for you.— A. Green Pond; read my own ticket.

Q. How many boxes were at the poll?—A. Two.

Q. State the name of the person who read your ticket to you, and to what political party he belongs.—A. J. H. Chapman; is a Republican.

Q. State what house or place the Federal election was conducted in, or any circumstances that are material to the election that day.—A. It was held in a middle room of the house, a room I took to be the dining-room, owned by J. S. Hickman. I do not know whether it was occupied or not. I arrived at the poll about daylight that morning. About an hour and a half after I was there I saw Mr. Strobel. the depot agent. go down to Mr. Sanders's store; I went down behind him; he called Mr. Sanders, who opened the store and opened a back room in the store, the same we voted in the election before, and a table was placed in a position as if the election would have been held the e. I was informed that the election would be held there. About half past six I see no boxes, neither the managers; I felt somewhat uneasy in regard to it being held there. I saw that Mr. Strobel and Sanders were also uneasy; I think either Messrs. Strobel or Sanders told me the election would be held at Sanders's store. I noticed Mr. Strobel walking out of the back door into the back yard, and being informed that the managers were all at Mr. Hickman's house I walked out of the front door. The crowd followed me, Mr. Strobel goes through into his (S.) yard, then into Mr. Hickman's yard and into the back door of Mr. Hickman's house, the crowd and I following along the R. R. track. When I was about 100 or 150 feet from Mr. Hickman's gate Mr. Strobel came out of the front door of Hickman's house and announced that the poll was opened. I then entered the building and found the managers and M. A. Draudy, the supervisor, at the box; it was then fifteen minutes to seven by my time. I then asked the managers to exhibit the box before voting commenced; they announced the poll had been opened and they could not do it. A dispute arose between the managers and myself in regards to the time, after which I asked him that if they would not exhibit the boxes to give me the names of the persons who had voted. Manager Rice gave me the names of N. V. Robertson and E. G. Strobel as persons who had voted; I took a seat at a table they had prepared for me, about 4 or 5 feet from the table on which the boxes stood. Everything went on quietly after that until about 8 o'clock in the morning, then Manager Rice commenced shifting or changing the boxes around. I called his attention to the fact that he ought not to do it; he replied that all I could do "Report;" after then I said no more about the changing of the boxes. About 10 o'clock he called our attention to the fact that the people had found a way to vote by a split on top of the Federal box near the hole, and that he would remedy it; he goes over to Mr. Strobel, borrowed mucilage, came back and took a Democratic ticket from the table and placed it on the split.

Q. Did you keep a poll-list, and have you got it ?—A. I kept a poll-list, and here it is.

Q. From the poll-list you kept state how many white voters' names are on it.—A. There are fifteen names on here that I am positive are white, and the name N. V. Robertson, the first name given me and whom I did not see vote; I don't know whether he is white or colored.

Q. The persons whose names appear on your poll-list other than N. V. Robertson and Strobel deposited their ballots in your presence ?—A. They did.

Q. How many names have you on that poll-list ?—A. Two hundred and sixty-eight (268).

Q. Place the said poll-list in evidence.

(Paper placed in evidence purporting to be the poll-list kept by supervisor at Green Pond, and attached to this testimony.)

Q. Is this paper with the 268 names, beginning with the name of N. V. Robertson and ending with the name of James Campbell, and marked on first page "Poll-list," the list of the voters who appeared and cast their ballots at Green Pond precinct, in Colleton County, on the 6th of November last, at the Federal poll where you acted as U. S. supervisor ?—A. It is.

Q. Did you make this list of voters in the presence of the managers of election for Green Pond precinct on the 6th of Nov. last, and is it the original and official poll-list ?—A. This is the original list I made in the presence of the managers, and the managers and myself were very careful during the day to see that the two lists tallied, and I have made a copy of this poll-list and sent it to Charleston with my report to the chief supervisor.

Q. State what was the condition of the ballot-boxes when they were opened after the polls were closed, and how the tickets or ballots contained therein compared with the poll-lists kept by you and the managers ?—A. When the boxes were opened they were full of votes; they opened the Congressional box first, and counted all the votes out of that box except seventy-three that they torn up as being deposited in the wrong box, and placed them in a large box, that is, the untorn ballots; those placed in the large box were (586) five hundred and eighty-six votes or ballots. When they commenced counting them out of the box I stood near enough to look into the box, and the ballots in the bottom of the box appeared to have been newly folded and laid in; the rest of the ballots appeared as after they were folded they had been held in the hands some time before they were voted; I saw the names on some of these newly folded ballots in the box as they were taken out, and the name I saw was that of Wm. Elliott. They then commenced to draw out the excess ballots; Mr. Blanchard commenced drawing, I noticed him; he drew from the top of this large box. After he was drawing for some time, about 100 or 125, Mr. Rice winked at him and told him if he was tired drawing let him (R.) draw. Mr. Blanchard then moved away from the box; then Rice commenced drawing; I noticed him in drawing; he drew the votes that were in the bottom of the box, and continued to draw until he drawn out all the excess votes. Then they counted the votes and gave candidates credit for the first time. They gave Wm. Elliott 216; T. E. Miller, 52.

Q. Did you know or did you have any way of knowing during the day how many persons at Green Pond voted for Wm. Elliott for Congress ?—A. I know this, that when I went into the room in the morning I found the tickets or some tickets for Wm. Elliott on the table by the Congressional box, and the Democratic electoral tickets by the box for Presidential electors, and every white man that voted the Democratic ticket that day in my presence took the ticket from that table, folded and deposited them in the box, voting for Wm. Elliott and the Presidential electors, Democratic.

Q. Will you take the poll-list placed in evidence and state therefrom the names of the white men who took the Wm. Elliott tickets from the table and voted that day as you described?—A. They are S. B. Sanders, Jas. Gahagan, D. J. Chaplin, J. B. Hickman, B. P. Hooker, R. P. Sanders, Wm. Fuller, Wm. Sallibank, H. D. Bodiford, J. P. Slattery, R. B. Grant, C. A. Savage, C. C. Jones. I have stated that there were 16 white men who voted at Green Pond, but on going over the list again I found that I was mistaken; there are only fifteen white men's names on the list, and I do swear, to my knowledge, that fourteen of them are white. I do not know the fifteenth man, N. V. Robinson, as I did not see him vote.

Q. As to the colored voters who voted there that day, state if any of them voted the Elliott ticket and their names.—A. After I found the Elliott tickets on the table I sat there the entire day to see whether any colored voter would have taken any of the Elliott's tickets from the table and voted it. One man, John Lessington, came into the room without a ticket; the managers asked him if he wanted to vote; he said yes, but had no ticket. We asked him then whether he wanted to vote a Democrat or Republican ticket; he said he wanted to vote a Republican ticket; this was after he was already sworn; the managers thereupon allowed him to go out and get the Republican ticket, and he came back and voted it. Later on John Mustipher, a colored man, took a Democratic ticket from the table and voted it, and he is the only colored man that I saw who voted the Democratic ticket that day, that is, taking it from the table.

The testimony shows that the election was held at a private house, a different place from that at which it had been held at previous elections; that the poll was opened before the legal hour; that the managers of election refused to exhibit the inside of the box to the United States supervisor; that unregistered Democrats were permitted to vote; that the total number of names on the poll-list of those voting was 286, and that there were, at the close of the polls, 659 ballots in the Congressional box, 73 being Presidential tickets, and 586 Congressional tickets. Of these, the 73 Presidential tickets were destroyed, and 300 ballots were drawn out.

That these ballots were placed in the box before the election commenced admits of no reasonable question. They were so folded as to be easily known. The managers were all friends and partisans of contestee. They resorted to stratagem to have the polls declared open before the United States supervisor could get into their presence, and so have an excuse for not exhibiting the box to him. Only 2 votes are claimed to have been cast previous to the demand of the supervisor to have the box opened. One of them, that of Strobel, the decoy, and the other, that of Robertson, an unregistered voter.

The United States supervisor is on hand an hour and a half before the time for opening the polls. When the time approaches he is told that the election will be held at Saunders's store, the usual place; Strobel goes to the store, opens the door, places a table in position for the boxes, and arranges things preparatory for the election; he then steps out through the back door, into a back yard, and then into the back door of Hickman's house, where the election was actually held. The supervisor, on the watch for tricks, follows as fast as possible, followed by the voters; before he reaches Hickman's, Strobel comes out of the front door and announces that the polls are open, and the election managers announce that Strobel and Robertson have voted. All of the election managers, the clerks, and the marshals, all Democrats, went to the polling place the night before, and remained in Hickman's house over night.

The managers of the election were called as witnesses, and while claiming that the box was exhibited to the voters present they confirm

fully the testimony of Brown. The "voters present" were these Democratic election officers, who no doubt did exhibit the box to each other.
The action here is almost identical with that at Gloverville. In addition to the testimony of Brown, the supervisor, contestant introduced
Singleton (p. 92), Scott (p. 94), Myers (p. 284), and two hundred and
thirty-three others, whose testimony may be found on pages 91 to 93
and 162 to 285, from which it clearly appears that Miller received 252
votes at this precinct and Elliott but 16. Restating the vote according to the facts we have up to this point:

Elliott ....8,245—200=8,045
Miller ....7,983+200=8,183

     Miller's majority 138

Jacksonboro Precinct.—The returns from this precinct gave—

Elliott.. 68
Miller 45

     Total 113

An excess of 70 ballots at this poll was destroyed by the managers.
Here the ballot-box was not stuffed, but what was the equivalent of
ballot-box stuffing was done. The managers emptied the box on the
heads of some barrels standing behind the counter, where the supervisor had not been permitted to go during the day. The extra ballots
were undoubtedly on the heads of these barrels. When the count was
made it was found that there was an excess of 70 ballots in a poll of
113. Under pretense of complying with the law these 70 extra ballots
were eliminated by the usual method. Such method of disposing of
extra ballots is provided for mistakes, and not for frauds. We quote
the testimony of the supervisor, L. D. Smalls (page 116), who, after the
usual preliminary questions, says:

Q. What official position did you hold in connection with the election, if any?—A.
United States supervisor.

Q. Where were you during the day of election; that is, on the 6th day of last November?—A. I was in B. Sauder's building, where the election was held for Congressman from the 7th district and Presidential electors.

Q. State how many boxes were in said building and where they were placed during
said day.—A. There were two boxes situated on a counter; the box for Presidential
electors was on the left of any one coming in the door with his face to the boxes, and
the box for Congressman was on the right.

Q. Who was the other U. S. supervisor for Jacksonboro'?—A. C. W. Butler.

Q. Did you keep a poll-list of those who voted on said day at said election?—A. I
did, and I now have it with me.

Q. Please produce it and place it in evidence.

(Objected to on the ground that the law does not require the U. S. supervisor of
election to keep a poll list.)

A. Poll-list, marked with Maj. Howell's initials, placed in evidence [marked Exhibit A].

Q. How many names are there on said poll-list?—A. 113.

Q. Were you present when the votes were canvassed at the close of the election?—
A. Yes, sir.

Q. Were there as many votes or more votes in the Congressional box than there
were names on the poll-list at said count?—A. Yes; there were seventy (70) more
ballots in the box than there were names on the poll-list.

Q. Do you know how the seventy (70) extra votes got in said box?—A. I do not.

Q. Was there any difference between the paper on which the name of T. E. Miller
was printed and the paper on which the name of William Elliott was printed?—A.
No, sir; but in the printing the words on the Miller ticket were far apart and on the
Elliott ticket they were close together.

Q. Where were the boxes and votes placed during the count?—A. After they commenced to count there were two barrels behind the counter, and they emptied all the
votes on the barrel heads and commenced to count from there.

Q. How far were the barrels from the counter where the boxes were during the day?—A. About three (3) feet from the counter.

Q. How wide was the counter?—A. About two feet and a half wide.

Q. Were you behind the counter during the day?—A. No; I was on the opposite side from the barrel all day.

Q. Did you ask permission to go behind the counter during the count?—A. Yes, I did; but the managers objected to my doing so.

Cross-X:

Q. Could you see all that was going on during the count?—A. I could see the counting, but could not see the names on the tickets.

Q. How far were you from the managers while the count was going on?—A. I was about five feet from the managers during the count.

Q. Were you present when the result of the election was declared?—A. Yes, sir.

Q. Did you sign the Federal supervisor's return?—A. I signed it under protest.

Q. Were you forced to sign it; did any say that you had to sign it?—A. Yes, sir; L. B. Ackerman, one of the managers at said election, said I must sign the return, that the law required it, and I told him I had not seen the names on the tickets as they were being counted, and Mr. Butler said I could sign and say that I signed under protest. (Mr. Butler was the Democratic supervisor.) A man by the name of Simmons, a State constable, when I said to Mr. Ackerman that I could not see the names on the tickets, said, "Go on with the count, and if this damn supervisor says much I will put him in jail." For that reason I said no more.

Q. Did you say that you could read and write?—A. Yes, I can.

Q. Were you not furnished with the law informing you of the duties of the supervisor?—A. Yes, sir.

Q. Did you read them?—A. Yes, I read them, and called the managers' attention to them, too.

Q. What were your duties?—A. My duty was to keep a strict notice and see that no violation of law while in counting the votes.

Q. Did you make any report to the chief supervisor of any wrong that took place under your observation during the day of the election?—A. I did make a report to the supervisor, but not informing him of the wrong.

Q. Then your report to the supervisor was the same as the managers of election?—A. Yes.

Q. Did you have a full turn-out of the Republican voters of this poll on the day of the election?—A. Not as general.

The validity of the count and return having been destroyed each party is left to prove his own vote, so far as he is able. Contestant proves by calling the voters (pp. 97–124) that 67 of them, whose names all appear on the poll-list, voted for him. Under a strict rule of law the whole return would be rejected, and 67 votes allowed to contestant on the proof. In his original brief filed with the committee, contestant conceded to contestee 46 votes, the remainder of the 113 not proven to have voted for contestant; and for that reason, and because it is now only a question of the amount of contestant's majority, we state the vote as in this brief:

Elliott's vote by last statement... 8,045
Deduct difference between vote as returned, and as stated in brief............. 22

And we have for Elliott... 8,023
Add 22 to Miller (8183 + 22).... 8,205

Miller's majority 182

Counting the vote according to the strict rule of law, under the evidence, would make Miller's majority 228.

BEAUFORT COUNTY.

Port Royal.—The returns from Port Royal are:

Elliott.. 199
Miller.... 14

Total.. 213

Fifty-one witnesses (pp. 128–160) testify that they voted for Miller, and their names are all on the poll list as having voted. This evidence stands uncontradicted. Duly qualified voters were refused permission to vote, and names of Democrats are on the poll-list as having voted who had moved away, and were not present at the election, thus further discrediting the returns.

Giving Miller the 37 votes proved and not credited, and deducting a like number from the 199 returned for Elliott, as the vote is stated in contestant's original argument, and we have:

Elliott.. 8023 — 37 = 7986
Miller... 8205 + 37 = 8242

Miller's majority **256**

Counting, according to the strict rule of law, only such votes as are proven by the evidence, Miller's majority would be 464.

<h4 style="text-align:center">BERKELEY COUNTY.</h4>

St. Stephen's.—The poll-list of St. Stephen's shows that 310 persons voted. Only 285 are returned as voting for Representative in Congress, and a like number for Presidential electors (pp. 600, 602, 603).

It is evident that 25 votes have been lost here by being deposited in the wrong box. Eighty-one qualified voters, whose names appear on the poll-list, testify that they voted for Miller (pp. 52–68 and 74–86). No attempt is made to sustain this return, and, under the evidence, Miller is entitled to be credited with 81 votes, or 75 more than were given him in the returns. Deducting 75 from Elliott's vote, according to the statement in contestant's brief, we have:

Elliott .... 7986 — 75 = 7911
Miller .... 8245 + 75 = 8317

Miller's majority **406**

Following the strict rule of law, and allowing only the vote proven after rejecting the returns, makes Miller's majority 818.

<h4 style="text-align:center">ORANGEBURGH COUNTY.</h4>

Evans's Mill precinct.—At Evans's Mill the managers return 415 votes cast, crediting Elliott with 390 and Miller with 25.

According to the testimony for contestant there were over 100 more ballots in the box than names on the poll-list.

The testimony of T. T. Green (p. 316) shows that the box had been stuffed by the managers or some other person. The managers were all partisan friends of contestee. According to Green's testimony the managers knew without counting that there was an excess of tickets, for they immediately destroyed 125, and then, upon counting the remainder, found that they had destroyed 7 too many. To restore the 7 which were necessary to make up the full vote, 7 each of Democratic and Republican tickets were put into a box, and 7 of these 14 were drawn out and put with the other tickets.

The managers of the election are called, and acknowledge the destruction of some tickets, and the unlawful method of making up the deficiency after too many were destroyed, but deny that there were so many as stated by Green ; upon this question there is a conflict, but upon another there is not. One hundred and forty-two of the voters, whose names all appear on the poll-list, were called as witnesses (pp.

414–476) and 136 of them testify to having voted for Miller, conclusively proving the falsity of the return and the fraud perpetrated by the managers. This would give Miller 111 more than are credited to him, and conceding to Elliott the remainder of the votes cast in accordance with contestant's brief we have:.

```
Elliott........................................................... 7911—111=7800
Miller ........................................................... 8317+111=8428
                                                                    ————
    Miller's majority.......................................................  628
```

Or, rejecting the fraudulent return, and counting only the votes proven, and we have Miller's majority 1,319.

RICHLAND COUNTY.

Eastover precinct.—No returns were made from this precinct, and it was not included in the certified result. M. Johnson, the Republican supervisor, testifies (p. 319), that the Miller tickets were printed on coarser and darker paper than the Elliott tickets, and that when folded by the ticket distributors, Miller's name could be seen; that the name was printed in larger letters than Elliott's name; that he watched the voting and kept a tally of the voters, and that Miller's vote was not less than 248, nor more than 257 (some tickets not certain), and that Elliott's vote was from 83 to 92. The managers shifted the boxes two or three times, and in doing so removed them from the sight of the supervisor, to which he objected; and he believes other boxes were substituted at one of these shiftings.

H. W. Woodard (321) testifies to folding the Miller tickets so that the name was in sight and to the description of the tickets, the same as Johnson.

One hundred and ninety-seven colored voters testify to having voted for Miller (pp. 478–570). Forty-two affidavits of other voters were filed with the committee to the same effect. These voters' names are all on the poll-list kept by the supervisor, showing 385 votes cast, 298 by colored men, 11 of which were Democratic. Aside from the testimony of the supervisor, which shows pains-taking care, there is positive testimony taken in due process of law, of 197 voters who cast their ballots for Miller. As we have said, no return for this precinct ever reached the county board.

J. C. Eason (332), the Democratic supervisor, confirms Johnson as to the managers shifting the boxes, as to the whole number of votes cast, and as to Johnson's keeping a poll-list, and as to his being present, all the time, and in a position to see each vote when deposited. He also says that the colored voters in this district largely preponderate, at least two to one, and that when the colored men vote they mostly vote the Republican ticket. He did not keep a tally when the vote was counted, did not keep a poll-list, did not watch the tally nor notice the names on the tickets when they were being counted; in other words, did nothing that was required of him as a supervisor, but, after the managers had made up their return, he took the tally and made his return from that, without any knowledge whether it was right or wrong. According to his report the vote was:.

```
Elliott............................................................. 262
Miller.............................................................. 87
Simmons............................................................ 36
                                                                    ———
    Total........................................................... 385
```

H. Mis. 137——34

The commissioner of elections says that no return was made, but that an unsigned statement was found in the box returned, which was not counted. This statement was sent to the secretary of state, with all the papers except ballots, which he did not consider it his duty to count.

C. U. Marshall (335) testifies to the same vote as that given by the Democratic supervisor.

Says he made out the return on the back of an envelope, put it in his pocket, and has kept it there ever since. He testifies to destroying some votes, and then having as many left as there were names on the poll-list. We give some extracts from his testimony, illustrating his idea of an honest election:

Q. For what purpose were these boxes transposed and in what manner?—A. When we made the first change Meshoch Johnson, the Republican supervisor, spoke to a voter and told him to tell them outside about the position of the boxes. I called his attention to the State law forbidding any one to speak to voters. He then got to sending notes out by voters, trying to give them to voters surreptitiously. The boxes were changed several times in consequence of this U. S. supervisor trying to defeat the election laws, thus trying to give his party an undue advantage.

Q. In making these shiftings or transpositions of the boxes how much time was required to do so?—A. It was instantaneously. Often we would say aloud, "Let's change position of these boxes."

*   *   *   *   *   *   *

Q. Did you reside in the 7th Congressional district at the time of the election spoken of?—A. No, sir; on the edge of it.

Q. Did you ever live there?—A. No; a road divides me.

Q. How far is your residence from Eastover?—A. It was 20 miles.

Q. Who were the other managers of election with you?—A. W. S. Taylor and J. E. Touchberry.

Q. You were all Democrats?—A. I think so.

Q. What concern was it of yours as a manager of election if one of the supervisors did write notes to persons outside of the room?—A. If as an officer he had the right as a partisan in the interest of his own party, I think I had a right to upset his plans and transposed the boxes.

Q. Was it your place as a sworn officer of the election to make yourself a partisan for the purpose of counteracting the partisan action of any one else?—A. No; transposing boxes affected both parties; there were many negroes who couldn't read that voted the Democratic ticket. The law requires the managers to read to the elector when he goes to vote the name on the box if he demands it. On one or more occasions during that day I was called upon to read them, and did so for the voter, and nobody else was allowed to give any information.

Q. If the changing of boxes would make no difference in the relative vote of the parties, why did you transpose them for the purpose of antagonizing the Republican supervisor?—A. It was a matter—a byplay between, and we made it a matter of joke.

Dealing with this vote in the manner most liberal to contestee, the least we can give Miller is 239, and the most we can give Elliott is 110.

Elliott ....7800+110=7910
Miller ....8428+239=8667
                                                                              ————

Miller's majority... 757

Or by the count made by the strict construction of the law, Miller's majority is 1,448.

BERKELEY COUNTY.

Ben Potter precinct.—In this precinct there is a difference between the return of the United States supervisors and that of the precinct managers; the supervisors returning 41 as voting, and the managers 141. The evidence here is conflicting, and we do not find it necessary to decide which is the true return. The same is true of Privateer precinct, Sumter County, where Elliott is returned by the managers as receiving 130 votes, and by the supervisors as receiving 88.

Cooper's Store precinct.—Here the managers counted 94 for Miller and 96 for Elliott. The evidence satisfies us that the count was a gross fraud boldly perpetrated, by which a large number of Miller tickets were counted and tallied for Elliott by the managers of the election, but it is impossible to ascertain the amount of the fraud from the evidence and we can only reject the whole return, which only changes the result two votes.

Other allegations are made, and proof taken in regard to them, such as failing to hold election at large Republican precincts, etc., but we do not deem it nesessary to make further comment on the record. The frauds, false returns, and ballot-box stuffing which we have detailed are so conclusively proven, and the true vote so well established in the various precincts noticed, that there is left no room to doubt that Thomas E. Miller was legally elected, and was, through the crimes of election managers in the Seventh district of South Carolina, deprived of a certificate of election. We therefore recommend the adoption of the following resolutions:

Resolved, That William Elliott was not elected a Representative in the Fifty-first Congress from the Seventh Congressional district of South Carolina, and is not entitled to retain a seat therein.

Resolved, That Thomas E. Miller was duly elected a Representative in the Fifty-first Congress from the Seventh Congressional district of South Carolina, and is entitled to his seat as such Representative.

VIEWS OF THE MINORITY.

(1) **Registration and election law.**

The registration and election laws of South Carolina are reasonable and constitutional, and there is nothing in the evidence to sustain the conclusion of the committee that they are executed in an unfair or partisan manner.

(2) **Shifting of ballot boxes justifiable.**

The section of the election law which provides for a number of ballot boxes plainly labeled for the different offices, and requires that the voter shall be separated from others, and not spoken to by anyone except the judges while at the polling place depositing his vote, is well calculated to carry out the provision of the constitution that the voter shall be protected from "An undue influence from power, bribery, tumult, or improper conduct" and to protect him in his right to a secret ballot. If the voters were found to be receiving information from outsiders which they were required to receive from the judges, "If the wise provisions of this law were being interfered with, and rendered nugatory by any outsider at any poll, or if it came under the observation of those selected to supervise the execution of this law that its letter or intention or spirit was being violated, we submit it was the duty of the managers to shift the boxes, or perform any other legal act, to subserve its proper execution."

(3) The evidence relied on by the committee to establish the true vote in the boxes alleged to have been stuffed is untrustworthy and insufficient, and in some cases incompetent.

VIEWS OF THE MINORITY.

JULY 1, 1890.—Mr. WILSON, of Missouri, from the Committee on Elections, submitted the following as the views of the minority:

The undersigned, minority of the Committee on Elections, being unable to agree with the majority of the committee in their conclusions in this case, dissent therefrom, and present the following views.

At the general election in South Carolina for President and members of Congress on the 6th day of November, 1888, William Elliott was the Democratic, and Thomas E. Miller was the Republican candidate for Representative in Congress from the seventh district in that State, and the former was declared elected, having received 1,353 more votes than Miller, and having been granted the certificate of election now represents that district in the House of Representatives. The counties comprising that district, and the number of votes cast for each of the candidates, appears in the following table:

Election returns, seventh Congressional district.

Counties.	William Elliott.	Thomas E. Miller.	Robert Simmons.
Beaufort	898	2,056	....
Berkeley	1,753	1,547	54
Charleston	45	143	....
Colleton	652	210	....
Georgetown	821	957	....
Orangeburgh	987	310	....
Richland	367	222	2
Sumter	1,782	933	18
Williamsburgh	1,053	624	....
	8,358	7,003	74

The first of the many errors contained in the report of the majority of the committee are found in the following statement on page 2:

An examination of the description of the district in the Congressional Directory will show that its contiguity is secured by putting into it the sea beach of Charleston County, a strip of sand a few feet wide and many miles long, covered half of every day by the waters of the Atlantic Ocean and incapable of human habitation. All the habitable main-land of this county is in another district.

As to the point of contiguity an examination of the map will show that all the land on the south side of Charleston harbor, consisting chiefly of James Island, is in the seventh district, while directly opposite, on the northern side of the harbor, lies Berkeley County, all of which, excepting the village of Mount Pleasant, is in that district. With

535

equal force might the majority claim that each of the many navigable rivers flowing through the district destroys its contiguity.

More striking is the error of the majority as to none of the "habitable" part of Charleston County being in the seventh district. Immediately before this assertion appears a statement of the vote in the last election, and we find the following:

County.	William Elliott.	Thomas E. Miller.
Charleston	45	142

ELECTION BY CENSUS.

In proceeding to elect the contestant by the census the majority gives the population and voting strength of the district in 1880, and making out a colored majority of 25,000 votes, say:

> It is therefore safe to say, unless the mass of colored voters have ceased to take an interest in political matters, that with laws bearing equally on white and black, and with anything like a fair election, the Republicans of the seventh district would poll four times as many votes as the Democrats, and would have anywhere from 15,000 to 20,000 majority. -
> The history of the district as it has come before former Congresses, and as it is presented in this record, precludes the belief that its colored men have to any considerable extent ceased to be interested in elections, especially Presidential and Congressional elections.

Apart from the otherwise well-established fact that "the mass of colored voters have ceased to take an interest in political matters," the census, in connection with the vote in this case, gives irresistible force to that conclusion. Take Georgetown County, for example. The census gives:

Population and number of males of voting age classified by race according to census of 1880.

County.	Total.	White.	Colored.	Males 21 years of age and over. White.	Colored.
Georgetown	19,613	3,466	16,147	852	3,449

The vote was as follows:

County.	Elliott.	Miller.	Total.
Georgetown	821	957	1,778
Not voting			2,523
Total voting population			4,301

Now, in contestant's notice of contest Georgetown is not mentioned. There is no complaint that the supervisor of registration neglected or refused to register any applicant, nor that the managers of election, one of whom was a Republican at each precinct, refused any one the right to vote, and yet we find that out of 4,301 persons of voting age, in a county where there are five times as many colored as white people, no less than 2,523 failed to vote. No explanation can be given of this extraordinary result except that the mass of colored voters have ceased to take an interest in political matters.

In addition to this there is abundant proof throughout the testimony that colored men voted for contestee.

As to the table of population and men of voting age given by the majority, a careful examination of the books of the last census fails to disclose any such table.

THE ELECTION LAW.

In speaking of the election and registration of South Carolina, the majority say—

That this law was enacted for the deliberate purpose of indirectly disfranchising, so far as possible, the colored voters of the State, admits of no serious question.

We deny the allegation, and on our part allege that there is nothing in the law itself, nor in the evidence in the case from beginning to end, to justify it. Let it be remembered in this connection that the constitution of that State was framed by a Republican convention in 1868; that it required the legislature to enact a registration law, which the Republicans of that State for more than five years prior to their being driven from power in 1876 by the honest people of that Commonwealth, irrespective of party, utterly refused to pass, because, we presume, it would be an obstacle in the way to retention of power and the further wrecking of the State.

THE LAW CONSTITUTIONAL.

It is also held by the majority of the committee that "there is no valid registration law in South Carolina;" that the said laws are unconstitutional for various reasons stated in their report, and in support of this theory substantially alleges: (1) That as the letter of the law prescribes but one time for a qualified voter to register, he is disfranchised if he fails to obey the law; and the like is the case as to minors coming of age, and others afterwards becoming qualified voters, and who decline to obey the law as to the time required to register.

Now, a sufficient answer to all this, so far as the determination of this case is concerned, is that section 105 of the Revised Statutes requires the contestant to give notice of contest and "shall specify particularly the grounds upon which he relies in the contest." It has been determined over and over again that no point not made in the notice can be considered by the House. No such ground was specified, and it can not now be relied on, and its introduction here does but encumber the record and is wholly irrelevant.

It may further be answered that in the evidence taken herein there is no proof that this law was acted upon in the strict interpretation given, and therefore there is no proof that this requirement lost to either party a single vote.

The majority of the committee can hardly be serious in its declaration that the law is unconstitutional because it affixes "a like penalty for parting with or destroying a registration certificate;" the law carries upon its face a sufficient refutation of the charge, if seriously made. The majority say:

But they give such latitude to the supervisor of registration as will enable him to take good care that none of his political friends shall suffer the penalty.

The implication contained in this paragraph is altogether gratuitous, and as such we dismiss it.

OBSTRUCTION TO REGISTRATION.

Under this head the majority says:

In many counties a diligent search on the part of Republicans fails to discover the supervisor's office, or, when it is found, so many hindrances and obstructions are interposed that voters fail to get transfers or registry, although they apply at every opportunity, during every month of registration in the year of a general election. In some large precincts no one has been able to secure a transfer since the general registry in 1882.

We challenge contradiction of the assertion that in no county but Colleton is any charge made by the testimony that the supervisor's office could not be found. As to that county, the majority cite the testimony of N. F. Myers (p. 95), I. H. Chapman (p. 92), and W. B. Scott (p. 94).

Myers says:

I inquired at the offices located in the court-house, but none could or would say where he was located, excepting Auditor Smith, who said he (meaning the supervisor) came into his (Smith's) office, but he could not tell me if he had a permanent office.

It will be noted that Myers did find the office, but was not satisfied unless it was a "permanent" one. He does not claim to have gone on any day fixed by law for the supervisor to be at his office, and hence did not find him.

W. B. Scott says:

I went there the first Monday in last March, and as I went I took my registration certificate with me to see whether I could get it changed from Jacksonboro to Green Pond, and as I went up I ask Jackson Grant what time the supervisor will be in and whereabout he held his office; he told me to go to the court-house and I would find out, and I went over and saw the auditor; Mr. Smith told me where the office of the supervisor was; he said sometimes he comes in here, and moreover I have not time to bother with you. Then I came on back home and after I came back I wrote a letter to Major Myers.

So it seems Jackson Grant knew where the office was, and Mr. Smith told Scott where it was, just as he had previously told Myers.

Now, when I. H. Chapman testifies, he says:

I inquired for the office of the supervisor of registration; I inquired of Mr. Myers and Jackson Grant, but I could not find the office.

He inquired of both Myers and Jackson Grant, who knew that the office was the same as Auditor Smith's, and they must have told him where it was, and he did go to the court-house, but does not say a word about going to the auditor's office, contenting himself with looking for a "sign" and looking into some of the rooms, without ever asking any one which the office was.

As to the general charge of obstructing the registration of Republicans while facilitating that of Democrats, a careful examination of the testimony of these witnesses shows that not a name of a Republican denied registration is given except that of W. B. Scott, who says he wanted his certificate changed from Jacksonborough to Green Pond, and could not get it done, but it appears by the poll-list of Jacksonborough, p. 627, that Scott was the ninety-first voter at that precinct, which establishes, first, that his vote was not lost, and secondly, that he had no right to a transfer to Green Pond. No other name is given. Myers says he had the affidavits of one hundred and fifty persons desiring registration, and Scott says he had forty, but the law requires that the applicant must "appear," and no one can seriously contend that any registration law should allow registration upon affidavit. As to favoring Democrats, Myers says on cross-examination :

Q. Do you know of your own knowledge any Democrats who registered at any time other than the time provided for by law ?—A. Of my own knowledge I can not say.

Q. Who were the parties that told you that they had urged to register just prior to the day of election ?—A. I decline to give their names for the reason that under the intolerent system practiced they would be doomed to social as well as political ostracism.

Q. Do you know of any one in Colleton County who has been doomed socially or politically on account of their politics ?—A. If I can not a particular one, through the teachings of leading Democratic orators made on the husting, they have taught members of their party to believe that in the South, at least, it is a social question and all others are subservient.

Q. Does the Republican practice the same ostracism ?—A. So far as I know they do not, for in the town in which I live their are colored Democrats with whom I and other Republicans are on the most pleasant terms.

G. A. Beach, the supervisor, says (p. 293) :

Q. Have you during the last four years opened your books for registration at any of the precincts named in your examination and notified the citizens of either of those precincts of your appointment to appear before you as supervisor of registration for the purpose of renewing, transferring, or for original registration ?

(Objected to on ground that there is no provision of law by which any such appointments could have been made.)

A. I have not, but did open my office at the C. H., as required by law, for registration and renewal of certificates. 　　＊　　　　＊　　　　＊　　　　＊　　　　＊

X ex.:

Q. You have stated that no renewals have been made by you of registration cfts. of voters at the precincts named. Will you state whether any applications have been made for such renewals ?—A. There haven't been any made.
＊　　　　＊　　　　＊　　　　＊　　　　＊

Q. Did you have an office at the court-house ?—A. I did.
Q. What office did you use ?—A. The auditor's office.
Q. Were you in your office every day that you were required to be there by law for the purpose of attending to the duties of registration ?—A. I was, except one day I was sick.

At page 374 he further testifies :

Q. State your age, occupation, residence, and where you were on the 6th day of Nov. last.—A. Age, 30 years ; lawyer, and resides about 6 miles from Walterboro.

Q. Do you hold any official position in the county of Colleton ?—A. I do ; I am supervisor of registration.

Q. Have you an office at the court-house ? If so, state where it is located.—A. I have one, and hold it at the auditor's office in the court-house.

Q. Why did you occupy the county auditor's office ?—A. Because it had been occupied by the other supervisor, and there was no other office that I could get at the court-house, and the auditor offered me his office.

Q. Did you open said office for the business pertaining to your duties on each and every day required of you by law ?—A. I did, except one day that I was sick.

Q. Do you remember what day that you were sick ?—A. I do not ; it was the first Monday in March or the first Monday in April.

Q. How long have you held the office of supervisor of registration ?—A. Between three and four years.

Q. Have you always, and since your appointment to said office, occupied county auditor's office ?—A. I have.

Q. Have you always kept your records and books in said office ?—A. I have.

Q. Have you, since your appointment to said office, offered every facility for the registration and renewal of lost certificates to voters ?—A. I have so far as the law required.
＊　　　　＊　　　　．　　　　＊　　　　＊

Q. When you were at Walterboro, on the days required of you by law, and when you were not in the office, were you around on the court hill where you could be seen by any person who may have had business with you ?—A. I was ; during the time I was absent from my office I was around the court hill where I could be seen.

Q. Then no one was turned off by you from the seventh Congressional district who desired to register or have their certificates renewed ?—A. No one at all.

So much for Colleton County.

As to Orangeburgh County the majority rely on the testimony of E. A. Webster, a part of which they give. A careful examination of his whole testimony shows that, happening to meet the supervisor on the street after the first Monday in August, when he admits that by law the books were then closed, he applied for transfer and renewal certificates for other persons, which he also knew was illegal. Much of his testimony is admittedly hearsay, and his cross-examination closes as follows:

Q. Give me the name of any Republicans who applied for registration from the first Monday in Jan'y, 1887, to the first Monday in July, 1888, who were rejected, and when, in the 7th Cong. dist.—A. I will give one as a special case; Gadsden McFadden, a voter in first dist. I can not give the names now, nor date, but I have them on record at my home in Orangeburg.

Q. Then you can not swear, on personal knowledge, to one who was rejected before June, 1888, who applied in person, according to law?—A. As above stated, I can not give the names now. I can not give the name.

E. A. WEBSTER.

The only person named was a voter in the first—not the seventh—district. The foregoing four witnesses are all whom the majority refer to, and yet they do not hesitate to say:

By means detailed by these witnesses, thousands of Republicans of the seventh district were deprived of such certificates of registration as the managers would recognize.

BALLOTS IN WRONG BOX.

We come now to the consideration of that clause of the statute of South Carolina providing for the labeling of the ballot-boxes, and the numbers thereof, and in this connection to the allegation "that it makes an educational test, and therefore is in direct violation of the constitution of the State." It is proper here to observe that the law in reference to the number of boxes prevailed in that State prior to 1861, and therefore it will hardly answer the purpose of the majority of the committee in this case. The proof shows that the law was strictly complied with in labeling the boxes for President and member of Congress in plain and distinct Roman letters.

There was no dishonesty proved; no failure to discharge their duty on the part of any of the election officers, the only complaint being that the tickets for member of Congress found in the Presidential box were destroyed, no matter who they were cast for, contestant or contestee, as appears in the evidence of one of contestant's witnesses, one Lawrence Brown, page 14 of the record. He was interrogated on cross-examination by Mr. Gilland:

Question. How many of Mr. Elliott's votes were found in the Presidential box?—Answer. Twenty-one.

Q. Those were thrown out and not counted?—A. Yes, sir.

It seems there was no deviation from this rule, and the law was enforced to the letter in this regard with the utmost impartiality.

The impression is sought to be made that there were six or seven boxes all together at the same place, and the managers kept moving them about, and mixing and shuffling them up like a deck of cards, and the managers, when called on to know the boxes by the ignorant voter, so as to know where and in what box to deposit his ballot, as he was bound to do under the law, utterly refused to read to him the names on the boxes. The evidence fails to support this. As a matter of fact, there were but two boxes at the places designated for the reception of votes for President and members of Congress.

The constitution of South Carolina, section 33, article 1, heretofore cited, requires that the right of suffrage shall be protected by laws regulating elections, and prohibiting, under adequate penalties, all undue influences from "bribery, power, tumult, or improper conduct." It also provides that right of suffrage shall be exercised by ballot. The object in the laws in all the States which provide for the ballot is to have the exercise of the right to vote a secret, unknown to any but the voter himself, and for the best of reasons. The fact that the intention of this law is often thwarted in the heat of a political campaign is unfortunately true, but not more so in South Carolina than in Massachusetts or Illinois; in fact, we feel justified in affirming that the election laws of the former State are better calculated to protect the voter in the free exercise of the right to vote a secret ballot and thus express his own preference to the exclusion of that of others, than in most of the States of the Union.

It would be difficult to design an election law better calculated to protect the voter from "an undue influence from power, bribery, tumult, or improper conduct" than the law of the State now under consideration. It was mandatory on the legislature of that State to do so, and in so doing it devised a code of rules most admirably adapted for the purpose.

The law requires the voter to go alone to the polls, unattended by the worker, and protected from the bulldozer and the heeler, paid possibly to force him to express by his ballot another's will, and not his own. On reaching the polls he does so a free man, relieved from all coercing influences; no one is permitted even to touch his white ballot but himself; the boxes are before him, properly labeled, and if he wants information on the subject there are sworn officers of the law there to give it to him under the mandates of the law; and then, with his own hand, he deposits his vote in a securely locked box, and thus, free and untrammeled, gives, expression to his own will. If the wise provisions of this law were being interfered with, and rendered nugatory by any outsider at any poll, or if it came under the observation of those selected to supervise the execution of this law that its letter or intention or spirit was being violated, we submit it was the duty of the managers to shift the boxes, or perform any other legal act, to subserve its proper execution.

The subject of a "free ballot and a fair count" has long engaged the anxious attention of those who view in the increasing prostitution of the ballot, year by year, a grave menace to republican institutions upon this continent. Scarcely a session of the legislature in the various States transpires, that this subject is not the object of serious consideration. The miserable spectacle presented at every Presidential election throughout the country, at thousands of its polling places, of long lines of men forced by dire circumstances to surrender their right of suffrage and their manhood to others, and permit themselves to be marched to the polls from workshop, forge, mine, and factory, and the unlimited employment of money and other modes and methods of the "greatest managing politicians of the land," is fast bringing about a revolution in the election laws of the country.

The election laws of South Carolina have blazed the way to genuine reform. It is the skirmish line behind which comes to do battle purer methods and greater protection from "all undue influence from power, bribery, tumult, or improper conduct." Many of its features have been adopted in the States where what is known as the Australian system of voting now by recent enactment obtains.

For the benefit of the majority and any others who may be horrified and indignant because the law of South Carolina refuses to permit the political bummer and hired swashbuckler to attend voters to the polls to help them vote, and makes him rely on himself, and protects him in so doing, we here quote some of the provisions of a law recently enacted in the State of Missouri and other States, and known as the Australian system of voting, and which justified in their practical operations the high encomiums passed upon them by those sincerely desirous for a "free ballot and a fair count."

SEC. 24. On any day of election of public officers in any election district, each qualified elector shall be entitled to receive from the judges of the election one ballot. It shall be the duty of such judges of election to deliver such ballot to the elector. * * *

SEC. 25. On receipt of his ballot the elector shall forthwith and without leaving the polling place retire alone to one of the places, booths, or compartments provided to prepare his ballot. He shall prepare his ballot by crossing out therefrom the names of all candidates except those for whom he wishes to vote, or in case of a ballot containing a constitutional amendment or a question to be submitted to the vote of the people, by crossing out therefrom parts of the ballot in such manner that the remaining parts shall express his vote upon the questions submitted. After preparing his ballot the elector shall fold the same so that the face of the ballot will be concealed, and the signatures or initials of the judges may be seen. He shall then vote forthwith and before leaving the polling place.

SEC. 26. Not more than one person shall be permitted to occupy any one booth at one time, and no person shall remain in or occupy a booth longer than may be necessary to prepare his ballot, and in no event longer than five minutes.

SEC. 28. Any elector who declares to the judges under oath that he can not read or write, or that by reason of physical disability he is unable to mark his ballot, may declare his choice of candidates to either one of the judges having charge of the ballots, who, in the presence of the elector, shall prepare the ballots for voting in the manner hereinbefore provided; or such elector, after making such oath, may require one of such judges to read to him the contents of the ballot, so that the elector can ascertain the relative position of the names of the candidates on each ballot, whereupon the elector shall retire to one of the places, booths, or compartments provided to prepare his ballot in the manner hereinbefore provided.

We direct special attention to the following sections:

SEC. 23. All officers upon whom is imposed by law the duty of designating polling places, shall provide in each place designated by them a sufficient number of places, booths or compartments, which shall be furnished with such supplies and conveniences as shall enable the voter conveniently to prepare his ballot for voting, in which compartment the electors shall mark their ballots, screened from observation, and a guard so constructed that only persons within the rail can approach within five feet of the ballot-boxes, or the places or compartments herein provided for. The number of places or compartments shall not be less than one for every hundred electors who voted at the last preceding general election in the district. No persons other than electors engaged in receiving, preparing, or depositing their ballots shall be permitted to be within said rail, except by authority of election, and except as now by law otherwise provided. The expenses of providing such places, or compartments, or guard-rails, shall be a public charge, and shall be provided for in each town and city, in the same manner as the other election expenses.

Now this law embodying the same ideas and principles as the law of South Carolina, has never been declared unconstitutional, nor has it so far as we know ever been questioned. The object of both laws is to separate the voter when he goes to deposit his ballot from all outside influence and dictation.

Both laws were made to place the voter on his own intelligence, or on such information as he obtained from the judges of election or managers, who are sworn officers of the law.

No better illustration of the wisdom of this law can be found than is furnished by the evidence in relation to Grahamville and Ladies' Island precincts in Beaufort County, where a large number of voters, under the instruction of contestant and others of those voting them, deposited a Miller ballot in both boxes.

This was a willful and corrupt violation of the law, knowingly committed, and the House of Representatives is gravely asked to sanction and condone it. Grahamville was the home of Miller. He was present at that precinct a large part of the day, with tickets in his hands and very active, and voted. The count of the boxes and returns showed that there were 237 votes polled. Miller received in the Congressional box 205 votes and in the Presidential 189 votes, and not one solitary vote was cast for the Republican Presidential ticket. Miller himself forgot to vote for Harrison and Morton, but manifestly cast two votes for himself.

I. C. Rue, who had charge of contestant's tickets, gives this explanation of the above—p. 452:

Q. Do you know if the Congressional ticket was voted in the Congressional and electors' boxes at Grahamville; if so, by whose dictation?—A. In the morning when I went to the polls and began distributing tickets, I only gave one ticket to each voter. Some of the voters called my attention to the fact that there was also a Presidential box, whereupon I gave them another Congressional ticket and told them they just as well vote that one also, for luck, and continued to do so the rest of the day, as they did not seem satisfied in voting the one ticket.

The majority of the committee, in speaking of "ballots in wrong boxes," uses the following language:

As has been noted, managers of elections are prohibited from counting any ballots found in the wrong box. At the Federal polls, at this election, there were two boxes, one for Presidential electors and one for Congressmen. Under the peculiar wording of the statute unlettered voters are obliged to rely upon those of their associates who can read to learn how to deposit their tickets so as not to get them in the wrong box, and so lose their votes. If the two boxes are put into position before the voting commences, and are permitted to remain during the day, there is little danger of mistake, all the voters being instructed as to their position by those in whom they have confidence. But if the boxes are shifted about at intervals during the day it follows, as a matter of course, that every unlettered voter who goes to the poll after the change, and before its discovery deposits his ballot in the wrong box, loses his vote, so far as the count of the managers is concerned. There is no prohibition in the statute against shifting the boxes, and so it is assumed by the managers of elections that they have the right to shift the boxes as often as they please, for the express purpose, as they acknowledge, of confusing the voters and causing them to deposit their ballots in the wrong box.

We submit that the majority of the committee entirely misconceives the spirit and meaning of the law. The law on this subject reads as follows:

At each precinct a space, or inclosure, such as the managers of election shall deem fit and sufficient, shall be railed off, or otherwise provided, with an opening at one end or side for the entrance of the voter, and an opening at the other for his exit, as a polling-place in which to hold the election for the State, circuit, and county officers. A similar, but distinct, space or inclosure shall be railed off, or otherwise provided, as a polling-place for the election of Congressman and Presidental electors, at such distance from the polling-place for State officers as the commissioners of election for each county shall determine and appoint for each election precinct. *But one voter shall be allowed to enter any polling-place at a time*, AND NO ONE EXCEPT THE MANAGERS SHALL BE ALLOWED TO SPEAK *to the voter while in the polling-place casting his vote.*

The italics are our own. Now, what is the object of this law? Manifestly the very same that the Australian system has in view, and which has been heretofore cited, and which is attracting such favorable attention in the various States, to throw the protecting arm of the law around the voter, especially the weak and timid; enable him to give expression to his own will at the polls, and not that of others; in other words, to shield him, and, in the language of the constitution of South Carolina, "prohibit all undue influence from power, bribery, tumult, or improper conduct." Incredible as it may seem, yet our friends of the majority, because the managers refused to permit the voters to be SPOKEN to, and directed how to vote by "those in whom they had confidence," propose to repeal the law here, ignore the constitution of a State under the provisions of which this law was passed, and count against their political enemy, and in favor of their political friend, one thousand votes cast at the various polls in the district.

One of the witnesses testified that at one of the precincts a man climbed a tree, and from his perch among the branches directed men how to vote. Another witness, cited by the majority at page 13, testifies that at a different precinct, Eastover, one of the United States supervisors spoke to and wrote notes to the voters telling them how to vote; and all that in the very teeth of the law providing for a barricade to protect the voters from just such interference, providing but one man should be in there at the same time, and further providing that no one should speak to the voter while in the polling-place casting his vote, except the managers. The indictment thus preferred against the election and registration laws of South Carolina, and also against the managers, presumes guilt instead of innocence. And the statement that "the managers acknowledged that they shifted the boxes for the express purpose of confusing the voters and causing them to deposit their ballots in the wrong box," is not borne out by the testimony; nor is the further statement that in every instance where the boxes were shifted "the purpose was unlawful," borne out either by the law or the facts.

As the majority virtually decides this case against contestee by giving to contestant 1000 votes alleged to be found in the wrong box, we think it necessary to examine carefully the testimony. Speaking generally, we claim, first, that the testimony relied on by the majority is very unsatisfactory in character, and was given under very suspicious circumstances. It was taken about four months after the election, and in one case only did the witness pretend to rely on anything but his memory; and yet, as a rule, the witness as to each precinct undertakes to give from memory the precise vote cast, with exact numbers in the wrong box. When it is remembered that contestant's attorneys had in every case certified copies of the manager's returns and poll-lists, it can very easily be seen how the testimony relied on by the majority could be obtained. Here is a sample. B. I. Fortune, as to Corbett's store (p. 21):

Q. How many ballot-boxes were at that poll?—A. Two.
Q. How many persons voted at that precinct that day?
(Objected to on the ground that it does not call for the best evidence.)
A. 199.
Q. How many votes were returned by the managers of election for T. E. Miller?
(Objected to on the same ground.)
A. 79.
Q. How many for Wm. Elliott?—A. 91.
Q. How many for both?—A. 170.
Q. What became of the other 29 ballots?—A. They were destroyed by the managers.
Q. Why were they destroyed?—A. Because they were placed into the wrong box.
Q. What box?—A. Into the Presidential box.
Q. Whose names did these ballots bear?—A. T. E. Miller.

How easy for the witness to give a perfectly satisfactory answer when the attorney put the question, "what became of the other 29 ballots?" On the other hand, it was almost impossible to contradict the witnesses as to details by men having strict regard for the obligation of an oath and for the very reasons above alleged. It was four months after the election, and they could not undertake to swear to exact figures. Coming to the several precincts at which the majority gives contestant votes under this head, we note the following points: At Gourdin's they give contestant 22 votes. The only witness, Daniel Ravanell (p. 8), says: The votes in the wrong box "were about 21 or 22." On this testimony contestant, in his brief (p. 18), did not venture to claim more than 21, but the majority unhesitatingly gives him 22. Not very material, to be sure, in point of numbers, but it indicates the tendency of the report throughout. We give the following from the testimony of the managers. W. M. O'Bryan (p. 412):

Q. How did the ignorant voters distinguish the boxes?—A. They asked the managers.

Q. Did the managers tell them?—A. They did.

Q. I understand you to say that the managers would tell the voters which was the electoral box and which was the Congressional box.—A. Exactly.

Q. Were there votes for both Miller and Elliott in the wrong boxes?—A. There were.

Q. Can you say how many for each?—A. I can not.

Q. Do you know Daniel Ravanel?—A. I do.

Q. What was he doing there that day?—A. He was supervisor.

Q. Did Ravanell keep any account of any votes that day?—A. He did not, to the best of my belief; I was standing where I could see him when the votes were counted and he took no account then.

A. M. Gorden (p. 413) says:

Q. How did the ignorant voters distinguish the boxes?—A. They asked the managers.

Q. When asked did the managers tell them?—A. Yes.

Q. Were there any votes in the wrong boxes that day?—A. Yes.

Q. For whom were those votes?—A. There were some for Elliott and some for Miller.

Q. How many for each?—A. I have no idea; I kept no record of them.

Q. Where was Ravanell's position while the votes were being counted?—A. Standing right by me.

Q. Could he see the votes as they were read?—A. He could.

Q. Did he keep any kind of tally?—A. He kept no record at all; he had neither paper nor pencil in his hand during the entire counting of the votes.

Cross-examined by S. J. LEE, Esq.:

Q. Did Ravanell make a return as supervisor?—A. He did.

Q. May he not have kept account of the number of Miller's ballots in the wrong box in his head?—A. I don't think it was possible for him to have done it.

Q. There were not more than twenty-five or thirty ballots found in the wrong box, were there?—A. I don't know how many.

Q. Your return shows one hundred and fifty-one votes as being cast in the proper box that day for Congressman, while the poll-list shows one hundred and seventy-three persons voted, a difference of twenty-two. Ravanell says these twenty-two were Miller's ballots found in the electoral box. Can you say that this is untrue?—A. I can.

Q. Please explain?—A. I called the votes myself, and saw that there were Elliott votes in the wrong box.

Q. How many?—A. I kept no account of how many.

Q. How many Congressional ballots were found in the electoral box?—A. Don't know; there were some; kept no count.

A. M. GORDON.

SALTERS.

This is the poll already mentioned at which the Republican supervisor, Lawrence Brown, proves that Miller lost 23 and Elliott 21 in the wrong box.

KINGSTREE (66).

These votes are given on the testimony of M. M. Morzon, Republican supervisor (p. 13), who says that the vote was as follows:

Miller	66
Elliott	133
Miller in wrong boxes	66
Total	320

H. Mis. 137——35

and that "the others" were cast for Dargan. By his return made to the chief supervisor on the night of the election, he gave the vote as follows (p. 664):

Miller	159
Elliott	133
Dargan	56
Whole number for Congress	348

The total is 28 more than he swore to, and Miller's vote is 27 greater than he swore he got in all boxes, $66 + 66 = 132$. In his return he said not a word about votes in wrong boxes but gave Miller 27 more than he swears he got in all boxes. Did he know most about the vote on the night of the election, November 6, 1888, or on February 11, 1889, the day he testified? His testimony certainly shows that he knew nothing about it on the night of the election; how did he afterwards acquire more correct information? The mystery is explained when we find that the poll list introduced by contestant (p. 639), shows only 320 votes cast. Before his examination he had the privilege of seeing it, and shaped his testimony accordingly. This conclusion is irresistible, and clearly establishes the unreliable character of this whole line of testimony. And yet it is upon such proof that the majority gives contestant 1,000 votes and a seat in Congress.

INDIANTOWN.

Upon the testimony of Jesse S. Fulmore, Republican supervisor (p. 14), the majority gives contestant 81 votes at this poll. All that Fulmore can say is that that was the number "as well as I can remember." There is no other testimony to sustain it. On the night of the election he made his return as follows (p. 664):

Miller	82
Elliott	30
Whole number for member of Congress	112

His duty was to report anything wrong, and yet not a word is said about votes for contestant not being counted.

LYNCHBURG (29).

The witness is I. R. Smith (p. 27), and he swears to the following vote:

Total	181
Miller	18
Elliott	134
Miller in Presidential box	29
	181

We give his testimony in full on this point.

Testimony of I. R. SMITH, sworn:

Q. State your name, age, residence, and occupation.—A. I. R. Smith; 36 years old; Lynchburg Township, and a farmer.

Q. Where were you on the 6th day of November, 1888?—A. I was at Lynchburg polls.

Q. What official position did you hold?—A. I was a U. S. supervisor.

Q. Were you at the polls during the entire day?—A. I was.

Q. Did you see the votes counted?—A. I did.

Q. How many ballot-boxes were there?—A. Two; the Congressional and Presidential boxes.

Q. How many persons voted at that box on that day?

(Objected to as not calling for the best evidence.)
A. 181.
Q. How many votes were returned for T. E. Miller ?
(Objected to as above.)
A. 18.
Q. How many for Mr. Elliott ?
(Objected to as above.)
A. 134.
Q. How many for the two ?—A. 152.
Q. What became of the other 29 ?—A. They were counted out.
Q. Where were the other 29 ballots ?—A. In the Presidential box.
Q. Whose names did these ballots bear ?
(Objected to as being secondary evidence.)
A. Thos. E. Miller.
(Objected to as above.)

This reads very nicely, and is perfect in arithmetic. It was very easy for the witness, in answer to the suggestive question " What became of the other 29" to say "They were counted out," and had the name of "Thos. E. Miller" on them. But unfortunately for the witness, he, too, made a return on the night of the election, and here it is (p. 662):

Miller	18
Elliott	134
Robert Simmons	15
Scattering	14
Whole number for member of Congress	181

On the night of the election he gave Robert Simmons 15 votes and reported 14 as scattering, but when he came to testify on February 9, 1889, he utterly ignored this return, probably had forgotten all about the figures, and boldly gave the whole 29 to contestant as being cast in the wrong box. We think further comment is unnecessary.

BETHEL CROSS-ROADS (5).

G. W. Michau (p. 34) is the witness relied on to give contestant these 5 votes. On his cross-examination he says:

Q. In what box were they found, Congressional or President ?—A. 2 in the Presidential and 3 in the Congressional box.

G. W. MICHAU.

The result is, therefore, that the majority give contestant 3 votes found in the Congressional box, on the ground that they were not in that box, but in some other box.

MAYESVILLE (40).

x. C. McCall (p. 36) is the witness. He swears to the following vote

Total	220
Miller	58
Elliott	122
Miller, in wrong box	40
Making	220

He, too, made a return on the night of election (p. 662), as follows:

Miller	58
Elliott	122
Simmons	3
Whole number for member of Congress	183

Not a word is said about any votes for contestant in the wrong box, but, in his testimony, he gives him 40 votes, including those cast for Simmons, whom he does not mention.

FORT MOTTE (16).

R. M. Claffy (p. 381) is the witness. He says:

Q. Were any ticket with the name of Miller on them for Congress found in the Presidentiul box?—A. I think there were.
Q. Were they counted for Miller ?—A. No.
Q. Were they destroyed by managers ?—A. Yes.
Q. Can you state about how many ?—A. There were about fifteen or sixteen in both boxes altogether; there were some for Presidential electors and some for Miller.

On this testimony contestant's counsel (p. 14) had the modesty to claim only fifteen votes, but the majority increase it to sixteen.

BIGGIN CHURCH (18).

Carolina Holmes (p. 18) gives the vote as follows:

Miller	83
Elliott	26
Miller, in wrong box	18
Simmons	17
Total	144

His return as supervisor on night of the election is (p. 667):

Elliott	26
Miller	83
Robert Simmons	17
Whole number for member of Congress	126

BLACK OAK (44).

The witness Sampson Flowers (p. 43) gives the following vote:

Miller	66
Elliott	21
Miller, in wrong box	44
Total	131

His return as supervisor, signed also by the Democratic supervisor, is (p. 66):

Miller	66
Elliott	21
Whole number for member of Congress	87

CALAMUS POND (32).

M. P. Richardson, Republican supervisor (p. 48), swears to the following vote:

Total	259
Miller	166
Elliott	61
Miller in wrong box	32
	259

Both supervisors made the following return (p. 665):

Whole number for member of Congress... 227

=====

Elliott... 61
Miller 166

227

STRAWBERRY FERRY (21).

Contestant claims nothing at this poll, and very properly, because there is no proof that any of his tickets were found in a wrong box. The supervisor, Edward A. Jenkins, page 41, says, "21 Presidential electors Republican tickets were found in the Congressional box." On this the majority give contestant 21 votes that he never claimed.

We now call attention to some errors in statements made by the majority. At foot of page 13 they say :

- In every instance but one the shifting of boxes is shown.

In the following instances there is either direct proof by Republican supervisors that the boxes were not shifted, or there is an entire absence of proof on the subject, to wit:

Bloomingdale, Cades, Black Mingo, Bethel Cross Roads, Fort Motte, Ten Mile Hill, Adams Run, Calamus Pond, and Haut Gap. This does not include cases where the shifting was denied by the managers.

Another statement of the majority (p. 14):

The United States supervisors, present at all the polls when this destruction occurred, *kept an account of the number*, and by that means we are able to ascertain with reasonable certainty the whole number lost.

The majority say the supervisors "kept an account of the number." Out of the twenty-seven precincts there are just two, Camp Ground and Haut Gap, at which the testimony shows a tally was made at the time, with no proof that it was preserved, and *one only*, the majority's precinct, Strawberry Ferry, at which an account was kept and used at the examination, and at that precinct there was no proof of Congressional votes being in the wrong box. Upon a review of the whole testimony we can not believe that the House will sustain the majority in giving contestant these 1,000 votes, or any part of them.

GLOVERVILLE.

The majority next rejects the whole vote at Gloverville precinct, in Colleton County, because "the box was dishonestly stuffed by somebody," and though there is no competent evidence on this point as to who did it, yet, taking it for granted that the sworn officers of the law were the culprits, puts on the stand E. M. Chisholm, one of the United States supervisors at that precinct, and who Mr. J. H. Dodd, a merchant of Centerville in that precinct and county, says, "is looked upon by the leading men of the neighborhood as the most notorious liar in it," and by his unsupported evidence alone deprives Elliott of 113 votes and Miller 20 votes, notwithstanding the following evidence from reputable sources:

J. H. DODD, a witness in behalf of the contestee, being duly sworn, says:
Question. State your age, occupation, residence, and where you were on the 6th day of Nov. last.—Answer. I am 36 years old ; merchant, and reside at Centerville ; I was at Gloversville voting precinct.
Q. Did you vote at the election held at the Gloversville precinct on the 6th day of Nov. last for a Representative in Congress ?—A. I did.

Q. Did you act in any official capacity that day? If so, state in what capacity.—
A. I was one of the managers of the Congressional box.

Q. At what time was the polls opened?—A. At 7 o'clock in the morning.

Q. Was the voting during the day peaceable and unmolested?—A. Yes.

Q. Who was the other two managers?—A. C. P. Chisholm and J. E. J. Bryant.

Q. Did you open and expose the box before the voting commenced, as required by
law?—A. We did.

Q. Were you present and did you assist in the canvass of the votes at the close of
the polls?—A. I was present and assisted in the canvass of the votes.

Q. Please state how the votes were canvassed, and with what result.—A. The first
thing we done was to open the boxes and count the votes, putting them in a pile on
the table. Finding there was more votes than there was names on the poll-list, we
put all the votes back into the box. One manager turned his back and drew out the
overplus and destroyed them. Then the remainder was taken from the box and
counted, showing a hundred and thirteen for William Elliott and, I think, twenty-
one for Miller.

Q. In the examination of the votes that you found in the box, did you find any
folded together? If so, state what you found and the kind of tickets you so found.—
A. I found the Congressional ticket with Miller's name on it folded with the Presidential ticket.

Q. From the appearance of those tickets would you say that they had been voted
by the same man?—A. I should say that they were voted by the same person.

Q. Who acted as supervisor of the Republican party at Gloversville precinct?—A.
E. M. Chisolm.

Q. Was he present when the polls were opened?—A. He was not.

Q. Do you know where he was?—A. Yes; he was across the road, standing around
the fire, about 50 yards away.

Q. Did you know before the polls were opened who the Republican supervisor was?
A. I did not.

Q. When were you first informed that E. M. Chisolm represented the Republican
party in the capacity of supervisor? A. Some little time after the voting had started
I walked out to the fire and asked E. M. Chisolm if he knew who was the supervisor.
He said that he was supervisor. I then asked him why he did not go to his post. He
said he would be in after a little.

Q. Did he come in after a little? A. He did.

Q. What did he say when he came in? A. He asked me if I refused to let him see
in the box. I told him I could not let him see in the box, as the voting had started.
He said that was all right, and that he would make a note of it. I then invited him to
take a seat at the table, which he did, and staid there the greater part of the day ;
at times he put another man in his place and went out, as he said he wanted to take
a little exercise.

Q. Then the poll-list kept by the supervisor was the work of others as well? A. It
was, as several had a hand in keeping Chisolm's poll-list.

Q. Did Chisolm occupy a place in the room while the votes were being counted?—
A. Yes; and also Abram Smalls.

Q. Do you know A. B. Smalls?—A. Yes.

Q. Was he at the polls that day ; if so, what did he do?—A. He stood outside at
the window, and folded tickets and gave them to voters as they came up.

Q. Did he remain at the window during the entire day?—A. No; he was only
there a portion of the time.

Q. Did you see Elliott tickets in circulation among the voters that day?—A. I did.

Q. Did you see any colored men distributing Elliott tickets?—A. Yes; there was
three or four colored men that were working in that direction that day.

Q. Were these colored men that you saw distributing Elliott tickets men of some
influence with the colored people?—A. They were the leading colored men in that
section of country.

Q. During the day did A. B. Smalls apply to any one of the managers for the correct
time of day?—A. He asked me three times during the day to let him set his watch
by mine. One time I took his watch in my hand and it was four hours out of the way.

Q. Do you or do you not know whether the number of white voters residing in
Glover Township largely exceeds twenty-five?—A. I think the white voters in Glover
Township number about 38 or 40.

Q. Are you not intimately acquainted with the white men who voted at Gloversville precinct that day?—A. I am personally acquainted with every one.

Q. Did any white man vote for State and county officers on the 6th of Nov. last
and refuse to vote for William Elliott for Congress?

(Counsel for contestant objects to the question because witness was not at the State
polls in any official capacity, and can not state except on information given by the
voters.)

A. That there was no white man who refused to vote for William Elliott that day.
I can not say as to the State and county polls, as I was not a manager there.

Q. Do you or do you not know that every white man that you saw at the precinct that day who was legally entitled to vote voted for Elliott?—A. I know they did.

Q. Do you know a white man residing in Gloversville Township by the name of H. B. Ackeman?—A. I do.

Q. Did he not vote at Gloversville precinct for William Elliott on the 6th of Nov. last?

(Counsel for contestant objects to the question upon the ground that the testimony of the voter mentioned is the best evidence.)

A. He did.

Q. Did any white man offer to vote for William Elliott that day and was rejected by the managers?—A. Yes; William Holts.

Q. When the tickets were given to the colored voters on the outside of the building by A. B. Small, was it possible for E. M. Chisolm to have watched the people to whom they were given and see that the same tickets were deposited in the box by the people to whom they were given?—A. It was impossible; it was on account of the position he occupied in the room, and further that the tickets were given out at the window, and the voters very often took the ticket and went off in the crowd and knocked about awhile and then came back and voted.

Q. After the polls had been closed and the Congressional box had been opened were any tickets found folded with a twist which could not have been voted through the opening in the lid of the box?

(Counsel for the contestant objects upon the ground that the question is leading.)

A. No, none.

Q. Did you find any tickets twisted at all?—A. None; the tickets were all folded.

Q. When the polls were formally closed was anybody, white or colored, ordered to leave the room?—A. No one was ordered to leave the room, but just requested that the crowd should fall back so as to give them room to work. I invited A. B. Small to come up to the table and witness the count.

Q. Is it true that you or any one of the managers told the white men present to crowd around the table?—A. We did not; there was no such language used that night.

Q. Is it true that the managers indulged in a general drunk while the count was being conducted and endeavored to get the Republican supervisor drunk?—A. There was no one under the influence of liquor that day except A. B. Smalls. I gave him nothing but one glass of ginger ale. Neither of the managers invited E. M. Chisolm to drink.

Q. After the polls were closed is it true that yourself and C. P. Chisolm went off and had a private consultation as to how the votes were to be counted?—A. We did not.

Q. While Chisolm was calling the names from the tickets did he at any time throw one of the tickets over his ear and then pretend that it was a mistake?—A. He did not.

Q. Did you at any time during the day see A. B. Smalls at the State and county polls?—A. I did; he voted a man at the Congressional poll and then told him that he must go to the Democratic boxes and vote there. I followed Smalls and the voter to the State and county polls, and saw Smalls folding the Democratic tickets and the voter putting them in.

Q. Is it true that when C. P. Chisolm drew the tickets from the box that he turned his back but not his eyes?—A. His face was turned away from the box.

Q. What opportunities were offered the Republican supervisor for witnessing the voting during the day and the count after the polls had closed?—A. He was invited to take a seat at the table on which the ballot boxes were placed, and when we went to count the votes he occupied the same position at the table as he had at times during the day. As I called out the votes I asked him to notice each vote and to see if it was right. He told me that he could see, and Abram Smalls was in a foot of my elbow and saw every vote as I called them out to the tally-keeper.

Cross-examined by W. F. MYER, counsel for contestant:

Q. How long have you been living in Gloversville Township?—A. I have been living on the township line all my life.

Q. Are you a voter at Gloversville precinct?—A. I am.

Q. Are you or not an officer in the Democratic Club in Gloversville?—A. I am an executive officer, if you call that an officer.

Q. Keeping stores at two most popular points in the precinct you know pretty well the white and colored voters of the precinct, do you not?—A. I do.

Q. Who were present when you asked Chisolm who was Republican supervisor?—A. C. P. Chisolm, A. B. Small and his brother.

Q. As the poll was open, there being but three managers, a majority of them then was interviewing Chisolm, the Republican supervisor, away from the poll?—A. The place that the boxes were arranged were in full view of the fire. All persons having voted that were present, white and colored, C. P. Chisolm and myself walked out to the fire.

Q. The boxes being in full view of those who were standing at the fire, do you mean to say that the men at the fire did not know the polls were open and voting going on until said voting was over and you went out to them?—A. I take it as a matter of course that they knew that voting was going on as several persons had come in and voted.

Q. State how many up to this time had voted?—A. About four, or maybe five.

Q. Please name them.—A. I think Nero Williams was one, my brother and myself. I was not acting as secretary, therefore did not charge my memory with it.

Q. Whose store was it, and who occupied it at the time?—A. It was my store, in partnership with Hill.

Q. Did you or not stay at the store on the night preceding the election?—A. I did.

Q. Who stayed with you?—A. The clerk, W. F. Hill, J. B. Dodd, and C. P. Chisolm.

Q. Was not Nero Williams in there?—A. Not until the polls had been opened next morning.

Q. Do the men above named always sleep there, or was it the custom at the time mentioned for them to do so?—A. No. Myself and brother had been on business down to Cottageville, and until a late hour in the night. As it was nearer to my Gloversville store than to my home, and knowing that we would have to go down there early next morning, we called in and spent the night with the clerk at the store.

Q. Then you can name those only who were in the store that voted before E. M. Chisolm was notified?—A. I told you that Nero Williams came as soon as the poll was opened. He did not stay there that night.

Q. What direction did he come from, and what direction did he go after voting?—A. I did not see where he came from or where he went to.

Q. How did the voters approach the poll to vote, through the store or at the window?—A. Most of them voted at the window. Some came inside and voted.

Q. You say you know all of the white Democratic voters of Gloversville. Will you please give the names of all or some of them who voted that day?—A. H. B. Ackeman, T. S. Ackeman. I can't remember all the names except referring to the list, but they were nearly all present.

Q. As you can not tell all who voted, can you tell all who were not present?—A. I don't remember who was not present of the white Democrats.

Q. You stated that you know pretty well white and colored voters of this precinct. Will you state the names of the colored Democrats?—A. I don't wish to do so, as it would only bring down the wrath of the Republican leaders upon their heads.

Q. Are these colored Democrats members of your club, or are they organized into a separate club?—A. Some of them are; others are not. I mean our club; other colored Democrats are not members.

Q. Are not C. P. Chisolm and Nero Williams Democrats and known to your community?—A. They are.

Q. They being known as Democrats by white and colored, never have been molested or wrath brought down upon them, why can not you give the names of other colored Democrats?—A. Because I have been informed that they—Chisholm and Williams—have been threatened with lynching by the Republican leaders in the neighborhood.

Q. Did you ever hear a Republican leader make this threat, or are only giving what you heard others say?—A. I am telling what I know to be true.

Q. How do you know it to be true?—A. By information received from responsible parties.

Q. Will you name them?—A. I will not name them unless I am forced to do it.

Q. Have these men ever been lynched?—A. No; but they have been cussed and abused and threatened with lynching.

Q. Do they not live in the most thickly-populated settlement of the colored people in Grover Township?—A. No; they live in the upper part of the township, and most of their neighbors are near relatives.

Q. Then I suppose these two men have to be accompanied with a guard to protect them from lynchers?—A. No; they do not. I have known them to go around together for protection to each other, and have been forced to carry arms for their protection.

Q. Is Chisolm not an active worker for the Democratic party?—A. Yes; he expresses his opinion generally.

Q. Name the colored men whom you saw going amongst the colored voters with Elliott tickets on election day last trying to induce them to vote the Democratic ticket?—A. I can not give their names in justice to those colored men.

Q. You said in your direct that those men were openly working amongst the colored voters for the Elliott ticket; they were not molested then; why do you refuse now to give their names?—A. Because at that time all the white strength was out as a reason why they were not molested; things are quiet now, and I don't wish to bring them to any trouble this late day

Q. Did not the Republicans down there know these men?—A. I don't know whether they did or not, but I did.

Q. Please state if Smalls or Chisolm did not compare time with your watch when you went to the fire.—A. Nothing said about time at the fire; but when E. M. Chisolm came he said it lacked 15 minutes to six by A. B. Small's watch; and then it was some time after seven by mine.

Q. Was that the time Small's watch was four hours behind?—A. No.

Q. What manager drew the votes from the box while counting them?—A. C. P. Chisolm.

Q. Did he lay them on the table, or put them in another box?—A. He drew them out, called the name, passed them on to me and A. B. Smalls, and the two of us looked over them.

Q. When you requested the crowd to fall back or withdraw, what was the language used by you?—A. I do not remember the exact language, but wanted Smalls and Chisolm to take seats at the table and assist in counting the votes.

Q. Were they, or either of them, a manager?—A. They were not, but I wanted to show the Republicans present a free ballot and a fair count.

Q. As you wanted to show them a free ballot and a fair count, how is it that, of the number of Republicans around the poll, and the very few Democrats, only one Republican was admitted and all the Democrats who were present?—A. The Republicans all congregated in front of the store, and did not seem to want to come in. There was only one or two white Democrats that staid in the room when we first started to count; but when the managers of the State and county boxes got through they came in and took back seats.

Q. Did you and the other managers sit at the same table with E. M. Chisolm?—A. We did.

Q. Did the managers have a good view of the voters as they approached the window to vote?—A. Those of us who sat at the side of the table had full view of the voters as they came to the window.

Q. The managers having been able to see the voters sitting at the same table with E. M. Chisolm, how do you account for his inability to see as well as you?—A. Because I sat at the side of the table, while he (E. M. Chisolm) sat at the end of the table, which put him two feet away from the window.

Q. Are you well acquainted with E. M. Chisolm?—A. I have known him all my life.

Q. He is very active and earnest as a Republican, is he not?—A. I can't say. He is so tricky that I don't know.

Q. Being tricky, as you say, yet with this qualification, standing in full view of a lone building where every voter's attention was centered, the early morning being the most interesting time of voting, with men passing in and out, Chisolm, as you say, did not see or know the poll was open. Am I to understand that you outtricked him on that occasion?—A. No; you did not understand me to say so. I think he lies when he says he did not know the poll was open.

Q. Though a manager at the Congressional poll, you actively extended to the State and county poll the scrutinizing of voters and rallies, the knowledge of colored men being openly Democrat and rallying for the Democratic ticket, but you refuse to tell the name or names of colored men who voted for Elliott on the 6th of Nov. last, excepting Nero Williams and C. P. Chisolm, do you?—A. The colored men who voted the Democratic ticket that day made me promise faithfully that I would not give them away, as they did not want the ill will of their neighbors, and at the same time wanted to do what they thought was to their best interest. At the time I went out to the State and county boxes and saw A. B. Smalls voting a colored man, there was no voting going on at that time at the national box and the boxes were left in charge of two managers and the Republican supervisor.

Re-direct:

Q. E. M. Chisolm, a witness on the part of the contestant, heretofore testified that when he entered the poll in the morning the name of W. F. Hill was given to him by the managers as the one who had already voted, and that later during the day the said Hill presented himself and said that he had not voted, and was then permitted to vote by the managers; is that true?—A. That is not true; Hill did not vote but once, as will be seen by the poll-list.

Q. How long have you known Mr. Chisolm?—A. I have known him all my life.

Q. Are you intimately acquainted with the general reputation for truth of E. M. Chisolm in the community in which he lives?—A. I am.

Q. What is that reputation?—A. As I have before stated, his is tricky and not to be trusted; he is looked upon by the leading men in the neighborhood as the most notorious liar in it.

Q. Being a merchant and residing in the immediate vicinity of Gloversville precinct do you not know the sentiment of the colored voters regarding their political leaders?—A. I do.

Q. Was T. E. Miller popular or unpopular with the colored people of that commu.
nity?—A. From what I have learned from leading Republicans in the township, I
suppose he was very unpopular.

Q. Do you know the reasons which they assigned for his unpopularity?—A. Those
whom I heard say anything about it seemed to think that he had not dealt fairly with
Rob't Smalls, ex-Congressman, and they did not like a mulatto nohow.

Q. Do you not know that a great many colored people at that precinct remained
away from the polls for the reasons above given?—A. That is what I have been informed, and know there was nothing like a full vote polled.

Cross-examination:

Q. Who were the colored men that said they were down on Miller because of his
treatment to Smalls and his condition birth?—A. I don't think that I am liberty to
make public the parties who held this conversation in my store, as I think what one
hears under his own roof is sacred.

Q. You claim now to be scrupulous of telling conversation because of their sacred-
ness; why did you tell of the sacred conversation that occurred in your store by two
leading colored men in reference to Miller under your own declaration; is it less
sacred to give the name as I asked?—A. I have only made public what I believe to
be the general sentiment of the colored people, but at the same time, not having di-
vulged the names of the parties holding the conversation, I have done them no harm.

Q. As the men held the conversation in a public store, asking no .injunction as to
secrecy, how came you to regard it more sacred than they?—A. They were the only
persons in the store at that time. I was in the office writing, and I don't suppose
they intended me to hear what they were talking about.

Q. Seeming to be an expert in matters relating to the standing of men and the sentiments of the people in your community, you mean to say that the opinion of the
entire Republican vote down there must be governed by the sacred conversation had
in your store by two men?—A. As political leaders always understand the sentiment
of their party, I took it for granted the two leading Republicans know the sentiment
of their township.

Q. Are you or are you not postmaster at the Round or Centerville P. O.?—A. I am
postmaster at Round.

Q. Is that now in the district represented by W. Elliott in Congress?—A. I think
it is.

Q. You have expressed a thorough knowledge of things in Glover precinct; I desire
you to state if the Round P. O. is not in the Seventh Congressional District, now
represented by William Elliott?—A. I told you it was.

J. B. DODD, being duly sworn, says:

Question. State your age and residence.—Answer. I am 28 years old and reside at
Gloversville precinct.

Q. Where were you on the 6th day of Nov. last?—A. At Gloversville voting precinct.

Q. Were you at the precinct at the time that the Congressional poll was opened?—
A. I was; I was in the room when the poll was opened.

Q. Were the boxes opened for the scrutiny of those who wished to see before the
voting commenced?—A. Yes.

Q. Did you vote in the Congressional box that day, and if so, whom did you vote
for for Congress?—A. I did; and voted for Elliott.

Q. Did you, at any time during the day, see A. B. Smalls at the State and county
poll?—A. Yes; I was manager of that poll.

Q. What was A. B. Smalls doing there when you saw him?--A. He came to that
poll with a colored, who seemed to be a very ignorant man, and told him he must
vote in all of those boxes, and folded Democratic tickets, giving him one to poll into
each box, which the man did; stated as he left that he was going to bring more
votes to the boxes at which he was manager. He was about, the State and county
polls several times that day, but never brought any more voters.

Q. When you voted for William Elliott at the national poll did you not have your
registration certificate?—A. Yes; I had.

Q. Have you that certificate with you now?—A. I have not; as I never carry it except to elections.

Q. Do you remember about how long ago it was issued to you?—A. Not exactly;
about four years, I think.

Q. Do you remember its serial number?
(Counsel for contestant objects, as the original certificate is the proper evidence.)
A. No. 90, I think.

Cross-examination:

Q. Who acted with you as managers at the State and county precinct on election
day last?—A. T. S. Ackerman, and H. B. Ackerman a portion of the time. The reg·

ular manager did not come, and as soon as H. B. Ackerman got there we appointed him to act with us.

Q. You say a portion of the time H. B. Ackerman acted; that is, when did he reach the poll to act with you?

(Counsel for contestee objects to the question upon the ground that it is irrelevant; this examination has reference to the conduct of the election at the Federal poll, and not the State and county.)

A. About ten o'clock, as well as I remember.

Q. When you opened the State and county poll, did you open the boxes to allow the voters to see that they were all right?

(Objection as above.)

A. Yes.

Q. At what time or what o'clock was this done?—A. About 7 o'clock.

Q. How far was the State and county poll from that of Congressional?—A. From 75 to 100 yards.

Q. Am I to understand that you got up, dressed, and voted at the Federal poll in the building in which you slept the night preceding, saw the managers examine box or boxes, you and others voted then, and yet you got to the State and county poll and opened at 7 o'clock a. m.?—A. In the first place I did not say I opened at 7, but about 7, and further I did not wait to see anybody vote but myself, and the time that it took me to walk 75 yards could not be considered difference enough to make the time illegal.

Contestant's case, as heretofore stated, rests on the testimony of E. M. Chisolm, who, as J. H. Dodd says, "is looked upon by the leading men in the neighborhood as the most notorious liar in it." In one place he says about his report as supervisor:

I simply could make one reference, and that was that the poll-list only called for 134 votes, and that there were 229 ballots in the box.

In another place he says:

I reported several objections; one is that the manager, while pretending to scratch his head, threw a vote over his back.

Again he says:

I remember giving the total number of votes cast, and at the bottom I made a statement as to how the true number of votes were not given, making a statement of the irregularities.

And here is the return that he did make (p. 661):

EXHIBIT A.

Return of the election held at Gloverville precinct, Colleton County, November 6, 1888.

The whole number of votes given for member of Congress was 134
Of which William Elliott received... 113
Of which Thomas E. Miller received... 21
Of which   received ....
Of which   received ....

We, the undersigned supervisors, certify that the above is a correct return of the votes cast at the election held at Gloverville precinct, of Colleton County, on the 6th day of November, 1888.

E. M. CHISOLM,
Supervisor.

I certify that the foregoing is a true copy of the original return now on file in my office.

SAMUEL T. POINIER,
Chief Supervisor.

According to his own account he did not before election day notify the managers that he was supervisor, and even on election day did not notify them until "some time" after he had seen one of them, but contented himself with hanging around a fire, when, according to J. H. Dodd, he had to be asked who was supervisor, and even after being told that the polls were opened, and asked why he did not go to his post, said "he would be in after a little." When the ballots are being counted he does not examine them because he was "keeping a poll-list." The testimony indicates very strongly that Chisolm was simply laying the foundation for the charge that he was not allowed to examine the box, and thereby defeat the election. If his demand to examine the box after the voting had commenced had been complied with, then we would have had a fervid complaint based on that fact. The only testimony explaining the surplus of ballots in the box shows that Republican tickets were found folded together, Congressional and electoral. Nothing is said about the vote in the electoral box. After the performance at Grahamville, under contestant's eye, what may not be expected from Republican leaders in South Carolina? Uncontradicted testimony shows that leading colored men at the precinct were favoring contestee's election, on account of contestant's treatment of ex-Congressman Smalls, and two uncontradicted witnesses prove that A. B. Smalls, possibly a relative, who was relied on to distribute contestant's tickets, was openly pushing the Democratic ticket at the State polls. Contestant undertook to swear the voters as to their votes, but gave up the attempt after examining three witnesses.

GREEN POND.

The returns in this precinct gave Elliott 216, Miller 52.

Notwithstanding these returns by the sworn officers of the law, the majority, on the strength of the testimony of one Brown, who was one of the United States supervisors at that poll, and against the testimony of five reputable citizens, managers and clerks of the election, 200 votes are taken from Elliott and 200 added to Miller, thus giving Miller 400 votes off hand at that precinct.

In order that the House may have a just conception of the character of evidence employed in this case to unseat Mr. Elliott, we give here some sample extracts:

Cross-examination of Emanuel Youton (p. 186):

Question. When were you born; what year?—Answer. I can not tell the year.
Q. How many ballot-boxes were at the poll that day?—A. There were two.
Q. Did each of the boxes have labels on them?—A. Yes.
Q. What did those labels contain?—A. Don't know.
Q. Then you don't know whether you put your ticket for T. E. Miller in the box labeled Presidential electors or the box labeled Representative in Congress?—A. I do not know.

Cross-examination of July Gadsden (p. 187):

Q. How many tickets did you vote on the 6th of Nov. last?—A. I voted one ticket.
Q. How many ballot-boxes were at the precinct at which you voted?—A. Two.
Q. Then you did not vote in but one of them?—A. But one.
Q. Did you vote that one ballot in the box labeled Rep. in Congress or the box labeled Presidential electors?—A. In the Congressional box.
Q. Who did you vote for President?—A. Harris.
Q. Now, you testified a few minutes ago that you did not vote but one ballot on Nov. 6th last, and that you voted that one ballot for T. S. Miller for Congress in the box labeled Rep. in Congress, and now you say that you voted for Harris for President. How do you account for that?—A. Singleton read the ticket that Miller was on it for Congress, and I voted that.

Cross-examination of Prince Warley (p. 201):

Q. Did you notice any difference in the construction in the two boxes of the precinct?—A. I notice that one hole was large and the other small in the two boxes.
Q. On which side was the box located containing the large hole?—A. On the right.
Q. How many ballots did you vote on that day?—A. Two.
Q. For what officers were those two ballots voted?—A. One was for President and the other for Miller.

Q. What was Miller running for, governor?—A. He did not run for governor; I have forgotten what he ran for.

Cross-examination of Bristow Mitchell (p. 208):

Q. Did you see Chapman vote on on that?—A. I saw him vote.

Q. Did you read the ticket that Chapman voted for President?—A. Yes; I read his ticket.

Q. Did he vote for Grant or Garfield for President?—A. Yes; he did vote for Garfield.

Q. Did the boxes at the precinct that day have labels on them?—A. Yes; they had labels.

Q. What did these labels contain?—A. The labels was to show you the difference for Presidential electors and Congressman.

Q. Will you swear of your own knowledge that you voted for Miller in the box labeled Presidential electors?—A. No; I voted for Miller in the one on the right with the large hole.

Q. Did you vote for the same man for President that Chapman voted for?—A. I did not vote for the same man.

Q. Did you vote for Grant or Sherman for President?—A. No.

Q. Who did you vote for for President?—A. I can not remember the names that were on the ticket, but I voted for the electors on the ticket.

Q. Are you willing to swear of your own knowledge that the word Republican was printed on your ticket?—A. No; that was not there.

Q. Did you vote for Cleveland for President?—A. I did.

Cross-examination of Wm. Alston (p. 208):

Q. Who did you vote for for President, Cleveland or Conklin?—A. I voted for President at large.

Q. Then you just went it blind, for nobody in particular?—A. No; I voted for nobody in particular.

Q. You voted for Congressman in the same way, did you not?—A. Yes.

Q. How many ballots did you vote on that day?—A. I voted two.

Q. Did you vote them both for the same officer?—A. Yes.

Q. Did you vote them both in the box on the right with the big hole in it?—A. No, I did not.

Q. Did you vote them both in the box on the left with the little hole in it?—A. No, sir; I put one in each box.

Q. Which box had Miller's name for Congress on it, the one on the right or left?—A. The one on the left with the small hole for Miller.

Q. Then you voted for Miller in the small hole?—A. Yes.

Q. In which box did you vote for Miller, on the right or on the left?—A. I voted in the right for Miller.

Q. For what office was the President running?—A. For Senator.

Q. In which box did you vote for Senator?—A. In the right-hand box.

Cross-examination of Jeffrey Smith (p. 204):

Q. You really did not have but one ballot that day?—A. Only one.

Q. You have already sworn that you did not vote but one ballot that day, and that was for Congressman. Why did you not vote for President also?—A. May have been two tickets in one for what I know; he gave me the ticket, saying it was Republican, and I voted it.

Q. What did you put in the other box—the box with the little hole?—A. I put them in just as they were given to me; if there were two tickets I put them in the box with the big hole.

Cross-examination of Paris Smalls (p. 205):

Q. What office was Harrison running for?—A. I understand he was running for President.

Q. What office was T. E. Miller running for; was he running for U. S. Senator?—A. I do not know.

Q. If you do not know what office he was running for, how did you testify a few minutes ago that you voted for him for Congress?—A. By Chapman's instructions.

Cross-examination by W. B. Gruber, esq., of Jake Brown (p. 206):

Q. Who did you vote for for President on November 6th last?—A. I voted for Miller.

Q. Who did you vote for for Congress on November 6th last?—A. I voted for nobody but Miller.

Q. How many ballots did you vote on November 6th?—A. Two.

Q. Did you vote both of those ballots in the same box for the same candidate?—A. One on the right and one on the left.

Q. You have already testified that you saw but one box, and that you voted in that for Miller; now in what kind of a machine did you deposit your other ballot? A. There were two holes there.

Cross-examination of Denibo Washington (p. 210):

Q. How many ballots did you vote that day?—A. I voted two.

Q. Did you vote for President?—A. I voted for Miller at large.

Q. Did you vote for Miller for President?—A. Yes, sir.

Q. How many ballots did you vote for Miller for President?—A. I cast two, but I had an understanding of the difference.

Q. Did you vote for Elliott or Smalls as Representative in Congress?—A. I voted for Smalls.

Q. Who did you vote for for Vice-President, Cleveland or Thurman?—A. I did not vote for either.

Q. Who did you vote for for Vice-President?—A. I do not understand the men's names, as I can not read.

Q. Didn't you vote for Miller for Vice-President?—A. I cast my vote for Miller, but as I can not read myself I do not know.

Q. If you can not read yourself how did you happen to testify just now that you voted for Miller for President?—A. So far as I got the ballot to cast I ask the name, and they gave me Miller's name.

Cross-examination of George Morgan (p. 212):

Q. Did you notice any difference in the construction of the two boxes?—A. No, sir.

Q. Then how did you know which box in which you should deposit your ticket for Congressman?—A. I know by instruction; I put it in on the right.

Q. Was that the box in which you were instructed to vote for Presidential elector? A. Yes, sir.

Q. Was that also the box in which you were instructed to vote for Congressman? A. Yes, sir.

Q. Did you vote as you were instructed?—A. Yes, sir.

Q. Did you vote for Miller for President?—A. Yes, sir.

Q. Did you vote for Miller for U. S. Senate?—A. Yes, sir.

Cross-examination by W. B. Gruber, esq., of P. Cattles (p. 219):

Q. Then you did not know whether you were voting correctly or not?—A. I voted, as I think was proper to my advantage.

Q. Did you vote for T. E. Miller as a presidential elector?—A. That's what I did.

Q. Did you notice any difference in the construction of the boxes?—A. I did; one box had a small hole and the other hole was larger.

Q. Was the small hole on the right or left?—A. On the left.

Q. Did you vote for T. E. Miller in the small or large hole?—A. In the large hole.

Q. Did you vote in the large hole for President Sherman?—A. In the large hole for President Sherman.

Q. Did you vote in the large hole or the small for V. President Cleveland?—A. In the small hole.

Cross-examination of Sam Rutledge (p. 220):

Q. Will you swear that you actually voted for Miller as Presidential elector?—A. Yes, sir.

Q. Will you swear that you actually voted for Harrison for Congress?—A. No, sir.

Q. Did you vote for Morton for Vice President?—A. No, sir.

Q. Did you vote for Harrison for President?—A. Yes, sir.

Q. Did you notice any difference in the construction of the boxes?—A. Yes; one box had a larger hole than the other.

Q. Did you vote for Harrison for Congress in the big or the little hole?—A. Vote for Harrison in small hole, but did not vote for him for Congress.

Q. Was the small hole on the right or the left?—A. On the left when I voted.

Q. Will you swear, of your own knowledge, that that was the box in which you voted for Miller?—A. Yes.

Cross-examination of Charles Nichols (p. 221):

Q. Will you swear that you voted for Miller for President?—A. I did not know what he was running for. I took the ticket and voted as instructed.

Q. For whom did you vote for President—Elliott or Miller?—A. Miller.

Q. Did you vote two ballots or tickets in each of the boxes at the precinct?—A. One in each.

Q. Did you notice any difference in the construction of the boxes at the precinct?—A. One box had a larger hole than the other. The right-hand box I voted for Miller in.

Q. Having voted for Miller in the right-hand box, will you swear that you voted for Elliott in the left?—A. I voted in the right-hand box.

Q. In which of them did you vote for Elliott—the right or the left?—A. The left.

Q. For what office did you vote for Miller—President or Senator?—A. President.

Q. For what office did you vote for Sherman—President or Congress?—A. I don't know what office he ran for, but I vote two papers.

Q. What kind of papers did you vote—registration certificates or letter receipts?—A. I voted a paper like print.

Cross-examination of Sam Frazer (p. 222):

Q. Did the boxes at the precinct have labels on them?—A. Yes; some were torn.

Q. Did those labels indicate in which box you were to deposit your ballot for the officers for whom you were voting?—A. No; it did not. I was looking for that purposely.

Q. If the labels did not indicate in which box you were to deposit your ballots it was therefore impossible for you to vote correctly, was it not?—A. They told me before going in that the box with the small hole was for Congress and the big hole for President.

Q. In which hole did you vote for Miller, the big or the little hole?—A. I voted for Miller in the big hole.

Q. Miller was running for President, was he not?—A. Miller was running for President.

Cross-examination of Ben Green (p. 225):

Q. In which box did you vote for Miller for Presidential elector, the right or the left, the big or the little hole?—A. In the large hole.

Q. Then if you voted for Miller for Presidential elector in the big hole, in which hole did you vote for Elliott for Congress?—A. Did not vote in either for Elliott.

Q. For what office was Miller running, President or Senator?—A. Miller was running for President.

Q. Did you vote for him for that office?—A. 'Twas my intention to vote for him for what he was running for.

Q. For whom did you vote for Congressman, Sherman or Harrison?—A. I voted for Miller.

Q. Are you willing to swear that you voted for Elliott or Sherman for President?—A. I voted for Miller.

Q. How many ballots did you vote that day?—A. I voted one ticket that day.

Q. Did you vote that one ticket for President?—A. Yes.

Q. Did you vote for Miller for President?

(Objected to on ground that witness has fully answered the question; it is misleading and intended to materially injure contestant.)

A. I voted for Miller for President.

Cross-examination of Sharper Gillings (p. 228):

Q. Were you born in 1784 or 1785?—A. In 1775; but you must speak plain, I am an Englishman.

Q. Did you come over to this country in the Mayflower or originally with Christopher Columbus?—A. I was born right here.

Q. How is it then that you call yourself an Englishman?—A. Because that's the way my mother and father learn me the English language and in politics.

Q. Did you vote for Miller for President in the big or little hole?—A. I voted for Miller for President in the big hole.

Q. In which hole did you vote for Elliott, in the big or little one?—A. I voted for all who was along with Mr. Miller; they just told me and I voted.

Q. In which hole did you vote for Mr. Sherman for President, the big or the little hole?—A. All what was with Mr. Miller went in the big hole.

Q. Then you did not vote in the little hole at all, did you?—A. I voted in the big hole on the right and the little one on the left.

Q. Did you vote for Miller in the little hole on the left?—A. I voted for Miller on the right.

Q. Who did you vote for on the left and what office was he running for?—A. I don't know.

Cross-examination of Jackson Pinkney (p. 233):

Q. To what religious denomination does the Republican party belong—African,

560 :MILLER VS. ELLIOTT.

Methodist, or Baptist ?—A. I believe the Republican party belong to every denom-
ination.
Q. Are you willing to testify that the words "Republican party" were printed on
the ticket that you voted that day ?—A. Yes, the word was printed on the ticket.
Q. Who did you vote for for President, Beck or Elliott?—A. Beck and Harrison.
Q. Did you vote for both Beck and Harrison for President?—A. The same ticket I
voted for Beckman for V. President I voted for Harrison.
Q. What did you vote for Mr. Sherman for, Congressman or governor?—A. I vote
for Mr. Miller for Congressman.
Q. Who did you vote for governor ? Did you not vote for Sherman ?—A. I did not
vote for any governor.
Q. You know who you voted for, do you not?—A. I do.
Q. For what office, then, did you vote for Sherman ?—A. I did not vote for Sherman
for any office.
Q. In which box did you deposit your ballot for Miller ?—A. The one to the right,
with the big hole, for Miller.
Q. Was that the box labelled "Representative in Congress?"—A. Yes, that is the
box.
Q. Are you willing to testify that the name of Beck and Harrison were printed on
the ticket which you voted ?—A. I am willing.

Cross-examination of Sam Simmons (p. 230):

Q. In which hole did you vote for Miller for President—the big or the little one?—
A. The large one on my right.
Q. In which hole did you vote for Elliott for Congress—the big or the little one ?—
A. I voted in the little hole.

Cross-examination of April Ford (p. 233):

Q. How many ballots did you vote that day ?—A. Two.
Q. Did you vote them for Miller for Congress ?—A. I vote them for Miller for Con-
gress.
Q. Did you notice any difference in the construction of the boxes at the precinct ?—
A. No.
Q. For what office was Wm. Elliott running ?—A. I do not know.
Q. Did you not vote for him for President ?—A. No ; I did not.
Q. Are you willing to testify that you actually voted for Miller as Presidential
elector ?—A. Yes.
Q. Who did you vote for as Representative from this district in the 51st Congress—
Harrison or Cleveland?—A. I did not vote for Harrison or Cleveland for Congress.
Q. Are you willing to swear that you did not vote for Harrison or Cleveland on
that day ?—A. Yes; I am willing to swear I did not.
Q. Did you vote in both of the boxes at the precinct that day ?—A. Yes.
Q. Did you vote two ballots in each of the boxes?—A. No ; one.
Q. And each of these ballots contained the name of your friend, T. E. Miller ?—A.
Yes.

Cross-examination of Baalam Burnet (p. 234):

Q. If I were to call the name of the man for whom you voted for Congressman
from this district, would you know it ?—A. Yes.
Q. Was it Harrison ?—A. Yes, sir.
Q. If I were to call the name of the man for whom you voted in the box for Presi-
dent, would you know it ?—A. Yes.
Q. Was it Sherman ?—A. No.
Q. Was it Garfield ?—A. No, sir.
Q. Was it Miller?—A. Yes, sir.

Cross-examination of Philip Robinson (p. 236):

Q. Did you read Harrison's name on your ticket ?—A. No, sir.
Q. Then you did not vote for Harrison on that day ?—A. Yes, I voted for Harrison.
Q. Then you were mistaken were you not when you said just now that you did not
read his name on your ticket ?—A. I am not mistaken, because I did not read his
name.
Q. When Chapman read your ticket to you did he read the name of Harrison ?—A.
Yes, sir.
Q. Are you willing to testify, of your own knowledge, that you voted for Miller in
the box labeled Presidential electors ?—A. Yes, sir.

Cross-examination of Baalam Ford (p. 238):

Q. Who did you vote for for President, Sherman or Rob't Smalls ?-
vote for either one-

Q. Are you willing to swear that you voted for Miller in the box labeled for Presidential electors?—A. Yes, sir.

Cross-examination of Simon Fraser (p. 242):

Q. If you voted for Miller for Congress, for what office did you vote for W. F. yers, governor or President?—A. I can not read and can not tell.

Q. Will you swear that the words Republican party were printed on the ticket which you voted for Miller for Presidential elector?—A. Yes, sir.

Q. Will you swear that you voted for Miller in the box labeled Presidential electors?—A. Yes, sir.

Cross-examination of Bencher Morgan:

Q. Who did you give the tickets to that Smith gave to you?—A. I put them in the box.

Q. Are you willing to testify that the words, "Republican Party Rally 'round the Poll" was printed on the ticket you voted?—A. I can not tell.

Q. Are you willing to swear that nobody read your ticket to you?—A. No one read them.

Q. Then you don't know who you voted for for Presidential electors and Representative in Congress?—A. I do not.

Cross-examination of Ben Harlbeck (p. 244):

Q. If you voted for Miller for Congress, for what office did you vote for W. F. Myers, governor or President?—A. President.

Q. Are you willing to swear that you voted for Miller for Presidential elector in the box with the large hole?—A. No.

Q. Are you willing to swear that you voted for him for Presidental elector in the box with the small hole?—A. Yes.

Cross-examination of Tony Robinson (p. 248):

Q. Are you willing to swear that you didn't vote but one ticket on the day of election?—A. I voted two tickets.

Q. Are you willing to swear that you voted for Miller for Presidential elector?—A. For President.

Q. If you voted for Miller for President, for what office did you vote for Cleveland; gov. or senator?—A. None.

Cross-examination by W. B. Gruber of Bob Robinson (p. 249):

Q. Are you willing to swear that you actually voted your registration certificate for Tom Miller? A. Yes. sir.

Q. Are you willing to swear that you voted for Miller in the box for Presidential electors?--A. Yes, I did.

Cross-examination of John Lessington (p. 250):

Q. Will you swear, on your honor as a man, that you did not vote but one ballot on the 6th of Nov. last? A. One.

Q. In which box, the right or the left, did you vote for Miller for Presidential elector, the big or the little hole?—A. There were two boxes, one on the right and the other on the left, and just as Chapman gave me the tickets I voted them, as he instructed; I don't know whether I voted for him in big or little hole.

Q. Will you swear that you actually voted for him that day for Presidential elector?—A. Yes, sir.

Q. If you voted for Miller in one of the boxes, who did you vote for in the other?—A. I did not hear the name of the man.

Q. Did you vote in both of the boxes?—A. Yes, sir.

Q. You have already sworn that you did not vote but one ballot that day, now you swear that you voted in both boxes; will you explain how you voted one ballot in two boxes?—A. I don't know how.

Cross-examination of Jackey Wragg (p. 253):

Q. Will you swear positively that you did not vote but one ballot that day?

(Objected to on the ground that the question is irrelevant to the issue and intended to prolong the examination for the benefit of the contestee.)

A. I voted two tickets.

(Counsel for contestee objects to counsel for contestant stating that witness can answer as he answered before.)

Q. For whom did you vote for President, Col. Wm. Elliott or T. E. Miller?—A. I voted for Harrison and Miller.

H. Mis. 137——36

Q. Will you swear of your own knowledge that you voted for both Harrison and Miller for President?

(By contestant.—Objected on the ground that the witness has already answered the question; the question is irrelevant to the issue, as the witness has testified already that he voted for Miller for Congress and Harrison for President.)

(By contestee.—Objection is made to above objection on ground that it is unfair to recall to recollection of witness what he has formerly testified to for the purpose of enabling witness to answer correctly, and for the further reason that the witness has not answered that he voted for Harrison for President separately, but both Miller and Harrison together for the office of President.)

A. I voted for Harrison for Congressman.

Cross-examination of Wm. Boggs (p. 254):

Q. Will you swear that you voted for Sherman for President in the left-hand box with the small hole?

(Objected to on ground that the question will benefit neither contestant nor contestee, and is irrelevant to the issue.)

A. Miller for President.

Cross-examination of Anthony Bartlett (p. 265):

Q. Will you swear that you voted for Miller in the box labeled Presidential electors on the right-hand side with the big hole?—A. Yes, sir.

Q. Will you swear that the words Republican party were printed on your ticket A. Yes, sir.

Q. Will you swear that you voted for Grant, the Republican nominee for President?—A. I don't know anything about him.

Q. If I were to call the name of the person for whom you voted for President would you know it?—A. I don't know, because I can't read.

Q. Did you ever hear his name?—A. No, sir.

Cross-examination of Moses Field (p. 266):

Q. Will you swear that you voted but one ticket that day?—A. Voted one ticket.

Q. Will you swear that that one ticket contained the name of Benj. Harrison for President?—A. Yes, sir.

Cross-examination of Scipio Campbell (p. 268):

Q. Will you swear that the name of T. E. Miller was not printed on the ticket for Presidential elector?—A. I don't know whether it was on there for President, Senator, or not.

Q. Will you swear that you voted for Miller for Senator?—A. Yes, sir.

Q. Will you swear that you voted for Harrison in the box labelled or marked Representative in Congress?—A. Yes, sir.

Cross-examination of Toby Elliott (p. 269):

Q. Will you swear that you voted for T. E. Miller in the right box for V. Presd't?—A. Yes, sir.

Q. Will you swear that you voted for T. E. Miller in the box labelled Presidential elector?—A. Yes, sir.

Cross-examination of Aaron Judge (p. 270):

Q. For whom did you say you voted for President that day?—A. Miller.

Q. Are you willing to swear that that is true?—A. Yes, sir.

Q. Are you willing to swear that you put the ticket containing Miller's name in the box labelled Presidential electors?—A. Yes, sir.

Cross-examination of Chas. Mitchell (p. 270):

Q. Are you willing to swear that the name of T. E. Miller was actually printed on the ticket you voted for Vice-President?—A. Yes.

Q. Are you willing to swear that you voted for Mr. Miller in the box labelled for that officer?—A. I voted for Miller in the left box.

Q. Are you willing to swear that that was the box labelled or printed Presidential electors?—A. Yes, sir.

Cross-examination of Titus Wright (p. 271):

Q. Are you willing to swear that you voted for T. E. Miller for Presidential elector, in the right-hand box with a big hole?—A. Yes, sir.

Cross-examination of Ambrose Morgan (p. 271):

Q. Are you willing to swear that Dan'l Fields read the words "Republican party" on your ticket?—A. Yes, sir.

Q. Are you willing to swear that he read those words on the ticket which you voted for Miller, and that you put that ticket in the box labelled or marked "Presidential electors?"—A. Yes, sir.

Cross-examination of Wm. Huguinin (p. 272):

Q. Are you willing to swear that the words Republican party were on the ticket which you voted for Miller?—A. Yes, sir.

Q. Are you willing to swear that you voted for Miller for Presidential elector in the right-hand box with the big hole?—A. Yes, sir.

Cross-examination of Smith Bowan (p. 273):

Q. Will you actually swear that you threw two tickets in the box?—A. I threw one.

Q. Will you swear that that ticket was voted in the box for Presidential electors?—A. Yes, sir.

Cross-examination of Mooner Washington (p. 273):

Q. Did you have your specks on day of election, but haven't got them to-day?—A. Yes, and I can not read without them.

Q. Will you swear that you voted the ticket with Miller's name on it in the box labelled Presidential electors?—A. Yes.

The contestee examined O. P. Williams (p. 369), manager; M. A. Draudy, clerk (p. 371); Sam'l Driggs, constable (373); B. H. Padgett (375); J. T. Blanchard, manager (376). In order to show that this poll was honestly conducted, and everything on the part of managers was legal and fair, their testimony will be given:

O. P. WILLIAMS, a witness in behalf of the contestee, being duly sworn, says:

Question. State your age, occupation, residence, and where you were on the 6th day of Nov., 1888.—Answer. Age, 33 years; merchant; residence at White Hall, and was at Green Pond.

Q. In what capacity, if any, were you at Green Pond on that day?—A. I was one of the managers of election at the Federal box.

Q. At what hour were the boxes opened?—A. At seven o'clock a. m.

Q. At what place at Green Pond were the polls held?—A. At Hickman's Hotel.

Q. Did the managers expose the boxes to those present when they opened the polls?—A. Yes.

Q. Did the voters have free access to the polls during the entire day, and did everything pass off peaceably and without hindrance?—A. Yes.

Q. Were you present when the polls closed?—A. Yes.

Q. Was the canvass of the votes made in accordance with law?—A. Yes.

Q. Did you find in the canvass more votes in the box than there were names upon the poll-list?—A. Yes.

Q. How did you dispose of the excess of votes?—A. Mr. Blanchard and Mr. Rice counted the votes and disposed of the excess.

Q. Did they blindfold or did some one turn their back and draw the excess?—A. Yes; Mr. Draudy drew them with his back turned to the box.

Q. At the close of the polls, who were permitted to remain in the building during the count and canvass of the votes?—A. The managers were present and the supervisor, J. F. Brown, and some others; I do not now remember their names. The room was very small and would not admit of many persons being in there.

Q. It has been testified to that Mr. Rice, one of the managers, during the count took quantities of the tickets or ballots and tore them up. Is that true?—A. No, it is not.

Q. Do you know that a quantity of tickets with the name of William Elliott were distributed and given out on the day of election?—A. Yes.

Q. Are you well acquainted with the colored people who live in that vicinity and vote at the Green Pond precinct?—A. I am.

Q. Did you, prior to the last election, know that there was a strong sentiment existing amongst the colored people against Thomas E. Miller? If so, state their reasons as gathered by you from your intercourse and dealings with them?

(Objected to as leading.)

A. Well, the sentiment was this, that they preferred Smalls; if not Smalls, they wanted a white man, as Miller was neither one nor the other, and they frequently cited Mackey.

Q: Then you know that the colored people did not desire Miller to represent them in Congress ?—A. That is my impression, gathered from my dealings with them.

Q. Did you find on opening the Congressional box any tickets folded together ?—A. Mr. Blanchard and Mr. Rice took them out; I did not.

Q. How long after the polls had opened was it before J. F. Brown, the supervisor, made his appearance ?—A. I don't remember the exact time, but it was after the polls had opened; I sent for him; I thought he was in the house.

Q. Did he, Brown, make a demand on the managers to open the boxes and let him see in them ?—A. He did not; I suggested to him that if he desired it I would let him see in the boxes; that the hour had arrived for opening the polls and I could not wait. Brown replied and said it made no difference and declined to insist on the boxes being opened.

Cross-examined:

Q. Did you or not stay in the house in which the voting was held the night preceding said voting ?—A. We got there very late that night and laid down and took a rest.

Q. Who else besides you were in the house that night ? Please name them.—A. Mr. Rice, Mr. Blanchard, Draudy, and Dreggers. If there was any one else in the house I don't know.

Q. What relation had these gentlemen or any of them to the election that was conducted the next day ?—A. Mr. Blanchard and Rice were managers and Mr. Draudy was acting as clerk; the others I don't think had anything to do with it.

Q. Who was the Democratic supervisors ?—A. We had none.

Q. Did you and the other managers stay in the house until time to open the poll at seven o'clock ?—A. I did, but Mr. Rice and Blanchard were out a few moments and returned immediately.

Q. Locking yourselves up in the polling place the night preceding the election and opening the doors that morning without publicly notifying the voters who had gathered around, and taking care not to notify J. F. Brown, the supervisor, until after the voting had commenced, will you here under oath say that you were carrying out the laws governing you as manager.

Q. As you did not admit citizens to the room during the count because it was small, why did you and other managers order the windows and doors closed, thus shutting out the view of a number of citizens who were quietly looking on ?—A. I did not order the windows shut, nor do I think any of the managers ordered them shut. As to the doors, they had to be closed to prevent the crowd from coming and disturbing us during the count.

Q. Will you deny that the window was closed and the back door opening into the room in which you were conducting the count ?—A. I don't know that the windows were closed; I won't say they were not closed.

Q. Do you not know that the front door was open and a constable placed thereat during the count ?—A. I do not know. I don't think there was any one at the door during the count.

Q. This front door led through a passage to the room in which you conducted the count ?—A. Yes.

Q. Do you know the number of Democratic votes at the Green Pond poll ?—A. I do not.

Q. Are you not largely acquainted down there ?—A. I am very well known down there.

Q. Can't you give an approximation of the vote ?—A. I can not.

M. A. DRAUDY, being duly sworn, says:

Q. State your age, occupation, residence, and where you were on the 6th day of Nov. last ?—A. Age, 36; farmer; reside at Cook's Hill, Verdur Township, and was at Green Pond polling precinct on the 6th day of Nov. last.

Q. In what capacity, if any, did you act in the election held on that day ?—A. I was clerk of the board of managers at Green Pond.

Q. At what time were the polls opened on that day ?—A. Well, sir, when we opened the polls on that day it was 10 minutes past 7 in the morning.

Q. Were the boxes opened and exposed before the voting commenced ?—A. Yes, they were.

Q. Do you know J. F. Brown ?—I do.

Q. How long after the polls had opened was it before he came in ?—A. I suppose about 5 or 10 minutes. I don't know exactly how long.

Q. Did the voters have free access to the building and box for the purpose of voting during the entire day ?—A. They did.

Q. Were you present when the polls were closed ?—A. I was.

Q. Did you assist in canvassing the vote and declaring the election ?—A. I did.

Q. After opening the box did you find more than one ticket folded together ? If so, state how many and whose name appeared on said tickets ?—A. Well, I found, on drawing the tickets from the box from one to five folded together. Thomas E. Miller's name was on all of them that were folded together.

Q. After you had counted the votes did you find more tickets in the box than there were names on the poll-list?—A. We did.

Q. Who destroyed the excess of ballots, and how were they destroyed?—A. Mr. Blanchard and Mr. Rice destroyed them. I don't know whether they tore them up or threw them on the ground.

A. They blindfolded me and asked me to turn my back and draw, which I did.

Q. Did you prevent any person or persons from entering the building during the count?—A. We did. We were in a small room and the weather was pretty warm. We also had the train lying over waiting for us, and we could not have been bothered with everybody and have been ready for the train.

Q. It has been testified to here that Rice, one of the managers, during the count would take tickets out of the box and tear them up. Is that true?—A. I deny any such charges. It is not true.

Cross-examination:

Q. Where did you stay the night preceding the election?—A. I staid in Mr. Hickman's house, the place where the voting was held.

Q. I suppose you did that for the purpose of being early to open the polls, did you not?—A. I did not.

Q. Why did you stay there that night?—A. Well, because I went down on the train that night and found no other place to stay. Mr. Hickman is a particular friend of mine, and I always stop with him when I go to Green Pond.

(Counsel for contestant objects to the latter clause of answer, as it is stated under direction of counsel for contestee, and not the original words of the witness.)

Q. Who else staid with you there that night, and what relation had they to the conduct of the election at Green Pond?—A. Charley Rice, Oliver Williams, T. J. Blanchard, Samuel Driggers, Rhitt Hickman, Noel Robinson. Myself was clerk for the Democratic party; Mr. Rice, Mr. Blanchard, Oliver Williams was managers. Mr. Driggers, Mr. Hickman, they were marshals on the election grounds.

Q. Did these parties above named, or either of them, vote at Green Pond on that day?—A. I can not say.

Q. You say you were clerk; having kept a poll-list, and knowing these parties intimately, you can not tell whether or not they voted?—A. I never kept a personal poll-list, but put all of my returns in the box.

Q. Did you keep a poll-list at all?—A. Of course I kept a poll-list; I did not write it all.

Q. Did you write any of it, and how much?—A. I don't remember how much.

Q. Who else kept the poll-list with you?—A. Charley Rice; he acted in my place a good deal of the time.

Q. Who acted as clerk that night after the poll was closed and the canvass was being made?—A. Charley Savage done that.

Q. Then you did very little work yourself, but relied on others?—A. I did a heap of writing during the day, but was only excused for about 5 minutes.

Q. Can you read and write sufficient to keep a poll-list?—A. I can.

Q. How long after the boxes were put on table before front door was opened?—A. From 2 to 5 minutes.

Q. What was then done after the door was open; did you swear and vote men?—A. We did.

Q. That was the very next thing in order then?—A. It is reasonable that that was the next thing in order.

Q. Where do Mess. Rice, Blanchard, O. P. Williams, Samuel Driggers, Rhett Hickman, Noel Robinson, and yourself reside? Do you or any of you live in the precinct of Green Pond?—A. Rice and Blanchard reside in Walterboro'; myself, I reside about 6 miles below Walterboro', on the Cook's Hill place; Mr. Diggers reside about 4 miles below Walterboro'; as to O. P. Williams I don't know where he was living at that time; Noel Robinson at that time was living at Green Pond. It is a hard matter to tell where Rhett Hickman was living; I think somewhere near Walterboro.

Q. Where did you vote on election day last?—A. I did not vote.

Q. Why did you not vote at Green Pond, having been there?—A. The reason why I did not vote at Green Pond was because my certificate was not for Green Pond precinct. I am a citizen of the precinct of Walterboro'.

Q. You being a citizen of the precinct of Walterboro', Mess. Rice and Blanchard, two of the managers, living in that precinct, Mess. Driggers and Hickman, two marshals, living in Walterboro' precinct—all of you acting at Green Pond on election day, seems that there were no Democrats, or not enough to even fill the few election positions; how do you explain such a transfer?—A. Well, I don't know.

Q. You said, amongst other reasons for not admitting citizens or some of them to witness the count, as the law requires, that the train was waiting and you all did not want to be bothered, or words to that effect. I suppose you attached more importance to getting on train than in having the votes publicly counted?—A. No, we did not.

Q. Then why did you so state in your direct testimony?—A. Well, because in a close room a man don't want to be smothered down by the heat of other men.

Q. You want to avoid being smothered by the heat of these men; that being the case, under what sanitary laws did you find authority for closing the back door and windows that night of election?—A. I don't know, on that occasion, that any doors or windows were closed.

Q. Will you under oath say positively that these places were not closed during the counting that night?—A. I don't think they were.

Q. Do you know that they were not closed?—A. If I were called on to say positively whether they were or not I should say they were not.

Q. Will you swear positively that they were not?—A. I can say that they were not closed as long as I paid any attention.

Q. Will you swear positively that those windows were not closed that night during the count?—A. I refuse to swear any further.

Q. Do you refuse to answer the question above propounded?—A. I do.

Redirect:

Q. Do you refuse on the grounds as explained by you to the several questions relating thereto?

(Objection by counsel as being leading and not in reply to anything newly brought out.)

A. Yes, I do.

Q. You stated awhile ago that you did not know exactly where O. P. Williams resided on the 6th of Nov. last. Do you not know as a fact that he lived in the immediate neighborhood of Green Pond station and was merchandizing near there for a number of years?—A. Well, I did know some time back, but right at that time I did not know.

Q. You don't know that Blanchard, one of the managers, was conductor on the G. P. and W. Railroad and spent a large part of his time at Green Pond prior to and after Nov. the 6th last, do you?—A. I do.

(Counsel for contestant objects to question and answer as not being pertinent, no question having been raised as to Manager Blanchard's occupation, but to his place of residence, which this witness has already answered, that he lived at Walterboro' precinct.)

SAMUEL DRIGGERS, being duly sworn, says:

Question. State your age, occupation, residence, and where you were on the 6th day of Nov. last.—Answer. Age 37 years; I reside 3 miles and a half below Walterboro'; farmer; I was at Green Pond on the 6th day of Nov. last.

Q. In what capacity, if any, did you act at the election held at Green Pond precinct on that day?—A. I was constable.

Q. Were you present when the polls were closed?—A. I was at the front door, just a few steps from the box.

Q. Did you prevent the crowd from passing or going in the room when the count was going on? If so, state what you done and what was done.—A. Yes, I did; and kept them out. I did not do anything, but kept them out—from going in on the managers.

Q. Did you prevent whites as well as blacks from crowding around the managers?—A. I did.

Q. Do you know that a number of Elliott tickets were in circulation at the precinct on the day of election?—A. Yes, sir; I saw some come in with the voters, and that they voted them as they said they were going to do.

Q. Were they white or colored people?—A. They were colored, and there was a few whites voted that day.

Q. Did you have any conversation with the colored voters that day in reference to Elliott and Miller; if so state what was said?—A. I saw some of them with whom I talked. I asked them who they were going to vote for, and some of them said they were going to vote for Elliott and some for Miller, I believe.

Q. Do you believe this or do you know it?—A. I know it.

Cross-examination:

Q. In what voting precinct do you reside, and where did you live on the 6th of November last?—A. I lived in the Walterboro' precinct, and lived there on election day.

Q. Do you know the citizens of Green Pond, generally?—A. No.

Q. Name the men who said they were going to vote for Elliott.—A. I don't know their names.

Q. Are you not frequently in and around Green Pond?—A. No; but I go there sometimes, once or twice a year.

Q. You said some colored men said to you they were going to vote for Elliott. What office did they say?—A. They did not say what office.

Q. Was Elliott really a candidate that day, and what office was he running for?—A. He was a candidate, and he was running for office of Congress, I think.

Q. From what district was he running?—A. Seventh, I think.

Q. Do you know the relative strength—voting strength, I mean—of the Democrat and Republican parties at Green Pond poll?—A. No, I dont.

Q. You said you saw some of the men with Elliott tickets. How do you know they were Elliott tickets?—A. They had them open in their hands and I saw them.

Q. Do you mean to say that you read them yourself?—A. I did read them all myself; I saw Elliott's name on some of them.

Q. Can you read?—A. I can read a little.

Q How long were you acting marshal at the door or in the building; were you there continually during the day?—A. I was there acting from seven o'clock until six in the evening. I went one time to the depot and right back. Another time I went in the kitchen to eat my dinner. Those are the only times I left my post.

Q. State what time of day you went to the depot, and what time of day you took dinner.—A. I suppose it was about 10 o'clock when I went to the depot; about two o'clock I took dinner.

Q. When you went to the depot, did you pass by many people to get there?—A. No.

Q. How near did you pass to any persons in going to the depot?—A. I passed some in two or threee feet of me, the others were further.

B. H. PADGETT, a witness in behalf of contestee, being duly sworn, says:

Question. State your age and occupation, and where you reside.—Answer. Age, 33; I am a physician, a merchant, and treasurer and business manager of the Green Pond, Walterboro' and Branchville Railroad; I reside at Walterboro'.

Q. Were you at any time on the 6th of November last at Green Pond?—A. I was there at nine in the morning and staid until about eleven; and from about five in the afternoon until the polls were closed and the votes had been counted.

Q. Did you at any time after the polls had been closed, and before the count of the ballots had been finished, enter the room in which the poll was held?—A. I did; and a few others.

Q. Were you permitted by the managers to remain in that room?—A. I was not; the managers were counting the votes when I reached the door, and others crowded in, and we were ordered out, the managers stating that the train was waiting for them, and they wanted the crowd to disperse so that they could get through counting the votes.

Q. At what time was the train scheduled to have left Green Pond?—A. The train was scheduled to have left Green Pond at 5.30 p. m., Charleston time, and the managers did not finish canvassing the votes until about 9 o'clock.

Q. Was there any distinction made between white and colored on the part of the managers in ordering the crowd to leave the room?—A. If there was I did not notice it. I noticed colored people in the room when I was in there.

Cross-examined:

Q. In what precinct do you reside, and to what party do you belong?—A. I reside at Walterboro precinct, and belong to the Democratic party.

Q. Were you and others not in the room when W. F. Myers asked for admission and was refused?—A. I was, but had been ordered out, and was on my way out when I heard them talking to him.

Q. You stated that colored men were in the room when you were there. How many of them did you see, and who were they?—A. There were two or three: I did not know them but one—Brown.

Q. Do you know the relative strength of the Democratic and Republican parties at Green Pond poll?—A. I do not.

T. J. BLANCHARD, a witness in behalf of the contestee, being duly sworn, says:

Question. What is your age?—Answer. Thirty-three years of age.

Q. Where do you reside?—A. Walterboro.

Q. What is your occupation?—A. I am conductor of the Walterboro Railroad, running between Walterboro and Green Pond.

Q. Where were you on the 6th day of November last?—A. I was at Green Pond.

Q. In what capacity, if any, did you act at the election held for Congressman on that day?—A. One of the managers.

Q. At what time were the polls opened?—A. Seven o'clock, some time.

Q. Do you know J. T. Brown?—A. I know Brown who acted as supervisor.

Q. Was he there when the polls were opened ?—A. I did not see him.

Q. Was he there during the day ?—A. Yes; I suppose it was five minutes after voting had commenced, as several had come in and voted.

Q. Was he present when the polls closed, and did he remain in the room when the canvass of votes was made ?—A. Yes.

Q. Did the managers exclude colored people and white people alike from the room while the count was going on ?—A. Well, we did not at first, but after we had started to count found it impossible to get along without having them removed from where we were counting, as the entry where we were counting was very small, and the talking and noise was so great that you could not hear anything, and we were anxious to get through and get back on the train: the train had been already waiting at least two hours.

Q. Do you know what became of the poll-list kept at the poll that day ?—A. It was put in the box after we got through counting and locked up and brought to the commissioner.

Q. Did the voters have free access to the building in which the election was held during the day for the purpose of voting ?—A. Yes.

Q. At the close of the polls was the canvass made, the excess of tickets, if any, destroyed, according to law ?—A. They were.

Q. Do you know O. P. Williams, who acted as one of the managers ?—A. Yes, sir.

Q. Do you know where he resided at that time ?—A. White Hall Station, about four-and-a-half miles from Green Pond.

Q. Do you know that White Hall is in the Seventh Congressional district ?—A. Yes.

Q. Is it in the Green Pond voting precinct ?—A. Yes.

Q. Do you know that tickets bearing the name of William Elliott for Congress was circulated at the precinct on the day of election among the voters ?—A. Yes.

Cross-examination:

Q. At what time did you reach the poll, or reach the place where the voting was conducted, and who accompanied you ?—A. Between twelve and three in the morning; there was myself, Mr. Rice, O. P. Williams; there was four colored men who pulled the crank car from Walterboro to Green Pond.

Q. Did you all stay at the house in which the voting was to be conducted next day ?—A We staid in the house where it was conducted.

Q. What relation or connection the others had to conduct of election ?—A. There were at least a dozen who staid in the house who were not connected with the conduct of election; Mr. Rice and Mr. Oliver Williams; I am not sure all the managers slept in the same room.

Q. Where did the voters come from who voted before the supervisor appeared; were they those in the house or some of them ?—A. They came from the outside; they did not sleep in the house, what I saw of them.

Q. Who were they ?—A. I don't remember their names or who they were.

Q. Will you testify that none who slept in house the night preceding voted before the supervisor appeared ?—A After the poll were opened and the voting had commenced I went to wash my face.

Q. And yet you can not tell who or how many had voted ?—A. I was so worn out from the loss of rest I did not pay any attention to who had voted.

Q. All the managers having slept in the house in a room of which the voting was conducted did they announce publicly to the large number of voters on the outside, including J. F. Brown, supervisor, that they were ready to receive votes ?—A. The voting was not conducted in the room in which we slept, but in the entry. Yes, they were all notified; don't know who was among them, don't know whether Brown was there or not. I found him there when I came from washing.

Q. This house being used as private quarters for the managers, do you mean to say that Brown, as supervisor, and other voters could have gone in until they were invited, or notified that the voting was to be conducted there.—A. They were invited as soon as the polls were open. The house was unoccupied at the time, but I think Mr. Hickman's clerk slept there.

Q. Was it not occupied, the night preceding the election, as a lodging place for the three managers ?—A. It was the only place we could get.

Q. Do you know the relative strength of the Democratic and Republican parties at Green Pond precinct?—A. No.

Q. Your being a citizen of Walterboro' precinct and another of the managers living there, also the entire board being Democratic, was it for the want of material down there that they had to deprive a majority of the board the right to vote at home?—A. No.

Q. You said you saw Elliott tickets in circulation that day; was it not in the entry and on the table or box where the voting was being conducted?—A. All around the precinct.

Q. You saw them circulated; are you prepared to swear that they were voted?—
A. Some of them were.

Q. You say the room was so crowded that they, the outsiders, were ordered to leave. About how many was in there, and who were they?—A. They were not ordered to leave, but simply to move back—Mr. May and several others, white and black.

Q. Who was clerk that day?—A. Mr. Rice, Mr. Williams, and Drawdy, who relieved them.

Redirect:

Q. Do you not know that Mr. Drawdy was regarded as the clerk?
(Objected to as leading.)
A. Yes.

Q. What was the location of the building in which the election was held?—A. It was right in the center of the town, in the most public place in the town, and the only place that could have been gotten that I know of. The building was about five steps from the railroad track.

Q. Is not that railroad track used as a thoroughfare or walkway for almost if not every colored man who goes to Green Pond?—A. Yes; and white, too.

Q. What was the situation of the passage-way in relation to the railroad track?—A. The house and passage-way fronted the railroad track.

In reply:

Q. State what part of the entry-way the boxes were located. Was it not in the extreme rear, leading to the kitchen?—A. About the center.

Q. About how many feet from the back door was the table?—A. About ten or twelve feet.

Now where is the truth? With the five unimpeached witnesses or with the man Brown? The bare suggestion, it seems to us, will suggest the answer without allusion to the law of evidence touching the preponderance of the testimony. The evidence discloses that there were from 1 to 5 ballots with Miller's name on them, folded together and stuffed in the box. Who did it? There is no doubt that Miller's adherents were the ballot-box stuffers there.

JACKSONBORO PRECINCT.

At this poll it is charged that there were 183 ballots, and about 70 were in excess of the poll-list. On the evidence of one witness, the United States supervisor, L. D. Smalls, who testified that he signed the returns and reported the same as the managers, and who says he objected to signing at the start because he could not see the names on the tickets when they were counted, and for that reason only, but finally signed them all, declares the validity of the return to have been destroyed, and with great reluctance conceding to Elliott 46 votes (because Miller in his brief gives them to him), places all the balance to the credit of Miller.

Somewhat taken aback, however, it seems, by their own liberality in allowing to Elliott what Miller himself admits the majority deem it necessary to apologize for the same, which it naïvely does in the following language:

In his original brief filed with the committee, contestant conceded to contestee 46 votes, the remainder of the 113 not proven to have voted for contestant; and for that reason, *and because it is now only a question of the amount of contestant's majority*, we state the vote as in this brief, etc.

The italics are ours. It is a noticeable fact in the record that very few, only 14, of the witnesses for contestant, who say they voted for him, can read or write, and most of them in the density of their ignorance, such as we have heretofore illustrated herein, evidently knew as little about what they were doing as the common run of ten-year-old children.

W. F. Myers, contestant's chief witness, swears (p. 95) that the Democratic voting strength at Jacksonboro' is "about 70." Contestee got 68.

PORT ROYAL, BEAUFORT COUNTY.

The return shows—

Elliott 199
Miller 14
                                                                                          ——
    Total 213

All the proof as to this poll is summed up as follows by the majority (p. 22):

> Fifty-one witnesses (pp. 128–160) testify that they voted for Miller, and their names are all on the poll-list as having voted. This evidence stands uncontradicted. Duly qualified voters were refused permission to vote, and names of Democrats are on the poll-list as having voted who had moved away and were not present at the election, thus further discrediting the returns.

And the majority adds 37 to contestant's vote and deducts that number from contestee. Taking first the statement that "duly qualified voters were refused permission to vote," what is the testimony? Two men only were rejected—John Hicks and Benjamin Wroten. John Hicks says (p. 156):

> Q. Did you offer to vote at the last election; and, if yes, were you objected to, and at what precinct?
> (Objected to on the ground that the poll-list is the best evidence.)
> A. Yes, sir; but I was objected to because they said my register certificate was not dated right at Port Royal precinct.

On cross-examination he says:

> Q. Where is your registration certificate?—A. At home.
> Q. Who said it was dated wrong?—A. Mr. Rodgers was there at the box, also Mr. Stickney and Mr. Bull. I don't remember who said it was wrong. I think it was Mr. Stickney.
> Q. How was it dated?—A. I can't tell; I don't remember.
> Q. Was it somebody else's certificate?—A. No, sir; I went there and got it myself and put it away until the day of election; nobody had anything to do with it.

He had the certificate at home and yet could not produce it. What proof is there that he was registered at all? Is it possible to consider this as "discrediting" the returns? The other rejected voter is Benjamin Wroten, who says he was rejected because the name on his certificate did not correspond with the registration book used by the managers.

On cross examination he says (p. —):

> Q. Where is your registration certificate?—A. I have it at home.
> Q. How do you spell your name?
> (Objected to on the ground that voters are not required by law to spell their names neither at the time of registering, nor at the poll, to enable them to register or vote. The supervisor of registration is supposed to spell each person's name correctly on the registration certificate, and to so copy it on the registration list.)
> A. Benjamin Wroten, but I find most people here spell it Roten.

Again the certificate was not produced, and for no earthly good reason. By referring to the two notices of deposition at page 162 it will be found that in one his name is spelt "Rhoten" and in the other "Roden," while he was sworn as "Roten." It is upon the foregoing testimony that the majority finds that "duly qualified voters were refused permission to vote."

Now as to the next statement, that Democrats who had moved away were on the poll-list as voters. John McClellan, p. 142, swears there were two, J. W. Barnes and T. E. Barnes. On cross-examination he says:

> Q. Do you mean to swear that neither J. W. or T. E. Barnes were in Port Royal on election day, or do you mean to swear that you did not see them?—A. T. E. Barnes

was not in this town on that day, and if J. W. Barnes was here I did not see him, nor for weeks before.

Q. Will you swear that I was not here on election day?—A. No, but I can swear I did not see you.

Q. Did you vote in the Presidential box?—A. No, sir; I did not.

JOHN (his x mark) McCLELLAN.

Why was McClellan, who can not sign his name, relied on to prove this instead of the Republican supervisor, who could certainly have proved that these men did not vote? We submit that there is nothing in this testimony to overthrow the presumption of the correctness of the return, so as to admit proof as to how each voter voted, as the majority decides. Of the witnesses who swear they voted for Miller, twenty-four made their mark. They got their tickets chiefly from John McClellan, who himself had to make his mark. Fourteen of them were examined without notice—Kit Chisolm, Cicero Lawton, F. Brown, A. Black, W. Stelling, H. Jourdan, S. Anderson, W. Flowers, D. Johnson, J. Toomer, A. Green, Rich Heyward No. 1, J. Jones, and A. Moye, p. 162. They were all objected to on this ground; and each is styled in the depositions "voluntary."

ST. STEPHEN'S, BERKELEY COUNTY.—The objection to this precinct is that eighty-one persons say they voted for Miller. There was no proof to overthrow the presumption of the correctness of the managers' return. Of the eighty-one, fifty-six made their marks to their depositions. Every one swears that he got his ticket from one Tobe Price, and the great majority that they relied entirely on his representation as to its kind. We call especial attention to the following testimony (page 75):

JINGO DINGLE, sworn:

Q. State your name, age, residence, and occupation.—A. Jingo Dingle; age, 37; residence, Old Field Plantation; occupation, laborer.

Q. Where were you on the 6th of November, 1888, the day of the last general election?—A. At St. Stephen's.

Q. Did you vote there that day?—A. Yes, sir.

Q. For whom did you vote as candidate for Congress?—A. Mr. Miller.

Q. Who gave you your ticket?—A. Mr. Price.

Cross-ex.:

Q. Can you read and write?—A. No sir.

Q. Then you know you voted for Miller because Price told you so?—A. Yes, sir; he read the ticket to me and told me so.

(Same objection as to last witness.)

Redirect:

Q. Did you vote the ticket Price gave you?—A. Yes, sir; the same he gave me.

Q. What is that?

(Counsel hands witness a ticket, T. E. Miller, Representative for 51 Congress.)

A. That was not the kind of a ticket he read to me.

Q. What kind of a ticket did he read to you?

(Objected to.)

A. He read Mr. Miller's name to me for Congress.

JINGO (his x mark) DINGLE.

when contestant's counsel showed witness the ticket " T. E. Miller, Representative for Fifty-first Congress," he answered " *that was not the kind of ticket he read to me.*"

Now it is very strange, in this connection, that Price, who gave out all these tickets, was never sworn to tell what tickets he did distribute. No explanation is given of this failure. As to most of the witnesses, therefore, there is absolutely no proof what ticket they voted. We give the following testimony,

572 MILLER VS. ELLIOTT.

JACOB CAMPBELL, sworn (p. 52):

Q. State your name, age, residence, and occupation.—A. Jacob Campbell; age, 50 years; residence, Jervey's Chapel; occupation, laborer.
Q. Where were you on the 6th November, 1888, the day of the last general election?—A. At St. Stephen's voting precinct.
Q. Did you vote there that day?—A. I did.
(Objected to, as the poll-list is the best evidence.)
Q. For whom did you vote as candidate for Congress?—A. I voted for Smalls.
Q. Who gave you your ticket?—A. Tobe Price.
Q. How many tickets he gave you?—A. One.
Q. Can you read and write?—A. No, sir.
Q. Who was the Democratic candidate for Congress?—A. That man that ran against Smalls; can't think of his name.
Q. Do you know if Thomas E. Miller was a candidate for Congress?
(Objected to as leading question.)
A. Yes, sir.
Q. Was Thomas E. Miller the Republican or Democratic candidate that day?—A. I could not exactly tell; he seem to be pressing very hard for Small.

JACOB (his x mark) CAMPBELL.

SHIRER MIDDLETON, sworn (p. 80):

Q. State your name, age, residence, and occupation.—A. Shirer Middleton; age, 57; residence, Gillinsville; occupation, farmer.
Q. Where were you on the 6th November, 1888, the day of the last general election?—A. St. Stephen's.
Q. Did you vote there that day?—A. Yes, sir.
Q. For whom did you vote as candidate for Congress?—A. Thomas E. Miller.
Q. Who gave you your ticket?—A. Tobe Price.
Q. Can you read?—A. I can read enough to find the name of Thomas E. Miller.

Cross-ex.

Q. You said you can read, read this [hands witness printed paper and asks him to read a line thereon].—A. I can not read it, sir.
Q. Can you read that line [shows witness first line of the heading of the answer of Wm. Elliott, which read: "Thomas E. Miller vs. Wm. Elliott"]?—A. I can't read it.

JERRY MAURICE, sworn (p. 54):

Q. State your name, age, residence, and occupation.—A. Jerry Maurice; age, 45; residence, Speir's Still; occupation, farmer.
Q. Where were you on the 6th November, 1888, the day of the last general election?—A. At St. Stephen's voting precinct.
Q. Did you vote there that day?—A. Yes, sir; at the county and State poll, but not at the Congressional poll.
Q. For whom did you vote as candidate for Congress?—A. Thomas Miller, but I did not vote for Congressman.

BEN WILSON, sworn (p. 77):

Q. State your name, age, residence, and occupation.—A. Ben Wilson; age, 32; residence, Buck Hall; occupation, farmer.
Q. Where were you on the 6th November, 1888, the day of the last general election?—A. At St. Stephen's voting precinct.
Q. Did you vote there that day?—A. No, sir; they would not let me vote.
Q. For whom did you vote as a candidate for Congress?—A. Did not vote.
Q. Who gave you your ticket?—A. B. T. Price.
Q. Did you go to the polls to vote?—A. Yes, sir.
Q. Who were you going to vote for?—A. I was going to vote for Miller.
Q. Did you have your registration certificate with you?—A. Yes, sir.

Cross-examined:

Q. Why was it they would not let you vote?—A. They said my certificate was not right.
Q. What was wrong about it?—A. They never said what was wrong about it.
Q. Where were you living on the day of election?—A. At Buck Hall.
Q. Did the managers ask you any questions?—A. No, sir; just asked me where I was living.

BEN (his x mark) WILSON.

All these witnesses are included in the 81 allowed contestant, although several say they did not vote for him. The majority refrain from depriving contestee of his entire vote only because contestant's counsel did not demand it, they say.

EVANS' MILLS, ORANGEBURGH COUNTY.

At this poll the majority, while admitting that "there is a conflict" as to the facts, say the box was stuffed. A careful examination of the testimony will show that this is not so. The only witness (T. T. Green, p. 316), speaking of ballots being torn up, says:

> For the right number, I can not exactly tell. I suppose about 125, or more, taken from the three different piles.

The Republican precinct chairman came in just after, but Green did not report a word of the destruction to him. Hazard Barden, Democratic supervisor, says (p. 386):

> When we went to count the Congressional box we proceeded in like manner. After tearing up all the Presidential tickets found therein there was an excess in the box of tickets. I don't remember how many, but a few ; and on the tally which three kept—myself, Dr. Lawton, an I T. T. Green—there was a difference in the tally of all three of some few votes. We decided to take the tally of T. T. Green, the Republican supervisor, and the ballots were all put back in the box and stirred up thoroughly. Dr. A. C. Baxter, jr., was blindfolded and requested to draw out the excess and tear up in the presence of all without knowing what he tore up ; then we proceeded to count. After the count we found that there had been seven tickets too many drawn out and torn up, and to make it fair we put in seven Democratic and seven Republican tickets, and we blindfolded a colored man by the name of Wm. Hilliard to draw out the seven tickets, and Hilliard, to the best of my knowledge, drew out five for Elliott and two for Miller.
>
> *   *   *   *   *   *
>
> Q. From whence did you obtain the seven Miller tickets, and to whom did you first apply for them ?—A. I applied to Wm. Hilliard for them ; he was a ticket distributer for the Republican party. He gave me seven tickets and I went to hand them to the managers, and I looked at the tickets and found them to be Elliott tickets ; I then applied for more Miller tickets, and they were handed to me by some one, Baldrick, I think, and they were placed in the box.

Dr. Lawton says (p. 387):

> Q. Can you state how many ballots were found in excess ?—A. About seventeen, according to Green's tally; that number was drawn out the box, and then votes were counted and found to be seven less than poll-list.
> Q. Can you state the number of votes Miller received as member for Congress ?—A. I don't remember; neither Mr. Elliott's.
> Q. Did Mr. Miller receive no more votes at that poll than those you gave him in your official return as manager of election at that precinct ?—A. All Miller tickets found in Congressional box were counted for Miller.
> Q. Were any found in any other box ? — A. There were ; some were found in the Presidential box.
> Q. Can you state how many ?—A. I can not.
> Q. Did Mr. Miller receive the benefit of those tickets found in Presidential box ?—A. He did not; neither did Elliott receive the benefit of his tickets found in same box.
> Q. Are you a Republican or Democrat ?—A. A Democrat.
> Q. Were the other managers Democrats or Republicans ?—A. They were Democrats.

W. H. LAWTON, M. D.

So stood the matter when contestee closed his case, his testimony being strictly in reply to contestant's. In rebuttal, however, contestant called a large number of witnesses to prove how they had voted (pp. 414–476), whereupon contestee's counsel filed the following:

> Mr. Dautzler, attorney for Wm. Elliott, makes the following objections :
> 1st. That the notice to take testimony is illegal, having been served before the time of Mr. Elliott in reply had expired.

2d. That objection is made to taking testimony before John H. Ostendorff as notary public, his name being on the record in the case as one of the attorneys of the contestant.

3. That the evidence taken is not in rebuttal..

The objection to Mr Ostendorf being notary while being contestant's attorney on record was certainly valid. He was not only attorney and notary but also a witness (p. 69), not an uncommon occurrence in this case. The testimony was certainly not in rebuttal, and should be ruled out. (See Posey *vs.* Parrott, page 1 of Report.) Of the 142 who testified, 109 made their mark. The great majority of them say they got their tickets from Bill Green, the remainder from Tom Allen, Edward Hartwell, Wesley Shuler, Rufus Felder, Lee Williams, and William Hilliard. Strange to say neither Bill Green, Tom Allen, Wesley Shuler, nor Lee Williams is sworn, neither as to the tickets they distributed and not even that they themselves voted. Edward Hartwell and Rufus Felder say they voted, but say nothing about the tickets they distributed. Here is Hartwell's cross-examination (p. 444):

Q. Will you read this paper? [Hands witness copy of newspaper.]—A. I decline to read the newspaper.

He had sworn he could read. The other distributer was Bill Hilliard, who, as testified to by Mr. Hazard Bardin, had Elliott tickets and not Miller's. We note the following testimony (p. 420):

STEPHEN WASHINGTON, who being sworn, says:

Q. State your age, occupation, residence, and where you were on the 6th day of November, 1888.—A. Age, 26; farmer; Floods; Evans Mill.

Q. State for whom you voted as member of Congress from the 7th district on the 6th of November, 1888.—A. Green.

Q. Who did you vote for?—A. Mr. Elliott.

Q. State from whom did you get your ballot, if you can read, and how many ballots or tickets did you vote for Congressman at the last election.—A. Mr. Green; can't read; one.

Q. State at what precinct did you vote, and if any one read your ticket for you.—A. Vance's.

Q. State the name of the person who read your ticket to you, and to what political party he belongs.—A. Green; Republican party.

STEPHEN (his x mark) WASHINGTON.

He got his ticket from Green and voted for Elliott. Numbers of the voters swear they received and voted only one ticket. We note three of these in succession on page 418—Wellfare, Gettress, and Oliver. Perry Dun (p. 415) says:

Cross-ex'd by Mr. DAUTZLER

Q. How many tickets did he give you?—A. One.
Q. Where did you vote it?—A. In the *Presidential* box.

Time and again witnesses who swore they could read refused the test on cross-examination. Here are samples:

Cross-ex. (p. 438):

Q. Did you read your ticket?—A. Yes, sir.
Q. Tell me exactly what was on that ticket?—A. 7th Congressional and Miller.
Q. Is that all?—A. That is all I can remember just now.
Q. What Miller was that?—A. T. B. Miller.
Q. You say you can read; read this [hands witness copy of newspaper].—A. I refuse to read for you.

(Same objections.)

ELLISON (his x mark) HUGGINS.

Cross-ex. (p. 439):

Q. For what Miller did you vote?—A. T. A. Miller.

Q. Can you read [offers paper to read]?—A. Yes, I can read, but I decline to read. (Same objections.)

BRANTLY (his x mark) MOORER.

Cross-ex.:

Q. For what Miller was it that you voted?—A. Thomas Miller.

Q. You stated you can read a little, read this for me? [Hands witness copy of newspaper.]—A. I am a little hungry; don't feel like reading now. (Same objections.)

DUDLEY (his x mark) EVANS.

EASTOVER, RICHLAND COUNTY.

The return from this precinct not having been sent up in time the votes were not canvassed and not included in the result. The majority say:

M. Johnson, the Republican supervisor, testifies (p. 319) that the *Miller tickets were printed on coarser and darker paper than the Elliott tickets, and that when folded by the ticket distributors, Miller's name could be seen;* that the name was printed in larger letters than Elliott's name; that he watched the voting and kept a tally of the voters, and that Miller's vote was not less than 248 nor more than 257 (some tickets not certain), and that Elliott's vote was from 83 to 92.

It was upon this kind of proof as to the vote cast that the supervisor made his return, and it is substantially the only proof as to the vote cast introduced by contestant in chief, no voter being called to prove his vote. Contestee then had the manager's return and poll list proved and had the ballots in the box produced and counted, which verified the return, thus:

Elliott 262
Miller 87
Simmons 36

Total.. 385

On November 21, 1888, contestant had filed the following with the State board of canvassers:

EXHIBIT C.—J. T. B.

In the matter of the election of a Representative to the 51st United States Congress in the Seventh Congressional district of the State of South Carolina.

To the honorable the Board of State Canvassers.

The undersigned, a candidate for Representative to the 51st Congress in the Seventh district for the State of South Carolina, begs leave to suggest and give information to your honorable board that in respect to the statement and return of the county board of canvassers for Federal elections for Richland County, the said board has not included in their statement the poll cast at the precinct of Eastover, in said county and in the Seventh Congressional district, upon the ground, as the undersigned is informed, that the return from said precinct had been defectively made; that the undersigned was not aware of such fact while said board was in session, and has just come into possession of such information long after said board had finally adjourned; that it appears by a statement made by the managers on the poll-list of said box, but not signed by the managers, that the undersigned, William Elliott, received 262 votes, Thomas E. Miller 87 votes, and —— Simmons 36 votes, giving the undersigned a majority over Thomas E. Miller of 175 votes; that the undersigned is informed and believes that votes cast and in the box at said precinct exactly correspond with the statement of the vote made upon the poll-list and now in your possession. All of which facts and things may be verified by an inspection of the papers sent down to your body and the votes in said box.

The undersigned therefore respectfully begs that this suggestion may be filed by your board in the records of the election in the Seventh Congressional district.

WILLIAM ELLIOTT,
Per B. L. ABNEY,
Att'y for Wm. Elliott.

Nov. 21, 1888.

After all of contestee's testimony was in, contestant, in violation of the law, as at Evans Mill, took in rebuttal and against objection the testimony of 197 witnesses to swear to their vote, the same not being in rebuttal. He also gave contestee's attorney notice of deposition before three notaries at the same place, at the same hour, to which objection was made, as well as to the questions being printed instead of written, which was common on the part of contestant. The testimony is of the same general character as that heretofore noted. We call attention to the following ruling of N. F. Myers, notary (p. 526):

Q. When you voted that day did you show your registration ticket ?—A. Yes, sir.
Q. Have you that ticket, now ?—A. Yes, sir.
Q. Let me see it.
(Notary public refuses to let the witness produce registration ticket, as counsel for contestee is not a judge as to competency of voters.
Counsel for contestee objects to ruling on the following grounds: That the witness has stated that he voted at the Congressional election and it is desired to show whether or not he was legally qualified to vote; 2d, that the notary has no right to rule on questions of law, as he has already ruled himself that his duties were purely ministerial and not judicial in their character.)

Myers, as will be remembered, was an important witness for contestant as well as notary in Colleton County. To show how he was influenced as notary by his interest for contestant we refer to his ruling in Colleton County, already mentioned, where he declined to exclude from the room witnesses for examination on the ground that his was "merely a clerical position with not a *shadow of judicial powers.*"

In this connection we call attention to the fact that in addition to the above and that John H. Ostendorf was contestant's attorney, notary, and witness, there were these other witnesses: J. F. Brown was notary, page 92; witness, page 294. Jno. C. Rue was notary, page 97; witness, page 452. T. J. Reynolds was notary, page 543; attorney, page 128. H. D. Edwards was attorney, page 459; witness three times, pages 302, 310, 324.

BEN POTTER'S PRECINCT.

The majority say:

Ben Potter precinct.—In this precinct there is a difference between the return of the United States supervisors and that of the precinct managers; the supervisors returning 41 as voting, and the managers 141. The evidence here is conflicting, and we do not find it necessary to decide which is the true return.

In order to show the facts as to this precinct we quote from contestee's brief, p. 131, the following which is sustained by the testimony:

The managers' return gives Elliott 141 votes, Miller none. Contestant attacks this return, alleges that 103 votes were illegally and fraudulently given contestee, and contends that the true return should have been—

Elliott.. 38
Miller 3
                                                                              ——
    Total 41

To sustain this he relies on the testimony of J. H. Johnson, supervisor (p. 46), who swears that but 41 votes were cast; that Elliott got 38 and Miller 3, and that he and the Democratic supervisor, W. H. Parsons, signed such a return and forwarded it to the chief supervisor. Instead of making out a case of fraud against the Democratic officials the testimony discloses a disgraceful series of crimes on the part of contestee's adherents.
In the first place, Parsons was not the Democratic supervisor, but W. P. Gardner was. (See certificate of clerk of U. S. Circuit Court, p. 667.) The copy of Johnson's return put in evidence was not certified to by the chief supervisor, but by contestant's notary (p. 661). When the original return was examined by contestee's attorney, it was found that there had been a clumsy attempt at changing the figures—

changing the total vote from 141 to 41, and changing Elliott's vote from 141 to 38, and giving Miller 3 votes. Thereupon, contestee had the paper examined by E. H. Sparkman, cashier, and gave notice of his examination at the office of the clerk of U. S. Circuit Court, when the original was filed, *on 2d April.* The return was seen and examined on 1st April by both Sparkman and Hon. H. K. Jenkins, contestee's attorney; but *it had disappeared during the night*—all the custodians being Republicans—and *on the 2d could not be produced,* having been sent out of the State for no reason whatever. Sparkman was examined as to the above changes and testified to them. Contestant was present and *objected to Sparkman's testifying as to the forgeries without the paper being produced.* He subsequently admitted to Mr. Jenkins that he had "got information yesterday that you were going to examine an *expert as to erasures and forgeries.*"

We give the following testimony:

E. H. SPARKMAN, sworn (p. 395):

1. Q. State your name, age, occupation, and residence.—A. E. H. Sparkman; 43 years; cashier in bank; Charleston.

2. Q. Does your occupation require that you should pay particular attention to written instruments, with a view to detecting forgeries, alterations, erasures, etc ?—A. It does.

3. Q. Did you examine the return of a supervisor of elections which was on file in this office, or in this room or building for Ben Potter's precinct on yesterday ?

(T. E. Miller objects to the above question on the ground that there is no proof of there being any return on file in any room or any building anywhere in the world in these records.)

A. I examined a paper which was submitted to me, and which, I think, I could identify if produced again.

4. Q. Where did you examine this paper ?—A. In this room, clerk's office of the United States circuit court.

5. Q. Do you remember anything peculiar about the appearance of that paper; if so, state what ?

(T. E. Miller objects on the ground that the paper is the best evidence of its peculiarity, and witness is not competent to testify about its condition until the said paper has been produced or it is proven that the said paper is not in existence.)

A. The paper bore evidence of alteration in some of the figures and erasures in others.

6. Q. Can you state what those alterations and erasures were ? If you can please do so.

(T. E. Miller objects because the paper or supervisor's report is the best evidence of its condition.)

A. I would say that in my opinion the original returns called for 141 votes, and was so altered as to read 41. Lower down on the same paper the same figures, 141, were changed to read 38; next lower, comes the figure 3, representing the vote for somebody, who, I don't remember. On the next two succeeding lines below, on each, there is the figure 3 with a line drawn horizontally through each.

Cross-examined by T. E. MILLER:

The cross-examination consists chiefly of elaborately prepared questions as to forgeries, of which we give the following:

12. Q. Are you an expert in handwriting ?—A. I have been examined as such.

13. Q. Can you distinguish between the writing that is intended to mislead, or to make one believe that it is done by one and the same person ?—A. I have found differences in handwriting by comparison which detected the forgery.

14. Q. I have here a paper with the name of Thomas E. Miller written forty-nine times, the key to which is in an envelope. Please tell me, if you can, whether all of the forty-nine names were written by one and the same person, and I state that No. 2 on this paper is a [H. K. Jenkins objects to this question until he can see what the key is or how it is intended to be used] genuine signature, and you will so find it stated in the key.—A. In the forty-nine signatures submitted there is an evident attempt to mislead, which makes it quite possible that they were all written by the same person.

We give a part of the testimony of H. K. Jenkins, contestee's counsel, who was compelled to testify later as to the abstraction of the record.

HAWKINS K. JENKINS sworn (p. 400):

My name is Hawkins King Jenkins; my age, 29 years; occupation, attorney and counsellor at law, and I reside in Mt. Pleasant, S. C. I am one of the counsel for Col. Elliott in this contest. As such counsel, on the 30th day of March last, I served

H. Mis. 137——37

Genl. S. J. Lee, who accepted service as attorney for the contestant, with notice that I would examine Mr. E. H. Sparkman on the Tuesday succeeding, at the custom-house in Charleston, at 2 o'clock p. m., on behalf of Col. Elliott. During a short conversation which I had with Genl. Lee at that time, he said that he would like to know what I was going to examine Mr. Sparkman about, and asked who Mr. Sparkman was. I replied, "I will tell you at the examination. I am going to examine him as to Ben Potter's. On Monday, the 1st of April, Mr. Sparkman was taken into the office of clerk of the circuit court of the United States for the purpose of having him examine the return of the United States supervisor for Ben Potter's precinct. This return, along with the others, had been kept in that office, where I had examined it carefully on two occasions. I had noticed that the figures on this return had been changed and erasures had been made, so as to show a total vote of 41 instead of 141, and a vote of 38 for Col. Elliott instead of 141. I therefore determined to call an expert, and summoned Mr. Sparkman, who I knew had been used as such on former occasions in the State court. On Tuesday, at the hour appointed, I went to the custom-house with Mr. Sparkman and S. Porcher Smith, notary public. After a few moments Mr. Miller and W. H. Berney, esq., his notary, came in. I asked Col. Hagood, the clerk of the circuit court, from whom I had gotten them on former occasions, to let me have or see the supervisor's return for Ben Potter's. He said they were not there. I asked him where they were. He said, "I have sent them to Washington." I replied, "Why, they were here yesterday, for Mr. Sparkman examined the returns for Ben Potter's at that time." Mr. Hagood replied, "I know that, but I sent all of the supervisors' returns to Washington by this morning's mail." I think he said that he had sent them to Col. Poinier. We then examined Mr. Sparkman. At the close of his testimony I remarked to the contestant, "You seem to have expected evidence as to forgeries." He replied, "Yes, I did." I asked him, "What made you expect it?" He replied, "Well, the examination is over now, and we are talking as men, and I don't mind telling you that I got information yesterday evening that you were going to examine"—I don't remember whether he said Mr. Sparkman or an expert— I think he said an expert "as to erasures and forgeries." Mr. Hagood is a Republican, and so is Col. Poinier, the chief supervisor. In the conversations given above I think I have given the exact words. I have certainly given the exact meaning or import thereof.

(All of the above testimony is objected to by counsel for contestant as irrelevant, hearsay, and inadmissible, who gives notice that at the proper time and place he will move to strike the same out of the record.)

Cross examined by S. J. LEE.

2. Q. Do you know at whose request those records were sent to Washington?—A. I know that Col. Hagood was informed by Col. Elliott (or at least I do not know of my own knowledge), upon the authority of a letter from Col. Poinier addressed to Col. Elliott, which I have in my possession, that it was not necessary to forward the original returns to Washington or to him, but that Col. Elliott might have copies made of any which he needed, and that if Col. Hagood would write out the certificate and forward the copies with the certificates so written, he would cheerfully sign the same.

3. Q. You have not answered my question. With Col. Poinier's letter in your possession did you call on Col. Hagood and ask him to make the copies referred to, and forward them to Col. Poinier?—A. I did not intend to evade answering your question, and will now state that I do not believe that Col. Hagood was requested by any Democrat or by Col. Poinier to forward the records or any part of them to Washington; he was certainly not requested to do so either by Col. Elliott or myself, as we both knew that we would need this particular return on Tuesday for the purpose of submitting it to an expert. In reply to your last question I would say that I did not; I believe that Col. Elliott asked that copies should be made and forwarded with certificates as directed in Col. Poinier's letter to him, but "Ben Potter's" was not among the number asked for. I say this because I was present when Col. Elliott made a list, in Col. Hagood's office, of differerent records of which he desired copies. He took the "Ben Potter's" return out of the package; we examined it together; I reminded him that contestant had put in a certified copy of it, and he replaced it in the package, and said, "we would not need a copy." At that time I did not have Col. Poinier's letter in my possession.

4. Q Who were present when you and Col. Elliott examined that return?—A. Col. Hagood's clerk was in the room, and a part of the time, I think, a gentleman named Seignious. Col. Elliott and myself examined the papers at Col. Poinier's desk in one corner of the room; several people passed through the room while we were there.

5. Q. Who was present with you when you first examined that return?—A. Col. Elliott was with me.

On 13th of April, after contestee's time to take testimony had expired, the return is produced by contestant's witness B. A. Hagood, deputy clerk United States circuit court (p. 455). *Not a word of ex-planation is given of its disappearance, nor of its restoration.* Mr. Hagood, on cross-examination, testifies that there had been an erasure of one figure before the figures 41—the whole vote for member of Congress and that under the figures 38—the vote given Elliott—he could see 41, and that there was an erasure before 38, showing undoubtedly that the vote originally given Elliott was 141. Although contestee was thus prevented from showing by an expert this forgery, yet it is as clearly proved as if a hundred experts had testified to it.

So stood the matter at the close of the taking of testimony and after contestee's brief had been filed. When contestant put in his brief in reply the following appeared therein, dated six months after the testimony had been closed:

UNITED STATES OF AMERICA,
   District of South Carolina:

   Personally appeared B. A. Hagood, deputy clerk of the United States circuit court for the district of South Carolina, who deposes and says: That the returns of the Federal supervisors of election for the precinct of Ben Potter's, in the county of Berkeley, in the Seventh Congressional district of the State of South Carolina, were in the custody of the clerk of this court, and were never out of the office of the clerk except when on the 2d of April, 1889, they were, with other returns, sent by the clerk to the chief supervisor of elections, who at that time was in the city of Washington, D. C., in order that the said chief Supervisor might, under his hand and seal, certify to the correctness of certain copies thereof forwarded with said originals at the same time, said copies being made for and at the request of William Elliott, contestee. That they were sent in pursuance to a letter received from the chief supervisor of elections, which said letter contained the following:

"WASHINGTON, D. C., *March 28,* 1889.

   "Be kind enough to let Mr. Elliott have free access to all the records of the supervisor's office. If he finds any that will be of service to him in his contest *let him have copies made of them. If you or your father will write the certificates, that they are true copies and will forward them to me, I will sign them.*"

   Copies of returns having been made they were, in accordance with directions from chief supervisor, forwarded to him at Washington, D. C., and but for the aforesaid request the returns would have been in the office of the clerk.

   Sworn and subscribed to before me this 15th day of November, 1889.

   [SEAL.]
                                                B. A. HAGOOD,
                                          Dep'ty Cl'k U. S. Ct. Court Dist. S. C.
JULIUS SEABROOK,
   Dep. C. D. C. U. S. S. C.

   The italics are ours.

   As already stated, Mr. Hagood had been examined in the case, and had said not a word about the disappearance of the return, which he then produced, but six months afterwards he made this affidavit. But it does not at all help the matter, because the letter of the chief supervisor says distinctly that the *copies*, with the certificates written out, were only to be sent. In fact, it proves beyond a doubt, and by written testimony, that the originals were not to be sent from the office. Moreover, Mr. Jenkins testified that contestee did not want a copy of the return from this precinct and had not asked for it, because contestant had already put it in evidence. We have not time to comment further upon the foregoing testimony, the true character of which every one must understand.

PRIVATEER, SUMTER COUNTY.

   The majority say :

   The same is true of Privateer precinct, Sumter County, where Elliott is returned by the managers as receiving 130 votes, and by the *supervisors* as receiving 88.

That is, "the evidence is conflicting and we do not find it necessary to decide which is the true return." In the first place this charge was never made in the notice of contest. In the second place, there is no evidence whatever, except the return of the Republican supervisor, not *supervisors*, as the majority say, and that of the managers. Contestant did call a witness who was "distributing tickets and keeping a memo-randum of the voting" at this very place, R. C. Andrews (p. 31), and yet he was never asked a word about this charge. The managers' return and poll-list will be found at pages 652, 653. Contestant in his brief (p. 53) asserts that the return was that of the "Democratic supervisor." The record shows (p. 668) that he was not the Democratic but the Republican supervisor. Why was not this alleged fraud made a ground of contest, or why was not this supervisor called to prove it ?

COOPER'S STORE.

We dissent entirely from the conclusion of the majority as to this precinct, but as their action only makes a difference of two votes we will not discuss it.

We have considered all the cases in which the majority has made any change in the vote as returned and have given our views thereon, together with the testimony. We do not agree with the majority in their conclusion, but conceding, for the purpose of the argument, that they are correct in all respects excepting as to the 1,000 votes alleged to be found in the wrong box and given contestant, still the contestee would have a majority of 243.

We would therefore offer the following substitute for the resolutions of the majority:

Resolved, That Thomas E. Miller was not elected a Representative from the Seventh district of South Carolina to the Fifty-first Congress.

Resolved, That William Elliott was duly elected, and is entitled to retain his seat.

R. P. C. WILSON.
C. F. CRISP.
CHARLES T. O'FERRALL.
LEVI MAISH.
L. W. MOORE.
J. H. OUTHWAITE.

FRED S. GOODRICH vs. ROBERT BULLOCK.

SECOND FLORIDA.

The grounds of contest set out in the notice are, in general, refusal to receive legal votes tendered, false counting, false returns, destruction of ballot boxes, and the commission of various other frauds by the election officers.

The committee find that by the illegal action of registering officers in refusing qualified voters permission to register, or arbitrarily striking their names from the list, and of election officers in refusing to receive legal votes tendered, as well as by some instances of the other frauds charged, the contestant was deprived of a sufficient number of votes legally cast or tendered for him to have given him a majority had they been counted.

The minority find some votes illegally rejected, but that most of the votes in question were properly rejected, the voters having failed fully to comply with the registration and election laws of Florida. The evidence relied on to sustain the other charges is insufficient, and the number of voters illegally rejected being much less than the majority returned, contestee is still entitled to the seat.

This case was never reached by the House.

(1) **Registration.** *When new certificate necessary under Florida law.*

A new certificate of registration is not a condition-precedent to voting, under the Florida law, when a voter has moved from one house to another within a voting district. "While the law provides for issuing a new registration certificate to a voter who has changed his residence, either within the precinct or to another one, it does not require such a new certificate as a condition-precedent to voting when the change of residence is within the precinct or voting district. On the contrary, it expressly provides that a new certificate shall be necessary if the change of residence is from one voting district to another, thus implying that it shall not be necessary if the change is not from one voting district to another. *Inclusio unius, exclusio alterius.*"

(2) **No registration.** *In a county, vote counted.*

Where the governor failed to appoint a supervisor of registration for a county, and there was consequently no registration as provided by law, but the election was held under the old registration, and no harm appears to have been done, *held*, that the vote of the county should be counted. "The committee are clearly of opinion that voters complying with all other requirements of the law can not be disfranchised by the neglect of public officials to furnish them opportunity to register."

(3) **Ballots.** *Distinguishing mark.*

Where the statute provides that "The voting shall be by ballot, which ballot shall be plain white paper, clear and even cut, without ornaments, designation, mutilation, symbol, or mark of any kind whatever, except the name or names of the person or persons voted for and the office to which such person or persons are intended to be chosen, which name or names and office or officers shall be written or printed, or partly written and partly printed, thereon in black ink or with black pencil, and such ballot shall be so folded as to conceal the name or names thereon, and so folded shall be deposited in a box to be constructed, kept, and disposed of as hereinafter provided, and no ballot of any other description found in any election box shall be counted," *held*, that an asterisk, so small as to escape attention, printed on the lower corner of the ticket, did not constitute a distinguishing mark within the meaning of the statute.

(4) **Ballots.** *Distinguishing mark.*

Where certain tickets were "scratched" in red or purple ink, instead of the black ink required by law, the colored ink being the only ink to be had in the only store in the place, *held*, that the votes should be counted. "The committee do not think that under the circumstances these voters should be disfranchised, notwithstanding the terms of the statute, as the marking was not done for any improper or unlawful purpose and the use of this ink was, in a manner, compulsory. (See McCrary on Elections, sections 400, 401, 404.)"

(5) **Ballots.** *Distinguishing mark.*

Ballots rejected because of scarcely visible specks, and those rejected because of a printer's dash in a place where no person was named for a particular office, were improperly rejected.

(6) **Ballots.** *Distinguishing mark.*

Ballots rejected because the name of a candidate for justice of the peace was written in with a red pencil should be counted.

(7) **Ballots.** *Distinguishing mark.*

Ballots rejected because of a printer's dash separating each name on the ticket should be counted.

(8) **Ballots.** *Distinguishing mark.*

Ballots rejected because of pencil marks on them made by the judges of election in pushing them into the box with a pencil should be counted.

(9) **Ballot boxes.** *Stolen.*

Where the ballot boxes were stolen and no returns were made the committee count the votes upon satisfactory proof of how they were cast.

REPORT.

AUGUST 4, 1890.—Mr. ROWELL, from the Committee on Elections, submitted the following report:

The Committee on Elections, having had under consideration the contested-election case of Fred S. Goodrich *vs.* Robert Bullock, from the
second Congressional district of Florida, submit the following report:

The second district of Florida is composed of the following counties:
Madison, Hamilton, Suwannee, Columbia, Baker, Nassau, Duval, Clay,
Bradford, Alachua, Putnam, Marion, Sumpter, Lake, Orange, Osceola,
Dade, Brevard, Volusia, and St. John's.

The contest in this case is confined to the following eleven counties:
Dade, Columbia, Putnam, Volusia, Orange, Marion, Nassau, Alachua,
Hamilton, Duval, and Madison.

The grounds of contest, set out in the notice, are, in general: refusal
to receive legal votes tendered, false counting, false returns, destruction
of ballot-boxes, and the commission of various other frauds by the
election officers.

Under the constitution of Florida residence in the State one year, in
the county six months, registration, and the age of twenty-one years are
the qualifications for native-born electors. Foreigners are placed on
the same footing as natives after having declared their intention to become citizens. There is the usual disqualification for conviction of
crime.

The result of the election in the second district, as declared by the
State canvassing board, was:

Robert Bullock 20,012
Fred. S. Goodrich 16,813

Majority for Bullock 3,195

The first general question necessary to be examined, in order to arrive
at a correct understanding of this case, is that of registration.

At its session in 1887 the legislature of Florida enacted a new registration and election law, copied largely from the South Carolina election law, but in many respects more just and equal in its provisions,
and, when executed according to its letter and spirit, calculated to secure reasonably fair elections. Some of its provisions would, in a proper
case, be held to be inoperative, as going beyond the constitutional limit,
but these provisions are not involved in this case to any material extent, and will not be discussed here. The complaint in this case is not
against the laws, but against the manner of executing them.

The registration is, in a manner, permanent; one registered for any
particular county and precinct is permanently registered for that precinct
until, by removal or conviction of crime, he forfeits his right to remain

583

on the registry. The new law of 1887 preserves the registration then existing.

A registered voter may apply for and receive a certificate of registration, but it is not necessary for him to have such certificate to entitle him to vote. It is evidence of his right, but it need not be presented at the polls except when, for any reason, his name does not appear upon the registry book in the hands of the precinct managers of election.

Each county has a supervisor of registration, having an office at the county seat which he is required to keep open at least three days in each week, from 9 to 12 a. m. and from 1 to 5 p. m., from the first Monday in August to the last Saturday preceding the first Monday in October in each year in which there is a general election. The supervisor is required to appoint a district registering officer for each election district, whose duty it is to register the votes of his district and who is required to keep his books open at some convenient place in his district, at least two days in each week, between the same hours as provided for the supervisor, during the month of September in each year of general election. Voters may register either with the district registering officer or with the supervisor. On removing from one residence to another voters are entitled, on application, to receive a transfer of registration and a certificate of transfer. This right is not confined to the days of registration or to the months in which original registration may be had.

The county commissioners are required at their October meeting to review the work of the supervisor of registration and to hold special meetings for that purpose. They are required to publish the names of all persons stricken from the rolls, and the supervisor is required to restore to the rolls all names ordered by the commissioners to be so restored.

Much of the evidence in this case is directed to the misconduct of supervisors of registration and of district registering officers. Other portions of the evidence are directed to the misinterpretation of the law by managers of election. The misconduct of registering officers consisted in unlawfully striking from the books large numbers of duly registered voters, in refusing or neglecting to restore the names ordered to be restored by county commissioners, in keeping their offices closed on days of registration, in unreasonably delaying applicants, in unlawfully requiring colored applicants to prove their places of residence by white witnesses known to the registering officers, in unlawfully refusing or neglecting to make transfers on due application, in furnishing unequal facilities for registration, as between their party friends and their party opponents, and in fraudulently registering persons not qualified.

Complaint is made, in some instances, against county commissioners for failing to meet to revise the work of the supervisors, and to order restored those names that had been unlawfully stricken from the books.

Managers of election unlawfully refused to receive the ballots of colored Republican voters who were duly registered, and whose names were on the registry books in the hands of the managers, because they did not present their registration certificates. They also refused to accept such certificates as proof of the right to vote of voters whose names had been unlawfully stricken from the rolls.

They also refused to accept the tendered votes of Republicans who were marked as having moved within the precinct in which they were registered. In many instances this removal had not, in fact, taken place, and when it had it did not disqualify the voter, under the law, from voting. While the law provides for issuing a new registration certificate to a voter who has changed his residence, either within the precinct or to another one, it does not require such a new certificate as a condition precedent to voting when the change of residence is within the precinct or voting district. On the contrary, it expressly provides that a new certificate shall be necessary if the change of residence is from one voting district to another, thus implying that it shall not be necessary if the change is not from one voting district to another. *Inclusio unius, exclusio alterius.*

The evidence in the case is voluminous, covering all the irregularities which are noted, and which will be referred to more in detail as we consider the vote in the various counties and precincts.

DADE COUNTY.

The vote in Dade County was: Bullock, 95; Goodrich, 45. It is claimed by contestant that this whole vote should be rejected, because no registration was had in the county under the statute. It appears that no supervisor of registration was appointed in this county until after the election. This was not the fault of the voters, and we do not think they should be disfranchised because of the failure of the governor to commission a supervisor of registration, as required by law. The old registration was in existence, and the election was held under it in full compliance with the law, with the exception noted. The committee are clearly of opinion that voters complying with all other requirements of the law can not be disfranchised by the neglect of public officials to furnish them opportunity to register.

COLUMBIA COUNTY.

District No. 7.—Ten duly registered and legally qualified voters tendered ballots for contestant and were rejected. (Record, pp. 184, 189.)

District No. 4.—Twenty legally qualified and duly registered voters tendered their ballots for contestant and the ballots were rejected. They were then handed to the United States supervisor, were preserved, and are in evidence. (Record, pp. 184, 185.)

District No. 5.—Thirty-three qualified voters tendered ballots for contestant, which were rejected by the inspectors, but were received and preserved by the United States supervisor. (Record, pp. 186, 188.)

District No. 10.—Forty ballots tendered for contestant by qualified voters were rejected. They were then delivered to the Democratic county judge, and by him preserved. All these voters were duly registered and their names were on the registry list in the hands of the inspectors. (Record, pp. 86, 87.)

District No. 8.—Thirteen ballots tendered for contestant by qualified voters were rejected by the inspectors, and then received and preserved by the United States supervisor. (Record, pp. 181, 182.)

District No. 2.—Three ballots tendered for contestant by duly qualified voters were rejected. (Record, p. 183.)

District No. 6.—Five ballots tendered for contestant by duly qualified voters were rejected. (Record, pp. 183, 184.)

District No. 3.—Three ballots tendered for contestant by duly qualified voters were rejected. (Record, p. 189.)

These 127 voters were all residents of the several precincts at which they offered to vote, had been duly registered, tendered their votes, and were refused the right to vote under various pretexts, none of which were valid. No attempt has been made to rebut the evidence proving the above facts. One hundred and twenty-seven votes should be added to the vote of contestant in Columbia County.

PUTNAM COUNTY.

District No. 1.—Fifteen witnesses swear to tendering their votes for contestant and that their ballots were refused. They had also duly applied for registration and had been refused. They were qualified for registration and were illegally rejected. Fifteen votes should be added to the vote of contestant in Putnam County. (Rec., pp. 75–79.)

VOLUSIA COUNTY.

In Volusia County thirty-one qualified voters tendered their ballots for contestant and were rejected. Some of these voters were duly registered and then, in violation of the law and without notice, their names were stricken from the registry. Others had applied for registration and had been informed by the supervisor of registration that their names were already on the list. Others, under various pretexts, were illegally refused registration. The evidence in regard to these votes is conclusive and uncontradicted, and contestant's vote in Volusia County should be increased by 31. (Rec., pp. 17–63, 199–207, 219–221.)

ORANGE COUNTY.

In District No. 3, Orange County, 31 ballots cast for contestant were not counted, on the ground that there was a distinguishing mark upon them. On the lower right-hand corner of these ballots was a printed star (*), so small as not to attract attention. Careful voters, on examining their tickets, would scarcely notice it. The ballots were printed in a Democratic newspaper office, and the star was undoubtedly placed there for the purpose of deception and to secure the rejection of these ballots by the precinct inspectors. This was not such a distinguishing mark as, under the circumstances, authorized the inspectors to refuse to count these ballots. (Rec., pp. 251–254.)

In this county, also, nine duly qualified voters tendered their ballots for contestant and were rejected. (Rec., pp. 256–266.) The committee add 40 votes to contestant's vote in Orange County.

MARION COUNTY.

In Fauntville precinct, Marion County, 83 ballots for contestant were thrown out on the ground that names on the ticket for justice of the peace and constable were scratched off and other names written on in red or purple ink. Persons desiring to vote for these officers applied at the only store in the place for ink and could only get the kind of ink used in scratching these tickets, and hence the use of the red or purple ink. The committee do not think that under the circumstances these voters should be disfranchised, notwithstanding the terms of the statute, as the marking was not done for any improper or unlawful purpose and the use of this ink was, in a manner, compulsory. The committee count the 83 votes for contestant. (See McCrary on Elections, sections 400, 401, 404.)

In Marion County large numbers of duly registered voters were unlawfully stricken from the registration lists by E. M. Gregg, supervisor of registration, in reckless disregard of the law, and, as your committee believe, with the deliberate and criminal purpose of depriving the Republican voters of the county of their rights.

In Ocala precinct, No. 1, one hundred and ten duly registered voters had their names stricken from the registry list after having registered under the new law and without any legal authority for such action. These one hundred and ten voters tendered their ballots for contestant and were refused the right to vote.

In Fantville precinct, No. 20, twenty-nine voters were in like manner stricken from the registry.

In Millwood district, No. 2, fifty-one names were stricken from the registry.

In Reddick precinct ten names were stricken from the registry.

In Flemington precinct, No. 3, forty-two names were stricken from the registry.

In Cotton Plant district, No. 4, nineteen were stricken from the registry and seven on the registry were rejected at the polls, making twenty-six.

In Summerville district, No. 8, seven were stricken from the registry.

In Blichville precinct one was stricken from the registry.

In Shady Grove district, No. 7, nineteen were stricken from the registry and five whose names remained on the registry were rejected at the polls, making twenty-four.

In Whitesville precinct, No. 8, nine were stricken from the registry.

In Citra precinct, No. 16, twenty-four were stricken from the registry.

In Anthony district, No. 17, nine were stricken from the registry.

In McIntosh district, No. 2, thirty-three were stricken from the registry and fifteen others were rejected at the polls whose names were on the registry list.

In Silver Springs precinct eight were stricken from the registry and three registered voters were rejected.

In Silver Springs Park precinct, No. 24, three were stricken from the registry and ten registered voters were rejected at the polls.

In Camden district, No. 25, two registered voters were rejected.

In Spar precinct, No. 27, twelve voters were rejected and two were stricken from the registry.

In Belleview district, precinct No. 26, twenty-one registered voters were rejected, and eleven were stricken from the registry.

In Lake Weir precinct one was stricken from the registry.

In Stanton precinct three were stricken from the registry.

The above account of persons stricken from the registry includes only those who were lawful voters, had been registered under the new law, tendered ballots for contestant at their proper voting places, and were unlawfully rejected.

These 466 rejected voters in Marion County had all been duly registered. Some 366 of the number had their names stricken from the registry rolls just previous to the election. The supervisor of registration refused to allow the Republican campaign committee to have a copy of the registration list, or to inspect the list. He also refused to restore names that he had stricken from the rolls, after having been ordered by the county commissioners to restore them. He closed his office on the day before election, and thus prevented a large number of applicants from obtaining transfer certificates. He refused to submit his registration books to the county commissioners, as the law required.

These 466 duly qualified voters appeared at their proper polling places and tendered their votes for contestant, which votes were rejected. The names of 100 of them were still on the registry lists, and yet the precinct inspectors rejected the votes, either saying that they could not find the name on the registry, or setting up some frivolous pretext for rejection. Voters duly registered were required, in violation of law, to present their registration certificates. Others, who presented registration certificates, were rejected because their names had been stricken from the registry. The illegal action of Supervisor Gregg can not be permitted to disfranchise these voters.

Most of the tickets in these various precincts were preserved in Republican side boxes, and the names of the various voters so disfranchised, with the pages of the record establishing their right to vote, and the tender of their ballots, will be found on pages 15 to 28 of contestant's brief.

These 466 rejected votes, added to the 83 votes not counted in Fauntville, make 549 votes to be added to contestant's vote in Marion County.

NASSAU COUNTY.

District No. 5.—The registration and election in this district were wholly fraudulent. The return shows that there were 141 votes polled in this precinct, and the evidence conclusively establishes that there were but 58 qualified voters then residing in the district. The poll-list of those voting was destroyed, but it sufficiently appears that more than half of the persons voting were strangers in the precinct, and had no residence therein. A fraudulent registration was made up for the precinct, and it is impossible, from the evidence, to ascertain the legal vote cast. The returns gave 121 to contestee and 13 to contestant. The committee reject the poll, and deduct 121 from contestee's vote, and 13 from contestant's. Eight qualified voters testify that they voted for contestant. These are the only votes proved, and, under the rule of law that when the return is impeached only such votes as are proved *aliunde* can be counted, we give these 8 votes to contestant, reducing the amount to be deducted from his vote in this precinct to 5. (Rec., pp. 577–579, 587.)

District No. 1.—In district No. 1 one qualified voter, who tendered a vote for contestant, had his vote rejected.

District No. 12.—In district No. 12 eighteen qualified voters tendered their votes for contestant, and the votes were rejected.

District No. 3.—In district No. 3 an election was held as provided by law, but no return was made. (Rec., p. 593). Twenty-four duly qualified voters are proved to have voted for contestant in this district, and that number should be credited to him.

District No. 9.—The returns from this precinct give contestee 221, and contestant 38 votes. The election was held three-quarters of a mile from the established polling place without notice to the voters. It does not appear in evidence that there was general knowledge of the change. It does appear, however, that the registering officer of the precinct was taken sick and that during his illness and in his absence his deputy refused to register any Republican voters. On the last day of registration the registrar returned, but, after a few minutes, closed his registration office, went away, and staid away all day, thereby preventing a large number from registering.

It further appears that this same registering officer placed Democrats upon the registration who were not qualified. While the holding of the election at a different place from that provided by law would not vitiate the poll, provided due notice was given of the change, so that knowledge of the fact would come to both political parties, yet, in this case, the change without notice, added to the conclusive evidence of the fraudulent acts of the registrar and his deputy in closing the registration office against Republican voters, and in illegally registering unqualified Democrats, so vitiate the integrity of the poll as to destroy the value of the return and make it impossible to say that the election at this poll was a fair one. The committee, accordingly, reject the poll and deduct from contestee and contestant the 221 and 38 votes returned for them, respectively.

District No. 13.—In District No. 13, Briceville, 79 votes are returned, all for contestee. Nineteen of this number are proved to have been non-residents and to have been fraudulently registered. (Rec., pp. 586, 587, 596). The least that we can do with this precinct is to deduct from the vote of contestee the nineteen fraudulent votes proved to have been cast for him.

Summing up the above-noted changes in Nassau County, the committee find 43 votes to be added to and 43 votes to be deducted from contestant's vote, and so make no change in it. Three hundred and sixty-one votes should be deducted from contestee..

ALACHUA COUNTY.

Aredondo District, No. 12.—There were returned from this poll for contestee 222 votes and for contestant 59. One hundred and sixty-nine voters testify to having voted for contestant. Twenty-four others testified that they tendered votes for contestant and that their votes were rejected. Thirty-one others are proved to have tendered votes for contestant and their votes were rejected. All these voters were either registered or had applied for registration and been fraudulently refused. N. A. Collison, United States supervisor, was not permitted to act, under the pretense that he lived in a quarantined town, although it appears from the evidence that there was free intercourse between the two towns. A person designated by him and not subject to the same objection was also refused permission to act in the supervisor's place, though it had been agreed that he might act. (Rec., pp. 319, 320.)

The inspectors did not commence canvassing the votes until over an hour after closing the polls, and pistol firing was indulged in, evidently with the intention of keeping witnesses away from the count. Every conceivable obstruction was interposed in this district to prevent Republicans from registering. The names of a large number of Republican voters were arbitrarily stricken from the registration books, and the names of those so stricken were not published, as required by law. The evidence conclusively shows that the return from the district is fraudulent and false. The 222 votes returned for contestee should be deducted from his vote, as there is no proof of contestee's vote aside from the vitiated returns; and contestant should be credited with 224 votes actually cast or tendered for him, or 165 more than were given him in the returns. The names of the voters in district No. 12 will be found on pages 51 to 56 of contestant's brief.

Hayne Station, District No. 17.—Sixty-four votes duly tendered for contestant were rejected and should be counted for him. (Rec., pp. 331–370.)

District No. 7.—Seventy-two legally qualified voters tendered their votes for contestant and were refused. Nearly all of these voters were registered and the remainder had made due effort to be registered.

District No. 20.—Forty-nine duly qualified electors tendered their votes for contestant and were refused.

District No. 10.—Thirty-three duly qualified voters tendered their votes for contestant and were refused.

District No. 6.—Fifty duly qualified electors tendered their votes for contestant and were refused.

District No. 2.—Forty-six legally qualified electors tendered ballots for contestant and were rejected.

District No. 16.—Six legal voters tendered ballots for contestant and were refused.

District No. 11.—Ninety legally qualified voters tendered their ballots for contestant and were rejected.

District No. 3.—Ten legally qualified electors tendered their ballots for contestant and were refused.

District No. 19.—Seventeen qualified voters tendered ballots for contestant and were rejected.

District No. 1, *Waldo.*—Twenty-three duly qualified voters tendering their votes for contestant were rejected.

District No. 15.—Fifty qualified electors tendering their votes for contestant were rejected.

It appears from the evidence that nearly all these voters had been registered under the old registry; that they applied for registration under the new law and were either told that they were already registered or were denied the opportunity of getting transfers; that those who failed to get on the registry or to get proper transfers appeared at the time and place advertised for the meeting of the county commissioners, whose duty it is, under the law, to correct all errors of registration, and that only one of the county commissioners appeared, and he, not being a quorum, refused to act. In this county, therefore, there was an entire failure on the part of the county officers to discharge their duty with reference to registration.

They had no meeting, as the law required, to perfect the registration lists and they did not publish the names stricken from the registry. The supervisor of registration neglected to perform the duties of his office, so far as Republican voters were concerned. The registration lists of the county were, therefore, of little value, not because of the neglect of the Republican voters, who were thoroughly organized and made every effort to get their names properly on the registration lists, but because of the negligent and unlawful acts of the officers charged with the duty of registration. Under these circumstances the committee hold that the proof of the qualification of the before-mentioned voters who sought to cast their ballots for contestant is satisfactory, and the votes should be counted as if cast.

The committee accordingly add to contestant's vote in Alachua County 677 votes, and deduct from contestee's vote 222 votes.

HAMILTON COUNTY.

District No. 3.—Thirteen votes, duly tendered for contestant by legal voters, were rejected on the ground that the voters were charged with having changed their residences from one place to another in the same voting precinct. This, if true, would not interfere with their right to vote.

District No. 2.—One hundred and four votes cast for contestant and 2 for contestee were not counted on the ground that there was a printer's dash under the names of some of the candidates on the tickets. We do not think that this was such a distinguishing mark as authorized the rejection of these ballots. One hundred and four votes should be added to contestant's vote and two to contestee's.

In this district there were also 18 votes tendered for contestant refused which should be counted.

District No. 1.—Sixteen votes are claimed in district No. 1, but the evidence in regard to them is not quite conclusive.

District No. 7.—Forty-eight votes for contestant were not counted because of a printer's dash (- ——) separating each name on the ticket. These votes should be counted. (See McCrary on Elections, 2d ed., § 104.)

District No. 5.—Eighteen duly qualified voters tendered votes for contestant and were rejected. They should be counted.

The committee accordingly add 199 votes to contestant's returned vote in Hamilton County.

DUVAL COUNTY.

District No. 2.—Thirty-two persons tendered votes for contestant, and were rejected. It does not appear from the evidence for what reason they were rejected, or that they had made efforts to be registered, and therefore we do not count them.

District No. 8.—Twelve of the 14 claimed legal voters were duly qualified, tendered their votes for contestant and were rejected, and 13 ballots for contestant were illegally rejected on the claim that they had some specks on them. One Democratic ticket was rejected in the same way. One witness testified that he could discover nothing on them, another that there appeared to be small ink spots. These tickets ought not to have been rejected.

District No. 21.—Eight out of the 14 claimed legal voters who tendered their votes for contestant should be counted, and 9 votes for contestant not counted under pretense that they were marked should be counted for him. The rejection of these 9 ballots was on the ground that there was a printer's dash on the ticket in a place where no person was named for a particular office.

District No. 23.—One qualified elector was illegally denied the right to vote for contestant.

District No. 17.—Twenty-nine qualified voters tendered their votes for contestant and were rejected. They should be counted.

District No. 18.—Three legally qualified voters who tendered their votes for contestant were rejected.

District No. 20.—Of the 57 who tendered their votes for contestant 39 were duly registered and qualified voters and should be counted.

District No. 6.—Three qualified voters were illegally denied the right to vote for contestant, and 45 votes cast for contestant were not counted because the name of a candidate for justice of the peace was written on the ticket with a red lead-pencil. We think these votes should be counted.

District No. 12.—Twelve votes cast for contestant were illegally not counted, on the ground that they were marked. There were pencil-marks on the tickets made by the judges pushing them into the box with a pencil.

District No. 15.—Seventeen qualified voters tendered their votes for contestant and were rejected, and 9 votes cast for contestant were illegally not counted.

District No. 7.—Three qualified voters tendered ballots for contestant, and their ballots were not received.

District 16, *or ward No.* 2.—Seventy-five duly qualified and registered voters tendered their votes for contestant, and were refused; they should be counted. The others claimed in this district the committee do not allow.

District No. 19.—Twenty-eight legally qualified electors tendered their votes for contestant, and were rejected.

District No. 22.—Sixty-two qualified voters tendered ballots for contestant, and were rejected.

District No. 13.—Eighteen qualified voters tendered their votes for contestant, and were rejected.

In this county the supervisor of registration resorted to dilatory tactics to prevent Republicans from registering, and thereby prevented a large number of qualified voters from being registered. (Record, pp. 116–18.)

The committee add 385 votes to the vote returned for contestant in Duval County.

MADISON COUNTY.

Cherry Lake district, No. 7.—At this district the regularly appointed Democratic election inspectors appeared at the polling place, but having in some way received notice of an intended raid on the ballot-box, declined to hold an election. Thereupon the voters present proceeded to elect a board of inspectors. These inspectors refused to hold the election at the place, fearing danger, and so adjourned the election to a point three-quarters of a mile distant. The Democrats refused to participate in this election although they had due notice of it. One hundred and thirty-one votes were cast for contestant, canvassed, and duly returned to the supervisor of elections for the county, but the canvassing board of the county refused to consider the return. It was the fault, first, of the Democratic election inspectors, and second, of the Democratic voters themselves, that the few Democratic votes there were in the precinct were not cast. The committee count for contestant the 131 votes cast for him in this precinct.

Madison district, No. 1.—At this district an election was duly held, as provided by law, and 615 votes were cast. After the close of the polls, the Democratic inspectors delayed for some two hours the counting of the vote, and then proceeded very slowly, occupying two hours more in counting some seventy votes. When they had proceeded thus far, an armed body of white Democrats appeared at the polls, and forcibly carried off the ballot box. Consequently, no return was made of this vote.

There was a side election held, by Democrats alone, at the same poll, to inform the governor whom the Democratic voters desired for county commissioners. This box was undisturbed, and return was duly made of the result to the Democratic chairman of the county. Two hundred and six votes were cast at the side box. Presumably all, or nearly all, of the Democrats voting in the precinct voted at this side box. There is evidence that some four did not. Inasmuch as the party friends of contestee destroyed the evidence of the result of the election at this precinct, and because of the disturbed condition in the county at the time this contest was pending, making it dangerous to attempt to take testimony in the county, the committee take the result at the side box and the other evidence in regard to the vote as the best evidence attainable as to the result at this precinct. Accordingly, they count 210 votes for contestee, and 405 votes for contestant.

Hickstown district.—Here an election was regularly held, and, after the polls were closed, the Democratic inspectors refused to canvass the votes, fearing, or pretending to fear, violence. The ballot-box, and the tickets, however, were preserved. At this district contestant received 100 votes, and contestee 30 votes, and the committee count the votes as cast.

Greenville district, No. 5.—The election was regularly held in this district; 215 votes were cast, of which contestant received 130, and contestee 85. The box and returns were delivered by the Democratic inspectors to J. A. Redding, a Democrat, who assisted, as clerk, at the counting of the vote, to be by him delivered to the county supervisor of election. He took it to his store and late at night, while he was engaged in putting up his books, a body of armed white men came to his store and by deception gained access to the store room and forcibly carried away the box so that no return was made. The committee count for contestant the 130 votes cast for him and for contestee the 85 votes cast for him at this precinct. They also count 19 additional votes for contestant, tendered and illegally rejected at this poll.

Hamburg district, No. 6.—At this district an election was held in an orderly manner, but just before the closing of the polls an armed body of mounted men, variously estimated at from forty-four to ninety, rode down upon the polls and seized and carried away the ballot-box. They were white men and friends of contestee. The evidence shows that 259 Republicans voted there that day. There is no evidence as to what the Democratic vote was. The committee accordingly count 259 for contestant.

Elaville district, No. 2.—The returns from this district gave contestant only 29 votes. J. H. Stripling, United States supervisor, was refused admission to the polling place by the precinct inspectors, which refusal discredits the return. Being refused permission to act as United States supervisor, he took his place outside of the polling place, distributed Republican tickets, and kept account of the number voted. From his evidence it appears that 97 instead of 29 Republican votes were cast for contestant. No attempt is made to refute or discredit this testimony, and the unlawful action of the inspectors of election leaves it as the only valid evidence of the vote. Counting the vote, however, as claimed in contestant's brief, which is the method most liberal to contestee, the committee add 68 to contestant's vote and deduct a like number from the vote of contestee.

Macedonia district.—In Macedonia district, No. 11, twenty-nine votes only are returned for contestant. The proof shows that he received at least 65 votes at this poll. The committee add 36 to contestant's vote and deduct a like number from that of contestee, following the liberal method of counting conceded in contestant's brief.

The committee add 1,147 votes to contestant's vote in Madison County and 325 to contestee's, and deduct from contestee's vote 104, making a net change of 926 in contestant's favor.

To sum up the result in all the counties:

Net changes in favor of contestant in—

Columbia County	127
Putnam County	15
Volusia County	31
Orange County	40
Marion County	549
Nassau County	361
Alachua County	899
Hamilton County	199
Duval County	385
Madison County	926
Total	3,532
Bullock's returned majority	3,195
Majority for Goodrich	337

H. Mis. 137——38

The committee recommend the passage of the following resolutio

Resolved, That Robert Bullock was not elected a Representative in Fifty-first Congress from the second Congressional district of Flori and is not entitled to retain a seat therein.

Resolved, That Fred. S. Goodrich was elected a Representative in Fitty-first Congress from the second Congressional district of Flori and is entitled to the seat.

(1) **Registration law.** *Power of legislature to enact.*

"The right of suffrage is regulated by the States, and while the legislature of a State can not add to, abridge, or alter the constitutional qualifications of voters, it may and should prescribe proper and necessary rules for the orderly exercise of the right resulting from these qualifications. It can not be denied that the power to enact a registration law is within the power to regulate the exercise of the elective franchise and preserve the purity of the ballot."

(2) **Return.** *Evidence necessary to overthrow.*

"Before the official return can be properly rejected, there must be satisfactory proof that the proceedings in the conduct of the election or in the return of the vote were so tainted with fraud that the truth can not be correctly ascertained from the returns. In other words, the returns must be accepted as true until they are clearly shown to be false."

(3) **Registration.** *When new certificate necessary under Florida law.*

Registration is not necessary when a voter has changed his residence from one place to another in the same voting precinct. "While section 8 of the act of June 7, 1887, may possibly admit of a different construction, we are inclined to the opinion that a mere change of residence from one house to another in the same voting precinct should not deprive an elector of his right to vote."

(4) **Ballot.** *Distinguishing mark.*

A printer's dash separating the names of candidates on a ticket is not a distinguishing mark which would justify the rejection of the ballots under the Florida statute.

(5) **No registration.**

The opinion of the committee as to the votes of the county where there was no registration is concurred in.

(6) **Votes not registered.** *Presumed to be properly rejected.*

Certain votes "were rejected by the inspectors because the names of the persons offering them were not found on the registration list. In the absence of proof to the contrary there is a legitimate presumption that they were properly rejected. It has been repeatedly decided by the House of Representatives that the acts of proper officers, acting within the sphere of their duties, must be presumed to be correct, unless shown to be otherwise."

(7) **Ballot.** *Distinguishing mark.*

The ballots partly written in red ink or red pencil were properly rejected, their rejection being directly required by the law of Florida.

(8) **Votes rejected.** *Most of them properly so.*

"We submit that a careful examination of the testimony will show that from want of sufficient intelligence to understand the registration laws a large majority of the persons whose votes were rejected for failure to register properly had not complied with the requirements of the law in obtaining transfers, in having themselves reregistered after a change of residence, and in giving attention to other matters absolutely necessary to render them qualified electors in the State of Florida.

VIEWS OF THE MINORITY.

Mr. MAISH presented the following as the views of the minority:

The undersigned, dissenting from the conclusions reached by the majority of the Committee on Elections in the above-cited case, submit herewith the reasons for their dissent, as follows:

The Second Congressional district of Florida is composed of the following counties, to wit: Madison, Hamilton, Suwannee, Columbia, Baker, Nassau, Duval, Clay, Bradford, Alachua, Putnam, Marion, Sumter, Lake, Orange, Osceola, Dade, Brevard, Volusia, and St. John's. At the election for Representative in Congress, which was held on the 6th of November, 1888, Robert Bullock was the Democratic candidate and Frederick S. Goodrich was the Republican candidate. The result of the election, as certified by the secretary of state, was as follows:

Counties.	Robert Bullock.	Fred. S. Goodrich.	Counties.	Robert Bullock.	Fred. S. Goodrich.
	Votes.	*Votes.*		*Votes.*	*Votes.*
Alachua	2,067	1,362	Marion	1,938	1,780
Baker	378	152	Nassau	975	901
Bradford	1,007	361	Orange	1,849	1,552
Brevard	472	232	Osceola	434	224
Clay	565	480	Putnam	1,170	1,340
Columbia	1,039	977	St. John's	1,049	1,634
Dade	95	45	Sumter	784	308
Duval	1,406	2,688	Suwannee	1,008	784
Hamilton	741	353	Volusia	982	1,175
Lake	1,330	900			
Madison	723	179		20,015	16,817

It thus appears that according to the official result of the election as ascertained and declared, according to law, the contestee received a majority of 3,195 votes. Before proceeding to consider the testimony as disclosed by the record, it may not be inappropriate to state that, according to the census of 1880, the population of the counties composing this district consisted of 70,947 whites and 65,040 colored, thus showing a majority of 5,907 white people. In addition we call attention to the fact that at the Congressional election held in this district in 1884 the Democratic candidate received 17,248 votes, and the Republican candidate received 15,857 votes, showing a majority of 1,391 for the Democratic candidate. At the Congressional election held in 1886 the Democratic candidate in this district received 18,892 votes, and the Republican candidate received 15,763 votes, showing a majority of 3,129 votes in favor of the Democratic candidate. There was no contest made either in 1884 or 1886, and the result of the election in each year was accepted as fair by all concerned.

As the principal ground of contest in this case is the alleged refusal of the inspectors to receive votes tendered, because the persons tendering them had not been duly registered, we deem it proper to call attention to certain provisions of the election laws of Florida. The right of suffrage is regulated by the States, and while the legislature of a State can not add to, abridge, or alter the constitutional qualifications of voters, it may and should prescribe proper and necessary rules for the orderly exercise of the right resulting from these qualifications. It can not be denied that the power to enact a registration law is within the power to regulate the exercise of the elective franchise and preserve the purity of the ballot. The law of Florida in force on the 6th day of November, 1888, contained, among others, the following provisions:

First. No persons can vote unless they are duly registered according to law.

Second. The elector is required, under oath, to give such description of himself as will be sufficient to identify his person with the act of registration.

Third. The governor appoints a supervisor of registration in each county, who appoints a registration officer for each election district, whose duty it is to attend to the registration of electors in such district.

Fourth. It is the duty of the board of county commissioners to divide the county into election districts, which said districts may be changed by the board at any time at least three months before any general election, designating each district by a number, and at the most suitable point to establish a voting place or a precinct.

Fifth. Immediately upon the expiration of the time for registration at the several precincts, each district registration officer shall subscribe in his book an oath that he has faithfully executed his duties as the registration officer at such precinct, and shall deliver his book and all blanks left in his possession to the supervisor of registration, and thereupon the supervisor shall proceed to make up the registration lists for the several precincts.

Sixth. Each elector upon being registered shall be furnished by the registration officer with a certificate, which shall be numbered by consecutive numbers for each district, and shall contain a statement of his name, age, color, occupation, place of residence, and date of registration as entered in the registration book, which certificate shall be signed by the registration officers. No person shall be allowed to vote in any other election district than the one for which he is registered nor shall any person whose name does not appear upon the registration list be allowed to vote, unless he produces and exhibits such certificate to the managers of election.

Seventh. When the name of any elector shall have been wrongfully erased the same may be restored by order of the county commissioners if the supervisor on application and proper proofs fails so to do.

Eighth. In case of the removal of an elector from one residence to another in the same district, or from one district to another district in the same county, such elector shall notify the supervisor of registration and shall surrender his certificate of registration to such officer, who shall enter the fact upon the registration book and shall give such elector a new certificate in accordance with such change of residence.

Ninth. No elector removing from one residence district or ward to another shall be allowed to register or vote without a transfer of registration, as above provided.

Tenth. It is made the duty of the county commissioners to examine and revise the list of registered electors, erasing therefrom the names of such as have died or removed from the county, or who are otherwise disqualified to vote, and restoring such names as have been improperly taken off by the supervisor of registration.

Eleventh. At each election the supervisor of registration shall furnish the inspectors of election at each election district with a copy of the registration book for such district, the names in which have been arranged alphabetically and certified by him to be correct, for the care and custody of which the inspectors receiving the same shall be responsible, and which they shall return to the supervisor of registration within three days after the close of the election.

We submit that a careful examination of the testimony will show that from want of sufficient intelligence to understand the registration laws a large majority of the persons whose votes were rejected for failure to register properly had not complied with the requirements of the law in obtaining transfers, in having themselves reregistered after a change of residence, and in giving attention to other matters absolutely necessary to render them qualified electors in the State of Florida.

ALACHUA COUNTY.

It is claimed by the majority of the committee that in Arredonda district No. 12 in this county the official returns should be rejected as fraudulent; that the 222 votes returned for contestee should be deducted from his poll, and that the contestant should be credited with 224 votes as actually cast or tendered for him, making 165 more than he received by the official returns. Before the official return from this election precinct can be properly rejected, there must be satisfactory proof that the proceedings in the conduct of the election or in the return of the vote were so tainted with fraud that the truth can not be correctly ascertained from the returns. In other words, the returns must be accepted as true until they are clearly shown to be false. As specimens of the testimony introduced by contestant to impeach the returns from this precinct, we extract the following:

Joseph Williams testifies, p. 271:

Q. Who was the Republican or Democratic candidate for Congress in this county?—A. I can not remember, as there was so many of them.

Q. Is it not a fact that you never inquired or asked on the day you got your ticket and did not know when you went to vote whether there was a candidate for Congress that year or not?—A. No, sir; I did not exactly know.

Q. Do you know what Congress is? Is Congress a man or a woman?—A. It is a man, I suppose.

Q. Is it an old man or a young man; black or white?—A. I could not tell.

Q. What was the name you remembered on your ticket?—A. I do not remember any name on my ticket but Goodrich; I know them, but do not remember now. I do not know whether he was running for governor; they told me so.

Q. You remember distinctly that Goodrich's name was on your ticket for governor; because you had it read to you was the reason why you remember it so distinctly; because you wanted to vote for him for Congress, so as to have the State have a Republican governor once more?—A. Yes, sir.

Monroe Welsh testifies, p. 272:

Q. Who was running for governor on your ticket?—A. F. S. Goodrich.

Q. Was he the man you wanted for Governor?—A. Yes, sir.

Fortune Sturks testifies, p. 287:

Q. Was Mr. Barnes on your ticket for Congress, and did you meet anybody this morning and tell them so?—A. Yes, sir.

Q. What Mr. Barnes was it; the Mr. Barnes that lives at Gainesville and who used to be sheriff?—A. I don't know; I voted the Republican ticket.

Q. The parties who you spoke to on the road this morning, did you not tell them that you did not know what ticket you voted, only that you know you voted for Mr. Barnes for Congress, and that they told you so, and that is all you know about the ticket?—A. Yes, sir; that is all I know about it, and my privilege was to vote, and that is all I know about it.

William Starks testifies, p. 292:

Q. Who did you vote for for governor?—A. Mr. Goodrich.

Q. Why did you want to vote for Mr. Goodrich for governor; was it so you could have a Republican governor once more in this State, and have the control of the courts and the counties; is that so?—A. Yes, sir.

Q. Are you positive he is the man you wanted for governor?—A. According to the nominees I am going by.

Bernett Kelly testifies, p. 301:

Q. Did you vote at the last election at Arredonda?—A. Yes, sir.

Q. Who did you vote for Congress, the Republican or Democratic candidate?—A. I don't know, sir.

Perry Luker testifies, p. 302:

Q. Can you read or write?—A. A little.

Q. Did you read the ticket you voted at the last election?—A. Yes, sir.

Q. Are you a Democrat or a Republican ?—A. From the ticket I voted I must be a tie of both.

Q. Was Bullock a candidate for Presidential elector on the ticket you voted ?—A. It was stated that Bullock was a candidate for Congress on the ticket I voted.

As to the testimony of the fifty-four witnesses for contestant found in the record from page 307 to page 320, inclusive, we submit that it can not be considered, for the reason that it was taken after the expiration of the forty days allowed by law. If, however, said testimony should be considered at all, it shows that some of the witnesses did not vote because their names were not found on the registration list; some of them are not able to state for whom they voted, and others testify that they voted for the contestee. To show the insufficiency of the testimony found in the record, from page 339 to page 359, inclusive, we present the following:

Jessie Owens testifies on cross-examination that if from any cause his name was erased from the Arredonda precinct registration list, he did not apply to the supervisor of registration of Alachua County to have his name restored before he offered to vote.

Charles Yorick testifies on cross-examination, p. 343, that he could not read the name of the candidate for Congress on his ballot, and does not in reality know whose name was on his ballot.

James Bullock testifies on cross-examination, p. 344, that when he offered his ballot to the inspectors they gave as a reason for not receiving it that they could not find his name on the list, and that he did not apply to the supervisor of registration of Alachua County to have his name restored.

Henry Adams testifies on cross-examination, p. 345, that his name was not on the registration list at the Arredonda precinct; that it was on the list at the Jonesville precinct, and that he did not apply to Mr. Saddler, the supervisor of registration, to have his name transferred on account of the yellow fever.

Isaac Thompson testifies on cross-examination, p. 346, that he did not notify the supervisor of registration of his change of residence, and did not ask him to note the same on the registration books and give him a certificate.

Lewis McCray testifies on cross-examination, p. 347, that he does not know who the candidates for Congress were at the last general election, and does not know for whom he voted.

David Simmons testifies on cross-examination, p. 349, that he really does not know whose name was on his ticket for Congress.

Jordan Perry testifies on cross-examination, p. 350, that he does not know how many Congressional candidates there were, and does not know whose names were on his ticket for Congress at the last election.

Cubner Johnson testifies on cross-examination, p. 351, that he does not know whether he voted the Congressional ticket and does not know whose name was on his ticket.

Bill Neal testifies on his direct examination, p. 352, that he did not vote at the last general election, but offered to vote at Arredonda. It appears from the registration list, p. 323, that his name had been erased.

Joe Bradley testifies on his direct examination, p. 353, that he does not know what State he lives in.

Shedrick Bell testifies on cross-examination, p. 364, that he does not know what State officers or what candidate for Congress he voted for.

The testimony of the witnesses to be found in the record from page 381 to page 398, inclusive, is not sufficient to justify the rejection of the official returns. The contestant claims that C. H. DeBose distributed tickets to thirty-one persons at this precinct, who offered to vote for the contestant, and whose votes were refused, but it appears from an examination of his testimony (pp. 331, 382, and 383) that he does not know how many persons to whom he distributed tickets actually voted or how they voted.

Moses Duncan testifies on cross-examination, p. 386, that he does not know whether the name of Robert Bullock was on the ticket for Congress which he voted or not.

Ned Baskins testifies on cross-examination, p. 387, that he does not know whether the name of Robert Bullock for Congress was on his ticket or not, and that he does not know for whom he voted.

Nelson Johnson testifies on cross-examination, p. 388, that the name of the man for whom he voted is spelled "G-w-a-r-r-e-t."

Richard Clark, sr., testifies on cross-examination, p. 389, that L. A. Barnes was his choice for Congress, and that he voted for him.

Simon Phillips, p. 391, testifies on cross-examination, that he was told L. A. Barnes was on the ticket for Congress, and that he desired to vote that ticket.

John Burnett testifies on cross-examination that he voted for Shipman for Congress.

Ben Clifton testifies on cross-examination that Shipman was running for Congress and that he voted for him.

Joseph Davis testifies on cross-examination, p. 394, that he does not know who was the Republican or Democratic candidate for Congress, and does not know for whom he voted.

Solomon Harris testifies on cross-examination, p. 394, that he voted for Mr. Shipman for Congress.

Murray Bullard testifies on cross-examination, p. 397, that he voted for L. A. Barnes for Congress, and that he was his choice.

Aleck Brown testifies on cross-examination, p. 398, that he believes he voted for Mr. Shipman as a Republican candidate for Congress.

The testimony of the witnesses to be found in the record from page 426 to 450, inclusive, is equally unsatisfactory.

George Hall testifies on cross-examination, p. 427, that he voted for V. J. Shipman as a Republican candidate for Congress.

Echard Doley testifies on cross-examination, p. 429, that he is unable to state positively for whom he voted.

Peter Davis testifies on cross-examination, p. 429, that he voted for Mr. Goodrich, but does not know for what office.

Lewis Spell testifies on cross-examination, p. 429, that he would not know the names of the persons on his ticket, or for what offices they were candidates, if he should hear them called.

Abram Young testifies on cross-examination, p. 430, that he voted for Mr. Goodrich for governor.

Charles Neal testifies on cross-examination, p. 433, that he voted for Goodrich for governor.

Wilson Douglass testifies on cross-examination, p. 437, that he does not know how many candidates there were for Congress in the Second Florida district in the last election or for whom he voted.

Dick Mavins testifies on cross-examination, p. 438, that he does not remember a single name on the ticket, and would not remember them even though they were mentioned to him.

Solomon Joshua, sr., testifies on cross-examination, p. 438, that he voted for Mr. Goodrich and Mr. Shipman as Presidential electors.

Isam Cunningham testifies on cross-examination, p. 439, that he voted for Mr. Shipman for Congress.

Robbin Clifton testifies on cross-examination, p. 439, that Mr. Goodrich was on the ticket for Presidential elector and that he voted for him as such.

George Bessant testifies on cross-examination, p. 442, that in truth and in fact he does not know whose name was on his ballot for Congressional and national positions.

Vanus White testifies on cross-examination, p. 442, that he does not know and will not swear for whom he voted.

James Certain testifies on cross-examination, p. 443, to the same effect.

July Belton testifies on cross-examination, page 444, that as a matter of fact he can not swear anything about the ticket he voted or what names were on it, or whether there was anything on it about Congress or not.

Benjamin Drayton testifies on cross-examination, p. 445, that as a matter of fact he could not swear who were on his ticket when he voted it and what offices they were candidates for.

Charley Drayton testifies on cross-examination, p. 446, to the same effect.

R. M. Witt testifies on his direct examination, p. 446, that he was not a registered voter of Arredonda district No. 12; that he did not offer to register before the registration officer during the month of September, 1888, when the books were opened for registration; that he went to the supervisor of registration to secure a transfer from District No. 7 to District No. 12, but he was unable to fix the date; that the supervisor told him that he would have to go to the commissioners, who were to meet at Doig's Mill, and that when he went to Doig's Mill there was only one of the commissioners present, and he did not succeed in getting a transfer.

William Reuben testifies on cross-examination, p. 448, that he does not know anything about the ticket he voted so as to be able to swear what it was.

James Porter testifies on cross-examination, p. 448, that, with the exception of Martin's name on his ticket, he can not tell what it was or anything about it.

William Woods testifies on cross-examination, p. 449, to the same effect.

The testimony of the witnesses found in the record from page 450 to 454, inclusive, can not be considered for the reason that it was taken after the expiration of the forty days allowed by law and when there was no one present to cross examine the witnesses on behalf of the contestee. As to the construction of contestant that obstructions were interposed to prevent Republicans from registering at this precinct, we submit that the testimony relied upon does not support the charge.

Mr. E. P. Axtell says on cross-examination, p. 366, that he is not able to give the name of a single person who went in his individual capacity before the supervisor and was refused registration after complying with the requirements of the law.

Mr. James Hearns testifies on cross-examination, p. 372, that he does not know anything about the evidence offered by the parties which entitled them to registration or transfer.

It appears from the testimony of contestant's own witnesses that if at any time the registration books were not open at the supervisor's office on the day appointed by law, or of the board of county commissioners failed to meet to hear applications for the corrections of the books, according to the notice given, such failure was due entirely to the prevalence of the yellow fever in that community. We submit that the testimony relied upon is altogether too vague and indefinite to justify the rejection of the official return from this precinct.

It is claimed by the majority that 64 votes duly tendered for contestant were rejected at Hague Station, No. 17, and that they should be counted for him. In our opinion the testimony relied upon is not sufficient to sustain this claim.

As to the claim of the majority that 72 legally qualified voters tendered their votes for contestant in district No. 7, and were improperly rejected, we think the testimony relied upon shows that the persons referred to had failed to comply with the requirements of the law in regard to registration. In answer to the claim that Republican voters were excluded from the polls at this precinct by force, we invite attention to the following testimony:

M. J. MADDOX, being duly sworn as a witness for contestee, deposes as follows:

Question. What is your name, age, and profession?—Answer. M. J. Maddox; age, 32; profession, teacher.

Q. Are you a white or colored person?—A. Colored man.

Q. What election precinct in Alachua County do you live in?—A. Precinct No. 7.

Q. Did you go to the polls at the last general election in Precinct No. 7?—A. I did.

Q. While there did you see any armed parties around or about the polls or any other evidence of intimidation of voters?—A. Certainly I saw nothing of the kind; I saw a gun on the ground; it did not occur to me at the time that it was there for the purpose of intimidation; it was in the possession of a colored man in a buggy; I talked with him about it.

Q. Are you a Republican or a Democrat in politics?—A. I am a Republican.

Q. How long have you resided in the Gainesville precinct, Alachua County?—A. More than four years.

Q. At the regular Republican county convention called for the nomination of Republican candidates for the different county offices, were there any colored men nominated by that convention for any office; and, if yea, what were their names and for what offices were they nominated?—A. There were; M. M. Lewey for county judge and I. C. Sebastion for county assessor.

Q. Were they regarded as good citizens, well qualified to discharge the duties of the offices for which they were nominated?—A. They were both regarded as good citizens, and one of them, Mr. Lewey, was pre-eminently qualified for the position, but the other, Mr. Sebastion, was by some regarded as not qualified.

Q. Was there any charge or complaint that the nomination of Lewey and Sebastion had been procured by any unfair or improper methods?—A. None whatever, to my knowledge.

Q. Were you present and had full opportunity to observe the proceedings of that convention?—A. I was present, and did have full opportunity to observe the proceedings.

ED. FRAZIER, being sworn, says:

Question. What is your name, age, place of residence, and occupation?—A. Edward Frazier; age, 28; I reside in Gainesville; an a common laborer.

Q. Are you a white or colored man?—A. I am a colored man.

Q. In what election precinct in Alachua County do you live?—A. Gainesville precinct.

Q. Were you present throughout the day of the election held in Precinct No. 7, on November 6, 1888?—A. I was.

Q. State whether or not it was quiet and peaceable.—A. Yes; it was.

Q. Did you take an active part on election day among the voters of your color?—A. Yes, sir.

Q. Did you distribute any tickets on election day; if so, about how many?—A. I distributed about 58 to colored voters.

Q. Do you know how many of these tickets were voted by colored men on that day?—A. Yes; 54 were voted.

Q. Did not a great many more colored people vote the Democratic ticket at the last election than at former political elections?—A. Yes, sir.

Q. Do you know of any special reasons why so many colored voters voted the Democratic ticket at the last election?—A. Yes, sir; the reason was that there was a split among the colored people, and they declared before they would vote the split ticket that they would vote a straight Democratic ticket.

Q. Were these 54 tickets that you say were voted by colored voters and the ticket you voted yourself straight Democratic tickets or not ?—A. They were straight Democratic tickets.

B. F. DAWKINS, being duly sworn for contestee, deposes and says :

Question. State name, age, occupation, and place of residence.—Answer. B. F. Dawkins ; 39 years old ; policeman ; Gainesville, Fla.

Q. Were you at the election held in Gainesville precinct in November last ; and, if so, in what capacity did you act ?—A. I was ; a quarantine officer at the time, and ordered at the polls by the chief quarantine officer of the county.

Q. State what your instructions were and what you did on that day.—A. My instructions were to keep the crowd from crowding the polls or the piazza, which I did.

Q. What was the reason for keeping the people from crowding together at the polls or elsewhere ?—A. There were two reasons ; 1st, the inspectors said that they could not conduct the election with such crowded windows, and asked me to keep them from off the piazza and allow only two up at the window at one time ; 2d, they did not want the people living in the town at that time to mix with the people that had refuged from here on account or the yellow-fever epidemic.

Q. You were at the polls throughout the day ; did you see any persons, armed or not armed, interfere, or attempt to interfere, with the right of any elector to vote for the candidate of his choice ?—A. I was at the polls from the time they opened in the morning until eleven o'clock at night ; I did not see any one armed, nor any one interfered with from voting for any one he chose.

Q. Was it or was it not an exceptionally quiet and peaceable election ?—A. The most peaceable I ever saw with such a crowd.

Q. Was there more or less electioneering going on on the ground ?—A. There was.

Q. Did you see any colored men electioneering for the success of the Democratic ticket ?—A. I did ; I saw several around electioneering for the success of the Democratic ticket.

Q. Did you hear any colored men express an opinion how the box was going ?—A. I did ; I heard a good many say that they thought it would go Democratic.

Q. Did you hear them assign any reason why the colored voters were changing from the Republican to the Democratic ticket ?—A. They said they were not satisfied with the Republican candidates.

J. C. BAILIS, being duly sworn for the contestee, deposes and says :

Question. State your name, age, occupation, and residence.—Answer. J. C. Bailis ; 48 years old ; clerk ; Gainesville, Fla.

Q. Were you present at the election held in the Gainesville precinct in November last, and, if so, in what capacity ?—A. I was ; in the capacity of poll clerk.

Q. Mr. Drake, a witness for the contestant, has stated in his opinion an error was made by you in the transposition of the two Congressional candidates' names, Bullock and Goodrich ; state if any transposition was necessary ; if so, was any error made therein ?—A. There was no transposition made ; none was necessary. No, there was no error made ; there was no chance for any error in the way of transposition.

Q. The returns show that the Republican Presidential electors received more votes at the Gainesville box than the Republican Congressional candidates ; Mr. Drake attempts to account for this by a supposed error of yours in transposition ; you say there was no error in transposing the name ; how do you account for the difference in the vote ?—A. Well, I account for it from the fact that Mr. Bullock would naturally draw some votes from the Republican votes ; there are of my own knowledge Northern men here who told me that they voted for the county Democratic and Congressional candidates, Robert Bullock ; in other words, voted the whole Democratic ticket except the Presidential electors ; that they were National Republicans, but could not vote with the negro.

Q. What State are you a native, and how long have you resided in Florida ?—A. Native of New York State, and resided in Florida about seven years.

Q. State, if you know, what action was taken by the sheriff on the day of the election to keep the poll from being too crowded, and at whose request, and for what reason ?—A. The room was very dark, and that it was a dark day ; the police were unable to keep the door and window clear ; at the general request of the managers of the election the sheriff was asked to clear the yard, and admit voters only in groups of two and three, in order to give all an opportunity to vote without crowding, and to lessen the danger of infection from yellow fever, as it was reported that several suspected cases were present on the grounds ; no objections were made to this action on the part of the sheriff, and the voting proceeded in an orderly manner till the closing of the polls, and more rapidly than previous to this action. It is a fact, too, that the yellow fever broke out in the house in two days after the election in which the polling-place was held.

Q. Was any rioting or intimidation of voters, or was the election a quiet and peaceable one ?—A. There was no rioting or intimidation, and I never saw a more quiet and peaceable election.

Q. Electors, then, were allowed to deposit their ballot for the candidates of their choice without hindrance or interference from any one ?—A. I saw nothing that could be construed as a hindrance or interference.

HART JOHNSON, a witness for the contestee, being sworn, says :

Question. What is your name, age, and place of residence ?—Answer. Hart Johnson ; aged 30 years ; reside in Gainsville, Fla.

Q. Where were you on the 6th day of November, 1888 ?—A. I was in Gainsville.

Q. Were you at the polls of district No. 7 that day ?—A. I was.

Q. Did you see Mr. Wienges, the sheriff, or any of his deputies around with Winchester rifles or other guns on that day ?—A. I did not.

Q. Were you at the polls all day ?—A. I was.

Q. If there was any intimidation there that day, and if there had been any persons armed with Winchester rifles or other guns, would you have seen them ?—A. I would.

Q. And you say you did not see anything of the kind that day ?—A. No, sir ; I did not.

Q. Describe the manner in which the election was conducted as to voting.—A. They were placed two to two ; there was a line struck from the gate and orders given for them to go up two and two.

Q. Why were the people placed in line this way ? Was it to keep the people from crowding up to the polls ?—A. It was.

Q. Did the voting go on more rapidly after this line was made than before ?—A. There was more quietness kept after it was struck ; they voted more regular than before.

Q. Were all voters, white and black, Democrats and Republicans, required to conform to this rule as to going up and voting two by two ?—A. They were.

Q. It is not a fact that the county board of health gave Mr. Wienges, the chief quarantine officer of this county, orders to keep the people from crowding together as much as possible on account of the prevalence of yellow fever in Gainsville at that time, so as to prevent the yellow fever from spreading ?—A. It is a fact.

Q. Is it not a fact that the white and colored voters were joking and jesting with each other in regard to the result of the election on that day ?—A. They were.

Q. How long have you been a member of the Republican party in Alachua County ?—A. About twenty-four years.

Q. Are you a white man or a black man ?—A. I am a black man.

Q. Is it not a fact that two colored men, Lewey and Sebastian, were nominated for the offices of county judge and county tax assessor by the regularly called Republican county convention in this county previous to the last election ?—A. This is a fact.

JAMES B. CULLEN, being duly sworn for the contestee, deposes and says :

Q. State your name, age, occupation, and place of residence.—A. James B. Cullen; 48 years old ; deputy sheriff, Gainesville, Fla.

Q. State how long you have been a resident of Florida, and where you came from, and what brought you here.—A. I have been [here] over twenty-three years; from New York State; I was brevet major in the 7th Infantry United States Army, and was ordered here, and resigned from the Army in 1868, and have remained here ever since.

Q. State whether or not you were at the polls at the last election held in November in this precinct, number 7, and whether there was any intimidation of voters at the polls.—A. I was at the polls from the time they opened until they closed. There was no intimidation ; the colored men were by themselves; the whites kept from them on account of hearing of suspects of yellow fever among them, and the election was as quiet as any I ever saw. I was at the polls in the capacity of deputy sheriff and assistant quarantine officer. Our orders were from the board of health to keep the crowd from gathering in large numbers. I saw no guns nowhere on the grounds.

Q. State whether or not the orders of the board, above referred to, in keeping the crowd from gathering in large numbers, prevented any person in any way, shape, or form, or in any way hindered or delayed them from voting.—A. It did not.

Q. State whether you saw any colored people working in the interest of the Democratic ticket; and, if they gave any reasons in your presence for so doing, state them.—A. There was a good many working for the success of the Democratic party. The reason of this action of the voters was that the Republican county executive had displaced two regularly Republican nominees, colored men, and put two white men on in their place. The colored people were very much incensed about the two colored men being taken down. This incense was shown on the streets of Gainsville before the day of election, and they did not intend to vote the Republican ticket.

Q. State if you are familiar with the elections in Florida for the past eighteen or twenty years; and, if so, whether you did not observe a greater disposition on the part of the colored voters to break away from party lines at the last election and vote for whom they please than ever before.—A. I have been here ever since the first election was held here after the war, and at most every election as deputy sheriff. I did observe a greater disposition to break away from party lines than heretofore, and think one reason was that they was left to some extent without leaders on account of the yellow fever.

Q. State what the reason was, if the inspectors gave you any, for keeping the crowd from the window.—A. It was so dark is one reason, and nearly suffocating on account of heat, being only one window by which we could vote or get light. After that they were put outside of the gate, and the election or voting proceeded very rapidly by letting two go to the polls to vote without one pushing the other, as was done heretofore.

ARCH GREEN, being duly sworn as a witness for contestee, deposes as follows:

Question. What is your name, age, place of residence, and occupation?—Answer. Arch Green; age, 35; Gainesville, Fla.; occupation, teamster.

Q. Are you a white man or colored man?—A. Colored man.

Q. What election precinct in Alachua County do you live in?—A. Gainesville precinct No. 7.

Q. Were you present throughout the day at the election held in precinct No. 7 on November 6, 1888?—A. I was.

Q. State whether or not the election was quiet and peaceable?—A. It was peaceable.

Q. Did you see Mr. Wienges, the chief quarantine officer and sheriff, or any of his deputies, on that day with Winchester rifles and threatening to interfere with the right of any person, white or black, to vote?—A. No; I did not.

Q. So, then, if there had been any intimidation of voters by these officers on that occasion you would certainly have known it?—A. I would.

Q. Were you at the polls that day distributing tickets; and, if so, what was the character of the tickets?—A. I was there distributing tickets; I had some Democratic tickets and some Republican tickets.

Q. About how many straight Democratic tickets did you distribute to colored voters on that day?—A. About fifty or seventy-five, I suppose.

Q. About how many of these Democratic tickets that you distributed to colored voters on that day you have reason to believe were voted?—A. I suppose about fifty that I was sure were voted.

Q. Why is it that you think that so many colored men voted the straight Democratic ticket at the last election ; was it because some of the white Republican nominees refused to run on the ticket with the colored Republican nominees?—A. That is the very reason they did it; because we had some white nominees on the ticket who said they would not run with the colored nominees.

S. H. WIENGES.

Question. What is your name and place of residence?—Answer. S. H. Wienges Gainesville, Fla.

Q. Did you hold any official position in Alachua County on the 6th day of November, 1888; if so, what was it?—A. I did; I was sheriff of Alachua County and chief quarantine officer.

Q. Where were you and what doing on the 6th of November, 1888?—A. I was at the voting place of precinct 7, Alachua County, and acting under instructions from the board of health principally.

Q. On that day and at that place were there any armed men around the polls of precinct 7?—A. I did not see any myself, but heard there was one party with a gun before I got there.

Q. Was this person who you heard had a gun a white man or a black man, Republican or Democrat?—A. He was a black man, and I presume a Republican.

Q. Did you have any deputies there who were armed with rifles on that day?—A. I did not.

Q. You have stated that you were acting principally as chief quarantine officer under the board of health; state what your instructions were from said board?—A. My instructions were not to allow crowds to congregate for fear of spreading the fever.

Q. Please state the condition relative to the health of Gainesville at that time.—A. We had the yellow fever here.

Q. Had the yellow fever been epidemic in Gainesville at that time by the duly constituted officers?—A. It was declared epidemic.

Q. In the discharge of your duties as health officer was there any discrimination made by you or those acting under you in favor of or against either the Democratic or Republican electors?—A. There were none, only in one case; a colored man who claimed to be sick **asked** if I would not get him to the polls so that he could vote and get out of the rain, that it was raining; I got the crowd to open a way for him and passed him inside of the line; with this one exception, whenever there was a white man there, my instructions was to my deputy, who was at the gate, to pass one white and one colored at a time; if no white man was present, then two colored men was to pass at a time.

Q. State the order or manner of voting that day, as to placing the crowd as they approach the polls.—A. The crowd was outside of the yard, about 60 or 70 feet from the house; they were allowed to come in two at a time; two at the piazza, two were held back at the gate inside of the line, until one who was in the piazza had voted; then the two who were in line at the gate were permitted to go to the polls, and two more were taken inside of the line.

Q. Prior to the adoption of this method had the voters crowded the polling place or not?—A. They had; they were crowded into the piazza so that the inspectors called on me to remove them from the window so as to allow them to get some fresh air.

Q. Please give a description of the room in which they voted, the number of windows, and what effect crowding around the voting place produced?—A. The room was a front room of the house, with two doors leading into it, one from an entry and another from a back room; the voting was done from the window on the south side of the house; I don't know whether or not there was any other window to the house.

JOSEPH SHANNON, being duly sworn for the contestee, says:

Question. What is your name, age, occupation, and residence?—Answer. Joseph A. Shannon; 47; farmer; Gainesville, Alachua County, Florida.

Q. Were you present at the general election held in November last at precinct number 7, Alachua County?—A. I was.

Q. State whether or not the election was quiet and peaceable?—A. It was.

Q. Were you there throughout the day, and did you see any intimidation of voters by members of either political party?—A. I was there and saw no intimidation.

Q. Did you see any parties there armed with Winchester rifles or other guns?—A. I saw a negro there with a double-barrel shotgun.

Q. If there had been armed parties there, interfering with the right of any person to vote, you would certainly have seen and known, would you?—A. Yes; I would known it.

Q. You state positively that there was no such occurrence at the polls on that day.—A. I do.

W. A. WALTERS, being duly sworn for contestee, says:

Question. State your name, age, and profession.—Answer. W. A. Walters; 39 years old; minister of the gospel.

Q. Are you a white man or a colored man?—A. Colored man.

Q. Are you a Democrat or Republican in politics?—A. Republican.

Q. What election precinct in Alachua County do you live in?—A. Gainesville, precinct number 7.

Q. Were you present throughout the day at the election held in precinct number 7, in Alachua County, in 1888?—A. I was from 10 o'clock until the polls closed.

Q. State whether the election was quiet and peaceable or not.—A. It was; appeared so to me.

Q. Did there seem to be a friendly feeling between the white and colored voters, and were they not laughing and jesting about the election with one another?—A. They were.

Q. Did you see any armed parties there threatening to interfere with the right of any persons, either Republicans or Democrats, to vote?—A. I did not.

Q. Did you see Mr. Winges, the sheriff and quarantine officer, or any of his deputies there on that day; and, if so, state what they did as far as under your observation?—A. I saw Mr. Winges and his deputies there keeping peace and everything quiet.

Q. Did they have Winchester rifles or any other arms?—A. If they did I did not see it. and I was there all day long.

Q. So, then, if there had been any intimidation of voters by these officers on that occasion you would have certainly known it?—A. Yes; I would.

Q. State, if you know, whether it was not the understanding among the electors that on account of the prevalence of yellow fever in precinct No. 7 they were expected and required to go to the polls singly, deposit the ballot, and retire without intermingling more than possible?—A. They were.

Q. Did you see the sheriff and his deputies make an effort to keep the people from massing together in crowds at any one point, and did these officers state why they did so?—A. They did. Mr. Winges and his officers stated why they were at the gate, and told them it was on account of yellow fever, and they must not assemble too much together; that they could not all vote at once.

It is claimed by the majority in their report that in—

District No. 20, forty-nine duly qualified electors tendered their votes for contestant and were refused.

District No. 10, thirty-three qualified electors tendered their votes for contestant and were refused.

District No. 6, fifty qualified electors tendered their votes for contestant and were refused.

District No. 2, forty-six qualified electors tendered their votes for contestant and were refused.

District No. 16, six legal voters tendered ballots for contestant and were refused.

District No. 11, ninety qualified electors tendered their ballots for contestant and were refused.

District No. 3, ten legally qualified voters tendered their ballots for contestant and were rejected.

District No. 19, seventeen qualified voters tendered their ballots for con-. testant and were refused.

District No. 1 (Waldo), twenty-three qualified voters tendered their votes for contestant and were refused.

District No. 15, fifty qualified electors tendered their votes for con- testant and were refused.

Without undertaking to make here a critical examination of the tes- timony relating to the several claims hereinbefore mentioned, we deem it sufficient to say that we can not concur with the majority in holding that the proof of the qualification of the voters referred to is satisfac- tory, and that their votes should be counted as if cast. The testimony shows that as a general rule the witnesses did not know the sections, township, and range included in said districts so as to enable them to state positively that the persons claiming to be voters were legally qualified to vote in said districts; it shows in many instances that the persons claiming to be voters had not applied to the supervisor of reg- istration as the law requires to have their names placed upon the reg- istration lists; it shows that the supervisor of registration was inter- rupted in the discharge of his duties by the prevalence of the yellow fever, and that the board of county commissioners were prevented . from meeting at the time and place designated by the same cause; it shows that in many instances the persons referred to failed to do what they were required to do in order to register, or to have their names restored to the registration lists if they had been improperly stricken off.

We submit that the burden of proof is upon the contestant, and that the testimony adduced by him is not sufficient to impeach the official conduct of sworn officers, charged with the duty of ascertaining and declaring the result of the election in this county.

When it is remembered that in the county of Alachua at the Con- gressional election held in 1886 the Democratic candidate received 1,900 votes, and the Republican candidate received 1,742 votes, and when we take into consideration the complete disorganization of the Republican party in that county in the contest of 1888, it can not be a matter of surprise that the county gave a Democratic majority for the contestee. Indeed, no other result could have reasonably been anticipated.

It appears from the record that there was an open rupture in the ranks of the Republican party, and, as a natural result, many colored Republicans voted the Democratic ticket and contributed largely to the increase of the Democratic vote. The testimony shows that two colored Republicans, who were men of character and extensive influence in the county and had been fairly nominated by the regular Republican convention, were unceremoniously stricken from the Republican county committee because they were colored men, and that J. T. Watts, a prominent colored man, who formerly represented the district in Congress, was summarily removed by the same committee as county chairman. To show the state of feeling existing among Republicans in that county we present the following testimony:

HENRY C. DENTON, a witness for contestee, being duly sworn, deposes as follows:

Question. State your name and residence.—Answer. Henry C. Denton; Gainsville, Fla.

Q. Was you present at the polls at precinct No. 7 at any time during the day on the day of the last general election?—A. I was; in the afternoon.

Q. Did you see any colored men on that day and at that place distributing Democratic tickets and otherwise electioneering for the success of the Democratic party?—A. I can't say that I did, as I was there only a short while. I went there to vote and drove back to Arredonda, and did not have time to see how things were going.

Q. Were you present at the election at Arredonda? And, if so, state whether you saw any colored men there working in the interest of the Democratic party.—A. I was present there on election day and saw a good many colored men working in the interest of the Democratic party. I distributed tickets at both Gainesville and Arredonda. There were a good many colored men at Gainesville who promised me to vote the Democratic ticket, and waited until I came up and distributed tickets before they voted. I saw several colored men vote the Democratic ticket at Arredonda, but did not at Gainesville, as I came up in a borrowed vehicle and could not remain long.

Q. You say that you distributed Democratic tickets to the colored voters at Gainesville box, and that these electors waited until you came in the afternoon in order to obtain their tickets from you. Did they say to you that they intended to vote the Democratic ticket, and did they ask you for that kind of a ballot?—A. They did.

Q. You say that you distributed Democratic tickets at the Arredonda box. Was this near the polls, and did you see any colored voters who obtained their tickets from you go immediately to the polls with their folded ballot?—A. I did distribute tickets at the Arredonda box; was right at the polls and saw them put them in. Collison and Martin, Republican distributors of tickets, were some distance off in the woods distributing tickets, and we changed quite a number of them.

Q. You have heretofore resided at Arredonda and was temporarily living there during the prevalence of yellow fever in Gainesville. State whether or not there was great dissatisfaction among the colored Republicans there growing out of the action of the county Republican executive committees removing two colored county nominees and substituting in their place two white Republicans. State fully what result this action had upon the colored Republican voters in that precinct.—A. I resided in Arredonda from 1875 to 1881, and was temporarily living there when the election took place. The action of the county Republican executive committee in removing two colored nominees and substituting two white Republicans caused great dissatisfaction among the colored voters at that precinct.

Q. Was or was it not common talk among the colored Republicans at Arredonda before and on election day that they would pay off the Republican party for ignoring their race at the polls?—A. Yes.

Q. Is it not a fact that the action of the Republican county executive committee caused many colored voters to vote the Democratic ticket at the last election at that precinct?—A. That is a fact that can not be denied.

Q. Did not kicking of Gen. J. T. Walls out of the chairmanship of the Republican county executive committee also add to their dissatisfaction and determination for revenge upon their white Republican friends?—A. It certainly did.

Q. Is it not within your knowledge by experience, as well as observation, that colored men who voted the Democratic ticket at former as well as at the last election, who are so desirous of concealing the fact by fear of some of their own race that they would bitterly deny it, and some even to the extent of denying it under oath?—A. I have known many instances of that kind. I mean to convey the idea that they voted the Democratic ticket and deny it, but so far as denying it under oath I could not say.

Q. You say you were distributing Democratic tickets at Arredonda. Did you give any colored men tickets to distribute, and do you know whether they distributed them or not?—A. I did distribute tickets to colored voters at Arredonda, and know of several colored men who were distributing them also.

JOSIAH T. WALLS, being duly sworn as a witness for contestee, deposes as follows:

Question. What is your name; in what election district in Alachua County,

H. Mis. 137——39

Florida, did you reside and vote at the election held November 6, 1888 ?—A. Josiah T. Walls; 1 voted at Arredonda Precinct No. 12. and reside there.

Q. How long have you been a resident and voter of No. 12 district ?—A. Since 1877.

Q. Were you present at or near the polls on November 6, 1888, at Arredonda No. 12; if so, how long ?—A. I was; from about 7 a. m. to 10 p. m.

Q. What official position in the Republican party did you hold in this State on that day ?—A. I was a member of the State central committee.

Q. Were you or not a delegate to the county Republican convention that met in Gainesville, Alachua County, Florida, to put a county ticket in the field, and did you take part in said convention, and did said convention nominate and put a ticket in the field or not ?—A I was, and they did put a ticket in the field.

Q. Did said convention make an executive committee for the county; and, if so, who was the chairman of said committee ?—A. It did, and I was elected chairman of the committee.

Q. Did you as chairman call the committee together the next day ?—A. I did not call the committee together; the convention passed an order for committee to meet, and I was elected chairman at that time.

Q. Were you present at the meeting of the committee held in pursuance of the resolution passed by the convention ?—A. I was.

Q. What was the object for which said committee was called together ?—A. It was ordered by the convention that the committee meet the next morning at 9 o'clock and organize by electing a chairman and secretary; that was all the resolution embodied.

Q. What, if anything else, was done by said committee when it met and organized the day after the convention adjourned ?—A. After the committee had organized Mr. Barnes, J. E. Webster, and Mr. Callison appeared before the committee and stated that they declined to run as candidates on the county ticket if Mr. Lewey and Mr. Sebastion, two colored men, remained on the ticket.

Q. Did the committee take any action that you thought they were empowered to do under any resolution, call, or authority, or precedent at said meeting ?—A. They did not.

Q. Were Lewey and Sebastion, the two colored candidates nominated by the convention, displaced from said ticket at said meeting of the committee ?—A. They were.

Q. Was there not protest made by you and others in said committee meeting against said action, and did you and others point out that the drawing of the color line by Barnes, Webster, and Callison would lead to a rupture and the disintegration of the Republican party in this county ?—A. We did.

Q. Were you not called away a few days afterward to go on the State canvass with the Republican candidate for governor, V. J. Shipman ? · A. I was.

Q. Upon your return from the canvass were you not taken sick with what was at that time reported yellow fever, and upon your recovery did you or not address a letter to Webster and Barnes in relation to the removal of Lewey and Sebastion from the county ticket, and was it an open letter or not ?—A. I was taken sick, as stated, and on my recovery did address a letter to Webster and Barnes in reference to the removal of Lewey and Sebastion; the letter was dated September 22, 1888.

Q. As a result, then, there were two Republican county tickets in the field on the day of the election ?—A. There was.

Q Did not the action of Barnes, Webster, and Callison engender a very bitter feeling among the white and colored Republicans, and did not a considerable number of the colored people, including many of the old leaders in the party in the different precincts, regard it as an insult to their rights and their intelligence to be told by white men that to be a colored man was a disqualification to be a candidate on the Republican ticket for a county office ?—A. It did create considerable feeling; the people resented it by their votes, and it certainly changed the result of the election in this county, and there were not less than 700 colored voters in Alachua County who voted the Democratic ticket for county officers.

Q. From your knowledge of the politics of this county are you able to say that this bitter feeling between the white and colored Republicans did affect the entire Republican ticket throughout the county ?—A. It affected it to some extent.

Q. Was not there more interest displayed and taken by the colored people at the last election in district No. 12 in the election of the Democratic county ticket and the defeat of Webster and Barnes than there was about any other part of the ticket ?—A. There was.

Q. Were you in Arredonda the night preceding the election, and did you see Mr. L. A. Barnes, the chairman of Republican State campaign committee, and also of the county campaign committee, and candidate for clerk of the court, and did he have any conversation with you an. others; if so, state as near as you can what that conversation was ?—A. Yes; I was at Arredonda, at Chesnut & Stringfellow's store; I met Mr. Barnes there, and the following conversat on took place: He requested me to support him for clerk of the court; that he had always been my friend; that he did not care anything about the rest of the ticket; and whether he was elected or not he wanted Henry Denton elected as tax collector, and he seemed to be excited, and says: "In short, I do not care a damn just so Bill Sheats was defeated as superintendent of schools."

Q. Was Henry Denton the candidate on the Democratic ticket for tax collector at the last election or not?—A. Yes.

Q. From th; best of your information, knowledge, and belief did not a larger number of colored people vote the Democratic ticket at the last election than at any election prior thereto? Was not that defection caused, in your opinion, by the drawing of the color line for candidates?—A. Yes; and it was caused by drawing the color line.

VIRGIL GEORGE, being sworn, says:

Question. What is your name, age, and place of residence?—Answer. Virgil George; aged 66 years of age; reside at Arredonda Precinct No. 12.

Q. Are you a white man or a colored man?—A. I am a colored man.

Q. Where were you and what were you doing on the 6th day of last November, 1 88, the day of the last general election?—A. I was in Arredonda Precinct, No. 12, Alachua County, Florida, and one of the managers of the election in precinct No. 12.

- Q. Were you a Republican or Democrat manager of the election?—A. I was a Republican manager.

Q. Were you in the room where the ballot-box was kept where the election was carried on during that day and all of the time up to the end of the counting of the ballots?—A. I was.

Q. Did you and the other inspectors keep the ballot-box on the table by the window in full view of the public?—A. Yes; we did.

Q. Did you keep the ballot-box by the window and keep the window open all during the day and up to the time the counting was commenced?—A. Yes; we did.

Q. As an inspector will you swear that you, together with other inspectors, counted the ballots as cast in that ballot-box, and returned them as they were counted; and is it not a fact that you can read and write and kept a tally-sheet of the counting?—A. Yes; that is a fact.

Q. Is it not a fact that the ballot-box remained on the table with the window open after the polls had closed till a light was obtained to commence the counting?—A. It is a fact.

Q. Were there any colored and white people standing outside watching the box all this time to see that everything was kept straight?—A. There was during this time.

Q. Were they Republicans or Democrats or both?—A. Both Democrats and Republicans.

Q. Did you or any of the other inspectors allow any person to come inside the room where the ballot-box was during the day and up to the time you commenced counting the ballots or not? A. We did not.

Q. You say you staid in the room all day and up to the time the ballots were counted; were you very careful to keep your eyes on the ballot-box and watch it all during the day and up to the time the count was commenced, so as to perform your full duty as an inspector?—A. Yes, sir; I did.

Q. Are you willing to swear, as an inspector, that there was no tampering with the ballot-box done, and that the votes were counted as cast?—A. Yes, I am.

Q. It has been charged, and attempted to be proved, by the contestant, that you were in a state of intoxication that day and disqualified as an inspector to discharge your duty. Is this charge true or false?—A. It is false; I neither tasted or smelled or saw a drop of liquor that day, and I discharged my duty as an inspector to the best of my ability, so help me God.

Q. Then the charge that you were intoxicated with liquor on that day, while you were acting as inspector, is absolutely false and without foundation, is it?—A. It is false.

Q. How long have you been a member of the Republican party in this county; and have you always voted the straight Republican ticket up to the time of the last election?—A. 24 years; always voted the straight Republican ticket until the last election.

AMOS GEORGE, a witness for contestee, being sworn, deposes as follows:

Question. State your name, place of residence, and color.—Answer. Amos George; live at Arredonda precinct, Alachua County, District No. 12; black man.

Q. Where were you on the 6th day of November last, and what were you doing on said day, the same being general election?—A. I was at Arredonda trying to cast my vote.

Q. Were you engaged in distributing tickets on that day at that precinct; and, if so, what sort of tickets?—A. I distributed a good deal of tickets among my friends, who said they were going to vote them.

Q. Were the tickets you distributed among your friends Republican or Democratic tickets?—A. They said they were Democratic tickets. I am a Democrat myself.

Q. Did those persons to whom you distributed these Democratic tickets tell you

that they intended to vote the same?—A. Yes, sir; all of them said they were going
to vote same ticket I did.

Q. Were these per-ons to whom you distributed tickets white or black persons?—
A. They were all colored, like myself.

Q. Do you know of any other colored man who was distributing Democratic tickets
that day at Arredonda?—A. I do not know positively of any colored man distributing Democratic tickets that day. A heap of them used Democratic tickets that day,
but would not own to it.

Q. Do you mean to say that a good many colored men at Arredonda that day voted
the Democratic ticket, but do not now own to the same?—A. Yes, sir; lots of them
there voted the Democratic ticket, but are ashamed to own it now.

Q. Did you hear any of these colored persons at Arredonda that day say that they
had voted the Democratic ticket?—A. Yes, sir; I heard lots of them say it.

Q. Do they now deny it because they are afraid of the colored Republican leaders?—A. Yes; the colored people are afraid of one another, and go and vote the
Democratic ticket, and now they don't own it; I voted the Democratic ticket and
they did it.

Q. Were these tickets you distributed the straight Democratic ticket, containing
the names of all the Democratic nominees?- A. They told me they were straight
Democratic tickets; I told them I wanted nothing but straight Democratic tickets.

So far as Alachua County is concerned, we submit in view of all the
testimony that the official returns have not been successfully assailed,
and that the vote should be counted as returned.

HAMILTON COUNTY.

We concur with the majority in holding that the 13 votes in district
No. 3, duly tendered for contestant and rejected upon the ground that
the voters had changed their residences from one place to another in
the same precinct, should be counted for him. While section 8 of the
act of June 7, 1887, may possibly admit of a different construction, we
are inclined to the opinion that a mere change of residence from one
house to another in the same voting precinct should not deprive an
elector of his right to vote. We also concur with the majority in holding that the 104 votes cast for contestant and the 2 votes cast for contestee in district No. 2, which were thrown out because there was a
printer's dash under the names of some of the candidates on the tickets,
should be counted. We do not believe that this was such a distinguishing mark as justified the rejection of these ballots.

The same remark may be made as to the 48 votes claimed for contestant in district No. 7. We also agree with the majority in holding
that 18 additional votes should be counted for contestant in district
No. 5; but we do not think that the 18 additional votes claimed in
district No. 3 should be allowed to the contestant. It will be noticed
that the witness relied upon to establish this claim does not pretend to
know that the persons referred to were legally qualified voters under
the laws of Florida.

As to the result of our examination, we have come to the conclusion
that 183 additional votes should be counted for the contestant in this
county, and 2 additional votes for the contestee.

DUVAL COUNTY.

We concur with the majority in the opinion that the 13 ballots for
contestant in district No. 8 and the 1 ballot for contestee, which were
rejected on the claim that they had specks on them, should be counted.
We also think that the 9 ballots for contestant in district No. 21, which
were thrown out on the ground that there was a printer's dash on them,
should be counted; but we think that the 45 votes for contestant in
district No. 6 were properly rejected, because the name of one of the

candidates on the ticket was written with a red lead pencil. We also agree that the 12 additional votes claimed for contestant in district No. 12 should be counted. We do not agree to the claim made for contestant of 12 additional votes in district No. 8, 8 additional votes in district No. 21, 1 additional vote in district No. 23, 29 additional votes in district No. 17, 3 additional votes in district No. 18, 39 additional votes in district No. 20, 3 additional votes in district No: 6, 26 additional votes in district No. 15, 3 additional votes in district No. 7, 75 additional votes in district No. 16, 28 additional votes in district No. 19, 62 additional votes in district No. 22, and 18 additional votes in district No. 13.

An examination of the testimony relied upon to establish these several claims will show, we think, that it is legally insufficient for the purpose intended. It is not the best evidence which could have been produced. The persons themselves should have been called and required to testify. Such hearsay evidence as is relied upon is not admissible; but if it should be accepted, it proves that the votes of nearly all the persons referred to were rejected because they failed to produce the certificate of registration required.

As the result of our investigation, we credit contestant with 34 additional votes in this county and the contestee with 1.

DADE COUNTY.

There was no charge of fraud in this county, and it appears that the vote returned was about the usual vote as cast in preceding elections. We concur with the majority that the vote as returned from this county should be counted.

COLUMBIA COUNTY.

We concur with the majority that 127 additional votes should be counted for the contestant in this county.

PUTNAM COUNTY.

We concur with the majority in the opinion that 15 additional votes should be counted for contestant in this county.

VOLUSIA COUNTY.

As to the 31 votes claimed in this county for contestant, it appears from the testimony that they were rejected by the inspectors because the names of the persons offering them were not found on the registration list, and in the absence of proof to the contrary there is a legitimate presumption that they were properly rejected. It has been repeatedly decided by the House of Representatives that the acts of proper officers, acting within the sphere of their duties, must be presumed to be correct, unless shown to be otherwise.

ORANGE COUNTY.

We concur with the majority of the committee in the opinion that 31 additional votes should be counted for contestant in this county, but we do not think that the 9 votes claimed should be allowed, because it appears that the names of eight of the persons referred to had been stricken from the registration list, and that the other one had been convicted of larceny.

MARION COUNTY.

We differ from the majority in holding that the 83 ballots for contestant at Fautville precinct, thrown out because certain names were written in red ink, should be counted. It appears from the testimony that the inspectors were unanimous in the rejection of those ballots; that it was not known at the time of their rejection whether they had on them the names of the Democratic or Republican candidates, and they were rejected solely for the reason that they were written in red ink. Section 23 of the Florida election laws of 1887 provides as follows·

The voting shall be by ballot, which ballot shall be plain white paper, clear and even cut, without ornaments, designation, mutilation, symbol, or mark of any kind whatever, except the name or names of the person or persons voted for and the office to which such person or persons are intended to be chosen, which name or names and office or officers shall be written or printed, or partly written and partly printed, thereon in black ink or with black pencil, and such ballot shall be so folded as to conceal the name or names thereon, and so folded shall be deposited in a box to be constructed, kept, and disposed of as hereinafter provided, and *no ballot of any other description found in any election box shall be counted.*

We do not concur with the majority in the opinion that, in addition to the 83 votes referred to, 466 votes should be counted for the contestant in this county. A careful examination of the testimony relied upon can not fail to impress the impartial reader with the idea that many of the witnesses did not know what they were testifying about. As an illustration, we furnish from numerous examples the following:

Elias Jackson testifies, p. 856, as follows:

Q. What is Congress?—A. Mr. Williams told me to vote for the Pugrakin nominee.
Q. Is Congress a man or a woman?—A. I think it is a woman, a black woman.

Henry White, p. 842, testifies as follows:

Q. Who was the Republican nominee for Congress in the Second Congressional district of Florida at the election held November 6, 1888. and who was the Democratic nominee?—A. Bob Ingersoll, Republican, and John Sherman was the Democratic nominee.

As to the suggestion of the majority that E. M. Gregg, supervisor of registration, was actuated by a deliberate and wicked purpose to deprive Republican voters of their rights, we submit that it is not sustained by the evidence. To sustain this charge the testimony of one Jesse Reddick has been offered. An examination of his testimony will show that it bears upon its face internal evidence of falsehood, and that it can not be accepted as true. As further proof that the statement of the said Reddick is utterly unworthy of credit, we call attention to the affidavits which have been furnished and filed with the committee, and appended to this report.

As to the "side boxes" referred to in the testimony of Monroe, Tidwell, and Robinson, we submit that they were used without any authority of law, and that the so-called returns made from them are entirely worthless for the purpose of setting aside the official returns made from the ballot-boxes provided by law and by the sworn officers of the election. We call attention to the testimony of E. M. Gregg, supervisor of registration, as a complete refutation of the charges preferred against him, and as showing that he made no discrimination whatever between Republicans and Democrats in the discharge of his official duties

To sustain the testimony of Mr. Gregg upon the issue referred to we present the following :

July Brown, colored, p. 976, testifies that he acted on the police force in the city of Ocala five years, and also as deputy sheriff at different times during the past seven years; that he is personally acquainted with the colored men whose names are enumerated; that he knows said persons changed their places of residence betw_·en September 3, 1887, and November 6, 1888, and that he notified the registration officer of said change of residence.

J. D. Williams, deputy sheriff, testifies, p. 977, that he was well acquainted with the persons whose names are given; that they changed their residences within the Ocala precinct between the 3d day of September, 1887, and 6th day of November, 1888, and that he so notified E. M. Gregg, the registration officer.

E. L. Ferguson testifies, p. 979, that the persons whose names are given changed their places of residence from one point to another in the same district, or from one district to another, between the 3d day of September, 1887, and the 6th day of November, 1888, and that he so notified the supervisor of registration.

So far as this county is concerned, we submit that the contestee has more cause of complaint than the contestant. The testimony shows that at Ocala precinct the friends and supporters of the contestant adopted the most unwarrantable methods to prevent the free exercise of their rights and privileges by the voters. (See testimony of B. F. Lyons, p. 966, and J. T. Lancaster, p. 967, and E. S. Williams, p. 967.)

MADISON COUNTY.

We can not agree with the majority of the committee as to the result reached in this county. Without undertaking to make a critical examination in this report of all the testimony relating to the county of Madison, we adopt as substantially correct the following views of the contestee's attorney as contained in his brief:

We propose to notice briefly his claim in the several districts. In the Cherry Lake district, No. 7, he claims one hundred and thirty-one (131) votes upon the ground that the regularly appointed officers of the election were so intimidated that they refused to open the polls, and that under the circumstances the Republicans elected a board of election officers, who held an election at a different place from that appointed by law, at which place one hundred and thirty-one (131) votes were cast for contestant.

The testimony of M. H. Waring, p. 225, shows that an election was held about a quarter of a mile from the regular polling place by inspectors chosen by the bystanders, all of whom were Republicans; that said election was not recognized by the Democrats as valid, and that none but Republicans participated in it.

Charles Hayes testifies, p. 236, that none but Republicans took part in the so-called election in the Cherry Lake precinct, that all of the inspectors were colored men, and that they had no registration list showing who were the legally qualified voters.

J. F. Livingston testifies, p. 238, that some colored man, whose name he does not know, brought to him as supervisor of registration a ballot-box purporting to come from Cherry Lake precinct, and that he had opened the ballot box to get a book from it.

The testimony of H. B. Coffee, G. W. Barnard, J. L. Edwards, W. Townsend, and Richard Boyd, taken by contestee and found in the supplemental record showing the "Testimony from Madison County," proves that no election was held at the regular polling place in Cherry Lake precinct, that the regularly appointed inspectors were apprehensive of an attack at night from the colored people, who had collected and deposited guns near to the regular polling place, and that the inspectors, fearing that their lives would be endangered, declined to open the polls. Whatever may be thought of the reasonableness of the apprehension of personal danger, which they evidently felt, and their failure to perform the duties required of them by law, we submit that the vote claimed for the contestant at this precinct can not properly be counted for him. There was no election held in this precinct. The persons who undertook to conduct an election had no authority whatever to open polls at a place different from that appointed by law, and the Democratic voters, well knowing that fact, declined to recognize or to participate at all in the so-called election. The provisions of law which fix the time or place of holding elections are to be construed as mandatory and not as merely directory. The reason for this is obvious. Every voter is presumed to know the law, and to be thereby informed as to the time when and the place where he may deposit his ballot; but if that time or place be changed without proper authority and due notice, no voter can be held as legally bound to take notice of the change. (See McCrary on American Law of Elections, sec. 114.)

As to Madison district No. 1, the testimony shows that the ballot-box and ballots were taken and carried away about ten o'clock at night, while the inspectors were in the act of canvassing the votes. No return whatever has been made from this district, and yet the contestant's attorney claims that of the six hundred and fifteen (615) votes said to have been cast two hundred and six (206) should be counted for contestee and four hundred and nine (409) for contestant. The best evidence would of course be that of the voters themselves, but instead of producing that, an effort is made to show the Democratic vote by proving the number of votes cast for county commissioners at an informal election held on the same day. We submit that, according to contestant's own testimony, the vote given for the county commissioners can not be accepted as a fair test of the Democratic strength in that precinct, while the testimony of contestee shows that very little interest was felt by the Democrats in that matter, and that a great many of them would not vote, because they regarded it as a farce. (See Testimony of R. M. Witherspoon, p. 12, "Testimony from Madison County;" also Testimony of James N. Adams, p. 5.)

There is no legal evidence in the record to show what vote the contestant received in Madison district No. 1, and he can not expect the committee to guess at it and to assume that he received four hundred and nine (409) votes because two hundred and six (206) Democrats by an informal vote recommended to the governor the appointment of certain county commissioners.

It is claimed by contestant's attorney that in Hickstown district No. 10 one hundred (100) votes should be counted for contestant and thirty (30) for contestee. It appears from the testimony, pp. 232, 233, 234, that there was no registration list used at this precinct, and that after the inspectors had canvassed about thirty (30) votes they refused to proceed further, left the polling place, and abandoned the ballot-box, which was afterwards carried to Mr. Henderson's store by a little negro boy.

The testimony of Elza McCraine, p. 6, and Rufus E. Dickinson, p. 12, "Testimony from Madison County," shows that the inspectors at this precinct, after the closing of the polls, were frightened off by thirty (30) armed negroes, who made a hostile demonstration in front and in rear of the house. Whatever may be thought of the conduct of the inspectors in thus abandoning their post of duty, this committee can not determine how many votes were given for the rival candidates at Hickstown precinct No. 10 in the absence of any reliable information whatever upon that subject.

The contestant's attorney claims that twenty-three (23) votes should be added to contestant's vote and a like number deducted from contestee's vote at Norton's Creek district No. 3, and he relies upon the testimony of John Wilkins, p. 236. It will be seen, however, that while this witness testifies that he distributed twenty-six (26) ballots to Republican voters, he is not willing to swear that they voted the Republican tickets.

The contestant's attorney claims in his brief that thirty-six (36) votes should be added to contestant's vote and a like number deducted from contestee's vote in Macedonia district No. 11. Instead of producing the voters themselves, whose evidence would be the best the case admits of, it seems that the contestant is content to rely upon the testimony of one Patrick Warock, who testifies, p. 242, that he distributed sixty-five (65) ballots to persons claiming to be Republicans, and that he went to the polls with these persons and saw them vote. Surely no argument is necessary to prove that official returns made by sworn officers of the election can not be changed by such testimony as that relied upon here.

It is claimed by contestant's attorney that one hundred and thirty (130) votes were cast for contestant and not returned from Greenville, district No. 5, and that nineteen (19) votes were illegally rejected which should be added to contestant's vote. The testimony, pp. 244, 245, 250, 251, shows that no return of the vote was made from this district or canvassed by the board of county canvassers. It shows that the ballot-box was entrusted by the officers of election to one J. H. Redding, who was not acting in any official capacity and had no authority to receive it. According to the statement of Redding the ballot-box was forcibly seized by armed men and taken from his custody. He testifies that the aggregate vote cast at this precinct was about two hundred and fifteen (215), and of this number he thinks the contestant received one hundred and thirty (130). In the absence of the official returns, we insist that the voters themselves should have been called to testify how they voted. This would undoubtedly have been the best evidence, and as it was not produced the contestant has failed to establish his claim.

In addition to the one hundred and thirty (130) votes above referred to, it is claimed upon the testimony of Thomas Greenwood, p. 248, that nineteen Republican votes were illegally rejected at this poll. We submit that the testimony relied upon is not sufficient to establish the claim. On the contrary, it appears from the statement of the witness himself that the votes of the nineteen persons referred to were rejected because they had no certificates of registration, and it does not appear that they had been properly registered. It is claimed by contestant's attorney in his brief that sixty-eight (68) votes should be added to contestant's vote, and a like number deducted from contestee's vote at Ellaville, district No. 2, upon the ground that twenty-nine (29) votes were returned and canvassed for contestant, and that ninety-seven (97) votes were cast for him at this poll. To establish this claim he relies upon the testimony of J. H. Stripling, p. 249, but we submit that it is not sufficient for that purpose. The witness testifies that he distributed ninety-seven (97) ballots to Republicans but he admits, upon cross-examination, that he does not know and can not swear that these persons cast the identical ballots which he distributed to them.

In addition to the official returns from this precinct we rely upon the testimony of William P. Denham and J. A. M. Brown, p. 11, "Testimony from Madison County," who testify that the election at this precinct was fairly and properly conducted. It is claimed by contestant's attorney in his brief that two hundred and fifty-nine (259) votes should be added to contestant's vote at Hamburg, district No. 6. The testimony shows that the ballots were seized and destroyed by a band of armed men, and that no return of the vote was made from this precinct. It appears that Reuben Haines and Austin Hays distributed two hundred and fifty-nine (259) ballots to persons claiming to be Republicans, but they do not know and do not pretend to know that these persons voted the identical ballots that were given to them. The committee can not count votes for the contestant upon such hearsay evidence as is relied upon here. The contestant has failed to produce the best evidence that was attainable; that is, the evidence of the voters themselves.

The authority quoted by contestant's attorney (McCrary on Elections, Sec. 293) shows that "where a voter refuses to disclose or fails to remember for whom he voted, it is competent to resort to circumstantial evidence to raise a presumption in regard to that fact."

The contestant's attorney, after figuring out a majority in Madison County of four hundred and thirty-seven (437) votes for contestant, suggests that the vote as thus *corrected* by him approximates very closely the vote as cast in the Congressional election of 1882 when (as alleged) Mr. Bisbee, the Republican candidate, received in that county a majority of four hundred and seventy-six (476) votes. In reply to that suggestion we call attention to the testimony of J. P. Perry, p. 240, showing that in the Congressional election of 1886, Mr. Dougherty, the Democratic candidate, received in the county of Madison twelve hundred and eighty-one (1,281) votes, and Mr. Greeley, the Republican candidate, received four hundred and twelve (412) votes.

J. F. Livingston, a witness for contestant, testifies, p. 241, that in his opinion the county would have been Democratic if there had been a fair election last fall.

Cornelius T. Coyle, witness for contestant, testifies, p. 245, that in his opinion at the last election if the votes cast had been counted there would have been a majority of from forty (40) to sixty (60) in favor of the Democratic nominee, and that the county has on several occasions given a Democratic majority. He further testifies that, according to the best of his knowledge, from one hundred and forty (140) to one hundred and sixty (160) negroes in Madison County voted the Democratic ticket at the election of 1888.

We submit, with confidence, that so far as the county of Madison is concerned, the contestant has failed to establish his claim.

NASSAU COUNTY.

As to this county we adopt the views of contestee's attorney, as follows:

The contestant's attorney, in his brief, claims that the return from district No. 5 in Nassau County, which return gives to contestee one hundred and twenty-one (121) votes, and to contestant thirteen (13) votes, should be rejected upon the ground that more than eighty (80) persons were allowed to vote who were not residents of the said district. To establish this claim the testimony of David B. Hudson and others, p. 577, *et seq.*, is referred to, but we submit that the registration lists furnish the best evidence as to the residence of the voters, and that they must be accepted as true unless they are corrected in the mode provided by law.

The testimony of S. D. Swann, supervisor of registration in Nassau County, p. 586, shows that a list of all the persons entitled to vote in district No. 5, made from the registration books in his office, was furnished to the inspectors of the election in that district.

It appears from the testimony of William Green, Republican inspector in district No. 5, that the names of the persons voting were on the registration list.

As to the claim of contestant's attorney in his brief that nineteen (19) persons, whose names are enumerated, offered to vote for contestant in district No. 1 and district No. 12, and were illegally rejected, we submit that the testimony relied upon is altogether too vague and indefinite.

The witnesses state that they offered to vote for contestant and that their votes were refused, but, with one or two exceptions, they fail to state why their votes were rejected by the inspectors.

In the absence of any testimony on the subject how can the committee say that said votes were illegally and improperly rejected?

The contestant's attorney in his brief claims that the returns from district No. 9, according to which contestee. received two hundred and twenty-one (221) votes and contestant received thirty-eight (38) votes, should be rejected and no votes therein stated should be counted, on the ground that no election was held at the place designated by law. It appears from the testimony that the election in district No. 9 was held at Booth's Mill, about three-quarters of a mile distant from the town of Callahan, the usual place of voting; but it is not shown that the change of place was not legally made, that it was not duly advertised, or that the Republican voters had no notice of the change of place. On the contrary, it appears that the Republican voters did have notice, because they appeared at the polls and participated in the election. In the absence of any proof in the record, it is fair to presume that the change of place was legally made by the board of county commissioners, and that it was duly advertised according to law. We understand the fact to be that the voting place was changed by the board of county commissioners because there was yellow fever at Callahan, and the quarantine regulations prevented persons from going into the town, and that legal notice of the change was published in the "Florida Mirror," the only newspaper published in the county. We submit that the committee may take notice of this fact without formal proof. However that may be, the courts have held that "the voice of the people is not to be rejected for a defect or even a want of notice if they have in truth been called upon and have spoken." In this case, whether there was notice or not, there was an election, and the people of the district voted, and it is not alleged that any of them failed to vote for the want of notice.

The contestant's attorney claims in his brief that the return from district No. 13, or Bryceville, should be rejected and no votes counted for either party, on the ground that it is tainted with fraud, and a large number of persons were allowed to vote who had never resided in the district. John A. Ellerman testifies, p. 586, that there are nineteen (19) names of persons on the poll-list of district No. 13, known as Bryceville, who were not residents of that district at the time of the election, but he does not know for whom they voted. The presumption is that their votes would not have been received unless they were duly registered, and that they would not have been registered unless they had been legally qualified voters.

Upon a review of the whole case we are of opinion that the result in this district should be stated as follows:

Net changes in favor of contestant in—

	Votes.
Hamilton County	1×3
Duval County	34
Columbia County	127
Putnam County	15
Orange County	31
Total	390
Returned majority for Bullock	3,195
Net change in his favor in Hamilton County	2
In Duval	1
	3,198
Deducting	390
Bullock's majority is	2,808

We therefore submit the following resolutions in lieu of those offered by the majority:

Resolved, That Frederick S. Goodrich was not elected a Representative in the Fifty-first Congress from the Second Congressional district of Florida, and is not entitled to a seat therein.

Resolved, That Robert Bullock was duly elected a Representative in the Fifty-first Congress from the Second Congressional district of Florida, and is entitled to retain the seat he now holds.

LEVI MAISH.
CHARLES F. CRISP.
CHARLES T. O'FERRALL.
JOSEPH H. OUTHWAITE.
L. W. MOORE.
ROBERT P. C. WILSON.

APPENDIX.

WASHINGTON, D. C., *April* 22, 1890.

The Chairman of the House Committee on Privileges and Elections:

SIR: On the 8th of April, 1890, Hon. F. S. Goodrich submitted to the committee of which you are chairman, certain correspondence between himself and D. M. Rodeffer and H. L. Anderson; also the affidavits of Jesse Reddick and of the said Rodeffer and the said Anderson, for the purpose of showing that the said Jesse Reddick did give the testimony purporting to have been given by him and found on page 893 of the printed record.

In reply to the said correspondence and affidavits, I have the honor to submit herewith the following affidavits, which have been furnished to me for the use of the committee:

(1) Affidavit of Jesse Reddick, bearing date April 17, 1890, and also the accompanying affidavit of H. W. Chandler, G. A. Dwelly, and E. Van Hood (marked Exhibit I).

(2) Affidavit of F. E. Pritchett, bearing date April 12, 1890 (marked Exhibit II).

(3) Affidavit of E. M. Gregg, bearing date April 12, 1890 (marked Exhibit III).

(4) Affidavit of D. A. Miller, bearing date April 12, 1890 (marked Exhibit IV).

(5) Affidavit of S. F. Sistrunk, bearing date April 12, 1890 (marked Exhibit V).

(6) Affidavit of Louis Fox, a notary public, bearing date April 12, 1890 (marked Exhibit VI).

(7) Affidavit of Ben Cody, bearing date April 9, 1890, accompanied by the certificate of J. R. Wilmer and J. M. Gates (marked Exhibit VII).

(8) Another affidavit of Ben Cody, bearing date April 11, 1890, accompanied by the certificate of John C. Graham, E. G. Smith, John H. Welsh, D. E. Eichelberger, and G. U. Saussy, and also the certificate of R. E. Davidson and S. S. Burlingame (marked Exhibit VIII).

(9) Affidavit of S. S. Burlingame, a notary public, bearing date April 12, 1890 (marked Exhibit IX).

(10) Affidavit of Henry W. Chandler, bearing date April 8, 1890 (marked Exhibit X).

I respectfully submit that the affidavits herewith presented require no extended comment from me. They speak for themselves. All that I ask is that the committee will give them a fair and impartial consideration. If they will do so, they must inevitably reach the conclusion, not only that the deposition purporting to have been given by Jesse Reddick, as found on page 893 of the record, has been fabricated, but that a conspiracy has been entered into between H. L. Anderson, the contestant's attorney, and D. M. Rodeffer, the notary public, to perpetrate a wrong upon the contestee in this contest, against the people whose representative he claims to be.

Jesse Reddick swears positively that the affidavit he made before Louis Fox, a notary public, in November, 1889, was true; that he had at no time any conversation with E. M. Gregg, the registration officer of Marion County. It further appears from the affidavit of the said Jesse Reddick that on the 4th day of April, 1890, he was sent for to go to the office of the said H. L. Anderson, where the said Anderson had already prepared a certain affidavit which he wished him to make to the effect that some time during the registration of electors for Marion County, during the year 1888, he, the said Reddick, had seen a pistol lying on the table of E. M. Gregg. That the affiant, knowing that fact to be true, agreed to make such affidavit; whereupon the said Anderson informed him that such were the contents of the affidavit which he had prepared and wished him to sign. That relying upon and believing the statement of the said Anderson in relation to the contents of the said affidavit, he signed the same without having it read to him by Anderson, by the notary public, or by any other person.

The affidavit of F. E. Pritchett shows that no such conversation ever took place in his presence with E. M. Gregg, as appears in the pretended testimony of the said Jesse Reddick, as reported on page 893 of the record, and that he never heard any conversation of any character whatever between the said Reddick and the said Gregg.

It appears from the affidavit of E. M. Gregg that he utterly denies ever having

619

had any such conversation with the said Jesse Reddick or any other person. He indignantly repudiates any such statement as is attributed to him in the pretended conversation referred to.

D. A. Miller swears that sometime in the year 1889, he heard Jesse Reddick say in the most positive terms that he never gave any testimony whatever in the contested election case of Goodrich *vs.* Bullock, and that he never knew that said testimony was reported until it was shown to him by the contestee. He further states that Reddick said that he would give the contestee an affidavit to that effect. That the conversation between the contestee and Reddick took place in his, the said Miller's office, in Ocala and at the time his deputy clerk, S. T. Sistrunk, was present; that said conversation was conducted pleasantly and agreeably and with no manifestation of feeling on the part of the contestee; that the said testimony was simply read to Reddick and that he made the statements as hereinbefore given in a quick, calm, and deliberate manner.

S. F. Sistrunk, the deputy clerk, testifies that in the latter part of the year 1889 he was present at a conversation that took place in the clerk's office between the said Reddick and the said contestee; that the said Reddick said most positively and emphatically that he never gave any testimony whatever in the said contested-election case; that he never knew or heard of any such testimony as given by himself until it was read to him by the contestee; and that he would make an affidavit to that effect. This witness further states that the conversation between the two was in an ordinary tone, the contestee simply asking Reddick if he had testified in said case and Reddick answering that he had not and knew nothing about it at all.

Louis Fox, a notary public, swears that he has known Jesse Reddick for a number of years; that on or about the ——— day of November, 1889, the said Reddick appeared before him and made the affidavit attached marked "Louis Fox" in red ink; that he read the said affidavit over to the said Reddick and explained the contents thereof to him; that the contestee was not present in the room when the said affidavit was made; and that the said Jesse Reddick swore before him, the said Louis Fox, as notary that the contents of the affidavit were true.

The first affidavit of Ben Cody shows that sometime during the taking of the testimony in this contest H. L. Anderson, attorney at law, procured him to testify for the contestant; that at the instance of the said Anderson he went to Anderson's law office, where Anderson requested him to hold up his hand to be sworn before him, the said Anderson; that Anderson and none other administered the oath to him; that Anderson then reduced his testimony to writing; that he is unacquainted with D. M. Rodeffer, who reported his testimony as it appears in the record at pages 840, 841; that he has never seen the said Rodeffer to his knowledge, and would not know him if he should see him.

In his second affidavit Ben Cody reiterates the statement contained in his first affidavit and declares it to be absolutely true. He further testifies that on the evening of the next day after his first affidavit was made, the said Anderson came to him and complained that he had made an affidavit against him and threatened if he did not change it at once he would have him put in jail, notwithstanding he had already stated to him that he had simply sworn to the truth. It appears that this second affidavit of Ben Cody was read over to him by the notary and fully explained to him before signing it in the presence of John C. Graham, E. G. Smith, John H. Welsh, D. E. Eichelberger, G. Saussy, who certify that the affidavit was signed in their presence and that they know Cody and have known him for several years to be an honest, truthful, upright, and good citizen. S. S. Burlingame, the notary public, certifies that John C. Graham and E. G. Smith are both colored men, that John H. Welsh is a white man, all of whom are prominent leading Republicans in the county of Marion; that they and the others who certify to the good character of Cody are known to him as good, worthy, and highly respected citizens of that county.

Another affidavit of S. S. Burlingame, notary public, is exhibited, in which it appears that on Friday, the fourth day of April, 1890, Jesse Reddick produced to him a paper writing to be sworn to; that he asked Reddick if the said paper writing had been read to him; whereupon said Reddick answered in the affirmative and said that Mr. H. L. Anderson had read the same to him; that believing said Reddick was fully aware of the contents of said paper, he administered the oath to him and attached his signature and seal of office; that he did not read the said affidavit to Reddick; did not read it himself and was not aware of its contents; that the said affidavit was taken by him in the office of H. L. Anderson, whither he had been called and in the presence of the said H. L. Anderson and D. M. Rodeffer.

The only other affidavit exhibited is that of Henry W. Chandler, the Republican candidate for secretary of state and a colored man. This testimony, while not strictly relevant to the present issue, is offered for the purpose of rebutting the statements in the correspondence and affidavits filed with the committee by the contestant since the oral argument, with reference to the methods in office of E. M. Gregg, supervisor of registration. This testimony shows that prior to the election held on the 6th day of November, 1888, the said Henry W. Chandler and David S. Williams, who was a candidate for the office of county judge, were accorded the courtesies of and had seats in the office of Mr. Gregg while the voters were being registered.

I have thus called attention, as briefly as possible, to the contents of the affidavits herewith exhibited, and confidently submit that they are absolutely conclusive and overwhelming as to the issue which has been raised in regard to the testimony of Jesse Reddick. They not only prove beyond question that no such testimony was ever given by Jesse Reddick, as is reported on page 893 of the record, but they furthermore show that a system of forgery and deliberate manufacture of testimony has been resorted to in this case, which not only merits the emphatic condemnation of this committee, but of honorable and fair-minded men everywhere.

In conclusion, I deem it not inappropriate to invite the attention of the committee to the marked contrast between the methods adopted by myself and my adversaries in the procurement of the affidavits of Jesse Reddick. I desire also to place upon record my emphatic denial of the statement made by H. L. Anderson as to the agreement between us for the taking of testimony in our absence. It is not true that I entered into any such agreement as is claimed by him. The committee will observe that his statements as to this matter are contradictory and wholly inconsistent. Especial attention is invited to the postscript to his letter addressed to Mr. Goodrich, bearing date April 4, 1890, and his affidavit of the same date. In the one he states as follows:

"About the question of notice. I always had a notice served on Bullock from day to day. It was not necessary to give him names of all the witnesses."

In his affidavit he states as follows: "Affiant further says that said contestee in the beginning waived all formal notice of taking from day to day the testimony in said cause but agreed that after commencement the taking should proceed without further notice."

Apologizing to the committee for the length of this communication, and hoping that they will properly appreciate my motives,

I am, very respectfully,

R. BULLOCK.

No. 1.—*Affidavit of Jesse Reddick before Fox denying testimony as appears in record of contest testimony made at request of Bullock.*

STATE OF FLORIDA, *Marion County:*

On this the —— day of November, A. D., 1889, personally appeared Jesse Reddick, who, being duly sworn, says that he had read to him from the printed testimony taken before D. M. Rodeffer, a notary public, in the contest case of F. S. Goodrich vs. Robert Bullock, for a seat in Congress, wherein he, the said Jesse Reddick, on page 893, of said printed testimony purports to have sworn before the said Rodeffer to a conversation he had with E. M. Gregg, registration officer for Marion County, Florida, prior to the election on the 6th of November, 18-8, when the said E. M. Gregg admitted, among other things, that he was hired by the county commissioners to strike off Republicans from the registration list, etc., etc.

This deponent solemnly swears that he never at any time had any conversation with the said registration officer, nor did he ever make any such testimony before the said Rodeffer as aforesaid, and that he, the said Jesse, is the only person in this community bearing the name of Jesse Reddick, and that he has been living in this community a number of years, and knows there is no other Jesse Reddick living in this community.

JESSE (his X mark) REDDICK.

Sworn to and subscribed, day and year above written.

[SEAL.]   LOUIS FOX,
                    Notary Public, Marion County, Fla.

No. 2.—*Affidavit of Jesse Reddick made at request of Anderson denying affidavit made at request of Bullock.*

THE STATE OF FLORIDA, *Marion County:*

Personally appeared before me Jesse Reddick, who, being duly sworn, says: That he is the same person who made affidavit in the contest election case of Fred S. Goodrich vs. R. Bullock, for a seat in the Fifty-first Congress of the United States, representing the second Congressional district of Florida, which affidavit is printed on the record of said contested election case at page 893.

Affiant further states positively that on the 26th day of February, A. D. 1889, he went to the office of the commissioners appointed to take the testimony in said case for Marion County, to wit, the office of D. M. Rodeffer, at Ocala, Fla., and then and there made the statements contained in his said affidavit printed on said page 893, and swore to the same before D. M. Rodeffer, the commissioner appointed to take testimony for contestant, Goodrich.

Affiant further says that he does not remember whether the attorneys for the respective parties were present or not, but affiant states that he did make the affidavit verbatim as the same appears in said record, and affiant further states that the facts related in said affidavit are true as therein stated, and that the conversation related therein between affiant and said E. M. Gregg, actually occurred, and that said Gregg made to affiant the statement in said affidavit contained.

Affiant further says that if he ever signed any paper containing a statement in denial of said affidavit that he signed same in ignorance of its contents and without knowing what it contained.

Affiant says that he is a man of limited education and unable to read writing, but that this affidavit has been read over to him and its contents fully explained before he signed same.

JESSE (his x mark) REDDICK.

Sworn to and subscribed before me this 4th day of April, 1890.
[SEAL.]   S. S. BURLINGAME,
Notary Public.

No. 3.—*Affidavit of Jesse Reddick explaining how Anderson fooled him into making affidavit denying his affidavit to Bullock denying testimony attributed to him in the record of contest testimony.*

STATE OF FLORIDA, *Marion County:*

Personally came Jesse Reddick, who, being duly sworn, says: That he is the identical Jesse Reddick who made the affidavit before Louis Fox, notary public, in November, 1889, in which affidavit he stated, amongst other things, that he had heard read from the printed testimony taken in a case wherein F. S. Goodrich was contestant and Robert Bullock was contestee for a seat in the Fifty-first Congress of the United States, in which affidavit, before the said Fox, this deponent stated that he had at no time any conversation with E. M. Gregg, registration officer, and wherein he further said that he did not make any testimony bef re D. M. Rodeffer, a notary public, taking testimony on the part of said contestant, all of which affidavit made at said time was true, and he now states the same to be true. Affiant further says that on Friday, April 4, 1890, one H. L. Anderson, of Ocala, Fla., sent a carriage to the East Florida Ice Manufacturing Company, where this affiant was at work, with the request that this affiant should come up town. This affiant, being engaged at the time, could not go in response to the request; that afterwards, later in the afternoon, said H. L. Anderson came to the ice factory in person and requested this affiant to come up town, that he wanted him to make an affidavit; that affiant, after working hours, did go up to the office of said H. L. Anderson, where the said Anderson had already prepared, before this affiant arrived, a certain affidavit; that he, the said Anderson, wanted him to swear that some time during the registration of electors for Marion County for the year 1888 this affiant had seen a certain pistol lying on the table of E. M. Gregg, supervisor of registration. This affiant knowing said fact to be true, stated that he would make such affidavit, whereupon said H. L. Anderson informed him that such statement was the contents of the affidavit which he had prepared and wished him to sign. That this affiant is a colored man and can neither read nor write and that, relying upon and believing the statement of said Anderson in relation to the contents of said affidavit signed the same. This affiant then appeared before one, S. S. Burlingame, a notary public, for the purpose of swearing to said affidavit before said Burlingame; that the said Burlingame asked this affiant if he knew the contents of this affidavit; that this affiant informed said Burlingame that he did, believing said affidavit to contain only the one fact in relation to said pistol mentioned by said Anderson; that the said Burlingame then requested this affiant to hold up his hand, and asked this affiant if he swore that the contents of this affidavit were true, whereupon this affiant answered in the affirmative. This affiant further states that in making this affidavit he intended and believed that he was only swearing to the one fact in relation to the said pistol. Affiant further states that he has heard read to him the affidavit which he is informed and believes is the affidavit that he signed, which affidavit is as follows.

THE STATE OF FLORIDA, *Marion County:*

Personally appeared before me Jesse Reddick, who, being duly sworn, says: That he is the same person who made affidavit in the contest election case of Fred S. Goodrich *vs.* R. Bullock for a seat in the Fifty-first Congress of the United States, representing the second Congressional district of Florida, which affidavit is printed on the record of said contested election case, at page No. 893.

Affiant further states positively that on the 26th day of February, 1889, he went to the office of the commissioner appointed to take the testimony in said case for Marion County, to wit, the office of D. M. Rodeffer, at Ocala, Florida, and then and there made the statement contained in his said affidavit printed on said page No. 893 and swore to the same before D. M. Rodeffer, the commissioner appointed to take testimony for the contestant, Goodrich. Affiant further states that he does not remember whether the attorneys for the respective parties were present or not, and affiant states that he did make the affidavit verbatim as the same appears in said record and affiant further states that the facts related in said affidavit are true as therein stated; and that the conversation related therein between affiant and said E. M. Gregg actually occurred, and said Gregg made to affiant the statement in said affidavit contained.

Affiant further says that if he ever signed any paper containing a statement in denial of said affidavit, that he signed same in ignorance of its contents, and without knowing what it contained.

Affiant says that he is a man of limited education, and unable to read writing, but that this affidavit has been read over to him and its contents fully explained before he signed the same. JESSE (his x mark) REDDICK.

Sworn to and subscribed before me this 4th day of April, 1890.
S. S. BURLINGAME,
Notary Public.

And this affiant now states that no such affidavit was ever read to him by H. L. Anderson, S. S. Burlingame, or any other person, and that he had not intended to make any such statements as are contained in said affidavit. Affiant further states that he has heard read to him from the printed record in said contest case on page 893, and again repeats that the same is absolutely and unconditionally false and fraudulent and that he gave no such testimony, or testimony of any character whatever before said D. M. Rodeffer or any other person.

Affiant further states that, as to the said conversation which said record reports that he had with E. M. Gregg, supervisor of registration for Marion County, in the presence of Mr. Pritchett, it is absolutely untrue, and that he had no such conversation with said E. M. Gregg at said time or any other time.

JESSE (his x mark) REDDICK.

Subscribed and sworn to before me this 17th day of April, 1890.
[SEAL.]
R. A. BURFORD,
Notary public, State of Florida at large.

STATE OF FLORIDA, *Marion County:*

Personally came H. W. Chandler, G. A. Dwelley, E. Van Hood, who, being severally sworn, say that they were each one present and heard the foregoing type-printed affidavit on three sheets of paper read over to and explained to Jesse Reddick, in our presence, that he, the said Reddick, knew contents thereof and that it was true, and that he fully understood the same.

H. W. CHANDLER,
G. A. DWELLEY,
E. VAN HOOD, M. D.

Sworn and subscribed before me on this April 17th, 1890.
[NOTARY SEAL.]
R. A. BURFORD,
Notary Public, State of Florida at large.

I certify that the foregoing affidavit printed with type-writter on three pieces of paper, was read over to Jess. Reddick by me in the presence of H. W. Chandler, a leading Republican and candidate for secretary of state on Republican ticket in 1888, G. A. Dwelley, a well-known Republican, and commander of Post No. 17, Grand Army of the Republic, and E. Van Hood, before he signed the same and it was explained to him, and he declares that he fully understands the same, and contains what he intends to say.

In testimony whereof I set my hand and official seal at Ocala on this 17th day of April, A. D. 1890. Each of said parties are personally known to me.
[SEAL.]
R. A. BURFORD,
Notary Public, State of Florida at large.

*Affidavit of Louis Fox and copy of affidavit of Jesse Reddick explaining under what cir-
cumstances he took Reddick's first affidavit at my instance.*

THE STATE OF FLORIDA, *County of Marion:*

Personally appears Louis Fox, who, being duly sworn, says that he is a citizen of
Ocala for thirteen years; that he has personally known one Jesse Reddick for a number of years; that on about —— day of November, 1889, in the city of Ocala, said
Jesse Reddick appeared before him and subscribed to the following affidavit, which
is hereunto attached, marked "Louis Fox," in red ink, with his notarial seal there-
under, and made part of this affidavit. Affiant further swears that he read the
said affidavit to Jesse Reddick and explained the contents thereof to him, at which
time no other person, that this affiant remembers, was present; that the affiant is
positive that General Robert Bullock was not present in the room when this affidavit
was made, and that the said Jesse Reddick swore before him that the contents to his
affidavit were true; that to the best of the knowledge and recollection of this affiaut
the affidavit hereto attached signed by Jesse Reddick, and sworn to before him, is a
true copy of the affidavit that Jesse Reddick signed and swore to before him on the
day therein mentioned.

LOUIS FOX.

Sworn to and subscribed before me on this 12th day of April, A. D. 1890.
[SEAL.]   S S. BURLINGAME,
Notary Public.

STATE OF FLORIDA, *Marion County:*

On the —— day of November, A. D. 1889, personally appeared Jesse Reddick, who,
being duly sworn, says that he had read to him from the printed testimony taken before D. M. Roddeffer, a notary public in the contest case of F. S. Goodrich *vs.* Robert
Bullock for a seat in Congress, wherein he, the said Jesse Reddick, on page 893 of said
printed testimony, purports to have sworn before the said Roddeffer to a conversation he had with E. M. Gregg, registrating officer for Marion County, Fla., prior to
the election on the 6th day of November, 1888, when the said E. M. Gregg admitted, among other things, that he was hired by the county commissioners to strike off
Republicans from the registration list, etc. This deponent solemnly swears that he
never at any time had any conversation with the said registration officer, nor did he
ever make any such testimony before the said Roddeffer as aforesaid, and that he,
the said Jesse, is the only person in the community bearing the name of Jesse Reddick, and that he has been living in this community a number of years and knows
there is no other Jesse Reddick living in this community.

JESSE (his x mark) REDDICK.

Sworn and subscribed to day and year above written.
[SEAL.]   LOUIS FOX,
Notary Public, Marion County, Fla.

---

*Affidavit of S. T. Sistrunk, showing how I approached Reddick about his testimony in
printed testimony contest.*

STATE OF FLORIDA, *Marion County:*

Personally came S. T. Sistrunk, who, being sworn, says that he is and has been
deputy clerk of the circuit court for Marion County, Fla., for about three years
continuously last past. That he is personally acquainted with one Jesse Reddick, a
colored man. That some time during the year 1889, in the latter part of it, that he
was present at a conversation between the said Reddick and General R. Bullock that
took place in said clerk's office; that said Reddick most positively and emphatically
said that he never gave any testimony whatever in the contested-election case
wherein F. S. Goodrich was contestant and Robert Bullock contestee. The said
Reddick stated at the same time that he never knew nor heard of any testimony
given by himself until it was shown or read to him by General Bullock, and stated that
he would make an affidavit to General Bullock stating that he had never testified before
D. M. Rodiffer in said contest case. That the said conversation was in ordinary con-
versational tone and manner. General Bullock simply asking Jesse Reddick if he had
testified in said case, and Reddick answering that he had not, and knew nothing
about it at all. General Bullock read the testimony to Reddick, and after hearing it
Reddick denied ever hearing or having testified to any such thing.

S. T. SISTRUNK.

Sworn and subscribed before me on this the 12th day of April, A. D. 1890.
[SEAL.]   RICHARD MCCONATHY,
County Judge.

Affidavit of E. M. Gregg as to testimony of Reddick in the printed contest testimony.

STATE OF FLORIDA, *Marion County:*

Personally came E. M. Gregg, who, being sworn, says: That during the year 1888 he was the supervisor of registration of electors for Marion County, Fla.; that his office was in the southwest corner room of the court-house in Ocala. That said room is a small room of the dimensions of ten by twelve feet; that in said room is a large iron safe, a flat top desk, an ordinary table of three by six feet, some small file cases, etc.; that affiant is also deputy clerk of the board of county commissioners; that said office is entirely too small to comfortably accommodate the incumbent of the office; that there is no private railing in any portion of the office, but the whole an open room, in which the officer, visitors, and those on business, and loafers are all promiscuously mixed. Affiant further states that the registration books of Marion County, Fla., consist of fifty-six small books, and during the registration of electors of Marion County, Fla., for the year 1888 it was very difficult to prevent persons in the office from handling and marking the books. Being so many small books, it was difficult for this affiant to furnish information to those inquiring and take care of the other books; that when affiant would put down one book, some restless, impatient persons who could not wait their turn would be pulling at the books to get his information for himself, and a half dozen making different requests at the same time.

That affiant discharged the duties of said office honestly, faithfully, and justly, seeking and obtaining the best opinion of lawyers, whether Republican or Democrat, as to my duties under the law, and then pursued them to the very utmost of my capacity and ability.

Affiant further states that he extended the courtesies of the office as much to one party as another; that it would have been utterly impossible for this affiant, or any other person, to proclaim an invitation to the public to come into the office and for him to have transacted any business whatever; that the privileges of the office were extended to Mr. Henry W. Chandler, a colored man and a candidate on the Republican ticket for the office of secretary of state, as a representative of the colored people and the Republican party of the State, and Mr. D. S. Williams, who is a white man and was a candidate for the office of judge of the county court for Marion County, Fla., on the Republican ticket, and to others without regard to party to the full extent that it was possible for me to do and attend to the duties of the office.

Affiant states that he has read from the printed record of the testimony in the contested-election case of Hon. F. S. Goodrich *vs.* Hon. R. Bullock, on page 893, what purports to be the testimony of one Jesse Reddick, before D. M. Rodiffer, in which said Reddick testifies to a conversation that he had with this affiant. This affiant, in the most positive, emphatic, absolute, and direct manner, denies the same to be absolutely and wholly untrue; that no such conversation was ever had between this affiant and Jesse Reddick, or any other person; nor any conversation of any such character whatsoever with any person whomsoever. Affiant further states that not only does he deny the conversation, or any other such conversation at any time, but most positively denies the existence of the facts stated in said conversation, and says that such statement is the conception of a villanous, dishonest, lying mind, and the production of a corrupt, depraved, unscrupulous, and wicked heart.

E. M. GREGG,

Sworn to and subscribed to before me this 12th day of April, 1890.
[SEAL.] S. S. BURLINGAME,
Notary Public.

Affidavit of Ben Cody as to how Anderson personated the officer, having no authority himself, and administered an oath to Cody, a colored man.

THE STATE OF FLORIDA, *County of Marion:*

Before me personally came Ben Cody, who, being by me duly sworn, says: That he knows of no other Ben Cody in said county; that he has resided in said county for about six years; that some time during the taking of testimony in the contested election case wherein F. S. Goodrich was contestant and Robert Bullock was contestee for a seat in the Fifty-first Congress of the United States, H. L. Anderson, esq., attorney-at-law, procured this affiant to testify on the part of the contestant; that this affiant at the instance of the said Anderson went to the law office of the said Anderson where said Anderson requested this affiant to hold up his hand to be sworn, before him the said Anderson, and he the said Anderson, and none other, administered the oath to him this affiant; that said Anderson then reduced to writing the evidence of this affiant; that there were no other persons present during the whole time this affiant was in the office of the said Anderson except this affiant, H. L. Anderson, and an old colored man with whom this affiant is unacquainted; and this affiant states that he is unacquainted with D, M, Roddeffer, the notary public, who reported the testimony of this affiant as the same appears in the record of said testimony on pages 840 and 841; that should this affiant see the said Roddeffer now he would not know him; that he has never seen the said Roddeffer that he knows of.

BEN CODY.

Sworn to and subscribed to in my presence by the said Ben Cody, and I certify that I have heard read the above affidavit over to him and he says he fully understands the same, this April 9th, 1890.

[SEAL.]
LOUIS FOX,
Notary Public.

We certify that the above affidavit was read over to Ben Cody in our presence and he acknowledged to us that he fully understands the same, to which we swear to be true.

J. R. WILMER.
J. M. GATES.

Sworn to before me this April 9th, 1890.

[SEAL.]
LOUIS FOX,
Notary Public.

Affidavit of Ben Cody as to how Anderson, by threats, tried to make him, Cody, change his affidavit as to Anderson's personating an officer.

STATE OF FLORIDA, *Marion County:*

Personally came Ben Cody, who, being sworn, says: That he is a colored man, and politically a Republican; that on the 9th day of April, 1890, in the city of Ocala, and in the county of Marion, he made an affidavit before Louis Fox, as notary public, in which affidavit I stated substantially that when I appeared as a witness in the Congressional contest in a case wherein F. S. Goodrich was contestant and Robert Bullock contestee for a seat in the Fifty-first Congress of the United States; that one Mr. H. L. Anderson, of Ocala, on the occasion of my testifying administered the oath, and wrote down my testimony, and that no one was present except this affiant, H. L. Anderson, and one old colored man, whose name I do not know, and that I was unacquainted with one D. M. Rodeffer, had never seen him, and would not know him if I was to see him. I again repeat the truthfulness of said statements contained in said affidavit as being absolutely true. This affiant further states that on the evening of the next day after said affidavit was made, the same H. L. Anderson came to this affiant and inquired of this affiant if he had made such an affidavit, whereupon affiant informed him that he had. Anderson then said "Ben, why did you make this affidavit against me?" Affiant then stated to said Anderson, "that I did not make it against you, but simply swore to the truth." Whereupon said Anderson told affiant, "Ben, you go and change that affidavit; if you do not I will be damned if I don't have you put in jail, so go on now at once and do it."

BEN CODY.

Sworn and subscribed before me on this the 11th day of April, 1890.

[SEAL.]
S. S. BURLINGAME,
Notary Public.

Witness to signature of Ben Cody:
    JNO. C. GRAHAM.
    R. E. DAVIDSON.

I, S. S. Burlingame, notary public, do certify that the foregoing affidavit of Ben Cody was read over to him in the presence of John E. Graham and R. E. Davidson, and by me explained to him before signing, and that he signed the same in this presence and swore to me before said parties that the contents thereof was true.

In testimony whereof I have hereunto set my hand and official seal at Ocala on this the 11th day of April, 1890.

[SEAL.]
S. S. BURLINGAME,
Notary Public.

We, John C. Graham, E. G. Smith, John H. Welsh, D. G. Eichelberger, and G. N. Saussy, certify that we are, each one of us, personally acquainted with Ben Cody, a colored man, who signed the foregoing affidavit, and state we have known him for several years and know him to be an honest, truthful, upright, and good citizen.

JOHN C. GRAHAM.
E. G. SMITH,
JOHN H. WELSH.
D. G. EICHELBERGER.
G. N. SAUSSY.

Signed in the presence of us as witnesses.
    R. E. DAVIDSON.
    S. S. BURLINGAME.

Personally came R. E. Davidson and S. S. Burlingame, who being sworn, say they saw John C. Graham, E. G. Smith, John H. Welsh, D. G. Eichelberger, and G. N. Saussy sign the above certificate of character of Ben Cody, and we witnessed their signatures.

R. E. DAVIDSON.
S. S. BURLINGAME.

Sworn to and subscribed before me this 11th day of April, 1890.
[SEAL.]

LOUIS FOX,
Notary Public.

STATE OF FLORIDA, *Marion County :*

I, S. S. Burlingame, a notary public for Marion County, do certify that the above-named John C. Graham and E. G. Smith are both colored men, and John H. Welsh is a white man, all of whom are prominent leading Republicans in this county; that D. G. Eichelberger and G. N. Saussy are white men and Democrats in this county; that all of said persons are personally known to the undersigned, and all of them are good, worthy, and highly-respected citizens of the county; that during the reading of the foregoing affidavits in the front of the store that fronts the public square of the city of Ocala these gentlemen, E. G. Smith, John C. Graham, and John H. Welsh, were called to witness the reading and signing thereof.

In testimony whereof I set my hand and official seal at Ocala, on this the 11th day of April, A. D. 1890.
[SEAL.]

S. S. BURLINGAME,
Notary Public.

Affidavit of T. E. Pritchett.

STATE OF FLORIDA, *County of Marion :*

Personally came T. E. Pritchett, who, being duly sworn, says that during a part of the time for the registration of electors in Marion County, Fla., for the year 1888, he was in the office of E. M. Gregg, supervisor of registration for Marion County, Fla., as his deputy. Affiant further states that he is not acquainted with one Jesse Reddick. Affiant states that he has read the testimony of said Jesse Reddick as the same appears on page 893 of the record in the contested-election case of F. S. Goodrich against R. Bullock. Affiant further states that the conversation as reported in said record as given by Jesse Reddick never took place at any time in the office of the supervisor of registration or anywhere else, to his knowledge, between E. M. Gregg and said Reddick within the hearing of this affiant that he never heard said conversation or any other conversation of any character whatsoever between said Reddick and Gregg. Affiant states that on the 22d day of September, 1888, he left the said registration office and during the month of October, 1888, and at least a month before the election of November 6, 1888, he left the city of Ocala in said Marion County and went on the Ocklawaha River, where he resided continuously ever since and did not return to the said city of Ocala until the month of February, 1890

T. E. PRITCHETT.

Sworn to and subscribed before me this 12th day of April, A. D. 1890.
[SEAL.]

S. S. BURLINGAME,
Notary Public.

Affidavit of D. A. Miller.

STATE OF FLORIDA, *Marion County :*

Before me, the undersigned authority, personally came Dan A. Miller, who, being duly sworn, says upon oath: That he is clerk of the circuit court in and for the county of Marion; that he is personally acquainted with one Jesse Reddick; that some time during ——, 1889, he heard Jesse Reddick say in the most positive terms that he never gave any testimony whatever in the contested-election case of F. S. Goodrich, contestant, against Robert Bullock, contestee; that he never knew that said testimony was reported until it was shown to him by General Bullock. And affiant further states that he heard the said Jesse Reddick say that he would, and intended to give General Bullock an affidavit denying ever having given such testimony as was reported by D. M. Rodeffer. Affiant further states that said conversation between General Bullock and Jesse Reddick took place in his office in Ocala, and at the time thereof there was present his deputy clerk, S. T. Sistrunk; that said conversation was conducted pleasantly and agreeably, and with no manifestation of feeling on the part of General Bullock; that said testimony was simply read to Reddick, and he made the statements, as hereinbefore stated, in a quiet, calm, and deliberate manner.

D. A. MILLER.

Sworn to and subscribed before me this 12th day of April, 1890.
[SEAL.]   RICHARD McCONATHY,
County Judge.

Affidavit of Henry W. Chandler, colored man and candidate for state secretary, corroborating Gregg, registration officer.

STATE OF FLORIDA, *County of Marion :*

Before me personally came Henry W. Chandler, who, being by me duly sworn, says upon his oath that he was the Republican candidate for secretary of state of the State of Florida, in the election held on the 6th day of November, 1888, at which election a Representative to the Fifty-first Congress of the United States was voted for. That prior to said election he and David S. Williams, who was a candidate for the office of county judge of said county at said election, were accorded the courtesies of and had seats in the office of the supervisor of registration for said county while voters were being registered.

HENRY W. CHANDLER.

Sworn to before me this the 8th day of April, 1890, and in my presence subscribed to by the above-named Henry W. Chandler.
[SEAL.]   LOUIS FOX,
Notary Public.

Affidavit of Sol Benjamin, showing the conduct of Anderson and Rodiffer in going together to get the colored man Reddick to fool him into making a false affidavit. Contrast this with my method.

STATE OF FLORIDA, *Marion County:*

Personally came Sol Benjamin, who, being sworn, says that on Friday evening, April 4, 1890, late in the evening, a carriage came down to the East Florida Ice Manufacturing Company's building, of which company affiant is the president, and the driver announced that Mr. H. L. Anderson had sent him for Jesse Reddick, a colored man, in the employ of said company; that affiant sent Mr. Anderson word that Reddick was at work and could not leave then. Later, on the same evening, Mr. H. L. Anderson and D. M. Rodiffer came in person, and after making some little apology to affiant for not requesting him to allow said Reddick to leave, Mr. Anderson then had some private interview with Jesse Reddick; that next morning affiant asked said Reddick what Mr. Anderson wanted with him; that said Reddick replied he wanted him to sign an affidavit about him (Reddick) seeing a pistol lying on the table of the supervisor of registration for Marion County, and that he signed it, and that was all of the contents of said affidavit; that said Reddick has repeatedly made same statement in the presence of many persons, and continues up to this time to make the same statement.

Affiant states that at one time, to wit, April 5, 1890, when Reddick made the statement as to contents of the affidavit he made for H. L. Anderson, on April 4, 1890, before S. S. Burlingame, there was present Mr. R. B. Bullock, secretary of the Withlacoochie Phosphate Company; W. A. Smith, engineer at the East Florida Ice Manufacturing Company, and this affiant; and he has made the same statement on a great many other occasions, in the presence of different persons, both white and colored.

SOL BENJAMIN.
W. A. SMITH.

Sworn to and subscribed before me on this 17th day of April, A. D. 1890.
[SEAL.]   WM. FOX,
Notary Public.

Personally came R. B. Bullock and W. A. Smith, persons mentioned in above affidavit, and all of them to me personally known, who, being each duly sworn, say they have read said affidavit of Sol Benjamin, and say that so much thereof as states that they were present and heard Jesse Reddick state the contents of the affidavit made by him on April 4, 1890, before S. S. Burlingame, is true, and they each swear they were present and heard same statement of said Jesse Reddick, and the same was made as set forth in said affidavit.

R. B. BULLOCK.

Sworn to and subscribed before me on this April 17th, 1890.

[SEAL.]
WM. FOX,
Notary Public State of Florida.

Affidavit of S. S. Burlingame, showing that he only administered the oath taken by Reddick, without reading the same to him, as he said it had been read to him by Anderson and only related to a pistol.

STATE OF FLORIDA, *Marion County*:

Personally came S. S. Burlingame, who, being duly sworn, says that he is a citizen of Ocala, Marion County, Fla., and the clerk of the city of Ocala, notary public, and also a clerk in the dry goods and clothing store of Benjamin & Fox; that he is a northern man by birth; that he has resided in Ocala since May, A. D. 1880; that on Friday, April 4, 1890, one Jesse Reddick, a negro man, who is well known to affiant, and who is in the employ of the East Florida Ice Manufacturing Company, did, between the hours of 6 and 7 o'clock p. m. on said day, produce to him a paper-writing, to be sworn to by said Reddick before the affiant; that affiant asked said Jesse Reddick if said paper-writing had been read to him; whereupon said Reddick answered in the affirmative, and said that Mr. H. L. Anderson had read the same to him; that this affiant, believing that said Reddick was fully aware of the contents of said paper-writing, asked said Reddick if he did swear that the contents thereof were true, whereupon said Reddick said that he did; and that this affiant then administered the oath to him on the faith of this statement, and attached his signature and seal of office thereto; that this affiant did not read said affidavit to Reddick, nor did he read it himself, nor was he, this affiant, aware of the contents of said paper-writing, signed by said Reddick on April 4, 1890; that the said affidavit of said Reddick was taken by me in the office of H. L. Anderson, whither I was called by him for that purpose, and in the presence of H. L. Anderson and D. M. Roddeffer. And affiant further states that said paper-writing was not read in his presence by any other person, and that he does not know the contents thereof.

S. S. BURLINGAME.

Sworn to and subscribed before me on this 12th day of April, A. D. 1890.

[SEAL.]
LOUIS FOX,
Notary Public.

JAMES H. McGINNIS vs. JOHN D. ALDERSON.

THIRD WEST VIRGINIA.

The governor of West Virginia declared the result and issued the certificate to Alderson on the basis of the returns from all the counties except Kanawha, omitting the latter return on account of legal proceedings in which it had become involved. McGinnis claimed to be entitled to the certificate in the first instance, he being elected on the face of the returns including that from Kanawha County, and also to be elected if all illegal votes cast on both sides be deducted. Alderson claimed that the return from Kanawha County was properly omitted by the governor; that if said return were correctly made out, including the results of recounts legally had, it would show that he was elected on the face of all the returns, and that his returned majority would be still further increased by deducting from both sides the illegal votes cast for them respectively. The committee in general sustain the claims of McGinnis, as above stated, the minority those of Alderson. The case was never reached by the House.

(1) Certificate of election. *Force of.*

"A certificate of election showing upon its face that nearly 8,000 votes were wholly ignored in the count can have no binding force and effect in a contest of this character. * * * * * When his title is assailed in a direct proceeding by way of a contest, we think that a certificate showing the above facts gives the contestee no superior standing over the contestant as to burden of proof. For the purposes of the contest a certificate which, on its face, shows that a large vote was wholly ignored, and giving no data from which the true results could be ascertained, ought not to be considered as binding upon anybody."

(2) Burden of proof. *When contestant elected on face of returns.*

When it is shown that the contestant was elected on the face of the returns, the burden is cast upon the contestee to overcome the prima facie right which the returns give to the contestant.

(3) Recount.

In order to justify a recount it ought to appear that the statutory requirements have been complied with, "or clearly shown that the failure to comply therewith has resulted in no injury. If proper care is not taken to so preserve the ballots that they may not be changed they will always be the subject of a natural suspicion, and when a material difference appears between the original count and the recount the weight to be given to the recount must depend wholly upon the methods used in preserving the ballots free from suspicion or opportunity to do wrong. In a conflict between the first and second count it is evident that the one or the other does not show the true result.

If every opportunity to change the ballots has been prevented, and if the law in relation to a recount has been complied with, the recount becomes entitled to the greater credit and should prevail. But if, on the other hand, the ballots have been so kept that they may be readily changed, our observation upon this committee would hardly justify us in indulging in the conclusion presumptive that no one had been found wicked enough to make the change."

REPORT.

JULY 23, 1890.—Mr. LACEY, from the Committee on Elections, submitted the following report:

As in the case of Smith *v.* Jackson from West Virginia, decided by this committee and their findings approved in the present Congress, the first important question to determine is as to whether the contestee or contestant was entitled to the certificate of election.

THE PRIMA FACIE CASE.

In the present case the returns certified to the governor in due form of law as to all the counties except Kanawha are as follows:

Third Congressional district.

Counties.	John D. Alderson.	James H. McGinnis.	C. W. Henson.	W. D. Sanford.	Frank Burt.	J. H. Higgins.
Logan	1,508	416	....	....	....	....
Wyoming	500	565	....	....	....	....
McDowell	409	583	....	....	....	....
Mercer	1,371	1,406	3	4	....	1
Raleigh	888	842	13	....	....	....
Boone	742	512	1	....	....	....
Kanawha	....	....	....	....	....	....
Fayette	1,854	2,685	19	150	4	....
Clay	415	463	....	4	....	....
Nicholas	1,101	690	12	11	....	....
Greenbrier	2,072	1,394	5	....	....	....
Monroe	1,324	1,225	23	....	....	....
Summers	1,356	1,277	10	....	....	....
Webster	666	276	....	....	....	....
Pocahontas	898	580	6	....	....	....
Upshur	840	1,717	18	5	....	....
Total	15,944	14,631	110	174	4	1

The foregoing statement is copied from the executive order of the governor of West Virginia, and it will be observed that he treats the county of Kanawha as a blank.

The reason for thus ignoring the county of Kanawha is set out in the executive order of his excellency, the governor, in the following language:

EXECUTIVE DEPARTMENT, *February 28, 1889.*

The governor having received from the commissioners of the county courts of the several counties of the Third and Fourth Congressional districts of the State of West Virginia, excepting the county of Kanawha, certificates of the result of the vote cast at the election held on the Tuesday next after the first Monday in November, 1888, for Representative in the Congress of the United States, and it being apparent, for the reasons hereinafter stated, that the returns from Kanawha County can not now be made befóre the beginning of the Congressional term on March 4, 1889, this day proceeded to ascertain and declare the result of said election in said Congressional districts.

The county commissioners declared the result of the election in Kanawha County *December* 15, 1888. The certificate was mailed in this city on the 17th of said month, *and received in this office late in the afternoon.*

On the same day a writ of *certiorari* was awarded by the circuit court of Kanawha County on the petition of John D. Alderson, who claimed to be elected to said office, against the said commissioners, and against James H. McGinnis, who also claimed to be elected to said office. The order awarding the *certiorari* provided for a *supersedeas* to the judgment and decision of said commissioners upon the execution of bond, as required by statute. The bond was forthwith executed, and said judgment and decision suspended. A certified copy of the record in the *certiorari* proceedings shows that said commissioners, in declaring the result of the election in said county, excluded from the recount, had, under the statute, on the demand of said Alderson, a sufficient number of ballots in his favor to have secured his election to said office.

I have time and again personally urged counsel on *both sides* of this controversy to insist upon a prompt decision by the circuit court, in order that a final conclusion might be reached before the 4th of March next, the beginning of the Congressional term. I can see no reason why it should not have been done. The circuit court aforesaid on the 23d inst. entered judgment reversing the entire proceedings and finding of said commissioners, and remanding the cause. Upon inquiry, I find that no steps have yet been taken for the reassembling of said commissioners to ascertain the election result, and it is evident that such result can not now be ascertained before the beginning of the Congressional term.

Therefore, I believe it to be my duty to certify an election *on the returns now in* this office.

E. W. WILSON.

By the governor:
HENRY S. WALKER,
    Secretary of State.

It thus appears affirmatively from the record before the committee that because of the legal proceedings referred to above the governor certified the "election on the returns *now* in this office" on the 28th of February, 1889, although the governor had ineffectually urged "*both* sides" to secure a prompt decision from the courts.

The fact that the contestee, Mr. Alderson, had attempted to supersede the returns by the legal proceedings gave him no right to have the certificate, based upon a count of the district, omitting the most important county therein. The county of Kanawha cast a vote larger than the average of three of the other counties in the district. That county cast an undisputed majority of over 1,300 in favor of the contestant.

A certificate of election showing upon its face that nearly 8,000 votes were wholly ignored in the count can have no binding force and effect in a contest of this character. It is true that it has been sufficient to entitle the contestee to sit in the House, to take part in its organization, and to perform all the duties of a member of Congress whether elected or not. But when his title is assailed in a direct proceeding by way of a contest, we think that a certificate showing the above facts gives the contestee no superior standing over the contestant as to burden of proof. For the purposes of the contest a certificate which, on its face, shows that a large vote for the contestee was wholly ignored, and giving no data from which the true results could be ascertained, ought not to be considered as binding upon anybody.

As the governor did not decide the result and issue the certificate upon the returns from the whole district, the first duty devolving upon the committee was to take the returns and make a statement of the same.

The corrected returns, so far as certified by the governor, showed the following result:

For Alderson	15,944
For McGinnis	14,631
Plurality for Alderson	1,313

Returns from Kanawha County:

For McGinnis	4,658
For Alderson	3,329
Majority in Kanawha County for McGinnis	1,329

The original returns gave McGinnis 1,344 majority in this county (2d Rec., 108), but this excluded Coalburgh which we will show should not be excluded.

The net majority for McGinnis in the district is 16.

Upon the face of the returns, McGinnis was entitled to the certificate by a majority of 16.

In the county of Boone there was an error in the footing or else an accidental transposition of figures.

The figures certified to the governor for contestant were 512 instead of 521, making a difference of 9 votes. Three witnesses show that this error occurred (Rec., 34, 35). Leftwich, McNeeley, and Smoot all testify as to the error. Their evidence is confirmed by the tally-sheet, page 36.

No attempt is made to contradict this tally-sheet or the evidence of these witnesses. We do not think that a clerical error of this character ought to stand uncorrected where it is practically undisputed. It is claimed that the evidence showing this fact should not be considered because the notice to take depositions did not give the names of the witnesses. But J. B. Hayger appeared as attorney for Mr. Alderson at the taking of this evidence; and besides, no objection was made to the printing of this evidence at the time that it was opened by the clerk. (Lowry v. White, 50th Cong., and Featherstone v. Cate, 51st Cong.) By correcting this clerical error in the returns it appears that contestant was elected by a plurality of 25 over the contestee on the face of the returns. If these returns remain unimpeached the tables are turned and the burden is cast upon the contestee to overcome the prima facie right which the returns give to the contestant.

To meet this question the contestee asserts that under the laws of West Virginia he was entitled to a recount of the ballots, and that upon such recount in Kanawha County this result was changed and that the contestee gained 12 votes and the contestant lost 20, making a change of 32 votes, which would give him a majority of 7 upon the basis above set out.

THE RECOUNT.

The recount in Kanawha County showed a change of 9 votes in Alum Creek precinct, and 25 votes in Charleston precinct.

In the West Virginia election cases in the present Congress, and in the famous case in the gubernatorial contest between Fleming and Goff, we have had striking illustrations of the dangers of a recount of the ballots, where a change of a few tickets may affect the result. The law of West Virginia, whilst it provides for such recount, attempts to throw around the recount such elements of safety as will prevent a fraudulent change of the ballots. Such recount is always viewed with suspicion and is full of danger.

The law of West Virginia is as follows:

They shall, upon the demand of any candidate voted for at such election, open and examine any one or more of the sealed packages of ballots and recount the same, but in such case they shall seal up the same again, along with the original envelope, in another envelope, and the clerk of the county court shall write his name across the place or places where it is sealed, and indorse on the outside: Ballots of the election held at ——, the district of —— and county of ——, etc.

The law also provides that the original packages shall be sealed up at the place of voting, as follows:

When the said certificates are signed, the ballots shall be inclosed by the commissioners in an envelope, which they shall seal up, and write their names across the place or places where it is sealed, and indorse on the outside of the said envelope as follows: " Ballots of the election held at ——, in the district of ——, and county of ——, the —— day of ——," etc.

In order to justify a recount it ought to appear that these requirements have been complied with, or clearly shown that the failure to comply therewith has resulted in no injury. We are constrained to find that in the present case there was not that care of the ballots contemplated by this statute, nor such care of the same as would justify us in overturning the count made at the time by the judges of the election.

The ballots of Alum Creek precinct were put in a paper package and the package placed in a bag and carried to the court-house where the bag was thrown up over a storm-door at the clerk's office.

When the recount was commenced this package was found broken open, or else it had never been sealed.

J. A. Jones, witness for contestee, says that when the ballots were laid before the court for recount the Alum Creek package was unsealed, and it had the appearance of not having been sealed at any time, though it showed that an effort had been made to seal it. (Rec., 159.)

From Thursday after the election until the following Monday this package was lying unsealed in a bag on top of the storm door. It had been sealed with mucilage, which did not stick. (Rec., 193.) About half the returns came in wholly unsealed, with a string tied around them. (Rec., 192.)

Goshorn and Quarrier show clearly that the law was not complied with by sealing up the returns.

This is not a mere unimportant requirement. The sealing up and proper care of the ballots is an essential requisite to an honest and correct recount of the ballots.

If proper care is not taken to so preserve the ballots that they may not be changed they will always be the subject of a natural suspicion, and when a material difference appears between the original count and the recount the weight to be given to the recount must depend wholly upon the methods used in preserving the ballots free from suspicion or opportunity to do wrong. In a conflict between the first and second count it is evident that the one or the other does not show the true result.

If every opportunity to change the ballots has been prevented, and if the law in relation to a recount has been complied with, the recount becomes entitled to the greater credit and should prevail. But if, on the other hand, the ballots have been so kept that they may be readily changed, our observation upon this committee would hardly justify us in indulging in the conclusion presumptive that no one had been found wicked enough to make the change.

Where party spirit runs high, and a Congressional election depends upon the substitution of a few votes, and opportunity for the change is afforded, and the recount of two precincts like Alum Creek and Court-House show an error of 32, we must give the greater credit to the first count.

At Alum Creek 3 votes more for Alderson were found on the recount and 6 votes were counted for McGinnis less than the judges of the precinct counted for him. Such an error in a vote of 194 is very improbable. In Court-House precinct Alderson gained 12 and McGinnis lost 13. McGinnis has taken testimony to show specifically 143 votes for him instead of the 138 shown by the recount, thus showing the recount to be wrong. This evidence shows clearly that the recount was erroneous. But aside from all questions of probability or improbability, we think the only safe rule of law in relation to a recount of the ballots is to require that the ballots should be preserved in the manner pointed out by law, or clearly shown not to have been tampered with, in order to render a recount of any validity. The same statute which provides for a recount also provides a method to make such recount worthy of credit.

The ballots at Charleston were placed in a cracker-box, and nailed up, sealed, and indorsed. The box showed chisel marks in the bottom where it had been opened. (Rec. 76). The change of 25 votes in the count in this box can be accounted for in two ways. The first count was inaccurate, or the ballots were changed. The county commissioners were notified that there was something wrong about the recount, and refused to certify it, and legal proceedings were instituted to compel them to adopt the recount, which they declined to do, and while these proceedings were pending the executive cut the Gordian knot by leaving Kanawha out of the count altogether, and thus giving to the contestee a majority of over 1,300 votes. One Montague was in charge of the clerk's office a part of the time. Mr. Montague was an intemperate man and had been on a spree. He got ten cents of the deputy clerk to get some whisky with to steady his nerves while he made some copies of some papers.

One Forsythe testifies to seeing Montague apparently tampering with the ballots. (Rec. 67.) Forsythe's character and evidence are bitterly assailed, and it is claimed that he could not have seen Montague on the date at which he claims to have seen him in the clerk's office, but it clearly appears, at least, that Montague had ample opportunity to change the ballots. Montague's character and habits are shown by one of contestee's witnesses, Mr. Quarrier. (Rec. 208.):

Q. 17. Please state what part of the week on which the election was held was the said Montague employed in or about said office?

A. He worked on Monday and Tuesday the day of the election, and came back to the office on Saturday evening at about 3 o'clock and asked for his two days' pay. I told him that I would not pay him unless he went to work to make a copy of a deed for Wm. S. Edwards, who desired the same to be copied by nine o'clock that night in order that he might proceed to New York City to raise money for the Paint Creek Railroad Company. Montague said that he was in no condition to make the copy, and asked me to send for Mr. A. P. Fry to make the same. I told him that if he did not make the copy I would not pay him for the two days' work; he was at the time very tremulous, having been on a spree. It was a very long deed, the copy of which the fee amounted to four dollars. He began working in a few minutes in the back room; after working some half hour he came to the front room, and said it was impossible for him to proceed with the work on account of his nervousness, and asked me to get some one else to do the work; I replied that if you do not make that copy I will not pay you a cent, and gave him ten cents to go and get a drink of whisky with; he then returned and went to work again. I staid in the office until about dark, locked the front door, and left Montague therein. I fixed the shutters on the front side of the office so that any person could look in the office where he was working, with instructions to him to allow no one to come into the office except the said Wm. S. Edwards, who said to me that he would be down to the office about dark to get his copy. I went to supper and returned in about 40 minutes, and saw the shutter ajar as I had left it, and invited John T. Dudding to go in the office with me. Montague showed me the amount of work he did since I left, and requested that I would give him money to get his supper, and said that Edwards had not been to the office. I gave him ten cents to get a drink with; he finished the copy about half past eight o'clock; I then locked up the office and went home.

Forsythe and other Republicans were engaged in watching the clerk's office, fearing that the ballots might be tampered with, and the date at which the occurrence was seen may have been misstated. At any rate, a drunken penitentiary convict was not a proper person to put in control of such documents under the circumstances. (Rec., 458.)

Mr. Goshorn, the county clerk, testifies that Montague had served a term in the penitentiary and that he was a Democrat (Rec., 198). **Mr.** Goshorn says that Montague was an intemperate man but reliable. Montague's antecedents and habits caused him to be the natural object of suspicion.

Montague is now dead, and was not a witness in the case.

The cracker-box showed the chisel marks where it was opened at the bottom. Whether the suspicions naturally attaching to Montague were well founded or not, it is very probable that the box was opened. A board was taken off the bottom and again nailed up. Sealing up the top lid of the box was no protection against removing a board from the bottom. The statute requires that the ballots should be "sealed up in an envelope and the envelope indorsed," etc.

This requirement is not met by merely nailing up the ballots in a wooden box and sealing up one side of the box.

We think the recount should not be considered and that the examination of the case should therefore proceed upon the assumption that contestant was entitled to the certificate of election, and that he should be seated, and that he should retain his seat unless his plurality of 25 votes shall be overcome by the investigation of the alleged illegal votes cast for the contestant.

FAILURE OF ELECTION OFFICERS TO BE SWORN.

At Coalburg precinct, contestant claims that the officers were not sworn. Section 8, chapter 3, of the code of West Virginia, provides as follows:

The said oath shall appear properly certified on one of the poll-books of every election, and in no case shall the vote taken at any place of voting be counted unless said oath so appears, or unless it be proved to the satisfaction of the commissioners of the county court, convened at the court-house as hereinafter required, that said oath was taken before said commissioners, canvassers, and clerks entered upon the discharge of the duties of their appointment.

Contestee claims that this law, which in terms is mandatory, should be held unconstitutional.

If the commissioners of the county court had counted this precinct it would be presumed that the proof of the oath was made to their satisfaction as provided in the statute. (See Smith vs. Jackson, 51 Cong.) It may well be doubted whether such a statute could be held to be other than merely directory in any event. As the general result arrived at would not be changed by excluding the Coalburg vote we refrain from directly passing upon the question.

Whilst it might be very proper to punish the officers in some way for violating a duty imposed by statute it would be manifestly a dangerous thing to disfranchise a precinct because the officers of the law through accident, oversight, or design fail to take the prescribed oath of office.

Such a construction would place it in the power of the officers to have their return rejected at will if the majority should be contrary to their political preferences.

There is some evidence to show that a part of the officers were sworn and we do not feel willing to so construe this law as to disfranchise the voters of Coalburgh, where Mr. Alderson had a majority of 20. The supreme court of the State has never passed upon the question.

ILLEGAL VOTES CHALLENGED.

· Having thus reported our views upon the election and as to the right of the contestant to the seat upon the face of the returns we will next review the question as to illegal voters challenged on both sides. This is a laborious and difficult task and we have endeavored to consider the evidence as to each particular vote. ·

The following is the constitutional requirements of the State (Art. IV., sec. 6) :

The male citizens of the State shall be entitled to vote at all elections held within the counties in which they respectively reside, but no person who is a minor, or of unsound mind, or a pauper, or who is under conviction of treason, felony, or bribery in an election, or who has not been a resident of the State for one year and of the county in which he offers to vote for sixty days next preceding such offer shall be permitted to vote. Const. W. Va., Art. I, sec. 6.

BOARD CAMP PRECINCT, MERCER COUNTY.

Contestee challenges this precinct because the poll-books do not show that all the judges were sworn, and that one judge was not sworn.

What we have said as to precincts where the same point is made by contestant is sufficient answer to this claim.

DISPUTED VOTES.

Assailed by L. D. Solomon (Rec. 233) in Mercer and McDowell counties:

E. I. Edwards,	Bowers Darby,	Jno. Kirby,
Lee Kirby,	Wm. Mays,	Jos. Ballard,
Jno. Jackson,	Juo. Terry,	Sperill Wilcher,
Juo. Locher,	M. C. Bodkin,	Wm. Old,
Thos. Chandler,	Ed Waller,	Beverly Sanders,
Monno Kent,	Pleasant Lee,	Monro Wonack,
Bill Nowlen,	And. Bowen,	Wm. Lee.
Total 21.		

Mr. Solomon was one of the judges of election at the Peery Bottom precinct, McDowell County, and in his official capacity received the votes cast by these electors. It does not appear that he objected to any of them, although he was well acquainted with them, and if they were illegal voters, should have known it at the time that he received their votes. His action as an election officer is utterly at variance with his testimony as a witness, and we do not believe that we would be justified in excluding these votes upon such testimony.

C. E. Rusmeisel (Rec. 325, 326) unsuccessfully assails the following names: John Jackson, Pleas. Lee, George Clark, Albert Clark. He shows that Jackson was working at Shamokin Works in October, 1887. He does not know personally where any of them came from.

Madison Radford unsuccessfully assails the followin g parties at Mill Creek, Mercer County : A. J. Kinsey, A. F. Kinsey, E. J. Kinsey, Milton Otey, Armstead Otey, and David Sales. (Page 277 of the record, and pay-roll 303 to 307.)

Armstead Otey had been working there more than a year. The time of the residence of the Kinseys is stated from their declarations. Milton Otey had stated that he had been away to Alabama. This evidence wholly fails to show that these men were not competent voters. As to Sales, the witness says he did not look old enough to vote. A. J. Kinsey does not appear on Mill Creek poll-list. (Rec. 341.)

L. A. Conner unsuccessfully assails the following parties (Rec. 270) at Simmons Creek, Mercer County : James Clemens, Peter Hartsook, F. D. Holland, James Hackney, Caleb Welcher, George Price, and David E. Bishop.

His statement is based wholly upon vague declarations of the voters made before the election, and which declarations are inconsistent with their subsequent action in casting their votes.

James Arnold, Honaker's Mill, Mercer County, unsuccessfully assails Junius Cook.

Witness says the voter did not look to be of age. The witness proves the vote by hearsay from the voter. Knows nothing of the length of the voter's residence in West Virginia.

W. A. Davidson unsuccessfully assails at Bluefield, Mercer County, Charles Lee, G. B. Smith, and John Martin.

Says he does not know of a single illegal vote (Rec. 333). The fact that a voter had worked in Virginia did not show loss of residence in West Virginia.

D. S. Ratcliffe assails the following at Oak Vale, Mercer County : Isaac Porterfield, Thomas Saunders, George Saunders, James Wall, and W. D. Melvin. (Rec. 248.)

Mr. Ratcliffe was one of the judges of election, and the same reasons already assigned for ignoring the testimony of Solomon apply with equal force to him. Two of the judges were Democrats and one Republican. Melvin's vote was challenged on the ground of minority; his father was present and the vote was received. Witness made no objection to the voting of the other parties.

W. P. Boggess, Oak Vale, Mercer County, unsuccessfully assails I. Porterfield, Joseph Wall, Charles Robinson, and W. B. Melvin. (Rec., 346.)

The witness was a candidate for office, and he importuned these men to vote for him, and they claimed not to be voters. Declarations of this character are proverbially unreliable.

W. A. Young assails (Rec. 301) at Mill Creek, Simmons Creek, and Honaker's Mills, Mercer County :

Dan'l Barbour,	Randall Cook,	Jno. Heil,
Ed. Hampton,	Jas. Jarvis,	E. J. Kinsey,
Mack Lee,	Ambrose Mills,	Thos. Mertin,
Armsted Ottey,	Wm. Brown,	Moses Johnson,
Silas Johnson,	Elijah Perkins,	Peter Perkins,
Green Sheppard,	W. J. Thornhill,	Granville Toller.
Phillip Turner,	J. H. Bramwell,	
Total, 20.		

His testimony is simply to the effect that many of these men brought their families to West Virginia within a year, but does not go to the time when the men themselves became residents, and is insufficient to overturn a presumption arising out of their votes having been received by the duly appointed election officers. We may further add that Mr.

Young was one of the clerks òf the election; that he was a Democrat, and registered all those whose votes were cast, and challenged none of them but Bramwell (Rec. 307).

The evidence is very wholesale in its character. Hampton was working there November, 1887 (Rec. 302); Barbour was working there November, 1887 (Rec. 302); Armstead Otey was working there November, 1887 (Rec. 302); Silas Johnson was working there November, 1887 (Rec. 302); Green Sheppard was working there November, 1887 (Rec. 302); William Brown was working there September, 1887 (Rec. 302); Elijah Perkins was working there November, 1887 (Rec. 302); W. J. Thornhill was working there November, 1887 (Rec. 302); Thomas Merton was working there September, 1887 (Rec. 302); Granville Toler was working there November, 1887 (Rec. 302).

- A. I. Godfrey assails at Simmons Creek, Mercer County, James Cook and John L. Smith (Rec. 358).

He bases his evidence upon the fact that taxes for 1887 were collected from voters in West Virginia and afterwards paid back, because they had been taxed in Virginia. It by no means follows that because these men had not been in West Virginia long enough to be taxable for the year 1887, that they were not there in time to be legal voters in the eleventh month of the year 1888.

C. M. Kyle, (Rec. 279 and 281) testifies as to sundry parties, but his evidence proves nothing except the time that they worked at that particular place, and he does not recollect where the voters had previously worked. He sets out a list of workmen at Caswell Coal Company's Works.

L. Schereschewsky, Simmons Creek, Mercer County, assails Joseph Ward unsuccessfully.

Ward has resided a year and a half in the county.

J. H. Hetherman assails James Cook, Ed. Spinner, at Simmons Creek, Mercer County. (James Cook, No. 87, page 388, and Ed. Spinner, No. 294, page 339.)

Spinner's vote was challenged, as appears by the poll list. This evidence is not sufficient to overcome the ruling of the election officers on the challenge. As to Cook the witness says he was living in McDowell County at time of election, and had previously resided in Mercer County; that he had resided in McDowell less than sixty days. The question of their residence was argued before the judges of the election and determined that it had not been lost. The evidence of error on the part of these officers ought to be clear to justify a change of ruling. Perdue, a Democratic election officer, says that the voters were challenged and sworn (Rec. 238); that after examination he and the other judges thought they ought to vote. In many instances other proof was furnished as to their residence.

W. A. Thompson assails at Cross Roads, Mercer County—

D. M. Jones.	Jos. Williams.	Jas. Craft.
C. B. Smith.	Hy. Lessen.	Jno. Griffith.
Jerry Davis.	Jas. Glenn.	Rob't. Craft.
J. C. Simpson.	Jno. Marlin.	Lewis Troy.
Ben. Peery.	Gus. Hale.	Han'l Smith.
Total, 15.		

He was commissioner of election, the judges being two Democrats and one Republican. All these votes were received by these parties, and what we have said of Solomon applies here also.

Pleas. Robinson assails, at Mill Creek, Mercer County, the follow-

H. Mis. 137——41

ing (Rec. 287): Ambrose Mills, James Jarvis, Armstead Otey, Bird. Wright, David Sales, and Jim Mowgrass.

Otey had lived there over a year but did not have his family with him. As to Sales' age, he simply repeats what he says Sales' mother told him. This is not sufficient. As to Ambrose Mills, James Jarvis, Bird. Wright, and Jim Mowgrass, witness shows that they came from Virginia in the spring of 1888, but Mills worked at Mill Creek three years ago. Jarvis he says he understood worked at Mill Creek before, but witness did not know him. As to Wright and Mowgrass, witness shows their residence at Pocahontas, Va., and these two votes should be held illegal.

Thomas Falconbridge assails the following parties (Rec. 312) at Maybery, McDowell County:

Alex. Stokes.	J. H. Tate.	Jos. Napor.
W. T. Smith.	Henry James	J. W. Marshall.
Clem Green.	Geo. Wade.	A. L. Calhoun.
Jno. Saunders.	Wm. Hardy.	Wm. Wooten.
Hardy Green.	Robt. Lemen.	Wash Hardy.
Wm. Old.	M. Robinson.	
Total, 17.		

This witness seems to be quite an enthusiastic one. He is impeached as to many of the parties named, and such doubt is cast upon his testimony that it ought not to be allowed to supersede the action of the election officers and the presumption which attaches to the receipt of a vote. For impeachment of this witness' testimony see as follows:

Rolls, p. 326, shows Hardy was working for Shamokin Coal Company October 1, 1887, more than a year before the election. He changed to Elkhorn Coal Company August, 1888. (Rec. 329.)

J. W. Marshall (Rec. 326) was working in October, 1887, for Shamokin Coal Company.

Wm. T. Smith is shown by Mr. Hegg to have worked two years in the State for Freeman & Jones. (Rec. 448.)

J. H. Tate worked for Houston Coal Company from August, 1888, to October, 1888. (Rec. 334.) Falconbridge says this man came direct from Virginia to him in August, 1888. (Rec. 313.) He is charged to have voted at Peery Bottom (Rec. 29), but his name is not on the Peery Bottom list. (Rec. 350.)

Robert Lemen did not vote (Rec. 350), though he worked for Shamokin Coal Company from October, 1887. (Rec. 326.)

Joseph Napor was working for witness in October, 1888, he says. Hewitt says Napor lived at Elkhorn. (Rec. 453.)

W. R. Jacobs assails (Rec. 367) unsuccessfully at Peery Bottom and Mayberry, McDowell County—

Geo. Brown.	C. S. Calloway.	Wm. Nowlin.
Geo. Brown.	Jacob Dennis.	Hy Gardner.
Geo. Allen.	Rich'd Britton.	Jno. Crenshaw.
Calvin Green.	Hy Holly.	Jno. Mitchell.
Chas. Folk.	Gus Thompson.	Allison Toller.
Polk Burman.	Anthony Wyatt.	Wm. Brown.
Thad Brown.	Thos. Edwards.	Wm. Holland.
Tom Martin.	Ambrose Mills.	Jno. Patterson.
Bird Wright.	Sam'l Wheeler.	Jacob Witters.
Total, 27.		

These parties are assailed on the ground that within a year's time they had been working in an adjoining county. This witness's evidence is insufficient to exclude these votes.

Mr. Bloch (Rec., 368), registrar at Pocahontas, assails :

Mill Creek, Mercer Co.

1 Brown, Wm.(colored).
2 Edwards, Thos. (white).
3 Evans, Lee (colored).
4 Lee, M. (colored).

5 Patterson, Jno. W. (colored).
6 Smoot, Bullet (colored).
7 Williams, Addison (colored).

Simmons Creek, Mercer Co.

1 Allen, Geo. (colored).
2 Bailey, Jno. (white).
3 Bagley, David (colored).
4 Chambers, Soloman (colored).
5 Chetam, John (colored).
6 Dromnie, J. W. (white).
7 Duncan, John (white).
8 Davis, Wm. (colored).
9 Green, Calvin (colored).
10 Hackney, Jas. (colored).

11 Harman, Lewis (colored).
12 Jones, Fred. (colored).
13 Lucky, Frank (colored).
14 Lee, James (white).
15 Powell, W. A. (white).
16 Polk, Chas. (colored).
17 Robertson, Jno. (colored).
18 Thompson, Gus. (colored).
19 Williams, Geo. (colored).
20 Weatherford, Wm. (colored).

Peery's Bottom, McDowell Co.

1 Brown, Geo. (colored).
2 Callaway, S. C. (white).

3 Davis, Wm. (colored).
4 Harriss, Reuhin (colored).

Mayberry, McDowell Co.

1 Brown, Jim (colored).
2 Brown, Geo. (colored).
3 Debnan, Wm. (colored).

4 Price, Wm. (colored).
5 Scott, Green (colored).
6 Smith, George (colored).

These voters are objected to on the ground that they were registered at Pocahontas. This is not sufficient to overcome the presumption attaching to the receipt of the votes by the election officers, for the reason that under the law of Virginia the registration is permanent, and there is nothing inconsistent in the prior registry of these parties at Pocahontas and actual citizenship in West Virginia at the time the votes were cast.

J. M. Myles (Rec., 266), at Mill Creek, Mercer County, assails (see Time-book, 302):

Wm. Brown, Sept. 15, '87.
Green Sheppard, Nov., '87.
Ray Fitzgerald, Nov., 1887.
Joe Colliver, Nov., 1887.
Jas. Harvey, Dec., '87.
Lip Starling, not on roll.
Thos. Bibb, not on roll.
D. W. Figgins, not on roll.
W. Rice, not on roll.
Sam. Davis, not on roll.
Jno. Guy, not on roll.
J. H. P. Prior, Nov., 1887.
Jas. Prior, not on roll.
Squire Young, not on roll.
And. Ross, not on roll.
Wm. Bruce, not on roll.
Rob't Simmons, not on roll.
Fount Black, not on roll.
Thos. Chambers, not on roll.
Geo. Redd, not on roll.
Peyton Simmons, Sept., '88.
Wm. Gather, not on roll.
Henry Watkins, not on roll.
King Stovall, not on roll.
W. H. Nicewander, not on roll.
Jno. Dickerson, Nov., 1887.
Albert Garrison, Nov., 1887.
Jno. Watkins, not on roll.

Anderson Price, not on roll.
Oscar Holmes, not on roll.
Dan Franklin, not on roll.
Jas. Jeffries, not on roll.
O. Lewis, not on roll.
George Ray, not on roll.
Wash. Pennell, Oct. 3, '87.
Geo. Johnson, not on roll.
W. H. Hastin, not on roll.
Rob't Franklin, not on roll.
Ed. Fullen, Nov., '87.
Oliver Dillard, Mch., '88.
Jno. Daniels, not on roll.
Chas. Harvey, not on roll.
Sam. Wheeler, Sept., '88.
And. Jeffries, not on roll.
E. P. Alley, not on roll.
Phil. Turner.
Jud. Coles, Jan., '88.
Geo. Johnson, not on roll.
Jno. Douglass, not on roll.
Ed. Ford, not on roll.
Ed. Dillard, not on roll.
Peter Parker, Nov., '87.
Henry Woodson, not on roll.
Jas. Giles, not on roll.
Ed. Ford, not on roll.

The evidence of this witness is wholly unreliable. The foundation of it as given by himself is the time-book found upon page 302 of the record. An examination of this time-book will disclose the fact that a very large number of the parties as to whom he testified were not to be found upon the roll at all, their names are so noted above. With respect to others as to whom he testified his testimony is contradicted by the evidence of other parties, showing the residence of the voters assailed in West Virginia at times different from those given by the witness. His testimony as a whole is vague and indefinite and given in wholesale. It is founded, furthermore, upon declarations, many of them made subsequent to the election, and which, under the rules of law adopted by the committee heretofore, have been declared incompetent. There are in fact no declarations testified to by this witness which, in the judgment of your committee, have sufficient weight to overcome the judgment of the election board that received the votes.

King Stoval is on Cooper's roll, p. 303, November, 1887; Green Shepherd worked for Cooper November, 1887. (Rec., 303.)

George Booth assails, at Mill Creek, Mercer County (Rec., 284):

Jas. R. Booth,	Jno. W. Booth,	Thos. Booth,
Thos. Myles,	Jeff. Willis,	Wilson Booker,
Moses Johnson,	Jno. Loch,	Jas. Jarvis,
Thos. Saunders,	Duke Cobbs,	Elijah Perkin.
Chas. Toller,	Granville Toller.	
Total, 14.		

This witness's evidence is not sufficient to overcome the right of any of these men to vote. It fails to prove the beginning of their residences, and the presumption arising from the reception of their votes has not been overcome.

W R. Johnston assails, at Mill Creek, Mercer County, the following (Rec., 321):

Wilson Booker,	Overton Mead,	Sam'l Mayberry,
Peter Parker,	Sheridan Reed,	Hy Woodson,
Kelton Winston	Addison Williams,	J. T. Smith,
Jas. Davis,	Wm. Estes,	Sam'l T. Hunter.
Total, 12.		

S. C. Bernheim (432) supports the right of the following voters: Willis Hayden, Mason Thornton, Jeff. Shelton, Thos. Hightower.

W. R. Johnson is a somewhat interesting example of the testimony by which large masses of voters have been sought to be disfranchised or their votes excluded in this district. He swears that his family reside in Salem, Roanoke County, Va. He also swears that these various voters, or a considerable portion of them, were not residents of West Virginia, but were in fact residents of Virginia because their families resided in Virginia, but it appears on page 341 that said Johnson, notwithstanding the residence of his family at Salem, Roanoke County, Va., voted for Alderson at Mill Creek, Mercer County, and his vote has been counted for Alderson. He now seeks to disfranchise twelve other persons upon grounds which, if tenable, disfranchise himself. He voted under the same circumstances which he claims disfranchises the others. He voted after being challenged, and swore his vote in. A man whose family lived in Virginia and who swore his vote in in West Virginia, should hardly be accepted as a witness to disqualify a large number of other voters situated precisely as he was. Johnson was living at Flat Top Tunnel, W. Va. By a misprint (p. 321) it is stated as Flat Top Tunnel, Va. (See map, p. 245.) His working residence was in West Virginia, and he voted there, notwithstanding the residence of his family at Salem, Va.

Witness says he does not know whether the men came directly from Virginia. (Rec., 322.)

S. M. Williamson assails (Rec., 290) at Simmons' Creek, Mercer County, Perry Bottom poll-list, p. 350:

Monroe Wammick,	W. H. Smith,	Kelton Winston,
Jno. Jankin,	C. S. Calloway,	G. B. Smith,
Rob't Tanner,	Dick Woods,	C. M. Spencer,
Green Scott,	Spencer Witcher,	Dan Dickenson,
Geo. Brown,	Edw'd Johnson,	A. C. Patterson,
Mack Robinson,	Mason Thornton,	Thos. Clark,
Abe Helm,	Henry Janies,	Jno. L. Waite,
Marshall Clark,	J. W. Marshall,	W. T. Smith,
J. A. Williams,	J. A. Napor,	Smith Russell,
Chas. Hardy,	Geo. Helm,	Jno. Patterson,
Jno. Lewis,	Henry Taylor,	Jno. Bolling,
Lee Kirby,	Chas. H. Howard,	Wm. Lee,
Jerry Richardson,	Rob't Saunders,	G. W. Wilson,
Marshall Stoball,	Wm. Caldwell,	Chas. Clark,
J. J. Scott,	Henry Woodson,	Ben Wade.
David M. Jones,	Wm. Brown,	
Jas. Weaver,	Chas. Johnson,	

S. M. Williamson assails these parties upon the ground that they were not qualified voters by reason of lack of sufficient time of residence in West Virginia. As to a very large number of the parties so assailed, there is contradictory testimony out of the mouths of other witnesses. This is true probably as to seventeen or eighteen of the 49 voters assailed. In other words, Mr. Williamson is by the testimony of witnesses upon the contestee's side of the case proven to have been mistaken, to put it mildly, in at least that many cases. With respect to the other voters, as to whom he is not directly contradicted, his testimony is of such a vague and indefinite character as to render it worthless to disfranchise these parties. In not a single instance, if the inquiry were being made as to the legality of the particular vote cast, could its illegality be proven by the testimony of Mr. Williamson. This is an example of testimony by wholesale, and it is insufficient to affect individual votes. After testifying as to the names given, he qualifies his evidence by confining it to "most of them."

Solomon (235) says Womack came from Virginia in November or December, 1887; Williamson claims that he came in May, 1888.

Robert Lemon, witness says, came in July, 1887, and worked till fall; then went home, and did not come back till July, 1888, whereas it appears from the Shamokin pay-roll (326) that he was working for that company in October and November, 1887.

Green Scott, witness says, came from Virginia in February, 1888, but the Caswell Creek Company's rolls show that he was working for that company almost continually from October, 1887, to August, 1888.

John Lewis, witness says, came from Virginia in April, 1888, but it appears from Cooper's rolls (p. 303) that he was working from January to November, inclusive, for Cooper.

Lee Kerby, witness says, came from Virginia November 17, 1887, while Solomon swears (p. 234) that Lee Kerby came with John Kerby in July or August, 1887.

Mason Thornton, witness says, came from Virginia in November, 1888, while S. C. Bernheim (p. 432) swears that he had lived on Simmons' Creek three years.

J. W. Marshall, witness says, came from Virginia in January, 1888, but pay-roll (p. 326) of Shamokin Company shows that he was working for that company in October, November, and December, 1887.

J. A. Napor, witness says, came from Virginia in February, 1888, but

John D. Hewitt (p. 453) swears that he had been in West Virginia two years before the election.

Charles H. Howard, witness says, came from Virginia in January, 1888, but Rev. John M. Douglass (p. 441) says he had been in West Virginia about two years before election; and John Cooper's pay-roll (p. 302) shows that he had been working for him from September, 1887, to November, 1888, continuously, except in June, July, and August, 1888.

John Patterson, witness says, came from Virginia in February, 1888; by Cooper's pay-roll (p. 303) shows that he worked for Cooper from November, 1887, to November, 1888, without interruption.

William Lee, witness says, came from Virginia in March, 1888, but Shamokin Coal Company's roll shows (p. 326) that he was working for that company in August and October, 1887.

To undertake to disfranchise voters—whose votes had been accepted by an election board—with testimony such as that of Williamson would be to render elections a farce.

Sam'l Beckett assails at Simmons' Creek, Mercer County, the following (Rec., 228):

Thos. Ingram,	Willis Hayden,	Wiley Morton,
York Scales,	King Lee,	Woodey Dews,
F. D. Holland,	Jeff Shelton,	Harris Boyd,
Geo. Price,	Sam'l Wilburn,	Chas. E. Holloway,
Jas. Hackney,	Caleb Wilcher,	Mason Thornton.
Total, 14.		

It appears that the votes of these parties were challenged at the polls, which were presided over by two Democratic judges and one Republican judge, and the challenge was overruled. The testimony of this witness is against the judgment of the election board, rendered in the exercise of its proper functions, and is not sufficient, in the judgment of your committee, to exclude the votes of the parties assailed.

The witness concedes a four years' residence in the State to Thomas Ingram.

York Scales, the witness says, came from Virginia about six months before the election. On the contrary, he came from Simmons' Creek in October (p. 281), and had been working for the Caswell Creek Coal Company from October, 1887 to April, 1888, and in August and September, 1888.

Caleb Wilcher, witness says, came from Virginia about three months before the election; but Jno. D. Hewitt (p. 453) says he had been working at Simmons and Flipping's for about two years, part of the time at one place and part at the other.

J. H. Clare assails (Rec., 250) at Peery's Bottom, McDowell County:

Robt. Good.	Geo. Smith.	L. M. Burwell.
Alex. Stokes.	J. Naper.	Lewis Law.
Jno. Crider.	Tas. Dillard.	Wm. Simpson.
Minnis Wade.	Wm. Price.	J. W. Marshall.
Jno. Kerby.	Bowles Darby.	Robt. Jones.
Wm. Lee.	Joshua Green.	Pleasant Lee.
Monroe Kent.	J. L. Kinner.	Sam. Eckers.
Jno. Jackson.	Fry Wade.	W. T. Smith.
Wm. Nowlin.	W. C. Botkins.	
Total 26.		

Mr. Clare was a detective employed in the interest of the contestee at $2.50 a day to travel around and hunt up illegal votes. His evidence is mainly based upon conversations had with the parties named, after the election, and this testimony generally is of such a character as to carry but little weight. We do not think that this testimony overcomes the presumption arising from the reception of any of these votes.

R. L. Weaver (page 282) also assails at Mayberry, McDowell County, Robert Law, Lewis Law, James Dillard, J. H. Mosely, Lowne Jones, Morris Wade, Smith Russell, and J. W. Marshall.

This witness testifies to declarations of the voters as to their residence. These declarations are insufficient to overcome the presumption of legality as to the reception of their votes.

J. C. Freeman (Rec., 371) assails William Lee and Wesley Wagner.

Wesley Wagner did not vote, and there is no proof that William Lee, who voted, is the same man referred to by this witness, and we have already seen that William Lee, who voted at Peery's Bottom, was a legal voter (p. 326), as Lee commenced work at Shamokin County, August 29, 1887.

M. C. Franklin assails the following in Mercer and McDowell Counties (Rec., 333):

Sam Akers.	Joe Ballard.	Jno. Dooley.
Ed Harmon.	Jas. Hackley.	Sam'l Lambert.
Geo. Marsh.	Jake Prillerman.	H. C. Patterson.
W. T. Smith.	Wylie Smith.	W. H. Terry.
Jno. Terry.	Frye Wade.	J. S. Wade.

This witness only knows where these men come from by report. p. 335. This is not sufficient.

J. R. Jewell assails the following parties: Richard Holloway, William Johnson, George Johnson, and Philip Williams, at Alderson, Monroe County.

The right of these voters to vote is assailed on the ground of non-residence. The proof of non-residence is very vague, and is mainly based on declarations made by the voters that in going back to Virginia they were "going home," an expression which is in common use by men living in a State different from that of their birth. Besides, these votes were challenged and passed upon by the judges of election.

We find the following illegal votes cast for the contesting parties.

Illegal votes for McGinnis.

1 Taz Brown (Rec., 152, 159, 173, 174, 179, 180, 197).
2 Joseph Robinson (Rec., 159, 173, 174, 197, 209).
3 Augustus Higginbotham (Rec., 175, 176, 178, 180, 197).
4 Wesley Moyes (Rec., 184, 186, 187).
5 Robert Riley (Rec., 164, 184, 186, 187, 213).
6 Frank Frame (Rec., 163, 213).
7 Dan'l Casdorf (Rec., 164, 213).
8 Geo. Hughes (Rec., 115).
9 J. W. Moore, minor (Rec., 115, 116, 119, 121).
10 F. M. Norman (Rec., 185, 204, 214).
11 H. C. Patterson (Rec., 334, 293, 294.
12 Tim Mowgrass (Rec., 287).
13 Bird Wright (Rec., 287).

Jacob Judy was a legal voter and offered to vote and his vote was excluded. He had the same right to vote as two Democrats named Quick. Their votes were received and his was excluded. His vote should be counted for McGinnis. (Rec., 49, 50, 52.)

Rhodes D. Trent (misprinted Friend, Rec., 89) went to the polls at 4.30 p. m. to vote for McGinnis and his vote was refused, the polls being closed that early. This vote was tendered and refused during voting hours and should be counted for McGinnis.

Illegal votes for Alderson.

1 M. A. Bell (Rec., 37, 38).
2 Luther P. Fleming (Rec., 42, 44).
3 J. Traineor (Rec., 53, 54, 55).
4 Christopher Burnes (Rec., 56, 57, 146).
5 John R. McCoy (Rec., 89, 93).
6 J. R. Presley (Rec., 90).
7 Captain Newsome (Rec., 89, 93).
8 Isaac Brown (Rec., 89, 90, 93).
9 Wm. J. Wyant (Rec., 97, 98).
10 Riley Gilpin (Rec., 97).
11 Elmore Ross (Rec., 99).
12 Wm. Bittinger (Rec., 101, 103).
13 John Parke (Rec., 102).
14 Archibald Ganoe (Rec., 103).
15 Kelley Broyles (Rec., 104).
16 James H. Crawford, jr. (Rec., 9

SUMMARY.

Majority for McGinnis on returns ....
Deduct illegal votes...

Add votes illegally rejected...

Majority for McGinnis..
Add illegal votes, lost to Alderson..

Net majority for McGinnis...

We recommend the passage of the following resolutions :

Resolved, That Jno. D. Alderson was not elected to the office of .
resentative in Congress for the Third Congressional district of 1
Virginia.

Resolved, That James H. McGinnis was duly elected as Represe
tive in the Fifty-first Congress for the said district and is entitle
his seat as such Representative.

VIEWS OF THE MINORITY.

_ The return of Kanawha County was properly omitted by the governor; indeed, in technical strictness, there is even yet no legal return from this county. But counting the vote of said county as shown by recounts lawfully had, contestee has a plurality on the face of the returns. The precautions taken pending the recount were sufficient to make it trustworthy. Of the illegal votes charged, a very much larger number is proved to have been cast for McGinnis than for Alderson, and contestee's plurality is considerably increased thereby.

VIEWS OF THE MINORITY.

AUGUST 2, 1890.—Mr. OUTHWAITE, from the Committee on Elections, submitted the following as the views of the minority:

For the purpose of attempting to shift the burden of proof in this case, the majority set out to show that the contestant was entitled to the certificate of election. The report presents a tabulated statement made by the governor of the vote cast in the district, from which he omits the vote of Kanawha County. It insinuates that some great wrong was done by omitting this county that "cast an undisputed majority of over 1,300 in favor of the contestant," and gravely states that—

A certificate of election showing upon its face that nearly 8,000 votes were wholly ignored in the court can have no binding force and effect in a contest of this character.

The statement of the governor clearly shows that it was by no fault of his, nor of the contestee's, that the vote of this county was omitted at the time he issued the certificate. He says:

The county commissioners declared the result of the election in Kanawha County *December* 15, 1888. The certificate was mailed in this city on the 17th of said month, *and received in this office late in the afternoon.*

On the same day a writ of *certiorari* was awarded by the circuit court of Kanawha County on the petition of John D. Alderson, who claimed to be elected to said office, against the said commissioners, and against James H. McGinnis, who also claimed to be elected to said office. The order awarding the *certiorari* provided for a *supersedeas* to the judgment and decision of said commissioners upon the execution of bond, as required by statute. The bond was forthwith executed, and said judgment and decision suspended. A certified copy of the record in the *certiorari* proceedings shows that said commissioners, in declaring the result of the election in said county, excluded from the recount, had, under the statute, on the demand of said Alderson, a sufficient number of ballots in his favor to have secured his election to said office.

The circuit court aforesaid on the 23d inst. entered judgment reversing the entire proceedings and finding of said commissioners, and remanding the cause.

It will thus be seen that no hardship resulted to contestant, no injustice to Kanawha County, no evil to the people of the district, and no wrong to the country by this omission of Kanawha County. The first certificate of election issued by the Kanawha County commissioners was annulled by the judgment of the circuit court of Kanawha County, entered on the 23d day of February, 1889, the judge thereof being a Republican (see Rec., p. 221). The second certificate of the result of the election in said county, issued by said commissioners, if they issued one, is now inoperative and suspended by an order made by the same circuit court entered on the 3d day of January, 1890 (see additional testimony printed in this case, pp. 93, 94); and, in truth and in fact, there is to-day existing no legal return of the election in said county. If a

technical rule was to be applied in this case, it might be claimed that
this controversy should be determined without considering the vote of
Kanawha County at all.

Yet, including this county, Mr. Alderson has a clear majority of 16 in
the district. Even if the correction of the error claimed to have been
made against contestant in Boone County were conceded, all votes cast
counted gives contestee a clear majority of 7 in the district. But we
can not concede this claim. It is sufficient reason to call attention to the
unsatisfactory testimony by which the certified vote of that county is
sought to be changed favorably for the contestant. No explanation is
attempted to be given, no error is pointed out, to account for it. The
officers having in charge the poll-books and tally-sheets are not called
to account for their proper keeping, nor to explain the reasons for the
desired change. The witnesses were examined without due legal notice
to contestee as required by law. It is a " recount" of a nature not authorized by law. The men who made the mistake, if any was made, are
kept off the witness stand. Yet the committee insist upon giving contestant 9 votes. No suspicion, no danger of fraud (in their view), seems
to attach to such unwarranted change of the legally ascertained vote of
a county. It is for the interest of the contestant.

The contestee claims and proves that a large number of illegal votes
were cast and counted for contestant. Contestant sets up a similar
claim as to a small number of votes given for contestee, but, as he says
in his brief, " has taken but little testimony." Before examining into
these illegal votes upon either side, we shall consider the recount in
Kanawha County, which was taken under the following provisions of
the law of West Virginia as to the duties of the county commissioners
when acting as a canvassing board :

> They shall, upon the demand of any candidate voted for at such election, open and
> examine any one or more of the sealed packages of ballots and recount the same, but
> in such case they shall seal up the same again, along with the original envelope, in
> another envelope, and the clerk of the county court shall write his name across the
> place or places where it is sealed, and endorse on the Outside : Ballots of the election
> held at ——, the district of ——, and county of ——, etc.

THE RECOUNT.

Contestee made a demand, in writing, before the commissioners of
the county court of Kanawha County for a recount of the ballots cast
at said election at all the precincts of said county, at the meeting of
said commissioners held to ascertain the result of said election in said
county on the 12th day of November, 1888, that being the time fixed
by law for the ascertaining and certifying of the result of the election in
each county. On this day the said court took charge of all the ballots
cast in said county, and the election of contestee was then conceded.
The said commissioners were all Republicans; and in the progress of
said recount their actions and rulings were so partisan, corrupt, and
biased in favor of contestant that they refused to allow contestee to
appear before them in person or by counsel. They denied him the
process of the court, refused to permit him to introduce any testimony,
or to cross-examine the witnesses who were put upon the stand to testify in respect to the regularity of the returns from the various precincts in said county. And they further refused to settle and sign bills
of exceptions certifying their illegal and partisan action aforesaid until
they were compelled to do so by the peremptory writ of mandamus
issued by the supreme court of appeals of the State. (See record in
case of J. D. Alderson vs. Commissioners of County Court of Kanawha

County, filed in this case, marked "Record No. 1," and also the opinion of the supreme court of appeals in said case, W. Va. Rep, vol. 31, p. 633.)

After the said order of the supreme court made in said case, requiring said commissioners to settle and sign bills of exception to their rulings in making the recount and requiring them to allow contestee to appear by himself or attorney to said proceedings, they continued their partisan and illegal actions and committed very many wrongs, to the prejudice of the contestee, in ascertaining the result of said election in said county upon his demand for the recount aforesaid. *In the precincts where the recount of the ballots showed gains for the contestant, they adopted the recount, and where gains were made for the contestee they rejected the recount and certified from the poll-books rather than from the ballots.* They rejected the recount of the ballots at St. Albans precinct of said county, where contestee made a gain of one vote and contestant sustained a loss of three votes, without any evidence or facts appearing to warrant them in doing so. They rejected the recount at Alum Creek precinct, where contestee made a gain of three votes and contestant sustained a loss of six votes, against the evidence received and considered by them and without authority of law. They likewise rejected the recount at Charleston precinct, where contestee made a gain of twelve votes and contestant sustained a loss of thirteen votes, without any evidence to sustain them in their action. But they were careful to accept the recount in West End precinct, where contestee sustained a loss of two votes and contestant made a gain of two votes; in Malden precinct, where contestee sustained a loss of one vote; at Thaxton's, where contestee sustained a loss of one vote; at Field's Creek, where contestant made a gain of one vote; at Clifton, where contestant made a gain of one vote, and at Cannelton, where contestee sustained a loss of one vote. All of the facts and rulings of said commissioners, herein referred to in respect to said recount, are contained and set out in Record No. 2, filed in this case (p. 41 to 86, additional testimony).

The following tabulated statement, as appears upon page 36 of said Record No. 2, shows the vote as it was certified upon the poll-books from each and every precinct in said county, and also the result of the recount of the ballots cast at said precincts made by said commissioners, as hereinbefore stated, as between contestant and contestee:

Precincts.	Original count.		Recount.	
	Alderson.	McGinnis.	Alderson.	McGinnis.
Upper Pinch	14	55	14	55
West End	153	229	151	231
Malden	264	320	263	320
St. Albans	228	234	220	231
Thaxton's	88	163	87	163
Alum Creek	50	144	53	138
Island Branch	17	77	17	77
Kendall's Mills	25	40	25	40
Dry Ridge	16	26	16	26
Brownstown	92	70	92	70
Smith's Creek	58	40	58	40
Coalburg	124	104	124	104
Spring Hill	47	69	47	96
Lewiston	79	88	79	88
Big Sandy	82	211	82	211
Kelley's Creek	69	15	69	15

Precincts.	Original count.		Recount.	
	Alderson.	McGinnis.	Alderson.	McGinnis.
Cross Lanes	121	53	121	53
Tyler Creek	60	44	60	44
Sissonville	91	331	91	334
Conley's	101	179	101	179
Shrewsbury	36	40	36	40
Danaville	52	154	52	154
Upper Falls	23	22	23	22
Field Creek	49	179	49	180
Fairfield	19	82	19	82
Clifton	113	134	113	135
Kanawha Mines	64	84	64	86
Pine Grove	100	82	101	81
Cannelton	64	61	63	61
City of Charleston	840	864	852	851
Alden City	27	51	27	50
Big Chimney	74	162	74	162
Poca Fork	37	138	37	138
Givens	52	110	52	110
Total	3,329	4,658	3,341	4,638

The contestant received in all of the counties of said district, other than the county of Kanawha, 14,631 votes, and contestee received in same counties 15,944 votes. If the election is determined in Kanawha County as certified upon the poll-books, contestant has a plurality in the district of 16 votes. If, however, it is determined upon the recount of the ballots cast in said county, then contestee has a plurality of 16 votes.

Can it be this result which leads the committee to the conclusion that "such recount is full of danger?" There were two precincts in which the changes were largely against the contestant. The changes in the other precincts were in his favor as much as they were against him. The recount in those is not attacked; but the recount in Alum Creek and Charleston is objected to by the committee, also by the contestant. By counting the ballots the county commissioners found that the judges or clerks of election had mistakenly counted 3 votes less for Alderson than he had received and 6 votes more for McGinnis than he had actually received at Alum Creek precinct.

In the same way we learn that the election officers in the Charleston precinct had erroneously counted 12 votes less for Alderson than there were ballots cast for him, and 13 more for McGinnis than there were ballots cast for him. An examination of the circumstances under which the election officers made their count will show that such mistakes could easily have occurred. We shall draw no inference from the fact that two of the judges of election at Alum Creek were Republicans to account for the mistakes there.

But we here call attention to the evidence upon the matter of said recount.

AT ALUM CREEK PRECINCT.

It appears from the evidence of J. B. Holstein, J. C. Holstein, J. W. Goshorn, W. A. Griffith, and W. McCorkle that the said W. A. Griffith, who was one of the commissioners of election at Alum Creek precinct, was drinking and under the influence of liquor on the day of said election while ballots were being received by him, and that night, while same were being counted; that there was whisky in bottles and in a jug there, being passed around generally during that time; that the ballot-box at that precinct was opened, contrary to law, during the day while ballots were being received, and the same counted on certain candidates voted for; that the said Griffith was asleep from the influence of liquor during a portion of the night when the ballots were being counted. (See Rec., pp. 61, 172, 211, 191, and 194.)

It appears from the evidence that on the morning after the election - the said Griffith took the package of ballots which, he states, were sealed up, put it in one end of a sack and a rock in the other, threw the sack across a horse, and rode upon the same 12 miles to the city of Charleston and delivered said package, so sealed up, to J. W. Goshorn, clerk of the county court of said county. This certainly afforded an opportunity for said package to be defaced or broken open. And the evidence further shows that said package was carefully and properly preserved, with all the other packages of ballots, until same were laid before the commissioners of the county court on the 12th day of November, 1888; that the said commissioners of the county court then and there took all the packages of ballots, including the package from Alum Creek, and placed them in a bag and carefully tied and sealed up the same, and wrote their names across said seal. This bag, under the directions of the said commissioners, was placed over the storm-door to the clerk's office of said county court. It further appears that said bag was thrown down from the top of the said storm-door, a distance of 7 feet, upon the stone floor in said clerk's office, several times while said packages of ballots were still in said bag.

The package which contained the Alum creek ballots was made of thick manilla paper of the same kind and quality as the one filed with the proof in this case. Considering the character of the package and tha manner the same was handled while in said bag, it is not improbable that the seal was broken or torn by reason thereof, especially when the proofs show that same was not well sealed by the precinct commissioners. When the commissioners of said county court proceeded to recount the ballots, upon the demand for same, which was about ten days after they were returned to said clerk's office, the said bag was found in the same condition in which it was left when first sealed up, with the seal unbroken. It also appears from the evidence that a number of the packages of the ballots from various precincts in said county were returned to said clerk's office unsealed, before the Alum Creek package was so received. These open packages were never sealed up, except in the bags before stated, until after the ballots were recounted by the commissioners of the county court.

If it had been desired by any one to tamper with any of the ballots so returned to said clerk's office, it is unreasonable to assume that a sealed package would have been broken when it thus appears to have been unnecessary. We refer to the depositions of J. W. Goshorn, Joel S. Quarrier, and W. E. G. Gillison; also to the deposition of J. A. Jones, pp. 159, 204, and 203, Record:

When the vote was all counted it was near daylight in the morning.

Were these ballots properly kept until they were recounted by the county commissioners?

The law provides that the original packages shall be sealed up at the place of voting, as follows:

When the said certificates are signed, the ballot shall be inclosed by the commissioners in an envelope, which they shall seal up, and write their names across the place or places where it is sealed, and indorse on the outside of the said envelope as follows: "Ballots of the election held at ——, in the district of —— and county of ——, the —— day of ——, etc.

As soon as the result of the recount was discovered to be adverse to the contestant, his political friends set about to destroy the legal effect thereof by questioning the care taken of the ballots since they were miscounted. The three precinct commissioners in their testimony show that the ballots were put on a string as they were taken out of the ballot-box; after the vote was counted the ballots were put in an envelope or manilla-paper box, they send a clerk to get some mucilage to seal this box up, and do seal it up with mucilage, and it was cared for and disposed of as we have just set forth.

The circumstances surrounding the disposition of thes·· ballots and the preservation of them is such as might ordinarily occur in a great many precincts. Nowhere is there any evidence tending to show, in any degree, that the ballots were tampered with. The law was substantially complied with up to the hour the county commissioners took the ballots into their charge and possession—and they left them in the custody of the county clerk. This county clerk was a Republican and so were the county commissioners, and up to the time in which they took possession of all the precinct returns the election of contestee had not been questioned; rather had it generally been accepted. No one has testified that the envelope was torn open when these county commissioners came to make their recount. Mr. Jones testifies that—

This package did not appear to have been torn open. It showed an effort had been made to seal it.

Mr. Goshorn, the Republican clerk (Rec., 193), testifies that—

It had not been torn open, but looked, upon close examination, like it had been glued, but the glue did not stick.

In fact the package, newly mucilaged and carried to town as described, had become loosened, or from the subsequent tossing down from above the storm-door in the bag with thirty-two other packages, had pulled apart. There is no room for even a "natural suspicion" that the ballots from Alum Creek had been tampered with. No opportunity is shown for it to have been done. The fourteenth, fifteenth, and sixteenth questions to J. W. Goshorn, the Republican clerk, and his answers are here given.

Q. 14. At the time you speak of the returns from the various precincts being put in the sack and sealed-up and the sack placed over the storm-door, what question was there about the election of Fleming for governor and Alderson for Congress?—A. There was none whatever, as we had not heard from the remote or back counties, and it was confidently believed that Fleming and Alderson were both elected by good and safe majorities, and not until the returns from these back Democratic counties, where the Republicans made heavy gains and this changed the result, which was ten days after the election.

Q. 15. Were you present when the sack you spoke of was presented to the county court to make the recount? If so, state in what condition it was?—A. I was; it was examined by the court and the attorneys, and they decided that it was in the same condition that it was on the Monday after the election, as the seal was unbroken and no holes in the sack or any indication of any having been made in the sack.

Q. 16. Please state in what condition the package from Alum Creek precinct was when it was taken out of the sack for the recount?—A. The red string or tape was tied around the paper box; when we examined the box closely it looked like there had been mucilage or glue used to stick it together. My impression, or the way I account for it, was, that there had been a little glue put on and had not had time to dry, as the box was so thick that the mucilage or glue would not stick unless it was perfectly dry. If it was stuck when Mr. Griffith left home, the ride of twelve miles horseback, with the returns in one end of sack and a rock in the other, would be almost certain to break the box open. If the box was fastened when it came to the clerk's office, the simple fact of putting it in a sack with 32 others would make a weight of about 60 pounds; throwing that sack up and down on and from the storm-door on to the rock floor would have surely broken the glue. I do not think that any one of the 33 packages which was sealed up in like manner as the Alum Creek package was claimed to be, but what the glue or mucilage had broken loose. Those that did hold were sealed up with a piece of paper round the outside of the envelope or box.

Q. 17. When the said Alum Creek package was produced on the recount was the same torn open or did it appear that mucilage or glue had come apart?—A. It had not been torn open, but looked, upon close examination, like it had been glued but the glue did not stick.

CHARLESTON PRECINCT.

An attempt is made to discredit the recount of the vote for Congress-man at Charleston precinct because it gives Alderson a gain of 12 and McGinnis a loss of 13. Before considering the claim that these ballots were not preserved in the manner pointed out by law let us see how they were counted by the precinct commissioners and clerks of election, two-thirds of whom were Republicans.

It appears that, at Charleston precinct, a very large number of votes were polled at said election, to wit, 1,758; that, in order to make proper tally of all persons voted for at said precinct at said election, a column was kept for each one of one hundred and two names upon tally-sheets, each 3½ feet by 4 feet in size, by each of the clerks who kept said tally. More than 500 votes having been polled at this precinct, it was unnec-essary, under the law, to wait until the polls were closed to begin the counting of the vote, and about 8 or 9 o'clock on Tuesday morning of the said election the canvassers and clerks commenced to count this said vote, and were engaged continuously, without intermission, both day and night, until the hour of 11 o'clock on Friday night following in com-pleting said count. The canvassers who read the ballots were old men, and most of them required the use of glasses to aid their eye-sight. The count was made in the court-room of the county court-house, which was very poorly lighted, there being in the night-time what was called a ".cross-light." That it is probable that mistakes were made by these canvassers and clerks is shown by the fact that they frequently discov-ered each other in so doing. They necessarily were inaccurate because of their long engagements, growing tired, and the loss of sleep, as stated by them.

After the count was completed the ballots were strung and, to-gether with the tally-sheets, were placed in a cake or cracker box selected for the purpose—it having been necessary from the bulk made by said ballots and tally-sheets—and the box nailed up, sealed, and in-dorsed by said commissioners of election at said precinct, as required by law. The box was procured by Joel S. Quarrier from S. S. Smith, a clerk in the store of A. C. Orcutt.

The only ground upon which the rejection of the recount of the said ballots can be justified is the untenable one that the ballots in said box so sealed up were tampered with after the same were placed in the hands of the clerk of said county court and before the same were laid before the said commissioners of the county court on the 12th day of November, 1888. To support this contention an effort is made to prove, by Thomas Y. Jarrett, T. J. Rocky, and John Slack, jr., that the con-dition of said box, when the same was laid before said commissioners on November 12, 1888, was different from what it was when the said ballots and tally-sheets were placed therein on the Friday night pre-vious.

Mr. Jarrett testified (p. 65) that he was one of the commissioners at said election; that he looked at said box before the ballots were placed in it; that it appeared to be sound; did not notice any crack or chisel-mark on the bottom thereof, but declined to state that the condition of

the box was changed. Mr. Rocky (p. 73) testified that he examined
the box before the ballots were put in it; that the box was turned upside down; he discovered no defects in box, and considered it in good
condition; that the other canvassers and commissioners examined the
box at the same time and appeared to be satisfied with its condition;
that none of them mentioned the discovery of any defects; that the
next time he saw the box was when he was summoned before the
commissioners of the county court to testify in regard to the condition
of the box, when they were making the recount. This witness didn't
think the box was in same condition then as when ballots were put in
it; that a board on bottom of box was split; there were three indentures, as if made by chisel or other instrument in attempt to pry board
off of bottom of box; direction of split in board corresponded with direction of pressure as indicated by indentures. On cross-examination (p.
75) the following question was propounded to witness, who made the
subjoined answer thereto:

Question 20. Did you not state on your examination before the county court, in
answer to a question as to the condition of said box, that you had not made an examination of the box and could not say whether said marks were on said box at said
time or not, or words to that effect? —Answer. I believe I stated before the county
court that I did not turn the box over myself, but that some one else did; that I saw
the box; that I thought the box in good condition; that I noticed no split or defect
in the box. I may have stated that the chisel-marks might have existed at that time
and I not have noticed them.

Mr. Slack (p. 76) testifies that he examined box at time of recount;
it had every appearance of bottom being taken off; marks of chisel that
had pried bottom off were plain to be seen; nails had every appearance of having been taken out and driven back; a small splinter had
been broken loose, evidently done when bottom was taken off.

The testimony of T. J. Rocky is not to be relied upon in this case.
He has impeached himself by his own statements, independent of the
evidence on that subject to which we will hereafter call attention. It
appears he was summoned before the commissioners of the county
court of said county when they were engaged in making said recount
on the 6th day of December, 1888, and testified as follows:

Q. Did you examine the box in which the ballots were put?—A. I did not examine
the box.
Q. Did not examine the bottom of it?—A. No, sir; I did not. (See Record No.
2, pp. 67, 68.)

The foregoing is all the testimony of the said Rocky given before
said commissioners with reference to his examination of said box.

He testifies emphatically before the commissioners that he did not
examine said box before the ballots were put in it; yet he testifies in
this case that he did make such examination, and in his answer to question No. 20 of his cross-examination he stated what must be construed
to mean that he formerly testified that he did make such examination.

On page 365 of record J. A. Hutchison testifies that he was the stenographer who took the testimony of the said Rocky given before said
commissioners with reference to the condition of said box before the
ballots were placed therein. We quote from said Hutchison's testimony:

Q. 6. Was he asked as such witness (meaning said T. J. Rockey) in respect to box
in which the ballots cast at Charleston precinct, in said county, were placed by the
election commissioners of said precinct after said ballots had been strung by them?—
A. He was.
Q. 7. What did he say in respect to the condition of the box? -A. He said, "I did
not examine the box or the bottom of it before the ballots were placed in it," or after
they were placed in it, and before the box was delivered to the county court clerk of
Kanawha County.

James A. Mahan testified in this case (p. 209) that he was one of the canvassers of said election at Charleston precinct; that Joel S. Quarrier brought the box into the court-house in which said ballots were placed; that he was the only one of the election officers who took hold of the box before the ballots and tally-sheets were placed therein, but that no examination whatever was made of the box by any one after the box was brought in and before the ballots were put in it; and that he examined box at the time the said commissioners of the county court were taking testimony about it and saw no difference in its condition then than when it was brought into the court-house by Mr. Quarrier.

Here is a witness directly contradicting Rocky.

E. M. Senter, J. D. Shumate, and I. E. Christian, on pages 426–429, all testify that they are acquainted with the general reputation of said Rocky for truth and veracity, and from that reputation would not believe him on oath. It appears from the evidence of A. P. Fry, J. D. White, James H. Fry, and J. A. Jones that said Rocky did not make the examination of the box, as stated by him before the ballots were put in it.

Mr. Rocky is shown to have been a Republican at the time of said election; so partisan in his friendship for contestant in this contest that, although not a public officer, he traveled many miles to serve notices upon contestee to take depositions in this case. Under this state of facts is it not fair to assume that Mr. Rocky's testimony in this case is wholly unreliable and should be disregarded; and in view of the fact that Mr. Slack states in his deposition, exultingly, that he was a Republican and devoted his time solely for ten days prior to the election in the interest of the Republican party, that he, too, may have been somewhat biased in his statement in reference to said box? But, even if his statement is true, it by no means proves that the condition of the box was changed. He had never seen the box until during the recount.

But the testimony of unimpeached witnesses entirely destroys the last vestige of this subterfuge to avoid the recount of Charleston precinct.

J. W. Goshborn deposes and says:

A. When they got thro' counting on Friday night about 11 o'clock, after the election, Mr. Quarrier, my deputy clerk, got a cake or cracker box from Mr. Orcutt's store, across the street from the court-house, and the ballots and tally-sheets were put into that box; Mr. Quarrier took charge of the box and put it in the corner of the back room of the clerk's office and covered it over with some papers, and there it staid until it was put into the strong wooden box we had made to keep all the ballots in, which was about three days afterwards.

Q. 25. Please state how the said cake or cracker box in which said ballots and tally-sheets were kept was secured?—A. There was a piece of paper pasted over it and sealed, with the commissioners' names written across it, and it was never broken until the county court commenced the recount, when they broke it.

Q. 26. Please state when you first heard the charge made that said box had been tampered with, and from whom did it proceed?—A. The morning after the recount was completed; I could not find out, as it was talked about by irresponsible Republicans; when I heard there was an intimation of that kind I inquired of Mr. Quarrier where he got the box. He told me that he got it across the street, from Mr. Orcutt's store; I went across the street and got Mr. Orcutt and Mr. Smith, his clerk, from whom the box was procured, and we examined the box; they both stated that there was no indications that the box had been tampered with. Mr. Smith stated that the wholesale houses were in the habit of opening that kind of box from the bottom to sample, as the top was put on with hinges and nailed. We went over to Mr. Orcutt's office and examined a box of the same make and from the same firm, which was split in identically the same place as the ballot-box. I went to Messrs. Cunningham and Staunton, two of the county commissioners, and told them that some irresponsible scamps were intimating that the ballot-box had been tampered with in my office, and that I wanted them to put Mr. Quarrier, Mr. Orcutt, and Mr. Smith on the stand; they would testify that the box was in the same condition as it was when they brought it to Mr. Quarrier. They both told me that it wasn't necessary, as they would a resolution exonerating me and my office from all blame.

Q. 27. Were you present in the court-house when the said box was brought from Mr. Orcutt's store and the ballots placed in it?—A. Yes, sir; I was.

Q. 28. What examination was made of that box by any person interested before ballots were placed in it?—A. Mr. Quarrier brought the box, set it down on the court-house floor, Mr. Mahan picked up the box and turned it over and set it again; Mr. White and Mr. Jarrett looked in the box; the tally-sheets and were put in, I think, by Mr. Jarrett; there was no critical examination of that by any one, as it was nearly 12 o'clock, and the commissioners, canvassers, and had been working for four days and nights and were anxious to get home and get rest.

Q. 29. In what way was it charged that said box had been tampered with? There never was any charge that the box had been tampered with, but there intimations from irresponsible scamps that part of the bottom had been taken.

Q. 30. Please state, after such intimations were made, if you noticed any or splits on the bottom of the box; if so, state what they were?—A. The bottom the box had either two or three (I think three) planks in it, and one of the was split. I am of the impression this was caused by the sun, or a sun crack not believe that plank could be taken off without splitting out the nail holes plank is very thin and the nails are very close to the edge.

Q. 31. Was there any signs of freshness about the splits?—A. None whatever.

Joel S. Quarrier, another witness of lawful age, being first sworn, deposes and says:

Q. 1. (By M. Jackson, attorney for J. D. Alderson.) State your name, residence, and occupation.—A. Joel S. Quarrier; 57 years; Charleston, W. Va.; clerk county court.

Q. 2. Please state if you were employed in the county clerk's office at the of the election, November 6th, 1888, and how long you have been employed there? was so employed at the time of said election, and have been in the office about and one-half years as deputy clerk.

Q. 9. Please state if your attention was called to the box in which were placed ballots cast at the Court-House precinct. If so, when, and in what condition did you find it?—A. My attention was called to it after the recount was had; am not that I knew the ballots were in a box before that time. I found it all right, apparently, except that there seemed to be a small abrasure or something on one side or the bottom, which, in my opinion, did not amount to anything; one of the planks in the bottom was cracked or split, which did not seem to be of recent date; pieces or plank of the box seemed to be all well nailed, as far as I observed; the plank at one end of the box, by reason of its thinness and not being nailed near the end it should have been, seemed to have sprung a little and left a small crack, increased I have no doubt, by frequent manipulations of prying fingers, as I saw many persons examining the place with their fingers.

Q. 10. Did you see any signs of freshness about the abrasure you speak of, or any or anything suspicious in the appearance of the box?—A. I did not.

Q. 19. What have you to say as to the truth of the evidence of one W. A. Forsythe given in this cause, about seeing said Montague engaged after night in said office said work, and the statements made by said Forsythe, and in connection therewith?—A. I have read the statements made by said Forsythe, and know that the same is an infamous lie.

Q. 20. Did you in any manner change, alter, or tamper with the ballots or election returns of said election, or do you know of any one who did, or have you any reason to believe the same were changed, altered, or tampered with?—A. I did not, and know of no person who tampered with the ballots of said election. I have no reason to believe they were tampered with, from the fact that I was in said office every day and night during the period from the election to the end of the recount.

Q. 21. Did you get the box in which were placed the ballots cast at the Court-House voting precinct; if so, from whom did you get it?—A. I got it from A. C. Orcutts, at his store, which is opposite the court-house, and delivered the same to the commissioners of election on Friday evening after the election; I assisted in placing in said box the ballots and tally-sheets; I sealed it securely with mucilage (it being a box with a lid), and the same was delivered to me in said clerk's office by T. Y. Jarrett, one of the officers of the election.

Q. 22. What examination, if any, was made of said box before said ballots and tally-sheets were placed in it?—A. Some of the officers examined—turned it over to get some dirt out of it—but I made no examination of it.

A. P. Fry testifies that he was present when the box was brought into the court-house by Mr. Quarrier; that no special examination was made of it by any one before the ballots were put in it, and that it was sealed up and delivered to the clerk; that his attention was called to the box while the county commissioners had it under examination, and it seemed to be in the same condition it was when he first saw it; that he saw no evidence that it had been tampered with, or anything to raise a suspicion of that kind (p. 206).

The evidence of Mr. Fry in this matter is corroborated by the evidence of J. H. Fry, J. D. White, and J. A. Jones (pp. 159, 210, 217).

The true explanation of the condition of said box is that it appears to have been a cracker or cake box. It was the custom or habit of dealers in that class of goods to open such boxes on the bottom for the purpose of sampling the goods therein, and it was evidently done so with this box before the ballots were first placed in it, as is fully explained by the depositions of A. C. Orcutt, S. S. Smith, and S. M. Snyder, here copied from record in this case.

A. C. Orcutt, another witness of lawful age, and for contestee, being first duly sworn, deposes and says:

Q. 2. (By M. Jackson, counsel for J. D. Alderson.) State your name, age, residence, and occupation.—A. A. C. Orcutt; near Charleston, W. Va.; 44 years; merchant and timber dealer.

Q. 2. Please state where you were doing business at the time of the election held in Kanawha County on the 6th of November, 1888.—A. At 205 Kanawha street, Charleston, W. Va., opposite the old court house.

Q. 3. State who furnished the box in which were placed the tally-sheets and ballots cast at the Court-House precinct at said election.—A. It was furnished from my store.

Q. 4. Who was your clerk at that time?—A. S. S. Smith and W. A. Mahan.

Q. 5. Please state what kind of a box it was and where it came from?—A. It was a cracker or cake box, and it came from my store.

Q. 6. Please describe said box, and where you kept your empty boxes.—A. It was a box with lid fastened on with hinges; empty boxes were usually kept in cellar under store.

Q. 7. State if your attention was called to said box after it was said to have been tampered with. If so, where and in what condition did you find it?—A. It was at the clerk's office of Kanawha County. I saw nothing about the box that would arouse my suspicions that it had been tampered with.

Q. 8. State if your attention was called to any splits or marks on the bottom of said box. If so, what were they?—A. I saw a split in the bottom of the box; it was split clear across the bottom; it was an ordinary split in the wood; I saw what they said was the marks.

Q. 9. Did you see any signs of freshness about the split or mark spoken of?—A. I did not; nothing that would arouse my suspicions, for I went immediately across to my store and examined a box of the same kind, and found identically the same split and marks on it.

Q. 10. Please state, if you can, from your own knowledge of the trade, how such splits and marks happen in those boxes?—A. I think it was from sampling or examining the contents of the box before shipping, by the wholesaler or dealer.

Q. 11. Please state the object of sampling from the bottom?—A. In order to save the lid, which is put on with hinges.

Q. 12. Mr. Orcutt, if you have no objection, will you please state your politics?—A. I am a Republican.

S. S. Smith, another witness of lawful age and for the contestee, being first duly sworn, deposes and says:

Question 1. (By M. Jackson, attorney for Alderson). State your name, age, residence, and occupation.—A. S. S. Smith; age, 37; State of Ohio; in mercantile business.

Q. 2. (By same.) State what occupation you were engaged in, and where, at the time of the election held in Kanawha County on the 6th day of November, 1888?—A. I was here in Orcutt's store.

Q. 3. State, if you know, who furnished the box in which were placed the tally-sheets and ballots cast at the Court-House precinct at said election?—A. I furnished the box to Joel S. Quarrier.

Q. 4. Please state what kind of a box it was and where you got it?—A. It was a cake box; I got it out of the cellar under the store-room.

Q. 5. Please describe the size of the box, the kind of material, and its construction.—A. It was about 2 feet long, ten or twelve inches deep, about twelve or fourteen inches wide, made of poplar lumber; the plank was about ¼ of inch thick, and the lid was put on with hinges and when the box was filled with cakes the lid was nailed down.

Q. 6. Please state if your attention was called to said box after it was charged it had been tampered with; if so, when and where and in what condition did you find it?—A. Yes; my attention was called to it a short time after the polls were counted; a day or two after it was reported the box had been tampered with. I suppose it was in the clerk's office. My attention was called to some marks on the box that looked like it had been made with an edged tool, and a split in the bottom of the box which was nothing more than a wind-shake in the plank in the bottom of the box of which it had been made. The marks to which my attention was called that looked like they had been made with an edged tool were old marks. I saw nothing suspicious about the box.

Q. 7. Did you observe any signs of freshness about the split you mention?—A. No, sir.

Q. 8. State if you made any comparison of the said box with any other box?—A. Yes, sir; I went to the cellar and got another box of same size, made of same material, made by the same company or manufacturers, and had been filled with cakes by the same cake company; it had the same marks between the edge of the bottom plank and the lower edge of the end plank, and the same crack in the bottom of the box as the box to which my attention was called.

S. M. Snyder, a witness in this cause, being first duly sworn, deposes and says:

Q. 1. (By M. Jackson.) Was your attention ever called to the box in which were put the ballots and tally-sheets of the election held at the Court-House precinct at the election held November 6th, 1888, after it was said to have been tampered with?—A. Yes. On the morning after the ballots were placed in the clerk's office I went over and examined the box carefully; the splits were old, and it would have been impossible to have drawn the nails in the ends of the box without splitting the boards. There was a mark in the end of the box as though made by some sharp instrument, but the mark looked old; nothing fresh looking about it.

Q. 2. Did you see anything suspicious looking or unusual about said box?—A. I did not.

Q. 3. Please state what kind of a box that was?—A. Cracker or cake box.

Q. 4. Have you ever been in the grocery business?—A. Yes; about two years.

Q. 5. Please state in what manner boxes filled with cakes or crackers are sampled?—A. I understand they are sampled from the bottom, in order not to disfigure the appearance of the goods, and that they may open up nicely.

See also the deposition of James H. Fry, p. 210.

At the time the commissioners of the county court took charge of the ballots returned to the said clerk's office, viz, on Monday, November 12, 1888, the result of the election in the other counties of the Congressional district was not known at Charleston.

Mr. J. W. Goshorn testifies (p. 193):

We had not heard from the remote or back counties, and it was confidently believed that Fleming and Alderson were both elected by good and safe majorities. There was no question about the election until the returns came in from these back Democratic counties, where the Republicans made heavy gains, which was ten days after the election. Mercer and McDowell Counties had for years been largely Democratic. No one could anticipate the results in those counties.

It is apparent, then, that prior to November 12, 1888, no one could have had any possible motive for tampering with the ballots, nor could any one possibly guess how much of a change would be required to affect the result in the district.

It will be observed that no officer or officers who had possession of said box and ballots, after the same were sealed up and delivered to the county clerk, were political friends of or belonged to the same political party as the contestee. The clerk and his two deputies, all Republicans, testify that there was no opportunity for the ballots to be tampered with.

Charleston precinct was the last to be recounted. The completion of this recount disclosed that the contestee had received a plurality of all the votes cast for Representative in Congress for that district. When the partisan and corrupt county commissioners found that contestee was elected they began to look around for some pretext to deny him the result of said recount. The subterfuge resorted to as to Alum Creek would not sufficiently help them. At this point the old marks on the box were discovered, and that was enough. When this contest was brought in the evidence to sustain contestant is found in this statement:

W. A. Forsythe, being duly sworn, deposed as follows:

Question 1. State your name, residence, and occupation.—Answer. W. A. Forsythe; Charleston, W. Va.; lumberman.

Question 2. State where you were on or about Nov. 6th, 1888, and what precautions, if any, were taken to protect the ballots and poll-books of Charleston precinct and Kanawha County, by the county court of said county or by any one else, after the said general election of Nov. 6th, 1888, and to prevent fraud and tampering with the returns of said election for said county. State in this connection all you may know about the same.—Answer. I was in Charleston during the election and the day after election. I think I suggested to several Republicans the propriety of selecting a Republican and a Democrat to take charge of the returns from the several precincts of Kanawha County until the county court met and not permit the said returns to go into the hands of the county clerk, for fear that he might tamper with or deface them; that I talked the matter over from the day after election until the next Friday. On Friday I was solicited to keep a watch on the clerk's office that night. On that night I went down to the clerk's office not far from seven o'clock in the evening, where I saw the clerk, Joel S. Quarrier, and deputy clerk, Phil. Montague, and a man I did not know, all in the office. About half past seven o'clock the man I did not know and Mr. Gashorn left the office. Mr. Quarrier and Mr. Montague stayed on until nine o'clock or after, when Mr. Quarrier left, leaving Mr. Montague alone in the office. Mr. Montague closed the blinds of the office, except one blind which he left open for a space of two and a half or three inches wide. Mr. Montague sat at a table in the south room of the clerk's office and seemed to be copying from a book of record which he had before him on the table. He continued at this until perhaps ten o'clock or after, when he did something with the book, took it out of sight. He got up and went to the south side of the room. I didn't see him when he again returned to the table, until after he had returned and sat down. When I again saw him sitting at the table he had several packages of papers which seemed to be different in size and shape from other packages which were lying on the table when I first saw him sitting at the table. He was examining the first packages spoken of and had a pen or a pencil in his hand. He examined two or three packages. He finally got up and shut the blind so I could see nothing more except to distinguish a light in the room. The light continued to show until eleven o'clock or after. I watched the next evening (Saturday) until three o'clock in the morning. I saw nothing worthy of observation. This is all I know. I may state more fully on cross-examination.

This witness is totally discredited in every way possible to destroy the credibility of a man.

First. Several reputable citizens each testify that they are acquainted with his reputation for truth and veracity in the neighborhood where he resides; that it is bad, and that he would not believe him (Forsythe) under oath because of such bad reputation. (See Rec., pp. 159, 160, 162, 165, 196, 205, 210, 212.)

Second. Upon cross-examination he is asked to tell to whom he made known the discoveries of the night. He answers Colonel Patton, who was acting as attorney for some of the Republican candidates, and then admits that Colonel Patton testified he did not remember the witness telling him of all the details of things that he saw there. He answers also "Mr. Burlew," another Republican lawyer and counsel for Mr. McGinnis, contestant. That gentleman testifies (Rec., 458) as follows:

Answer. Shortly after the election in Nov., W. A. Forsyth told me that he had seen Montague, one of the clerks employed in the county clerk's office, quite late in the evening after dark one night engaged in some kind of work; the shutters were closed

and the light was dim; therefore, Forsyth said he could not see what he was doing.
I recollect of him saying that Montague wasn't engaged in writing at a table, as if
doing office work, but seemed to be moving considerable; I know that Forsyth said
in that conversation that he believed that Montague was the man that interfered with
the ballots and packages filed there of the election had in Nov., and that he did it that
night. He seemed to be quite earnest about it and a little excited; Forsythe with
other Republicans were watching the county clerk's office.

Neither of these attorneys corroborates him, but rather contradict.
Neither of them used the story before the county commissioners to
attack the recount. Why?

Third. Mr. Goshorn testifies in respect to Forsythe's statement:

It is a lie made from the whole cloth.

Quarrier testifies:

I have read the statement made by said Forsythe and know that the same is an
infamous lie.

Both of them give other evidence showing that Montague was not in
the clerk's office at the time at which Forsythe professed to have seen
him there. The witness' manner of testifying would destroy his credibility with most honest, impartial, sensible men. Had he seen Montague tampering with those ballots he would have known it before
morning. Yet he was never called upon to testify as a witness during
the recount when contestant's counsel were putting before the commissioners all the testimony possible to provide an excuse for them to
avoid doing what the facts of the ballots required—render a judgment
which would leave no question as to the right of the contestee to his
seat.

Montague was never in charge of the clerk's office so as to have tampered with the ballots. Forsythe, even, does not testify to seeing Montague apparently tampering with the ballots. The ballots were never
tampered with. The recount should stand. Contestee was thus entitled to the certificate by a plurality of 25 upon the proper returns. We
shall now proceed to show that the honest plurality of contestee should
be largely increased because of the illegal votes cast and counted for
contestant. The latter in his brief says " this case will show about as
many illegal votes cast for one party as the other."

This might be true if both parties had been equally diligent and had
taken testimony as to an equal number of suspected illegal votes. But
contestant, as he says on page 2 of same brief, "relying upon that well-
settled principle of law that the election officers to whom the law con-
fides the duty of determining who are qualified legal voters are
presumed to have done their duty," * * * has taken but little
testimony and has sought out and charged as illegal voters against
himself only about 200 and took testimony as to the qualifications of not
more than 50 voters. The contestee has found nearly 400 illegal voters
who voted for contestant and has taken a great deal of testimony to
sustain his charges, examining one or more witnesses about each voter.
The number of illegal votes cast for one party will not be shown to be
as many as those cast for the other when such a state of facts exists.
Some of the witnesses contestant called sustained the claims of contestee. A different reason from that given by contestant clearly appears for taking little testimony as to a large number of his alleged
illegal voters.

The committee have adopted a queer plan to dispose of the testimony
of contestant sustaining the charges of illegal voting made by him.
For example, they have in many instances made statements of votes
assailed by a particular witness, as if he were the only one who had

testified to the illegality of their votes, when in fact several witnesses have sworn to facts tending to prove that the voters named were not entitled to vote. Further along in their report some mention may be made of other witnesses whose testimony assailed the legality of these same voters. But it is presented in such a way as to hide or weaken the force of their evidence.

If the purpose of the committee was to discourage and prevent members from investigating for themselves, it certainly has been successfully effected. Many illegal votes for contestant are refused to be rejected, because the witness against them was one of the judges of election who received the votes cast by those electors, while the facts to which he swears are nowhere controverted, but are corroborated by other witnesses. More than once the proposition is advanced that certain testimony does not overcome the presumption arising from the reception of any of these votes, when that testimony is but a part of a chain of evidence establishing beyond all question that many of the voters were not legal voters in West Virginia at the time of that election. The committee concedes that 13 of the 361 voters directly challenged by contestee for being illegal were so and were cast for contestant.

The names of the 13 are given, and the pages of the record on which the testimony concerning said voters may be found.

The committee claim that 16 of 50 voters investigated by the contestant were illegal and cast for contestee, and therefore should be deducted from his total. A fair comparison of the testimony upon which the 13 are conceded or the 16 claimed with the evidence against each of 300 others who voted for contestant will show that every one of them ought to be rejected. Take, for instance, from the table in the report of "Illegal votes for Alderson," No. 9, William J. Wyatt (Rec., 97, 98). This is the testimony of John Buckland:

Question 3. Do you know where the said Wm. J. Wyatt voted on the 6th day of November, 1888?—Ans. I understand he voted in Talcott district, Summers Co., W. Va.

Ans. to Quest. 4. He lives in Greenbrier district, said county of Summers, and has lived there all his life.

Ans. to Q. 6. He belongs to the Democratic party.

Ans. to X-Q. 1. I understand he voted there (at Talcott), but don't know it of my own knowledge.

Re-ex. Yes; he lives in Greenbrier, in about 30 yards from the line.

John P. Buckland testifies as to William J. Wyatt:

I don't know whether he voted at Talcott or not. My understanding is he voted there. He always made a habit of voting there.

The committee reject this voter and take 1 from Alderson. Is any comment necessary?

1. M. A. Bell (Rec., 37, 38) on that list. This vote is assailed by one of the two Republican judges who permitted him to vote. The question was as to residence and a county line. Why did the committee violate its own astute ruling as to the evidence of Mr. Solomon and other Democratic judges?

4. Christopher Burns (Rec., 56, 57, 146). A question of the county lines arises.

This man's vote is taken from Mr. Alderson's majority upon the testimony of George H. Surber, about two brothers, James Burns and Christopher Burns, as follows:

They voted at White Sulphur Springs at said election.

They voted the Democratic ticket. The two Burnses lived in Alleghany County, Va. He is contradicted by William H. Mann (146):

I have known Christopher and James Burns for a number of years. I was at their home some years ago; was informed by Mr. Burns yesterday that they still resided at the same place in White Sulphur district, Greenbrier County, W. Va. When I was at the Burns house I was shown a line between the two counties (Greenbrier, W. Va., and Alleghany, Va.), and from what Mr. Burns showed me, he lived in Greenbrier Co., W. Va. I am informed that the sons reside in the old home house. I was informed by one of them yesterday that he did not vote.

By what process of ratiocination did the committee evolve that it was Christopher not James who should be taken? Why should either be selected to be rejected?

Mr. Mann, who says he has lived in that precinct all his life—forty-three years—was one of the commissioners of election, also said he had seen Mr. James Burns frequently at that precinct on election days.

10. Riley Gilpin (Rec., 97). This voter is deducted by the committee from contestee's majority upon the following evidence of John S. Gilpin:

Q. Did your son Riley Gilpin vote at Hinton, Summers County, W. Va., on the 6th day of Nov., 1888?—A. I think he did.
Ans. to Q. 3. He was 20 years old.
Ans. to Q. 4. He was a Democrat.

11. Elmore Ross (Rec., 99) goes off the poll for contestee upon the story of Mr. W. F. Arter, a lumber dealer, who resides in Cleveland, Ohio, as follows:

Q. 2. Do you know one Elmer Ross?—Ans. I do.
Q. 3. Do you know whether he voted at Talcott?—Ans. I am informed that he did.
Q. 4. Was he entitled to vote?—Ans. He was not.
Ans. to Q. 5. He claimed to be a Democrat.
Ques. 1st. How do you know said Ross was not a voter in the county of Summers at the election held Nov. 6th, 1888?—Ans. He came from Texas about the 20 of Nov., 1887, and the following spring and summer was gathering fruit and berries and having his sister to can them to take back to Texas, and said he had no right to vote, but if here on election day he intended to vote.
Do you know that said Ross did vote?—Ans. No; I was not at the election. I have been told so and seen his name on a copy of the poll-books.
And further this deponent saith not.

                                                        W. F. ARTER.

15. Kelly Broyles (Rec., 104), in the same list, did not vote at all. According to his own story perhaps he should be counted for McGinnis. The committee say Jacob Judy's vote should be counted for McGinnis. As there is a question of a line between precincts it may be it should. He says "they would not let him vote at Livesay's Mills precinct because he lived in Falling Springs district." He did not try the latter. "He did not know the correct location of the line between the two districts." The committee have compared his treatment with that of the Quicks. He, in his evidence, says he lived in Falling Springs. W. N. Neal (53) one of their witnesses and the Republican judge at that precinct, says:

Judy resides farther over in the district (Falling Springs) than the Quicks.

According to Judy's own testimony he was not entitled to vote at the precinct he went to November 6, 1888.

Rhodes D. Trent (Rec., 89) says he went to the polls "about half after 4 o'clock, or it may have been a little later."

I did not vote; I went up into the yard where the election was held; I can't say that I offered to vote for this reason, I met Joe Peck and John Vance in the yard and they told me that I was too late, as the polls were closed. I am a Republican and would have voted for McGinnis.

He don't say the polls were closed. He was too lazy to go see for himself. Why should he be counted for any one?

Before considering the individual cases of the large number of illegal votes cast and counted for contestant, a careful survey of the situation of that part of the district in which the wholesale frauds were perpetrated and the circumstances under which they were committed is advisable.

A large number of witnesses have testified in this case in such manner as to make their evidence apply generally to the persons who voted illegally, as charged, at the precincts of Mill Creek and Simmons Creek, in Rock district, and at Cross Roads precinct, Beaver Pond district, in Mercer County, and at Mayberry and Peerey Bottoms precincts, in Elkhorn district, in McDowell County, both as to their right to vote and the person for whom they voted. It appears that the county of Mercer, and especially that part of it which constitutes the mining district, lies immediately upon the borders of the State. McDowell County is also a border county.

The Norfolk and Western Railroad is the only thoroughfare leading into this section of the country. These counties lie in the extreme southern part of the State and many miles distant from any West Virginia railroad proper. The only connection possible to be made, by way of the Norfolk and Western Railroad, leading from this locality, with any other railroad is to pass through the southwestern portion of the State of Virginia. The proof shows that it is but a mile and a half from Mill Creek voting precinct, 3 miles from Simmons Creek voting precinct, and not to exceed 7 miles from the most remote of the McDowell precincts by the route of said railroad to the Virginia line. The town of Pocahontas, which has a mining population of not less than 5,000, two-thirds of whom are negroes, is situated just across the Virginia line and but 2 miles from Mill Creek voting precinct. A like proportion of the persons who are employed to labor in and about the mines in Mercer and McDowell Counties were negroes at the time of said election. These negroes, so employed, were extremely migratory and, in the language of many of the witnesses, "coming and going all the time." None of them had acquired, either in Mercer or McDowell County, residences or homes of their own, or lived in any other than the tenement houses of their employers. These facts are clearly and conclusively demonstrated by the copies of the pay-rolls, running over a period of twelve months next preceding said election, of all the colliery companies in both said counties, and printed in the record of this case.

The first of the collieries in Mercer County started upon development after 1883. They were the plants of John Cooper & Co. at Mill Creek, Freeman & Jones, afterwards the Caswell Creek Coal and Coke Company, and William Booth & Co., afterwards the Booth-Bowen Coal and Coke Company. The other mines in Mercer County were developed at a later date. The branch of the Norfolk and Western road, extending from Mill Creek into McDowell County, was not completed until August, 1888, and none of the collieries in that county began operations until that time, and but three of them during that year. There were no negroes in Rock district, Mercer County, or in Elkton district, McDowell County, prior to these mining developments.

It also appears from the evidence that these various colliery companies build tenement houses upon their properties to be occupied exclusively by their own employés; and, that whenever a person was engaged by them in any of the departments of their business, he contributed to the rent-roll of such company by occupying one of its tenements. Said companies kept pay-rolls upon which were entered the names of all per-

sons employed by them and which showed the days or months they
were engaged at work for them. It is also shown by the evidence that
there were no negroes living within either of the said voting precincts
in Mercer or McDowell Counties at the time of said election who were
not then employed by some one of said colliery companies. It appears
from an inspection of said pay-rolls that every negro who voted at any
precinct in either of said counties, whose vote is challenged by contestee and concerning whose right to vote specific evidence was taken,
was employed by some one of said collieries for some time during the
year preceding the election, but none of them, with but three exceptions,
were employed in all the colleries taken together for the whole of the
twelve months.

All of these negroes who are charged to have voted illegally at one
or the other of these precincts came direct from the State of Virginia
or the State of North Carolina when they entered the service of those
coal companies. Therefore, if it be true, as the evidence discloses,
that all the male negroes who were in Rock district of Mercer County and
Elkhorn district of McDowell County at the time of said election were in
the employ of said colliery companies and had been so employed during their stay there, and it does not appear from all of said pay-rolls
taken together that they had been employed for the period of the twelve
months next preceding said election, it follows, necessarily, that they
had not been in the State of West Virginia during all of that time
and had not, therefore, acquired under the laws of said State the right
to vote at said election.

This argument applies with equal force to the persons hereinafter
referred to in connection with McDowell County, charged by contestee
to have voted illegally at one or the other of said precincts in McDowell
County, and who had not been employed by either or all of said companies for sixty days next preceding said election.

It also appears from the evidence that all of the seven colliery companies in McDowell County were owned and re-operated by incorporated
companies; and, as we have heretofore stated, the law of West Virginia, in defining the right of franchise in said State, provides:

* * * Nor shall any person in the employ of any incorporated company, or of
this State, be deemed a resident of any county, or of any district therein, by reason
of being employed in said county or district.

It is shown by Samuel Beckett that he was at Simmons Creek precinct during all the day of said election; that he saw Republican
tickets there on that day and being distributed among the negroes by
Republican leaders and workers, among whom were Mr. John D.
Hewett, a member of the State central committee and of the Congressional and county executive committees of the Republican party, superintendent and part owner of one of the collieries, and Mr. J. B. Kremer,
book-keeper for another colliery and a Republican campaign orator.
Mr. Hewett admits himself in his testimony that all the negroes in
Rock District were Republicans; that he knew of but one Democrat
among them, to wit, Pleas. Robinson, and states that 150 negroes, all
Republicans, went in a body with a brass band at their head to within
100 yards of the polls at Simmons Creek precinct, there broke ranks,
and voted. (See p. 454.)

In this connection it may not be improper to remark that it appears
from the testimony that the owners of the collieries, in the vicinity of
all these precincts, and the persons who controlled the laborers, with
power to employ or discharge them, were, almost without exception,
Republicans, prominent and active workers for their party; that they

employed in their mines negro labor almost exclusively, in opposition
to the general rule in respect to employment of mine labor (for party
purposes no doubt); that we find the gentlemen before named and other
operators at the polls on election day distributing tickets among their
employés and influencing them, challenging white voters, but never once
questioning the right of any negro to vote, and where a negro's vote
was questioned advocating his right to vote. These facts are significant.

The West Virginia law requires the assessors of the various counties
to list for taxation as of April 1 of each year "every male inhabitant
who has attained the age of twenty-one years"

James B. Cyphers, deputy assessor of McDowell County, testifies
that he was very active, careful, and diligent about the listing of persons above twenty-one years of age in the mining section in 1888;
that we went to the collieries and where the hands were at work; and
listed all persons that he could find liable to such taxation, swore the
negroes, and used every possible effort, and yet it appears from his testimony that one hundred and thirty-four persons (and the evidence shows
that they were negroes almost without exception) voted at Peery Bottoms and Mayberry precincts, in Elkhorn district, in McDowell County,
not listed by him for taxation in said county (pp. 252–254).

Only eighteen of the persons voting at said precincts, whose votes are
questioned by contestee, were assessed for taxation in 1888 in said
county, and their names are stated by said witness.

Votes.

In 1888 (November 6) Republican nominee for Representative in Congress received, in Rock district, Mercer County 737
In 1886 the Republican nominee received in same district 121

Increase of Republican vote in Rock district in two years 616
Or above 600 per cent. (See deposition of H. B. Barber, pp., 344, 345.)

These men were not assessed, either, because they were not there or
claimed non-residence if there.

The assessor of Mercer County listed of such persons in Rock district, in 1888, 61 blacks and 564 whites; total 625. (See testimony of
W. H. H. Witten, assessor, p. 245.)

Vote cast in Rock district, November 6, 1888, 1,145; number of persons voting, not listed for taxation, 520. But 61 negroes, bear in mind,
were listed for taxation in 1888, and the testimony shows that more
than 600 voted at said election in said district. W. H. H. Witten, assessor, testifies that he was very careful and diligent about the discharge of his duty, and listed, for such taxation, all persons he could
find in Rock district, where the mines were located and negroes were;
that many of them claimed not to live in West Virginia. Negroes said,
"We do not live here. We do not claim this as our home and we do
not pay taxes here." and that they lived in Virginia and paid taxes
and voted there. (See p. 246.)

In 1886 total vote cast in Mercer County was 1,564
In 1888 total vote cast in Mercer County was 2,777

Increase in two years (nearly 80 per cent.) 1,213

In May, 1889, total vote cast.. 1,608
Decrease in vote from November, 1888, until May, 1889 (nearly 80 per cent.).. 1,169

From these facts and from the testimony showing that not more than
one in twenty of the male negroes employed in the mines of Rock district was married, with a family residing in said State (see p. 308); that
there were no negroes in said section when the mines were developed;

that said district borders on Virginia; that there was railroad communication between said district and Virginia; that such negro employés were migratory in their habits, and invariably claimed Virginia as their homes, and were sending money continually and going to Virginia themselves, many of them back and forth; that they were working sometimes at one colliery, and then at another; sometimes in Mercer County; sometimes in McDowell County, W. Va.; sometimes at Pocahontas, Va.; it must be accepted as true that not only a most inviting opportunity existed for fraud, and that grossest frauds were committed in the casting of illegal negro votes in Rock district, Mercer County; at Simmons Creek, Mill Creek, and Honaker's Mills precincts; at Cross Roads, Beaver Pond district, Mercer County, and at Mayberry and Peery Bottoms precincts, in Elkhorn district of McDowell County, at or contiguous to which precincts the mines of Mercer and McDowell Counties are situated and around, and at which the negro population was on November 6, 1888; but also that a vast number of negroes voted illegally at said precincts. In this connection it should also be remembered that the owners and persons controlling these mines and employés were almost, without exception, Republicans (one of them, John Cooper, was chairman of the Republican county executive committee, and another, John D. Hewett, member of the Republican State executive committee), and took active parts on the day of and before the election in behalf of the Republican ticket; and that there is no registration of voters in West Virginia.

The mine-owners, who were Republicans and employed the negro miners, were in a position to know all about the residence of their employés. The contestee offered evidence to prove that a large number of such employés were not residents of West Virginia at the time of said election. If contestee's position and evidence was not true, then it would have been easy for contestant to show its falsity by producing the voters challenged or some one who knew of their residence in the State of West Virginia as witnesses to testify. It is a significant fact that no such witness was produced, except J. M. Douglas. Mr. Hewett himself, a superintendent of a mine and prominent in the councils of his party and an active worker for its success, was a witness, but failed to say a word to contradict the testimony of contestee. If the negroes whose votes were attacked by contestee had been residents of West Virginia for one year before November 6, 1888, it is probable that they would have been such residents when contestant took his testimony in rebuttal. It is also significant that no one of these negroes was examined as a witness by contestant. Contestee could not be expected, even if any of said negroes could have been found by him, to have committed himself to the evidence of persons who had systematically, willfully, and palpably broken the laws of the State.

J. M. Douglas, a negro minister, could not tell when a single one of those to whom his attention was called first came to the State, and he did not show that a single one was a bona fide resident of the State on November 6, 1888. The fact that he had seen them around there does not establish that they were residents; and five of the persons whom he states to have lived in Mercer County at the time of the election are proven to have voted in McDowell.

It is not important to the contention made by contestee concerning the negroes who voted in these counties whether or not the Republican mine-owners were privy to the casting of illegal votes by negroes. Mr. Hewitt shows that there were a large number of negroes who were not legal voters in said counties at the time of the election; and the proof discloses that the negroes were determined to vote, whether entitled to do so or not, as was naturally the case; and illegal votes would have been cast by negroes in these counties even if the persons on both sides having in charge the campaign had united in a common effort to preserve the purity of the ballot.

For the purpose of abridging the abstract of this testimony in regard to each case, let us say:

First. That each witness testifying in regard to any of the alleged illegal voters of these two counties testifies that he is a negro, and a miner or laborer by occupation, unless otherwise expressly stated.

Second. That all of the alleged illegal voters are shown to have voted at the respective precincts at which they are charged to have voted by the poll-lists (pp. 252, 254, 338, et seq., 350.)

Third. That the charge in regard to each is that he was not a resident of the State of West Virginia for one year preceding said election, or of the county in which he voted sixty days prior thereto, and was not a resident of State, county, or district in which he voted, unless otherwise expressly stated.

Fourth. That the names of none of these persons hereafter named as having voted illegally in McDowell County were upon the assessor's books of said county (see testimony of J. B. Cyphers, p. 253 et seq.) except James Hackey, and his name does not appear on the assessor's books of Elkhorn district. (J. D. Christian, p. 360). And that said Cyphers took the precaution and care to list all male residents over twenty-one years of age, as above stated.

Fifth. That the contestant was the candidate of the Republican party, and his name was on the Republican tickets voted.

Sixth. That the time about which witnesses testify refers to time of election (November 6, 1888).

Seventh. That in connection with the statement made of the testimony of S. M. Williamson in regard to each alleged illegal voter, concerning whom he testifies, in these two counties, the following facts are to be applied to each case without further statement thereof, viz:

He was book-keeper and paymaster for Henry Fairfax, who was engaged in grading a railroad from Mill Creek, in Mercer County, to Elkhorn, and in the building on the line of railroad the flat-top tunnel, from 8th of March, 1887, to August, 1888; and also was grading at the town of Bluefield, in Mercer County, from January, 1888, to April, 1888, for said railroad; that the labor employed was nine-tenths negroes; that they were engaged in Virginia, where they lived, by the foremen, in different counties; their transportation was paid for them to place of working, and that they claimed Virginia as their home and came for the purpose of working on the road; entry of the date of their employment was made upon the books kept by the witness, which show the date of their arrival and the length of time they worked. The voters he testifies in relation to were brought to West Virginia under the circumstances above stated, and each was brought inside year of election.

We have not cited the witnesses nor quoted the testimony to establish the foregoing general propositions in every instance. These propositions are not controverted, and could not be with the overwhelming proof there is in the record to sustain them. The committee have seen proper to ignore them, possibly so as not to call attention to the strength of the contestee's case with respect to the multitude of illegal votes cast for contestant with a brass band accompaniment. The contestee proves that 345 illegal votes were cast for contestee. We select a large number of these which will bear the comparison we have before

asserted. In addition to the witness cited in each individual ca:
the surroundings of the voter, which we have fully set forth, mi
borne in mind.

MONROE WOMACH (voter):

Witness, Solomon (R., 235), foreman Powhattan Coal and Coke Co.. W
claimed his home in Pittsylvania County, Va.; came here from Pittsylvania C
Va., latter part of November or December, 1887; married man; family live
never been here; would send money to them; voted the Republican ticket at el
Witness, Williamson (R., 291), book-keeper and paymaster Elkhorn extension.
ach came from Virginia in May, 1888, and commenced work for us on Elkhorn
sion; name on the poll-books.

SAM AKERS:

J. H. Clare's testimony (p. 250) shows he was a young man and his home
Virginia. M. C. Franklin (p. 334-5) shows he came from his home in Fi
County, Virginia, to McDowell County, and commenced to work for the H
Coal and Coke Company April 23, 1888.

JOSEPH BALLARD:

First came to W. Va. from North Carolina in March, 1888, and stayed two da
returned to North Carolina, came back again in April, 1888 (L. D. Solomon, 1
He worked for Houston Coal and Coke Co. (Franklin's testimony p. 334-5
voted the Republican ticket (pp. 350, 235). Returned to N. Car. after electio
been back since.

M. C. BOTKIN, white:

It is shown by L. D. Solomon (p. 235) that he is a white man; lived with his
in Pocahontas, Virginia, until January or February, 1888. By J. H. Clare (
that he had lived with his family in Pocahontas until nine months before ele
that he was a Republican and voted that ticket.

ANDREW BOLIN:

It is shown by L. D. Solomon (p. 254-5) that he came, in December, 188:
Cripple Creek, Virginia, at which place he claimed his home. He voted the 1
lican ticket (p. 235).

BOWLES DARBY:

L. D. Solomon testifies that voter lived in Campbell County, Virginia; firs
to West Virginia in August, 1888, and worked at different places until Oct
1888, when he returned home to Virginia; came again to Elkhorn, Octobe
1888; that he voted the Republican ticket (p. 234-5). See also J. H. Clare'
mony (p. 250), name on poll-lists (p. 350) is misprinted, "Bolen Darly."

JOHN KIRBY:

Solomon testifies that he is married; his family lived in Virginia, where :
property, until shortly before election; he voted Republican ticket (p. 234-5).
menced work for Crozier Coal & Coke Co. January 31, 1888 (p. 363). He tol
Clare he had voted the Republican ticket; that his home was in Virginia. (1

WM. LEE:

L. D. Solomon testifies that voter was never in the State of West Virgini.
summer of 1888, when he came from Virginia, where he claimed his hom
voted the Republican ticket (pp. 234-5). J. H. Clare's testimony as to vo
same effect, and voter's home was in Virginia. (p. 250.)

Williamson shows that he was brought from his home in Virginia, in Marcl
and worked for Mr. Fairfax at Bluefield, Mercer Co.; was one of those who we
ployed in Virginia and brought out to work on railroad (p. 291).

WM. MAYS:

L. D. Solomon testified that voter voted the Republican ticket. Came to W
ginia first in October, 1888, from Virginia, and claimed that his home and res
was there (p. 234).

JOHN JACKSON:

L. D. Solomon testifies that voter was a married man and lived with his fai
Pocahontas, Virginia, until about January, 1888, when he moved to Elkhor
voted the Republican ticket (p. 234); J. H. Clare testifies that voter's home
Virginia, &c. (p. 250).

SPENCER WITCHER:

Williamson (p. 291) came from Virginia December, 1887. The evidence of Mr. Solomon (p. 234), Clare (p.. 250), are the same as in regard to Wm. Mays, above; in addition he was married and lived with his family in Virginia. Solomon is corroborated by Eugene Robertson (p. 358). He never moved his family into West Virginia.

JOHN LOCKETT:

The evidence of Solomon as to this voter is the same as to Wm. Mays (above). In addition, he was married and lived with his family in Virginia (p. 234). Solomon is corroborated by Eugene Robertson (p. 358).

FRY WADE:

Mr. Clare's testimony (p. 250) is the same as in regard to Robert Jones. In addition thereto, M. C. Franklin (p. 334-5) testifies that said Wade was a negro, and came from Franklin County, Virginia, in October, 1888, and entered the employment of the Houston Coal and Coke Company. In the printed record a typographical error occurs in saying "West Virginia" instead of "Virginia," there being no Franklin County, West Virginia.

ED. WALLER:

In regard to him Mr. Solomon testifies substantially the same as in regard to Wiliam Mays (p. 234). J. J. Davidson shows that Waller was employed by the Turkey Gap C. & C. Co.; had a family in Virginia, and referred to Virginia as his home at the time ofthe election (p. 324). Brought his wife to West Virginia in Nov., 1888.

BEVERLY SAUNDERS:

It is shown by Mr. Solomon's testimony (p. 234) that he came from his home in Virginia and commenced work for the Turkey Gap C. & C. Co. September 5, 1888.

MONROE KENT:

J. H. Clare shows that voter claimed Virginia as his home, and is a Republican (p. 250). It is shown by Mr. Solomon that he came from Pittsylvania County, Va., the latter part of November or December, 1887, and that he voted and was a Republican (p. 234).

PLEASANT LEE:

It is shown by Mr. Solomon that Lee came from Virginia the latter part of November or December, 1887; claimed that as his home. He commenced work for the Turkey Gap Coal and Coke Co. Sep. 10th, 1888 (p. 324). J. H. Clare testifies to the same facts in regard to him as in regard to John Kirby (p. 250).

WILLIAM NOWLIN:

L. D. Solomon testifies that voter came from Virginia and claimed that his home; worked a great deal in Pocahontas, Virginia (p. 235). Mr. Clare testifies in regard to him the same as in regard to John Kirby (p. 250). W. R. Jacobs shows that he worked at Pocahontas, Virginia, from February, 1888, to June, following (p. 367). Mr. Jacobs being clerk of the Southwestern Virginia Improvement Company, doing business and located at Pocahontas, Virginia.

J. JENKINS:

It is shown by S. M. Williamson's testimony that he came from his home in Virginia, to work at Bluefield, Mercer County, November 25, 1887, and was imported to work on railroad grading (p. 290-91).

ED. JOHNSON:

The same facts are shown by same witness as in regard to the last voter (p. 290-91).

ROBERT LEMON:

Mr. Williamson shows (p. 290-1) that he was brought from his home in Virginia in 1887 to work on the railroad; that he went home—claiming Virginia his home—and again came back to work in May, 1888. Thomas Falconbridge's testimony shows that he was a Republican, and voted at the precinct; claimed Virginia as his home; frequently went home, and was gone two or three months (p. 312). Falconbridge was section foreman, Norf. & West.; had been foreman, Shamokin Coal & Coke Co.

DAN. DICKINSON:

Mr. Williamson shows that voter was brought from his home in Virginia to work on the railroad, and first came to West Virginia in August, 1888, working at Bluefield, Mercer County (p. 290-91).

H. Mis. 137——43

W. T. SMITH:

J. H. Clare shows that Smith voted; claimed Virginia his home (p. 250); Mr. Williamson testifies that he was brought from his home in Virginia to work on railroad in March, 1888 (p. 290–91); M. C. Franklin shows that Smith is married, had a family living in Virginia at the time of the election; that he is a Republican, and commenced work for the Houston Coal and Coke Company in April, 1888 (p. 234–5). T. Falconbridge (p. 213) corroborates above. Smith admitted voting illegally. Ran away for fear of getting into trouble. Not seen there since.

C. S. CALLAWAY:

It is shown by Mr. Williamson that voter first came from his home in Virginia to work on railroad in August, 1888, and claimed Virginia as his home (p. 290–91).

DICK WADE:

Is shown by Mr. Williamson to have been brought from Virginia, his home, to work at Bluefield, Mercer County, in February, 1888 (p. 290–91).

H. C. PATTERSON:

Is shown by Dr. Jeter to be non-resident, and to have voted the Republican ticket. He came to Elkhorn in January, 1888—his family lived in Botetourt County, Virginia. The doctor knew his family in Virginia (p. 294). This is confirmed by Franklin's testimony (p. 334–5).

JAMES HACKLEY:

By Mr. Franklin it is shown that he came from his home in Botetourt County, Virginia, in April, 1888, and commenced work for the Houston Coal and Coke Company, and was a Republican (p. 334–5). Mr. Franklin was book-keeper in above company, and a Republican.

JAKE PRILLMAN:

Mr. Franklin shows that voter came from Franklin County, Virginia [misprinted "West Virginia"] in May, 1888, and was employed by the Houston Coal and Coke Company (p. 334–5).

GEORGE BROWN:

By W. R. Jacobs it is shown that Brown worked at Pocahontas, Virginia, where he resided, from November, 1887, to May, 1888 (p. 369). By M. Bloch, that he was registered as a voter in Virginia in 1888 (p. 369).

SAM ROSS:

It is shown by J. M. Myles, foreman Cooper Company, that voter was a Republican; voted that ticket; that he came in the early part of the year 1888 from Virginia, where he claims his home (p. 266–7; returned home to Virginia in December, 1888.

WILEY SMITH:

It is shown by M. C. Franklin that voter came from Virginia, his home, in August, 1888, and entered the employment of the Houston Coal and Coke Company (p. 334–5).

WM. H. TERRY:

The same facts are shown, as are shown in regard to Smith, above, by same witness (p. 266–7).

JOHN TERRY:

Substantially the same facts shown to exist as in regard to the last voter by same witness (p. 266–7). In addition Mr. Solomon testifies that he is a single man, and came from Virginia in October, 1888 (p. 234).

J. S. WADE:

Williamson shows (p. 291,) that he was brought from his home in Virginia in March, 1888. In April following it is shown by Mr. Franklin (p. 334–5) that he claimed Virginia as his home and was employed by the Houston Coal and Coke Company.

WM. DAVIS:

Mr. Bloch shows that voter was registered as a voter in Virginia in 1888 (p. 369); it is also shown by R. J. Jennings (p. 369–70) that he resided in Virginia during the twelve months. It is shown by B. F. Hodge voter resided in Pocahontas, Virginia, shortly before July 1st, 1888 (p. 370). Mr. Hodge was mayor of Pocahontas,

J. H. TATE:

It is proven by Thos. Falconbridge that Tate voted the Republican ticket, that he came direct from Pocahontas, Virginia, where he lived, and cOmmenced work August 23, 1888, his home being previously in Virginia (p. 312).

WESLEY WAGNER: '

J. C. Freeman (pp. 371-2), testifies that Wagner voted at this precinct; was a Republican, and had not been in the State for twelve mOnths; having come first in February, 18c8.

These voters names are all found ou the poll-book of Perry Bottoms precinct. Taking into consideration the facts proved generally pertaining to these voters and those relating to them individually and we have satisfactory proof that these 36 votes should be deducted from contestant's vote, thus increasing Alderson's plurality by that number. Starting then with his majority of 7 on the corrected returns, adding the 13 illegal votes conceded and this illegal 36, and we have 56. If we deduct from this the 16 claimed by the committee to have been illegally cast for contestee and he still has 40 plurality before proceeding to consider some 300 other illegal votes cast for contestant. From this time on we shall give only the names of such illegal voters, the names of the witnesses, pages of the record on which their testimony is found.

Mayberry precinct, poll-list of 350.

No.	Voters.	Witnesses.	Page of record.
56	Robert Law	R. L. Weaver	283
55	Lewis Law	do	283
123	T. H. Mosely (misprint, Mosen)	do	283
71	Lowry Jones	do	283
90	William Price	J. H. Clare	250
		Wm. Block	369
72	Abe Helm	Wm. Williamson	290
77	Marshall Clark	do	290-299
4	Thomas Clark	do	290-299
20	M. C. Clark	do	290-299
122	G. W. Wilson	do	290-299
129	Minnis Wade	do	292
		do	292
		R. L. Weaver	283
7	Mason Thorpton	S. Bechek	330
		S. C. Bernheim	432
		S. M. Williamson	290, 291
9	Green Scott	Williamson	290
		Block	369
124	Laz Dillard	Clare	250
		Weaver	282, 283
46	Alex. Stokes	Clare	250
		Falconbridge	312
65	J. Napor	Clare	250
		Falconbridge	312, 313
126	J. W. Marshall*	Clare	250, 251
		Weaver	282
		Williamson	290, 291
		Falconbridge	312, 313
85	Wm. Old (misprint, Oes)	Solomon	234
		Falconbridge	312
100	Wm. Hardy	do	312
47	Clem Green	do	312
43	Wm. Wooton	do	313
86	Wash. Hardy	do	312
120	Thomas Chanler	Solomon	234
66	George Brown	Williamson	290
		Jacobs	367
		Block	369
61	M. Robinson	Williamson	290
		Falconbridge	312

* No one can examine the testimony in this case without being convinced beyond a reasonable doubt that the vote should be rejected from contestants; yet the committee have overlooked it, along with many others equally as well impeached. This instance will do for the comparison heretofore suggested.

Mayberry precinct poll-list of 350—Continued.

No.	Voters.	Witnesses.	Page of record.
13	Henry James...............................	Williamson...........................	291
		Falconbridge	312
41	Hardy Green *.............................	... do	312, 313
33	A. L. Calhoun	...do	312, 313
75	Geo. Helm	Williamson..........................	290, 291
53	Geo. Clark	C. E. Rusmisell.....................	327
42	Albert Clark	...do	327
102	Jeff. Shelton	Bechet	229, 230
		Bernheim............................	432
98	C. E. Goodwin	Young...............................	308, 309
		Pay-roll	303
		...do	329

* This man confessed that he had voted when he had no right to, and ran away to avoid trouble and has never been back since.

Here are 33 more illegal votes proven to have been cast for contestant. Their rejection increases the plurality of contestee to 73. Having established the election of the sitting member beyond a reasonable doubt, the only illegal voters hereafter cited out of some 146 others, which are clearly proven to have been cast for contestant, will be such as afford striking instances for the comparison with the findings of the committee. We shall give the references to the particular testimony in each case, again calling attention to the general testimony which must be applied also :

Mercer County—Mill Creek Precinct.

Voter.	Record.
173. William Brown.....................................108, 266, 267, 302, 291, 366	
186. E. J. Kinsey ⎱ 277, 303–307	
104. A. F. Kinsey ⎰	
14. Milton Otrey..277, 284, 303	
209. Armistead Otrey...277, 284, 287, 307	
23. Ambrose Mills...287, 303, 307, 368	
145. David Sales 277, 287, 289	
97. Charles H. Howard...284, 291, 303	
34. Charles Johnson 290, 362	
214. John Saunders 312, 313	
31. James Jarvis...287, 303–305, 384–385	
48. Tom Morton 303–307, 368	
61. Moses Johnson...285, 303–307	
141. Silas Johnson *	
55. Bullet Smoot *...	
77. Peter Parker *...	
62. Elijah Perkins *...:............	
26. Green Sheppard *..	
144. Granville Toler *...	
182. Philip Turner *...	
112. William Anthony*...	
117. Jerry Richardson............................284, 290–291–292, 302–305–306	
74. George Shazier..284	
211. Thos. Saunders..284	
16. J. H. Bramwell 234, 285, 307, 335, 353	
170. Duke Cobbs...284, 302–307	
Wilson Booker..303–306–307, 321	
Henry Woodson...290–321	
Wm. Estis 304, 322	
Green Shephard...268, 306–307	
Keaton Winston 284, 290–291–292, 304–306–321	

* The same witnesses testifying as to Moses Johnson testify substantially the same as to these voters, only differing in regard to dates. In addition, R. W. Jacobs testifies in regard to the last (Anthony) that he worked in Virginia during the month of December, 1888. In regard to Bullet Smoot, M. Block testifies he was registered as a voter in Virginia for 1888 (p. 369).

Simmons Creek Precinct.

Samuel Willburn	229, 230
John L. Smith	359
York Scales	229, 230, 338
Caleb Wilcher	229, 230, 338, 270, 271
J. D. Holland	229, 230, 271
Geo. Price	229, 230, 338, 270, 271
James Hackney	229, 230, 338, 270, 271, 369
Harris Boyd	229, 230, 338
Willis Hayden	229, 230, 338
George Williams	304, 307, 369
Chas. E. Hallowell	229, 230
King Lee	230
John Crenshaw*	368
Ernest Freeman, alien	265
Thomas Hightower	273, 275, 289
Chas. Polk	275, 302, 307, 368, 369
James Cook	262, 359

Cross Roads Precinct, Beaver Pond District.

David M. Jones	239, 290, 291
G. B. Smith	239, 240, 290, 291, 332
James Glover	239, 240, 243, 331, 354
Ben Perry	239, 240, 354
Hannibal Smith	230, 240, 258, 354, 355
James Weaver	239, 240, 290, 291
C. M. Spencer	239, 240, 290, 291
W. H. Smith	239, 240, 290, 291
Chas. Lee	332, 354, 356, 431

Oak Vale Precinct.

Isaac Porterfield	248, 337, 346, 347
George Saunders	248, 256, 237
Thos. Saunders	248, 256, 237
James Wall	248, 249, 346, 347

These 61 illegal votes cast for contestant should be deducted from his vote, which increases the certain plurality of the sitting member to 134. There are still a large number that should be treated in the same way.

Monroe County.

Alexander Haines, felon	380
W. L. Ballantine	375, 376, 377
James McDaniel	378
Philip Williams	373, 374

Nicholas County.

W. E. Camp	116, 117, 386
George A. Rennick	392, 393, 394
J. A. Martin (five witnesses)	381, 382, 385
James Lea (five witnesses)	389, 390
A. L. Godfrey (four witnesses)	390, 391
J. H. Props (three witnesses)	386, 387

Raleigh County.

James Kidwell (Ridwell)	395, 396, 399, 400
Wm. Kidwell (Ridwell)	395, 396, 399, 400
George E. Fisher	395, 396, 398, 399
James C. Maynor	398, 399, 400
Clark E. Stover	397, 398, 399, 400, 401

---

* Also pay-rolls.

Summers County.

Anthony Rollins, J. B. Chapman, W. M. Wright, G. W. Given, H. D. Richards, Robert Brown, Wash. Jackson, Howard White, Wash. Carter, J. W. Wood 404, 407, 408, 413, 414
L. L. James, S. D. Henderson, Peyton Williams 404, 405, 406, 407, 408, 413, 414
Tom Worley, Robert Berkley, Robert Carter, Wyatt Wingfield, Elijah Berkley..405, 406, 407, 408, 413, 414
A. L. Moody, John Johnson, Powell Booker, Wash. Taylor, Jos. Smith, D. T. Nicholas, Lewis Lee, and Lewis Paine.

By L. T. Marshall, that said voters, except Powell Booker and Wash. Taylor were brought from Frederick's Hall, Virginia, on March 8, 1888, where their homes were and where they lived. Said Booker and Taylor came from Kentucky inside of the year preceding said election; that all of said voters were negroes and laborers on the construction force of the C. and O. R. R. at time of said election; they lived in a box-car wherever they stopped along the line (p. 410). By G. D. Haynes and N. J. Lute that same facts existed as to these voters as to L. L. Jones (pp. 405,–6–7). By E. H. Peck and Walter Bonde (see note pp. 404,–7–8 and pp. 413, 414).

In this county the illegal voters are grouped together because the testimony so groups them. The committee speaks of this evidence as wholesale. It is appropriate that the testimony should be of the same character as the frauds perpetrated. Careful scrutiny will show no defect in the proof that at least 26 illegal votes were cast in this county for McGinnis.

Upshur County.

Andrew Grubb 415–17–20–22
B. W. Phillips...417–20
E. L. Smith..416–17–18–21

Webster County.

Wm. R. Hosey (five witnesses)..424–25
W. A. Gawthrop (four witnesses)..424–25

Kanawha County.

Obadiah Bayes, Thomas Bayes, Rhodes Bayes.....................................216, 223
Lemuel Stricklin 188, 215–216
Albert Ross..187–9, 203

We have now shown that the sitting member has a clear plurality of at least 174 votes. To reach this conclusion we have not claimed for him the benefit of a large number of illegal votes cast for contestant, and fairly proved. We have insisted upon no technicalities to enable us to effect this result. We submit the passage of the following resolutions as substitutes for those recommended by the committee.

Resolved, That James H. McGinnis was not elected as a Representative in the Fifty-first Congress for the Third Congressional district of West Virginia, and is not entitled to a seat as such Representative.

Resolved, That John D. Alderson was duly elected to the office of Representative in the Fifty-first Congress for the Third Congressional district of West Virginia, and is entitled to retain his seat as such Representative.

JOS. H. OUTHWAITE.
C. F. CRISP.
CHAS. T. O'FERRALL.
LEVI MAISH.
L. W. MOORE.

JOHN M. CLAYTON vs. C. R. BRECKINRIDGE.

Clayton served a notice of contest on Breckinridge, charging that the result of the election was obtained by ballot-box-stealing, intimidation, and false counting, and took some testimony, but while still in process of taking testimony he was assassinated by some one. A subcommittee of the Committee on Elections was appointed to proceed to Arkansas and take testimony "in regard to the methods of said election, to the contest, and all events relating thereto or arising therefrom after said election, and as to whether the contestant or the contestee, or either of them, was lawfully elected."

Acting under the terms of the resolution, the subcommittee took testimony in regard to the killing of Mr. Clayton, and a number of other murders and disturbances alleged to have been connected with the election or contest, and a discussion of the facts of these cases will be found in the report. Upon the question of the contest proper, the committee find that by counting the votes in the Plummerville box, which was stolen, as they are proved in the evidence to have been cast, the majority of Breckinridge is considerably reduced, and that the remainder of his majority is overcome, and a majority shown for Clayton by rejecting the returns of other precincts proved to be fraudulent, and counting the votes proved *aliunde*.

The minority find that, except as to Plummerville, the evidence is insufficient to establish the charges, but that, even if the testimony of the voters who testify as to how they voted is to be believed, all the votes in the boxes attacked, which are not proved to have been cast for Clayton, should be counted for Breckinridge. This rule should be applied because of the unfairness of the investigating committee in not taking the testimony of the voters who voted for Breckinridge, as well as of those who voted for Clayton, and because this is not a contested election case, and the rules of evidence established in contested election cases do not apply.

The resolutions presented by the committee, declaring that Clayton was elected and recommending that on account of his death the seat be declared vacant, were adopted by the House September 5, 1890, by a vote of 105 to 62. The debate will be found on pages 9559 to 9751 of the Record.

(1) Effect of court trials.

The result of a trial in a criminal case where parties were charg
with election frauds is not an adjudication binding on·the House in
case involving the same frauds.

(2) Impeached returns.

When returns are impeached they can not be received for any pu
pose, but only those votes proved *aliunde* can be counted.

"If the returns have been falsified by the election officers it is a we
settled rule 'of law that they cease to have any *prima facie* cffect, a
each party can only be credited with such votes at the box in questi
as he may show by other evidence. This rule is one of long standin
It works no hardship upon contestee which does not fall as heavily
the contestant. The contestant is required in the first instance to she
the fraud in the return, and then must follow that up by proving h
vote; or, in some instances, the proof of the fraud is connected wi
the proof of his vote."

(3) Estoppel by swearing in of contestée.

No sort of estoppel can arise from the fact that contestee was swo
in with other members at the beginning of the session.

REPORT.

AUGUST 5, 1890.—Mr. LACEY, from the Committee on Elections, submitted the following report:

A subcommittee was appointed to take testimony in this cause, consisting of Messrs. Lacey, Cooper of Ohio, Bergen, Maish, and Wilson of Missouri. Most of the evidence was taken by them in Arkansas.

After the evidence had been reported, the case was argued before the full committee. We will endeavor to embrace the action of the full committee and of the subcommittee in one report.

At the November election, in 1888, Hon. C. R. Breckinridge, of Jefferson County, Ark., and Hon. John M. Clayton, of the same county, were the nominees of their respective parties for Representative in Congress from the second Arkansas district. Major Breckinridge, the Democratic nominee, was a member of the Fiftieth Congress, and was well known in the district and in the nation at large. Colonel Clayton, the Republican nominee, had been sheriff of his county and State senator, and was well and favorably known in this district. Colonel Clayton was a vigorous and skillful campaigner, and the interest attendant upon a Presidential election and the uncertainty of the result excited active efforts, and rendered the return of Major Breckinridge uncertain. The result in the gubernatorial contest, in September, previous, when the Farmers' Alliance or "Wheelers" had nominated a ticket which was indorsed by the Republicans, and at which it was confidently claimed that the fusion ticket had been elected and counted out, had excited high party feeling. The fact that Norwood, the fusion candidate, had run ahead of Eagle, Democrat, for governor, by 3002 votes in the district led the Republicans to hope for and the Democrats to fear the result.

Charges of fraud in the September State election were freely made, and Federal supervisors were selected to watch the election and returns at the November election.

The contestee received the governor's certificate by a majority certified as amounting to 846, and has not only taken part in the organization of the House, but has during this contest filled the exalted place of a member of the Committee on Ways and Means. It is undisputed that between 400 and 500 of Clayton's majorities were lost to him by the forcible stealing of a ballot-box, and that the results were certified by the governor with this box wholly ignored. These facts would reduce the claimed majority of the contestee to somewhere between 300 and 400. The men who stole the ballot-box were white men, whose faces were partly masked. That there was a very large majority for contestant in the stolen box is nowhere denied.

The contestant charged very many frauds and irregularities in the conduct of the election, and the contestee denied the same, and they proceeded to take testimony to prove up their allegations.

The Plummerville stolen box could not well be disputed, although at the September election, where there were no Federal supervisors, and where the judges were all Democrats, the vote was returned as giving a Democratic majority of 76.

Conway County was the most excited scene of the contest, and the methods of the election and the dangerous practices there used have, in the light of the subsequent events attracted the attention of the nation. Before the September election Conway County was well known to be strongly Republican. The county officers were all Republican. An organized effort was made to carry the county for the Democracy. One Stowers, who had recently come from Mississippi, organized a militia company, which was not only armed by the governor but furnished with an abundance of ammunition. It was composed exclusively of Democrats. The report was current that it was organized to advance the interests of the party to which all of its members belonged. The Republican majority in the county was largely composed of colored men, who became timid and fearful that these arms were to be used at the election, and the belief became prevalent that force and fraud were to be used to carry the county against the unquestioned majority of Republican voters.

At Plummerville, which was the Republican stronghold, Democratic judges and clerks obtained control of the election, and at a previous election an attempt was made to knock over and steal the box by Democrats in the room, one Dr. White actively participating in the attempt. On that occasion the lights were extinguished with the exception of one, and the attempt to prevent the counting of the vote was defeated by the one light being sufficient to enable witnesses to identify the wrong-doers. This wrongful attempt was made wholly by Democrats, and in view of the previous frauds the Republicans entertained and expressed great fears of a theft of the ballot box in November. Boxes had been stolen in other counties at the September election, the thefts in *every* case inuring to the benefit of the Democracy, and it was but natural that a crime of this character should be anticipated and feared.

M. D. Shelby obtained the office of sheriff of the county at the September election, and had entered on his duties before the Congressional election. He professed much anxiety to have "a fair election and an honest count" at Plummerville, and for that ostensible purpose appointed from 12 to 20 deputy sheriffs, all Democrats, to attend, and see that such a desirable result might be accomplished. He appointed as deputy at Plummerville one of the men who attempted to steal the box on the occasion referred to, and one of the others who took part in this attempt was made one of the judges of election. He appointed among this list Robert Pate, a saloon-keeper at Plummerville, and Bert Wally, his bar-tender, and a number of strong Democratic partisans from Morrilton, the county seat, which is about 7 miles distant from Plummerville.

These men appeared upon the scene in time for the opening of the polls, which, under the Arkansas law, is 8 o'clock a. m. The judges of the election consisted of two Republicans and one Democrat. The Democrat, Thomas C. Hervey, had been appointed by the county judge in vacation, and to set at rest all questions as to the validity of his appointment the county judge had suggested that Mr. Hervey's appointment should be confirmed by the voters at the time of opening the polls. Accordingly, one of the Republican judges nominated Hervey as a judge of the election, and the assembled voters, regardless of party, voted for him and confirmed his appointment. Mr. Hervey then announced that this was an attempt to question his authority, and that he would also submit to the voters who the other judges should be, and nominated Mr. Hobbs and Mr. Palmer as judges, both Democrats, and put it to vote, calling for the affirmative, and declining to put the negative, and at once declared the Republican judges ousted, who had without question been lawfully selected by the county court.

The Republican judges objected to this summary ejectment from office, and insisted on taking part in the election. The purpose and character of the deputy sheriffs at once became manifest. They took the matter in hand, and prevented the two Republican judges from exercising their rights. The election was, therefore, held by three Democratic judges and two Democratic clerks. These Democratic deputy sheriffs, though actively present in the morning and taking part in the unlawful eviction of the Republican judges, claim to have been absent when most needed in the evening to search for the ballot-box thieves. The disappearance of the deputies before the masked men made their appearance, and the fact that some of them returned in the rain to Morrilton, about dark, and there changed hats and returned to Plummerville, remaining only a few minutes, and disappearing just before the box was stolen; the fact that they rode home again in the rain and dark, one of them losing his hat on the way, very naturally led to the suspicion that the sheriff's organized posse of deputies were parties or privies to the stealing of the box.

Mr. Wahl, the Federal supervisor, seems to have been a man of much nerve and presence of mind; he watched the box constantly, and accompanied Mr. Hervey, the same man who had taken part in a previous trouble about the Plummerville ballot-box, and who was one of the judges, when he took the box to supper. Hervey complained that Wahl "watched him like a thief," and subsequent events justified Wahl in his so doing.

The judges separated, and left Wahl and one of the judges in charge of the box. After dark, some one came to the room where the box was and, looking into the door, asked if they had commenced counting. Mr. Wahl answered that they had not. Mr. Hobbs, the judge, whose back was turned at the time, asked Wahl who that was, and Wahl replied that it was O. T. Bentley.

This same Bentley is still the deputy sheriff of the county, and the duty of capturing the murderers of Clayton and thieves of the ballot-box has been largely intrusted to him. He has been in a position to know all that the governor and other State officials have been doing to disclose the crimes in Conway County. A few minutes after Bentley, or the man whom Wahl recognized as Bentley, disappeared, four men with handkerchiefs over their faces and with revolvers in hand entered and took the ballot-box and poll-books away by force. Mr. Hobbs says that they had white faces, and there was no evidence to the contrary. In the light of these well-known facts it is strange that contestee should have charged that the ballot-box with nearly 500 Republican majority was stolen by Republicans. But he does so in his answer in the following language:

I deny that the poll-books and ballot-box were taken by partisans of mine, and charge that they were taken by partisans of yours.

After the contest was commenced, a number of persons were indicted for violating the election laws at Plummerville, and among them said O. T. Bentley.

Rewards were offered for the conviction of the thieves, and much apprehension prevailed among them, for, although they manifested but little fear of the local authorities, they did not relish a contest in the Federal courts. Mr. Bentley opened up negotiations for a settlement of the indictments by having the amount of Clayton's majority at Plummerville conceded. He assumed to act for the thieves, and was evidently in communication with them. The attempted settlement failed, and Colonel Clayton proceeded to take his testimony at Plummerville.

However, before proceeding to this part of the transaction, let us return to some other events.

MURDER OF JUDGE BENJAMIN.

Hon. M. W. Benjamin, a well-known Republican of Little Rock, was sent to Morrilton the day before the election to confer with the Republicans there, and to arrange, if possible, to prevent the anticipated frauds. His coming was announced, and as he got off the train a mob stood ready to receive him. He was knocked down, beaten, and shot in the head with a leaden ball from what is called in Conway County a "bean-shooter." These "bean-shooters" are a dangerous device, and, when used by a skillful hand, may kill birds and squirrels, or even men. The ball entered Mr. Benjamin's head over the eye, but did not fracture the skull. It was cut out by a surgeon.

Mr. Benjamin returned home to Little Rock, complaining of his bruises and wounds, and, in three weeks after, died of "heart failure" produced by the shock, as his physician testifies. Though a large crowd was present, no one has ever been punished for this crime.

ATTEMPTED MURDER OF SUPERVISOR WAHL.

After the theft of the ballot-box Wahl remained in the neighborhood. He was an important witness in the Federal prosecutions. One night he was playing cards in a doctor's office at Plummerville, the same Dr. White before referred to being one of the players. Wahl changed places with White at the table after playing until a late hour of the night. When he had changed his place at the table he was near a glass door leading outside from the office. Some one shot him through the door from the outside, inflicting a dangerous wound in his neck and head. The aim was slightly imperfect, or the ball glanced in passing through the glass, or he would have been instantly killed. In the light of these events the temerity of Colonel Clayton in going to Plummerville to take testimony is somewhat surprising.

MURDER OF COLONEL CLAYTON.

Colonel Clayton had with him at Plummerville a notary, Mr. Allnutt, from Morrilton, and also Mr. Middlebrook, a colored deputy sheriff from Pine Bluff. His baggage was taken from the depot to the village hotel, but the landlord, although furnishing room and board to Mr. Breckinridge's attorney, Armstrong, refused to entertain him, placing his refusal on the ground of illness in his family. Colonel Clayton then procured boarding at the residence of a widow, Mrs. McCraven, who lived in the woods in the outskirts of the town. Middlebrook, the colored deputy sheriff, insisted that there was great danger, and declined to stay at Plummerville, leaving only Clayton and the notary. Colonel Clayton remained four days, taking testimony and sleeping in a room which had no windows.

On the night of January 29, 1889, his room was changed, and he and Mr. Allnutt were occupying a room on the ground floor that had a window curtained with calico, a slit of a few inches being open in the middle of the curtain. After dark Colonel Clayton spent some time in walking backward and forward in this room. As the tracks subsequently showed, his murderers stood for some time at the window, watching his motions. He finally sat down at a table to write, and the instant that he was seated the fatal shot came crashing through the window. A load of buckshot penetrated his neck, almost severing the head from the body.

The State and nation were horrified. Rewards were offered, and the community at Morrilton, near which the murder occurred, passed appropriate resolutions, but no earnest attempt to aid in bringing the murderers to justice has been made by the local authorities. The efforts of the governor have been in vain. Much of the work done has been upon a mistaken line, and without giving due weight to the suspicion that should naturally attach to the ballot-box thieves.

The object of the sub-committee was dual, to report upon the issue as to who was elected, and to inquire as fully as possible into the murder itself; and they took all the testimony available upon both questions.

KILLING OF SMITH, THE NEGRO DETECTIVE.

We may add that two other deaths have occurred that were the proper subjects of inquiry connected with or growing out of the murder of Colonel Clayton. One Joseph Smith, a negro, was acting as a detective in Conway County, and was killed by a young man named Richmond. Richmond was the son of Republican parents, and was about nineteen years old. The grand jury of Conway County refused to indict him. Ordinarily there would be nothing in the facts and circumstances surrounding this homicide to necessarily connect it with the Clayton case, but the manner of the killing of Smith was involved in much obscurity, and the fact that Smith had been communicating and acting as a detective with the Pinkerton Agency, and the further fact that another detective had been driven out of Plummerville, could not fail to lead the sub-committee to inquire into and suspect the probability that the killing of this detective had some bearing on the Clayton murder. The failure to indict young Richmond had prevented any very thorough investigation of the facts.

KILLING OF GEORGE BENTLEY.

George Bentley, the town marshal of Morrilton, a brother of O. T. Bentley, was suspected of being one of the ballot-box thieves. He was one of the parties who went from Morrilton to Plummerville on the night of the election. He opened communication with the Pinkerton Agency, and during the time he was negotiating to become a Government witness and expose the guilty parties he too was killed. A strange fatality seemed to attend persons who communicated with the detectives. He was said to have been accidentally shot by O. T. Bentley, his brother.

There is no direct evidence to show that there was anything criminal in the killing of Bentley by his brother, as the shooting was done in the presence of a single witness, Wells, who was also one of the parties indicted for the ballot-box theft; and it was claimed that O. T. Bentley was handling a breech-loading revolver at the time. It is unfortunate that George Bentley should have been killed before making the full disclosures which were expected, and that the negro Smith should have been killed while making investigations and reports to the detectives. In the light of the other murders and attempted murders the coincidence of the killing of these two men can not be viewed without suspicion. With all these circumstances disclosed the sheriff of Conway County has subjected himself to severe criticism, to say the least of it, by retaining O. T. Bentley as his deputy during the whole time that has elapsed since the murder and during the time when the sheriff was claiming to be on the hunt of the criminals.

THE HOOPER THEORY OF THE MURDER.

Upon the arrival of. the subcommittee at Little Rock they found just published dispatches and interviews in which the contestee claimed that the whole case would be made clear, and it was claimed that a man named Thomas Hooper, now dead, who recently lived in Los Angeles County, Cal., had killed Colonel Clayton for revenge. Thomas Hooper had some difficulty with the State militia during the reconstruction troubles, and his father was killed in 1868, and Hooper had not lived in Arkansas for about twenty years. He appears to have entertained personal enmity to Governor Powell Clayton, because of the transactions of the militia, and had made threats against Governor Clayton in his conversation with different persons. Hooper died some time after the murder of Colonel Clayton. His violent talk in regard to Clayton led one Sater to suspect him of the murder, and he communicated his suspicions to Governor Eagle in the summer of 1889.

Mr. Breckinridge accepted this theory as one which relieved his partisans in Arkansas from the charge, and on the arrival of the subcommittee at Little Rock they found that contestee had, in a published interview, announced that the secret of the murder would be made known. The Hooper theory of the murder had been kept a secret by the friends of contestee, and was brought to the notice of the committee after the investigation had commenced. Mr. Sater was sent for, and his evidence taken, and telegraphic communication had with Los Angeles to ascertain whether Hooper had been absent from California at the time of the murder. Hooper's family returned to Arkansas after his death and they were examined and testified that Hooper was sick with dropsy on his farm in Los Angeles County, Cal., in January, 1889.

Reports from Los Angeles to different persons showed that no credence was attached by the people there to the theory that Hooper had been away from home in January, 1889. The St. Louis Republic, a Democratic newspaper of great enterprise, had adopted this theory of the murder, and had sent a correspondent immediately to Hooper's neighborhood, and the correspondent telegraphed the result of his inquiries. We quote from the record, page 460.

JOHN T. GINOCCHIO.

Direct ex.:

Mr. LACEY. Would it be anything improper to furnish the telegram you received from St. Louis in regard to this Hooper matter?
A. No, sir; not if the gentleman is willing.
Q. Produce it, please.—A. I will explain how I came to receive this. I will state in the evidence of Mrs. Hooper there was some mention, it will be remembered, by

her, of names of several gentlemen in Los Angeles, that would corroborate her statement in many particulars; so I wired the editor of the Republic, Col. Jones, to instruct his Los Angeles correspondent to see those parties and see if they would corroborate what Mrs. Hooper stated; he did so, and to-day he sent me the result of that work. Shall I read it?

Mr. LACEY. Well, if you please.

A. (Reading):

LOS ANGELES, CAL., May 1st.

Careful canvass of the neighborhood of Tom Hooper fails to disclose any individual who can say positively that Hooper was at home in January, 1889, but all are morally certain that he was there. For three years previous to his death he suffered from dropsy and could move only with difficulty. Those knowing him think the report of he having murdered Clayton is absurd.

GEORGE W. BARTON.

The governor and Major Breckinridge had been working on this supposed clue for ten months or more, but had kept it secret, so that Colonel Clayton's friends had had no chance to investigate the truth of it. No one had been sent to California to see whether the story was true or not and Sater claimed to have had conversations with Hooper before his death which would arouse suspicion as to Hooper. The theory was naturally a pleasing one to contestee, and no one would blame him for following such a clue, though the friends of Colonel Clayton very justly complained that so important information should have been known for ten months by contestee and concealed from them until the day of commencement of the Congressional investigation.

Mr. Breckinridge in his argument before the committee says:

He (Governor Eagle) said General Clayton and his brother had had one of Pinkerton's best men there a long time, and were reported to have spent large sums in aiding him; that they, at least General Clayton and the detective, had talked to him from time to time, and he was satisfied they had done so without reservation.

It would seem that equal frankness ought to have been manifested in informing Governor Clayton of this important clue.

The adoption of this theory would only, in any event, have partly solved the mystery, for there were at least two persons present at the murder, as the tracks of two persons at the window fully showed.

The subcommittee followed up this clue. They summoned Sater, now in Indiana, and all persons who would likely know if Mr. Hooper had been in Arkansas at any time during the winter of 1888-'89. But it clearly appears that Hooper was not only in California, but was ill with dropsy at the time, and has since died.

No reasonable explanation of the murder of Colonel Clayton appears except that some of the ballot-box thieves, finding the taking of the testimony progressing, killed him, and we believe the attempt to kill Wahl was made by parties to the same conspiracy. No Clayton militia theory would explain the attempt upon Wahl's life, and the evidence clearly disproves any such an explanation as to Colonel Clayton's death.

The necessity for the enactment of some laws which will prevent ballot-box stealing and murder from conferring a *prima facie* title to a seat in Congress is evident from the result in this contest. Had such laws been in force as would have prevented the contestee from taking his seat with such a title, no one would have attempted to confer such title by stealing the ballot-box.

Evidently ballot-box stealing was looked upon as a joke in that community until the awful consequences that have resulted have appalled the good people of the county. It was talked of and laughed about on the streets of Plummerville the night of the election.

Major Breckinridge, in his conversation with the chairman of the Democratic committee of the county, and Bob Pate, has given us an idea of the jocular view of such proceedings taken by them.

Maj. C. R. Breckinridge:

Mr. McCain. I would like to say that I call Maj. Breckinridge without his request.

Q. I would like to have you state to the committee whether you stated anything during the campaign in 1888, whether you stated just before the election for Congress in that campaign anything to either encourage or discourage fraud or any kind of interference in the election.—A. The only conversation I had was with Mr. Armstrong.

Q. What official position did he hold in the party?—A. He was chairman of the Democratic committee of Conway Co., and I believe when Col. Clayton and I came to Ft. Smith I wrote Mr. Armstrong to meet us at Conway, and we all went up towards Morrilltown together. At Plummerville Mr. Pate, as I remember, and one or two others got on the cars. Mr. Pate was the only name I recollect now. Mr. Armstrong and I were sitting together and these two gentlemen took seats in the rear of us. Mr. Pate was telling, as if giving an account of some horse-play, as I understood, about the ballot-box at Plummerville at the Sept. election which he was referring to and speaking of it as a joke of some kind. I then remarked to Mr. Armstrong, and turned around a little so the other two gentlemen could hear what I said, that I had heard some reports about the ballot-box in the Sept. election, that they were indefinite, and I knew nothing of them, but I had seen some complaints about the ballot-boxes at perhaps 2 or 3 localities in previous elections, with regard to the county officers and so on. I called their attention to the fact that in the three Congressional races I had made before there had never been complaints in any newspaper on the part of any individual about any precinct in the second Congressional district, or about any citizen in the second Congressional district, and I was acquainted, with the conversations, and with the public press, and with the talk of the people I associated with; that there might be something or there might be nothing in these reports that I had heard. I had just come back to the State. I had been in the Presidential canvass in the State of New York, and had come back in obedience to a telegram from Mr. Hudson, chairman of the committee, to devote a couple of weeks to my district, and I trusted that nothing in jest or otherwise—I told him I hoped that nothing in jest or otherwise would take place that could be susceptible of any misconstruction in the Federal election about to occur. I told them that of course they would realize that it would not do to have any performance of that kind. That if a box was taken, there was, I believe, no instance where a certificate framed upon such a basis was ever permitted to stand by the Democratic House; and that if the House were Republican, of course it would not be permitted to stand in a Republican House in favor of a Democrat. And there was more; that if my election should hinge upon any occurrence of that sort, that I could not afford to take the certificate. And that, therefore, as there had been some reports—the truth of which, I repeated, I did not pretend to vouch for, and there might be something or there might be nothing in them for all I knew—I said to them and told them I wanted them to understand I meant that in a different spirit from the laughter they had just been engaged in—that I meant it serious, and under those circumstances did I want any such thing to occur. That was the substance of my remark and almost the exact words.

Mr. Lacey. Did you think Mr. Armstrong and the party looked upon the ballot-box steal as a matter of no importance?

A. By no means.

Q. They were treating the knocking of the ballot-box over and the lights over as a joke?—A. It was Bob Pate who was speaking and telling about it.

Q. I understood Armstrong was laughing about it to Pate?—A. Oh, no; Pate was telling it and they was all perhaps laughing. He was not telling it as serious; he was telling it as horse-play. I never heard it spoken of afterwards.

No doubt some of these men would have been deterred from taking the first step in their crimes if they had realized that murder would be the end, but they crossed their Rubicon. Breckinridge got the seat in Congress, and one crime followed in the footsteps of the other. The least guilty of the criminals dare not expose the more guilty lest the fate of Clayton should overtake them, and Taylor, one of the parties who went to Plummerville for the ballot-box, having turned States evidence, is a fugitive from his State. In fact, the only person who seems to have been punished by the local authorities is Wahl, the Federal supervisor.

The murderers of Benjamin must be well known, for a large number of persons were present but they are not indicted, no indictments have been found under the State election laws for these crimes, the murderer of Smith is discharged without a trial; the killing of Bentley is not investigated, and the only man whose crime has received full attention at the hands of the local authorities is Wahl, who was indicted for playing the game of cards at the time that he was shot. Where public officers receive their offices as the result of criminal or fraudulent methods of elections, it is not to be expected that they will render active service in punishing men who have committed like offenses in other elections. But the great misfortune is that the worthy and honorable people of all parties in Conway County must bear the stigma that such actions, by a few violent and wicked men, cast over the whole community.

A striking illustration of the cowed and timid feeling of good and worthy people was shown at Plummerville on the day after the assassination of Clayton. We can not believe that the people of that village all united in sympathizing with the assassins, but yet it appears that they shunned Clayton's friends who went to Plummerville after the dead body, and when a few faithful and sympathizing negroes carried the coffin to the cars there was no one of the town to turn out and manifest his sympathy for the victim, or his abhorrence of the crime.

EFFECT OF THE TRIALS IN THE FEDERAL COURT.

Contestee claims in his application for further time, and also upon the floor of the House, and more surprising still, his counsel, General Garland, also claims that the acquittal of the judges and others charged with frauds in this election is a fact binding upon this House and the committee; that such result in a criminal case before a jury is practically an adjudication that there was no such fraud, and that such adjudication should be so accepted by Congress. It is a common saying in criminal proceedings that it is better that ninety-nine guilty men should escape than that one innocent man should be convicted.

All of the Woodruff County officials who were indicted were convicted. In fact, all the persons who were indicted were convicted, except the persons indicted for the crime against Wahl, and those for the stealing of the Plummerville box. Two persons were indicted and convicted on one trial, and acquitted on a new trial. - This only shows that the evidence in the cases of conviction satisfied the minds of the jurymen to the exclusion of every reasonable doubt. Upon the new trial when there was an acquittal, no one can say whether it was a difference in the evidence or a difference in the character of the jury. It is sufficient for us to determine this proceeding upon the evidence introduced before us, without speculating upon the causes that might have led an Arkansas jury to acquit or convict.

The distinction between the rules governing juries in criminal cases and those prevailing in civil proceedings is well known, and we can not but express surprise at the persistence with which the contestee and his counsel cling to this theory that the verdict of the Arkansas juries upon the indictments for violating the election law should be treated as an adjudication that contestee is entitled to his seat. It might as properly be contended in an action of replevin, brought by the owner of a stolen horse against a party claiming title through the thief, that the thief had been able to prove an alibi on a criminal trial, and that therefore this should be regarded as an adjudication divesting the true owner of his title, although the owner was not a party to the criminal proceeding, and had no right to cross-examine witnesses or produce testimony in his own behalf, nor to appeal from an adverse decision.

Such a legal proposition could only excite attention by its entire novelty in a court of justice, where rights of property were involved. But when it is seriously contended that a seat in Congress obtained by fraud and ballot-box stealing, can not be contested unless the Government authorities have been able to convict the parties charged upon indictment, we can only express our surprise at the persistence with which contestee insists upon so evident an error. The rule contended for in behalf of contestee does not apply even in small matters, involving only the rights of property, and to allow the control of the legislative branch of the Government to be thus decided would be monstrous. The Constitution, in express terms, declares that Congress shall judge of the qualifications and election of its members; and the right to exclude from its body men whose title is procured by crime does not depend upon the ability of the Department of Justice to capture and punish the criminals.

The receiver of stolen goods, even though innocent of all guilty knowledge, can not claim title based upon the failure to catch or punish the thieves. Only the seriousness with which it is urged justifies any extended notice of so evident an error.

The converse of the contestee's proposition, if he is right, must also be true. If so, the conviction of Dansby would conclusively invalidate the Kingsland returns, and the conviction of the various judges who did not escape would be conclusive against Mr. Breckinridge, although he was not a party to the proceedings. Let us analyze for a moment this proposition, upon which Mr. Breckinridge seems to have rested his case.

Reed, Lucas, and Blakeley, were indicted for interfering with election officers. Their acquittal does not show that the ballot-box was not stolen.

Hervey was indicted for interfering with the election officers, and convicted. This surely does not defeat Major Breckinridge's right to his seat. White, McCullough, Watson, Dunham, and Palmer were indicted for conspiracy to murder the Federal witness, Wahl. They were acquitted; but Wahl was nevertheless shot. How does this acquittal adjudicate that the Plummerville box was not stolen?

Roddy was convicted of ejecting the Federal supervisors from the room at Augusta. Is this an adjudication that Clayton was elected?

Jones, Mann, and Smith were indicted for violating the election law at Augusta. They were all convicted.

Reed, Ward, Bentley, W. P. Wells, Woods, Heard, and Thad R. Wells were indicted for stealing the Plummerville ballot-box, and were all acquitted. But it is undisputed that the box was in fact stolen by somebody. It by no means follows that because the jury acquitted these men therefore the ballots in the box should not be counted upon proper proof. In fact, Major Breckinridge in his answer conceded that the vote of this precinct should be ascertained and counted.

Ferguson ejected the supervisor at Augusta, and was indicted and convicted. Is this an adjudication that Breckinridge was not elected?

Hopkins, Davenport, and Hickerson violated the election laws at Augusta Township, Woodruff County. They were convicted.

Martin, Hignight, and Anthony were indicted for stuffing the White River ballot-box and the jury disagreed. Afterwards they were convicted on one count of the indictment, for separating and not making return and proclaiming the result. They were acquitted of stuffing the box. But some one stuffed the box. These men violated the election law, and were convicted. The jury evidently gave them the benefit of the doubt as to who it was that took out Clayton's tickets and put in Breckinridge's.

We have given the list of cases so confidently relied on as an adjudication, and it appears that most of these indictments in the United States courts resulted in convictions.

THE VALUE OF IMPEACHED RETURNS.

Contestee complains that the committee may refuse to accept the impeached returns as of any validity, and thus work a hardship upon him.

If the returns have been falsified by the election officers it is a well-settled rule of law that they cease to have any *prima facie* effect, and each party can only be credited with such votes at the box in question as he may show by other evidence. This rule is one of long standing, and one of which contestee, as an old member of Congress, must have had notice. It works no hardship upon contestee which does not fall as heavily on the contestant. The contestant is required in the first instance to show the fraud in the return, and then must follow that up by proving his vote; or, in some instances, the proof of the fraud is connected with the proof of his vote.

In the present case the fraud is in a large degree shown by proving that votes cast for Clayton were substituted by ballots for Breckinridge, and in proving the fraud the votes for contestant are proved at the same time. Contestant is required to go outside of the returns to prove up his vote, because the judges of the election have falsified the returns. It is no more a hardship upon the contestee to prove up his vote by outside evidence than it is upon the contestant. If contestee's partisans had perpetrated no fraud, the returns would be accepted as true on both sides. His friends having falsified the returns and substituted his ballots for those of his opponent, there is no return at all of any legal effect. He might as well complain of the hardship of being compelled to prove up his vote at Plummerville, where his adherents stole the ballot-box before the vote was counted. No doubt contestee received some votes at the boxes where the returns were falsified, which votes he wholly failed and neglected to prove whilst he had the opportunity in Arkansas.

If the holder of a promissory note alters the note and raises the amount from $1,000 to $2,000, he is met in court with the rule of law which prevents him from using the fraudulent instrument in evidence. It is not even good proof as to the $1,000. The same principle is applied to fraudulent election returns. Courts can not take the fraudulent statements of the election officers and analyze them, and select the true from the false. The whole stream is sullied by the impurity, and all that can be done is to reject the returns altogether and seek other sources of evidence.

ESTOPPEL BY SWEARING IN OF BRECKINRIDGE.

Upon the hearing before the full committee the contestee presented a brief from ex-Attorney-General Garland. He claims that by reason of the swearing in of Major Breckinridge at the organization of the House some sort of an estoppel arises by which no contest can be afterwards carried on. Such is not the rule as to living contestants.

They or their friends are neither required nor permitted to object to the swearing in of a member who holds the formal certificate.

No estoppel will arise against the dead. Clayton could not object to Breckinridge taking the disputed seat. No one else had a right to appear for him. Other members present at the time had no apparent title higher than that of Major Breckinridge. The House was in the process of organization, and the members were sworn in by groups. There were eighteen cases of contest. If it was proper to exclude Major Breckinridge because of the contest, the other seventeen contestees would, in like manner, have been subject to exclusion. Notwithstanding the high standing of the counsel who makes this singular claim, we can not but feel that a mere statement of the proposition carries with it its own refutation.

APPLICATION OF CONTESTEE FOR FURTHER TIME.

The subcommittee examined at Little Rock about twelve hundred witnesses, and there closed the case so far as the evidence in that region is concerned, but with the understanding that the parties might take some special testimony at Washington. The day before the committee left Washington for Arkansas they were notified that Mr. Rowell, and some other members of Congress, would be examined by Mr. Breckinridge, and it was anticipated that they would be called when the subcommittee returned. The contestee, after returning from Little Rock, demanded to reopen the case and take the evidence of Governor Clayton and Dr. Taylor, of Arkansas, and also of the voters in several precincts. To have granted this request fully would have involved the return of the subcommittee to Little Rock, which they did not think was proper to do under the circumstances.

After the case in Arkansas had been closed, and the subcommittee had returned to Washington, contestee then asked to go on and prove up his votes, in the following language:

He asks, therefore, to prove up his vote at these precincts, provided it is contemplated by the committee to refuse the reports of the officials and the findings of the United States court, which tried and acquitted these officials upon the charge that they had tampered with the ballots, which court had the ballots and poll-books, and all other evidence before it. (Rec., p. 379.)

Mr. Breckinridge had expressed a desire to take some testimony at Washington, and it was announced that the evidence in Arkansas was closed, but that the subcommittee would hear some further testimony in Washington. The subcommittee declined to reopen the case as to witnesses in Arkansas. But Dr. Taylor and Governor Clayton happened unexpectedly to appear in Washington, and the subcommittee informed contestee that they would hear these witnesses as their examination would not involve delay or a return to Little Rock. After the leave was granted contestee declined to take the testimony of these witnesses. Dr. Taylor's evidence was assumed to be very important, but when he happened to appear in the city, contestee no longer desired to take it; and so also with that of Governor Clayton.

He also asked to take further testimony in regard to what has been referred to as the Hooper theory of the murder. But in the light of the investigation of this theory at Little Rock, and in the absence of any new discovery, or claim of anything new on the subject, it did not seem reasonable to send to California for other witnesses upon that question. Contestee requested it in his application, but did not show any informa-

tion to base any belief that any witnesses in California would testify
that Hooper was not at his home at the time of the murder. There
were at least two of the murderers, as the tracks showed, and the theory
that Thomas Hooper fired the shot at a man whom he did not know,
and against whom he had no complaint in connection with some one
else, whose name and purpose were unknown, seemed very unreasonable. Governor Eagle, who had attached much importance to the
Hooper clue, after full investigation gave it as his opinion to the subcommittee that it was unfounded. We quote his language:

As to the other matter of offering a reward for the ballot-box thieves, I want to say,
as I said then, I say now, that I believe, I believed then and I believe now, that the
men who stole the ballot-box were implicated in the murder. I will not state that
it was done with a view of putting Clayton out of the House of Representatives, or
with a view of keeping him out and putting Breckinridge in; but because they were
conscious, probably, of having committed a crime against the law and that there was
an investigation going on there, and they were feeling that probably they would be
overtaken in the crime and be punished.

If Mr. Breckinridge had any new information which would have justified the subcommittee in returning to the investigation of this clue
he should have made it known to the subcommittee in his application.

As to Major Breckinridge's claim that he has not had ample time in
Arkansas, we refer to the record of the stenographer as to the adjournment. By some oversight this was not inserted in the transcript
and printed, and we here insert it:

At the close of the examination of Governor James P. Eagle, on recall, on the
night of May 8, 1890, the following proceedings were had, to wit:
Mr. LACEY. Now, gentlemen, are there any other witnesses to be examined?
Mr. McCLURE. I have none.
Mr. McCAIN. We had thought of offering some further evidence, and bringing some
other witnesses, but we have concluded to accommodate the committee as you are
anxious to get away and get back to Washington, and we will say we are through.
Mr. LACEY. We want to take all the evidence you have to offer, and are willing to
stay until you are through, but if you have nothing further to offer we will adjourn
sine die.
The committee adjourned *sine die.*

It is well to observe, before leaving this branch of the matter, in regard
to the voters in Arkansas and the great desire of contestee, as shown
in his application, to take their evidence, that he waited until he got
1,500 miles away from them before manifesting any such disposition.

DANSBY'S CASE.

In Cleveland County one Dansby appeared at the polls, and, bringing
two shot-guns, announced his purpose of taking an active interest in
the proceedings. He was under the influence of liquor. He threatened
Monk Williams, the Republican colored supervisor, and Williams, under
Dansby's threat, abandoned the polls and did not supervise the count
as provided by law.

Dansby is a married man, and his age is given variously by the witnesses, but he appears to be from thirty to thirty-five years old. He is
the nephew of the chairman of the Democratic Congressional district
committee. Mr. Dansby is a strong Democrat, and was a partisan of
contestee. His high connections, instead of being treated as an aggra-
vation of his gross violation of both State and Federal law, is rather
urged as an excuse for shielding him from punishment, and his fine of
$500, inflicted by the United States court, was paid by the chairman of
the Democratic district committee, assisted by Mr. Breckinridge. Mr.

Breckinridge makes the following statement in regard to the payment of this fine:

> Mr. Dansby's punishment was quite severe, $500 and costs, for an offense that usually would not have been punished with 10 per cent. of that amount; but no particular complaint was made of it. The fact that Hon. J. M. Hudson, chairman of the district Democratic committee, helped Mr. Dansby pay his fine, is mentioned as very significant. It might have been added that I helped Hudson help Dansby. Somebody had to help Dansby pay his fine or he had to go to jail. Mr. Hudson is his uncle, and Dansby is a young man and an orphan.

A man of thirty or thirty-five years of age got drunk, took guns to the polls, and drove away a Federal supervisor from the discharge of his duty, and made the most outrageous threats against Republican voters. He was fined $500, and the contestee insists that 10 per cent. of that sum was the "usual" amount, and concedes that the fine was paid by his district chairman and by himself. But contestee says that Dansby was an "orphan." He was a tolerably mature "orphan." Contestee in rendering pecuniary aid to so old an orphan as Dansby has subjected himself to the natural criticism of sympathizing with the act rather than with the youth and inexperience of the actor. If Dansby's crime had been against some other law than that protecting elections, we might well surmise that the party committee and nominee for Congress benefited by the present crime would have hardly felt called upon to pay his fine for him.

That the nominee of a great political party should accept a certificate of election to a seat to which he was clearly not elected, when the certificate was obtained by the well-known larceny of a ballot-box, and at the same time openly aid in the payment of a fine imposed upon another violator of the election laws who had driven an election officer from his post, and that such conduct should not be met with anything but commendation and approval by his political followers, shows a state of disregard for the principles of popular government which may well make us look with apprehension upon the future of our country. That men may be found lawless enough to commit these crimes is to be deplored, but when men of high character and standing complacently avail themselves of the fruits of such crime and the control of the National House of Representatives is made to turn upon such methods, it no longer remains a mere matter of local concern, but arises to the magnitude of a national calamity.

FREEMAN TOWNSHIP.

In Freeman Township, Woodruff County, no election was held. This failure was occasioned by the act of the Democratic sheriff in furnishing the poll-books locked up in the ballot-box and with no key. The Republican supervisor was informed that if he would break open the box they would hold the election, but not otherwise, as the act, it was suggested, involved a penitentiary offense. Though anxious to hold the election, the supervisor did not deem it prudent to incur this risk, and the election was not held. The precinct had been a very close one, according to the returns at the State election, but the Republicans claimed that with the aid of proper supervision, so as to insure a fair count, there would be a good majority for their ticket.

In fact but few Democrats of this precinct appeared at the polls, whether because they knew there would be no election or not does not appear, and the proof did not show how many Democrats were prevented from voting at this box by the failure of the election officers to hold the election. Eighty-three persons made proper effort to vote for the contestant and were prevented by the failure to open the polls. We attach a list with the other lists in the appendix. This state of facts raises an interesting question upon the law of elections, to which we have given some attention, and which, under the peculiar facts of this case, appears not yet to have been heretofore directly decided. It becomes, however, an important fact as bearing upon the issue of a concerted plan to prevent a fair election. If this vote claimed be counted it would only increase the majority of contestant, and its omission from the count would not change the result, and therefore we do not deem it necessary to pass upon the question.

Notwithstanding the murder of the contestant, the contestee appeared and took the contested seat. The present case has attracted national attention, not because it stands alone, as a startling and striking incident of dangers ahead to our form of government, but because it appears to be one of the worst of a very bad kind. Other ballot-boxes have been stolen in other districts, other ballot-boxes have been stuffed, other returns have been falsified, other voters have been intimidated, other political murders have been committed, but now for the first time a member of Congress elected by a fair and full majority of his people has been foully murdered while preparing his case for presentation to this House, and a new element of settlement of political contests is introduced.

In the old days of the code of honor, political antagonists often met face to face and eye to eye, and sought their adversary's life. This method of settling political differences has become obsolete, and we frequently congratulate ourselves upon the improved moral tone of our day and generation. But, never before has a contest for a seat in Congress been terminated by the bullet of an assassin. If such methods are submitted to in silence, the party benefited by the crime of his partisans quietly and without dispute retaining the benefits of the death of his competitor, we would find that a new element would be introduced into our form of government.

Complaint against those who object to fraud and murder in elections, as constituting an assault upon the "people" of Arkansas, is the most cruel form of attack upon the people of that State. This indirect recognition of the criminals as the "people" and the constant and repeated complaint that reference to such methods is a libel upon the "people" of any State, coming as it does from persons high in influence and authority, is calculated to convey the impression that the people are in general sympathy with such methods, and we protest against it, and believe that such defense of the people of Arkansas is the grossest of libels against them.

THE RESULTS.

The following is the vote as returned to the governor:

Counties.	Breckinridge.	Clayton.
Cleburne	536	266
Stone	509	98
Van Buren	561	278
Pope	1,733	890
Conway	1,377	1,837
Faulkner	1,337	1,119
White	1,995	795
Woodruff	1,327	1,107
Lonoke	1,480	1,106
Prairie	828	668
Monroe	811	1,161
Arkansas	912	1,091
Jefferson	1,953	5,377
Grant	707	208
Lincoln	766	1,182
Cleveland	1,031	403
Total	17,847 17,011	17,011
Majority for Breckinridge	846	

Mr. Breckinridge, by the suppression of the Plummerville vote, was returned by a majority of 846.

Under the well-settled law, as decided in this House repeatedly, when a return is found to be tainted with fraud it ceases to have any binding force whatever, and we must look to other evidence for the vote. A number of precincts were attacked in the evidence, and in all of them material changes were shown to have been fraudulently made in the interest of the contestee. Ballots were suppressed or substituted, and if the same percentage of fraud was committed throughout the district, Mr. Clayton might have had as large a majority as Norwood had over Eagle in the same counties in September. To have gone through the other precincts in the same way would have involved the examination of several thousand more witnesses, and a few precincts were singled out by the parties representing the contestant, and the attack confined to them.

WHITE RIVER TOWNSHIP, WOODRUFF COUNTY.

The return shows:

Breckinridge 210
Clayton 44

Under the laws of Arkansas, the judges are required to mark a number on the outside of the ballot, before putting it in the box, and such number corresponds with the number opposite the voter's name on the poll-list. In this precinct 62 persons who swear they voted for Clayton, deny that they cast the tickets numbered as having been cast by them. The original tickets were presented to them before the committee, and are shown to be the opposite of what they voted. These 62 tickets were evidently changed by or with the connivance of the Democratic judges of the election, and when corrected make a difference of 62 off of Breckinridge's vote, and 62 to be added to that of Clayton.

These ballots had manifestly been substituted after they were deposited, and this could not have been done if the judges had not either permitted it or committed the act themselves. This change of 124 invalidates the return. A fraudulent return of this character can have no effect, and as a matter of law we must deduct from—

Breckinridge's reported majority of... 846
The votes so fraudulently returned 210
                                                                              ——
     Leaving a majority of... 636

In counting Clayton's vote, 44 votes were credited to him in making Breckinridge's original majority. The proof shows that he got 62 votes where the tickets were changed, 39 votes where his tickets were not changed, as shown by the voters themselves, and 5 others where the proof is that the voters were furnished with and cast Clayton tickets, and that the voters were Republicans. Total vote proved for Clayton 106. He has already been credited with 44, so he should now be credited with the balance, 62. There were also two names of voters not on the book, who voted for Clayton. We will insert the names of all these voters in an appendix, which we think will be more convenient for reference than to incorporate them here. Deducting from Breckinridge's returned majority 64, leaves 572.

COTTON PLANT TOWNSHIP, WOODRUFF COUNTY.

In this precinct there were returned for—

Breckinridge... 186
Clayton... 132

The fact that the ballots were changed after being cast is not only sworn to by the voters at this precinct, but, in many instances, the ballots introduced in evidence appears to have been folded after they were numbered. The judges are required to put the number on the ballot before depositing it, and the numbers in many instances showed that they must have been written on the ballot before folding, the crease of folding running through the number on the back of the ticket. This was utterly at variance with the contestee's theory that Republican colored voters were secretly voting the Democratic ticket. If these men voted for Breckinridge at all they voted an open ticket.

Deduct the vote returned for Breckinridge, the return being set aside for fraud, 186; leaving Breckinridge's majority 386.

There were returned for Clayton 132; 48 voters swear they voted for Clayton, but are returned as voting for Breckinridge; this fraud invalidates the return. These 48 votes should be counted for Clayton; also 104 tickets in the returns proved to have been cast as returned, the voters being called as witnesses; also 23 voters whose names are entered in the poll-books, and who are shown to have voted for Clayton; also 30 voters whose names were not on the poll-books; total, 205. Of this 205, 132 are already counted for Clayton, leaving to be deducted 73; leaving Breckinridge's majority 313.

TOWN OF AUGUSTA, WOODRUFF COUNTY.

The returns show—

Breckinridge... 98
Clayton... 34

The evidence of the voters shows that 8 ballots were changed from Clayton to Breckinridge, and 7 persons swear they voted for Clayton, and are voters, and their names are not on the poll-lists; 26 persons swear that they voted for Clayton, and are so returned; 10 persons are shown by other evidence to have voted for Clayton, and are so returned ; also one ticket is shown to have been voted for Clayton, and Clayton's name afterwards erased, making a total for Clayton of 52. Deduct the returned vote for Breckinridge, 98; balance Breckinridge's majority, 215. Clayton is already credited with 34. Deduct the difference between 34 and 52—18. Balance Breckinridge's majority, 197.

RIVERSIDE, WOODRUFF COUNTY.

Returned for Breckinridge 197
Returned for Clayton 59

It appears from testimony of the voters that 29 Clayton tickets were changed and Breckinridge tickets substituted, thus invalidating the returns.

Deduct vote for Breckinridge, 197; majority for Breckinridge, 0. The 29 persons whose tickets were so changed should be counted for Clayton ; also 32 others appear and testify that they voted for Clayton, and their tickets so appear; also 25 persons admitted in the record to have voted for Clayton, whose tickets are so returned ; also 4 persons who voted for Clayton, but whose names do not appear on the poll-list; also one vote with no ticket preserved in the box; total 90. Already returned for Clayton 59; balance to be counted to him 31; total Clayton's majority, 31.

Breckinridge did not attempt to prove up his vote at these boxes, but incidentally some of them were proved up, and the lists are attached to the Appendix.

Proved in Augusta for Breckinridge.. 3
Proved in Cotton Plant for Breckinridge.. 1
Proved in White River for Breckinridge.. 3
                                                                                    ——
    Total... 7

The balance of Clayton's majority, without taking into account Freeman Township, Woodruff County, or the Plummerville vote in Conway County is 24.

HOWARD TOWNSHIP, CONWAY COUNTY.

Total vote for Clayton... 560
For Breckinridge... 125
                                                                                        ——
    Majority for Clayton... 435
Total majority for Clayton in the district... 459

There are in addition to this 83 votes which were not cast at Freeman Township, Woodruff County, by reason of the failure to open the polls.

The above is the computation upon the settled rules of election law in this House. We will now state the return upon the most favorable view that contestee could claim, under the case of Jones vs. Glidewell, Supreme Court of Arkansas, A. D. 1890. If we were to throw out the whole vote in the impeached precincts, and inasmuch as Breckinridge has not proved his vote there, to ignore the proof of Clayton's vote, it would show the following results:

Breckinridge's majority.. 846
Deduct Howard Township, Conway County, majority shown...................... 435
                                                                                        ——
    Majority remaining... 411

Now deduct the vote returned for both parties in the disputed precincts:

Precincts.	Breckinridge.	Clayton.
White River	210	44
Cotton Plant	186	132
Augusta	98	34
Riverside	197	59
Total	691	269

By thus considering the proof for the purpose of showing fraud alone, and not for the purpose of counting the votes, Breckinridge would lose the difference between 691 and 269, or 422, which would leave Clayton elected by 11 majority without taking into consideration Freeman Township. But this method, so favorable to contestee, is not the rule of this House, and we only make the computation in this form to show that by the most favorable method of calculation the contestee is not entitled to the seat which he holds, after the proof is adduced as to the Plummerville box.

We recommend the adoption of the following resolutions:

"*Resolved*, That Clifton R. Breckinridge was not elected to the seat which he now holds as Representative in Congress from the Second Congressional District of the State of Arkansas,

"*Resolved*, That John M. Clayton was elected as Representative in Congress from the Second Congressional District of the State of Arkansas, and because of his death the seat is declared vacant."

The committee do not feel called upon to offer any resolution in regard to the "methods of the election" referred to. It is a proper subject for legislation, but has been anticipated in the House by the Federal election law just passed.

APPENDIX.

CLAYTON v. BRECKINRIDGE CONTEST FROM SECOND ARKANSAS DISTRICT.

LIST OF VOTERS AND THE PAGES OF THE RECORD WHERE THE EVIDENCE MAY BE FOUND.

WHITE RIVER TOWNSHIP, WOODRUFF COUNTY.

Names of persons appearing on the poll-book of said township who are returned as voting for Breckinridge who have testified they voted for Clayton.

	Page.		Page.
1. Anthony, Armstead	17	32. Jones, C. P	16
2. Anthony, J. W	20	33. Jones, Jim	21
3. Anthony, C. H	21	34. Johnson, Geo	33
4. Anderson, Geo	26	35. Montgomery, Geo	14
5. Anthony, J. T	26	36. McDonald, Josey	14
6. Anderson, Lewis	29	37. Minor, Jessee	17
7. Anthony, Ruben	32	38. McCoy, Allen ....1st Rec.	86
8. Bledsoe, Wash ....1st Rec.	93	39. McCoy, Ben............86, 1st Rec.	19
9. Butler, Frank............1st Rec.	90	40. McCoy, Levey	20
10. Brown, Harry	16	41. McDonald, Lewis	24
11. Briscoe, William............1st Rec.	88	42. McDonald, Mans	24
12. Boon, Tony	24	43. McCoy, Clint	25
13. Briscoe, Ed............1st Rec.	90	44. Magnus, Frank	28
14. Campbell, Isom ....1st Rec.	94	45. Moore, Henry	31
15. Campbell, Albert ....1st Rec.	94	46. Miller, Joe	32
16. Curry, Willis ....1st Rec.	90	47. Murray, Allen	34
17. Curry, Bud	27	48. Nelson, Alex	31
18. Curry, Ike	28	49. Owen, Charles	19
19. Eden, Sam............1st Rec.	88	50. Pranty, John	30
20. Eaton, Jessee	18	51. Roddy, Lewis ....1st Rec.	80
21. Fulton, David............1st Rec.	90	52. Simpson, Ben ....1st Rec.	92
22. Felton, William	23	53. Simpson, F ....1st Rec.	95
23. Freeman, Rufus	23	54. Thompson, F ....1st Rec.	94
24. Greenwood, James ....1st Rec.	87	55. Thompson, T ....1st Rec.	86
25. Graham, Armond	25	56. Tucker, Dan	33
26. Hodges, Nick............1st Rec.	90	57. Vaughn, J. A ....1st Rec.	90
27. Haigh, Alex ....1st Rec.	95	58. Wise, John ....1st Rec.	83
28. Henderson, J. U	22	59. Ward, J. H	20
29. Hughes, Tom ....1st Rec.	90	60. Williams, Joe ....1st Rec.	90
30. Houston, Henry ....1st Rec.	96	61. Warren, Ike	21
31. Hodge, Nick............1st Rec.	92	62. Wright, Alfred ....1st Rec.	95

Names of persons appearing on the poll-book of said township who are returned as voting for Clayton who appeared and testified they so voted, or whose votes were shown by other evidence.

	Page.		Page.
1. Anthony, Andy	22	21. McCoy, M. W	25
2. Anthony, Willis	28	22. McKenzie, And	29
3. Anthony, H. A	32	23. McDonald, Dan	192
4. Anthony, Paul	190	24. Pitts, Pompey............1st Rec.	89
5. Anthony, R. B............1st Rec.	92	25. Pussell, It ....1st Rec.	87
6. Bridges, Louis ....1st Rec.	85	26. Rozzell, Ed ....87, 1st Rec.	39
7. Butler, H. F ....1st Rec.	94	27. Ross, H ....1st Rec.	89
8. Beverly, G. W	26	28. Runyan, S. C ....1st Rec.	88
9. Beal, S. A	191	29. Stewart, Sam	18
10. Corley, Sherwood............1st Rec.	86	30. Stewart, Joe	31
11. Corley, Wm	30	31. Tripp, J ....1st Rec.	89
12. Conch, Anthony	191	32. Tripp, I ....1st Rec.	87
13. Davis, David	27	33. Thompson, A. L	192
14. Davis, Wyatt	32	34. Watson, S ....1st Rec.	95
15. Ellis, W. L	191	35. Williams, Oscar ....1st Rec.	96
16. Graham, Sam	40	36. Westmoreland, D	26
17. Lowe, Marshal ....1st Rec.	86	37. Briscoe, E ....1st Rec.	90
18. Martin, J. M ....1st Rec.	89	38. Briscoe, Wm............1st Rec.	88
19. Martin, Sam'l............1st Rec.	88	39. Watson, Gus ....1st Rec.	90
20. Martin, Thomas	22		

Names of persons appearing on the poll-book of said township who are returned as voting for Clayton who were not found, but who are proven to be Republicans and to have been furnished with a Clayton ticket.

	Page.		Page
1. Jelks, Rich'd	191	4. Young, J. W.	25
2. Richards, Wm	192	5. Ayres, S. E	192
3. Slocum Madorn	192		

Names of persons whose names do not appear on the poll-book, but who swear they were at the election and voted for Clayton.

	Page.		Page.
1. Danshee, Wash	15	2. Neal, Tobe	96, 1st rec. 14

Total number of names on poll-book 257
Return shows Breckinridge 210
Clayton 44
Tickets show Breckinridge 209
Clayton 45

WHITE RIVER TOWNSHIP, WOODRUFF COUNTY.

Names of persons shown to have voted for Breckinridge.

	Page.		Page.
1. McNealy, George	656	3. Harris, Rufus	658
2. Hutchinson, J. A	657		

COTTON-PLANT TOWNSHIP, WOODRUFF COUNTY.

List No. 1.—Names of persons appearing on the poll-book of said township who are returned as voting for Breckinridge, who have testified they voted for Clayton.

	Page.		Page.
1. Brown, Julius	68	25. Laimer, Jacob	83
2. Campbell, Henry	62	26. Nixon, Dunk	81
3. Childers, Peter	61	27. Nowling, E.	74
4. Carter, George	60	28. Phillips, James	61
5. Copland C E	63	29. Pearson, L	77
6. Chunn D	86	30. Reynolds, G.	97
7. Davis, John	68	31. Richards, G	91
8. Floyd. L	94	32. Roland, Ruben	79
9. Floyd, B.	78	33. Razor, Joe	93
10. Finley, Ben	65	34. Sloan, Z. L	66
11. Folsom, Harry	90	35. Sanders, M	76
12. Greer, Will	92	36. Sawyers, G	86
13. Giles, Henry A	67	37. Smith, Neath	87
14. Halland, Chas	59	38. Sampson, Sandy	63
15. Hibler, Austin	64	39. Turner, Henry	79
16. Hall, Theo	100	40. Tiggs, Pleasant	61
17. Hall, Sam	95	41. Thompson, Mack	69
18. Hardin, Jeff	74	42. Taylor, L. S	66
19. Johnson, John	73	43. Wilson, D. H	58
20. Johnson, R.	110	44. Walton, Wm	60
21. Johnson, C	70	45. Wilson, Mack	64
22. Jones, Charley	75	46. Woods, C.	79
23. Kaiser, John	93	47. Walker, James	71
24. Leech, Dan	76	48. Young, Jack	65

List No. 2.—Names of persons appearing on the poll-books of said township who are returned as voting for Clayton, who appeared and testified they so voted.

	Page.		Page.
1. Anderson, A	74	18. Chunn, Will	65
2. Ashley, H	78	19. Drummond, Pink	69
3. Brown, R. H	62	20. Davis, J	68
4. Buchanan, Isaac	91	21. Davis, Bill	86
5. Blackman, B	63	22. Elmer, Bob	76
6. Bostick, Esau	92	23. Hampton, Geo	92
7. Brunston, A	90	24. Holliday, G	79
8. Briggs, Sam	69	25. Horton, B	81
9. Black, John	88	26. Horton, F	97
10. Crutchmer, R. G	84	27. Harvey, Denis	67
11. Childers, Joe	69	28. Haskins, Pink	85
12. Chunn, Rix	96	29. Hall, Sam	95
13. Chunn, Mark	95	30. Hancock, C	83
14. Chunn, F	82	31. Hunter, A. H	71
15. Chunn, Alex	91	32. Jenkins, P	81
16. Chunn, Jake	89	33. Johnson, Aaron	73
17. Clark, Chas	73	34. Jones, Wash	77

List No. 2.—Names of persons appearing on the poll books of said township who are returned as voting for Clayton, etc.— Continued.

	Page.		Page.
35. Johnson, J	72	70. Russell, Joe	75
36. Jones, Mat	64	71. Roberts, Lee	93
37. Jones, Sandy	77	72. Roland, R	101
38. Johnson, Dave	72	73. Rogers, Ned	67
39. Jains, Jasper	63	74. Slaughter, Bob	66
40. King, Geo.	81	75. Settle, Ben	95
41. Laird, Jeff	96	76. Shelton, Sam	77
42. Lard, Barney	87	77. Summers, W	91
43. Lester, Charley	93	78. Shelton, Jacob	83
44. Leek, J	83	79. Slay, Adolphus	109
45. Leek, Will	76	80. Sutton, Smith Ben	107
46. Locke, Will	65	81. Shelton, Henry	64
47. Locke, H.	82	82. Sledge, Jos	72
48. Lapier, Will	77	83. Shelton, Frank	105
49. Locke, Sam	73	84. Shelton, Osborn	93
50. Locke, Mat	82	85. Trent, R	93
51. Lock, Lon	87	86. Thompson, Richard	81
52. Lard, Kearney	88	87. Taylor, Nelson	72
53. Madden, Milton	87	88. Taylor, Green	72
54. McGee, Sam	71	89. Woods, Remus	70
55. Merritt, Nick	82	90. Williams, Henry	75
56. McDaniel, W	75	91. Watters, Bill	87
57. Mayo, Lee	90	92. Woods, Robt	95
58. Morris, W. A	101	93. Williams, Jas	74
59. McCoy, Sam	80	94. Williams, Buck	87
60. Morris, Alex	67	95. Woods, Spence	88
61. Monroe, Wynn	70	96. Wilson, Geo	76
62. McNeeley, Henry	80	97. Woods, Jeff	108
63. Nesbitt, Berry	69	98. Woods, Dick	81
64. Nixon, G	80	99. Walker, A	107
65. Paul, Aaron	96	100. Woodsmith, Haywood	80
66. Philip, Andrew	107	101. Hollins, W. T	109
67. Perkins, W	79	102. James, Nill	109
68. Pier, W. La	76	103. Sutton, B. S	107
69. Perkins, Bob	71		

List No. 3.—Names of persons appearing on the poll-book of said township who are returned as voting for Clayton, who were not found, but are proven to be Republicans and to have been furnished with Clayton tickets.

	Page.		Page.
1. Ackal, Jack	108	12. Irwin, P. J	109
2. Bates, G. H	108	13. Irwin, Tobe	109
3. Clemings, R. N	108	16. Jenkins, R	109
4. Dossen, J. M	109	17. Lard, Barney, No. 2	109
5. Featherston, A. G	109	20. Morgan, T. J	109
7 Gathing	109	21. Sikes, W	110
9. Hollins, W. P	109	22. Slay, Adolphus	110
10. Henry, Wm	109	23. Shaw, Mack	110
11. Hardin, Henry	109		

List No. 4.—Names of persons whose names do not appear on the poll-books, but who swear they were at the election and voted for Clayton.

	Page.		Page.
1. Arnold, Peter	83	16. Marshal, Henry	90
2. Barnea, Jerry	89	17. Otem, Freeman	111
3. Beckham, Ruben	106	18. Otem, David	112
4. Clark, Nick	94	19. Reeve, Morrison	96
5. Chaffin, Geo	103	20. Robinson, A	99
6. Gregory, Heuston	106	21. Runnels, H. R.	106
7. Harshaw, J. W	80	22. Simon, Joseph	86
8. Hughes, John	88	23. Slayton, Lucius	98
9. Henderson, Thos	95	24. Thompson, Henry	91
10. Jenkins, Paul	92	25. Vincent, J. M	71
11. Jarmin, Peter	101	26. Wilson, H	78
12. Locke, Lew	87	27. Weaver, Claib	80
13. Moran, Henry	83	28. Woods, Noah	89
14. Madden, Chris	84	29. Woods, Alex	96
15. Musgrave, Dock	85		

Total number of names on poll-book 319
Return shows Breckinridge 186
          Clayton 132
Tickets show Breckinridge 174
          Clayton 134

There are eleven less tickets than there are names on the poll-book.

List No. 1.. 48
List No. 2.. 105
List No. 3.. 23
List No. 4.. 31

       Total 207
Below 2
                                                               209

Names of voters who testify they voted for Clayton and are on poll-list, but no ticket in box.

	Page.		Page.
1. Buford, Bob	70	2. Miller, Calvin	110

COTTON PLANT TOWNSHIP, WOODRUFF COUNTY.

List of voters shown to have voted for Breckinridge.

	Page.
Hennigdon, James	678

TOWN OF AUGUSTA, WOODRUFF COUNTY.

List No. 1.—Names of persons appearing on the poll-books of said precinct who are returned as voting for Breckinridge who have testified they voted for Clayton.

	Page.		Page.
1. Aultevery, A	52	5. James, Napoleon	49
2. Burfoot, Emmet	45	6. Johnson, Granville	54
3. Price, Moses	46	7. Moore, Thomas	44
4. Hampton, Sam	47	8. Williams, Mose	47

List No. 2.—Names of persons appearing on the poll-book of said precinct who are returned as voting for Clayton who appeared and testified they so voted.

	Page.		Page.
1. Bobo, A. E	51	14. Martin, John	46
2. Cartner, Warren	46	15. Malone, William	52
3. Cook, J. J	55	16. Montgomery, C	47
4. Cook, W. A	55	17. Martin, Lewis	56
5. Chambers, W. H	52	18. Roddy, Jerry	51
6. Derain, C. H	46	19. Roddy, Alex	52
7. Davis, William	48	20. Rider, Ed	57
8. Harris, Henderson	47	21. Rodgers, J. H	53
9. Harris, Tom H	54	22. Reese, Mark	48
10. Hinkston, Geo	51	23. Williams, Jim	47
11. Hardy, Albert	48	24. Wilson, H. H	49
12. Hamlet, Ike	54	25. White, Charley	52
13. Knox, Henry	53	26. Willis, E. J	57

List No. 3.—Names of persons appearing on the poll-book of said precinct who are returned as voting for Clayton who were not found, but are proven to be Republicans and to have been furnished with Clayton tickets.

	Page.		Page.
1. Battle, L	57	6. Leach, D. D	58
2. Ford, R. H	45, 57	7. Lock, Henry	58
3. Jackson, J	57	8. McGloflin, J. T	58
4. Kerr, C. M	57	9. Pettigrew, Dan	58
5. Knox, Geo	58	10. Knox, Geo	58

List No. 4—Names of persons whose names do not appear on the poll-books of said precinct who swear they were at the election and voted for Clayton.

	Page.		Page.
1. Allen, Lewis	52	5. Woods, N. W	54
2. Curry, Dock	48	6. Davis, Wm. (no ticket in box)	48
3. Chambers, D. W	53	7. Reese, M. (no ticket in box)	48
4. Smith, Harvey	48		

Total number of names on poll-book............................... 134
Return shows Breckinridge.. 98
              Clayton.. 34
Tickets show Breckinridge... 94
              Clayton.. 34

Names of voters whose tickets were scratched, but who swear they voted an unscratched ticket for Clayton.

Page.

1. J. W. Nelson... 55

List of voters who swear they voted for Breckinridge.

1. J. W. Headen.. 56

AUGUSTA, WOODRUFF COUNTY.

List of voters shown to have voted for Breckinridge.

Page.

1. Henderson, John (convicted of felony)... 658
2. Moore, W. M. 660

RIVERSIDE PRECINCT, WOODRUFF COUNTY.

List No. 1.—Names of persons appearing on the poll-book of said precinct, who are returned as voting for Breckinridge, who have testified they voted for Clayton.

	Page.			Page.
1. Anderson, John	120	16. Kendrick, F		116
2. Beverly, Henry	131	17. Miller, Joe		115
3. Beverly, A. H	122	18. Patterson, A		124
4. Barton, Bob	119	19. Partee, R. M		116
5. Campbell, H	62	20. Parmer, Barney		122
6. Cole, George	120	21. Russell, E. J		114
7. Compton, Green	124	22. Russel, Harry		115
8. Eason, John	129	23. Rollins, Andrew		114
9. Gilchrist, Fred	117	24. Roddy, Mace		114
10. Hunt, Jim	122	25. Haugbter, Alex		118
11. Haywood, Fred	130	26. Simpson, Jim	118,	131
12. Henderson, Lewis	119	27. Williams, Gus		122
13. Jones, Ross	117	28. Walton, Bew		122
14. Jackson, Allen	123	29. Wess, Jessie		133
15. Johnson, Geo	113			

List No. 2.—Names of persons appearing on the poll-book of said precinct, who are returned as voting for Clayton, who appeared and testified they so voted.

	Page.			Page.
1. Allen, John	120	17. Massey, E		123
2. Buggs, George	121	18. Miller, Charles		121
3. Brewster, Tony	122	19. McPheters, B. Y	125,	133
4. Coy, Hamil	120	20. Penn, Christopher		118
5. Cariker, Bill	120	21. Page, Monroe		116
6. Calvin, John	116	22. Palmer, Barney		122
7. Cariker, Arthur	122	23. Rawlins, Sam		117
8. Billard, Allen	131	24. Redden, Alf		121
9. Freeman, Jeff	114	25. Redden, Henry		116
10. Golightly, A. D	113, 131	26. Roddy, Lewis		117
11. Gray, Felix	132	27. Still, Lee		130
12. Jackson, George	119	28. Spiller, Henry		115
13. Jones, Mack	117	29. Tallman, Alf. (no ticket in box)		119
14. King, Manuel	117	30. Westmoreland, Claud		121
15. Little, Joe	116	31. White, Jim		131
16. Morgan, William	131	32. Jones, Ross		117

List No. 3.—Names of persons appearing on the poll-book of said precinct, who are returned as voting for Clayton, who were not found but are proven to be Republicans and to have been furnished with Clayton tickets.

	Page.			Page.
1. Adams, James	133	14. Morgan, Bunch		133
2. Austin, Ben	133	15. Matheny, Tom		133
3. Bobo, L	133	16. Massey, Jack		133
4. Chassy, W	133	17. Miller, Alfred		133
5. Chase, W	133	18. Miller, Louis		133
6. Chase, Asbury	133	19. Robinson, Mack		133
7. Davis, Simon	133	20. Roddy, Chas		133
8. Epps, Archie	133	21. Sheppard, Anthony		133
9. Epps, James	133	22. Veeder, S		133
10. Freeman, James	133	23. Wesley, John		133
11. Forbes, Lewis	130, 133	24. Watson, L. A		133
12. Henry, Clayburn	133	25. Watson, S. W		133
13. Johnson, O. D	133			

NOTE.—It is admitted of record by Breckinridge that these persons were at the election and voted for Clayton (p. 133).

List No. 4—Names of persons whose names do not appear on the poll-book of said precinct who swear they were at the election and voted for Clayton.

	Page.		Page.
1. Allen, Freeman	121	3. Roddy, Rance	132
2. Forbes, Lewis		4. Snoddy, J. A	132

Names of voters who voted for Clayton, but no ticket in box.

	Page.
1. Tolman, Alfred	119

Total number of names on poll-book	257
Return shows Breckinridge	197
Clayton	59
Tickets show Breckinridge	192
Clayton	52

There are *thirteen* less tickets than there are names on the poll-book.

List No. 1	29
List No. 2	32
List No. 3	28
List No. 4	4
Total	89

PLUMMERVILLE VOTE, CONWAY COUNTY.

Names of persons who have testified they were at the election in Howard Township, Conway County, Ark., on November 6, 1888, and voted for John M. Clayton; or whose votes were otherwise proved.

	Page.		Page.
1. Acklin, W. R	197	51. Birdle, Morgan	218
2. Albright, Henry	203	52. Bloom, Gus	550
3. Alexander, W. M	482	53. Burt, Alex	199
4. Adams, Willis	216	54. Broton, James P......1st Rec.	60
5. Andrew, Ned ....74, 1st Rec.	457	55. Bell, Robert	248
6. Alexander, Alfred	266	56. Booker, Ben ....1st Rec.	64
7. Allen, J	248	57. Booker, Aaron	271
8. Armstead, E	195	58. Bradford, John ....1st Rec.	61
9. Arthur, Charles	250	59. Barnes, Lewis	223
10. Anthony, H. A	240	60. Bowair, F. Pierce	253
11. Atkinson, T. J	489	61. Bowgan, Isaac	234
12. Armstead, Levy ....1st Rec.	59	62. Blassingame, John ......1st Rec.	66
13. Alexander, John	252	63. Bowsir, James.........1st Rec.	81
14. Allington, John	206	64. Bradley, Charles	459
15. Adams, Amos ....1st Rec.	77	65. Bowlin, Jack	236
16. Addison, J. A ....1st Rec.	76	66. Butler, Harry ....1st Rec.	45
17. Alexander, Fenton ....1st Rec.	49	67. Byrum, John	221
18. Acklin, W. R, jr .....1st Rec.	50	68. Cox, Albert	203
19. Atkinson, J. M	478	69. Cox, Garrett	471
20. Alexander, E. D ....1st Rec.	43	70. Cox, Tolbert	268
21. Ackron, W. R	225	71. Cox, Green ....1st Rec.	55
22. Albright, Wm	258	72. Carter, Jonas.........1st Rec.	60
23. Alexander, Henry	245	73. Carter, Dock	268
24. Aaron, Isaac	208	74. Carter, Robert	361
25. Brown, W	240	75. Carter, Gus	200
26. Brown, Sam	489	76. Carter, Jacob	480
27. Brown, John	200	77. Carter, James	220
28. Brown, Cager ....1st Rec.	71	78. Carter, Dock, No. 2	453
29. Brown, Daniel	237	79. Clifton, Henry	253
30. Brown, French	457	80. Compton, D	205
31. Brown, W. H	459	81. Compton, John ....1st Rec.	58
32. Brown, R. B	197	82. Compton, S. C ....1st Rec.	58
33. Brown, H. B	216	83. Cook, Wm	210
34. Black, Wash	452	84. Clark, Ned	215
35. Brown, Sam, No. 2	550	85. Clark, David	245
36. Black, P. B ....1st Rec.	48	86. Clark, Thomas	447
37. Black, Wm...........1st Rec.	294	87. Champon, Dan'l ......1st Rec.	57
38. Black, Sylvester	472	88. Cartwright, Geo	204
39. Black, Robert	247	89. Clements, Jack	477
40. Black, J. B	293	90. Culp, R. A...........1st Rec.	62
41. Blair, Van	227	91. Colcord, David	476
42. Berry, Peter	267	92. Carrington, Sam'l C	256
43. Bowling, J. M	256	93. Colcom, R. C	256
44. Baldwin, Monroe	457	94. Chappl, E. R	202
45. Burks, W	244	95. Coy, Frank	198
46. Bailey, Jack	473	96. Chase, Danl ....1st Rec.	62
47. Bailey, Geo	268, 473	97. Coles, James	341
48. Bailey, Thomas........1st Rec.	46	98. Call, Nelson	243
49. Blackburn, Wilson	203	99. Cash, Mike	241
50. Belden, Toll	473	100. Calvin, John	242

Names of persons who have testified they were at the election in Howard Township, Conway County, Ark., on November 6, 1888, etc.—Continued.

Names of persons who have testified they were at the election in Howard Township, Conway County, Ark., on November 6, 1888, etc.—Continued.

	Page.			Page.
269. Jones, Isom, No. 2	473	353. McMurray, Richd		450
270. Jones, S. H	359	354. Morgan, Wash		258
271. Jones, Henry	234	355. Majors, Cupid	1st Rec.	50
272. Jones, D. S	215	356. Manning, Robt	1st Rec.	73
273. Johnson, C. T	234	357. Metchum, Lewis		478
274. Johnson, Ford	360	358. McKinney, S		489
275. Johnson, M	479	359. McHinney, S		255
276. Johnson, Jerry	245	360. Macklin, David	1st Rec.	65
277. Johnson, Richd	1st Rec. 49	361. Matthews, I. C		452
278. Johnson, Bailey	221	362. Matthews, Philip		475
279. Johnson, Albert	1st Rec. 55	363. Mitchell, Henry		454
280. Johnson, Isaac	219	364. Madlock, Bob		473
281. Johnson, Frank	244	365. Mitchell, L. M		242
282. Johnson, Henry	1st Rec. 59	366. Mayburn, Wiloy	1st Rec.	56
283. Johnson, Isaac	219	367. Mattox, Clark		242
284. Johnson, Isaac, No. 2	221	368. McCully, John		447
285. Johnson, Isaac S	451	369. McCully, E. D		232
286. Jenkins, Peter	225	370. Neely, Jim		480
287. Jenkins, Raymond	1st Rec. 56	371. Owens, Geo	1st Rec.	50
288. James, Thomas	1st Rec. 65	372. Oten, John		364
289. Jamison, John R	233	373. Ostler, Alex		477
290. Jamison, Jacob	1st Rec. 58	374. Oslee, Richd		360
291. Jamison, J. W	250	375. Ostler, James		459
292. Jamison, Isaac	208	376. Parrott, M		551
293. Jordan, Jacob	453	377. Parrot, Frank		477
294. Jordan, William	271	378. Parrot, Bryant		473
295. Jennings, Nathl	359	379. Parker, A	1st Rec.	73
296. Kirtland, G. W	255	380. Adams, Joshua		549
297. Kennedy, Wm	242	381. Parker, Arthur		235
298. Kennedy, Henry	220	382. Parker, Wm		447
299. Kelsey, Henry	263	383. Parker, Wm., No. 2		553
300. King, David	256	384. Potter, Dick	1st Rec.	71
301. King, William	241	385. Payne, Bedford		521
302. Kimp, A	49, 1st Rec. 478	386. Payne, Squire		489
303. Kieth, A	213	387. Payne, Sam		249
304. Kennedy, Jerry	552	388. Page, Frank B		231
305. Kelly, Mose	552	389. Page, W. I		237
306. Levels, King	246	390. Phillips, H		358
307. Levels, A	457	391. Perry, W. T		553
308. Levels, Robt	1st Rec. 44	392. Parry, Isom		475
309. Lambert, Ranzo	1st Rec. 77	393. Pope, John		239
310. Lewis, Charles M	200	394. Pope, James		262
311. Littlefield, L	251	395. Pope, Theopolis		215
312. Livingston, Adam	1st Rec. 46	396. Pope, Peter		361
313. Long, Alfred	245	397. Powell, Lewis		236
314. Lackey, David	79, 1st Rec. 479	398. Patterson, N		341
315. Lindsley, Perry	448	399. Peoples, Geo		248
316. Lambert, Jordan	1st Rec. 82	400. Price, Ben		257
317. Lucas, Frank	1st Rec. 45	401. Price, Albert		246
318. Lucas, J	266	402. Patterson, Dan		476
319. Lane, Ike	453	403. Reese, Tobe	1st Rec.	57
320. Lewis, Thomas	245	404. Rivers, E	48, 1st Rec.	479
321. Leslie, W. D	199	405. Rivers, Dave		472
322. Leverett, C	269	406. Richardson, W. R		265
323. Lindsley, Al	458	407. Richardson, Clem		458
324. Moore, Sylvanus	210	408. Randolph, W. M		269
325. Moore, Samuel	254	409. Ridley, Roy		456
326. Moore, Gen'l	1st Rec. 61	410. Richello, Richd		197
327. Moore, Monroe	1st Rec. 62	411. Rozelle, J. R		459
328. Moore, John H	343	412. Rice, Charles	1st Rec.	52
329. Moore, John H., No. 2	201	413. Rowley, Eph		489
330. Moore, Dan	218	414. Ragland, Charles		246
331. Moore, Washington	269	415. Raglen, Lewis		226
332. Moore, Frank	271	416. Rice, Milton		448
333. Moore, Geo. H	343	417. Rye, Scott		365
334. Moore, Miles	255	418. Raglen, Stephen		226
335. Moore, John W	341	419. Reed, James	1st Rec.	57
336. Moore, Joseph	1st Rec. 46	420. Rainwater, J. D	1st Rec.	54
337. Miller, Harry, No. 2	259	421. Robinson, A. R		204
338. Miller, Wesley	294	422. Reasoner, Armstead	78, 1st Rec.	477
339. Miller, Harry	240	423. Rothwell, Alex. A		216
340. Miller, Anthony	264	424. Raglan, Lee	1st Rec.	73
341. Morris, Gus	251	425. Smith, Thomas		268
342. Martin, D. N	472	426. Smith, Alex		359
343. Mormon, Lewis	480	427. Smith, Saul		272
344. McCollough, Al	75, 1st Rec. 244	428. Smith, W. B		218
345. McCollough, Gabe	480	429. Smith, Ed		246
346. Mason, Jerry	255	430. Smith, Wade		222
347. McDaniel, Bob	552	431. Smith, Thomas, jr		270
348. McDaniel, Napoleon	226	432. Smith, A		201
349. McDaniel, Wm	448	433. Smith, John		241
350. Buchanan, Nelson	550	434. Smith, J. P	1st Rec.	49
351. McDaniel, James	217	435. Smith, Sam'l	1st Rec.	70
352. Mitchell, R. A	215	436. Adams, Joshua		549

Names of persons who have testified they were at the election in Howard Township, Conway County, Ark., on November 6, 1888, etc.—Continued.

No.	Name		Page.
437.	Buchanan, N		549
438.	Smith, C. J		458
439.	Sunderland, Jack		482
440.	Strickland, L. R		200
441.	Stricklin, James M		217
442.	Slayton, John		270
443.	Slayton, John, No. 2	1st Rec.	67
444.	Sanders, Henry		456
445.	Sanders, Lewis		270
446.	Sloan, Geo. D		553
447.	Sloan, Marion		553
448.	Sheppard, Sam		553
449.	Street, Felix		270
450.	Shaw, Haywood		232
451.	Stevens, Cager	1st Rec.	56
452.	Stubbs, Jacob		452
453.	Spivey, Watt		225
454.	Snipes, John		296
455.	Snipes, T. C		259, 296
456.	Snipes, Sam'l		247
457.	Shelton, Robt		449
458.	Steele, Henry		451
459.	Stephenson, Henry		224
460.	Seadan, Ben		473
461.	Scott, Ruben		231
462.	Smiles, William		453
463.	Salters, John A		264
464.	Talley, Ed. jr		238
465.	Talley, Ed		231
466.	Thornton, E. D		204
467.	Thornton, Hiram		248
468.	Tolliver, H		224
469.	Thomas, Geo		456
470.	Thomas, Carolina	1st Rec.	54
471.	Thomas, F. M		264, 265
472.	Turner, Anthony		240
473.	Thompson, R. S		452
474.	Tesezivan, Wm		476
475.	Taylor, Virgil		478
476.	Thompson, J		219
477.	Tyler, Jacob		225
478.	Trent, Peter	1st Rec.	78
479.	Taylor, R		343
480.	Taylor, Geo. H		479
481.	Turner, Sam		554
482.	Thompson, Thomas		471
483.	Thompson, Ross		238
484.	Thornton, Andover		216
485.	Thornton, Hiram, No. 2		257
486.	Tucker, Jacob		342
487.	Tharp, Silas		222
488.	Taylor, William		263
489.	Taylor, Arthur		222
490.	Thompson, Charles		472
491.	Taylor, Jerry		213
492.	Thurman, Wm. M		249
493.	Theaman, Will		476
494.	Taylor, Doc		452
495.	Thompson, Alex		364
496.	Venable, Alex		294
497.	Vernen, Ben		342

No.	Name		Page.
498.	Vernen, Prince		
499.	Vernon, Bill		
500.	Vernen, Ed		
501.	Vernen, Barney		
502.	Vick, J. B		
503.	Williams, Henry		
504.	Williams, E. D	1st Rec.	73
505.	Williamson, James	1st Rec.	74
506.	Williams, E. M	1st Rec.	67
507.	Williamson, A.		
508.	Williams, Wm		477
509.	Williams, Amos		451
510.	Williams, Sam		452
511.	Williams, Loomis		249
512.	Williams, Thompson		265
513.	Williams, J. W		251
514.	Williams, Henry		294
515.	Williams, Irwin		451
516.	Williams, James		247
517.	Williams, Henry		219
518.	Washington, Alex		199
519.	Washington, Geo		222
520.	Washington, Sam		418
521.	Washington, Willie		452
522.	Washington, Manson		343
523.	Wilson, Anderson		475
524.	Wilson, Alfred		343
525.	Wilson, Peter	1st Rec.	80
526.	Wilson, Jeff		472
527.	Wilson, Henry		554
528.	Wilson, Thomas		296
529.	Wilson, Jesse		451
530.	Wilson, W. M		201
531.	Worship, Ben		296
532.	Wallace, John	1st Rec.	73
533.	Woodson, J. W		297
534.	Woodson, A		344
535.	Wiley, Wesley		251
536.	Wahls, Charles		344
537.	Wisham, E. W		531
538.	White, James C		297
539.	Watson, Richard, jr		258
540.	Winn, George		400
541.	Wagner, Ned		222
542.	Watson, R		258
543.	Winston, Richard W		713
544.	Watson, Joe		490
545.	Woods, George W		222
546.	Wright, H. W		302
547.	Walker, William		298
548.	Winston, F. I		294
549.	Wallace, Matt		250
550.	Wright, Madison		251
551.	Wilson, Belfield		257
552.	Walls, Henry		221
553.	Walls, Alex		253
554.	White, Sam	1st Rec.	92
555.	Walls, Alfred		342
556.	Wilson, H. W		218
557.	Yancy, Bragg		343
558.	Jones, Milton		478

Names of persons who have testified they were at the election in Howard Township, Conway County, Ark., on November 6, 1888, and voted for C. R. Breckinridge, or whose votes were otherwise proved.

	Page.
1. Allgood, S. E	821
2. Branson, E. B	821
3. Branson, D. B	829
4. Belcher, R. J	759
5. Binkley, J. W	761
6. Brinkley, K. H	762
7. Burns, Aaron	762
8. Bradley, A. R	712
9. Baldwin, R. D	782
10. Burchett, J	793
11. Boyett, Frank	829
12. Bowdre, A. R	830
13. Butram, Ben	711
14. Boren, W. T	708
15. Croley, J. P	762
16. Crawford, W. R	762
17. Crawford, J. C	821
18. Crawford, R. L	825
19. Churchwell, J. R	823
20. Cullina, C	718
21. Collins, W. A	700
22. Crissenberry, G. F	789
23. Cross, H	761
24. Cash, John	760
25. Christenberry, M	778
26. Chambers, W. C	777
27. Dean, A. C	821
28. Dean, R. H	823
29. Dixon, T. P	778
30. Deaver, Nathan	698
31. Deaver, Sam	697
32. Edwards, John	829
33. Evans, J. M	717
34. Fields, W. J	709
35. Ford, George W	684
36. Ford, J. F	711
37. Ford, G. W	694, 705
38. Ford, D. C	825
39. Gwynn, Wm	759
40. Garret, J. W	710
41. Garrett, W. F	707
42. Garrett, C. M	708
43. Garrett, John	841
44. Gardner, W. J	717
45. Gordon, J. M	759
46. Gordon, J. W	770
47. Hobbs, R. K. John	789
48. Hobbs, W. T	718
49. Hervey, Thos. C	802
50. Higginbottom, B. W	831
51. Jones, J, W	829
52. James, Henry	693
53. Johnson, W. T	789
54. Johnson, D. Y	795
55. Ketchy, S. R	789
56. Kemp, James	697
57. King, J. R	757
58. King, R. M	795
59. Lacefield, S. S	824
60. Lacefield, W. P	757
61. Lambert, Peter	826
62. Landers, S. W	796
63. Lindsay, Carroll	778
64. Littlejohn, John H	831
65. Long, J. C	828
66. Miller, John W	711

	Page.
67. Miller, T. J	842
68. Miller, Lewis	788
69. Miller, J. B	761
70. Miller, G. T	841
71. Miller, G. J	756
72. Miller, J. W	795
73. Miller, W. W	842
74. Miller, J. D	757
75. Mason, J. T	824
76. Malone, A. D	691
77. Morgan, Clay	762
78. Martin, Bemar	762
79. Martin, J. F	771
80. Moore, Harry	696
81. Mitchell, J. N	693
82. Matlock, J. W	826
83. Miles, John	767
84. McGehee, Frank	606
85. McCullough, C. H	784
86. May, Wm. J	762
87. Nesbitt, B. F	705
88. Osborn, J. E	827
89. Osborn, E. A	825
90. Owens, Jack	841
91. Overstreet, J. H	795
92. Oliver, W. T. (voted in wrong township by mistake)	756
93. Oola, G. J	756
94. Overton, J. M. (voted at Morrillton for Breckinridge, but lived at Plummerville; knew he was voting in wrong place)	757
95. Palmer, W. C	700, 708
96. Palmer, D. J	842
97. Palmer, J. J	782
98. Powell, Wesley	759
99. Pullman, Pat	759
100. Parker, Riley	707
101. Plummer, Thos	693
102. Parsley, S. S	823
103. Pate, J. A	823
104. Pate, R. L	691
105. Roe, Isaac	692
106. Rice. J. A	608
107. Rambo, J. E	829
108. Sims, J. M	692
109. Stacks, B. R	756
110. Smith, G. W	718
111. Smith, T. S	695
112. Solomon, C. B	710
113. Vance, W. J	693
114. Vann, E. D	717
115. Watson, Russell	827
116. Watkins, Bob	762
117. Wells, W. T	777
118. Williams, Mack	760
119. Williams, J. N	758
120. Wilson, C. M	825
121. Wilson, Geo	698
122. White, B. G	762, 782
123. White, E. W	762
124. White, Robert	747
125. Wilder, J. A	694
126. Wolley, T. B	825
127. Armstrong, C. D	840

Vote of J. M. Overton should be deducted from above, because he voted at Morrillton; and also from above return as illegal, reducing same to 125.

FREEMAN TOWNSHIP, WOODRUFF COUNTY.

List of names of voters who went to the polls to vote for Clayton and were prevented by the failure to open the polls.

VIEWS OF THE MINORITY.

The testimony taken is insufficient to sustain the charges, except as to the conceded Plummerville box, the manner in which it was taken and abruptly closed by the investigating committee was grossly unfair, and it is misrepresented and misstated in the committee report. But even if the testimony of the voters who testify as to how they voted is to be believed, all the votes in the boxes attacked which are not proved to have been cast for Clayton should be counted for Breckinridge. This rule should be applied because of the unfairness of the investigating committee, and the exceptional character of the case.

VIEWS OF THE MINORITY.

AUGUST 18, 1890.—Mr. MAISH, from the Committee on Elections, submitted the following as the views of the minority:

This case arises out of an election held in the Second Congressional district of Arkansas for the position of Representative in this Congress. Hon. Clifton R. Breckinridge was the Democratic candidate, and Col. John M. Clayton was the Republican candidate, and there was no other candidate. On the 19th of December, 1888, notice of contest was served on Mr. Breckinridge by Colonel Clayton, and it was duly answered. On the 29th of January, 1889, Colonel Clayton, while engaged in taking testimony at Plummerville, in Howard Township, Conway County, met with a violent death. This put an end to the contest in the form it then had, and referred the whole matter in its incomplete stage to the House of Representatives.

On March 10, 1889, the House adopted the following resolution:

That, owing to the alleged assassination of Colonel Clayton, whereby the contest has been suspended, it is of the highest importance that the facts in the case should be thoroughly investigated, and recommend the passage of the following resolution:

Resolved, That a subcommittee of five be appointed by the chairman of the Committee on Elections to make a full and thorough investigation of the contested-election case of Clayton *vs.* Breckinridge; to take and report all the evidence in regard to the methods of said election; to the contest and all events relating thereto or arising therefrom after said election, and as to whether the contestant or the contestee or either of them was lawfully elected, and report such evidence to the Committee on Elections, and said committee will report said evidence and its findings to the House for further action.

Said subcommittee is empowered to issue subpœnas for witnesses; to send for persons and papers; to employ a stenographer and deputy sergeant-at-arms, and to sit during session of the House. Said subcommittee may proceed to Arkansas, if deemed necessary by them, to take any part of said testimony.

That all expenses of said committee shall be paid out of the contingent fund of the House. That all vouchers or expenditures shall be certified by the chairman of the subcommittee of the Committee on Elections. The Clerk of this House is authorized to advance the necessary funds to the chairman of said subcommittee upon his drafts therefor in sums not exceeding $1,000 at any one time, to be accounted for under the terms of this resolution, under the supervision of the Committee on Accounts.

In this resolution the duty and powers of the committee are accurately defined. In it the status of the case is clearly stated; and to it we must continually refer in order to learn the proper order of proceedings.

The printed matter in this case is in four parts, to all of which reference must be had for a clear understanding of the case.

This case comes from a district which has always gone Democratic in national elections, and in which the white population is about double that of the blacks. Once or twice, in State elections, the aggregate

713

vote in the sixteen counties comprising this district has shown a majority for the "wheel" or farmers' ticket, when it secured the Republican vote. But only once in a State election did it ever show a Republican majority, and then it was a small one, of only about 1,000 votes, when the certainty of the result, it being determined by the vote of the whole State, caused great apathy in many Democratic localities. The presumptions, therefore, as usually calculated, are all in favor of the Democrats and against the Republicans.

Of the rumors and charges regarding the local contests of this people we know nothing reliable beyond their official reports; and over their local affairs we have no jurisdiction. Although in all their previous national elections no complaint has ever been brought before Congress, and not even a rumor of wrong-doing has ever been spoken or published, so far as we know, yet in this election it was stated and acknowledged upon every hand that one of their ballot-boxes had been stolen. This was followed by a deplorable and shocking tragedy, resulting in the death of the contestant.

While the theft of the ballot-box did not, upon any possible hypothesis, change the result of the election or alter the right of the Democratic candidate to the certificate, for the maximum voting strength of the precinct was known and not disputed, and the returns showed that the Democrats had carried the district by a majority of 149 votes even if the Republicans had obtained every vote in the township, which they did not claim and did not do, yet this event gave a striking feature upon which to base a contest, and the two events gave abundant food for speculation, crimination, and charges.

Whatever might be the hasty or passionate view of these matters, we have had time for reflection. Whatever might be the vulgar, sordid, and unpatriotic view, we know that these questions and this case involve the memory of a gentleman whose death was deplored by good men throughout the Union, and nowhere so deeply as by the people with whom he lived; that they involve the rights of a member of this House, a gentleman of long service and honorable life, the representative rights, the honor and the good name of an American constituency, and the rights, dignity, and honor of the American House of Representatives itself. These considerations, at once tragic, pathetic, personal, patriotic, and rising to the highest dignity of judicial duty, would move men, if any power on earth could do so, to measure well their course. The case is exceptional. The eyes of the whole country have been directed to it.

No people have ever been called upon to pass through a more trying ordeal than this people; no men through one more trying than these men; no committee and no Congress has ever been put to a severer test; and to neglect the duty of fair and impartial work, to stoop to speculate upon a people's honor, to prostitute the power, functions, and dignity of the House, to work palpable injustice, and to make merchandise of human blood is to degrade the House in the estimation of all good men. This the House seemed fully to appreciate, judging by the full and accurate instructions it gave to the committee.

Astonishing as it may seem, respecting a district with the past record of this one, a district where, with the exception of two or three counties out of the sixteen that compose it, there is hardly a saloon in it, yet the notice of contest, with which we will show Colonel Clayton had substantially nothing to do, was filled with hundreds of statements and charges of the most serious character, covering every county and perhaps every township and precinct in it. This was evidence of either the most serious matters for the attention of the committee, as respects the methods of the election, or of the most abandoned recklessness of statement as respects the contest. In addition to this most extensive ground and material of the suspended contest there had been extensive and unusual proceedings in the Federal court, all throwing light from the highest source upon the methods of the election; and the other events charged as "relating thereto or arising therefrom," in addition to the foregoing, all made a volume of work unequaled in extent as it is unsurpassed in importance by any case the House has ever had to deal with.

In regard to all this the House said "it is of the highest importance that these matters be thoroughly investigated." * * * The committee was instructed to "make a full and thorough investigation." * * * It was instructed "to take and report all the evidence." * * * It was instructed to "make" this investigation and to take "all the evidence," not only in regard to the "case," but also "in regard to the methods of said election;" also in regard "to the contest;" and in regard to "all events relating thereto or arising therefrom after said election," etc.

It will be seen that all the points enumerated are clearly and forcibly embraced in the positive instructions of the House. It is known also that Colonel Clayton had only just begun to take his testimony, and at only two places, when he was killed, and the contest was suspended. Therefore the whole case and all the subsequent events and proceedings, so complicated and important and all covered by the instructions of the House, fell to the consideration of the committee.

It is something of a guide in forming a judgment of the thoroughness with which the committee has discharged its duties in regard to these matters of so much more than ordinary extent and complexity, to consider what time is deemed necessary and usually consumed in taking testimony in ordinary cases. The time fixed by law for taking testimony in an ordinary election case is ninety days (Revised Statutes U. S., sec. 107). If exceptional circumstances arise this is sometimes extended. All other proceedings connected with an election case come out of other time. Ninety days, then, is the least time provided by the laws of the United States and the custom of the House for taking testimony alone in an ordinary contested-election case.

What has the committee done in this cause, so extensive, so complicated, and demanding so especially fair and careful treatment? The House might have directed the attorneys for contestant and contestee to complete the taking of testimony in the usual way, but it did not. Then the time for taking this testimony, under the law and under universal usage would have been ninety days, or, say, at the least, eighty-seven days, as three days had already been consumed by contestant. The House could then have provided otherwise for taking evidence in regard to the other features now embraced in the case. But it did not do this. It considered this case so important that it concluded to order a special proceeding in regard to the whole matter.

Thus instructed and empowered, the committee has taken evidence all told not quite twelve days. It was fifteen days at Little Rock, it had, say, eleven working days there, and it took the testimony of one witness for the Government, here in Washington, consuming perhaps a couple of hours. The report of the majority appeared in the press before it was submitted to the House, before it was submitted to the committee, before it was authorized by the committee to be commenced or it was ordered to be favorable or adverse, and before all the evidence called for by the committee was printed or submitted to the committee in any form, and this without complaint or ground for complaint of delay in its submission.

From these extraordinary proceedings the House may judge of how its instructions have been carried out. It may judge from this, and it will be called upon to judge from proceedings still more extraordinary, how this case has been handled. Every facility has been granted to the committee. Every process has been obeyed, every question has been promptly and frankly answered, and every request the majority has made to perfect and facilitate their examinations and inquiry has been fully granted. They have then no denial or obstruction to complain of anywhere.

It is far otherwise as to them. They say on page 1:

The fact that Norwood, the fusion candidate, had run ahead of Eagle, Democrat, for governor, by 3,002 votes in the district led the Republicans to hope for and the Democrats to fear the result.

Charges of fraud in the September State election were freely made, and Federal supervisors were selected to watch the election and returns at the November election.

Norwood, it is well known, was a one-legged ex-Confederate soldier, and uniformly claimed to be " a better Democrat than Eagle." This, however, did not prevent his getting the Republican support, as his general attitude was that of an independent or bolter. This the people had a right to do, and it furnishes no just ground of complaint or suspicion on the part of the House. Nor do we think his majority of 3,002 votes in the counties comprising this district is any evidence of fraud on the part of his opponents. Nevertheless the fact, with characteristic logic, is cited by the majority as reason for public distrust of the way these Democrats conducted that election.

The State election of September, 1888, was not simply a contest between Norwood and Eagle for the position of governor; it was for the election of all the other State officers except judges of the supreme court. Members of both branches of the legislature were voted for, as well as all the country officers. This election was, of course, solely under State control. It was for a very large number of positions, and it embraced all those matters which are nearest to the people. Under the State law the question of temperance is also involved at every State election in every county and separately at every precinct. If license is not affirmatively voted, then there is prohibition. Nearly every county and precinct in this district of sixteen counties rigidly enforces prohibition. So it will readily be seen that at a State election the supervision of the election is the least and the inducements to commit fraud are the greatest. Only the State courts have jurisdiction over offenses in this election, and if persons encourage fraud or crime for office or advantage there is always interested local influence and power to protect the guilty.

As a rule, candidates for all these positions are selected on party lines, and their names placed on party tickets. Consequently, if there be fraud it is likely to be by the substitution of party tickets, or by some other mode that will equally effect the whole list. The majority report selects the vote for governor as the test. We abide by it. We have brought out these associated facts to show how much it proves, and we think we have clearly shown the character of what it proves. Having done this in a somewhat comprehensive way we pass over minor details alluded to in the majority report for the present, at least, as they fall to the ground as gross exaggerations and perversions of incidents. Norwood was strikingly successful in getting his vote in this district, and there is a cry of fraud. We presume if he had come out behind the majority would have cited that as evidence of fraud as zealously as they do the fact that he came out ahead. We can not prevent the complaint. We can only show that it is ridiculous.

But they are not going to run these risks again, and so, out of abundant caution, " Federal supervisors were selected to watch the election and returns at the November election."

These supervisors were carefully selected by the Republican managers, and the men of their selection were duly appointed by Judge Caldwell, of the Federal bench, an able judge and a zealous Republican. The November election was held. It was under the " watch" of these chosen officials of the Federal court Very many officers, close to the people, were to be chosen before. Only national positions, few in number and remote from the people, were voted for this time. The same State laws operating in September were operating now. No powerful local friends or influences were here to shield wrong-doers as before. The restraining terrors of a distant Federal court, occupied by an able, bold, aggressive Republican judge, were now joined to the local courts under which alone the September election had been conducted, and the Federal court had its chosen " watch" and argus eyes at every precinct.

The November election was held, and what were the tidings and result ? The large vote polled by the Republicans shows there was none of the suppression of negro voters of which we have so much talk, concerning some localities, and so little proof. Fortunately no allegation of that is made as to this district, and we have never heard that it was ever made by any man. As to rioting, a Mr. Benjamin, of Little Rock, went to Morrillton with a detective the day before the election to see about the election. He did not live in this district, and a number of the people, being advised of his coming in this manner, evidently thought he was coming there for bad and not good purposes. Giving way to their indignation, most improperly, of course, they hooted him and jostled him as he alighted from the cars, and a boy, it is supposed, as only boys handle such things, struck him over the eye with a shot from what is known as a " bean-shooter." He was badly frightened and received a severe nervous shock, but his family physician denies that he was bruised in the least, except the slight injury received from the " bean-shooter."

We may refer to this again further on, but so far as this election is concerned the majority do not allege nor attempt to prove, nor has it ever been alleged by any one, unless perhaps in the notice of contest, that the vote at Morrillton next day was other than full and fair and honestly returned. The significance of this incident, then, is difficult to perceive, though dwelt upon by the majority with great stress. They evidently think it indispensable to show that the election at Morillton was unfair, though it is universally admitted to have been perfectly fair, and they do not attempt to show that the Republican vote fell off or that a single man or vote was in any manner restrained or interfered with.

From Cleveland County it was reported that a young man named Dansby had been drunk and disorderly, but that he was taken away by his personal friends, put to bed and kept away. We will refer to this again, as the majority lays great stress upon it, though the evidence shows that a negro disarmed him, and he was no more potent than one drunken man would be in a numerous community anywhere. That he affected a single vote is ridiculous to assume, as shown by the circumstances and evidence; and the majority, much as they dwell upon the drunkenness of this young man, do not attempt to carry it to an effect upon the vote. Yet they dwell upon it and seem unable to turn it loose. If it did not affect the vote we can not see that it affected the election.

We will consider the matter of the Plummerville box, the maximum vote of which is conceded to be accurately known, and hence its maximum possible effect upon the election, later on. But we affirm that with the exception of this box (Plummerville) what we have related is the sum total of rumors, charges, newspaper reports or reports of any kind of wrong or disorder of any kind on the part of any Democrat, citizen or official, that ever arose or was heard of that have come to our notice from or about any county, precinct, or locality in this district until the 19th day of December, 1888, several weeks after Congress met and long after the certficate was issued, when Judge John McClure presented his remarkable notice of contest. We say his notice of contest, for we will show that Colonel Clayton had nothing to do with it, except to consent to it with great reluctance and after long delay.

There was no evidence, then, ot any wrong affecting a single vote except that relating to the Plummerville box. We will show that Colonel Clayton knew of none; that Judge McClure knew of none, and that there was none. One man was drunk in Cleveland County, the only drunken white man ever alluded to by anybody or heard of on the day of that election in the district. One man jostled and maltreated the night before the election at Morrillton, a hundred miles away, and this was the only man struck a blow in the district. The election at both places proceeded orderly, and resulted fairly, as conceded, and yet the House and the country are led to believe that it was an election of great and general excitement and violence.

We deal at present with the vote at Plummerville, Howard Township, Conway County, and with its effect on the general result of the election. All the officers of election say that the total vote cast was 697. No question is raised that this was a very full vote. Mr. Breckinridge's majority upon the face of the returns was 846. If Colonel Clayton had received the entire vote at Plummerville Mr. Breckinridge would still have had a majority of 149. The Republican supervisor, Wahl (p. 335), says the total vote was 697. But no one pretended that all the votes were Republican. Wahl estimated at the time (p. 336) that the Democratic vote was 120 or 125. According to Wahl's smaller estimate the Republican majority here would have been 577. Then by the Republican estimate at the time Breckinridge's majority in the district, including the Plummerville box, was 369.

In the notice of contest the total vote is stated as 697, and it is there claimed that the Democratic vote was only 75. Of course Judge McClure had no such information, but he did not write the notice on information. But according to this the Republican majority would have been 547 at this box, leaving Breckinridge a majority in the district of 299. Then the committee polled the vote of this township. It found a total Republican vote, according to the majority report (pp. 29 and 30,) of 558 and a Democratic vote of 125, making a Republican majority at Plummerville of 433. According to the majority report, then, Breckinridge had a majority in the district, including this box of 413.

These are all the proofs and estimates of the result of the election, if the vote of this box (Plummerville) has been included in the returns, that are of record. They include the highest and the lowest of the Republican estimates, as well as the proof obtained by the majority. By every one of them Mr. Breckinridge was elected, even if every possible vote in the township had been cast against him.

Mr. Breckinridge uniformly declared that if by any possible construction the vote in this box could have changed the result of the election he would not accept the certificate of election. Beyond this there was no other known crime against the ballot. Colonel Clayton alleged no other (p. 848 and later in this report), and Mr. Breckinridge and the chairman of the Democratic committee at once repudiated the result of this wrong (p. 848), and offered to prove the vote by any one he (Colonel Clayton) might select (p. 848). Yet knowing all this, and knowing that this is the only box stolen or alleged to have been stolen, and that the election was held on the 6th day of November, 1888, and Colonel Clayton was killed on the 29th of January, 1889, nevertheless the majority has the hardihood to say:

The necessity for the enactment of some laws which will prevent *ballot-box stealing and murder* from *conferring* a *prima facie* title to a seat in Congress is evident from the result in this contest. Had such laws been in force as would have prevented the contestee from taking his seat with such a title, no one would have attempted to *confer* such title by stealing *the ballot-box.* (Report, p. 7.)

Again they say:

The certificate was *obtained* by the well-known larceny of *a* ballot-box. (Report, p. 14.)

And although they know all the foregoing, and also that no objection was raised by Colonel Clayton or by Judge McClure or by any one to the certificate being issued, nevertheless the majority say, in terms of affected reprobation and censure:

Notwithstanding the *murder* of contestant, the contestee appeared and took his seat. (Majority Report, p. 15.)

The parts emphasized by italics are so marked by us.

These extracts convey in clear and unmistakable terms to the House and the country the assertion that if the vote of "the box" and if the vote of "a box" which was stolen had been included in the returns then those returns would not have shown a majority for Mr. Breckinridge; but, upon the contrary, that they would have shown a majority for Colonel Clayton. And also that if Colonel Clayton had not been killed in January, 1889, then these events would have been different in November and December, 1888. Such bold, illogical, and unwarranted statements are an insult to the intelligence of the House to which they are addressed and are a suitable illustration of the manner in which the majority have argued and treated this case and in which they expect to get the support of the House.

Now this is not a matter of opinion. It is a plain question of fact. The majority report deliberately affirms to the House and the country that but for the theft of this box on the night of November 6, 1888, and the death of Colonel Clayton on January 29, 1889, the certificate of election, which was duly issued without protest on the 12th of December, 1888, would have been reversed from Breckinridge to Clayton.

There is no room for ignorance here. Such boldness of misstatement in the report is simply amazing. Here is the question, apart from all others that are considered in turn, of who was elected according to the effect of these three matters, first, the returns; second, the Plummerville vote; third, the death of Colonel Clayton. The country has been made to ring with the assertion that the theft of this box and the death of Colonel Clayton so changed the face of the returns as to secure the certificate of election for Breckinridge instead of Clayton. The majority, after proving it to be false and utterly impossible by every line of testimony on these topics, and after stating the contrary as to the box on the first page of their report, yet on the subsequent pages quoted solemnly avow it and give their official sanction to what they had already shown to be, in the very nature of the case, impossible and untrue; and which was originally coined and circulated as a political lie to defame a State and its officials, to create sectional animosities, to excite the prejudices and to inflame the party passions of the majority of this House so that this seat might be declared vacant and the mind of the North prepared for the consummation of the greater conspiracy for the perpetuation of the worst elements of the Republican party in power.

The majority seemingly loses all guide and restraint, and they become as dangerous to their friends as to their foes. On page 1 of the report they say:

> The contestee received the governor's certificate by a majority certified as amounting to 846, and has not only taken part in the organization of the House, but has during this contest filled the exalted place of a member of the Committee on Ways and Means.

And again, on page 15, the majority say:

> Notwithstanding the murder of the contestant, the contestee appeared and took his seat.

These remarks are either meant as personal attacks on Mr. Breckinridge, or they are offered as reasons why he should not have taken his seat, should not have taken part in the organization of the House, should not have been appointed on the Ways and Means Committee, and should not now be declared to have been elected. Perhaps they are meant as all. At all events these are the only deductions that can be made from them, except such as may relate to their being used at all in connection with this case.

The effect of a murder in January, 1889, upon an election held in November, 1888, has already been discussed. The effect upon embittered partisan minds, if Mr. Breckinridge had resigned, may be discussed later on. But what information did Mr. Breckinridge have that was not also possessed by the House? The House knew that Colonel Clayton was dead, and that he had, apparently, been intentionally killed. The House knew that a ballot-box had been stolen, and it accurately knew its total contents. No one disputes either of these facts. Who knew anything more? There was no report, official or otherwise, of anything more that could possibly affect a vote, except what Judge McClure had alleged for Colonel Clayton in the notice of contest.

The House let Mr. Breckinridge participate in the organization. The Speaker appointed him on the Ways and Means committee, and the House acquiesced in it. The House has let Mr. Breckinridge sit in his place and participate fully as a member for more than eight months. The House was Republican when it organized and it has been Republican ever since it organized. The Speaker was elected as a Republican and he has been a Republican ever since he was elected. These are Republican acts and not the acts of Mr. Breckinridge in any sense except in a receptive sense, and by and with Republican consent. We do not say this to the reproach of the Speaker or the House. Both did right, as we affirm and as they will admit. Then why is this either a reproach to Mr. Breckinridge, or a reason why he was not elected, or that he should now be turned out?

Why this illogical vindictiveness now? Is it pertinent to the election, or is it meant to unjustly defame a Democrat and to help pass the force bill? This is the line of reasoning and policy adopted by the majority; and the House can judge of the merits of the cause which needs it.

But let us inquire further into the sources and extent of this early information. It is pertinent here and it will also throw light upon that which is to come. Nothing could more severely rebuke the policy of proceeding upon assumption than the facts in this particular. Hon. J. M. Hudson, although a Democrat, was the warm and intimate personal friend of Colonel Clayton. His high standing and character puts his testimony beyond question. The House having gone Republican there was some talk, on account of the capital that could be made out of the affair of the Plummerville box, of a contest. Mr. Hudson asked Colonel Clayton—

what he was going to do? And it was a long time before he made any direct answer. He told me he didn't want to make the contest; but finally he told me he had concluded to make the contest at the earnest solicitation of the leaders of the Republican party. I then said to him, "You will have no trouble about Howard township (Plummerville); you recollect my proposition?" He said, "Yes, but I will take the testimony in the regular way, the way they generally do in Congress to take testimony." That is the conversation I had with him on that particular subject. (Testimony, p. 848.)

The following letter, from Judge W. E. Hemingway, now a member of the supreme court of Arkansas, but who at the time of Colonel Clayton's death was his law partner, throws conclusive light upon this subject:

SUPREME COURT OF THE STATE OF ARKANSAS,
Little Rock, March 16, 1890.

DEAR MAJOR: I see that some of our Republican friends are intimating that the contest for your seat will be embarrassed by the loss of information within the exclusive knowledge of Colonel Clayton. This I know is not well founded. He had no definite information of facts that would have tended to change the result outside of the Plummerville box, of which everybody was advised. He so told me the evening before he left home to begin taking his depositions; as he had taken no depositions elsewhere, he could have acquired no other information that was definite or satisfactory to him. Although his conversation was confidential, it does not seem to me improper that I write you of it. I do not know that it will be material, but you are at liberty to consider it and make use of it if you think it material.

Yours, truly,

W. E. HEMINGWAY.

Hon. C. R. BRECKINRIDGE, *Washington, D. C.*

On the first page of the brief (committee print) of Judge McClure, counsel for Colonel Clayton, he denies that he had anything to do with " inducing John M. Clayton to institute a contest," * * *. That is not the question. That point was not raised and it is of no consequence in any sense. The sole question in this connection was and is what was known beside the affair of the Plummerville box, and who knew it, what was asserted, and by whom asserted, and what credence properly attached thereto? That the numberless charges were neither affirmed nor believed by John M. Clayton we think is conclusively shown. That they are the fictions of his counsel is, in our opinion, being shown with equal clearness. Certain it is that neither Mr. Breckinridge, nor the Republican House, nor the Republican Speaker had any other basis than his affirmation to go upon, and this has not been deemed trustworthy by any of them. Yet all of them come under the reckless criticism of the majority of this committee, who in the same spirit have treated all the other features of this case.

But there has been another test to all this and to all the majority say of the result of this election, and that is a most extraordinary series of trials before the Federal court. While this contest was being brewed

H. Mis. 137——46

by the "leaders of the Republican party," careful inquiry was made, not only into the single case of "drunk and disorderly" conduct of young Dansby, and into the offense against the ballot-box at Plummerville; but this form of inquiry was also made into all the little omissions or breaches of the many technical and inconsequential rules of proceedings in the conduct of the election by officials. Our present Federal election laws, not to speak of those proposed, are very comprehensive and quite intricate.

In an agricultural district like this one, which is composed of sixteen counties, many of the election officials are necessarily plain men, not skilled in the law; and it is not infrequent in every State that such men do not do everything in precisely the way and at precisely the time laid down in the minute manuel of the laws. But true as this is this district had gone through two previous Congressional elections, this being the third one since its formation, and no occasion had ever arisen before to indict any one. Judge Caldwell, a strong Republican, was on the Federal bench all the time, and the first election was under a Republican administration (Arthur's), and the present Republican United States district attorney, Mr. Waters, was the United States district attorney then.

In the Plummerville case in this election there is no allegation that the election was not conducted honestly. All the judges and clerks of election at that box were Democrats, and the box was stolen by other and unknown parties. But now people were indicted by wholesale. It is well known that indictments are easy to procure from a pliant or conscientious grand jury if men can be persuaded to make sworn allegations, whether they be true or false. At all events the grand jury was secured just as every grand jury in such cases is. They showed that they were willing, pliant, or conscientious, it matters not which, so far as the fact of willingness to indict is concerned. There was no fear or hinderance as to allegations or witnesses. The only question, then, was the question of innocence or guilt.

But to further show the zeal of the officials, the jurors, and all people, regardless of party, to make these tests full and ample, covering as they did all things imaginable and all men in the district against whom rumor, slander, or just suspicion pointed or could be made to point, we quote the following from the brief of Judge McClure, page 4, committee print:

Every one of the prosecutions against persons in Conway and Woodruff Counties, except the persons who were charged with the theft of the Howard Township box, and those who were charged with a conspiracy to injure Wahl, a United States witness, was instituted before a United States commissioner, under the direction and supervision of a Democratic district attorney, at a time when the gentleman's present counsel was Attorney-General of the United States. In every one of the cases so instituted the defendants had been bound over to answer, by the action of a Democratic officer, before I was employed to prosecute.

Again he says, on the same page:

Out of all the cases instituted in the Second district, and of which so much complaint is made, two cases, and only two, were instituted under Republican officers. What amount of money was spent in the prosecution of these cases, I am not prepared to say. Whatever sum it may be, it is to be hoped it will be as bread cast on the waters.

These cases, as we have stated, extended over many weeks, consuming a great part of two terms of the court, the spring and fall term of 1889. Judge Caldwell, now circuit judge of the United States court; Judge Brewer, now of the United States Supreme Court, and Judge Shiros, of the United States district court of Iowa, all presided in the course of the trials of these cases. When the present administration came into power and it was intimated that the Democratic marshal and the Democratic United States district attorney, whose fidelity and zeal the boastful allusion to the prosecutions by Judge McClure is ample assurance, would not be earnest in further prosecution, they resigned, and the entire machinery was promptly turned over to the Republicans. The trials all came on then under these Republican authorities.

The former Republican district attorney, Charles C. Waters, was in office again. He had an assistant in S. R. Allen, a prominent Republican attorney, and Judge John McClure was made "special district attorney" (page 578, *et seq.* testimony). Rewards were offered and paid for testimony (page 179, testimony); the inducements of mileage and Federal fees was of moment to the blacks, and it is alleged negroes filled the yard and building of the Federal court as if an army were gathered. It is stated that these vast proceedings must have cost not less than $80,-000, and Judge McClure in alluding to this feature, in an extract quoted, refrains from an estimate. He is "not prepared to say," yet no man is in better position to know than he. His attention had long been called to it. A cursory glance at the reported expenditures of the Department of Justice and an examination of "costs" as assessed in the cases (page 588, *et seq.* testimony) now show that far the greater part of these great outlays did not come out of the Federal Treasury. They could only have been met, then, out of some other funds not indicated by the testimony.

We are not complaining of the exhaustiveness or character of these vast proceedings. We are simply calling attention to the facts. These evidently were not political trials, with the ordinary purpose to punish election crimes, with the exception of course of what might have been reasonably suspected of the parties charged, but acquitted, of the theft of the box at Plummerville, and the same may be said of the parties accused and acquitted of shooting Supervisor Wahl some time after the election. It is true that no election was held at two remote precincts in the overflowed region of the White and Mississippi River bottom, one a Democratic precinct and one Republican. The day was cold, wet, and raining hard. The country low, flat, and muddy. No election was held at these two remote points. The officers admitted it, and it had been this way before under such circumstances, and the court, with a full knowledge of the facts and motives, fined them, on their own frank confession, $10 each.

But these are not the precincts nor are these the cases where the votes are to come or go that are to decide this case, even upon the most extreme theories advanced by the majority.

We make no mistake about the results of trials upon criminal accusation in their application in a civil case involving the same issue as to the result produced by the alleged acts. We know that the doctrine of doubt properly figures more largely in the former than in the latter case. We know also that the power of the House in a question of the election of one of its members is, under the Constitution, exclusive. Hence to the House, in point of fact, all evidence is simply persuasive. These, however, were not ordinary trials. They were political and party prosecutions in the broadest and most comprehensive sense, manifestly originated by a party, and for a party, and unexampled in the efforts to prove that which would unseat a Democrat and help pass a force bill. Democratic officials gave due credence to allegations and secured indictments. The grand jury, before Cleveland went out of office, gave due credence to allegations, and the willingness of the juries to convict, as well as to indict, is a subject of boasting by Judge McClure (his brief, p. 4, committee print) and of exultation by the majority report, which says, pages 9 and 11:

All of the Woodruff County officials who were indicted were convited. In fact, all the persons who were indicted were convicted, except the persons indicted for the crime against Wahl and those for the stealing of the Plummerville box.

And

We have given the list of cases so confidently relied on as an adjudication, and it appears that most of these indictments in the United States courts resulted in convictions.

The trouble with the majority is that it is not uniform in its practice or in its use of evidence.

If convictions in the Federal court are potential and adequate as evidence in this case, why are not acquittals in the same court and by the same juries equally potential and adequate? No one ever denied that there were convictions; but convictions of what? conviction of one man being drunk and disorderly. He was disorderly to a supervisor, but also to others. He was taken away. Was this a calm, cool, premeditated plot against the ballot? No. Did it affect a single vote? No. It is most improbably alleged that one voter was scared, but the fellow was disarmed by a negro and laughed at, taken away and put to bed. (Testimony, pp. 178, 184, 631, et seq.)

A supervisor was told by a sheriff that his place was on the outside, thinking his duty was to keep order. The matter was referred by the sheriff by telegraph to the United States judge—Judge Caldwell, a strong Republican. Judge Caldwell was absent, and the telegram was replied to by Mr. Cooper, the chairman of the Republican State committee (Testimony, p. 663), and Mr. Cooper's telegram was promptly obeyed. In a sense and in fact the sheriff was guilty. He acted honestly and never denied anything. He was convicted and fined $10. Was this a plot against the ballot? Did it, could it possibly affect a vote? Election officers of both parties were in the room or by the box. The supervisor promptly returned and did as he pleased. How could there be any foul play or intention of it here? The testimony is singularly straightforward and from men of undoubted honesty.

The point is that every Democrat was, by these same juries of the Federal court, acquitted of any offense and of every charge that involved, directly or indirectly, the corrupting of the ballot, or affecting the free casting, fair counting, and honest returning of the vote. While convicted on some they are acquitted on these counts. Mr. Breckinridge, in his argument before the committee, distinctly asked Judge McClure to name any instance, when his time came to close the argument, in which the finding of the court was not that the vote was counted and returned as cast, and he did not attempt to name one. Among other comments he used the following language:

There were various charges. Men were charged with technical violations of law and with consequential violations of law. Judge Caldwell took the position that these trials were not simply to punish crime affecting the ballot, but as educational to the general masses upon the technical ministerial features. I referred specifically to those charges or counts affecting the integrity of the vote, and I challenge the gentleman to produce to this committee a single instance where a man in all those proceedings was not vindicated by acquittal of any act affecting or intending to affect a single vote. The juries convicted the accused of such offenses as they were guilty of, and exposed them to the severest penalties where no real wrong had been either contemplated or done, showing they were willing to convict them even where they are not guilty of any real wrong. I say the gentleman can not find a single instance where a charge affecting the integrity of the ballot was not dismissed by the judge from the bench as being untenable, or instructions given to the jury to acquit, or withdrawn by himself; not one. Therefore it is not a conviction of a technicality that does not affect the integrity of the vote that I spoke of as a vindication, as he states; but it is the action I have cited and his own action upon all those charges which affect the integrity of the vote.

The gentleman dwelt with great stress yesterday about feloniously doing so and so. He did not reveal the real act or the penalty until asked. Feloniously doing what? Why, going to supper before counting the vote. It is denounced in the law, and I suppose that is the usual phraseology that is used. The law does not permit them to separate, but he can not say, and he does not, that they separated under circumstances or in a way that could possibly contaminate the ballot. You know, gentlemen, perfectly well, that at these country precincts these mere ministerial or technical features and modes are frequently overlooked by the people. They make mistakes some times by thinking the Federal supervisor is the man to preserve order, but these disputed precincts were all held under the supervision of both parties, and there is nothing to justify an attack upon the result; a mere mistake of that sort can not hold against the integrity of the result. The case where that view was held of a supervisor by the sheriff at a Woodruff County precinct, what did the sheriff do? He telegraphed instantly for instructions to Judge Caldwell, the Republican United States judge, or rather for a statement of the law, and he at once obeyed the Republican reply.

Not only, then, in every case affecting or calling in question a single vote cast, excepting of course the Plummerville box, have you the sworn statement in every case of the election officials of both parties that the election was fair, peaceful, and honest, and that the vote was counted and returned just as it was cast; but you have in addition to this the finding of the Federal court, covering every one of these precincts. The court had the ballots and poll-books, some of them I know, and I know it had access to all of them. I asked Judge Rose, of counsel for the defense, to see to it that the court had a full and fair offer of all the records, and you see in the testimony where they called at least for some of them and had them in possession. The question was, was the vote cast as counted and returned, and was it counted and returned as cast? In every instance the court said it was.

No reply was made to this and none to the special request, and the House is referred to the court records, page 588 *et seq.*, testimony.

Attention is called to an error in the index that might mislead upon a hasty examination. It is stated in the index, page 876, that Martin, Hignight, and Antony are convicted of making a false certificate of election. Reference to pages 603 and 607 shows that they were acquitted of all charges except the one involving their going to supper before casting up the vote. Two judges were Democrats, one a Republican, and the Republican supervisor staid with the judge that had the box and with the box all the time.

The majority indulges in the following line of reasoning:

Reed, Lucas, and Blakely were indicted for interfering with election officers. Their acquittal does not show that the ballot-box was not stolen.

Of course not. But, does it not show quite conclusively that the charge that they intefered with election officers is not true? Again they say:

Reed, Ward, Bentley, W. P. Wells, Woods, Heard, and Thad. R. Wells were indicted for stealing the Plummerville ballot-box, and were all acquitted. But it is undisputed that the box was in fact stolen by somebody.

Certainly it is. Nobody denies that the Plummerville box was stolen. But is not this very good evidence that these men did not steal it? There must be a stop somewhere. What more evidence do you want? What better can you have? Some of these men at least appeared before the subcommittee at Little Rock. They could have plead acquittal and refused to testify on this subject, but they did not. They answered every question frankly and promptly; they were asked for specimens of their writing. They wrote out at once every dictation given to them. It is perfectly plain from this line of reasoning that the majority will accept as good only that evidence which tends to prove what they want to prove, and reject any, however good, which opposes their wishes and intentions.

But take the cases now of the election officers at the various Woodruff County precints, and these embrace every vote except that of the Plummerville box that the majority passes judgment upon. In every instance the election officials, including the supervisors, were of both parties. In no instance do any of them fail to certify officially and without complaint that the votes and returns were fair in every way. A lot of charges were gotten up; a lot of indictments are secured; " the leaders of the Republican party " have brought great inducements and pressure to bear *after* the election, and *after* the returns are all in. They are going to override Colonel Clayton's convictions by their "earnest solicitations."

We make no complaint of this. In one sense this is their right. These officials are charged with all manner of offenses, great and small. One or two errors and misunderstandings as to the exact meaning of the law are found as to some of them. The prosecutions are vigorous and they are fined $10 each and costs, which are somehow vastly below the actual outlay. Most of the outlay in the prosecution is concealed. No one is punished for his unintentional and inconsequential violation of law more than this, and no other convictions of these men were had. What does this show? In this case, under the extraordinary circumstances we have related, what does it conclusively show?

Colonel Clayton had been killed, for the purpose, as charged, of "quieting a contest." This is the theory of the murder (good enough if sustained by evidence) of those who think that such an act would commend men, already indicted, to the clemency of the Federal court. This is the theory of those who think it would close the investigation and secure the good graces of a Republican House, already elected. But under the fierce heat engendered by this sad event all of these men were still acquitted of any corrupt dealing with the ballots or with the returns. This certainly does not show that Colonel Clayton was not killed. Nor does it show that the Plummerville box was not stolen, for it is not related to either of those events. We know that both of these events occurred. Neither does it prove who killed Colonel Clayton nor who stole the Plummerville box, two events remote from this county and in no wise connected with the charges tested by the trials of these election officers. This does show, however, and under all the circumstances of the case it conclusively shows that these officials did not do those things of which they were acquitted.

These charges were presented in every form and phase that ingenuity could suggest. It is all given in the records of the court, page 574 *et seq.* of the testimony.

Then what follows? It is not asserted or pretended that any other persons had a chance to stuff these ballot-boxes or to falsify these returns except the election officials. If they did not do this, then nobody did it; and the judgment of the court, the unanimous verdict of juries composed of Republicans as well as Democrats, a judicial outfit which was wholly under Republican control, was that these votes were cast as they were counted, and that they were honestly counted and honestly returned. This all took place also before Mr. Breckinridge took his seat in the House.

Whatever may be said of these being criminal cases and of the greater operation of doubt in favor of the accused in criminal than in civil cases, is fully and fairly offset by the *extraordinary* circumstances attending these trials—*all* being adverse to the accused—and the *complete failure* of Judge McClure, his assistants, and "the leaders of the Republican party" to cast a shadow of doubt or discredit upon the ballot at these boxes.

These proceedings, we repeat, embrace every box and every vote that the committee takes from or counts adversely to Mr. Breckinridge, except that of the Plummerville (Howard Township) box, which, after proof, left him a majority, by the figures of the committee itself, of 413 in the district. Therefore, these two heads, the Woodruff County boxes and the Plummerville box, cover the whole case as presented by the majority as respects votes.

It is the returns from these boxes that they overthrow. They overthrow them in the face of these certificates from officials of both political parties, and in the face of the findings, under even the exceptional circumstances stated, of the Federal court. The supreme purpose was to get convictions of a character that would give them some color under which to claim votes.

But they signally failed ; and now, after these extraordinary cases and proceedings, the committee says, when it suits them, that this is all of no consequence or moment; it is no proof; and at the same time they use events and convictions that have no earthly relation to the vote as evidence of the highest consequence.

Before commenting on other features of this case we wish to remark that we are not to be understood as objecting to those cases which looked to punishment for the crime of stealing the Plummerville box, or for any other crime. Democrats as well as Republicans offered a reward for the arrest and conviction of those unknown parties (page 869, testimony). The acquittal of those tried by the Federal court for this crime, and the non-arrest by the officers of the same court of any others, is sufficient refutation of the complaint of the majority of no one being punished for it by the State. Judge W. H. H. Clayton says on page 432 of the testimony:

The Arkansas Gazette, which was then under a different management than it is now, was standing very nobly upon the right side of the wall.   *   *   *

The Gazette at that time, in its issue of March 3, 1889, used this language:

A reward of $1,200 is outstanding for the arrest and conviction of the ballot-box thieves, and the rewards for the conviction of the assassins aggregate about $10,000. If these are not sufficient to punish these crimes it is doubtful if any sum of money can do it. There is danger in over stimulus.

Neither have we any objection to make to indictments or convictions for errors or omissions that contravene the law, or to proceedings upon any reasonable grounds of belief of guilt of any kind. We assent to the rod of the court being used, with tempered severity, even in an educational way, to rebuke ignorance, to check carelessness, and thus to prevent growth to a more serious condition. Nor are we passing any criticism upon the able and honorable court, which, although it punished a drunken and disorderly Democrat (Dansby), whose conduct did not affect a vote, with a fine of fifty times the amount imposed upon the Republican judges of Richland Township, who confessed to knowingly permitting illegal voting, yet they imposed punishment upon the guilty, and they fairly earned for themselves and their juries full faith in the innocence of those who were acquitted, and in all that logically and inevitably follows therefrom.

What we do complain of is, the majority of the committee, after all these efforts by their party and by the Federal court, and the complete failure of every feature as alluded to instituted to get votes, still coming here and saying this is all of no force or effect, not entitled to credence, and at the same time making up the greater part of their report in support of their case in erroneous statements of what occurred in the State and apart from the election, even if it were as they gave it, and in erroneous statements in support of their case of the findings of the very court they elsewhere reject.

The majority report asserts that there were frauds in the State election in Conway County, which the committee has not attempted to prove. It appears in the testimony that the Republicans had two tickets then in the field in that county, and the result was the Democrats carried the county. The Democrats estimate the county at from 300 to 350 Republican majority if they are united and there is a full vote. In the State election of 1886, Cunningham, a Union Labor candidate, got 158 votes in Conway County, mostly Democrats, and that enabled Gregg, the Republican candidate for governor to carry the county by 401 votes more than were cast for Eagle, the Democratic candidate. In 1888 it was Norwood, Union Labor and Fusion, claiming to be a Democrat, and Eagle, the regular Democratic candidate for governor, with a bad split in the Republican party for the local offices. This time Eagle, the Democrat, carried the county by a majority of 475. This obviously very reasonable result is called a fraud without adducing any proof. Then, in the Congressional election of 1888—

	Votes.
Clayton got	1,119
Add his vote in Plummerville box	558
Total	1,677
Breckinridge got	1,337
Add his Plummerville vote	125
Total	1,462
Take this from Clayton's vote	1,462
And Clayton carries the county by	215

Breckinridge, with a united Democratic party, and when fraud is charged, gets only 37 more votes than Hughes got with a divided party in 1886, when no fraud is charged. And he gets 506 less votes than Eagle got with a divided and rent Republican party in 1888, and yet fraud is charged now also against the Democrats. Clayton gets in 1888 184 more votes than his party was able to run up for their fusion candidate, Norwood.

We now invite attention to some general facts and features about elections in Woodruff County. There is no charge of fraud, nor has there ever been in the State election of 1886. In that election the vote for governor in the county was:

Eagle, Democrat	1,289
Gregg, Republican	1,109
Democratic majority in 1886	180

But Cunningham, Union Labor, drew off 53 votes, perhaps every one of them Democratic on a straight party issue. Add this 53 and the real Democratic majority, with no charge of fraud anywhere, is 233 in Woodruff County in 1886.

We know of no charge of fraud in this county in the race for governor in 1888. Then the vote was:

Eagle, Democrat	1,548
Norwood, Fusion	1,375
Democratic majority over the Fusion ticket in 1888	173

Next take the vote in this county in the race for supreme judge in 1888. Taking the highest vote on each side and it is as follows:

Sanders, Democrat... 1,222
Hill, Republican... 1,037

Democratic majority 185

This vote has been cited by the other side as an evidence of the result of a perfectly fair vote between the parties in this district. We accept it as such. If the Democrats did not turn out in all the counties they need not have expected to carry the part of the State embraced in this district. They did not turn out, and the counties of this district gave a Republican majority of say 1,000.

. To show the apathy in the mountain and other remote counties, all strongly Democratic: In Van Buren County only 240 Democrats voted, and they carried the county by only 9 votes; in Cleburne County only 232 Democrats voted, and they carried the county by only 130 votes; in Stone County only 146 Democrats voted, and they carried the county by only 76 votes. The normal Democratic majority in these counties alone would have given the portion of the State embraced in this district to the Democracy. Although this election was held April 3, 1889, after the contest of this case was begun and after Colonel Clayton was killed, no effort was made to bring out the vote and carry these counties or the counties of this district. That was all looked upon as " stage" work that men confident of a good cause would not stoop to.

Perhaps it is well now in every way that this was not done, for as this is cited as a perfectly fair election in the whole district, it follows that it was perfectly fair in every county and at every precinct of the district. The result then is that the Democracy, with conceded fairness, carried Woodruff County at this election by 180 majority. Now what did they carry it at when Breckinridge ran against Clayton ? Breckinridge's majority was only 220. It was only 40 votes more than it is conceded the Democracy carried it at fairly in the supreme court election. And yet the one is boasted of as fair and the other as horribly unfair.

Yet these are the people held up to the House and the country as ballot-box stuffers, thieves, aiders, abettors, and sympathizers with such practices. It should take very strong evidence to convict these people of such charges and to overturn the official returns of their election corroborated in the many ways we have cited.

Consider now the character of the testimony in opposition to all this and the means employed to procure it.

They offer the inducement of $2 a day and mileage to a few negro voters to deny after the election how they voted. What is the central idea of the secret ballot now so warmly urged all over the country ? It is not all men who need it. Not even all negroes who vote the Democratic ticket. But surely if men will not vote freely when exposed to influences in the act of voting, then these same men will deny that they did or that they intended to so vote when offered money or confronted with influences by the exposure of their ballot *after* they have voted. Are they weaker before than after ? If the vote is to be cast in secret and the act of the voter is to remain a secret, then what are we to rely upon as good and sufficient evidence of the result ? Obviously upon the returns as certified by the election officials. Were there ever returns more reliably certified than these from Woodruff County ? Were they ever more reliably borne out by the results of past elections, not only admitted to be fair, but especially that for supreme judges boasted of as fair ? And here, too, they have been further accredited by the result of the remarkable trials in the Federal court. It is alleged too that the Republican party was not in good accord with Colonel Clayton in this county.

Mr. Breckinridge asked to have Mr. Leach summoned, the leading Republican then living in the county. He was the Republican candidate for Congress in 1886. It was desired to show that with the sentiment among Republicans in this county towards Colonel Clayton it was remarkable that Mr. Breckinridge did not run far ahead of the acknowledged honest majority of the Democrats in this county instead of only 40 votes ahead of it. Mr. Leach had gone to Oklahoma to live It was promised that he should come to Washington to testify, and then it was refused after the subcommittee got to Washington. We will say more of this and of similar acts of bad faith later on. We wish however, to impress upon the House that even allowing all thus claimed Breckinridge is still elected. Only by allowing such evidence as this to overbalance that in favor of the honesty of the returns—a most impotent conclusion—and by permitting it to overturn and not to correct the returns, and also by refusing to poll the vote for Mr. Breckinridge at these precincts as it was polled for the other side, can his majority possibly be overcome.

To show how the majority really estimate their negro testimony, which here they take above that of the best officials, courts, juries, and all evidence by past elections of the fairness of the result, we recall the instance where two negroes, as respectable looking as any who appeared, testified that they saw Dr. White and Wm. Palmer in the latter's blacksmith-shop, burning up the Plummerville ballots and ballot-box. Judge McClure, without even being sworn, contradicted them. The subcommittee accepted this off-hand and single statement as fully satisfactory and dismissed the matter at once.

This ignorant and characterless testimony is brushed aside when contradicted in a certain matter by a Republican, although the former are under oath and the latter is not. But the same kind of testimony, even more ignorant and evidently more destitute of character, is in every instance accepted at once when it relates to a vote as against the sworn testimony of election officials of both political parties. One such negro comes and now says he didn't intend to vote the way he is recorded. All the election officials contradict him, and they are brushed aside and he is accepted. It is solely upon such testimony that the majority has changed votes, and upon the same testimony they cast out Democratic votes.

OMISSIONS FROM THE RECORD AND REFUSALS TO TAKE TESTIMONY.

On page 11 of the majority report is the following alleged extract of proceedings at Little Rock:

At the close of the examination of Governor James P. Eagle, on recall, on the night of May 8, 1890, the following proceedings were had, to wit:

Mr. LACEY. Now, gentlemen, are there any other witnesses to be examined?

Mr. McCLURE. I have none.

Mr. McCAIN. We had thought of offering some further evidence, and bringing some other witnesses, but we have concluded to accommodate the committee as you are anxious to get away and get back to Washington, and we will say we are through.

Mr. LACEY. We want to take all the evidence you have to offer, and are willing to stay until you are through, but if you have nothing further to offer we will adjourn *sine die.*

The committee adjourned *sine die.*

There is no account of any such proceedings in the record. The ma jority says:

By some oversight this was not inserted in the transcript and printed, and we here insert it.

In every other instance the adjournment is duly noted and inserted in the record. Reference to the record will show that in every other instance the proceedings are all taken down in the order in which they occur and the final words are a statement of the fact of adjournment or recess, as the case may be, and of the hour to which it is taken. For instance, on page 536, the last words in the proceedings of a sitting are as follows:

The committee adjourned to 9 o'clock a. m., May 8, 1890.

Again on page 555, the presence of certain witnesses is ascertained and then the committee takes a short adjournment for supper, and the facts are recorded in the following closing words:

Witnesses * * * were called * * * the committee adjourned until 7 p. m., May 8, 1890.

In no instance is the date of the meeting of the committee brought down at the hour of adjournment. That is inserted at the beginning of the sitting, not at the close. But it will be observed that not only is there nothing in the record of a *sine die* adjournment but the extract given by the majority is not in the form in which such action or any adjournment would be recorded. The very first lines of what purports to be an account of what took place, and of a transcript at the time of what took place, shows that it is composed wholly as it written from memory. That it is an incomplete and incorrect statement of what took place, as we shall conclusively show, is by far the most important fact, especially in view of the very important character of those proceedings and of subsequent events in connection therewith. But we wish to fix the responsibility clearly.

Mr. Maish (a Democratic member of the subcommittee) especially impressed upon the stenographer at the time to take down the full and exact terms and conditions of the last adjournment at Little Rock. This was perhaps the only part of the entire proceedings that was so specially and emphatically directed to be taken down and inserted in the record; though it was several times impressed that all proceedings should be taken down and reported. But here were agreements of the most important character. It was with great astonishment, therefore, that it was found that every word of the final agreements and proceedings had been omitted from the record. When Mr. Maish called attention to this fact, Mr. Lacey, the chairman of the subcommittee, said:

The omission is that the reporter probably failed to take that.

Then, again, Mr. Lacey said:

I will telegraph him in regard to it.

A reply was received from the stenographer and shown to Mr. Maish, in which he stated that he had not taken down these proceedings. Then, we ask, why did he omit to take down a part of the proceedings? Why so important a part? Why that part which he was directed above all other parts by a member of the committee to take down? By whose orders was this most important data omitted? And if not taken down, where does this extract inserted in the majority report come from?

As the stenographer states he did not take this down, by whose order was this pretended transcript prepared? It was not any official order

of the Committee on Elections or of the subcommittee on this case.'
When and where was this pretended transcript prepared? That stenographer remains at his home in Iowa, has not been to Washington,
nor submitted to any examination so far as the minority of the committee is aware. Nor has the minority been consulted as to the accuracy
or propriety of this alleged transcript or as to the mode of obtainment.

It is a fabrication. Not only has the record been mutilated by the
omission of most essential matter, which stamps the subsequent, as other
things do the former, proceedings of the majority with prejudice and un-
fairuess, but a fabricated and false account has been reported to the House.
In order to get at the truth of the agreements and proceedings of the
committee in regard to the taking of testimony, we insert the following
official report of the colloquy in the course of Mr. Breckinridge's argument before the full committee, July 16, 1890. It gives the distinct admission by Mr. Lacey of every statement we make.

Mr. LACEY. I would like to ask if you challenge the fairness of the sub committee?

Mr. BRECKINRIDGE. I do most emphatically. This, of course, is Mr. Garland's
argument, but I do charge unfairness.

Mr. LACEY. I would like to ask if on the night we left there it was not asked if any
more testimony was necessary, and your counsel said they would take no more testimony there that night.

Mr. BRECKINRIDGE. On conditions covering two things: first explicit promises,
not one of which has been complied with, as to the taking of testimony in Washington ; and next, that the whole question was just as open in Washington as it was in
Little Rock, and inquiry was not to be construed at all as closed.

Mr. LACEY. What specific promises?

Mr. BRECKINRIDGE. Well, at the request of the subcommittee, we deferred summoning parties from St. Louis, in connection with the Meecham Arms Company. It
was suggested by you, Mr. Chairman, that we have a meeting in St. Louis, but afterwards preferred to bring them to Washington, that you declined here afterwards. And
as regards Mr. Wood, it was stated and admitted by yourself, and apparently assented
to by the committee, that it would be more convenient to have Mr. Wood come to
Washington than Little Rock. I think you will remember you said his coming to
Little Rock was inconvenient. I offered to pay his way there and you promised he
would be in Washington, which was specifically denied afterwards. Then in regard
to Mr. Coblentz, it was stated that it was easier to call him to Washington than
Arkansas.

Mr. LACEY. That is three; what others?

Mr. BRECKINRIDGE. I will not pretend to call them all off.

A MEMBER. We would like to have it because it seems to be a matter of controversy.

Mr. MAISH. I would suggest I was sorry to see that that part of the proceedings
which related to the taking of testimony subsequent to the adjournment there is not
in the record. I think Mr. Breckinridge would be sustained entirely if it was there.
I was very particular that that should not be waived at all, and I discovered afterwards they quit taking testimony. There is not a single thing in the record about it.

Mr. LACEY. The omission is that the reporter probably failed to take that.

Mr. MAISH. I had personally requested the reporter to take down everything.

Mr. LACEY. I think it is important we should have these names.

Mr. CRISP. Who was the reporter?

A MEMBER. Some one from the West.

Mr. CRISP. He must be required to produce it.

Mr. LACEY. I shall telegraph him in regard to it.

Mr. BRECKINRIDGE. My distinct understanding with the chairman was that any of
these witnesses that I desired should be brought to Washington, and therefore I did
not enumerate them all to the chairman.

Mr. LACEY. Did you not on that occasion say there were about twenty-five witnesses whose testimony you desired to take in relation to these votes?

Mr. BRECKINRIDGE. Not at all. That related to another matter. I stated, Mr.
Chairman, distinctly, that if you were going to adjourn I would like to get the power
to have depositions taken, and that I might want to take the depositions of a large
number of witnesses as to how they voted, etc., but that until I had opportunity to
confer with counsel, I could not tell definitely. The chairman knows how brief the
time was, everything was under whip and spur, and we had no previous notice in the
way matters are usually conducted. That was denied me, and it was stated in that
connection that the whole question was just as open in Washington as in Little Rock.

Well, I said, "if it is just as open in Washington as in Little Rock, it does not make any difference to me whether we sit at Washington or Little Rock." What I wanted to know was, whether it was entirely open. I said, "You have the power to close it here, but I want you to understand you do not close it at this time or at this place with my consent."

Mr. LACEY. There is no controversy about that.

Mr. BERGEN. I want to enter right here a denial of the statement as made by Mr. Breckinridge and I want to state that this question was not to be opened in full committee or in Washington.

Mr. BRECKINRIDGE. That relates to the business of the subcommittee and the full committee, and they can attend to it at any time.

Mr. MAISH. I state that it was understood it should not be closed and we might determine and take testimony just as we saw fit.

Mr. BRECKINRIDGE. It was as open here as there. Those are the exact words of the chairman.

Mr. BERGEN. I do not think there will be any controversy between Mr. Maish and myself about it. I am sure——

Mr. MAISH. Certainly not.

Mr. HAUGEN and several members. Suppose we go on with Mr. Garland's brief, Mr. Chairman.

Mr. LACEY. Mr. Breckinridge, there is no controversy between you and myself in regard to the witnesses referred to in that way. I thought it was but just to the committee that he give us the names so we may have them in the record.

Mr. BRECKINRIDGE. You refused to summon them after an express agreement that you would do so.

A MEMBER. Suppose, Mr. Chairman, we go on hearing Mr. Garland's brief now.

What stronger evidence could there be of the incomplete and prejudiced character of this so-called investigation, and of the utter unreliability of the findings and statements of fact by the majority.

The subcommittee dispersed, after adjourning on the 8th of May, some going to their homes, and they assembled here slowly afterwards. Mr. Breckinridge remained a few days in Arkansas. The time when the subcommittee was ready to proceed to the completion of the investigation is indicated by the time they had their witness, Warren Taylor, here to meet them and testify. He was an alleged State's witness in one of the prosecutions before the Federal court. The subcommittee was ready to hear him and to resume on the 21st of May, 1890, less than two weeks after their adjournment at Little Rock.

On the 23d of May, 1890, ex-Attorney-General Garland, counsel here for Mr. Breckinridge, promptly met the subcommittee (p. 377) in regard to taking the additional testimony. He also called attention to the fact that he had addressed a note to the chairman during the previous week upon this subject. Mr. Lacey said it was thought important to take Taylor's testimony here (the prosecuting witness); "but," said he, "the other witnesses, I am informed, are not to be called." Who informed him of this he does not state, nor have we ever been able to ascertain.

Then he alludes to the application Mr. Breckinridge made two or three days before the subcommittee started for Arkansas, and which was not only not granted but was not even replied to, asking that certain members of the House, four of them members of the Committee on Elections, be called upon to testify before the subcommittee left. These were Mr. Rowell, chairman of the full committee, Mr. Haugen, Mr. Dalzell, and Mr. Greenhalge. All of these gentlemen had argued from this case to show why other Democrats should be unseated before they had entered upon the investigation.

It is difficult to conceive upon what grounds of justice or propriety gentlemen will cite in argument the assumed character or facts of a case before any evidence therein was taken. Especially is this so when the case had been referred to them for judicial investigation and consideration; and still more especially if they knew nothing about it. These gentlemen of matured judgment and training, and occupying the positions they did, were not to be presumed to be thus bold unless they had peculiar information not possessed by others, and no positive information was known to be possessed by any one as to the mooted points in controversy.

Hence it was desirable in the interest of justice that the subcommittee get their testimony *before* going to Arkansas. And even had these gentlemen spoken in ignorance, and hence in blindness and prejudice, it was equally desirable to expose that fact, if rights are to be equally guarded, in order that they might take warning before being called upon to pass final judgment, and that the House and the country might have this suitable test of their fairness. But it was ignored and not even laid before the subcommittee. Why not? Is it presumptious to suppose that in this case the sitting member or his constituents have any rights? Ordinarily in a case of the gravity of this one, we would expect the majority to be exceedingly careful to avoid even the appearance of unfairness, in order that no man could say that they were disposed to fasten upon innocent men or upon a people the guilt of an "alleged assassination," to use the language of the House, or that they were disposed to make political capital out of blood. Nothing can be so potent in a case like this as the truth fairly found and fairly told.

It was agreed that Mr. Garland should present an application setting forth what he deemed necessary to complete the case and properly exhaust the parts that had been hurriedly or insufficiently examined into.

The subcommittee had been authorized to " proceed to Arkansas, if deemed necessary by them, to take any part of said testimony." The House had only instructed it to "*make* a full and thorough investigation." * * * It had not instructed it to go to Arkansas; it said it "*may* proceed to Arkansas to take any *part* of said testimony." It had not instructed it to complete anything *there*, or fixed any limitation upon it except that it must be "full and thorough;" and we have seen from Mr. Lacey's own admission that "*everything* was to be just as open at Washington as there," and that "any of these witnesses were to be brought to Washington."

Pages 377 and 388 of the testimony will show how members of the committee viewed this matter upon its casual introduction before this ampler statement of the facts was concurred in by Mr. Lacey. Mr. Garland submitted his statement. Nothing in it called for the absence of the subcommittee again. Mr. Breckinridge had witnesses in attendance near midnight, when the Little Rock adjournment took place, unexamined, but which he thought, under the agreement, it would be cheaper and better to defer to Washington or to take by deposition than to longer detain the committee. It will be seen that most of the testimony here called for could be easily taken by the usual mode of deposition, quickly prepared and quickly taken. The application was as follows:

IN THE MATTER OF THE INQUIRY INTO THE ELECTION OF CLIFTON R. BRECKINRIDGE FROM THE SECOND CONGRESSIONAL DISTRICT OF ARKANSAS.

To the Committee on Elections in the House of Representatives in the Fifty-first Congress:

The said Breckinridge moves the committee to prolong this investigation and give him time to take the testimony of the following witnesses to prove what is set forth and mentioned in connection with the names of each, viz:

It is understood the vote of the Plummerville box, as proved up, leaves the defendant's majority in the district something less than 500 votes.

Certain precincts in Woodruff County, viz, Augusta Town, Augusta Township, Riverside, and White River precincts, have been dealt with by the committee. Defendant has rested secure as to these, as the United States court, as well as the election officials of both parties, have declared that the votes were counted as cast and were cast as counted. Defendant had not presumed that an attempt would be made to deprive him of the small contingent of colored votes received there.

As the proceedings of the committee, however, indicate an intention to reverse the findings of the election officials of the United States district court by the testimony of the few negroes defendant had voting for him, now exposed to the proscription of their church and race if they confessed in public how they voted, and to cast out these precincts except in so far as the votes may be proved up anew, it is desired to prove up the defendant's vote. It is true the change in the small Democratic negro vote, apparently proposed by the committee, does not defeat defendant; but if they propose to cast out the white vote and only hold on to the Republican vote, that would defeat him. He asks, therefore, to prove up his vote at these precincts, provided it is contemplated by the committee to refuse the reports of the officials and the findings of the United States court which tried and acquitted these officials upon the charge that they had tampered with the ballots, which court had the ballots and poll-books and all other evidence before it.

The committee also took proceedings as to the Cotton Plant box, in Woodruff County, and it is asserted they found certain ballots which the majority considered suspiciously numbered, and also that a few negroes were returned as voting for defendant who denied it when asked in public. If it is contemplated to cast out the Democratic vote here and count only the Republican vote as thus proved, it is asked to poll the Democratic vote at this box.

The Freeman Township box in Monroe County appears to be attacked because no election was held there. If it is proposed to count the Republicans who did not vote, it is requested to similarly poll the Democrats there who failed to vote. Defendant claims that this is a Democratic precinct by a small majority, and that the failure to hold an election was due to the Republicans; the only lawyer on the ground being a Republican. and he also a United States election official.

It is asked that Mr. Leach be summoned to prove that the Republican party was not well organized in Woodruff County in 1888, and that under such circumstances the Democratic party usually can and does receive about 10 per cent. of the colored vote, as in 1888.

It is requested that Dr. C. M. Taylor, of South Bend, Ark., be examined to testify that he could have voted thirty-two colored laborers on his farm if the "church" had not been brought to bear on them. He lost all their votes, and if they had voted for Breckinridge and had been called on afterwards to confess it under proscriptive conditions, they would have denied it.

Wood—Pinkerton detective—to prove the course of proceedings to detect the murderer of John M. Clayton.

Produce the reward proclamation of Democratic county committee of Conway County to catch ballot-box thieves at Plummerville.

To produce the letter from a widow lady, name not remembered, to Governor Eagle to show persistency of Democrats in aiding him to catch the murderers, upon the theory that the ballot-box thieves or any citizens of Conway County committed the murder.

Also the letter of C. R. Breckinridge to Carroll Armstrong, relating to duty of Conway County and Armstrong's reply to Breckinridge.

To produce the proceedings of coroner's jury in Conway County in case of Joe Smith, colored, killed, and politics of jury.

To produce the communication from the colored man Jordan in Conway County, showing how and why that county went Democratic in September State election in 1888.

The testimony of Judge Cunningham, now in Guthrie, Oklahoma, to show why he resigned as circuit judge, or accept a copy of his letter to the Gazette on that subject.

The testimony of Carter, prosecuting attorney of judicial circuit Conway County is in, to show why no indictment was found for the killing of Clayton.

Testimony of Eagle Club (colored and Democratic) Cornerstone, Ark., to show difficulty of colored men who wanted to vote the Democratic ticket.

The testimony of Logan H. Roots, as to his article in the North American Review last spring on the subject of the killing of Clayton and politics in Arkansas.

The testimony of William M. Fishback as to the character of the people making the wholesale charges of wrong and crime against the people of that district, and his theory, after investigation, of the killing of Clayton.

The testimony of Powell Clayton as to his letter requesting all such troubles to be reported to him, to be used for campaign purposes, or a copy of the letter be admitted in evidence; and also a copy of his letter and other official proceedings approving the murder of Hooper and others in Conway County; and also his letter, or a copy, to Major Hunn, at Pine Bluff, asking for money from Democrats to aid his private detectives in finding out the murderer of his brother.

The testimony of the sheriff of Los Angeles, Cal., to show on what he based his unqualified statement that Hooper was absent from California some time before and after Clayton was killed.

The testimony of Dr. Greene, of Los Angeles, Cal., who was Hooper's family physician continuously.

The testimony of the citizens referred to by Sater and Mrs. Hooper, who, he said, told him of Hooper's absence, as stated above.

The testimony of the man Lewis, referred to by the California sheriff, whose evidence was reported to Governor Eagle.

The production of the confession of the colored man Parks as to the real murderer of Clayton.

The testimony of D. H. Womack, for the further statement of the particulars of the killing of Clayton, not distinctly brought out in his former examination.

The testimony of E. C. Meacham, of the E. C. Meacham Arms Company, St. Louis, Mo., with his sales-books from April 24. 1888, to January 29, 1889, as to the pistol alleged to have been sold by his company, and supposed to be the pistol found on the ground or place of the killing of Clayton.

And the testimony of C. H. Jones, of St. Louis, and Samuel W. Fordyce, of the same place, as to their inquiries on this same subject of the pistol, or the production of their correspondence with the defendant touching the same.

And the testimony of Judge W. S. Hemmingway, law partner of John M. Clayton, to show Clayton had no information upon which to base a belief of his election, or the production of Judge H.'s letter on this point, written about the close of last winter.

The testimony of C. R. Breckinridge himself as to the steps taken to detect the person or persons engaged in killing Clayton.

The testimony referred to to be taken in such manner as may best suit the convenience of the committee.

He believes and so avers the same is essential to a clear and proper understanding of the merits of his case, as charged and brought before the committee by the inquiring party.

He does not ask for the taking of this testimony for delay, but because he has not had the opportunity to present the facts fully, which he expects to prove as aforesaid. The investigation has not proceeded, as is usual in such cases, but each party has been allowed to bring in testimony at will, without waiting for the case to be closed on the one side, and then for the other to rebut, a mode protested against by defendant, and manifestly unfair to him. Occupying the position of defendant in this inquiry, he could not be expected to present his case entire until the contestant, or the inquiring party, had concluded the case against him.

He did not, nor does he now, understand that the case was closed when the subcommittee ended its sitting at Little Rock, Ark., and certainly nothing he and his counsel there said or did would warrant such an impression, but quite the contrary. His belief was, that on the adjournment of the subcommittee at Little Rock, Ark., this defendant would be allowed here or elsewhere, as it pleased the committee, to bring in the testimony above indicated to rebut, as far as may be, the testimony produced by the other side.

He does not feel that it is fair and just to his constituents and to the very right of his claim, as the legal representative of such district, to proceed to a hearing of the case without this testimony.

While he by no means concedes the testimony already taken in any manner impeaches his right to the seat contested, yet, to refute and clear up certain points made as charges against the people he represents, he deems it right that this testimony be adduced.

Wherefore, etc.

Very respectfully,

C. R. BRECKINRIDGE.

A. H. GARLAND,
H. J. MAY,
Attorneys.

UNITED STATES OF AMERICA.
    District of Columbia:

I, Clifton R. Breckinridge, named in the foregoing motion, do solemnly swear the facts therein stated are true, to the best of my knowledge and belief. So help me God.

CLIFTON R. BRECKINRIDGE.

Sworn to and subscribed before me, May 26, 1890.
[SEAL.]

WILLIAM W. MOFFETT,
Notary Public.

To this the majority of the subcommittee, through its chairman, made the following reply, so strangely at variance from the promises and agreements upon which an adjournment was made at'Little Rock, so at variance from what is said on pages 377 and 378, from the duty of the committee, and from the admission of Mr. Lacey in his colloquy with Mr. Breckinridge and Mr. Maish before the full committee:

JUNE 3, 1890.

The subcommittee having examined the application of contestee in relation to the taking of further testimony in the case of Clayton *vs.* Breckinridge, make the following ruling:

The application of the contestee to take further testimony in Arkansas is denied. Full opportunity was given to take such testimony at Little Rock, and the case was there closed as to such testimony with the consent of the contestee. The closing of the case, however, at that point only related to taking testimony at Little Rock, leaving the subject of further testimony at Washington to be considered on arrival here. As to three of the witnesses, Dr. C. M. Taylor, C. R. Breckinridge, and Powell Clayton, while the committee know of no reason why their testimony was not sufficiently taken at Little Rock, yet as all three of said witnesses are in Washington to-day, the committee will hear their further testimony if contestee desires to have same taken.

As to all documentary evidence called for, the committee will receive same and place same in the record, subject to all proper objections as to relevancy, materiality, or competency, provided the same is furnished before the evidence is fully printed. The record is now being printed and the committee suggest that evidence of this character shall be presented at an early day if contestee desires to have same printed in the record.

As to the Meacham Arms Company evidence, the committee have fully examined the correspondence of said company. The application to take such testimony does not disclose its materiality or relevancy, but the committee deem it proper to say that from such correspondence they are informed that the company did not keep the numbers of the revolvers sold at that time, and had no record by which the sale of this revolver could be traced. A revolver of the same pattern, however, seems to have been sold to one Vandermeulen, and by him sold to a party whose name was to him unknown, and who was en route to Montana, and there is no way of ascertaining whether the revolver was or was not the one in question, it merely being one of the same pattern.

As to the testimony of Mr. Fishback and Mr. Roots, they were both present during a considerable portion of the hearing at Little Rock, and no reason is given why the testimony was not there taken if desired.

As to the testimony of Judge Cunningham, whilst the subject of his resignation was discussed before the committee, it was not explained by testimony, and there is no showing as to its relevancy or materiality.

The other witnesses living in Arkansas could have been examined there.

As to the recalling of Mr. Wonark, no reason is given as to why his evidence and that of Mr. Alnutt, already taken, did not fully describe the particulars of the killing of Mr. Clayton.

As to the testimony of parties in California, there is no showing as to the character of their testimony, as to its relevancy or materiality, nor is there anything to indicate that the testimony would in any manner conflict with the testimony already taken as to the whereabouts of Hooper at the time of the murder. There is no showing that such testimony would conflict with that of the Hooper family taken at Little Rock. Owing to the fact that the so-called Hooper theory was brought out about the time that the investigation commenced at Little Rock there had been no previous opportunity to investigate the same upon the part of persons representing the contestant. Telegraphic communication was at once had with parties at Los Angeles, the results of which are not set out in this application, although exhibited to the committee.

In the absence of any showing whatever that the proposed testimony will throw any light upon that theory of the case the committee do not deem it proper to delay the case to take the proposed testimony of California witnesses.

As to the testimony of Jones and Fordyce in regard to the revolver, there is no showing that the same would throw any light upon the identity of the revolver.

As to Judge Hemmingway's testimony, we do not believe it to be competent or material, and if contestee desires to take the testimony, there is no reason why the same was not taken in Arkansas.

If contestee desires to take the testimony of Dr. Taylor or Mr. Breckinridge or General Clayton, the witnesses now present in the city, he should so notify the committee immediately.

H. Mis. 137——47

To this proposition to violate agreements and to dismember Mr. Breckinridge's presentation of his case the following reply was made:

WASHINGTON, D. C., *June 4*, 1890.

To the Committee on Elections in the House of Representatives in the Fifty-first Congress :

In response to the communication of yesterday from your subcommittee touching the application of Clifton R. Breckinridge, filed before you on the 27th ult., for the taking of additional testimony in the matter of inquiry into his right to the seat in the present Congress as Representative of the Second Congressional district of Arkansas, the said Breckinridge would respectfully say :

His said application was made in good faith, and as the first step towards a methodical procedure in this investigation, presenting for the first time in its progress the names of witnesses, what was expected to be proved by each of them, with dates and points all attached. Heretofore, as suggested in such application, the inquiry proceeded in no fixed or connected manner, and he knew not exactly what he was called upon or expected to rebut. In fact, he was without information on this subject until the witnesses were being examined on the stand. Making the application as he did to meet certain vague and undefined charges and assertions as a whole, his request stands as a whole, and not a fragment. Every part and parcel of it is a link to be connected with other facts and circumstances that make up his case to meet such charges and assertions of the party inquiring, whoever he may be. There is nothing to be found in the record, directly or indirectly, that precludes respondent from the exercise of this right. Had the investigation at Little Rock, Ark., been conducted according to the usages in judicial or quasi-judicial controversies, with ample time therefor, this application would not have been necessary.

Respondent is compelled to accept the overruling of this application, with the three exceptions of the testimony of Dr. Taylor, Powell Clayton, and respondent; and, so far as these are concerned, their testimony, standing unconnected with the other testimony asked for in the application, would be of no avail. And as to what is termed documentary evidence in the ruling of the subcommittee the same reason applies: all that is a portion of an entire defense, suggested and indicated by the motion or application, and of itself and by itself, without the other facts to be established, as set forth in such application, are valueless.

The concession of the committee to the respondent that he may take the testimony of Dr. Taylor and Powell Clayton because they are here present must not be based upon the assumption that they are here at the request or by the procurement of respondent, for, so far as he is concerned, their presence is entirely accidental. They were not brought here by any act or suggestion of this respondent. He asks no further delay of the committee since this ruling upon his application, but leaves it free to proceed with the case as it may deem best, requesting that his motion for the taking of more testimony, with the ruling of your subcommittee on it and this response to such ruling, be made a part of the record of this case and printed therein ; and also that the names of the witnesses, voters at the election inquired into in the State of Arkansas, be printed in the record in alphabetical order, as a matter of convenience to all.

Very respectfully,

C. R. BRECKINRIDGE.
A. H. GARLAND,
H. J. MAY,
                                Counsel.

DEATH OF JOHN M. CLAYTON.

Without discussing the question of the Federal Government inquiring into the criminal affairs of a State, we will simply say that the direction of the committee to inquire thoroughly into everything relating to the death of Clayton was perhaps the one part of the instructions that the public expected and desired to be carried out the most exhaustively. In order that there might be no misunderstanding about the authority and duty to do this, Mr. Breckinridge had the order of inquiry enlarged by an amendment which clearly embraced it, and the instructions, as thus amended, were unanimously adopted by the House.

Citizens, authorities, all have responded to every call and assisted every effort. Every process has been promptly obeyed. Every question promptly answered. Every test, such as writing from dictation, or any other the committee saw fit to, impose, was promptly responded to by every party suspected or accused. If, then, there has been failure to examine important witnesses, to exhaust any and every theory, if there has been any halting in proceedings and any suppression of testimony, any effort to confuse the case, to shield the guilty, to accuse or besmirch the innocent, or to place a cloud needlessly and hence unjustly upon any one, or any effort in any way to handle this case badly for mere political purposes, the House will know where the responsibility lies.

John M. Clayton was killed at a little place called Plummerville, in Conway County, Ark., on the night of January 29, 1889. Two men were in the room with him at the time he was shot. One of them was Mr. W. D. Allnutt, a lawyer and notary public, and a Republican. He was assisting Colonel Clayton in conducting his contest at this point, acting, however, simply in his capacity as a notary public, Colonel Clayton himself doing the legal part of the work, advising, however, with Judge John McClure, his attorney, at Little Rock. The other man was Mr. E. H. Womack, misspelled in the testimony and index as Wamuck. He was a salesman for a pottery concern, was at Plummerville on business connected with his concern, was stopping that night at the same house as Colonel Clayton and Allnutt, was a stranger to both Clayton and Allnutt. Womack is said to be a Democrat. The testimony of these two men is most important for any speculation upon the case, and we here insert it:

W. D. ALLNUTT, called, sworn, examined, and testified.

Direct ex.:

Q. Where do you reside?—A. Clarksville, Johnson County.
Q. Where were you on the night of January 29th, 1889?—A. Plummerville.
Q. Where had you been in business and how was you engaged prior to that day?—A. I had been down there taking depositions between Clayton and Breckinridge.
Mr. COOPER. Were they being taken before you or were you acting as attorney?
A. I was notary public; they were being taken before me.
Mr. McCLURE. About what time in the evening did you and Mr. Clayton get your supper?
A. I suppose somewhere about 7 o'clock.
Q. At whose place did you get supper?—A. Mrs. McCraven's.
Q. About how long was you getting your supper?—A. I couldn't tell you about that; I didn't pay any particular attention to the time; I suppose we were at the table about as long as it usually takes a man to eat a meal.
Q. 15 or 20 minutes?—A. Yes, sir.
Q. Did you take supper at Mrs. McCraven's house?—A. Yes, sir.
Q. After you got your supper where did you go next?—A. We went back to the front room where we were before and where Mr. Clayton was killed.
Q. How long did you remain there?—A. We remained there all night.
Q. All the balance of the evening?—A. Yes, sir, excepting a few minutes when I went out of the room after he was shot and sent somebody down after a doctor.
Q. Do you know a man named Wamuck?—A. Yes, sir.
Q. Was he in the room the time Clayton was shot?—A. Yes, sir.
Q. How long had he been in the room prior to the shot?—A. He been there ever since supper; he went in about the time we did, I think.
Mr. COOPER. Is that a sort of a sitting-room for the house as well as a bed-room?
A. Yes, sir.
Q. That is the reason the other folks were in there as well as him?—A. Yes, sir. I will not say Wamuck came in with us; it is possible he didn't come until after we had been to supper, but I am under the impression he was there before that.
Mr. McCLURE. Tell how you spent the early part of the evening; what were you doing after supper?
A. We were in the room talking.
Q. Were you engaged at work there in the preparation of any papers?—A. I was not.
Q. Was he?—A. I don't remember that he was now.
Q. You were just holding a casual conversation?—A. When we first went into the room after supper I sat down and commenced reading a paper, and I think I read there probably 15 or 20 minutes, and I got up from there and went across on the op-

posite side of the fire-place, and Mr. Wamuck sat down in the chair and he had a
little memorandum book he was figuring in.

Q. How long would you think Wamuck was there?

Mr. COOPER. There is a diagram Mr. Wamuck made this morning which is in use;
it shows the house and the surroundings.

Mr. McCLURE. Is this paper now shown you approximately[a correct diagram of
the house of Mrs. McCraven?

A. Yes, sir; the shape of the house.

Q. And the surrounding grounds?—A. Yes, sir.

Q. Mark the sitting-room, dining-room, and Mrs. Craven's room, etc.; mark them
1, 2, 3, 4, 5, 6, and so they can be identified.

(Witness does so.)

Q. Now, about what time in the evening was it that Mr. Clayton was shot?—A.
Well, sir, as near as I can get at it it was about 10 minutes before 8 o'clock.

Q. Before 8?—A. Yes, sir.

Q. How do you fix the time?—A. I started to tell awhile ago.

Q. Well, go on.—A. When we first came out from supper I sat down to the table,
took a newspaper, and read there probably 10 or 15 minutes, or maybe a little longer;
then I got up and went over on the other side of the fire-place and Wamuck sat down
and figured a little while, probably as much longer; then when he got up to walk
across to the fire-place where I was sitting in the chair I got up and invited him to
take a seat, and I went over on the other side, and just as I got up to go Mr. Clayton
was shot, and I am satisfied it was in about that time. I gather it from that, and
when the doctor came up there the first thing was to take out Clayton's watch and
look at it.

Q. Was the watch going?—A. Yes, sir.

Q. What time of day was it by the watch?—A. 5 minutes after 8, and he had been
dead then, I suppose, 10 or 15 minutes.

Q. Who was in the house when he was shot; was there any other man?—A. There
was no man in the house except Mr. Wamuck and myself; Mrs. McCraven's grandson had gone down town; Wamuck was a stranger; I didn't feel like going down there.

Mr. COOPER. You had no watch?

A. No, sir.

Mr. McCLURE. Wamuck had no watch?

A. I don't know about that. I went into Mrs. McCraven's room and took a lamp
and went back into the room where he was, and about the time we got back in these
young men came in, and so we sent them down town after the doctor, and by the
time they got down there and back they told anybody else they saw that Mr. Clayton had been killed; they went down there and got Dr. Allgood, and when he got up
there Mr. Clayton had been dead, I suppose, 10 or 15 minutes.

Q. What examination, if any, was made that night, if any?—A. Out of doors, do
you mean?

Q. Oh, no; but in the house, of the body.—A. They examined the body, and took
what he had on his person, his watch and money and papers and letters. Dr. Allgood took them off and turned them over to me; we raised him up from where he
was lying in the blood and laid him over a little closer to the wall, and put a pillow
or something under his head and put a sheet over him and let him lie there all
night. Some of them suggested that we take him up and put him on the bed, but I
suggested we had better let him stay where he was until the inquest was held. I
told them I thought probably it would be better to let him stay there where he was
until the coroner's jury viewed the remains or until somebody would come and take
charge of it.

Mr. MAISH. If I understand you correctly you say you removed the remains of Mr.
Clayton?

A. Yes, sir; we just picked him up out of the blood and laid him over a little nearer
to the wall.

Q. Did you take him off of the chair where he was lying?—A. Yes, sir; we took
his feet down off there and straightened him out, took his shoes off, and put a sheet
over him.

Q. And that was done on your suggestion?—A. Yes, sir.

Mr. McCLURE. Who were the first persons that came to the house after the firing;
that is strangers, persons who were not in the house when it occurred?

A. The first persons came in there was Mrs. McCraven's and son or stepson, or whatever it is, and another young man that was boarding there.

Q. How long was it after that shot was fired until they came to the house?—A. I
suppose 5 or 6 minutes.

Q. Was it as much as that?—A. I guess it was; I will say 5 minutes anyhow.

Q. Which way did they enter that house?—A. They came in through that side
gate at the back end of the house, and went into the doorway into Mrs. McCraven's
room.

Q. Before entering the house in the manner you have described would they have to pass the window through which Clayton was shot ?—A. No, sir; they come in at the other end of the house.

Q. Did they come that way ?—A. No, sir.

Q. Of that you are positive ?—A. I am sure of that; these two fellows didn't. When the other fellows come afterwards they come in around that way as well as other ways.

Q. When these two young fellows went down after the doctor and they told the people what had happened, who do you recollect of being the first persons that returned up to the house on account of the news being spread down town ?—A. Well, sir, it was Dr. Allgood, and I don't remember who else, until Mr. Armstrong come directly a few minutes after that.

Q. Gen. Armstrong ?—A. Carroll Armstrong.

Q. How long was it after the shooting before he was there ?—A. Carroll Armstrong ?

Q. Yes, sir.—A. I suppose it was 20 minutes, and maybe a little longer—about 20 minutes, I should judge.

Q. Now, what took place after that ?—A. Well, I don't know; Mr. Armstrong came there and he and I sat up the greater part of the night, and Mr. Wamuck sat up awhile with us. If my memory serves me I went to bed about 11 o'clock, and I think Mr. Hobbs came up there and Armstrong, and I was up there until about 3 o'clock in the morning, and Mr. Wamuck and Mr. Hobbs, and Hobbs and this young boy was staying there.

Q. Was there any dispatches sent off that night at your instance or suggestion ?—A. Yes, sir; there was some sent; I don't remember it was at my suggestion, but as soon as the doctor made the examination of Mr. Clayton's body and straightened him out Mr. Armstrong said he would go down to the telegraph office and telegraph some of his friends, and he asked me if I knew where Powell Clayton was, and I think he said he would telegraph to Little Rock or to Washington, and he went and said something about telegraphing to him, and I understood he did so.

Q. How long was this conversation about sending off the dispatches after the death of Clayton ?—A. He had been dead then half an hour.

Q. Mr. Armstrong then, as I understand you, went off to send dispatches ?—A. Yes.

Q. How long was he gone ?—A. He was gone some considerable time; he had some trouble about finding the operator; he had left the office—at least that's my impression now. When he came back he told me he had to go to the operator's house or had sent somebody there after him.

Q. Something has been said about a blanket being up at that window ?—A. Yes, sir; Mr. Armstrong and I had it put up there; I suggested it, that we were both sitting there, and I called his attention to the looks of the window and that curtain, and I said I didn't like it, and he said he didn't like it very well himself, and I suggested that something ought to be up there. And I went out and saw Mrs. McCraven, and she came in with a blanket.

Mr. COOPER. That was to prevent persons from seeing in ?

A. It was a blanket or quilt, I forget which, and I think Mr. Wamuck helped me to hang it up. Yes, sir; it was to close the window so people couldn't see in.

Mr. McCLURE. You put it up over the window ?

A. Yes, sir.

Q. What time of night was it hung up ?—A. I don't know; perhaps an hour and a half after Clayton was killed.

Q. Something has been said about that window curtain that was there before you put up the blanket across it; state whether that was a perfect curtain ?—A. Yes, sir, it was a calico curtain, a thin curtain, but there was no holes in it. It was one of those curtains strung on a string at the top of the window and the curtain slide back and forth on the string; there was two curtains, one slides one way and the other the other, and they separated in the middle, leaving a little crack.

Q. It didn't cross all the way ?—A. No, sir.

Q. It was in a condition that persons on the outside could see through the curtain ?—A. Yes, sir; but I didn't notice until after the shooting.

Q. What sort of a hole was made in the curtain by that shot ?—A. I suppose it was a hole tore in one edge of it; probably I could put my fingers through it that way. [Bunched together.]

Q. What took place the next morning now, so far as making examinations as to tracks was concerned ?—A. The first thing next morning when I got up, about sunrise or a little before, it is my impression Mr. Wamuck went with me, and I went out to look for tracks. I first called Mr. Armstrong and woke him, and said we would go out and see if we could see any of these tracks, and after he had dressed he made the remark he would go down to the telegraph office and see if any telegrams had come for him, and for me to go out and look for tracks, and I think Mr. Wamuck went with me, and part way anyhow. He was out to that gate and went in through the gate. I don't remember now, but think he went back to the house,

and I went out there to that hole where they come through, and there I turned
around and came back.

Q. What did you see in the way of tracks?—A. I saw some tracks of two men
coming in and two men going out.

Q. So they returned by the same path they came in?—A. Yes, sir; they went right
back the same way, but they didn't strike the same place in the fence. One of them
ran right against the fence and knocked off a picket or two from the looks of the
hole; he had run over something and fell through the hole.

Q. There was a hole in the fence? Was that hole made prior to that time?—A.
Yes, sir; there was an opening in the fence before that I think.

Q. When they went away from the house they didn't seem to strike the same
place?—A. No, sir; one of them struck the opening in the fence, and the other
didn't; he struck the fence.

Q. One of them made his exit through the hole where he came in?—A. Yes, sir.

Q. And the other one went through where he knocked the pickets off?—A. Yes, sir.

Q. You didn't go beyond the garden fence?—A. No, sir; I didn't go over on the
other side.

Q. Where did you go then?—A. I went back to the house.

Q. It is said there is another window in the room, and some steps or marks were
found about that end of the house also?—A. Well, the two windows are right close
together, one at the end of the house and the other at the side of it. One is here [in-
dicating], and the other is right around the corner. I didn't see any steps under the
window, but I seen the place out by a little tree.

Q. Some persons seem to have been standing at that little tree?—A. Yes, sir.

Q. Were those tracks by the tree independent tracks or were they the same?—A.
No, sir; them tracks were the tracks that went out through the little gate.

Q Were they all the same tracks?—A. Yes, sir; they were.

Q. Were you before the coroner's inquest?—A. Yes, sir.

Q. In what capacity did you act there that day, if any?—A. The day after Clayton
was killed?

Q. Yes, sir.—A. Not any.

Q. Who wrote the testimony was taken at the coroner's inquest?—A. I couldn't
tell you.

Q. Did you?—A. I got the impression I wrote down some of it, maybe—I believe I
did. After we went down to the house where we took the depositions I think I wrote
part of it.

Q. Can you tell how many witnesses were examined there that day?—A. No, sir.

Q. Were you?—A. Yes, sir.

Q. But you don't know who else was?—A. No, sir.

Q. About what time were the duties of the coroner completed?—A. Somewhere
about 10 or 11 o'clock, or maybe later.

Q. Was the inquest concluded before W. H. H. Clayton got up there with the coffin?—A. I think so.

Q. That is your impression?—A. That is my impression.

Mr. COOPER. Do you know how heavy that load was; was it a shotgun and shot?
A. It was loaded with powder and buck-shot. I don't know what the gun was.

Q. Whereabouts did it hit him?—A. Right under the ear; right there [indicating].

Q. Do you know how many buck-shot entered his neck there?—A. No, sir; I don't
know how many there were and I did hear Mr. Cook, the undertaker, say too. I
don't think he found the whole lot. I think some buck-shot was in his body when
he was taken away; it nearly shot his ear off, it was hanging by the skin.

Q. Did Wamuck state that his first impression was the lamp had exploded?—A.
Yes, sir; he said, My God, that lamp has exploded and killed Mr. Clayton. And I
said to him, some fellow had shot him through the window. I used a very ugly
word.

Q. He said you used the word, "as I expected." Did you say that?—A. I don't
remember about that, but it's very probable I did say it.

Q. Did you have any reason to expect or to suspect he would be shot?—A. No, sir;
but I felt just all the time I was down there that it was a dangerous piece of business; I can't tell why, but I felt that way.

Q. Where did you live at that time?—A. I lived up at Morrillton at that time.

Q. Where did you sleep that night?—A. I slept there in the room where Mr. Clay
ton's body was lying.

Where did Mr. Wamuck sleep?—A. Now, I can't say whether Wamuck slept in the
room or whether he slept in that little hall room in the bed where Mr. Clayton had
been sleeping; I am under the impression he slept in that hall room.

Q. How many other people slept in that house on that night?—A. There was myself, Mr. Armstrong, Mr Wamuck, Mrs. McCravens' grandson, and another young
man, I do not know his name, and I think he stayed there and Mr. Hobbs.

Mr. BERGEN. Will you put on this map the window through which he was shot; put a "W" right in that place on this diagram?

(Witness does so.)

Q. Now be kind enough to put on the map the letter "P" at the place where the pistol was found, if you can tell us?

(Witness does so.)

Q. Now is there anything between the pistol and the window?—A. Yes, there is two fences there.

Q. Something has been said about some paling that were broken off?—A. Yes.

Q. How near was that to where the pistol was found?—A. The pistol was found right on the opposite side of the fence across where the paling was broken. I wasn't there and didn't see where it was picked up, but I know where it was found.

Q. Mr. Coblentz was the man that picked it up?—A. Yes, sir.

Q. There are two crosses there to the right seemingly in the fence?—A. That nearest one to the house is the gate to the garden. Where the other crossed out in the lane is where the fellow stumbled against the fence.

Q. And seemingly dropped the pistol just beyond it?—A. Yes, sir.

Q. You have made little marks there?—A. That represents the pickets. The pickets on the fence; it is a picket fence.

Q. But these little dots? Do those represent the tracks?—A. They represent the tracks; that is the road they came in and went out.

Q. Up beyond here put an "R" where the rose-bush was?—A. It wasn't a rose-bush, it was a cedar-tree. There was several of them about in this yard.

Q. Why did they seem to have skulked; is that right?—A. Yes, sir.

Q. Well, put that there?—A. I will just write the word tree there.

Q. Now, who had called on Mr. Clayton that night?—A. Up there at the house?

Q. Yes, sir.—A. No, sir; there had been no one to see him.

Q. Where were you going to take testimony?—A. We was continuing it the next morning; we had been at it for 3 or 4 days.

Q. Whose testimony was you going to take next day?—A. I don't know, sir; I was only the notary. Mr. Armstrong and Mr. Clayton was taking the investigation and they never said anything about what they would put on the stand.

Q. The records show what you have taken?—A. Yes, sir.

Q. Was this room the room in which you were—who was going to sleep in that room?—A. That night?

Q. Yes.—A. I don't know, sir; I was not, and neither was Mr. Clayton. Mr. Clayton slept in the hall room—in the little room—and Mrs. McCraven came in there just after supper and said to me I could sleep with Mr. Clayton, and I told her I was rather a bad bedfellow and that I would probably annoy him, and I would rather she would arrange me a bed somewhere else; she said she would; and there was a little shed room there was closed in, and she went in there and prepared me a bed there, and that is where I was going to sleep, but I didn't sleep there.

Q. Was Mr. Wamuck going to sleep there?—A. Yes, sir.

Q. Then he was going to sleep in one end of the room and yourself in——?—A. Yes, sir.

Mr. MAISH. Was there any dog about the house?

A. No, sir.

Mr. McCLURE. Did you know a man by the name of Cap. Matthews?

A. Yes, sir.

Q. The Cap. Matthews spoken of by Mr. Sater here as being one of the men that Hooper claims to have killed? Do you know when Matthews departed this life?—A. Yes, sir; I believe I do. I remember the circumstances of his death.

Q. In what year was it?—A. To the best of my recollection that was in 1878 or 1879, I said it was, but I believe I am mistaken about that. I have got the matter fixed in my mind and I know very well where he was killed at.

Q. Where was he killed?—A. At Perryville. They had him indicted down there at one time for something concerning the murder of old man Hooper; I think he was indicted at the time Charley Reed was prosecuting attorney.

Q. Was Matthews killed in the day-time or night-time?—A. In the night-time.

Q. Did you know this Thomas Hooper that went to California?—A. Yes, sir; I went to Louisville the same time he went to Cal.

Q. What year was that?—A. In 1870.

Q. How many years do you know Hooper had been gone when Matthews was killed?—A. He went in 1870, and I think Matthews was killed along in 1876, 1877, 1878, or 1879.

Q. Anyway this was some years after Hooper had left the country?—A. Yes, sir.

Q. Do you know a man by the name of N. N. Conway who got killed?—A. No, sir; I was only told of a man got killed by that name.

Q. Did you know a man by the name of Capt. Gibbon or some such name as that?—A. Yes, sir.

Q. Do you know whether he died before or after Hooper left this country to go to Cal. ?—A. Gibbons died after that.

Q. Long after that ?—A. Yes, sir.

Q. Something has been said about Mr. Hooper having been hung; did you know Mr. Hooper in his life-time ?—A. The old man ? I have seen him.

Q. Did you know him ?—A. I can't say that I knew him.

Q. Did you know him by sight ?—A. Yes, sir; Hooper was killed in 1868. I went down there in that year. I came to this country with C. C. Reed. Reed seems to have known Mr. Hooper or had met him; I don't remember where it was, but it was at the landing on the river here some place, and went up there over on a steamboat. I wrote to his mother after that, and told her he was shot, and I knew it to be the old man Hooper at that time. I didn't live in this country then. I went up to Johnson County, the place where I live now, and the place where I was when Hooper was killed.

Q. Do you know how he met his death ?—A. Well, I have always been under the impression or told that the militia killed him.

Q. Then he wasn't hung ?—A. I don't know how they killed him—whether they shot him or hung him.

Mr. MAISH. You are a lawyer ?—A. Yes, sir.

Q. How long have you been a lawyer ?—A. I was admitted to the bar in 1868 as well as I remember.

Q. You were a personal friend of John M. Clayton in his life-time ?—A. Yes, sir; I suppose you can say that I was. But I had never met him very frequently.

Q. Both members of the same political party and of the same political sympathy ?—A. I suppose so, sir.

Q. You was engaged at that time taking depositions for him ?—A. Yes, sir.

Q. You was in attendance at the coroner's inquest all the time, was you, whilst it was going on ?—A. Yes, sir.

Q. How many jurors composed the inquest ?—A. I don't remember now whether we had 12 or not.

Q. What is your best recollection ?—A. My best recollection is there was 12 of them.

Q. Where were they selected from ?—A. From among the citizens there at Plummerville.

Q. In the town of Plummerville ?—A. Yes, sir; there may have been one or two men on the jury from the country.

Q. Do you remember who they were ?—A. Why, no; I couldn't tell you now; I know several of them.

Q. Mention those you remember.—A. I can not remember their names now; what I mean to say is I know several of the names who lived there, but I can't remember now who they were.

Q. Were there a great many people there ?—A. Yes, sir.

Q. Whilst the inquest was going on ?—A. Yes, sir; there was a large crowd there.

Q. All the time ?—A. I think so. Yes, sir; there was a grea many people around the house, and a great many came to the hall and about the room where they could be, and after adjournment we left the house and went to the hall.

Q. There was a great many at the house when Mr. Clayton was killed in the first place ?—A. Yes, sir.

Q. How many ?—A. I suppose at one time—there was over 100 people at one time, I reckon.

Q. How many people did you see at the inquest down there?—A. I don't remember.

Q. Will you state if there were about 2,000 at the house, do you think ?—A. Well, there was a large crowd there all day.

Q. As many as 100 ?—A. Yes, sir; half the colored people of the township were there.

Q. Were there a great many white people ?—A. I don't think there was; that's not my recollection.

Q. Were there not white people there ?—A. Yes, sir; some white men there.

Q. Were there some white men at the house ?—A. Yes, sir.

Q. In the crowd there ?—A. Yes, sir.

Mr. LACEY. Do you remember who those white men were ?

A. No, sir; I don't.

Mr. MCCAIN. How many people gathered in there that night of the killing ?

A. Nearly everybody in Plummerville gathered in there that night.

Q. Was the house packed ?—A. Yes, sir; the house was full. They came in there and looked around there until we laid Mr. Clayton out and covered him up, and they all went off.

Q. Except you watchers ?—A. Yes, sir.

Q. Four of you watched ?—A. Yes, sir.

Q. Was there anything that could be done that you all could have done there that night that yOu did not do?—A. I don't know anything else that I could have done.

Q. Did everybody else do everything that you thought they might have done?—A. I think so. We notified the authorities. Mr. Armstrong telegraphed to the sheriff or clerk or some of them up at Morrilltou; notified them; notified the governor and I think notified Mr. Clayton.

Q. Was there any courtesies or assistance amOng the citizens there in anything you needed done? I don't mean in regard to authorities, but about the house there that night or the next morning. Did you have any help?—A. Oh, yes; there was nothing to do but lay him out of that blood and lay him back against the wall. While the people were up there I didn't see any indications from any of them at all that they would object to helping.

Q. Well, the people seemed to be interested in the occurrence there?—A. Well, I don't know; they wouldn't talk much about it.

Q. They would not talk much about it?—A. No, sir.

Q. They gathered about there quite a large crowd, you say?—A. Yes, sir; the people right there in Plummerville seemed to be very reticent about it and would not talk.

Q. You were a little reticent yourself, were you not?—A. Yes, sir.

Q. Were they any more reticent than you?—A. I don't know that they were. I didn't talk.

Q Well, didn't you get the impression of it, and didn't you have an impression there that you needed to act with some prudence to be there at that time?—A. Yes, sir.

Q. But so far as taking care of and lOoking after Col. Clayton was concerned there was no backwardness about that on the part of anybody?—A. No, sir; none that I saw.

Q. This old lady you were stopping with, did she seem to be a poor old lady, or well-to-do?—A. Well, she was rather a poor woman.

Q. Didn't fix up in much style?—A. No, sir.

Q. Well, were the colored people attentive about there?—A. Yes, sir.

Q. Did Judge Clayton or Gov. Clayton send any of you any telegrams of any kind?—A. He didn't send any to me. I don't know whether there was any sent to Mr. Armstrong or not. There was no telegrams sent in my name. He done all the telegraphing.

Q. What time of day did you have that inquest?—A. We commenced it in the morning.

Q. What time did you get through?—A. I was asked that awhile ago, and gave it about 11 o'clock; but I wish to state I suppose it was about 10 o'clock or 11 when we commenced.

Q. What time of day did you get through?—A. I suppose it was an hour or two hours.

Q. You hadn't got through when the train arrived?—A. I don't know whether we had or not, but it seems to me we had; but I am not sure of that.

Q. What was the reasOn you didn't go to the train that day?—A. Me?

Q. Yes, sir.—A. I don't remember why it was I didn't go.

Q. You didn't go to meet Judge Clayton?—A. No, sir; I didn't go to the train. And that makes me think now whether they hadn't got through with the inquest when the train come, but I can't remember about that. I don't remember what I was doing at the time the train came.

Q. You know yOu was there and you did not meet him?—A. No, sir; I did not.

Q. And you think yOu was there and taking testimony?—A. Yes, sir; I think so now.

Q. Were you engaged after the coroner's jury had rendered its verdict to put matters in shape and kept you longer than you would have been?—A. It seems to me that I wrote some after that. I picked up a pencil and wrote some for the coroner, but I do not remember what.

Q. Who was on that jury?—A. I couldn't name a man that was on it; I knew several of the men, but I can't tell now.

Q. See if you can't call some of them; who summOned the jury?—A. I think Mr. Bently summoned the jury. Yes, sir; I remember one man was on there is man named Patterson was on the jury, and a man named Pate, Robert Pate, and probably a man named Sagg was on it. I am not sure about him, but I rather think he was.

Q. Is that all you remember now?—A. Yes, sir.

Q. Your impression is they were Plummerville people?—A. Yes, sir; there might have been one or two or two or three from the country; that man Sagg I think was from the country and perhaps two or three.

Q. Were they all white?—A. I think there were some colored men on it, is my recollectiOn now.

Q. Who were the colored men ?—A. I couldn't say ; I don't know that I knew any of them.

Mr. McCain. Could you get any information before the coroner's jury at all as to who he was killed by ?

A. No, sir.

Q. Or how it happened ?—A. No, sir.

Q. You couldn't learn anything yourself on that question ?—A. No, sir.

Q. Well, did the people—did any of them seem to have any opinion about that—the people that lived out there ?—A. I didn't talk to but one or two men about it, and they didn't have any opinion.

Q. You didn't talk with them ?—A. No, sir ; they didn't seem to want to talk, and I didn't talk much either.

Q. Is that the only reason why they were reticent—because you didn't want to talk ?—A. I don't know that it was ; I couldn't tell you.

Q. Why didn't you want to talk to them ?—A. I didn't want to talk about that matter ; that is, simply because I was afraid to talk about it was why.

Q. Well, neither you nor anybody else seemed to have any opinion about how that crime was perpetrated or who perpetrated it, and could get no information about it ?—A. No, sir ; I got no information and got no opinion, and I am satisfied if I had went to any man in Plummerville and asked him if he knew, I don't think he would have said ; and I don't suppose any man in Plummerville knew.

Q. Well, that wasn't very remarkable ; they would be backward in saying who they thought did it if they didn't know ?—A. That is my idea ; they thought so.

Q. It was just prudence that everybody exercised on such occasions ?—A. I thought it was a fact that they didn't know.

Mr. Bergen. You were away from home ?

A. Yes, sir.

Q. Where is your home ?—A. I lived at that time in Morrillton, and that was the first night I had staid down there. I had been riding down there on horseback and going back at night, and Mr. Clayton suggested I should stay all night with him, and we could get to work that much earlier. I didn't want to stay anyway.

After the introduction of testimony for contestee from Augusta precinct, Woodruff County, the committee adjourned to 9 o'clock a. m. May 7, 1890.

The following is the testimony of Womack :

E. H. Wamuck, called, sworn, examined, and testified.

Direct-ex. :

Q. Where do you reside ?—A. I live out here in Benton, Saline County.

Q. Were you in Plummerville on the 29th of January, 1889 ?—A. Yes, sir.

Q. What time in the evening did you go there ?—A. I think it was about 7 o'clock at night ; just about dusk.

Q. By what species of conveyance did you go there ?—A. I came down on a freight from Roselle.

Q. Where did you go when you got there ?—A. I went to Mr. Simms's hotel.

Q. How long did you remain there ?—A. I wanted to get a bed and sleep, and Simms told me his beds were all taken up and he didn't have any bed for me, and he told me where I might go over to Mrs. McCraven's. I went straight across to where Mr. H—— kept, and went to go across the creek on a log, and I went back down and got a man to show me the way up there, some time about dark.

Q. What time in the night did you get to Mrs. McCraven's house ?—A. I think it was about 7 o'clock, or a little after 7. I know it was pretty late when the train got up there.

Q. Did you get supper then ?—A. No, sir.

Q. Where did you get supper then ?—A. I got it from Mrs. McCraven.

Q. How long after you got there until you got supper ?—A. Just a few minutes. She told me she would fix me supper. They had all been to supper.

Q. She did fix you up some supper ?—A. Yes, sir.

Q. After you got your supper where did you go ?—A. I went into the room where Allnutt and Mr. Clayton was.

Q. Had you been in the room in the early part of the evening ?—A. No, sir.

Q. Your first appearance there was after supper ?—A. Yes, sir.

Q. Were you acquainted with either of these people ?—A. No, sir.

Q. Were you introduced to either of them ?—A. Well, not in there ; there—they was busy talking. Mrs. McCraven said she would introduce me to them, but they was busy talking, and I just sat down ; I didn't have anything to say.

Q. Did you know either of them at that time ?—A. No, sir.

Q. They were both strangers ?—A. Yes, sir : but I had learned their names ; Mrs. McCraven had told me at supper that Mr. Clayton and Mr. Allnutt were there ; she told me she would go in there and introduce them, but they was busy.

Q. What were they doing?—A. I believe then—I don't think they was doing anything but just sitting talking. They was very busy at their books, maybe, and was sitting down. I was sitting down near the table and Mr. Allnutt and Mr. Clayton was close to me, and they were talking.

Q. How long did they remain in that position?—A. I don't remember, but I think Mr. Clayton got up and Mr. Allnutt picked up a paper and was reading a paper.

Q. Sitting near the window?—A. Sitting near the table where the lamp was, right close the window.

Q. How long did they remain there at the table?—A. Well, I don't know exactly; within some 20 or 30 minutes, maybe longer; I couldn't tell exactly.

Q. What was Clayton doing during that interval?—A. Well, now I think I know he was walking the floor for some time.

Q. Was he talking to anybody?—A. Yes, sir; he was talking to Mr. Allnutt as he walked.

Q. Was any portion of their conversation addressed to you?—A. No, sir.

Q. What did he appear to be talking to Allnutt about?—A. Well, he was talking about the election, in the conversation, one thing and another in Conway Co. Well, Allnutt was telling him how they had conducted the election.

Q. In that tp. or some other?—A. In that tp. I don't know of any other, but I think may be somebody spoke about Woodruff; I paid no attention.

Q. Where did you say Allnutt was sitting?—A. By the table near the window.

Q. About how late in the evening was Allnutt sitting reading the paper?—A. Well, I expect it was something like half after 7 maybe. Of course it may not be just correct, but something a little after or half after 7 when I went in there, and I sat down there and they sat and talked some, and Clayton got up and Allnutt got the paper and sat down and was reading. He was sitting down there reading a newspaper.

Q. Well, what then?—A. Well, I, after I sat a while I said I had some writing to do, had some figuring to do. My business was stoneware business, and I had delivered some of my wares at Russell, and was shipping some back from Plummerville to Russell and had to go back there to collect, and get down next day to Little Rock. I had some figuring to do, and when he got up I sat down and was figuring some 20 or 30 minutes, and was writing. It was about 9 o'clock and I was tired and I concluded to go to bed. During that time I was there, almost all the time, Mr. Clayton was walking to the door, and then to the bed and then back to the door, so he walked and turned around back and forth. When I got up out of the chair, he come and didn't get more than half way sat down in the chair until the gun was fired, and I said to Mr. Allnutt the lamp had exploded, and he said no it was somebody had killed Clayton. And I said let's pick him up, maybe he ain't dead, and he said somebody shot him through the window. He said "That is just as I expected." He said he was looking for something like that. I said "Is that so?" to Mr. Allnutt, and he said "of course, don't you hear the blood running there. The blood is running just like water out of a jug," and I noticed it after he called my attention to it; at the time I didn't know. The concussion had blowed the lamp out and there was just a little fire in the fire-place. We could just see the body of the man to see he was lying there. We just walked into the other room where Mrs. McCraven was and she asked what was the matter, and we said somebody had shot Clayton. And just about that time there was three persons came in, she said they were her boarders, and we got a lamp and walked back, and we found he had fallen right back with his feet hanging over his chair; I don't think be ever moved at all.

Q. His feet were hanging over a chair?—A. The chair he was sitting down on. He fell right over and the back of his head struck the floor.

Q. His body fell over the chair?—A. Yes, sir.

Q. His feet were lying up over the chair?—A. Yes, sir; there was just enough fire for us to see his legs where they hung up over the chair.

A. You went back into the room?—A. Yes, sir, and he was lying there just as we left him.

Q. His life was extinct?—A. Yes, sir; we didn't see any signs of life.

Q. What time elapsed from the time the gun was fired until you went back in the room?—A. Oh, I suppose 5 minutes. I was afraid to go back there right quick. I didn't know whether they was gone or would shoot again, but I hesitated to go back, but finally we went back.

Q. Who went back?—A. Well, Mr. Allnutt I know he was in front and I know I was behind, and I think a man they call Mundon had come in. They had a lantern. It was not over three minutes that they come after he was shot.

Q. They came right past the window through which Clayton was shot?—A. That is the way I think they come. Of course I was listening for everything made any noise and I could hear them walking right round, and when they come we didn't know hardly whether to let them in or not, but Mrs. Cravens knew their voice.

Q. Did you hear anybody immediately after the report of the gun—did you hear anybody going away from the outside?—A. No, sir; I didn't hear a thing.

Q. At the time that you were sitting there at the window writing at the table, you didn't hear anything?—A. I hadn't noticed any noise.

Q. No noise from the outside there? How long after you left that seat before Clayton was killed?—A. I don't think it could have been more than a minute or two minutes; that is my recollection.

Q. Had you just gotten out of your seat?—A. I just walked off in front of the fireplace and was a little chilly, and I just started to the fireplace and he went and sat down in the chair, and before he got himself seated, he was just about in a stooping position, a sort of half-sitting down position, talking to Allnutt. He was talking to Allnutt all the while. He was in this position when he was sitting down, stooping, and had his hands in his pockets, and he had been walking the floor with his fingers in his pockets.

Q. Did you remain there the balance of that night?—A. Yes, sir.

Q. Do you recollect what kind of a *curtain* hung over the window?—A. Yes, sir; it was just a calico curtain; it lacked about two inches I suppose of covering the window where it parted.

Q. Do you recollect that curtain, what its condition was there?—A. I think the curtain had a hole that was left there as it hung, separated but not far. It lacked an inch and a half I suppose of covering the window at the bottom; it spread apart a little.

Q. Did the shot destroy the curtain in any way?—A. It tore a hole in the side near the middle of the window. I don't think it tore it to the edge. You could put your fist through the hole.

Q. The curtain separated of its own volition?—A. Yes, sir.

Q. Where did you remain the balance of the night?—A. Well, I stayed up with the corpse until about 1 o'clock, or I reckon it was about 12 or 1 when I went to bed.

Q. Did you hear anybody around there during the balance of the night while you were staying up?—A. No, sir.

Q. Something has been said about a blanket having been put up at the window?—A. I think Mr. Allnutt put it up some time after; he said he didn't like the looks of that window. He put up the blanket over it; I think he did; I won't say. It may be Mr. Armstrong put it up; I ain't positive. Somebody put up that blanket and he suggested to somebody to help to put it up.

Q. Something has been said about some tracks being about there around the window next morning.—A. There was.

Q. Did you have any occasion to look at them?—A. Yes, sir; I got up and looked at them.

Q. Before many people had been about the door?—A. There was a few had been about the door. Those who stayed about there all night probably had been out.

Q. What tracks at the window did you discover?—A. I looked; there had been two persons around there, walking, and there was, it looked, about a No. 8 shoe, and I didn't notice the length of it.

Q. Now did you make any observation under both windows?—A. No, sir, I didn't; only the window where the shot was fired.

Q. That was the window near the chimney?—A. Yes, sir.

Q. Did you make any attempt to trace these tracks?—A. I did, just to the garden gate. I was—I saw it, walked up right to a little garden gate and went through that garden gate and I didn't follow that up any further than the first gate in the garden; but some parties had passed out where there was some palings off the fence, and I think they come and went back the same way, from the looks of the tracks.

Q. Was there any path which led from the garden gate?—A. I don't think there was any track.

Q. No track?—A. There was tracks, but no regular path where the people went in and out.

Q. Was that a dark night?—A. I think it was starlight; there was no moon, it was tolerably dark, I think, is my recollection.

Q. How wide was that gate?—A. I suppose 3 feet to three and a half.

Q. Had it any fastening?—A. I don't remember now whether there was any shut to the gate or not; it was wide open.

Q. In passing through that *gate* going out towards the *garden* what point would that run to, the road?—A. No, sir.

Q. That is not the point that runs out to the road?—A. No, sir; there is *woods* back of the garden.

Q. I understand your best impression is these tracks came through that gate originally?—A. From the signs it appeared to me that it looked like the same tracks had come there.

Q. And the persons who came through were familiar with the opening of the fence ?—A. That's the way I think they came from what I could see. I don't know whether they was familiar with it or not. I just went to the first gate.

Q. How long did you remain at Plummerville after that ?—A. I left and came down when the corpse come. I got through with my business and came down.

Cross-ex:

Q. There was no one in the room but Allnutt and yourself ?—A. No, sir.

Q. Did Allnutt stay all night ?—A. Yes, sir ; he stayed all night.

Q. Who else was there during the night ?—A. There was nobody, until after the shooting several came in. Mr. Armstrong came in there—was staying up with the corpse. Several I didn't know came in when they heard of it.

Q. What did you do with the body ?—A. Well, we moved it back out of the blood, and I think they put a quilt under him and one under his head, they got a double quilt and put it under his head, and laid one over him and moved him out of the blood.

Q. Was he straightened out ?—A. Yes, sir.

Q. You think there was a quilt under him and may be something over him ?—A. I think there was. I know there was a quilt doubled up and put under his head.

Q. There was a watch kept up all night ?—A. Yes, sir ; Mr. Armstrong staid up awhile, and some others after I went to bed.

Q. Was there a quilt laid under him, and something over him, or just something under him ?—A. I think there was something over him ; I don't remember particularly.

Q. There was several came in there, but only four of you kept watch ?—A. Yes, sir.

Q. Who kept watch with you ?—A. Mr. Armstrong was up as long as I staid there.

Q. Then you went to bed, and who got up, Mr. Allnut ?—A. Mr. Allnut, I think, stayed ; he was staying up after I went to bed ; I think he stayed up all night, but I don't know.

Q. Where were you next morning ?—A. After breakfast I went down to finish delivering my ware.

Q. Did W. T. Hobbs keep watch that night ?—A. I don't know. I know Mr. Hobbs very well, but there was so many and I was kind of excited.

Q. Did everybody seem to be very attentive in doing what they could that night ?—A. Yes, sir ; Mr. Armstrong said he would go right off and send off some dispatches as soon as he could, and we stayed there and he went off to send off some dispatches and was moving around pretty pert.

Q. Did everybody seem to be attentive ?—A. Why, they appeared that way to me.

Q. Did you see any difference between the attention given there and what is ordinarily given when anybody is dead and the people gather about ?—A. They seemed to be all right smart excited about it.

Q. Who took charge of his effects, if you remember ?—A. Next morning ?

Q. Well, any time there ; who took charge of his pocket-book, or anything of the kind ; did anybody look after that ?—A. Well, it seems to me like the marshal did ; I forget his name. I think somebody spoke about getting the marshal. Perhaps Mr. Carroll Armstrong was there present.

Q. Who seemed to superintending it or to be in charge ?—A. Mr. Armstrong.

Q. Do you know whether Mr. Allnut took charge of his satchel, or anything, or what Mr. Allnut did about there ?—A. I think probably he did take charge ; yes, sir, I think he did.

Q. Did he seem to be interesting himself ?—A. He seemed like he was interested right smartly, so far as going out of doors and running around is concerned ; I think Mr. Armstrong did most of that ; I didn't think Mr. Allnut went out that night.

Q. Was there any pursuit organized that night by any one that you know of ?—A. By Mr. Allnut ?

Q. By anybody ?—A. No, sir ; I don't know that there was.

Q. What did Mr. Allnut do in the way of finding out who did the shooting ? Did he do anything ?—A. No, sir ; he never went out of the house up to the time I went to bed.

Q. Did he ask anybody else to go out around ?—A. Not that I heard of.

Q. Do you know that he took any steps or have any of the officers to do anything ?—A. I don't know but he did.

Q. You think he didn't go out of the house ?—A. I am satisfied he didn't go out as long as I was up ; I heard him say he wouldn't go out.

Q. You think he was a little alarmed ?—A. Yes, sir ; he was a right smartly scared, and so was L

Q. You don't know of his asking any one else to go ?—A. No, sir.

Q. You know whether he requested anybody to send for any officer ?—A. I don't remember of hearing him request anybody at all ; I don't remember of hearing him say anything about it.

Mr. BERGEN. How long had you been in Plummerville ?

A. I just came that night about dark, I reckon.

Q. Who had you seen after you arrived in Plummerville ?—A. I hadn't seen anybody, except I went to Mr. Sims at the hotel, and he told me he didn't have any bed for me, and told me I could get a bed over at Mrs. McCravens's.

Q. Who did you see before you left Plummerville, in a business way ?—A. I saw all the merchants; I had a bill of crockery there to deliver to most all the merchants.

Q. What was the object of your visit to Plummerville ?—A. It was to deliver stoneware; I was in the crockery business.

Q. Did you represent a mercantile business ?—A. No, sir; I represented stoneware and crockery; I represented that business down there.

Mr. LACEY. How high above the window-sill did the shot come in ?

A. Well, sir, I think about a foot or a little over.

Q. Did it go in through the second pane of glass ?—A. I think the second pane.

Q. Very near the center of the window ?—A. Yes, sir; it came in between where the curtains were apart.

Q. Did some of the shot go through both curtains ?—A. No, sir; it seemed to me the shot was slanted and just put a hole through one curtain.

Q. Suppose the window was where I am, it was just about this way from the window ?—A. The window was right here, and he shot him as he came along and sat down.

Q. How was his face; was it turned towards the window as yours is towards me ?—A. No sir; but about this way; he was looking towards Mr. Allnut.

Q. So that the murderer had apparently fired the shot into his ear ?—A. Yes, sir; he shot him as he was sitting down.

Q. In the act of sitting down ?—A. Yes, sir.

Q. You heard no confusion nor anything of the kind ?—A. No, sir.

Q. Did you notice the tracks next morning ?—A. Yes, sir; I noticed the tracks.

Q. Did you see where the man had fallen down ?—A. No, sir.

Q. Did you hear since any one saw where a man had fallen down ?—A. No, sir; I heard where they had went against the fence and went out at the gate.

Q. Did you notice tracks at the window looked as though a man had been moving around ?—A. Yes, sir; it appeared so.

Q. Was it a single track ?—A. It appeared to me he had been tramping around a little; several tracks together.

Q. As though these men had to stand there and watch him for awhile ?—A. It looked like they had been moving around there a little.

Mr. COOPER. The tracks of two different men ?

A. It looked to me like it was.

Q. Different size tracks or different foot-gear ?—A. Yes, sir; I think it appeared they both had on overshoes, if there was two of them. Of course one man could have made those tracks.

Q. What was your opinion at the time ?—A. My opinion was there was two.

Mr. MAISH. Did you notice whether one of them had new rubbers on ?

A. I don't know whether they was new rubbers or not.

Q. You could tell it from the marks ?—A. I could tell they was rubber overshoes, but I don't know whether they was new or not.

Mr. McCAIN. Did you inquire to see if you could get any clew as to who had perpetrated that act the next morning ?

A. No, sir; I did not.

Q. You didn't hear of anything you would regard feasible ?—A. Not a word. Everybody seemed to be astonished, and everybody of course was excited, and didn't know hardly what to do. That was the fact about it. It appeared to me that way—that they didn't know what to do or what steps to take the next morning.

Q. Didn't Maj. Breckinridge write you once to get the particulars ?—A. Well, yes. I didn't get the letter direct from Breckinridge; Armstrong wrote me.

Q. Did you write to Breckinridge ?—A. Yes, sir.

Q. You say you wrote to him ?—A. No; I didn't write to Breckinridge; I just answered Carroll Armstrong's letter. It was a request of Breckinridge to know the particulars.

Q. Do you know that Mr. Armstrong received the letter ?—A. Yes, sir; I think he did. I think he told me so. I know it was a request of Mr. Breckinridge; he sent the letter to Morrilton.

Q. Did you see the people there next morning ?—A. Yes, sir.

Q. How did the people talk about it next morning, or did you hear anybody talk about it ?—A. No; I did hear people talk about it some. They seemed to regret it very much that it had happened.

Q. Did they seem to feel considerable interest in the occurrence ?—A. Yes, sir; they talked that way.

Q. Did you get from them any idea of how that had occurred or anything ?—A. Well, no, sir; I didn't. They seemed to be astonished.

It will be seen that all the evidence so far is circumstantial. The people were almost stupefied with astonishment, and when Mr. W. H. H.
Clayton arrived next morning they were nearly all at the building
where the coroner's inquest was held or was being held. Even Mr. Alnut was there, and he was held there by his deep interest in the tragedy
and proceedings until after the body was taken away.

To still further show the state of public sentiment there at the time, a
very important feature in guiding suspicion, we call attention to the
statements and complaints upon this score of Mr. W. H. H. Clayton
and to such as have been circulated generally.

It has been said that Col. Clayton was forced to go to Mrs. McCravens's house, on the edge of the little town, being suspiciously denied
lodging at the stopping place near the railroad. Mr. Womack had to
do the same, for the assigned reason that the other place was full or the
man's wife was sick. Mrs. McCravens was a sister of a brave officer in
the Union army, and could hardly be looked upon with suspicion. No
suspicion is attached by any one, except in this alleged connection, to
the keeper of the other boarding-house. Mr. Clayton says the people
did not come about him. As Alnut did not come, the reasons that kept
him where the coroner's jury was must be accepted as sufficient to keep
the others. Besides, neither he nor they knew of his coming. All were
absorbed in the proceedings at and about the coroner's place of inquiry.

He says the people of the town put Mrs. McCravens up to charging
him a big bill for damages. She and her daughter both deny it. He
holds Mr. Armstrong responsible for what he considers the neglect of
his brother's body. Mr. Alnut shows that the body was decently and
tenderly cared for, and, while covered and arranged, was left on the
floor at *his* suggestion, Mr. Armstrong having desired to place it on the
bed. All the arrangements met the approval of Mr. Alnut and the attending physician, and Mr. Alnut took charge of the effects. He complains that no ladies met him. Mrs. McCravens and her daughter, Mrs.
Hall, were in the house, and Mrs. Hall explains that she was so frightened that she didn't know what to do, and she thought the gentlemen
would attend to the body. It is fair to conclude that the other women
of the place were shocked and startled and thought and felt pretty
much as Mrs. Hall did.

Plummerville is a little trading place on the Little Rock and Fort
Smith railroad, with but few inhabitants, and the township, including
the town, if it may be called a town, has a population of four or five
negroes to one white person.

The facts utterly discredit the idea that the community was "terrorized" or anything of that sort, as is so frequently expressed. As Mr.
Alnut says, the people were "astonished," and they evidently "didn't
know" anything. They evidently acted as such a community would
naturally act in perfect innocence, and yet in the immediate presence
of such a tragedy. It shows that the community was both ignorant and
innocent of the crime, and that hence we must look to individuals alone
for guilt, or, if we still suspect a community, then to some other community than the one in which the crime was committed. It remains to
be seen whether the deed points to the collective sympathy and guilt
of any other community, or simply to the guilt of individuals. This
character may be clearly determined while the actual perpetrators may
still remain wholly undetected.

We forbear any criticism upon the statements of W. H. H. Clayton.
They evidently were born almost solely of his feelings, and hence are unreliable as evidence. John M. Clayton was his twin brother, and the

grief and shock of his death can readily account for his conceptions. He was at one time very bitter in his views about the Hooper theory of the murder, thinking the governor had been misled, and that he was not properly justified in giving it the attention he did. This he has already corrected when the governor said to him (page 555 testimony):

After reading the Sater letters and hearing the testimony, he said in his testimony that he believed that I was misled in some way to go off after a clew which would probably lead away fr m rather than t0 the murderers. Now, after reading the letters, and having a full statement of the facts connected with it, I would be glad if he would state now whether he now thinks that I had justifiable grounds for pursuing that clew or not.

W. H. H. CLAYTON. You had, sir.

We mention this, not as additional evidence of the unreliability of his statements and opinions upon this subject, for it shows that he is beginning to see the unreasonableness of some of his expressions, but we do it as an exhibition of his sincerity and to prevent our judgment of his statements from being construed as any reflection upon his veracity. His condition and the circumstances account for his errors, which call for sympathy rather than strictures. We doubt not the errors will soon appear as apparent to him as they must be to others. Censure here is only appropriate for those who knowing better continue to use these misstatements as facts.

But to fully present the preliminary basis of all right reasoning about this matter, we insert the testimony of Mrs. McCravens, and her daughter, Mrs. Hall, at whose house Colonel Clayton was killed.

Mrs. MARY ANN McCRAVENS, called, sworn, examined, and testified:

Q. Where do you reside now ?—A. Plummerville.

Q. Where did you reside on the 29th day of January, 1889 ?—A. Plummer.

Q. How long have you resided there prior to that time ?—A. 10 years.

Q. In what business were you engaged ?—A. Keeping boarders.

Q. State if on that 29th day of January John M. Clayton was b0arding at your house ?—A. Yes, sir.

Q. It was in your house he was killed ?—A. Yes, sir; me and my daughter live together.

Q. State what time in the evening the killing took place; if you know ?—A. About 9 o'clock; it lacked 5 minutes of 9 by our time-piece.

Q. Do you know whether your time-piece was approximately correct ?—A. I don't know. I can't say.

Q. How was it as compared with the town time ?—A. I don't know whether they had a time-piece in town, but I saw it lacked 5 minutes of 9 by our clock there.

Q. At what time do you usually have your meals ?—A. Well, about 6 o'clock.

Q. About 6 o'clock in the morning ?—A. About 6 o'cl0ck in the evening; I am speaking about supper.

Q. How about noon time ?—A. At 12 o'clock.

Q. Well, now, when your boarders come in there, did they c0me about when your clock was 12 and 6 ?—A. Yes, sir; generally.

Q. It seemed to be your clock was then about like it was in town ?—A. Yes, sir, it is.

Q. You say you think it was about 5 minutes of nine ?—A. Before 9.

Q. How many beds was there in the room in which Mr. Clayton was killed ?—A. Two.

Q. What number of pieces of furniture were in the r00m ?—A. Bureau, table, and chairs.

Q. How many chairs, do you recollect ?—A. I don't remember.

Q. Is there a fireplace in that room ?—A. Yes, sir.

Q. At which end of the house is it ?—A. The north end of the house.

Q. How wide is that fireplace ? What size stick of w00d will it take in ?—A. About that long, 2 or 3 feet; I reckon about two and a half.

Q. How many windows were in the room ?—A. Two.

Q. Where were they ?—A. One in the north end of the house and one in the east end.

Q. In the same room ?—A. Yes.

Q. What kind of a table was there ?—A. Just a c0mmon, plain table to set a candle on.

Q. Round or square?—A. It was kind of square at the corners.

Q. About how large was it across the top?—A. I reckon about that wide across. [Indicating.]

Q. You mean in length, or that much square?— A. Square.

Q. Was that a square table?—A. Yes, sir.

Q. How many days was Mr. Clayton in your house down there?—A. I declare I don't remember how many days he did stay there.

Q. You don't recollect?—A. No, sir.

Q. Now you ought to know.—A. I tell you I have been so confused, but I want to tell the truth; but I disremember how many days he staid there.

Q. Didn't he go there on Thursday evening before that?—A. I ain't going to say positively, for I don't recollect. I want to tell the truth about everything. The first was a gentleman with him, and they took dinner and in the evening they came over to our house.

Q. On Thursday?—A. I believe it was.

Q. Did Mr. Clayton and the gentleman who was with him—do you recollect whether they remained at your house during that time?—A. They came and spoke for boarding.

Q. Who was the man that first spoke for boarding?—A. He spoke for boarding himself; he never called Mr. Clayton's name; he just spoke for himself and another gentleman, and I took him in, and he said they would be there for some 8 or 10 days.

Q. How many parties were in the room when he came to see you about getting board in the house?—A. Well, I will tell you the room they occupied together had but one bed in it, and they slept together. It was a hall; there was just one bed in it they occupied to sleep in.

Q. Is that the room in which Mr. Clayton was killed?—A. No, sir; he was killed in the room where the fire-place was.

Q. Did they sleep in the room where the fire-place was?—A. No, sir; he slept in the place where the hall was I speak of.

Q. Was there any window in that room?—A. No, sir.

Q. Now as to the furniture in the other room where the fire-place was, how many beds were there when this first gentleman went over there?—A. Just the two beds.

Q. Who did you say it was spoke for boarding there; what was his name?—A. Mr. McCord.

Q. Did you change the position of the beds in that room at any time after Mr. McCord engaged rooms of you over there?—A. No, sir; not any.

Q. They remained precisely the same?—A. Yes, sir; the same.

Q. Did they remain in the same place?—A. Yes, sir.

Q. The table was in the same place?—A. Yes, sir.

Q. There had been no movement or moving of the furniture from the time he went there?—A. No, sir; not any.

Q. Can you tell me what happened immediately or what you did upon hearing the shot?—A. Well, I can't tell you nothing, only we was all scared to death when we heard the shot. I can't tell you much about it. Me and my daughter was just there alone and Mr. Wamuck and Mr. Allnutt was in the room with Mr. Clayton, and Mr. Allnutt came running in and we said the lamp was exploded, and he said no, somebody had shot Mr. Clayton, but none of us ever went into the room; I went to see if the lamp had exploded and set the building on fire; we never went in the room.

Q. How long was it after the shot was fired before anybody went in that room?—A. Just a short time.

Q. Who went into it first; do you recollect about that?—A. I don't recollect.

Q. Do you recollect who took the light in there?—A. I don't know.

Q. Who were the first persons that came to your house immediately after the shooting?—A. Well, I can't tell you; there was three gentlemen, but they didn't go into the room at all; they came in the gangway, in the door.

Q. Who were the first persons you saw there?—A. I don't know.

Q. It has been stated that some members of your family were the first persons there—who boarded there, came shortly after?—A. They came in a few minutes. Mr. Mundon and Mr. Elihu Durham and my grandson.

Q. How long was that after the shot was fired?—A. Just a few minutes; I couldn't tell exactly. They said they was about half way from our house and town where Mundon kept store when they heard the shot.

Q. They came on up there?—A. Yes, sir; but they said they never thought about it.

Q. How did they come into your house?—A. They came in another way; they came in at the south end. They didn't go in the room where Mr. Clayton was.

Q. What become of these people after they had come in the house; where did they go to?—A. They went to town to report the news of what had occurred.

Q. You knew then that Clayton had been killed before anybody entered the room?—A. Oh, yes; them gentlemen said so, Mr. Wamuck and Mr. Allnutt.

Q. Had either of them at that time been in there?—A. They left there as quick as

H. Mis. 137——48

they could, but if they went back afterwards before Mr. Mundon and them gentlemen come I don't know it; I was so frightened myself.

Q. You recollect who came up there that night after that, after those people that belonged to your family ?—A. I don't think anybody else belonged to the family.

Q. I meanyafter those people that stayed in your family ?—A. I don't know; we never left our room.

Q. So you don't really know who came there ?—A. Oh, no, sir; there were a great many people passing in and out.

Q. Was you in and out of the room before that ?—A. I had been in and out of the room about 20 minutes before that.

Q. You had been talking in there ?—A. Yes; I went into the room to ask Mr. Clayton if Mr. Allnut could sleep with him. Mr. Allnutt had never stayed there with us until that night. Mr. Clayton said yes he could sleep with him, but Mr. Allnutt made so much fuss in his sleep Mr. Clayton couldn't sleep, and then I fixed a bed off in a side room for Mr. Allnutt, and then I went off around into the gallery and told my daughter we had to fix a bed up for Mr. Allnutt and I went back to tell Mr. Allnutt he could have the door open from Mr. Mundon's room to go into the room; I stayed there a little bit and talked and I had been out of there perhaps 20 minutes when I heard the gun.

Q. You speak about going into the gallery.—A. I went out into the gallery to her room.

Q. Did you see or hear anybody around there that night ?—A. No, sir; not at all.

Q. Where was the gallery ?

Mr. LACEY. The gallery is the same as the porch.

A. Yes, sir; it is a porch, and there was a side room on the north end of it.

Q. The gallery is on the south side of the house ?—A. No; it is on the west.

Q. While you had been out in the gallery could you have seen through the window into the room where Mr. Clayton was shot ?—A. No, sir.

Q. If there had been anybody out there they could not have seen in ?—A. No, sir.

Q. Had you any occasion to go to the door or to pass where you could have seen any person if they had been at that window that night ?—A. No, sir.

Q. Did you see anybody going away or running away from there ?—A. No, sir.

Q. Did you hear anybody running away from there that night ?—A. No, sir.

Q. Something has been said of some palings being broken off the garden fence.—A. Yes, sir; there were a couple of places.

Q. Were those places broken in the fence that night, or were they old openings in the fence that existed there before ?—A. No, sir; if it had been done before it was by some person unbeknowns to us.

Q. It hadn't been done in the day time the day before he was killed ?—A. No; I never noticed the side of the house, for our cookingyroom and dining-room are around on the west side of the house, and we never went around; sometimes it would be 3 or 4 days we wouldn't go around there.

Q. In tending to the ordinary cares of the house would you be apt to be around there to see them, or in that direction ?—A. No, sir; we hadn't been for a great while.

Q. You don't know when those palings were taken off ?—A. No, sir; I never knew they was off until the next morning after he was killed.

Q. What time in the morning did you discover them ?—A. The gentleman who was there found them before I did.

Q. Did you go out there ?—A. No, I didn't go out.

Q. Do you know whether the palings were lying there or had been broken off that gate-way ?—A. I couldn't say; I don't know.

Q. What condition was that ground out there as to decayed vegetation ?—A. There wasn't any thing there.

Q. Was there no weeds standing ?—A. Not to amount to anything.

Q. What had been kept in that garden—any cattle of any sort ?—A. No, sir.

Q. How came it to be eaten off ?—A. The calves had been in there; they got in at night; and we had it plowed up, and that killed the vegetation off; and we sowed mustard and turnips in there. There was no weeds

Q. Had they come up ?—A. Yes, sir; it came up—the mustard; the weeds and every thing was killed out nearly; there was no weeds in there.

Q. Did you ever have any occasion to examine tracks that have been spoken of here—to look at them ?—A. I looked at the tracks under the window.

Q. Something has been said about the tracks in the vicinity of the tree ?—A. That is right at the window.

Q. How far ?—A. As far as from here to this gentleman.

Q. 4 or 5 or 6 feet ?—A. Yes, sir; but it wasn't the window he was shot at; it was the north window, right at the chimney.

Q. You know whether those are the same tracks that had been there at the window, were afterwards discovered at that one ?—A. I don't know whether it was the same tracks or not; people had been around the house so much before I went out doors.

Q. This tree or rose bush was at what windOw ?—A. The nOrth window.

Q. There was tracks where the chimney was ?—A. Yes, sir.

Q. You don't know whether they was the same tracks on the other side or not ?—A. No, sir; for I never went tO look.

Q. Well, I dOn't know as I have anything else to ask.—A. Well, I don't know, but I want to tell everything as correct as I can.

Mr. McCAIN. There was no occasion or any hostility on your part or in your family ?

A. What's that ?

Q. You were all friendly to Mr. Clayton ?—A. Why, now——

Q. You had nothing against him ?—A. There was nobody with me but my daughter there of the family; we had nothing against him.

Q. Your family were Union people during the war ?—A. My husband was a Democrat.

Q. Some of yOur folks were in the Union Army ?—A. Yes, sir; my brOther. We all lived in the North. I havn't gOt no relatiOns in this cOuntry to amount to anything.

-Mrs. ELIZABETH HALL, called, sworn, examined, and testified.

Direct ex.:

Q. Where do you reside ?—A. At Plummerville.

Q. Where did you reside on the 29th day of January, 1889 ?—A. At Plummerville.

Q. How long did you reside there before that ?—A. Nearly 10 years.

Q. In what business were you engaged there in January, 1889 ?—A. Keeping boarders; a boarding-hOuse.

Q. State whether or not John M. Clayton was a bOarder in your family in the month of January, 1889 ?—A. Yes, sir; he was.

Q. Do you recOllect what time in the month he came there ?—A. No, sir; I don't.

Q. Do yOu recollect the day of the week ?—A. As well as I recollect it was on Thursday.

Q. State who came first, himself or who else to see about it ?—A. A gentleman came with him, McCord, I think was his name.

Q. Well, what length of time did he engage bOard for ?—A. I don't recollect, exactly.

Q. In which room of the hOuse did Mr. Clayton sleep ?—A. He slept in the middle room.

Q. In the middle one ?—A. Yes, sir.

Q. Was there anybody else in the room ?—A. No, sir.

Q. Was there a fire-place in it ?—A. No, sir.

Q. What Opening, if any, was there Out of that room intO what we call the north room ?—A. A door.

Q. How many pieces of furniture were on that north room where the fire-place is ?—A. At that time ?

Q. Yes, ma'am.—A. There was two bedsteads, a bureau, and a stand table.

Q. Was there a wash-stand in the roOm, or did they go outdoors ?—A. They went out on the porch to wash.

Q. Who made the beds in that house, principally ?—A. My daughter.

Q. Did you ever assist in that ?—A. No, sir.

Q. Were you familiar with the conditiOn of the furniture in these rooms ?—A. Yes, sir.

Q. How frequently did you visit them; once a day ?—A. Yes, sir.

Q. You must have been in the room as much as Once a day ?—A. Yes, sir.

Q. From the time Mr. Clayton came there until he was killed, had there been any change in the position of furniture in that room ?—A. No, sir.

Q. It was precisely the same the day he came there as it was the day he was killed ?—A. Yes, sir.

Q. You heard the shot fired ?—A. Yes, sir.

Q. Where were you then ?—A. I was in my roOm.

Q. What did you do then ?—A. What did I do; I didn't do anything; I just sat in my chair.

Q. Where did you think it was ?—A. Well, I didn t know where it was.

Q. When did you learn first where it was ?—A. From the gentleman who came in.

Q. How long after the firing of the shot before they came in or before they come tO you ?—A. It wasn't but a few minutes.

Q. What did they say ?—A. Mr. Wamuck said he thought the lamp had exploded, and Mr. Allnutt said some one had killed Mr. Clayton.

Q. Did any of you go intO the room to ascertain how that was ?—A. No, sir; we were afraid to go into the room for a short time.

Q. How long afterwards was it before you went in there ?—A. I didn't go in at all. I went to the door after——

Q. Was there a light in the room ?—A. No, sir; the explosion put the lamp out.

Q. COuld you see ?—A. Yes, sir; I cOuld see frOm the fire.

Q. There was a fire-light?—A. Yes, sir.

Q. In what position was Mr. Clayton?—A. I couldn't see his body; I could see his feet lying on the chair.

Q. His feet were lying upon a chair?—A. Yes, sir.

Q. Was the chair sitting up or lying down?—A. Lying down.

Q. And his feet were on top of it?—A. Yes, sir.

Q. How long was it before that or after that your son came up?—A. Well, it wasn't but a short time; I couldn't tell.

Q. Had you gone to the door at the time your son came up?—A. No, sir; they come up on the porch; I didn't know who was there, or whether it was some of the same ones, and I wanted to know who it was; Mr. Mundon called me and asked me what I wanted, and I knew his voice.

Q. Who is Mr. Mundon?—A. He is a gentleman from Alabama.

Q. What kind of a man is he; what nationality?—A. He had the appearance of being——

Q. Is he American born?—A. I think he is.

Q. Who suggested the propriety of your son and young Durham going down into the village to inform the neighbors?—A. I don't know who.

Q. Did they go?—A. Yes, sir; I think my son, Mr. Durham, and Mr. Mundon all went down, as near as I remember.

Q. Did you have any curiosity at any time to examine the tracks said to have been about the window?—A. No, sir; I did not.

Q. How long was it from the time your son and Durham went away until they returned to the house?—A. I wouldn't know; but a short time. Just as soon as they could go down and back.

Q. How long do you think that was?—A. I couldn't tell you.

Q. Did the people of the town begin to come there before they returned from the village?—A. I couldn't tell you, for I never left my room.

Q. You didn't go out?—A. No, sir; I didn't.

Q. Had you been out around the house that evening at all?—A. No, sir.

Q. Was there a fire-place in the room in which yourself and your mother occupied?—A. Yes, sir.

Q. You stayed there most of the time?—A. Yes, sir.

Q. Had you been in the room in which Mr. Clayton was killed at any time during the evening of the 29th of January?—A. No, sir; I was in there about noon.

Q. You have no recollection of being in there after dinner?—A. No, sir.

Q. What kind of a curtain was over that window through which the shot was fired?—A. A dark calico curtain.

Q. Of what thickness was it?—A. It was of thin, common calico; it wasn't very thick.

Q. Was it a perfect curtain?—A. No, sir; it wasn't a regular window curtain.

Q. Had it been torn?—A. No, sir.

Q. Was it wide enough to cover the entire width of the window?—A. Yes, sir.

Q. Did you look to see whether that window curtain was down or not that night?—A. The way it looked next morning it was down; it was down that evening when she went in there to fix the room, and it looked next morning as if it was down.

Q. What was over the window the next morning?—A. That curtain was over it, and a blanket.

Q. When was the blanket put up?—A. It was put up during the night.

Q. Who put it up?—A. I can't tell you; I was up in my room.

Q. Why was it put up?—A. I don't know.

Q. Do you know anything about that?—A. No, sir.

Q. Did you know it before morning, that it was put up?—A. Somebody called for a blanket to be put over the window.

Q. After Mr. Clayton was killed the blanket was put over the window in addition to the curtain?—A. Yes, sir.

Q. Did you see the curtain next morning?—A. Yes.

Q. Was the curtain in perfect condition or was it torn?—A. It was torn where the shot went through it.

Q. Was that the only place?—A. Yes, sir.

Q. Where did the lamp sit in the room at the time Mr. Clayton was shot?—A. It stood by that window.

Q. Was Mr. Clayton sitting at the time or going to sit at the writing table so that lamp would reflect his position on that curtain?—A. Well, I don't know.

Q. Is it not true that the table was so close to the wall that it would have been possible for any person standing out there north of the table to have seen Mr. Clayton's form reflected on the curtain?—A. Well, I couldn't tell you; I never noticed.

Q. How close was that table to the wall?—A. It was sitting by the wall.

Q. Then Mr. Clayton couldn't have been between the table and the wall?—A. No, sir.

Q. How close was the table to the window?—A. Well, the table was right at the fire-place, as close as it could be put in, and right in the corner of the room. It had been sitting there all winter.

Q. Now, to get that fixed in your mind, could that lamp have been so placed on that stand as to reflect the shadow of any person on the curtain of that window ?—A. I don't know.

Q. Think it over in your mind.—A. I couldn't tell you that.

Q. I understand you to say this table here was up in the corner of the room?—A. Yes, sir.

Q. Right in the corner of the room ?—A. Yes, sir.

Q. In which corner ?—A. The north corner.

Q. The north corner of the room ?—A. Yes, sir.

Q. How wide is that table and how long ?—A. It is about square.

Q. A couple of feet across ?—A. As wide as 2 feet or two and a half—it is about 2 feet, I think.

Q. That occupied the north and east corner of the room ?—A. Yes, sir.

Q. The table, then, was up in the corner ?—A. Yes, sir.

(The witness here illustrated by a square piece of paper the location of the furniture in the room.)

Q. How wide is that window ?—A. It is just a small window.

Q. Did you ever observe that the curtain was torn before or until after Mr. Clayton was killed?—A. No, sir.

Q. Do you think it had been torn before that time?—A. No, sir.

Q. Do you think if it had been torn you would have seen it or noticed it?—A. I think I would.

Q. How long had the furniture in that room occupied the position it did when he was killed?—A. We took the carpet up immediately after it.

Q. Then the position of the furniture had been changed?—A. Yes, sir, we changed it.

Q. After the shooting?—A. Yes, sir.

Q. Now, do you recollect what day that was?—A. It was the next day after he was taken home.

Q. Where was the bureau ?—A. We stood the bureau over then by the window.

Q. Where was the table placed ?—A. As well as I remember we stood the table there where the bureau was.

Q. The bureau was placed where the table was?—A. Yes, sir.

Q. And the table was placed where the bureau was ?—A. Yes, sir.

Q. The bed remained without change?—A. Yes, sir.

Q. No change was made in the position of the bed ?—A. No, sir.

Q. I am not certain, but think you told me you had been out during the evening ?—A. No, sir; I hadn't been out.

Q. To look out around the house ?—A. No, sir.

Q. Where did you get the wood you had been burning in this fire-place ?—A. Out on the south side of the house.

Q. I thought perhaps in the course of the evening you had been out around that place where you could have seen the window through which Mr. Clayton was shot?—A. No, sir.

Q. You are usually in the opposite side of the house ?—A. Yes, sir.

Q. In the performance of household duties did you see the north side of the house ?—A. No, sir; not a great deal.

Q. The wood-pile is on the other side of the house ?—A. Yes, sir.

Q. In entering the house did you enter on the south or north ?—A. The south side.

Q. So that the young men from town came in from the south side ?—A. Most always.

Q. Did the neighbors coming from beyond you; did they come by that window or pass by it?—A. No, sir.

Q. They passed by the south side too ?—A. Some come from the front or east side of the house.

Q. I understood you to say the next morning you saw a hole in the curtain—the curtain was torn?—A. Yes, sir; where the shot went through.

Q. What kind of a hole did it make, if you remember?—A. I don't remember.

Q. Did it frizzle it out and make a hole through it?—A. It frizzled it out, as well as I remember.

Q. What was the size of the hole, as near as you remember?—A. I couldn't tell you. It was a great size of a place.

Q. As big around as your hand ?—A. No, sir.

Q. It cut out to the lower part of the curtain ?—A. It jutted through over the lower point of the crease.

Q. I mean did the hole cut out through the lower part of the curtain ?—A. No, sir.

Q. It just made a hole, but didn't tear it out all the way down ?—A. No, sir.

Q. Was that curtain powder-burnt any ?—A. Not as I ever seen.

Q. I understood you to say the furniture hadn't been changed in the room until what time? Until the time after he was shot ?—A. No, sir; it was not.

Q. It remained in the same precise place ?—A. Yes, sir.

Q. What number of persons have boarded in the house during that time that Mr. Clayton had been there, McCord, Mundon, Durham, Wamuck, Allnutt?—A. I couldn't tell you.

Q. Any strangers?—A. No, sir; only some Mr. Clayton brought there.

Q. Where did you reside before you come to Plummer?—A. I resided in Portland.

Q. In what county and State is that?—A. Conway Co.

Q. What direction?—A. South.

Q. Were you acquainted with Thomas Hooper in his life-time?—A. No, sir.

Q. The one who went to Cal.?—A. No, sir.

Q. You never seen him?—A. No, sir.

Cross-ex.:

Q. How many people were in the room at the time this occurred? You say there were three?—A. Boarding there?

Q. Well, no. How many were in the house when the shot was fired; how many of the family?—A. There was Mr. Allnutt, and Mr. Wamuck was there in the room, and they came into our room after the assassination.

Q. Did anybody give any attention of any kind to the body of Mr. Clayton?—A. I couldn't tell you; I never left my room.

Q. You didn't?—A. No, sir.

Q. Why did you not give him some attention?—A. I was so frightened that I didn't know what to do. and I thought the gentlemen would attend to that.

Q. Well, how much did you charge Judge Clayton for the damage done there?—A. For the damage done there?

Q. Yes.—A. $15.

Q. You wanted him to pay some more than that?—A. Yes, sir.

Q. How much did you want him to pay?—A. As well as I remember, it was $30.

Q. Don't you think it was a little steep?—A. No, sir, I don't; of course we wasn't the cause of it, and our house was awfully torn up.

Q. You finally had him pay you $15?—A. Yes, sir.

Mr. COOPER. Did you advise with anybody as to how much you should charge?—A. No, sir.

Q. Did your mother advise with any body down town as to how much you should charge?—A. Not that I know of.

Mr. McCAIN. Do you think $15 didn't overpay you a little.

A. No, sir; I don't.

Mr. McCLURE. Do you recollect when Gov. Clayton came down there?—A. To our house?

Q. Yes.—A. No, sir.

Q. Do you recollect, perhaps the day after Clayton's body was taken away, that the train came by and a gentleman came up?—A. Yes, sir.

Q. Was that curtain in the same condition then as it was the next morning after the deed had been done?—A. Yes, sir.

Q. It was the same curtain that hung there then?—A. Yes, sir.

Q. Was it the same curtain that was there when the people came up after his body; the undertaker and Mr. Clayton's brother?—A. Yes, sir.

Q. It was in that condition that you speak of?—A. Yes, sir.

Mr. McCAIN. How far was the shot from the edge of the window sash?

Q. Well, it didn't seem to be——

Q. Was it through the middle pane or one of the side panes?—A. There was but two panes in the sash in the small window.

Q. What was the size of the pane the shot passed through?—A. I declare I couldn't tell you.

Q. Was it about 12 inches long?—A. Yes, sir; I think it would measure that.

Q. About as wide as this pencil, say 6 inches wide or wider than that?—A. I think they were wider than that.

Q. Did it go through the middle of one of those panes or through the edge of one of those panes?—A. I couldn't tell you.

Q. Did it break the entire pane out?—A. Yes, sir; it shattered it all to pieces.

Q. Did it spread the curtain or go through the edge of the curtain; or did it go through the middle of the curtain?—A. Well, there is two pieces of the curtain—two widths, and it went through one width of the curtain.

Q. It went through but one width of the curtain?—A. Yes, sir.

Mr. COOPER. Did it make a hole through the curtain, or just a niche in the curtain?

A. It just cut a niche in the curtain.

Q. It didn't cut a hole?—A. There was some of both sides, as well as I remember.

Q. Both sides had a hole?—A. Yes, sir.

Q. Where the shot went through?—A. Yes, sir.

Mr. McCAIN. You think it went through the outer part of the curtain there and at cut a notch?

A. That curtain is two widths of calico, and it wasn't sewed up all the way.

Q. It just went through one of the widths?—A. There was a piece taken out of the other width, as well as I remember.

Q. Now, did it cut through the edge near the window, or through the edge near the outside of the window, or the middle of the window?—It went through that edge?—A. Yes, sir.

Q. Do you remember whether it took a part of that edge, or did it make a hole in the middle of that curtain, or a piece of that part?—A. It was through the middle of the curtain.

Q. Supposing you had two curtains, it hung this way, didn't it? [Illustrating.]—A. Yes, sir.

Q. Now it went through that part and not through this part?—A. Yes, sir.

Q. It went through this part in the middle?—A. Yes, sir.

Q. It struck both parts?—A. Yes, sir. It took a little piece out of one side.

Q. And something more out of the other?—A. Yes, sir.

Q. Just the one place it took out; or did the shot go through a number of places?—A. It seemed to be all in one place.

Q. How big a place did it tear out, was it as much as 2 inches or 4 inches across it?—A. It wasn't that.

Q. Was it more than 2 inches?—A. I think it was.

Q. Was it as much as 3 inches?—A. I think it was. It was quite a large place.

Mr. McCLURE. I understand you to say, in the explanation you are now making, that the curtain was not all in one piece?

A. No, sir; it was sewed up part way down.

Mr. COOPER. Was it sewed up part way from the bottom or the top?

A From the top.

Mr. McCLURE. How near was it sewed up from the top to the bottom?

A. About midway from the top down.

Q. Was that the curtain you had at the time—it was in that condition at that time?—A. Yes, sir.

Q. Now when it separated, state whether it was closed to prevent people from seeing from the outside?—A. Yes, sir; whenever it was let down it was closed.

Q. How much did it pass below the window-sill?—A. When it was let down it came most to the floor.

Q. You don't know whether it made an opening there near the bottom?—A. No, sir; I don't think it did.

Q. I understand you then to say the curtain had not been sewed up all the way down?—A. No, sir.

Q. It was in two pieces of cloth?—A. Yes, sir, and when it was let down it all come together.

Q. How was it sewed together?—A. On the machine.

Q. Down to that point?—A. Yes, sir.

Q. How much did that lap in; you say it come together; how much did it lap, one piece on the other?—A. We just put the two pieces together.

Q. How big a seam did you take about?—A. I couldn't tell you; a common size seam.

Q. Just an ordinary sized seam, perhaps that distance from the edge [illustrating]?—A. Yes, sir.

Q. One-third of an inch, perhaps?—A. Yes, sir.

Q. Now, when that was put up there and hung down would that curtain come together and cover the edges?—A. It always come together.

Q. It always went together when it was let down?—A. Yes, sir.

Q. So that a person standing on the outside when the curtain was let down couldn't see through the window at all?—A. I don't think he could.

Q. Had either one of those pieces been torn?—A. Before the shot went through?

Q. Yes.—A. No, sir.

Q. Did you have that window up at any time during the 29th of January?—A. No, sir.

Q. Was that a window that could be raised?—A. Yes, sir.

Q. You could raise it to let in the air?—A. Yes, sir.

Q. Was it raised any on the 29th of January?—A. No, sir.

Q. Was it raised on the 28th?—A. No, sir.

Q. Do you think that window had been up at all?—A. No, sir.

Q. The window had a sash to it so you could raise it up and down that way?—A. Yes, sir.

Q. How many panes of glass were there in the sash?—A. There were two in the sash—four in the sash.

Q. So then there was 8 lights in that window?—A. Yes, sir.

Q. And you say neither one of those pieces of that curtain had been torn before that?—A. No, sir.

Q. If they had been you didn't notice it?—A. No, sir.

Q. Nobody had access to that window that day except Mr. Allnut, Mr. Womuck, and Mr. Clayton?—A. All the boarders were in there.

Q. That is a sort of sitting-room for the gentlemen? A place they went in during the day?—A. Yes, sir.
Q. While they were waiting for their meals?—A. Yes, sir.
Mr. BERGEN. How long had Mr. Clayton been at your house?
A. Well, I couldn't tell you the day of the month he came there.
Q. He had been there some days?—A. How many days?
Q. Yes, sir.—A. He had been several days.
Q. Who had been in your house that day?—A. Well, I couldn't tell you, there was so many of them there.
Q. I wish you would name them.—A. Well, all the boarders went there.
Q. Name them.—A. Mr. Mundon, Durham, I suppose went in there, and J—— and Mr. W. T. Hobbs, I suppose they had all been in there during the day.
Q. They were boarders?—A. They were at that time.
Q. Were those all the boarders you had at that time?—A. All the regular boarders we had.
Q. In addition to that you had Mr. McCord there, Mr. Clayton, and Mr. Allnutt. Did you have anybody else boarding there at that time?—A. Mr. Wamuck came there and stayed all night.
. When did he come there?—A. He came there for supper.
. Is that the first night he came there?—A. Yes, sir.
. He hadn't been there the night before?—A. No, sir.
. He took supper there on the night of the 29th of January?—A. Yes, sir.
Q. Who else called on you during the day?—A. No one that I remember of.
Q. Nobody else had been there during the whole day?—A. No, sir.
Q. I thought you stated a few minutes ago there had been so many there you couldn't remember who?—A. Well—during the day?
Q. Yes.—A. I think Mr. Clayton, as well as I remember, brought two gentlemen up there for dinner.
Q. Two came with him?—A. Yes, sir.
Q. Who were they?—A. I don't know.
Q. Now, who else?—A. That's all I remember of.
Q. Is that all you can remember, the two?—A. Yes, sir.
Q. Now, you have mentioned all the persons that came to your house during the 29th of January, have you?—A. All that I remember of.
Q. Was this house a one-story house?—A. One story.
Q. Which way does it face, north, south, east, or west?—A. East.
Q. It faces east?—A. Yes, sir.
Q. Has it a double front?—A. No, sir; it has a porch in front and a portico.
Q. Has it two rooms?—A. Yes, sir.
Q. And a hall between them?—A. Yes.
Q. And the parlor is on one side of the hall?—A. We don't have no parlor.
Q. Did Mr. Clayton occupy a room on one side of the hall?—A. He occupied the little hall to sleep in, he occupied the sitting-room during the day.
Q. You had no intercourse with anybody while Mr. Clayton was there at your house?—A. No, sir.
Q. How long had this curtain been up at this window?—A. It had been up a good while.
Q. How long had it been there at the time Mr. Clayton was killed?—A. 4 or 5 months.
Q. Had you been expecting Mr. Clayton to come to your house for a long time?—A. No, sir.
Q. When were the rooms engaged for Mr. Clayton?—A. Mr. McCord engaged the rooms for himself and a partner; he didn't call Mr. Clayton's name.
Q. With whom did you talk about the bills presented to Judge Clayton after the death—with whom did you talk about that bill you made out of $30 you said, who told you how much to make it out for?—A. Ma said she thought it would be little enough.
Q. You consulted with your mother?—A. Yes, sir.
Q. Who else did you consult, or any one else?—A. No, sir.
Mr. McCAIN. You say you hadn't seen anybody there that evening?
A. Any stranger?
Q. Yes.—A. Nor neighbors.
Q. There was no one you wasn't accustomed to about the house?—A. No, sir.
Q. No unusual visitor had been there during the day?—A. No, sir.
Mr. LACEY. Did you know of a barber stopping at your mother's a short time after the murder—a stranger?
A. Yes, sir.
Q. How long did he board there?—A. I couldn't tell you; just a few days.
Q. What was his name?—A. I couldn't tell you that.
Q. How old a man was he?—A. He didn't not look to be very old.
Q. Was he a young man 20 or 25 years or younger?—A. He looked to be of that age.

Q. Do you know why he left?—A. No, sir.
Q. Did anybody talk to your mother about him?—A. No, sir.
Q. And advise you not to keep him?—A. How is that?
Q. Did anybody come to the house and advise you not to keep him?—A. No, sir.
Q. You didn't hear anything of the kind?—A. No, sir.
Q. Did you learn afterwards he was a detective?—A. No, sir.
Q. Did you learn that while he was there or did you hear it at any time?—A. No, sir.

Mrs. MARY ANN McCRAVEN, recalled.

Mr. BERGEN. With whom did you consult about making out your bill?—A. With no person at all.
Q. It has been stated here that you consulted with some person out in town about making out your bill?—A. No, sir.
Q. Who did you say you consulted with?—A. Nobody.
Q. You didn't?—A. No, sir; I will tell you just what I thought; I just thought we was damaged that much. I had all new carpets and paid $31 for them, and it never looked like they could be cleaned up, and they were spoiled. I didn't go to see people to consult; I have just got a mind of my own. That's the way. I just thought I was injured that much.
Q. What did you give for your carpet?—A. I gave $31 for that carpet and the one that was on the hall, and the other was on the room, and they were just as muddy; I never did see such a looking house in my life.
Q. How much was your carpet destroyed?—A. It was destroyed and it spoiled the looks of it.
Q. The blood didn't cover the whole of it?—A. No, sir.
Q. Only a few feet of it, I suppose?—A. I seen there wasn't.
Q. Who came to your house during that day?—A. Nobody specially at all, but the boarders.
Q. Nobody came around there to inquire about Clayton?—A. No, sir; I never heard a person speak about him.
Q. Who stayed there the night before?—A. No person but the boarders, I don't think.
Q. Are you sure of that?—A. I tell you I couldn't state positively, but I am going to tell everything just as straight as I can. If any person stayed there but the boarders I don't know it. After Mr. Clayton was killed Mr. Wamuck stayed there and Mr. Allnutt; that was the first night Mr. Allnutt came there to stay. He was working for Mr. Clayton, so he said.
Q. How long had you had t ose curtains?—A. We had them a year or two.
Q. How long had you had that curtain put up to that window in that room as it was put up?—A. 3 or 4 or 5 months; I couldn't tell you the time exactly, because it was a dark window curtain and it didn't require much washing, and it had just been hanging there ever since away along in the summer.
Mr. LACEY. Now, when that barber boarded at your house how long did he stay there?
A. Why, he stayed two nights and a day and then eat his dinner and had to leave there in the evening, and he left.
Q. Did you learn that he was a detective or hear that he was?—A. I heard it said, but didn't know it.
Q. Did you know of his having any trouble there?—A. I heard he had.
Q. What was the trouble?—A. Well, now, I will tell you, you will have to get other folks; I wasn't there.
Q. You only know from hearsay?—A. It is all hearsay.
Q. Did any body make complaint to you about him?—A. No, sir.
Q. Did you have any talk with Mr. Pate about him?—A. I heard that, but it ise't so. I have heard a great many stories ain't so, too.'
Q. You only know how he came to leave there from what somebody else told you?—A. Well, he came to the house and told me that somebody had disturbed him; and I told him I would rather he would leave there; that I didn't want him to stay there; I didn't want anything that would cause any hardness; and he eat his dinner and never came back any more until they arrested him and brought him back
Q. Who was it first said anything about causing any hardness?—A I just stated that. You know we was in so much trouble and I wanted everything quiet at our house.
Q. Wasn't you afraid the person who committed the crime would make some trouble?—A. I have been in so much trouble about that. He went off withotu paying his board bill, but he paid it after he came back. He didn't pay the money, but he just gave me a pair of pitchers and towel and a razor and I sold them and got the money.
Mr. McCAIN. Who was that man?
A. He called himself Wilson, but I don't know his name.

Q. What was his occupation?—A. He said he was a barber. I don't know what he followed, but he didn't stay there at the house only about meal time.

Q. Who was it complained of him?—A. Nobody complained of him to me. He only come and told me and I didn't know; I can't tell nothing only what I know. If I hear what ain't so, but what I know I tell, and that's all.

Q. Was that a man somebody had arrested for stealing a razor? Was there any such thing as that? What did he say his trouble was? What was that about?—A. I didn't ask him.

Q. You don't know anything about that?—A. No, sir; I didn't ask him.

Q. You don't know anything about any complaint being made?—A. No, sir; they didn't make no complaint to me.

Q. You suggested to him to go away; why was that?—A. Because he said he had got into trouble and I didn't want him to stay.

Q. Was that about selling a razor?—A. No, sir; it was something about a letter; I think he said something about his mail; but now I don't know nothing about that, only just what he said, and I told him I would rather he would leave and that I didn't want him any——

Q. What did he say?—A. He just said he had got into trouble, and I said if that was the case I wanted him to go somewheres else.

Q. He didn't tell you what the trouble was about?—A. No, sir.

Q. Well, did he tell you it was about a letter, or did you hear that from some other source?—A. He said it was about his mail; that's what he said; but I never asked him in what way, or in any way.

Q. He didn't explain the details to you?—A. No, sir; I never asked him, only when he said that, I said I would rather he would go somewhere else.

Q. Who was it that the trouble with the razor was about, if you remember?—A. A colored man, I think.

Q. A colored barber?—A. Yes, sir; I think so. Well, I am satisfied that is what they arrested him and brought him back for, but I don't recollect the darkey's name.

We herewith give the diagram of Mrs. McCraven's house as published on page 610 of the testimony.

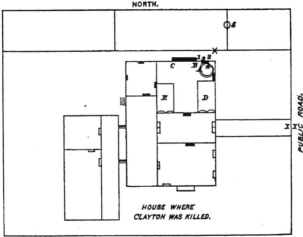

1 and 2 Where men were standing.
3. Spot from which shot was fired.
4. Window through which shot was fired.
XX Garden gate where they entered.
O. Hole in the garden fence where they entered; they returned the same way.
5. Where the pistol was found.
A. Clayton's position when shot, 6 feet from window.
B. Where Allnut was standing, about 3 feet in front and to Clayton's left.
C. Where D. H. Womack was sitting.
D Bed.
E. Bed.

We have given, then, the full testimony, as printed, of the four persons in the house at the time Colonel Clayton was killed, as indispensable to a beginning of any reasonable speculations upon the subject of his death.

So far as we know all the theories of the killing of Colonel Clayton are as follows:

First. That he was killed by the men who stole the ballot-box.

Second. That he was killed by the men who were under indictment.

Third. That he was killed by men who wanted to stop inquiry into the right of Mr. Breckinridge to hold his seat.

Fourth. That he was killed out of some grudge arising out of the murders committed before and during the period of martial law under his brother Powell Clayton's administration as governor.

Fifth. That he was killed out of rivalries and factional hatreds existing in the Republican party.

Sixth. That he was killed in an attempt to manufacture a mock outrage, and hence not intentionally.

None of these theories have been intelligently, systematically, or exhaustively inquired into by the committee, and some of them have not been inquired into at all. At a glance one can see from the status of the question as left by the testimony of the four witnesses who were in the house at the time of the killing that the most careful, intricate, and extensive inquiry would, in all probability, be necessary. The difficulties the case had presented to the State authorities, to individual efforts, notably to those of the brothers of Colonel Clayton, and to the intelligent inquiries of special agents of great metropolitan newspapers, all pointed to the necessity of great thoroughness if any reliable conclusions were to be reached. It was known that all these efforts had been baffled; and now a special committee, backed by all the power and resources of the Federal Government, was to give the matter an exhaustive and supreme overhauling.

They seem to have been dominated by the unfortunate sentiment and policy of General Powell Clayton, who, when governor of the State and engaged in torturing a previously quiet and peaceful people into outbreaks, wrote A. M. Merrick, as shown by the official letter-copy book:

Report to me every violation of law and every Outrage, giving all the facts, as we intend using them as political capital to influence Northern elections.

When men once engage in the "outrage" business as a species of political merchandise, they seldom take much interest in any discoveries which will stop the source or use of the supply.

In this way there appears to be a settled purpose to "work" John Clayton's death "for all it is worth;" and the State, the people, and parties whom it is of interest to accuse are assailed without testimony.

The best refutation possible, however, to the allegations of the majority is a plain statement of the facts as shown by the record. The first features to note are the expressions of public sentiment and the forms of public and popular action in the premises. Page 562 of the record discloses the following information, which the majority had to guide them:

In the first place, immediately upon hearing the report, Governor Eagle wired Sheriff Shelby to this effect: "Inform me at once as to the truthfulness of the report of murder of Clayton last night, giving particulars."

To this Jeff Wright, clerk of Conway County, in the absence of Sheriff Shelby, wired: "Clayton was shot through a window in the early part last night and killed; perpetrators of crime not known."

Governor Eagle then issued the following proclamation:

PROCLAMATION BY THE GOVERNOR.

Whereas it has been made known to me that on or about the 29th day of January 1890, in the county of Conway, State of Arkansas, John M. Clayton was foully slain by an assassin at the village of Plummerville, in this State, and that the perpetrator of this fearful crime has not as yet been discovered, but is now at large:

Now, therefore, be it known that I, James P. Eagle, governor of Arkansas, by virtue of authority vested in me by the constitution and laws of said State, do offer a reward of $1,000 for the arrest and conviction of the perpetrator, or perpetrators, of said crime.

In witness whereof I have hereunto set my hand and caused the great seal of the State to be affixed, at Little Rock, this 30th day of January, A. D. 1890.

JAMES P. EAGLE, Governor.

By the GOVERNOR:
BEN B. CHISM,
  Secretary of State.

The governor then wrote Sheriff Shelby as follows, indorsing a copy of the proclamation, viz:

STATE OF ARKANSAS, EXECUTIVE OFFICE,
Little Rock, Jan. 31, 1889.

Mr. M. D. SHELBY,
 Sheriff Conway County, Morrillton, Ark.:

DEAR SIR: Inclosed I hand you proclamation for reward for the apprehension and conviction of the assassin or assassins of Hon. John M. Clayton, and hope it will serve to cause the utmost effort to be made to ferret out the perpetrator of this crime.

Arkansas can not afford to rest quietly under this foul blood, and it is not right that the officers should do so, nor do I believe you will in this case, but I trust you will spare no effort to ascertain some clew that will enable you to locate the man who has committed this greatest of crimes.

Report to me from time to time any news you may obtain concerning this matter.

Very truly,

JAMES P. EAGLE, Governor.

MESSAGE TO THE LEGISLATURE.

The governor sent this message to the legislature:

EXECUTIVE OFFICE,
Little Rock, January 31, 1889.

To the General Assembly of the State of Arkansas:

I am officially informed that on the night of the 29th inst. John M. Clayton was foully slain by an assassin at the village of Plummerville, in this State, and that the perpetrator of this fearful crime, which has shocked the whole community, has not as yet been discovered. At the time the deceased was thus murdered in cold blood, he was engaged in taking testimony in reference to a contest for a seat in Congress, in which he was the moving party. He was, therefore, in the exercise of an inalienable right of citizenship, which none could have any disposition to thwart, except the most abandoned of men. He was a man of most unquestioned integrity and honor, standing high in the esteem of all classes of men; a man whose personal conduct could not have given well-grounded offense to any one.

Under these circumstances, this revolting crime, if suffered to go unpunished, is of a kind to bring the administration of justice into disgrace and to stain the good name of the State.

Going so far as the law would allow me, I have issued a proclamation offering $1,000 for the arrest and conviction of the perpetrator of this lawless deed; but I have felt that the unprovoked and flagrant atrocity of the act calls for unusual efforts for this conviction, and the enforcement of the utmost penalty of the law.

I therefore recommend that I, as governor of the State of Arkansas, and in her name, be authorized to offer a reward sufficient to induce the making of every possible effort to bring said offender to speedy justice.

JAMES P. EAGLE, Governor.

The legislature took up the matter immediately and the following bill was passed

THE BILL PASSED.—Act X.

AN ACT to increase the governor's contingent fund

Be it enacted by the General Assembly of the State of Arkansas :

SECTION 1. That the sum of $5,000 be, and the same is hereby, appropriated as a part of the governor's contingent fund, to be used in his discretion in the procuring the apprehension of any notorious criminal who has been guilty of recent brutal murder or assassination in the State of Arkansas.

Approved, February 13th, 1889.

When the bill was passed the following was issued :

PROCLAMATION BY THE GOVERNOR.

Whereas it has been made known to me that on or about the 29th day of June, 1889, in the county of Conway, State of Arkansas, John M. Clayton was foully slain by an assassin, at the village of Plummerville, in said county and State and that the perpetrator of this fearful crime has, as yet, not been arrested but is now at large ; and, whereas, on the 30th day of June, ult., a proclamation was made by the undersigned offering a reward of $1,000 for the arrest and conviction of the perpetrator or perpetrators of said crime: and, whereas, since said proclamation was issued a bill has been passed by the general assembly, now in session, authorizing the governor to offer a reward of $5,000:

Now, therefore, be it known that I, James P. Eagle, governor of Arkansas, by virtue of authority vested in me by the constitution and laws of said State, in addition to the $1,000 heretofore offered, do hereby offer an additional reward of $4,000, making in all $5,000 offered for the arrest and conviction of the perpetrator or perpetrators of said crime.

In witness whereof I have hereunto set my hand, and caused the great seal of the State to be affixed at Little Rock, the 14th day of February, A. D. 1889.

JAMES P. EAGLE, *Governor.*

By the Governor :
BEN B. CHISM,
Secretary of State.

This proclamation was forwarded immediately to Sheriff Shelby, accompanied by the following letter :

STATE OF ARKANSAS, EXECUTIVE OFFICE,
Little Rock, Feb. 15, 1889.

M. D. SHELBY,
Sheriff Conway County :

SIR : I herewith inclose proclamation of reward of $4,000 for the assassin of John M. Clayton, which, together with the reward of $1,000 heretofore offered, makes $5,000.

Yours, truly,

JAMES P. EAGLE, *Governor.*

To this letter Sheriff Shelby replied, assuring the governor that he was doing everything he could in the matter. A few days later he came to Little Rock, and had an interview with the governor in which he again assured the executive that everything would be done that was possible.

The governor urged upon the sheriff the importance of having the grand jury make a thorough investigation of the matter, to try to arrest the evil-doers, not only the murderer, but the men who stole the ballot-box. The sheriff said he would leave nothing undone in his efforts to ferret out the criminals. A meeting of the governor, judge, and prosecuting attorney of the district was arranged, and took place at the governor's office where the whole matter was talked over, and fully and thoroughly agreed among the three officers that they were to enter into the fullest investigation possible.

In addition to this, public meetings were held at Morrilton, Plummerville, Fort Smith, Little Rock, Pine Bluff, and indeed all over the State, denouncing the crime and demanding the detection and punishment of the guilty parties. As to the press, Gen. Powell Clayton says :

All the Democratic journals of the State at the time were vigorously denouncing this thing in as strong language as I could possibly dictate, if I should dictate all of it, and urging that the men should be brought to justice. (Testimony, p. 557.)

But in addition to all this public sentiment otherwise manifested itself in the most practical manner. Voluntary rewards were offered; $1,000 by the people at Fort Smith; about $2,000 at Little Rock; over $2,000, all told nearly $2,500, at Pine Bluff; some hundreds in smaller amounts from other places, aggregating nearly or quite $6,000 in addition to the official reward offered by the State. This makes a total reward of say $11,000, $5,000 of which was by the State and $6,000 by voluntary subscription. While this action was totally non-partisan, yet it is known that the action of the State government was by a Democratic executive and a Democratic legislature, and the overwhelmingly larger part of the voluntary subscriptions was by Democrats. This should have tempered the subsequent partisan proceedings of Republicans, but it has not had any appreciable effect that way. Never before in the history of the State had exceeding $1,000 been offered for the arrest and conviction of a murderer.

Any amount necessary in the opinion of the governor could have been raised, but we have the evidence of General Clayton turning back money he could not use, and of the Gazette, whose management and policy at that time General Clayton speaks of so highly, protesting that more money would be injurious rather than beneficial. This stands out conspicuously then, as the one case in all our history where, upon the testimony of all, the amount offered exceeded the wants, with no sign of exhaustion in willingness to give, and in which more than half of it was by popular subscription, the State exceeding any former offer fivefold, the people exceeding t sixfold, the total elevenfold, and as much more in reserve if the governor would only say he needed it. This is the conduct of the governor, the legislature, and the people of a State that the majority tells you needs to be bound by new and coercive laws.

In the face of these proceedings there appeared a remarkable campaign document, signed by General Powell Clayton and Mr. W. H. H. Clayton. General Clayton says it was issued several days, "four or five," after the funeral. It appeared simultaneously in the leading newspapers of the country, evidently having been furnished to the "Associated Press," and as it was in the Washington Post of February 4, the sixth day after Colonel Clayton's death, it was issued on the 3rd, just three days after the funeral. The composition of it began, and, indeed, it was issued, before the term for the court had begun; before very exhaustive investigations could have been made, and before the "vigorous denouncing" by "all the Democratic journals of the State" and the ample rewards could have had a full opportunity for their full and fair effect. As this is a comprehensive and initial outline of a policy, we insert it in full:

Powell and W. H. Clayton tell the tale of John Clayton's murder—they stamp it a political crime, and recount the preceding incidents indirectly connected with it.

Gen. Powell Clayton and Judge W. H. H. Clayton, brothers of the Hon. John M. Clayton, who was assassinated on the night of January 29th, have furnished the following statement to the Gazette for the benefit of the public:

That the public may understand the circumstances leading up to and culminating in the assassination of our brother, John M. Clayton, we desire, over our own signatures, to make the following statement of facts:

All agree that this was a political assassination. It will be therefore necessary for us to refer to the political condition and circumstances surrounding it. We do this in no partisan spirit, but only that justice may be done to the memory of our brother, and that a knowledge of the facts which led to his assassination may induce the people of this State to correct the evils from which this and other great crimes have sprung, and that, however sad the circumstances may be to us, his martyrdom may result in good to the people of this and other States. Although since the commencement of the last political canvass for State officers in Arkansas many political crimes have been committed in different parts of the State. in this statement, however, we will confine ourselves to the limits of Conway County, within which Plummerville, the scene of this murder, is situated, and only to those circumstances which in our opinion led to the commission of the crime.

Prior to the September election and during the canvass a political club was organized at Morrillton, the county seat of Conway County, with one Stowers, fresh from Mississippi, at its head. The club soon after resolved itself into a militia company, and about two weeks before the election, at a time of profound peace in the county, the Hon. Simon P. Hughes, then governor, not only supplied it with State arms, but furnished it with a full supply of ammunition. This was the beginning of the trouble in Conway County.

From this time until the day of election Stowers, with his armed partisans, almost daily paraded the streets of Morrillton. On election day their guns were deposited, loaded and ready for action, in a convenient place in the building in which the election was held. On the morning of that day the Republican judge of election, on his way to assume the duties of his office, on a frivolous and preconcerted pretext, was arrested, whereupon Stowers with his men marched to the polls, and upon his nomination and their votes another person was declared elected to fill the vacancy.

By these unlawful proceedings the election board, composed of citizens representing both political parties, was made solidly Democratic.

Whether Stowers and his men at this time were acting as a political club or as a company of State militia we are not advised, but certain it is their loaded guns were near at hand.

While at Morrillton these things were being done the citizens of the town of Plummerville, who were nearly all politically opposed to our brother, while those of the farming parts of the precinct were his political friends (the latter greatly outnumbering the former), collected at the voting place long before the hour fixed by law for the opening of the polls, and organized a full set of election officers of their party. When the two Republican judges returned they found their places usurped and the election in full blast.

The result of the September election so conducted in Conway County was a complete change of its political status so far as its officers were concerned, but not as to the sentiments of its people under these changed conditions. About two months thereafter the Congressional election occurred, John M. Clayton being the Republican candidate and C. R. Breckinridge the Democratic. The day before this election M. W. Benjamin, a prominent Republican lawyer of Little Rock, and one of Arkansas's best citizens, was sent to Conway County by the Republican State central committee, with instructions to use his best endeavors to secure an honest election. On his arrival at the depot at Morrillton he was confronted by an infuriated mob of several hundred citizens, who threw him from the cars, assaulted and beat him, pulled from his face handfuls of beard, and met all of his appeals to their humanity with kicks and cuffs and by shooting him in the forehead with a weapon of sufficient force to embed and flatten a bullet on his skull. A short time after this Mr. Benjamin died, telling his wife before his death that his sufferings were due to the treatment received at the hands of the Morrillton mob.

On the following day, being the day of the election at Plummerville, at the hour for opening the polls, the two Republican judges were on hand ready to perform their duties, but were ignored by the Democratic judge, who put in nomination two members of his own party, and upon a mere affirmative vote, without putting the negative, declared them elected, and they were installed. The Republican judges, not being permitted to act, accompanied by the Republican United States supervisor, undertook to open polls elsewhere, but were notified by Democratic deputy sheriffs, five of whom were present, that they would not be permitted to do so. Under these and other threats, they abandoned their purpose, and the Republican supervisor returned to where the election, as first organized, was being held, where he remained in the faithful performance of his duty until the polls were closed; whereupon the election judge, by whose illegal action the board was organized, as before stated, took the ballot-box and carried it from place to place through the town, followed however, by the faithful supervisor, Charles Wahl. At last, finding that he could not shake him off, he and the supervisor returned about 9 o'clock at night to the voting place, finding one of the other judges there. Remaining a few minutes, he again left, attempting to carry the box with him, which he only desisted from doing by the emphatic insistance of the supervisor that the box should be left at the polling place, with the other judge who was there.

About one-half hour thereafter four masked and armed men rushed into the room and at the muzzles of their pistols compelled the remaining judge and supervisor to turn their backs, whereupon they seized the box and poll-books and carried them away. We are informed by Wahl and other credible persons that the box so stolen contained 697 ballots, of which at least 372 were cast for John M. Clayton.

Upon hearing of these unlawful acts, together with many others in different parts of his district, he, Clayton, felt it to be his duty to institute a contest for his seat in Congress, and for the purpose of ascertaining the actual vote cast for him at the Plummerville precinct, that he might ingraft that fact in his notice of contest, he employed a responsible citizen named Alexander, of the Plummerville precinct, to obtain the names of those who voted for him, who obtained the names of over 450 such voters, when on the 17th of September his work suddenly terminated by reason of the events which we now proceed to detail.

On the seventeenth of December Wahl, the aforementioned supervisor, was inveigled into a game of cards at night in the back room of a doctor's office in Plummerville, where he was seated in close proximity to a glass door, through which he was shot by a would-be assassin, the ball piercing the top of his left ear and cutting a gash in his neck about three inches long; Wahl fled to the house of the aforementioned Alexander, where he remained until daylight, after which he reached his home and soon after repaired to Little Rock, where he now remains for safety. This attempt on the life of Wahl so alarmed Alexander as to cause him to abandon his work and fly from the State.

For the crimes above enumerated no man has been arrested by State or county authorities, nor has any official reward been offered. John M. Clayton went to Plummerville unarmed and unescorted, recognizing the futility of such precautions against the stealthy assassin, and believing that his opponent, Mr. Breckinridge, who was aware of the condition of affairs in this county, would be willing and able to restrain his partisans. While passing through Little Rock on his way there he said to Hon. Henry M. Cooper, in response to a suggestion of danger: "I do not, believe that I will be harmed, but the men who voted for me believe I was elected and so do I, and I will go there even at the risk of my life." And so he went. After having engaged for several days in taking testimony, about 9 o'clock p. m. of January 29, while in his room at his boarding-house, in the act of sitting down at a table near a window to write to his motherless children, he was shot through the window by concealed assassins a few feet from him, and instantly killed. We were unable to remove his body until 3.30 o'clock p. m. of the next day, up to which time the sheriff of the county had not appeared, being, in the language of his deputy, engaged in the more important business of collecting taxes. Nor had any citizens of the town made the slightest effort to trace or apprehend his murderers. The foregoing facts we stand ready to substantiate in every essential particular, every one of which we believe to be a material link in the chain of circumstances surrounding and leading to the inhuman murder of our brother, John M. Clayton.

POWELL CLAYTON.
W. H. H. CLAYTON.

The first lines assume a comprehensive conspiracy spreading, inferentially, at least, over the county, district, and State, as a fact. Everything stated are "facts." The State authorities and the people are practically requested to give over any attempts to vindicate the memory of John M. Clayton. The reasonable suspicion that his death grew out of political difficulties that had arisen at that precinct is crystallized into the proposition in the broadest terms, and here given the broadest construction by application, that "all agree that this was a political assassination;" Mr. Breckinridge is accused of a lack of "ability to restrain his partisans;" a general reflection upon his supporters thus generally indicted, or of not being "willing" to do so; and on this broad and settled basis a general reform movement is started to cover "this and other States."

To such wrongs as existed—and governments always find something to do—the State, circuit, and county governments were addressing themselves with a zeal that gave security to capital and citizens, and remarkable and undiminished immigration and prosperity attest it. Even negroes have continued to come into the State as was never known before, so much so as to seriously disturb the supply of labor in eastward and older Southern States. No "official rewards" were offered for certain offenses when it is known that the law did not provide for rewards in such cases, half of which here are grossly exaggerated and the other half are false. Democratic and Republican rewards were out for the ballot-box thieves, and the then management of the Gazette protested against its being increased. Any careful reader of this report will see how many of these reckless and partisan statements have been proven before the Federal court and by overwhelming testimony before the subcommittee to be unfounded.

The citizens of the town are reflected upon as if all of them were Democrats and in sympathy with murder, when it was well known that the township is strongly Republican and that Republican officials and citizens had acted in the same way as the Democrats, and that all were bewildered and utterly without a trace except the tracks in the garden and the pistol that was found near by. Then it closes with these words:

The foregoing facts we stand ready to substantiate in every essential particular, every one of which we believe to be a material link in the chain of circumstances surrounding and leading to the inhuman murder of our brother, John M. Clayton.

And yet, when called upon to prove them, Mr. W. H. H. Clayton responded in the following language:

We have published the statement made by us of those facts, and it seems to us that the burden of proof to disprove them is upon the other gentlemen. (Testimony, p. 437.)

When General Clayton is similarly questioned about such matters it is:

Well, I don't know about that. It seems that even if evidence was procured it would be almost impossible to hang them in that county.

And,

Oh, I can't make any suggestions. Well, I don't know what the State has done. The State may have done everything it is required to do—I don't know. (Testimony, p. 559.)

And so it is. They all know it for politics, but none of them know anything for conviction.

We do not say that Powell Clayton, so potential with the majority, desired to prevent the detection and punishment of the supposed murderers of his brother, which of course would stop the use of that event as political capital; but we do say that this is exactly the kind of an address best calculated to insult the public, to cool and drive off popular support from him, if not from the whole question, and to thus leave the whole matter more exclusively in his own hands.

It was in the face of these features that the legislature passed the additional reward act approved February 13, 1889, and, handicapped by this injudicious quarrel, the efforts at detection began. The act was delayed by having first passed one house in a form of doubtful constitutionality, and this had to be considered and corrected. The law of the State does not provide for expenditures for detectives, but upon the theory of stimulating activity by a reward for "arrest and conviction." The private subscriptions had been made upon this customary theory.

Hence for the time-being the proceedings consisted of what took place under this theory of expenditure, and of the personal expenditures of General Clayton and his brother.

Whatever may have been the theories and suppositions previously held as to the stealing of the ballot-box, whether it was done by Democrats to prevent the counting of the vote, or by negroes, as they threatened to do, as the Democrats had all the clerks and judges of election at this box, and the negroes said they thought they were going to "stuff" it, or by white Republicans from the same fear or to make a pretext to start a contest in case the actual vote should run close

H. Mis. 137——49

and the new House should be .Republican; or whatever it may **have** been, the generally accepted idea was that the men who stole the box, or the men in that county and locality who were under indictments, to which reference has been made, were the parties guilty of the murder. In a political way sympathies, etc., were charged to extend further, as shown, but general suspicion located the actual doers of the deed in this group.

The first thing to determine, before relating subsequent proceedings, is this list of men. They come under two heads, the indicted men and the ballot-box thieves. The men under indictments are easy to identify, for their names appear in the court records. It is difficult to assume that the election officials stole their own box, for with the fondness for whisky that the Republican Supervisor Wahl relates of himself on page 347 of the testimony, it would have been easy to have disqualified him for inspection duty. Then, the officials, being all of one party, could, if they wanted to do wrong, have stuffed the box instead of stealing it. But if they are suspected they at least are known. The only other Democrats ever mentioned in this connection with suspicion, either direct or remote, so far as the record shows or we have any knowledge, are first, Dr. B. G. White and W. C. Palmer, citizens of Plummerville, and the posse that came to Plummerville that night from Morrillton. Various witnesses state who these men were. There was no concealment as to who composed the posse.

Some of the men charged with stealing the ballot-box were also under indictment upon other charges; but these two lists and these two citizens embrace every Democrat suspected of the killing under the two theories, if they may be separated, that he was killed by the ballot-box thieves or by the men laboring under indictments. If none of the Democrats enumerated stole the box, then presumably no Democrat stole it. That we conclude, and as the majority hold that some of these men did it, then they must hold the same belief. But all of these men are known. They are not numerous, and their names are all in the testimony. They are as well known and as clearly identified as if they had been convicted by the Federal court of the offenses charged, instead of having been acquitted, as they were. Of course their acquittal upon these charges does not prove that none of them committed the murder. But these charges were for offenses real or alleged along in November, 1888, and the killing was done on the 29th of January, 1889.

Other facts and circumstances must be established as a new crime was committed. They might have committed the first crimes and not the last one. They would have to be tried separately. Therefore their acquittal by the Federal court is no embarrassment to this inquiry, for all admit that this list of names includes all of those who could possibly have been guilty under these theories, for we can not assume that if Republicans stole the box *they* would on that account have killed Colonel Clayton; and no Republicans in this county were being either prosecuted or persecuted by indictment or otherwise. Hence, for the purposes of this inquiry let us assume that all these Democrats were guilty of the previous acts, real or alleged, as charged against them, and with these two lists we are as completely equipped as it is possible to be for this line of investigation. These facts were, of course, as well known to the detectives and the State as they are to us, and we must, judge of the results of their efforts in the light of them.

The rewards of course stimulated generally to suspicion and search; but firmly impressed with the foregoing theory, as General Clayton and his brother frequently say they were, and as nearly everybody was,

their efforts can best be stated in their own language. W. H. H. Clayton details the matter as follows:

After he was buried we, of course, took steps to ascertain who the murderers were.
My brother Powell and myself wrote a statement to give to the State press. We then
sat down to devise some method and some means by which we could apprehend who
the murderers were. At Pine Bluff, before we left there, we wrote to Pinkertons to
send us their best man. Before we left Pine Bluff I believe we received a letter from
Pinkerton stating that they would send a man by the name of Woods here, that they
regarded as one of the best men they had. He came to Little Rock, and when we
came over we found him here. We employed him and gave him unlimited charge.
We paid him at the rate of $8 a day, all his expenses, and we paid every necessary
expense, or every expense he thought necessary, such as employing other men, sending them into the country, sending them into Plummerville in a thousand different
ways, anything he might suggest; we gave him *carte-blanche* to go ahead and we
would pay the bill, make it whatever he pleased. He made his reports in the first
place to me and afterwards to to my brother. I sent those reports to my brother and
he sent them to Mr. McClure. Nothing was accomplished, however. In a short time
after that we saw him here. We revised our plans, my brother and I. My brother
and I called on Governor Eagle for the purpose of urging him to do whatever he
could; we received very kind attention at his hands, and thought at that time that
he would do everything that he could to assist us in the premises. I went and wrote
to Judge Cunningham, judge of the circuit court, and to Mr. Carter, the prosecuting
attorney, asking them to grant me an interview. They stated to me they would. I
went down and saw them, and I think—I thought—got their hearty co-operation as
far as those two officers were concerned; and I think those two gentlemen did all in
their power. From that time on we have done everything we could in our power to
find out who these men were. (Testimony, p. 424.)

Again he says, on page 435:

I have spent thousands of dollars in that direction.

As the result of all this he says:

Wherever we could find a clue we run it far enough to see there was nothing in it.
(Testimony, p. 440.)

Also:

Our theory has always been that the politicians of Conway County did this thing
(p. 440).

Also:

And all the facts we had pointed in that direction (p. 440).

Also:

But I will state now we have no sufficient proof, nor do we know of anybody who
does; we have a great many suspicious circumstances, and everything seem to point
in one direction (pp. 435 and 436).

Also:

A thousand little impressions have been made on my mind in the investigation of
this matter (p. 427).

He also says, on pages 426–7, that he thinks men in Little Rock were
concerned in it.

Again, on page 442, he refers to O. Bently and Robert Pate as

The two men we believed to be the murderers of my brother.

And on page 436, in speaking of the guilt of his brother's murder,
he says:

Perhaps it extended as far as Pine Bluff.

This testimony was nearly all in response to questions addressed by
Mr. Breckinridge, who concluded as follows:

Mr. BRECKINRIDGE. I will ask in a general way if you have the names of any parties that this committee can interrogate that can fix guilt on any body in regard to
this offense; and if so, if you will furnish them to the chairman.—A. We will see
what we can produce during the investigation; Judge McClure has that in hand.—
(P. 443.)

General Powell Clayton's responses, if not so scattering, were even more vague and general. The sum of it is about as follows:

I mean to say, if John M. Clayton had not been a Republican he would never have been assassinated. I mean to say if he hadn't been a candidate for Congress in that Second Congressional district, he would never have been assassinated. If he had not been investigating the stealing of the ballot-box and making a contest in that election there, he would not have been assassinated.--(P. 557.)

This is broad enough to cover anything you want, dexterous enough to point anywhere you want, and vague enough to keep you from catching anybody. He might have added with equal propriety that if he had not been at Plummerville he would not have been killed.

Judge McClure has taken no special action as indicated by Mr. W. H. H. Clayton, so far as we know.

The most important witness in connection with this theory, and indeed in connection with the whole case, would seem to be the chosen detective sent by the Pinkerton's, a man skilled above all others, who have been associated with the case, and who has been so abundantly supplied with facilities and money as Mr. Clayton describes. General Clayton speaks of him as "the best detective talent," on page 556. Then he says he then thought "the men who stole the ballot box were probably behind the offense covering their own transactions."

Nor had he any difficulty in getting men to work. Mr. Clayton says, page 440, that "a hundred men wanted to go into the field as detectives;" and elsewhere we quote him as to sending men everywhere for Wood. We don't know what the testimony of this detective who had "charge" of the case would be. Mr. Breckinridge says he doesn't know. But we presume it would be the truth. A full examination of him is indispensable to an exhaustion of the case. Mr. Breckinridge offered to pay his expenses to Little Rock. He was refused his urgent request to have him there, but was positively promised that he should be here. He is still refused. He is likewise promised and subsequently refused as to Mr. Carter, the prosecuting attorney, Judge Cunningham, the judge of the district, both so approvingly spoken of by the Claytons. Also as to Coblentz, the Republican who found the pistol, as to the Meacham Arms Company and their invoice books, from whom we know the pistol came. All of these, acknowledged at the time as most important witnesses, are promised to be called at Washington, as well as others, and they are afterwards refused. There is something very strange about all this. Wood seems to have found out something or to have formed some opinion that is not wanted. All the push seems to have been taken out of the majority. They won't go ahead. They won't even keep their promises which are already out. Is this "thorough?" Is it just to Mr. Breckinridge and others whom they fiercely accuse?

If other theories have failed does not that make this conduct all the more significant?

The proceedings of Governor Eagle and Sheriff Shelby, of Conway County, are so intimately connected that we will consider them together, and what we say under this head will comprise an account of all that remains to be said in connection with the killing of Colonel Clayton in the present incomplete state of the investigation. The governor's action upon the instant of hearing of the death of Colonel Clayton, previously related, was that of a good and capable man, and it has been most conscientious throughout. He has so far exhausted every possible resource, and he has done all that was possible for a law-abiding official to do. Those who go beyond the law evi-

dently do so for revenge or for political purposes, and, as in the case
of Governor Clayton's administration, they are compelled to have a special act of the legislature passed afterwards to condone their own lawlessness. If such men as Governor Clayton and Mr. W. H. H. Clayton
have had to acknowledge that they could find no fault with the governor, as they do, it comes with poor grace for the committee to censure
him.

The sheriff did not sufficiently appreciate the case at first; but we
think he did his full duty after the governor saw him and impressed
the case upon him. He should have broken his appointment at the
remote point where he was engaged and employed at the time. He
should have immediately left off the collection of taxes and hurried
instantly to Plummerville. His deputy, Ollie Bentley, who was accused, and whom the sheriff at one time suspected of killing Colonel
Clayton, was overwhelmingly shown to be innocent. The sheriff's conduct towards him was discreet. It met the approval of the governor;
and all the stories about his crying in talking to W. H. H. Clayton, and
saying that the sheriff " was engaged in more important business," and
that the accidental killing of his brother while handling a hammerless
pistol, was intentional, we believe to be utterly groundless.

Mr. Breckinridge has shown not only the utmost zeal in supporting
the governor, but also a spirit of comradeship in doing for the memory
of his opponent, who was also his personal friend, all that could possibly be expected from an honorable man. His entire course in this matter has been both in spirit and in fact the reverse of what in prejudice
and injustice has been attributed to him. After the Clayton statement,
assailing him so pointedly, and the people of his district so bitterly, he
refused to enter into the proffered quarrel, and only after these matters
were taken up officially, nearly a year afterwards, did he begin to reply.

Governor Eagle, having no money to employ detectives, could only
act upon such clues as the hope of the rewards or other causes might
bring to his notice. Say in March, 1889, he had a letter implicating
two men—Hervey, one of the indicted men, and a man named Alnut, a
guard on a convict farm. Mr. Breckinridge returned home from Washington about that time, Congress having adjourned, and calling at once
to see the governor, he supplied him with funds to follow this up. The
governor did so, and found there was nothing in it. Soon afterwards
Mr. Breckinridge, partly of his own means, and partly with that of
other citizens of Pine Bluff, gave the governor $500 additional to use
at his discretion for detective purposes.

Before going away for the summer, he asked the governor to name
any amount of money he thought he might need and he would see that
he was supplied. This is related by the governor (page 560 of the testimony, and at other places, and the Gazette), then under the management that General Clayton approved of so highly, commended all this
action in the highest terms, but from the report of the majority it
would not be supposed that it was even taken.

Without following minor matters we will relate that the first heard
of the Hooper theory was in a letter to Sheriff Shelby from Jared Sater,
of Jeffersonville, Ind., of July 1, 1890 (testimony, page 618). In this
he simply says he knows a man who said in November, 1888, that he
was going to kill John M. Clayton, and that he believes from other evidence he either did or had it done. This letter left so vague an impression upon the mind of the governor, Mr. Breckinridge, and others, that
we have to refer to the letters at the time to definitely fix it. It was
one of the batch of letters, etc., that the sheriff, through Mr. Armstrong,

sent Mr. Breckinridge to read, at the request of the governor. **Mr. Breckinridge** writes the governor his views about them July 9, 1889. The only reference he makes to the Sater or Hooper theory is this:

Jared Sater should be asked the name of his man and witnesses. (Testimony, p. 624.)

No more is heard of this until the last of July, when the governor wrote Mr. Breckinridge the following letter, relating to a fuller letter that had been received from Sater.

STATE OF ARKANSAS, EXECUTIVE OFFICE,
Little Rock, July 29, 1889.

MY DEAR SIR: I inclose herewith copy of a letter received by M. D. Shelby, the sheriff of Conway County, from one Jared Sater, of Jeffersonville, Ind. I am inclined to think that the contents furnish a clue which, if properly followed up, will result in the capture of the murderer of Clayton. The sheriff (Mr. Shelby) requested that I furnish a part of the money in my hands to be used in sending a man out to California to investigate the matter. I declined to do this without first submitting the letter received from Sater by Shelby to you and having your views as to the propriety of doing so.

You will see from the correspondence that Mr. Shelby has agreed with Sater to give him half of the reward offered for the arrest and conviction of Thomas Hooper, the supposed assassin. I desire your opinion as to whether it would be better to quietly work up the matter through some one in California or whether it would be better to furnish money to have some one go out there and investigate.

Awaiting your reply, I am, dear sir, yours, truly,

JAMES P. EAGLE,
Governor,
By C. W. WALKER,
Executive Clerk.

Hon. C. R. BRECKINRIDGE,
St. Paul, Minn.,

P. S.—If you are of opinion that some one had better go, how would it do to have the sheriff of Conway County go?

Yours,

J. P. E.,
By C. W. W.,
Clerk.

(Mr. Breckinridge's brief, p. 18.)

The governor is "inclined to think" that this "will result in the capture of the murderer of Clayton."

This was not viewed so hopefully by Mr. Breckinridge in his reply. The governor stated that he did not furnish that letter because in stating his grounds of doubt Mr. Breckinridge wrote confidentially his opinion or doubts as to certain individuals. This is related in the colloquy on page 18 of Mr. Breckinridge's brief; will be found in Governor Eagle's testimony, and is familiar to all the committee. Not until October 12, 1889, did Mr. Breckinridge feel any confidence in this clue. The governor had written him on the 4th of October, as follows:

STATE OF ARKANSAS, EXECUTIVE OFFICE,
Little Rock, October 4, 1889.

MY DEAR SIR: I herewith inclose to you papers, with stamps and indorsements as you see them. I telegraphed you on the 30th ultimo that I would send the papers, and really thought I had done so. I would be obliged to you for your views at length in regard to the matter, or, if you contemplate returning soon, we can have a personal interview. What do you think of the propriety of putting the matter in the hands of a Pinkerton detective? One-half of the reward according to agreement with Mr. Shelby goes to informer.

Very truly yours,

JAMES P. EAGLE,
Governor.
By WALKER,
Executive Clerk.

Hon. C. R. BRECKINRIDGE,
Washington, D. C.

To this Mr. Breckinridge replied on the 12th as follows:

HOUSE OF REPRESENTATIVES U. S.,
Washington, D. C., Oct. 12, 1889.

GOvernor JAMES P. EAGLE, *Little Rock, Ark.:*

MY DEAR SIR: Your favor of the 4th inst., with inclosure, was duly received. I expect Sheriff Shelby had better go to Calfornia. He will doubtless need the help of a shrewd official after he gets there to collect evidence. I take it that his departure should be secret, for there may be personal sympathizers who would give the party notice of Shelby's departure. This might lead to such deportment as to prevent the getting of evidence still needed. I should think an officer or a detective could do much more in California with Shelby on the ground, with his knowledge of Arkansas details and associations, than could otherwise be done. The letter from "Jack the Ripper" should be taken along and compared with his writing.

_ I have inquired of Sater, through a Mr. Ingram, of the Treasury Department, whose home is at Jeffersonville. Ingram is said to be a perfectly responsible man, and he says Sater and his family are people of veracity, and that they were in California at the time they speak of. I did not reveal the nature of the business in hand.

I shall be home in ten days or two weeks, and will you see as soon as I arrive. This trip will consume largely of the funds you have, I think I can promptly get more.

This clew certainly leads to what appeared to me to be an extremely improbable direction, but it takes on very decided and convincing scope. These matters, involving the life first of one and then of another, are very sad.

Sincerely, yours,

C. R. BRECKINBRIDGE.

(Record, p. 624.)

He had promised in his letter in August, from St. Paul, to make inquiries of Indianians at Washington about Sater's reliability, and this is the result of the inquiries.

On the 23d of December, 1889, the governor wrote Mr. Breckinridge as follows:

LITTLE ROCK, *December* 23, 1889.

DEAR SIR: I am directed by Governor Eagle to say, in reply to your favor of 19th inst., that he will write to St. Louis parties as you request. The governor further directs me to say that he has received another letter from the sheriff of Los Angeles County, Cal., and that he is now fully impressed with the belief that that is the right clue. The family of that California party has recently returned to Conway County, but report the man (i. e., supposed assassin) as dead. The sheriff of Conway County is now working up that clue, as is also the sheriff of Los Angeles County, Cal., and I will keep you advised as to developments.

Very truly,

JNO. C. ENGLAND,
Private Secretary.

Hon. C. R. BRECKINRIDGE,
Washington, D. C.
(Mr. Breckinridge's brief, p. 19.)

The governor was then "fully impressed with the belief that that is the right clue." This implied disbelief in all the other clues which had been so fully and so exhaustively explored.

Then on January 1, 1890, the governor got the following letter from the sheriff of Los Angeles County, Cal.—the law officer and a Republican:

LOS ANGELES, *Jan.* 1, 1890.

Hon. J. P. EAGLE, *Governor State of Arkansas:*

DEAR SIR: Yours of December 16, 1889, duly received; contents noted. Have been unable to reply ere this, owing to unusually heavy rains and washouts. We will, however, now give you a complete report in regard to the matter of Thomas Hooper. Something like eight or nine months ago one Chas. W. Lewis came into my office at night-time and gave the following information to W. A. Hammel, one of my deputies. That some time in latter part of 1888 he made the acquaintance of Thomas Hooper under the following circumstances: Hooper had been put out of the house in which he had been living for non-payment of rent, and that he (Lewis) took him into his own house and cared for him, as Hooper was quite sick at the time. The result was that Lewis and Hooper became quite intimate, and Lewis, observing that Hooper was moody and surly at times, finally asked Hooper what was the matter, when Hooper made the following statement: That in 1868 (supposed to be the same year in which Hooper's father was killed) Hooper intimated that he had killed two men, whose names Lewis understood to be Thomas and Mays (first names unknown), and Lewis was not sure of these names being right, but was sure of the circumstances. The men were ambushed in a corn-field in Conway County, Ark.; that these two men were two of three ringleaders of a mob that had lynched his father, and that the third man was Senator Clayton, and that he would kill him, too; that he could not rest in his grave if he did not kill him; that, in fact, it was his religion to revenge the death of his father; and if Lewis, ever heard of Clayton dying with his boots on, to just lay it to him. Lewis further stated that H. disappeared from Los Angeles the latter part of December, 1888, or the 1st of January, 1889; and when he heard of the murder of Senator Clayton, and also learning of H.'s absence from home, through H.'s own son, he finally thought it his duty to see me. I at once wrote to the authorities proposed by Lewis, but never received an answer, one letter having been returned; and until I received your first letter had taken no active steps in the matter.

I then, in conjunction with H. A. Hammel and A. W. Marsh, my deputies, and both in possession of these facts, we finally located H. at Los Netos Township, some fifteen miles from here. In the meantime Lewis left here, leaving no address, but we have now located him in Minneapolis, Minn., where he is now, or was, working in a laundry, as shirt ironer. We had taken steps to get Lewis' affidavit of these facts, but in the meantime Hooper died. Of this fact we could not get information, for the reason that it has been raining here for nearly a month, and he died just when the rain commenced, and as the ranchito where he lived was mostly surrounded by water, we made no attempt, knowing full well that he would not leave.

After Hooper returned here he purchased a ranch reported to be worth $10,000, although apparently poor a year before. I have been to considerable expense, and have made a thorough examination of the matter, and would be glad to hear from you. You can rely on the foregoing as a simple, unvarnished statement of the facts in this case.

Respectfully,

M. G. AGUIRRE,
Sheriff of Los Angeles County.

Here this Republican official produces a witness, presumably responsible, who confirms all that Sater had said. He proves from Hooper's son that the father was absent at the time of the killing, and no mention was made, or had ever been made, of ill-health. He closes by saying: "You can rely on the foregoing as a simple, unvarnished statement of the facts in this case."

Thus everything remained with only confirmatory details until the committee went to Little Rock. The evidence there was almost as confirmatory as contradictory. The dispatch received by the reporter of the St. Louis Republic, referred to on page 7 of the majority report, was in reply to one sent at the request of Mr. Breckinridge, who used every effort to exhaust every clue. We have seen how the committee refused to take depositions of parties in California to settle conflicting testimony at Little Rock; but the evidence procured lately by the governor, page 28 of Mr. Breckinridge's brief, indicates with reasonable certainty that this clue also is false.

A perusal of only the parts we introduce, all being of the same tenor, shows how conclusive the truth of this appeared at one time. If what the California sheriff said first and last was true, there was, under the circumstances, a reasonable certainty of its truth; but it is evident that he is not reliable, and yet that is the last thing to expect from the official chosen by the people to deal with criminal matters. How far the governor was from being beguiled into this is very apparent; that Mr. Breckinridge was the last and the most reluctant person to give credence to it is equally clear.

The committee complains that "no one was sent to California to see whether the story was true or not," and yet the matter was intrusted to the sheriff of their own political faith.

After the thousands of dollars spent by the Messrs. Clayton on the ballot-box theory, after the sifting of everything possible through the Federal court trials, after the undeviating attention of the governor to only this theory for six months, after the open rewards of about $11,000 for a year or more, the committee still say there has not been given "due weight to the suspicion that should naturally attach to the ballot-box thieves," and (p. 5) in the very next breath complain of the governor for not sending a man to California.

They take credit for sending for Sater (p. 3), when it was only by the most persistent efforts of Mr. Breckinridge that they consented to let him come to Little Rock, he or his friends advancing his expenses. We know from experience that if he had been deferred to be examined at Washington he would never have been examined at all.

They say (p. 5) "they took all the testimony available," and yet they violated their agreement to take testimony in many and most important instances.

They say (p. 6) " Mr. Breckinridge accepted this theory as one which relieved his partisans in Arkansas from the charge," in the face of the evidence that he was the last man to accept it.

- They say (p. 7) "the theory was a pleasing one to contestee, and no one would blame him for following such a clue," not only in the face of the facts we have given, but in the face of the additional fact that the conduct they impute and indorse would be highly dishonorable in Mr. Breckinridge.

They say (p. 7) "no reasonable explanation of the murder of Colonel Clayton appears, except that some of the ballot-box thieves, finding the taking of the testimony progressing, killed him," which clearly makes it a personal crime and personal to those men; and yet they argue all through that it was not of this nature, but to affect the election and not to prevent their own punishment, and then on page 15 they state a wholly different theory, as settling a mere personal rivalry and dispute, such as men have settled in duels. Their language is as follows:

In the old days of the code of honor political antagonists often met face to face and eye to eye and sought their adversary's life. This method of settling political differences has become obsolete, and we frequently congratulate ourselves upon the improved moral tone of our day and generation.

They also complain, on page 7, that "this theory would only, in any event, have partly solved the mystery, for there were at least two persons present at the murder." The logic of this is that if you don't know beforehand all there is in a clue you must not pursue it, and if a clue promises directly only to disclose the principal you must neglect it because it does not immediately discover the confederate.

Thomas Hooper was a Democrat. He had been a brave soldier all through the war, in Governor Eagle's regiment. The governor knew him well, and remembered him with strong personal attachment. The town of Morrilton, the county of Conway and adjoining counties, contained his brothers, nephews, and numerous other kinspeople. They are all Democrats, and many of them people of influence, one brother being, or has been, a member of the legislature. Who could have had more personal sympathy than this family? Who more dangerous to arouse in that community? If there were any "Democratic" secrets, who would be more likely than they to know something of them? The most casual reflection will convince that this strong and numerous connection could not be put to the distress they were without serious peril to any guilty people there who had secrets to keep. It put the most powerful internal influences at work to split the local Democracy into angry factions, to awaken crimination and recrimination, to bring out every latent suspicion, to bring out the truth if anybody there knew it. One of the most conclusive evidences of the innocence of those people of all knowledge or sympathy with this event is the failure of this fearful ordeal to develop a single fact. This makes the mystery of the killing of Clayton all the more strange. It is evident in every way that this clue was not in any sense a pleasing one, or one calculated to shield any guilty man.

Reference to the acquittal of the men tried before the Federal court for conspiring to injure Wahl, and to their testimony, Page — *et seq.*, shows clearly that no conspiracy existed against him, nor did these men try to harm him. He was one of the foremost men in getting up the game of cards, he was foremost in the drinking, and he testifies himself that the change of seats was made at his own request. The shot passed so close to others as to indicate that they might have been fired at, wounding the town marshal in the neck with a piece of glass, and it is most probable that the disturbance he had that day with drunken teamsters accounts for the whole matter. One or more of them had threatened to kill him, and they were still camping near by. The testimony is frank and full, and it is evident Wahl's companions were as much startled and alarmed as he. As to the statement that he, only, was indicted for playing cards, we did not look it up; but we would expect he testimony to show that there is no more in this than in the others features. The testimony of Captain Stowers, Dr. Sayle, and others, show conclusively that the militia talk is a gross exaggeration.

THE OUTRAGE BEFORE THE SUBCOMMITTEE, IN THE UNITED STATES COURT-ROOM, AT LITTLE ROCK, ARK.

A very significant event occurred in the United States court-room, at Little Rock, during the taking of testimony, on the night of the 5th of May, 1890. Had the acts of Republicans on this occasion been committed by Democrats the country would have rung with statements and charges, and we think the event would have occupied a most conspicuous place in the report of the majority. As it is, the matter is briefly and obscurely printed in the testimony and no mention is made of it in the report.

The various charges and insinuations of every conceivable character that had been made, especially against citizens of Conway County, were calculated to be very irritating. Mr. Carroll Armstrong, of that county, had been in attendance for some time. He is a small, frail man, weighing but little, if any, over 100 pounds, and of nervous temperament. Evidently laboring under a strong sense of injustice done to his neighbors and to the good name of his county, he for the first time indulged in language similar to that which had been used towards them and him, but of far less import than what he had been called upon to endure. While this does not justify an expression of resentment, especially at that time and place, still less is an assault to be justified at the same time and place and under far less provoking circumstances, and still less if by one most experienced in the proprieties and restraints appropriate to such a place and occasion. The latter offender was Judge John McClure, a large and powerful man, and the difference in their physical strength would alone suggest forbearance.

The Record is as follows:

Mr. CARROLL ARMSTRONG then addressed the committee as follows:

Mr. Chairman: There have been some foul charges made against the people of

Morrillton and of Conway County by the mouth-piece of Powell Clayton. I desire to enter an appearance for Conway County.

Mr. LACEY (to the stenographer). Note that Mr. Armstrong desires to enter an appearance for Conway County.

Mr. ARMSTRONG. I understand this committee intends in a short time to adjourn, after having received the testimony here that would cast a cloud upon the people of Conway County, and retire to the city of Washington for the purpose of making their report.

Here he was interrupted again by Mr. Lacey, who remarked:

Mr. LACEY. I think that is quite probable.

Mr. Armstrong was evidently stung by the confirmation of his worst fears of injustice to his county and by the interruptions, manner, and words of Mr. Lacey. He continued his application as follows:

Mr. ARMSTRONG. I insist that this committee shall subpœna witnesses from the people of Conway County, from the good people of Conway County, to refute the charges that have been made by this infamous slanderer.

At this instant Judge McClure rose from his seat and aimed a powerful blow at Mr. Armstrong's face, but he dodged it and received it only partially on the side of his head. Being thus assaulted Mr. Armstrong, as he dodged the blow, caught with his left hand at Judge McClure's beard, which is full and long. The earnestness and honesty of Mr. Armstrong's request and the nature of the interruptions had fastened the attention of every one.

The assault by Judge McClure, in the Federal court-room, in the presence of a Congressional committee, and in the presence of a number of ladies, was startling to all. Messrs. McCain and Harrod quietly and instantly stepped between the parties before McClure could follow up his blow. Mr. Armstrong stood where McCain and Harrod had pushed him, and a deputy United States marshal quickly drew his pistol and he held it on a level with about the middle of Mr. Armstrong's back, behind whom he was standing. Mr. Breckinridge, who had worked himself around near the group, while, like ourselves (Wilson and Maish), calling for order, ran instantly to Mr. Armstrong, and seizing him, pressed him back and down into a chair. Judge McClure, Armstrong being removed, and adjured and confronted by McCain, Harrod, and one or two others, sat down.

In the St. Louis Globe Democrat of May 13, 1890, there appeared the following, as coming from Mr. Lacey:

If Armstrong had drawn his pistol, said Mr. Lacey, he would undoubtedly have been shot immediately by the United States marshal, who stood in his rear prepared for emergencies.

This is the Nagle case reversed. The Supreme Court held that when a powerful man offered to strike a weak man (Judge Terry having approached Judge Field evidently for this purpose, in a dining-room), the United States marshal was justified in killing the strong man in defense of the weak man. Here it seems the marshal was also stationed upon the lookout, with instructions. The strong man was not to be killed in this case if he offered to strike the weak one, nor even if he struck him, nor did there seem to be the slightest indication of instructions to arrest an assailant, and thus to prevent a difficulty.

We did not see the slightest indication, nor is there any reason to believe that a single Democrat had a weapon of any kind; and Mr. Armstrong has stated personally that he was totally unarmed. But it has been stated and not denied, so far as we know, that Mr. W. H. H. Clayton threw his hand to his hip to draw his pistol, and he testifies on page 448 that General Powell Clayton habitually goes armed.

It was necessary for something to be alleged against their opponents that can be distorted; that can be used to "influence the elections in the North;" that can make up for the lack of evidence to declare this seat vacant; that can be used to obscure and overcome the fact that the testimony positively proves that Mr. Breckinridge was elected. Political capital must be had to help pass a force bill. But the obvious plot miscarried, and we see the whole matter placed with studied obscurity in the testimony, not indexed, and described in the following brief and colorless words:

(At this point in Mr. Armstrong's address a personal difficulty occurred between Mr. Armstrong and Judge McClure, occasioning considerable excitement for few minutes.)

This indicates the character of this whole contest, investigation, and proceeding; and we ask the House to weigh well all the facts we cite before it indorses the actions, assertions, and recommendations of the majority of the subcommittee or of the full committee.

THE RESULT OF THE ELECTION.

The minority do not find or believe that the election was affected in the least, or was intended to be affected, by but one event, and that was the theft, by unknown parties, of the Plummerville ballot-box. The count of this vote, however, upon the accepted proof of the majority of the committee, leaves Mr. Breckinridge a majority in the district of 413 votes, and this is his rightful majority. But to show that Mr. Breckinridge was elected upon every possible theory of the case, we give the following table:

	Breckinridge.	Clayton.
Total vote returned for Breckinridge	17,857	
Total vote returned for Clayton		17,011
Deduct the lesser from the greater	17,011	
Majority for Breckinridge	846	
Clayton's vote proved at Plummerville		558
Breckinridge's vote proved at Plummerville	125	
Deduct the lesser from the greater		125
Clayton's majority at Plummerville		433
Breckinridge's majority brought down	846	
Deduct the lesser from the greater	433	
Breckinridge's true majority in the district	413	
Town of Augusta, Woodruff County, 8 negroes who voted for Breckinridge testified they did not intend to so vote. Multiply by 2 and deduct	16	
Leaving majority for Breckinridge	397	
Riverside precinct, Woodruff County, 22 negroes testified as above; but the majority say 29. Multiply the latter by 2 and deduct	58	
Leaving majority for Breckinridge	339	
Cotton Plant, Woodruff County, 48 negroes testified as above. Multiply by 2 and deduct	96	
Leaving majority for Breckinridge	243	
White River, 21 negroes testify as above, but the majority say 62. Multiply the latter by 2 and deduct	124	
Leaving majority for Breckinridge	119	
They claim 29 negroes at Cotton Plant who did not vote (we make it 23) and are not recorded either way, but now come and say they did vote. Deduct this	29	
Majority left for Breckinridge	90	
Thirteen other negroes are brought up from the other precincts and made to swear they voted. Deduct	13	
Majority left for Breckinridge	77	
According to the figures as computed by McCain & Harrod, attorneys at Little Rock, for Mr. Breckinridge, the above final result, correctly computed from the testimony, exclusive of the negroes not voting at all, makes the majority for Breckinridge	226	

They make the number of those voters 23, instead of 29 and 13=52, as above. But this is immaterial as the highest and all the estimates of the committee are included above.

This includes every vote counted or claimed in any and every way by the majority. The result is that instead of showing that Mr. Breckinridge was not elected, the testimony shows most positively that he was elected.

The only way in which this can be overcome is by casting out Democratic votes which are conceded by the notice of contest to be fair. Or, if the committee is conducting an "investigation," then this is not to be treated as a contest, but as an inquiry; not as a statutory case, but as an investigation under a special resolution. Under this theory no evidence should be acceptable to the committee or the House except that which is procured by the same mode upon the one side as upon the other. To poll the vote upon one side and *not* to poll it upon the other is manifestly unfair,

The sub-committee was acting independently, for the House. The lawyers who appeared were employed and acting solely as the representatives and in the interest of other parties than the House. The policy of the committee seems to have been to follow the theory of the one side, and to exclude the testimony of the other side. But we are disposed to believe the refusal to poll the vote for Mr. Breckinridge at the Woodruff County precincts was caused by the astonishing result of the Plummerville vote when polled.

It was alleged in the notice of contest that he had only 75 votes there. The vote was polled and the committee concedes that he had 125 votes there, or more than 66 per cent. in excess of what the subcommittee expected. If this extended to the Woodruff County boxes, the result would be far more disastrous to Republican expectations or wishes than the present demonstrated majority for Breckinridge shows.

Believing from the testimony as developed in this case, that Mr. Breckinridge was fairly and honestly elected, we recommend the adoption of the following resolution:

"*Resolved*, That Clifton R. Breckinridge was elected to the seat which he now holds as Representative in Congress from the Second Congressional district of the State of Arkansas, and he is entitled to the same."

LEVI MAISH.
R. P. C. WILSON.
CHAS. F. CRISP.
CHAS. T. O'FERRALL.
J. H. OUTHWAITE.
L. W. MOORE.

HENRY KERNAGHAN vs. CHARLES E. HOOKER.

SEVENTH MISSISSIPPI.

———

Contestant charged partisan and illegal appointment of election officers, fraudulent registration, false counting, ballot-box-stuffing, interference with United States supervisors, violence, and intimidation. The committee find that all these practices were resorted to and that a considerable portion of contestee's majority is due to them ; but, the evidence failing to show that the frauds affected enough votes to overcome the entire majority returned for contestee, he is still entitled to the seat.

There is no minority report.

The case was not reached in the House.

REPORT.

FEBRUARY 25, 1891.—Mr. ROWELL, from the Committee on Elections, submitted the following report:

At the election held in the Seventh Congressional district of Mississippi on November 6, 1888, Henry Kernaghan and Charles E. Hooker were the Republican and Democratic candidates, respectively, for the office of Representative in Congress. According to the declared result of the election, Hooker received 8,491 majority.

In due time, and in accordance with law, Kernaghan filed his notice of contest, alleging, in substance, that the commissioners of election in the several counties of the district were not appointed, as provided by law, by the governor, lieutenant-governor, and secretary of state, but were in fact appointed by one D. P. Porter, deputy secretary of state and chairman of the Democratic executive committee of the Seventh Congressional district; that in making such appointments the recommendations of the Republican executive committees were ignored and boards were appointed either composed entirely of Democrats or with a Republican minority member who could be controlled by his Democratic associates; that in appointing precinct judges the county commissioners of election, in violation of law, either appointed boards composed entirely of Democrats or with one illiterate Republican; that in holding the election fraudulent registrations were made, false counting resorted to, ballot boxes stuffed, United States supervisors prevented from discharging their duty, violence and intimidation resorted to to keep voters from the polls, and that other like frauds were prevalent, with the result of changing a majority for contestant into a minority.

Answer was duly filed by Hooker denying the charges, and testimony was taken by both parties upon the issues joined.

While the committee have reached the conclusion that upon consideration of the whole evidence, and restating the result so far as the evidence enables us to do so, contestee has remaining a majority of the votes cast, yet the facts developed in the evidence are such as to require more than a formal report. The Seventh Congressional district of Mississippi is composed of the counties of Claiborne, Copiah, Franklin, Hinds, Jefferson, Lincoln, Madison, Rankin, and Simpson. According to the census of 1880 it appears that the population of the district was 179,484, of which 115,823 were colored and 63,632 were white, and that the adult males were 36,327; the colored majority being from 10,000 to 12,000, or not quite 2 to 1.

785

H. Mis. 137——50

At the election of 1872, prior to the historic "revolution," in which
was inaugurated what is known as the "shotgun policy" of carrying
elections, the vote in this district for secretary of state was as follows:

Counties.	Republican.	Democratic.	Total.
Claiborne	2,238	486	2,724
Copiah	1,811	1,900	3,711
Franklin	440	530	970
Hinds	4,011	354	4,365
Jefferson	1,698	454	2,152
Lincoln	824	640	1,464
Madison	2,601	48	2,649
Rankin	1,058	1,123	2,181
Simpson	307	508	815
	14,988	6,043	21,031

It is the concurrent testimony in this record and in other Mississippi
records examined by the committee that the great mass of colored voters are Republicans and vote the Republican ticket when they vote at
all. There are in this district a good many white Republicans, especially in the city of Jackson, the capital of the State. Upon that question the Ledger, a Democratic paper published at Tupelo, in this district, in its issue of November 15, editorially says:

> Their old and flimsy pretext heretofore for being Republicans—that they were fear-
> ful that they would be put back into slavery—was completely exploded by the present
> Democratic administration, which has been more friendly to the negroes' interest
> than the Republicans ever were. But with all this, the negroes in this State turned
> a deaf ear to their best interests and voted for Harrison for President, for the sole
> and express purpose of being in opposition to the white people of the south. * * *
> There are a few good and true negro Democrats in Mississippi, but a large majority
> of them are insolent, turbulent Republicans.

The whole article is printed in the Record, pp. 529, 530.
Judge Lee says:

> My opinion is that the negroes, if free to vote, would vote for a Republican against
> any Democrat, although there are a small number of them, comparatively, who vote
> the Democratic ticket. (Record, page 370.)

He also says:

> That there are a considerable number of white Republicans in the district, and that
> the negro voters largely outnumber the white.

In the light of recent events it will hardly be claimed anywhere that
any considerable number of negroes in the Seventh district of Mississippi, or, indeed, anywhere in that State, willingly vote the Democratic
ticket. It does not follow, however, that because they are in a majority
in the Seventh district, therefore the result of any election must necessarily be a victory for the Republicans. If, from lack of organization,
failure to register, or indifference as to results, they fail to vote, while
their opponents do not neglect this political duty, the result will necessarily be defeat. It is claimed by contestee in this case that these were
among the causes of the Republican defeat.

The record discloses that to some extent the Republicans of the Seventh
district were indifferent, that they lacked organization, and that many
of them neglected to see to it that they were properly registered. It is
claimed that this indifference resulted in part from a belief, based on
past experience, that their votes would not be counted even if they did
vote.

Charles W. Carraway, a leading planter and a friend of contestee, testified as follows (Record, pp. 495–497):

Int. 8. When fair elections are held at Dry Grove, what is the usual Democratic and Republican vote at that poll?
(Objected to as incompetent and irrelevant, for the reason that the answer is made to depend upon the witness's opinion of what is a fair election, and because a statement of fact of which better evidence exists.)
A. Can not recall but one fair election since I have been a voter, and can only judge from the registration books, knowing the politics of most of the people. As fair elections have so seldom been had there, no one could tell what the vote would be, *the majority knowing it would be useless to go and vote.*
(Objected to as incompetent and irrelevant, because, after saying that he does not know, the witness proceeds to give his opinion of the politics of and alleged majority that he says does not vote, and because of reference to the registration books, of which neither the original nor copies are produced.)
Int. 9. Why do they know it to be useless to vote there?
A. *Because the vote is never counted as cast.*
(Objected to as incompetent and irrelevant, stating the mere opinion of the witness.)
Int. 10. What is the number of Republican voters in that precinct?
(Objected to as incompetent and irrelevant, stating the mere opinion of the witness.)
A. Never counted them and could not guess within a hundred, some having left the county who have since returned, and a good many names having been erased from the poll-books for that reason, I suppose, but I believe *there are over nine hundred registered voters on the books now,* and, if they are correct, *ninety per cent. are Republicans.*

* * * * * *

X-int. 11. Why did they not provide a substitute for the box, as allowed by law, and vote?
A. It would have done no good; *the Democrats would have counted it to suit themselves, or the mules would have eaten the box the following night.*
(Objected to as not responsive to the interrogatory.)
X int. 12. Do you know of any other reason?
A. There are few white Republicans there, and *unless white men took hold on both sides, the negroes know it is of no use.* I would have insisted on voting, but I believe *the people would have objected and caused some trouble.* I was in no way interested, only to pacify the negroes and keep them from leaving, not knowing the Republican candidate, and *Col. Hooker being a personal friend, and whom I have always supported for Congress, regarding him as the only Democrat from the State that ever did us any good at Washington.* I mean in recent years.

Judge Lea, who was called on behalf of contestee, in response to a question asked by contestee's counsel, said (Record, p. 370):

A. Such is the belief of a number of the more intelligent Republicans of the State. The evils which have resulted from what is commonly called negro rule, which have existed in the past, *is the reason assigned by the Democrats in the State as justifying the lawless measures which have been resorted to for the purpose of preventing negro domination;* to which, I will add, I am as much opposed as anybody.

The result of the election as declared, together with the adult white and colored males in the district, is shown in the following table:

Counties.	Adult white males.	Adult colored males.	Votes returned for Kernaghan.	Votes returned for Hooker.
Claiborne	799	2,620	13	602
Copiah	2,560	2,842	458	2,269
Franklin	900	901	203	779
Hinds	2,593	7,166	945	2,215
Jefferson	837	2,559	363	684
Lincoln	1,504	1,139	211	851
Madison	1,214	4,036	343	2,031
Rankin	1,369	1,778	509	1,543
Simpson	947	571	193	755
Total	12,713	23,612	3,238	11,729
				3,238
Hooker's majority				8,491

The total vote for Congressman is seen to be less than 15,000. If this announced result is a correct exhibit of the vote as cast, and contestee was supported only by the whites, he received within 1,000 of the total white voting strength of the district, while 20,000 negroes failed to vote, counting the population as in 1880.

But this return does not show the true result of the election. The commissioner of election in many of the counties of the district did not have the confidence of the Republicans. When there was a Republican representative on the board he was not the man of their choice, was not trusted by the party, and in some instances was not regarded as a Republican. It should be borne in mind that—

The election commissioners hold in their hands the entire election machinery of their counties; they establish and abolish election precincts at will; they revise the registration and poll books, erasing names therefrom as occasion demands; they sit as a court to decide appeals from the circuit clerk when complaint is made that registration is improperly refused; they appoint all election officers in their counties, including peace officers to preserve order at the voting places; they receive, compute, and return the whole vote of their counties; and to exercise these great powers and delicate trusts the concurrence of only two of the three commissioners is required. (Buchanan *vs.* Manning, Digest Election Cases, 1882-'83, p. 307.)

In the appointment of precinct inspectors of election these commissioners in the main disregarded the law, and either appointed boards composed entirely of Democrats, or, in apparent compliance with the statute, appointed one illiterate Republican who was incompetent to discharge the duties of the office. It is impossible to resist the conclusion that these illegal appointments were not made in the interest of an honest election. It was said in the case of Buchanan *vs.* Manning, above cited :

The appointment of the managers of the election, in fairness and common decency, should be made from opposite political parties. A refusal to do so, in the face of a statute directing it to be done, may in some cases be evidence of fraud, and it might form an important link in a chain of circumstances tending to establish a conspiracy.

As showing the unlawful methods resorted to to diminish the Republican vote, we quote the following from the record.

W. H. Gibbs (Rec., p. 525) testifies as follows :

The meeting (held at Brandon, the home of the contestant, the day before election) was addressed by ex-Chief Justice H. F. Simrall. Mr. Kernaghan was present and presided. He introduced Judge Simrall. The speaker was interrupted in the progress of his speech by a young lawyer commonly known as "Coote" White, who said that as Judge Simrall had asked the question, "How long these ballot-box outrages and intimidations were to continue in this country?" he wanted to answer his question by saying that they would last just so long as such men as Judge Simrall went around organizing the negroes and urging them to vote against the white people of the country. That is about the substance of what he said, if not the exact language. Judge Simrall replied that he was not arraying the negroes against the whites or seeking to do so. He proceeded then to finish his speech, and had about concluded when he was again interrupted by another gentleman, Mr. Pat Henry, another lawyer, who asked Judge Simrall some question, which I don't now recollect, to which Judge Simrall replied very courteously, as I thought, but which Mr. Henry said was not an answer to the question he had asked, and then said that "we don't propose that this crowd shall leave this house till they have heard our side of the question. Upon this a crowd in the northeast corner of the court-house, probably fifteen or twenty, commenced to get upon the desk and shout, "Close the doors!" Several pistols were drawn, and "Coote" White presented a pistol at Mr. Kernaghan. Some of the crowd attempted to leave the building, but were prevented by the doors being closed and guards placed there to keep them in. "Coote" White then went up into the stand and commenced to try to make a speech. The noise and confusion was so great that he couldn't be heard until the sheriff was sent for, who came up, and after some time succeeded in restoring order. White then proceeded with his speech, in which he said that they had carried the elections by force in times past and they would do it again this time. The balance of his speech didn't amount to very much. He only spoke a few minutes. The doors were then opened and the crowd allowed to depart.

This testimony is corroborated by other witnesses; and "Coote" White, who was one of contestee's attorneys in taking testimony, was not put on the stand.

R. H. Truly, a lawyer and independent Democrat, testifies as follows: (Red. p. 480.)

Int. 1. State your name, age, residence, and occupation.—Ans. R. H. Truly; 55 years; Fayette, Jefferson Co., Miss.; lawyer.

Int. 2. If you were present at Fayette on the Tuesday preceding the Congressional election of 1888, state what you may know of any arrangement for a Republican meeting there on that day, and of any interference with any Republicans; state fully all you know of what happened there that day.—Ans. Yes, I was present; Mr. Kernaghan had given notice through the public prints and through posters that he would address the citizens of Jefferson County on that day at Fayette; Mr. Kernaghan came to town in a buggy with a colored man named Jones, from Claiborne County, I believe; four or five gentlemen, Democrats, waited on Jones and told him if he had any business of more importance anywhere else than there, that he had better get away; I went to those gentlemen, all being friends of mine, and asked them what they meant; they told me at first that Jones was there with the Republican tickets, to distribute it, and that they wanted him to leave; I told them that that was all foolishness; that there were hundreds of negroes there who could distribute their tickets as well as Jones, and that their actions were liable to injure Col. Hooker's cause; they then said that he was a rascal and a very disreputable character; I asked them if they knew him, and they said no, but that Mr. Spencer had told them so.

(The foregoing answer objected to as incompetent and irrelevant, constituting no evidence pertinent to the issue involved in this contest and in no wise showing that any fraud or intimidation occurred at the election in question.)

Inter. 2. State what you may know on information as to what the said Jones did after having been so notified:

(Objected to as irrelevant to the issue involved, and because the question calls for hearsay.)

Ans. I was told that Jones became very much frightened and immediately went to the depot to take the train to leave; there being no train, he walked out to Harriston, and that he burned the Republican tickets he had in his possession.

(Answer objected to as mere hearsay.)

Int. 3. If you were present at Fayette on election day, November 6, 1888, state whether or no there were any colored voters in attendance there; and if so, how many, and whether they voted or not; and if not, why not.

(Objected to as incompetent and irrelevant, as in no wise affecting the issue involved in this contest.)

Ans. I was present on that day; there was a considerable number of colored voters in attendance; I presume about 300, possibly more; out of that number there were, I think, three that voted the Democratic ticket; none of the others voted; there were no Republican tickets at that box is the reason, I presume, why they all didn't vote.

(Answer objected to as stating mere conclusion of the witness as to why the persons mentioned did not vote.)

Int. 4. Were the said voters who did not vote on said day solicited to vote the Democratic ticket; and if so, with what success,

(Objected to as incompetent, because the solicitation of votes is incidental to all elections, and the result of such solicitation upon those not voting being in no wise prejudicial to the result attained by those who do vote.)

Ans. Yes; there was a great deal of electioneering with the colored voters by the Democrats, and three of them voted the Democratic ticket.

Int. 5. To what political party do you belong?—Ans. I have always voted the Democratic ticket, but have been very independent in my views, and when the Democratic party's nominee didn't suit my views I didn't vote for either side; I have always voted for Col. Hooker, and warmly supported him, both against Maj. Barksdale and Mr. Kernaghan.

The testimony of Mr. Truly not only shows that the Republicans in Jefferson County did not have an opportunity to vote, because tickets were not distributed there, but it shows the Republicanism of the colored voters; that out of 300 present at Fayette, only 3 could be persuaded to vote the Democratic ticket, and the remainder refused to vote because there were no Republican tickets.

We also quote the testimony of E. W. Jones (Record, page 477).

Interrogatory 1. State your name, age, residence, and occupation.—Answer. E. W. Jones; 40 years; Jackson, Miss.; I have farming interests in Claiborne County.

Int. 2. How long have you resided at Jackson, Miss., and where was your residence before you came to Jackson ?—Ans. I have resided in Jackson about 10 or 12 months; I formerly lived at Port Gibson, Miss.; was born and raised there.

Int. 3. If you were present at the town of Fayette, Miss., a few days previous to the election of 1888, state with whom you went there, for what purpose you went there, and all that happened to you there that day.—Ans. I was at Fayette, Miss., a few days before the election; I went there in company with Mr. H. Kernaghan; we arrived at Fayette about 12 or 1 o'clock; a short time after our arrival a crowd of men, eight or ten in number, all white, came to Mike Howard's office; Mr. Kernaghan, myself, and Lewis Robinson, chairman of the Republican committee of Jefferson County, were in the office in consultation as to the best time to have our speaking at that point. We had gone there for the purpose of having a Republican meeting on that day. One of the crowd of men that came to the office spoke in a loud tone of voice, and said, "Come out here!" I was sitting near the door, and asked him, "Who?" "You, by God!" was the answer. I went out on the sidewalk and there found 10 or twelve men. They asked me what I wanted there; I told them I had come to accompany Mr. Kernaghan, at his request; they told me that I should leave that town on the first train, or they would make it red-hot for me; I asked what I had done, whether I was disturbing anybody or not. Several of the crowd spoke almost at once, and said, "By God, we don't care to debate it with you at all." At that time Mr. Kernaghan came to the door and said to the crowd, "Don't disturb this man; I brought him her ; I am the one if you want to disturb anybody, and not him." The reply was, "We are not going to have any Radical speaking here by anybody." Some one in the crowd said, "We propose to manage our own affairs," or words to that effect. I then went back into Mike Howard's office; Mr. Kernaghan went out, and said to me to stay there a few minutes till he came back; I went to the door a few seconds afterwards, the crowd of men having returned to the hotel, some 20 or 30 steps off.

I saw Col. Chas. E. Hooker sitting in a chair on the sidewalk at the hotel; these gentlemen were all standing around him; I came out of the office and started to go up to where he was; Lewis Robinson, the chairman of the committee, told me I had better not go up there, that I would get into trouble; I thought he knew best, and didn't go; I then sent a messenger to Mr. R. H. Truly, asking him not to let them interfere with me if he could help it; he sent me a message that he would do all in his power to see that I wasn't disturbed. Mr. Kernaghan returned in a short while, and said we would have to abandon the meeting; Mr. Lewis Robinson, chairman of the committee, agreed with us that we could not hold a meeting there. A short time afterwards a messenger came in and notified me that it had been asserted on the streets by white men that I had in my possession Republican tickets, and that was why they were after me. I will state that I had 2,000 Republican tickets for the Fayette box. I then went to the depot alone and on foot; I tried to get somebody to accompany me there, as I felt uneasy. When we first reached Fayette that day there were two or three hundred colored people in the street; in twenty minutes after the excitement I couldn't find a colored man to go to the depot with me; I met a friend while en route to the depot who advised me not to be caught with the tickets; I went to the residence of J. D. Weston, south of the depot; I had the tickets in my valise; I took them out and put them in the fire and burnt them up; the train came a short time afterwards and I got on it and went to Harriston; some of the same crowd who had ordered me from Fayette were at Harriston, and followed me around the depot and every other place that I went around there; commenced abusing me by cursing me, etc.; I tried to remonstrate with them by telling them I hadn't disturbed anybody; I met a white friend of mine there and appealed to him to go aboard of the train with me, and he did so; I there took the train and went through to Vicksburg.

(Objected to as incompetent and irrelevant, for the reason that the events related occurred some time prior to the election, and were not in themselves of the character to affect its validity.)

Int. 4. Who was this white friend who protected you at Harriston ?—Ans. M. R. Jones, of Carlisle, Miss.

Int. 5. Was the crowd who attacked you in Fayette quiet and peaceable in their behaviour, or boisterous and angry ?—Ans. They were apparently angry, using curse-words for almost every expression.

Int. 6. Were matters at that time on the streets of Fayette quiet or excited ?—Ans. Up to the time the crowd came to the office they were quiet. The moment I came to the door the negroes seemed to understand it and commenced squatting and dodging.

Int. 7. You have said that when you first went there there was a large number of colored people in the town, and that after this attack on you you could not find a colored man to go to the depot with you; what become of them?—Ans. They left the streets; I could not tell where they went.

Int. 8. Was there any noise, or disturbance, or shooting, or fast riding on the streets of Fayette that day?

(Objected to as leading and incompetent.)

Ans. I heard no shooting or fast riding, and know of no disturbance except that already told about.

Int. 9. At the time you came to the door of the office, when the crowd was standing on the sidewalk cursing, as you have described, was Col. Hooker then sitting on the sidewalk. at the place you have stated?

(Objected to as leading and incompetent.)

Ans. I don't think he was at that immediate time, but he was a few minutes afterwards, but he was sitting there, though, when the crowd went back.

Int. 10. You have stated that, up to a few months since, your home has been in Claiborne County. Were you in Claiborne County at any time previous to election day in 1888; if so, when and at what places?—Ans. I was at Port Gibson on the 29th of October, and attended a Republican meeting there that day.

Int. 11. Are you well acquainted with the colored people of Claiborne County?— Ans. I am; know almost the name of every man in the county.

Int. 12. What is the politics of the colored voters of that county?

(Objected to as incompetent and irrelevant, because it asks about the politics of the colored people in general, and this contest relates to a particular election, and because it calls for mere matter of opinion.)

Ans. Republican; and they vote the Republican ticket almost to a man.

Int. 13. State, if you can, what party has the majority of votes in Claiborne County when the elections are fairly held, and what its majority is in said county.

(Objected to as calling for mere matter of opinion, and because it is immaterial in contesting this particular election.)

Ans. The Republican party has a majority of 2,500 or 3,000; and it always went that way in fair elections.

Int. 14. What is the registered vote of Claiborne County, and what part of it is white and what colored?

(Objected to as incompetent and irrelevant, the registration books, or copies thereof, being the best evidence, and because the number of registered voters, as shown by the registration books, is no evidence of the number of votes actually cast, nor the candidate who received them.)

Ans. The registered vote is about 2,000 properly, about 700 of whom are white and the others colored. Only about half the voters are registered.

(Objected to because the witness assails in general terms the correctness of an official record prepared by competent authority under the laws of this State, without producing the records or a copy thereof, and without showing that any person entitled to registration has ever been refused.)

Int. 15. State why such a large part of the voters are not registered in said county, and how long such has been the condition of the registration there.

(Objected to as incompetent and irrelevant, as calling for mere matter of opinion about facts not affecting the validity of this particular election.)

Ans. It is because of the general methods of the Democrats of Claiborne County in carrying elections, no matter which way the votes are cast, that a large portion of the Republicans have refrained from registering on that account.

Int. 16. Have they had a new registration in Claiborne County of late years, and if so, in what year was it, or is the county using its old, original registration books?

(Objected to as incompetent and irrelevant, because neither of said books or copies thereof are introduced, and because the witness is in no way connected with said books, as custodian or otherwise.)

Ans. They have had a new registration in 1886 or 1887.

(Answer objected to because the fact that the county is using new registration books in no way affects the validity of the election in question.)

Int. 17. Did the Republican voters of Claiborne County generally vote in the last election, that of November, 1888, and if not, why not?

(Objected to as incompetent and irrelevant, because the mere failure of persons to vote does not prejudice an election, no matter what their politics is, and because the question calls for mere matter of opinion.)

Ans. They did not vote, but very few, at this last election. It was because the Republican executive committee had asked to have a county commissioner appointed and was refused. One Henry Weekly was appointed against their protest. It was then decided by the committee that we would have no show, that we would have no commissioner to look after our interests. I was at that time and still am a member of the committee, and recommended A. M. Addison as commissioner, but they refused to appoint him.

Int. 18. **Who was this Henry Weekly**, and what was his political status, and by whom was he nominated as the Republican county commissioner?

(Objected to as incompetent and irrelevant, the matter of the appointment of the election commissioners being a matter confided to the discretion of a State board that is in no way bound by outside nominations, suggestions, or interference.)

Ans. He is a colored man who has been always known to be a man used by the Democrats of Claiborne County, and who voted the Democratic ticket. I do not know by whom he was nominated, but not by the Republican executive committee, or any member of it, as far as I know.

Int. 19. What is his business, and can he read and write well?—Ans. He is a carpenter by trade, and can scarcely write his name; I don't know that he can read at all.

Int. 20. Can he read writing or only print?—Ans. My impression is that he can not read writing, as he has scarcely any qualifications at all.

Cross-examined:

X Int. 1. What is the nature of your farming interests in Claiborne County?—Ans. My mother lives there and has farming interests, and I assist her, and am interested with her.

X Int. 2. Have you no other occupation?—Ans. I have; I am engaged in selling lands, and have an intelligence office here.

X Int. 3. What is the nature of the intelligence office?—Ans. Furnishing labor to planters and others.

X Int. 4. What time in the day did Mr. Kernaghan tell you at Fayette that there would be no speaking?—Ans. It was probably as late as three o'clock in the evening or afterwards.

X Int. 5. How long was that before or after the party told you to leave?—Ans. The party had told me to leave at least an hour before that time.

X Int. 6. How long was it after Kernaghan told you there would be no speaking before you left on the train for Harriston?—Ans. About an hour.

X Int. 7. Who was the person who came and told you that you had been disturbed because you had Republican tickets for distribution?—Ans. His name I do not know; he was a colored man.

X Int. 8. Was he a Democrat or a Republican?—Ans. I couldn't say.

X Int. 9. Had you shown the tickets to any one that day?—Ans. I had only shown them to the chairman of the Republican executive committee, Lewis Robinson; a few others, whose names I don't know, were present when I showed them.

X Int. 10. Was any one present when you burnt them?—Ans. There was, Mrs. J. D. Weston.

X Int. 11. Had Col. Hooker spoken when you left Fayette, and if so, did you hear him?—Ans. I was informed that he was speaking when we reached Fayette; I did not hear him.

X Int. 12. What time did you reach Fayette?—Ans. Between 12 and 1 o'clock.

X Int. 13. Why did you not distribute the tickets during the several hours that elapsed before the men disturbed you?—Ans. It was because my intention to give them to Lewis Robinson, and he absolutely refused to take them, and said he wouldn't be caught with them for anything.

(So much of the answer as states what Lewis Robinson said objected to.)

X Int. 14. Were there no other persons there you could have left them with?—Ans. I saw no one else except Mike Howard, whom I met en route to the depot, and he refused to take them.

X Int. 15. Had you asked either Lewis Robinson, Mike Howard, or any one else to take them before the men waited on you?—Ans. I had told Robinson I had them, but did not offer them to him until I was about to start off. I did not offer them to any one else, except Howard, while going to the depot.

X. Int. 16. Did you know the men who disturbed you at Fayette?—Ans. I only knew one man in the crowd.

X Int. 17. Were any of the Harriston people in Fayette that day?—Ans. I couldn't say.

X. Int. 18. Did the people that you saw at Fayette and afterwards at Harriston go out on the same train with you?—Ans. Two of them did.

X Int. 19. Did not they live at Harriston or in the neighborhood?—Ans. My impression is that one of them lived at Red Lick, but I don't think the other did.

X Int. 20. Did General Hooker come out to Harriston on the same train with you?—Ans. I don't think he did; I didn't see him.

X Int. 21. When did you first see the men who disturbed you in Fayette?—Ans. They came up in a body in front of Mike Howard's door about half an hour after I reached Fayette.

X Int. 22. Had you seen them at all before you went to the door of the office to meet them?—Ans. I had not.

X Int. 23. Have you not related here this morning an incident that occurred during the present winter, in which a white planter, a Democrat, and socially and politically prominent, who had gone to Jefferson County to procure hands for his plantation in another county, was waited upon by residents of Jefferson County and told to leave?—Ans. I was informed that such an incident occurred, and told it here this morning.

X Int. 24. Was not Mr. Kernaghan invited to divide time with Colonel Hooker at Fayette that day?—Ans. I don't know that he was; Mr. Kernaghan has told me so since.

X Int. 25. Was not the meeting that Colonel Hooker addressed a general public meeting, at which persons of both parties and races were present?—Ans. I couldn't say; I was not present at any time during the speaking.

E. W. JONES.

We also quote the testimony of J. W. Cain:

- Int. 1. State your name, age, residence, and occupation.—Ans. J. W. Cain; 23 years; Jackson, Miss.; am on the police force of the city.

Int. 2. If you were present at a Democratic meeting held in the capitol on the night of the 5th of November, 1888, being the night before the election, state what arrangements or agreements were made there, or after said meeting, by the parties there assembled, in regard to the firing of cannon, and how the same was afterwards carried out.— Ans. It was proposed that we were to fire the cannon early next morning, and some of the boys proposed to carry it through "Nigger Town" that night. They fired it out there perhaps a dozen times or more; stopped in some places and fired it in front of the houses. They stopped once in front of the colored hall, where they were holding some sort of a meeting, and the reason they didn't fire it there was that it was in front of a house where a woman was about to die, and some one came out and begged us not to shoot. We went to West Jackson then, and stopped in front of the lunch stand, and then came back to the capitol.

Int. 3. Were there many or few people went with the cannon, and how did they act and what did they do and say?—Ans. There were about 12 or 15 went with it. Some made the remark that it would be a good thing to carry it out there to bluff the negroes and keep them away from the polls.

Int. 4. Were they noisy or quiet in their travels with the cannon?
(Objection by contestee's counsel that the question is leading.)
Ans. They were very noisy.

Int. 5. If they used any threatening language while passing through the colored neighborhood, state what it was.
(Objection by contestee's counsel that the question is leading, and assumes the existence of a state of facts about which there has been no proof.)
Ans. Some said: "You damned black sons of bitches, you wouldn't come to the door to see what this cannon was being fired for if you knew the effect they were trying to have on you," and, "You had better not come to the polls."

Int. 6. If you know of any act of intimidation or violence committed in Jackson on that night, state the same fully.—Ans. That night, I suppose it was about 11 or 12 o'clock, after the meeting adjourned, I was in company with some gentlemen, Mr. Walt. Hendricks was one of them, Mr. Horace Perry was another, and walking on the V. and M. Railroad towards West Jackson. There is a house near the railroad belongs to Mrs. Spengler. There were some men bursting in the door and cursing the niggers, telling them the damned sons of bitches had better keep away from the polls, if they didn't fire at every one of them would be killed, or language to that effect. They had some straps beating on the side of the house and said they wanted one of them out of that. Said they wanted Thornton Reynolds out of there. The men had handkerchiefs over their faces; they were masked. Some of them from the inside answered that the "nigger" was not in there. Then they commenced to burst in the window lights. After that they commenced a shooting. About 20 shots were fired into the house—at least that. The crowd dispersed after that. We started on towards West Jackson, and heard several shots in different portions of the the town. We then changed our minds—not to go to West Jackson—and came back up town.

Int. 7. Of what ward are you a voter?—Ans. Of the South ward.

Int. 8. If you were present when the polls were opened in that ward on the 6th day of November last, state what time of day they were opened.—Ans. About half past ten or eleven o'clock.

Int. 9. Were you about the polls at nine o'clock that morning and from that till the polls were opened?—Ans. Yes, sir.

Int. 10. What was the reason that the polls were not opened sooner?—Ans. The reason was that there was a gentleman's name on the ticket spelled wrong. His name was "Candler" and they had it "Chandler."

Int. 10. On which ticket was this, and how did that delay the election?—Ans. Democratic ticket; had to wait till they could print some new tickets.

Int. 11. What number of people assembled at the polls between the hours of nine and eleven o'clock, before the polls were opened?—Ans. There were a good many came there and went away; don't know the exact number.

Int. 12. Were those people who so came and went away Republicans or Democrats?—Ans. Most of them were negroes; I couldn't say; most every negro is a Republican, especially in Presidential elections.

Int. 13. If you know of any bogus Republican tickets being brought to those polls that day, state fully what instructions were given in regard to them, and by whom the instructions were given, and who brought them there.—Ans. Mr. R. H. Henry brought them there. He brought the ones he gave to me. He had a big roll of them; he said they were bogus tickets; I think that's all he said. I commenced dishing them out, swapping tickets with the negroes. I gave some of them to Jim Hardy, and I gave one or two to Col. Hamilton. Mr. Joe White took some of the tickets from negroes to whom I had given them and said he was going off to measure them. I told Mr. Henry and he said, keep quiet—say nothing about them.

Int. 14. If you know anything of any conspiracy or proposed plan on foot on the night before the election to commit any violence on the person of any Republican or Republicans here, state who it was that proposed it and all about it.—Ans. I don't know of any that night.

Int. 15. Do you know of any such plan or proposition on foot just before said election?—Ans. Mr. L. F. Chiles said that he and Gen. Wm. Henry had been talking, and said it would be a good idea to take Charlie Morgan down in the swamp and tie him to a tree till after the election, as he was a leader among the negroes, and put somebody to watch him.

Int. 16. Were any propositions made by him or any one else for you and your friends to carry out this plan?—Ans. Yes, sir.

Int. 17. Who made such proposition?—Ans. Mr. L. F. Chiles.

Int. 18. What offices, if any, did Mr. Chiles hold at that time and now?—Ans. He was a deputy sheriff and alderman of the city of Jackson, and holds both of those offices.

Int. 19. To what political party do you belong?—Ans. I am a Democrat; I have always been, and have never voted anything but a Democratic ticket.

And on cross-examination:

X Inter. 90. Give us the name, dimensions, carriage, and history of the cannon used on that occasion.—Ans. She is named "Little Moses;" size a little over two feet long; bore about 2½ inches in diameter; rigged on the wheels of a sulky plow; don't know its history; it is generally fired about election day, to let 'em know we are going to have a fair election and to announce meetings of the Democratic club.

*   *   *   *   *   *

Re-examined:

Int. 1. To whom does this cannon, "Little Moses," belong?—Ans. To a party of four—L. F. Chiles, A. G. Lewis, and A. J. Davis. I don't know who the other one is; may be Tuck Holland.

Int. 2. If Mr. Chiles holds any offices, state what they are.—Ans. Deputy sheriff of Hinds County, alderman of the city of Jackson, and secretary of the Mississippi State Fair Association.

Int. 3. If Mr. Lewis holds any office, state what that is.—Ans. Treasurer of Hinds County.

Int. 4. If Mr. Holland holds any office, state what that is.—Ans. I don't know whether he holds any office.

Int. 5. Where is Holland now?—Ans. In Salt Lake City, Utah.

Int. 6. Does he not hold some position under the Government there?—Ans. Not that I know of.

Int. 7. In your progress with the cannon, "Little Moses," that night, did you go up into the North ward and fire the same before the doors of any Democrats?—Ans. We did not.

Int. 8. Why didn't you do so?—Ans. We knew the cannon wouldn't have any effect on white men.

Int. 9. Did you go up there and do any cursing, swearing, and hallooing before the doors of any white Democrats?—Ans. We did not.

Int. 10. Why didn't you?—Ans. We didn't think it was necessary.

Int. 11. Did you then think it was necessary to go into the colored parts of the city and fire the cannon, and curse and swear, and halloo before the doors of the people there?—Ans. I did; to keep them away from the polls.

Int. 12. You have stated in your cross-examination that you are a policeman of the city of Jackson, and that while off duty the night before the election, you saw certain disorderly proceedings and did not interfere; was not the principal reason of your non-interference at that time because of a general understanding among Democratic city and county officials in this city and county, that at and just before election times Democrats are privileged to commit almost any acts they please, no matter how Outrageous or disorderly, which may tend to intimidate Republican votes from the polls. Was this not the real reason why you did not interfere?—Ans. Yes; it was.

Int. 13. Is it not a fact that the grand juries in this county never indict anybody for outrages cOmmitted at and just before election times?—Ans. I never heard of them doing it.

Int. 14. Do they ever indict any one for frauds on the ballot-box of this cOunty?—Ans. I never heard of any.

The witness here expressed a desire to make a correctiOn in his answer to interrogatory 12, last above given, and proceeding said: "I do not believe that every sort of outrage would be tolerated, but I believe that so far as intimidating niggers is concerned, that wOuld be winked at by the officers of the law."

- To what extent the frauds above recounted affected the result, it is impossible to ascertain from the evidence. It is evident, however, from the testimony of Cain, that there could be no such thing as a fair election in the city of Jackson. It is also evident from the testimony of Truly and Jones that contestant lost several hundred votes at Fayette because the conditions there were such that his tickets could not be distributed. The declarations of "Coote" White show a willingness at Brandon to resort to any methods to defeat the will of the people.

CLAIBORNE COUNTY.

In Claiborne County no Republican tickets were distributed and no Republican votes were cast anywhere in the county, except at Port Gibson, where 13 votes are returned for contestant, and exactly 13 colored voters are marked "voted" on the poll book. In the whole county there were but 722 registered white voters. Contestee was returned 602 votes, of which only 48 are claimed to have been cast by colored men. The concurrent testimony of a large number of witnesses is that there was very great indifference among both white and colored in this county in regard to the election and that many of both races remained away from the polls. Notwithstanding this indifference, if the returns are true, contestee got nearly 80 per cent. of the registered white vote, a suspicious showing when taken in connection with the evidence. But it is a significant fact that if these returns are correct only 48 colored men could be persuaded to vote for contestee in a county where no Republican tickets were to be had.

In district No. 2, 15 colored voters are marked "voted." It is in evidence that just 15 colored men, all Republicans, appeared at the polls, but none of them voted because there were no Republican tickets. The now famous process of counting persons "present and not voting" seems to have been anticipated and somewhat advanced upon in this precinct.

COPIAH COUNTY.

In Copiah County there were counted for contestee 2,269 votes, and for contestant 458 votes. In the following-named precincts the returns have been proved to be fraudulent by calling the individual voters, viz.: *Heath's store, Crystal Springs west, Crystal Springs east, Hopewell, Brower's store, Mount Hope, Green's store, and Rockport.* For example, at *Heath's store* 52 witnesses testify that they voted for contestant; only 11 were returned for him.

Other evidence shows that many others in addition to these 52 voted for contestant. At Rockport 9 witnesses testify that they voted for contestant; none were returned for him. Those who testified were only a portion of those who cast Republican votes at this precinct. In nearly every precinct of this county the election boards were composed entirely of Democrats.

There are 22 precincts in Copiah County; the returns in 8 are conclusively proved to have been fraudulent; suspicion attaches to the others, but, in the absence of evidence sufficient to overturn the prima facie correctness of the returns, we do not disturb the count in them. Eliminating the fraudulent returns and restating the vote of Copiah County, so far as the evidence enables us to do so, we find the majority for contestee in this county reduced from 1,811 to 808.

HINDS COUNTY.

The official returns from Hinds County give contestee 2,215 votes, and contestant 945 votes. In this county the colored vote outnumbers the white vote nearly three to one. The testimony of Cain, already quoted, shows the means used to prevent a fair election in the city of Jackson, the capital of the State. Frauds are proved to have been committed in other precincts in this county, as follows: At *Liberty Grove*, 19 more votes were in the box than there were names on the poll list. The whole vote was counted, and both United States supervisors joined in a report that the return was fraudulent. This was a large Republican precinct, and the fact that the returns showed a Democratic vote in excess of the Democratic voters of the precinct, shows that these extra votes counted were Democratic.

At *Bolton* precinct a comparison of the poll book with the registration book shows that 74 names in the poll book had been changed, thus resulting in the disfranchisement of 74 duly registered voters.

In *Utica* precinct 368 votes were returned for contestee and none for contestant. Reuben Adams was appointed United States supervisor. His commission was forwarded to him by mail and arrived at his postoffice on the 31st day of October, as shown by the postmark on the envelope produced in evidence. He called at the post-office twice during the week preceding the election and received letters, but his commission was not delivered to him until the 17th of November. The check marks on the poll book show that only 266 persons voted, though contestee is generously returned as having received 368 votes.

At *Auburn* box 223 votes are returned for contestee and none for contestant. Fifty-three persons only are marked on the poll list as "voted" at this precinct. Similar fraud is shown at the *Cayuga* box.

At the *Raymond* box contestee was credited with 198 votes and contestant with 70, yet one of the inspectors of the election testifies that the number of whites who voted was only slightly greater than the number of colored. The Republican vote greatly exceeds the Democratic in this precinct, but either through a feeling that it was unsafe, owing to past practices, or for some other reason not disclosed, a comparatively small number of the 600 colored voters in this precinct cast their ballots.

At *Dry Grove* no election was held. There were present at the polling place about 400 Republicans and 50 Democrats. A Republican United States supervisor was present. Charles W. Carraway, whose testimony has already been referred to, gives the reason for not holding an election; he says: "I did not ask the reason why, but it is well known the Democratic party desired no election held there, as the box, on a fair count, is overwhelmingly Republican."

Jackson, north ward.—In the north ward of the city of Jackson the man appointed as Republican inspector voted the Democratic ticket. The ballot box was removed from the polling place before counting, and then counted in secret.

Jackson, south ward.—In the south ward Republican tickets prepared by the Democrats, not in conformity to the requirements of the law, were distributed.

MADISON COUNTY.

Canton, west ward.—In the west ward, precinct of Canton, 531 votes were returned for contestee and 17 for contestant. This return has been proved to be fraudulent by calling the individual voters, and should be rejected. In addition to the individual voters who testified, and conclusively proved the falsity of the return, from 300 to 400 Republican voters entered the polling place to vote. The method of voting in this ward and the arrangements for receiving ballots tend to the conviction that fraud was deliberately planned. The poll list of the ward was refused to contestant.

Canton, east ward.—At the east ward in Canton, 368 votes were returned for contestee and 10 for contestant. The election was held upstairs, and Republicans were prevented from going up to vote unless they would take Democratic tickets. On the night previous to the election a crowd of roughs broke into the house of a Republican voter and terrorized him, so that he kept away from the polls. A number of railroad men, not residents of the district and not registered, voted the Democratic ticket, the inspectors deciding that they had the right to vote for President and member of Congress anywhere in the State.

In *Camden precinct,* where the evidence indicates that twice as many Republicans as Democrats voted, the ballot box was carried away from the polls at dinner time, and when the count was made it showed 68 Democratic majority.

At *Sulphur Springs* precinct the ballot box was carried off, and kept away about 2 hours against the protest of the United States supervisor. The evidence tends to show that more Republicans than Democrats voted at this precinct, yet the returns give contestee 124 and contestant 32. In this county the action of the majority of the election commissioners in the selection of precinct inspectors was a violation of the letter and spirit of the law, and, to say the least, showed a willingness to prepare the way for fraudulent returns.

RANKIN COUNTY.

At *Steen's Creek* precinct, Rankin County, 230 votes were returned for contestee and 63 for contestant. The testimony of T. J. Cooper, United States supervisor, shows that the ballot box was taken from the polling place against his protest, both at noon and in the evening after the close of the election and before the commencement of the count. When the counting commenced, one of the inspectors took a lot of Republican tickets from the box and put them into his pocket.

Threats were freely made against the supervisor, and he was induced to leave the polling place and go home before the count was completed. Sometime during the night a gang of men went to his house and induced him by threats to sign a return corresponding to the return made by the inspectors. One of them said to him, "We'll outswear you if you should live to make your report, but you can't live to make it."

This supervisor followed the box when it was taken from the polling place, and seemed determined to discharge his whole duty, but while it was being carried from the polling place and back again, after supper, it was dark, and the box was kept out of his sight. If this witness is to be believed, of course there is no validity to the return from this precinct. It further appears that a large number voted at this precinct who were not registered.

At *Brandon* precinct the United States supervisor was ejected from the polls. He appealed to the governor of the State, who was present, and the governor advised him, against the plain letter of the statute, that he could only stay outside to aid in keeping the peace. In this precinct Mr. Pickett, one of the Democratic inspectors, carried off the ballot box both at dinner and supper time. The count was not completed that night, and this same Mr. Pickett took the box away and said he would sleep with it. The polling place was upstairs, and the colored people were let in at the front door very slowly, while the white voters were let in at the back door and had no difficulty in voting. Pickett is shown to have had both the disposition and the opportunity to subvert a fair election. Inspector McBeth testified that the colored vote seemed to be more solid that day than usual. The returns for the precinct gave contestee 244 and contestant 101.

Pisgah.—The conduct of Democrats at Pisgah precinct is best shown by quoting the testimony of some of the witnesses.

Henry Turnage (pp. 261–262) testified:

When I got there Mr. Miller and Mr. Ed. Davis come and met us and asked us if we come to vote. I told him yes, and he asked me did I have a ticket, and I told him yes, sir. He asked me to let him see it, and I give it to him, and he told me that wasn't the ticket to vote, and I asked him why, and he went on to tell me, and he said he would give me a ticket to vote, and I told him I didn't want his, and he said he didn't want mine. He asked me would I vote the ticket he give me. I told him "no, sir." He said, "If you don't vote this one you won't vote any." I told him all right; there was a heap of men there that wasn't voting, and I reckon I could do without too. He said, "All right; *if you vote this ticket you can vote, and if you don't, God damn you, can't vote narry one.*" I said "all right," and walked off from him. I went on 'round to the wagon where there was some fellows talking, and left him. I don't know where he went or what he done after that. My father come to me and told me to less go home. I told him, "No, sir; I am going to stay here a while longer; *I think I will vote directly.*" Mr. Davis walked up and said : "*No, you won't here to-day unless you take this ticket and some white man side of you, and walk up with you and put it in for you.*" I said: "No, sir; I won't do that;" and he said,"You had just as well go home, then; *before you or any other God damn nigger shall go up there and vote, unless he vote this ticket he will walk in blood knee-deep.*" I told him all right and walked off and got on my horse and went home.

A. G. McKoy testified (p. 263):

I issued until I saw things were getting brash; then I thought, from the appearance I saw, and actions, it would be better for me to stop; I heard several remark that *those tickets were going to cause hell here.*

Wiley Boyd (pp. 269-270) testified:

I went up to the polls to vote and they said I couldn't vote there; said no nigger couldn't vote except they would bring a white man with him; said we had to vote their way; that this was their country and they were going to rule it. Nat Polk and Will Buckner; Nat Polk had a stick and Will Buckner had a brickbat. They stood up to the dead-line and said no nigger couldn't cross the dead-line unless he carried a white man in with him. And George Denson he took me off behind the church and asked me what ticket I was going vote, and I told him I was going to vote the Republican ticket; and he asks me to let him scratch it, and I told him no, I didn't vote a scratched ticket. He said then, "By God, *we have been begging you all to vote with us,* and if you don't vote with us to-day we are going to *make* you vote with us." And about that time Joe Boyd was standing off in the road talking to Van Thornton, and he hollowed then, "This is our country, by God, and we are going to rule it." Then the crowds all broke to him, and about 20 or 30 was standing waiting to vote, and they got in behind them and told them *to get out and leave there*, and *got in before them* and *they were in behind them*, and Geo. Denson *shot off his pistol* and made them leave, and Will Buckner pulled off his coat, and several more others, and said *not another nigger should vote there that day*. And saw Will Buckner take a double-barrel shotgun out of the hind part of a buggy and turn it around and cover it up, and I heard Mr. Andrews and Nat Polk say *before any other nigger voted there they would wade in blood knee-deep*.

At Shiloh, where the return shows 106 for contestee, and 20 for contestant, the ballot-box was carried away from the polling place, and kept away nearly two hours.

Irregularities of a similar character took place in other precincts of this county. Precinct inspectors asked for by the Republican commissioner of elections to represent the Republicans on the election boards, were refused, and taking into consideration all the evidence, the committee are convinced that frauds sufficient to invalidate the returns were committed in the precincts noted and some others in this county, but, inasmuch as these frauds do no not affect a sufficient number of votes to overcome the majority returned for contestee, the committee do not attempt to restate the vote in full, and determine what reductions ought to be made from contestee's returned majority.

Taken altogether, the record discloses a deplorable condition of affairs in the Seventh Mississippi district, such as can neither be excused nor palliated. For the reason that the frauds developed in the evidence and described in this report are insufficient in amount to overcome all the majority returned for contestee, the committee recommend the adoption of the following resolutions:

Resolved, That Henry Kernaghan was not elected a Representative in the Fifty-first Congress from the Seventh Congressional district of Mississippi, and is not entitled to a seat therein.

Resolved, That Charles E. Hooker was elected a Representative in the Fifty-first Congress from the Seventh Congressional district of Mississippi, and is entitled to retain his seat therein.

JAMES HILL vs. T. C. CATCHINGS.

THIRD MISSISSIPPI.

The notice of contest alleges fraudulent refusal to receive the ballots of legal voters; fraudulent refusal to hold elections in several large Republican precincts; that the whole election machinery of the district was in the hands of friends of contestee, in violation of the statutes; that the United States supervisors were prevented from discharging the duties imposed upon them by law; and that the returns transmitted to the secretary of state are fraudulent.

The committee find frauds of various sorts, but that they are not shown to have affected enough votes to overcome the whole of the majority returned for contestee. A letter written by contestee is in evidence which the committee find to be a suggestion to hinder unlawfully the taking of testimony in the case, but it does not appear that the suggestions were acted on.

Mr. Lacey files a minority report contending that the above-mentioned letter constructively connects contestee personally with the frauds found to have been practiced at the election, and that under such circumstances the rule *ought to be* to declare the seat vacant. The case was never reached by the House.

(1) Election officers. *Partisan appointment of.*

"A statutory provision for allowing opposing parties to have representation on all election boards having charge of the conduct of elections is usually deemed necessary to secure honest results, and when fairly executed in letter and spirit may as a rule be relied on, at least so far as counting and returning the vote is involved. A general and willful disregard by the appointing power either of the letter or spirit of the law raises a strong presumption of an intent on the part of the appointing officers to afford opportunity for fraud. * * * While the statute does not direct how the appointing bodies shall make selections, its spirit clearly requires that in selecting representatives of the different parties the wishes of those representing the party organization shall be considered, and that the appointees shall be men having the confidence of their political associates. The selection of men to represent a political party on an election board who habitually vote the opposite ticket, who are not trusted in their party, or who are notoriously

H. Mis. 137———51

incompetent, is not a compliance either with the letter or the spirit of the statute." * * *

"While suspicion attaches to all such precincts, such suspicion is not sufficient to invalidate the return, in the absence of other evidence, but it does have the effect of requiring less evidence to overturn the prima facie correctness of the returns."

(2) **United States Supervisor.** *Interference with.*

"In every instance where a United States supervisor is prevented from discharging his duties, as provided by statute, the committee hold that such fact destroys the validity of the return and requires its rejection, leaving the parties to prove the vote by other competent evidence."

(3) **United States Supervisors.** *Duties of.*

Section 2029 of the Revised Statutes is not a repeal of sections 2016, 2017, and 2018, and in no way changes the duty of the supervisors "to be and remain where the ballot boxes are kept at all times after the polls are opened until every vote cast at such time and place be counted, the canvass of all votes polled wholly completed, and the proper and requisite certificates or returns made."

"By section 2029 the power to order arrests is taken from United States supervisors in all places other than in cities of 20,000 inhabitants or upwards, and their duties are limited to witnessing the conduct of the election, the counting and making return of the result. This includes the power and duty to be present at all times and to scrutinize the count and return."

(4) **Ex parte affidavits.**

Ex parte affidavits filed by the contestant were not considered by the committee, there being nothing in the record to justify the resort to this kind of proof.

REPORT.

FEBRUARY 25, 1891.—Mr. ROWELL, from the Committee on Elections, submitted the following report:

The Committee on Elections, having had under consideration the contested-election case of Hill *vs.* Catchings, from the Third Congressional district of Mississippi, submit the following report:

At the election held November 6, 1888, for Representative in Congress from the Third Congressional district of Mississippi, James Hill was the Republican and T. C. Catchings the Democratic candidate. Catchings received the certificate of election, his majority according to the returns being 7,011.

We insert the returns by counties:

Counties.	T. C. Catchings.	James Hill.
Bolivar	1,673	951
Coahoma	945	1,257
Sharkey	662	185
Quitman	130	144
Sunflower	379	2
Warren	2,745	585
Washington	2,603	613
Issaquena	779	275
Tunica	879	600
Le Flore	829	1
Total	11,624	4,613

Catchings's reported majority, 7,011.

The notice of contest alleges fraudulent refusal to receive the ballots of legal voters; fraudulent refusal to hold elections in several large Republican precincts; that the whole election machinery of the district was in the hands of friends of contestee, in violation of the statutes; that the United States supervisors were prevented from discharging the duties imposed upon them by law; and that the returns transmitted to the secretary of state are fraudulent.

The population of the district is largely colored, the proportion of colored to white being about 4 to 1. The evidence discloses the fact that a large majority of the colored voters are Republicans, and a large majority of the white voters are Democrats. On a fair election, with both parties equally well organized and with equally acceptable candidates, there is no question but that the district would go Republican by a very large majority.　　803

The committee, however, are of opinion, from the evidence presented to them, that T. C. Catchings was elected by a majority of all the legal votes cast, but by a much less majority than was returned for him. He was popular with his party, was believed to be especially efficient in representing the interests of his district, and to be able to do more in the way of securing Government aid in protecting the lands of the district from the ravages of the Mississippi River than was his opponent. He was stronger than his party, and was supported in some parts of the district by influential colored Republicans. In addition, his party was well organized and more fully registered than the opposition.

Mr. Hill was popular with the colored Republicans in most of the district, but failed to secure the active support of the white Republicans. In a portion of the district his adherents were not organized, and in only a small portion of the whole district did he have that kind of effective organization which would enable his followers to poll anything like a full vote.

In reporting that contestee was duly elected, as shown by the evidence, we by no means mean to be understood as saying that the election as a whole was free and fair. On the contrary, we are satisfied that preparation was made to commit fraud if necessary to secure the election of contestee, and that in some instances the preparation ripened into action. By the statutes of Mississippi the election machinery of the State is primarily in the hands of the governor, lieutenant-governor, and secretary of state. Previous to each general election these State officers are required to appoint three commissioners of election for each county, not all of whom shall be of the same political party. These commissioners appoint the precinct inspectors, with a like limitation as to party affiliation.

Such a statutory provision for allowing opposing parties to have representation on all election boards having charge of the conduct of elections is usually deemed necessary to secure honest results, and when fairly executed in letter and spirit may as a rule be relied on, at least so far as counting and returning the vote is involved. A general and willful disregard by the appointing power either of the letter or spirit of the law raises a strong presumption of an intent on the part of the appointing officers to afford opportunity for fraud. In this case it clearly appears that the State officers in appointing county commissioners intentionally disregarded the spirit of the law, and in some instances violated its letter. In like manner the county commissioners quite generally violated the letter and spirit of the law in appointing precinct inspectors, Republican committees were ignored, their wishes disregarded, and their recommendations rejected.

While the statute does not direct how these appointing bodies shall make selections, its spirit clearly requires that in selecting representatives of the different parties the wishes of those representing the party organization shall be considered, and that the appointees shall be men having the confidence of their political associates. The selection of men to represent a politcal party on an election board who habitually vote the opposite ticket, who are not trusted in their party, or who are notoriously incompetent, is not a compliance either with the letter or the spirit of the statute. We are glad to note some honorable exceptions to the general rule in this district, in the selection of precinct inspectors, and to commend the effect in producing confidence in the returns from such boards.

In a majority of the precincts, about which evidence was taken, we find that the precinct inspectors appointed to represent the Republicans were either Democrats in fact, or were incompetent and untrustworthy. While suspicion attaches to all such precincts, such suspicion is not sufficient to invalidate the return, in the absence of other evidence, but it does have the effect of requiring less evidence to overturn the prima facie correctness of the returns. In regard to a few of the precincts this evidence is not wanting, while in others there is an entire absence of evidence tending to impeach the validity of the returns. In some instances there is affirmative proof sustaining the correctness of the returns.

In several large Republican precincts no elections were held, and it is manifest that the neglect to hold elections was intentional and for the purpose of depriving contestant of the votes which he otherwise would have received. In one instance the poll books were carried off to prevent the holding of an election. While there is some conflict in the evidence, we are convinced that the whole matter was arranged at a Democratic meeting the night before the election.

In district No. 2, Sharkey County, Hill received 129 votes and Catchings 25. When the returns came in the vote was found to be reversed. All the inspectors of the election testify to the correct returns, and are at a loss to explain how the change took place. The error is conceded. The committee have no doubt that the change was intentionally made by some one connected with the election. In five or six instances United States supervisors were prevented from discharging their duties according to law, either by being refused admission to the polling place, or by being prevented from witnessing the count, or by the removal of the ballot box from their presence.

In every instance where a United States supervisor is prevented from discharging his duties, as provided by statute, the committee hold that such fact destroys the validity of the return and requires its rejection, leaving the parties to prove the vote by other competent evidence.

After allowing such correction of the vote as the evidence requires, and after rejecting all the returns which have been proved to be untrustworthy, and even conceding to contestant such majority as he might have received in the districts where no election was held, there is still left to contestee a good majority.

Previous to the election one J. S. McNeily, chairman of the Democratic Congressional Committee, issued a circular of instructions to the inspectors of elections, in which occurs the following (Record, 193, 194):

Here I had intended closing this paper, when I read a copy of the instructions issued to the Federal supervisors by R. H. Winter, chief supervisor of elections for the southern district of Mississippi. To my utter surprise I discovered that he had, through ignorance, I presume, under cover of "instructions," grossly misled these officials by quoting for their guidance law wholly inapplicable to their office and its functions. The sections of the U. S. Statutes comprised in those instructions, sections 2016, 2017, 2018, 2019, and 2029, are, with the exception of the last, expressly applicable to cities alone of 20,000 inhabitants and over. This production of the chief supervisor embodies the outrageous proposition that the Federal dark-corner appointees shall by authority of a false quotation of law usurp and exercise the lawful duties of the State officials. While it is charitable to allow that Mr. Winter has done this thing in ignorance, there is beyond question a wicked design behind it. Of this I have evidence that it is a part of Jim Hill's contest programme to use it as a means of creating an embroilment between the Federal and the State officials. Knowing that he is beaten at the polls, this is his only purpose. Be this as it may, you will on no account permit your lawful conduct, as defined above, and more particularly in the code of 1880, to be interfered with. The Federal supervisors, you will see to it, shall restrict their acts to section 2029 U. S. Statutes. This section is the law, and the sole law, for their guidance as laid down by U. S. Judge R. A. Hill in his rebuke of a former similar attempt at usurpation. If they do not, if they attempt to interfere with the executive duties imposed upon you by assuming "to personally scrutinize, count, and canvass each ballot" as they are misdirected to do, you will resolutely and promptly hand them over to the proper peace officer on the charge of unlawful interference. If trouble arises, if any of these Federal appointees have the hardihood to attempt to carry out this illegal direction, the responsibility w rest with Mr. Winter and those who have inspired his most mischievous circular

I have taken the highest legal advice as to my warrant in issuing this paper. I address it to the Democratic election inspectors, perfectly confident that they will, at all hazards, carry out its lawful substance and meaning. I furthermore appeal to the Democrats, and all good men of the district, to rebuke this effort upon their rights, and to see in it a true reflection of the vile and reckless nature of this contest against them, of the character of the movement to which they are called upon to surrender their largest material interest. Let the full strength of your manhood come forth on election day and inflict upon this nefarious scheme utter and overwhelming defeat.

Mr. Winter has had his attention directed, by telegraph, to the error of his action and the probable consequence thereof if he does not promptly revoke his circular, and that in any event the Democratic skirts may be clear Judge Hill will be asked, by telegraph, to order its revocation. But in any event the course of the State officials is clear.

I hereto append the opinion upon this question, often quoted and uniformly coincided in by legal authorities, of Ex-Attorney-General Catchings.

J. S. McNEILY,
Chairman.

This language is based upon an opinion given by contestee when attorney-general of the State. It assumes that section 2029 of the Revised Statutes alone defines the rights and duties of supervisors of election in counties and parishes, and is in effect a repeal of all of sections 2016, 2017, and 2018 so far as such supervisors are concerned.

This is a mistake; section 2029 in no way changes the duty of the supervisors

To be and remain where the ballot boxes are kept at all times after the polls are opened until every vote cast at such time and place be counted, the canvass of all votes polled wholly completed, and the proper and requisite certificates or returns made.

By section 2029 the power to order arrests is taken from United States supervisors in all places other than in cities of 20,000 inhabitants or upwards, and their duties are limited to witnessing the conduct of the election, the counting and making return of the result. This includes the power and duty to be present at all times and to scrutinize the count and return.

The McNeily instructions spoke of the supervisors as "Federal dark corner appointees" and directed:

If they attempt to interfere with the executive duties imposed upon you by assuming "to personally scrutinize, count, and canvass each ballot." * * * You will resolutely and promptly hand them over to the proper peace officers on the charge of unlawful interference.

This was not only a direction to violate the United States statute, but was in other respects calculated to cause a breach of the peace and prevent an orderly election. Had this advice been generally followed the committee would reject all returns of elections held under such circumstances.

Ex parte affidavits were filed in the case by contestant, which, if considered by the committee, would materially change the result; but the committee find nothing in the record to justify the resort to this kind of proof, and reject all the affidavits as not being legitimately in the record.

After the election and pending the contest General Catchings, the contestee, wrote a letter to Chairman McNeily, in which occurs the following language:

After his (Hill's) time is out we have so many days in which to take testimony, and will have to give him similar notice. *I do not think it would hurt at all if one or two of them should disappear. It might have a very happy effect on Hill, his witnesses, and lawyers.*

General Catchings filed the following written acknowledgment with the committee, submitting the above quotation from his letter:

The following extract from a letter written to J. S. McNeily, chairman Congressional committee, Third Mississippi district, by Hon. T. C. Catchings, contestee, under date December 28, 1888, is admitted as having been written and delivered to J. S.Mc-Neily, chairman Democratic Congressional committee, Third Mississippi district, and is admitted in evidence in this case by agreement.

T. C. CATCHINGS,
JAMES HILL,
Per DUDLEY & THOMAS,
Att'ys for Contestant.

The language speaks for itself. It was a suggestion to hinder unlawfully the taking of testimony in the case. Had the advice been acted upon the committee would have had more difficulty in reaching the conclusion that contestee was elected. But so far as appears in the evidence the suggestions of the letter were not acted upon in any instance, and it is a reasonable conclusion that they were not approved by Chairman McNeily. Such suggestions, coming from a reputable source, but emphasize the truth of the charge that the public sentiment of the dominant race in this district is hostile to the exercise by the colored voter of the rights granted him by the Constitution, and looks with leniency upon crimes against the purity of the ballot box.

As further showing the state of public opinion on this question we quote from the testimony.

Mr. Martin Marshall, a lawyer of character, says on page 306 of the record:

As to whether such rascally tricks would be a preferable, though bad, alternative to avoid misrule and public thievery and the destruction of the material interests of the country, I am not casuist enough to decide; whether a people reduced to that bad alternative are to be condemned for resorting to that sort of defense of their interests, let those who never were reduced to it be bold enough to answer.

Chairman McNeily says, on page 195:

Would the fact that a man had ever stuffed a ballot box cause him to forfeit either his social or business standing?
If he had [been] convicted, sentenced, and punished, yes.
In that case would the ostracism be due to the crime or because he had been fool enough to be caught?
I don't think I would ostracise him.
In a choice between negro rule and ballot-box stuffing which would you choose?
I would do like the old darky preacher, I would take to the woods.

Mr. John Finlay, a druggist of Greenville, says, on page 368:

Do you consider ballot-box stuffing a crime, in view of the peculiar surroundings in the county and the South generally?
No, I don't; I consider it a necessity at times.
In a contest where it was a question of race supremacy rather than one of party politics, would a man who stuffed the ballot box forfeit either his social or business standing?
No, sir; he would not.
Is not ballot-box stuffing looked upon by the best element in the South as the choice between necessary evils?
It is so far as I know.

Matthew F. Johnson, a planter and a member of the Democratic executive committee of the district, says, on page 339:

What is your opinion of ballot box stuffing?
I believe if necessity required it, to protect the property interest of the white people in this county, and if I did it, I don't think it would affect my chances for heaven one particle, and I would stuff a ballot box if required to do it to put a good Republican in office as I would a Democrat, as my object is to have good honest government.

Inasmuch as the committee are of the opinion that after making all legitimate deductions required by the evidence from the majority returned for contestee, he still has a majority of the votes, it is not deemed necessary to review in detail the evidence in regard to the several precincts where frauds were perpetrated sufficient to cause the rejection of the returns.

The committee recommend the adoption of the following resolutions

Resolved, That James Hill was not elected a Representative in the Fifty-first Congress from the Third Congressional district of Mississippi and is not entitled to the seat as such Representative.

Resolved, That T. C. Catchings was elected a Representative in the Fifty-first Congress from the Third Congressional district of Mississippi, and is entitled to retain his seat as such Representative.

VIEWS OF MR. LACEY.

(1) **Fraud or bribery.**—*Committed by a candidate, should invalidate his election.*

"The law ought to be held as follows:

Where the friends of a successful candidate, without collusion or combination with such candidate, engage in fraud, bribery, intimidation, or other violations of law to influence the election, and the number of votes affected thereby is insufficient to change the result, the election will not be invalidated thereby; but if such candidate takes part in such wrongs, or confederates with those engaged therein, and it does not appear that the election has been changed in its results thereby, the election should be held void, and a new election ordered. * * *

In order to give the seat to the contestant, it should be necessary to prove that the results were changed by the transactions in question, but to unseat the participant a less amount of proof should be sufficient."

(2) **Suppression of testimony.**

The attempt of contestee, as shown in his letter, to suppress the evidence of the frauds committed, connects him with those frauds and brings him within the scope of the above rule.

809

VIEWS OF MR. LACEY.

Mr. LACEY submits the following as the views of the minority:

The report of the majority of the committee concedes that the district has a large Republican majority. The majority report further concedes that there were gross frauds, and that when these frauds are eliminated from the count the majority of the contestee would be greatly reduced. I will not recite these frauds fully, as they are for the purpose of this report sufficiently set out in the report of the majority.

It appears, however, that in selecting the officers to hold the election neither the letter nor spirit of the law was complied with, and the Republican party had no fair representation upon the election boards. In some precincts where there was a Republican majority no election was held. The returns showing a majority for Hill were fraudulently reversed, showing a like majority for the Democratic nominee. Federal supervisors were interfered with in the discharge of their duties. In short, there were frauds of various kinds, materially affecting the result, but the evidence does not show enough in detail to change the result and give a majority for the contestant.

Mr. Hill contended that the occurrence of certain political murders and outrages in other localities justified him in not incurring the danger of taking further testimony in his case, and that if the evidence had been fully taken his election would have been clearly shown. That his fears were not groundless is shown by well-known bloody occurrences which have startled the whole country. But I agree with the majority in their conclusion that the contestant has not introduced enough testimony to show that he did in fact receive a majoriy of the legal votes cast. This, however, leaves for discussion the question as to whether enough has been shown to require that the election should be held void.

I think that the law ought to be held as follows:

Where the friends of a successful candidate, without collusion or combination with such candidate, engage in fraud, bribery, intimidation, or other violations of law to influence the election, and the number of votes affected thereby is insufficient to change the result, the election will not be invalidated thereby; but if such candidate takes part in such wrongs, or confederates with those engaged therein, and it does not appear that the election has been changed in its results thereby, the election should be held void, and a new election ordered.

The question as to the effect of connivance with or participation in such wrongful acts by a candidate is one in which the law ought to be clearly laid down and unhesitatingly enforced.

I concede that the preponderance of the authorities hold to the effect that such acts upon the part of the contestee will not render the election void unless it appears affirmatively that such unlawful acts changed

811

the result. The effect of bribery in parliamentary elections has been settled by statute in Great Britain, and renders the election void although the votes affected were insufficient to change the result. The interests of good government and the importance of purity of elections require that the rule should be laid down and enforced against every candidate that he should not participate in or incite any violations of the laws under which the election is held.

Whilst a candidate should not be held accountable for the acts of his partisans, committed in the heat of a political campaign, yet he should be held to instigate or participate in such acts at his peril. He should understand that in case of his instigation of violations of the law or of his participation in such violation he shall not be permitted to hold his seat. A contestant should not be compelled to prove just how many votes were affected by such wrongful acts of the contestee in order to have the election declared void. The full effect of such wrongs may often be hard to prove. The sitting member should have his skirts clear of all participation.

In order to give the seat to the contestant, it should be necessary to prove that the results were changed by the transactions in question, but to unseat the participant a less amount of proof should be sufficient.

A vigorous contest was made in this district, which was naturally a Republican stronghold. The contestant and the contestee took an active interest and participated in the campaign pending the election. It is not probable that any wide-spread and obviously preconcerted violation of the election law, such as is shown, should have occurred against the wishes of the contestee.

But after the election, and while the contest was in progress, it appears that the contestee wrote to the chairman of his party a letter in which appears the following language:

After his (Hill's) time is out we have so many days in which to take testimony, and will have to give him similar notice. I do not think it would hurt at all if one or two of them should disappear. It might have a very happy effect on Hill, his witnesses, and lawyers.

In the light of the deplorable events which have occurred in some parts of Mississippi in connection with elections and election contests, it is unnecessary to discuss the full scope and meaning of this letter. The language is of contestee's own choosing and speaks for itself. General Catchings had a full opportunity to explain this letter before the committee, but wholly failed to avail himself of that opportunity. He argued his own case in person, and when the letter was read to the committee an opportunity was given him to contradict or explain, but he did not see fit to do so.

Does the fact of writing such a letter, under the circumstances, sufficiently connect the contestee with the various frauds described in the majority report? I think it does. Where the recipient of the benefits of such a fraud not only accepts its advantages, but attempts to suppress the testimony of the crime, such attempted suppression, or attempted suppression when unexplained and uncontradicted, ought to be regarded as sufficient to show the contestee's original connection with these various wrongs. The frauds are general and widespread, the party of the contestee were acting in concert, and a just suspicion will always attach to a leader where his followers are so generally guilty of offenses against fair elections. But when such acts are followed by active attempts at suppression of the evidence, such as appears in the letter to McNeily, the inference is irresistible. Taking the letter of the contestee into consideration, in the light of all the surrounding circumstances, the conclusion follows that the contestee is responsible in some degree for the acts of his party and partisans, as set out in the majority report.

The seat ought, therefore, to be declared vacant and an election stained with so much fraud and corruption ought to be set aside. I recommend the adoption of the following substitute for the resolution reported by the majority:

·   *Resolved*, That T. C. Catchings was not elected as Representative in the Fifty-first Congress from the Third Congressional district of Mississippi, and that the seat is hereby declared vacant.

L. B. EATON vs. JAMES PHELAN.

TENTH TENNESSEE.

Contestant charged repeating, illegal voting, corruption, and fraud in the city of Memphis, and ballot-box-stuffing and false counting in the county of Fayette and portions of other counties. A large amount of testimony was taken, and the case argued before the committee.

The seat became vacant by the death of Mr. Phelan before the expiration of Congress. No report was ever made or decision reached upon the question of the right of Mr. Eaton to fill the vacancy.

DIGEST—INDEX.

Abbreviation. *The word "twe."*

    Where the statute requires the return to set forth the number of votes received "in words at length," the word "*twe*" can not be construed to mean twelve or twenty without evidence. It should either be counted as two, or the ambiguity explained by evidence.

        Smith *vs.* Jackson...   17

Ballots. *Best evidence.*

    The ballots, when clearly shown to be the identical ballots cast, are the best evidence of the vote.

        Mudd *vs.* Compton (minority report).................................   165

As evidence.

    Best evidence, and none other admissible.

        McLean *vs.* Broadhead (minority), Forty-eighth Congress (Mobley, 389).

        McDuffie *vs.* Davidson, Fiftieth Congress (Mobley, 579).

        Craig *vs.* Shelley (minority), Forty-seventh Congress (2 Ells., 48).

    Can not be contradicted even by testimony of voters themselves.

        Otero *vs.* Gallejos, Thirty-fourth Congress (1 Bart., 184).

        Van Rensselaer *vs.* Van Allen, Third Congress (C. & H., 76).

        (*See* Evidence and Recount.)

    Not best evidence when fraud is alleged.

        Bisbee *vs.* Finley, Forty-seventh Congress (2 Ells., 180).

        Reed *vs.* Julian, Forty-first Congress 2 (Bart., 822).

(For cases where other evidence was received see *Returns.*)

Distinguishing mark.

    An asterisk so small as not to be noticeable, printed in the lower corner of a ticket, does not constitute such a distinguishing mark as to require the ballot to be rejected under the Florida statutes.

        Goodrich *vs.* Bullock   586

    Where the statute provided that ballots should be written or printed in black ink or black pencil, and that no ballot of any other description should be counted, and certain ballots were partly written, in red ink, it being impossible to procure any other ink in the only store in the place, *held*, that the votes should be counted on a contest, notwithstanding the terms of the statute.

        Goodrich *vs.* Bullock   586

    Ballots rejected because the name of a candidate for justice of the peace was written in with a red pencil should be counted.

        Goodrich *vs.*, Bullock   591

    Ballots rejected because of scarcely visible specks, and those rejected because of a printer's dash in a place where no person was named for a particular office, were improperly rejected.

        Goodrich *vs.* Bullock   591

    Ballots rejected because of a printer's dash separating each name on the ticket should be counted.

        Goodrich *vs.* Bullock   591

    Ballots rejected because of pencil marks on them made by the judges of election in pushing them into a box with a pencil should be counted.

        Goodrich *vs.* Bullock   591

    The ballots partly written in red ink or red pencil were properly rejected, their rejection being directly required by the law of Florida.

        Goodrich *vs.* Bullock (minority).....................................   614

Ballot box. *Removal of.*

Where the poll was closed for dinner, and the box removed from the presence of the United States supervisors, *held,* that "but for the strong affirmative proof that no wrong was intended or done in this case, the committee would unhesitatingly reject the return."

Adjournment for dinner held not sufficient of itself to reject a poll.

Shifting of.

The shifting of ballot boxes for the purpose of deceiving voters and enforcing on them an educational test not permitted by the constitution of the State, is an unlawful and fraudulent proceeding. "An act may not expressly be forbidden by law, but if it is done with an unlawful purpose, and succeeds in accomplishing that purpose, the act is thereby made unlawful." Under such circumstances the votes found in the wrong boxes should be counted. "It is no answer to say that the counting of such ballots is prohibited by statute (even admitting that the statute is a reasonable regulation, which, under the peculiar circumstances in South Carolina, we do not), when the mistaken deposit has resulted from the active deception of the managers. It is a crime at common law to enter into a conspiracy to commit an offense against the purity and fairness of a public election (Paine on Elections, section 496, and authorities cited)."

Shifting of, justifiable.

The section of the election law of South Carolina which provides for a number of ballot-boxes, plainly labeled, for the different offices, and requires that the voter shall be separated from others and not spoken to by any one except the judges while at the polling place depositing his vote, is well calculated to carry out the provisions of the Constitution—that the voter shall be protected from "an undue influence from power, bribery, tumult, or improper conduct," and to protect him in his right to a secret ballot. If the voters were found to be receiving information from outsiders which they were required to receive from the judges, "if the wise provisions of this law were being interfered with and rendered nugatory by any outsider at any poll, or if it came under the observation of those selected to supervise the execution of this law that its letter or intention or spirit was being violated, we submit it was the duty of the managers to shift the boxes or perform any other legal act to subserve its proper execution."

Irregularities. *Their effect on the prima facie of the returns.*

"Mere irregularities in the conduct of the election, where it does not appear that the legally expressed will of the voter has been suppressed or changed, are insufficient to impeach officially declared votes. But a succession of unexplained irregularities and disregard of law on the part of intelligent officials removes from the ballot-box and the official returns that sacred character with which the law clothes them, and makes less conclusive evidence sufficient to change the burden upon the party who maintains the legality of the official count."

(*See Return*, irregularities in.)

Irregularity *in one portion of a return does not affect the rest.*

Where a precinct return was irregular as to votes cast for Presidential electors, and had been rejected entire by the county commissioners, the committee counted the vote for Representative in Congress, which was regularly returned.

In a county return does not cause its rejection.

Clark *vs.* Hall, Thirty-four{ . Congress (1 Bart., 215).

Mistake. *Power of board to correct.*

There is inherent in every body charged with the ascertainment of the popular will, whether its functions be judicial or ministerial, the power to correct an error when discovered, and to make its conclusions conform to the facts.

Where a county returning board in making out their abstract accidentally omitted one precinct, but before forwarding their return discovered and corrected their mistake, *held*, that this was just what ought to have been done, and if this precinct return had been omitted it would have been the duty of the committee to include it in the total vote. The vote of a county cannot be thrown out for such an informality.

Allowed to be corrected.

Root *vs.* Adams, Fourteenth Congress (C. & H., 271).
Guyon *vs.* Sage, Sixteenth Congress (C. & H., 349).
Colden *vs.* Sharpe, Seventeenth Congress (C. & H., 369).
Adams *vs.* Wilson, Eighteenth Congress (C. & H., 375).
Sleeper *vs.* Rice, Thirty-eighth Congress (1 Bart., 473).
Archer *vs.* Allen, Thirty-fourth Congress (1 Bart., 169).

Notice of contest.

The recitals in the notice can have none of the sanctity and binding force of an agreement or stipulation, and can not be construed into a concession.

Parties should be bound by.

If any question had been raised in the notice of contest in regard to the precinct from which the returns were not signed, and no evidence taken to show their correctness, the committee would be right in rejecting them, but there being no mention of this precinct in the notice, contestee should not be required to produce any evidence in regard to it.

Same principle.

Leib,. Ninth Congress (C. & H., 165).
Stoval *vs.* Cabell, Forty-seventh Congress (2 Ells., 667).
McKenzie *vs.* Braxton, Forty-second Congress (Smith, 19).
Finley *vs.* Walls, Forty-fourth Congress (Smith, 367).

Officers of election. *Not sworn.*

When all the officers are not shown to have been sworn, but no harm has resulted, it will not vitiate the election, they being *de facto* officers. And in West Virginia, where it is provided that the fact of taking the oath must either appear on the poll-books or be proved to the satisfaction of the commissioners of the county court before they can count the vote of a precinct, and the county commissioners did count the vote of a precinct when the oath was not sufficiently certified on the poll-book, it will be presumed that they had satisfied themselves of the fact by other evidence before counting the vote.

Vitiates return.

Blair *vs.* Barrett, Thirty-sixth Congress (1 Bart., 315).
McFarland *vs.* Purviance, Eighth Congress (C. & H., 131).

Return. *Irregularities in*—Continued.

Evidence necessary to overthrow.

"Before the official return can be properly rejected, there must be satisfactory proof that the proceedings in the conduct of the election or in the return of the vote were so tainted with fraud that the truth can not be correctly ascertained from the returns. In other words, the returns must be accepted as true until they are clearly shown to be false."

Statutes. *Directory and mandatory.*

Statutes directing the mode of proceeding of public officers are directory merely unless there is something in the statute itself which plainly shows a different intent.

Supervisors of election.

(See United States Supervisors).

Suppression of testimony.

Where one party suppresses testimony, strict and technical proof will not be required of the other.

By dilatory cross-examination.

Where in one precinct contestant began taking testimony twenty-three days before the expiration of his time, in pursuance to a notice containing the names of 292 persons who, it is claimed, would have testified that they voted for him in said precinct, and the first two witnesses, the ticket distributers, were cross-examined by the contestee throughout the entire twenty-three days, *held* that the contestee is estopped from claiming that the evidence of these ticket distributers is insufficient unless corroborated by that of the voters themselves, he having by his own act prevented the latter testimony from being taken.

For minority views, *see* Evidence.

Smalls *vs.* Elliott (minority), Fiftieth Congress (Mobley, 728).

The attempt of a successful candidate to suppress the evidence of frauds committed to secure his election connects him with the frauds, and brings him within the scope of the rule that fraud committed by a successful candidate invalidates the election.

Tender. *What is.*

The ability to reach the window and actually tender the ticket to the judges is not essential in all cases to constitute a good offer to vote. From the time the voter reaches the polling place and takes his position in line to secure his orderly turn in voting, he has commenced the act of voting.

What necessary.

"To hold that anything short of an actual tender of the ballot to the election officers and a rejection by them was an offer to vote would be a most dangerous and uncertain rule, and one to which we can not give our sanction. Where the evidence plainly establishes the fact that a legal voter

Lightning Source UK Ltd.
Milton Keynes UK
UKHW011102211118
332724UK00009B/214/P